W9-AOB-136

This modern text is designed to prepare you for your future professional career. While theories, ideas, techniques, and data are dynamic, the information contained in this volume will provide you a quick and useful reference as well as a guide for future learning for many years to come. Your familiarity with the contents of this book will make it an important volume in your professional library.

EX LIBRIS

Accounting Principles

Accounting Principles

ROGER H. HERMANSON, Ph.D., C.P.A.
Research Professor of Accounting
Georgia State University

JAMES DON EDWARDS, Ph.D., C.P.A.
J. M. Tull Professor of Accounting
School of Accounting
The University of Georgia

R. F. SALMONSON, Ph.D., C.P.A.
Professor of Accounting
Michigan State University

1983 • REVISED EDITION

Business Publications, Inc.
Plano, Texas   75075

ISBN   0-256-02872-9

Library of Congress Catalog Card No. 82–72759

Printed in the United States of America

3 4 5 6 7 8 9 0 K 0 9 8 7 6 5 4

Preface

Accounting Principles is intended for use in first-year introductory accounting courses. The text includes both financial and managerial accounting topics. The authors recognize that students taking the first-year accounting course seek various careers. Some may choose accounting as a major, while others will choose another aspect of business or a nonbusiness major. All of these students will find the ability to use and interpret accounting information valuable both in their careers and in their personal lives.

Accounting Principles serves as a foundation for subsequent courses in accounting and business. The authors assume that students using this text will have a limited understanding of business concepts. Thus, new terms and concepts are defined and fully explained when introduced.

Features of the revised edition

1. A portion of Chapter 1 in the first edition is an *introduction* to the entire text in the revised edition. The purpose is to shorten Chapter 1 and to give the instructor material to discuss on the first day of class.
2. The first six chapters are thoroughly rewritten and reorganized. A *building-block approach* is used in presenting the accounting cycle. For example, information for the same company is used in Chapters 2, 3, and 4.
3. *Two comprehensive review problems* are included, one after Chapter 4 and one after Chapter 6. These comprehensive problems allow the student to review all concepts covered to that point by working the problems.
4. All discussion of adjusting entries is delayed until Chapter 3.
5. The *closing process* in Chapter 5 is simplified by treating the "closing" of all merchandise-related accounts as part of the closing process rather than as adjusting entries.

6. All discussion of bad debts expense and interest computation on notes is delayed until Chapter 8.

7. All discussion of *perpetual inventory* procedure is delayed until Chapter 9.

8. The material on accounting theory and *inflation accounting* is covered at a level appropriate for the first-year course and is presented in Chapter 13.

9. The statement of changes in financial position material is revised and clarified to emphasize the cash definition of funds, a concept which is coming into widespread usage.

10. Chapter 21 on manufacturing accounting is thoroughly revised and includes a work sheet using periodic inventory procedure.

11. The managerial portion of the book is reorganized to make it more teachable.

12. All coverage of income taxes now appears in Chapter 28. Features of the 1981 Economic Recovery Tax Act and the 1982 Tax Equity and Fiscal Responsibility Act are included.

13. A new appendix on *international accounting* appears at the end of the text.

14. All *questions, exercises,* and *problems* have been traced back to the text to ensure that nothing is asked of a student which does not appear in the preceding portion of the text.

15. *Chapter goals* appear at the beginning of each chapter.

16. The terms used in the text are the most commonly used accounting terms, such as balance sheet, income statement, net income, Income Summary account, and cost-volume-profit.

17. *Demonstration problems* and *business-decision problems* are included in each chapter.

18. Fresh problems have been added to each chapter. *Series A* and *Series B problems* in each chapter cover common concepts but are not always identical in format.

19. Many of the above features resulted from following the advice of numerous reviewers who were retained by the publisher to comment on the teachability of the previous edition.

20. A professional editor with an accounting background thoroughly edited the entire manuscript.

Supplementary materials—learning aids for students

Study guides. Two study guides are available, one for each half of the book. The study guides were developed by Professor Gayle Rayburn, Memphis State University. Included for each chapter are chapter goals; reference outline; chapter review; matching, true-false, multiple-choice, and fill-in-the-blank questions; demonstration problem; exercises; and answers.

Working papers. Two sets of working papers are available for working assigned problems and business decision problems, one set for each half of the text. The working papers in many instances are partially filled in to reduce the "pencil pushing" required to solve the problems. *The format and spacing used in the working papers are identical to the Instructor's Solutions Manual and to the transparencies.* This feature makes it easier to compare students' solutions to the authors' solutions.

Practice sets. Four practice sets are available. Practice Set I, developed by Professor Margaret Mills, Tidewater Community College, Virginia, illustrates special journals and includes a work sheet for a retailing company. Practice Set II illustrates the accounting system used by a manufacturing company and was developed by Herbert A. O'Keefe, Georgia Southern College. Practice Set III illustrates the use of business papers for a retailing company. And Practice Set IV is a microcomputer practice set which can be used with the Apple and IBM personal microcomputers. Practice Sets I, III, and IV may be used any time after Chapter 8 has been covered. Practice Set II may be used any time after covering Chapter 21.

Check figures. The list of check figures gives key amounts for the A and B Series problems in the text. Students can determine whether they are "on the right track" when working a problem by comparing their solutions with the key amount given for a particular problem.

Supplementary materials—teaching aids for instructors

Instructor's guide. The instructor's guide is a new feature with this edition. For each chapter, the guide contains a summary of major concepts; chapter goals; lecture notes; and the estimated time, level of difficulty, and content of exercises and problems.

Instructor's solutions manual. The instructor's solutions manual contains sample syllabi for both quarter- and semester-basis courses. For each chapter the manual contains an outline and answers to the questions, exercises, Series A and B and comprehensive review problems, and business decision problems. The spacing and format are identical to the work papers used by the students.

Transparencies. Very clear transparencies of solutions to problems are available to adopters. These transparencies can be especially useful when covering problems involving work sheets and in large classroom situations.

Achievement tests. Three series of achievement tests—A, B, and C—are available in bulk to adopters. Each series consists of six one-hour exams and two two-hour final exams. In each series, three of the one-hour exams and a final exam cover Chapters 1–14, and the other three one-hour exams and a final exam cover Chapters 15–28. All questions in the exams are multiple-choice for ease in grading.

Examination booklet.   An examination booklet contains true-false questions, additional multiple-choice questions, and short problems for each chapter. The true-false questions are ideal for quizzes. The multiple-choice questions may be used to freshen up the achievement tests, and the short problems can be used to supplement or replace the multiple-choice questions on the achievement tests for those who object to the sole use of such questions.

Computer data bank of examination questions.   A test generator software package which can be used to prepare examinations by selecting questions on a random basis is available to all adopters. A data base of approximately 2,000 multiple-choice questions is included.

We are indebted to many individuals for reviewing the manuscript of the revised text. In addition to those on the acknowledgments page, we are especially indebted to colleagues and students at our respective universities for their helpful suggestions.

> **Roger H. Hermanson**
> **James Don Edwards**
> **R. F. Salmonson**

Note to students

Letricia Gayle Rayburn has written a two-volume Student Study Guide to assist you in understanding the material in this text. Each chapter of the Study Guide is keyed to a chapter of the text and provides a reference outline, a detailed chapter review, matching questions containing important new terms and concepts, demonstration problems and answers, true-false questions, completion questions, multiple-choice questions, and exercises. Answers to all questions are included in the Study Guide to provide you with immediate verification of your responses. Explanations are also given for the answers to the true-false and multiple-choice questions. This Student Study Guide, published by Business Publications, Inc., is available through your college bookstore. If it is not in stock, please ask your bookstore manager to order a copy for you.

> **R. H. H.**
> **J. D. E.**
> **R. F. S.**

Acknowledgments

We are grateful to many individuals who have contributed to the development of this text. Special appreciation is due: Lane K. Anderson, Texas Tech University; Lloyd Badgett, University of Central Arkansas; Edgar T. Bitting, Elizabethtown College; Sallie Branscom, Virginia Western Community College; Trudy Chiaravalli, Lansing Community College; Charles Coleman, Bellvue Community College; G. Michael Crooch, Arthur Andersen & Co.; Lawrence Curbo, Memphis State University; Nita Dodson, East Texas State University; Linda Dykes, Oglethorpe University; Russell T. Gingras, Saginaw Valley State College; Raymond Green, Texas Tech University; Jean Gutman, University of Southern Maine; James T. Hood, Northeast Louisiana University; the late Rita Huff, Sam Houston State University; Marty Jagers, University of South Carolina; Robert A. Kelley, Corning Community College; Anthony T. Krzystofik, University of Massachusetts, Amherst; Donald E. MacGilvera, Shoreline Community College; Thomas E. McLeod, University of Alabama, Birmingham; Patricia H. Michel, Loyola College; Margaret Mills, Tidewater Community College; John L. Nabholtz, Southern Methodist University; Herbert A. O'Keefe, Georgia Southern College; Douglas Pfister, Lansing Community College; Cecily Raiborn, Texas Women's University; L. Gayle Rayburn, Memphis State University; Arthur T. Roberts, University of Baltimore; David E. Rogers, Mesa College; Virgil E. Stone, Texas A & I University; Mary J. Swanson, Mankato State University; Deborah Turner, Georgia State University; James J. Wallace, Rochester Institute of Technology; Penny Wardlaw, University of Georgia; and Jackson A. White, University of Arkansas, Little Rock.

The publisher owes a debt of gratitude to the late Dr. Rita Huff of Sam Houston State University for her professional help and her personal friendship. She profoundly influenced those who knew her.

R. H. H.
J. D. E.
R. F. S.

Contents

Other assumptions or concepts. Measurement in accounting: *Measuring assets. Measuring liabilities. Measuring changes in assets and liabilities.* The major principles: *The exchange price (or cost) principle. The matching principle. Revenue recognition. Exceptions to the realization principle. Expense and loss recognition.* Modifying conventions: *The conceptual framework project.* Inflation—a serious reporting problem: *The nature and measurement of inflation. Consequences of ignoring effects of inflation. Accounting responses to inflation.* Constant dollar accounting: *Constant dollar accounting—pro and con.* Current cost accounting: *Current cost accounting—pro and con.* The FASB requirements.
Appendix: The conceptual framework project. Objectives of financial reporting. Qualitative characteristics: *Relevance. Reliability. Comparability (and consistency). Pervasive constraints.* The basic elements of financial statements.

The partnership agreement. Characteristics of a partnership: *Voluntary association. Mutual agency. Limited life. Unlimited liability.* Advantages of a partnership. Disadvantages of a partnership. Unique features in partnership accounting: *The partners' capital accounts. The partners' drawing accounts. End-of-period entries.* Division of partnership income or loss: *Illustrations of distributions of partnership income.* Financial statements of a partnership: *Partnership income statement. Partnership balance sheet. Statement of partners' capital.* Changes in partnership personnel: *Admission of a new partner. Retirement of a partner.* Liquidation of a partnership: *Partnership liquidations illustrated.*

PART FIVE

CORPORATIONS

The corporation: *Advantages of a corporation. Disadvantages of the corporation. Incorporating. Articles of incorporation. Bylaws. Organization costs. Directing the corporation.* Documents, books, and records relating to capital stock: *Stockholders' ledger. The minutes book.* Capital stock authorized. Capital stock outstanding. Par value and no par value capital stock: *Par value stock. No par value stock. No par value stock with a stated value.* Other values commonly associated with capital stock: *Market value. Liquidation value. Redemption value. Book value.* Classes of capital stock: *Common stock. Preferred stock.* Types of preferred stock: *Stock preferred as to dividends. Stock preferred as to assets. Convertible preferred stock. Callable preferred stock.* Balance sheet presentation of stock. Stock issuances for cash: *Capital stock with par value. Capital stock without par value. Shares without par value or stated value.* Recording capital stock issues by subscription: *The stock subscribed account. Issuance by subscription of par value stock. Issuance by subscription of no par value stock. Balance sheet presentation of subscriptions receivable and stock subscribed. Balance sheet presentation of paid-in capital in excess of par (or stated) value—common or preferred. Defaulted subscriptions.* Capital stock issued for property or services. Book value.

Paid-in (or contributed) capital: *Paid-in capital—recapitalization. Paid-in capital—treasury stock transactions. Paid-in capital—donations.* Retained earnings. Paid-in capital and retained earnings in the balance sheet. Retained earnings appropriations: *Retained earnings appropriations in the balance sheet.* The statement of retained earnings. Dividends: *Cash dividends. Stock dividends.*

Recording stock dividends. Stock splits. Legality of dividends. Liquidating dividends. Treasury stock: *Acquisition and reissuance of treasury stock. Treasury stock in the balance sheet. Stockholders' equity in the balance sheet.* Net income inclusions and exclusions: *Extraordinary items. Accounting changes. Prior period adjustments. Accounting for tax effects. Summary of illustrative financial statements.* Earnings per share.

Bonds: *Comparison with stock. Issuance. Characteristics of bonds. Advantages of issuing debt. Disadvantages of issuing debt. Accounting for bonds. Bond prices and interest rates. Computing bond prices. Discount/premium amortization. Redeeming bonds payable. Serial bonds. Bond redemption or sinking funds. Convertible bonds. Long-term mortgage notes payable.* Bond investments: *Short-term bond investments. Long-term bond investments. Sale of bond investments. Valuation of bond investments.* Stock investments: *Accounting for stock investments. Valuation of stock investments.*
Appendix: Future worth and present value. Interest. Future worth. Present value: *Present value of an annuity.*

Parent and subsidiary corporations: *Eliminations.* Consolidated balance sheet at time of acquisition: *Acquisition of subsidiary at book value. Acquisition of subsidiary at a cost above or below book value. Acquisition of less than 100 percent of subsidiary.* Accounting for earnings, losses, and dividends of a subsidiary: *Cost method. Equity method.* Consolidated financial statements at a date after acquisition. Purchase versus pooling of interests. Uses and limitations of consolidated statements.

PART SIX

ANALYSIS OF FINANCIAL STATEMENTS

The concept of funds: *Funds defined as working capital. Funds defined as cash. Major sources and uses of funds. Funds from operations.* Statement of changes in financial position—working capital basis: *Determining the change in working capital. Analyzing the noncurrent accounts.* Statement of changes in financial position—cash basis: *Cash provided by operations. Cash basis statement preparation.* A comprehensive illustration: *Completing the working paper. The formal statement. Losses on the working paper. Working paper for statement of changes on a working capital basis.* Uses of the statement of changes in financial position: *Management uses. Creditor and investor uses.* Working capital or cash flows: *The shift toward cash flows.*

Objectives of financial statement analysis. Financial statement analysis. Horizontal and vertical analysis: An illustration: *Analysis of balance sheet. Analysis of income statement.* Trend percentages. Ratio analysis: *Liquidity ratios. Equity or solvency ratios. Profitability tests. Market tests.* Final considerations in financial statement analysis: *Sources of comparative standards. Need for comparable data. Influence of external factors.*

PART SEVEN

ACCOUNTING IN MANUFACTURING COMPANIES

PART EIGHT

PLANNING, CONTROL, AND DECISION MAKING

Cost behavior patterns: *Methods for analyzing costs.* Cost-volume-profit (CVP) analysis: *Break-even chart. Changing the break-even point. Margin of safety. Assumptions made in cost-volume-profit analysis. Cost-volume-profit analysis illustrated. Calculating the break-even point for a multiproduct firm.* Differential analysis: *The nature of fixed costs. Product pricing. Special orders. Elimination of products, segments, or customers. Joint products. Make-or-buy decisions.* Absorption versus direct costing: *Absorption costing. Direct costing. Comparing the two methods.*

Capital budgeting defined. Project selection: A general view: *Time value of money. Net cash benefits.* Project selection: Payback period. Project selection: Unadjusted rate of return. Project selection: Net present value method and the profitability index. Project selection: The time-adjusted rate of return. Investments in working capital. The postaudit.

Personal federal income taxes: *Who must file a return. Gross income. Adjusted gross income. Taxable income. Exemptions. Computing tax liability. Capital gains and losses. Taxation of capital gains. Tax credits. Filing the tax return.* Comprehensive illustration—personal income taxes. Corporate federal income taxation: *Taxable income. Tax loss carry-backs and carry-forwards. Depreciation methods used for tax purposes.* Income tax allocation: *Permanent differences. Timing differences.*
Appendix: Accelerated cost recovery system depreciation allowance tables.

Accounting Principles

Part One

Introduction

The accounting environment

Chapter 1
Accounting and its use in business decisions

The accounting environment

Accounting is an interesting field of study that has many uses in society. In fact, accounting is useful in every organization that has economic resources such as money, machinery, and buildings. One such organization is the business firm. While accounting has been called the language of business, it also serves as a language to provide financial information about other types of organizations, such as governments, churches, fraternities, and hospitals. This text will concentrate on the use of accounting as it relates to the business firm.

ACCOUNTING DEFINED

Accounting is the process used to measure and report to various users relevant financial information regarding the economic activities of an organization or unit. The information is primarily financial and is generally stated in money terms.

Accounting is often confused with bookkeeping. Bookkeeping involves the recording of economic activities and is a very mechanical process. Accounting includes bookkeeping, but goes well beyond it in scope. Accountants prepare financial statements, conduct audits, design accounting systems, prepare special business and financial studies, prepare forecasts and budgets, do income tax work, and analyze and interpret financial information.

Specifically, accounting consists of a number of functions. Accountants *observe* many events and *identify* those events that are considered evidence of economic activity. The purchase and sale of goods and services are examples. Then accountants *measure* these selected events in financial terms. As the next step, the events are *recorded* to provide a permanent history of the financial activities of the organization. Accountants *classify* these measurements of recorded events into meaningful groups and *summarize* the information for conciseness. Accountants *report* on business activity by preparing financial statements and other reports. Finally, accountants may be asked to *interpret* these statements and reports for various groups such as management and creditors. Interpretation may involve explanation of the uses, meanings, and limitations of accounting information. The functions performed by accountants are summarized in the accompanying illustration.

The *accounting system* may be viewed as an *information system* designed to provide relevant financial information through the use of financial statements. In designing the system, accountants consider the types of users of the information, such as owners and creditors, and the kinds of decisions they make that require financial information. Usually, the information provided relates to the economic resources owned by an organization, claims against these resources, changes in both resources and claims, and results of using these resources for a given period of time.

EMPLOYMENT OPPORTUNITIES IN ACCOUNTING

Accountants typically are employed in (1) public accounting, (2) private industry, or (3) the not-for-profit sector. Specialization is possible in accounting

Accounting functions performed by accountants

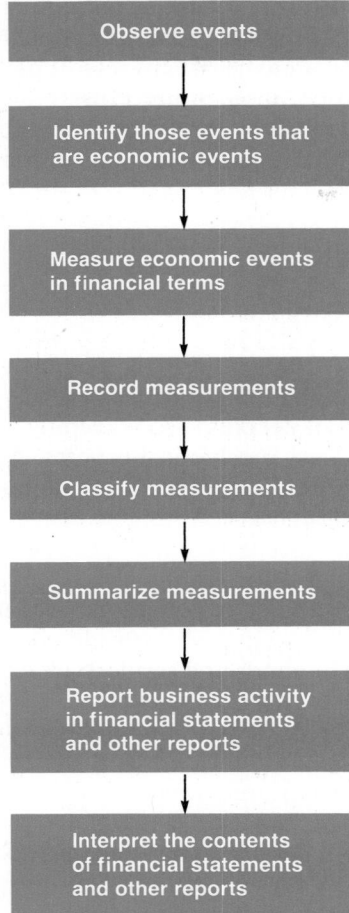

in areas such as auditing, systems development, budgeting, cost accounting, or tax accounting.

Public accounting

An accountant may become a *certified public accountant (CPA)*. A CPA is an accountant who has passed an examination prepared and graded by the *American Institute of Certified Public Accountants (AICPA)* and has met certain other requirements. These requirements vary by state but may include having a certain number of years of experience in accounting, having had certain courses in accounting, and having lived in that state a certain length of time before taking the exam. When all requirements are met, the accountant may be licensed by the state to practice. A CPA is an independent professional who may offer auditing, consulting, and tax services to clients such as businesses, individuals, and not-for-profit organizations.

Auditing. When a business seeks a loan or seeks to have its securities traded on a stock exchange, it is usually required to provide statements concerning its financial affairs. Users of these statements may accept and rely upon them more freely when they are accompanied by an *auditor's opinion or report*. An auditor's opinion or report contains the opinion of the CPA regarding the fairness of the client's financial statements. To have the knowledge necessary for an informed opinion, the CPA conducts an examination of the client's accounting and related records; this is referred to as an audit. Supporting evidence from external sources is sought. For instance, the accountant may contact a bank to verify cash balances of the client.

Management advisory services. From knowledge gained in an audit, CPAs often offer suggestions to their clients on how to improve their operations. From these and other contacts, CPAs may be engaged to provide a wide range of consulting services. These services are likely to be accounting related, such as the design and installation of an accounting system, the electronic processing of accounting data, inventory control, budgeting, or financial planning. Although these services are available from CPAs, other accountants provide similar services.

Tax services. CPAs often provide expert advice for the preparation of federal, state, and local tax returns and for tax planning. The objective in tax preparation is to use legal means to minimize the amount of taxes paid. *Tax planning* is also important to clients because of high tax rates and complex tax laws. Proper tax planning requires that the tax effects of every business decision be known and considered before a financial decision is made.

Private or industrial accounting

Accountants employed by a single business are called private or industrial accountants. A given company might employ only one private accountant or many. Private accountants may or may not be CPAs. If these accountants have passed an examination prepared and graded by the National Association of Accountants (an organization for accountants employed in private industry) and met certain other requirements, they will possess a *Certificate in Management Accounting* (*CMA*).

Industrial accountants may be specialists in providing certain services. They may, for example, be concerned with recording events and transactions involving outsiders and in the preparation of financial statements. Or they may be engaged in gathering and controlling the costs of goods produced by their employer. They may be specialists in budgeting—that is, in the development of plans relating to future operations. Many private accountants become specialists in the design and installation of systems for the processing of accounting data. Others are internal auditors and are employed by a firm to see that its policies and procedures are followed in its departments and divisions. These latter individuals may earn the designation, *certified internal auditor (CIA)*. This certificate is granted by the Institute of Internal Auditors after the individual has successfully completed an examination prepared and graded by the Institute.

Accounting in the not-for-profit sector

Many accountants, including CPAs, are employed by not-for-profit organizations, including governmental agencies at the federal, state, and local levels. The governmental accountant often is concerned with the accounting for and control of tax revenues and their expenditure. Some accountants become FBI agents and find their accounting background useful in investigating criminal activities. Accountants are also employed by governmental agencies whose task is the regulation of business activity—for example, the regulation of public utilities by a state public service commission.

Accountants (including CPAs, CMAs, and CIAs) are also employed in the academic segment of the profession. These accountants perform two major functions: teaching accounting to students who will become professionals and conducting research on the uses, limitations, and improvement of accounting information.

MANAGERIAL ACCOUNTING VERSUS FINANCIAL ACCOUNTING

Accounting is often divided into two categories—managerial accounting and financial accounting. The distinction between managerial and financial accounting will now be discussed.

Managerial accounting

Managerial accounting provides special information and analyses for internal uses. The information may range from very broad long-range planning to very detailed explanations of why costs varied from planned amounts. Managerial accounting information must meet *two tests:* (1) it must be useful and (2) it must not cost more to gather than it is worth. The information generally relates to a specific part of a firm, such as a plant or a department, since decisions are made at operating levels of management. Managerial accounting information also is used to measure a manager's performance in such areas as cost control and profit margins. Managerial accounting information often is forward-looking, involving planning for the future. For instance, a budget may be prepared that shows financial plans for the coming year.

Types of internal decisions. In most companies, persons at various levels of management make decisions that require managerial accounting information. Internal management decisions can be classified into four major types:

1. *Financial decisions*—deciding what amounts of capital (funds) are needed and whether these funds are to be secured from owners or creditors.

Capital used in this sense means *money* to be used by the company to purchase resources such as machinery and buildings and to pay expenses of conducting the business.

2. *Resource allocation decisions*—deciding how the total capital of a firm is to be invested, such as the amount to be invested in machinery.
3. *Production decisions*—deciding what products are to be produced, by what means, and when.
4. *Marketing decisions*—setting selling prices and advertising budgets; determining where a firm's markets are and how they are to be reached.

Management accounting can provide information for each type of management decision.

Financial accounting

Financial accounting differs from managerial accounting in that the information is for use by persons outside the firm. Financial accounting information relates to the firm as a whole. Outsiders can make decisions only on matters pertaining to the entire firm, such as whether to extend credit and whether to make an investment in the firm.

Financial accounting provides statements on a firm's financial position, changes in this position, and on the results of operations (profitability). Many companies publish these statements in an *annual report.* The annual report also contains the auditor's opinion as to the fairness of the financial statements and other information about the company's activities, products, and plans.

Financial accounting information is historical in nature, reporting upon what has happened in the past. This information must conform to certain standards or methods of presentation called *generally accepted accounting principles (GAAP)* in order to facilitate comparisons between companies. These generally accepted accounting principles have developed largely in accounting practice or have been established by an authoritative organization.

External users and their decisions. There are different types of external users of accounting information. Each group has certain types of questions for which answers are sought. Examples are:

1. *Owners and prospective owners.* Has the firm had satisfactory earnings on its total investment? Can the firm install costly pollution control equipment and still remain profitable? Should an ownership interest be acquired in this firm? Should an existing ownership interest in the firm be increased, decreased, or retained at its present level?
2. *Creditors and lenders.* Should a loan be granted to the firm? Will the firm be able to pay its debts as they become due?
3. *Employees and their unions.* Does the firm have the ability to pay increased wages? Is the firm financially able to provide permanent employment?
4. *Customers.* Does the company offer good products at fair prices? Will the firm survive long enough to honor its product warranties?

5. *Governmental units.* Is this public utility earning a fair return on its capital investment?
6. *The general public.* Is the profit margin on products reasonable?

Most of the information needs of the above users are met by providing a set of general purpose financial statements. These statements are the end product of the process known as financial accounting.

THE DEVELOPMENT OF FINANCIAL ACCOUNTING STANDARDS

As noted earlier, the financial statements a business firm issues to external parties must conform to generally accepted accounting principles. These principles have been developed largely in accounting practice or have been established by an authoritative body. Brief mention is made at this point of four prominent accounting authorities.

American Institute of Certified Public Accountants (AICPA)

The *American Institute of Certified Public Accountants (AICPA)* has been the dominant organization in the development of accounting standards over the past half century. In a 20-year period ending in 1959, the AICPA Committee on Accounting Procedure issued 51 *Accounting Research Bulletins* recommending certain principles or practices. From 1959 through 1973, the committee's successor, the *Accounting Principles Board (APB)*, issued 31 numbered *Opinions* which CPAs generally were required to follow. Through its monthly magazine, the *Journal of Accountancy,* its research division, and its other divisions and committees, the AICPA continues to influence the development of accounting standards and practices.

Financial Accounting Standards Board (FASB)

The *Accounting Principles Board (APB)* was replaced in 1973 with a new, independent, seven-member full-time *Financial Accounting Standards Board (FASB)*. The FASB has issued numerous *Statements of Financial Accounting Standards* and interpretations of those standards. The FASB is widely accepted as *the major influence, in the private sector,* in the development of new financial standards.

U.S. Securities and Exchange Commission (SEC)

Created under the Securities and Exchange Act of 1934, the *Securities and Exchange Commission (SEC)* administers a number of important acts dealing with the interstate sale of securities. The SEC has the power to prescribe accounting practices to be followed by companies under its jurisdiction. This includes virtually every major U.S. business corporation. But rather than exercise this power, the SEC has adopted a policy of working closely with the accounting profession, especially the FASB, in the development of accounting standards. The SEC indicates to the FASB the accounting topics it believes should be addressed.

American Accounting Association (AAA)

Consisting largely of accounting educators, the *American Accounting Association (AAA)* has sought to encourage research and study at a theoretical level into the concepts, standards, and principles of accounting. It publishes statements on such matters and supports the research efforts of individuals. Statements of the AAA are not required to be followed in the preparation of financial statements. In recent years, its quarterly magazine, the *Accounting Review,* has carried many articles reporting on research into the uses of accounting information.

CONCLUDING NOTE

You may decide to pursue a career in accounting. There are many accounting positions which offer stimulating challenges and attractive financial rewards. Even if you decide not to pursue an accounting career, you will find your knowledge of accounting useful in whatever career you do decide to follow. You are encouraged to put forth the necessary time and effort to gain a strong foundation in this important subject.

Chapter 1

Accounting and its use in business decisions

CHAPTER GOALS

After study of this chapter, you should be able to:

1. Identify the forms of business organization and describe their characteristics.
2. Describe the nature of the different types of businesses including service, merchandising, and manufacturing companies.
3. Analyze business transactions and determine their effects on items in the financial statements.
4. Prepare basic financial statements, such as a balance sheet and income statement, for a business firm.
5. Define and use correctly the new terms in the glossary.

In our free enterprise society, there are three basic forms of business organizations. These forms are the *single proprietorship, partnership,* and *corporation.* The proprietorship form is the simplest and most common form of business organization. The corporation is the form of organization used for the largest, most complex businesses in the United States.

Single proprietorship. A *single proprietorship*[1] *is a business owned by an individual and often managed by that same individual.* Many small service-type businesses such as physicians, lawyers, barbers, electricians, and small retail establishments are single proprietorships. There are no legal formalities in organizing such a business, and usually only a limited investment is required to begin operations. In a single proprietorship, the owner is solely responsible for all debts of the business. Financial activities of the business, such as the receipt of fees from selling services to the public, are kept separate from personal financial activities of the owner. An example of a personal financial activity is the owner making a payment on an auto used exclusively for nonbusiness purposes. The business is considered an entity separate from the owner. An *entity* is a unit that is considered to have an existence separate from its owner(s), creditors, employees, and other interested parties and for which an accounting is undertaken. The business entity concept applies to all three forms of business organizations—single proprietorship, partnership, and corporation.

Partnership. A *partnership is a business owned by two or more persons associated as partners.* It is often managed by those same persons. The partnership is created by a partnership agreement setting forth the terms of the partnership. This agreement is the only legal formality in organizing a partnership. Included in the agreement will be such things as the initial investment of each partner, the duties of each partner, the means of dividing profits or losses between the partners each year, and the settlement to be made upon the death or withdrawal of a partner. Each partner may be held liable for all the debts of the partnership and for the actions of each partner within the scope of the business.

Corporation. A *corporation is a business that may be owned by a few persons or by thousands of persons and is incorporated under the laws of one of the 50 states.* A corporation is managed by officers of the corporation. The officers are often individuals other than the owners.

Accounting is necessary for all three forms of business organizations, and generally accepted accounting principles (GAAP) are applicable to each. In the early chapters of this text, the single proprietorship will be used, since it most easily illustrates basic accounting principles.

---

[1] When undertaking the initial study of any discipline, new terms are encountered. To aid in becoming familiar with the language of accounting, these terms (at their first occurrence in each chapter) are set in boldface italic type and are also listed and defined at the end of the chapter.

Types of businesses

The three basic types of businesses are service, merchandising, and manufacturing companies. Service companies perform services such as accounting, legal, cleaning, or repairs for a fee. Merchandising companies purchase goods that are ready for sale and sell them to customers. Merchandising companies are also known as wholesalers and retailers and include companies such as auto dealerships, clothing stores, and supermarkets. Manufacturing companies buy materials, convert them into products, and sell the products to other manufacturing companies or to final customers. Examples of manufacturing companies are steel mills, auto manufacturers, and clothing manufacturers.

The first several chapters of this text will deal only with service companies. Then, accounting for a merchandising company is illustrated. Manufacturing companies are discussed in the last part of the text, since these businesses are more complex and therefore require more detailed accounting records.

FINANCIAL STATEMENTS OF BUSINESS ENTERPRISES

Although a modern business firm has many objectives or goals, the two primary objectives of every business firm are *profitability* and *solvency*. *Profitability* is the ability to generate earnings. *Solvency* is the ability to pay debts as they become due. Unless a firm can produce satisfactory earnings and pay its debts as they become due, any other objectives a firm may have will never be realized simply because the firm will not survive. The financial statements that reflect a firm's solvency (the balance sheet) and its profitability (the income statement) are illustrated and discussed below.

The balance sheet

The *balance sheet,* sometimes called the statement of financial position, presents a listing of (including dollar amounts) the firm's assets, liabilities, and owner's equity *as of a specific moment in time.* The balance sheet is like a still photograph; it only captures reality for a particular point in time. Should any event happen which affects the business, the balance sheet would change.

Assets are things of value that are owned by the business. They are also known as the *resources* of the business. Assets have value because of the uses to which they can be put or the things that can be acquired by exchanging them for something else. Examples of assets include money, machines, and buildings.

Liabilities are the debts owed by a firm. Typically, they must be paid by certain dates. Liabilities typically are incurred through purchasing something on credit and promising to pay for it later, or by borrowing. Examples of liabilities are charge account balances and notes payable.

Owner's equity is the proprietor's (owner's) interest in the business. Owner's equity is equal to assets minus liabilities. Owner's equity consists of the

Illustration 1.1:   Balance sheet

BRENT'S POOL SERVICE COMPANY
Balance Sheet
December 31, 1984

Assets		Liabilities and Owner's Equity*		
Cash	$15,500	Liabilities:		
Accounts receivable	700	Accounts payable ...	$ 600	
Truck	6,000	Loan payable	6,000	
Cleaning equipment	14,000	Total liabilities ..		$ 6,600
Office equipment	2,500			
		Owner's equity:		
		William Brent, capital		32,100
		Total liabilities and		
Total assets	$38,700	owner's equity		$38,700

* The liabilities and owner's equity portion of the balance sheet may be shown directly beneath the assets instead of to the right of them as shown in the illustration. When liabilities and owner's equity are placed under the assets, it is called the *vertical format*. The vertical format is as acceptable as the *horizontal format* used above.

owner's investment in the business plus profits made from the business that were not withdrawn from the business.

A brief example of the three types of balance sheet items may be helpful. Assume that Kathy Rice purchased an automobile which cost $8,000 for her business. She made a down payment of $2,500 and borrowed the rest. Kathy has an asset worth $8,000, a liability of $5,500, and owner's equity of $2,500. Another way of stating this is: what you own minus what you owe is what you are worth.

Illustration 1.1 shows the balance sheet of Brent's Pool Service Company on December 31, 1984. All financial statements have headings which include (1) the name of the organization, (2) the title of the statement, and (3) the date of or period covered by the statement. The assets of Brent's Pool Service amount to $38,700. These consist of cash, *accounts receivable* (amounts due from customers for services already provided), and various types of equipment. Brent's liabilities consist of *accounts payable* (amounts owed to suppliers for goods or services purchased on credit) and a *loan payable* (an amount owed to someone who loaned the firm money). Brent's owner's equity is $32,100; this is shown on the balance sheet or could be calculated as the difference between assets of $38,700 and liabilities of $6,600. Although it is not specified on the statement, there are two items which constitute owner's equity: investment and cumulative net income earned and retained by the business. If Brent's investment is assumed to be $30,000, income earned and retained by the business is $2,100.

The income statement

The purpose of the *income statement* is to report the profitability of a business organization *for a stated period of time.* It is often called an earnings

Illustration 1.2: Income statement

BRENT'S POOL SERVICE COMPANY
Income Statement
For the Month Ended December 31, 1984

Service revenues	. . . .		$5,700
Expenses:			
Wages	. . . .	$2,600	
Rent	. . . .	400	
Gas and oil	. . . .	600	
Total expenses	. . . .		3,600
Net income	. . . .		$2,100

statement. In accounting, profitability is measured in a given period by comparing the revenues generated with the expenses incurred to produce those revenues. *Revenues are defined as the inflow of assets resulting from the sale of products or the rendering of services to customers. Expenses are the costs incurred to produce revenues.* Expenses are measured by the assets surrendered or consumed in serving customers. If revenues exceed expenses, *net income* results. Net income is often referred to as the earnings of the company. If expenses exceed revenues, the business is said to be operating at a *net loss*.

Illustration 1.2 contains the income statement of Brent's Pool Service for the month of December 1984. Notice the difference in the headings between the balance sheet and income statement due to the fact that a balance sheet is for a specific point in time and an income statement is for a specified period of time. The income statement for Brent's shows revenues generated by serving customers for December totaled $5,700. Expenses for the month amounted to $3,600. As a result of these business activities, Brent's net income for the month of December was $2,100. This amount is determined by subtracting expenses of $3,600 from revenues of $5,700 to arrive at net income.

THE FINANCIAL ACCOUNTING PROCESS

The remainder of the chapter is concerned with the process of accumulating the data to include in financial statements.

The accounting equation

The balance sheet is made up of three essential elements—assets, liabilities, and owner's equity. The relationship of these three elements make up what is known as the accounting equation. Understanding the accounting equation is essential to understanding accounting. The basic *accounting equation* is:

$$\text{Assets} = \text{Liabilities} + \text{Owner's Equity}$$

Substituting the amounts from Illustration 1.1 for these terms results in:

$$\begin{array}{ccccc} \text{A} & = & \text{L} & + & \text{OE} \\ \$38,700 & = & \$6,600 & + & \$32,100 \end{array}$$

This equation must *always* be in balance. The left-hand side of the equation shows the assets, which are things of value owned by the business. The right-hand side of the equation shows the *equities,* made up of liabilities plus owner's equity. Liabilities could be viewed as creditor's equity. Equities are interests in, or claims upon, assets. For instance, in Brent's Pool Service Company there are $38,700 of assets. Creditors have a claim to, or interest in, those assets of $6,600, the amount of the liabilities. The owner's interest is $32,100, the amount of owner's equity. The right side of the equation above is also looked upon in another manner—namely, it shows who provided the funds to acquire the existing assets. Creditors provided $6,600 of the funds and the owner provided $32,100. The funds to acquire the assets are provided by either creditors or owners.

As a business engages in economic activity, the dollar amounts and the *composition* of its assets, liabilities, and owner's equity *change. But the equality of the basic equation always holds.*

Transaction analysis

Our society is characterized by *exchange.* That is, the bulk of the goods and services produced are exchanged rather than consumed by their producers. From this, it follows that economic activity can be observed from the exchanges that take place. In accounting, these exchanges of goods and services are called *transactions.* Transactions provide much of the raw data entered in an accounting process. There are two reasons for this. First, an exchange is an observable event providing evidence of business activity. Second, an exchange takes place at an agreed-upon price, and this price provides an *objective* measure of the economic activity that has occurred. These two factors—evidence and measurement—allow the recording of a transaction.

Underlying assumptions. Some underlying assumptions or concepts are used by the accountant in recording business transactions. For instance, data gathered in an accounting system are assumed to relate to a *specific business unit* or entity. This *entity,* as noted earlier, is assumed to have an existence separate from its owners, creditors, employees, and other interested parties.

Also, every transaction has a two-sided or dual effect upon each party involved. This two-sided effect is referred to as *duality.* Consequently, if information is to be complete, both sides or effects of every transaction must be included in the accounting system.

Economic activity is initially recorded and reported in terms of a *common*

unit of measure—in the United States, this is the dollar. This form of measurement is referred to as ***money measurement.*** Most of the amounts entered in
an accounting system are the objective prices determined in the exchange
process. The result is that most assets are recorded and reported at their
acquisition cost. *Cost* is the sacrifice made or the resources given up to acquire
some desired thing such as an asset.

Unless strong evidence exists to the contrary, the accountant assumes
that the entity will *continue* operations into the indefinite future; this is referred
to as the ***continuity*** or ***going-concern*** assumption.

Specific transactions. The analysis of transactions and their effects
upon the basic accounting equation will now be illustrated. The activities of
Brent's Pool Service Company that occurred in November 1984 are presented
below.

1a. Owner invested cash. Assume that Brent's Pool Service Company
was formed on November 1, 1984. The owner invested $30,000 cash in the
business. The transaction increased assets (cash) of the company by $30,000
and increased owner's equity by $30,000. Consequently, the transaction yields
a basic accounting equation containing the following:

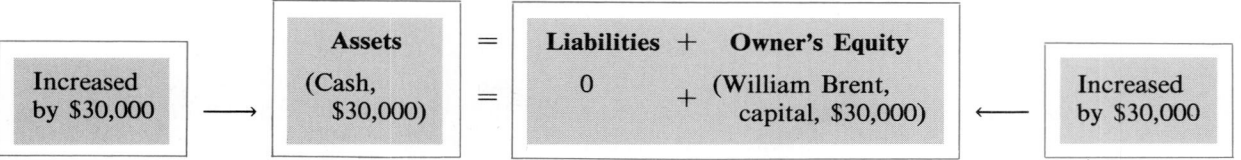

2a. Borrowed money. The company borrowed $6,000 from Mrs.
Brent's father. After including the effects of the second transaction, the basic
equation is:

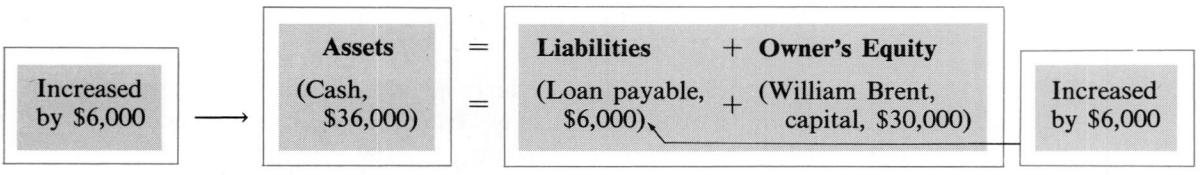

3a. Purchased equipment for cash. Brent's Pool Service Company
spent $6,000 for a truck, $14,000 for cleaning equipment, and $1,500 for
some office equipment. *This transaction does not change the totals in the basic
equation; it merely changes the composition of the assets.* Cash was decreased
and other types of assets were increased. The equation is now as follows:

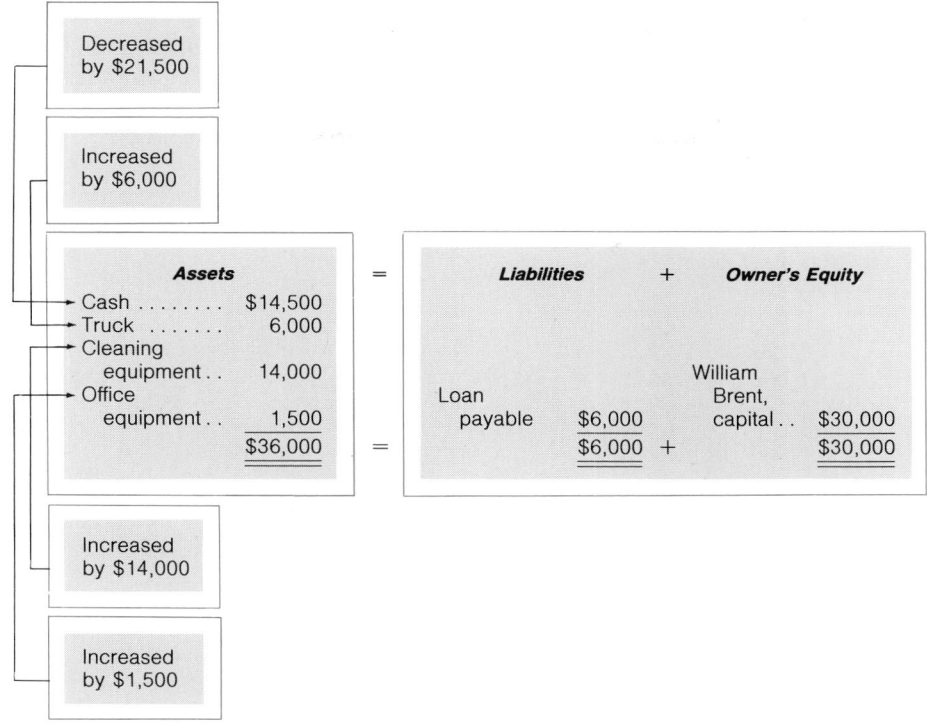

4a. Purchased equipment on account (for credit). Brent's Pool Service Company purchased $1,000 of office equipment on account, agreeing to pay within 10 days after receiving a bill. To purchase an item "on account" means to buy it on credit. This transaction increases liabilities in the form of accounts payable by $1,000. Accounts payable are amounts owed to creditors for items purchased from them. The items making up the totals in the accounting equation now appear as follows:

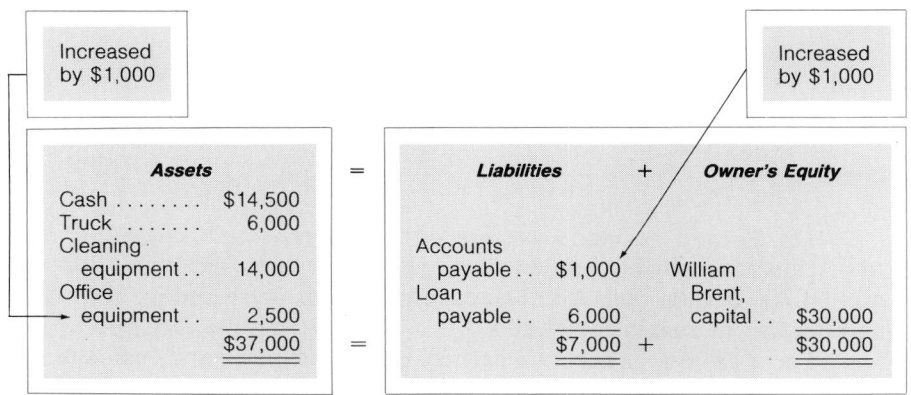

5a. **Paid an account payable.** Next, the company paid the $1,000 balance due on the purchase of the office equipment (transaction 4*a*). This reduced cash by $1,000 and reduced the debt owed to the equipment supplier by $1,000. Thus, assets and liabilities are both reduced by $1,000. After this transaction, the totals in the accounting equation are as follows:

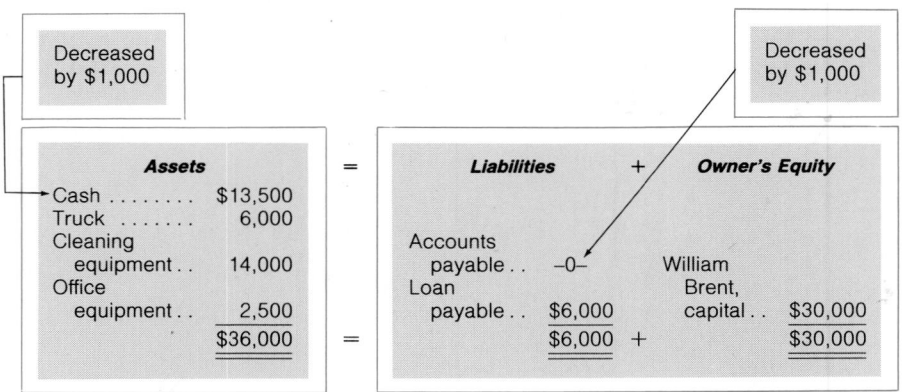

A summary of transactions prepared for the month of November appears in Illustration 1.3 in accounting equation form. You can see how the totals at the bottom of Illustration 1.3 tie into the balance sheet shown in Illustration 1.4. The balance sheet in Illustration 1.4 is dated November 30, 1984. These totals become the beginning totals for the month of December 1984.

Revenue and expense transactions

Thus far all transactions have consisted of exchanges or acquisitions of assets either by borrowing or by owner investment. This procedure was used so that you could focus on the accounting equation as it relates to the balance sheet. But a business is not formed merely to hold present assets. Rather, *a business seeks to use its assets to generate greater amounts of assets.* A business increases its assets by providing goods or services to customers. The expectation is that the value of the assets received from customers will exceed the cost of the assets consumed in serving them. The assets received are usually in the form of cash or accounts receivable.

Assume that the company engaged in the following transactions in December 1984.

1b. **Earned service revenue and received cash.** Assume that as its first transaction in December, cleaning services are performed for customers and $4,800 cash is received. The cash balance is increased by $4,800. Owner's capital also increases by $4,800.

The $4,800 is a revenue earned by the business and, as such, increases owner's equity because the owner is the one to prosper as a result of the

Illustration 1.3: Summary of transactions

BRENT'S POOL SERVICE COMPANY
Summary of Transactions
Month of November 1984

Trans-action	Explanation	Assets					=	Liabilities		+	Owner's Equity
		Cash	Accounts receivable	Truck	Cleaning equipment	Office equipment		Accounts payable	Loan payable		William Brent, capital
	Beginning balances	$ –0–	$–0–	$ –0–	$ –0–	$ –0–	=	$ –0–	$ –0–		$ –0–
1a	Owner invested cash	+ 30,000									+30,000
		$30,000					=				$30,000
2a	Borrowed money .	+6,000							+6,000		
		$36,000					=		$6,000	+	$30,000
3a	Purchased equipment for cash ..	−21,500		+6,000	+ 14,000	+ 1,500					
		$14,500		$6,000	$14,000	$1,500	=		$6,000	+	$30,000
4a	Purchased equipment on account					+ 1,000		+ 1,000			
		$14,500		$6,000	$14,000	$2,500	=	$1,000	$6,000	+	$30,000
5a	Paid on account payable	− 1,000						− 1,000			
	End of month balances	$13,500		$6,000	$14,000	$2,500	=	$ –0–	$6,000	+	$30,000

Illustration 1.4: Balance sheet

BRENT'S POOL SERVICE COMPANY
Balance Sheet
November 30, 1984

Assets		Liabilities and Owner's Equity	
Cash	$13,500	Liabilities:	
Truck	6,000	Loan payable $6,000	
Cleaning equipment	14,000	Total liabilities ...	$ 6,000
Office equipment	2,500	Owner's equity:	
		William Brent, capital ..	30,000
		Total liabilities and owner's	
Total assets	$36,000	equity	$36,000

business earning profits. The owner, in the long run, is the one who will receive the rewards if the business is profitable or will sustain the losses if the business fails.

The effects of this transaction upon the financial status of Brent's Pool Service Company yield the following amounts in the basic equation:

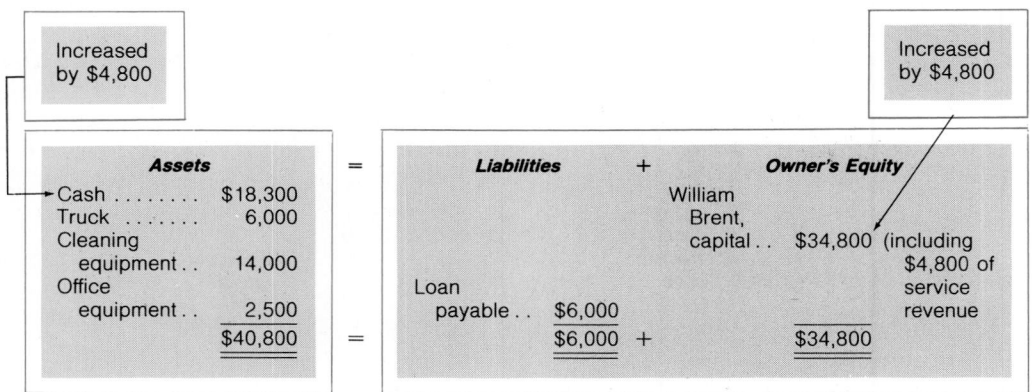

The expectation is that the amount of revenues will exceed the amount of expenses and will yield net income. If net income is not withdrawn by the owner, it becomes *an addition* to the owner's capital balance. Later chapters will show that because of complexities in handling large numbers of transactions, revenues will be shown as affecting the owner's capital only at the end of an accounting period. The procedure shown above is a shortcut used to explain why the accounting equation remains in balance.

2b. **Earned service revenue on account (for credit).** The company performs services for customers who agree to pay $900 at a later date. To earn revenue "on account" means the company granted credit rather than requiring the customer to pay cash immediately. The transaction consists of an exchange of services for a promise by the customer to pay later. This transaction is similar to the preceding transaction in that owner's equity is increased because revenues have been *earned*. But it differs because although cash has not been received, another asset has been. This asset, an account receivable, is the legal right to collect from the customer in the future. The important point is that accounting recognizes such claims as *assets* and records them. The accounting equation, including this $900 item, is as follows:

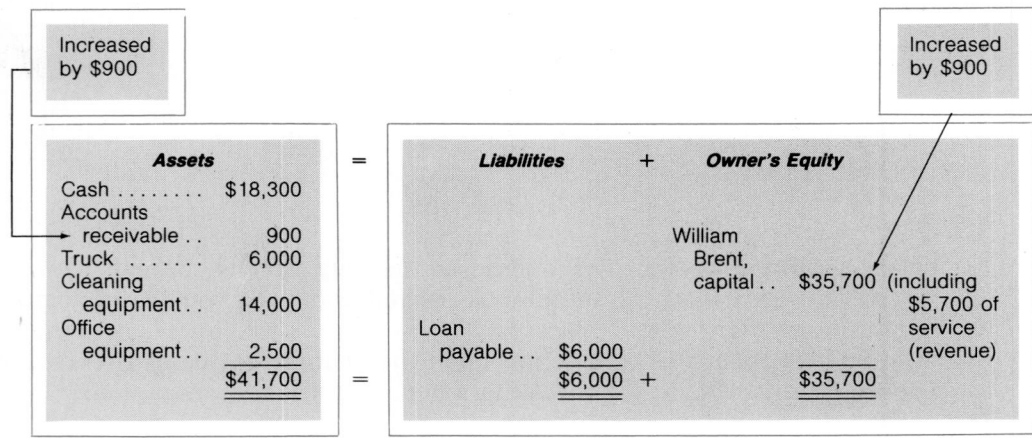

3b. Collected cash on accounts receivable. Assume that $200 is collected from customers "on account." The transaction consists of the giving up of claims upon customers in exchange for cash. The effects of the transaction are to increase cash by $200 and to decrease accounts receivable by $200. *Note that this transaction consists solely of a change in the composition of the assets,* not of an increase in assets resulting from the generation of revenue. The revenue was recorded when the services were rendered; that is, when it was earned.

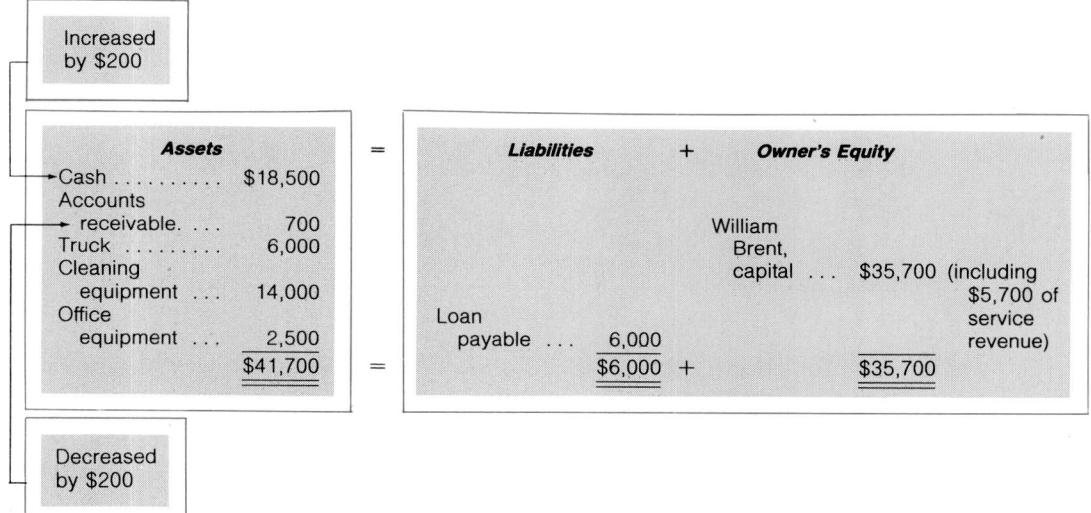

4b. Paid wages. The payment of $2,600 of wages consists of an exchange of cash for employee services. Typically, employee services have been received by the time payment is made. Thus, the accountant treats the transaction as a decrease in an asset (cash) and a decrease in owner's equity because an expense has been incurred. Expense transactions will reduce net income. Since net income becomes a part of the owner's capital balance, expense transactions reduce the owner's capital.

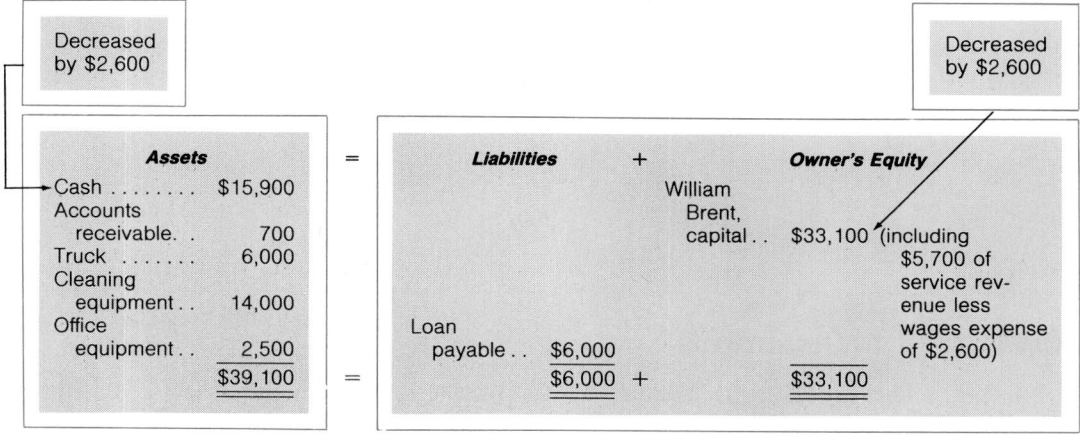

5*b*. **Paid rent.**   In December, the company paid $400 cash for office space rent. This transaction causes a decrease in cash of $400 and a decrease in the owner's equity of $400 because of the incurrence of rent expense.

Transaction 5*b* has the following effect on the amounts in the accounting equation:

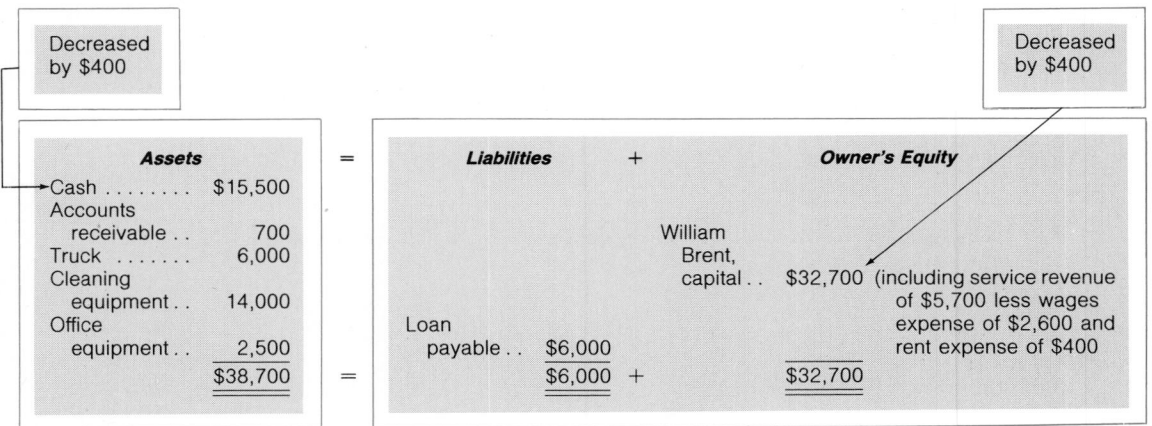

Paying cash for other expenses would be recorded in the same way as transactions 4*b* and 5*b* were recorded.

6*b*. **Received bill for gas and oil used.**   At the end of the month, the company received a bill for gasoline, oil, and other supplies consumed during the month in the amount of $600. This transaction involves an increase in a liability, accounts payable, and a decrease in owner's equity because of the incurrence of an expense. The accounting equation of Brent's Pool Service Company now reads:

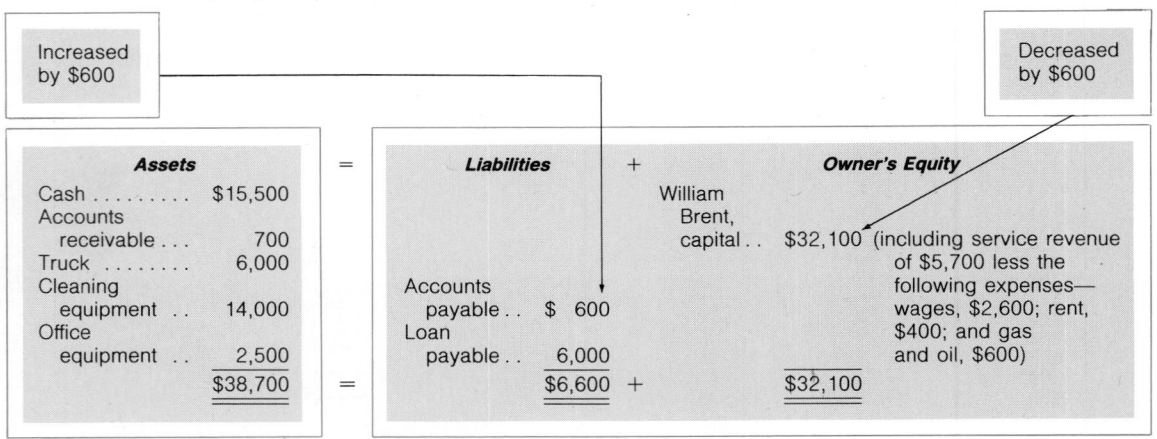

SUMMARY OF TRANSACTIONS

The effects of all the preceding transactions upon the assets, liabilities, and owner's equity of Brent's Pool Service Company in its second month of

Illustration 1.5:   Summary of transactions

BRENT'S POOL SERVICE COMPANY
Summary of Transactions
Month of December 1984

		Assets					=	Liabilities	+	Owner's Equity
Trans-action	Explanation	Cash	Accounts receiv-able	Truck	Cleaning equip-ment	Office equip-ment	=	Accounts payable	Loan payable	William Brent, capital
	Beginning balances (Illustration 1.3) ..	$13,500	$-0-	$6,000	$14,000	$2,500	=	$-0-	$6,000 +	$30,000
1b.	Earned service revenue and received cash ...	+4,800								+4,800 (service revenue)
		$18,300		$6,000	$14,000	$2,500	=		$6,000 +	$34,800
2b.	Earned service revenue on account		+900							+900 (service revenue)
		$18,300	$900	$6,000	$14,000	$2,500	=		$6,000 +	$35,700
3b.	Collected cash on account	+200	−200							
		$18,500	$700	$6,000	$14,000	$2,500	=		$6,000 +	$35,700
4b.	Paid wages	−2,600								−2,600 (wages expense)
		$15,900	$700	$6,000	$14,000	$2,500	=		$6,000 +	$33,100
5b.	Paid rent	−400								−400 (rent expense)
		$15,500	$700	$6,000	$14,000	$2,500	=		$6,000 +	$32,700
6b.	Received bill for gas and oil used							+600		−600 (gas and oil expense)
	End of month balances	$15,500	$700	$6,000	$14,000	$2,500	=	$600	$6,000 +	$32,100
			$38,700					$6,600		$32,100

Illustration 1.6:   Balance sheet

BRENT'S POOL SERVICE COMPANY
Balance Sheet
December 31, 1984

Assets		Liabilities and Owner's Equity	
Cash	$15,500	Liabilities:	
Accounts receivable	700	Accounts payable	$ 600
Truck	6,000	Loan payable	6,000
Cleaning equipment	14,000	Total liabilities	$ 6,600
Office equipment	2,500	Owner's equity:	
		William Brent, capital ..	32,100
		Total liabilities and owner's	
Total assets	$38,700	equity.......	$38,700

Illustration 1.7:   Income statement

BRENT'S POOL SERVICE COMPANY
Income Statement
For the Month Ended December 31, 1984

Service revenue		$5,700
Expenses:		
Wages	$2,600	
Rent	400	
Gas and Oil	600	
Total expenses		3,600
Net income		$2,100

operations are summarized in Illustration 1.5. The beginning balances are those shown as ending balances in Illustration 1.3. The summary shows subtotals after each transaction; these subtotals are optional and may be omitted. Notice how the accounting equation remains in balance and assets do equal liabilities plus owner's equity.

The totals shown at the bottom of Illustration 1.5 are the amounts reported in the balance sheet in Illustration 1.6. Illustration 1.7 shows the revenue and expense items listed in the owner's equity column of the transaction summary. Brent's capital account on the balance sheet consists of his $30,000 investment plus the $2,100 earned during the month of December.

Withdrawals by owner

A *withdrawal* is cash or other assets taken out of the business by the owner for personal use. Withdrawals differ from expenses due to the entity concept; if the business is the entity for which the accounting records are being maintained, personal bills should not be included in determining the entity's income for a period. An example of a withdrawal would be if William Brent took $50 from the Pool Service cash register to pay his home utility bill. Mr. Brent has every right to the money, but the bill does not relate to the business. This transaction would be recorded as a decrease in cash and a decrease in owner's equity or capital. It would be included in the transaction summary as a reduction in the owner's capital account balance, but it would not appear on the income statement of the business. A withdrawal is considered a distribution of earnings to the owner.

NEW TERMS INTRODUCED IN CHAPTER 1

Accounting equation
Assets = Liabilities + Owner's Equity.

Accounts payable
Amounts owed to suppliers for goods or services purchased on credit.

Accounts receivable
Amounts due from customers for services already provided.

Assets
Things of value that are owned by the business. Examples include money, machines, and buildings. They possess service potential or utility to their owner that can be measured and expressed in money terms.

Balance sheet
Also called a statement of financial position. Presents a listing of (including dollar amounts) the firm's assets, liabilities, and owner's equity as of a specific moment in time.

Continuity (going concern)
The assumption by the accountant that, unless specific evidence exists to the contrary, a business firm will continue to operate into the indefinite future.

Corporation
A business that may be owned by a few persons or by thousands of persons and is incorporated under the laws of one of the 50 states.

Cost
The sacrifice made or the resources given up to acquire some desired thing such as an asset.

Duality
The assumption by the accountant that every transaction has a dual or two-sided effect upon the party or parties engaging in it.

Entity
A unit that is deemed to have an existence separate and apart from its owner(s), creditors, employees, and other interested parties and for which an accounting is undertaken.

Equities
Broadly speaking, all claims to or interest in assets (liabilities and owner's equity).

Expenses
The costs incurred to produce revenues.

Going concern
See continuity.

Income statement
Reports the profitability of a business organization for a stated period of time. Also called an earnings statement.

Liabilities
Debts owed by a firm.

Loan payable
An amount owed to someone who loaned the firm money.

Money measurement
Recording and reporting economic activity in terms of a common monetary unit of measure, such as the dollar.

Net income
The amount by which the revenues of a period exceed the expenses of the same period.

Net loss
The amount by which the expenses of a period exceed the revenues of the same period.

Owner's equity
The proprietor's interest in the business. It is equal to assets minus liabilities.

Partnership
A business owned by two or more persons associated as partners.

Profitability
The ability to generate earnings.

Revenues
The inflow of assets resulting from the sale of products or the rendering of services to customers.

Single proprietorship
A business owned by an individual and often managed by that same individual.

Solvency
The ability to pay debts as they become due.

Transactions
Exchanges of goods and services. Transactions affect the assets, liabilities, owner's equity, revenues, or expenses of an entity.

Withdrawal
Cash or other assets taken out of the business by the owner for personal use.

DEMONSTRATION PROBLEM

On June 1, 1984, Barbara Macon formed the Huntcliff Riding Stable. The following transactions occurred during June:

Transactions:

June 1 The owner invested $10,000 cash in the business.
 4 A horse stable and riding equipment were rented (and paid for) for the month at a cost of $1,200.
 8 Horse feed for the month was purchased on credit, $800.
 20 Miscellaneous expenses of $600 for June were paid.
 24 The owner withdrew $500 cash.
 29 Land was purchased for use in the business by borrowing $40,000 from a relative. The loan is due to be repaid in five years.
 30 Salaries of $700 for the month were paid.
 30 Riding and lesson fees were billed to customers in the amount of $2,400. (They are due on July 10.)
 30 Fees of $3,000 for the month were charged to those owning horses who were boarding their horses at the stable. (This amount is due on July 10.)

Required:

a. Prepare a summary of the above transactions (Illustration 1.5). Use columns headed Cash, Accounts Receivable, Land, Accounts Payable, Loan Payable, and Barbara Macon, Capital. Determine balances after each transaction to show that the basic equation is in balance.

b. Prepare an income statement for the month of June 1984.

c. Prepare a balance sheet as of June 30, 1984.

Solution to demonstration problem

a.

HUNTCLIFF RIDING STABLE
Summary of Transactions
Month of June 1984

			Assets		=	Liabilities		+	Owner's Equity
Date	Explanation	Cash	Accounts receivable	Land		Accounts payable	Loan payable		Barbara Macon, Capital
June 1	Owner investment	$10,000			=				$10,000
4	Rent expense	−1,200							−1,200
		$ 8,800			=				$ 8,800
8	Feed expense					$+800			−800
		$ 8,800			=	$ 800		+	$ 8,000
20	Miscellaneous expenses	−600							−600
		$ 8,200			=	$ 800		+	$ 7,400
24	Owner withdrawal	−500							−500
		$ 7,700			=	$ 800		+	$ 6,900
29	Purchased land by borrowing			$+40,000			$+40,000		
		$ 7,700		$ 40,000	=	$ 800	$ 40,000	+	$ 6,900
30	Salaries paid	−700							−700
		$ 7,000		$ 40,000	=	$ 800	$ 40,000	+	$ 6,200
30	Riding and lesson fees billed		$+2,400						+2,400
		$ 7,000	$ 2,400	$ 40,000	=	$ 800	$ 40,000	+	$ 8,600
30	Boarding fees		+3,000						+3,000
	Month-end balances	$ 7,000	$ 5,400	$ 40,000	=	$ 800	$ 40,000	+	$11,600

b.

HUNTCLIFF RIDING STABLE
Income Statement
For the Month Ended June 30, 1984

Revenues:
Horse boarding fees $3,000
Riding and lesson fees 2,400
    Total revenues $5,400
Expenses:
Rent.................................. $1,200
Feed 800
Salaries 700
Miscellaneous 600
    Total expenses 3,300
Net income $2,100

c.

HUNTCLIFF RIDING STABLE
Balance Sheet
June 30, 1984

Assets

Cash	$ 7,000
Accounts receivable	5,400
Land	40,000
Total assets	$52,400

Liabilities and Owner's Equity

Liabilities:

Accounts payable	$ 800
Loan payable	40,000
Total liabilities	$40,800

Owner's equity:

Barbara Macon, capital	11,600
Total liabilities and owner's equity	$52,400

QUESTIONS

1. Identify and briefly describe the three forms of organization for a business entity.

2. Identify and briefly describe the three types of businesses.

3. What is a balance sheet? This statement generally seeks to provide information relative to what aspect of a business?

4. Define asset, liability, and owner's equity.

5. How do liabilities and owner's equity differ? In what respects are they similar?

6. What is an income statement? This statement generally provides information on what aspect of a business?

7. What are revenues?

8. Define expenses. How are expenses measured?

9. What is the accounting equation? Why must it always balance?

10. What is the accounting entity assumption? Why is it needed?

11. What is the duality assumption of accounting? Why is it needed?

12. What is a transaction? What use does the accountant make of transactions? Why?

EXERCISES

E–1. Collins Company, engaged in a service business, completed the following selected transactions during the month of July 1984:

  a. Purchased office equipment on account.
  b. Paid an account payable.
  c. Earned service revenue on account.
  d. Borrowed money from a relative to use in the business.
  e. Paid wages for month to employees.
  f. Received cash on account from charge customers.

    g. Received gas and oil bill for month.
    h. Purchased truck for cash.

Using a tabular form similar to Illustration 1.5 of the chapter, indicate the effect of each transaction on the equation using (+) for increase and (−) for decrease. No dollar amounts are needed and you need not fill in the Explanation column.

E–2.   Indicate the immediate amount of change (if any) in the owner's equity balance based on each of the following transactions:

    a. The owner invested $15,000 cash in the business.
    b. Land costing $2,500 was purchased by paying cash.
    c. The company performed services for customers who agreed to pay $4,000 in one month.
    d. Paid wages for the month, $3,600.
    e. Paid $1,250 on an account payable.

E–3.   Give examples of transactions that would have the following effects upon the elements in a firm's accounting system:

    a. Increase cash; decrease some other asset.
    b. Decrease cash; increase some other asset.
    c. Increase an asset; increase a liability.
    d. Increase an expense; decrease an asset.
    e. Increase an asset other than cash; increase revenue.
    f. Decrease an asset; decrease a liability.

E–4.   Assume that owner's capital increased because of net income by $32,000 from June 30, 1984, to June 30, 1985. Assume expenses for the year were $80,000. Compute the revenue for the year.

E–5.   On December 31, 1984, P Company had assets of $460,000, liabilities of $260,000, and owner's equity of $200,000. During 1985, it earned revenues of $130,000 and incurred expenses of $102,000. Compute the owner's equity amount as of December 31, 1985.

E–6.   For each of the following transactions present an analysis showing clearly its two sides or dual nature:

    a. Purchased land for cash, $4,000.
    b. Purchased a truck for $20,000; payment to be made next month.
    c. Paid $400 cash for the current month's utilities.
    d. Paid for the truck purchased in (*b*).

E–7.   Which of the following transactions result in an increase in an expense? Why?
    a. Cash of $30,000 was paid to employees for services received during the month. yes
    b. Cash of $1,200 was paid to a supplier for some advertising supplies used during the month. -yes
    c. Paid $10,000 on a loan payable. no is intrest yes
    d. Paid $150 cash in payment of an account payable. no
    e. The owner withdrew $500 cash. no

E–8.   At the start of a year, a company had liabilities of $36,000 and owner's equity of $120,000. Net income for the year was $50,000, and $15,000 cash was withdrawn by the owner. Compute owner's equity at the end of the year and total assets at the beginning of the year.

E–9. From the following selected data for the York Company compute net income for *expenses and revenues only* 1984:

Revenue from services rendered on account ..	$ 75,000
Revenue from services rendered for cash	15,000
Cash collected from customers on account . . .	42,000
Owner's equity, January 1, 1984	81,000
Expenses incurred on account	50,000
Expenses incurred for cash	20,000
Cash withdrawn by owner	6,000
Additional cash investment by owner	10,000
Owner's equity, December 31, 1984	105,000

PROBLEMS, SERIES A

P1–1–A. The Brent Lawson Company engaged in the following transactions in January 1984, its first month of operations:

Transactions:

1. The owner, Brent Lawson, invested cash of $50,000 in the business.
2. The owner borrowed $20,000 from his brother-in-law to use in the business.
3. The following assets were purchased for cash: truck, $8,000; cleaning equipment, $4,000; and office equipment, $5,000.
4. Office equipment was purchased on account, $6,000.
5. The account payable in (4) was paid, $6,000.

Required:

a. Prepare a summary of transactions using a format similar to Illustration 1.3 in the chapter. Include money columns for Cash, Truck, Cleaning Equipment, Office Equipment, Accounts Payable, Loan Payable, and Brent Lawson, Capital. Determine new balances after each transaction.

b. Prepare a balance sheet as of the end of January.

P1–2–A. The Sam Young Company completed the following transactions in July 1984:

Transactions:

1. The company was organized and received $20,000 cash investment from the owner.
2. The company bought equipment for cash at a cost of $15,300.
3. The company performed services for customers who agreed to pay $2,000 in one week.
4. The company received the $2,000 from transaction (3).
5. Equipment which cost $1,000 was acquired today; payment was postponed until August 28.
6. $600 was paid on the liability incurred in transaction (5).
7. Employee wages for the month were paid, $1,200.

Required:

a. Prepare a summary of transactions (Illustration 1.5) for the company for the above transactions. Use money columns headed Cash, Accounts Receivable, Equipment, Accounts Payable, and Sam Young, Capital. Determine balances after each transaction.

b. Prepare an income statement for July 1984.

c. Prepare a balance sheet as of July 31, 1984.

P1–3–A.   The following is a list of balances for the Winston Company. The revenues and expenses are for the month of December 1984. The asset and liability balances are as of December 31, 1984. Edward Winston's equity balance on December 1, 1984, was $16,225.

Office equipment	$ 3,000	Cash	10,950
Wages expense	2,900	Gas and oil expense ...	425
Accounts payable	850	Loan payable	3,100
Service revenue	5,800	Accounts receivable ...	2,400
Truck	5,900	Rent expense	400

Required:

  a.   Prepare an income statement for the month ended December 31, 1984.

  b.   Prepare a balance sheet as of December 31, 1984. You will need to calculate the December 31, 1984, balance in the owner's capital account.

P1–4–A.   The transactions shown below are for the Joseph Cantrell Company for the month of June 1984. This was the first month of operation of the business.

Transactions:

1. Owner invested cash, $60,000.
2. Borrowed $10,000 from a relative to use in the business.
3. Purchased office equipment for cash, $12,000.
4. Earned service revenue and received cash, $8,000.
5. Paid wages, $4,000.
6. Paid rent, $1,000.
7. Received bill for gas and oil used, $700.
8. Made a $5,000 payment on loan payable.

Required:

  a.   Prepare a summary of transactions using a format similar to Illustration 1.5 in the chapter. Determine new balances after each transaction.

  b.   Prepare an income statement for June 1984.

  c.   Prepare a balance sheet as of June 30, 1984.

P1–5–A.   The Sally Meadows Company completed the following transactions in June 1984:

Transactions:

June	1	The company was organized and received $80,000 cash investment from the owner.
	4	The company paid $32,000 cash for land.
	7	The owner of the company borrowed $20,000 cash from a relative to use in the business.
	9	Cash received for services performed to date was $3,000.
	12	Rent for the month was paid in cash, $2,000.
	18	Services performed for customers who agree to pay within a month amounted to $3,600.
	30	Wages for the month were paid, $2,550.

Required:

  a.   Prepare a summary of transactions (Illustration 1.5). Determine balances after each transaction. Include money columns for Cash, Accounts Receivable, Land, Loan Payable, and Sally Meadows, Capital.

  b.   Prepare an income statement for June 1984.

  c.   Prepare a balance sheet as of June 30, 1984.

P1–6–A.   The following selected transactions are data for the Harvey Mailer Company, a parking ramp operator, for the month of May 1984:

Transactions:

May 1 Paid May rent on the parking structure, $10,000.
8 Cash was received for parking services, $24,500.
17 Received cash from additional investment by owner, $5,000.
19 Paid advertising expenses for May, $800.
30 Purchased motorized sweeper to clean parking structure, $6,000. Payment will be made next month.
31 Paid wages for May, $5,400.

Required:

a. Prepare a summary of transactions (see Illustration 1.5 except do not bother to include subtotals after each transaction). Include money columns for Cash, Equipment, Accounts Payable, and Harvey Mailer, Capital. Beginning balances were Cash, $20,000, and Harvey Mailer, Capital, $20,000.

b. Prepare an income statement for May 1984.

c. Prepare a balance sheet as of May 31, 1984.

P1–7–A. The following data are for the McDonald Olson Company:

MCDONALD OLSON COMPANY
Balance Sheet
September 30, 1984

Assets

Cash	$68,000
Accounts receivable	6,000
Total assets	$74,000

Liabilities and Owner's Equity

Liabilities:

Accounts payable	$18,000

Owner's equity:

McDonald Olson, capital	56,000
Total liabilities and owner's equity ...	$74,000

Transactions:

Oct. 1 The accounts payable owed as of September 30 ($18,000) were paid.
2 The company paid rent for the premises for October, $6,400.
7 The company received cash of $1,400 for parking by daily customers during the week.
10 The company collected $5,000 of the accounts receivable in the balance sheet at September 30.
14 Cash receipts for the week from daily customers were $2,200.
15 Parking revenue earned but not yet collected from fleet customers was $1,000.
16 The company paid wages of $1,000 for the period October 1–15.
19 The company paid advertising expenses of $400 for October.
21 Cash receipts for the week from daily customers were $3,000.
24 The company incurred miscellaneous expenses of $280 which will be paid November 10.
31 Cash receipts for the last 10 days of the month from daily customers were $2,800.
31 The company paid wages of $1,000 for the period October 16–31.
31 Customers were sent bills totaling $7,200 for parking services provided in October.

Required:

a. Prepare a summary of transactions (Illustration 1.5) using column headings for items given in the above balance sheet. Enter the balances shown in the September 30, 1984, balance sheet as beginning balances in the summary of transactions. Determine balances after each transaction.

    b.   Prepare an income statement for October 1984.

    c.   Prepare a balance sheet as of October 31, 1984.

PROBLEMS, SERIES B

P1–1–B.   The Howard Rand Company began operations on March 1, 1984. During March, it engaged in the following transactions:

Transactions:

1. Howard Rand invested cash of $100,000 in the business.
2. Howard's father loaned $50,000 to Howard to be used in the business.
3. The following assets were purchased for cash: truck, $12,000; cleaning equipment, $20,000; and office equipment, $25,000.
4. Office equipment was purchased on account, $15,000.
5. The account payable in (4) was paid, $15,000.

Required:

    a.   Prepare a summary of transactions using a format similar to Illustration 1.3. Include money columns for Cash, Truck, Cleaning Equipment, Office Equipment, Accounts Payable, Loan Payable, and Howard Rand, Capital. Determine new balances after each transaction.

    b.   Prepare a balance sheet as of March 31, 1984.

P1–2–B.   The Jim Sander Company, which provides financial advisory services, engaged in the following transactions during the month of October:

Transactions:

1. Received $60,000 cash investment from the owner.
2. The owner borrowed $8,000 from a friend for use in the business.
3. The company bought $50,000 of computer equipment for cash.
4. Cash received for services performed to date was $3,800.
5. Services performed for customers who agreed to pay within a month were $3,000.
6. Employee wages were paid, $3,300.
7. Customers paid $800 of the amount they owed the company.

Required:

    a.   Prepare a summary of the above transactions (Illustration 1.5). Use money columns headed Cash, Accounts Receivable, Equipment, Loan Payable, and Jim Sander, Capital. Determine balances after each transaction.

    b.   Prepare an income statement for October 1984.

    c.   Prepare a balance sheet as of October 31, 1984.

P1–3–B.   The following balances are for the Bently Company. All revenues and expenses are for the month of September. All asset and liability balances are as of September 30, 1984. The owner's equity balance is as of September 1, 1984.

Cash	$15,000
Service revenue	10,000
Accounts payable	1,800
Accounts receivable	2,600
Cleaning equipment	12,000
Office equipment	3,000
Gas and oil expense	700
Advertising expense	300
Wages expense	4,800
Ralph Bently, capital, September 1, 1984	25,240

Truck	6,000
Loan payable	8,000
Rent expense	600
Miscellaneous expense	40

Required:

      a.   Prepare an income statement for the month ended September 30, 1984.

      b.   Prepare a balance sheet as of September 30, 1984. You will need to calculate the September 30, 1984, balance in the owner's capital account.

P1–4–B.   The transactions appearing below are those of the Paul Fletcher Company for the month of April 1984. This was the first month of operation of the business.

Transactions:

1. Owner invested cash, $50,000.
2. Purchased cleaning equipment on account, $15,000.
3. Earned service revenue on account, $12,000.
4. Collected cash on account, $4,000.
5. Paid wages, $3,000.
6. Paid rent, $2,000.
7. Received bill for advertising for April, $600.
8. Paid an account payable, $15,000.

Required:

      a.   Prepare a summary of transactions using a format similar to Illustration 1.5 in the chapter. Determine new balances after each transaction.

      b.   Prepare an income statement for April 1984.

      c.   Prepare a balance sheet as of April 30, 1984.

P1–5–B.   The Cindy Thomas Company engaged in the following transactions in April of 1984:

Transactions:

Apr. 1   The owner invested $40,000 cash in the business.
      4   The company bought land for cash, $20,000.
    15   Cash received for services performed to date was $400.
    16   Amounts due from customers for services performed on account totaled $700.
    30   Collections on accounts receivable were $460.
    30   A bill was received for advertising expense, $800.

Required:

      a.   Prepare a summary of transactions (Illustration 1.5). Use money columns headed Cash, Accounts Receivable, Land, Accounts Payable, and Cindy Thomas, Capital. Determine balances after each transaction.

      b.   Prepare an income statement for April 1984.

      c.   Prepare a balance sheet as of April 30, 1984.

P1–6–B.   Following are the transactions for August 1984 of the Sunset Theater, a theater owned by Bob White:

Transactions:

Aug. 2   Paid current month's rent of building, $10,500.
    15   Cash withdrawal by owner was $1,000.
    24   Received and paid month's advertising bill, $3,800.
    27   Miscellaneous expenses paid, $1,400.
    31   Paid rental on films shown during month, $10,000.
    31   Received $12,400 cash as concession revenue from the operators of various concessions who sold candy, popcorn, and similar items in the theater during August.

Aug. 31 Cash ticket revenue for August was $23,300. (Actually cash would be received daily through-out the month, but we assume it was all received on August 31 to simplify the problem.)

31 Paid payroll for the month, $12,900.

Required:

a. Prepare a summary of transactions (see Illustration 1.5 except do not bother to include subtotals after each transaction). Include money columns for Cash and Bob White, Capital only. Beginning balances were Cash, $40,000, and Bob White, Capital, $40,000.

b. Prepare an income statement for August 1984.

c. Prepare a balance sheet as of August 31, 1984.

P1–7–B.   The balance sheet of the Marianne Mills Company as of April 30, 1984, was as follows:

MARIANNE MILLS COMPANY
Balance Sheet
April 30, 1984

Assets

Cash	$ 14,000
Accounts receivable	40,000
Land	150,000
Total assets	$204,000

Liabilities and Owner's Equity

Liabilities:

Accounts payable	$ 36,000

Owner's equity:

Marianne Mills, capital	168,000
Total liabilities and owner's equity	$204,000

Summarized, the transactions for the month of May 1984 were as follows:

Transactions:

1. The owner invested an additional $50,000 cash in the business.
2. Collected $30,000 on accounts receivable.
3. Paid $26,000 on accounts payable.
4. Sold land costing $50,000 for $75,000 cash. The gain of $25,000 increases owner's equity and is shown as a revenue in the income statement.
5. Decorating services were rendered to customers: for cash, $40,000; and on account, $30,000.
6. Employee services and other operating costs were incurred: for cash, $15,000; and on account, $40,000.
7. The owner withdrew $6,000 cash.

Required:

a. Prepare a summary of transactions (Illustration 1.5) using column headings for items appearing in the above balance sheet. Enter the balances shown in the April 30, 1984, balance sheet as beginning balances in the summary of transactions. Determine balances after each transaction.

b. Prepare an income statement for the month of May 1984.

c. Prepare a balance sheet as of May 31, 1984.

BUSINESS DECISION PROBLEM 1–1

Upon graduation from high school, Frank Patton went to work for a builder of houses and small apartment buildings. During the next six years, Frank earned a reputation as an excellent employee—hardworking, dedicated, and dependable—and as a very capable all-around employee in the light construction industry. He could handle almost any job requiring carpentry, electrical, or plumbing skills.

Frank then decided to go into business for himself under the name of Frank's Fix-It Shop. He invested cash, some power tools, and a used truck in his business. He completed many repair and remodeling jobs for both homeowners and apartment owners. The demand for his services was so large that he had more work than he could handle. He operated out of his garage, which he had converted into a shop, adding several new pieces of power woodworking equipment.

Two years after going into business for himself Frank is faced with a decision of whether to continue in his own business or to accept a position as construction supervisor for a home builder. He has been offered an annual salary of $25,000 and a package of "fringe benefits" (medical and hospitalization insurance, pension contribution, vacation and sick pay, and life insurance) worth approximately $5,000 per year. The offer is very attractive to Frank. But he dislikes giving up his business since he has thoroughly enjoyed "being his own boss," even though it has led to an average workweek well in excess of the standard 40-hour week.

Frank now comes to you for assistance in gathering the information needed to help him make a decision. Adequate accounting records have been maintained for his business by an experienced accountant.

Required:

Using logic and your own life experiences, indicate the nature of the information Frank needs if he is to make an informed decision. Pay particular attention to the information likely to be found in the accounting records for his business that would be useful. Does the accounting information available enter directly into the decision? Explain.

BUSINESS DECISION PROBLEM 1–2

Analysis of the transactions of the Summers Drive-In Theater, owned by Tom Summers, for the month of June 1984 discloses the following:

Ticket revenue	$35,500
Rent expense for premises and equipment	5,000
Film rental expense paid	8,900
Revenue received from operators of candy	
and popcorn concessions	5,000
Advertising expense	4,200
Wages and salaries expense	7,800
Utilities expense	2,500

Asset and liability amounts as of June 30 which the accountant has calculated include the following:

Cash	$50,000
Land	8,000
Accounts payable	10,400

The balance in the Tom Summers, Capital account on June 1 was $35,500.

Required:

a. Prepare an income statement for the month of June 1984.

b. Prepare a balance sheet as of June 30, 1984.

c. Did the month of June seem to be a beneficial month for this company?

Part Two

Processing accounting information

Chapter 2

Recording business transactions

CHAPTER GOALS

After study of this chapter, you should be able to:

1. Use the account as the basic classifying and storage unit for information.
2. Express the effects of business transactions in terms of debits and credits to specific accounts.
3. Record the effects of business transactions in a journal.
4. Post journal entries to the accounts in the ledger.
5. Prepare a trial balance to test the accuracy of the journalizing and posting process.
6. Define and use correctly the new terms in the glossary.

THE ACCOUNTING SYSTEM

This chapter introduces the basic components of the accounting system—the ledger (book of accounts) and the journal—and illustrates their use in recording business transactions. Knowledge of the underlying recording process will yield greater understanding of the end products—the financial statements.

In Chapter 1, the effects of transactions were shown as increases or decreases in the three elements in the basic accounting equation. The approach used in Chapter 1 was adopted solely to obtain an introductory understanding of some basic accounting relationships. But that approach is far too cumbersome to be used in actual practice, since even a small business enters into a large number of transactions every week, month, or year.

THE ACCOUNT

A business may engage in thousands of transactions during a period of time. The data in these transactions must be classified and summarized before becoming useful information. Making the accountant's task somewhat easier is the fact that most business transactions are repetitive in nature and can be classified into groups having common characteristics. For example, there may be thousands of receipts or payments of cash. As a result, a part of every cash transaction can be recorded and summarized in a single place called an account. An **account** is an element in an accounting system that is used to classify and summarize measurements of business activity. An account will be set up whenever it is necessary to provide useful information about a particular business item. Thus, every business will have a *Cash account* in its accounting system simply because knowledge of the amount of cash owned is useful information.

An account may take on a variety of forms, from a printed format in which entries are written by hand to an invisible encoding on a piece of magnetic tape. Every account format must provide for increases and decreases in the item for which the account was established. The account balance, the difference between the increases and decreases, may then be determined.

The number of accounts in a given accounting system will depend upon the information needs of those interested in the business. *The primary requirement is that the account provide useful information.* Thus, one account may be set up for all cash rather than having a separate account for each form of cash (coin, currency, deposits in banks). The amount of cash is useful information; the form of cash is not.

The T-account

The way an account functions is shown by use of a T-account. The *T-account* is used in textbooks for illustrative purposes only and derives its name because it looks like the letter T. The name of the item accounted for, such as cash, is written across the top of the T. Increases are recorded

41

on one side and decreases on the other side of the vertical line of the T, depending on the type of account. A T-account appears as follows:

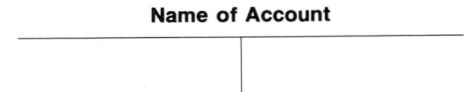

Name of Account

In Chapter 1, it was shown that each transaction affects at least two accounts. For instance, when the owner invested cash in the business, cash increased and the owner's capital account increased. These changes were shown in the summary of transactions schedule. Now these changes will be recorded in T-accounts.

Debits and credits

The accountant uses the term *debit* in lieu of saying "place an entry on the left side of the T-account" and *credit* for "place an entry on the right side of the T-account." *Debit* (abbreviated Dr.) simply means left side; *credit* (abbreviated Cr.) means right side. A *debit entry* is an entry on the left side of an account, while a *credit entry* is an entry on the right side of an account. Thus, for any account, the left side is the debit side and the right side is the credit side:

Any Account

Debit side	Credit side

A synonym for *debit* an account is **charge** an account.

Recording changes in assets, liabilities, and owner's equity. Increases in assets are recorded on the left (debit) side of the T-account; decreases on the right (credit) side of the T-account. The process is reversed for liability and owner's equity accounts. For liability and owner's equity accounts, increases are recorded on the right (credit) side and decreases are recorded on the left (debit) side. Thus, a company would record the receipt of $10,000 invested by its owner, John Stevens, as follows:

(Dr.)	Cash	(Cr.)	(Dr.)	John Stevens, Capital	(Cr.)
(1) 10,000				(1)	10,000

The transaction involves an increase in the asset, cash, which is recorded on the left side of the Cash account, and an increase in owner's equity, which is recorded on the right side of the John Stevens, Capital account.

Assume John Stevens went to the bank and borrowed $5,000 on a promissory note. A *promissory note* is a written promise to pay to another party (the bank) the amount owed either when demanded or at a certain specified date. The transaction would be recorded as follows:

(Dr.)	Cash	(Cr.)	(Dr.)	Notes Payable—Bank	(Cr.)
(2)	5,000			(2)	5,000

Notice that liabilities are increased by an entry on the right (credit) side of the account.

Recording changes in expenses and revenues. To understand the logic behind the recording of changes in expense and revenue accounts recall that all expenses and revenues *could be* recorded directly in the owner's capital account as was done in Chapter 1. But recording revenues and expenses directly in the owner's capital account is not recommended because of the volume of transactions. The *amounts* of *revenues* and *expenses* are needed to prepare the income statement. Thus, a separate account should be kept for each revenue and expense. The recording rules for these items are as follows:

1. Increases in revenues are recorded on the right (credit) side and decreases on the left (debit) side. The logic behind this is that revenues increase owner's equity and increases in owner's equity are recorded on the right side.
2. Increases in expenses are recorded on the left (debit) side and decreases on the right (credit) side. The logic behind this is that expenses decrease owner's equity, and decreases in owner's equity are recorded on the left side. Following these rules the receipt of $800 cash from customers for services rendered is recorded as follows:

(Dr.)	Cash	(Cr.)	(Dr.)	Service Revenue	(Cr.)
(3)	800			(3)	800

The payment of $600 cash to employees as wages would be recorded as follows:[1]

(Dr.)	Cash	(Cr.)	(Dr.)	Wages Expense	(Cr.)
		(4) 600	(4) 600		

Withdrawals by the owner. Withdrawals are a distribution of assets to the owner. Withdrawals have the same effect on owner's equity as an expense in that they reduce the owner's equity in the business. Just as investments increase owner's equity, withdrawals reduce it.

---

[1] Certain deductions are normally taken out of employees' pay for social security taxes, federal and state withholding, and so on. Those deductions will be ignored until the topic of payroll is covered in more detail (Chapter 12).

A withdrawal could be shown directly as a reduction of the owner's capital account balance by entering the amount on the left (debit) side of that account. But a clearer record of withdrawals is available if a separate drawing account is used to record all amounts withdrawn. Withdrawals are shown as debits to the owner's drawing account. The drawing account is increased by debits and decreased by credits.

A withdrawal of $100 cash by John Stevens would be shown as follows:

(Dr.)	Cash	(Cr.)	(Dr.)	John Stevens, Drawing	(Cr.)
	(5)	100	(5)	100	

Determining the balance of an account

The balance of any T-account is obtained by totaling the debits to the account, totaling the credits to the account, and subtracting the smaller sum from the larger. If the sum of the debits exceeds the sum of the credits, the account has a *debit balance.* For example, the Cash account shown below has a debit balance of $15,100, computed as total debits of $15,800 less total credits of $700.

(Dr.)		Cash		(Cr.)
(1)		10,000	(4)	600
(2)		5,000	(5)	100
(3)		800		
		15,800		700
Dr. bal.		15,100		

If, on the other hand, the sum of the credits exceeds the sum of the debits, the account will have a *credit balance.* For instance, assume that a company has an Accounts Payable account with a total of $10,000 in debits and $13,000 in credits. It will have a credit balance of $3,000 as shown in the following T-account:

(Dr.)	Accounts Payable	(Cr.)
10,000		7,000
		6,000
10,000		13,000
	Cr. bal.	3,000

Normal balances

Since asset, expense, and drawing accounts are increased by debits, they *normally* have debit (or left side) balances. Conversely, liability, owner's equity, and revenue accounts are increased by credits and *normally* have credit (or right side) balances.

The normal balances of accounts are as follows:

Accounts normally having a debit balance	Accounts normally having a credit balance
Assets	Liabilities
Expenses	Owner's equity
Owner's drawing	Revenues

Double-entry procedure

Business transactions are analyzed to determine the effects they have upon the assets, liabilities, owner's equity, revenues, or expenses of the business. These increase or decrease effects are then translated into debits and credits. For example, an increase in an asset is recorded as a debit in the proper asset account.

In each recorded transaction, the total amount of debits must equal the total amount of credits. This requirement means that when one account is debited for $100, another account (or accounts) must be credited for a total of $100. The requirement that each transaction be recorded by an entry that has equal debits and credits is called *double-entry procedure.* This double-entry procedure keeps the accounting equation in balance. The double-entry procedure is related to the duality concept discussed in Chapter 1. The duality concept is that every transaction has a dual or two-sided effect.

Rules of debit and credit summarized

The rules of debit and credit may be presented in account form as follows:

Debits	Credits
1. Increase assets.	1. Decrease assets.
2. Decrease liabilities.	2. Increase liabilities.
3. Decrease owner's equity.	3. Increase owner's equity.
4. Increase owner's drawing.	4. Decrease owner's drawing.
5. Decrease revenues.	5. Increase revenues.
6. Increase expenses.	6. Decrease expenses.

These rules may also be summarized another way. The summary shown below focuses on the five types of accounts and illustrates the effects of debits and credits on these accounts. Note the treatment of expense and drawing accounts as if they were subsets of the debit side of the owner's capital account.

Remember that increases in expenses reduce owner's capital. The opposite holds true for revenues. If revenues increase, owner's capital increases.

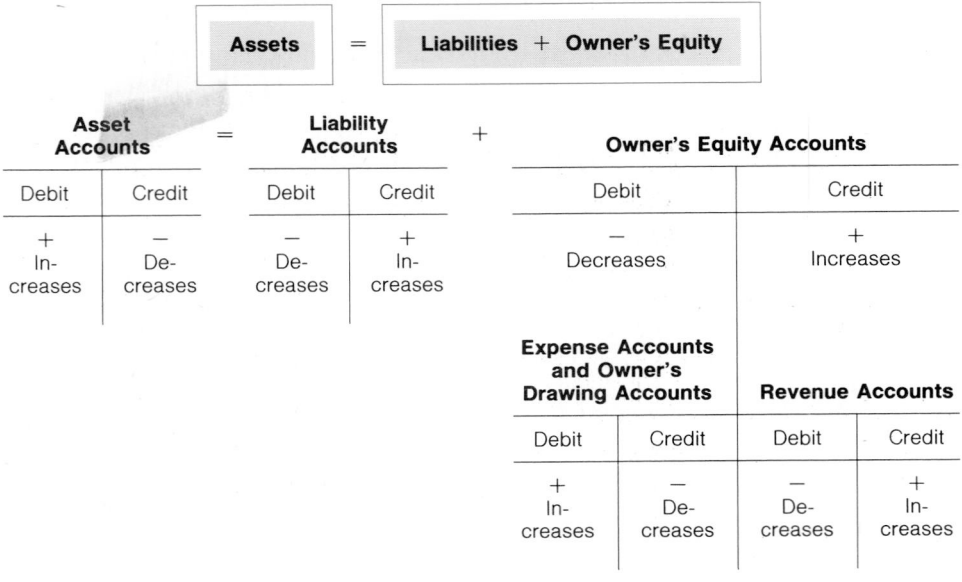

Assets	=	Liabilities + Owner's Equity

Asset Accounts		=	Liability Accounts		+	Owner's Equity Accounts	
Debit	Credit		Debit	Credit		Debit	Credit
+ In- creases	− De- creases		− De- creases	+ In- creases		− Decreases	+ Increases

Expense Accounts and Owner's Drawing Accounts		Revenue Accounts	
Debit	Credit	Debit	Credit
+ In- creases	− De- creases	− De- creases	+ In- creases

THE LEDGER

A *ledger* (general ledger) is the complete collection of all the accounts of a company. Accounts are classified into two general groups: (1) the *balance sheet accounts* (assets, liabilities, and owner's equity) and (2) the *income statement accounts* (revenues and expenses). Balance sheet accounts are also called *real accounts* because they are *not* subsets or subdivisions of any other account, while income statement accounts are also called *nominal accounts* because they *are* merely subsets of the owner's equity accounts. "Nominal" literally means "in name only." Nominal accounts temporarily contain the revenue and expense information which eventually becomes part of the balance of a real account, owner's capital. The ledger may be in loose-leaf form, in a bound volume, or in a computer memory.

A complete listing of account titles and account numbers of all of the accounts in the ledger is known as the *chart of accounts.* Each account typically has an identification number as well as a name to help locate accounts when recording data. For example, asset accounts might be numbered 100–199; liability accounts, 200–299; owner's equity accounts and drawing account, 300–399; revenue accounts, 400–499; and expense accounts, 500–599. Other numbering systems may be used. For instance, sometimes the accounts are numbered in sequence starting with 1, 2, and so on. *The important idea is that some numbering system typically is used.* The groups of accounts usually appear in the following order in the ledger—assets, liabilities, owner's equity, drawing, revenues, and expenses. Sometimes relatively minor revenues are placed last along with relatively minor expenses. Individual accounts are arranged in numerical sequence in the ledger.

Having completed this introduction to accounts and the recording process, attention is now directed to the journal and journal entries.

THE JOURNAL

So far in Chapter 2, transactions have been recorded directly in the accounts. Each ledger account shows only the increases and decreases in that account. Thus, all of the effects of a single business transaction would not appear in any one account. For example, the Cash account contains only data on changes in cash. It does not show how the cash was generated or what it was spent on. In order to have a permanent record of an entire transaction, the accountant uses a book or record known as a journal. A *journal is a chronological* (arranged in order of time) *record of business transactions*. A journal entry is the recording of a business transaction in the journal. A *journal entry* shows all of the effects of a business transaction as expressed in terms of debit and credit and may include an explanation of the transaction. Because each transaction is initially recorded in a journal rather than directly in the ledger, a journal is called the book of *original entry*.

The general journal. The basic form of journal is the *general journal.* As shown in Illustration 2.1, a general journal contains the:

1. *Date column.* The first column on each general journal page is for the date. For the first journal entry on a page the year, the month, and the day are entered here. For all other journal entries on a page, only the day of the month is shown, until the month changes.
2. *Account Titles and Explanation column.* The first line of an entry shows the account debited. The second line shows the account credited. Notice that the credit is indented to the right. For instance, in Illustration 2.1 the debit to the Cash account is shown first and the credit to the John Stevens, Capital account is shown next. Any necessary explanation of a transaction appears on the line(s) below the credit entry and is indented halfway between the debit and credit entries. A journal entry explanation should be complete enough to fully describe the transaction and prove the entry's accuracy, and yet should be concise. If a journal entry is self-explanatory, the explanation may be omitted.
3. *Posting Reference column.* This column shows the account number of the account that has been debited or credited. For instance, the number 100 in the first entry means that the Cash account number is 100. No number appears in this column until the information is posted to the appropriate ledger account.
4. *Debit column.* This column is where the amount of the debit is placed on the same line as the title of the account debited.
5. *Credit column.* The amount of credit is placed in this column on the

Illustration 2:1   General journal

| GENERAL JOURNAL | | | | Page 1 |

Date	Account Titles and Explanation	Post. Ref.	Debit	Credit
1984 Jan. 1	Cash	100	1 0 0 0 0	
	John Stevens, Capital	300		1 0 0 0 0
	The owner invested $10,000 cash in the			
	business.			
5	Cash	100	5 0 0 0	
	Notes payable—Bank	201		5 0 0 0
	Borrowed $5,000 from the			
	bank on a note.			

same line as the title of the account credited. A line is skipped between each journal entry.

Journalizing

Journalizing is the entering of a transaction in a journal. Business information comes from source materials or documents such as invoices, cash register tapes, timecards, and checks. The information appearing on these documents must be analyzed to determine the specific accounts affected and the dollar amounts of the changes. Then the proper journal entry must be recorded.

Posting

In a sense, a journal entry is a set of instructions. *The carrying out of these instructions is known as posting. Posting* is recording in the ledger the information contained in the journal. A journal entry directs the entry of a certain dollar amount as a debit in a specific account and directs the entry of a certain dollar amount as a credit in a specific account. In Illustration 2.2, the first entry directs that $10,000 be posted as a debit to the Cash account and as a credit to the John Stevens, Capital account. The arrows in the illustration show how these amounts have been posted to the correct accounts. The three-column balance type of account is shown in that illustration. In contrast to the two-sided T-account format shown so far, the three-column format has columns for debit, credit, and balance. One advantage of this form is that the balance of the account is shown after each item has been posted. This chapter indicates whether each balance is a debit or a

Illustration 2.2: General journal and general ledger; posting and cross indexing

GENERAL JOURNAL

Page 1

Date	Account Titles and Explanation	Post. Ref.	Debit	Credit
	Cash	100	1 0 0 0 0	
	John Stevens, Capital	300		1 0 0 0 0
	Owner invested $10,000 cash in business.			
5	Cash	100	5 0 0 0	
	Notes payable—Bank	201		5 0 0 0
	Borrowed $5,000 from the bank on a note.			

GENERAL LEDGER

Cash

Account No. 100

Date		Explanation	Post. Ref.	Debit	Credit	Balance
1984 Jan.	1	Owner investment	GJ1	1 0 0 0 0		1 0 0 0 0 Dr.
	5	Bank loan	GJ1	5 0 0 0		1 5 0 0 0 Dr.

Notes Payable—Bank

Account No. 201

Date		Explanation	Post. Ref.	Debit	Credit	Balance
1984 Jan.	5	Borrowed cash	GJ1		5 0 0 0	5 0 0 0 Cr.

John Stevens, Capital

Account No. 300

Date		Explanation	Post. Ref.	Debit	Credit	Balance
1984 Jan.	1	Cash from owner	GJ1		1 0 0 0 0	1 0 0 0 0 Cr.

credit. In subsequent chapters and in practice, the nature of the balance is not indicated since it is understood.

Postings to the ledger accounts may be made (1) at the time the transaction is journalized; (2) at the end of the day, week, or month; or (3) as each journal page is filled.

Cross-indexing

The account number of the ledger account to which the posting was made is placed in the Posting Reference column of the journal. In Illustration 2.2, notice the arrow from Account No. 100 to the debit in the first entry in the general journal. The number of the journal page *from* which the entry was posted is placed in the Posting Reference column of the ledger account. Notice the arrow from page 1 in the general journal to GJ1 in the Posting Reference column of the general ledger. The date of the transaction is also shown in the general ledger. Notice the arrows from the date in the general journal to the dates in the general ledger. Posting is always from the journal to the ledger account. *Cross-indexing is the placing of the account number in the journal and the placing of the journal page number in the ledger account,* as shown in Illustration 2.2.

Cross-indexing aids the tracing of any recorded transaction, either from journal to ledger or from ledger to journal. Cross-reference numbers are not placed in the Posting Reference column of the journal until the entry is posted. If this practice is followed, the cross-reference numbers indicate the entry has been posted.

An understanding of the posting and cross-indexing process can be obtained by tracing the entries from the journal to the ledger. The ledger accounts need not contain explanations of all the entries, since any needed explanations can be obtained from the journal.

Compound journal entries

The analysis of a transaction may show that more than two accounts are affected. In these cases, the journal entry will involve more than one debit and/or credit; such a journal entry is a *compound journal entry.* An entry with one debit and one credit is a *simple journal entry.*

As an illustration of a compound journal entry, assume that on July 1, 1984, John Stevens purchased $8,000 of machinery from the Myers Company, paying $2,000 cash with the balance due on open account. The journal entry for Stevens would be shown in the general journal as follows:

```
1984
July 1   Machinery ...........................................  8,000
            Cash ............................................           2,000
            Accounts Payable ...............................           6,000
         Machinery purchased from Myers Company, Invoice No. 42.
```

Summary of functions and advantages of a journal

The functions and advantages of using a journal are summarized below. The journal—

1. Sets forth the transactions of each day.
2. Records the transactions in chronological order.
3. Shows the analysis of each transaction in terms of debit and credit.
4. Supplies an explanation of each transaction when necessary.
5. Serves as a source for future reference to accounting transactions.
6. Removes lengthy explanations from the accounts.
7. Makes possible posting to the ledger at convenient times.
8. Assists in maintaining the ledger in balance.
9. Aids in the tracing of errors.
10. Promotes the division of labor (for example, one person may enter the journal entries and another may post them).

THE ACCOUNTING SYSTEM IN OPERATION

Presented below is an illustration of an accounting system that might be employed by a small delivery service company, the Rapid Delivery Company, owned by John Turner.

The ledger accounts that will be used for the Rapid Delivery Company in this chapter are as follows:

	Account No.	Account title	Description
Assets	100	Cash	Bank deposits and cash on hand.
	101	Accounts Receivable	Amounts owed to the company by customers
	102	Supplies on Hand	Items such as paper, envelopes, writing materials, rope, and other materials used in performing services for customers or in doing administrative and clerical office work.
	103	Prepaid Insurance	Insurance policy premium paid in advance of the periods for which the insurance coverage applies.
	104	Prepaid Rent	Rent paid in advance of the periods for which the rent payment applies.
	110	Delivery Trucks	Trucks used to perform delivery services for customers.
Liabilities	200	Accounts Payable	Amounts owed to creditors for items purchased from them.
	201	Unearned Delivery Fees	Amounts received from customers before the services have been performed for the customers.

	Account No.	Account title	Description
Owner's equity	300	John Turner, Capital	The owner's equity or interest in the business.
	301	John Turner, Drawing	The amount of withdrawals made by the owner this accounting period.
Revenues	400	Delivery Service Revenue	Amounts earned by performing delivery services for customers.
Expenses	500	Advertising Expense	The cost of advertising incurred in the current period.
	501	Gas and Oil Expense	The cost of gas and oil used in trucks in the current period.
	502	Salaries Expense	The amount of salaries incurred in the current period.
	503	Utilities Expense	The cost of utilities incurred in the current period.

Other accounts to be used for the Rapid Delivery Company will be introduced in the next chapter.

The company was formed in late November 1984 when John Turner invested $50,000 in the business. When the owner invested $50,000, the accounts were affected as follows:

(Dr.)	Cash	(Cr.)	(Dr.)	John Turner, Capital	(Cr.)
50,000					50,000

No other transactions occurred in November. The company prepares financial statements at the end of each month. The company's balance sheet at November 30, 1984, is shown in Illustration 2.3.

Illustration 2.3: Balance sheet

RAPID DELIVERY COMPANY
Balance Sheet
November 30, 1984

Assets		Liabilities and Owner's Equity	
Cash	$50,000	Owner's equity:	
		John Turner, capital	$50,000
Total assets	$50,000	Total liabilities and owner's equity	$50,000

The balance sheet reflects ledger account balances as of the close of business on November 30, 1984. These closing balances are the opening balances on December 1, 1984, and are shown as such in the ledger accounts.

Now assume the transactions below are entered into by the Rapid Delivery Company in December 1984. After each transaction, the proper recording of the transaction is shown in T-account form and a brief explanation is given. The purpose of using the T-account format is to help you analyze each transaction. Later, the journal entries and postings to ledger accounts will be shown.

Dec. 1 Paid cash for four delivery trucks, $40,000.

(Dr.)	Delivery Trucks	(Cr.)
1984		
Dec. 1	40,000	

(Dr.)	Cash	(Cr.)
1984		
Beg. bal.	50,000	Dec. 1 40,000

One asset, delivery trucks, is increased (debited); and another asset, cash, is decreased (credited) by $40,000.

Dec. 1 Purchased $2,400 of insurance on the trucks to cover a one-year period from this date. Payment will be made in January.

(Dr.)	Prepaid Insurance	(Cr.)
1984		
Dec. 1	2,400	

(Dr.)	Accounts Payable	(Cr.)
		1984
		Dec. 1 2,400

An asset, prepaid insurance, is increased (debited); and a liability, accounts payable, is increased (credited) by $2,400. The debit is to Prepaid Insurance rather than Insurance Expense because the policy covers more than the current accounting period (December). If the payment had covered only the current period, the debit would have been to Insurance Expense.

Dec. 1 Rented a building and paid $1,200 to cover a three-month period from this date.

(Dr.)	Prepaid Rent	(Cr.)
1984		
Dec. 1	1,200	

(Dr.)	Cash	(Cr.)
1984		1984
Beg. bal.	50,000	Dec. 1 40,000
		1 1,200

An asset, prepaid rent, is increased (debited); and another asset, cash, is decreased (credited) by $1,200. The debit is to Prepaid Rent rather than Rent Expense because the payment covers more than the current month. If the payment had just been for December, the debit would have been to Rent Expense.

Dec. 4 Purchased $1,400 of supplies on account to be used over the next several months.

(Dr.)	Supplies on Hand		(Cr.)
1984			
Dec. 4	1,400		

An asset, supplies on hand, is increased (debited); and a liability, accounts payable, is increased (credited) by $1,400. The debit is to Supplies on Hand rather than Supplies Expense because the supplies are to be used over several accounting periods.

(Dr.)	Accounts Payable		(Cr.)
		1984	
		Dec. 1	2,400
		4	1,400

In each of the preceding three entries, an asset was debited rather than an expense. The reason given was that the expenditure applies to (or benefits) more than just the current period. Whenever an item such as insurance, rent, or supplies will not be fully used up in the period in which purchased, an asset should be debited.

Sometimes prepaid expenses such as insurance, rent, and supplies are bought and will be fully used up within the current accounting period. For instance, the company may buy supplies during the first part of the month that it intends to fully consume during that month. If supplies will be fully consumed during the period of purchase, it is best to debit Supplies Expense rather than Supplies on Hand at time of purchase. This same advice applies to insurance and rent. If insurance is purchased that will be fully consumed during the current period, Insurance Expense rather than Prepaid Insurance should be debited at time of purchase. If rent is paid that applies only to the current period, Rent Expense rather than Prepaid Rent should be debited at time of purchase. As illustrated in the next chapter, following this advice simplifies the procedures at the end of the accounting period.

Dec. 7 Received $4,500 from a customer in payment for future delivery services.

(Dr.)	Cash		(Cr.)
1984		1984	
Beg. bal.	50,000	Dec. 1	40,000
Dec. 7	4,500	1	1,200

An asset, cash, is increased (debited); and a liability, unearned delivery revenue, is increased (credited) by $4,500. The credit is to Unearned Delivery Fees rather than Delivery Service Revenue because the $4,500 applies to more than just the current accounting period. If the payment had been for services to be provided in December, the credit would have been to Delivery Service Revenue.

(Dr.)	Unearned Delivery Fees		(Cr.)
		1984	
		Dec. 7	4,500

Dec. 15   Performed delivery services for customers for cash, $5,000.

(Dr.)	**Cash**		(Cr.)
1984		1984	
Beg. bal.	50,000	Dec. 1	40,000
Dec. 7	4,500	1	1,200
15	5,000		

An asset, cash, is increased (debited); and a revenue, delivery service revenue, is increased (credited) by $5,000.

(Dr.)	**Delivery Service Revenue**		(Cr.)
		1984	
		Dec. 15	5,000

Dec. 17   Paid the $1,400 account payable resulting from the transaction of December 4.

(Dr.)	**Accounts Payable**		(Cr.)
1984		1984	
Dec. 17	1,400	Dec. 1	2,400
		4	1,400

A liability, accounts payable, is decreased (debited); and an asset, cash, is decreased (credited) by $1,400.

(Dr.)	**Cash**		(Cr.)
1984		1984	
Beg. bal.	50,000	Dec. 1	40,000
Dec. 7	4,500	1	1,200
15	5,000	17	1,400

Dec. 20   Billed customers for delivery services performed, $5,700.

(Dr.)	**Accounts Receivable**		(Cr.)
1984			
Dec. 20	5,700		

An asset, accounts receivable, is increased (debited); and a revenue, delivery service revenue, is increased (credited) by $5,700.

(Dr.)	**Delivery Service Revenue**		(Cr.)
		1984	
		Dec. 15	5,000
		20	5,700

Dec. 24   Received a bill for advertising that appeared in a local newspaper in December, $50.

(Dr.)	Advertising Expense	(Cr.)
1984		
Dec. 24	50	

An expense, advertising expense, is increased (debited); and a liability, accounts payable, is increased (credited) by $50. The reason for debiting an expense rather than an asset is because the cost all pertains to the current accounting period, the month of December. Otherwise Prepaid Advertising (an asset) would have been debited.

(Dr.)	Accounts Payable		(Cr.)
1984		1984	
Dec. 17	1,400	Dec. 1	2,400
		4	1,400
		24	50

Dec. 26   Received $500 on accounts receivable from a customer.

(Dr.)	Cash		(Cr.)
1984		1984	
Beg. bal.	50,000	Dec. 1	40,000
Dec. 7	4,500	1	1,200
15	5,000	17	1,400
26	500		

One asset, cash, is increased (debited); and another asset, accounts receivable, is decreased (credited) by $500.

(Dr.)	Accounts Receivable		(Cr.)
1984		1984	
Dec. 20	5,700	Dec. 26	500

Dec. 28   Paid salaries of $3,600 to truck drivers for the first four weeks of December. (Payroll and other deductions are to be ignored since they have not yet been discussed.)

(Dr.)	Salaries Expense	(Cr.)
1984		
Dec. 28	3,600	

An expense, salaries expense, is increased (debited); and an asset, cash, is decreased (credited) by $3,600.

(Dr.)	Cash		(Cr.)
1984		1984	
Beg. bal.	50,000	Dec. 1	40,000
Dec. 7	4,500	1	1,200
15	5,000	17	1,400
26	500	28	3,600

Dec. 29 Received and paid the utilities bill for December, $150.

(Dr.)	**Utilities Expense**	(Cr.)
1984		
Dec. 29	150	

An expense, utilities expense, is increased (debited); and an asset, cash, is decreased (credited) by $150.

(Dr.)		**Cash**		(Cr.)
1984		1984		
Beg. bal.	50,000	Dec. 1	40,000	
Dec. 7	4,500	1	1,200	
15	5,000	17	1,400	
26	500	28	3,600	
		29	150	

Dec. 30 Received a bill for gas and oil used in the trucks for December, $680.

(Dr.)	**Gas and Oil Expense**	(Cr.)
1984		
Dec. 30	680	

An expense, gas and oil expense, is increased (debited); and a liability, accounts payable, is increased (credited) by $680.

(Dr.)		**Accounts Payable**		(Cr.)
1984		1984		
Dec. 17	1,400	Dec. 1	2,400	
		4	1,400	
		24	50	
		30	680	

Dec. 31 John Turner withdrew $3,000 cash to pay personal living expenses.

(Dr.)	**John Turner, Drawing**	(Cr.)
1984		
Dec. 31	3,000	

The owner's drawing account is increased (debited); and an asset, cash, is decreased (credited) by $3,000.

(Dr.)		**Cash**		(Cr.)
1984		1984		
Beg. bal.	50,000	Dec. 1	40,000	
Dec. 7	4,500	1	1,200	
15	5,000	17	1,400	
26	500	28	3,600	
		29	150	
		31	3,000	

The T-accounts shown above were only for analysis purposes. In the accounting records the transactions given above would first be entered in a journal and then posted to the ledger.

The general journal of the Rapid Delivery Company is presented below. The transactions just presented for the month of December have been entered in the journal.

GENERAL JOURNAL				Page 1
Date	Account Titles and Explanation	Post. Ref.	Debit	Credit
1984 Dec. 1	Delivery Trucks	110	4 0 0 0 0	
	Cash	100		4 0 0 0 0
	To record the purchase of four delivery			
	trucks.			
1	Prepaid Insurance	103	2 4 0 0	
	Accounts Payable	200		2 4 0 0
	Purchased truck insurance to cover a one-			
	year period.			
1	Prepaid Rent	104	1 2 0 0	
	Cash	100		1 2 0 0
	Paid three months' rent on a building.			
4	Supplies on Hand	102	1 4 0 0	
	Accounts Payable	200		1 4 0 0
	To record the purchase of supplies for			
	future use.			
Dec. 7	Cash	100	4 5 0 0	
	Unearned Delivery Fees	201		4 5 0 0
	To record the receipt of cash from a			
	customer in payment for future delivery			
	services.			
15	Cash	100	5 0 0 0	
	Delivery Service Revenue	400		5 0 0 0
	To record the receipt of cash for			
	performing delivery services for customers.			
17	Accounts Payable	200	1 4 0 0	
	Cash	100		1 4 0 0
	Paid the account payable arising from the			
	purchase of supplies on December 4.			

		GENERAL JOURNAL								*Page 2*		
Date		Account Titles and Explanation	Post. Ref.	Debit				Credit				
	20	Accounts Receivable	101	5	7	0	0					
		Delivery Service Revenue	400						5	7	0	0
		To record the performance of delivery										
		services on account for which customers										
		were billed.										
	24	Advertising Expense	500			5	0					
		Accounts Payable	200								5	0
		Received a bill for advertising for the month										
		of December.										
	26	Cash	100			5	0	0				
		Accounts Receivable	101							5	0	0
		Received $500 from customers as payments										
		on accounts receivable.										
	28	Salaries Expense	502		3	6	0	0				
		Cash	100						3	6	0	0
		Paid truck driver salaries for the first four										
		weeks of December.										
	29	Utilities Expense	503			1	5	0				
		Cash	100							1	5	0
		Paid the utilities bill for December.										
Dec.	30	Gas and Oil Expense	501			6	8	0				
		Accounts Payable	200							6	8	0
		Received a bill for gas and oil used in the										
		trucks in December.										
	31	John Turner, Drawing	301		3	0	0	0				
		Cash	100						3	0	0	0
		The owner withdrew $3,000 to pay										
		personal expenses.										

Presented below are the general ledger accounts of the Rapid Delivery Company after the journal entries have been posted. Each ledger account would appear on a separate page in the ledger. You should trace at least a few of the postings from the general journal to the general ledger to make sure you know how to post journal entries.

GENERAL LEDGER

Cash

Account No. 100

Date		Explanation	Post. Ref.	Debit	Credit	Balance
1984 Dec.	1	Beginning balance				5 0 0 0 0 Dr.
	1	Delivery trucks	GJ1		4 0 0 0 0	1 0 0 0 0 Dr.
	1	Prepaid rent	GJ1		1 2 0 0	8 8 0 0 Dr.
	7	Unearned delivery service revenue	CJ1	4 5 0 0		1 3 3 0 0 Dr.
	15	Delivery service revenue	GJ1	5 0 0 0		1 8 3 0 0 Dr.
	17	Paid accounts payable	GJ1		1 4 0 0	1 6 9 0 0 Dr.
	26	Collected accounts receivable	GJ2	5 0 0		1 7 4 0 0 Dr.
	28	Salaries	GJ2		3 6 0 0	1 3 8 0 0 Dr.
	29	Utilities	GJ2		1 5 0	1 3 6 5 0 Dr.
	31	Owner withdrawal	GJ2		3 0 0 0	1 0 6 5 0 Dr.

Accounts Receivable

Account No. 101

Date		Explanation	Post. Ref.	Debit	Credit	Balance
1984 Dec.	20	Delivery service revenue	GJ2	5 7 0 0		5 7 0 0 Dr.
	26	Collections	GJ2		5 0 0	5 2 0 0 Dr.

Supplies on Hand

Account No. 102

Date		Explanation	Post. Ref.	Debit	Credit	Balance
1984 Dec.	4	Purchased on account	GJ1	1 4 0 0		1 4 0 0 Dr.

Prepaid Insurance

Account No. 103

Date		Explanation	Post. Ref.	Debit	Credit	Balance
1984 Dec.	1	One-year policy on trucks	GJ1	2 4 0 0		2 4 0 0 Dr.

GENERAL LEDGER (*continued*)

Prepaid Rent   Account No. 104

Date		Explanation	Post. Ref.	Debit	Credit	Balance
1984 Dec.	1	Three-month payment	GJ1	1 2 0 0		1 2 0 0 Dr.

Delivery Trucks   Account No. 110

Date		Explanation	Post. Ref.	Debit	Credit	Balance
1984 Dec.	1	Paid cash	GJ1	4 0 0 0 0		4 0 0 0 0 Dr.

Accounts Payable   Account No. 200

Date		Explanation	Post. Ref.	Debit	Credit	Balance
1984 Dec.	1	Insurance	GJ1		2 4 0 0	2 4 0 0 Cr.
	4	Supplies	GJ1		1 4 0 0	3 8 0 0 Cr.
	17	Paid for supplies	GJ1	1 4 0 0		2 4 0 0 Cr.
	24	Advertising	GJ2		5 0	2 4 5 0 Cr.
	30	Gas and oil	GJ2		6 8 0	3 1 3 0 Cr.

Unearned Delivery Fees   Account No. 201

Date		Explanation	Post. Ref.	Debit	Credit	Balance
1984 Dec.	7	Received cash	GJ1		4 5 0 0	4 5 0 0 Cr.

John Turner, Capital   Account No. 300

Date		Explanation	Post. Ref.	Debit	Credit	Balance
1984 Dec.	1	Beginning balance				5 0 0 0 0 Cr.

GENERAL LEDGER (*concluded*)

John Turner, Drawing   *Account No. 301*

Date		Explanation	Post. Ref.	Debit	Credit	Balance
1984 Dec.	31	Cash	GJ2	3 0 0 0		3 0 0 0 Dr.

Delivery Service Revenue   *Account No. 400*

Date		Explanation	Post. Ref.	Debit	Credit	Balance
1984 Dec.	15	Cash	GJ1		5 0 0 0	5 0 0 0 Cr.
	20	On account	GJ2		5 7 0 0	1 0 7 0 0 Cr.

Advertising Expense   *Account No. 500*

Date		Explanation	Post. Ref.	Debit	Credit	Balance
1984 Dec.	24	On account	GJ2	5 0		5 0 Dr.

Gas and Oil Expense   *Account No. 501*

Date		Explanation	Post. Ref.	Debit	Credit	Balance
1984 Dec.	30	On account	GJ2	6 8 0		6 8 0 Dr.

Salaries Expense   *Account No. 502*

Date		Explanation	Post. Ref.	Debit	Credit	Balance
1984 Dec.	28	Cash paid	GJ2	3 6 0 0		3 6 0 0 Dr.

Utilities Expense   *Account No. 503*

Date		Explanation	Post. Ref.	Debit	Credit	Balance
1984 Dec.	29	Cash paid	GJ2	1 5 0		1 5 0 Dr.

The recording process yields two sets of accounts—those with debit balances and those with credit balances. If the totals of these two groups are equal, the accountant has some assurance that the arithmetic part of the recording process has been properly carried out. The *double-entry* system of accounting requires that the debits must equal the credits in every entry to record a transaction.

The equality of debits and credits provides an important means of control. If every transaction is recorded in terms of equal debits and credits, the total dollar amount of accounts with debit balances must equal the total dollar amount of accounts with credit balances.

THE TRIAL BALANCE

The accuracy of the recording process is generally tested by preparing a trial balance. A *trial balance* is a listing of the ledger accounts and their debit or credit balances to determine that debits equal credits in the recording process. The trial balance for the Rapid Delivery Company is shown in Illustration 2.4. Note the listing of the account titles on the left (account numbers could be included, if desired), the column for debit balances, the column for credit balances, and the equality of the two totals.

An inequality in the totals of the debits and credits would automatically signal the presence of an error. Errors that would cause the trial balance to be out of balance include:

1. Failing to post part of a journal entry.
2. Posting a debit as a credit or vice versa.
3. Incorrectly determining the balance of an account.
4. Recording the balance of an account incorrectly in the trial balance.
5. Omitting an account from the trial balance.
6. Incorrectly determining the totals of the two columns of the trial balance.

To find the cause of such an error, the accountant should work backwards through the steps in the accounting process (e.g., start by re-adding the trial balance columns, then compare the trial balance figures with the account balances, verify the balance of each ledger account, verify postings to the ledger, verify journal entries, and then review the transactions). The equality of the two totals does not necessarily mean that the accounting has been error-free. Serious errors may have been made, such as failure to record a transaction, or posting a debit or credit to the wrong account. For instance, if a transaction involving payment of a $100 account payable is never recorded, the trial balance totals will still balance, but at an amount which is $100 too high. Both cash and accounts payable would be overstated by $100.

A trial balance may be prepared at any time—at the end of a day, a week, a month, a quarter, or a year. Typically, one is prepared prior to the preparation of financial statements.

Illustration 2.4: Trial balance

RAPID DELIVERY COMPANY
Trial Balance
December 31, 1984

	Debits	Credits
Cash	$10,650	
Accounts receivable	5,200	
Supplies on hand	1,400	
Prepaid insurance	2,400	
Prepaid rent	1,200	
Delivery trucks	40,000	
Accounts payable		$ 3,130
Unearned delivery fees		4,500
John Turner, capital		50,000
John Turner, drawing	3,000	
Delivery service revenue		10,700
Advertising expense	50	
Gas and oil expense	680	
Salaries expense	3,600	
Utilities expense	150	
	$68,330	$68,330

Use of dollar signs

Dollar signs are not used in journals or ledgers. They may be used in trial balances, but are not required.

When amounts are in even dollar amounts, the cents column may be left blank, or zeros or a dash may be used. When lined accounting pads are used, there is no need to use commas or a period in recording an amount. When using unlined paper, both commas and a period should be used.

NEW TERMS INTRODUCED IN CHAPTER 2

Account
An element in an accounting system that is used to classify and summarize measurements of business activity. The three-column account is normally used. It contains columns for debit, credit, and balance.

Chart of accounts
The complete listing of the titles and account numbers of all of the accounts in the ledger; somewhat comparable to a table of contents.

Charge
Means the same as the word *debit*.

Compound journal entry
A journal entry with more than one debit and/or credit.

Credit
The right side of any account; when used as a verb, to enter a dollar amount on the right side of an account.

Credit balance
The balance in an account when the sum of the credits to the account exceeds the sum of the debits to that account.

Credit entry
An entry on the right side of an account; credits increase liability, owner's equity, and revenue accounts and decrease asset, expense, and owner's drawing accounts.

Cross-indexing
The placing of the account number in the journal and the placing of the journal page number in the ledger account.

Debit
The left side of any account; when used as a verb,

to enter a dollar amount on the left side of an account.

Debit balance
The balance in an account when the sum of the debits to the account exceeds the sum of the credits to that account.

Debit entry
An entry on the left side of an account; debits increase asset, expense, and owner's drawing accounts and decrease liability, owner's equity, and revenue accounts.

Double-entry procedure
The accounting requirement that every transaction be recorded in an entry that has equal debits and credits.

Journal
A chronological (arranged in order of time) record of business transactions; the simplest form of journal is the two-column general journal.

Journal entry
Shows all of the effects of a business transaction as expressed in terms of debit and credit and may include an explanation of the transaction.

Journalizing
A step in the accounting recording process that consists of entering a transaction in a journal.

Ledger
The complete collection of all of the accounts of a company; often referred to as the general ledger.

Nominal accounts
Income statement accounts (revenues and expenses).

Note (promissory)
A written promise to pay to another party the amount owed either when demanded or at a certain specified date.

Posting
Recording in the ledger the information contained in the journal.

Real accounts
Balance sheet accounts (assets, liabilities, and owner's equity).

T-account
An account resembling the letter T, which is used for illustrative purposes only. Debits are entered on the left side of the account and credits are entered on the right side of the account.

Trial balance
A listing of the ledger accounts and their debit or credit balances to determine that debits equal credits in the recording process.

DEMONSTRATION PROBLEM

The Huntcliff Riding Stable, owned by Barbara Macon, had the following balance sheet on June 30, 1984:

HUNTCLIFF RIDING STABLE
Balance Sheet
June 30, 1984

Assets

Cash	$ 7,000
Accounts receivable	5,400
Land	40,000
Total assets	$52,400

Liabilities and Owner's Equity

Liabilities:

Accounts payable	$ 800
Loan payable	40,000
Total liabilities	$40,800

Owner's equity:

Barbara Macon, capital	11,600
Total liabilities and owner's equity	$52,400

Transactions for the month of July 1984 were as follows:

Transactions:

July 1 The owner invested additional cash of $25,000.
1 Paid for a prefabricated building constructed on the land at a cost of $24,000.
8 Paid the accounts payable of $800.
10 Collected the accounts receivable of $5,400.
12 Horse feed to be used in July purchased on credit for $1,100.
24 Miscellaneous expenses of $800 for July were paid.
28 The owner withdrew $700 cash.
31 Salaries of $1,600 for the month were paid.
31 Riding and lesson fees for July were billed to customers in the amount of $3,600. They are due on August 10.
31 Boarding fees for July were charged to customers in the amount of $4,500. This amount is due on August 10.

Required:

 a. Prepare the journal entries to record the transactions for July 1984.

 b. Post the journal entries to the ledger accounts after entering the beginning balances in those accounts. Insert cross-indexing references in the journal and ledger. Use the following chart of accounts:

Account No.	**Account title**
100	Cash
101	Accounts Receivable
112	Land
114	Building
200	Accounts Payable
205	Loan Payable
300	Barbara Macon, Capital
301	Barbara Macon, Drawing
400	Horse Boarding Fees
401	Riding and Lesson Fees
501	Feed Expense
502	Salaries Expense
510	Miscellaneous Expense

 c. Prepare a trial balance.

Solution to demonstration problem

a.

| | | | | | | | GENERAL JOURNAL | | | | | | | | | | | | | | | | | | | Page 1 |

GENERAL JOURNAL   Page 1

Date		Account Titles and Explanation	Post. Ref.	Debit	Credit
1984 July	1	Cash	100	2 5 0 0 0	
		Barbara Macon, Capital	300		2 5 0 0 0
		Additional cash invested by owner.			
	1	Building	114	2 4 0 0 0	
		Cash	100		2 4 0 0 0
		Paid for building.			
	8	Accounts Payable	200	8 0 0	
		Cash	100		8 0 0
		Paid accounts payable.			
	10	Cash	100	5 4 0 0	
		Accounts Receivable	101		5 4 0 0
		Collected accounts receivable.			
	12	Feed Expense	501	1 1 0 0	
		Accounts Payable	200		1 1 0 0
		Purchased feed on credit.			
	24	Miscellaneous Expense	510	8 0 0	
		Cash	100		8 0 0
		Paid miscellaneous expenses for July.			
	28	Barbara Macon, Drawing	301	7 0 0	
		Cash	100		7 0 0
		Owner withdrew cash.			
	31	Salaries Expense	502	1 6 0 0	
		Cash	100		1 6 0 0
		Paid salaries for July.			
	31	Accounts Receivable	101	3 6 0 0	
		Riding and Lesson Fees	401		3 6 0 0
		Billed riding and lesson fees for July.			
	31	Accounts Receivable	101	4 5 0 0	
		Horse Boarding Fees	400		4 5 0 0
		Billed boarding fees for July.			

b.

GENERAL LEDGER

Cash

Account No. 100

Date		Explanation	Post Ref.	Debit	Credit	Balance
1984 June	30	Balance				7 0 0 0 Dr.
July	1	Owner investment	GJ1	2 5 0 0 0		3 2 0 0 0 Dr.
	1	Building	GJ1		2 4 0 0 0	8 0 0 0 Dr.
	8	Accounts payable	GJ1		8 0 0	7 2 0 0 Dr.
	10	Accounts receivable	GJ1	5 4 0 0		1 2 6 0 0 Dr.
	24	Miscellaneous expense	GJ1		8 0 0	1 1 8 0 0 Dr.
	28	Owner withdrawal	GJ1		7 0 0	1 1 1 0 0 Dr.
	31	Salaries expense	GJ1		1 6 0 0	9 5 0 0 Dr.

Accounts Receivable

Account No. 101

Date		Explanation	Post Ref.	Debit	Credit	Balance
1984 June	30	Balance				5 4 0 0 Dr.
July	10	Cash	GJ1		5 4 0 0	– 0 –
	31	Riding and lesson fees	GJ1	3 6 0 0		3 6 0 0 Dr.
	31	Horse boarding fees	GJ1	4 5 0 0		8 1 0 0 Dr.

Land

Account No. 112

Date		Explanation	Post Ref.	Debit	Credit	Balance
1984 June	30	Balance				4 0 0 0 0 Dr.

Building

Account No. 114

Date		Explanation	Post Ref.	Debit	Credit	Balance
1984 July	1	Cash	GJ1	2 4 0 0 0		2 4 0 0 0 Dr.

GENERAL LEDGER (*continued*)

Accounts Payable   *Account No. 200*

Date		Explanation	Post Ref.	Debit	Credit	Balance
1984 June	30	Balance				8 0 0 Cr.
July	8	Cash	GJ1	8 0 0		– 0 –
	12	Feed expense	GJ1		1 1 0 0	1 1 0 0 Cr.

Loan Payable   *Account No. 205*

Date		Explanation	Post Ref.	Debit	Credit	Balance
1984 June	30	Balance				4 0 0 0 0 Cr.

Barbara Macon, Capital   *Account No. 300*

Date		Explanation	Post Ref.	Debit	Credit	Balance
1984 June	30	Balance				1 1 6 0 0 Cr.
July	1	Cash	GJ1		2 5 0 0 0	3 6 6 0 0 Cr.

Barbara Macon, Drawing   *Account No. 301*

Date		Explanation	Post Ref.	Debit	Credit	Balance
1984 July	28	Cash	GJ1	7 0 0		7 0 0 Dr.

Horse Boarding Fees   *Account No. 400*

Date		Explanation	Post Ref.	Debit	Credit	Balance
1984 July	31	Accounts receivable	GJ1		4 5 0 0	4 5 0 0 Cr.

GENERAL LEDGER (*concluded*)

Riding and Lesson Fees

Account No. 401

Date		Explanation	Post Ref.	Debit	Credit	Balance
1984 July	31	Accounts receivable	GJ1		3 6 0 0	3 6 0 0 Cr.

Feed Expense

Account No. 501

Date		Explanation	Post Ref.	Debit	Credit	Balance
1984 July	12	Accounts payable	GJ1	1 1 0 0		1 1 0 0 Dr.

Salaries Expense

Account No. 502

Date		Explanation	Post Ref.	Debit	Credit	Balance
1984 July	31	Cash	GJ1	1 6 0 0		1 6 0 0 Dr.

Miscellaneous Expense

Account No. 510

Date		Explanation	Post Ref.	Debit	Credit	Balance
1984 July	24	Cash	GJ1	8 0 0		8 0 0 Dr.

c.

```
              HUNTCLIFF RIDING STABLE
                    Trial Balance
                    July 31, 1984

                               Debits      Credits
Cash ....................      $9,500
Accounts receivable .......     8,100
Land ....................      40,000
Building..................     24,000
Accounts payable ........                  $1,100
Loan payable ............                  40,000
Barbara Macon, capital .....               36,600
Barbara Macon, drawing ...       700
Horse boarding fees .......                 4,500
Riding and lesson fees .....                3,600
Feed expense ...........       1,100
Salaries expense ..........    1,600
Miscellaneous expense .....      800
                              $85,800      $85,800
```

QUESTIONS

1. Why are expense and revenue accounts used when all revenues and expenses could be shown directly in the owner's equity account?

2. What is the purpose of the owner's drawing account and how is it increased?

3. Which of the following cash payments would involve the immediate recording of an expense? Why?

    a. Paid an account payable.
    b. Paid for land to use as a future plant site.
    c. Paid the current month's rent.
    d. Paid salaries for the last half of the current month.

4. Define debit and credit. Name the types of accounts that are:

    a. Increased by debits.
    b. Decreased by debits.
    c. Increased by credits.
    d. Decreased by credits.

Do you think this system makes sense? Can you conceive of other possible methods for recording changes in accounts?

5. Are the following possibilities conceivable in an entry involving only one debit and one credit? Why?

    a. Increase a liability and increase an expense.
    b. Increase an asset and decrease a liability.
    c. Increase a revenue and decrease an expense.
    d. Decrease an asset and increase another asset.
    e. Decrease an asset and increase a liability.
    f. Decrease a revenue and decrease an asset.
    g. Decrease a liability and increase a revenue.

6. Describe a ledger and a chart of accounts. How do these two compare with a book and its table of contents?

7. Describe the nature and purposes of the general journal. What does "journalizing" mean? Give an example of a compound entry in the general journal.

8. Describe the act of posting. What difficulties could arise if no cross-indexing existed between the general journal and the ledger accounts?

9. What types of accounts appear in the trial balance? What are the purposes of the trial balance?

10. You have found that the total of the debit column of the trial balance of the Landers Company is $100,000, while the total of the credit column is $90,000. What are some of the possible causes of this difference?

11. Store equipment was purchased for $1,500. Instead of debiting the Store Equipment account, the debit was made to Delivery Equipment. Of what help will the trial balance be in locating this error? Why?

12. Differentiate between the trial balance, chart of accounts, balance sheet, and income statement.

13. A student remembered that the side toward the window in the classroom was the debit side of an account. The student took an examination in a room where the windows were on the other side of the room and became confused and consistently reversed debits and credits. Would the student's trial balance have equal debit and credit totals? If there were no existing balances in any of the accounts to begin with, would the error prevent the student from preparing correct financial statements? Why?

EXERCISES

E–1.   Below is a diagram of the various types of accounts. Indicate where pluses (+) or minuses (−) should be inserted to indicate what effect debits and credits have on each account.

Asset Accounts		=	Liability Accounts		+	Owner's Equity Accounts	
Debit	Credit		Debit	Credit		Debit	Credit

Expense Accounts and Owner's Drawing Account		Revenue Accounts	
Debit	Credit	Debit	Credit

E–2.   Using T-accounts show how the following transactions would be recorded.

a. Cash of $20,000 was invested in a business by its owner, Malcom Fisher.
b. Wages for the period were paid to employees, $2,500.
c. Services were performed for customers on account, $4,000.

E–3.   Give the journal entry required for each of the following transactions:

a. Will Britt invested $50,000 cash in his business.
b. A $30,000 loan was arranged with a bank. The bank increased the company's checking account by $30,000 after the owner signed a written promise to return the $30,000 in 30 days.
c. Cash was received for services performed for customers, $800.
d. Services were performed for customers on account, $1,200.

E–4. Prepare journal entries to record each of the following transactions for the Larry King Company. Use the letter of the transaction in place of the date. Include an explanation for each entry.

    a. The owner invested $80,000 cash in the business.
    b. Purchased delivery equipment on account, $50,000.
    c. Earned (but did not yet receive) delivery fee revenue, $1,000.
    d. Collected the account receivable for the delivery fees, $1,000.
    e. Paid the account payable for the delivery equipment purchased, $50,000.
    f. Paid utilities for the month in the amount of $500.
    g. Paid salaries for the month in the amount of $1,500.
    h. Incurred delivery expenses in the amount of $400, but did not yet pay for them.
    i. Purchased more delivery equipment for cash, $10,000.
    j. Performed delivery services on account, $5,000.

E–5. Using the data in Exercise E–4 record the transactions in T-accounts. Write the letter of the transaction in the T-account before the dollar amount. Determine a balance for each account.

E–6. Using your answer for Exercise E–5, prepare a trial balance. Assume the date of the trial balance is March 31, 1984.

E–7. Give the journal entry (without dollar amounts) for a transaction that would involve each of the following combinations of types of accounts:

    a. An asset and a liability.
    b. An expense and an asset.
    c. A liability and an expense.
    d. Owner's equity and an asset.
    e. Two asset accounts.
    f. An asset and a revenue.

E–8. Raymond Byars owns and manages a bowling center called Tri-Angle Lanes. He also maintains his own accounting records and was about to prepare financial statements for the year 1984. When he prepared the trial balance from the ledger accounts, the total of the debits column was $614,800 and the total of the credits column was $612,800. What are the possible reasons why the totals of the debits and credits are out of balance? How would you proceed to find the error?

PROBLEMS, SERIES A

P2–1–A. The following is a list of accounts and their balances for the Allen Company as of December 31, 1984:

Carla Allen, drawing	$ 2,000	Cash	8,000
Accounts payable	2,400	Rent expense	4,000
Salaries expense	30,000	Miscellaneous expense	1,500
Furniture and equipment	12,000	Supplies on hand	2,500
Accounts receivable	4,600	Prepaid insurance	3,800
Carla Allen, capital	13,700	Unearned service fees	6,300
Service revenue	46,000		

Required:

Prepare a trial balance as of December 31, 1984. Arrange the accounts in the order in which they would normally appear in the ledger.

P2-2-A. Joan Babfield prepared a trial balance for the Sterns Company and it did not balance. The trial balance she prepared was as follows:

STERNS COMPANY
Trial Balance
December 31, 1984

	Debits	Credits
Cash	$ 8,000	
Accounts receivable	5,100	
Equipment	20,000	
Accounts payable		$ 3,000
Harvey Sterns, capital		20,000
Harvey Sterns, drawing	2,000	
Service revenue		54,000
Advertising expense	150	
Salaries expense	22,000	
Rent expense	8,000	
Utilities expense	5,600	
	$70,850	$77,000

In trying to find out why the trial balance did not balance, Joan discovered the following errors:

1. Cash was understated (too low) by $1,000 because of an error in addition in determining the balance of that account in the ledger.
2. A credit of $600 to Accounts Receivable in the journal was not posted to the ledger at all.
3. A debit of $2,000 for a withdrawal by the owner was posted as a credit to the owner's capital account.
4. The balance of $1,500 in the Advertising Expense account was entered as $150 in the trial balance.
5. Miscellaneous Expense, with a balance of $400, was omitted from the trial balance.

Required:

Prepare a correct trial balance as of December 31, 1984.

P2-3-A. The transactions for October 1984 for the Delivery Services Company are given below. The owner of the business is Warren Childs.

Transactions:

Oct. 1 The owner invested cash, $16,000.
3 Borrowed $5,000 from the bank on a note.
4 Purchased a truck for $9,300 cash.
6 Delivery services were performed for customers who promised to pay later, $3,600.
7 Employee services received and paid for, $1,400.
10 Collections were made for the services performed on October 6, $800.
14 Office supplies were purchased for $500 on account. They will be paid for and used next month.
17 A bill for $500 was received for gas and oil used to date.
25 Delivery services were performed for customers who paid immediately, $4,500.
31 Wages paid were $1,500.
31 The owner withdrew $400.

Required:

a. Open T-accounts and record the transactions. Place the date of each transaction in the accounts. Determine the ending balance of each T-account where more than one dollar amount has been entered.

    b.   Prepare a trial balance as of October 31, 1984.

P2–4–A.   The transactions appearing below are those of the E-Z Appliance Repair Service Company for the month of July 1984. The company is owned by Arthur Oliver.

Transactions:

July 2 The owner invested $10,000 cash in the business.
      3 The company paid rent for July, $500.
      5 A truck was purchased for $3,000 cash.
      9 A bill for $500 for advertising for July was received and paid.
    14 Cash of $1,400 was received for appliance repair services performed.
    15 Wages of $400 for the first half of July were paid.
    20 The company performed appliance repair services on account for the Saunders Company, $400.
    22 Office furniture was acquired for $800 on account from the Olympic Company.
    25 The owner withdrew $300 cash.
    30 Cash of $2,250 was received for appliance repair services performed.
    31 Wages of $400 for the second half of July were paid.

Required:

    a.   Open T-accounts and record the transactions. Place the date of each transaction in the accounts. Determine the ending balance of each T-account where more than one dollar amount has been entered.

    b.   Prepare a trial balance as of July 31, 1984.

P2–5–A.   Presented below are the transactions (partially summarized for the sake of brevity) of the Trowell Realty Company, owned by Sandy Trowell, for the month of March 1984.

Transactions:

1. The owner invested $20,000 cash.
2. Paid $1,800 as the rent for March on an office building.
3. Billed clients for commissions revenue for March, $16,000.
4. Paid $200 for office supplies received and used in March.
5. Borrowed $5,000 from the bank on a note.
6. Collected $12,000 cash on accounts receivable.
7. Received a bill for $600 for advertising appearing in the local newspaper in March.
8. Paid cash for gas and oil consumed in March, $425.
9. Paid $16,000 to employees for services provided in March.
10. The owner withdrew $500 cash.

Required:

    Prepare the general journal entries that would be required to record the above transactions in the records of the Trowell Realty Company.

P2–6–A.   The Window Cleaning Company, owned by Tina Hightower, began business on July 1, 1984. The following account numbers and titles constitute the chart of accounts for the company:

Account No.	Account title	Account No.	Account title
101	Cash	332	Tina Hightower, Drawing
102	Accounts Receivable	441	Cleaning Service Revenue
111	Office Equipment	551	Salaries Expense
112	Cleaning Equipment	552	Insurance Expense
113	Service Truck	553	Gas and Oil Expense
221	Accounts Payable	554	Rent Expense
222	Notes Payable	555	Utilities Expense
331	Tina Hightower, Capital	556	Cleaning Supplies Expense

The company entered into the following transactions in July 1984:

Transactions:

July 1 The owner invested $60,000 cash in the business.
5 Office space was rented for July, and $600 cash was paid for the rental.
8 Desks and chairs were purchased for the office on account, $6,000.
10 Cleaning equipment was purchased for $8,400; a note was given, to be paid in 30 days.
15 Purchased a service truck for $18,000, paying $12,000 cash and giving a note for $6,000 to be paid in 60 days.
18 Paid for cleaning supplies for July, $300.
23 Cash received for cleaning service revenue earned, $3,600.
27 Insurance expense for July was paid, $900 cash.
30 Paid for gasoline and oil used by the service truck in July, $60.
31 Billed customers for cleaning services rendered, $4,200.
31 Paid salaries for July, $7,500.
31 Paid utilities bill for July, $550.
31 The owner withdrew $700 to make her house mortgage payment.

Required:

a. Open ledger accounts for all of the above accounts.

b. Journalize the transactions given above for July 1984.

c. Post the journal entries to the ledger accounts.

d. Prepare a trial balance.

P2–7–A. The Exceptional Lawn Care Company, owned by David Lee, was formed several years ago. The company's trial balance at the end of the first 11 months of its fiscal year is presented below.

EXCEPTIONAL LAWN CARE COMPANY
Trial Balance
June 30, 1984

Account No.	Account title	Debits	Credits
101	Cash	$ 49,160	
102	Accounts receivable	52,400	
110	Land	63,530	
201	Accounts payable		$ 22,400
301	David Lee, capital		85,690
302	David Lee, drawing	22,000	
400	Lawn care revenue		180,000
410	Shrubbery care revenue		67,340
510	Salaries expense	43,900	
520	Chemical supplies expense	49,600	
530	Advertising expense	12,200	
540	Truck operating expense	14,600	
550	Office rent expense	22,000	
560	Office supplies expense	800	
570	Telephone and utilities expense	1,540	
580	Customer entertainment expense	1,700	
590	Truck rent expense	22,000	
		$355,430	$355,430

Required:

a. Open three-column ledger accounts for each of the accounts in the trial balance. Place the word *balance* in the explanation space, enter the date July 1, 1984, on the same line, and enter the proper beginning balance in each account.

      b. Prepare general journal entries for the transactions given below for July 1984.

      c. Post the journal entries to the general ledger accounts.

      d. Prepare a trial balance as of July 31, 1984.

Transactions:

July 2 Paid office rent for July, $2,000.
      5 Paid the accounts payable of $22,400.
      8 Paid advertising for the month of July, $800.
    10 Purchased a small tract of land for cash, $700.
    13 Purchased on account $160 of office supplies for use in July.
    15 Collected cash from customers on account, $51,200.
    20 Paid for customer entertainment in July, $50.
    26 Paid for gasoline used in the trucks in July, $180.
    28 Billed customers for services; lawn care, $31,500; shrubbery care, $21,500.
    30 Paid for July chemical supplies, $13,200.
    31 Paid truck rent expense for July, $2,000.
    31 Paid July salaries, $10,200.
    31 The owner withdrew $2,000 cash.

PROBLEMS, SERIES B

P2–1–B.   The following is a list of accounts and their balances for the Baker Company as of December 31, 1984:

John Baker, drawing	$ 6,000	John Baker, capital	28,300
Accounts payable	10,000	Rent expense	3,600
Supplies expense	1,200	Delivery equipment	32,000
Office equipment	9,000	Delivery service revenue	37,000
Notes payable	15,400	Salaries expense	16,000
Accounts receivable	14,900	Prepaid insurance	1,800
Utilities expense	2,400	Unearned delivery fees	3,000
Cash	6,800		

Required:

    Prepare a trial balance as of December 31, 1984. Arrange the accounts in the order in which they normally would appear in the ledger.

P2–2–B.   Jim Bunch prepared the following trial balance from the ledger of the Grace Company. It did not balance. This fact caused Jim to examine the accounting records very carefully.

GRACE COMPANY
Trial Balance
December 31, 1984

	Debits	*Credits*
Cash	$ 7,400	
Accounts receivable	5,100	
Furniture and equipment	15,000	
Office fixtures	6,000	
Accounts payable		$ 2,800
Robert Grace, capital		30,000
Robert Grace, drawing	3,600	
Service revenue		45,000
Salaries expense	35,000	
Rent expense	5,000	
Miscellaneous expense	900	
	$78,000	$77,800

In searching back through the accounting records, Jim found that the following errors had been made:

1. One entire entry was never posted. It included a debit to Cash and a credit to Accounts Receivable for $600.
2. In computing the balance of the Accounts Payable account, a credit of $400 was omitted from the computation.
3. In preparing the trial balance, the Robert Grace, Capital account balance was shown as $30,000. The ledger account has the balance at its correct amount of $30,400.
4. One debit of $300 to the Robert Grace, Drawing account was posted as a credit to that account.
5. Office fixtures of $1,000 were debited to Furniture and Equipment when purchased.

Required:

Prepare a corrected trial balance for the Grace Company as of December 31, 1984. Hint: Some errors may not cause the trial balance to be out of balance.

P2–3–B.   The transactions listed below are those of the Wayne Pierce Company for the month of April 1984.

Transactions

Apr. 1 $60,000 cash was received as the owner's investment in the business.
     3 Rent was paid for April, $400.
     6 Delivery equipment was purchased and paid for, $7,000.
     7 Office equipment was purchased on account from the Norton Company for $4,800.
    14 Wages were paid, $1,400.
    15 $2,900 was received for services performed.
    18 An invoice was received from Pat's Gas Station for $50 for gas and oil used.
    23 Borrowed $5,000 from the bank on a note.
    29 Purchased delivery equipment for $9,200 on account.
    30 Wages of $1,800 were paid.

Required:

a.   Mentally analyze each transaction in terms of debit and credit and then enter them directly in suitable T-accounts. To identify each part of each transaction, also enter the date of the transaction in the accounts. Determine the ending balance in each T-account where more than one dollar amount has been entered.

b.   Prepare a trial balance as of April 30, 1984.

P2–4–B.   The transactions given below are for the Stay Trim Company.

Transactions:

Apr. 1 $50,000 cash was invested in the business by the owner.
     5 The company borrowed $25,000 from its bank and issued its note payable to the bank.
     9 Paid $20,000 cash for land and $47,500 cash for a building located on the land.
    14 Purchased $8,000 of exercise equipment on account.
    17 Paid $600 cash for supplies to be used in April.
    25 Sales of services on account were $5,000.
    30 Sales of services for cash for the month were $1,000.
    30 Paid salaries for April, $1,000.

Required:

a.   Set up the following T-accounts: Cash; Accounts Receivable; Land; Building; Exercise Equipment; Accounts Payable; Notes Payable, Bank; Beth White, Capital; Service Revenue; Salaries Expense; and Supplies Expense. Enter the transactions in the T-accounts.

Date each transaction entry as indicated. Determine the ending balance in each T-account where more than one dollar amount has been entered.

b. Prepare a trial balance after entering the last transaction.

P2–5–B. The Peachtree Laundry Company, owned by Chris Warden, entered into the following transactions in August 1984:

Transactions:

Aug. 2 The owner invested $60,000 cash in the business.
3 Paid rent for August on a building and laundry equipment, $1,050.
4 Purchased and paid for a delivery truck, $8,000.
6 Cash received for laundry services performed, $9,000.
13 Laundry services were performed on account for various customers, $8,000.
15 Received and paid a bill for $197 for gasoline and oil used in operations.
23 Cash collected from customers on account, $7,500.
31 Paid $2,700 to employees for services performed in August.
31 Received the electric and gas bill for the month of August, $155.

Required:

Prepare general journal entries for the above transactions.

P2–6–B. The Quick Delivery Company was formed on January 1, 1984, by its owner, Pat Hixon. Its chart of accounts is as follows:

Account No.	Account title	Account No.	Account title
101	Cash	332	Pat Hixon, Drawing
102	Accounts Receivable	441	Delivery Service Revenue
111	Delivery Trucks	551	Garage Rent Expense
112	Garage Equipment	552	Gasoline and Oil Expense
113	Office Equipment	553	Repairs Expense—Delivery Trucks
221	Accounts Payable	554	Salaries Expense
222	Notes Payable	556	Utilities Expense
331	Pat Hixon, Capital	557	Insurance Expense

The company had the following transactions in January 1984:

Transactions:

Jan. 1 The company received $50,000 cash and $20,000 of garage equipment as an original investment of the owner.
2 Paid garage rent for the month of January, $500.
4 Purchased office equipment on account, $2,900.
6 Purchased three delivery trucks at $7,500 each; payment was made by giving cash of $12,500 and a 30-day note for the remainder.
10 Paid $165 cash for repairs to the delivery trucks.
12 Purchased insurance for January on the delivery trucks. The $200 cost of the policy was paid in cash.
15 Received and paid January utility bills, $80.
20 Received bill for gasoline purchased and used in January, $60.
23 Purchased one delivery truck for cash, $9,000.
25 Cash sales of delivery services were $390.
27 Purchased a calculator on account, $300.
31 Paid salaries for January, $1,400.
31 Delivery services were performed on account, $950.
31 Paid for repairs to a delivery truck, $10 cash.
31 Pat Hixon withdrew $400 cash from the business.

Required:

a. Open ledger accounts for all the above accounts.

b. Journalize the transactions given above for January 1984.

    c.   Post the journal entries to the ledger accounts.

    d.   Prepare a trial balance as of January 31, 1984.

P2–7–B.   The trial balance of the Tennis Court at the end of the first 11 months of its fiscal year is given below.

TENNIS COURT
Trial Balance
May 31, 1984

Account No.	Account title	Debits	Credits
100	Cash	$ 54,120	
102	Accounts receivable	54,500	
121	Land	20,000	
210	Accounts payable		$ 12,500
220	Notes payable		10,000
310	Jo Stone, capital		71,200
320	Jo Stone, drawing	11,000	
400	Tennis lesson revenue		135,000
510	Tennis professionals' salaries expense ..	33,000	
520	Advertising expense	14,000	
530	Lesson supplies expense	1,500	
540	Equipment repairs expense	1,000	
550	Office salaries expense	11,000	
560	Building rent expense	22,000	
570	Utilities expense	1,400	
580	Entertainment expense	580	
590	Equipment rent expense	4,400	
600	Miscellaneous expense	200	
		$228,700	$228,700

Required:

    a.   Open three-column ledger accounts for each of the accounts in the trial balance. Place the word *Balance* in the explanation space, enter the date June 1, 1984, on the same line, and enter the proper beginning balance in each account.

    b.   Prepare general journal entries for the transactions given below for June 1984.

    c.   Post the journal entries to the general ledger accounts.

    d.   Prepare a trial balance as of June 30, 1984.

Transactions:

June 1 Paid building rent for June, $2,000.
      2 Paid accounts payable, $12,150.
      5 Purchased a small tract of land for cash, $1,500.
      7 Gave tennis lessons on account, $18,000.
    10 Paid the note payable of $10,000.
    13 Received cash from customers on account, $24,000.
    19 Received a bill for equipment repairs, $150.
    24 Paid the June telephone bill, $55, and the June electric bill, $65.
    28 Received a bill for June advertising, $1,100.
    30 Gave tennis lessons for cash, $3,000.
    30 Paid office salaries, $1,000, and tennis professionals' salaries, $3,000.
    30 Gave tennis lessons on account since June 7, $12,000.
    30 Costs paid in entertaining persons who subsequently became members, $170.
    30 Paid equipment rent expense for June, $400.
    30 The owner withdrew $1,000 cash.

BUSINESS DECISION PROBLEM

Steve Victor lost his job as a carpenter with a contractor when a recession hit the building trades industry. Steve had been making about $25,000 per year. He decided to form his own company and do home repairs.

The following is a summary of the transactions of the business during the first three months of operations in 1984:

Transactions:

Jan.	15	Steve invested $10,000 in the business.
Feb.	10	Owner withdrew $1,000 for living expenses.
	25	Received payment of $2,200 for remodeling a basement into a recreation room. The homeowner purchased all of the building materials.
Mar.	5	Paid cash for an advertisement that appeared in the local newspaper, $55.
	18	Owner withdrew $900 for personal living expenses.
Apr.	10	Received $3,200 for converting a room over a garage into an office for a college professor. The professor purchased all of the materials for the job.
Jan. 15–Apr. 15		Paid gas and oil expenses for automobile, $350.
Jan. 15–Apr. 15		Miscellaneous business expenses were paid, $225.
Jan. 15–Apr. 15		The owner withdrew $4,270 to pay various personal expenses.

Required:

a. Prepare journal entries for the above transactions.

b. Post the journal entries to T-accounts.

c. How is Steve doing in this new venture?

Chapter 3

Adjusting the accounts

CHAPTER GOALS

After study of this chapter, you should be able to:

1. Identify the reasons why adjusting entries must be made.
2. Describe the basic characteristics of the accrual basis and the cash basis of accounting.
3. Identify the major types of adjusting entries.
4. Prepare adjusting entries.
5. Define and use correctly the new terms in the glossary.

Previous chapters have discussed and illustrated how and why transactions are relied on as the basic source of input data for accounting. These chapters also have shown how transactions are analyzed, journalized, and summarized in accounts.

This chapter uses the Rapid Delivery Company illustration in the preceding chapter to show the need for adjusting entries. *Adjusting entries* are journal entries made at the end of an accounting period to change the balances of certain accounts to reflect economic activity that has taken place but has not yet been recorded. The reason the economic activity has not been recorded is because no business transaction concerning that activity has come to the accountant's attention to cause a journal entry to be prepared.

THE NEED FOR ADJUSTING ENTRIES

The income statement of an entity must report all revenues earned and all expenses incurred to generate those revenues during a given period. If the income statement does not report all revenues and expenses, it is incomplete, inaccurate, and possibly misleading. Similarly, a balance sheet that does not report all of an entity's assets, liabilities, and owner's equities at a point in time may be misleading.

Since interested parties need timely information, financial statements must be prepared periodically. To prepare such statements, the accountant arbitrarily divides an entity's life into *time periods.* Economic activity is then assigned to specific periods. The time periods are usually equal in length and are called accounting periods. An *accounting period* may be one month, one quarter, or one year long. An accounting period of one year is called an *accounting year* or fiscal year. A *fiscal year* is any 12 consecutive months, and it may or may not coincide with the *calendar year,* ending on December 31. Periodic reporting necessitates the preparation of adjusting entries. Adjusting entries bring the accounts to their proper balances before financial statements are prepared. That is, *adjusting entries convert the amounts that are actually in the accounts to the amounts that should be in the accounts for proper financial reporting.*

Cash versus accrual basis accounting

Some relatively small business firms and professional persons, such as physicians, lawyers, and accountants, may account for their revenues and expenses on a cash basis. The *cash basis of accounting recognizes revenues when cash is received and recognizes expenses when cash is paid out.* For example, under the cash basis, services rendered to clients in 1984 for which cash was collected in 1985 would be treated as 1985 revenues. Similarly, under the cash basis, expenses incurred in 1984 for which cash was disbursed in 1985 would be treated as 1985 expenses. Because of these improper assignments of revenues and expenses, the cash basis of accounting is generally considered unacceptable. It is acceptable only under those circumstances in which the results approximate those obtained under the accrual basis of accounting. The cash basis may also be used for income tax purposes under certain circumstances.

The **accrual basis of accounting** *recognizes revenues when sales are made or services are performed even though cash has not yet been received. Expenses are recognized as incurred regardless of whether or not cash has been paid out.* Revenue and expense transactions not involving cash may not have been recorded by the end of the period. Therefore, under the accrual basis, adjusting entries are needed to bring the accounts up to date for economic activity that has taken place but has not yet been recorded. Accurate financial statements can then be prepared.

Time of preparation of adjusting entries

Adjusting entries must be prepared whenever financial statements are to be prepared. Therefore, if monthly financial statements are prepared, monthly adjusting entries are required. By custom, and in some instances by law, business firms report to their owners at least annually. Accordingly, adjusting entries will be required at least once a year.

CLASSES OF ADJUSTING ENTRIES

Adjusting entries can be grouped first into broad classes. One class consists of those entries that relate to data previously recorded in the accounts. These entries involve the transfer of data from asset and liability accounts to expense and revenue accounts. The types of adjusting entries included within this class are entries for prepaid expenses, depreciation (to be explained

Illustration 3.1: Trial balance

RAPID DELIVERY COMPANY
Trial Balance
December 31, 1984

	Debits	Credits
Cash	$10,650	
Accounts receivable	5,200	
Supplies on hand	1,400	
Prepaid insurance	2,400	
Prepaid rent	1,200	
Delivery trucks	40,000	
Accounts payable		$ 3,130
Unearned delivery service revenue		4,500
John Turner, capital		50,000
John Turner, drawing	3,000	
Delivery service revenue		10,700
Advertising expense	50	
Gas and oil expense	680	
Salaries expense	3,600	
Utilities expense	150	
	$68,330	$68,330

later), and unearned revenues. The second class consists of entries relating to activity on which no data have been previously recorded in the accounts. These entries involve the initial recording of assets and liabilities and the related revenues and expenses. The types of adjusting entries included in this second class are entries for accrued assets and accrued liabilities. As will be illustrated later, *accrued assets and liabilities* are those that exist at the end of an accounting period, but have not yet been recorded.

Each type of adjusting entry will be illustrated in this chapter. Data relating to the Rapid Delivery Company example in the preceding chapter will be used. The trial balance of the Rapid Delivery Company at December 31, 1984, is shown in Illustration 3.1. Several of the accounts in the trial balance need to be adjusted. Each of these will be discussed and illustrated.

The additional accounts that will be used in this chapter for the Rapid Delivery Company are:

	Account No.	Account title	Description
Contra asset*	110A	Accumulated Depreciation—Delivery Equipment	Contains the total depreciation cost taken on delivery equipment. The balance of this account is deducted from Delivery Equipment on the balance sheet.
Liability	202	Accrued Salaries Payable	Shows the amount of salaries earned by employees but not yet paid by the company.
Expenses	504	Insurance Expense	The cost of insurance incurred in the current period.
	505	Rent Expense	The cost of rent incurred in the current period.
	506	Supplies Expense	The cost of supplies used in the current period.
	507	Depreciation Expense—Delivery Trucks	The cost of the portion of delivery equipment used up during the current period.

* A contra asset is deducted from an asset account on the balance sheet.

PREPAID EXPENSES

The prepaid expenses illustrated are prepaid insurance, prepaid rent, and supplies on hand.

(Prepaid insurance)

When an insurance policy premium is paid in advance of the period covered by the policy, an asset is created. The asset expires and becomes an expense with the passage of time. To illustrate this point, recall that the Rapid Delivery Company purchased on account an insurance policy on its delivery trucks that covers the period from December 1, 1984, to December 1, 1985. This purchase creates an asset called *prepaid insurance* on December

1, 1984. An asset exists because benefits—insurance protection—will be received in the future. The journal entry made on December 1 to record the purchase of the policy was:

```
1984
Dec.  1   Prepaid Insurance ......................................   2,400
              Accounts Payable ...................................            2,400
              Purchased truck insurance to cover a one-year period.
```

There are two accounts which relate to insurance, Prepaid Insurance (an asset) and Insurance Expense. After posting this entry, the Prepaid Insurance account has a $2,400 debit balance and the Insurance Expense account has a zero balance:

(Dr.)	Prepaid Insurance	(Cr.)	(Dr.)	Insurance Expense	(Cr.)
Bal.	2,400		Bal.	–0–	

By December 31, a part of the period covered by the policy has expired. Therefore, a part of the *service potential* (or benefits that can be obtained from the asset) has expired. The asset now provides less future benefits than when acquired. The future services that an asset can render are what make the asset "a thing of value" to a business. This reduction of the asset's ability to provide services must be recognized. The cost of the services received from the asset is treated as an expense. In this case, the service received was one month of insurance coverage. Since the policy provides the same services for every month of its one-year life, it seems logical to assign an equal amount ($200) of cost to each month. Thus, 1/12 of the annual premium is charged to insurance expense on December 31. The adjusting journal entry is as follows:

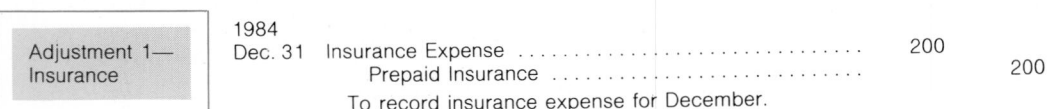

```
                              1984
  Adjustment 1—              Dec. 31   Insurance Expense ............................   200
  Insurance                                  Prepaid Insurance .........................           200
                                             To record insurance expense for December.
```

In T-account format, the accounts would appear as follows after posting the two entries:

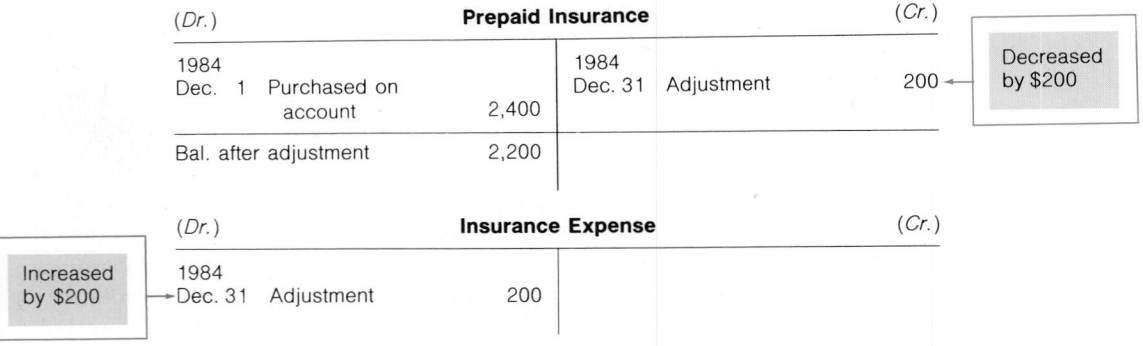

(Dr.)	Prepaid Insurance			(Cr.)	
1984			1984		
Dec. 1 Purchased on			Dec. 31 Adjustment	200	Decreased by $200
account	2,400				
Bal. after adjustment	2,200				

	(Dr.)	Insurance Expense		(Cr.)
	1984			
Increased by $200	Dec. 31 Adjustment	200		

T-accounts will sometimes be used to illustrate entries in the text. Normally they are not used in practice, since the three-column form has the advantage of showing a balance after each transaction.

The three-column ledger accounts after posting the two entries above appear as follows:

		Prepaid Insurance					Account No. 103	
Date		Explanation	Post. Ref.	Debit	Credit	Balance		
1984 Dec.	1	Purchased on account	GJ1*	2 4 0 0		2 4 0 0	Dr.	
	31	Adjustment	GJ3*		2 0 0	2 2 0 0	Dr.	

		Insurance Expense					Account No. 504	
Date		Explanation	Post. Ref.	Debit	Credit	Balance		
1984 Dec.	31	Adjustment	GJ3*	2 0 0		2 0 0	Dr.	

* Note: These posting references are assumed.

Before the adjusting entry was made, the entire $2,400 was a prepaid expense. The adjusting entry transferred $200 of the $2,400 to insurance expense. The insurance expense of $200 is reported in the income statement for the year ended December 31, 1984, as one of the expenses incurred in generating that year's revenues. The remaining amount of the prepaid expense, $2,200, is reported as an asset. This type of asset is often referred to as a prepaid expense. A *prepaid expense* is an asset that is awaiting assignment to expense. The $2,200 prepaid expense is a measure of the cost of the remaining asset, prepaid insurance. Prepaid insurance is an asset because it provides future benefits; in this case, there is insurance coverage for 11 more months.

Prepaid rent

Prepaid rent is another example of the continuous using up of a previously recorded asset. When rent is paid in advance to cover more than one accounting period, the prepayment is debited to the Prepaid Rent account (an asset account) at the date it is paid. Benefits resulting from the expenditure are yet to be received, thus the expenditure creates an asset. Services from the facilities being rented are received *continuously* through time. The expense is incurred *continuously* as time elapses. An entry could be made frequently, even daily, to record the expense incurred. But typically the entry is not made until financial statements are to be prepared. At that time, an entry is made transferring from the asset account to an expense account the cost of the portion of the asset that has expired.

The measurement of rent expense usually is quite simple. Generally, the rental contract specifies the amount of rent per unit of time. If the prepayment covers a three-month rental, one third of this rental is charged to each month. The same amount is charged to each month even though there are varying numbers of days in some months.

To illustrate, the Rapid Delivery Company paid $1,200 rent in advance on December 1, 1984, to cover a three-month period beginning on that date. The entry made at that time was:

```
1984
Dec.  1   Prepaid Rent .........................................  1,200
              Cash .............................................           1,200
          Paid three months' rent on a building.
```

The two accounts relating to rent are Prepaid Rent (an asset) and Rent Expense. After this entry has been posted, the Prepaid Rent account has a $1,200 balance and the Rent Expense account has a zero balance:

(Dr.)	Prepaid Rent	(Cr.)	(Dr.)	Rent Expense	(Cr.)
Bal.	1,200		Bal.	–0–	

On December 31, 1984, an adjusting entry must be prepared. Since one third of the period covered by the prepaid rent (one of three months) has elapsed, one third of the $1,200 of prepaid rent is charged to expense. The required adjusting entry is as follows:

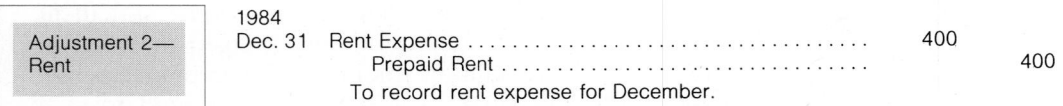

```
                          1984
Adjustment 2—             Dec. 31   Rent Expense .................................   400
Rent                                    Prepaid Rent ..............................        400
                                    To record rent expense for December.
```

The T-accounts would appear as follows after posting the adjusting entry:

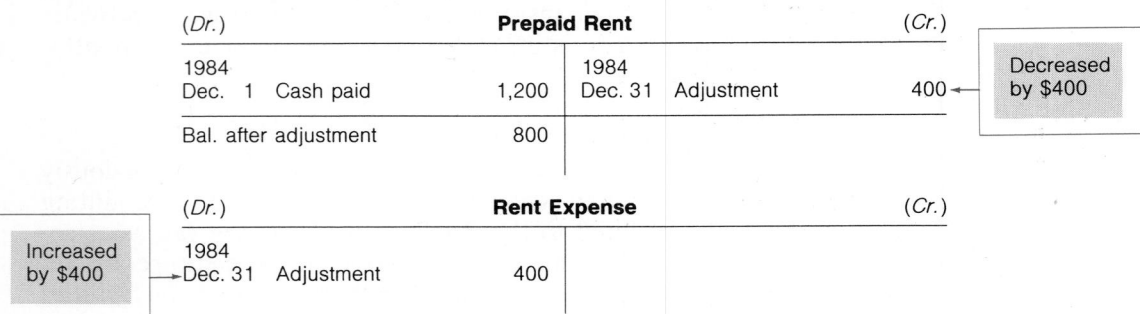

(Dr.)		Prepaid Rent		(Cr.)	
1984			1984		Decreased
Dec. 1 Cash paid	1,200		Dec. 31 Adjustment	400 ◄—	by $400
Bal. after adjustment	800				

(Dr.)		Rent Expense	(Cr.)
Increased	1984		
by $400	Dec. 31 Adjustment	400	

The $400 rent expense would appear in the income statement for the year ended December 31, 1984. The remaining $800 of prepaid rent is reported as an asset in the balance sheet for December 31, 1984.

Supplies on hand

Every business uses supplies in its operations. Supplies may be classified simply as supplies (to include all types of supplies), office supplies (paper, stationery, carbon paper, pencils), selling supplies (gummed tape, string, paper bags or cartons, wrapping paper), or, possibly, cleaning supplies (soap, disinfectants). Supplies are frequently bought in bulk and are an asset until they are used. The asset may be called *supplies on hand* or *supplies inventory*.

On December 4, 1984, the Rapid Delivery Company purchased supplies and recorded the transaction as follows:

```
1984
Dec. 4   Supplies on Hand .....................................   1,400
              Cash .........................................              1,400
         To record the purchase of supplies for future use.
```

The two accounts relating to supplies are Supplies on Hand (an asset) and Supplies Expense. After this entry has been posted, the Supplies on Hand account shows a debit balance of $1,400 and the Supplies Expense account has a zero balance as shown:

(*Dr.*)	**Supplies on Hand**	(*Cr.*)	(*Dr.*)	**Supplies Expense**	(*Cr.*)
Bal.	1,400		Bal.	–0–	

An actual physical inventory (a count of the supplies on hand) at the end of the month showed that only $900 of supplies were on hand. Thus, $500 of supplies must have been used in December. An adjusting journal entry is required to bring the accounts to their proper balances. The entry recognizes the reduction in the asset and the incurrence of an expense through the using up of supplies. From the information given, the asset balance should be $900 and the expense incurred, $500. By making the following adjusting entry, the accounts will be adjusted to those balances:

Adjustment 3— Supplies

```
1984
Dec. 31   Supplies Expense ............................   500
               Supplies on Hand...........................              500
          To record supplies used during December.
```

The T-accounts after posting the entry would appear as follows:

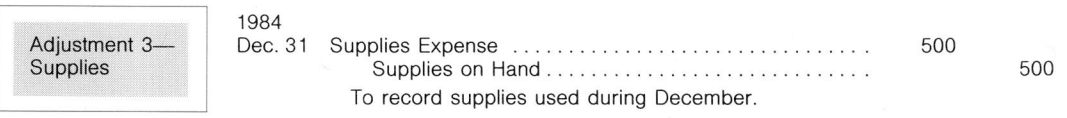

(*Dr.*)		**Supplies on Hand**		(*Cr.*)	
1984			1984		
Dec. 4	Cash paid	1,400	Dec. 31	Adjustment	500
Bal. after adjustment		900			

Decreased by $500

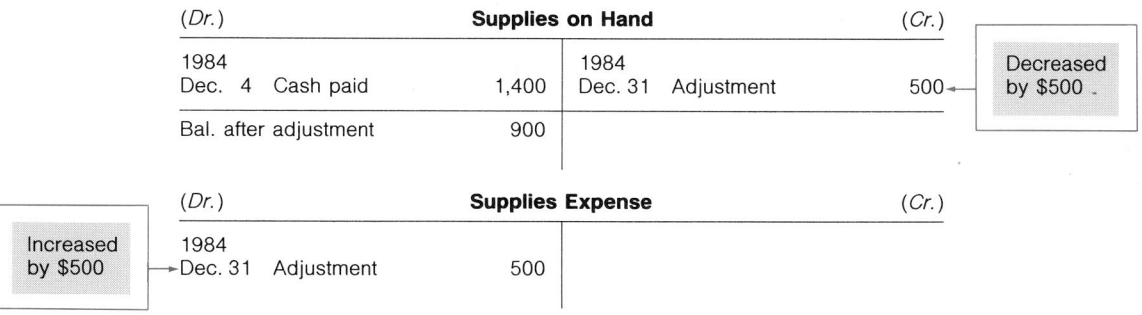

Increased by $500

(*Dr.*)		**Supplies Expense**		(*Cr.*)
1984				
Dec. 31	Adjustment	500		

While the entry to record the usage of supplies could be made when the supplies are issued from the storeroom, it is usually not worth the cost to account so carefully for such small items each time they are issued.

Supplies expense will appear in the income statement. Supplies on hand will be reported as an asset in the balance sheet.

Sometimes prepaid expenses such as insurance, rent, and supplies are bought and fully used up within one accounting period (usually one month or one year). If so, it is easier to debit an expense rather than an asset at the time of purchase. This procedure avoids having to make an adjusting entry at the end of the accounting period.

DEPRECIATION

Depreciation is another example of the *gradual using up* of a previously recorded asset. The overall period of time involved in using up an asset such as a building, for example, is much longer and less definite than for prepaid insurance or prepaid rent. A *depreciable asset* is a building, machine, vehicle, or piece of equipment on which depreciation expense is recorded. *Depreciation expense* is the amount of asset cost assigned as an expense to a particular time period.

To find the amount of depreciation expense for each time period, the asset cost less estimated salvage value is divided by the estimated number of periods in the asset's useful life. Estimated *salvage value* is the amount for which the asset can probably be sold at the end of its estimated useful life. The *useful life* of an asset is the estimated number of periods that a company can make use of an asset. Useful life must be *estimated* in advance. The degree of certainty as to useful life is reduced because individuals are not able to see 10 to 15 years into the future with precise accuracy. The process of recording depreciation expense is called *depreciation accounting.* The depreciation method discussed and illustrated here is known as the *straight-line method.* Other depreciation methods are discussed later in the text.

As stated above, there are three factors involved in the computation of depreciation:

1. Asset cost.
2. Estimated useful life.
3. Estimated salvage or scrap value.

The straight-line *depreciation formula* is as follows:

$$\text{Annual depreciation} = \frac{\text{Cost} - \text{Estimated salvage value}}{\text{Number of years of useful life}}$$

The Rapid Delivery Company purchased four trucks at a cost of $40,000. The entry made at that time was:

```
1984
Dec. 1  Delivery Trucks .......................................  40,000
             Cash ..............................................              40,000
        To record the purchase of four delivery trucks.
```

The estimated total salvage value of the four trucks was estimated at $4,000, and their useful life was estimated to be four years. Annual depreciation on the trucks is calculated as follows:

$$\text{Annual depreciation} = \frac{\$40,000 - \$4,000}{4 \text{ years}} = \$9,000$$

The amount of depreciation for one month would be 1/12 of the annual amount. Thus, depreciation expense for December is $9,000 \div 12 = \$750$.

The difference between an asset's cost and its estimated salvage value is sometimes referred to as an asset's *depreciable amount.* The depreciable amount must be allocated as an expense to the various periods in the asset's useful life.

The amount of depreciation for a period is debited to a depreciation expense account and credited to an accumulated depreciation account. The depreciation on the delivery trucks for December is $750 and is recorded as follows:

Adjustment 4—
Depreciation
	1984
	Dec. 31 Depreciation Expense—Delivery Trucks 750
	         Accumulated Depreciation—Delivery Trucks 750
	      To record depreciation expense for December.

The T-accounts would appear as follows after posting the adjusting entry:

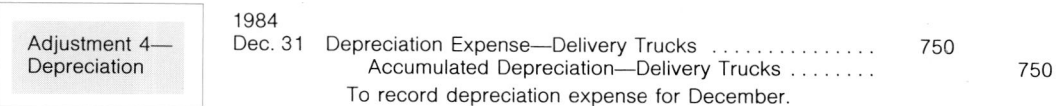

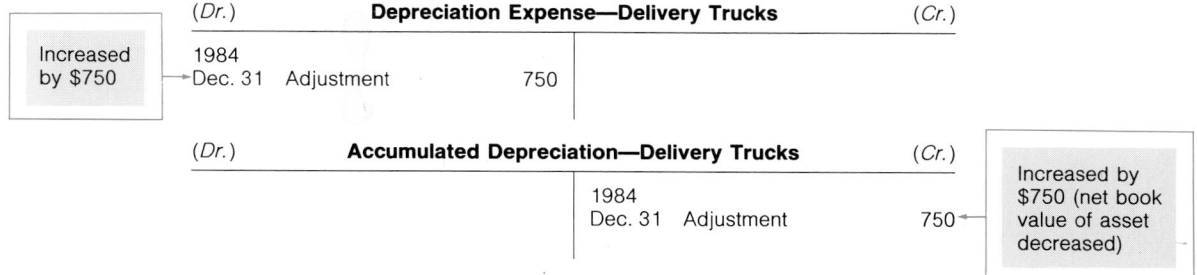

Depreciation expense is reported in the income statement. Accumulated depreciation is reported in the balance sheet as a deduction from the asset.

The *accumulated depreciation account* is a contra asset account that shows the total of all depreciation recorded on the asset up through the balance sheet date. A *contra asset account* is a deduction from the asset to which it relates in the balance sheet. The debit balance in the asset account minus the credit balance in the accumulated depreciation contra account equals the *undepreciated cost of the asset.* An asset's cost less accumulated depreciation is sometimes called *book value* (or net book value). Book value is the cost not yet allocated as an expense. In the above example, the book value of the delivery equipment after the first month is:

Cost	$40,000
Less accumulated depreciation	750
Book value or cost not yet	
allocated as an expense	$39,250

     The reason depreciation is credited to accumulated depreciation instead of directly to the asset is that recorded amounts of depreciation are inexact because of the use of estimates. No one is sure that the estimates are correct. To provide more complete balance sheet information by users of the financial statements, both original acquisition cost and accumulated depreciation are shown.

     The accumulated depreciation account balance increases each period by the amount of depreciation recorded until it finally reaches an amount equal to the original cost of the asset less estimated salvage value.

Accumulated depreciation in the balance sheet

     The accumulated depreciation is shown as a deduction from the asset in the December 31, 1984, balance sheet:

Assets

Delivery trucks	$40,000
Less: Accumulated depreciation—delivery trucks ...	750
	$39,250

UNEARNED REVENUES

     An adjustment involving unearned revenues covers those situations where the customer has transferred assets, usually cash, to the selling company prior to the receipt of merchandise or services. When assets are received before being earned, a liability called *unearned revenue* is created. Such receipts are debited to Cash. The liability account may be called Unearned Fees, Revenue Received in Advance, Advances by Customers, or some similar title. The seller is obligated either to provide the services or return the customer's money. By performing the services, revenue is earned and the liability is canceled.

     Advance payments are received for many items such as delivery services, tickets, and magazine or newspaper subscriptions. While only advance receipt of delivery fees will be illustrated and discussed, the other items are treated similarly.

Unearned delivery fees

     On December 7, the Rapid Delivery Company received $4,500 from a customer in payment for future delivery services. The entry was recorded as follows:

```
1984
Dec.  7  Cash .............................................  4,500
              Unearned Delivery Fees ............................        4,500
         To record the receipt of cash from a customer in payment for
         future delivery services.
```

The two T-accounts relating to delivery fees are Unearned Delivery Fees (a liability) and Delivery Service Revenue. These accounts appear as follows after this entry has been posted.

(Dr.)	**Unearned Delivery Fees**	(Cr.)		(Dr.)	**Delivery Service Revenue**	(Cr.)
	1984 Dec. 7	4,500			Bal.	–0–

The liability established when the cash was received will be converted into revenue as the delivery services are performed. An adjusting entry to update the accounts is usually required before financial statements are prepared in order to recognize the earning of revenue and the reduction of the related liability. Assuming that one third of the delivery services paid for in advance have been performed by the end of December, the required adjusting entry is:

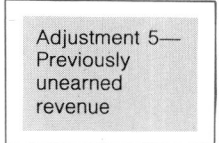

Adjustment 5—
Previously
unearned
revenue

```
1984
Dec. 31  Unearned Delivery Fees ........................  1,500
              Delivery Service Revenue .....................        1,500
         To transfer a portion of delivery fees from the liability
         account to the revenue account.
```

The T-accounts would appear as follows after the adjusting entry has been posted:

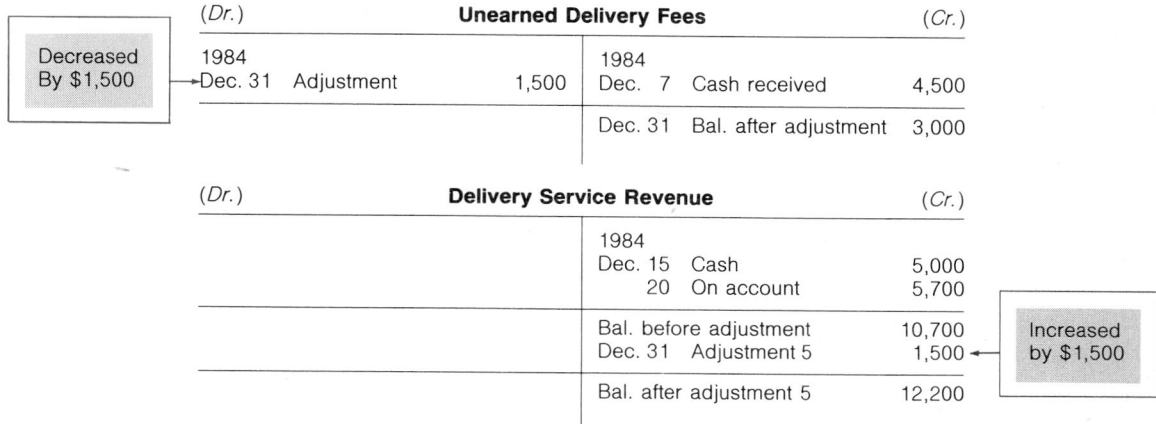

Decreased
By $1,500

(Dr.)	**Unearned Delivery Fees**			(Cr.)
1984 Dec. 31 Adjustment	1,500	1984 Dec. 7 Cash received	4,500	
		Dec. 31 Bal. after adjustment	3,000	

(Dr.)	**Delivery Service Revenue**			(Cr.)
		1984 Dec. 15 Cash	5,000	
		20 On account	5,700	
		Bal. before adjustment	10,700	
		Dec. 31 Adjustment 5	1,500	
		Bal. after adjustment 5	12,200	

Increased
by $1,500

The delivery service revenue is reported in the income statement for 1984. The $3,000 balance in the Unearned Delivery Fees account is reported as a liability in the balance sheet. In 1985, the $3,000 will be earned and transferred to a revenue account.

ACCRUED ASSETS

Accrued assets are those assets that exist at the end of an accounting period but have not yet been recorded. They represent rights to receive payments that are not legally due at the balance sheet date. At the end of an accounting period, any such rights must be recognized by preparing an adjusting entry. An example of this type of adjustment includes revenues earned that have not been billed or collected.

Unbilled delivery fees

Services may be performed for customers in one accounting period while the billing for those services is in a different accounting period. The Rapid Delivery Company performed $1,000 of delivery services on account for clients in the last few days of December. Because it takes time to do the paper work, the clients will be billed for the services in January. The necessary adjusting entry at December 31, 1984, is:

Adjustment 6— Unbilled revenues	1984
	Dec. 31 Accounts Receivable (or Accrued
	            Delivery Fees Receivable) 1,000
	               Delivery Service Revenue ....
		1,000

	To record unbilled delivery services performed in December.	

After posting the adjusting entry the T-accounts will appear as follows:

(Dr.)	Accounts Receivable		(Cr.)
Increased by $1,000	1984 Previous bal. Dec. 31 Adjustment	5,200 1,000	
	Bal. after adjustment	6,200	

(Dr.)	Delivery Service Revenue		(Cr.)
	1984 Dec. 15 Cash 20 On account	5,000 5,700	

	Bal. before adjustment
	Dec. 31 Adjustment 5—
	          previously unearned
	          revenue
	Dec. 31 Adjustment 6
		10,700
		
		1,500
		1,000
			Increased by $1,000

	Bal. after both adjustments	13,200	

The delivery service revenue will appear in the income statement, and the accounts receivable will appear in the balance sheet.

ACCRUED LIABILITIES

Accrued liabilities are those liabilities which exist at the end of an accounting period, but which have not yet been recorded. They represent obligations to make payments which are not legally due at the balance sheet date. At the end of an accounting period, any such obligations must be recognized by preparing an adjusting entry. Discussed below is the adjustment relating to salaries.

Salaries

The recording of the payment of employee salaries usually involves a debit to an expense account and a credit to cash. Unless salaries are paid on the last day of the accounting period for a pay period ending on that date, an adjusting entry will be required to record any salaries incurred but not yet paid.

The Rapid Delivery Company paid $3,600 of salaries on Friday, December 28, 1984, to cover the first four weeks of December. The entry made at that time was:

```
1984
Dec. 28  Salaries Expense  ....................................  3,600
             Cash  .........................................           3,600
         Paid truck driver salaries for the first four weeks of December.
```

If salaries are $3,600 for four weeks, they are $900 per week. Assuming a five-day workweek, daily salaries are $180. Since the last day of December 1984 falls on a Monday, the expense account does not show salaries earned by employees for the last day of the month. Nor does the account show the employer's obligation to pay these salaries. The accounts pertaining to salaries appear as follows before adjustment:

(Dr.)	**Salaries Expense**	(Cr.)	(Dr.)	**Accrued Salaries Payable**	(Cr.)
1984 Dec. 28 3,600				Bal. –0–	

The following adjusting entry is needed on December 31:

Adjustment 7—
Accrued
salaries
	1984
	Dec. 31 Salaries Expense 180
	              Accrued Salaries Payable 180
	          To accrue one day's salaries which were earned
	          but are unpaid.

The two accounts involved appear as follows after adjustment:

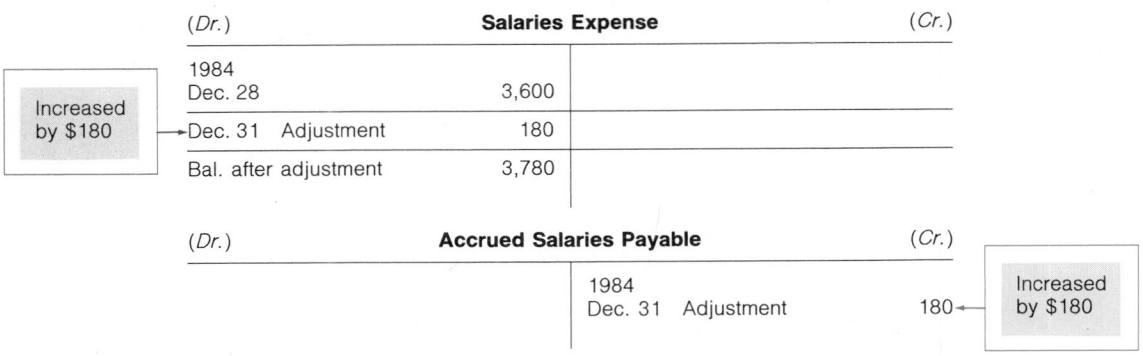

	(Dr.)	**Salaries Expense**	(Cr.)
Increased by $180	1984 Dec. 28	3,600	
	→Dec. 31 Adjustment	180	
	Bal. after adjustment	3,780	

	(Dr.)	**Accrued Salaries Payable**	(Cr.)	
			1984 Dec. 31 Adjustment	180→	Increased by $180

The debit in the adjusting journal entry brings the month's salaries expense up to its correct $3,780 amount for income statement purposes. The credit records the $180 salary liability to employees. The accrued salaries payable is shown as a liability in the balance sheet.

CONCLUDING NOTE

This chapter has discussed and illustrated many of the typical adjusting entries which companies must make at the end of an accounting period. The Rapid Delivery Company illustration was used. Certain types of adjusting entries were not discussed in this chapter. These other types of adjusting entries are covered in later chapters.

NEW TERMS INTRODUCED IN CHAPTER 3

Accounting period
A time period normally of one month, one quarter, or one year into which an entity's life is arbitrarily divided for reporting purposes.

Accounting year (fiscal year)
An accounting period of one year. The year may or may not coincide with the calendar year.

Accrual basis of accounting
Recognizes revenues when sales are made or services are performed even though cash has not yet been received. Expenses are recognized as incurred regardless of whether or not cash has been paid out.

Accrued assets and liabilities
Include those assets and liabilities which exist at the end of an accounting period, but which have not yet been recorded. They represent rights to receive, or obligations to make, payments which are not legally due at the balance sheet date. Exam-

ples are accrued fees receivable and salaries payable.

Accumulated depreciation account
A contra asset account which shows the total of all depreciation on the asset up to the balance sheet date.

Adjusting entries
Journal entries made at the end of an accounting period to change the balance of certain accounts to reflect economic activity which has taken place but has not yet been recorded. Adjusting entries are made to bring the accounts to their proper balances before financial statements are prepared.

Book value
For depreciable assets, book value equals cost less accumulated depreciation.

Calendar year
The normal year ending on December 31.

Cash basis of accounting
Recognizes revenues when cash is received and recognizes expenses when cash is paid out.

Contra asset account
An account shown as a deduction from the asset to which it relates in the balance sheet

Depreciable amount
The difference between an asset's cost and its estimated salvage value.

Depreciable asset
A building, machine, vehicle, or equipment on which depreciation expense is recorded.

Depreciation accounting
The process of recording depreciation expense.

Depreciation expense
The amount of asset cost assigned as an expense to a particular time period.

Depreciation formula (straight line)
$$\frac{\text{Annual}}{\text{depreciation}} = \frac{\text{Cost} - \text{Estimated salvage value}}{\text{Number of years of useful life}}$$

Fiscal year
An accounting year of any 12 consecutive months which may or may not coincide with the calendar year. For instance, a company may have an accounting or fiscal year which runs from April 1 of one year to March 31 of the next.

Prepaid expense
An asset which is awaiting assignment to expense. An example is prepaid insurance. Assets such as cash and accounts receivable are not prepaid expenses.

Salvage value (scrap value)
The amount for which an asset can probably be sold at the end of its estimated useful life.

Service potential
The benefits that can be obtained from assets. The future services that assets can render are what make assets "things of value" to a business.

Unearned revenue
Assets received from customers before services are performed for them. Since the revenue has not been earned, it is a liability, often called *revenue received in advance,* or *advances by customers.*

Useful life
The estimated number of periods that a company can make use of an asset.

DEMONSTRATION PROBLEM

The trial balance of the Korman Company at December 31 of the current year includes, among other items, the following account balances:

	Debits	Credits
Office supplies on hand	$ 3,000	
Prepaid insurance	3,900	
Prepaid rent	12,600	
Buildings	100,000	
Accumulated depreciation—buildings		$16,625
Salaries expense	62,000	

Additional data;

1. The inventory of supplies on hand at December 31 amounts to $1,200.
2. The debit balance in the Prepaid Insurance account is the advance premium for one year from October 1 of the current year.
3. The debit balance in the Prepaid Rent account is for a one-year period that began May 1 of the current year.
4. The annual depreciation for the buildings is based on the cost shown in the Buildings account less an estimated salvage value of $5,000. The estimated useful lives of the buildings are 40 years each.
5. Since the last payday, office employees have earned additional salaries of $3,000.

Required:

Prepare the adjusting journal entries at December 31, assuming adjusting entries are prepared only at year-end.

Solution to demonstration problem

KORMAN COMPANY
GENERAL JOURNAL

Date		Account Titles and Explanation	Post. Ref.	Debit	Credit
19—					
Dec.	31	Office Supplies Expense		1 8 0 0	
		Office Supplies on Hand			1 8 0 0
		To record office supplies expense			
		($3,000 − $1,200).			
	31	Insurance Expense		9 7 5	
		Prepaid Insurance			9 7 5
		To record expired insurance			
		($3,900 × 3/12).			
	31	Rent Expense		8 4 0 0	
		Prepaid Rent			8 4 0 0
		To record rent expense ($12,600 × 8/12).			
	31	Depreciation Expense—Buildings		2 3 7 5	
		Accumulated Depreciation—Buildings			2 3 7 5
		To record depreciation			
		[($100,000 − $5,000) ÷ 40 years]			
	31	Salaries Expense		3 0 0 0	
		Accrued Salaries Payable			3 0 0 0
		To record accrued salaries.			

QUESTIONS

1. Why are adjusting entries necessary? Why not treat every cash disbursement as an expense and every cash receipt as revenue when the cash changes hands?

2. "Adjusting entries would not be necessary if the cash basis of accounting were followed (assuming no mistakes were made in recording cash transactions as they occurred). Under the cash basis, receipts that are of a revenue nature are considered revenue when received and expenditures that are of an expense nature are consid-

ered expenses when paid. It is the use of the accrual basis of accounting, where an effort is made to match expenses incurred against the revenues they create, that makes adjusting entries necessary." Do you agree with this statement? Why?

3. Why don't accountants keep all the accounts at their proper balances continuously throughout the period so that adjusting entries would not have to be made before financial statements are prepared?

4. Identify the two major classes of adjusting entries and identify the types of adjusting entries that are included in each.

5. Give an example of an adjusting journal entry for each of the following:
   a. Increase of an expense and decrease of an asset.
   b. Earning of revenue that was previously recorded as unearned revenue.
   c. Equal growth of an asset and revenue.
   d. Equal growth of an expense and a liability.

6. You notice that the Supplies on Hand account has a debit balance of $3,700 at the end of the accounting period. How would you determine the extent to which this account needs adjustment?

7. It may be said that some assets are converted into expenses as they expire and that some liabilities become revenues as they are earned. Give examples of asset and liability accounts for which the statement is true. Give examples of asset and liability accounts for which the statement does not apply.

8. What does the term *accrued liability* mean?

9. What is meant by the term *service potential?*

10. Give the depreciation formula for straight-line depreciation.

11. When assets are received before they are earned what type of an account is credited? As the amounts are earned what type of an account is credited?

EXERCISES

E–1.   a. A one-year insurance policy was purchased on, and provides coverage from, October 1, 1984, for $3,600. The following entry was made at that time:

```
1984
Oct.  1  Prepaid Insurance . . . . . . . . . . . . . . . . . . . . . . . . . . . . . . . . . . . . .   3,600
              Cash . . . . . . . . . . . . . . . . . . . . . . . . . . . . . . . . . . . . . . . . . . . . .            3,600
         To record the purchase of insurance to cover a one-year period.
```

The company prepares financial statements once a year at year-end. What adjusting entry is necessary at December 31?
        b. Show how the T-accounts for Prepaid Insurance and Insurance Expense would appear after the two entries are posted.

E–2.   Assume that rent of $7,200 was paid on September 1, 1984, to cover a one-year period from that date. Prepaid Rent was debited. If financial statements are prepared only on December 31 of each year, what adjusting entry is necessary on December 31, 1984, to bring the accounts involved to their proper balances?

E–3.   Office supplies were purchased for cash on December 2, 1984, for $1,600. The supplies were to be used over the next several months. A physical inventory showed that $400 of the supplies were on hand on December 31, 1984. Show the entry for the purchase. What adjusting entry would be necessary at December 31 assuming that financial statements are prepared at that time?

E–4.   Assume that a company acquires a building on January 1, 1984, at a cost of $250,000. The building has an estimated useful life of 40 years and an estimated salvage value of $50,000. What adjusting entry is needed on December 31, 1984, to record the depreciation for the entire year 1984?

E–5.   A building is being depreciated by an amount of $28,000 per year. You know it had an original cost of $310,000 and was expected to last 10 years. How must the $28,000 have been determined?

E–6.   On September 1, 1984, the Randall Company received a total of $60,000 as payment in advance for a number of one-year subscriptions to a monthly magazine. By the end of the year, one third of the magazines paid for in advance had been delivered. Give the entries to record the receipt of the subscriptions fees and to adjust the accounts at December 31 assuming annual financial statements are prepared at year-end.

E–7.   Guilty and Innocent, a law firm, performed legal services in late December 1984 for clients. The $12,000 of services will be billed to the clients in January 1985. Give the adjusting entry which is necessary on December 31, 1984, if financial statements are prepared at the end of each month.

E–8.   West Company incurs sales salaries at the rate of $500 per day. The last payday in January is Friday, January 27. Salaries for Monday and Tuesday of the next week have not been recorded or paid as of January 31. Financial statements are prepared monthly. Give the necessary adjusting entry on January 31.

E–9.   State the effect that each of the following would have on the amount of annual net income reported for 1984 and 1985.

    a.   No adjustment was made for accrued salaries of $900 as of December 31, 1984.

    b.   The collection of $800 for services yet unperformed as of December 31, 1984, was credited to a revenue account and not adjusted. The services are performed in 1985.

PROBLEMS, SERIES A

P3–1–A.   The trial balance of the Tall Company at December 31, 1984, includes, among other items, the following account balances:

	Debits
Prepaid insurance	$25,000
Prepaid rent	28,800
Supplies on hand	6,600

Examination of the records shows that annual adjustments should be made for the following items:

1. Of the prepaid insurance in the trial balance, $10,000 is for coverage during the months after December 31 of the current year.

2. The balance in the Prepaid Rent account is for a 12-month period that started October 1 of the current year.

3. Supplies used during the year amount to $3,600.

Required:
        Prepare the annual adjusting journal entries at December 31.

P3–2–A.   The Summit Company acquired a new truck on January 1, 1984. The truck has a cost of $8,000, an estimated useful life of three years, and an estimated salvage value of $500.

Required:

    a. Prepare annual adjusting journal entries as of the end of 1984, 1985, and 1986 to record depreciation on the truck.

    b. Using T-accounts, show how the entries made in (*a*) would appear.

P3–3–A.

Required:

    For each of the following cases for the Ross Company:

    a. Prepare the annual adjusting journal entry, dating it December 31, 1984.

    b. Set up T-accounts, enter balances before adjustment as given, if any, post the adjusting entries made in part (*a*), and determine balances after adjustment.

    c. Show the data that would appear on the balance sheet.

    d. Show the data for the year that would appear on the income statement.

		Trial balance	Information for adjustments
Case 1:	Office Building	$850,000	The useful life is 50 years. Salvage value is esti-
	Accumulated Depreciation		mated at $50,000. The amount shown for Accu-
	—Office Building	160,000	mulated Depreciation—Office Building resulted
			from credits to that account made in adjusting
			entries for previous years
Case 2:	Salaries Expense	102,000	Salaries earned by employees since the last payday are $2,960. These have not been recorded.
Case 3:	Office Supplies on Hand ...	6,000	At the end of the period, office supplies on hand are $2,000.

P3–4–A.   Renwick Company has the following account balances, among others, in its trial balance at December 31, 1984:

	Debits	Credits
Accounts receivable	$25,000	
Supplies on hand	1,290	
Prepaid rent	2,400	
Service revenue		$87,000
Salaries expense	41,000	

Additional data:

1. The amount of supplies on hand at December 31 is $90.
2. The balance in the Prepaid Rent account is for a one-year period starting October 1 of the current year.
3. Since the last payday, the employees of the company have earned additional salaries of $2,030.
4. Services were performed in December which will not be billed until January, $6,000.

Required:

    a. Prepare the annual adjusting journal entries at December 31.

    b. Open three-column ledger accounts for each of the accounts involved, enter the balances as shown in the trial balance, post the adjusting journal entries, and show balances.

P3–5–A.   The reported net income amounts for the Wheeler Company for calendar years 1984 and 1985 were $80,000 and $102,000, respectively. No annual adjusting entries were made at either year-end for any of the transactions given below.

Transactions

a. A fire insurance policy to cover a three-year period from the date of payment was purchased on March 1, 1984, for $3,600. The Prepaid Insurance account was debited at the date of purchase.
b. Subscriptions for magazines in the amount of $72,000 to cover an 18-month period from May 1, 1984, were received on April 15, 1984. The Unearned Subscriptions account was credited when the payments were received.
c. A building costing $180,000 and having an estimated useful life of 50 years and a salvage value of $30,000 was purchased and put into service on January 1, 1984.
d. On January 12, 1985, wages of $9,600 were paid to employees. The account debited was Wages Expense. One third of the amount paid was earned by employees in December of 1984.

Required:

Calculate the correct net income for 1984 and 1985. In your answer start with the reported net income. Then show the effects of each correction (adjustment) using a plus or a minus to indicate whether reported income should be increased or decreased as a result of the correction. When the corrections are added to or deducted from the reported net income amounts, the result should be the correct net income amounts. The answer format should appear as follows:

Explanation of corrections	*1984*	*1985*
Reported net income	$80,000	$102,000
To correct error in accounting for:		
a. Fire insurance policy premium:		
Correct expense in 1984......	−1,000	
Correct expense in 1985......		−1,200

P3–6–A.   The Jane Geary Company adjusts and closes its books each December 31. Given below are a number of the company's account balances prior to adjustment on December 31, 1984:

	Debits	*Credits*
Prepaid insurance	$ 5,000	
Supplies on hand	2,150	
Building	85,000	
Accumulated depreciation—building ...		$34,000
Unearned delivery fees		1,800
Salaries expense	23,000	
Service revenue		92,500

Additional data (number your entries to match these items):

1. The Prepaid Insurance account balance represents the remaining cost of a four-year insurance policy dated June 30, 1982, having a total premium of $8,000.
2. The physical inventory of the supply stockroom indicates that the supplies on hand at December 31 had a cost of $750.
3. The building was originally acquired on January 1, 1967, at which time it was estimated that it would last 40 years and have scrap value of $5,000.
4. Salaries earned since the last payday but unpaid at December 31 amount to $2,500.
5. Of the delivery fees received in advance, $450 had been earned by year-end.

Required:

Prepare the adjusting entries indicated by the additional data. While explanations may be omitted, computations should be included.

PROBLEMS, SERIES B

P3–1–B.   The trial balance of the Dolly Barton Company at December 31, 1984, includes, among other items, the following account balances:

	Debits	Credits
Prepaid insurance	$ 6,000	
Buildings	100,000	
Accumulated depreciation—buildings ..		$32,000
Salaries expense	55,000	
Prepaid rent	12,000	

Additional data:

1. The debit balance in the Prepaid Insurance account is the advance premium for one year from September 1 of the current year.
2. The buildings have an estimated useful life of 25 years and an estimated salvage value of $20,000.
3. Salaries accrued at December 31 are $4,400.
4. The debit balance in Prepaid Rent is for a one-year period that started March 1 of the current year.

Required:

Prepare the annual adjusting journal entries at December 31.

P3–2–B. The Willie Rogers Company bought a new machine on January 1, 1984, at a cost of $20,000. The machine had an estimated life of three years and an estimated salvage value of $2,000.

Required:

a. Prepare annual adjusting journal entries as of the end of each of the three years of useful life to record depreciation on the machine.

b. Using T-accounts, show how the entries made in (a) would appear.

P3–3–B.

Required:

For each of the following cases for the Alice Company:

a. Prepare the annual adjusting journal entry, dating it December 31, 1984.

b. Set up T-accounts, enter balances before adjustment as given, if any, post the adjusting entries made in part (a), and determine balances after adjustment.

c. Show the data that would appear on the balance sheet.

d. Show the data for the year that would appear on the income statement.

	Account title	Trial balance	Information for adjustments
Case 1:	Equipment	$90,000	Depreciation is based on a five-year life and a $10,000 estimated salvage value. The amount shown for Accumulated Depreciation—Equipment resulted from credits to that account made in adjusting entries for previous years.
	Accumulated Depreciation—Equipment	32,000	
Case 2:	Salaries Expense	44,000	Unpaid salaries incurred amount to $2,000. The $2,000 is not included in the amount shown in the trial balance.
Case 3:	Prepaid Insurance	17,900	Of the prepaid insurance in the trial balance, only $5,400 is for additional protection after December 31.

P3–4–B.   Among the account balances shown in the trial balance of the Mark Snyder Company at December 31, 1984, are the following:

	Debits	Credits
Supplies on hand	$ 3,480	
Prepaid insurance	4,800	
Buildings	84,000	
Accumulated depreciation—buildings ..		$19,500

Additional data:

1. The amount of supplies on hand at December 31 is $600.
2. The balance in the Prepaid Insurance account is for a two-year policy effective on June 1 of the current year.
3. Depreciation for the buildings is based on an estimated salvage value of $9,000 and an estimated useful life of 50 years.

Required:

a.   Prepare the annual adjusting journal entries at December 31.

b.   Open three-column ledger accounts for each of the accounts involved, enter the balances as shown in the trial balance, post the adjusting entries, and show balances.

P3–5–B.   The reported net income amounts for the Nesbit Company were: 1984, $70,000; 1985, $85,000. No annual adjusting entries were made at either year-end for any of the transactions given below:

Transactions:

a.   A building was rented on April 1, 1984. Cash of $24,000 was paid on that date to cover a two-year period. Prepaid Rent was debited.
b.   The balance in the Office Supplies on Hand account on December 31, 1984, is $4,000. An inventory of the supplies on December 31, 1984, revealed that only $2,500 were actually on hand at that date. No new supplies were purchased during 1985. At December 31, 1985, an inventory of the supplies revealed that $500 were on hand.
c.   A building costing $500,000 and having an estimated useful life of 40 years and a salvage value of $100,000 was put into service on January 1, 1984.
d.   Services were performed for customers in December 1984. The $15,000 bill for these services was not sent until January 1985. The only transaction that was recorded was a debit to Cash and a credit to Service Revenue when payment was received in January.

Required:

Calculate the correct net income for 1984 and 1985. In your answer start with the reported net income amounts. Then show the effects of each correction (adjustment) using a plus or a minus to indicate whether reported income should be increased or decreased as a result of the correction. When the corrections are added to or deducted from the reported net income amounts, the result should be the correct net income amounts. The answer format should be as follows:

Explanation of corrections	1984	1985
Reported net income	$70,000	$85,000
To correct error in accounting for:		
a. Prepaid rent:		
Correct expense in 1984......	−9,000	
Correct expense in 1985......		−12,000

P3–6–B.   The Martha Hall Company occupies rented quarters on the main street of the city. In order to get this location, it was necessary for the company to rent a store larger than needed, so a portion of the area is subleased (rented) to Tim's Restaurant.

Required:

Present the adjusting entries required by the data presented below. Show your calculations of the amounts as explanations of your entries.

The following partial trial balance was taken from the company's ledger as of the close of business on December 31, 1984. You should study the partial trial balance to determine how certain transactions were originally recorded. Then you will be able to determine the necessary annual adjusting entry.

MARTHA HALL COMPANY
Partial Trial Balance
December 31, 1984

	Debits	Credits
Cash	$30,000	
Prepaid rent	1,000	
Prepaid insurance	2,700	
Store supplies on hand	500	
Store equipment	35,000	
Accumulated depreciation—store equipment		$ 3,000
Service revenue		225,000
Store salaries expense	36,750	
Rent revenue		5,500

Additional data to be considered:

1. The salaries of the store clerks amount to $135 per day and were last paid through Thursday, December 27. December 31 is a Monday. Saturday is a workday, and the store is closed on Sundays.
2. The equipment had a cost of $35,000, an estimated useful life of 20 years, and an estimated salvage value of $5,000.
3. The store carries one combined annual insurance policy which was taken out on August 1. The policy was new this year and costs $2,700 per year.
4. The store supplies on hand at December 31, 1984, have a cost of $230.
5. The prepaid rent applies to December 1984 and January 1985.
6. Services of $4,000 were performed in December which will be billed to customers in January.

BUSINESS DECISION PROBLEM

A friend of yours, Jeff Ward, is quite excited over the opportunity he has to purchase the land, building, equipment, and several miscellaneous assets of the Fairbank Bowling Lanes for $187,500. Jeff tells you that the owner (who is moving because of poor health) reports that the business had net income of $37,500 in 1984 (last year). Jeff believes that annual net income of $37,500 on an investment of $187,500 is a really good deal. But, before completing the deal, he asks you to look it over. You agree and discover the following:

1. The owner has computed his annual earnings for 1984 as the sum of his cash withdrawals plus the increase in the Cash account—withdrawals of $22,500 + increase in Cash account of $15,000 = $37,500 earnings.

2. As buyer of the business, Jeff will take over responsibility for repayment of a $150,000 loan owed to a relative of the previous owner. The land, building, and equipment were acquired seven years ago at a cost of $15,000, $400,000, and $160,000, respectively. The building has a useful life of 40 years and an estimated salvage value of $40,000,

while the equipment has an estimated useful life of 8 years and an estimated salvage value of $16,000.

    3. An analysis of the Cash account shows the following for 1984:

Revenues received		$210,000
Cash paid out in 1984 for—		
Wages paid to employees in 1984	$129,000	
Utilities paid for 1984	9,000	
Advertising expenses paid	7,500	
Supplies purchased and used in 1984 ...	12,000	
Payment on loan	15,000	
Owner withdrawals	22,500	195,000
Increase in cash balance for the year		$ 15,000

    4. You also find that the December utility bill of $1,500 and an advertising bill for December of $2,250 have not been paid.

Required:

    a. Prepare a written report for Jeff giving your appraisal of the offer to sell the Fairbank Bowling Lanes. Comment on the owner's method of computing the annual net income of the business.

    b. Determine the book value of the assets employed in the business and an approximate income statement for 1984.

Chapter 4

The work sheet, closing entries, and the classified balance sheet

CHAPTER GOALS

After study of this chapter, you should be able to:

1. Prepare a work sheet for a service company.
2. Prepare an income statement, statement of owner's equity, and balance sheet using information contained in a work sheet.
3. Prepare adjusting and closing entries using information contained in the work sheet.
4. Prepare a classified balance sheet.
5. Prepare reversing entries (covered in Appendix 4–A).
6. Define and use correctly the new terms in the glossary.

THE ACCOUNTING CYCLE

The *accounting cycle* consists of a series of steps performed during an accounting period related to gathering, classifying, and reporting useful financial information. Some of the steps in the accounting cycle were discussed in earlier chapters. These included journalizing transactions, posting entries to ledger accounts, preparing a trial balance, preparing adjusting entries, and preparing financial statements.

Additional steps in the accounting cycle are discussed in this chapter. These steps are the preparation of a work sheet and closing entries. Another optional step, preparing reversing entries, is discussed in Appendix 4–A. The Rapid Delivery Company example from Chapters 2 and 3 will be continued in this chapter.

In addition to discussing these additional steps in the accounting cycle, the chapter presents a more useful format for the balance sheet, a *classified balance sheet.*

THE WORK SHEET

A *work sheet* is a large columnar sheet of paper that offers a convenient means for entering and summarizing information needed for making adjusting and closing entries and for preparing financial statements. A work sheet may be prepared each time financial statements are to be prepared, usually monthly, quarterly, or at the end of the accounting year. Since a work sheet is only used internally and is not part of the formal accounting records, it may take on a variety of forms and is usually prepared in pencil so that errors can easily be corrected.

Illustrated in this chapter is the 10-column work sheet which includes sets of columns for a trial balance, adjustments, adjusted trial balance, income statement, and balance sheet. There will be two columns for each of the mentioned classifications—a debit column and a credit column. Illustration 4.1 shows the format of the work sheet for the Rapid Delivery Company, with only the Trial Balance columns filled in, using the facts presented in Chapters 2 and 3.

The Trial Balance columns

Instead of preparing a separate trial balance as was done in Chapter 2, the trial balance can be entered in the work sheet. As shown in Illustration 4.1, numbers and titles of ledger accounts are entered in the left-hand portion of the work sheet. Usually only those accounts with balances as of the end of the accounting period are listed. The balances of the accounts are entered in the Trial Balance columns of the work sheet, and the columns are totaled. If the debit and credit column totals are not equal, an error exists and will need to be found and corrected before proceeding with the work sheet.

Illustration 4.1: Partially completed work sheet—Trial Balance columns

RAPID DELIVERY COMPANY
Work Sheet
For the Month Ended December 31, 1984

Acct. No.	Account Titles	Trial Balance		Adjustments		Adjusted Trial Balance		Income Statement		Balance Sheet	
		Debit	Credit	Debit	Credit	Debit	Credit	Debit	Credit	Debit	Credit
100	Cash	10,650									
101	Accounts receivable	5,200									
102	Supplies on hand	1,400									
103	Prepaid insurance	2,400									
104	Prepaid rent	1,200									
110	Delivery trucks	40,000									
200	Accounts payable		3,130								
201	Unearned delivery fees		4,500								
300	John Turner, capital, 12/1/84		50,000								
301	John Turner, drawing	3,000									
400	Delivery service revenue		10,700								
500	Advertising expense	50									
501	Gas and oil expense	680									
502	Salaries expense	3,600									
503	Utilities expense	150									
		68,330	68,330								

The Adjustments columns

Adjustments are required to bring the accounts up to date prior to the preparation of financial statements. Adjustments are entered on the work sheet in the Adjustments columns (Illustration 4.2). The debit and credit parts of each entry are cross-referenced by placing a key number or letter to the left of each amount. For example, the adjustment debiting Insurance Expense and crediting Prepaid Insurance is identified by the number (1). Notice that the Insurance Expense account title needed to be written in below the accounts listed in the trial balance because it did not have a balance prior to adjustment. A brief explanation can be provided at the bottom of the work sheet for each keyed entry. These explanations are optional but provide valuable information for other people who may review the work sheet at a later time. The explanations will not be repeated in subsequent illustrations in this chapter.

Illustration 4.2:   **Partially completed work sheet—Adjustments columns**

RAPID DELIVERY COMPANY
Work Sheet
For the Month Ended December 31, 1984

Acct. No.	Account Titles	Trial Balance		Adjustments	
		Debit	Credit	Debit	Credit
100	Cash	10,650			
101	Accounts receivable	5,200		(6) 1,000	
102	Supplies on hand	1,400			(3) 500
103	Prepaid insurance	2,400			(1) 200
104	Prepaid rent	1,200			(2) 400
110	Delivery trucks	40,000			
200	Accounts payable		3,130		
201	Unearned delivery fees		4,500	(5) 1,500	
300	John Turner, capital, 12/1/84		50,000		
301	John Turner, drawing	3,000			
400	Delivery service				(5) 1,500
	revenue		10,700		(6) 1,000
500	Advertising expense	50			
501	Gas and oil expense	680			
502	Salaries expense	3,600		(7) 180	
503	Utilities expense	150			
		68,330	68,330		
504	Insurance expense			(1) 200	
505	Rent expense			(2) 400	
506	Supplies expense			(3) 500	
507	Depreciation expense—				
	delivery trucks			(4) 750	
110A	Accumulated depreciation—				
	delivery trucks				(4) 750
202	Accrued salaries payable				(7) 180
				4,530	4,530

Adjustments explanations:
    (1) To record insurance expense for December.
    (2) To record rent expense for December.
    (3) To record supplies used during December.
    (4) To record depreciation expense for December.
    (5) To transfer a portion of delivery fees from the liability account to the revenue account.
    (6) To record unbilled delivery services performed in December.
    (7) To accrue one day's salaries which were earned but are unpaid.

The adjustments for the Rapid Delivery Company were explained in Chapter 3 and are as follows:

Entry (*1*) records the expiration of $200 of prepaid insurance relating to coverage for the month of December.

Entry (*2*) records the expiration of $400 of prepaid rent relating to the month of December.

Entry (*3*) records the using up of $500 of supplies during the month. This amount was determined by taking a physical inventory of supplies, which came to $900, and deducting that amount from the balance in the Supplies on Hand account.

Entry (*4*) records depreciation expense on the delivery truck of $750 for the month.

Entry (*5*) records the earning of $1,500 of the $4,500 in the Unearned Delivery Fees account.

Entry (*6*) records $1,000 of unbilled delivery services performed in December.

Entry (*7*) records the accrual of $180 of salaries expense at the end of the month.

One advantage of a work sheet is that it assembles information about all of the accounts in one place where the accounts may be studied to determine the need for possible adjustment. Discovering all the adjusting entries that should be made is often a difficult task for the accountant. The following steps should aid in this task:

1. Examine adjusting entries made at the end of the preceding accounting period. The same types of entries often are necessary period after period.
2. Examine the account titles appearing in the trial balance. For instance, if there is an account entitled Delivery Trucks, an entry for depreciation must be made.
3. Examine various business papers to discover other assets, liabilities, expenses, and revenues that have not yet been recorded.
4. Ask the owner or other personnel specific questions regarding adjustments which may be necessary.

After all adjusting entries have been entered in the Adjustments columns, the two columns are totaled and their equality noted as a partial check of the arithmetic accuracy of the work completed thus far.

The Adjusted Trial Balance columns

After adjustments have been entered, the adjusted balance of each account is computed and entered in the Adjusted Trial Balance columns (Illustration 4.3). For example, Supplies on hand (Account No. 102) has an unadjusted balance of $1,400. Adjusting entry (*3*) credited the account for $500, leaving a debit balance of $900. This amount is shown as a debit in the Adjusted Trial Balance columns.

Illustration 4.3: Partially completed work sheet—Adjusted Trial Balance columns

RAPID DELIVERY COMPANY
Work Sheet
For the Month Ended December 31, 1984

Acct. No.	Account Titles	Trial Balance Debit	Trial Balance Credit	Adjustments Debit	Adjustments Credit	Adjusted Trial Balance Debit	Adjusted Trial Balance Credit
100	Cash	10,650				10,650	
101	Accounts receivable	5,200		(6) 1,000		6,200	
102	Supplies on hand	1,400			(3) 500	900	
103	Prepaid insurance	2,400			(1) 200	2,200	
104	Prepaid rent	1,200			(2) 400	800	
110	Delivery trucks	40,000				40,000	
200	Accounts payable		3,130				3,130
201	Unearned delivery fees		4,500	(5) 1,500			3,000
300	John Turner, capital, 12/1/84		50,000				50,000
301	John Turner, drawing	3,000				3,000	
400	Delivery service revenue		10,700		{ (5) 1,500 / (6) 1,000		13,200
500	Advertising expense	50				50	
501	Gas and oil expense	680				680	
502	Salaries expense	3,600		(7) 180		3,780	
503	Utilities expense	150				150	
		68,330	68,330				
504	Insurance expense			(1) 200		200	
505	Rent expense			(2) 400		400	
506	Supplies expense			(3) 500		500	
507	Depreciation expense—delivery trucks			(4) 750		750	
110A	Accumulated depreciation—delivery trucks				(4) 750		750
202	Accrued salaries payable				(7) 180		180
				4,530	4,530	70,260	70,260

All accounts having balances are extended to the Adjusted Trial Balance columns. Note carefully how the rules of debit and credit apply in determining whether an adjustment increases or decreases the account balance. For example, Salaries Expense has a $3,600 debit balance in the Trial Balance columns. This account is increased by a $180 debit adjustment, giving a $3,780 debit balance in the Adjusted Trial Balance columns.

Note also that some account balances do not change because no adjustments affected them. The balances in these accounts are simply extended to the Adjusted Trial Balance columns in the work sheet.

The Adjusted Trial Balance debit and credit columns are totaled, and the totals must be equal before taking the next step in completing the work sheet. If the Trial Balance columns and the Adjustments columns both balance but the Adjusted Trial Balance columns do not, a math error or an error in extension are the most likely causes.

The Income Statement columns

All revenue and expense account balances in the Adjusted Trial Balance columns are extended to the Income Statement columns (Illustration 4.4). Since revenues carry credit balances, they are extended to the credit column; expenses are extended to the debit column. Each column is then subtotaled. For Rapid Delivery Company, total expenses are $6,510 and total revenues are $13,200. Thus, net income for the period is $6,690 ($13,200 − $6,510). This amount is entered in the debit column in order to bring the two column totals into agreement. A *net loss* would be recorded in the opposite manner; expenses (debits) would have been larger than revenues (credits), so a net loss would be entered in the credit column in order to make the columns balance.

The Balance Sheet columns

Assets, liabilities, and owner's equity accounts listed in the Adjusted Trial Balance columns are extended to the Balance Sheet columns—assets as debits and liabilities and owner's equity amounts as credits (Illustration 4.5). Note that the beginning, rather than the ending, balance of John Turner's capital account is carried into the credit column. This is because the beginning balance is the dollar amount that is in the capital account until closing entries are prepared and posted.

Notice also that the net income which was determined in the Income Statement columns appears again in the Balance Sheet columns. The net income amount was shown as a debit in the Income Statement columns in order to force balance those columns. It is shown as a credit in the Balance Sheet columns because it increases owner's equity or capital, and increases in owner's equity are accounted for as credits. With the inclusion of the net income amount, the Balance Sheet columns balance.

If the balance sheet column totals do not agree on the first attempt, work backwards through the process used in preparing the work sheet. Specifically, the following steps should be taken *until* the error is discovered:

1. Retotal the two Balance Sheet columns to see if an error in addition was made. If the column totals do not agree, check to see if some balance sheet item was not extended from the Adjusted Trial Balance columns.

Illustration 4.4: **Partially completed work sheet—Income Statement columns**

RAPID DELIVERY COMPANY
Work Sheet
For the Month Ended December 31, 1984

Acct. No.	Account Titles	Trial Balance		Adjustments		Adjusted Trial Balance		Income Statement	
		Debit	Credit	Debit	Credit	Debit	Credit	Debit	Credit
100	Cash	10,650				10,650			
101	Accounts receivable	5,200		(6) 1,000		6,200			
102	Supplies on hand	1,400			(3) 500	900			
103	Prepaid insurance	2,400			(1) 200	2,200			
104	Prepaid rent	1,200			(2) 400	800			
110	Delivery trucks	40,000				40,000			
200	Accounts payable		3,130				3,130		
201	Unearned delivery fees		4,500	(5) 1,500			3,000		
300	John Turner, capital, 12/1/84		50,000				50,000		
301	John Turner, drawing	3,000				3,000			
400	Delivery service				(5) 1,500				
	revenue		10,700		(6) 1,000		13,200		13,200
500	Advertising expense	50				50		50	
501	Gas and oil expense	680				680		680	
502	Salaries expense	3,600		(7) 180		3,780		3,780	
503	Utilities expense	150				150		150	
		68,330	68,330						
504	Insurance expense			(1) 200		200		200	
505	Rent expense			(2) 400		400		400	
506	Supplies expense			(3) 500		500		500	
507	Depreciation expense—								
	delivery trucks			(4) 750		750		750	
110A	Accumulated depreciation— delivery trucks				(4) 750		750		
202	Accrued salaries payable				(7) 180		180		
					4,530		4,530	70,260	70,260	6,510	13,200
	Net income							6,690	
								13,200	13,200

2. Retotal the Income Statement columns and determine whether the correct amount of net income or net loss for the period was entered in the appropriate columns in the Income Statement and Balance Sheet columns.
3. Retotal the Adjusted Trial Balance columns. If the totals agree, check to see that each item was transferred to the correct Income Statement

Illustration 4.5: Completed work sheet—Balance Sheet columns

RAPID DELIVERY COMPANY
Work Sheet
For the Month Ended December 31, 1984

Acct. No.	Account Titles	Trial Balance		Adjustments	
		Debit	Credit	Debit	Credit
100	Cash	10,650			
101	Accounts receivable	5,200		(6) 1,000	
102	Supplies on hand	1,400			(3) 500
103	Prepaid insurance	2,400			(1) 200
104	Prepaid rent	1,200			(2) 400
110	Delivery trucks	40,000			
200	Accounts payable		3,130		
201	Unearned delivery fees		4,500	(5) 1,500	
300	John Turner, capital, 12/1/84		50,000		
301	John Turner, drawing	3,000			
400	Delivery service				(5) 1,500
	revenue		10,700		(6) 1,000
500	Advertising expense	50			
501	Gas and oil expense	680			
502	Salaries expense	3,600		(7) 180	
503	Utilities expense	150			
		68,330	68,330		
504	Insurance expense			(1) 200	
505	Rent expense			(2) 400	
506	Supplies expense			(3) 500	
507	Depreciation expense—				
	delivery trucks			(4) 750	
110A	Accumulated depreciation—				
	delivery trucks				(4) 750
202	Accrued salaries payable				(7) 180
				4,530	4,530
	Net income				

or Balance Sheet column. If the totals do not agree, make sure that each adjustment was properly added to or subtracted from the related amount in the Trial Balance column.

4. Retotal the Adjustments columns.
5. Retotal the Trial Balance Columns. If the totals do not agree, the ledger accounts must be reviewed to find the error.

Adjusted Trial Balance		Income Statement		Balance Sheet	
Debit	Credit	Debit	Credit	Debit	Credit
10,650				10,650	
6,200				6,200	
900				900	
2,200				2,200	
800				800	
40,000				40,000	
	3,130				3,130
	3,000				3,000
	50,000			.	50,000
3,000				3,000	
	13,200		13,200		
50		50			
680		680			
3,780		3,780			
150		150			
200		200			
400		400			
500		500			
750		750			
	750				750
	180				180
70,260	70,260	6,510	13,200		
		6,690			6,690
		13,200	13,200	63,750	63,750

PREPARING FINANCIAL STATEMENTS FROM THE WORK SHEET

When the work sheet has been completed, all the information needed to prepare the financial statements is readily available. The information only needs to be recast into a more appropriate format.

Illustration 4.6:   Income statement

```
                    RAPID DELIVERY COMPANY
                         Income Statement
                  For the Month Ended December 31, 1984

Revenue:
   Delivery service revenue  . . . . . . .          $13,200
Expenses:
   Advertising . . . . . . . . . . . . . . . . . .   $   50
   Gas and oil . . . . . . . . . . . . . . . . .        680
   Salaries . . . . . . . . . . . . . . . . . . .     3,780
   Utilities . . . . . . . . . . . . . . . . . . .      150
   Insurance . . . . . . . . . . . . . . . . . .        200
   Rent . . . . . . . . . . . . . . . . . . . . .       400
   Supplies . . . . . . . . . . . . . . . . . .         500
   Depreciation—delivery trucks  . . .                  750
      Total expenses  . . . . . . . . . . .           6,510
Net income . . . . . . . . . . . . . . . . . .      $ 6,690
```

Income statement

Information needed to prepare the income statement can be taken from the Income Statement columns in the work sheet. The income statement in Illustration 4.6 is based upon the information in Illustration 4.5.

Statement of owner's equity

The *statement of owner's equity* is a financial statement that summarizes the transactions affecting the owner's capital account balance. Such a statement (Illustration 4.7) is prepared by showing the beginning capital account balance, adding net income (or deducting net loss), and then subtracting the owner's withdrawals. The ending capital balance is then carried forward to the balance sheet. The statement of owner's equity helps to relate income statement infor-

Illustration 4.7:   Statement of owner's equity

```
                    RAPID DELIVERY COMPANY
                      Statement of Owner's Equity
                  For the Month Ended December 31, 1984

John Turner, capital, December 1, 1984  . . . .     $50,000
Net income for December  . . . . . . . . . . . . .    6,690
      Total . . . . . . . . . . . . . . . . . . . . . . .  $56,690
Less: Drawings  . . . . . . . . . . . . . . . . . . . . .    3,000
John Turner, capital, December 31, 1984  . . .      $53,690
```

mation to balance sheet information; it indicates how net income relates to the balance sheet account, owner's capital.

Balance sheet

The balance sheet is then completed from the information in the Balance Sheet columns of the work sheet. The balance sheet for Rapid Delivery Company is shown in Illustration 4.8.

Illustration 4.8:   Balance sheet

RAPID DELIVERY SERVICE
Balance Sheet
December 31, 1984

Assets

Cash		$10,650
Accounts receivable		6,200
Supplies on hand		900
Prepaid insurance		2,200
Prepaid rent		800
Delivery trucks	$40,000	
Less: Accumulated depreciation	750	39,250
Total assets		$60,000

Liabilities and Owner's Equity

Liabilities:		
Accounts payable		$ 3,130
Unearned delivery fees		3,000
Accrued salaries payable		180
Total liabilities		$ 6,310
Owner's equity:		
John Turner, capital		53,690
Total liabilities and owner's equity		$60,000

JOURNALIZING ADJUSTING ENTRIES

The financial statements have now been completed. Adjustments were entered on the work sheet and were used to determine proper account balances for inclusion in the financial statements. Adjusting entries must now be entered in the general journal and posted to the appropriate ledger accounts so the adjustment information will be recorded in the permanent accounting records. The preparation of a work sheet does *not* eliminate the need to prepare and post adjusting entries. The adjusting entries for Rapid Delivery Company appear as follows in the general journal:

GENERAL JOURNAL				Page 3

Date	Account Titles and Explanation	Post. Ref.	Debit	Credit
1984	*Adjusting Entries*			
Dec. 31	Insurance Expense	504	2 0 0	
	Prepaid Insurance	103		2 0 0
	To record insurance expense for December.			
31	Rent Expense	505	4 0 0	
	Prepaid Rent	104		4 0 0
	To record rent expense for December.			
31	Supplies Expense	506	5 0 0	
	Supplies on Hand	102		5 0 0
	To record supplies used during December.			
31	Depreciation Expense—Delivery Trucks	507	7 5 0	
	Accumulated Depreciation—Delivery Trucks	110A		7 5 0
	To record depreciation expense for December.			
31	Unearned Delivery Fees	201	1 5 0 0	
	Delivery Service Revenue	400		1 5 0 0
	To transfer a portion of delivery fees from the liability account to the revenue account.			
31	Accounts Receivable	101	1 0 0 0	
	Delivery Service Revenue	400		1 0 0 0
	To record unbilled delivery services performed in December.			
31	Salaries Expense	502	1 8 0	
	Accrued Salaries Payable	202		1 8 0
	To accrue one day's salaries that were earned but are unpaid.			

THE CLOSING PROCESS

After the financial statements for the period have been prepared, the revenue and expense accounts must be closed. The *closing process* is the act of transferring the balances in the revenue and expense accounts to a clearing account called Income Summary and then to owner's capital. The closing process reduces revenue and expense account balances to zero in order that information for the next accounting period may be accumulated. Without closing entries, revenue and expense information for the current period would be intermingled with similar information from all prior periods.

The balance in each revenue and expense account is transferred by journal entry to an Income Summary account. The *Income Summary account* is a clearing account used only at the end of an accounting period to summarize revenues and expenses for the period. After all revenue and expense account balances are transferred to Income Summary, the balance in the account represents net income or net loss for the period. This balance is then transferred to the owner's capital account. This leaves a zero balance in the Income Summary account.

The owner's drawing account is also closed at the end of the period. The owner's drawing account shows how many dollars of cash or goods the owner is taking out of the business each period. This account is closed directly to the capital account; it is not closed to Income Summary. The reason is that drawings have no effect on income earned or loss incurred for the period.

Therefore, the closing process consists of (1) transferring revenue and expense account balances to Income Summary, (2) determining income for the period and transferring that amount to owner's capital, and (3) reducing the drawing account balance to zero and at the same time reducing owner's capital by the amount of owner's drawings during the period. This process is often referred to as "closing the books." Remember, though, that not all accounts are closed; assets, liabilities, and owner's capital are *not* closed during the closing process.

Closing the revenue account(s)

The work sheet is useful in preparing closing entries. Revenues appear in the Income Statement credit column of the work sheet. The only revenue appearing in the Income Statement credit column for Rapid Delivery Company is delivery service revenue of $13,200 (Illustration 4.5). Since revenue accounts have credit balances, they must be debited for an equal amount to bring them to a zero balance. The credit in the closing entry is made to Income

	GENERAL JOURNAL				Page 4
Date	Account Titles and Explanation	Post. Ref.	Debit	Credit	
1984 Dec. 31	*Closing Entries* Delivery Service Revenue	400	1 3 2 0 0		
	Income Summary	600		1 3 2 0 0	
	To close the revenue account in				
	the Income Statement credit				
	column to Income Summary.				

Summary (Account No. 600). The entry on page 121 is made in the general journal to close the Delivery Service Revenue account.

After closing, the Delivery Service Revenue account (in T-account format) will appear as shown below. Notice the account now has a zero balance.

		Delivery Service Revenue		Account No. 400
Decreased by $13,200	1984 Dec. 31 To close to Income Summary 13,200	Bal. before closing		13,200
		Bal. after closing		–0–

The Income Summary account was credited for $13,200 as a result of the above entry. The Income Summary account will be shown later.

Closing the expense accounts

Expenses appear in the Income Statement debit column of the work sheet. There are eight expenses for Rapid Delivery Company appearing in the Income Statement debit column (Illustration 4.5). As shown by the column subtotal, they add up to $6,510. Since expense accounts have debit balances, *each one* must be credited to bring it to a zero balance. The debit in the closing entry is made to the Income Summary account for $6,510. The following entry is made to close the expense accounts:

GENERAL JOURNAL					
Date	Account Titles and Explanation	Post. Ref.	Debit	Credit	
1984 Dec. 31	Income Summary	600	6 5 1 0		
	Advertising Expense	500		5 0	
	Gas and Oil Expense	501		6 8 0	
	Salaries Expense	502		3 7 8 0	
	Utilities Expense	503		1 5 0	
	Insurance Expense	504		2 0 0	
	Rent Expense	505		4 0 0	
	Supplies Expense	506		5 0 0	
	Depreciation Expense—Delivery Trucks	507		7 5 0	
	To close the expense accounts				
	appearing in the Income Statement				
	debit column to Income Summary.				

The debit of $6,510 to the Income Summary account agrees with the Income Statement debit column subtotal in the work sheet. This shows another way in which the work sheet is helpful in preparing closing entries. It can serve as a check to make certain that all revenue and expense items are listed and have been closed; had the debit in the above entry been for a different amount than the column subtotal, there would be an error in the closing entry for expenses.

The expense accounts will appear as shown below after they have been closed. Notice that each account has a zero balance after closing.

Advertising Expense		*Account No. 500*
Bal. before closing	50	1984
		Dec. 31 To close to Income Summary 50 ◄— Decreased by $50
Bal. after closing	–0–	

Gas and Oil Expense		*Account No. 501*
Bal. before closing	680	1984
		Dec. 31 To close to Income Summary 680 ◄— Decreased by $680
Bal. after closing	–0–	

Salaries Expense		*Account No. 502*
Bal. before closing	3,780	1984
		Dec. 31 To close to Income Summary 3,780 ◄— Decreased by $3,780
Bal. after closing	–0–	

Utilities Expense		*Account No. 503*
Bal. before closing	150	1984
		Dec. 31 To close to Income Summary 150 ◄— Decreased by $150
Bal. after closing	–0–	

Insurance Expense		*Account No. 504*
Bal. before closing	200	1984
		Dec. 31 To close to Income Summary 200 ◄— Decreased by $200
Bal. after closing	–0–	

Rent Expense		*Account No. 505*
Bal. before closing	400	1984
		Dec. 31 To close to Income Summary 400 ◄— Decreased by $400
Bal. after closing	–0–	

Supplies Expense		*Account No. 506*
Bal. before closing	500	1984
		Dec. 31 To close to Income Summary 500 ◄— Decreased by $500
Bal. after closing	–0–	

**Depreciation Expense—
Delivery Trucks**   *Account No. 507*

Bal. before closing	750	1984	
		Dec. 31 To close to Income Summary 750	Decreased by $750
Bal. after closing	–0–		

Closing the Income Summary account

After the revenues and expenses have been closed, the total amounts that formerly were carried in those accounts now are carried in the Income Summary account.

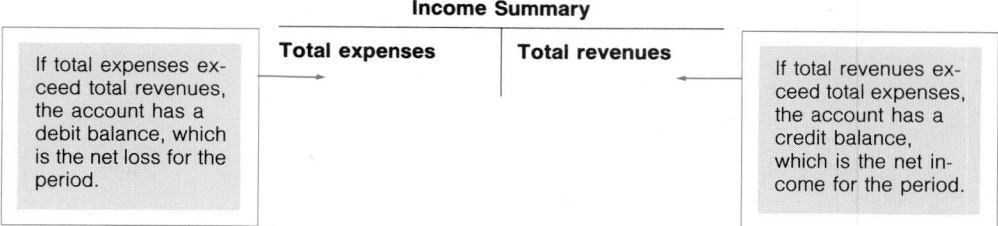

Income Summary

Total expenses	**Total revenues**

If total expenses exceed total revenues, the account has a debit balance, which is the net loss for the period.

If total revenues exceed total expenses, the account has a credit balance, which is the net income for the period.

For the Rapid Delivery Company, the Income Summary account appears as follows:

Income Summary   *Account No. 600*

1984		1984	
Dec. 31 From closing the expense accounts	6,510	Dec. 31 From closing the revenue account	13,200
		Bal. before closing this account (net income)	6,690

The credit balance of $6,690 is the net income for December.

Now the Income Summary account needs to be closed to the owner's capital account. The entry to do this is:

GENERAL JOURNAL

Date		Account Titles and Explanation	Post. Ref.	Debit	Credit
1984 Dec.	31	Income Summary	600	6 6 9 0	
		John Turner, Capital	300		6 6 9 0
		To close the Income Summary			
		account to the owner's capital			
		account.			

The Income Summary and John Turner, Capital accounts will appear as follows after the Income Summary account is closed:

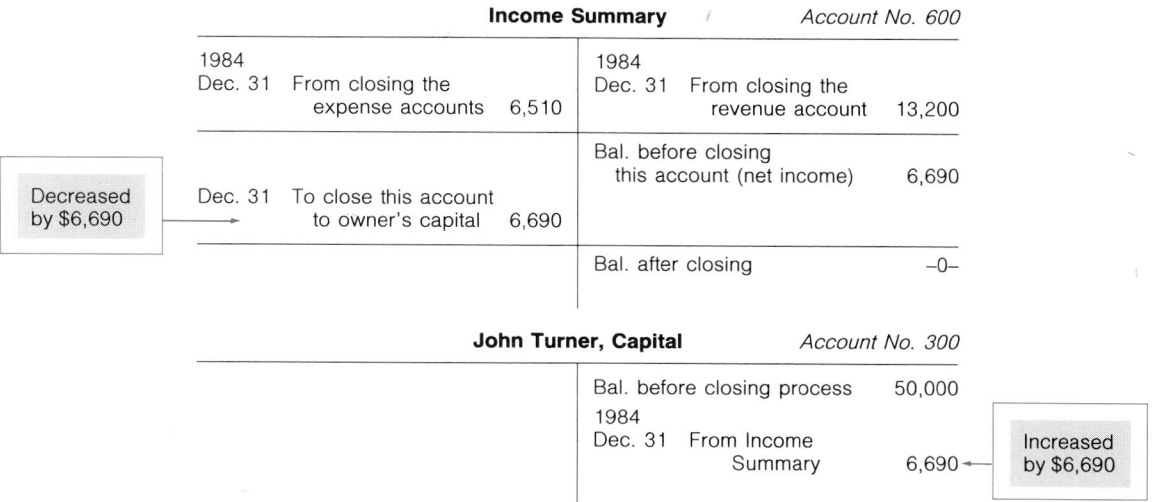

Income Summary / *Account No. 600*

1984		
Dec. 31	From closing the expense accounts	6,510

Decreased by $6,690

| Dec. 31 | To close this account to owner's capital | 6,690 |

1984		
Dec. 31	From closing the revenue account	13,200
	Bal. before closing this account (net income)	6,690
	Bal. after closing	–0–

John Turner, Capital *Account No. 300*

	Bal. before closing process	50,000
1984		
Dec. 31	From Income Summary	6,690

Increased by $6,690

Closing the owner's drawing account

The last closing entry that needs to be made is to close the owner's drawing account. This account has a debit balance before closing. To close the account, the owner's drawing account is credited and the owner's capital account is debited.

For the Rapid Delivery Company, the entry to close the owner's drawing account is:

GENERAL JOURNAL

Date		Account Titles and Explanation	Post. Ref.	Debit	Credit
1984					
Dec.	31	John Turner, Capital	300	3 0 0 0	
		John Turner, Drawing	301		3 0 0 0
		To close the owner's drawing			
		account to the owner's capital			
		account.			

The owner's drawing and capital accounts as they appear after the closing entry has been posted are:

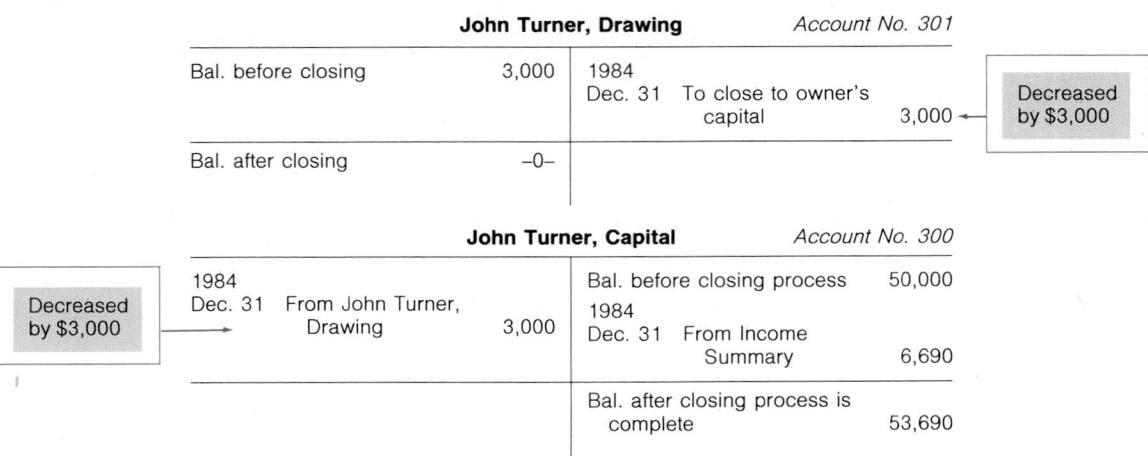

Closing process summarized

The closing process is the transferring of revenue and expense account balances to a clearing account called Income Summary and then transferring from Income Summary to Owner's Capital the amount of net income or net loss for the period. Closing also includes the elimination of the balance in the owner's drawing account by transferring that amount to owner's capital. A summary of the process used to close the Rapid Delivery Company accounts is as follows:

1. The revenue account appearing in the Income Statement credit column (revenues) was debited and the Income Summary account was credited for the amount of revenue earned for the period, $13,200. Notice that the credit to Income Summary is equal to the subtotal of the Income Statement credit column of the work sheet. This will be true no matter how many revenue accounts are closed.

2. Each expense account appearing in the Income Statement debit column (expenses) was credited for its balance and the Income Summary account was debited for the total amount of expenses incurred for the period, $6,510. Notice that the debit to Income Summary is equal to the subtotal of the Income Statement debit column of the work sheet.

3. The balance of the Income Summary account, $6,690, was closed to the owner's capital account. The Income Summary account balance was a credit (net income), so to close it the account was debited and owner's capital was credited. If a net loss had occurred, Income Summary would have had a debit balance and closing would have been through a credit to Income Summary and a debit to owner's capital.

4. The balance in the owner's drawing account was closed to the owner's capital account by debiting the capital account and crediting the drawing account. The balance in the drawing account is found in the Balance Sheet debit column of the work sheet.

The three-column ledger accounts for the Rapid Delivery Company, as they would appear after adjusting and closing entries have been posted, are shown in Appendix 4–B at the end of the chapter.

Post-closing trial balance

After closing has been completed, the only accounts in the ledger which have not been closed are the balance sheet accounts (the permanent or real accounts). Since these accounts contain the opening balances for the coming accounting year, they must, of course, be in balance. The preparation of a post-closing trial balance serves as a means of checking the accuracy of the closing process and ensures that the books are in balance at the start of the new accounting period.

A *post-closing trial balance* is a trial balance taken after the revenue, expense, and drawing accounts have been closed. The only accounts which should be open are assets, liabilities, and owner's capital. Account balances are listed in debit and credit columns and summed to prove the equality of the debits and credits.

A post-closing trial balance for the Rapid Delivery Company as of December 31, 1984, is shown in Illustration 4.9.

The amounts appearing in the post-closing trial balance would be taken from the ledger after the closing entries had been posted. You may want to verify this for yourself by comparing the above amounts with those appearing in the ledger accounts for the Rapid Delivery Company shown in chapter Appendix 4–B. *This concludes the Rapid Delivery Company illustration which has been used in Chapters 2, 3, and 4.*

Illustration 4.9:   Post-closing trial balance

RAPID DELIVERY COMPANY
Post-Closing Trial Balance
December 31, 1984

Account No.		Debits	Credits
100	Cash	$10,650	
101	Accounts receivable	6,200	
102	Supplies on hand	900	
103	Prepaid insurance	2,200	
104	Prepaid rent	800	
110	Delivery trucks	40,000	
110A	Accumulated depreciation—delivery trucks		$ 750
200	Accounts payable		3,130
201	Unearned delivery fees		3,000
202	Accrued salaries payable		180
300	John Turner, capital		53,690
		$60,750	$60,750

THE ACCOUNTING CYCLE SUMMARIZED

The financial accounting process consists of a number of functions beginning with observation of economic activity and ending with interpretation of reports and statements upon such activity. As mentioned at the beginning of the chapter, this process consists of a number of steps relating to the formal accounting system and its use in gathering, classifying, and reporting useful financial information. These steps, which have been illustrated and discussed in this and previous chapters, are referred to collectively as the accounting cycle. The accounting cycle consists of the following steps:

1. Journalize transactions in the journal.
2. Post journal entries to the accounts in the ledger.
3. Take a trial balance of the accounts and complete the work sheet.
4. Prepare financial statements.
5. Journalize adjusting entries.
6. Post adjusting entries to the accounts.
7. Journalize closing entries.
8. Post closing entries to the accounts.
9. Take a post-closing trial balance.

As shown in this chapter, completion of many of the steps at the end of an accounting period may be made somewhat easier through use of a work sheet.

THE CLASSIFIED BALANCE SHEET

All of the balance sheets presented so far in this text have been unclassified balance sheets. An *unclassified balance sheet* has only major categories labeled assets, liabilities, and owner's equity. As an example, the balance sheet in Illustration 4.8 grouped items only into these three major categories. A *classified balance sheet* subdivides at least some of the three major categories in order to provide useful information for interpretation and analysis by users of financial statements. Assets may be subdivided into many different categories; at this point, the classifications of current assets and property, plant, and equipment will suffice. Liabilities may be classified as either current or long term. Owner's equity for a single proprietorship cannot be subdivided into classifications.

An example of a classified balance sheet for the Jamestown Sports Arena is given in Illustration 4.10. The company rents its facilities for sporting events, concerts, and other activities. This balance sheet is presented in a vertical format (assets appearing above liabilities and owner's equity) rather than the horizontal format (assets on the left and liabilities and owner's equity on the right) which has been used previously in the text. Both formats are equally acceptable.

Each of the major categories included in Illustration 4.10 and items that may be included within those categories will now be discussed. Some of the

Illustration 4.10: A classified balance sheet

JAMESTOWN SPORTS ARENA
Balance Sheet
June 30, 1984

Assets

Current assets:

Cash	$ 40,000	
Accounts receivable	55,000	
Notes receivable	15,000	
Prepaid insurance	2,000	
Total current assets		$112,000

Property, plant, and equipment:

Land		$114,000	
Building	$300,000		
Less: Accumulated depreciation	100,000	200,000	
Sports equipment	$ 75,000		
Less: Accumulated depreciation	15,000	60,000	
Office equipment	$ 18,000		
Less: Accumulated depreciation	6,000	12,000	
Total property, plant, and equipment			386,000
Total assets			$498,000

Liabilities and Owner's Equity

Current liabilities:

Accounts payable	$ 25,000	
Notes payable	6,000	
Accrued salaries payable	800	
Unearned rental fees	1,100	
Total current liabilities		$ 32,900

Long-term liabilities:

Note payable, 15%, due in 1990	150,000
Total liabilities	$182,900

Owner's equity:

Andrews, capital	315,100
Total liabilities and owner's equity	$498,000

accounts have been explained briefly before but are described again here in more detail.

Current assets

Current assets are cash and other assets that will be converted into cash or used up by the business in a relatively short period of time, usually a year or less. Current assets commonly found in a service-type business include cash, accounts and notes receivable, and prepaid expenses. Current assets are normally listed in order of liquidity, or how easily they are convertible into cash.

Cash includes deposits in banks available for current operations at the balance sheet date, plus cash on hand consisting of currency, undeposited checks, drafts, and money orders. Normally, cash is the first current asset to appear on a balance sheet.

Accounts receivable (also called trade accounts receivable) are the amounts owed to a concern by customers. An account receivable arises when a service (or merchandise) is sold and cash is not received immediately. Normally, no written evidence of indebtedness is given by customers except by signing their signatures to sales invoices or delivery tickets.

A *note* is an unconditional written promise to pay a definite sum of money at a certain or determinable date, usually with interest (a charge made for use of the money) at a specified rate. A note is a *note receivable* on the balance sheet of the company to which the note is given. A note receivable arises (*a*) when a sale is made and a note is received from the customer, (*b*) when a customer gives a note for an amount due on an account receivable, or (*c*) when money is loaned and a note is received as evidence.

Prepaid expenses include items such as rent, insurance, and supplies that have been paid for but not yet used. If prepaid expenses had not been paid for in advance at the balance sheet date, they would require the disbursement of cash in the following period. Furthermore, prepaid expenses are current assets because they have service potential.

Property, plant, and equipment

Property, plant, and equipment are assets acquired for use in a business rather than for resale. Property, plant, and equipment also are termed *plant assets* or *fixed assets*. Property, plant, and equipment are called "fixed" assets because they are to be used for long-term purposes. Several types of property, plant, and equipment are described below.

Land is ground upon which the business buildings of the company are located. Land could also be used for outside storage space or a parking lot.

Buildings are structures in which business is carried out.

Machinery is heavy equipment such as a commercial press used in a laundry or a stamping machine used to punch out metal parts.

Sports equipment includes items such as hockey goals, basketball gear, and wrestling mats.

Store equipment, or *store fixtures,* includes items such as showcases, counters, stools, chairs, and cash registers.

Office equipment, or *office fixtures,* includes items such as file cabinets, calculators, typewriters, computers, desks, and chairs.

Delivery equipment includes autos, trucks, and vans used primarily in making deliveries to customers.

Accumulated depreciation is a contra asset account to depreciable assets such as buildings, machinery, and equipment. It shows total depreciation taken to date on the assets.

Current liabilities

Current liabilities are debts, usually due within one year, the payment of which normally will require the use of current assets. Examples of current liabilities follow.

Accounts payable are amounts owed to creditors for items or services purchased from them. Accounts payable are generally due in 30 or 60 days and do not bear interest.

Notes payable are unconditional written promises to pay a certain sum of money at a certain or determinable future date. The notes may arise from borrowing money from a bank, from the purchase of assets, or from the giving of a note in settlement of an account payable. Generally, only notes payable due in one year or less are included as current liabilities.

Accrued salaries payable are amounts owed to employees for services rendered, but for which payment has not been made at the balance sheet date. The salaries have not been paid at the balance sheet date because they are not due until later.

Unearned revenues result when payment is received before revenue has been earned, such as in a subscription to a magazine. Unearned revenues represent a liability to perform the agreed services or other contractual requirements or to return the assets received.

Long-term liabilities

Long-term liabilities are those not due for a relatively long period of time, usually more than one year. It is good policy to show maturity dates in the balance sheet for all long-term liabilities.

Notes payable with maturity dates at least one year beyond the balance sheet date are also long-term liabilities.

APPENDIX 4–A: REVERSING ENTRIES

For certain types of adjusting entries, reversing entries may be prepared as of the first day of the next accounting period. *Reversing entries* are so named because they reverse the effects of the adjusting entry to which they relate. The purpose of a reversing entry is to simplify the first entry relating to that same item in the next accounting period.

To illustrate, an example from the Rapid Delivery Company will be used. An adjusting entry was made at December 31, 1984, to recognize $180 of accrued salaries payable. The company pays salaries every four weeks. Thus, the next payday is Friday, January 25, 1985. Below are illustrated the entries from December 31, 1984, through January 25, 1985, assuming (1) no reversing entry is used and (2) a reversing entry is used.

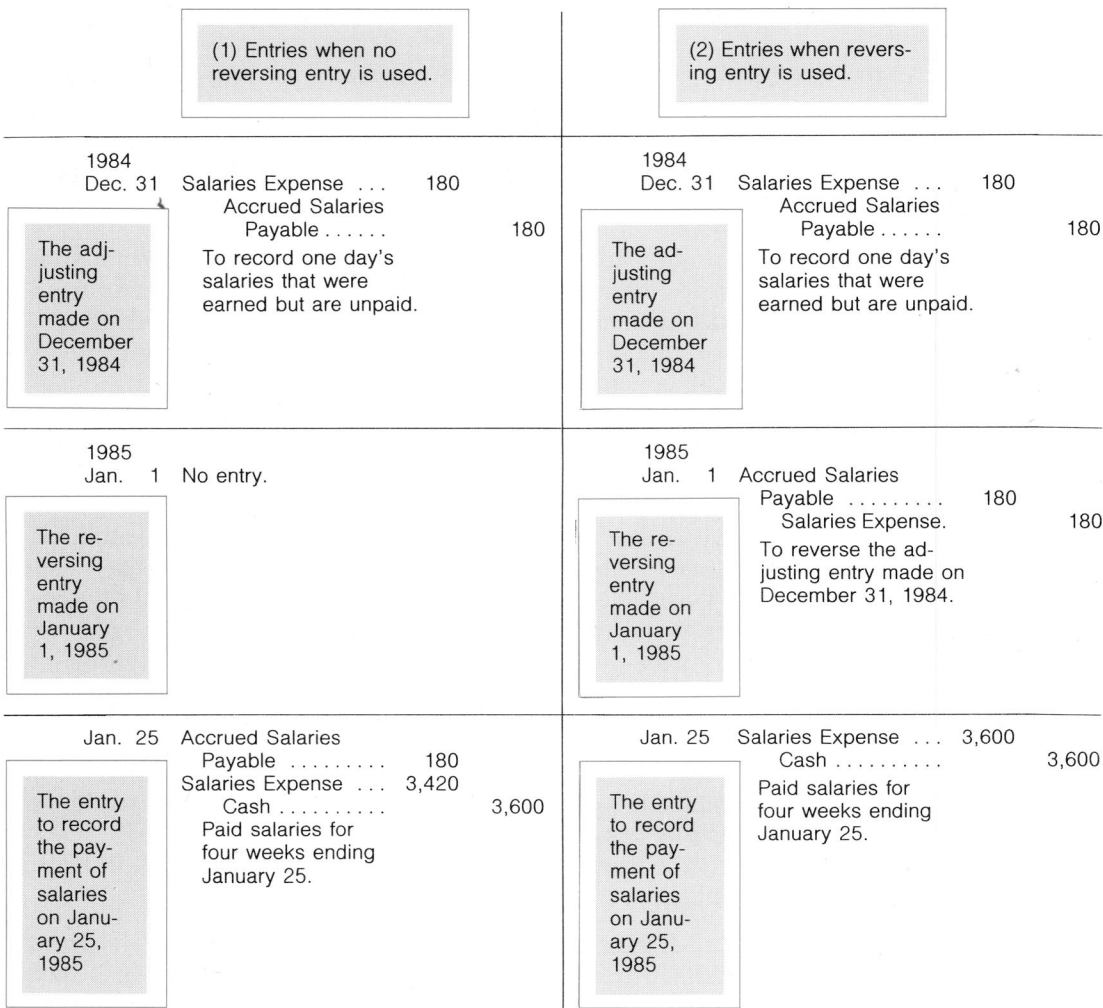

(1) Entries when no reversing entry is used.	(2) Entries when reversing entry is used.

The adjusting entry made on December 31, 1984

1984
Dec. 31   Salaries Expense ...   180
               Accrued Salaries
                  Payable   180
           To record one day's
           salaries that were
           earned but are unpaid.

1984
Dec. 31   Salaries Expense ...   180
               Accrued Salaries
                  Payable   180
           To record one day's
           salaries that were
           earned but are unpaid.

The reversing entry made on January 1, 1985

1985
Jan. 1   No entry.

1985
Jan. 1   Accrued Salaries
               Payable   180
                  Salaries Expense.   180
           To reverse the adjusting entry made on
           December 31, 1984.

The entry to record the payment of salaries on January 25, 1985

Jan. 25   Accrued Salaries
               Payable   180
           Salaries Expense ... 3,420
                  Cash   3,600
           Paid salaries for
           four weeks ending
           January 25.

Jan. 25   Salaries Expense ... 3,600
                  Cash   3,600
           Paid salaries for
           four weeks ending
           January 25.

Whether or not a reversing entry is used, the adjusting entries as of December 31, 1984, are the same. The reversing entry, dated January 1, 1985, shown in the second column above is the exact reverse of the debit and credit used in the adjusting entry. Use of the reversing entry simplifies the entry made on January 25. The accountant does not have to remember that accrued salaries payable of $180 have already been recorded. When the $3,600 payment is made, the entry is simply a debit to Salaries Expense and a credit to Cash for $3,600.

Another reason for using reversing entries is that when the accounts are maintained on a computer, the computer may have been programmed to debit Salaries Expense and credit Cash every time salaries are paid. The use of a reversing entry on January 1 permits the January 25 entry to be recorded in this way.

The end result in the accounts is the same whether or not a reversing entry is used. To prove this, the accounts as they would appear are shown below. The beginning balance in Accrued Salaries Payable results from the adjusting entry made on December 31, 1984. Adjusting entries from 1984 are not shown since they were the same under either method.

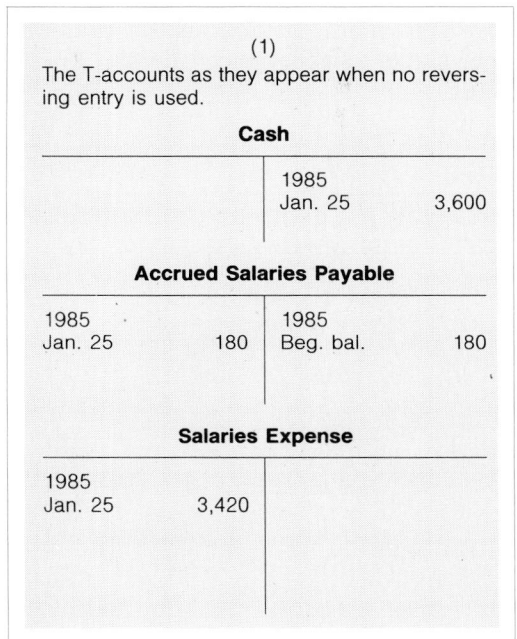

(1)
The T-accounts as they appear when no reversing entry is used.

Cash

| | | 1985 | |
| | | Jan. 25 | 3,600 |

Accrued Salaries Payable

| 1985 | | 1985 | |
| Jan. 25 | 180 | Beg. bal. | 180 |

Salaries Expense

| 1985 | | | |
| Jan. 25 | 3,420 | | |

(2)
The T-accounts as they appear when a reversing entry is used

Cash

| | | 1985 | |
| | | Jan. 25 | 3,600 |

Accrued Salaries Payable

| 1985 | | 1985 | |
| Jan. 1 Reversing entry | 180 | Beg. Bal. | 180 |

Salaries Expense

1985		1985	
Jan. 25	3,600	Jan. 1 Reversing entry	180
Bal.	3,420		

Not all adjusting entries may be reversed on the first day of the next accounting period. Ideal entries for reversal are those relating to situations where cash is going to be paid or received in the following period for an item which accrues and has resulted in an adjusting entry. Examples of such items would include accrued salaries and unbilled revenues. Adjustments for items which will not result in a subsequent receipt or payment of cash, such as the adjustment for depreciation, are not reversed. *A general rule to follow is that all adjusting journal entries that increase assets or liabilities may be reversed, but those adjusting journal entries that decrease assets or liabilities may not be reversed.* Thus, adjusting entries which involve accruals of assets (accrued receivables) and liabilities (accrued payables) may be reversed.

Reversing entries are optional and relate to bookkeeping technique. Whether or not they are used has no effect on the financial statements. Students may encounter the use of reversing entries in more advanced accounting courses or in actual practice. An understanding of reversing entries is not essential to understanding the remainder of this text since they will not be used.

APPENDIX 4–B: LEDGER ACCOUNTS AFTER CLOSING PROCESS COMPLETED

The ledger accounts for the Rapid Delivery Company after the adjusting and closing entries have been posted would appear as shown below. Adjusting entries appeared on page 3 of the general journal. Assume all closing entries were entered on page 4 of the general journal. The initial December 31 balances are before adjusting and closing entries have been posted. The balances are labeled as a debit or a credit to assist you in understanding the example. Normally this is not done in the ledger since an experienced person knows whether each balance is a debit or credit.

GENERAL LEDGER

Cash   Account No. 100

Date		Explanation	Post. Ref.	Debit	Credit	Balance
1984 Dec.	31	Balance				10 650 Dr.

Accounts Receivable   Account No. 101

Date		Explanation	Post. Ref.	Debit	Credit	Balance
1984 Dec.	31	Balance				5 200 Dr.
	31	Adjustment	GJ3	1 000		6 200 Dr.

Supplies on Hand   Account No. 102

Date		Explanation	Post. Ref.	Debit	Credit	Balance
1984 Dec.	31	Balance				1 400 Dr.
	31	Adjustment	GJ3		500	900 Dr.

Prepaid Insurance   Account No. 103

Date		Explanation	Post. Ref.	Debit	Credit	Balance
1984 Dec.	31	Balance				2 400 Dr.
	31	Adjustment	GJ3		200	2 200 Dr.

Prepaid Rent   *Account No. 104*

Date		Explanation	Post. Ref.	Debit	Credit	Balance
1984 Dec.	31	Balance				1 2 0 0 Dr.
	31	Adjustment	GJ3		4 0 0	8 0 0 Dr.

Delivery Trucks   *Account No. 110*

Date		Explanation	Post. Ref.	Debit	Credit	Balance
1984 Dec.	31	Balance				4 0 0 0 0 Dr.

Accumulated Depreciation—Delivery Trucks   *Account No. 110A*

Date		Explanation	Post. Ref.	Debit	Credit	Balance
1984 Dec.	31	Balance				– 0 –
	31	Adjustment	GJ3		7 5 0	7 5 0 Cr.

Accounts Payable   *Account No. 200*

Date		Explanation	Post. Ref.	Debit	Credit	Balance
1984 Dec.	31	Balance				3 1 3 0 Cr.

Unearned Delivery Fees   *Account No. 201*

Date		Explanation	Post. Ref.	Debit	Credit	Balance
1984 Dec.	31	Balance				4 5 0 0 Cr.
	31	Adjustment	GJ3	1 5 0 0		3 0 0 0 Cr.

GENERAL LEDGER (*continued*)

Accrued Salaries Payable   Account No. 202

Date		Explanation	Post. Ref.	Debit	Credit	Balance
1984 Dec.	31	Balance				– 0 –
	31	Adjustment	GJ3		1 8 0	1 8 0 Cr.

John Turner, Capital   Account No. 300

Date		Explanation	Post. Ref.	Debit	Credit	Balance
1984 Dec.	31	Balance				5 0 0 0 0 Cr.
	31	Net income	GJ4		6 6 9 0	5 6 6 9 0 Cr.
	31	Drawings	GJ4	3 0 0 0		5 3 6 9 0 Cr.

John Turner, Drawing   Account No. 301

Date		Explanation	Post. Ref.	Debit	Credit	Balance
1984 Dec.	31	Balance				3 0 0 0 Dr.
	31	To close	GJ4		3 0 0 0	– 0 –

Delivery Service Revenue   Account No. 400

Date		Explanation	Post. Ref.	Debit	Credit	Balance
1984 Dec.	31	Balance				1 0 7 0 0 Cr.
	31	Adjustment	GJ3		1 5 0 0	1 2 2 0 0 Cr.
	31	Adjustment	GJ3		1 0 0 0	1 3 2 0 0 Cr.
	31	To close	GJ4	1 3 2 0 0		– 0 –

Advertising Expense   Account No. 500

Date		Explanation	Post. Ref.	Debit	Credit	Balance
1984 Dec.	31	Balance				5 0 Dr.
	31	To close	GJ4		5 0	– 0 –

Gas and Oil Expense

Account No. 501

Date		Explanation	Post. Ref.	Debit	Credit	Balance
1984 Dec.	31	Balance				6 8 0 Dr.
	31	To close	GJ4		6 8 0	– 0 –

Salaries Expense

Account No. 502

Date		Explanation	Post. Ref.	Debit	Credit	Balance
1984 Dec.	31	Balance				3 6 0 0 Dr.
	31	Adjustment	GJ3	1 8 0		3 7 8 0 Dr.
	31	To close	GJ4		3 7 8 0	– 0 –

Utilities Expense

Account No. 503

Date		Explanation	Post. Ref.	Debit	Credit	Balance
1984 Dec.	31	Balance				1 5 0 Dr.
	31	To close	GJ4		1 5 0	– 0 –

Insurance Expense

Account No. 504

Date		Explanation	Post. Ref.	Debit	Credit	Balance
1984 Dec.	31	Balance				– 0 –
	31	Adjustment	GJ3	2 0 0		2 0 0 Dr.
	31	To close	GJ4		2 0 0	– 0 –

Rent Expense

Account No. 505

Date		Explanation	Post. Ref.	Debit	Credit	Balance
1984 Dec.	31	Balance				– 0 –
	31	Adjustment	GJ3	4 0 0		4 0 0 Dr.
	31	To close	GJ4		4 0 0	– 0 –

GENERAL LEDGER (*concluded*)

Supplies Expense
Account No. 506

Date		Explanation	Post. Ref.	Debit	Credit	Balance
1984 Dec.	31	Balance				– 0 –
	31	Adjustment	GJ3	5 0 0		5 0 0 Dr.
	31	To close	GJ4		5 0 0	– 0 –

Depreciation Expense–Delivery Trucks
Account No. 507

Date		Explanation	Post. Ref.	Debit	Credit	Balance
1984 Dec.	31	Balance				– 0 –
	31	Adjustment	GJ3	7 5 0		7 5 0 Dr.
	31	To close	GJ4		7 5 0	– 0 –

Income Summary
Account No. 600

Date		Explanation	Post. Ref.	Debit	Credit	Balance
1984 Dec.	31	Balance				– 0 –
	31	Revenue	GJ4		1 3 2 0 0	1 3 2 0 0 Cr.
	31	Expenses	GJ4	6 5 1 0		6 6 9 0 Cr.
	31	To close	GJ4	6 6 9 0		– 0 –

As each of the expense and revenue accounts is closed, its balance is reduced to zero. The balances formerly in those accounts are transferred to the Income Summary account. Note that the Income Summary account shows clearly the net income for the period—the final amount transferred, or closed, to the John Turner, Capital account. The balance in the John Turner, Capital account of $53,690 is the amount of capital shown in the balance sheet for December 31, 1984.

NEW TERMS INTRODUCED IN CHAPTER 4

Accounting cycle
Steps performed during an accounting period related to gathering, classifying, and reporting useful financial information. The steps include journalizing transactions, posting journal entries, taking a trial balance and completing the work sheet, pre-

paring financial statements, preparing and posting adjusting entries, preparing and posting closing entries, and taking a post-closing trial balance.

Buildings
Structures in which business is carried out.

Cash
Includes deposits in banks available for current operations at the balance sheet date, plus cash on hand consisting of currency, undeposited checks, drafts, and money orders.

Classified balance sheet
Subdivides the three major categories in order to provide useful information for interpretation and analysis by users of financial statements. Assets may be divided into current assets and property, plant, and equipment; and liabilities are divided into current liabilities and long-term liabilities.

Closing process
The act of transferring the balances in the revenue and expense accounts to a clearing account called Income Summary and then to the owner's capital account. The balance in the owner's drawing account is transferred to the owner's capital account.

Current assets
Cash and other assets that will be converted into cash or used up by the business during a relatively short period of time, usually a year or less.

Current liabilities
Debts, usually due within one year, the payment of which normally will require current assets.

Income Summary account
A clearing account used only at the end of an accounting period to summarize revenues and expenses for the period.

Land
Ground upon which the business buildings of the company are located. Land also could be used for outside storage space or a parking lot.

Long-term liabilities
Liabilities not due for a relatively long period of time, usually more than a year.

Machinery
Heavy equipment such as a commercial press used in a laundry or a stamping machine used to punch out metal parts.

Note
An unconditional written promise to pay a definite sum of money at a certain or determinable date, usually with interest at a specified rate.

Post-closing trial balance
A trial balance taken after the revenue, expense, and drawing accounts have been closed.

Property, plant, and equipment
Are acquired for use in a business rather than for resale. They are also called plant assets or fixed assets.

Reversing entries
Reverse the effects of the adjusting entries to which they relate. They are made on the first day of the next accounting period. Their purpose is to make easier the recording of subsequent transactions relating to those same items. Reversing entries may only be used for certain types of adjusting entries—usually those accruals where cash is to be paid or received in the next accounting period.

Statement of owner's equity
A financial statement that summarizes the transactions affecting the owner's capital account balance. The statement starts with the beginning capital account balance, adds net income or deducts a net loss, and then subtracts the owner's withdrawals to arrive at the ending capital account balance.

Unclassified balance sheet
One showing only major categories labeled for assets, liabilities, and owner's equity.

Work sheet
A large columnar sheet of paper that offers a convenient means for entering and summarizing information needed for making adjusting and closing entries and for preparing financial statements.

DEMONSTRATION PROBLEM

The demonstration problem for Chapters 1 and 2 used information for the Huntcliff Riding Stable to illustrate concepts. This problem illustrates the use of a work sheet for the same company for the month ended July 31, 1984. Financial statements are also prepared. Then the closing process is illustrated. The trial balance for the Huntcliff Riding Stable as of July 31, 1984, was as follows:

HUNTCLIFF RIDING STABLE
Trial Balance
July 31, 1984

	Debits	*Credits*
Cash	$ 9,500	
Accounts receivable	8,100	
Land	40,000	
Building	24,000	
Accounts payable		$ 1,100
Loan payable (due June 1989)		40,000
Barbara Macon, capital		36,600
Barbara Macon, drawing	700	
Horse boarding fees		4,500
Riding and lesson fees		3,600
Feed expense	1,100	
Salaries expense	1,400	
Miscellaneous expense	1,000	
	$85,800	$85,800

Additional data:

1. Depreciation expense for the month is $200.
2. Accrued salaries at the end of the month are $100.

Required:

a. Prepare a 10-column work sheet for the month ended July 31, 1984.

b. Prepare an income statement for the month ended July 31, 1984.

c. Prepare a statement of owner's equity for the month ended July 31, 1984.

d. Prepare a balance sheet as of July 31, 1984. (Classify the items to the extent possible.)

e. Journalize the adjusting entries.

f. Journalize the closing entries.

Solution to demonstration problem

a.

HUNTCLIFF RIDING STABLE
Work Sheet
For the Month Ended July 31, 1984

Account Titles	Trial Balance Debit	Trial Balance Credit	Adjustments Debit	Adjustments Credit	Adjusted Trial balance Debit	Adjusted Trial balance Credit	Income Statement Debit	Income Statement Credit	Balance Sheet Debit	Balance Sheet Credit
Cash	9,500				9,500				9,500	
Accounts receivable	8,100				8,100				8,100	
Land	40,000				40,000				40,000	
Building	24,000				24,000				24,000	
Accounts payable		1,100				1,100				1,100
Loan payable		40,000				40,000				40,000
Barbara Macon, capital		36,600				36,600				36,600
Barbara Macon, drawing	700				700				700	
Horse boarding fees		4,500				4,500		4,500		
Riding and lesson fees		3,600				3,600		3,600		
Feed expense	1,100				1,100		1,100			
Salaries expense	1,400		(2) 100		1,500		1,500			
Miscellaneous expense	1,000				1,000		1,000			
	85,800	85,800								
Depreciation expense—building			(1) 200		200		200			
Accumulated depreciation—										
building				(1) 200		200				200
Accrued salaries payable				(2) 100		100				100
			300	300	86,100	86,100	3,800	8,100		
Net income							4,300			4,300
							8,100	8,100	82,300	82,300

Adjustments:
    (1) To record depreciation of building for July.
    (2) To record accrued salaries.

b.

```
                    HUNTCLIFF RIDING STABLE
                        Income Statement
                 For the Month Ended July 31, 1984

Revenues:
    Horse boarding fees . . . . . . . . . . . . . . . .    $4,500
    Riding and lesson fees . . . . . . . . . . . . . .     3,600
        Total revenues . . . . . . . . . . . . . . . . .            $8,100
Expenses:
    Feed . . . . . . . . . . . . . . . . . . . . . . . . . . . .    $1,100
    Salaries . . . . . . . . . . . . . . . . . . . . . . . . .      1,500
    Miscellaneous . . . . . . . . . . . . . . . . . . . . .        1,000
    Depreciation—building . . . . . . . . . . . . . . .          200
        Total expenses . . . . . . . . . . . . . . . . .               3,800
Net income . . . . . . . . . . . . . . . . . . . . . . . . .          $4,300
```

c.

```
                    HUNTCLIFF RIDING STABLE
                     Statement of Owner's Equity
                 For the Month Ended July 31, 1984

Barbara Macon, capital, July 1, 1984 . . . . . . . . . . .    $36,600
Net income for July . . . . . . . . . . . . . . . . . . . . . . .       4,300
        Total . . . . . . . . . . . . . . . . . . . . . . . . . . . . . . .   $40,900
Less: Drawings . . . . . . . . . . . . . . . . . . . . . . . . .            700
Barbara Macon, capital, July 31, 1984 . . . . . . . . . . .   $40,200
```

d.

HUNTCLIFF RIDING STABLE
Balance Sheet
July 31, 1984

Assets

Current assets:			
Cash		$ 9,500	
Accounts receivable		8,100	
Total current assets			$17,600
Property, plant, and equipment:			
Land		$40,000	
Building	$24,000		
Less: Accumulated depreciation	200	23,800	
Total property, plant, and equipment			63,800
Total assets			$81,400

Liabilities and Owner's Equity

Current liabilities:		
Accounts payable........................	$ 1,100	
Accrued salaries payable	100	
Total current liabilities		$ 1,200
Long-term liabilities:		
Loan payable		40,000
Total liabilities		$41,200
Owner's equity:		
Barbara Macon, capital, July 31		40,200
Total liabilities and owner's equity		$81,400

e.

General Journal

Date		Account Titles and Explanation	Post. Ref.	Debit			Credit		
1984		*Adjusting Entries*							
July	31	Depreciation Expense—Building	503	2	0	0			
		Accumulated Depreciation—Building	115				2	0	0
		To record depreciation for July.							
	31	Salaries Expense	502	1	0	0			
		Accrued Salaries Payable	202				1	0	0
		To record salaries accrued at the							
		end of the period.							

f.

General Journal

Date	Account Titles and Explanation	Post. Ref.	Debit	Credit
1984	*Closing Entries*			
July 31	Horse Boarding Fees	400	4 5 0 0	
	Riding and Lesson Fees	401	3 6 0 0	
	Income Summary	600*		8 1 0 0
	To close accounts in the Income			
	Statement credit column of the			
	work sheet.			
31	Income Summary	600	3 8 0 0	
	Feed Expense	501		1 1 0 0
	Salaries Expense	502		1 5 0 0
	Miscellaneous Expense	510		1 0 0 0
	Depreciation Expense—Building	503		2 0 0
	To close accounts in the Income			
	Statement debit column of			
	the work sheet.			
31	Income Summary	600	4 3 0 0	
	Barbara Macon, Capital	300		4 3 0 0
	To close Income Summary account.			
31	Barbara Macon, Capital	300	7 0 0	
	Barbara Macon, Drawing	301		7 0 0
	To close the owner's drawing			
	account.			

* Assumed account number.

QUESTIONS

1. Describe the purposes for which the work sheet is prepared.

2. At what point in the accounting cycle is a work sheet usually prepared?

3. You have taken over a set of accounting books for a small business as a part-time job. At the end of the first accounting period, you have partially completed the work sheet by listing the proper ledger accounts and entering their balances in the Trial Balance columns. You turn to the manager and ask, "Where is the list of additional information I can use in entering the adjusting entries?" The manager indicates there is no such list. In all the textbook problems you have done, you have always been given this information. How would you obtain the information for this real-life situation? What are the consequences of not making all of the adjustments required at the end of the accounting period?

4. How are the amounts in the Adjusted Trial Balance columns of a work sheet determined?

5. After the Adjusted Trial Balance columns of a work sheet have been totaled, which account balances are extended to the Income Statement columns, and which account balances are extended to the Balance Sheet columns?

6. A company has net income of $2,500 for the year. In which columns of the work sheet would net income appear?

7. Describe the format of the statement of owner's equity.

8. Assuming that the closing process has been accomplished properly, which of the following statements is true? Why?

   a. After closing, expense and revenue accounts never have a balance other than zero.
   b. After closing, balance sheet accounts always have a balance other than zero.

9. In what important way do the pre-closing trial balance and the post-closing trial balance differ? Why is the post-closing trial balance prepared?

10. Your uncle knows you are taking a course in accounting in college, and he asks you to come over and help him. It seems his new bookkeeper has journalized all of the business transactions for the month and has posted the journal entries to the ledger accounts. The bookkeeper now admits a difficulty in knowing how to proceed in completing the accounting process for the month. Your uncle asks you to tell the bookkeeper what should now be done to complete the process.

11. Describe the differences between an unclassified balance sheet and a classified balance sheet.

12. (Based on Appendix 4-A) Describe the nature and purpose of a reversing entry.

EXERCISES

E-1. Three of the major column headings on a work sheet are Trial Balance, Income Statement, and Balance Sheet. For each of the following items, determine under which major column heading it would appear and whether it would be a debit or credit. (For instance, cash would appear under the debit side of the Trial Balance and Balance Sheet columns.)

	Trial Balance		Income Statement		Balance Sheet	
	Debit	Credit	Debit	Credit	Debit	Credit
a. Accounts receivable.						
b. Accounts payable.						
c. Service revenue.						
d. Advertising expense.		✓		✓		
e. T. P. Howse, capital.			✓			✓
f. Fees earned. (Revenue)						
g. Net income for the month.			✓			
h. Net loss for the month.					✓	

E-2. Ralph Reynolds was preparing the work sheet for the Davenport Company. He calculated the net income to be $20,000. When he totaled the Balance Sheet columns, the column totals were: Debit, $186,000; and Credit, $146,000. What was the probable cause of this difference? If this was not the cause, what should he do to find the error?

E-3. The first attempt at preparing the work sheet for the Johnston Company resulted in net income of $50,000 for the current year. Careful examination of the work sheet and supporting data indicated that the following items were ignored:

1. Accrued salaries were $3,000 at December 31.

2. Depreciation on equipment acquired on July 1 amounted to $4,000.

3. The amount of prepaid insurance which had expired by year-end was $1,000.

    a. Based upon the above information, what adjusting journal entries should be included to make the work sheet correct? Show them in journal entry form.
    b. What is the correct net income?

E–4.   The Income Statement column totals on a work sheet prepared at December 31, 1984, are: Debit, $80,000; and Credit, $100,000. In T-account format show how the postings to the Income Summary account would appear as a result of the closing process. Identify what each posting represents.

E–5.   After adjustment, selected account balances of the Redford Campground are:

	Debits	*Credits*
Campsite rental revenue		$60,000
Salaries expense	$21,000	
Depreciation expense	4,000	
Utilities expense	13,000	
Redford, drawing	2,000	
Redford, capital		40,000

In T-account format, give the entries required to close the books for the period. Enter the above balances in the accounts before doing so. Key the postings from the first closing entry with the number (*1*), the second with the number (*2*), and so on.

E–6.   Restructure the following unclassified balance sheet into a classified balance sheet.

CADIGAN TALENT AGENCY
Balance Sheet
December 31, 1984

Assets

Cash		10,000
Accounts receivable		15,000
Prepaid insurance		4,000
Land		25,000
Building	$100,000	
Less: Accumulated depreciation	40,000	60,000
Total assets		$114,000

Liabilities and Owner's Equity

Liabilities:

Accounts payable		$ 8,000
Note payable, due 1988.................		12,000
Total liabilities		$ 20,000

Owner's equity:

T. Cadigan, capital		94,000
Total liabilities and owner's equity .		$114,000

E-7.   (Based on Appendix 4–A) Assume that an adjusting entry made on December 31, 1984, was as follows:

```
1984
Dec. 31  Salaries Expense . . . . . . . . . . . . . . . . . . . . . . . . . . . . . . . . . . . . . .      800
              Accrued Salaries Payable . . . . . . . . . . . . . . . . . . . . . . . . . . .              800
         To accrue salaries for last four days of December.
```

Show how the January 3, 1985, payment of $1,200 of salaries would be recorded assuming (1) no reversing entry is used and (2) a reversing entry is used on January 1, 1985 (show this entry also). Then show by the use of T-accounts that the end result is the same whether a reversing entry is used or not.

PROBLEMS, SERIES A

P4–1–A.   The trial balance of the Reece Plumbing Company at December 31, 1984, is as follows:

REECE PLUMBING COMPANY
Trial Balance
December 31, 1984

	Debits	Credits
Cash	$ 45,000	
Accounts receivable	13,600	
Supplies on hand	2,000	
Prepaid insurance	1,800	
Building	70,000	
Accumulated depreciation—building		$ 12,500
Plumbing tools and equipment	18,000	
Accumulated depreciation—plumbing		
tools and equipment		4,500
Accounts payable		11,000
B. W. Reece, capital		52,100
B. W. Reece, drawing	20,000	
Plumbing service revenue		140,000
Salaries expense	48,000	
Utilities expense	1,700	
	$220,100	$220,100

Additional data:

1. Supplies on hand at December 31, 1984, have a cost of $600.
2. The balance in the Prepaid Insurance account represents the cost of a two-year insurance policy covering the period from January 1, 1984, through December 31, 1985.
3. Depreciation expense is $1,250 on the building and $900 on the equipment.

Required:

          Prepare a work sheet for the Reece Plumbing Company for the year ended December 31, 1984.

P4–2–A.   The following account balances appeared in the Income Statement columns of the work sheet prepared for the Reliable TV Repair Company for the year ended December 31, 1984:

	Income Statement	
	Debit	Credit
TV repair service revenue		352,000
Advertising expense	1,500	
Salaries expense	110,000	
Utilities expense	2,000	
Insurance expense	1,000	
Rent expense	6,000	
Supplies expense	2,000	
Depreciation expense—equipment	4,500	
	127,000	352,000
Net income	225,000	
	352,000	352,000

Required:

    a. Prepare the closing journal entries. Assume that on December 31, 1984, the J. M. Thompson, Drawing account had a debit balance of $25,000 and the J. M. Thompson, Capital account had a credit balance of $70,000 before the closing process began.

    b. Using T-accounts show how the accounts would appear after all of the closing entries have been posted.

    c. Prepare an income statement.

P4-3-A. Given below are the amounts appearing on the Adjusted Trial Balance columns of the June 30, 1984, work sheet for the Gardner Real Estate Company.

	Adjusted Trial Balance	
	Debit	Credit
Cash	80,000	
Accounts receivable	9,750	
Office equipment	35,000	
Accumulated depreciation—office equipment		14,000
Automobiles	55,000	
Accumulated depreciation—automobiles		20,000
Accounts payable		3,000
Michael Gardner, capital		155,400
Michael Gardner, drawing	5,000	
Sales commissions revenue		130,000
Office salaries expense	25,000	
Salespersons' commissions expense .	90,000	
Automobile operating expense	4,000	
Rent expense	4,250	
Supplies expense	900	
Utilities expense	2,000	
Depreciation expense—office equipment	3,500	
Depreciation expense—automobiles	8,000	
	322,400	322,400

Required:

      a.   Based on the above data, prepare closing entries. (You may want to mentally determine which of the above items would appear in the Income Statement columns of the work sheet.) In preparing the third closing entry, you will also need to determine whether there was net income or a net loss for the period.

      b.   Using T-accounts show how the accounts would appear after all of the closing entries have been posted.

P4–4–A.

Required:

      Using the following trial balance and additional information for the Hawkins Equipment Rental Company:

      a.   Prepare a 10-column work sheet for the year ended December 31, 1984.

      b.   Prepare the adjusting journal entries.

      c.   Prepare the closing journal entries.

HAWKINS EQUIPMENT RENTAL COMPANY
Trial Balance
December 31, 1984

	Debits	Credits
Cash	$ 64,000	
Accounts receivable	44,000	
Prepaid rent	7,200	
Prepaid insurance	3,600	
Equipment	120,000	
Accumulated depreciation—equipment		$ 40,000
Accounts payable		31,000
G. O. Hawkins, capital		139,200
G. O. Hawkins, drawing	24,000	
Rental service revenue		350,000
Salaries expense	250,000	
Travel expense	35,400	
Miscellaneous expense	12,000	
	$560,200	$560,200

Additional data:

1. The prepaid rent was for the period January 1, 1984, to December 31, 1985.
2. The depreciation on the equipment is $8,000 per year.
3. The prepaid insurance was for the period April 1, 1984, to March 31, 1985.
4. Accrued salaries payable total $3,000 at December 31.

P4–5–A.   The Adjusted Trial Balance columns of the work sheet for C. S. Berman, Attorney, at December 31, 1984, are as follows:

	Adjusted Trial Balance	
	Debit	Credit
Cash	58,400	
Accounts receivable	33,720	
Prepaid insurance	1,200	
Supplies on hand	1,000	
Land	16,000	
Building	95,000	
Accumulated depreciation—building		20,000
Office equipment	14,000	
Accumulated depreciation—office equipment .		4,000
Accounts payable		9,000
Accrued salaries payable		4,700
Notes payable (due March 1, 1985)		32,000
C. S. Berman, capital		90,980
C. S. Berman, drawing	20,000	
Legal service revenue		187,000
Travel expense	14,160	
Depreciation expense—building	4,250	
Depreciation expense—office equipment	1,400	
Salaries expense	81,200	
Supplies expense	1,900	
Insurance expense	1,800	
Building repairs expense	1,050	
Utilities expense	2,600	
	347,680	347,680

Required:

a. Prepare an income statement.

b. Prepare a statement of owner's equity.

c. Prepare a classified balance sheet.

d. Prepare the closing journal entries.

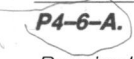

P4–6–A.

Required:

From the following trial balance and additional information for the Waldrop Cleaning Service Company, prepare:

a. A 10-column work sheet for the year ended December 31, 1984.

b. An income statement.

c. A statement of owner's equity.

d. A classified balance sheet.

e. Adjusting journal entries.

f. Closing journal entries.

WALDROP CLEANING SERVICE COMPANY
Trial Balance
December 31, 1984

	Debits	Credits
Cash	$ 29,000	
Accounts receivable	21,800	
Prepaid insurance	4,800	
Prepaid rent	9,000	
Supplies on hand	11,500	
Office equipment	10,000	
Accumulated depreciation—office equipment		$ 3,500
Cleaning equipment	30,000	
Accumulated depreciation—cleaning equipment		8,750
Service trucks	75,000	
Accumulated depreciation—service trucks		23,438
Accounts payable		7,000
D. L. Waldrop, capital		59,162
D. L. Waldrop, drawing	30,000	
Cleaning service revenue		240,000
Salaries expense	114,250	
Gas and oil expense	3,500	
Utilities expense	3,000	
	$341,850	$341,850

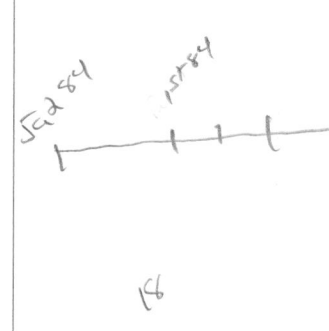

Additional data:

1. The balance in the Prepaid Insurance account represents the remaining cost of a five-year insurance policy purchased on January 2, 1983. The account was last adjusted on December 31, 1983.
2. The balance in the Prepaid Rent account represents the amount paid on January 2, 1984, to cover rent for the period from January 2, 1984, through June 30, 1985.
3. Depreciation on the plant assets is: office equipment, $1,000; cleaning equipment, $2,500; and service trucks, $9,375.
4. Accrued salaries at December 31, 1984, are $3,100.
5. A physical inventory shows that $2,000 of the supplies are on hand at December 31, 1984.

P4–7–A.

Required:

From the trial balance and additional data given below for the Letts Electrical Contracting Company, prepare:

a. A 10-column work sheet for the year ended December 31, 1984.

b. An income statement.

c. A statement of owner's equity.

d. A classified balance sheet.

e. The December 31, 1984, closing entries.

LETTS ELECTRICAL CONTRACTING COMPANY
Trial Balance
December 31, 1984

	Debits	Credits
Cash	$136,000	
Accounts receivable	15,760	
Prepaid insurance	2,400	
Prepaid rent—building	28,800	
Supplies on hand	2,680	
Equipment	84,000	
Accumulated depreciation—equipment		$ 8,800
Accounts payable		1,900
Letts, capital		276,000
Letts, drawing	15,000	
Electrician service revenue		238,680
Salaries expense	190,100	
Rent expense—truck	39,000	
Advertising expense	4,940	
Legal and accounting expense	4,500	
Miscellaneous expense	2,200	
	$525,380	$525,380

Additional data as of December 31, 1984:

1. Insurance expense is $1,700.
2. Supplies on hand are $850.
3. Rent expense on the building is $25,300.
4. Depreciation expense on the equipment is $4,400.
5. Accrued salaries are $3,500.

P4–8–A.

Required:

Given the following trial balance and additional information for J. Emory, CPA, prepare:

a. A 10-column work sheet for the year ended December 31, 1984.

b. An income statement.

c. A statement of owner's equity.

d. A classified balance sheet.

e. Adjusting and closing entries.

f. A post-closing trial balance. Normally the post-closing trial balance would be prepared from the ledger accounts, but use the information in the Balance Sheet columns of the work sheet to prepare it. You will have to determine the ending balance in the owner's capital account.

J. EMORY, CPA
Trial Balance
December 31, 1984

	Debits	Credits
Cash	$ 48,000	
Accounts receivable	9,600	
Supplies on hand	2,000	
Prepaid rent	6,120	
Prepaid insurance	3,640	
Office equipment	3,800	
Accumulated depreciation— office equipment		$ 1,380
Furniture and fixtures	14,600	
Accumulated depreciation— furniture and fixtures		4,140
Accounts payable		600
J. Emory, capital		64,300
J. Emory, drawing	21,260	
Accounting service revenue		100,000
Salaries expense	49,400	
Utilities expense	3,000	
Travel expense	7,000	
Miscellaneous expense	2,000	
	$170,420	$170,420

Additional data:

1. Supplies on hand at December 31, 1984, are $500.
2. $4,600 of the prepaid rent was consumed in 1984.
3. $1,200 of the prepaid insurance expired in 1984.
4. Depreciation expense is: office equipment, $400; and furniture and fixtures, $1,500.
5. Accrued salaries are $2,175.

PROBLEMS, SERIES B

P4–1–B. The trial balance of the Crow Travel Agency at December 31, 1984, contains the following account balances:

CROW TRAVEL AGENCY
Trial Balance
December 31, 1984

	Debits	Credits
Cash	$20,000	
Accounts receivable	5,000	
Supplies on hand	4,000	
Prepaid insurance	6,000	
Furniture and fixtures	14,000	
Accumulated depreciation—		
furniture and fixtures		$ 2,000
Accounts payable		2,000
A. B. Crow, capital		33,000
A. B. Crow, drawing	8,000	
Travel service revenue		45,000
Advertising expense	1,000	
Salaries expense	16,000	
Rent expense	5,000	
Miscellaneous expense	3,000	
	$82,000	$82,000

Additional data:

1. An inventory shows that $1,000 of the supplies are on hand at the end of the year.
2. The balance in the Prepaid Insurance account represents the cost of a three-year policy from January 1, 1984, through December 31, 1987.
3. The depreciation expense for the year on furniture and fixtures is $1,000.
4. Salaries accrued but unpaid at the end of the year are $1,200.

Required:

Prepare a work sheet for Crow Travel Agency for the year ended December 31, 1984.

P4–2–B.   The account balances below are for A. P. Apple, Architect, as they appeared in the work sheet for the month ended December 31, 1984.

	Income Statement	
	Debit	Credit
Architect service revenue		10,000
Salaries expense	2,000	
Advertising expense	400	
Insurance expense	50	
Supplies expense	170	
Depreciation expense—building	250	
Miscellaneous expense	200	
	3,070	10,000
Net income	6,930	
	10,000	10,000

Required:

    a. Prepare the closing journal entries. Assume that on December 31, 1984, the A. P. Apple, Drawing account has a debit balance of $4,000 and the A. P. Apple, Capital account has a credit balance of $50,000 before the closing process begins.

    b. Using T-accounts, show how the accounts would appear after all of the closing entries have been posted.

    c. Prepare an income statement for the month of December 1984.

P4–3–B.   Given below are the amounts appearing in the Adjusted Trial Balance columns of the December 31, 1984, work sheet for the Sloan Advertising Agency.

	Adjusted Trial Balance	
	Debit	Credit
Cash	35,000	
Accounts receivable	17,000	
Office equipment	100,000	
Accumulated depreciation— office equipment		60,000
Accounts payable		10,800
T. Sloan, capital		121,500
T. Sloan, drawing	28,000	
Advertising service revenue		110,000
Rent expense	12,000	
Travel expense	5,000	
Salaries expense	90,000	
Supplies expense	1,500	
Insurance expense	1,200	
Depreciation expense— office equipment	12,000	
Miscellaneous expense	600	
	302,300	302,300

Required:

    a. Based on the above data, prepare closing entries. (You may want to mentally determine which of the above items would appear in the Income Statement columns of the work sheet.) In preparing the third closing entry, you will need to determine whether there was net income or a net loss for the period.

    b. Using T-accounts show how the accounts would appear after all of the closing entries have been posted.

P4–4–B.

Required:

    Using the following trial balance and additional information for the Eckstein Auto Repair Company:

    a. Prepare a 10-column work sheet for the year ended December 31, 1984.

    b. Prepare adjusting journal entries.

    c. Prepare closing journal entries.

ECKSTEIN AUTO REPAIR COMPANY
Trial Balance
December 31, 1984

	Debits	*Credits*
Cash	$16,500	
Accounts receivable	2,800	
Prepaid rent	4,800	
Equipment	19,300	
Accumulated depreciation—		
equipment		$ 2,200
Accounts payable		4,500
Sam Eckstein, capital		20,500
Sam Eckstein, drawing	4,800	
Auto repair service revenue		67,000
Salaries expense	36,050	
Supplies expense	8,000	
Insurance expense	1,950	
	$94,200	$94,200

Additional data:

1. The prepaid rent is for the period July 1, 1984, to June 30, 1985.
2. The depreciation on the equipment is $1,330.
3. Salaries accrued as of December 31 are $3,000.

P4–5–B.   The Adjusted Trial Balance columns of the work sheet for the Libby Health Spa at December 31, 1984, is shown below.

	Adjusted Trial Balance	
	Debit	Credit
Cash	20,000	
Accounts receivable	14,050	
Prepaid insurance	480	
Prepaid rent	1,200	
Supplies on hand	300	
Land	22,000	
Exercise equipment	25,000	
Accumulated depreciation— exercise equipment		6,250
Building	60,000	
Accumulated depreciation— building		7,500
Accounts payable.........................		5,000
Accrued salaries payable		3,500
L. H. Libby, capital.......................		91,330
L. H. Libby, drawing	35,000	
Exercise service revenue		150,000
Insurance expense........................	960	
Rent expense	4,800	
Advertising expense.......................	900	
Depreciation expense— exercise equipment	1,250	
Depreciation expense— building	1,500	
Supplies expense.........................	1,140	
Salaries expense	75,000	
	263,580	263,580

Required:

a. Prepare an income statement.

b. Prepare a statement of owner's equity.

c. Prepare a classified balance sheet.

d. Prepare the closing journal entries.

P4–6–B.

Required:

From the following trial balance and additional information for Collins Printing Company, prepare:

a. A 10-column work sheet for the year ended December 31, 1984.

b. An income statement.

c. A statement of owner's equity.

d. A classified balance sheet.

e. Adjusting journal entries.

f. Closing journal entries.

COLLINS PRINTING COMPANY
Trial Balance
December 31, 1984

	Debits	Credits
Cash	$ 30,600	
Accounts receivable	6,750	
Prepaid insurance	1,500	
Supplies on hand	1,000	
Building	40,000	
Accumulated depreciation—building		$ 20,000
Printing equipment	20,000	
Accumulated depreciation—printing equipment		10,000
Accounts payable		5,000
R. P. Collins, capital		28,200
R. P. Collins, drawing	9,000	
Printing service revenue		80,000
Salaries expense	30,000	
Advertising expense	900	
Utilities expense	3,100	
Miscellaneous expense	350	
	$143,200	$143,200

Additional data:

1. Insurance expense for the year is $1,200.
2. A physical inventory shows that supplies costing $200 are on hand at December 31, 1984.
3. Depreciation expense on the building is $4,000.
4. Depreciation expense on the equipment is $1,250.
5. Accrued salaries are $3,000.

P4–7–B.

Required:

From the following trial balance and additional data, prepare:

a. A 10-column work sheet for the year ended December 31, 1984.

b. An income statement.

c. A statement of owner's equity.

d. A classified balance sheet.

e. The required closing entries.

RUSSELL PHOTOGRAPHY COMPANY
Trial Balance
December 31, 1984

	Debits	Credits
Cash	$ 70,250	
Accounts receivable	8,500	
Prepaid insurance	1,650	
Land	35,750	
Building	55,000	
Accumulated depreciation—building		$ 16,500
Photography equipment	27,800	
Accumulated depreciation—photography equipment		5,560
Accounts payable		2,950
Russell, capital		140,490
Russell, drawing	10,000	
Photography service revenue		119,450
Salaries expense	70,000	
Advertising expense	6,000	
	$284,950	$284,950

Additional data:

1. Depreciation on the building is $1,100 for the year.
2. Depreciation on the photography equipment is $2,780 for the year.
3. Accrued salaries are $700.
4. Prepaid insurance at year-end is $200.

P4–8–B.

Required:

Given the following trial balance and supplementary information, prepare:

a. A 10-column work sheet for the year ended December 31, 1984.

b. An income statement.

c. A statement of owner's equity.

d. A classified balance sheet.

e. Adjusting and closing entries.

f. A post-closing trial balance. Normally the post-closing trial balance would be prepared from the ledger accounts, but use the information in the Balance Sheet columns of the work sheet to prepare it. You will have to determine the ending balance in the owner's capital account.

OCEAN PROPERTIES REALTY
Trial Balance
December 31, 1984

	Debits	Credits
Cash	$20,000	
Prepaid rent	3,600	
Prepaid insurance on automobile	960	
Supplies on hand	300	
Office equipment	3,000	
Accumulated depreciation—		
office equipment		$ 720
Automobile	8,000	
Accumulated depreciation—		
automobile		2,000
Accounts payable		360
Unearned management fees		1,560
Al Olson, capital		44,580
Al Olson, drawing	23,500	
Sales commissions revenue		30,000
Management service revenue		2,400
Salaries expense	19,980	
Advertising expense	300	
Automobile expense	1,780	
Miscellaneous expense	200	
	$81,620	$81,620

Additional data:

1. Insurance expense on automobile for the year is $480.
2. Rent expense for the year is $2,400.
3. Depreciation expense is: office equipment, $360; and automobile, $1,600.
4. Salaries earned but unpaid at December 31 are $3,330.
5. Supplies on hand at December 31, $100.
6. The unearned management fees were received and recorded on October 1, 1984. The advance payment covered six month's management of an apartment building.

BUSINESS DECISION PROBLEM 4–1

Jane and Thomas Cassidy met while both were employed in the interior trim and upholstery department of an auto manufacturer. After their marriage, they decided to earn some extra income by doing small jobs involving canvas, vinyl, and upholstered products. Their work was considered excellent; and at the urging of their customers, they decided to go into business for themselves, operating out of the basement of the house they owned. To do this, they invested $10,000 cash in their business. They spent $7,000 for a sewing machine (expected life is 10 years) and $1,000 for other miscellaneous tools and equipment (expected life is 5 years). They undertook only custom work, with the customer purchasing the required materials other than miscellaneous supplies. An advance deposit was generally required on all jobs.

The business seemed to be successful from the start, but they felt something was wrong. They worked hard and charged competitive prices. Yet there seemed to be barely enough cash available for withdrawal from the business to cover immediate personal needs. Summarized, the checkbook of the business for 1984, their second year of operation, shows:

Balance, January 1, 1984		$ 1,600
Cash received from customers:		
For work done in 1983	$ 3,000	
For work done in 1984	48,000	
For work to be done in 1985	4,000	55,000
		$56,600
Cash paid out:		
Two-year insurance policy dated		
January 1, 1984	$ 1,600	
Utilities	4,000	
Supplies	12,000	
Taxes	2,200	
Miscellaneous	6,000	
Owner withdrawals	29,000	54,800
Balance, December 31, 1984		$ 1,800

The Cassidys feel, considering how much they worked, that they should have earned more than the $29,000 of cash they withdrew from their business. This is $18,000 less than their combined income when they were employed by the auto manufacturer. They are seriously considering giving up their business and going back to work for the auto manufacturer. They turn to you for advice. You discover the following:

1. Of the supplies purchased in 1984, $2,000 were used on jobs billed to customers in 1984; no supplies were used for any other work.
2. Work completed in 1984 and billed to customers for which cash had not yet been received by year-end amounted to $9,000 (which is considered fully collectible).

Required:

Prepare a written report for the Cassidys, responding to their belief that their business is not sufficiently profitable. (Hint: Prepare an income statement for 1984 and include it in your report.)

BUSINESS DECISION PROBLEM 4–2

On December 31, 1984, Jim Turner's bookkeeper quit his job without even notifying Mr. Turner of his net income for 1984. The bookkeeper had taken Mr. Turner's accounting records home with him the previous night and failed to bring them to work on December 31, 1984. But Mr. Turner found the following closing entries on a pad in the bookkeeper's desk:

1984			
Dec. 31	Service Revenue	90,000	
	Income Summary		90,000
	To close the revenue account appearing in the Income Statement credit column of the work sheet to Income Summary.		
31	Income Summary	37,600	
	Rent Expense		4,000
	Salaries Expense		24,000
	Advertising Expense		2,000
	Utilities Expense		2,400
	Depreciation—Automobiles		2,000
	Depreciation—Office Equipment		500
	Insurance Expense		2,520
	Miscellaneous Expense		180
	To close the expense accounts appearing in the Income Statement debit column of the work sheet to Income Summary.		

Mr. Turner knows that his capital account balance was $40,000 on January 1, 1984, and that he withdrew $20,000 for personal use during 1984.

Required:

a. Using the information given above, prepare an income statement and a statement of owner's equity for the year ended December 31, 1984.

b. What effect do the closing journal entries have on the income statement accounts?

c. What effect do the closing journal entries have on the balance sheet accounts?

d. Did the bookkeeper make all of the necessary closing entries? If not, what other entries should be made?

COMPREHENSIVE REVIEW PROBLEM 4–1

The Gutmann Delivery Service Company has the following chart of accounts:

Account no.	Account title	Account No.	Account title
100	Cash	301	J. E. Gutmann, Drawing
101	Accounts Receivable	400	Delivery Service Revenue
102	Supplies on Hand	500	Supplies Expense
103	Prepaid Insurance	501	Insurance Expense
104	Prepaid Rent	502	Rent Expense
110	Building	503	Depreciation Expense—Building
110A	Accumulated Depreciation—Building	504	Depreciation Expense—Trucks
111	Trucks	505	Salaries Expense
111A	Accumulated Depreciation—Trucks	506	Utilities Expense
200	Accounts Payable	507	Miscellaneous Expense
201	Accrued Salaries Payable	600	Income Summary
300	J. E. Gutmann, Capital		

The post-closing trial balance as of May 31, 1984, was as follows:

GUTMANN DELIVERY SERVICE COMPANY
Post-Closing Trial Balance
May 31, 1984

	Debits	Credits
Cash	$ 10,000	
Accounts receivable	15,000	
Supplies on hand	7,000	
Prepaid insurance	2,400	
Prepaid rent	6,000	
Building	160,000	
Accumulated depreciation—building		$ 18,000
Trucks	40,000	
Accumulate depreciation—trucks		15,000
Accounts payable		12,000
J. E. Gutmann, capital		195,400
	$240,400	$240,400

The transactions for June 1984 were as follows:

Transactions:

June 1 Performed delivery services for customers on account, $20,000.
　　3 J. E. Gutmann withdrew $5,000 to pay some personal bills.
　　4 Purchased a $10,000 truck on account.
　　7 Collected $11,000 of the accounts receivable.
　　8 Paid $8,000 of the accounts payable.
　11 Purchased $2,000 of supplies on account. The asset account for supplies was debited.
　17 Performed delivery services for cash, $16,000.
　20 Paid the utilities bills for June, $600.
　23 Paid miscellaneous expenses for June, $300.
　28 Paid salaries of $14,000.

Supplemental data needed to prepare adjusting entries:

1. Depreciation expense on the building for June is $400.
2. Depreciation expense on the trucks for June is $200.
3. Accrued salaries at June 30 are $1,000.
4. A physical count showed that there are $6,000 of supplies on hand June 30.
5. The prepaid insurance balance of $2,400 applies to a two-year period beginning June 1, 1984.
6. The prepaid rent of $6,000 applies to a one-year period beginning June 1, 1984.
7. Performed $6,000 of delivery services for customers as of June 30 which will not be billed to those customers until July.

Required:

a. Open three-column ledger accounts for the accounts listed in the chart of accounts.

b. Enter the May 31, 1984, account balances in the accounts.

c. Journalize the transactions for June 1984.

d. Post the June journal entries and include cross-references (assume all journal entries appear on page 10 of the journal).

e. Prepare a 10-column work sheet as of June 30, 1984.

f. Prepare an income statement, a statement of owner's capital, and a classified balance sheet.

g. Prepare and post the adjusting entries (assume they appear on page 11 of the general journal).

h. Prepare and post the closing entries (assume they appear on page 12 of the general journal).

i. Prepare a post-closing trial balance.

Chapter 5

Merchandising transactions and introduction to inventories

CHAPTER GOALS

After study of this chapter, you should be able to:

1. Record journal entries for sales and purchase transactions using periodic inventory procedure.
2. Describe the terms under which merchandise is sold, including freight terms, and distinguish cash discounts from trade discounts.
3. Prepare a classified income statement.
4. Prepare a work sheet and closing entries for a merchandising company.
5. Define and use correctly the new terms in the glossary.

Previous chapters dealt with accounting for companies that earned revenues by rendering services to customers for fees or commissions. In contrast to service-type businesses, *merchandising businesses acquire goods for resale to customers.* The fundamental accounting concepts applicable to service-type businesses also apply to merchandising businesses, but some additional accounts and techniques are needed to account for purchases and sales.

The main purpose of this chapter is to introduce, describe, and illustrate accounts and techniques used in merchandising businesses. Other purposes are to illustrate a classified income statement for a merchandising company and to show a work sheet and the closing process.

SALES REVENUE

In a merchandising business, revenue is earned from sales of merchandise to final consumers or to other companies that then sell the goods to final consumers. Companies that sell goods to final customers are called *retailers.* Companies that sell goods to other companies for resale to final consumers are called *wholesalers.*

Sales

A sales transaction consists of the transfer of legal ownership, or passage of title, of goods from one party to another. The sale is usually accompanied by physical delivery of goods. Each time a sale is made, a revenue account called Sales is increased (credited) by the selling price of the goods sold. The accompanying debit is to Cash if the terms of sale are cash or to Accounts Receivable if the goods are sold on account. For example, a $10,000 sale on account would be recorded as follows:

Accounts Receivable	10,000	
Sales		10,000
To record the sale of merchandise on account.		

Typically, the above entry will be based on a business document called an invoice (sometimes called a sales invoice by the seller and a purchase invoice by the buyer). An *invoice* is a document prepared by the seller of merchandise and sent to the buyer that contains the details of a sale, such as the number of units, unit price, total price billed, terms of sale, and manner of shipment. The invoice in a retail company is prepared at the point of sale. In a wholesale company that supplies goods to retailers, the invoice is prepared after the accounting department receives notification from the shipping department that the goods have been shipped to the retailer. Illustration 5.1 shows an invoice prepared by a wholesale company for goods sold to a retail company.

Illustration 5.1: Invoice

| BRYAN WHOLESALE CO. | | | Invoice No.: 1258 |
| 476 Mason Street, Detroit, Michigan | | | Date: Dec. 19, 1984 |

Customer's Order No.: 218
Sold to: Baier Company
Address: 2255 Hannon Street
              Big Rapids, Michigan
Terms: Net 30

Date Shipped: Dec. 19, 1984
Shipped by: Nagel Trucking Co.

Description	Quantity	Price per unit	Amount
True-tone CB radios Model No. 5868–24393	200	$50	$10,000
Total			$10,000

Revenue recognition.   Recording revenue at the time of sale is justified since:

1. *Legal title* to the goods has passed and the goods are now the responsibility and property of the buyer.
2. The selling price of the goods has been established.
3. The seller's part of the contract has been completed.
4. The goods have been exchanged for another asset such as cash or accounts receivable.
5. The costs incurred can be determined.

Determining sales price when there are trade discounts

A *trade discount* is a deduction from the list or catalog price of merchandise to arrive at gross invoice price. It is a means used to determine the actual gross selling price of an item. Trade discounts may be shown on the seller's invoice, but they will not be recorded in the seller's accounting records. Nor are they to be recorded on the books of the purchaser. Assume an invoice with the following data:

List price, 200 swimsuits at $6	$1,200
Less: Trade discount, 30%	360
Gross invoice price	$ 840

The vendor records the sale at $840. The purchaser records a purchase of $840.

Trade discounts are used to:

1. Reduce the cost of catalog publication. If separate discount lists are given the salespersons whenever prices change, catalogs may be used for a long period of time.
2. Grant quantity discounts.
3. Allow quotation of different prices to different types of customers, such as to retailers and wholesalers.

A wholesaler buying goods from a manufacturer may receive two trade discounts because of certain services performed, such as packaging and distributing, that the manufacturer would otherwise have to perform. The wholesaler may acquire the goods, package them, and then sell and ship them to retailers. A *chain discount* occurs when a list price is subject to several trade discounts.

An example of a chain discount is when an article with a list price of $100 is subject to trade discounts of 20 percent and 10 percent. The actual price is $100 − 0.2($100) = $80; $80 − 0.1($80) = $72. The same results can be obtained by multiplying the list price by the complements of the trade discounts allowed. For example, $100 × 0.8 × 0.9 = $72.

DEDUCTIONS FROM SALES REVENUE

Sales discounts and sales returns and allowances are recorded in *contra accounts* to the Sales account. These items are deducted from gross sales to arrive at net sales. Remember that contra accounts have normal balances that are opposite of the account they reduce. Since Sales has a credit balance, Sales Discounts and Sales Returns and Allowances have debit balances.

Sales discounts

Whenever goods are sold on account, terms of payment are clearly specified on the invoice. For example, in Illustration 5.1, the terms of payment are stated as "net 30." "Net 30" is sometimes written as "n/30." This means that the $10,000 amount of the invoice must be paid on or before 30 days after December 19, 1984, or on or before January 18, 1985. If the terms read "n/10/EOM" (EOM means end of month), the invoice would be due on the 10th day of the month following the month of sale—January 10 in the case of the invoice in Illustration 5.1. Credit terms vary from industry to industry according to trade practices.

In many instances, when credit periods are long, sellers will offer a cash discount in an attempt to induce early payment of an account. A *cash discount* is a deduction allowed from the gross invoice price to arrive at actual cost—the cash price—of the merchandise that can be taken only if the invoice is paid within a specified period of time. Discounts, usually ranging from 1 to 3 percent of the gross invoice price of the merchandise, may or may not be taken by the purchaser. To the seller, cash discounts are *sales discounts;* to the purchaser, they are *purchase discounts.*

Cash discount terms are often stated as follows:

2/10, n/30—means a discount of 2 percent of the gross invoice price of the merchandise may be taken if payment is made within 10 days following the invoice date. The *gross* invoice price is due 30 days from the invoice date.

2/EOM, n/60—means a 2 percent discount may be deducted if the invoice is paid by the end of the month. The gross invoice amount is due 60 days from the date of the invoice.

2/10/EOM, n/60—means a 2 percent discount may be deducted if the invoice is paid by the 10th day of the month following the date of sale. The gross invoice amount is due 60 days from the date of the invoice.

Recording sales discounts. The granting of sales discounts reduces the amount of cash actually collected from the sale of goods. To illustrate the usual manner for recording sales discounts, assume that a sale on account of $2,000 was made on July 12; terms are 2/10, n/30. A check in payment of the account was received on July 21 in the amount $1,960. The required entries are:

July 12	Accounts Receivable	2,000
	Sales	2,000
	To record sale on account; terms, 2/10, n/30.	
21	Cash	1,960
	Sales Discounts	40
	Accounts Receivable	2,000
	To record collection on account, less discount.	

The *Sales Discounts account* is a contra revenue account to Sales and is shown as a deduction from gross sales in the income statement. The amount of sales discounts is recorded in a separate account to provide useful information to owners in setting sales discounts policies. The Sales Discounts account is not an expense incurred in generating revenue. Rather, the purpose of the account is to reduce recorded revenue to the amount actually realized from the sale, which is the net invoice price.

Sales returns and allowances

Goods delivered to a customer may be returned to the seller for a variety of reasons. These reasons may include wrong color, wrong size, wrong style, wrong amounts, or inferior quality. In fact, in some firms, goods may be returned simply because the customer did not like them. The seller's policy may be "satisfaction guaranteed." A *sales return* is merchandise returned by a buyer and is considered a cancellation of a sale. It could be recorded as a debit to the Sales account. But the amount of sales returns may be useful information to owners. The amount of returns in relation to goods sold can be an indication of the quality of the goods (high return percentage, low quality) or of pressure applied by salespersons (high pressure sales, high returns). Thus, sales returns are recorded in a separate account entitled *Sales Returns and Allowances,* which is a contra revenue account to Sales.[1] For example, assume that $300 of goods sold on account are returned by a customer. If payment has not yet been received, the required entry is:

Sales Returns and Allowances	300
Accounts Receivable	300
To record sales return from a customer.	

---

[1] A contra revenue account is deducted from a revenue account in the income statement.

If the customer has already paid the account, the credit is to Cash rather than Accounts Receivable. A check will be sent to the customer for the amount of the credit. If a 2 percent discount was taken by the customer when the account was paid, only the net amount would be returned to the customer. The following entry would be made:

```
Sales Returns and Allowances ......................................    300
     Cash......................................................             294
     Sales Discounts...........................................             6
To record sales return from a customer who had taken a discount.
```

The credit to Sales Discounts reduces the balance of that account.

Sales allowances are deductions from original invoiced sales prices granted to a customer for any of a number of reasons, including inferior quality or damage or deterioration in transit. As was true for sales returns, sales allowances could be recorded directly as debits to the Sales account because they do cancel a part of the recorded selling price. But, because their amounts may be useful information in establishing policies regarding allowances, they are recorded in a Sales Returns and Allowances account. The Sales Returns and Allowances account is a contra account to Sales and is deducted from sales in the income statement.

To illustrate the recording of a sales allowance, assume that a $400 allowance is granted to a customer for damage resulting from improperly packed merchandise. If the customer has not yet paid the account, the required entry would read:

```
Sales Returns and Allowances ........................................    400
     Accounts Receivable .........................................             400
To record sales allowance granted for damaged merchandise.
```

If the customer has already paid the account, the credit is to Cash instead of Accounts Receivable. If the customer took a 2 percent discount when paying the account, only the net amount ($392) would be refunded, and Sales Discounts would be credited for $8.

Reporting net sales in the income statement

Illustration 5.2 contains a partial income statement showing how sales, sales discounts, and sales returns and allowances might be reported. Many

Illustration 5.2 Partial income statement

HANLON COMPANY
Partial Income Statement
For the Year Ended June 30, 1984

Operating revenues:		
Gross Sales		$282,000
Less: Sales discounts	$ 5,000	
Sales returns and allowances	15,000	20,000
Net sales		$262,000

times, the income statement will start with "Net sales" because the details of this computation are not important to financial statement users.

COST OF GOODS SOLD

Cost of goods sold is the next portion of the income statement for a merchandising business. *Cost of goods sold* shows the cost to the seller of buying the goods which it sold to customers. Computation of cost of goods sold involves knowing the cost of beginning and ending inventories of the accounting period and the cost of goods purchased during the period. *Inventory* (or *merchandise inventory*) is the quantity of goods on hand and available for sale at any given time. Each of the elements used in calculating cost of goods sold is discussed below. But first the two basic inventory procedures must be identified.

Two procedures for accounting for inventories

Basically, there are two procedures for accounting for inventory—*periodic inventory procedure* and *perpetual inventory procedure.* Only periodic inventory procedure will be dealt with in this chapter. Perpetual procedure will be covered in a later chapter.

Periodic inventory procedure is a method of accounting for merchandise acquired for sale to customers wherein the cost of merchandise sold and the cost of merchandise on hand are determined *only* at the end of the accounting period. Any goods not on hand at the end of the period are assumed to have been sold. Companies selling merchandise that has a low value per unit, such as nuts and bolts, nails, Christmas cards, pencils, and many similar items, tend to use periodic inventory procedure. More will be said about inventories after the other items comprising cost of goods sold have been presented.

Purchases of merchandise

The *Purchases account* is used under periodic inventory procedure to record the cost of merchandise purchased during the current accounting period. The Purchases account is increased by debits and is listed with the income statement accounts in the chart of accounts.

To illustrate the Purchases account, assume that Hollis Retail Food Stores made two purchases of merchandise from the Smith Wholesale Company. Hollis purchased $30,000 of merchandise on credit (on account) on May 4, and on May 21 purchased $20,000 of merchandise for cash. The purchases are recorded from the invoices at gross invoice price. The required entries are:

```
May  4  Purchases ........................................... 30,000
            Accounts Payable ...............................         30,000
        To record purchase of merchandise on account.

    21  Purchases ........................................... 20,000
            Cash ...........................................         20,000
        To record purchase of merchandise for cash.
```

Deductions from purchases

Purchase discounts, purchase returns, and purchase allowances are deducted from purchases to arrive at net purchases. These items are recorded in contra accounts to the Purchases account.

Purchase discounts. Merchandise is often purchased under credit terms that permit the buyer to deduct a stated discount if the invoice is paid within a specified period of time. Assume credit terms for Hollis's May 4 purchase were 2/10, n/30. If the merchandise is paid for by May 14, a 2 percent discount may be taken. Thus, only $29,400 must be paid to pay the $30,000 account payable. The entry to record the payment of the invoice on May 14 is:

```
May 14  Accounts Payable .................................... 30,000
            Cash ...........................................         29,400
            Purchase Discounts .............................            600
        To record payment on account within discount period.
```

The purchase discount is recorded only when the invoice is paid within the discount period and the discount is taken. The *Purchase Discounts account* is a contra account to Purchases which reduces the recorded gross invoice cost of the purchase to the price actually paid. The purchase discounts total is reported in the income statement as a deduction from purchases.

Purchase discounts are based on the invoice price of goods. If there were purchase returns or allowances, they must be deducted from the invoice price in calculating purchase discounts. For instance, if the invoice price of goods purchased from a supplier was $1,000 but $200 of the goods were returned, the purchase discount is calculated on $800.

Purchase returns and allowances. When a buyer returns merchandise to a seller, a purchase return results. When a seller grants an allowance or reduction in the price of goods shipped to the buyer, a purchase allowance results. Both returns and allowances serve to reduce the buyer's debt to the seller and to reduce the cost of the goods purchased. The buyer may be interested in knowing the amount of returns and allowances as the first step in controlling the costs incurred in returning unsatisfactory merchandise or negotiating purchase allowances. For this reason, purchase returns and allowances are recorded in a separate *Purchases Returns and Allowances account* as follows:

```
Accounts Payable .................................................   350
     Purchase Returns and Allowances ............................          350
     To record return of damaged merchandise to supplier.
```

If the company had already paid the account, the debit would be to Cash instead of Accounts Payable, since a refund of cash would be received. If the company took a discount at the time it paid the account, then only the net amount would be refunded. For instance, if a 2 percent discount had been taken, the entry for the return would be:

```
Cash ...........................................................   343
Purchase Discounts ..............................................     7
     Purchase Returns and Allowances ............................          350
     To record return of damaged merchandise to supplier and record receipt
     of cash.
```

Purchase Returns and Allowances is a contra account to the Purchases account and is shown on the income statement as a deduction from purchases.

Transportation costs

When goods are purchased, costs may be incurred to deliver them to the buyer. The term *FOB shipping point* means free on board at shipping point; that is, the buyer incurs all transportation costs after the merchandise is loaded on a railroad car or truck at point of shipment. The term *FOB destination* means free on board at destination; goods are shipped to their destination without charge to the buyer. The seller bears the transportation charges. Title to the goods passes from seller to buyer at the FOB point. Thus, when goods are shipped FOB shipping point, title passes at the shipping point. When goods are shipped FOB destination, title passes at destination. *Passage of title* is a legal term used to indicate transfer of legal ownership of goods.

When the seller pays the freight at the time of shipment, the term *freight prepaid* is used. When the buyer pays the freight bill upon the arrival of the goods, the term *freight collect* is used.

If goods are shipped FOB shipping point, freight collect, the buyer pays the freight bill and is responsible for the freight costs. Title passes at the shipping point. There is no entry for freight charges on the seller's books. Assuming a $100 delivery charge, the entry on the buyer's books is:

```
Transportation-In (or Freight-In) ...................................   100
     Cash ......................................................          100
     To record payment of freight bill on goods purchased.
```

The $100 transportation cost is recorded in the *Transportation-In account*, which is used to record transportation costs incurred in the acquisition of merchandise.

If goods are shipped FOB destination, freight prepaid, the seller pays the freight bill and is responsible for it. No separate transportation cost is billed to the buyer. No entry is required on the buyer's books. The transportation cost undoubtedly was taken into consideration by the seller in setting selling prices. The following entry is required on the seller's books:

Delivery Expense (or Transportation-Out Expense)	100	
Cash		100
To record freight cost on goods sold.		

Delivery expense is a selling expense recorded by the seller for freight costs incurred when terms are FOB destination; it is shown on the income statement with other selling expenses.

Purchase discounts and transportation charges.   Purchase discounts are not affected by transportation charges, regardless of whether the buyer or the seller is responsible for freight charges.

Merchandise inventories

Merchandise inventory is the quantity of goods on hand and available for sale at any given time. To determine the cost of goods sold in any accounting period, inventory information is needed. Cost of goods on hand at the start of the period (beginning inventory), purchases made during the period, and the cost of goods on hand at the close of the period (ending inventory) must be known. Since the ending inventory of the preceding period is the beginning inventory for the current period, the cost of the beginning inventory is already known. Purchases are recorded throughout the period. Therefore, only the cost of the ending inventory need be determined at the end of the period.

Taking a physical inventory.   Under periodic inventory procedure, ending inventory cost is determined by taking a physical inventory. Taking a *physical inventory* consists of counting physical units of each type of merchandise on hand. To calculate inventory cost, it is necessary to multiply the number of units of each kind of merchandise by its unit cost. Total costs of the various kinds of merchandise are then totaled to provide the total ending inventory cost.

In taking a physical inventory, care must be exercised to ensure that all goods owned, regardless of where they are located, are counted and included in the inventory. Thus, goods shipped to a potential customer "on approval" should not be recorded as sold. They should be included in inventory. Similarly, goods delivered on a *consignment basis,* which are goods sent by the owner to another party who will make an effort to sell the goods, should not be recorded as sold. Here the intent is that the goods remain the property of the owner (consignor) until sold by the consignee. Such goods must be included in the owner's inventory.

Merchandise in transit is merchandise in the hands of a transport company on the date of a physical inventory. Merchandise in transit at the end of the accounting period must be recorded as a purchase by the buyer and included in inventory if passage of title to the buyer has occurred. In general, the goods belong to the party who must bear the transportation charges.

Lack of control under periodic inventory procedure.   The periodic inventory method provides for little control over inventory. Any items not included in the physical count of inventory at the end of the period are assumed to have been sold. Thus, even if items have been stolen, the accountant would assume they had been sold and their cost would be included in cost of goods sold.

To illustrate, assume the cost of certain goods available for sale was $200,000 and the actual ending inventory is $60,000. This suggests that the cost of the goods sold to customers was $140,000. But assume further that it is known that $2,000 of goods were shoplifted. If such goods had not been stolen, the ending inventory would have been $62,000 and the cost of goods sold only $138,000. Thus, the cost of goods sold of $140,000 includes the cost of the merchandise delivered to customers and the cost of merchandise stolen.

Reporting ending inventory. Ending inventory cost is reported as a current asset in the end-of-period balance sheet. Ending inventory cost also appears in the income statement as a deduction from cost of goods available for sale in order to compute cost of goods sold.

Determining cost of goods sold

When beginning and ending inventories and the various elements making up the net cost of purchases are known, cost of goods sold can be determined.

Assume the ledger account balances as of December 31, 1984, for the following items were as follows:

Merchandise inventory, December 31, 1983 . . . . . $ 24,000 Dr.
Purchases . . . .   167,000 Dr.
Purchase discounts . . . .   3,000 Cr.
Purchase returns and allowances . . . .   8,000 Cr.
Transportation-in . . . .   10,000 Dr.

Merchandise inventory on December 31, 1984, was $31,000, determined by taking a physical inventory. Cost of goods sold would be determined as shown in Illustration 5.3. This computation appears in a section of the income statement directly below the calculation of net sales.

Illustration 5.3: Determination of cost of goods sold

Cost of goods sold:			
Merchandise inventory, December 31, 1983			$ 24,000
Purchases		$167,000	
Less: Purchase discounts	$3,000		
Purchase returns and allowances	8,000	11,000	
Net purchases		$156,000	
Add: Transportation-in		10,000	
Net cost of purchases			166,000
Cost of goods available for sale			$190,000
Less: Merchandise inventory, December 31, 1984			31,000
Cost of goods sold			$159,000

In Illustration 5.3, beginning inventory plus net cost of purchases is equal to cost of goods available for sale. Ending inventory cost is deducted from cost of goods available for sale to arrive at cost of goods sold. The relationship between items appearing in Illustration 5.3 is shown in the diagram below:

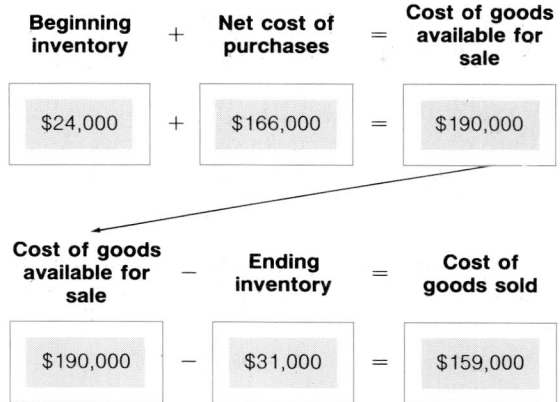

The calculation of net cost of purchases is shown in Illustration 5.3. Net cost of purchases is equal to purchases ($167,000), *less* purchase discounts ($3,000) and purchase returns and allowances ($8,000), *plus* transportation-in ($10,000).

CLASSIFIED INCOME STATEMENT

To this point, the text has only illustrated an unclassified income statement. The *unclassified income statement* has only two categories of items—revenues and expenses. Now a classified income statement will be introduced. A *classified income statement* divides both revenues and expenses into operating and nonoperating items. The statement also separates operating expenses into selling and administrative expenses. A classified income statement is also called a multiple-step income statement.

The previously presented data on sales (Illustration 5.2) and cost of goods sold (Illustration 5.3), together with additional assumed data on operating expenses and other expenses and revenues, are shown in the classified income statement in Illustration 5.4. Note that the income statement has four major sections:

1. Operating revenues.
2. Cost of goods sold.
3. Operating expenses.
4. Nonoperating revenues and expenses (other revenues and other expenses).

The term *operating revenues* refers to the revenues generated by the major activities of the business—usually the sale of products or services or both.

The cost of goods sold section of the classified income statement was shown in Illustration 5.3. The items used in calculating cost of goods sold have already been discussed in this chapter. Cost of goods sold is the major expense in merchandising companies. It is common to highlight the amount by which sales revenues exceed the cost of goods sold in the top part of the income statement. The excess of net sales over cost of goods sold is called *gross margin* or gross profit. Gross margin is often also expressed as a percentage rate and is computed by dividing gross margin by net sales. In Illustration 5.4, the gross margin rate is approximately 39.3 percent ($103,000/$262,000). This means that out of each sales dollar, approximately 39 cents is available to cover other expenses and produce income. This rate is watched closely, since a small fluctuation can cause a large change in net income.

Operating expenses for a merchandising company are those expenses, other than cost of goods sold, incurred in the normal buying, selling, and administrative functions of a business. Operating expenses are usually classified as either *selling expenses* or *administrative expenses*. *Selling expenses* are those expenses which are incurred in the selling and marketing effort. Examples include salaries and commissions of salespersons, salespersons' travel, delivery, advertising, rent on sales building, sales supplies used, utilities on sales building, and depreciation on equipment used in sales. *Administrative expenses* are those expenses incurred in the overall management of a business. Examples include executive salaries, rent on administrative building, insurance, administrative supplies used, and depreciation on office equipment.

Certain operating expenses may be related partly to the selling function and partly to the administrative function. For example, rent, taxes, and insurance on a building might be incurred for both sales purposes and administrative purposes. Expenses covering both the selling and administrative functions may be analyzed and prorated between the two functions in the income statement, or each such expense may be placed in the category to which it is more significant.

Nonoperating revenues (*other revenues*) are revenues not related to the sale of products or services regularly offered for sale by a business. An example of a nonoperating revenue is interest earned on notes receivable by a company.

Nonoperating expenses (*other expenses*) are those not related to the acquisition and sale of the products or services regularly offered for sale. An example of a nonoperating expense is interest incurred on borrowed money.

The more important relationships in the income statement of a merchandising firm can be summarized in equation form as follows:

1. *Net sales* = Gross sales − Sales discounts − Sales returns and allowances.
2. *Cost of goods sold* = Beginning inventory + Net cost of purchases − Ending inventory.
3. *Net cost of purchases* = Net purchases + Transportation-in.
4. *Net purchases* = Purchases − Purchase discounts − Purchase returns and allowances.
5. *Gross margin* = Net sales − Cost of goods sold.

Illustration 5.4:   Classified income statement for a merchandising company

HANLON COMPANY
Income Statement
For the Year Ended June 30, 1984

Operating revenues:			
Gross sales			$282,000
Less: Sales discounts		$ 5,000	
Sales returns and allowances		15,000	20,000
Net sales			$262,000
Cost of goods sold:			
Merchandise inventory, July 1, 1983		$ 24,000	
Purchases	$167,000		
Less: Purchase discounts	$3,000		
Purchase returns and			
allowances	8,000	11,000	
Net purchases		$156,000	
Add: Transportation-in		10,000	
Net cost of purchases			166,000
Cost of goods available for sale			$190,000
Less: Merchandise inventory,			
June 30, 1984			31,000
Cost of goods sold			159,000
Gross margin			$103,000
Operating expenses:			
Selling expenses:			
Sales salaries and commissions		$ 26,000	
Salespersons' travel		3,000	
Delivery		2,000	
Advertising		4,000	
Rent—store building		2,500	
Supplies used		1,000	
Utilities		1,800	
Depreciation—store equipment		700	
Other selling expense		400	$ 41,400
Administrative expenses:			
Salaries, executive		$ 29,000	
Rent—administrative building		1,600	
Insurance		1,500	
Supplies used		800	
Depreciation—office equipment		1,100	
Other administrative expense		300	34,300
Total operating expenses			75,700
Net income from operations			$ 27,300
Nonoperating revenues and expenses:			
Nonoperating revenues:			
Interest revenue			1,400
			$ 28,700
Nonoperating expenses:			
Interest expense			600
Net income			$ 28,100

6. *Net income from operations* = Gross margin − Operating (selling and administrative) expenses.

7. *Net income* = Net income from operations + Nonoperating revenues − Nonoperating expenses.

Future illustrations may vary somewhat in form, but the basic organization of the statement will be retained.

THE WORK SHEET FOR A MERCHANDISING COMPANY

Illustration 5.5 shows a work sheet for a merchandising company. To keep the illustration as simple as possible, a different company than the one used to this point will be introduced. The Lyons Company is a small sporting goods firm. The illustration for the Lyons Company focuses upon the merchandise-related accounts. For that reason, selling and administrative expenses have been grouped into two accounts rather than including all actual expense accounts. No adjusting entries were necessary at year-end. Except for the merchandise-related accounts, the work sheet for a merchandising company is the same as for a service company. Recall that use of a work sheet assists in the preparation of the adjusting and closing entries. The work sheet also contains all of the information needed for the preparation of the financial statements.

The trial balance is taken from the ledger accounts at the end of January. The $7,000 inventory in the trial balance is the beginning inventory. The sales and sales-related accounts and the purchases and purchases-related accounts summarize the merchandising activity for January 1984.

Completing the work sheet

All revenue accounts and contra purchases accounts in the work sheet are carried to the Income Statement credit column. All expense accounts, contra revenue accounts, beginning inventory, purchases, and transportation-in are carried to the Income Statement debit column. Ending merchandise inventory of $8,000 is entered in the Income Statement credit column *and* the Balance Sheet debit column. The reason both beginning and ending inventories are brought to the Income Statement columns is because they are both used to calculate cost of goods sold on the income statement. Net income or net loss for the period will balance the Income Statement columns. For the Lyons Company, the net income is $4,843 for the month of January. The net income amount is carried to the Balance Sheet credit column.

The reason the ending inventory is entered in the Balance Sheet debit column is that ending inventory is an asset which must appear on the balance sheet. All other assets are also carried to the Balance Sheet debit column, and the drawing account balance is carried to the Balance Sheet debit column. All liabilities and other owner's equity items are carried to the Balance Sheet credit column.

Illustration 5.5: Work sheet

LYONS COMPANY
Work Sheet
For the Month Ended January 31, 1984

Acct. No.	Account Titles	Trial Balance		Adjustments		Adjusted Trial Balance		Income Statement		Balance Sheet	
		Debit	Credit	Debit	Credit	Debit	Credit	Debit	Credit	Debit	Credit
1	Cash	18,663				18,663				18,663	
2	Accounts receivable	1,880				1,880				1,880	
3	Merchandise inventory	7,000				7,000		7,000	8,000	8,000	
4	Accounts payable		700				700				700
5	Lyons, capital		25,000				25,000				25,000
6	Lyons, drawing	2,000				2,000				2,000	
7	Sales		13,600				13,600		13,600		
8	Sales discounts	44				44		44			
9	Sales returns and allowances	20				20		20			
10	Purchases	6,000				6,000		6,000			
11	Purchase discounts		82				82		82		
12	Purchase returns and allowances		100				100		100		
13	Transportation-in	75				75		75			
14	Selling expenses	2,650				2,650		2,650			
15	Administrative expenses	1,150				1,150		1,150			
		39,482	39,482			39,482	39,482	16,939	21,782	30,543	4,843
	Net income							4,843			4,843
								21,782	21,782	30,543	30,543

Financial statements

Once the work sheet has been completed, the financial statements are prepared. Next, any adjusting and closing entries are entered in the journal and posted to the ledger. This process clears the accounting records for the next accounting period.

Income statement. The income statement in Illustration 5.6 is prepared from the work sheet in Illustration 5.5. The focus in this income statement is on the determination of the cost of goods sold. The other expenses are shown in summary form.

Statement of owner's equity. The statement of owner's equity, Illustration 5.7, shows the increase in equity resulting from net income and the decrease in equity resulting from the owner's withdrawals.

Balance sheet. The balance sheet, Illustration 5.8, contains the assets, liabilities, and owner's equity items taken from the work sheet. Note the

Illustration 5.6: Income statement for a merchandising company

LYONS COMPANY
Income Statement
For the Month Ended January 31, 1984

Operating revenues:			
Gross sales			$13,600
Less: Sales discounts		$ 44	
Sales returns and allowances		20	64
Net sales			$13,536
Cost of goods sold:			
Merchandise inventory, January 1, 1984		$ 7,000	
Purchases	$6,000		
Less: Purchase discounts	$ 82		
Purchase returns and allowances	100	182	
Net purchases		$5,818	
Add: Transportation-in		75	
Net cost of purchases		5,893	
Cost of goods available for sale		$12,893	
Merchandise inventory, January 31, 1984		8,000	
Cost of goods sold			4,893
Gross margin			$ 8,643
Operating expenses:			
Selling expenses (summary)		$ 2,650	
Administrative expenses (summary)		1,150	
Total operating expenses			3,800
Net income			$ 4,843

Illustration 5.7:　Statement of owner's equity

```
                    LYONS COMPANY
                 Statement of Owner's Equity
              For the Month Ended January 31, 1984

Lyons, capital, January 1, 1984 ......    $25,000
Net income for the month ...........        4,843
        Total ....................        $29,843
Lyons, drawing ...................          2,000
Lyons, capital, January 31, 1984 .....    $27,843
```

Illustration 5.8:　Balance sheet for a merchandising company

```
                       LYONS COMPANY
                        Balance Sheet
                       January 31, 1984

                           Assets
Current assets:
   Cash ..............................    $18,663
   Accounts receivable ...............      1,880
   Merchandise inventory .............      8,000
        Total assets .................    $28,543

               Liabilities and Owner's Equity
Current liabilities:
   Accounts payable ..................    $   700
Owner's equity:
   Lyons, capital ....................     27,843
        Total liabilities and owner's equity ...    $28,543
```

$8,000 ending inventory is shown as a current asset. The Lyons capital account balance comes from the statement of owner's equity.

Closing entries

Closing entries may be prepared directly from the work sheet using the same procedure as presented in Chapter 4. The first journal entry *debits* all items appearing in the Income Statement credit column of the work sheet and *credits* Income Summary for the total of that column, $21,782. The second entry *credits* all items appearing in the Income Statement debit column and debits Income Summary for the total of that column, $16,939. In the third entry, the credit balance in the Income Summary account of $4,843 is closed to the owner's capital account. In the fourth entry, the owner's drawing account balance of $2,000 is closed to the owner's capital account by debiting Lyons, Capital and crediting Lyons, Drawing. The entries to perform the closing process for the Lyons Company are:

1st entry	Merchandise Inventory	8,000	
	Sales	13,600	
	Purchase Discounts	82	
	Purchase Returns and Allowances	100	
	Income Summary		21,782
	To close accounts with a credit balance in the Income Statement columns and to establish ending merchandise inventory.		
2d entry	Income Summary	16,939	
	Merchandise Inventory		7,000
	Sales Discounts		44
	Sales Returns and Allowances		20
	Purchases		6,000
	Transportation-In		75
	Selling Expenses		2,650
	Administrative Expenses		1,150
	To close accounts with a debit balance in the Income Statement columns.		
3d entry	Income Summary	4,843	
	Lyons, Capital		4,843
	To close the Income Summary account to the owner's capital account.		
4th entry	Lyons, Capital	2,000	
	Lyons, Drawing		2,000
	To close the owner's drawing account.		

Notice how the closing entries tie into the totals shown in the Income Statement columns of the work sheet. In the first closing journal entry, the credit to the Income Summary account is equal to the total of the Income Statement credit column. In the second entry, the debit to the Income Summary account is equal to the subtotal of the Income Statement debit column. The difference between the totals of the two Income Statement columns ($4,843) represents net income and is the amount of the third closing entry.

The closing entries affect the accounts as shown in the following T-accounts:

Merchandise Inventory

| Bal. before closing | 7,000 | To close to Income Summary | 7,000 |
| To establish ending inventory | 8,000 | | |

Sales

| To close to Income Summary | 13,600 | Bal. before closing | 13,600 |
| | | Bal. after closing | –0– |

Sales Discounts

| Bal. before closing | 44 | To close to Income Summary | 44 |
| Bal. after closing | –0– | | |

Sales Returns and Allowances

Bal. before closing	20	To close to Income Summary	20
Bal. after closing	–0–		

Purchases

Bal. before closing	6,000	To close to Income Summary	6,000
Bal. after closing	–0–		

Purchase Discounts

To close to Income Summary	82	Bal. before closing	82
		Bal. after closing	–0–

Purchase Returns and Allowances

To close to Income Summary	100	Bal. before closing	100
		Bal. after closing	–0–

Transportation-In

Bal. before closing	75	To close to Income Summary	75
Bal. after closing	–0–		

Selling Expenses

Bal. before closing	2,650	To close to Income Summary	2,650
Bal. after closing	–0–		

Administrative Expenses

Bal. before closing	1,150	To close to Income Summary	1,150
Bal. after closing	–0–		

Income Summary

From closing accounts appearing in Income Statement debit column of work sheet	16,939	From closing accounts appearing in Income Statement credit column of work sheet	21,782
To close to owner's capital account	4,843	Bal. (net income) before closing this account	4,843
		Bal. after closing	–0–

Lyons, Capital

From closing owner's drawing account	2,000	Beg. bal.	25,000
		From closing Income Summary account	4,843
		End. bal.	27,843

Lyons, Drawing

| Bal. before closing | 2,000 | To close to owner's capital account | 2,000 |
| Bal. after closing | –0– | | |

After the entries have been posted, only the balance sheet accounts have balances. The revenue, expense, and drawing accounts have zero balances. The basic aspects of accounting for and reporting on merchandising activities have now been presented.

NEW TERMS INTRODUCED IN CHAPTER 5

Administrative expenses
Operating expenses incurred in the overall management of a business.

Cash discount
A deduction from the gross invoice price to arrive at actual cost that can be taken only if the invoice is paid within a specified period of time: to the seller, a sales discount; to the buyer, a purchase discount.

Chain discount
Occurs when a list price is subject to several trade discounts.

Classified income statement
Divides both revenues and expenses into operating and nonoperating items. The statement also separates operating expenses into selling and administrative expenses.

Consignment basis
Goods sent by the owner to another party who will make an effort to sell the goods for the owner.

Cost of goods sold
Shows the cost to the seller of buying the goods which it sold to customers; under periodic procedure cost of goods sold is computed as Beginning inventory + Net cost of purchases − Ending inventory.

Delivery expense
A selling expense recorded by the seller for freight costs incurred when terms are FOB destination.

FOB destination
Means free on board at destination; goods are shipped to their destination without charge to the buyer; the seller bears the transportation charges.

FOB shipping point
Means free on board at shipping point; goods are placed in the hands of the transport company, with the buyer responsible for all transportation costs that follow.

Freight collect
Terms that require the buyer to pay the freight bill upon the arrival of the goods.

Freight prepaid
Terms that indicate the seller has paid the freight bill at the time of shipment.

Gross margin
Net sales − Cost of goods sold.

Inventory
The quantity of goods on hand and available for sale at any given time.

Invoice
A document prepared by the seller of merchandise and sent to the buyer that contains the details of

a sale, such as the number of units, unit price, total price billed, terms of sale, and manner of shipment; a purchase invoice from the buyer's point of view and a sales invoice from the seller's point of view.

Merchandise in transit
Merchandise in the hands of a transport company on the date of a physical inventory.

Merchandise inventory
See inventory.

Net cost of purchases
Net Purchases + Transportation-in.

Net income
Net income from operations + Nonoperating revenues − Nonoperating expenses.

Net income from operations
Gross margin − Operating expenses.

Net purchases
Purchases − Purchase returns and allowances − Purchase discounts.

Net sales
Gross sales − Sales returns and allowances − Sales discounts.

Nonoperating expenses (other expenses)
Expenses incurred by a business that are not related to the acquisition and sale of the products or services regularly offered for sale.

Nonoperating revenues (other revenues)
Revenues not related to the sale of products or services regularly offered for sale by a business.

Operating expenses
Those expenses, other than cost of goods sold, incurred in the normal buying, selling, and administrative functions of a business.

Operating revenues
Those revenues generated by the major activities of the business.

Passage of title
A legal term used to indicate transfer of legal ownership of goods.

Periodic inventory procedure
A method of accounting for merchandise acquired for sale to customers wherein the cost of merchandise sold and the cost of merchandise on hand are determined only at the end of the accounting period by taking a physical inventory.

Physical inventory
Consists of counting physical units of each type of merchandise on hand.

Purchase discounts
See cash discounts.

Purchase Discounts account
A contra account to Purchases that reduces the recorded gross invoice cost of the purchase to the price actually paid.

Purchase Returns and Allowances account
An account used under periodic inventory procedure to record the cost of merchandise returned to a seller and to record reductions in selling prices granted by a seller because merchandise was not satisfactory to a buyer; viewed as a reduction in the recorded cost of purchases.

Purchases account
An account used under periodic inventory procedure to record the cost of merchandise purchased during the current accounting period.

Retailers
Companies which sell goods to final consumers.

Sales allowances
Deductions from original invoiced sales prices granted to a customer for any of a number of reasons, including inferior quality or damage or deterioration in transit.

Sales discounts
See cash discounts.

Sales Discounts account
A contra revenue account to Sales and is shown as a deduction from gross sales in the income statement.

Sales return
From the seller's point of view, merchandise returned by a buyer for any of a variety of reasons; to the buyer, a purchase return.

Sales Returns and Allowances account
A contra revenue account to Sales used to record the selling price of merchandise returned by buyers or reductions in selling prices granted.

Selling expenses
Those expenses which are incurred in performing and facilitating the selling and marketing effort.

Trade discount
A deduction from the list or catalog price of merchandise to arrive at the gross invoice price; granted

to particular categories of customers (e.g., retailers and wholesalers). Also see chain discount.

Transportation-In account
An account used under periodic inventory procedure to record transportation costs incurred in the acquisition of merchandise; a part of cost of goods sold.

Unclassified income statement
Shows only major categories for revenues and expenses.

Wholesalers
Companies which sell goods to other companies for resale to final consumers.

DEMONSTRATION PROBLEM

CAMP'S MUSIC STORE
Trial Balance
July 31, 1984

	Debits	Credits
Cash	$ 34,780	
Accounts receivable	4,600	
Merchandise inventory, 8/1/83	31,400	
Prepaid fire insurance	720	
Prepaid rent	4,800	
Office equipment	12,000	
Accumulated depreciation—office equipment		$ 4,500
Accounts payable		8,000
Clay Camp, capital		22,000
Clay Camp, drawing	20,000	
Sales		300,000
Sales returns and allowances	1,000	
Purchases	199,200	
Purchase returns and allowances		1,400
Advertising expense	1,000	
Supplies expense	1,800	
Salaries expense	23,200	
Utilities expense	1,400	
	$335,900	$335,900

Clay Camp has prepared the above trial balance for Camp's Music Store. The following information was gathered which will be used to prepare the work sheet.

1. A 12-month fire insurance policy was purchased for $720 on April 1, 1984, the date on which insurance coverage began.
2. On February 1, 1984, Camp paid $4,800 for the next 12 months' rent. The payment was recorded in the Prepaid Rent account.
3. Depreciation expense on the office equipment is $1,500.
4. Merchandise Inventory at July 31, 1984, was $26,400.

Required:

   a.   Prepare a 10-column work sheet for Camp's Music Store for the fiscal year ended July 31, 1984.

   b.   Prepare a classified income statement for the fiscal year ended July 31, 1984. Do not separate operating expenses into selling and administrative categories.

   c.   Prepare a statement of owner's equity for the fiscal year ended July 31, 1984.

    d. Prepare a classified balance sheet for July 31, 1984.

    e. Prepare closing entries.

Solution to demonstration problem

    a. See work sheet on following page.

    b.

CAMP'S MUSIC STORE
Income Statement
For the Year Ended July 31, 1984

Operating revenues:			
Gross sales			$300,000
Less: Sales returns and allowances			1,000
Net sales			$299,000
Cost of goods solds:			
Merchandise inventory, August 1, 1983		$ 31,400	
Purchases	$199,200		
Less: Purchase returns and allowances	1,400		
Net cost of purchases		197,800	
Cost of goods available for sale		$229,200	
Merchandise inventory, July 31, 1984		26,400	
Cost of goods sold			202,800
Gross margin			$ 96,200
Operating expenses:			
Advertising		$ 1,000	
Supplies		1,800	
Salaries		23,200	
Utilities		1,400	
Fire insurance		240	
Rent		2,400	
Depreciation—office equipment		1,500	
Total operating expenses			31,540
Net income			$ 64,660

CAMP'S MUSIC STORE
Statement of Owner's Equity
For the Year Ended July 31, 1984

Clay Camp, capital, August 1, 1983	$22,000
Net income for the year	64,660
Total	$86,660
Less: Drawings	20,000
Clay Camp, capital, July 31, 1984	$66,660

CAMP'S MUSIC STORE
Work Sheet
For the Year Ended July 31, 1984

Account Titles	Trial Balance		Adjustments		Adjusted Trial Balance		Income Statement		Balance Sheet	
	Debit	Credit	Debit	Credit	Debit	Credit	Debit	Credit	Debit	Credit
Cash	34,780				34,780				34,780	
Accounts receivable	4,600				4,600				4,600	
Merchandise inventory	31,400				31,400		31,400	26,400	26,400	
Prepaid fire insurance	720			(1) 240	480				480	
Prepaid rent	4,800			(2) 2,400	2,400				2,400	
Office equipment	12,000				12,000				12,000	
Accumulated depreciation—office equipment		4,500		(3) 1,500		6,000				6,000
Accounts payable		8,000				8,000				8,000
Clay Camp, capital		22,000				22,000				22,000
Clay Camp, drawing	20,000				20,000				20,000	
Sales		300,000				300,000		300,000		
Sales returns and allowances	1,000				1,000		1,000			
Purchases	199,200				199,200		199,200			
Purchase returns and allowances		1,400				1,400		1,400		
Advertising expense	1,000				1,000		1,000			
Supplies expense	1,800				1,800		1,800			
Salaries expense	23,200				23,200		23,200			
Utilities expense	1,400				1,400		1,400			
	335,900	335,900								
Fire insurance expense			(1) 240		240		240			
Rent expense			(2) 2,400		2,400		2,400			
Depreciation expense—office equipment			(3) 1,500		1,500		1,500			
			4,140	4,140	337,400	337,400	263,140	327,800		
Net income							64,660			64,660
							327,800	327,800	100,660	100,660

Adjustments:
(1) Expiration of prepaid fire insurance ($720 × 4/12).
(2) Expiration of prepaid rent ($4,800 × 6/12).
(3) Depreciation expense on office equipment for the fiscal year ended July 31, 1984.

d.

```
                        CAMP'S MUSIC STORE
                          Balance Sheet
                          July 31, 1984

                             Assets
Current assets:
  Cash .......................................................  $34,780
  Accounts receivable ........................................    4,600
  Merchandise inventory ......................................   26,400
  Prepaid fire insurance .....................................      480
  Prepaid rent ...............................................    2,400
      Total current assets ...................................            $68,660
Property, plant, and equipment:
  Office equipment ...........................................  $12,000
    Less: Accumulated depreciation ...........................    6,000
      Total property, plant, and equipment ...................              6,000
          Total assets .......................................            $74,660

                  Liabilities and Owner's Equity
Liabilities:
  Accounts payable ...........................................            $ 8,000
Owner's equity:
  Clay Camp, capital .........................................             66,660
      Total liabilities and owner's equity ...................            $74,660
```

e. Closing entries:

```
1984
July 31  Merchandise Inventory ..............................   26,400
         Sales ..............................................  300,000
         Purchase Returns and Allowances ....................    1,400
             Income Summary .................................              327,800
             To close accounts with credit balances
             in the Income Statement columns and to
             set up the ending merchandise inventory.

     31  Income Summary .....................................  263,140
             Merchandise Inventory ..........................               31,400
             Sales Returns and Allowances ...................                1,000
             Purchases ......................................              199,200
             Advertising Expense ............................                1,000
             Supplies Expense ...............................                1,800
             Salaries Expense ...............................               23,200
             Utilities Expense ..............................                1,400
             Fire Insurance Expense .........................                  240
             Rent Expense ...................................                2,400
             Depreciation Expense—Office Equipment ..........                1,500
             To close accounts with debit balances
             in the Income Statement columns.

     31  Income Summary .....................................   64,660
             Clay Camp, Capital .............................               64,660
             To close the Income Summary account
             to the owner's capital account.
```

July 31	Clay Camp, Capital	20,000	
	Clay Camp, Drawing		20,000
	To close drawing account.		

QUESTIONS

1. What account titles are likely to appear in the ledger of a merchandising company that do not appear in the ledger of a service enterprise?

2. What entry is made to record a sale of merchandise on account?

3. Describe trade discounts and chain discounts.

4. Sales discounts and sales returns and allowances are deducted from sales on the income statement to arrive at net sales. Why not deduct these directly from the Sales account by debiting sales each time a sales discount, return, or allowance occurs?

5. What are the two basic procedures for accounting for inventory?

6. How is cost of goods sold determined under periodic inventory procedure?

7. What useful purpose does the Purchases account serve?

8. Periodic inventory procedure is said to afford little control over inventory. Explain why.

9. How does the accountant arrive at the total dollar amount of the inventory after taking a physical inventory?

10. What do the letters FOB stand for? When terms are *FOB destination,* who incurs the freight?

11. What type of an expense is delivery expense? Where is it reported in the income statement?

12. Referring to Illustration 5.4, determine the effect on net income of each of the following:

 a. Ending inventory is overstated.
 b. Purchases are understated.
 c. Purchase discounts are overstated.
 d. Transportation-in is overstated.
 e. Beginning inventory is understated.

13. If at the end of a period the cost of goods available for sale and the cost of the ending inventory are known, how can this information be used?

14. What is gross margin? Why might management be interested in the percentage of gross margin to sales?

15. What are the major sections in a classified income statement for a merchandising company, and in what order do they appear?

EXERCISES

E–1.   In the following table, indicate how (debit or credit) each account shown is increased and decreased, and indicate the normal balance (debit or credit).

Title of account	Increased by (debit or credit)	Decreased by (debit or credit)	Normal balance (debit or credit)
Sales			
Sales Returns and Allowances			
Sales Discounts			
Accounts Receivable			
Purchases			
Purchase Returns and Allowances			
Purchase Discounts			
Accounts Payable			
Transportation-In			

E–2.   *a.*   The Crawley Company purchased merchandise from the Short Company on account. Before paying its account, the Crawley Company returned damaged merchandise with an invoice price of $2,100. Assuming use of periodic inventory procedure, prepare entries on both firms' books to record the return.

b.   Prepare the required entries assuming that the Short Company granted an allowance of $700 on the damaged goods instead of accepting the return.

E–3.   What is the last payment date on which the cash discount can be taken on goods sold on March 5 for $64,000; terms, 3/10/EOM, n/60? Assume that the bill is paid on this date and prepare the correct entry on both the buyer's and seller's books to record the payment.

E–4.   You have purchased merchandise with a list price of $4,000. Because you are a wholesaler, you are granted trade discounts of 30, 20, and 10 percent. The cash discount terms are 2/EOM, n/60. How much will you pay if you pay by the end of the month of purchase? How much will you pay if you do not pay until the following month?

E–5.   The P Company uses periodic inventory procedure. Determine the cost of goods sold for the company assuming purchases during the period were $8,000, transportation-in was $60, purchase returns and allowances were $200, beginning inventory was $5,000, purchase discounts were $400, and ending inventory was $2,600.

E–6.   The Jewel Company purchased goods for $4,600 on June 14 under the following terms: 3/10, n/30; FOB shipping point, freight collect. The bill for the freight amounted to $150.

a.   Assume that the invoice was paid within the discount period and prepare all entries required on Jewel Company's books.

b. Assume that the invoice was paid on July 11. Prepare the entry to record the payment made on that date.

E-7.   Given the balances shown in the partial trial balance, indicate how the balances would be treated in the work sheet. The ending inventory is $16. The amounts are unusually small for ease in rewriting the numbers.

Account Title	Trial Balance		Adjustments		Adjusted Trial Balance		Income Statement		Balance Sheet	
	Debit	Credit	Debit	Credit	Debit	Credit	Debit	Credit	Debit	Credit
Merchandise inventory	20									
Sales		140								
Sales discounts	3									
Sales returns and allowances	8									
Purchases	100									
Purchase discounts		2								
Purchase returns and allowances		4								
Transportation-in	6									

E-8.   Using the data in Exercise E-7:

a. Prepare closing entries for the accounts shown above. Do not close the Income Summary account.
b. Show in T-account format how the accounts would appear after this portion of the closing process has been completed.

E-9.   In each of the following equations supply the missing term(s):

a. Net sales = Gross sales − _____ _____ −
    Sales returns and allowances.
b. Cost of goods sold = Beginning inventory + Net cost of
    purchases − _____ _____ .
c. Gross margin = _____ _____ − Cost of
    goods sold.
d. Net income from operations = _____ _____
    − Operating expenses.
e. Net income = Net income from operations + _____
    _____ − _____ _____ .

E–10. In each case below use the information provided to calculate the missing information:

	Case 1	Case 2	Case 3
Gross sales	$100,000	?	?
Sales discounts	?	4,000	3,000
Sales returns and allowances	3,000	7,000	5,000
Net sales	95,000	189,000	?
Merchandise inventory, January 1	40,000	?	60,000
Purchases	60,000	120,000	?
Purchase discounts	1,200	2,100	2,000
Purchase returns and allowances	3,800	4,900	5,000
Net purchases	55,000	?	105,000
Transportation-in	4,000	6,000	5,000
Net cost of purchases	59,000	119,000	?
Cost of goods available for sales	?	169,000	170,000
Merchandise inventory, December 31	?	60,000	70,000
Cost of goods sold	50,000	?	100,000
Gross margin	?	80,000	50,000

PROBLEMS, SERIES A

P5–1–A. *a.* The Randolph Sporting Goods Company engaged in the following transactions in April 1984:

Transactions:

Apr. 1 Sold merchandise on account, terms 2/10, n/30, FOB destination, for $20,000.
  5 $3,000 of the goods sold on account on April 1 were returned for full credit. Payment for these goods had not yet been received.
  8 A sales allowance of $400 was granted on the merchandise sold on April 1 because the merchandise was damaged in shipment.
  10 Payment was received for the net amount due from the sale of April 1.

b. Andrews Stereo Company engaged in the following transactions during the month of July:

Transactions:

July 2 Purchased stereo merchandise on account at a cost of $3,000, terms 2/10, n/30, FOB destination.
  15 Sold $2,000 of the merchandise purchased on July 2 for $4,500, terms 2/10, n/30, FOB destination.
  16 Paid freight costs on the merchandise sold, $150.
  20 Andrews Stereo Company was granted an allowance of $200 on the purchase of July 2 because of damaged merchandise.
  31 Paid the amount due on the purchase of July 2.

Required:

Prepare journal entries to record the transactions.

P5–2–A. On July 2, 1984, the Melody Musical Instrument Company purchased merchandise with a list price of $10,000 from the Perma Company. The terms were 3/EOM, n/60, FOB shipping point, freight collect. Trade discounts of 15, 10, and 5 percent were granted by the Perma Company. The Melody Musical Instrument Company paid the freight bill of $230 on July 5. On July 6, it was discovered that merchandise with a list price of $800 had been damaged seriously in transit; these items were returned for full credit. Melody Musical Instrument Company made payment on the last day of the discount period.

Required:

Prepare all the necessary entries for the Melody Musical Instrument Company.

P5–3–A.

Required:

    a.   Journalize the following transactions for Company N.

    b.   Journalize the following transactions for Company O.

Transactions:

May 18 Company N sold to Company O merchandise with a sales price of $48,000; terms, 2/10/ EOM, n/60.

     29 Company O returned $3,000 of the merchandise to Company N.

June 3 Company O requested a gross allowance of $2,000 from Company N due to defective merchandise. Company N granted the allowance.

     10 Company O paid the net amount due.

P5–4–A.   The Bowman Ski Shop purchased merchandise on March 1, 1984, from the Biggs Company at a list price of $6,000, FOB shipping point. Trade discounts of 30, 25, and 5 percent were granted. Cash discount terms were 2/EOM, n/60. The buyer paid the freight of $124 on March 4, 1984. The buyer notified the seller that a $600 credit should be granted against the amount due because of damaged merchandise. The seller granted the allowance on March 25, 1984.

Required:

Record all entries, assuming payment on March 31, on the books of both the buyer and seller.

P5–5–A.   The Fitness Company sells exercise equipment to customers. The ending inventory on hand at December 31, 1984, had a cost of $24,200. The Adjusted Trial Balance columns of a work sheet prepared for the company is shown below.

Required:

    a.   Prepare a classified income statement for the year ended December 31, 1984.

    b.   Prepare a classified balance sheet as of December 31, 1984.

	Adjusted Trial Balance	
	Debit	Credit
Cash	11,000	
Accounts receivable	30,000	
Notes receivable	4,000	
Merchandise inventory	22,350	
Prepaid insurance	900	
Store supplies on hand	350	
Land.	40,000	
Accounts payable		7,550
Notes payable		13,500
Jones, capital		74,800
Sales		205,000
Sales discounts	3,650	
Sales returns and allowances	2,850	
Purchases	113,000	
Purchase discounts		2,050
Purchase returns and allowances		1,200
Sales salaries expense	32,000	
General selling expense	1,900	
Delivery expense	4,300	
Heat and light expense, selling	1,500	
Rent expense, selling	6,100	
Office salaries expense	20,250	
General administrative expense	3,950	
Telephone expense, administrative	700	
Rent expense, administrative	4,350	
Interest revenue		200
Interest expense	1,150	
	304,300	304,300

P5–6–A.

Required:

The Valley Western Wear Company is a wholesaler of western wear clothing. The company sells its merchandise to retailers. From the data given below for the Valley Western Wear Company:

a. Prepare journal entries for the transactions.

b. Post the journal entries to the proper ledger accounts.

c. Prepare a work sheet. (There were no adjusting journal entries.)

d. Prepare a classified income statement for the month ended May 31, 1984.

e. Prepare a classified balance sheet as of May 31, 1984.

Transactions:

1984

May 1 The Valley Western Wear Company was organized as a single proprietorship. Jo Valley invested the following assets in the business: $110,000 cash, $40,000 merchandise, and $25,000 land.

1 Paid rent on administrative offices for May, $6,000.

5 The company purchased merchandise from Wells Company on account, $45,000; terms, 2/10, n/30.

May 8 Cash of $2,000 was paid to a trucking company for delivery of the merchandise purchased May 5. Freight terms were FOB shipping point.
14 The company sold merchandise on account, $75,000; terms, 2/10, n/30.
15 Paid Wells Company the amount due on the purchase of May 5.
16 Of the merchandise sold May 14, $3,300 was returned for credit.
19 Salaries for services received were paid for the month of May as follows: office employees, $4,000; and salespersons, $8,000.
24 The company collected the amount due on $30,000 of the accounts receivable arising from the sales of May 14.
25 The company purchased merchandise on account from Alex Company, $36,000; terms, 2/10, n/30.
27 Of the merchandise purchased May 25, $6,000 was returned to the vendor.
28 A trucking company was paid $500 for delivery to the Valley Western Wear Company of the goods purchased May 25. Freight terms were FOB shipping point.
29 The company sold merchandise on open account, $3,600; terms, 2/10, n/30.
30 Cash sales were $17,640.
30 Cash of $24,000 was received from the sales of May 14.
31 Paid Alex Company for the merchandise purchased on May 25, taking into consideration the merchandise returned on May 27.

Additional data:

The inventory on hand at the close of business on May 31 is $71,200.

P5–7–A.

Required:

From the following information for the Northside Vitamin Supply Company:

a. Prepare journal entries for the summarized transactions for 1984. Omit explanations. Key your entries to the number of the transaction.

b. Set up T-accounts and enter the December 31, 1983, balances given below. Then post your journal entries to the T-accounts and calculate ending balances for those accounts having more than one entry in them.

c. Prepare a trial balance.

d. Prepare a classified income statement for the year ended December 31, 1984.

e. Prepare a classified balance sheet as of December 31, 1984.

NORTHSIDE COMPANY
Account Balances
December 31, 1983

	Debits	**Credits**
Cash	$ 48,000	
Accounts receivable	82,500	
Merchandise inventory	70,000	
Accounts payable		$ 52,500
Northside, capital		148,000
	$200,500	$200,500

Summarized transactions for 1984

1.	Cash sales	$170,000
2.	Sales on account at gross invoice prices	370,000
3.	Purchases on account at gross invoice prices	400,000
4.	Cash collected on accounts receivable (applied against $345,000 of accounts receivable on which sales discounts of $5,000 were taken)	340,000

5.	Sales returns (from credit sales)	$ 11,250
6.	Purchase returns	5,600
7.	Cash paid on accounts payable (applied against $328,500 of	
	accounts payable on which purchase discounts of $6,000 were taken)	322,500
8.	Selling expenses incurred and paid	49,000
9.	Administrative expenses incurred and paid	45,500

Additional data:

The merchandise inventory at December 31, 1984, is $85,400.

P5–8–A.

Required:

From the trial balance and additional data given below for the Peters Lumber Company, prepare:

    a.   A work sheet for the year ended December 31, 1984.

    b.   A classified income statement. The only selling expenses are sales salaries, advertising, sales supplies, and depreciation—store equipment.

    c.   A classified balance sheet.

    d.   The December 31, 1984, closing entries.

PETERS LUMBER COMPANY
Trial Balance
December 31, 1984

	Debits	*Credits*
Cash	$ 35,320	
Accounts receivable	79,760	
Merchandise inventory	142,600	
Sales supplies on hand	2,680	
Prepaid fire insurance	2,400	
Prepaid rent	28,800	
Store equipment	44,000	
Accumulated depreciation—store equipment		$ 8,800
Accounts payable		51,400
Peters, capital		209,820
Sales		561,180
Sales returns and allowances	2,580	
Purchases	250,420	
Purchase returns and allowances		2,020
Transportation-in	3,920	
Sales salaries expense	69,200	
Advertising expense	39,000	
General office expense	4,940	
Office salaries expense	40,400	
Officers' salaries expense	80,000	
Legal and auditing expense	5,000	
Telephone and telegraph expense	2,400	
Interest revenue		500
Interest expense	300	
	$833,720	$833,720

Additional data as of December 31, 1984:

1. Prepaid fire insurance expired, $1,700.
2. Sales supplies consumed, $1,830.
3. Prepaid rent expired during the year, $25,300.

4. Depreciation expense on store equipment, $4,400.
5. Accrued sales salaries, $2,000.
6. Accrued office salaries, $1,500.
7. Merchandise inventory on hand, $175,000.

PROBLEMS, SERIES B

P5–1–B.   *a.* The following transactions were entered into by the Dawson Carpet Company in August 1984:

Transactions:

Aug. 2 Sold merchandise on account, terms, 2/10, n/30, FOB destination, for $15,000.
  18 Received payment for the sale of August 2.
  20 A total of $500 of the merchandise sold on August 2 was returned, and a full refund was made because it was the wrong merchandise.
  28 An allowance of $800 was granted on the sale of August 2 because some merchandise was found to be damaged. $800 cash was returned to the customer.

  b. The Wyler Furniture Company engaged in the following transactions during August:

Transactions:

Aug. 4 Purchased merchandise on account at a cost of $7,000, terms, 2/10, n/30, FOB shipping point.
  6 Paid freight of $100 on the purchase of August 4.
  10 Sold goods with a total cost of $3,000 for $5,000; terms, 2/10, n/30.
  12 Returned $1,200 of the merchandise purchased on August 4.
  14 Paid the amount due on the purchase of August 4.

Required:
Prepare journal entries for the transactions.

P5–2–B.   The Reed Auto Parts Company purchased merchandise with a list price of $20,000, FOB destination, freight prepaid, from Grady Company, on August 15, 1984. Trade discounts of 20 and 10 percent were allowed, and credit terms were 2/10, n/30. Grady Company paid the freight charges of $250 on August 16. On August 17, Reed Company requested a purchase allowance of $470 because some of the merchandise had been damaged in transit. On August 20, the Grady Company granted the allowance. Payment was made on the last day of the discount period.

Required:
Record all the entries required on the books of both the buyer and the seller.

P5–3–B.

Required:

  a. Journalize the following transactions for Company X.

  b. Journalize the following transactions for Company Y.

Transactions:

Mar. 12 Company X purchased merchandise from Company Y, $14,000; terms, 2/10/EOM, n/60.
  20 Company X returned $4,500 of the merchandise to Company Y.
  30 Company X requested and received a gross allowance of $800 from Company Y, due to improper quality of merchandise purchased on March 12.
Apr. 10 Company Y received payment in full from Company X.

P5–4–B.   On August 1, 1984, the Patrick Hardware Store bought merchandise from the Jordon Company, $12,000 list price, FOB destination. (The seller prepaid the freight of $80 on August 1, 1984.) Other terms were trade discounts of 30 and 10 percent and cash discount of 2/10/EOM, n/60. On August 8, 1984, the Patrick Hardware Store returned $1,000 (at list price) of the merchandise. The balance due was paid on September 10, 1984.

Required:

Journalize all entries required on the books of both the buyer and the seller.

P5–5–B.

Required:

From the data given below for the King Building Supplies Company:

a.   Prepare journal entries for the summarized transactions. Omit explanations.

b.   Post the journal entries to the proper ledger accounts after entering the balances as of December 31, 1984.

c.   Prepare a classified income statement for the year ended December 31, 1985.

d.   Prepare a classified balance sheet as of December 31, 1985.

KING BUILDING SUPPLIES COMPANY
Balance Sheet
December 31, 1984

Assets

Cash	$ 51,000
Accounts receivable	33,000
Merchandise inventory	28,000
Total assets	$112,000

Liabilities and Owner's Equity

Accounts payable	$ 23,000
King, capital	89,000
Total liabilities and owner's equity	$112,000

Summarized transactions for 1985

1.	Sales for cash	$ 70,000
2.	Sales on account (gross)	148,000
3.	Purchases on account (gross)	160,000
4.	Cash collected on accounts receivable (applied against $139,500 of accounts receivable on which $2,000 of sales discounts were taken)	$137,500
5.	Sales returns (from credit sales)	4,500
6.	Purchase returns	2,400
7.	Cash payments on accounts payable (applied against $131,400 of accounts payable on which $2,400 of purchase discounts were taken)	129,000
8.	Land purchased for cash	62,000
9.	Selling expenses incurred and paid for	19,600
10.	Administrative expenses incurred and paid for	18,200

Additional data:

Merchandise inventory at December 31, 1985, is $35,200.

P5–6–B.   The Hughes Cabinet Company was organized May 1, 1984.

Required:

From the following information for the Hughes Cabinet Company:

a.   Journalize the transactions.

b.   Post the entries to the proper ledger accounts.

c.   Prepare a work sheet as of May 31. There were no adjusting entries.

d.   Prepare a classified income statement for May.

Transactions:

May 1   Ron Hughes invested $250,000 in his new business.
      1   Purchased merchandise on account from the Robertson Company, $13,000; terms, n/60, FOB shipping point.
      3   Sold merchandise for cash, $8,000.
      6   Paid transportation charges on May 1 purchase, $400 cash.
      7   Returned $1,000 of merchandise to the Robertson Company due to improper size.
     10   Requested and received an allowance of $500 from the Robertson Company for improper quality of certain items.
     14   Sale on account to Lewis Company, $5,000; terms, 2/20, n/30.
     16   Cash refund on returns of sales made on May 3, $50.
     18   Purchased merchandise on account from White Company invoiced at $8,000; terms, 2/15, n/30, FOB shipping point.
     18   Received a bill for freight charges of $250 from the Ace Trucking Company on the purchase from White Company.
     19   Lewis Company returned $100 of merchandise purchased on May 14.
     24   Returned $800 of defective merchandise to White Company. Received full credit.
     28   Lewis Company remitted balance due on sale of May 14.
     31   Paid White Company for the purchase of May 18 after adjusting for transaction of May 24.
     31   Paid miscellaneous selling expenses of $2,000.
     31   Paid miscellaneous administrative expenses of $3,000.

Additional data:

The May 30 inventory is $16,000.

P5–7–B.

Required:

From the following trial balance and additional data for the Wheeler Lamp Company, prepare:

a.   A work sheet for the year ended December 31, 1984.

b.   A classified income statement. The only administrative expenses are office salaries and insurance.

c.   A classified balance sheet.

d.   The required closing entries.

```
                        WHEELER LAMP COMPANY
                             Trial Balance
                          December 31, 1984
```

	Debits	Credits
Cash	$ 28,600	
Accounts receivable	24,150	
Prepaid insurance	1,450	
Merchandise inventory, 1/1/84	20,800	
Land	30,000	
Store building	55,000	
Accumulated depreciation—store building		$ 16,500
Store fixtures	27,800	
Accumulated depreciation—store fixtures		5,560
Accounts payable		18,950
Wheeler, capital		110,090
Sales		275,750
Sales discounts	1,850	
Sales returns and allowances	1,000	
Purchases	156,450	
Purchase discounts		1,300
Purchase returns and allowances		700
Transportation-in	3,650	
Sales salaries expense	32,000	
Advertising expense	6,000	
Delivery expense	2,300	
Office salaries expense	37,000	
Interest revenue		200
Interest expense	1,000	
	$429,050	$429,050

Additional data:

1. Depreciation expense on the store building is $1,100.
2. Depreciation expense on the store fixtures is $2,780.
3. Accrued sales salaries are $700.
4. Insurance expired in 1984 is $1,250. Insurance is an administrative expense.
5. Cost of merchandise inventory on hand December 31, 1984, is $27,750.

BUSINESS DECISION PROBLEM

Ron Day taught physical education classes at Riverwood High School for 20 years. In 1983, Ron's uncle died and left Ron $200,000. Ron quit his teaching job in December of 1983 and opened a hardware store in January of 1984. On January 2, 1984, Ron deposited $120,000 in a checking account opened in the store's name, Day's Hardware Store. During the first week of January, Ron rented a building and paid the first year's rent of $9,600 in advance. Also during that week, he purchased the following assets for cash:

Delivery truck	$20,000
Store equipment	10,000
Office equipment	6,000

During the remainder of the first six months of 1984, Ron received cash of $140,000 from customers and disbursed cash of $104,000 for merchandise purchases and $30,000 for operating expenses.

Ron had never had an accounting course, but he had heard the term *net income*.

He decided to compute his net income for the first six months of 1984 and prepared the following schedule:

Cash receipts		$140,000
Cash disbursements:		
Delivery truck..............	$ 20,000	
Store equipment	10,000	
Office equipment	6,000	
Prepaid rent	9,600	
Merchandise purchases	104,000	
Operating expenses	30,000	179,600
Net loss		$ (39,600)

Required:

    a.   Do you agree with Ron Day's statement that his hardware store suffered a net loss of $39,600 for the six months ended June 30, 1984? If not, show how you would determine the net income (or net loss).

    Assume that the depreciation amounts for the six-month period are as follows:

Delivery truck	$2,000
Store equipment	500
Office equipment	375

Also assume that you obtained the following information:

1. Day owes $16,000 to creditors for merchandise purchases.
2. Customers owe Day $20,000 on June 30, 1984.
3. Merchandise costing $12,000 is on hand at the end of the six months.

    b.   Is it possible to prepare a balance sheet on June 30, 1984, or does Mr. Day have to wait until December 31, 1984, to prepare a balance sheet? If a balance sheet can be prepared on June 30, 1984, prepare one.

Chapter 6

Internal control and accounting systems

CHAPTER GOALS

After study of this chapter, you should be able to:

1. Describe the necessity for and features of internal control.
2. Describe the relationship between subsidiary ledgers and control accounts.
3. Describe and use special journals in a manual accounting system.
4. Describe computer applications in business (covered in Appendix).
5. Define and use correctly the new terms in the glossary.

This chapter discusses internal control, subsidiary ledgers, and types of accounting systems. Internal control is covered first; then noncomputerized accounting systems are presented. Computerized systems for processing data are discussed in the chapter Appendix.

INTERNAL CONTROL

An internal control system provides direction to all activity within the organization and ensures that all units are functioning as intended. An *internal control system* is defined as the plan of organization and all the procedures and actions taken by an entity to (1) protect its assets against theft and waste, (2) ensure compliance with company policies and federal law, (3) evaluate the performance of personnel in all parts of the company so as to promote efficiency of operations, and (4) ensure accurate and reliable operating data and accounting reports.

Assets can be protected in a variety of ways. A different person should be responsible for safeguarding an asset from the person who is maintaining the accounting records for that asset; this is known as segregation of duties. Responsibility for related transactions should be divided between individuals so that the work of one person serves as a check on the work of others. In this way, collusion between at least two persons would be necessary to steal assets and cover up theft in the accounting records. For instance, a person could not steal cash from a company and have it go undetected unless the cash records can be changed to cover the shortage. Changing the records can only be accomplished if the person stealing the cash maintains the cash records, or is in collusion with the person who maintains the cash records.

After functions have been divided among employees, responsibility for a particular function is assigned to a specific person. In that way, a person is accountable for specific tasks, and in the event of a problem, that person can be located quickly. A problem does not have to be one of theft; it could simply be tracing a lost document or trying to find out how a particular transaction is accounted for. If one person is responsible for a task, that person will be best able to provide information of any kind about that task.

Employees' job assignments should be rotated when possible. Knowledge that rotation will occur may discourage some employees from engaging in long-term schemes to steal from the company. If theft does occur by an employee in a particular position, it may later be uncovered by the next employee who is assigned to that position. Related to job rotation is a company policy that all employees take an annual vacation. Many schemes that have been used by employees to steal from their company will collapse if not attended to on a daily basis.

Where feasible, mechanical devices may be used to help in asset protection. Check protectors (machines which perforate the check amount into the check), cash registers, and time clocks should be used so that documents and records cannot be altered by employees.

Policy and legal compliance

Well-conceived company policies will only have a beneficial effect on internal control if they are followed. Honest, competent people should be hired and then trained in company policies. The importance of following company policies should be communicated to employees so as to ensure an effective internal control system.

In December 1977, the Foreign Corrupt Practices Act was enacted by Congress. Under this law, publicly held corporations are *required* to devise and maintain an effective system of internal control and to keep accurate accounting records. The passage of this law came about partly because of the cover-ups in company accounting records of bribes and kickbacks made to foreign governments or government officials. This law made this type of bribery illegal.

Personnel performance evaluation

In evaluating how well company employees are doing their jobs, many companies use an internal audit staff. *Internal auditing* consists of investigating and evaluating compliance by employees regarding company policies and procedures. Internal audits are performed by company employees designated as internal auditors; these individuals should have been trained in their duties and in auditing techniques. The internal audit staff encourages operating efficiency throughout the company and is constantly alert for breakdowns in the system of internal control. The staff makes recommendations for the improvement of the system when necessary. Internal auditing is valuable in all companies but is especially necessary in large organizations.

Accuracy of reports

Complete and accurate accounting records should be maintained in the company. The best method for ensuring that this is done is to hire and train competent individuals. Each employee's work should be reviewed periodically by supervisors who can evaluate the proficiency of the employee at particular tasks. Inaccurate or inadequate accounting records serve as an invitation to theft by dishonest employees because the theft can be too easily concealed.

Another effective way to ensure the accuracy of the accounting records is through valid documentation of transactions. For example, in order for a merchandise transaction to be recorded, the following documents should be reviewed: purchase requisition, purchase order, invoice from vendor, and receiving report. A copy of each of these documents is sent to the accounting department, and together the documents serve as authorization to pay for merchandise. In the absence of these documents, a company might fail to pay a legitimate invoice, pay fictitious invoices, or pay an invoice more than once.

Almost all accounting transactions are supported by one or more business documents. These documents are an integral part of the system of internal control; source documents should be serially numbered for best control purposes. Transaction documentation and related aspects of internal control will be presented throughout the text.

Even a company which implements all of the above features in a system of internal control is not guaranteed a foolproof system. If collusion between dishonest employees exists, the system of internal control can be circumvented. Therefore, it is advisable to carry adequate casualty insurance on assets and fidelity bonds on employees handling cash and other negotiable instruments. With these coverages, the company can recover at least a portion of any loss from the insurance or bonding company.

THE PROCESSING OF DATA—MANUAL SYSTEM

The masses of raw data generated by even a small business are largely unintelligible until processed. Processing data includes analyzing, recording, classifying, summarizing, and reporting the data. The orderly and efficient processing of accounting data accomplishes the following:

1. Results of operations and financial position of the firm can be determined and reported on a timely basis.
2. Bills can be paid when due.
3. The proper quantities and items of inventory can be sent to customers.
4. Other aspects of business can be conducted in an orderly and purposeful manner.
5. Reports required by the government or regulatory agencies can be prepared efficiently.

CONTROL ACCOUNTS

In order to efficiently process information, a business needs the right information in the right form to process. Sometimes the business may need general information, and sometimes it may need specific information. For example, total amounts owed to and by the firm need to be presented on the balance sheet, but specific information is needed on customers and creditors in order to send out or pay bills. In order to provide both types of information, control accounts are maintained in the general ledger to provide necessary balance sheet data, and subsidiary accounts are maintained in subsidiary ledgers to provide specific information relating to customers and creditors. A *control account* is an account in the general ledger that shows the aggregate balance of all the subsidiary accounts to which it is related. A *subsidiary account* is the individual account the company maintains for each customer or creditor.

As an example of a control account, the general ledger account, *Accounts Receivable,* summarizes all of the amounts due to the firm. It would be impossible to send out customer statements based on the summary data provided in this account. Therefore, an account is created for each customer, detailing that customer's transactions with the firm. The sum of the subsidiary accounts should agree with the balance in the Accounts Receivable account when financial statements are to be prepared.

In T-account form, the principle of a control account and subsidiary accounts is as follows:

Control account in the general ledger	Subsidiary accounts in the accounts receivable subsidiary ledger	
Accounts Receivable	**Customer A**	**Customer C**
Bal. 1,000	Bal. 100	Bal. 400
	Customer B	**Customer D**
	Bal. 200	Bal. 300

Notice the sum of all balances in the subsidiary accounts ($1,000) on a given date is equal to the balance on that same date in the control account ($1,000).

All of the individual customers' accounts make up the *subsidiary accounts receivable ledger.* A *subsidiary ledger,* then, is a group of related accounts showing the details of the balance of a general ledger control account. Subsidiary ledgers are separated from the general ledger in order to (*a*) relieve the general ledger of a mass of detail and thereby shorten the general ledger trial balance, (*b*) promote division of labor in maintaining the ledgers, and (*c*) strengthen the system of internal control.

When a transaction occurs which affects a control account, some account(s) in the subsidiary ledger will also be affected. A journal entry will need to indicate which of the subsidiary ledger accounts is affected, and posting will be made to both the control account and the subsidiary ledger account. For example, if a $400 sale is made to Debbi Kahan on account, the journal entry would be:

```
Accounts Receivable—D. Kahan  ....................................    400
    Sales  .........................................................          400
  To record sale of merchandise on account.
```

The amount of the sale would be posted to the Accounts Receivable account in the general ledger, D. Kahan's account in the subsidiary ledger, and the Sales account in the general ledger.

Some examples of accounts which will frequently have backup subsidiary ledgers are:

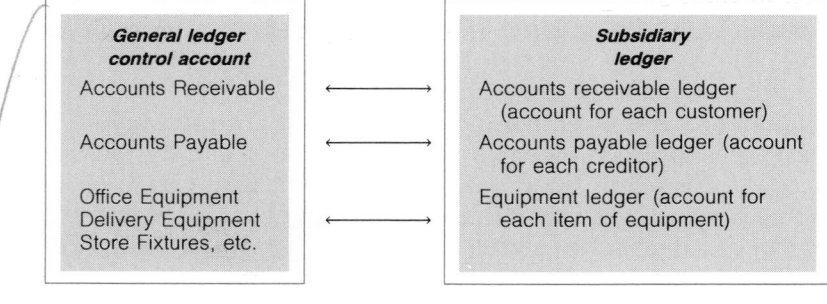

General ledger control account		Subsidiary ledger
Accounts Receivable	←——→	Accounts receivable ledger (account for each customer)
Accounts Payable	←——→	Accounts payable ledger (account for each creditor)
Office Equipment Delivery Equipment Store Fixtures, etc.	←——→	Equipment ledger (account for each item of equipment)

The number of subsidiary ledgers maintained will vary according to the information requirements of each company. Control accounts and subsidiary ledgers will generally be set up when there are many transactions in a given account and when information on the details of these transactions is needed on a continuing basis. This chapter focuses on the use of accounts receivable and accounts payable subsidiary ledgers.

SPECIAL JOURNALS

Until now, only one book of original entry, the general journal, has been used to record transactions. The first step toward more efficient processing of data usually consists of the development of several special journals to be used in addition to the general journal. The special journals will allow for a division or segregation of duties and a reduction in posting time. These advantages occur because special journals group similar types of transactions that can be handled by one employee and because some postings can be made as totals rather than individual amounts.

The special journals illustrated in this chapter are the *sales, cash receipts, purchases,* and *cash disbursements* journals. The number and format of the special journals actually used in a company will primarily depend on the nature of the transactions engaged in by the company.

Special journals are designed to systematize the original recording of major recurring types of transactions. The *sales journal* is used to record all sales of merchandise on account (on credit), while the *purchases journal* is used to record all purchases of merchandise on account. Merchandise refers to items of inventory being sold by the business. The *cash receipts journal* is used for all transactions involving the inflow of cash into the business; the *cash disbursements journal* is used for all payments of cash by the business. The *general journal* is *not* eliminated by the use of special journals; it is used to record all transactions that cannot be entered in one of the special journals.

All five of the journals are books of original entry. If a transaction is recorded in a journal, it will be posted and is part of the accounting records. Therefore, if a transaction is recorded in a special journal, it should *not* be recorded in the general journal also. To do this would be to double record the transaction.

Since the journals will be posted to ledger accounts, an indication needs to be given in the Posting Reference column as to the source of the posting. The following abbreviations are used for the journals:

	Abbreviation
Sales journal	SJ
Cash receipts journal	CRJ
Purchases journal	PJ
Cash disbursements journal	CDJ
General journal	GJ

Sales journal

Sales are normally made either for cash or on credit. The sales journal is used only for sales on account; cash sales would be recorded in the cash receipts journal. The simplest form of sales journal has only one money column which is entitled Accounts Receivable Dr. and Sales Cr. The headings in this form of sales journal might appear as follows:

| Date | Customer | Invoice No. | Accounts Receivable Dr. Sales Cr. | |
| | | | Amount | √ |

But variations in the sales journal can be made. For example, there could be a separate Sales column for each department in a company. If this is done, a separate column will be needed for Accounts Receivable Dr. The headings in a sales journal with separate columns for each department might appear as follows:

| Accounts Receivable Dr. | | Date | Customer | Invoice No. | Sales Cr. | | |
| Amount | √ | | | | Dept. A | Dept. B | Dept. C |

In either format, the customer's name is necessary in order to know which subsidiary ledger account is affected by the sales transaction. The invoice number simply provides documentation that a sale actually occurred. The column with the check mark is similar to a posting reference column; a check mark is placed in that column when the amount of the sale is posted to the customer's subsidiary ledger account. No posting reference column is needed because the column heading indicates to which account and in what manner (debit or credit) the column total will be posted.

Illustration 6.1 shows a sales journal with one money column for the John Mason Company, a retail clothing store. In Illustration 6.1, five credit sales transactions occurred in April.

Posting the sales journal. Individual amounts in the money column are posted daily to each individual customer's account in the subsidiary ledger. Daily posting is required to show the amount currently due from the customer. As each individual amount is posted, a check mark, √, is placed in the column headed √ opposite the amount to show that it has been posted. At the end of the month, the total of the money column, $290, is posted in the general ledger as a debit to the Accounts Receivable control account and as a credit to the Sales account. The posting reference of SJ1 (sales journal, p. 1) is entered in the Accounts Receivable and Sales accounts. The account numbers, 111 for Accounts Receivable and 301 for Sales, are written in the sales journal under the total of the money column to show that $290 was posted to those accounts.

Illustration 6.1: Sales journal

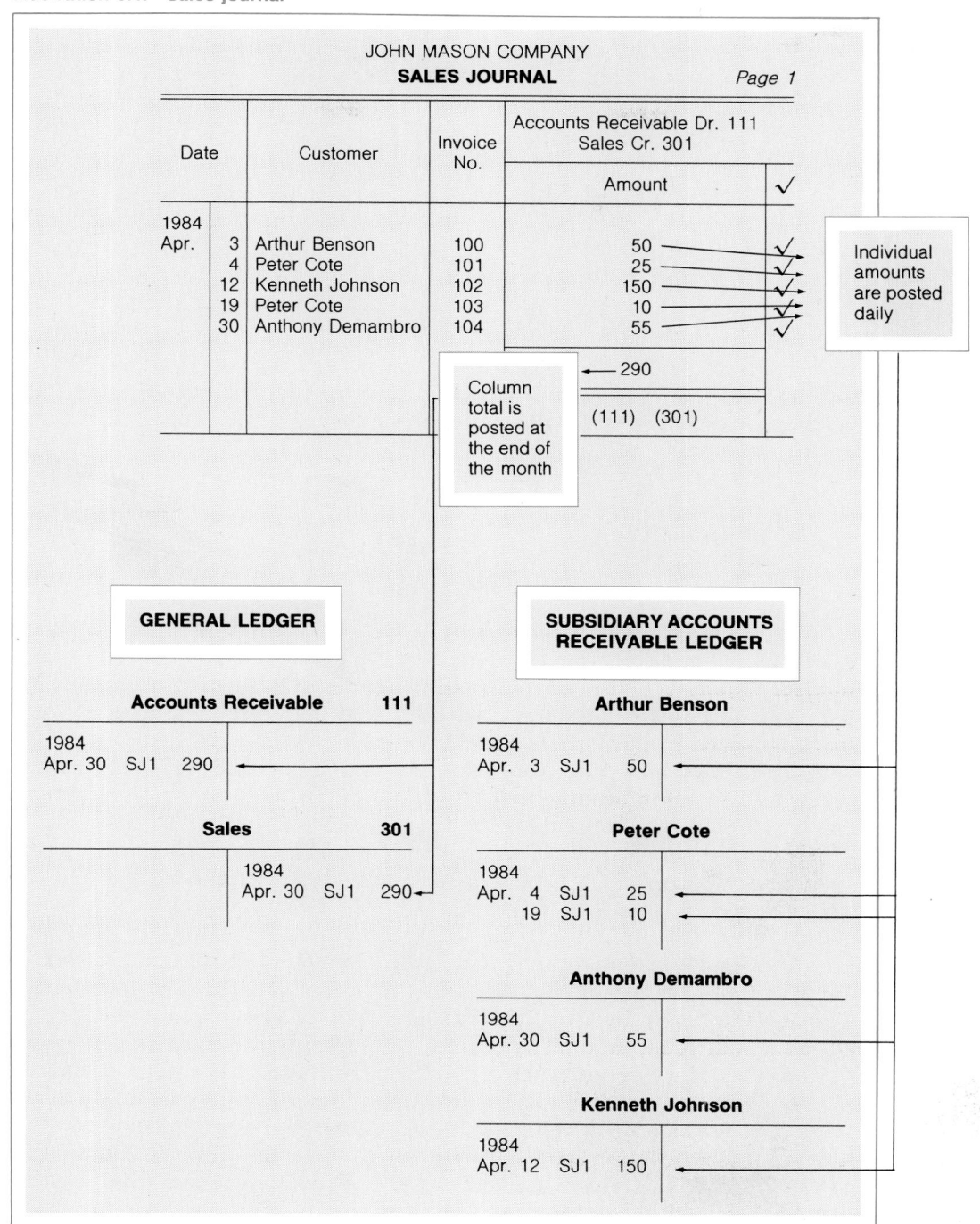

Illustration 6.2: Cash receipts journal

JOHN MASON COMPANY
CASH RECEIPTS JOURNAL

Page 5

101 Cash Dr.	302 Sales Discounts Dr.	Date	Description	310 Sales Cr.	111 Accounts Receivable Cr. Amount		Other Accounts Cr. Account Title	Acct No.	Amount	
		1984 Apr.								
5,000		1	Cash sales	5,000						
49	1	6	Arthur Benson—Invoice No. 100		50	✓				
8,000		7	Cash sales	8,000						
6,000		10	Sold land at cost to Wells Corporation				Land	138	6,000	✓
7,000		14	Cash sales	7,000						
25		19	Peter Cote—Invoice No. 101		25	✓				
147	3	20	Kenneth Johnson—Invoice No. 102		150	✓				
9,000		25	Cash sales	9,000						
200		26	Cash received from sale of scrap				Miscellaneous Revenue	303	200	✓
35,421	4			29,000	225				6,200	
(101)	(302)			(301)	(111)				(√)	

Individual amounts in Accounts Receivable Cr. and Other Accounts Cr. columns are posted daily

Total is not posted

Totals are posted at the end of the month

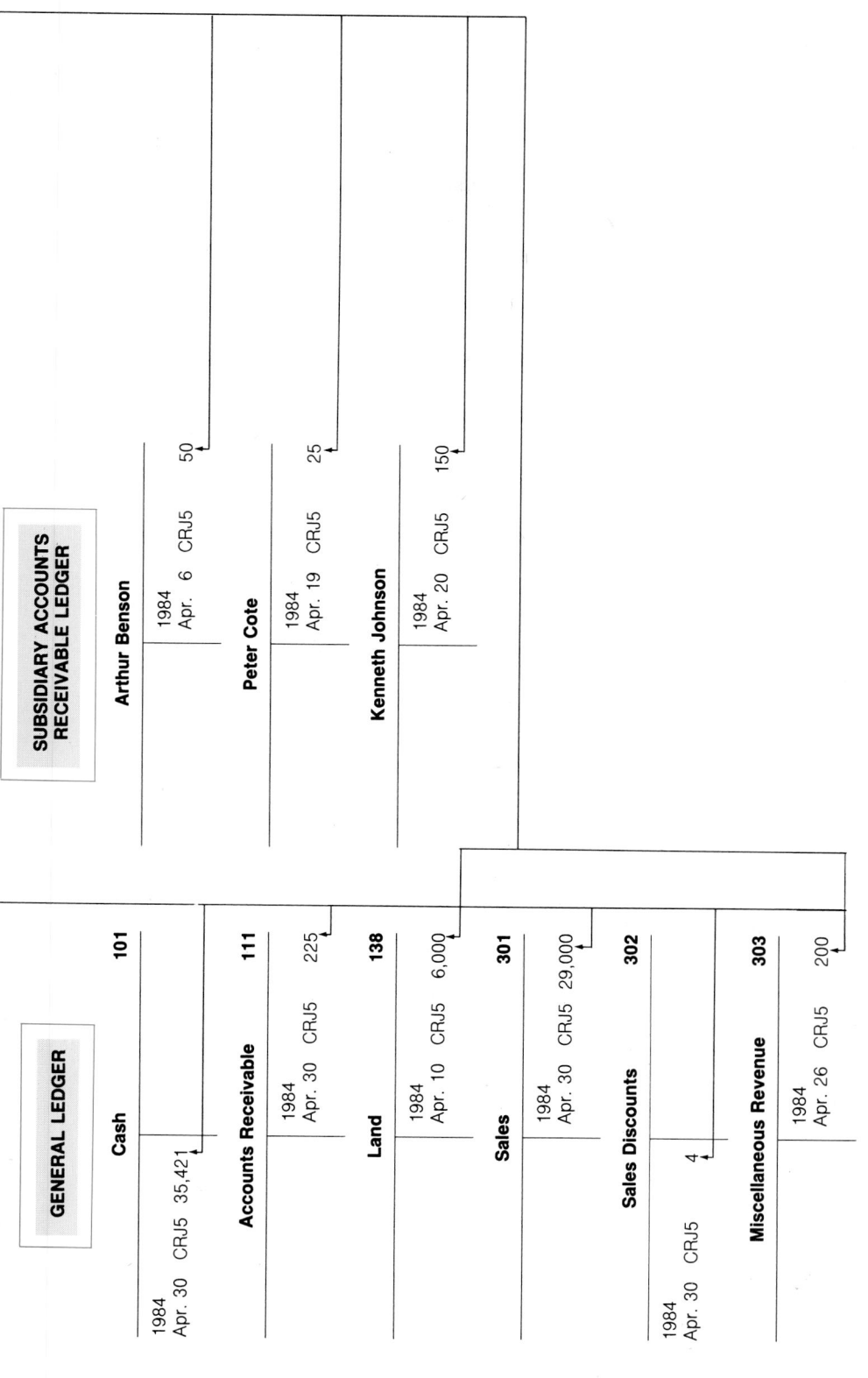

When posting of accounts receivable has been completed, the Accounts Receivable control account will show a balance of $290. This $290 is equal to the sum of the balances in the Accounts Receivable subsidiary ledger accounts, assuming there were no previous balances in the control account or the subsidiary accounts. Subsidiary ledger accounts, since their composition is constantly changing, usually are not numbered but are kept in alphabetical order. In a computerized system, they may be numbered.

Some companies do not use a formal sales journal for sales on account. Instead, the amount of each sales invoice is entered directly in the subsidiary ledger account of the customer. The sales invoices for a month are arranged in numerical order and fastened together. At the end of the month, all of the sales invoices for the month are totaled and an entry is made debiting the Accounts Receivable Control account and crediting Sales for the total amount. This procedure eliminates the need for separate recording of each credit sale in a sales journal.

Cash receipts journal

The cash receipts journal is used for all transactions involving the receipt of cash by the business. Cash sales and collections on accounts receivable are the most frequent types of cash receipts transactions. Therefore, separate credit columns appear for those items in the cash receipts journal shown in Illustration 6.2. Many other types of transactions may result in the receipt of cash by the business, but these transactions do not occur with enough frequency to warrant special columns. These transactions are accounted for in the *Other Accounts* (Miscellaneous Accounts) cr. column of the cash receipts journal.

If after several months or periods a certain transaction is appearing regularly in the Other Accounts Cr. column, the format of the cash receipts journal may be revised to provide a special column for that type of transaction. As an example, a firm that has several rental properties may wish to provide a column for Rent Revenue Cr. in the cash receipts journal.

Posting the cash receipts journal.   Individual amounts in the Accounts Receivable Cr. column are posted daily to customers' accounts in the subsidiary ledger in order to keep customer balances current. The items in the Other Accounts Cr. column are also posted daily to the individual accounts indicated (Account Nos. 138 and 303). The totals of the Cash Dr., Sales Discounts Dr., Sales Cr., and Accounts Receivable Cr. columns are posted at the end of the month to their respective general ledger accounts.

Since the amounts appearing in the Other Accounts Cr. column will normally pertain to different accounts, the column total is not posted and a check mark in parentheses ($\sqrt{}$) is placed immediately below the column total. This check mark in parentheses indicates that the amount shown as the column total is not posted to any account.

The ledger accounts in Illustration 6.2 show only the postings from the cash receipts journal.

The Accounts Receivable control account in the general ledger appears as follows after both the sales and cash receipts journals have been posted:

Accounts Receivable					Account No. 111
Date	Explanation	Post. Ref.	Debit	Credit	Balance
1984 Apr. 30		SJ1	2 9 0		2 9 0 Dr.
30		CRJ5		2 2 5	6 5 Dr.

Illustration 6.3 shows the subsidiary ledger accounts at the same point in time.

A schedule of accounts receivable is prepared at the end of the month in order to make certain that the total of the balances in the subsidiary ledger accounts agrees with the control account. This schedule is merely a listing of open account balances and appears as follows:

JOHN MASON COMPANY
Schedule of Accounts Receivable
As of April 30, 1984

Peter Cote	$10
Anthony Demambro	55
Balance in the controlling account ...	$65

Combined sales and cash receipts journal

It is possible to combine the sales and cash receipts journals. A combined sales and cash receipts journal is illustrated in Demonstration Problem 6–1 at the end of the chapter. In considering whether or not to combine these journals, posting and journalizing convenience is only one consideration. Remember that having separate sales and cash receipts journals allows more people to work with the data in the journals at the same time.

The purchases journal

The purchases journal is used to record all purchases of merchandise made on account. There are a number of designs which could be used for the purchases journal. A common form is one having only one money column,

Illustration 6.3: Subsidiary accounts receivable ledger

JOHN MASON COMPANY
SUBSIDIARY ACCOUNTS RECEIVABLE LEDGER
Arthur Benson

Date		Explanation	Post. Ref.	Debit	Credit	Balance
1984 Apr.	3		SJ1	5 0		5 0 Dr.
	6		CRJ5		5 0	– 0 –

Peter Cote

Date		Explanation	Post. Ref.	Debit	Credit	Balance
1984 Apr.	4		SJ1	2 5		2 5 Dr.
	19		SJ1	1 0		3 5 Dr.
	19		CRJ5		2 5	1 0 Dr.

Anthony Demambro

Date		Explanation	Post. Ref.	Debit	Credit	Balance
1984 Apr.	30		SJ1	5 5		5 5 Dr.

Kenneth Johnson

Date		Explanation	Post. Ref.	Debit	Credit	Balance
1984 Apr.	12		SJ1	1 5 0		1 5 0 Dr.
	20		CRJ5		1 5 0	– 0 –

headed Purchases Dr. and Accounts Payable Cr. The headings in a purchase journal with one money column might be as follows:

Date	Creditor	Terms	Invoice No.	Purchases Dr. Accounts Payable Cr.	
				Amount	√

If there are several departments for which purchases are made, a separate purchases column could be provided for each department. The headings in such a journal might appear as follows:

Purchases Dr.			Date	Creditor	Terms	Invoice No.	Accounts Payable Cr.	
Dept. A	Dept. B	Dept. C					Amount	✓

Illustration 6.4 shows a purchases journal having one money column. In Illustration 6.4, eight purchases of merchandise on account were made during the month.

Posting the purchases journal.　Individual amounts in the money column are posted daily to the accounts payable subsidiary ledger so the subsidiary accounts will be current at all times. The money column total is posted to the Purchases account as a debit and to the Accounts Payable account as a credit at the end of the month.

Cash disbursements journal

The cash disbursements journal is used to record all transactions that involve the payment of cash. The management of most businesses is aware that in order to have an acceptable level of control over cash disbursements, all bills should be paid by check. Therefore, the cash disbursements journal (Illustration 6.5) contains a column in which to record the number of the check written for the disbursement.

Payments on accounts payable constitute a major type of cash disbursement transaction. Thus, a column entitled Accounts Payable Dr. is provided. Many payments on account will involve a purchase discount, so a separate column is provided for discounts. The John Mason Company also purchases numerous supplies by writing a check; and, therefore, the journal has a separate column for Supplies Expense.

Posting the cash disbursements journal.　As shown in Illustration 6.5, individual items in the Accounts Payable Dr. column are posted daily to accounts in the accounts payable subsidiary ledger. Individual items in the Other Accounts column are posted daily to the appropriate accounts in the general ledger. The column totals for Accounts Payable Dr., Supplies Expense Dr., Cash Cr., and Purchase Discounts Cr. are posted at the end of the month to accounts in the general ledger. The total of the Other Accounts Dr. column is not posted. The only amounts shown in the accounts in Illustration 6.5 are those from the posting of the cash disbursements journal to make it easier to trace the postings.

Illustration 6.4: Purchases journal

JOHN MASON COMPANY
PURCHASES JOURNAL   Page 10

Date		Creditor	Terms	Invoice No.	Purchases Dr. 401 Accounts Payable Cr. 201	
					Amount	✓
1984 Apr.	1	Smith Corporation	2/10, n/30	862	200	✓
	7	Lasky Company	1/15, n/60	121	100	✓
	12	Booth Corporation	2/10, n/60	561	5,000	✓
	15	Gooch Corporation	2/10, n/30	1042	3,000	✓
	21	Wyngarden Company	3/15, n/60	633	10,000	✓
	26	Mertz Company	2/10, n/30	734	300	✓
	30	Nelson Company	2/10, n/30	287	4,000	✓
	30	Booth Corporation	2/20, n/60	568	1,500	✓
					24,100	
					(401)(201)	

Individual amounts are posted daily

Total is posted at end of month

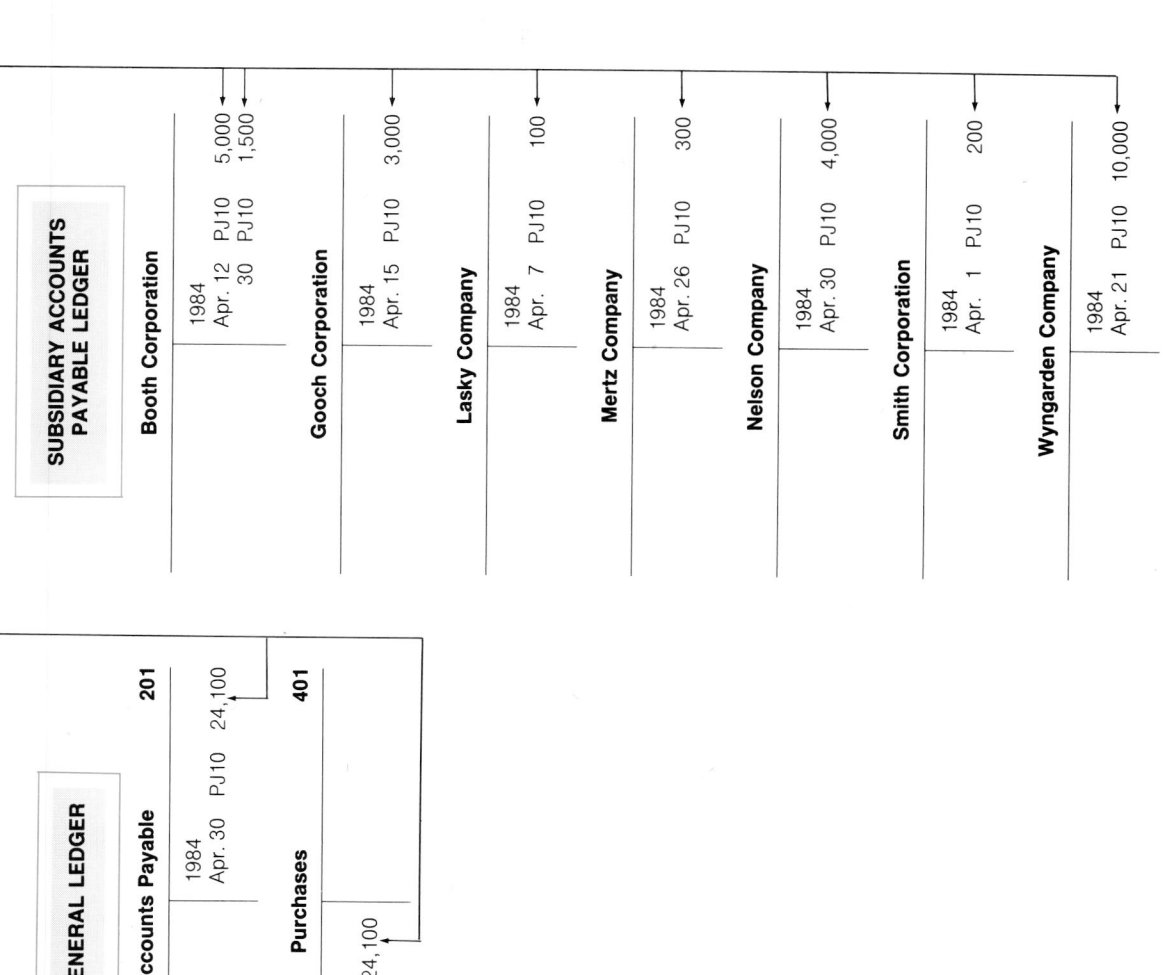

SUBSIDIARY ACCOUNTS
PAYABLE LEDGER

Booth Corporation

1984		
Apr. 12	PJ10	5,000
30	PJ10	1,500

Gooch Corporation

1984		
Apr. 15	PJ10	3,000

Lasky Company

1984		
Apr. 7	PJ10	100

Mertz Company

1984		
Apr. 26	PJ10	300

Nelson Company

1984		
Apr. 30	PJ10	4,000

Smith Corporation

1984		
Apr. 1	PJ10	200

Wyngarden Company

1984		
Apr. 21	PJ10	10,000

GENERAL LEDGER

Accounts Payable   **201**

1984		
Apr. 30	PJ10	24,100

Purchases   **401**

1984		
Apr. 30	PJ10	24,100

Illustration 6.5: Cash disbursements journal

JOHN MASON COMPANY
CASH DISBURSEMENTS JOURNAL

Page 7

201 Accounts Payable Dr. Amount	✓	422 Supplies Expense Dr.	Other Accounts Dr. Account Title	Acct. No	Amount	✓	Date	Description	Check No.	101 Cash Cr.	402 Purchase Discounts Cr.
		42					1984 Apr. 2	Brooklyn Square Paint Company	524	42	
			Prepaid Insurance	123	1,200	✓	3	Insurance policy to cover May 1 1984—April 30, 1985	525	1,200	
			Furniture and Equipment	140	500	✓	4	Furniture—office	526	500	
			Rent Expense	423	200	✓	4	Rent for April 1984	527	200	
200	✓						8	Smith Corporation—Invoice No. 862	528	196	4
		10					14	Allan Park Stationery Company	529	10	
100	✓						18	Lasky Company—Invoice No. 121	530	99	1
5,000	✓						21	Booth Corporation—Invoice No. 561	531	4,900	100
10,000	✓						27	Wyngarden Company—Invoice No. 633	532	9,700	300
3,000	✓						28	Gooch Corporation—Invoice No. 1042	533	3,000	
18,300		52			1,900					19,847	405
(201)		(422)			(✓)					(101)	(402)

Individual amounts in the Accounts Payable Dr. and Other Accounts Dr. columns are posted daily

Total is not posted

Totals are posted at the end of the month

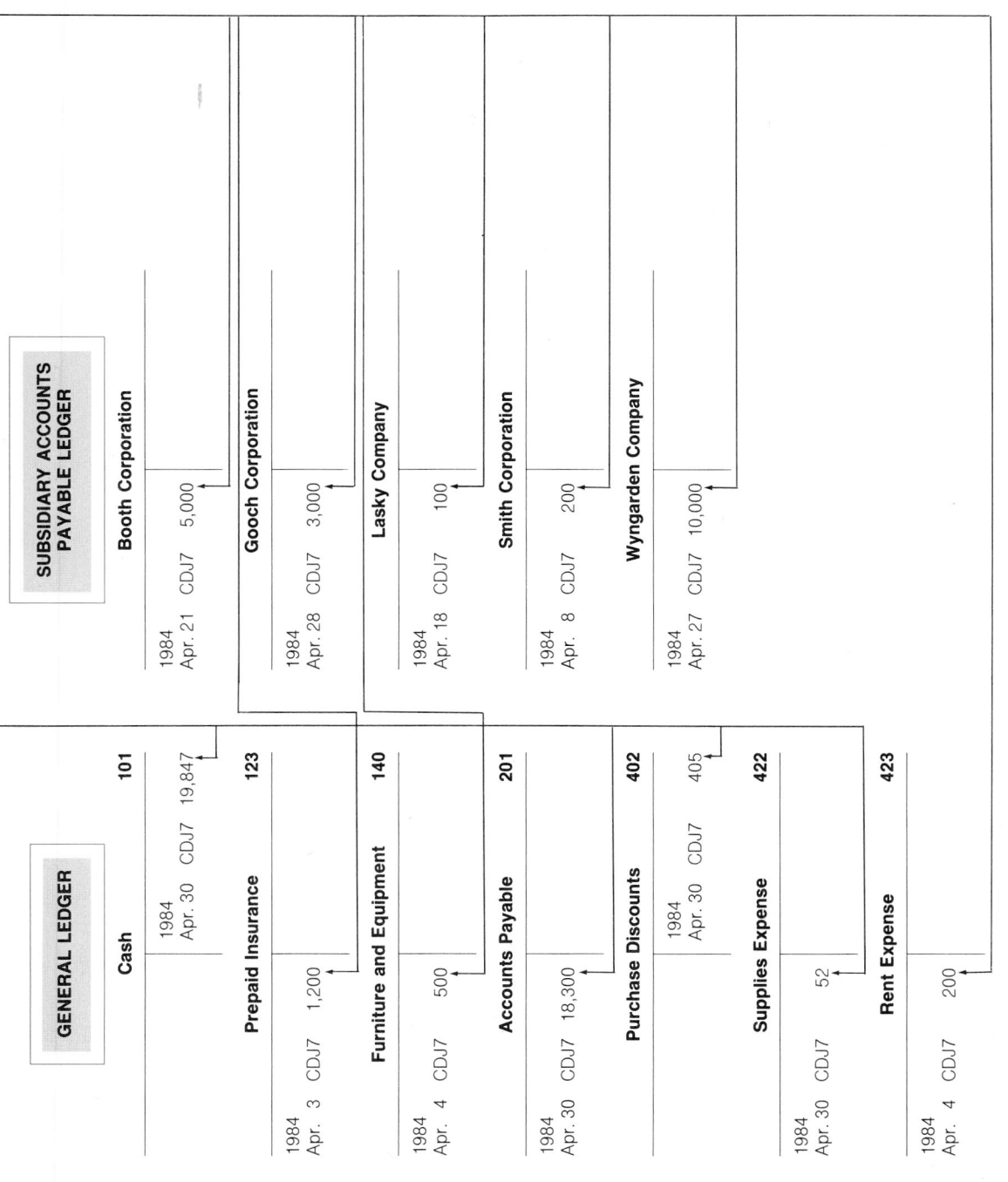

SUBSIDIARY ACCOUNTS PAYABLE LEDGER

GENERAL LEDGER

Booth Corporation

1984
Apr. 21   CDJ7   5,000

Gooch Corporation

1984
Apr. 28   CDJ7   3,000

Lasky Company

1984
Apr. 18   CDJ7   100

Smith Corporation

1984
Apr. 8   CDJ7   200

Wyngarden Company

1984
Apr. 27   CDJ7   10,000

Cash   101

1984
Apr. 30   CDJ7   19,847

Prepaid Insurance   123

1984
Apr. 3   CDJ7   1,200

Furniture and Equipment   140

1984
Apr. 4   CDJ7   500

Accounts Payable   201

1984
Apr. 30   CDJ7   18,300

Purchase Discounts   402
                                            405

1984
Apr. 30   CDJ7

Supplies Expense   422

1984
Apr. 30   CDJ7   52

Rent Expense   423

1984
Apr. 4   CDJ7   200

The general ledger Accounts Payable control account appears as follows after both the purchases and cash disbursements journals have been posted.

		Accounts Payable					Account No. 201
Date	Explanation	Post. Ref.	Debit	Credit	Balance
1984 Apr. 30		PJ10		2 4 1 0 0	2 4 1 0 0 Cr.
30		CDJ7	1 8 3 0 0		5 8 0 0 Cr.

The subsidiary accounts payable ledger, Illustration 6.6, appears as follows after both the purchase journal and the cash disbursements journal have been posted.

Illustration 6.6: Subsidiary accounts payable ledger

JOHN MASON COMPANY
SUBSIDIARY ACCOUNTS PAYABLE LEDGER
Booth Corporation

Date	Explanation	Post. Ref.	Debit	Credit	Balance
1984 Apr. 12		PJ10		5 0 0 0	5 0 0 0 Cr.
21		CDJ7	5 0 0 0		– 0 –
30		PJ10		1 5 0 0	1 5 0 0 Cr.

Gooch Corporation

Date	Explanation	Post. Ref.	Debit	Credit	Balance
1984 Apr. 15		PJ10		3 0 0 0	3 0 0 0 Cr.
28		CDJ7	3 0 0 0		– 0 –

Lasky Company

Date		Explanation	Post. Ref.	Debit	Credit	Balance
1984 Apr.	7		PJ10		1 0 0	1 0 0 Cr.
	18		CDJ7	1 0 0		– 0 –

Mertz Company

Date		Explanation	Post. Ref.	Debit	Credit	Balance
1984 Apr.	26		PJ10		3 0 0	3 0 0 Cr.

Nelson Company

Date		Explanation	Post. Ref.	Debit	Credit	Balance
1984 Apr.	30		PJ10		4 0 0 0	4 0 0 0 Cr.

Smith Corporation

Date		Explanation	Post. Ref.	Debit	Credit	Balance
1984 Apr.	1		PJ10		2 0 0	2 0 0 Cr.
	8		CDJ7	2 0 0		– 0 –

Wyngarden Company

Date		Explanation	Post. Ref.	Debit	Credit	Balance
1984 Apr.	21		PJ10		1 0 0 0 0	1 0 0 0 0 Cr.
	27		CDJ7	1 0 0 0 0		– 0 –

A schedule of accounts payable is prepared at the end of the month as follows:

JOHN MASON COMPANY
Schedule of Accounts Payable
As of April 30, 1984

Booth Corporation	$1,500
Mertz Company	300
Nelson Company	4,000
Balance in the controlling account	$5,800

A combined purchases and cash disbursements journal

It would be possible to combine the purchases and the cash disbursements journals. A combined purchases and cash disbursements journal is illustrated in Demonstration Problem 6–2 at the end of the chapter. But use of a combined journal limits the number of persons who can work with the data in the journals at any one time.

General ledger illustrated

After all four special journals have been posted, the general ledger appears as shown in Illustration 6.7.

Illustration 6.7: General ledger

JOHN MASON COMPANY
GENERAL LEDGER
Cash   *Account No. 101*

Date		Explanation	Post. Ref.	Debit	Credit	Balance
1984 Apr.	1	Beginning balance (assumed)				1 0 0 0 0 Dr.
	30		CRJ5	3 5 4 2 1		4 5 4 2 1 Dr.
	30		CDJ7		1 9 8 4 7	2 5 5 7 4 Dr.

Accounts Receivable   *Account No. 111*

Date		Explanation	Post. Ref.	Debit	Credit	Balance
1984 Apr.	30		SJ1	2 9 0		2 9 0 Dr.
	30		CRJ5		2 2 5	6 5 Dr.

Prepaid Insurance   *Account No. 123*

Date		Explanation	Post. Ref.	Debit	Credit	Balance
1984 Apr.	3		CDJ7	1 2 0 0		1 2 0 0 Dr.

Land   *Account No. 138*

Date		Explanation	Post. Ref.	Debit	Credit	Balance
1984 Apr.	1	Beginning balance (assumed)				1 8 0 0 0 Dr.
	10		CRJ5		6 0 0 0	1 2 0 0 0 Dr.

Furniture and Equipment   *Account No. 140*

Date		Explanation	Post. Ref.	Debit	Credit	Balance
1984 Apr.	4		CDJ7	5 0 0		5 0 0 Dr.

Accounts Payable   *Account No. 201*

Date		Explanation	Post. Ref.	Debit	Credit	Balance
1984 Apr.	30		PJ10		2 4 1 0 0	2 4 1 0 0 Cr.
	30		CDJ7	1 8 3 0 0		5 8 0 0 Cr.

John Mason, Capital   *Account No. 250*

Date		Explanation	Post. Ref.	Debit	Credit	Balance
1984 Apr.	1	Beginning balance (assumed)				2 8 0 0 0 Cr.

Illustration 6.7 (*concluded*)

GENERAL LEDGER (*concluded*)

Sales
Account No. 301

Date		Explanation	Post. Ref.	Debit	Credit	Balance
1984 Apr.	30		SJ1		290	290 Cr.
	30		CRJ5		29000	29290 Cr.

Sales Discounts
Account No. 302

Date		Explanation	Post. Ref.	Debit	Credit	Balance
1984 Apr.	30		CRJ5	4		4 Dr.

Miscellaneous Revenue
Account No. 303

Date		Explanation	Post. Ref.	Debit	Credit	Balance
1984 Apr.	26		CRJ5		200	200 Cr.

Purchases
Account No. 401

Date		Explanation	Post. Ref.	Debit	Credit	Balance
1984 Apr.	30		PJ10	24100		24100 Dr.

Purchase Discounts
Account No. 402

Date		Explanation	Post. Ref.	Debit	Credit	Balance
1984 Apr.	30		CDJ7		405	405 Cr.

Supplies Expense					*Account No. 422*
Date	Explanation	Post. Ref.	Debit	Credit	Balance
1984 Apr. 30		CDJ7	5 2		5 2 Dr.

Rent Expense					*Account No. 423*
Date	Explanation	Post. Ref.	Debit	Credit	Balance
1984 Apr. 4		CDJ7	2 0 0		2 0 0 Dr.

The general journal and other journals

Each transaction that does not belong in a special journal is entered in the general journal. All adjusting and closing entries would be made in the general journal. For instance, the general journal would be used to record depreciation expense of $1,500 on an office building as follows:

```
Depreciation Expense—Office Building .............................    1,500
      Accumulated Depreciation—Office Building. ......................          1,500
   To record depreciation expense.
```

The general journal could also be used to record the receipt of a note from a customer in settlement of an account receivable. A note would allow the company to begin earning interest on the amount due. An example of such an entry would be as follows:

```
Notes Receivable .............................................    2,000
      Accounts Receivable—A. Smith .................................          2,000
   To record the receipt of a 60-day, 12 percent note from Alex Smith
   in settlement of his account receivable.
```

Other types of transactions which would be recorded in the general journal include the purchase of equipment or some other asset by giving a note, the payment of an account payable by giving a note, sales returns and allowances, and purchase returns and allowances. For instance, the entry to record a sales allowance of $100 granted to John Burke for damaged merchandise is:

```
Sales Returns and Allowances .......................................     100
      Accounts Receivable—J. Burke .................................          100
   To record a sales allowance of $100 to John Burke for
   damaged merchandise.
```

Advantages of special journals

To summarize, the following advantages are obtained from the use of special journals.

a. *Time is saved in journalizing.*   Only one line is used for each transaction; usually a full description is not necessary. The amount of writing is reduced because it is not necessary to repeat the account titles printed at the top of the special column or columns.

b. *Time is saved in posting.*   Many amounts are posted as column totals rather than individually.

c. *Detail is eliminated from the general ledger.*   Column totals are posted to the general ledger, and the detail is left in the special journals.

d. *Division of labor is promoted.*   Several persons can work simultaneously on the accounting records. This specialization and division of labor pinpoints responsibility and allows for more rapid location of errors.

e. *Use of accounting machines is facilitated.*   The mass of routine transactions recorded in special journals frequently makes the use of accounting machines economical.

f. *Management analysis is aided.*   The journals themselves can be useful to management in analyzing classes of transactions, such as credit sales, because all similar transactions are in one place.

ALTERNATIVE METHODS OF PROCESSING DATA

The range of equipment that the accountant may be working with in a business situation is extensive, ranging from hand-posted special journals to use of a large computer. Some of the available alternatives for processing data are discussed briefly.

Hand-posted system

All accounting entries are recorded by hand; journals are summarized and posted to the general ledger. This system is typical of many of today's smaller businesses in which the accounting function is handled by the accountant and possibly one or two clerks. Such a system was illustrated in this chapter.

Bookkeeping machine system

The basic nature of a bookkeeping machine system is not much different from the hand-posted system. The bookkeeping machine system is generally set up in such a way that those transactions recurring most often are recorded on bookkeeping machines. The machines can post transactions to the general ledger and subsidiary ledger accounts and compute new balances. Typical applications include sales and receivables postings.

Mini-computers

Mini-computers are available which can be used to maintain the accounting records for a small business. These small business computers also have many other uses. Since the cost of these computers is so low, they have replaced many hand-posted and bookkeeping machine systems.

Service bureaus

Many firms have found it economical to have certain transactions (e.g., payroll, inventory, and accounts receivable) processed by a local service bureau. A *service bureau* is a large computer facility that rents out computer time to clients. Service bureaus usually can meet the specific output requirements of a firm if some advance planning is done.

Time-sharing terminals

Significant advances have been made in the field of computer time sharing. *Time sharing* occurs when several users utilize the same host computer to process data. The users literally share time on the computer. It is now possible to have a remote terminal in almost every business firm. The terminals are connected through telephone lines or radio waves to a host computer operated by an independent company. The host computer can be called up by the person operating the remote terminal. Typical applications involve large amounts of transactions data (e.g., printing and summarizing sales invoices, updating inventory records, and updating accounts receivable and accounts payable records). Note that the remote terminal must serve as both an input and output device. Thus, the amount of time before output is received may be longer than with a computer which has separate input and output equipment.

In-house computer

Many business firms purchase their own computer to process data. Where the volume of transactions is very large, the decision to purchase a computer is often justified. The Appendix contains more information about computers.

APPENDIX: THE PROCESSING OF DATA—ELECTRONIC SYSTEM

THE COMPUTER

The search for greater speed, accuracy, and storage capacity has presented a persistent challenge to both the designers of information systems and the accounting profession. This challenge has been met over the years through the increasing use of more sophisticated devices. The most recent device has been the computer. Use of the computer has permitted human participation in the processing function to be limited to the preparation of input (transaction) data and the set of instructions telling the computer how these data should be processed. If properly programmed, the computer is capable of journalizing and posting transactions with great speed and a high degree of accuracy.

The distinguishing features of a computer are its ability to accept instructions for the processing of transaction data, store those instructions, and execute them any number of times precisely in the desired sequence. The computer uses elementary numerical logic to alter the sequence of instructions by observing the outcome of a numeric or alphabetic comparison. An example of the use of such a comparison is an instruction to test whether the cash balance is zero before each transaction and to continue processing cash disbursements only if the balance is greater than zero. The computer has the capability to remain exceedingly accurate even at very high calculating speeds. Since sets of operating instructions are given to the computer at the outset, human effort is conserved. Performance of repetitive tasks, routine numerical decision making, and certain types of logical decision making are taken over by the computer.

COMPUTER COMPONENTS

The computer consists of three basic components: *a storage unit, an arithmetic unit,* and *a control unit.* The **storage unit** (sometimes called core storage) of a computer is its internal *memory* system. It is the most expensive component of the computer. To determine the optimum size of internal core storage, speed and cost factors must be considered. Generally, the greater the speed and storage required, the greater the cost. Problems requiring more storage space than originally provided in the computer can be solved by utilizing peripheral devices such as disks, drums, or tape units for temporary external storage.

The **arithmetic unit** of a computer contains devices that perform computations and comparisons.

The **control unit** of a computer is the unit that interprets the **program** (the set of **instructions** submitted to the computer that specifies the operations to be performed and the correct sequence), assigns storage space, and alters the sequence of operations if so instructed by the program. This unit can do only what it is told to do by the program. If the unit encounters a situation for which it has been given no explicit instructions, it will instruct the computer to halt operations. After finding and correcting the problem situation, the computer operator can restart the processing by means of a **console** that allows the operator to exercise control over the computer when necessary.

Peripheral equipment can be attached to the computer and used mainly to feed unprocessed information into and receive processed information from the computer. Examples of peripheral equipment are tape drives, card readers, and printers. The way in which these components are connected and controlled varies from computer to computer.

Illustration 6.8:   Main elements of a computer

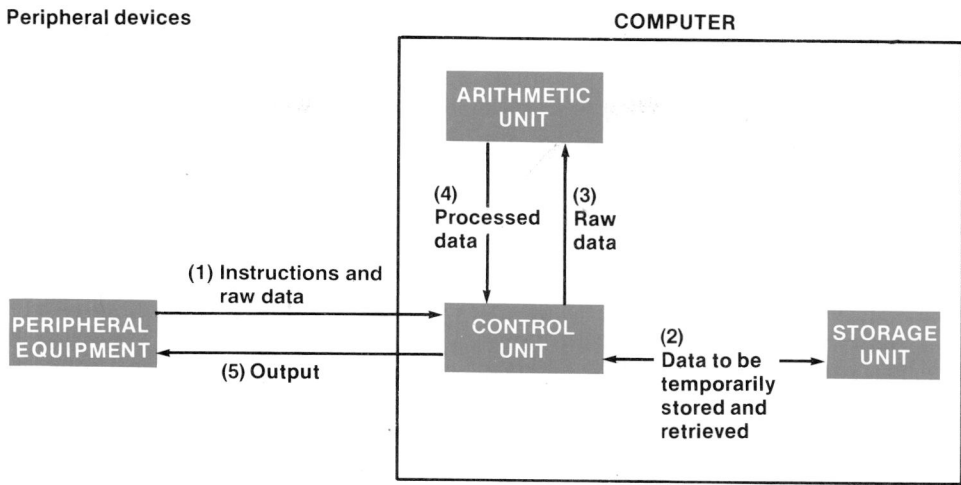

Illustration 6.8 shows a schematic design of a simple computer system. The control unit controls operation of the system. The peripheral equipment is not part of the computer but is used to transmit data into and out of the computer as directed by the control unit. The control unit sends the data to the storage unit until there is time available to process the data. At that time, the data are recalled from storage and transferred to the arithmetic unit where the required arithmetic operations are performed. Upon completion, processed data are sent by the control unit either to the peripheral equipment or, if there is more processing to be done using the data, the data will be sent back to storage. The peripheral equipment will display the processed output in a predefined format.

APPLICATIONS OF ELECTRONIC DATA PROCESSING TO ACCOUNTING

Typical accounting examples of electronic data processing applications are in the areas of payroll, accounts receivable, accounts payable, and inventory.

Nearly all applications of data processing, and particularly those that involve the accounting process, make considerable use of *files*. A *file* is any grouping of similar data arranged in an identifiable order. For example, the accounts receivable ledger is a file: data are the individual invoices and other open items, and the data may be stored by customer number. As transactions with customers occur, processing is undertaken to update this file; the end result is a new, updated accounts receivable file created by the computer. Other files include accounts payable and inventory.

NEW TERMS INTRODUCED IN CHAPTER 6

Arithmetic unit
A central component of a computer; it performs computations and comparisons.

Cash disbursements journal
A special journal used for all payments of cash by the business.

Cash receipts journal
A special journal used for all transactions involving the inflow of cash into the business.

Console
The component of an electronic computer system that enables an operator to communicate manually with the system and start, stop, or alter operations.

Control account
An account in the general ledger that shows the aggregate balance of all the subsidiary accounts to which it is related.

Control unit
The unit of a computer that interprets the program, assigns storage space, and alters the sequence of operations if so instructed by the program.

File
A group of related data treated as a separate unit. This may be a group of cards or a reel of magnetic tape.

General journal
A general purpose journal used to record all transactions that cannot be entered in one of the special journals.

Instructions
Coded information that causes the computer's control unit to perform specified operations.

Internal auditing
Consists of investigating and evaluating compliance by employees regarding company policies and procedures. Internal auditing is performed by company personnel.

Internal control system
The plan of organization and all the procedures and actions taken by an entity to (1) protect its assets against theft and waste, (2) ensure compliance with company policies and federal law, (3) evaluate the performance of personnel in all parts of the company so as to promote efficiency of operations, and (4) ensure accurate and reliable operating data and accounting reports.

Mini-computers
Small computers that can be used to maintain the accounting records for a small business.

Other accounts
Miscellaneous accounts.

Peripheral equipment
Can be attached to a computer and used mainly to feed unprocessed information into and receive processed information from the computer.

Program
The set of instructions submitted to the computer that specifies the operations to be performed and the correct sequence.

Purchases journal
A special journal used to record all purchases of merchandise on credit.

Sales journal
A special journal used to record all sales of merchandise on credit

Service bureau
A large computer facility that rents out computer time to clients.

Storage unit
A computer's internal memory system; it serves to record and retain data until they are required by and transferred to other areas of the computer.

Subsidiary account
The individual record a business maintains for each customer or creditor.

Subsidiary ledger
A group of related accounts showing the details of the balance of a general ledger control account.

Time sharing
A system whereby several users utilize the same computer to process data.

DEMONSTRATION PROBLEM 6–1

The chapter mentioned, but did not illustrate, that the sales journal and cash receipts journal could be combined.

Required:

Using the data in illustrations 6.1 and 6.2, prepare a combined sales and cash receipts journal for the John Mason Company. Show all the posting marks as they would be made.

Solution to demonstration problem 6–1

COMBINED SALES AND CASH RECEIPTS JOURNAL

101 Cash Dr.	302 Sales Discounts Dr.	✓	111 Accounts Receivable Dr. Amount	✓	Date	Description	Invoice No.	301 Sales Cr.	111 Accounts Receivable Cr. Amount	✓	Other Accounts Cr. Account Title	Acct. No.	Amount	✓
					1984 Apr.									
5,000					1	Cash sales		5,000						
		✓	50		3	Arthur Benson	100	50						
		✓	25		4	Peter Cote	101	25						
49	1				6	Arthur Benson	100		50	✓				
8,000					7	Cash sales		8,000						
6,000					10	Sold land at cost to Wells Corporation					Land	138	6,000	✓
		✓	150		12	Kenneth Johnson	102	150						
7,000					14	Cash sales		7,000						
		✓	10		19	Peter Cote	103	10						
25					19	Peter Cote	101		25	✓				
147	3				20	Kenneth Johnson	102		150	✓				
9,000					25	Cash sales		9,000						
200					26	Cash received from sale of scrap					Miscellaneous Revenue	303	200	✓
		✓	55		30	Anthony Demambro	104	55						
35,421	4		290					29,290	225				6,200	
(101)	(302)		(111)					(301)	(111)				(✓)	

DEMONSTRATION PROBLEM 6–2

The chapter mentioned, but did not illustrate, that the purchases journal and the cash disbursements journal could be combined.

Solution to demonstration problem 6–2

COMBINED PURCHASES AND CASH DISBURSEMENTS JOURNAL

401 Purchases Dr.	201 Accounts Payable Dr. Amount	✓	422 Supplies Expense Dr.	Other Accounts Dr. Account Title	Acct. No.	Amount	✓
200							
			42				
				Prepaid Insurance	123	1,200	✓
				Furniture and Equipment	140	500	✓
				Rent Expense	423	200	✓
100							
	200	✓					
5,000							
			10				
3,000							
	100	✓					
10,000							
	5,000	✓					
300							
	10,000	✓					
	3,000						
4,000							
1,500							
24,100	18,300		52			1,900	
(401)	(201)		(422)			(✓)	

Required:

Using the data in Illustrations 6.4 and 6.5, prepare a combined purchases and cash disbursements journal for the John Mason Company. Show all the posting marks as they would be made.

Date	Terms	Invoice No.	Description	Check No.	101 Cash Cr.	402 Purchase Discounts Cr.	201 Accounts Payable Cr. Amount	✓
1984								
Apr. 1	2/10,n/30	862	Smith Corporation				200	✓
2			Brooklyn Square					
			Paint Company	524	42			
3			Insurance policy to					
			cover May 1, 1984—					
			April 30, 1985	525	1,200			
4			Furniture—office	526	500			
4			Rent for April 1984	527	200			
7	1/15,n/60	121	Lasky Company				100	✓
8			Smith Corporation—					
			Invoice No. 862	528	196	4		
12	2/10,n/60	561	Booth Corporation				5,000	✓
14			Allan Park Sta-					
			tionery Company	529	10			
15	2/10,n/30	1042	Gooch Corporation				3,000	✓
18			Lasky Company—					
			Invoice No. 121	530	99	1		
21	3/15,n/60	633	Wyngarden Company				10,000	✓
21			Booth Corporation—					
			Invoice No. 561	531	4,900	100		
26	2/10,n/30	734	Mertz Company				300	✓
27			Wyngarden Company—					
			Invoice No. 633	532	9,700	300		
28			Gooch Corporation—					
			Invoice No. 1042	533	3,000			
30	2/10,n/30	287	Nelson Company				4,000	✓
30	2/20,n/60	568	Booth Company				1,500	✓
					19,847	405	24,100	
					(101)	(402)	(201)	

QUESTIONS

1. What purposes should a system of internal control accomplish?

2. Identify some features that, if present, would strengthen the internal control system.

3. Why might a firm, even if its management knew how to set up a foolproof system of internal accounting control, not choose to do so?

4. Name some control documents that are used in merchandise transactions.

5. The processing of data is usually very costly. Why bother with this task?

6. Is the balance of a controlling account equal to the total of its subsidiary accounts at all times? Explain.

7. In a hand-posted system, the subsidiary accounts receivable and accounts payable accounts usually do not have account numbers. Why?

8. How can you tell whether a special journal has been completely posted? Describe the posting marks.

9. Describe the purpose of each of the following journals by giving the types of entries that would be recorded in each: sales, purchases, cash receipts, cash disbursements, and general.

10. Identify the alternative methods of processing data.

EXERCISES

E–1. State whether each of the following statements about internal control is true or false:

a. Those responsible for safeguarding an asset should maintain the accounting records for that asset.

b. Complete and accurate accounting records should be maintained on a current basis.

c. Whenever possible, responsibilities should be assigned and duties subdivided in such a way that only one person is responsible for a given function.

d. Employees should be assigned to one job and should remain in that job so that skill levels will be as high as possible.

e. The use of check protectors, check registers, and time clocks is recommended.

f. An internal auditing function should not be implemented because it leads the employees to believe that management does not trust them.

g. One of the best protections is to hire honest, competent employees.

h. A foolproof system of internal control can be devised if management puts forth the effort.

E–2. Concerning internal control, which one of the following statements is correct? Explain.

a. Broadly speaking, internal control is only necessary in very large organizations.

b. The purposes of internal control are to check the accuracy of accounting data, safeguard assets against theft, promote efficiency of operations, and ensure that management's policies are being followed.

c. Once an internal control system has been established, it should be effective as long as the formal organization remains unchanged.

d. An example of internal control is where one individual counts the day's cash receipts and compares the total with the total of the cash register tapes.

E–3. The correct accounts receivable subsidiary ledger account balances for a company are as follows on a given date:

```
Apple . . . . . . . . .    $300
Crandle . . . . . . .      400
Rogers . . . . . . . .     600
Taylor . . . . . . . .     500
```

Using T-accounts, show how these accounts would appear and what the balance on this same date would be in the controlling account in the general ledger. If the balance in the controlling account is $2,000, what should be done?

E–4. You are employed by a company that has three selling departments. You are asked to design a sales journal that will provide a departmental breakdown of credit sales. Give the column headings that you would use and describe how postings would be made.

E–5. The column totals of a cash receipts journal were as follows:

```
Cash Dr. . . . . . . . . . . . . . . . . . . . . .    $39,400
Sales Discounts Dr. . . . . . . . . . . . . .          200
Sales Cr. . . . . . . . . . . . . . . . . . . . . .     20,000
Accounts Receivable Cr. . . . . . . . . .     10,000
Other accounts Cr. (sold land
  at cost for $9,000 and
  sold scrap for $600) . . . . . . . . . .       9,600
```

Using T-accounts, post the amounts which appear in the cash receipts journal. How would the individual amounts in the Accounts Receivable Cr. column be posted? How would the information in the Other Accounts Cr. column be posted?

E–6. Match each transaction in column A with the appropriate journal in which it would be recorded in column B. Assume each of the journals listed is used as a book of original entry and is designed as illustrated in the chapter.

Column A	*Column B*
1. Acquired merchandise on account.	a. Sales journal.
2. Recorded depreciation expense.	b. Cash receipts journal.
3. Sold merchandise on account.	c. Purchases journal.
4. Sold merchandise for cash.	d. Cash disbursements journal.
5. Collected cash on account.	e. General journal.
6. Gave a note to a trade creditor.	
7. Received cash for services performed.	
8. Granted a sales allowance to a customer.	
9. Paid rent for the month.	
10. Received notice of a purchase allowance from a trade creditor.	
11. Paid a trade creditor.	
12. Recorded closing entries at the end of the period.	

E–7. Which of the following figures would be posted to the general ledger?

a. The Cash Cr. column total in the cash disbursements journal.

b. The Other Accounts Dr. column total in the cash disbursements journal.

c. The individual items in the purchases journal.

d. The individual items in the sales journal.

E–8.   (Based on the Appendix)   Match each description in column A with the appropriate term in column B.

Column A	Column B
1. A computer's internal memory system.	a. Program.
2. Equipment that is attached to the computer.	b. Arithmetic unit.
3. A part of the computer that interprets the program.	c. Service bureau.
4. Any grouping of similar items of data arranged in some identifiable order.	d. Peripheral equipment.
5. A part of a computer that does the computing.	e. Mini-computer.
6. A set of instructions submitted to a computer that specifies the operations to be performed and their correct sequence.	f. File.
7. A large computer facility that rents out time for data processing.	g. Storage unit.
8. A small computer that can be used to maintain the accounting records for a small company.	h. Control unit.

PROBLEMS, SERIES A

P6–1–A.   a. The Clark Clothing Store sold goods on account to the following persons on the dates indicated:

Date	Customer	Invoice No.	Amount
1984			
June 1	John James	200	$300
4	Peter Cool	201	200
12	Joseph Branch	202	400
18	Jerry Inglema	203	600
29	Craig Jacobi	204	500

Required:

Record the transactions on page 1 of a sales journal. Then, using T-accounts, post the data to accounts in the general ledger and subsidiary accounts receivable ledger.

b. The Walker Book Store purchased merchandise from the following companies on the dates indicated:

Date	Customer	Terms	Invoice No.	Amount
1984				
July 3	Able Company	2/10, n/30	240	$2,000
5	Crane Company	1/15, n/30	360	1,000
14	Greer Company	2/20, n/30	142	4,000
22	Rextex Corporation	2/20, n/60	58	5,000
30	Zeetex Corporation	2/10, n/30	410	7,000

Required:

Record the transactions on page 10 of a purchases journal. Then, using T-accounts, post the data to accounts in the general ledger and subsidiary accounts payable ledger.

P6–2–A. On August 31, 1984, the Accounts Receivable control account on the books of the Wholesale Furniture Store was equal to the total of the accounts in the subsidiary accounts receivable ledger. The balances were as follows: Accounts Receivable control account (Account No. 120), $90,000; Battle Corporation, $36,000; Ferguson Company, $30,000; and East Corporation, $24,000.

Required:

Prepare a sales journal (Illustration 6.1) and cash receipts journal (Illustration 6.2). Also set up a general journal. Then using the following information:

    a. Completely journalize the transactions in the appropriate journals.

    b. Post only the amounts pertaining to accounts receivable to the subsidiary accounts and to the control account. You will have to prepare additional subsidiary accounts and should keep them all in alphabetical order. You will need additional accounts for Miles Corporation, Newton Company, and Oliva Company.

    c. Prepare a schedule of accounts receivable at September 30, 1984, and compare it with the balance of the control account at the same date.

Transactions (ignore the fact that normally the terms to all customers are the same):

Sept. 1 Received $13,720 from the Ferguson Company. A discount of $280 had been taken.
2 On this date, merchandise was sold on account for $22,000 to the Oliva Company; Invoice No. 501; terms, 2/20, n/30.
4 Cash sales, $50,000.
7 Received $18,000 on account from the Battle Corporation. No discount was taken.
8 Received $40,000 cash for land sold at cost.
12 Sold merchandise on account to the Ferguson Company, $18,000; Invoice No. 502; terms, n/30.
15 Received payment for $10,000 of the merchandise purchased on September 2 by the Oliva Company. The discount was taken on this payment.
18 Sold merchandise on account to the Miles Corporation, $68,000; Invoice No. 503; terms, n/30.
21 Cash sales, $114,000.
23 Allowed credit to Miles Corporation for $2,000 for goods returned.
26 Sold merchandise on account to the Newton Company, $20,000; Invoice No. 504; terms, 2/20, n/30.
29 Received $20,000 cash from the Miles Corporation to apply against the amount due on Invoice No. 503.
30 Cash sales were $78,000.

P6–3–A. On August 31, 1984, the Accounts Payable control account on the books of the Wholesale Furniture Store was equal to the total of the accounts in the subsidiary accounts payable ledger. The balances were as follows: Accounts Payable control account (Account No. 220), $72,000; Helzburg Company, $32,000; Zales Corporation, $24,000; and Bond Corporation, $16,000.

Required:

Prepare a purchases journal (Illustration 6.4) and cash disbursements journal (Illustration 6.5). Also set up a general journal. Then using the following information:

    a. Completely journalize each of the transactions in the appropriate journals.

    b. Post only the amounts pertaining to accounts payable to the subsidiary accounts and to the control account. You will have to create some additional subsidiary accounts.

You should arrange all subsidiary accounts in alphabetical order. You will need additional accounts for Jane Company, New Point Corporation, Quarter Company, Werling Company, and York Corporation.

    c. Prepare a schedule of accounts payable at September 30, 1984, and compare it with the balance of the control account at the same date.

Transactions:

Sept. 1 Purchased merchandise on account costing $30,000 from the Werling Company; Invoice No. 542; terms, 2/10, n/30.

       3 Paid the Bond Corporation $16,000 with Check No. 451. The original discount of 2 percent was not taken, as the discount period had expired.

       4 Paid rent for the month of September, $1,000, with Check No. 452.

       5 Paid the Helzburg Company $18,000 on account with Check No. 453. No discount was offered.

       6 Gave the Helzburg Company a $14,000, 30-day, 12 percent note for the balance due.

       7 Purchased merchandise on account costing $16,000 from the York Corporation; Invoice No. 982; terms, 2/10, n/30.

       8 Purchased merchandise on account costing $18,000 from the Bond Corporation; Invoice No. 1522; terms, 2/10, n/30.

       9 Received credit from the York Corporation for returning $2,000 of the $16,000 of merchandise purchased.

     12 Paid the Werling Company the amount due on the purchase of September 1 with Check No. 454.

     15 Purchased merchandise on account costing $24,000 from the New Point Corporation; Invoice No. 841; terms, n/30.

     17 Paid Bond Corporation the amount due on the purchase of September 8 with Check No. 455.

     20 Purchased merchandise on account costing $26,000 from the Bond Corporation; Invoice No. 1566; terms, 2/10, n/30.

     22 Purchased merchandise on account costing $14,000 from the Quarter Company; Invoice No. 1910; terms, n/30.

     25 Paid $16,000 on account to the New Point Corporation on the purchase of September 15 with Check No. 456.

     29 Received credit for $6,000 from the Bond Corporation for returning part of the merchandise purchased on September 20.

     30 Purchased merchandise on account having a cost of $10,000 from the Jane Company; Invoice No. 2125; terms, n/60.

P6–4–A.   Demonstration Problem 6–1 of this chapter illustrated a combined sales and cash receipts journal, and Demonstration Problem 2 illustrated a combined purchases and cash disbursements journal.

Required:

    a. Set up a *combined* sales and cash receipts journal similar to that shown in Demonstration Problem 6–1.

    b. Set up a *combined* purchases and cash disbursements journal using Demonstration Problem 6–2 as a guide. Include only those columns which are needed. No column is needed for Supplies Expense Dr.

    c. Set up a general journal.

    d. Journalize the transactions shown in both Problems P6–2–A and P6–3–A in the journals you have created.

    e. Post the amounts to the general ledger accounts shown below after entering the August 31, 1984, balances. Use three-column format for the accounts. You do not have to post to subsidiary accounts, but place the appropriate posting marks in the journals as if you had.

      f. Prepare a trial balance as of September 30, 1984.

      g. Why are combined journals not always used?

Account No.	Account title	Assumed balances after closing on August 31, 1984
110	Cash	$ 80,000
120	Accounts Receivable	90,000
150	Land.....................................	40,000
220	Accounts Payable	72,000
221	Notes Payable	–0–
250	K. Mustang, Capital	138,000
300	Sales	–0–
303	Sales Discounts	–0–
307	Sales Returns and Allowances	–0–
400	Purchases	–0–
404	Purchase Discounts	–0–
406	Purchase Returns and Allowances	–0–
407	Rent Expense	–0–

P6–5–A.   The West Department Store uses five journals as records of original entry. They are as follows: sales journal, cash receipts journal, purchases journal, cash disbursements journal, and general journal. At December 31, 1984, the column totals in the sales journal were as follows:

Accounts Receivable Dr.	Sales Cr.					
	Men's Clothing	Women's Clothing	Shoes	Cosmetics and Jewelry	Sporting Goods	Miscellaneous
81,000	20,000	25,000	8,400	8,000	15,600	4,000

The totals of the cash receipts journal columns were as follows:

Cash Dr.	Sales Discounts Dr.	Sales Cr.							Accounts Receivable Cr.	Other Accounts Cr.
		Men's Clothing	Women's Clothing	Shoes	Cosmetics and Jewelry	Sporting Goods	Miscel-laneous			
140,200	1,120	12,000	16,000	6,600	12,000	6,400	8,000		72,000	8,320

The entries in the Other Accounts Cr. column result from the sale of land at cost of $6,320 (December 4) and $2,000 of revenue from the operation of a delivery service for other companies (December 31).

    The column totals in the purchases journal were as follows:

Purchases Dr.						Accounts Payable Cr.
Men's Clothing	Women's Clothing	Shoes	Cosmetics and Jewelry	Sporting Goods	Miscellaneous	
28,000	38,000	12,000	15,000	27,800	8,000	128,800

The column totals of the cash disbursements journal columns were as follows:

Accounts Payable Dr.	Supplies Expense Dr.	Other Accounts Dr.	Cash Cr.	Purchase Discounts Cr.
117,000	19,400	15,800	149,400	2,800

The entries in the Other Accounts Dr. column result from the payment of $1,920 for a delivery truck (December 7) and $13,880 for the purchase of a garage (December 15).

The two-column general journal includes the following entry during the month:

Dec. 21 Buildings 17,400
              Notes Payable   17,400

An abbreviated trial balance of the general ledger immediately prior to posting the above journals for the year was as follows:

WEST DEPARTMENT STORE
Trial Balance
December 31, 1984

	Debits	Credits
Cash	$ 35,000	
Accounts receivable	24,000	
Inventory—men's clothing	12,000	
Inventory—women's clothing	20,000	
Inventory—shoes	2,000	
Inventory—cosmetics and jewelry ...	8,000	
Inventory—sporting goods	11,000	
Inventory—miscellaneous	2,600	
Office equipment	10,000	
Accumulated depreciation—office equipment		$ 3,400
Land	6,320	
Buildings	80,000	
Accumulated depreciation— buildings		19,400
Accounts payable		20,200
Notes payable		2,000
A. West, capital		165,920
	$210,920	$210,920

Required:

a.   Present the general ledger of the West Department Store, including the balances in the above trial balance and postings based on the other data given in the problem. Use three-column format. After posting, prepare a trial balance.

b.   Assuming the following ending inventory amounts, prepare a statement showing the gross margin of each department (ignore sales discounts and purchase discounts).

Department	Ending inventory
Men's clothing	$15,000
Women's clothing	10,000
Shoes	4,000
Cosmetics and jewelry	14,000
Sporting goods	20,000
Miscellaneous	2,000

P6–6–A.   The Bush Microcomputer Store uses special journals for sales, cash receipts, purchases, and cash disbursements, as well as a general journal. These journals follow the same general design as those illustrated in this chapter.

Required:

a.   Enter the following transactions for August 1984 in the proper journals. All journal pages are to be numbered page 5.

b.   Post the entries to the general ledger accounts shown below. There would usually be beginning balances in the accounts but they may be ignored.

c.   Prepare a trial balance as of the end of the period. General ledger accounts are:

1. Cash.
2. Accounts Receivable.
3. Notes Receivable.
4. Office Equipment.
5. Accounts Payable.
6. Notes Payable.
7. Sales.
8. Sales Discounts.
9. Purchases.
10. Purchase Discounts.
11. Delivery Expense.
12. Advertising Expense.
13. Rental Revenue.

Transactions:

Aug. 1 Sold Cod, Inc., a $6,000 computer on account; terms, 2/10, n/30; Invoice No. WI-A1.
     3 Bought computer merchandise on account from the Brad Company; Invoice No. 33-NP; terms, n/10, $4,200.
     5 Cash sales, $19,000.
     9 Rent revenue received, $800.
    11 Received amount due from Cod, Inc., for sale of August 1. The discount was taken.
    11 Paid for office equipment received today, $2,400 (Check No. 132). The equipment was for the company's own use.
    12 Paid Brad Company for purchase of August 3 (Check No. 133).
    14 Sold a $4,000 computer on account to McGuinn, Inc.; Invoice No. WI-A2; terms, 2/10, n/30.
    15 Sold a $1,400 computer on account to Franks Company; Invoice No. WI-A3; terms, 2/10, n/30.
    15 Bought computer merchandise on account from Brad Company, $1,980; Invoice No. 34-NP; terms, n/10.
    17 Bought computer merchandise on account from Brown Company, $3,000; Invoice No. 98-VX; terms, 2/10, n/30.
    18 Bought office equipment today for $1,900 and gave a 30-day, 12 percent note in payment. The equipment was for the company's own use.
    19 Received a 90-day, 12 percent note receivable for an account receivable (Paul McAllister) in the amount of $700.
    19 Cash sales of computer software, $3,600.
    20 Collected $1,540 on account from Charles Barfield.
    21 Cash sales of computer software, $2,240.
    22 Cash sales of computer software, $600.
    23 Collected net amount due from McGuinn, Inc., on sale of August 14.
    24 Collected net amount due from Franks Company on sale of August 15.
    25 Paid Brad Company on invoice of August 15 (Check No. 134).
    26 Paid Brown Company on invoice of August 17 (Check No. 135).

Aug. 28   Paid delivery expense in cash, $800 (Check No. 136).
28   Paid advertising expense in cash, $1,600 (Check No. 137).
29   Sold two computers for $7,400 on account to the Franks Company; Invoice No. WI-A4; terms, 2/10, n/30.
30   Sold three computers for $9,800 on account to McGuinn, Inc.; Invoice No. WI-A5; terms, 2/10, n/30.
31   Bought computer merchandise on account from the Brad Company, $1,780; Invoice No. 137-NP; terms, n/10.

P6–7–A.   Bill Clark, the golf professional at the Evergreen Country Club, has been using a general journal to record all business transactions. The volume of business has been increasing, and now he seeks your assistance in devising some special journals. He wants his wife to keep track of all receipts, disbursements, and adjusting entries in her office at home. He and his assistant are to record all credit sales and purchases at the golf shop.

Sales are classified as follows: Golf Equipment, Golf Supplies, Apparel, Lessons, Cart Rental, and Miscellaneous Services. Sales are made for both cash and on account. No sales discounts are offered.

Purchases are made from many different suppliers. Items purchased include apparel, golf supplies, and golf equipment. Periodic inventory procedure is used.

Required:

   a.   Determine which special journals should be used.

   b.   Show the column headings which could be used in each of the special journals. Illustrate the use of each special journal by journalizing enough assumed transactions for 1984 so that at least one number appears in each of the columns you have designed.

   c.   Describe the posting of each of the special journals you have designed.

PROBLEMS, SERIES B

P6–1–B.   *a.*   The Dixson Stereo Store sold merchandise on account to the following customers on the dates indicated:

Date	Customer	Invoice No.	Amount
1984			
Dec. 2	Susan Moore	300	$100
8	Margarett Allen	301	800
14	Barbara Malloy	302	600
21	Janet Gibson	303	400
31	Susan Miller	304	300

Required:

Record the transactions on page 5 of a sales journal. Using T-accounts, then post the data to accounts in the general ledger and subsidiary accounts receivable ledger.

   b.   The Dana Appliance Store purchased merchandise from the following companies on the dates indicated:

Date	Creditor	Terms	Invoice No.	Amount
1984				
Sept. 2	Baker Company	2/20, n/60	642	$10,000
7	Dexter Company	2/10, n/30	441	12,000
15	Hanley Corporation	2/EOM	543	4,000
23	Stanton Company	1/15, n/30	286	9,000
28	Welker Corporation	2/10, n/30	324	15,000

Required:

Record the transactions on page 20 of a purchases journal. Using T-accounts, then post the data to accounts in the general ledger and subsidiary accounts payable ledger.

P6–2–B.   On June 30, 1984, the Accounts Receivable control account on the books of the Graves Wholesale Shoe Company was equal to the total of the accounts in the subsidiary accounts receivable ledger. The balances were as follows: Accounts Receivable control account (Account No. 131), $17,180; Billings, Inc., $6,600; Haygood Products, Inc., $3,080; and Johnson Company, $7,500.

Required:

Prepare a sales journal (Illustration 6.1) and cash receipts journal (Illustration 6.2). Also set up a general journal. Then using the following information:

a.   Completely journalize each of the transactions in the appropriate journal.

b.   Post only the amounts pertaining to accounts receivable to the subsidiary accounts and to the control account. You will have to set up some additional subsidiary accounts. Keep all subsidiary accounts in alphabetical order. You will need additional accounts for the Glasco Company, May Company, and Wilson Company.

c.   Prepare a schedule of accounts receivable at July 31, 1984, and compare it with the balance of the control account at the same date.

Transactions (ignore the fact that usually the terms to all customers are the same):

July 1   Sales of merchandise on account to Johnson Company, $1,200; Invoice No. 306; terms, n/30.
   3   Cash sales, $3,450.
   5   Received cash for land sold at its original cost of $5,000.
   5   Received $4,500 cash as partial collection of amount due today from Billings, Inc. No discount was allowed.
   9   Sold merchandise on account to the Glasco Company, $900; Invoice No. 307; terms, 3/10, n/30.
   11   Received $3,018.40 from Haygood Products, Inc. A discount of 2 percent of the account balance was granted.
   16   Sold merchandise on account to the Wilson Company, $1,000; Invoice No. 308; terms, n/30.
   18   Sold merchandise on account to Haygood Products, Inc., $1,800; Invoice No. 309; terms, n/30.
   20   Allowed Haygood Products, Inc., credit for $250 on goods returned to Graves on Invoice No. 309.
   22   Sold $1,200 of merchandise to Billings, Inc.; Invoice No. 310; terms, n/10.
   23   Received cash of $4,000 on balance due today from Johnson Company. No discount was taken.
   25   Sold $1,500 of merchandise on account to Billings, Inc.; Invoice No. 311; terms, n/10.
   27   Allowed Billings, Inc., credit of $100 on goods sold July 25 and damaged in transit due to faulty packing by Graves Company.
   31   Sold $1,300 of merchandise on account to the May Company; Invoice No. 312; terms, 2/10, n/30.
   31   Cash sales, $20,600.

P6-3-B.   On June 30, 1984, the Accounts Payable control account on the books of the Graves Wholesale Shoe Company was equal to the total of the accounts in the subsidiary accounts payable ledger. The balances were as follows: Accounts Payable control account (Account No. 201), $15,500; Gate Company, $7,050; Jones Corporation, $2,450; and White Company, $6,000.

Required:

Prepare a purchases journal (Illustration 6.4) and a cash disbursements journal (Illustration 6.5). Also set up a general journal. Then using the following information:

a.   Completely journalize each of the transactions in the appropriate journal.

b.   Post only the amounts pertaining to accounts payable to the subsidiary accounts and to the control account. You should arrange all subsidiary accounts in alphabetical order. You will need additional accounts for Andrews Corporation, Hall Company, Dodge Company, and Sand Corporation.

c.   Prepare a schedule of accounts payable at July 31, 1984, and compare it with the balance of the control account at the same date.

Transactions:

July 1   Purchased merchandise on account costing $5,000 from the Hall Company; Invoice No. 562; terms, 2/10, n/30.
      2   Paid the Gate Company $5,000 on account with Check No. 101. No discount was available when the purchase was originally made.
      3   Paid rent for the month of July with Check No. 102, $600.
      5   Gave the Jones Corporation a 60-day, 12 percent note for the amount owed.
      6   Purchased merchandise on account costing $2,500 from the Gate Company; Invoice No. 261; terms, 2/10, n/30.
      9   Paid $4,900 to the Hall Company on the July 1 purchase with Check No. 103.
     11   Paid $2,000 for a life insurance policy on top executives to cover the period from August 1, 1984, to July 31, 1985. Used Check No. 104.
     17   Purchased merchandise on account costing $4,000 from the Hall Company; Invoice No. 581; terms, 2/10, n/30.
     21   Received credit from the White Company for $1,000 on merchandise returned to it. No discount was available as of the date of purchase.
     23   Purchased merchandise on account costing $1,500 from the Andrews Corporation; Invoice No. 1031; terms, n/30.
     25   Paid $3,000 to White Company with Check No. 105. No discount was allowed as of the date of purchase.
     27   Purchased merchandise on account costing $3,500 from the Sand Corporation; Invoice No. 328; terms, 2/10, n/30.
     29   Paid the Hall Company $2,000 on the purchase of July 17, Check No. 106.
     31   Purchased merchandise on account costing $4,000 from the Dodge Company; Invoice No. 168; terms, 2/20, n/60.

P6-4-B.   Demonstration Problem 6-1 of this chapter illustrated a combined sales and cash receipts journal and Demonstration Problem 6-2 illustrated a combined purchases and cash disbursements journal.

Required:

a.   Set up a *combined* sales and cash receipts journal similar to that shown in Demonstration Problem 6-1.

b.   Set up a *combined* purchases and cash disbursements journal using Demonstration Problem 2 as a guide. Include only those columns which are needed. No column is needed for Supplies Expense Dr.

c.   Set up a general journal.

d. Journalize the transactions shown in both Problems P6–2–B and P6–3–B in the journals you have created.

e. Post the amounts to the general ledger accounts shown below after entering the June 30, 1984, balances. Use three-column format for the accounts. You do not have to post to subsidiary accounts, but place the appropriate posting marks in the journals as if you had.

f. Prepare a trial balance as of July 31, 1984.

g. Why are combined journals not always used?

Account No.	Account title	Assumed balances after closing on June 30, 1984
130	Cash	$15,000
131	Accounts Receivable	17,180
133	Prepaid Insurance	–0–
150	Land....................................	5,000
201	Accounts Payable	15,500
202	Notes Payable	–0–
250	B. Graves, Capital	21,680
300	Sales	–0–
304	Sales Discounts	–0–
307	Sales Returns and Allowances	–0–
400	Purchases	–0–
405	Purchase Discounts	–0–
406	Purchase Returns and Allowances	–0–
407	Rent Expense	–0–

P6–5–B. The Hunnicut Department Store uses five journals as records of original entry. They are as follows: sales journal, cash receipts journal, purchases journal, cash disbursements journal, and general journal. At December 31, 1984, the column totals in the sales journal were as follows:

Accounts Receivable Dr.	Sales Cr.					
	Men's Clothing	Women's Clothing	Appliances	Furniture	Bargain Basement	Other Departments
112,750	20,000	22,500	17,500	30,000	15,000	7,750

The column totals of the cash receipts journal columns were as follows:

Cash Dr.	Sales Discounts Dr.	Sales Cr.						Accounts Receivable Cr.	Other Accounts Cr.
		Men's Clothing	Women's Clothing	Appliances	Furniture	Bargain Basement	Other Departments		
166,500	1,538	11,250	12,500	10,000	16,250	6,000	6,750	96,413	8,875

The entries in the Other Accounts Cr. column result from the collection of $6,500 of rental revenue (December 8) and $2,375 of miscellaneous revenue from the sale of scrap (December 14).

The column totals in the purchases journal were as follows:

Purchases Dr.						Accounts Payable Cr.
Men's Clothing	Women's Clothing	Appliances	Furniture	Bargain Basement	Other Departments	
26,250	27,000	13,750	25,500	18,750	10,875	122,125

The column totals of the cash disbursements journal columns were:

Accounts Payable Dr.	Supplies Expense Dr.	Other Accounts Dr.	Cash Cr.	Purchase Discounts Cr.
96,500	13,750	11,388	120,888	750

The entries in the Other Accounts Dr. column result from the payment of $638 for ordinary repairs to the buildings (December 15) and $10,750 for the purchase of a warehouse (December 22).

The general journal includes the following entry at the date indicated:

Dec. 18	Office Equipment	2,000	
	Notes Payable		2,000

An abbreviated trial balance of the general ledger immediately prior to posting the above journals for the year was as follows:

HUNNICUT DEPARTMENT STORE
Trial Balance
December 31, 1984

	Debits	Credits
Cash	$ 17,500	
Accounts receivable	13,750	
Notes receivable	1,250	
Inventory—men's clothing	3,750	
Inventory—women's clothing	4,500	
Inventory—appliances	3,000	
Inventory—furniture	7,000	
Inventory—bargain basement	1,750	
Inventory—other departments	1,250	
Office equipment	5,000	
Accumulated depreciation—office equipment		$ 2,000
Buildings	70,000	
Accumulated depreciation—buildings		13,750
Accounts payable		10,875
L. Hunnicut, capital		102,125
	$128,750	$128,750

Required:

a.   Present the general ledger of the Hunnicut Department Store including the balances in the above trial balance and postings based on the other data given in the problem. After posting, prepare a trial balance.

b.   Given the following data, compute the gross margin for each of the departments (ignore sales discounts and purchase discounts).

Department	Ending inventory
Men's clothing	$5,000
Women's clothing	3,750
Appliances	1,250
Furniture	2,500
Bargain basement	750
Other	1,000

P6–6–B.   The McGuire Wholesale Food Company uses special journals for sales, cash receipts, purchases, and cash disbursements, as well as a general journal. These journals follow the same general design as those illustrated in this chapter.

Required:

   a.   Enter the following transactions for December 1984 in the proper journals. All journals are to be numbered page 4.

   b.   Post the entries to the general ledger accounts shown below. There would be beginning balances in the accounts, but they may be ignored.

   c.   Prepare a trial balance as of the end of the period: General ledger accounts:

1. Cash.
2. Accounts Receivable.
3. Office Equipment.
4. Accounts Payable.
5. Notes Payable.
6. Sales.
7. Sales Discounts.
8. Purchases.
9. Purchase Discounts.
10. Advertising Expense.
11. Rental Revenue.

Transactions:

Dec. 1 Purchased merchandise on account from Dixon Company, $5,600; Invoice No. C1109; terms, 2/10, n/30.
2 Purchased merchandise on account from Bailey Company, $3,200; Invoice No. 1888Z; terms, n/10.
3 Bought office equipment from Harrell Company, $7,760; Invoice No. 854. Gave a 30-day, 12 percent note in payment.
5 Purchased merchandise on account from Abel Company, $4,400; Invoice No. X9784; terms, 2/10, n/30.
6 Cash sales, $5,680.
7 Collected rent revenue for December, $7,600.
8 Sold $4,000 of merchandise on account to David, Inc.; Invoice No. 3345; terms, 2/10, n/30.
9 Collected $6,000 on an overdue account receivable from R. Ray.
10 Sold $5,600 of merchandise on account to Potts Company; Invoice No. 3346; terms, 2/10, n/30.
11 Sold $6,400 of merchandise on account to Zap Company; Invoice No. 3347; terms, 2/10, n/30.
12 Paid Dixon Company for purchase of December 1 with Check No. 201.
12 Paid Baily Company for purchase of December 2 with Check No. 202.
14 Paid Abel Company for purchase of December 5 with Check No. 203.
16 Cash sales, $15,760.
18 Collected amount due on sale of December 8 to David, Inc.
20 Collected amount due on sale of December 10 to Potts Company.
21 Collected amount due on sale of December 11 to Zap Company.
23 Cash sales, $10,000.
24 Paid *The Newton News* for advertising expense, $600 (Check No. 204).
26 Sold $4,800 of merchandise on account to Zap Company; Invoice No. 3348; terms, 2/10, n/30.
26 Sold $11,200 of merchandise on account to Dee Company; Invoice No. 3349; terms, 2/10, n/30.

Dec. 27 Sold $23,760 of merchandise on account to Kote Company; Invoice No. 3350; terms, 2/10, n/30.

P6–7–B. Mike David, the owner and operator of Mike's Bowling Lanes, has been using a general journal to record all business transactions. The posting task has taken an increasing amount of his time. He asks your assistance in designing special journals which would make the task less time consuming.

His wife is to handle all of the credit purchases, cash disbursements, and adjusting entries in her office at home. Mike or his assistant will record all sales and cash receipts at the bowling lanes.

Sales are classified as follows: Bowling Fees, Equipment, Supplies, Shoe Rental, and Miscellaneous Services. (The adjoining restaurant and bar are owned and operated by another party.) Sales are made for both cash and credit. No sales discounts are offered.

Purchases are made from various suppliers. Periodic inventory procedure is used.

Required:

a. Determine which special journals should be used.

b. Show the column headings that could be used in each of the special journals. Illustrate the use of the special journals by journalizing a sufficient number of assumed transactions for 1984 so that at least one number appears in each of the columns you have designed.

c. Describe the posting of each of the special journals you have designed.

BUSINESS DECISION PROBLEM 6–1

During World War II, a managerial accountant in the United States was called back to active duty with the Army. An acquaintance of the accountant forged papers and assumed the identity of the accountant. He obtained a position in a small firm as the only accountant. Eventually he took over (from the manager) the functions of approving bills for payment, preparing and signing checks, and almost all other financial duties. On one weekend, he traveled to some neighboring cities and prepared and mailed invoices made out to the company he worked for. On Monday morning, he returned to work and began receiving, approving, and paying the invoices he had prepared. The following weekend he returned to the neighboring cities and cashed and deposited the checks in bank accounts under his own signature card. After continuing this practice for several months, he withdrew all of the funds and never was heard from again.

Required:

Discuss some of the steps which could have been taken to prevent this theft. Remember that it is a small firm with limited financial resources.

BUSINESS DECISION PROBLEM 6–2

You are the manager of a restaurant which has an ice cream parlor as a separate unit. Your accountant comes in once a year and prepares financial statements and the tax return. In the current year you have a feeling that even though business seems good, net income is going to be lower. You ask the accountant to prepare condensed statements on a monthly basis. All sales are priced to yield an estimated gross margin of 40 percent. You and your accountant and several of the accountant's assistants take physical inventories at the end of each of the four months indicated below. The resulting sales, cost of goods sold, and gross margins are as follows:

	March		April	
	Restaurant	Ice cream parlor	Restaurant	Ice cream parlor
Sales	$36,300	$53,000	$39,050	$42,750
Cost of goods sold	23,275	31,500	23,800	31,000
Gross margin	$13,025	$21,500	$15,250	$11,750

	May		June	
	Restaurant	Ice cream parlor	Restaurant	Ice cream parlor
Sales	$38,100	$39,000	$41,250	$35,500
Cost of goods sold	22,975	30,750	25,500	31,125
Gross margin	$15,125	$ 8,250	$15,750	$ 4,375

Required:

What would you suspect after analyzing these reports? What sales control procedures would you recommend to correct the bad situation?

BUSINESS DECISION PROBLEM 6–3

Cite some of the factors that you feel would be important in deciding whether a company should utilize an accounting (bookkeeping) machine, a time-sharing facility, a service bureau, or a computer system installed at the firm.

COMPREHENSIVE REVIEW PROBLEM

The Sportswear Outlet Store sells sporting equipment, clothes, and shoes for use in sports such as tennis, golf, skiing, jogging, racketball, and so on. The company, which has been in business for about five years, is owned and operated by Jack Springs. Most sales are for cash, but some are on credit. Financial statements are prepared at the end of each month. The post-closing trial balance as of November 30, 1984, appears as follows:

SPORTSWEAR OUTLET STORE
Post-Closing Trial Balance
November 30,1984

Account No.		Debits	Credits
1	Cash	$18,000	
2	Accounts receivable	5,000	
3	Prepaid insurance	700	
4	Supplies on hand	1,200	
5	Merchandise inventory	25,000	
6	Office furniture	4,000	
7	Accumulated depreciation— office furniture		$ 1,770
8	Store equipment	10,000	
9	Accumulated depreciation— store equipment		4,720
10	Accounts payable		4,500
11	Jack Springs, capital		52,910
		$63,900	$63,900

The chart of accounts for the Sportswear Outlet Store is as follows:

Account No.	Account title	Account No.	Account title
1	Cash	15	Sales Returns and Allowances
2	Accounts Receivable	16	Miscellaneous Revenue
3	Prepaid Insurance	17	Purchases
4	Supplies on Hand	18	Purchase Discounts
5	Merchandise Inventory	19	Purchase Returns and Allowances
6	Office Furniture	20	Transportation-In
7	Accumulated Depreciation—Office Furniture	21	Rent Expense
8	Store Equipment	22	Insurance Expense
9	Accumulated Depreciation—Store Equipment	23	Supplies Expense
10	Accounts Payable	24	Depreciation Expense—Office Equipment
11	Jack Springs, Capital	25	Depreciation Expense—Store Equipment
12	Jack Springs, Drawing	26	Income Summary
13	Sales		
14	Sales Discounts		

Schedules of accounts receivable and accounts payable prepared at November 30, 1984, are as follows:

SPORTSWEAR OUTLET STORE
Schedule of Accounts Receivable
As of November 30, 1984

Sallie Branscom	$ 800
Cindy Carrel	900
Charles Coleman	750
John Grant	1,100
James Hood	1,000
V. P. Stone	450
	$5,000

SPORTSWEAR OUTLET STORE
Schedule of Accounts Payable
As of November 30, 1984

Athletic Shoe Corporation	$ 900
Rackets, Inc.	1,500
Sports Clothes, Inc.	2,100
	$4,500

The company uses a sales journal, cash receipts journal, purchases journal, cash disbursements journal, and general journal.

Required:

a. Enter the beginning balances for December 1984 into the general ledger accounts, the subsidiary accounts receivable ledger accounts, and the subsidiary accounts payable ledger accounts.

b. Journalize in the appropriate journal the transactions given below for the month of December. All special journal pages should be identified as page No. 6.

c. Post the data in the journals to the appropriate general ledger and subsidiary ledger accounts.

d. Prepare a work sheet as of December 31, 1984. Use the additional data given below to prepare the necessary adjustments on the work sheet.

e. Prepare a classified income statement and balance sheet. Rent expense, depreciation expense—store equipment, and supplies expense are the only selling expenses.

f. Journalize in the general journal the adjusting entries and closing entries. The adjusting entries are to be entered on page 6 of the general journal, and the closing entries are entered on page 7 of the general journal.

g. Post the adjusting entries and closing entries to the general ledger accounts.

h. Prepare a post-closing trial balance.

i. Prepare a schedule of accounts receivable and a schedule of accounts payable at December 31.

Transactions:

Dec. 1 Paid rent for use of the sales building for the month of December, $1,600; Check No. 200.
2 Cash sales were $4,200.
4 Sold merchandise on account to Sallie Branscom, $250; Invoice No. 512; terms, 2/10, n/30.
5 Received payment on account from the following customers:

Name	Gross amount	Discount taken	Net amount received
Cindy Carrel	$ 900	$18	$ 882
Charles Coleman ..	750	15	735
John Grant	1,100	22	1,078
James Hood	1,000	20	980

7 Paid Rackets, Inc., $1,500 on account after deducting a 2 percent discount; Check No. 201.
8 Paid Sports Clothes, Inc., $2,100 on account after deducting a 2 percent discount; Check No. 202.
10 Cash sales were $7,200.
12 Granted a sales allowance to Sallie Branscom for $100 because of damaged merchandise.
14 Received payment from Sallie Branscom, $700. No discount was taken.
15 Paid the Athletic Shoe Corporation $900; Check No. 203. No discount was involved.
17 Purchased $2,800 of sports equipment on account from Rackets, Inc.; Invoice No. 210; terms, 2/10, n/30, FOB destination.
19 Cash sales were $6,600.
20 Purchased $1,700 of sports clothing on account from Sports Clothes, Inc.; Invoice No. 620; terms, n/30, FOB shipping point.
20 Paid freight charge of $60 to the Rapid Delivery Company on today's purchase from Sports Clothes, Inc., Check No. 204.
21 The owner withdrew $1,000 to cover living expenses; Check No. 205.
22 Received payment on account from V. P. Stone, $450. No discount was taken.
23 Purchased $1,000 of sports shoes on account from the Athletic Shoe Corporation; Invoice No. 125; terms, n/30, FOB destination.
24 Sold merchandise on account to John Grant, $850; Invoice No. 513; terms, 2/10, n/30.
26 Paid the invoice for the purchase on December 17 after taking the discount; Check No. 206.
26 Sold merchandise to James Hood, $900; Invoice No. 514; terms, 2/10, n/30.
27 Cash sales were $4,500.
28 Sold merchandise on account to Janice Thompson, $910; Invoice No. 515; terms, 2/10, n/30.
29 Purchased $2,400 of clothing on account from Sports Clothes, Inc.; Invoice No. 1006; terms, n/30, FOB shipping point.
29 Paid freight of $40 to the Rapid Delivery Company for today's purchase from Sports Clothes, Inc., Check No. 207.

Dec. 30 Sold merchandise on account to Jim Westerling, $1,200; Invoice No. 516; terms, 2/10, n/30.
   31 Received a $200 allowance on the purchase of December 29 because some of the merchandise was damaged.
   31 Cash sales were $2,100.
   31 Received $100 from the sale of scrap materials located on the premises.

Additional data:

1. Of the prepaid insurance, $150 expired in December.
2. The supplies on hand at December 31 were $900.
3. Depreciation expense on the office furniture for December was $30.
4. Depreciation expense on the store equipment for December was $80.
5. The merchandise inventory on December 31 was $20,000.

Part Three

Assets and liabilities

Chapter 7

Control of cash

CHAPTER GOALS

After study of this chapter, you should be able to:

1. Define cash and list the objectives sought by management in handling the company's cash.

2. Identify procedures for controlling cash receipts and disbursements.

3. Prepare a bank reconciliation statement and make necessary journal entries based on that statement.

4. Explain why a petty cash fund is used, describe its operation, and make the necessary journal entries.

5. Apply the net price method of handling purchase discounts.

6. Describe the operation of the voucher system and make entries in its special journals—the check register and the voucher register.

7. Define and use correctly the new terms in the glossary.

Cash includes currency, coins, undeposited negotiable instruments such as checks, bank drafts, and money orders, amounts in checking or savings accounts, and demand certificates of deposit. A *certificate of deposit* is an interest-bearing deposit at a bank that can be withdrawn at will (demand CD) or at a fixed maturity date (time CD). Cash does not include postage stamps, IOUs, or notes receivable. For general ledger purposes, generally two cash accounts are maintained: Cash (bank checking account balance) and Petty Cash. For financial reporting purposes, the two cash balances are combined into one amount and reported as "Cash."

Management must control and account for cash carefully. Many business transactions involve cash, making it a vital factor in business operations. Cash is also easily mishandled through either theft or carelessness. Management's objectives in regard to cash are to:

1. Account for all cash transactions accurately so that correct information will be available regarding cash flows and balances.
2. Make certain there is enough cash available to pay bills as they come due.
3. Avoid holding too much idle cash because excess cash could be invested to generate income, such as interest.
4. Prevent loss of cash due to theft or fraud.

Most of a firm's cash transactions involve a checking account. The firm deposits cash receipts in a checking account and writes checks to pay its bills. The firm receives a bank statement each month. A reconciliation between the firm's Cash account balance and the bank's balance is prepared to determine if any corrections or adjustments are needed in either balance. Considerable attention is devoted in this chapter to the bank reconciliation statement; but, first, procedures used to control cash receipts and disbursements are discussed. Later in the chapter petty cash and the voucher system are discussed.

CONTROLLING CASH RECEIPTS

From the moment cash is received until it is deposited in the bank, it should be carefully safeguarded. All assets need to be protected from theft or mishandling, but cash is more likely to be the object of theft because it (1) is easily concealed, (2) is not readily identifiable, and (3) can be quickly spent to acquire other things of value.

Although the specific procedures for controlling cash receipts vary with each business, several basic principles are:

1. A record of all cash receipts should be prepared as soon as cash is received. Most thefts of cash occur before a record is made of the receipt. Once a record is made, it is easier to trace improper uses.
2. All cash receipts should be deposited on the day received or the next business day. Cash disbursements should not be made from cash receipts but only by check or from petty cash funds. In many retail stores, refunds

for returned merchandise are made from the cash register. If this practice is followed, refund tickets should be prepared and approved by a supervisor.

3. The person who handles cash receipts should not record them in the accounting records.

4. If possible, the person receiving cash should be a different person than the one who is disbursing cash. This control feature is possible in all but the very smallest firms.

CONTROLLING CASH DISBURSEMENTS

Controls are also needed over cash disbursements. Since most of a firm's cash is spent by check, many of the controls deal with checks and authorizations for cash payments. Many are also applications of the basic principle of separation of duties. Following are some of the basic control procedures for cash disbursements.

1. All disbursements should be made by check or from petty cash.

2. All checks should be serially numbered, and access to checks should be limited.

3. Preferably, two signatures should be required on each check.

4. If possible, the person who authorizes payment of a bill should not be allowed to sign checks.

5. Approved invoices or vouchers should be required to support checks issued.

6. The person authorizing disbursements should be certain that payment is appropriate and is made to the proper party.

7. When invoices and vouchers are paid, they should be stamped "paid," with the date and number of the check issued indicated. These procedures lessen the chance of paying the same debt more than once.

8. The person(s) who signs the checks should not have access to canceled checks and should not prepare the bank reconciliation.

9. A bank reconciliation should be prepared each month, preferably by a person who has no other cash duties.

10. All voided and spoiled checks should be retained and defaced to prevent their unauthorized use.

11. A voucher system may be needed in large firms for close cash control.

12. Use of the net price method of recording purchases helps avoid loss of purchase discounts through planned timing of cash payments.

THE BANK CHECKING ACCOUNT

A bank is a business entity that seeks to earn income by providing a variety of services. One such service is a checking account. A *checking account* is a balance maintained in a bank that is subject to withdrawal by the depositor on demand. To provide accurate records of depositor funds received and disbursed, a bank uses the business documents discussed below.[1]

The signature card

A bank requires a new depositor to complete a *signature card* that provides the signatures of persons authorized to sign checks drawn upon an account. The card is retained at the bank to identify signatures on checks paid by the bank. The bank does not compare the signature on the check with the card for every check but makes the comparison only when the depositor disputes the validity of a check paid by the bank.

Deposit ticket

When a bank deposit is made, the depositor prepares a deposit ticket or slip. A *deposit ticket* is a form, often preprinted to show the depositor's

Illustration 7.1:   Deposit ticket

CHECKING ACCOUNT DEPOSIT		DOLLARS	CENTS
NAME **R. L. LEE COMPANY**	CURRENCY	140	—
	COINS	15	50
ADDRESS 1021 Roy Lane, East Lansing, Mich. 48823	CHECKS AS FOLLOWS PROPERLY ENDORSED		
ACCOUNT NUMBER 0936 162 01 DATE May 3 19	*Adams*	200	50
	Baker	170	—
East Lansing State Bank East Lansing, Michigan			
CHECKS AND OTHER ITEMS ARE RECEIVED FOR DEPOSIT SUBJECT TO TERMS AND CONDITIONS OF THIS BANK'S COLLECTION AGREEMENT.	TOTAL DEPOSITS	526	00

⑆072409927⑆   0930616211⑈01

name, address, and number of the account into which the deposit is made, that shows the date and the items comprising the deposit. Items comprising the deposit—cash and a list of checks—are entered on the ticket when the deposit is made. A deposit ticket is shown in Illustration 7.1. Upon making a deposit, the depositor is given a receipt showing the date and amount deposited. Deposit tickets are retained by the bank until returned to the depositor with the bank statement.

---

[1] Due to relaxed federal regulations, various institutions now offer checking account services, including savings and loan associations and credit unions. Since all function somewhat similarly, only banks will be discussed.

Check

A *check* is a written order on a bank to pay a specific sum of money to the party designated as the payee by the party issuing the check. Thus, there are three parties to every check transaction: the bank, the *payee*—party to whom the check is made payable—and the *drawer* (depositor). Most checks are serially numbered and preprinted with information about the depositor, such as name, address, and telephone number. Often a business check will have an attached remittance advice. A *remittance advice* is a form attached to a check informing the payee why the drawer of the check is making this payment; it is detached from the check before the check is cashed or deposited

Illustration 7.2:   Check with attached remittance advice

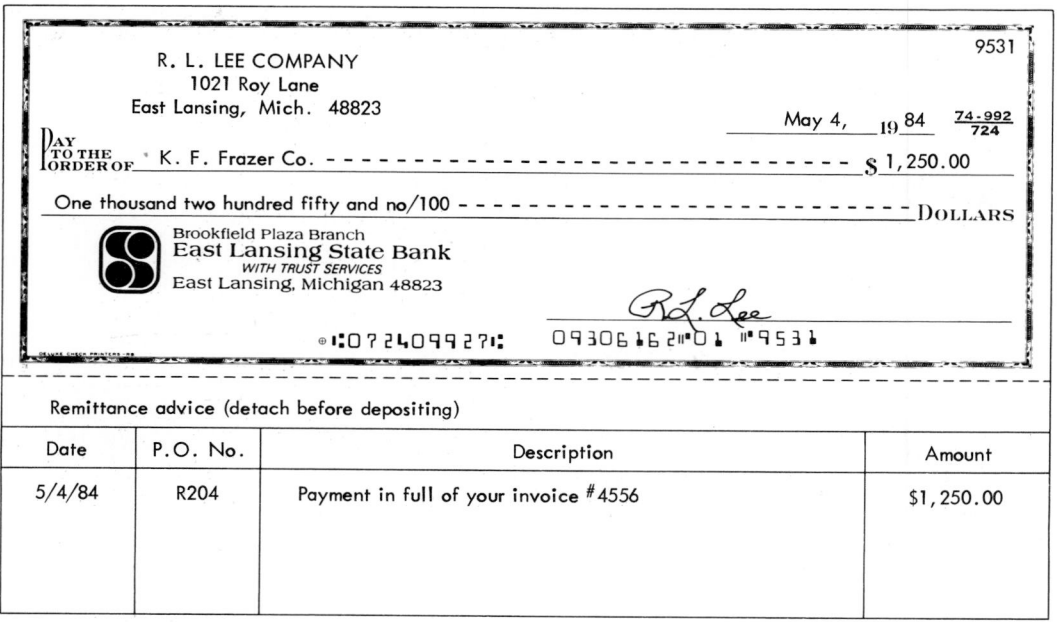

Date	P.O. No.	Description	Amount
5/4/84	R204	Payment in full of your invoice #4556	$1,250.00

in the payee's account. Illustration 7.2 shows a check with an attached remittance advice.

Bank statement

A *bank statement* is a statement issued (usually monthly) by a bank describing the activities in a depositor's checking account during the period. Illustration 7.3 shows a bank statement that includes the following data:

1. Deposits made during the period.
2. Checks paid out of the depositor's account by the bank during the period. These checks have "cleared" the bank and are "canceled."

Illustration 7.3: Bank statement

STATEMENT OF ACCOUNT

East Lansing State Bank

EAST LANSING, MICHIGAN

R. L. Lee Company
1021 Roy Lane
East Lansing, MI 48823

CUSTOMER NUMBER	
09306 162 2	Page 1
April 30 - May 31, 1984	
STATEMENT PERIOD	

CHECKING ACCOUNT SUMMARY

Balance forward	Number/Credits		Number/Debits		Fees	Closing balance
$2,248	23	$12,358	22	$11,331	$23	$3,252

Date	Description	Amount	Date	Description	Amount	Daily	balance
5/01	Deposit	$ 624	5/02	Deposit	$ 776	4/30	$ 2,248
5/03	Deposit	526	5/04	Deposit	474	5/01	2,872
5/07	Deposit	631	5/08	Deposit	608	5/02	3,648
5/08	Note collected	1,225	5/09	Deposit	667	5/03	3,669
5/10	Deposit	514	5/11	Deposit	401	5/04	4,143
5/14	Deposit	702	5/15	Deposit	303	5/07	3,974
5/16	Deposit	471	5/17	Deposit	653	5/08	4,146
5/18	Deposit	414	5/21	Deposit	419	5/09	4,813
5/22	Deposit	333	5/23	Deposit	407	5/10	5,327
5/24	Deposit	371	5/25	Deposit	331	5/11	5,728
5/28	Deposit	507	5/29	Deposit	601	5/14	6,430
5/30	Deposit	400	5/30	NSF Check	102	5/15	5,008
5/31	Box rent	15	5/31	Service charges	8	5/16	5,479
						5/17	5,902
						5/18	5,899

Check Number	Date	Amount	Check Number	Date	Amount	5/21	6,149
9515	5/03	$ 351	9519	5/03	$ 154	5/22	6,371
9527	5/07	208	9528	5/07	467	5/23	4,707
9529	5/07	125	9530	5/08	411	5/24	5,078
9531	5/08	1,250	9532	5/15	800	5/25	2,898
9533	5/15	925	9534	5/18	417	5/28	3,405
9535	5/17	230	9536	5/21	169	5/29	2,977
9537	5/22	111	9538	5/23	2,071	5/30	3,275
9539	5/25	413	9540	5/25	1,093	5/31	3,252
9541	5/25	1,005	9542	5/29	818		
9543	5/25	211					

3. Other deductions from the account for items such as service charges and
   check printing fees.
4. Other additions to the account for items such as proceeds of a note collected for the depositor and interest earned on the account.[2]

   Canceled checks and original deposit tickets generally have been returned
by the bank with the bank statement. But return of these items is not likely

---

[2] Effective January 1, 1982, revised federal regulations permit banks to pay interest on depositor's
checking account balances.

to continue because it is expensive to sort, handle, and mail these items. When checks and deposit tickets are not returned, the bank will provide listings as shown in Illustration 7.3. These documents may be stored on microfilm at the bank, with photocopies available if needed for any reason.

Copies of debit memos and credit memos also may be returned with the bank statement. A *debit memo* is a form used by a bank to explain a deduction from the depositor's account, while a *credit memo* explains an

Illustration 7.4:   Credit memorandum (top) and debit memorandum (bottom)

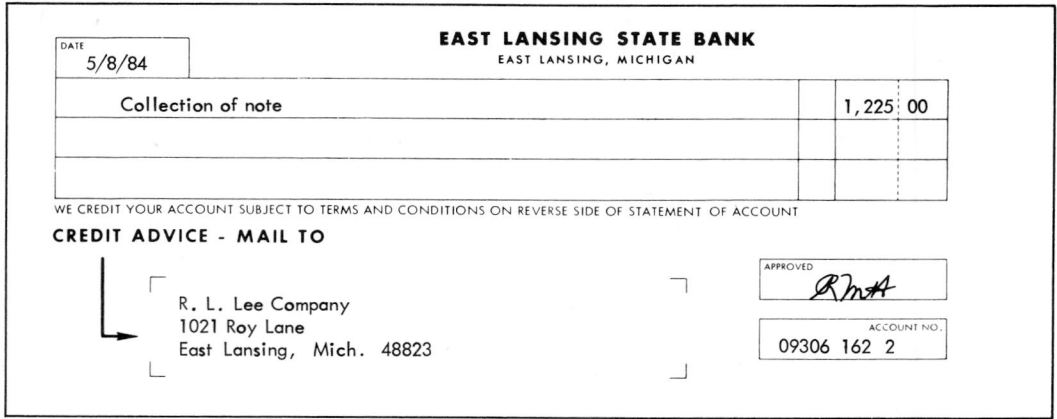

addition to the account. Such procedures may seem to be reversed, but bear in mind that the depositor's account is a liability—an account payable—of the bank. So, when the bank seeks to reduce a depositor's balance, a debit memo is prepared. To increase the balance, a credit memo is prepared. Examples of debit and credit memos are shown in Illustration 7.4. Banks are also trying to eliminate the mailing of these documents and to rely instead upon explanations on the bank statement.

Reconciling book and bank balances

The bank statement balance usually differs from the balance in the depositor's ledger account for cash. Having a difference is normal because neither the depositor or the bank has all the information about the depositor's account at the same time. For example, the bank may not know about the following:

1. *Outstanding checks,* which are checks issued by the depositor that have not yet been presented to the bank for payment. When a check is outstanding for many months and the drawer has received no further billings from the payee, the check is probably lost. Possibly the payee cannot be contacted. In such an instance, an entry should be made debiting Cash and crediting Miscellaneous Revenue. After the entry has been made, the check is no longer considered outstanding.

2. A *deposit in transit,* which is cash receipts of the depositor that are recorded in the books in one period but recorded as a deposit by the bank in the succeeding period. Such deposits usually are in transit only briefly before they are recorded by the bank.

3. Bank errors in the depositor's account. Even with modern, computerized equipment, errors can be made. For example, scanners can misread the account number printed in magnetic ink on the check and subtract the amount of the check from the wrong account. Human errors can arise when a bank employee encodes on the check an amount that differs from the check's actual amount.

No entries are required on the depositor's books for the above items. The depositor has already recorded the outstanding checks and the deposits in transit. The depositor will call bank errors to the bank's attention for correction.

Until the bank statement is received, the depositor may be unaware of:

1. *Service charges* assessed on the depositor by the bank to cover the cost of handling the account. Examples are charges for checks clearing the account, safety deposit box rental, and collection of a note for the depositor.

2. Deductions for not sufficient funds (NSF) checks. An *NSF check* is a check received from a customer that the customer's bank has refused to pay because the customer's checking account balance was not large enough to cover the check. The customer's bank returned the check to the depositor's bank, which deducted it from the depositor's account balance. Since the customer still owes the depositor money, the depositor will restore the amount of the NSF check to the customer's account receivable.

3. Nonroutine deposits in the depositor's account by the bank. For example, the bank may have collected a customer's note or received a wire transfer of funds for the depositor. A *wire transfer of funds* is an interbank transfer of funds by telephone.

A company operating in many widely scattered locations is likely to have accounts with many local banks. Special procedures should be set up to avoid accumulating too much idle cash. One such procedure involves the use of special-instruction bank accounts. For example, *transfer bank accounts* may be set up so that local banks automatically transfer to a central bank (by wire or bank draft) all amounts on deposit in excess of a stated amount. In this way, funds not needed for local operations are sent quickly to company headquarters where the funds can be used or invested as the company deems necessary.

4.   Errors made by the depositor. A common error involves recording a check in the accounting records at an amount that differs from the check's actual amount. For example, a $47 check may be recorded at $74. The check will clear the bank at the proper $47 amount and the error will be noticed when the canceled checks are reviewed.

Information the depositor did not know prior to receipt of the bank statement will require journal entries. After entries have been made to record the new information, the balance in the Cash account is the actual cash available to the company.

BANK RECONCILIATION STATEMENT

A *bank reconciliation statement,* or briefly, a *bank reconciliation,* is a statement that explains the difference between the cash balance shown on the books and the cash balance on the bank statement. The statement serves to determine the firm's actual cash balance. Adjustments are made to both balances, and after adjustments, both adjusted balances should be the same. An example of a bank reconciliation is shown in Illustration 7.5.

The first step in preparing the bank reconciliation is to enter the bank and book balances on the form. Next, examine the debit and credit memos, if any, returned or listed on the bank statement. Determine if the items referred to in the memos have been recorded in the accounting records. If not, note their effects upon the cash book balance on the reconciliation. See Illustration 7.5 for examples of a note collection, an NSF check, box rental, and service charges.

If canceled checks are returned with the bank statement, sort them into numerical order. The outstanding checks are determined by a process of elimination. The numbers of the checks that have cleared the bank are compared

Illustration 7.5:   Bank reconciliation statement

R. L. LEE COMPANY
Bank Reconciliation Statement
May 31, 1984

Balance per bank statement, May 31, 1984		$3,252	Balance per ledger, May 31, 1984		$1,891
Add: Deposit in transit		452	Add: Note collected		1,225
		$3,704			$3,116
Less: Outstanding checks:					
No. 9544	$322		Less: NSF check	$102	
No. 9545	168		Box rent	15	
No. 9546	223	713	Service charges	8	125
Adjusted balance, May 31, 1984		$2,991	Adjusted balance, May 31, 1984		$2,991

with the numbers of the checks issued. Tick marks ($\checkmark$) are used to identify those checks returned by the bank. Checks issued which have not yet been returned by the bank are the outstanding checks. If only a listing of the cleared checks is provided on the bank statement, outstanding checks will be determined by comparing this list with the record of checks issued.

Checks outstanding at the beginning of the month will be listed on the prior month's bank reconciliation. Some of these will have cleared during the current month; those that have not cleared will be shown as still outstanding on the current month's reconciliation.

Next, deposits in transit are determined. Deposits in transit normally occur only near the end of the period covered by the bank statement. For example, a deposit made in a bank's night depository on May 31 would be recorded by the bank on June 1. Thus, it would not appear on a bank statement for the month ended May 31. A missing deposit from other than the end of the period should be investigated immediately. To find deposits in transit, use the same elimination process as used for outstanding checks. Normally, the only deposit in transit will be the cash receipts of the last business day of the month.

Deposits in transit, outstanding checks, and bank service charges will often account for the entire difference between the Cash account and bank balances, especially for personal checking accounts. All items shown as adjustments of the book (ledger) balance on the reconciliation will require journal entries to adjust the Cash account. Items which appear on the bank side of the reconciliation do not require entries by the depositor. Any bank errors noted are called to the bank's attention.

To illustrate the preparation of the bank reconciliation shown in Illustration 7.5, assume the following information:

1. On May 31, 1984, R. L. Lee Company showed a balance in its Cash account of $1,891. On June 2, Lee received its bank statement for the month ended May 31, which showed an ending balance of $3,252.
2. Included with the bank statement was a credit memo for $1,225 for collection of a note owed to Lee by Shipley Company. Lee did not earn interest on the note.[3] Such a note is called a noninterest-bearing note.
3. Included with the bank statement is a $102 debit memo for an NSF check deposited by Lee which had been returned by the customer's bank.
4. Charges had been made to Lee's account for $15 safety deposit box rent and $8 service charges.
5. Examination of checks issued and checks cleared showed three checks outstanding:

No. 9544	$322
No. 9545	168
No. 9646	223
Total	$713

---

[3] Normally, interest is earned on notes, but this topic is not covered until the next chapter; a discussion of interest on notes is avoided here.

6.   A matching of debits to the Cash account with deposits on the bank statement showed that the $452 receipts of May 31 are included in Cash but not included as a deposit on the bank statement.

After reconciling the book and bank balances, Lee Company finds that its actual cash balance is $2,991. The following entries are needed to record information from the bank reconciliation:

Cash	1,225	
Notes Receivable		1,225
To record note collected.		
Bank Charges	23	
Cash		23
To record bank charges.		
Accounts Receivable	102	
Cash		102
To charge NSF check back to customer.		

The income statement for the period ending May 31, 1984, would include the $23 bank service charges as an expense. The May 31 balance sheet will show $2,991 cash.

As previously mentioned, no entries are made on the depositor's books for adjustments to the bank balance. The deposit in transit and the outstanding checks will be handled routinely when they reach the bank.

When more than one checking account is maintained by a company, each account must be reconciled separately with the balance on the bank statement for that account.

Certified checks

To avoid receiving a check which may later become an NSF check, a payee may demand that the check be certified. A *certified check* is a check drawn by a depositor and taken to its bank for certification. The bank will stamp "certified" across the face of the check and insert the name of the bank and the date; the certification will be signed by a bank official. The check will be certified only after it is determined that the depositor's balance is large enough to cover the check. The amount of the check will be deducted immediately from the depositor's account. The check now is a liability of the bank rather than the depositor. As a result, the check usually will be accepted without question.

PETTY CASH FUNDS

While it is best to make all disbursements by check, most firms find it convenient to make certain small payments in cash. Disbursements for delivery charges, postage stamps, taxi fares, supper money for employees working overtime, and other small items usually require a small amount of cash on hand.

To permit such disbursements to be made in cash and still maintain adequate control over cash, firms often establish a *petty cash fund* of some round dollar amount such as $50 or $100. One individual, sometimes called the petty cash cashier, is responsible for the operation of the fund.

Establishing the fund

Assume a $100 petty cash fund is to be set up. A check in that amount is drawn, payable to cash or the fund cashier. The following entry is required:

```
Petty Cash . . . . . . . . . . . . . . . . . . . . . . . . . . . . . . . . . . . . . . . . . . . . . . . . . . . . . . . . .   100
    Cash  . . . . . . . . . . . . . . . . . . . . . . . . . . . . . . . . . . . . . . . . . . . . . . . . . . . . . . .          100
    To establish petty cash fund.
```

The check is cashed, and the money turned over to the custodian. Disbursements can now be made from the fund. The fund should be large enough to take care of disbursements for a reasonable period, such as a month.

Operation of the fund

As payments are made from the fund, no journal entries are required. When the fund is reimbursed, an entry will be made for petty cash transactions. Thus, using a petty cash fund avoids the need for many entries for small amounts.

Illustration: 7.6   Petty cash voucher

PETTY CASH VOUCHER NO. 359		
To Local Cartage, Inc. Date June 29, 1984		
EXPLANATION	ACCT. NO.	AMOUNT
Freight on parts	27	2 27
APPROVED BY a. E. S.	RECEIVED PAYMENT Ken Black	

Petty cash voucher. A *petty cash voucher* (Illustration 7.6) is a document or form which indicates the amount and reason for a petty cash disbursement. A voucher should be prepared for each disbursement from the fund. If an invoice for the expenditure is provided, it should be stapled to the petty cash voucher. The person responsible for petty cash is at all times accountable for having cash and petty cash vouchers equal to the total amount of the fund.

Replenishing the fund

Whenever petty cash runs low, it is replenished. The petty cash vouchers are presented to the person having authority to order their reimbursement.

If all is in order, a check is drawn for the amount that will restore the cash in the fund to its original amount. Petty cash vouchers are summarized according to the reasons for expenditure. The journal entry to record replenishing the fund would debit various accounts and credit Cash. The petty cash vouchers are stamped or mutilated to prevent reuse.

For example, assume the $100 petty cash fund currently has a money balance of $7.40. A summary of the vouchers shows payments of $22.75 for transportation-in, $50.80 for stamps, and $19.05 for delivery expense for a total of $92.60. After the vouchers have been examined and approved, a check is drawn for $92.60 which, when cashed, restores the cash in the fund to its $100 balance. The entry to record replenishment is:

Transportation-In	22.75	
Postage Expense	50.80	
Delivery Expense	19.05	
Cash		92.60
To replenish petty cash fund.		

At the end of the accounting period, petty cash disbursements for which the fund has not been replenished must be recorded. A failure to do so could cause errors in both the income statement and balance sheet. The easiest way to record these disbursements is to replenish the fund. Replenishing the fund at year-end is handled exactly as at any other time.

If after some experience a petty cash fund is found to be larger than needed, the excess petty cash will be deposited in the company's checking account. The required entry debits Cash and credits Petty Cash for the amount returned and deposited. On the other hand, a petty cash fund may be too small, requiring replenishment every few days. The entry to record an increase in the size of the fund debits Petty Cash and credits Cash for the amount of the increase.

Cash short and over

Errors can be made in making change from the petty cash fund. In such cases, the amount of cash in the fund will be more or less than the amount of the fund less the total vouchers. The fund must always be restored to its set amount, so the credit to Cash will always be for the difference between the set amount and the actual cash in the fund. Debits will be made for all items vouchered. Any discrepancy will be debited or credited to an account called Cash Short and Over. The Cash Short and Over account is an expense or a revenue, depending upon whether it has a debit or credit balance.

Assume in the preceding example that the cash balance in the fund was only $6.10 instead of $7.40. To restore the fund to $100, a check for $93.90 is needed. Since the petty cash vouchers sum to only $92.60, the fund is short $1.30. Now the entry for replenishment is:

Transportation-In	22.75	
Postage Expense	50.80	
Delivery Expense	19.05	
Cash Short and Over	1.30	
Cash		93.90
To replenish petty cash fund.		

Entries in the Cash Over and Short account may be entered from other change-making activities. For example, assume that a clerk accidentally short-changes a customer $1. Total cash sales for the day were $740.50. At the end of the day, actual cash will be $1 over the sum of the sales tickets or the total of the cash register tape. The journal entry to record the day's cash sales is:

Cash	741.50	
Sales		740.50
Cash Short and Over		1.00
To record cash sales for the day.		

NET PRICE METHOD

A firm with good internal control over cash disbursements will normally take advantage of all discounts offered. Even with today's high interest rates, a firm may find it advisable to borrow to pay invoices within the discount period. For example, assume goods are purchased for $10,000 under terms, 2/10, n/30. The buyer is unable to pay at the end of 10 days, but expects to be able to pay at the end of 30 days. To take the $200 discount offered, the buyer needs a $9,800 loan for 20 days, beginning on the last day of the 10-day discount period. The buyer would benefit if the interest cost of such a loan was less than $200. (Short-term loans and interest computations are discussed in the next chapter.)

To emphasize the importance of taking discounts, purchases may be accounted for under the *net price method* rather than the *gross price method* illustrated in Chapter 5. The net price method has two advantages: (1) it is better theory and (2) it provides better cash control.

Using the net price method, a purchase is recorded in Purchases and Accounts Payable "net" of the discount. In other words, the discount is *deducted* from gross invoice price *before* entering the transaction in the accounts. To illustrate, assume a $1,500 purchase was made on May 14 under terms, 2/10, n/30. The invoice was paid on May 24, and the discount taken. Under the net price method, the entries are:

May 14	Purchases	1,470	
	Accounts Payable		1,470
	Purchased goods under terms, 2/10, n/30.		
24	Accounts Payable	1,470	
	Cash		1,470
	Paid account within discount period.		

These entries are theoretically preferable to those recorded under the gross price method because the goods are recorded at their actual cash cost. Thus, the cost principle has been applied. Also, the liability is shown in the accounts at the amount for which it could be settled.

Notice that the above example does not show discounts taken. But if the invoice had not been paid within 10 days, the method would have shown discounts lost. Assume that the invoice in the above example was paid on May 28 instead of May 24. The entry needed would read:

```
May 28   Accounts Payable . . . . . . . . . . . . . . . . . . . . . . . . . . . . . . . . . . . . . . . . . . . . .   1,470
         Discounts Lost  . . . . . . . . . . . . . . . . . . . . . . . . . . . . . . . . . . . . . . . . . . .        30
            Cash  . . . . . . . . . . . . . . . . . . . . . . . . . . . . . . . . . . . . . . . . . . . .                    1,500
                 Paid account and recorded discount lost.
```

Here is where the internal control advantage appears. The only time discounts appear under the net price method is when they are *lost*. With discounts of 2 percent or more, good cash management generally calls for procedures that make sure that all invoices on which discounts are available are paid within the discount period. The failure to take a discount should be highlighted as a deviation from company policy. The Discounts Lost account directs management's attention to such departures from company policy. The Discounts Lost account actually contains losses from inefficiency. It is reported among nonoperating expenses near the bottom of the income statement.

THE VOUCHER SYSTEM

There have been many instances where business firms suffered substantial losses from the embezzlement of cash. In most of these cases, the firm paid fictitious invoices. Thus, every business must make sure that its cash payments are proper and timely. This may not be a problem in very small firms because the owner has personal knowledge of all transactions and personally signs all checks. In larger companies where owners and high-level officers have no direct part in the payment process, cash payments can be controlled by a voucher system.

A *voucher system* is a set of procedures, special journals, and authorization forms designed to provide control over cash payments. The special journals used are the voucher register and the check register. The basic authorization form is the voucher. See Illustration 7.7.

The system works as follows: Each transaction that will involve a cash payment is entered on a voucher and recorded in a voucher register prior to payment. An invoice or other business document is the basis for preparing a voucher. A voucher is the basis for making a journal entry in the voucher register. A *voucher* is a form with spaces provided for data about a liability that must be paid. The data include such items as creditor's name and address, description of the goods or services received, invoice number, terms of payment, due date, and amount due. The voucher also has spaces for signatures of those approving the liability for payment. The voucher usually forms a "jacket"

Illustration 7.7: A voucher

ATWELL   SUPPLY   COMPANY
Atwell Plaza
Atwell, Texas 78712

VOUCHER

VOUCHER NO.   141
OUR P.O. NO.   2514
VENDOR'S INVOICE   416
PAID BY CHECK NO.   587
DATE PAID   7/18/84

Payable To: Gregory Corporation
48 Cadillac Square
Detroit, Michigan 48226

DATE	ACCT. NO.	DESCRIPTION	QUANTITY	UNIT PRICE	TOTAL
July 14	126	X-16 Transistors	100	$2.00	$200.00
		TOTAL			$200.00
		DISCOUNT	2%		4.00
		NET PAYABLE			$196.00

TERMS 2/10, n/30
EXPLANATIONS:

AUDITED AS TO CORRECTNESS a.T.	APPROVED FOR PAYMENT L.J.W.	ENTERED IN VOUCHER REGISTER R.E.J	DATE ENTERED 7/14/84

for the invoice and supporting documents, such as the receiving department's report. Each voucher undergoes careful examination and receives either approval or disapproval for payment. By the time a voucher is approved for payment, one can be quite sure that the payment is valid, since various persons have confirmed that the claim being paid is proper and accurate.

When a voucher system is used, the term *vouchers payable* replaces *accounts payable* in the ledger. When financial statements are prepared, the more common term *accounts payable* is used.

The voucher system relies heavily upon the separation of duties for its effectiveness. For instance, vouchers should be authorized only after receipt of goods or services has been verified. Those who authorize a voucher should not prepare and issue checks. Persons who sign checks should do so only when approved vouchers are presented. These procedures lower the risk of errors and of making improper cash payments.

Types of vouchers

The voucher system gets its name from the fact that *every check issued is authorized by a voucher*. In a broad sense a voucher is any written form that serves as a receipt or as evidence of authority to act. In a narrow sense—as applied to the voucher system—a voucher is a form that confirms a liability and thus serves as the basis for an accounting entry.

In some businesses, discount and payment terms run from invoice date. Here a voucher should be prepared for each invoice, as in Illustration 7.7, and should be filed according to the date on which the discount period terminates or payment is due.

When discount and payment terms are computed from the end of the month, it is possible to modify the form of the voucher so as to reduce the number of vouchers prepared and, therefore, reduce the number of entries made in the voucher register. All invoices received from a particular creditor may be accumulated and listed on one voucher at the end of the month, since all invoices will probably be paid by one check. The details of the various invoices may be summarized on one voucher. The vouchers will be filed by due dates.

Special journals used

Voucher register. A *voucher register* is a multicolumn special journal. It normally has special debit columns for accounts most frequently debited when a liability is incurred. The credit to each entry is to Vouchers Payable. Thus, the voucher register contains a record of all vouchers prepared, listed in order by date and voucher number. A brief explanation of each transaction also may be included.

As shown in Illustration 7.8, each voucher is debited to a special column or to an account named in the Other Accounts Dr. column. At the end of each month, the Vouchers Payable Cr. column total is posted to the general ledger control account, Vouchers Payable. In Illustration 7.8, a voucher is prepared for each invoice. Notice that the vouchers are recorded net of purchase discounts allowed. If a discount is missed, another voucher is prepared for the discount lost (see line 13 of Illustration 7.8). The total of each of the specifically titled columns is posted to the account named. The debits in the Other Accounts Dr. column are posted individually to the accounts named, usually on a daily basis. The total of the Other Accounts column is, of course, not posted.

Check register. A *check register* is a special journal showing all checks issued, listed by date and check number. One line is allotted each check. No check may be issued unless authorized by an approved voucher.

The check register in Illustration 7.9 shows the entry and procedure when a check is issued in payment of a voucher. When invoices are entered in the voucher register using the net price method, the check register normally has only one column. The column total is posted as a debit to Vouchers

Payable and a credit to Cash. Notice that check number 1352 is marked "void." This notation usually means a mistake was made in writing the check and another check had to be prepared.

If invoices had been entered gross (before discount deductions) in the voucher register, a Purchase Discounts Cr. column should be included in the check register. Separate columns would be needed for the debit to Vouchers Payable and the credit to Cash, since the dollar amounts posted to these two accounts would differ by the amount of the discount taken.

In a voucher system, the voucher register and the check register are the two primary journals from which postings are made to the Vouchers Payable control account. When a voucher system is used, these two journals replace the traditional purchases and cash disbursements journals.

Files maintained in a voucher system

Unpaid and paid voucher files. The *unpaid voucher file* contains all vouchers that have been prepared and approved as proper liabilities but which have not yet been paid. They are filed according to their due dates. The unpaid voucher file takes the place of the subsidiary accounts payable ledger. The total of the vouchers in the unpaid vouchers file should equal the total of the "open" items (those not paid) in the voucher register and also equal the balance in the Vouchers Payable account.

The *paid voucher file* contains all vouchers which have been paid. They are filed by voucher number in numerical order. Filed in this manner, they constitute a permanent and convenient reference for anyone who wants to check the details of previous cash disbursements.

Procedures for preparing a voucher

The preparation of a voucher begins with the receipt of an invoice from a creditor or with approved evidence that a liability has been incurred and cash will be disbursed. The procedures followed from that point typically are as follows: Basic data are entered on the voucher from the invoice. The invoice, voucher, and receiving report are sent to the persons responsible for verifying the correctness of the description of the goods as to quantity and quality, the dollar amounts, and other details. Each person initials the voucher when satisfied as to its correctness. When the voucher and accompanying documents are received by the accounting department, a notation is made on the voucher as to the proper accounts to be debited and credited. After a final review by an authorized person, the proper entry is made in the voucher register and the voucher is filed in the unpaid voucher file.

Procedures for paying a voucher

When a voucher is due for payment, it is removed from the unpaid voucher file. A check is prepared for the amount payable. The check, voucher, and supporting documents then typically are sent to the treasurer. The trea-

Illustration 7.8:   A voucher register

VOUCHER REGISTER

Line No.	Voucher Date 1984		Voucher No.	Payee	Explanation	Terms	Date Paid		Check No.	Vouchers Payable Cr. 101
1	May	2	223	Hanley Company	Ring binders	2/10,n/30	May	12	1350	980.00
2		4	224	Moore Transport	Transportation, binders			5	1347	13.00
3		6	225	White Stationery Company	Office supplies	2/10,n/30		12	1351	102.00
4		8	226	Specialty Advertisers	Advertising			8	1348	1,200.00
5		10	227	Blanch Company	Office equipment and supplies			10	1349	1,010.00
6										
7		14	228	Swanson Company	Filler paper	2/10,n/30		26	1356	3,920.00
8		16	229	Rizzo Company	Office desk	n/30		25	1355	640.00
9		18	230	Warren Company	Spiral binders	2/10,n/30		28	1357	4,900.00
10		20	231	First National Bank	Mortgage payment			20	1353	154.00
11		22	232	Falcone Company	Books	n/30				10,000.00
12		24	233	Petty cash	Reimbursement			24	1354	132.00
13		26	234	Swanson Company	Discount lost (No. 228)			26	1356	80.00
14		28	235	Celoron Company	Drawing sets	2/20,n/30				9,800.00
15		31	236	Payroll account	Salaries and wages			31	1358	24,000.00
16										
										56,931.00

surer examines all of the documents. If they are found to be in order, the treasurer initials the voucher to show that final approval has been given and signs the check. The treasurer then mails the check, and usually a remittance advice, to the creditor. The voucher is then returned to the accounting department.

Page No. *15*
Month *May 1984*

Dis-counts Lost Dr. 122	Mer-chandise Purchases Dr. 131	Transpor-tation in Dr. 144	Salaries and Wages Dr. 158	Office Expense Dr. 175	Advertising Expense Dr. 262	Other Accounts Dr.			
						Account Name	Acct. No.	Amount Dr.	✓
	980.00								
		13.00							
				102.00					
					1,200.00				
						Office Equipment	42	1,000.00	
						Office Supplies	33	10.00	
	3,920.00								
						Office Equipment	42	640.00	
	4,860.00	40.00							
						Mortgage Note Payable	151	154.00	
	10,000.00								
		31.88		60.12	40.00				
80.00									
	9,800.00								
			24,000.00						
80.00	29,560.00	84.88	24,000.00	162.12	1,240.00			1,804.00	

On receipt of the voucher, the accounting department makes an entry in the check register showing the date paid, check number, voucher number, and amount paid. The check number and date paid are also inserted in the voucher register and on the voucher itself. Note that by inserting the check number and date paid in the voucher register, the same data are included

Illustration 7.9:   Check register

	CHECK REGISTER			Page No. *24* Month *May, 1984*

Line No.	Date 1984		Payee	Voucher No.	Check No.	Vouchers Payable Dr., Cash Cr.
1	May	5	Moore Transport	224	1347	13.00
2		8	Specialty Advertisers	226	1348	1,200.00
3		10	Blanch Company	227	1349	1,010.00
4		12	Hanley Company	223	1350	980.00
5		12	White Stationery Company	225	1351	102.00
6		20	VOID		1352	
7		20	First National Bank	231	1353	154.00
8		24	Petty Cash	233	1354	132.00
9		25	Rizzo Company	229	1355	640.00
10		26	Swanson Company	228} 234}	1356	4,000.00
11		28	Warren Company	230	1357	4,900.00
12		31	Payroll account	236	1358	24,000.00
						37,131.00

in the voucher register as are included in the check register. The voucher then is filed in the paid voucher file.

NEW TERMS INTRODUCED IN CHAPTER 7

Bank reconciliation statement
A statement which shows the items and amounts which cause a bank's record of a depositor's account balance to differ from the depositor's record.

Bank statement
A statement issued (usually monthly) by a bank describing the activities in a depositor's checking account.

Cash
Currency, coins, undeposited negotiable instruments (such as checks, bank drafts, and money orders), amounts in checking or savings accounts at a bank, and demand certificates of deposit at a bank.

Certificate of deposit
An interest-bearing deposit in a bank that can be withdrawn at will (a demand CD) or at a fixed date (time CD).

Certified check
A check drawn by a depositor and taken to its bank for certification. The check is deducted from the depositor's balance immediately and becomes a liability of the bank. Thus, it usually will be accepted without question.

Check

A written order on a bank to pay a specific sum of money to the party designated as the payee by the party issuing the check.

Checking account

A balance maintained with a bank subject to withdrawal on demand.

Check register

A special journal containing a chronological and serial record of all checks issued.

Credit memo

A form used by a bank to notify a depositor that the depositor's account balance has been increased.

Debit memo

A form used by a bank to notify a depositor that the depositor's account balance has been decreased.

Deposit in transit

Cash receipts of a depositor recorded as receipts in the books of one period but recorded as a deposit by the bank in a succeeding period.

Deposit ticket

A form showing the name and number of the account into which the deposit is made, the date, and the items comprising the deposit.

Drawer

The party (depositor) writing a check.

Net price method

An accounting procedure in which purchases and accounts payable are initially recorded at net invoice price—gross price less discount offered for prompt payment. Records discounts lost rather than discounts taken.

NSF check

A check which the bank has refused to pay because the writer of the check does not have sufficient funds in its checking account to cover the check.

Outstanding checks

Checks issued by a depositor which have not yet been paid by the bank upon which drawn.

Paid voucher file

A permanent file where vouchers which have been paid are filed in numerical sequence.

Payee

The party to whom a check is made payable.

Petty cash fund

A usually nominal sum of money established as a separate fund from which minor cash disbursements for valid business purposes are to be made. The cash in the fund plus the vouchers covering

disbursements must always equal the balance at which the fund was established and at which it is carried in the ledger accounts.

Petty cash voucher

A form with spaces provided for recording data about disbursements from the petty cash fund. The data recorded often include the amount and purpose of the disbursement, to whom it was made, and a signature authorizing the disbursement.

Remittance advice

A form attached to a check informing the payee why the drawer of the check is making this payment.

Service charges

Charges assessed a depositor by a bank to cover the cost of handling the account.

Signature card

Provides the signatures of persons authorized to sign checks drawn upon an account.

Transfer bank account

A bank account controlled by special instructions that require the bank to forward immediately any funds in excess of a stated amount to a central bank.

Unpaid voucher file

Serves as a subsidiary accounts payable ledger under a voucher system; unpaid vouchers are filed according to their due dates.

Voucher

A form with spaces provided for data concerning the liability being recorded (such as invoice number, invoice date, creditor's name and address, terms, description of the goods or services, and amount due); also has spaces for approval signatures, the date of the check used for payment, and the check number.

Voucher register

A special journal in which prenumbered vouchers are recorded in numerical sequence. In addition to a credit column for Vouchers Payable, it normally has various columns for debits such as Merchandise Purchases, Salaries, and Transportation-In. See Illustration 7.8.

Voucher system

A procedure used to ensure tight internal control over all cash disbursements.

Wire transfer of funds

Interbank transfers of funds (in the form of accounting debits and credits) which are relayed by telephone.

DEMONSTRATION PROBLEM 7–1

The following data pertain to the Nunn Company:

1. Balance per bank statement, dated March 31, 1984, is $8,900.
2. Balance of the Cash account on the company's books as of March 31, 1984, is $8,938.
3. The $2,600 deposit of March 31 was not shown on the bank statement.
4. Outstanding checks as of March 31 totaled $2,100.
5. Service and collection charges for the month were $20.
6. The bank erroneously charged the Nunn Company account for the $400 check of another company. The check was included with the canceled checks returned with the bank statement.
7. The bank credited the company with the $2,000 proceeds of a noninterest-bearing note that it collected for the company.
8. A customer's $150 check marked NSF was returned with the bank statement.
9. As directed, the bank paid and charged to the company's account a $1,015 noninterest-bearing note of the Nunn Company. This payment has not been recorded by the company.
10. An examination of the cash receipts and the deposit tickets revealed that the bookkeeper erroneously recorded a customer's check of $263 as $236.
11. The bank credited the company for $20 of interest earned on the company's checking account.

Required:

a. Prepare a bank reconciliation statement as of March 31, 1984.

b. Prepare the necessary journal entries to adjust the account.

Solution to demonstration problem 7–1

a.

NUNN COMPANY
Bank Reconciliation Statement
March 31, 1984

Balance per bank statement, March 31, 1984		$ 8,900
Add: Deposit in transit	$2,600	
Check charged in error	400	3,000
		$11,900
Less: Outstanding checks		2,100
Adjusted balance, March 31, 1984		$ 9,800
Balance per ledger, March 31, 1984		$ 8,938
Add: Note collected	$2,000	
Interest earned on checking account	20	
Error in recording customer's check	27	2,047
		$10,985
Less: Service and collection charges	$ 20	
NSF check	150	
Nunn Company note charged against account	1,015	1,185
Adjusted balance, March 31, 1984		$ 9,800

b. Cash

Accounts Receivable ($150 − $27)	123	
Notes Payable	1,015	
Bank Charges	20	
Notes Receivable		2,000
Interest Revenue		20
To record adjustments to Cash account.		

Alternatively:

Cash	2,047	
Accounts Receivable		27
Notes Receivable		2,000
Interest Revenue		20
To record additions to Cash account.		
Notes Payable	1,015	
Accounts Receivable	150	
Bank Charges	20	
Cash		1,185
To record deductions from Cash account.		

DEMONSTRATION PROBLEM 7–2

The Blankenship Company uses a voucher system to control cash disbursements. Purchases are recorded at gross invoice prices. As of April 30, 1984, two vouchers are unpaid: Voucher No. 404 payable to Akers Company for $850 and Voucher No. 405 payable to Hanson Company for $50.

The Blankenship Company engaged in the following transactions affecting vouchers payable:

Transactions:

May 1 Prepared Voucher No. 406 payable to Carol Company for merchandise purchased; price on invoice dated April 30 is $400; terms, 2/10, n/30, FOB destination.

      2 Issued Check No. 385 in payment of Voucher No. 405; no discount was offered on this purchase.

      4 Received a credit memo for $100 for merchandise returned to Akers Company. Purchase was originally recorded in Voucher No. 404. (Record in general journal with notation of return on Voucher No. 404.)

      5 Prepared Voucher No. 407 payable to Allen Brothers for merchandise with an invoice price of $950 on invoice dated May 3; terms, 2/10, n/30, FOB shipping point, freight prepaid. Supplier paid $50 freight bill and added $50 to the invoice for a total billing of $1,000.

      6 Prepared Voucher No. 408 payable to API, Inc., for cost incurred to deliver merchandise sold, $120; terms, n/10.

      8 Issued Check No. 386 to pay Voucher No. 404, less return and less a 2 percent discount.

      9 Issued Check No. 387 to pay Voucher No. 406.

    12 Prepared Voucher No. 409 payable to Ames Insurance Company for $300, the three-year premium on an insurance policy. Issued Check No. 388 to pay Voucher No. 409.

    13 Issued Check No. 389 to pay Voucher No. 407.

    15 Prepared Voucher No. 410 payable to Cash for $2,000 salaries for the first half of May. Issued Check No. 390 in payment of Voucher No. 410. Cashed the check and paid employees in cash.

    16 Issued Check No. 391 to pay Voucher No. 408.

    23 Prepared Voucher No. 411 payable to Manders Company for merchandise with an invoice price of $300 on invoice dated May 22; terms, 2/10, n/30, FOB shipping point, freight collect.

    24 Prepared Voucher No. 412 payable to Short Lines, Inc., for $50 freight on merchandise purchased on May 23.

    26 Prepared Voucher No. 413 payable to Bell Telephone Company for $125 for monthly telephone service.

    28 Prepared Voucher No. 414 payable to We-Deliver, Inc., for costs incurred to deliver merchandise sold, $80; terms, n/30.

    31 Prepared Voucher No. 415 payable to Cash for salaries for the last half of May $2,200. Issued Check No. 392 in payment of Voucher No. 415. Cashed the check and paid employees in cash.

Required:

a. Prepare a voucher register, check register, and a general journal and record the above transactions.

b. Prepare a Vouchers Payable account and post the portions of the entries that affect this account.

c. Prepare a schedule (list) of unpaid vouchers to prove the accuracy of the balance in the Vouchers Payable account.

Solution to demonstration problem 7–2

a.

VOUCHER REGISTER*   *Page 12*

Date 1984	Vouch-er No.	Payee	Paid Date	Ck. No.	Vouchers Payable Cr.	Pur-chases Dr.	Freight-In Dr.	Delivery Expense Dr.	Salaries Expense Dr.	Other Accounts Dr. Account Name	Post. Ref.	Amount Dr.
May 1	406	Carol Company	5/9	387	400	400						
5	407	Allen Brothers	5/13	389	1,000	950	50					
6	408	API, Inc.	5/16	391	120			120				
12	409	Ames Insurance Company	5/12	388	300					Unexpired Insurance		300
15	410	Cash	5/15	390	2,000				2,000			
23	411	Manders Company			300	300						
24	412	Short-Lines, Inc.			50		50					
26	413	Bell Telephone Company			125					Telephone Expense		125
28	414	We-Deliver, Inc.			80			80				
31	415	Cash	5/31	392	2,200				2,200			
					6,575	1,650	100	200	4,200			425

* A column for terms could have been included.

CHECK REGISTER

Page 5

Date 1984		Payee	Voucher No.	Check No.	Vouchers Payable Dr.	Purchase Discounts Cr.	Cash Cr.
May	2	Hanson Company	405	385	50		50
	8	Akers Company	404	386	750	15	735
	9	Carol Company	406	387	400	8	392
	12	Ames Insurance Company	409	388	300		300
	13	Allen Brothers	407	389	1,000	19	981
	15	Cash	410	390	2,000		2,000
	16	API, Inc.	408	391	120		120
	31	Cash	415	392	2,200		2,200
					6,820	42	6,778

GENERAL JOURNAL

Page 17

Date		Account Titles and Explanation	Post. Ref.	Debit	Credit
1984 May	4	Vouchers Payable		1 0 0	
		Purchase Returns and Allowances			1 0 0
		To record receipt of credit memo for merchandise			
		returned. Voucher No. 404.			

b.

GENERAL LEDGER

Vouchers Payable

Account No. 201

Date		Explanation	Post. Ref.	Debit	Credit	Balance
1984 Apr.	30	Beginning balance				9 0 0
May	4	Credit memo; Voucher No. 404	J17	1 0 0		8 0 0
	31		VR12		6 5 7 5	7 3 7 5
	31		CR5	6 8 2 0		5 5 5

C. **SCHEDULE OF UNPAID VOUCHERS**

Voucher No.	Amount
411	$300
412	50
413	125
414	80
Total	$555

QUESTIONS

1. What are the four objectives sought in effective cash management?

2. Why might a company's managment wish to determine the daily cash position?

3. List four essential features in a system of internal control over cash receipts.

4. The bookkeeper of a given company was stealing cash received from customers in payment of their accounts. To conceal the theft, the bookkeeper made out false credit memos indicating returns and allowances made by or granted to customers. What feature of internal control would have prevented the thefts?

5. List six essential features in a system of internal control over cash disbursements.

6. "The difference between a company's Cash account balance and the balance on its bank statement is usually a matter of timing." Do you agree or disagree? Why?

7. Explain how transfer bank accounts can help bring about effective cash management.

8. Describe the operation of a petty cash fund and cite the advantages from its use. Indicate how control is achieved over petty cash transactions.

9. Explain how the net price method of accounting for purchases can improve internal control.

10. What can be accomplished with a voucher system that is not accomplished through use of a purchases journal and a cash disbursements journal?

11. What should be the relationship between the balance in the Vouchers Payable account, the "open" items in the voucher register, and the total of all vouchers in the unpaid vouchers file?

12. You are the chief accountant of the Magnuson Company. An invoice has just been received from the Arnott Company in the amount of $2,000, with credit terms of 2/10, n/30. List the procedures you would follow in processing this invoice through the point of filing it in the unpaid vouchers file.

13. Refer to the situation described in Question 12. Assume that the time for payment of the voucher has arrived and the payment is to be made within the discount period. List the actions that would be taken if the company uses a Discounts Lost account.

14. What would the procedures be if the discount period had elapsed before payment was made in Question 13?

15. List the posting steps that would be used to post the data shown in Illustration 7.8. How many numbers would actually be posted?

EXERCISES

E–1.   The bank statement for the Cook Company at the end of August showed a balance of $68,600. Checks outstanding totaled $21,000, and deposits in transit were $31,950. If these are the only pertinent data available to you, what was the adjusted balance of cash as of the end of August?

E-2.   From the following data prepare a bank reconciliation statement and determine the correct available cash balance for Unisco, Inc., as of October 31, 1984.

Balance per bank statement, October 31, 1984	$4,658
Ledger account balance, October 31, 1984	2,696
Noninterest-bearing note collected by bank not yet	
entered in ledger	2,000
Bank charges not yet entered by Unisco, Inc.	6
Deposits in transit	560
Outstanding checks:	
No. 327	218
No. 328	96
No. 329	130
No. 331	84

E-3.   The following is a bank reconciliation statement for Frank Company as of August 31, 1984:

Balance per bank, August 31, 1984		$2,490
Add: Deposit in transit		1,892
		$4,382
Less: Outstanding checks		2,007
Adjusted balance, August 31, 1984		$2,375
Balance per books, August 31, 1984		$2,416
Add: Error correction		18
		$2,434
Less: NSF check	$50	
Service charges	9	59
Adjusted balance, August 31, 1984		$2,375

The error occurred when the bookkeeper debited Accounts Payable and credited Cash for $75, instead of the correct amount, $57.

Prepare the journal entry needed to adjust or correct the Cash account.

E-4.   As of March 1 of the current year, the Paul Company had outstanding checks of $15,000. During March, the company issued an additional $57,000 of checks. As of March 31, the bank statement showed $48,000 of checks had cleared the bank during the month. What is the amount of outstanding checks as of March 31?

E-5.   The Druid Company's bank statement as of August 31, 1984, shows total deposits into the company's account of $25,670 and a total of 14 separate deposits. On July 31, deposits of $1,350 and $1,050 were in transit. The total cash receipts for August were $32,920, and the company's records show 13 deposits made in August. What is the amount of deposits in transit at August 31?

E-6.   On August 31, 1984, the Meds Company's petty cash fund contained coins and currency of $41.20, an IOU from an employee of $5, and vouchers showing expenditures of $20 for postage, $8.50 for taxi fare, and $23 to entertain a customer. The Petty Cash account shows a balance of $100. The fund is replenished on August 31 because financial statements are to be prepared. What journal entry is required on August 31?

E-7.   Use the data in Exercise E-6. What entry would have been required if the amount of coin and currency had been $43.50? Which of the accounts debited would not appear in the income statement?

E–8.   Seyforth Company has a $200 petty cash fund. The following occurred in December:

Transactions:

Dec. 2   The petty cash fund was increased to $300.
       8   Petty Cash Voucher No. 318 for $5.38 of delivery expense was prepared and paid. The fund was not replenished at this time.
      20   The company decided that the fund was too large and reduced it to $250.

Prepare any necessary entries for December for the above.

E–9.   Keystone Company uses the net price procedure for handling purchase discounts. Prepare the journal entries necessary to record the following 1984 transactions:

Transactions:

Oct. 6   Purchased $600 of merchandise; terms, 2/10, n/30.
       7   Purchased $2,000 of merchandise; terms, 2/10, n/30.
      17   Paid the invoice for the October 7 purchase.
      31   Paid the invoice for the October 6 purchase.

E–10.   Refer to Illustration 7.8.

                    a.   Assuming that all vouchers written before May 1, 1984, have been paid, what is the balance in the Vouchers Payable account on May 31, 1984?

                    b.   All checks written in May were in payment of May vouchers. What is the total dollar amount of vouchers paid in May?

                    c.   Explain how it is possible to determine the cash paid out in May to pay May's vouchers without looking at the check register.

E–11.   Ulray Company deposits all cash receipts intact each day and makes all payments by check. On October 31, after all posting was completed, its Cash account had a debit balance of $1,730. The bank statement for the month ended on October 31 showed a balance of $1,595. Other data are:

1.   Outstanding checks, $170.
2.   October 31 cash receipts of $335 were placed in bank's night depository and do not appear on the bank statement.
3.   Bank service charges for October, $6.
4.   Check No. 772 for store supplies was entered at $162, but paid by the bank at its actual amount of $126.

                    Prepare a bank reconciliation statement for Ulray as of October 31. Also prepare any needed journal entries.

E–12.   Arto company uses a voucher system. Selected recent transactions are: (*a*) prepared Voucher No. 801 for purchase of merchandise from Balke Company, $500; (*b*) issued Check No. 723 to pay Voucher No. 801; (*c*) prepared Voucher No. 802 to set up a petty cash fund, $150; (*d*) issued Check No. 724 to pay Voucher No. 802; (*e*) prepared Voucher No. 804 for $20 freight on merchandise in Voucher No. 801; (*f*) prepared Voucher No. 805 to replenish petty cash when it contained cash of $29 and receipts for postage, $65, supplies, $34, and miscellaneous expense, $21; and (*g*) issued Check No. 725 to pay Voucher No. 805.

                    Prepare entries in general journal form to record the above transactions. Identify the journal or book of original entry in which each transaction would normally appear.

E–13.   Assume that Job Company uses a voucher register and a check register exactly like Illustration 7.8 and Illustration 7.9. On May 1, Job Company purchased merchandise from Baird Company, $500; terms, 2/10, n/30. Job prepared Voucher No. 567 for $490.

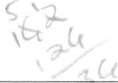

On May 29, Job paid for the merchandise purchased from Baird Company and missed the discount (Check No. 489).

State what would be entered in the voucher register and the check register to record the payment of May 29. Assume that the last voucher used was 598.

PROBLEMS, SERIES A

P7–1–A. The bank statement for P.C.C., Inc., showed a balance of $5,850.95 on July 31, 1984. On the same date, the company's Cash account balance was $4,129.65. Returned with the bank statement was a credit memorandum for $1,025 for a noninterest-bearing note that was collected by the bank for the company. There were two debit memoranda—one for service charges of $9.50 and one for an NSF Check of Greene Company for $35. By comparing the canceled checks with the check register, it was found that $2,430.80 of checks were outstanding. The deposit made after banking hours on July 31 of $1,690 was not listed on the bank statement.

Required:

a. Prepare a bank reconcilation statement for July 31, 1984.

b. Prepare any necessary journal entries.

P7–2–A. The following data pertain to the petty cash fund of the Krause Company:

Transactions

Nov. 2 A $300 check is drawn, cashed, and the cash placed in the care of the assistant office manager to be used as a petty cash fund.

Dec. 17 The fund is replenished. An analysis of the fund shows:

Coins and currency	$ 98.27
Petty cash vouchers for—	
Delivery expenses	115.65
Freight-in	74.08
Postage stamps purchased	10.00

31 The end of the accounting period falls on this date. The fund was replenished. Its contents on this date consist of—

Coins and currency	$234.70
Petty cash vouchers for—	
Delivery expenses	21.10
Postage stamps	24.20
Employee's IOU	20.00

Required:

Present journal entries to record the above transactions. Use the Cash Short and Over account for any shortage or overage in the fund.

P7–3–A. The following data relate to the petty cash fund of the Daniel Wrecking Company:

Transactions:

1984

Apr. 1 The petty cash fund is set up with a $50 cash balance.

19 Because the money in the fund is down to $10.40, the fund is replenished. Petty cash vouchers are as follows:

Flowers for hospitalized employee	
(miscellaneous expense)	$12.50
Postage stamps	20.00
Office supplies	6.92

30 The cash in the fund is $26.75. The fund is replenished to include petty cash payments in this period's financial statements. The petty cash vouchers are for the following:

Freight-in .... $ 9.50
Office supplies 13.75

May 1 The petty cash fund balance is increased to $75.

Required:

Prepare the journal entries to record the above.

P7-4-A. The bank statement for Leas Company's account with the First National Bank for the month ended April 14, 1984, showed a balance of $10,886. On this date, the company's Cash account balance was $8,990. Returned with the bank statement were (1) a debit memo for service charges of $13; (2) a debit memo for a customer's NSF check of $100; and (3) a credit memo for a $2,200 wire transfer of funds on April 14 from the State Bank, the local bank used by the company in another city. Further investigation revealed that outstanding checks amounted to $1,840, the cash receipts of April 14 of $1,621 did not appear as a deposit on the bank statement, and the canceled checks included a check for $410 (drawn by the president of the company to cover travel expenses on a recent trip) that the company has yet to record.

Required:

a. Prepare a bank reconciliation statement for the month ended April 14, 1984.

b. Prepare any necessary journal entries.

P7-5-A. The following information pertains to the Snell Company. The June 30 bank reconciliation statement was as follows:

		Cash account	Bank statement
Balances on June 30		$25,524.48	$24,859.08
Add: Deposit not credited by bank ...			1,256.80
Total			$26,115.88
Deduct: Outstanding checks:			
No. 724.........................	$ 24.60		
No. 886.........................	20.00		
No. 896.........................	191.40		
No. 897.........................	250.20		
No. 898.........................	105.20		591.40
Adjusted cash balance, June 30		$25,524.48	$25,524.48

The July bank statement was as follows:

Balance on July 1		$24,859.08	
Deposits during July		7,255.92	$32,115.00
Canceled checks returned:			
No. 724.........................	$ 24.60		
No. 896.........................	191.40		
No. 897.........................	250.20		
No. 898.........................	105.20		
No. 899	25.14		
No. 900.........................	1,799.40		
No. 902.........................	1,262.56		
No. 904.........................	58.68	$ 3,717.18	
NSF check of Manley Company		186.64	3,903.82
Bank statement balance, July 31			$28,211.18

The cash receipts deposited in July, including receipts of July 31, amounted to $6,904.40. Checks written in July:

No. 899 . . . . . $ 25.14
No. 900 . . . . .   1,799.40
No. 901 . . . . .   37.00
No. 902 . . . . .   1,262.56
No. 903 . . . . .   79.60
No. 904 . . . . .   58.68
No. 905 . . . . .   1,458.00
No. 906 . . . . .   20.00

The cash balance per the ledger on July 31 was $27,688.50.

Required:

Prepare a bank reconciliation statement and any necessary entries.

P7–6–A.   The Grimm Company was organized January 1 of the current year, 1984. It uses a voucher register and a check register with the same column headings as in Illustrations 7.8 and 7.9, except that there are only four voucher register debit columns headed Merchandise Purchases, Transportation-In, Discounts Lost, and Other Accounts.

Required:

Enter the following approved transactions for the month of January in these registers and total and rule the registers. Start with Voucher No. 1 and Check No. 1. Vouchers are prepared for the net amount of the invoice. For discounts lost, a new voucher is prepared for the amount of the discount.

Transactions:

Jan. 2   Received merchandise from the Lind Company on terms of 2/10, n/30. The invoice received was in the amount of $10,400.
      3   Paid transportation charges to Moyer Trucking Company on purchase of January 2, $174.
      6   Paid Wilson Display Company $6,600 for billboard advertising for a three-month period beginning February 1, 1984.
     15   Paid the Lind Company for the purchase of January 2.
     17   Received merchandise from Bradly Company on terms of 2/10, n/30. The invoice received was for $8,400.
     18   Received merchandise from Casp Company on terms of 2/10, n/30. The invoice received was for $35,500. Paid net amount today to establish a good credit rating.
     23   Received invoice for $3,600 from Office Equipment, Inc., for office equipment recently received. Terms are 2/10, n/30.

P7–7–A.   The following information pertains to the bank reconciliation statement to be prepared for the Boyle Company as of May 31, 1984:

Transactions:

1. Balance per bank statement as of May 31, 1984, was $10,980.
2. Balance per the Boyle Company's Cash account at May 31, 1984, was $11,222.
3. A late deposit on May 31 did not appear on the bank statement, $950.
4. Outstanding checks as of May 31 totaled $1,692.
5. During May, the bank credited Boyle Company with the proceeds, $1,510, of a noninterest-bearing note which it had collected for the company.
6. Service and collection charges for the month amount to $4.
7. Comparison of the canceled checks with copies of these checks reveals that one check in the amount of $234 had been recorded in the books at $342. The check had been issued in payment of an account payable.
8. A review of the deposit slips with the bank statement showed that a deposit of $500 of a company with a similar account number has been credited to the Boyle Company account in error.
9. A $60 check received from a customer, R. Perry, was returned with the bank statement marked NSF.

10. During May, the bank paid a $3,030 noninterest-bearing note of the Boyle Company and charged it to the company's account per instructions received. Boyle Company had not recorded the payment of this note.
11. An examination of the cash receipts and the deposit tickets revealed that the bookkeeper erroneously recorded a customer's check of $324 as $432.
12. The bank statement shows a credit to the company's account for interest earned on the account balance in May of $100.

Required:

a. Prepare a bank reconciliation statement as of May 31, 1984.

b. Prepare the journal entries necessary to adjust the accounts as of May 31, 1984.

P7–8–A. The Steele Company has been organized for several years and uses a voucher register and a check register with the same column headings as in Illustrations 7.8 and 7.9, except that there are only four voucher register debit columns headed Merchandise Purchases, Transportation-In, Discounts Lost, and Other Accounts. The last voucher used was No. 432, and the last check issued was No. A727. As of December 31, 1984, there were three vouchers in the unpaid voucher file:

Voucher No. 388	$ 5,760
Voucher No. 401	11,200
Voucher No. 431	3,280
	$20,240

The total of the unpaid voucher file agreed with the credit balance in the Vouchers Payable control account. The following transactions occurred during January 1985. Vouchers are prepared for the net amount of the invoice. For discounts lost, a new voucher is prepared for the amount of the discount.

Transactions:

Jan. 2 An invoice in the amount of $5,600 was received from the Drake Company for office equipment already received. Terms were 2/10, n/30, FOB shipping point.
3 Paid a $3,264 noninterest-bearing note that matured this date. Payee: Citizens' Bank. (Hint: Has a voucher been prepared to authorize this cash payment?)
4 Received an invoice for $4,000 from the Dundee Company for merchandise recently received. Terms were 2/10, n/30.
5 Paid Voucher No. 388 to the Engle Company, $5,760.
7 Paid $560 to the Rapid Service for transportation. Of this amount, $160 applied to the purchase from the Dundee Company and the balance applied to the purchase of office equipment from the Drake Company.
11 Paid the Drake Company for the purchase of January 2.
14 Paid Voucher No. 431 to the Baker Company, $3,280.
15 Paid $880 to the Ericson Company for advertising services received in January.
20 Paid the Dundee Company for the purchase of January 4.
22 Received an invoice for $12,000 from the Dundee Company for merchandise; terms, 2/10, n/30.
31 Received an invoice from Hanson Company for $73,200. This included $1,200 chargeable to Transportation-In and $72,000 for merchandise with credit terms, 2/5, n/30. Since the discount period is short, the invoice was paid immediately with a check for $71,760.

Required:

Set up a voucher register and a check register as described and enter the above transactions. Total and rule the registers at January 31. List the unpaid vouchers at January 31 and compare the total with the balance in the Vouchers Payable control account (Account No. 250) at that date, after posting has been completed.

PROBLEMS, SERIES B

P7–1–B.   From the following information for the Clank Company:

a.   Prepare a bank reconciliation statement as of September 30, 1984.

b.   Give the necessary journal entries to correct the accounts.

Balance per bank statement, September 30, 1984	$16,300
Ledger account balance for cash on September 30, 1984	14,150
Note collected by bank	1,000
Bank charges	10
Deposits in transit	924
NSF check deposited and returned	84
Outstanding checks	1,718
Bank error—deducted $50 from Clank account for check actually written for $500.	

P7–2–B.   Following are selected transactions of the Groves Company during 1984:

Transactions:

Mar. 1   Established a petty cash fund of $500 which will be under the control of the assistant office manager.

Apr. 3   Fund is replenished on this date. Prior to replenishment, the fund consisted of the following:

Coin and currency	$296.42
Payroll check issued by Richter Company to part-time office boy, Joe Johnson, properly endorsed by Johnson	31.28
Petty cash vouchers indicating disbursements for—	
Postage stamps	54.00
Supper money for office employees working overtime	24.00
Office supplies	21.80
Window washing service	40.00
Flowers for wedding of employee	10.00
Flowers for hospitalized employee	10.00
Employee IOU	10.00

The employee's IOU is to be deducted from the employee's next paycheck.

Required:

Present journal entries for the above transactions. Use the Cash Short and Over account for any shortage or overage in the fund.

P7–3–B.   The Arthur Company has decided to use a petty cash fund. Following are transactions made in 1984:

Transactions:

June 4   Set up a petty cash fund of $150.
    22   When the fund had a cash amount of $20.90, the custodian of the fund was reimbursed for expenditures made, including:

Transportation-in	$55.00
Postage	18.00
Office supples	54.50

    30   The fund was reimbursed so as to include petty cash items in the financial statements prepared for the fiscal year ending on this date. The fund currently has the following:

Coin and currency		$114.60
Employee IOU		10.00
Petty cash vouchers for:		
Postage	$18.00	
Office supplies	7.40	25.40

July   1   The fund balance was raised to $200.

Required:

Prepare journal entries for all of the above.

P7–4–B.   The bank statement for the Lynx Company's general checking account with the First National Bank for the month ended August 12, 1984, showed an ending balance of $5,309, service charges of $10, an NSF check returned of $183, and the collection of a $1,010 noninterest-bearing note. Further investigation revealed that a wire transfer of $1,800 from the bank account maintained by the company in City Bank in another city had not been recorded by the company as having been deposited in the First National Bank account. In addition, a comparison of deposits with receipts showed a deposit in transit of $2,100. Checks outstanding amounted to $1,479, while the cash ledger balance was $3,313.

Required:

a.   Prepare a bank reconciliation statement for the Lynx Company account for the month ended August 12, 1984.

b.   Prepare all necessary journal entries.

P7–5–B.   The following data pertain to the Munn Company:

Transactions:

1.   Balance per the bank statement dated June 30, 1984, is $40,760.
2.   Balance of the Cash in Bank account on the company books as of June 30, 1984, is $11,980.
3.   Outstanding checks as of June 30, 1984, are $19,954.
4.   Bank deposit of June 30 for $3,140 was not included in the deposits per the bank statement.
5.   The bank had collected a $30,150 noninterest-bearing note that it credited to the Munn Company account. The bank charged the company a collection fee of $20 on the above note.
6.   The bank erroneously charged the Munn Company account for a $14,000 check of another company that has a similar account number.
7.   Bank service charges for June, exclusive of the collection fee, amounted to $100.
8.   Among the canceled checks was one for $690 given in payment of an account. The bookkeeper had recorded the check at $960 in the company records.
9.   A check of Crosley, a customer, for $4,154, deposited on June 20, was returned by the bank marked NSF. No entry has been made to reflect the returned check on the company records.
10. A check for $1,680 of Moran, a customer, which had been deposited in the bank, was erroneously recorded by the bookkeeper as $1,860.

Required:

Prepare a bank reconciliation statement as of June 30, 1984. Also prepare any necessary journal entries.

P7–6–B.   The Nilson Company was organized January 1 of the current year. It uses a voucher register and a check register with the same column headings as in Illustrations 7.8 and 7.9, except that there are only four voucher register debit columns headed Merchandise Purchases, Transportation-In, Discounts Lost, and Other Accounts.

Required:

Enter the following approved transactions for the month of January in these registers. Total and rule the registers. Start with Voucher No. 1 and Check No. 1. Vouchers are prepared for the net amount of the invoice. For discounts lost, a new voucher is prepared for the amount of the discount.

Transactions:

Jan. 1 Received an invoice from the Modern Company in the amount of $2,400 for office equipment. Terms were 2/10, n/30, FOB shipping point.

3 Received an invoice from the Bailey Company for merchandise in the amount of $4,200. Terms were 2/10, n/30.

5 Received an invoice from the Simpson Company for merchandise in the amount of $3,100. Terms were 2/10, n/30.

7 Paid $360 to the Lund Advertising Service for services received in January.

10 Paid $270 of freight charges to the James Company. Of this, $60 was applicable to the office equipment received on January 1 and the rest to merchandise received from the Bailey Company.

14 Paid the Simpson Company the amount due.

20 Paid the Bailey Company the correct amount due.

31 Paid the Thomas Company the net amount of $24,210 for merchandise received today. (Hint: Has the voucher authorizing this payment been prepared?)

31 The January 1 Modern Company voucher was misfiled and had not been paid as of the end of the month. A voucher was prepared for the discount missed.

P7–7–B. The bank statement of the Lanard Company's checking account with the First National Bank shows:

Balance, June 30, 1984		$24,610
Deposits		36,400
		$61,010
Less: Checks deducted	$36,000	
Service charges	10	36,010
Balance, July 31, 1984		$25,000

The following additional data are available:

Transactions:

1. A credit memorandum included with the canceled checks returned indicates the collection of a note by the bank for the Lanard Company, $2,000.

2. An NSF check in the amount of $920 is returned by the bank and included in the total of checks deducted on the bank statement.

3. Deposits in transit as of July 31, $5,000, and as of June 30, $2,400.

4. Checks outstanding as of June 30, all of which cleared the bank in July, $3,400; checks outstanding as of July 31, $8,200.

5. Balance per ledger account as of July 31, $18,994.

6. The bank added the $4,300 deposit of another company to Lanard's account in error.

7. The bank deducted one of Lanard's checks as $3,000 instead of the correct amount of $300.

8. Deposit of July 21 was recorded by the company as $637 and by the bank at the actual amount of $673. The receipts for the day were from collections on account.

9. The deposits amount shown on the bank statement includes $100 of interest earned by Lanard on its checking account with the bank.

Required:

a. Prepare a bank reconciliation statement as of July 31, 1984, for the Lanard Company.

b. Prepare any journal entries needed at July 31, 1984.

P7–8–B. The Hilt Company has been organized for several years and uses a voucher register and a check register with the same column headings as in Illustrations 7.8 and 7.9, except that there are only four voucher register debit columns headed Merchandise Purchases, Transportation-In, Discounts Lost, and Other Accounts. The last voucher number used was 9743, and the last check issued was No. 2096. As of August 31, 1984, there were three vouchers in the unpaid voucher file:

Voucher No. 9696	. . . . .	$ 660
Voucher No. 9741	. . . . .	1,330
Voucher No. 9742	. . . . .	570
		$2,560

The total of the unpaid voucher file agreed with the credit balance in the Vouchers Payable control account.

The following transactions occurred during September 1984. Vouchers are prepared for the net amount of the invoice. For any discounts lost, a new voucher is prepared for the amount of the discount.

Transactions:

Sept. 3 Paid Citizens Bank $610 for a noninterest-bearing note that matured on this date.
5 Received an invoice for $850 from the Reese Company for merchandise. Terms were 2/10, n/30.
6 Paid Voucher No. 9696 to the Tims Company, $660.
10 Received an invoice for $294 from the Zink Company for merchandise. Terms were 2/10, n/30.
15 Paid the Reese Company the amount owed it on its invoice of September 5.
17 Paid $130 to the Jacklin Company for advertising appearing in September.
30 Paid $8,900 to the Arlin Company. This included $178 chargeable to the Transportation-In account. The balance paid was the net cost of merchandise received today. Terms were 2/10, n/30.
30 Paid the Zink Company the amount due on the purchase of September 10.

Required:

Enter these transactions in the voucher register and the check register. Total and rule the registers as of September 30. List the unpaid vouchers at September 30 and compare the total with the balance in the Vouchers Payable control account (Account No. 250) at that date after posting the proper amounts thereto.

BUSINESS DECISION PROBLEM 7–1

Walter Green was set up in business by his father, who purchased the business of an elderly acquaintance wishing to retire. One of the few changes in personnel made by Walter was to install a college classmate as the office manager–bookkeeper–cashier–sales manager.

During the course of the year, Walter found it necessary to borrow money from the bank (with his father as co-signer) because, although the business seemed profitable, there was a continuous shortage of adequate cash. The investment in inventories and receivables grew substantially during the year. Finally, after a year had elapsed, Walter's father employed a certified public accountant to audit the records of Walter's business. The CPA reported that the office manager–bookkeeper–cashier–sales manager had been stealing funds and had been using a variety of schemes to cover his actions. More specifically, he had—

1. Pocketed cash receipts from sales and understated the cash register readings at the end of the day or altered the copies of the sales tickets retained.
2. Stolen checks mailed to the company in payment of accounts receivable, credited the proper accounts, and then debited fictitious receivables to keep the records in balance.
3. Issued checks to fictitious suppliers and deposited them in accounts bearing these names with himself as signer of checks drawn on these accounts; the books were kept in balance by debiting the Purchases account.
4. Stolen petty cash funds by drawing false vouchers purporting to cover a variety of expenses incurred.

5. Prepared false sales returns vouchers indicating the return of cash sales to cover further thefts of cash receipts.

Required:

For each of the above items, indicate at least one feature of a good system of internal control which would have prevented the losses due to dishonesty.

BUSINESS DECISION PROBLEM 7–2*

The outstanding checks of the Barnes Company at November 30, 1984, were:

No. 229	$250.00
No. 263	272.25
No. 3678	169.75
No. 3679	201.00
No. 3680	350.00

During the month, checks numbered 3681–3720 were issued and all of these checks cleared the bank except Nos. 3719 and 3720 for $240.75 and $181.50, respectively. Check Nos. 3678, 3679, and 3680 also cleared the bank.

The bank statement on December 31 showed a balance of $5,986. Service charges amounted to $5, and two checks were returned by the bank, one marked NSF in the amount of $28.50 and the other marked "No account" in the amount of $500.

Salinas recently retired as the office manager–cashier–bookkeeper for the company and was replaced by Clark. Clark noted the absence of a system of internal control but was momentarily deterred from embezzling for lack of a scheme of concealment. Finally, Clark hit upon several schemes. The $500 check marked "No account" by the bank is the product of one scheme. Clark took cash receipts and replaced them with a check drawn upon a nonexistent account to make it appear that a customer had given the company a worthless check.

The other scheme was more subtle. Clark pocketed cash receipts to bring them down to an amount sufficient to prepare the following reconciliation statement:

Balance, Cash account December 31, 1984		$6,806.70
Deduct:		
Worthless check	$500.00	
NSF check	28.50	
Service charges	5.00	533.50
Adjusted balance		$6,273.20
Balance per bank statement, December 31, 1984 ..		$5,986.00
Add: Deposit in transit		709.45
		$6,695.45
Deduct: Outstanding checks:		
No. 3719	$240.75	
No. 3720	181.50	422.25
Adjusted balance		$6,273.20

Required:

a. State the nature of the second scheme hit upon by Clark. How much in total does it appear Clark has stolen by use of the two schemes together?

b. Prepare a correct bank reconciliation statement as of December 31, 1984.

* Note: This is the challenging problem that was not specifically illustrated in the chapter, but it can be worked by applying the principles illustrated in the chapter.

    c. Suggest procedures which would have defeated the attempts of Clark to steal funds and conceal these actions.

BUSINESS DECISION PROBLEM 7–3

    Carol Bell recently acquired an importing business from a friend. The business employs 10 salesclerks and four office employees. A petty cash fund of $500 has been established. All of the 14 employees are allowed to make disbursements from the fund. Vouchers are not used, and no one keeps a record of the disbursements. The petty cash is kept in a large shoe box in the office.

Required:

    Discuss the operation of the petty cash fund from an internal control point of view. Indicate the weaknesses that currently exist and suggest how the internal control system can be improved.

Chapter 8

Receivables and payables

CHAPTER GOALS

After study of this chapter, you should be able to:

1. Account for uncollectible accounts receivable.
2. Record credit card sales and collections.
3. Account for notes receivable and payable, including calculation of interest.
4. Record the discounting of a customer's note at a bank.
5. Define and use correctly the new terms in the glossary.

In accounting, the term *receivable* describes any sum of money due from any party for any reason. The term *payable* similarly describes any sum of money to be paid to any party for any reason.

This chapter deals primarily with receivables arising from the sale of goods and the rendering of services, paying particular attention to the accounting for uncollectible receivables. Also discussed are short-term notes receivable and payable, including the recording of interest on them, and their payment or dishonor.

ACCOUNTS RECEIVABLE

The term *accounts receivable* or **trade receivables** refers to amounts due from customers for goods sold and services rendered on open account. When goods are sold on open account, customers do not sign formal, written promises to pay. Rather, they agree to abide by the seller's customary credit terms. In some cases, they may sign a sales invoice to acknowledge purchase of goods. Thus, a firm that has accounts receivable is extending credit to its customers. For most firms, the granting of credit is a business necessity simply because competitors extend credit. Payment terms typically run from 30 to 60 days. Interest usually is not charged on amounts owed, except in some cases on past-due amounts.

The Accounts Receivable account should contain only amounts due from customers. The total amount due from customers is used to develop certain ratios that are used in financial statement analysis. Loans to officers, claims for tax refunds, interest receivable, and amounts due from sales of plant assets are classified as other receivables, not as accounts receivable.

Accounts receivable should contain only customer accounts with debit balances. Credit balances in customers' accounts should not offset accounts with debit balances. Credit balances may develop from advance payments by customers or from credit granted for returns after an account has been paid. Such credit balances should be reported as current liabilities under titles such as Advances from Customers or Credit Balances in Customers' Accounts. Similarly, advance payments to vendors should be reported as current assets under titles such as Advances to Creditors or Debit Balances in Creditors' Accounts and not be offset against accounts payable nor added to accounts receivable.

Recording revenue

For firms selling goods, accrual basis accounting generally requires the recording of revenue when a sale is made because the revenue is earned and realized. The revenue is earned because the seller has completed its part of the sales contract by delivering the goods. The revenue is realized because goods have been exchanged for the customer's promise to pay. The promise to pay is an account receivable.

Recording revenue upon receipt of an account receivable gives rise to an accounting problem not faced if sales are recorded only when cash is received. That problem is bad debts or uncollectible accounts.

Bad debts or uncollectible accounts

In seeking to increase sales and net income, firms extend credit to their customers. Doing business on a credit basis leads to an inescapable fact—some customers' accounts will prove uncollectible no matter how carefully a firm screens its applicants for credit. These credit losses are called bad debts expense. *Bad debts expense* is an operating (usually a selling) expense a business incurs when it sells on credit, and is also called uncollectible accounts expense.

Because bad debts expense is considered an operating expense, the matching principle requires that the expense be matched against the revenues it generates. Thus, a bad debt arising from a sale made in 1984 must be treated as a 1984 expense even though to do so requires the use of estimates. Estimates are necessary because the specific customer accounts from 1984 sales that will prove uncollectible will not be known until 1985 or later.

When bad debts are estimated, the company makes a periodic adjusting entry. The debit is to Bad Debts Expense to get the expense in the proper period. But the credit cannot be to Accounts Receivable. Since the company is estimating bad debts, it does not know which specific customer accounts will be uncollectible. If the uncollectible accounts were known, they would be written off now. Since they are not known, credits cannot be entered in customers' accounts. The credit is entered in an account called *Allowance for Doubtful Accounts* (also called *Allowance for Bad Debts* or *Allowance for Uncollectible Accounts*). The allowance is a contra account to accounts receivable used to value accounts receivable at their net realizable value. The allowance lets the firm recognize, for financial statement purposes, that some of the accounts receivable will not be collected without crediting the Accounts Receivable control account. If the control account were credited without crediting specific customers' accounts, the control account balance would not agree with the subsidiary ledger.

To illustrate, assume that a company estimates its bad debts expense for a given year at $4,000. The required year-end adjusting entry is:

```
Dec. 31  Bad Debts Expense........................................  4,000
             Allowance for Doubtful Accounts ........................          4,000
         To record estimated bad debts.
```

The debit to Bad Debts Expense brings about the desired matching of expense and revenue. The credit to the allowance reduces the recorded amount of accounts receivable to their net realizable value. *Net realizable value* is the amount expected to be collected from accounts receivable. It is equal to the total recorded amount of accounts receivable less the allowance for doubtful accounts. Bad Debts Expense will be closed to Income Summary when the books are closed. The allowance will be reported on the balance sheet as a reduction from accounts receivable.

To summarize: Recording the estimated amount of bad debts accomplishes two goals: (1) proper matching—bad debts expense is matched against revenues in the year of sale rather than being recorded in a future year when the accounts are actually found to be uncollectible—and (2) accounts receivable are properly valued on the balance sheet at their net realizable value.

Estimation methods

There are two basic methods of estimating periodic bad debts. One method focuses attention on the income statement and the relationship of bad debts to sales. The other method focuses attention upon the balance sheet and the relationship of the allowance for doubtful accounts to accounts receivable.

Percentage of sales. The *percentage-of-sales method* is a method of estimating uncollectible accounts from a given year's credit sales and, indirectly, of determining the balance in the Allowance for Doubtful Accounts. The method is based upon a ratio of prior years' actual bad debt losses to prior years' credit sales. This percentage is reviewed annually to see if it is still valid; if not; it will be increased or decreased to reflect changed conditions. For example, in periods of inflation and high interest rates, the rate may have to be increased to reflect decreased customer ability to pay. Alternatively, the rate may be decreased if fewer uncollectible accounts are expected because of a more stringent credit granting policy adopted. *If cash sales are small or a fairly constant percentage of total sales, the calculation can be based on total sales.*

To illustrate, assume that uncollectible accounts from 1982 sales were 1.1 percent of credit sales. It does not matter when the accounts were found to be uncollectible, they still arose from 1982 sales. A similar calculation for 1983 showed a loss ratio of 0.9; the average for the two years is 1 percent. The rate may be increased or decreased if future conditions are expected to differ.

Assume that these data apply to the Rankin Company which does not expect 1984 to differ from the previous two years. Credit sales for 1984 were $600,000; receivables at year-end were $100,000; and the allowance for doubtful accounts had a zero balance. Rankin would make the following adjusting entry for 1984:

```
Dec. 31  Bad Debts Expense .......................................  6,000
             Allowance for Doubtful Accounts ........................          6,000
                 To record estimated bad debts ($600,000  ×  0.01).
```

Bad Debts Expense would be closed to Income Summary, and the accounts receivable and allowance would be reported among current assets in the balance sheet as follows:

```
Accounts receivable ........................  $100,000
    Less: Allowance for doubtful accounts .......    6,000    $94,000
```

A more likely presentation in a published balance sheet is:

Accounts receivable (less estimated uncollectible
   accounts, $6,000) $94,000

The allowance usually has a balance prior to year-end adjustment. *Under the percentage-of-sales method, any existing balance in the allowance generally is ignored in calculating the amount of the year-end adjustment.* The expense and addition to the allowance are based on the past average relationship of actual losses to credit or total sales. Any given year can be expected to vary from the average. Hence, minor balances are ignored. Assume, in the example, Rankin's allowance had a $300 credit balance prior to adjustment. The adjusting entry would be the same as given for the preceding illustration. But the balance sheet would show $100,000 accounts receivable less a $6,300 allowance for net receivables of $93,700. Bad Debts Expense would still appear on the income statement as 1 percent of credit sales or $6,000.

While minor balances in the allowance are ignored, substantial balances cannot be ignored. For example, if Rankin had a $7,000 debit balance in its allowance prior to adjustment, the $6,000 adjustment made above would leave the allowance with a $1,000 debit balance. A revised adjustment is obviously needed. Such an adjustment might be calculated using the percentage-of-receivables method.

Percentage of receivables. The *percentage-of-receivables method* is a method of determining the desired size of the allowance for doubtful accounts and, indirectly, the bad debts expense for the period. The method uses as an estimation basis only those accounts from a given years' sales that might be uncollectible, that is, those still uncollected. One overall rate may be used in this method, or a different rate may be used for each age category of receivables.

Using the same information as before, Rankin will make an estimate of bad debts at the end of 1984. The balance of accounts receivable is $100,000, and the allowance has no balance. If Rankin estimates that 6 percent of the receivables will be uncollectible, the entry is the same as before:

Dec. 31   Bad Debts Expense 6,000
         Allowance for Doubtful Accounts 6,000
       To record estimated bad debts ($100,000 × 0.06).

If there was a $300 credit balance in the allowance, the entry would be the same as the one just given, except that the amount would be for $5,700.

The difference in amounts arises because the firm wants the allowance to contain a balance equal to 6 percent of the outstanding receivables when the two accounts are presented on the balance sheet. *Thus, under the percentage-of-receivables method, any balance in the allowance must be considered when adjusting for bad debts.* As another example, if Rankin had a $300 *debit* balance in the allowance prior to adjustment, a credit of $6,300 would be necessary to get the balance to the required $6,000. In this instance, T-accounts would show:

Bad Debts Expense		**Allowance for Doubtful Accounts**	
Dec. 31 Adjustment 6,300		Bal. before adjustment 300	Dec. 31 Adjustment 6,300
			Bal. after adjustment 6,000

No matter what the preadjustment allowance balance was, using the above information should lead Rankin to report Accounts Receivable of $100,000 and an Allowance for Doubtful Accounts of $6,000—which is 6 percent of the $100,000.

Aging schedule. An *aging schedule* is a means of classifying accounts receivable according to their age in appraising the accounts for purposes of establishing or adding to the Allowance for Doubtful Accounts. An aging schedule reflects the fact that the older a receivable is, the more likely it will not be collected. The aging schedule presented in Illustration 8.1 shows how the age of each customer's account is determined. The age of the accounts is the basis for estimating uncollectibility. For example, only 1 percent of the accounts not yet due (sales made less than 30 days prior to the end of the accounting period) is expected to be uncollectible. At the other extreme, 50 percent of all accounts over 90 days past due is expected to be worthless. The journal entry to record bad debts is affected by the balance in the allowance prior to adjustment because a percentage-of-receivables method is being applied. For example, Illustration 8.1 shows that $24,400 is needed in the allowance. If the allowance currently has a $5,000 credit balance, the adjustment will be for $19,400.

The information contained in an aging schedule may be useful to manage-

Illustration 8.1: Accounts receivable aging schedule

			Number of Days Past Due			
Customer	Debit Balance	Not Yet Due	1–30	31–60	61–90	Over 90
DARCY COMPANY Accounts Receivable Aging Schedule December 31, 1984						
X	$ 8,000					$ 8,000
Y	16,000		$ 12,000	$4,000		
Z	4,000				$800	3,200
All others	800,000	$560,000	240,000			
	$828,000	$560,000	$252,000	$4,000	$800	$11,200
Estimated uncollectible percentage		1%	5%	10%	25%	50%
Amount uncollectible	$ 24,400	$ 5,600	$12,600	$ 400	$200	$ 5,600

ment for purposes other than estimating bad debts. Visible information on collection patterns of accounts receivable may suggest the need for changes in credit policies or for added financing. For example, if the age of many customer balances has increased to fall in the 61–90 days past due category, collection efforts may have to be strengthened. Or management may have to find other sources of cash to pay the firm's debts.

Either of the two methods of estimating bad debts is acceptable. Some accountants prefer the percentage-of-sales method on the grounds that it does a better job of matching expenses with revenues. While bad debts expense under this method does have a specific relationship to sales, the results obtained under both methods are likely to be quite similar over time.

Write-off of receivables

When a specific customer's account is considered uncollectible, it must be written off. Under the allowance method, such write-offs are debited to the allowance, not to bad debts expense. Bad debts expense was recorded on an estimated basis in the year of sale. When the estimated expense was recorded, Accounts Receivable (the general ledger control account) could not be credited because the specific bad accounts were not known. The credit was entered in an allowance account. Now that a specific uncollectible account is known, the credit to the allowance can be transferred to the Accounts Receivable control account and to the customer's subsidiary ledger account. Thus, the entry to write off Smith's $750 account as uncollectible is:

```
Allowance for Doubtful Accounts .....................................   750
    Accounts Receivable—Smith ......................................          750
  To write Smith's account off as uncollectible.
```

This entry does not "double count" an expense. No expense is recorded in the entry. Expense was debited when the allowance was credited. The balance in the allowance represents potential bad debts whose negative impact upon income has been recognized in the year of sale. Debiting the allowance shows that a particular uncollectible account has been identified. If an expense was recognized at the time of write-off of the account, a reduction in total assets would be expected. But note that total assets are not reduced by the write-off. If total accounts receivable were $50,000 and the allowance was $3,000 before the above entry, the net realizable value of the accounts receivable was $47,000. After posting the above entry, accounts receivable are $49,250 and the allowance is $2,250. Net realizable value is still $47,000.

The Allowance for Doubtful Accounts may have a debit balance before adjustment if it is adjusted only at year-end. Companies do not often carry accounts receivable that are more than one year old in their records. Consequently, by the end of 1984, all accounts from 1983 sales will have either been collected or written off. If estimates were exact, the allowance would have a zero balance. But it may develop a debit balance if estimates were less than actual write-offs. Also, some accounts from 1984 sales probably have been charged off. The result is very likely to be a debit balance in the allowance before annual adjustment.

Also, after a company has used the allowance method for a few years, the balance in the allowance consists of the net amount of inadequate or excessive estimates of bad debts of prior years. Errors in estimating preceding years' uncollectibles are corrected by increasing or decreasing the current year's estimate.

Bad debts recovered

A company usually learns that an account has been charged off erroneously when a check applying to that account is received in the mail. The receipt of the check makes it obvious that the account should not have been charged off. The account should be reinstated by reversing the original write-off entry. Accounts Receivable—Smith is debited and the Allowance for Doubtful Accounts is credited. The check will be recorded in the cash receipts journal with a debit to Cash and a credit to Accounts Receivable—Smith. The credit is posted to both the general ledger and to the customer's subsidiary ledger account.

To illustrate, assume that on May 17 a $750 check is received from Smith in payment of an account that was previously written off. The entries required are:

May 17	Accounts Receivable—Smith	750	
	Allowance for Doubtful Accounts		750
	To reverse original write-off of Smith's account.		
17	Cash	750	
	Accounts Receivable—Smith		750
	To record collection of account.		

If only a part of a previously written off account is collected, the preferable procedure is to reinstate only that portion of the account actually collected unless there is evidence that the entire account will be collected.

Direct write-off method

The *direct write-off method* is a way of accounting for uncollectible accounts receivable in which such accounts are charged directly to an expense account. The method is used in some firms where accounts receivable and bad debts are immaterial. Under this method, no adjusting entry is made to record estimated bad debts. Rather, accounts receivable considered uncollectible are debited directly to Bad Debts Expense. To illustrate, assume that Robert Hill's $200 account is written off, with $125 subsequently collected. The entries are:

Bad Debts Expense	200	
Accounts Receivable—Robert Hill		200
To write off uncollectible account.		
Accounts Receivable—Robert Hill	125	
Bad Debts Expense		125
To reinstate portion of account written off.		

```
Cash .................................................. 125
     Accounts Receivable—Robert Hill ...............................        125
     To record collection on account.
```

Although acceptable for income tax purposes, the direct write-off method is not acceptable for financial accounting in most cases because (1) it does not properly match expenses and revenues and (2) it overstates accounts receivable in the balance sheet because the allowance for doubtful accounts is not used.

Credit cards

Credit cards are charge cards such as VISA, American Express, and MasterCard which are used by customers to charge their purchases of goods and services. For many businesses that now accept such cards, bad debt losses and other costs of extending credit to customers had become a significant burden. As a result, many of these firms elected to pass these costs on to banks and other credit agencies issuing national credit cards. For a fee ranging from 2 percent to 8 percent of sales price, credit card agencies absorb the bad debts and the costs of extending credit and maintaining records previously borne by the firm.

The credit card agencies issue credit cards, often at an annual fee, to approved credit applicants. A firm that contracts to accept a credit card in payment of a sale agrees to pay the fee mentioned above. Upon making a credit card sale, the seller checks the customer's card against a list of canceled cards and calls the credit agency for sale approval if the sale exceeds a prescribed amount, such as $50. These procedures are followed so that the seller does not accept a lost, stolen, or canceled card and so that the sale does not run the credit extended the customer over a specified limit. From this point on, the procedures differ depending upon whether a bank or a nonbank card is accepted.

To illustrate, assume that a restaurant has Diners Club invoices amounting to $1,400 at the end of a day. The following entry is needed:

```
Accounts Receivable—Diners Club ................................. 1,400
     Sales ........................................................        1,400
     To record credit card sales.
```

The invoices are mailed to Diners Club. Assume that payment is received from Diners Club some time later with a 5 percent service charge or fee deducted. The entry is:

```
Cash .................................................. 1,330
Credit Card Expense .....................................   70
     Accounts Receivable—Diners Club .............................        1,400
     To record remittance from Diners Club.
```

Credit card expense is the credit card agency's fee for services rendered in processing credit card sales.

To illustrate the use of bank credit cards, assume that a retailer made sales of $1,000 for which VISA cards were accepted. The VISA service charge is 5 percent. VISA sales are treated as if they were cash sales. The sales invoices are deposited in a checking account maintained in a bank just as checks are deposited in a regular checking account. The entry needed is:

Cash	950	
Credit Card Expense	50	
Sales		1,000
To record VISA credit card sales.		

The credit card company bills the customer for all charges made during the month. If the customer fails to pay, the credit card company suffers the loss, not the retailer.

NOTES RECEIVABLE AND PAYABLE

A *promissory note* is a written promise by a borrower (maker) to pay a certain sum of money to the lender (payee) on demand or on a specific date. Since the note is negotiable, the payee may transfer it to another party who then receives payment from the maker. An example of a promissory note is shown in Illustration 8.2.

A company may have notes receivable or payable arising from transactions with customers or suppliers. Notes may also arise from loans involving a bank or an individual. The accounting for note transactions is covered in this section of the chapter.

Interest calculation

Most notes have an explicit interest charge. Interest is the fee charged for use of money through time. It is an expense to the maker and a revenue to the payee of the note. For convenience, interest is commonly calculated on the basis of a 360-day year. To calculate the number of days in a stated period, count the exact number of days by omitting the day the money is borrowed (or the date of the note) but counting the day it is repaid. For example, a note dated May 15 which matures on July 14 runs for 60 days

Illustration 8.2: Promissory note

$ 2,000.00	June 1 , 19 84

Sixty days- -AFTER DATE We PROMISE TO PAY TO

THE ORDER OF **MOTOR WHEEL CORPORATION**

Two Thousand and no/100- **DOLLARS**

AT Motor Wheel Corporation, Lansing, Michigan

FOR VALUE RECEIVED WITH INTEREST AT THE RATE OF 10% PER ANNUM FROM June 1, 1984

This note is one of a series of 1 notes of even date herewith, numbered 487 to -- inclusive, and all of said notes shall become immediately due and payable at the option of the holder hereof on default being made in the payment of any one at maturity.

NO. 487 DUE July 31, 1984 THE PETERSON COMPANY

John J. Lucia, Treasurer

(16 days in May, 30 days in June, and 14 days in July for a total of 60 days). A note falling due on a Sunday or a holiday is due on the next business day.

The basic formula for computing interest is:

$$\text{Interest} = \text{Principal} \times \text{Rate} \times \text{Time}$$

Principal is the face value of the note. The rate is the stated interest rate on the note; interest rates are generally stated on an annual basis. Time is the amount of time the note is to run; it can be expressed in either days or months. An example of interest calculation is given with a $20,000, 15 percent, 90-day note:

$$\text{Interest} = \$20,000 \times 0.15 \times 90/360$$
$$\text{Interest} = \$750$$

Determination of maturity date

The maturity date may be found by one of several methods depending on the wording used in the note:

1. *On demand.* "On demand, I promise to pay. . . ." In this case, the maturity date is at the option of the holder and cannot be computed. The holder is the payee or another person who legally acquired the note from the payee.
2. *On a stated date.* "On July 18, 1983, I promise to pay. . . ." The date is designated, and a computation is not necessary to determine it.
3. *At the end of a stated period.*
   a. "One year after date, I promise to pay. . . ." If the maturity is expressed in years, the note matures on the same day of the same month as the date of the note in the year of maturity.
   b. "Four months after date, I promise to pay. . . ." If the maturity is expressed in months, the note will mature on the same date in the month of maturity. For example, one month from July 18, 1983, is August 18, 1983, and two months from July 18, 1983, is September 18, 1983. If a note is issued on the last day of a month and the month of maturity has fewer days than the month of issuance, the note matures on the last day of the month of maturity. A one-month note dated January 30, 1983, matures on February 28, 1983.
   c. "Ninety days after date, I promise to pay. . . ." If the maturity is expressed in days, the exact number of days must be counted. The first day (date of origin) is omitted and the last day (maturity date) is included in the count. For example, a 90-day note dated October 19, 1983, matures on January 17, 1984.

Life of note (days)		90 days
Days remaining in October not counting date of origin of note:		
Days to count in October (31–19)	12	
Total days in November	30	
Total days in December	31	73
Maturity date in January		17

To illustrate, assume that Cooper (in the above example) has a fiscal year ending on October 31. On that date, Cooper would make the following adjusting entry relative to the Price note:

```
Oct. 31   Accrued Interest Receivable . . . . . . . . . . . . . . . . . . . . . . . .      187.50
                Interest Revenue ($18,000  ×  0.15  ×  25/360)  . . . .                              187.50
                To record accrued interest earned for the period October
          6 through October 31.
```

Accrued Interest Receivable is an account showing the asset for interest revenue earned but not yet collected. It is reported as a current asset since it will be collected in 35 days. Interest revenue will be reported in the income statement.

When Price pays the note on December 5, Cooper will make this entry:

```
Dec.  5   Cash  . . . . . . . . . . . . . . . . . . . . . . . . . . . . . . . . . . . . . . .   18,450.00
                Notes Receivable—Price . . . . . . . . . . . . . . . . . . . . . . .               18,000.00
                Accrued Interest Receivable  . . . . . . . . . . . . . . . . . . . .                   187.50
                Interest Revenue . . . . . . . . . . . . . . . . . . . . . . . . . . . . .               262.50
          To record collection of Price note and interest.
```

This entry records collection of the note's principal and interest, a part of which was accrued in the prior accounting period.

Assuming Price's accounting year ends on November 30, Price's accounting records would be incomplete unless an adjusting entry is made to record the liability owed for the accrued interest on the Cooper note. The required adjusting entry is:

```
Nov. 30   Interest Expense ($18,000  ×  0.15  ×  55/360) . . . . . . . .      412.50
                Accrued Interest Payable . . . . . . . . . . . . . . . . . . . . . . .                   412.50
                To record accrued interest on Price note.
```

Accrued Interest Payable is an account showing the liability for interest expense incurred but not yet paid. It is reported as a current liability in the balance sheet because it will be paid in five days. Interest expense will be reported in the income statement.

Price will make this entry when the note is paid:

```
Dec.  5   Notes Payable—Cooper . . . . . . . . . . . . . . . . . . . . . . . . . . .   18,000.00
          Accrued Interest Payable . . . . . . . . . . . . . . . . . . . . . . . . .      412.50
          Interest Expense . . . . . . . . . . . . . . . . . . . . . . . . . . . . . . .       37.50
                Cash . . . . . . . . . . . . . . . . . . . . . . . . . . . . . . . . . . . . . . .            18,450.00
          To record payment of principal and interest on Cooper
          note.
```

Dishonored notes

A *dishonored note* is a note which the maker failed to pay at maturity. The payee of the note should debit Accounts Receivable for the maturity value of the note, crediting Notes Receivable for face value and Interest Revenue for the interest. Since the note has matured, it is no longer negotiable and must be removed from Notes Receivable but retained as an asset in Accounts Receivable. The maker of the note is now obligated to pay principal plus interest. If the interest has not been accrued, the maker should record interest expense for the life of the note. The full liability on the note is then included in the accounts.

To illustrate, assume that Price did not pay the note at maturity. The entries on each party's books are:

Cooper, payee

Dec. 5	Accounts Receivable—Price	18,450
	Notes Receivable—Price	18,000
	Interest Revenue	450
	To record dishonor of Price note.	

Price, maker

Dec. 5	Interest Expense	450
	Interest Payable	450
	To record interest on note payable.	

Sometimes when the maker of a note is unable to pay at maturity, the maker pays the interest on the original note or includes it in the face value of a new note given to replace the old note. The new note is accounted for in the same way as the old note.

If it becomes clear that the maker of a dishonored note will never pay, the payee should write off the account with a debit to Bad Debts Expense or Loss on Dishonored Notes and a credit to Accounts Receivable. If notes receivable were given consideration when the annual provision for bad debts was made, the debit should be to the Allowance for Doubtful Accounts.

Notes payable from short-term financing

There are several reasons why a business may need short-term financing. Two of these reasons are: (1) cash receipts are delayed because of credit terms granted customers and (2) cash is needed to finance the buildup of seasonal inventories such as that occurring in department stores prior to Christmas. Short-term financing may be secured by issuing interest-bearing notes, by issuing noninterest-bearing notes, and by discounting customers' notes which the firm holds.

Interest-bearing notes. A company may borrow money from a bank by issuing an interest-bearing note. The note will carry a stated interest rate and mature on a specific date. For example, assume that Needham Company issued a $10,000, 90-day, 18 percent note on August 18. The following entries would be made to record the loan and its payment on November 16:

Aug. 18	Cash..	10,000
	Notes Payable	10,000
	To record 90-day bank loan.	

Nov. 16	Notes Payable	10,000
	Interest Expense	450
	Cash	10,450
	To record principal and interest paid on bank loan.	

If the term of the note extended beyond a balance sheet date, an adjusting entry would be needed on the balance sheet date to record the accrued interest payable.

Noninterest-bearing notes. A company may borrow from a bank by issuing its own noninterest-bearing note. A noninterest-bearing note does not have a stated interest rate that is applied to face value to calculate interest. Instead, the note is drawn for a maturity amount from which bank discount is deducted and the proceeds given to the borrower. *Bank discount* is the difference between the maturity value of a note and its proceeds. It follows then that the *proceeds* are equal to maturity amount of a note less bank discount. The entire process is referred to as discounting a note payable. The purpose of the process is to introduce interest into what appears to be a noninterest-bearing note. Because interest is related to time, bank discount is not interest on the date the loan is made; but it will become interest expense to the company and interest revenue to the bank. To illustrate, assume that on December 1, 1984, Needham Company discounted its $10,000, 90-day, noninterest-bearing note at the bank at 18 percent. The discount is $450 ($10,000 × 0.18 × 90/360), and the proceeds to Needham are $9,550. The entry required is:

```
Dec.  1  Cash ...................................................   9,550
         Discount on Notes Payable ..............................     450
            Notes Payable .......................................            10,000
         Issued 90-day note to bank.
```

With Notes Payable recorded at face value, as is traditional in accounting, a Discount on Notes Payable must be recorded. *Discount on Notes Payable* is a contra account used to reduce Notes Payable from face value to the net amount to show on the balance sheet. The account is reported on the balance sheet as a deduction from the Notes Payable account. Over time, the discount becomes interest expense. If the note was paid before the end of the fiscal year, the entire $450 of discount would be charged to Interest Expense and credited to Discount on Notes Payable when the note was paid. If Needham's fiscal year ended on December 31, the required adjusting entry would read:

```
Dec. 31  Interest Expense ........................................   150
            Discount on Notes Payable .............................            150
         To record interest on note payable.
```

This entry records the interest expense incurred by Needham for the 30 days the note has been outstanding. The expense can be calculated as $10,000 × 0.18 × 30/360, or 30/90 × $450. No separate accrued interest payable account is needed. The notes payable account already contains the total liability that will be paid at maturity, $10,000. Rather, the liability grows by reducing the contra account. Thus, the current liability section of the December 31, 1984, balance sheet would show:

```
Notes Payable .....................  $10,000
   Less: Discount on notes payable ....     300   $9,700
```

The $9,700 is the amount that would have to be paid to the bank if the company wished to repay the loan on December 31 rather than at maturity date if interest rates have not changed. It is also the original amount borrowed, $9,550, plus the accrued interest for 30 days, $150.

When the note is paid at maturity, the entry is:

Mar. 1	Notes Payable	10,000	
	Interest Expense	300	
	Cash		10,000
	Discount on Notes Payable............................		300
	To record note payment and interest expense.		

This entry reduces Notes Payable to a zero balance and records the remaining discount as interest expense of the current period.

Care must be exercised when dealing with interest and discount rates. In both of the above examples, the quoted rate was 18 percent, which was the actual rate on the interest-bearing note. But the actual interest rate when a noninterest-bearing note was used was 18.8 percent. The borrower paid $450 for use of $9,550—not $10,000—for 90 days. Using the interest calculation formula of $I = P \times R \times T$, P is $9,550, I is $450, T is 90 days, and we solve for R:

$$\$450 = \$9,550 \times R \times 90/360$$
$$\$450 = \$2,387.50 \times R$$
$$R = \$450/\$2,387.50$$
$$R = 0.188, \text{ or } 18.8 \text{ percent}$$

Bank discount rates must be converted into actual interest rates before being compared with interest rates quoted by alternative sources of borrowed money.

Discounting notes receivable.   Rather than issue its own note payable, a company may discount a note received from one of it customers. Since a note is a negotiable instrument, it does not matter who holds the note at maturity; as long as the holder has obtained the note legally, it will be paid to the holder. *Discounting a note receivable* is the act of transferring a note receivable *with recourse* to a bank. *With recourse* is a legal term which means that the bank can collect from the company which transferred the note to the bank if the maker does not pay at maturity.

The party discounting the note has a contingent liability, or is said to be contingently liable on the note. A *contingent liability* is a condition that may become an actual liability if a specific action does or does not occur. In the case of a discounted note receivable, the contingent liability becomes an actual liability if the maker of the note does not pay at maturity date.

The bank may charge a different rate of interest (discount) than is stated on the note receivable. The discount rate must be used to compute the amount of bank discount on maturity value. The payee of the note may have been satisfied with a 9 percent rate, while the bank now seeks a 10 percent discount rate. The bank discount will be computed using the 10 percent rate. Cash proceeds from discounting a note receivable are determined as follows:

1. Determine maturity value of the note (face value plus interest).
2. Determine the discount period. Count the exact number of days from the date of discounting to maturity date. Exclude the date of discounting but include maturity date in the count.
3. Using the bank's discount rate, compute bank discount on maturity value for the discount period.
4. Deduct bank discount from maturity value to get cash proceeds.

Example. Assume that on May 4, 1984, Clark Company received a $10,000, 9 percent, 60-day note, dated May 4, 1984, from Kent Company. On May 14, 1984, Clark Company discounted the note at the Michigan National Bank at 10 percent. The discount and the cash proceeds are determined as follows:

Face value of note	$10,000.00
Add: Interest at 9% for 60 days	
($10,000 × 0.09 × 60/360)	150.00
Maturity value	$10,150.00
Less: Bank discount on $10,150 at 10 percent for 50 days	
($10,150 × 0.10 × 50/360)	140.97
Cash proceeds	$10,009.03

The entry needed is:

May 14 Cash	10,009.03	
Notes Receivable Discounted		10,000.00
Interest Revenue		9.03
To record discounting of notes receivable.		

The contingent liability is shown in the accounts by recording the note discounted in a Notes Receivable Discounted account at face value of the note, even though the contingent liability includes the interest also. *Notes Receivable Discounted* is a contra account to Notes Receivable and is used to show the contingent liability for customers' notes that have been discounted.

The proceeds received from discounting a note receivable will rarely, if ever, equal the amount at which the note is carried in the accounts—usually face value. Any difference between proceeds and face value of the note is recorded as interest expense or interest revenue. If proceeds are less than face value, interest expense is recorded. The bank's discount rate was higher than the interest rate in the note. Thus, the company incurred a cost to get cash now. If proceeds are greater than face value, interest revenue is recorded. Interest revenue results from the fact that the company held the note for some time before discounting it, or the interest rate on the note is higher than the bank's discount rate.

The discounting of a note can be presented graphically as is shown in Illustration 8.3. The $10,000 face amount of the note is increased to maturity value by the addition of interest at 9 percent. The $10,150 maturity value is reduced by the discount calculated at 10 percent for 50 days to obtain the proceeds of $10,009.03. Note that if the discount rate was greater than 10 percent, the proceeds would be smaller—dotted line *a*. If the rate was lower, the proceeds would be larger—dotted line *b*.

Illustration 8.3:   Discounting a note

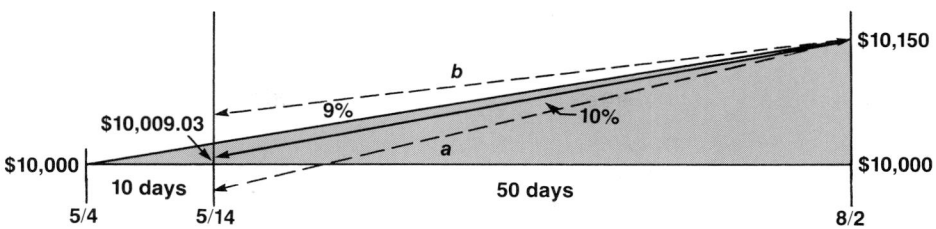

Balance sheet presentation of notes receivable discounted.   In the Clark Company example, a balance sheet prepared for Clark Company as of June 30, 1984, should show a contingent liability in the amount of $10,000 for notes receivable discounted. Assume that the total of all notes receivable is $70,000. An acceptable method of presenting this information in the balance sheet is:

Assets

Current assets:
Cash	$xx,xxx
Accounts receivable	xx,xxx
Notes receivable (Note 1) . . .	60,000

Notes to Financial Statements:
Note 1: At June 30, 1984, the company is contingently liable for $10,000 of customers' notes receivable that it has endorsed and discounted at the local bank.

An alternative balance sheet presentation of the above data where brevity is not so highly desired is:

Notes receivable	$70,000	
Less: Notes receivable discounted . . .	10,000	$60,000

Discounted notes receivable paid by maker.   When a note receivable has been discounted, it is usually the duty of the endorsee (the holder) to present the note to the maker for payment at maturity. If the maker pays the endorsee (the bank in the above illustration) at maturity, the endorser (the company which discounted the note) is thereby relieved of its contingent liability. If the note is not paid at maturity, the endorsee can collect from the endorser which, in turn, can try to collect from the maker. In this case, the contingent liability is also removed because payment was made, but a receivable exists for the amount of the note and interest from the maker.

Assume that in the above example, Kent Company pays the $10,000 note plus interest of $150 to the Michigan National Bank on July 3, 1984, the note's maturity date. Clark Company, which discounted the note at the bank, can no longer be held liable on the note and, therefore, will make the following entry:

July 3	Notes Receivable Discounted	10,000	
	Notes Receivable—Kent		10,000
	To remove the note and the contingent liability from the accounts.		

This entry reduces the balance of each of these accounts to zero.

Discounted notes receivable not paid by maker. If Kent Company dishonors its note, the Michigan National Bank will collect the principal ($10,000) and interest ($150) from Clark Company. Clark Company will have to make two entries as follows:

July 3	Notes Receivable Discounted	10,000	
	Notes Receivable—Kent		10,000
	To remove note and contingent liability from the accounts.		
3	Accounts Receivable—Kent	10,150	
	Cash		10,150
	To record cash paid to bank for Kent's dishonored note.		

Clark Company will then try to collect $10,150 from Kent Company. If these efforts prove unsuccessful, the $10,150 will be removed from Accounts Receivable and treated as a loss from bad debts.

NEW TERMS INTRODUCED IN CHAPTER 8

Accrued interest payable
An account showing the liability for interest expense incurred but not yet paid.

Accrued interest receivable
An account showing the asset for interest revenue earned but not yet collected.

Aging schedule
A means of classifying accounts receivable according to their age in appraising them for purposes of establishing or adding to the balance in an Allowance for Doubtful Accounts.

Allowance for doubtful accounts
A contra account to accounts receivable used to value accounts receivable at their net realizable value. Also called Allowance for Bad Debts or Allowance for Uncollectible Accounts.

Bad debts expense
An operating (usually a selling) expense a business incurs when it sells on credit. Also called uncollectible accounts expense.

Bank discount
The difference between maturity value of a note and its proceeds.

Contingent liability
A condition that may become an actual liability if a specific action does or does not occur.

Credit card expense
The credit agency's fee for services rendered in processing credit card sales.

Credit cards
Charge cards such as VISA, American Express, and MasterCard which are used by customers to charge their purchases of goods and services.

Direct write-off method
A way of accounting for uncollectible accounts receivable in which such accounts are charged directly to an expense account.

Discount on notes payable
An account used to reduce Notes Payable from face value to net amount to show in balance sheet.

Discounting a note receivable
The act of transferring a note receivable with recourse to a bank. With recourse means that the bank can collect from the company which transferred the note to the bank if the maker does not pay at maturity.

Dishonored note
A note which the maker failed to pay at maturity.

Maturity value
The amount that the maker must pay on the note on its maturity date.

Net realizable value
The amount expected to be collected from accounts receivable.

Notes receivable discounted
A contra account to Notes Receivable used to show the contingent liability for customers' notes that have been discounted.

Payable
Any sum of money due to be paid to any party for any reason.

Percentage-of-receivables method
A method of determining the desired size of the allowance for doubtful accounts and, indirectly, the bad debts expense for the period.

Percentage-of-sales method
A method of estimating the expected amount of uncollectible accounts from a given period's credit sales and, indirectly, of determining the balance in the Allowance for Doubtful Accounts.

Proceeds
Maturity amount of a note less bank discount.

Promissory note
A written promise by a borrower (maker) to pay a certain sum of money to the lender (payee) on demand or at a specific date.

Receivable
Any sum of money due from any party for any reason.

Trade receivables
Amounts due from customers for goods sold or services rendered on open account. Also called accounts receivable or trade accounts receivable.

With recourse
Legal term meaning the holder (e.g., a bank) can collect from the company which transferred a note to the holder if the maker does not pay at maturity.

DEMONSTRATION PROBLEM

Part a. A $15,000, 90-day, 12 percent note dated June 15, 1984, was received by the Long Company from the Short Company in payment of its account.

Required:

Prepare the journal entries in the records of the Long Company for each of the following:

1. Receipt of the note, June 15, 1984.
2. The Long Company discounted the note on July 15, 1984, at 10 percent at the Citizens' National Bank.
3. The Short Company paid the note at maturity.
4. Assume that the Short Company did not pay the note at maturity. The Citizens' National Bank charged the note to the Long Company. The Long Company decided that the note was uncollectible.

Part b. The Best Company estimates its bad debts expense to be 1 percent of sales. Sales in 1984 are $750,000.

Required:

Prepare the journal entries for the following transactions:

Transactions:

1. The company prepares the adjusting entry for bad debts for the year 1984.
2. On January 15, 1985, the company decided that the account for James Ryan in the amount of $500 is uncollectible.
3. On February 12, 1985, James Ryan's check for $500 arrives.

Solution to demonstration problem

Part a.

```
1.  1984
    June  15  Notes Receivable ...........................   15,000.00
                  Accounts Receivable ......................              15,000.00
              To record receipt of a note from Short Company.

2.  July  15  Cash .......................................   15,192.50
                  Notes Receivable Discounted ..............              15,000.00
                  Interest Revenue .........................                 192.50
              To record the discounting.
```

Computation of cash proceeds:
Maturity value (Days until
   maturity = 60) $15,450.00
   Discount = $15,450 × 10% × 60/360   257.50
                                    $15,192.50

3.	Sept. 13	Notes Receivable Discounted	15,000.00	
		Notes Receivable		15,000.00
		To remove the note and contingent liability.		
4.	Sept. 13	Notes Receivable Discounted	15,000.00	
		Notes Receivable		15,000.00
		To remove the note and contingent liability.		
	13	Accounts Receivable	15,450.00	
		Cash		15,450.00
		To record the charge made against our account for the Short Company note of $15,000 and interest of $450.		
	13	Allowance for Doubtful Accounts*	15,450.00	
		Accounts Receivable		15,450.00
		To write off the Short Company note as uncollectible.		

* This debit assumes that notes receivable were taken into consideration when an allowance was established. If it has not, a debit to Bad Debts Expense or Loss from Dishonored Notes Receivable should be made.

Part b.

1.	1984			
	Dec. 31	Bad Debts Expense	7,500	
		Allowance for Doubtful Accounts		7,500
		To record estimated bad debts for the year.		
2.	1985			
	Jan. 15	Allowance for Doubtful Accounts	500	
		Accounts Receivable, James Ryan		500
		To write off the account of James Ryan as uncollectible.		
3.	1985			
	Feb. 12	Accounts Receivable, James Ryan	500	
		Allowance for Doubtful Accounts		500
		To correct the write-off of James Ryan's account on January 15.		
	12	Cash	500	
		Accounts Receivable, James Ryan		500
		To record the collection of James Ryan's account receivable.		

QUESTIONS

1. What are the two major purposes to be accomplished in establishing an allowance for possible uncollectible accounts?

2. In view of the fact that it is impossible to estimate the exact amount of uncollectible ac-

counts receivable for any one year in advance, what exactly does the Allowance for Doubtful Accounts account contain after a number of years?

3. How might information in an aging schedule prove useful to management for purposes other than estimating the size of the required allowance for doubtful accounts?

4. In view of the difficulty in estimating future events, would you recommend that accountants wait until collections are made from customers before recording sales revenue? Should they wait until known accounts prove to be uncollectible before charging an expense account?

5. The credit manager of a company has established a policy of seeking to eliminate completely all losses from uncollectible accounts. Is this a desirable objective for a company? Explain.

6. For a company using the allowance method of accounting for uncollectible accounts, which of the following affects its reported net income: (1) the establishment of the allowance, (2) the writing off of a specific account, or (3) the recovery of an account previously written off as uncollectible?

7. Explain why an account receivable might

have a credit balance. What is the proper treatment of such an item in the financial statement?

8. Why might a retailer agree to sell by credit card when such a substantial discount is taken by the credit card agency in paying the retailer?

9. Explain why the direct write-off method of accounting for uncollectible accounts is generally unacceptable.

10. How do a dishonored note receivable and a discounted note receivable differ? How is each reported in the balance sheet?

11. Under what circumstances does the account Discount on Notes Payable arise? How is it reported in the financial statements? Explain why.

12. Why might a situation arise where the bank discount rate is less than the rate in a customer's note which the holding company discounts at the bank?

EXERCISES

E–1. How should the following situation be shown in the balance sheet? The subsidiary accounts receivable ledger of the Maroon Company shows a total of $267,000 of accounts owed to the company. An examination of the accounts shows one account of $39,000 due from the general manager of the company. This account consisted of:

    a. Due from sale of merchandise, $9,000.
    b. A loan of $30,000.

E–2. How should the following appear in the balance sheet of the Brown Company on December 31, 1983? Why?

Accounts receivable (after deducting credit balances of $600)	$117,600
Accounts payable (after deducting advance payments to vendors of $300)	76,700

E–3. On December 31, 1983, Roberts Company received a check for $3,600 as a 20 percent down payment on an order for merchandise from the Argonne Company. Argonne is not indebted to Roberts at this time. Roberts debited the $3,600 to Cash and credited Argonne's Accounts Receivable account. The merchandise was not delivered until January 5, 1984. On December 31, 1983, the trial balance amount of accounts receivable was $157,000. Indicate the proper balance sheet presentation of the above data.

E–4. The accounts of the Red Robin Company as of December 31, 1983, show Accounts Receivable, $110,000; Allowance for Doubtful Accounts, $700 (credit balance); Sales, $725,000; and Sales Returns and Allowances, $13,000. Prepare journal entries to adjust for possible uncollectible accounts under each of the following assumptions:

    a. Uncollectible accounts are estimated at 1 percent of net sales.
    b. The allowance is to be increased to 3 percent of accounts receivable.

E–5.   On April 1, 1984, Johnson Company, which uses the allowance method of accounting for uncollectible accounts, wrote off Bill Comb's $264 account. On December 14, 1984, the company received a check of that amount from Combs marked "in full of account." Prepare the necessary entries for all of the above.

E–6.   Compute the required balance of the Allowance for Doubtful Accounts for the following receivables:

Accounts receivable	Age (months)	Probability of collection
$110,000	Less than 1	0.95
55,000	1–3	0.85
26,000	3–6	0.75
7,000	6–12	0.35
1,500	12 and over	0.10

E–7.   Because its credit sales are immaterial in amount, the Shady Tree Company accounts for its uncollectible accounts using the direct write-off method. During 1984, the following accounts were written off as uncollectible:

Apr. 10   J. Jones $125
July 17   B. Smith 240
Oct. 11   L. Jackson 170

On December 10, payment in full is received from J. Jones. Prepare journal entries for the above.

E–8.   Hobo's Inc. sold $11,000 of goods to customers in May who charged them using their Carte Blanche credit cards. Such sales are subject to a 3 percent discount by Carte Blanche. Prepare journal entries to record the sales and the subsequent receipt of cash from the credit card company.

E–9.   Brown gave a $20,000, 120-day, 12 percent note to Lewis in exchange for merchandise. Prepare journal entries needed at maturity for both parties, assuming payment is made.

E–10.   Prepare the entries that Brown and Lewis (Exercise E–9) would make at maturity date assuming Brown defaults.

E–11.   Determine the maturity date for each of the following notes:

Issue date	Life
January 13, 1984	30 days
January 31, 1984	90 days
June 4, 1984	1 year
December 1, 1984	1 month

E–12.   On May 7, 1984, Able Company gave a 180-day, $7,500, 14 percent note to Ready Company. On August 20, Ready Company discounted the note at 14 percent. Prepare the entries each company would make on the discounting date.

E–13.   If in Exercise E–12 Able Company fails to pay the note, prepare the entries that would be recorded on the books of each company.

E–14.   Day Kreuzburg is negotiating a bank loan of $10,000 for 90 days. The bank's current interest rate is 16 percent. Prepare entries to record the loan under each of the following assumptions:

    a.   Day signs a note for $10,000. Interest is deducted in calculating the proceeds turned over to him.
    b.   Day signs a note for $10,000 and receives that amount. Interest is to be paid at maturity.

E–15.   Prepare the entry or entries that would be made at maturity date for each of the alternatives in Exercise E–14 assuming the loan is paid before the end of the accounting period.

PROBLEMS, SERIES A

P8–1–A.   As of December 31, 1983, Topes Company's accounts prior to adjustment show:

Accounts receivable	$ 184,000
Allowance for doubtful accounts	7,000
Net sales	1,500,000

    Topes Company follows a practice of estimating uncollectible accounts at 3 percent of net sales.
    On February 23, 1984, the account of Don Cole in the amount of $2,300 was considered uncollectible and written off. On August 12, 1984, Cole remitted $800 and indicated that he intends to pay the balance owed as soon as possible. By December 31, 1984, no further remittance had been received from Cole.

Required:

    a.   Prepare journal entries to record all of the above transactions and adjusting entries.

    b.   Prepare the journal entry as of December 31, 1983, if Topes estimated its uncollectible accounts at 11 percent of outstanding accounts receivable rather than 3 percent of net sales.

P8–2–A.   At the close of business on a certain date, Harry's Bar and Grill had credit card sales of $2,400. Of this amount, $1,600 were VISA sales invoices which can be deposited in a bank for immediate credit, less a discount of 3 percent. The balance of $800 consisted of American Express charges. These invoices were mailed to American Express. Shortly thereafter, a check was received for $776.

Required:
    Prepare journal entries for all of the above.

P8–3–A.   The following data pertain to the Donlow Company which began operations in 1983:

	1983	1984	1985
Total sales	$120,000	$105,000	$140,000
Credit sales	80,000	70,000	110,000
Accounts receivable balance, December 31	35,000	40,000	60,000
Actual accounts written off during the year and year of write-off:			
From 1983 sales	1,000	700	300
From 1984 sales		600	800
From 1985 sales			1,200

For parts (*a*) and (*b*) below, assume that the write-offs were made during the year and that the company expected to use the allowance method and make a year-end adjustment for bad debts.

Required:

      a.   Prepare journal entries for 1983, 1984, and 1985 to record the bad debts expense for the year using the percentage-of-sales method with bad debts estimated at 2 percent of credit sales. Also prepare the entries that were made to record the actual accounts written off in each year.

      b.   Repeat part (*a*) using the percentage-of-receivables method with the allowance adjusted to 5 percent of year-end receivables.

      c.   Prepare journal entries to record bad debts expense for 1983, 1984, and 1985 using the direct write-off method.

      d.   Compute the balance in the Allowance for Doubtful Accounts as of December 31, 1985, for each method.

P8–4–A.   The accounts receivable (all arising under sales terms of n/30) of the Spitz Company as of December 31, 1984, total $400,000. The age composition of $360,000 of these accounts is:

Age	Amount
Not yet due	$285,000
Past due:	
1–30 days	40,000
31–60 days	15,000
61–90 days	10,000
91–120 days	3,000
Over 120 days	7,000
	$360,000

      Given below are the three other accounts which account for the remaining $40,000 of accounts receivable:

Jones, Inc.

Date		Explanation	Post. Ref.	Debit	Credit	Balance
1984						
Jan.	1	Balance forward				3,000
		(12/28/83 sale)				
	8		CRJ2		3,000	–0–
	11		SJ1	4,000		4,000
Feb.	5		CRJ2		4,000	–0–
Sept.	18		SJ9	5,000		5,000
	26	Adjustment granted ($300 still in				
		dispute)	GJ9		700	4,300
Oct.	5		CRJ10		4,000	300
	8		SJ10	2,500		2,800
Nov.	3		CRJ11		2,500	300
	15		SJ11	3,200		3,500
Dec.	4		CRJ12		3,200	300
	18		SJ12	4,300		4,600
	21		SJ12	7,000		11,600

Kale Company

Date		Explanation	Post. Ref.	Debit	Credit	Balance
1984						
Apr.	5		SJ4	2,200		2,200
May	5		CRJ5		2,200	–0–
Aug.	3		SJ8	2,100		2,100
Sept.	5	Return	GJ9		500	1,600
	11		CRJ9		1,600	–0–
Oct.	15		SJ10	6,300		6,300
Nov.	7		CRJ11		500	5,800
	10		SJ11	1,500		7,300
Dec.	15		CRJ12		1,000	6,300

Rowbloch Company

Date		Explanation	Post. Ref.	Debit	Credit	Balance
1984						
Jan.	1	Balance forward				6,200
	8		CRJ1		6,200	–0–
Feb.	18		SJ2	11,000		11,000
Mar.	6		CRJ3		11,000	–0–
May	19		SJ5	2,200		2,200
June	1		SJ6	1,100		3,300
	7		CRJ6		2,200	1,100
	23		SJ6	20,500		21,600
July	5		CRJ7		21,600	–0–
Oct.	15		SJ10	23,000		23,000
Nov.	3		CRJ11		4,000	19,000
	9		SJ11	5,400		24,400
	18	Return 10/15 sale	GJ11		300	24,100
Dec.	5		CRJ12		5,000	19,100
	17		SJ12	3,000		22,100

Note: The abbreviations in the Posting Reference column stand for the following: CRJ = Cash Receipts Journal; SJ = Sales Journal; and GJ = General Journal. These journals are illustrated in Chapter 6.

Required:

   a. Prepare an aging schedule classifying the accounts as per the age groups given above. (Assign credits in the accounts to the oldest balance unless evidence indicates otherwise.)

   b. Assuming the Allowance for Doubtful Accounts has a debit balance of $3,400, prepare the necessary adjusting journal entry for estimated uncollectible accounts as of December 31, 1984, if the amount of uncollectible accounts is estimated at ½, 1, 2, 5, 10, and 25 percent, respectively, of the age groups given above.

   c. What has apparently happened with regard to $300 of the balance of the Jones, Inc., account? What is the probability of collecting this balance?

P8–5–A.   The Lemons Company discounted its own $15,000, noninterest-bearing, 60-day note on November 16, 1984, at the Chautauqua County Bank at a discount rate of 12 percent.

Required:

Prepare dated journal entries for—

a. The original discounting on November 16.

b. The adjustment required at the end of the company's calendar-year accounting period.

c. Payment at maturity.

P8–6–A.   On June 1, 1984, the Potts Company received an $18,000, 90-day, 16 percent note from the Thomas Company dated June 1, 1984. On August 15, 1984, the note was discounted at the bank. The rate of discount was 18 percent.

Required:

Determine:

a. The maturity value of the note.

b. The number of days from the discount date to the maturity date.

c. The dollar amount of the discount.

d. The cash proceeds received by the company.

e. The entry to record the receipt of proceeds at the date of discount.

f. The entry required on Potts' books when Thomas paid the note at maturity.

P8–7–A.   Following are selected transactions of the Blue Thumb Company for 1984:

Transactions:

Oct. 31   Discounted its own 30-day, $12,000, noninterest-bearing note at the First State Bank at 12 percent.
Nov. 8   Received an $8,000, 90-day, 9 percent note from the Worst Company in settlement of an account receivable. The note is dated November 8.
      15   Purchased merchandise by issuing its own 120-day note for $8,400. The note is dated November 15 and bears interest at 10 percent.
      20   Discounted the Worst Company note at 12 percent at the First State Bank.
      30   The First State Bank notified the Blue Thumb Company that it had charged the note of October 31 against the company's checking account.

Required:

Assume that all notes falling due after November 30 were paid in full on their due dates by the respective makers. Prepare dated journal entries for the Blue Thumb Company for all of the above transactions (including the payment of the notes after November 30) and all necessary adjusting entries assuming a fiscal year ending on November 30.

P8–8–A.   The Grisley Company is in the chain saw manufacturing business. As of September 1, the balance in its Notes Receivable account was $59,000. The balance in the Notes Receivable Discounted account was $24,000, and the balance in Accounts Receivable included $15,150 for Yahoo's dishonored note. A schedule of the notes (including the dishonored note) is as follows:

Face amount	Maker	Date	Life	Interest rate	Comments
$20,000	A. Box Co.	6/1/84	150 days	12%	
15,000	C. Davis Co.	6/15/84	90 days	8	
24,000	Chase Co.	7/1/84	90 days	10	Discounted 8/16/84 at 9%
15,000	Yahoo Co.	7/1/84	60 days	6	Dishonored, interest, $150
$74,000					

Required:

Prepare dated journal entries for the following 1984 transactions:

Transactions:

Sept. 5 The A. Box Company note was discounted at the Fulton County Bank. The discount rate was 10 percent.

10 Received $7,150 from the Yahoo Company as full settlement of the amount due from it. The company charges losses on notes to the Allowance for Doubtful Accounts account.

? The C. Davis Company note was collected when due.

? Chase Company paid its note at maturity.

? The A. Box Company note was not paid at maturity. The bank deducted the balance from the Grisley Company's bank balance.

Oct. 30 Received a new 60-day, 12 percent note from the A. Box Company for the total balance due on the dishonored note. The note was dated as of the maturity date of the dishonored note. The Grisley Company accepted the note in good faith.

PROBLEMS, SERIES B

P8–1–B.   Presented below are selected accounts of the Winston Company as of December 31, 1984. Prior to closing the books, the $4,000 account of the Park Company is to be written off (this was a credit sale of February 12, 1984.)

Accounts receivable	$ 210,000
Allowance for doubtful accounts (debit balance)	3,000
Sales	2,100,000
Sales returns and allowances	50,000

Required:

a.   Present journal entries to record the above and to record bad debts expense for the year, assuming the estimated expense is 1 percent of net sales.

b.   Give the entry to record the estimated expense if the allowance is to be adjusted to 7 percent of outstanding receivables instead of as in (a) above.

P8–2–B.   The cash register at Archie's Place at the close of business on a certain date showed cash sales of $1,800 and credit card sales of $2,200—$1,200 VISA and $1,000 American Express. The VISA invoices were discounted 5 percent when they were deposited. The American Express charges were mailed to the company. A few days later, a check was received for the amount of the charges, less a discount of 5 percent.

Required:

Prepare journal entries to record all of the above.

P8–3–B.   The following data pertain to the Easy Credit Company:

	1983	*1984*	*1985*
Total sales (net)	$200,000	$220,000	$250,000
Credit sales (other than VISA)	135,000	150,000	220,000
Credit sales (VISA)	65,000	70,000	30,000
Accounts receivable balance, December			
31 (excluding VISA)	45,000	24,000	30,000
Actual accounts written off and year			
of write-off:			
From 1982 sales	1,000		
From 1983 sales	1,600	1,800	
From 1984 sales		600	1,200
From 1985 sales			1,300

        For parts (*a*) and (*b*) below assume that the Allowance for Doubtful Accounts had a balance of $1,100 when properly adjusted on December 31, 1982.

Required:

        a.   Prepare journal entries for 1983, 1984, and 1985 to record the bad debts expense for the year using the percentage-of-sales method with bad debts estimated at 2 percent of credit sales (other than VISA). Also prepare the actual entries that were made to record the accounts written off in each year.

        b.   Repeat part (*a*) using the percentage-of-receivables method with the allowance adjusted to 5 percent of year-end receivables (excluding VISA).

        c.   Prepare journal entries to record bad debts expense for 1983, 1984, and 1985 using the direct write-off method.

        d.   Compute the balance in the Allowance for Doubtful Accounts as of December 31, 1985, for each method.

P8–4–B.   The accounts receivable (all arising under sales terms of n/30) of the Hinckley Company at December 31, 1984, total $300,000. The age composition of $275,000 of these accounts is:

Age	*Amount*
Not yet due	$203,000
1–30 days past due	36,000
31–60 days past due	18,000
61–90 days past due	8,000
91–120 days past due	4,000
Over 120 days past due	6,000
	$275,000

Given below are the four other accounts which account for the remaining $25,000 of accounts receivable:

Company E

Date		Explanation	Post. Ref.	Debit	Credit	Balance
1984						
Jan.	1	Balance forwarded (12/27/83 sale)				2,000
Feb.	7		SJ14	10,000		12,000
	10		CRJ3		2,000	10,000
Mar.	1		CRJ6		2,000	8,000
July	5		SJ17	2,200		10,200
	8		CRJ20		2,000	8,200
Nov.	3		CRJ31		400	7,800

Company G

Date		Explanation	Post. Ref.	Debit	Credit	Balance
1984						
Jan.	10		SJ5	5,000		5,000
Feb.	1		CRJ3		2,500	2,500
Mar.	4	Allowance granted 1/10 sale	GJ5		1,000	1,500
June	2		CRJ16		500	1,000
	6		SJ16	300		1,300
July	3		CRJ19		500	800
Sept.	12		SJ30	1,400		2,200
	15		CRJ22		200	2,000
Nov.	30		CRJ32		400	1,600

Company L

Date		Explanation	Post. Ref.	Debit	Credit	Balance
1984						
July	5		SJ17	1,500		1,500
Aug.	2		CRJ20		500	1,000
	28		SJ28	1,000		2,000
Sept.	5		CRJ21		500	1,500
Oct.	5		CRJ28		500	1,000
	6		SJ32	12,700		13,700
Nov.	3		CRJ31		1,000	12,700

Company Z

Date		Explanation	Post. Ref.	Debit	Credit	Balance
1984						
Aug.	22		SJ26	1,000		1,000
Sept.	5		CRJ21		1,000	–0–
	12		SJ30	1,200		1,200
	30		SJ31	500		1,700
Oct.	5		CRJ28		1,700	–0–
	28		SJ34	1,500		1,500
Nov.	2	Adjustment granted ($400 still in dispute)	GJ17		100	1,400
	7		CRJ31		1,000	400
	10		SJ36	1,800		2,200
Dec.	5		CRJ34		1,800	400
	11		SJ38	2,500		2,900

Note: The abbreviations in the Posting Reference column stand for the following: CRJ = Cash Receipts Journal; SJ = Sales Journal; and GJ = General Journal. These journals are illustrated in Chapter 6.

Required:

      a.   Prepare an aging schedule for the accounts receivable of the Hinckley Company. (Assign credits in the accounts to the oldest balance unless evidence indicates otherwise.) Compute the required Allowance for Doubtful Accounts balance assuming estimated percentages of uncollectible accounts of ½, 1, 2, 5, 10, and 25 percent, respectively, for the six classifications given above.

      b.   Prepare the necessary adjusting journal entry assuming the allowance has a debit balance of $900.

P8–5–B.   On November 1, 1984, the Byron Company discounted its own $30,000, 180-day, noninterest-bearing note at its bank at 18 percent. The note was paid on its maturity date. Byron Company uses a calendar-year accounting period.

Required:

      Prepare dated journal entries to record (*a*) the discounting of the note, (*b*) the year-end adjustment, and (*c*) the payment of the note.

P8–6–B.   The Limerick Company received on July 24, 1984, a note from the Able Company with the following description:

Face amount	$40,000
Life of note	120 days
Date of note	7/24/84
Interest rate on note	12%
Date of discounting note at the bank	8/23/84
Rate of discount charged by the bank	15%

Required:

      Determine:

      a.   The maturity date of the note.

      b.   The maturity value of the note.

      c.   The number of days from the discount date to the maturity date.

d. The dollar amount of the discount.

e. The cash proceeds received by the company.

f. The entry to record the receipt of the proceeds at the date of discount.

g. The entry needed on the maturity date assuming Able paid its note.

P8–7–B.   The Berry Company engaged in the following transactions in 1984:

Transactions:

May 31 Discounted its own 30-day, $24,000, noninterest-bearing note at the First National Bank at 12 percent.

June 8 Received a $16,000, 90-day, 9 percent note from the Second Company in settlement of its account balance. The note is dated June 8.

15 Issued a $16,800, 120-day, 10 percent note, dated today, to purchase merchandise.

20 Discounted the Second Company note at 12 percent at the First National Bank.

30 The bank notified Berry Company that it had charged the note of May 31 against the company's checking account balance.

Required:

Assume that all notes falling due after June 30 were paid in full on their due dates by their respective makers. Prepare dated journal entries for the Berry Company for all of the above transactions (including the payment of the notes after June 30) and all necessary adjusting entries for accrued interest assuming a fiscal year ending on June 30.

P8–8–B.   The Tweet Company has a fiscal year ending on July 31. On July 1, 1984, the balances of certain ledger accounts are Notes Receivable, $24,800; Notes Receivable Discounted, $18,000; and Notes Payable, $60,000. The balance in Notes Receivable consists of the following:

Face amount	Maker	Date of note	Life	Interest rate	Date discounted	Discount rate
$18,000	Good Co.	5/15/84	60 days	14%	6/1/84	12%
2,000	Bad Co.	6/1/84	60 days	14	—	—
4,800	Rugly Co.	6/15/84	30 days	12	—	—
$24,800						

The note payable is a 60-day bank loan dated May 20, 1984. Interest Expense was debited for the discount of $600 because the note will become due before the end of the accounting period.

Required:

Prepare dated journal entries for the following transactions and necessary July 31 adjustments for accrued interest:

Transactions:

July 1 The Tweet Company discounted its own $22,000, 90-day, noninterest-bearing note at the State Bank. The discount rate was 12 percent, and the note was dated today.

3 Received a 20-day, 12 percent note, dated today, from the Jones Company in settlement of an account receivable of $3,600.

6 Purchased merchandise from the Hood Company, $21,900, and issued a 30-day, 12 percent note, dated today, for the purchase.

8 Sold merchandise to the Brass Company, $6,000. A 45-day, 8 percent note, dated today, was received to cover the sale.

14 The $18,000 note discounted on June 1, 1984, was paid by the Good Company directly to the holder.

July 15 The Rugly Company sent a $3,000, 30-day, 12 percent note, dated today, and a check to cover its note of June 15, 1984, and interest in full to this date.
   18 The Brass Company note of July 8 was discounted at the State Bank for the remaining life of the note. The discount rate was 14 percent.
   19 The note payable dated May 20, 1984, was paid in full.
   23 The Jones Company dishonored its note of July 3, due today.
   26 The Jones Company sent a check for the interest on the dishonored note and a new 30-day, 12 percent note dated July 23, 1984.
   30 The Bad Company note dated June 1, 1984, was paid with interest in full.

BUSINESS DECISION PROBLEM 8-1

Larry Johnson runs an appliance store, selling items for both cash and on account. During 1983, which seemed to be a typical year, some of his operating and other data were as follows:

Sales
For cash	$250,000
On credit	350,000
Cost of obtaining credit reports on customers	750
Cost incurred in paying a part-time bookkeeper to keep the accounts receivable subsidiary ledger up to date	2,500
Cost associated with preparing and mailing invoices to customers and other collection activities	4,000
Bad debts arising from uncollectible accounts	11,000
The average outstanding accounts receivable balance (on which Larry estimates he could have earned 10% if it had been invested in other assets)	27,000

A national credit card agency has approached Larry and tried to convince him that instead of carrying his own accounts receivable he should only accept its credit card for sales on credit. The agency would pay Larry within two days after he submits sales charges. It would deduct 4 percent from the amount and pay him 96 percent.

Required:

a.   Using the data given, prepare an analysis showing whether or not it would pay Larry to switch to the credit card method of selling on credit.

b.   What other factors should be taken into consideration?

BUSINESS DECISION PROBLEM 8-2

Jim Bell operates a large garden supplies store on the outskirts of a city. In a typical year he sells $2,000,000 of goods to regular customers. His sales are 35 percent for cash and 65 percent on credit. He carries all of the credit himself. Only after a customer has a total of $200 unpaid balance on which no payments have been made for two months does he refuse that customer credit for future purchases. His income before taxes is approximately $650,000. The total of uncollectible accounts for a given year is about 10 percent of credit sales, or $130,000.

You are one of Jim's regular customers. He knows that you are taking a course in accounting in college and has asked you to tell him your opinion of several alternatives which have been recommended to him to reduce or eliminate $130,000 per year bad debt loss. The recommended alternatives are as follows:

1.   Do not sell on credit.
2.   Sell on credit by national credit card only.
3.   Allow customers to charge only until their account balance reaches $50.

4. Allow a bill collector to "go after" bad debts. He would keep half of what he collects.
5. Require all credit customers to sign a note so that Jim can discount these at the local bank.

Required:

Using your own logic and experiences, plus the information in this chapter, give Jim your opinion as to the advisability of following any of these alternatives.

Chapter 9

Measuring and reporting inventories

CHAPTER GOALS

After study of this chapter, you should be able to:

1. Indicate what costs are properly included in inventory.
2. Calculate the effects of inventory errors on certain financial statement items.
3. Calculate cost of ending inventory, cost of goods sold, and effects on net income under four major inventory cost methods.
4. Indicate the advantages and disadvantages of the four major methods.
5. Apply the lower-of-cost-or-market method to inventory.
6. Estimate cost of ending inventory using the gross margin and retail methods.
7. Record merchandise transactions under perpetual inventory procedure.
8. Define and use correctly the new terms in the glossary.

Previous chapters, especially Chapter 5, discussed and illustrated the accounting for a firm that earned its revenues by selling merchandise. Merchandise inventory was defined as the quantity of goods on hand and available for sale at any given time; such inventories were valued at cost. Also discussed were routine inventory transactions, such as purchases, purchase discounts, purchase returns and allowance, and transportation-in. The computation of cost of goods sold under periodic inventory procedure was also illustrated.

This chapter takes a closer look at some of the problems of accounting for inventories, seeking answers to questions such as: What costs should be included in inventory? Why is a proper determination of inventory so important? How is inventory cost determined when goods are purchased at varying prices? What are the effects of using different inventory methods? Are departures from the cost basis of inventory measurement proper? If so, under what conditions? How might a firm estimate its inventory if it does not wish to take a physical inventory? Most of this chapter is devoted to providing answers to these questions.

INVENTORIES IN GENERAL

Inventory is often the largest and most important asset owned by a merchandising or manufacturing firm. In some companies, inventory may be several times the size of any other asset. Cost of goods sold, the expense related to inventory, is often the largest expense on the income statement. As a result, improper accounting for inventory may have a material effect upon other reported financial statement items.

Types of inventories

The type of inventory carried by a firm will vary with the nature of a firm's operations. Retailers and wholesalers buy merchandise and sell it in the condition in which it was acquired. Such firms have only one major type of inventory—*merchandise held for resale.* Manufacturers, on other hand, generally have three types of inventory: *raw materials, work in process,* and *finished goods.* Raw materials will undergo processing into finished goods. While the goods are in a state of production and are, as yet, incomplete, they are referred to as work in process. Finished goods of a manufacturer are those goods held for sale to customers. A manufacturer's customers usually are retailers and wholesalers.

The cost concepts applied to merchandise inventories are also applicable to a manufacturer's finished goods inventory. But manufacturers do face some additional problems accounting for processing of raw materials into finished goods. Accounting for the manufacture of goods is discussed in Chapters 21–23.

Both manufacturers and merchandisers normally have certain supplies on hand that are used in operations. These supplies may be reported as supplies on hand or supplies inventory. In this text they are referred to as supplies on hand.

Inventory thus consists of those items of tangible property that (1) are held for sale in the ordinary course of business, (2) are in process of production for sale, or (3) are to be currently consumed in production of goods or services which will be available for sale.[1] The discussion in this chapter will focus only on the first type.

Reporting Inventories

Inventories usually are reported on the balance sheet as current assets because they will be consumed or converted into cash within a year or an operating cycle, whichever is longer. Current assets are reported in descending order of liquidity. Thus, inventories are reported after accounts receivable because they are a step further away from cash.

Importance of proper valuation

The primary objective sought in *accounting for inventory is the proper determination of income by matching appropriate costs with revenues.* The matching process has been discussed and illustrated repeatedly in prior chapters. As applied to inventory, matching involves determining how much of the cost of goods available for sale during the period should be deducted from current revenues and how much should be allocated to goods on hand and carried forward to be matched against future revenues.

Ending inventory is subtracted from cost of goods available for sale in order to compute cost of goods sold. Cost of goods sold is deducted from sales revenue to compute gross margin. Other expenses are then subtracted from gross margin in order to compute net income for the period. Thus, a highly significant relationship exists: *net income for a period depends directly upon the valuation of ending inventory.* More specifically, any change in the calculation of ending inventory will be reflected, dollar for dollar, in net income. Any change in inventory amount will also be reflected on the balance sheet in current and total assets.

Therefore, it is essential that ending inventory be properly valued for both balance sheet and income statement purposes. If ending inventory is overstated, current and total assets will be overstated; additionally, cost of goods sold is understated with a resulting overstatement of gross margin and, therefore, net income and owner's equity (Illustration 9.1).

When ending inventory is misstated in the current year, that misstatement is carried forward into the next year. The error is carried forward because the ending inventory amount of the current year is the beginning inventory amount for the next year. To continue Illustration 9.1, assume a correct ending inventory is taken for the year ended December 31, 1985 (Illustration 9.2).

---

[1] Committee on Accounting Procedure, American Institute of Certified Public Accountants, "Accounting Research Bulletin No. 43," *Accounting Research and Terminology Bulletins, Final Edition* (New York, 1961), p. 27.

Illustration 9.1

	For year ended December 31, 1984		
		Ending inventory correctly stated	Ending inventory overstated by $10,000
Sales		$800,000	$800,000
Cost of goods available for sale	$600,000		$600,000
Ending inventory	70,000		80,000
Cost of goods sold		530,000	520,000
Gross margin		$270,000	$280,000
Other expenses		170,000	170,000
Net income		$100,000	$110,000
Beginning owner's equity		$240,000	$240,000
Net income		100,000	110,000
Ending owner's equity		$340,000	$350,000

A comparison of Illustrations 9.1 and 9.2 shows that an overstated beginning inventory has the opposite effect on financial statement items from an overstated ending inventory. Cost of goods available for sale is overstated, and cost of goods sold is then overstated. Gross margin and net income are understated. When net income in the second year is closed to owner's equity, the owner's equity account will be stated at its proper amount. The overstatement of net income in the first year was offset by the understatement of net income in the second year. For the two years combined, net income is correct,

Illustration 9.2

	For year ended December 31, 1985		
		Beginning inventory correctly stated	Beginning inventory overstated by $10,000
Sales		$850,000	$850,000
Beginning inventory	$ 70,000		$ 80,000
Purchases	580,000		580,000
Cost of goods available for sale	$650,000		$660,000
Ending inventory	90,000		90,000
Cost of goods sold		560,000	570,000
Gross margin		$290,000	$280,000
Other expenses		107,000	107,000
Net income		$183,000	$173,000
Beginning owner's equity		$340,000	$350,000
Net income		183,000	173,000
Ending owner's equity		$523,000	$523,000

and, therefore, owner's equity is correct at the end of the second year. Also, assets on the balance sheet are properly stated at the end of the second year.

Since inventory errors affect gross margin and many other items reported in the financial statements, accountants proceed carefully in valuing inventory. Further, an error in one period's ending inventory automatically causes an error in the opposite direction in the next period. After two years, though, the error will "wash out" and owner's equity will be properly reflected.

INVENTORY COST

One aspect of the inventory valuation problem involves the question of what costs are included. Generally, inventory cost includes all necessary outlays to obtain the goods and place them in condition and in the desired location for sale to customers. Thus, inventory cost includes:

1. Seller's invoice price less purchase discount.
2. Cost of insurance on the goods while in transit.
3. Transportation charges when borne by the buyer.
4. Handling costs, such as cost of pressing clothes wrinkled during shipment.

In theory, then, the cost of each unit of inventory should include its net invoice price plus its share of the other costs listed. Some difficult problems are faced in assigning these other costs to units of inventory. For example, the freight bill on a shipment of clothes does not state separately the cost of shipping one shirt. If freight cost is to be included as part of the inventory cost of the shirt, it would have to be *allocated* in some manner because it cannot be measured directly. As a practical matter, allocations of freight, insurance, and handling costs to the units of inventory acquired are often viewed as not worth the cost incurred to make them. Consequently, such costs are often omitted from inventory in many firms. The effect upon income for a period is minimized when such costs are omitted from both beginning and ending inventories.

Even if a cost is derived for each unit in inventory, the inventory valuation problem is not solved. Still to be resolved are two problems:

1. How should cost of goods available for sale be allocated between the units sold and those that remain in inventory if goods were purchased at varying unit costs?
2. Does the fact that market prices are less than cost for some units in inventory have any bearing upon the inventory's cost?

Inventory valuation under changing prices

Inventories generally should be accounted for at historical cost. But this general rule does not indicate how the cost of goods available for sale should be assigned to ending inventory and cost of goods sold when goods have been acquired at different unit costs. For instance, suppose a retailer has three units of a given product on hand. One unit was acquired at $20, another at $22, and the third at $24. Now the retailer sells two of the units for $30 each. What is the cost of the two units sold? Is it $42, the cost of the first and second units; $44, the cost of the first and third units; or $46, the cost of the second and third units? Or is it $44, determined as two units at an average cost of $22? Four inventory costing methods have been developed to solve this type of problem. They are: (1) specific identification; (2) first-in, first-out (Fifo); (3) last-in, first-out (Lifo); and (4) average cost.

Assumed data for purchases, sales, and beginning inventory in Illustration 9.3 are used to illustrate the use of each of these four methods. Total goods available for sale consist of 80 units with a total cost of $690. Sixty units were sold generating $780 sales revenue. Twenty units were left in inventory. The questions to be answered are: What is the cost of the 20 units in inventory? What is the cost of the 60 units sold?

Illustration 9.3:   Beginning inventory, purchases, and sales

Beginning inventory and purchases				Sales			
Date	Units	Unit cost	Total cost	Date	Units	Price	Total
Beginning inventory	10	$8.00	$ 80	March 10	10	$12.00	$120
March 2	10	8.50	85	July 14	20	12.00	240
May 28	20	8.40	168	September 7	10	14.00	140
August 12	10	9.00	90	November 22	20	14.00	280
October 12	20	8.80	176				
December 21	10	9.10	91				
	80		$690		60		$780

Ending inventory = 20 units (80 available less 60 sold).

Methods of determining inventory cost

Specific identification.   *Specific identification* is an inventory pricing method that attaches a known actual cost to an identifiable unit of product. The method is easily applied when large inventory items such as autos are purchased and sold. When the method is used, unless each unit in inventory is basically unique, it is identified by means of a serial number plate or identification tag.

To illustrate, assume 20 units on hand at year-end in Illustration 9.3 can be identified as 10 units from the August 12 purchase and 10 units from the December 21 purchase. The ending inventory is computed as shown in Illustration 9.4. *The $181 ending inventory cost is subtracted from the total cost of goods available for sale of $690 to get the $509 cost of goods sold.* Note that it would have been quite easy to determine the cost of goods sold for the year by recording the cost of each unit sold.

The $509 cost of goods sold would be an expense in the income statement, and the $181 ending inventory would be a current asset on the balance sheet.

Illustration 9.4: Ending inventory under specific identification

Purchased	Units	Unit cost	Total cost
August 12	10	$9.00	$ 90
December 21	10	9.10	91
Total	20		$181
Cost of goods available for sale			$690
Ending inventory			181
Cost of goods sold			$509

Fifo (first-in, first-out). *Fifo* is a method of inventory pricing under which the costs of the *first* goods acquired are the first costs charged to cost of goods sold when goods are actually sold. In other words, it is assumed that the first goods acquired are the first goods sold. In many businesses, the first units "in" (acquired) must be the first units "out" (sold) to avoid large losses from spoilage. Fresh dairy products and fresh fruits and vegetables are excellent examples. In such cases, an assumed first-in, first-out flow would correspond with the actual physical flow of goods.

When Fifo is used, inventory consists of the newest units and their related costs. The older units are the first units out, that is, they have been sold, while the newer units are still on hand.

Since the inventory contains the costs of the latest purchases, the most recent purchases are listed first in applying Fifo. If inventory contains more units than purchased in the most recent purchase, include units from the next to the latest purchase at the unit cost incurred. Continue to list units from the latest purchases until the number of units listed agrees with the number in inventory. Illustration 9.5 shows that the 20 units in inventory under Fifo consist of 10 units from the December 21 purchase and 10 units from the October 12 purchase. The inventory has a cost of $179. Subtracting the $179 from the $690 leaves $511 as the cost of goods sold. The $179 is, of course, the cost of a current asset—inventory—and is reported on the balance sheet.

Illustration 9.5: Fifo cost of ending inventory under periodic procedure

Purchased	Units	Unit cost	Total cost
December 21	10	$9.10	$ 91
October 12	10	8.80	88
Total	20		$179
Cost of goods available for sale			$690
Ending inventory			179
Cost of goods sold			$511

Lifo (last-in, first-out). *Lifo* is a method of pricing inventory under which the costs of the *last* goods acquired are the first costs charged to cost of goods sold when goods are actually sold. Since the latest costs are the first costs removed from inventory and charged to cost of goods sold, the inventory must consist of the older costs. Application of Lifo to the basic data is shown in Illustration 9.6. The oldest units and their costs are listed first. The 20 units in ending inventory are assigned the cost of the 10 units in beginning inventory plus the costs of the 10 units purchased on March 2. Inventory cost is $165, and cost of goods sold is $525.

Illustration 9.6: Lifo cost of ending inventory under periodic procedure

Purchased	Units	Unit cost	Total cost
Beginning inventory	10	$8.00	$ 80
March 2	10	8.50	85
Total	20		$165
Cost of goods available for sale			$690
Ending inventory			165
Cost of goods sold			$525

Weighted-average method. The *weighted-average method* is a means of pricing inventory under which the total of the number of units purchased plus those in beginning inventory is divided into total cost of goods available for sale to arrive at a weighted-average unit cost. The ending inventory is carried at this cost per unit. The weighted-average method is applied to determine a unit cost for units that are basically the same. Since the units are alike, they are assigned the same unit cost. Application of the method to the basic data is shown in Illustration 9.7.

Illustration 9.7: Application of weighted-average method

	Units	Unit cost	Total cost
Beginning inventory	10	$8.00	$ 80.00
Purchased			
March 2	10	8.50	85.00
May 28	20	8.40	168.00
August 12	10	9.00	90.00
October 12	20	8.80	176.00
December 21	10	9.10	91.00
Total	80		$690.00
Weighted-average unit cost is $690 ÷ 80, or $8.625.			
Ending inventory then is $8.625 × 20			172.50
Cost of goods sold			$517.50

Weighted-average cost per unit is computed by dividing the total cost of units available for sale, $690, by total units available for sale, 80. Weighted-average cost per unit is $8.625. Each unit sold or remaining in inventory is valued at $8.625. The method is called a weighted-average method because the average unit cost computed is affected by the number of units purchased at various costs.

All of the above computations were made assuming use of periodic inventory procedure. Perpetual inventory procedure is discussed later in this chapter.

Cost flows and goods flows

The inventory methods described and illustrated above involve assumptions about how costs flow through a business. In some instances, assumed cost flows correspond with actual physical flow of the goods. For example, fresh meats and dairy products must flow in a Fifo manner to avoid spoilage losses. Lumber or coal stacked in a pile will be used in a Lifo manner. New shipments will be unloaded on top of the pile and will be used first. Gasoline held in a tank is a good example of an inventory which has an average physical flow. As the tank is refilled, the new gasoline is mixed with the old and an amount used will consist of a blend of the old with the new gas.

Although sometimes cited as support for an inventory method, accountants now recognize that an inventory method's assumed cost flows need not necessarily correspond with the actual physical flow of the goods. In fact, there are good reasons for simply ignoring physical flows. Cost flows and the flow of goods are discussed further below.

Advantages and disadvantages

Specific identification. Under specific identification, cost of goods sold and ending inventory are stated at actual cost of specific units sold and on hand. Some accountants feel that this method provides the most precise matching of costs and revenues and is, therefore, the most theoretically sound method. Indeed, in some cases such as an auto dealer or a dealer in real estate, use of any method other than specific identification seems completely illogical.

Other accountants criticize the method because it results in identical units being included in inventory at different costs. For example, television sets differing only in their serial numbers may be included in inventory at different costs if purchased at different times.

A further disadvantage of the specific identification method is that its use permits the manipulation of income. For example, assume that a firm has three identical units of a given product that were acquired at different prices. One unit cost $2,000, the second cost $2,100, and the third cost $2,200. One unit is sold for $2,800. Since the units are alike, the customer does not care which of the identical units is shipped. But gross margin on the sale could be either $800, $700, or $600 depending upon which unit is shipped.

Notes from normal business transactions

Sometimes a note results from the conversion of an open account. To illustrate, assume on October 6, 1984, Cooper (payee) received a note from Price (maker). Price had purchased $18,000 of merchandise on September 6 from Cooper on open account. The normal credit period had elapsed, and Price could not pay the bill. Cooper agreed to accept Price's $18,000, 15 percent, 60-day note to settle Price's open account. Assuming the note was paid at maturity, the entries for the maker and the payee are as follow:

Price, maker

Sept.	6	Purchases	18,000	
		Accounts Payable—Cooper		18,000
		To record purchase of merchandise on account.		
Oct.	6	Accounts Payable—Cooper	18,000	
		Notes Payable—Cooper		18,000
		To record exchange of note for open account.		
Dec.	5	Notes Payable—Cooper	18,000	
		Interest Expense	450	
		Cash		18,450
		To record payment of note and interest.		

Cooper, payee

Sept.	6	Accounts Receivable—Price	18,000	
		Sales		18,000
		To record sale of merchandise on account.		
Oct.	6	Notes Receivable—Price	18,000	
		Accounts Receivable—Price		18,000
		To record exchange of note for open account.		
Dec.	5	Cash	18,450	
		Notes Receivable—Price		18,000
		Interest Revenue		450
		To record receipt of note principal and interest.		

The $18,450 paid by Price to Cooper is called the maturity value of the note. *Maturity value* is the amount that the maker must pay on a note on its maturity date. Maturity value typically includes principal and accrued interest, if any.

Accruing interest

Interest accrues on an interest-bearing note on a day-to-day basis, although it is usually recorded only at maturity date unless the time it is outstanding overlaps the end of an accounting period. If a note is outstanding at the end of an accounting period, an adjusting entry must be made to record the accrued interest to state the proper assets and revenues for the payee or the proper liabilities and expenses of the maker. The failure to record accrued interest would understate payee's assets and revenues by the amount of interest earned but not collected. Similarly, the failure would understate the maker's expenses and liabilities by the interest expense incurred but not yet paid.

If higher income is desired, ship the unit costing $2,000; if lower income is desired, ship the unit costing $2,200.

The main disadvantage of specific identification is that it is simply too difficult to apply in most situations due to the quantities and types of inventories carried. For example, it would be impossible for a hardware store to determine the specific cost of 20 nails sold that were purchased in 100-pound kegs. Similarly, it would be difficult to use the method in an ice cream parlor that buys its ice cream in five-gallon cans and sells it in cones, sundaes, shakes, pints, and quarts. The difficulties in applying the method have led to the development of other methods that are based on assumed cost flows rather than actual physical product flows.

Fifo. The major advantages of Fifo are: it is easy to apply, inventory values are the same under periodic and perpetual procedure, the assumed flow of costs corresponds with the physical flow of goods, no manipulation of income is possible, and balance sheet amounts for inventory are likely to approximate current market values. All of the advantages of Fifo stem from the fact that the oldest unit costs are the first costs removed from inventory when goods are sold. Income cannot be manipulated by choosing which unit to ship because the cost of a unit sold is not determined by a serial number. The cost attached to the unit sold is always the oldest cost. Thus, purchases made at the end of the period have no effect on cost of goods sold or income under Fifo, whereas they do under Lifo and weighted average.

Disadvantages of Fifo include the recognition of "paper profits" and a heavier tax burden if used for tax purposes. These are discussed below as advantages of Lifo.

Lifo. Lifo's advantages are directly related to the fact that prices have risen almost constantly in this country for decades. The upward trend in prices leads to *inventory* or *"paper" profits.* Inventory or paper profits consist of the increase in cost to acquire a unit of inventory at time of sale over the unit's historical cost. For example, assume that a firm has three units of product on hand, each acquired at a different cost: $12, $15, and $20 (the most recent cost). The sales price of the unit will rise because its replacement cost is rising. Assume the firm sells one unit for $30. Fifo gross margin would be $18 ($30 − $12), while Lifo would show gross margin of $10 ($30 − $20). Lifo supporters would say that the extra $8 gross margin shown under Fifo represents inventory or paper profit because that "profit" is merely the additional amount that must be spent over cost of goods sold to acquire another unit of inventory ($8 + $12 = $20). Thus, the profit is not real; it exists only on paper. The $8 cannot be distributed to owners but must be retained in the firm if the firm is to continue handling that particular product. Lifo shows the actual profits that can be distributed to the owners while still replenishing inventory.

Lifo also shows the largest cost of goods sold of any of the methods in periods of inflation because the newest costs that are charged out of inventory are also the highest costs. The larger the cost of goods sold, the smaller net income will be. If Lifo is used for income tax purposes, the resulting lower income means lower income taxes to be paid. Many companies have begun using Lifo for this very reason. An example may be helpful.

Suppose Company B has one unit of product Y on hand which cost $20. The unit is sold for $30; other selling expenses total $7. The tax rate is 50 percent. The unit is replaced for $22 before the end of the accounting period. Using Fifo, net income is computed as follows:

Net sales	$30.00
Cost of goods sold	20.00
Gross margin	$10.00
Expenses	7.00
Net operating margin	$ 3.00
Federal income taxes (50% rate)	1.50
Net Income	$ 1.50

According to the above schedule, the company is selling product Y at a price which is high enough to produce net income. But consider the following:

Cash secured from sale	$30.00
Expenses and taxes paid ($7.00 + $1.50)	8.50
Cash available for replacement	$21.50
Cost to replace	22.00
Additional cash required to replace inventory	$ 0.50

Thus, Company B is reporting net income of $1.50, but it cannot replace its inventory unless it obtains more cash. Note the different results when Lifo is used to measure inventory.

Net sales	$30.00
Cost of goods sold	22.00
Gross margin	$ 8.00
Expenses	7.00
Net operating margin	$ 1.00
Federal income taxes (50% rate)	0.50
Net earnings	$ 0.50

Cash secured from sale	$30.00
Expenses and taxes paid ($7.00 + $0.50)	7.50
Cash available for replacement	$22.50
Cost to replace	22.00
Cash available after replacement	$ 0.50

Note that inventory profits are $2 in this case, and that the tax savings under Lifo are equal to the tax rate applied to the inventory profits (0.5 × $2 = $1) which Lifo does not include in income.

Those who favor Lifo argue that its use leads to a better matching of costs and revenues than the other methods. When Lifo is used, the income statement reports sales revenue in current dollars and cost of goods sold also in current dollars. The resulting gross margin is a better indicator of management's ability to generate income than is gross margin computed using Fifo, which may include substantial inventory profits.

Supporters of Fifo argue that Lifo matches the cost of goods *not* sold against revenues, grossly understates inventory, and permits income manipulation. The first criticism is an extension of the debate over whether the assumed flow of costs should agree with the flow of physical products. The second criticism is valid. Lifo inventory may be reported at a fraction of its current replacement cost, especially if the historical costs included are from several decades ago. Lifo supporters contend that the increased usefulness of the income statement more than offsets the negative effect of this undervaluation of inventory on the balance sheet.

Income manipulation is possible under Lifo. As an example, if management wished to reduce income, an abnormal amount of goods would be purchased near the end of the current period, at current high prices, for sale next period. Under Lifo, these higher costs will be charged to cost of goods sold in the current period, resulting in a substantial decline in reported net income. To obtain higher income, management delays making the normal amount of purchases until next period and in this way includes some of the old, lower costs in cost of goods sold.

Weighted average. When the weighted-average method is used and prices are rising, cost of goods sold is stated at an amount less than obtained under Lifo but more than obtained under Fifo. Inventory is not as badly understated as under Lifo, but not as up to date as under Fifo. Average costing takes a "middle-of-the-road" approach. Although income can be manipulated under average costing by buying or failing to buy goods near year-end, the effects of buying or not buying are muted by the averaging process.

Differences in cost methods summarized. Again using data from Illustration 9.3, Illustration 9.8 shows cost of goods sold, inventory cost, and gross margin for each of the four basic cost methods of inventory determina-

Illustration 9.8: Summary of effects of employing different inventory methods with same basic data

	Specific identification	Fifo	Lifo	Weighted average
Sales	$780.00	$780.00	$780.00	$780.00
Cost of goods sold:				
Beginning inventory	$ 80.00	$ 80.00	$ 80.00	$ 80.00
Purchases	610.00	610.00	610.00	610.00
Cost of goods available for sale	$690.00	$690.00	$690.00	$690.00
Ending inventory	181.00	179.00	165.00	172.50
Cost of goods sold	$509.00	$511.00	$525.00	$517.50
Gross margin	$271.00	$269.00	$255.00	$262.50

tion. Because the inventory method used affects these three financial statement items, as well as net income, companies are required to disclose the inventory method used. These differences are caused by different prices paid for goods purchased and would disappear if purchase prices were constant.

Which is the "correct" method?   All four methods are acceptable; there is no single correct one. Different methods look attractive under different conditions. If a company wanted to match sales revenue with current cost of goods sold, it would use Lifo. Lifo would also be used for tax purposes if the business sought to reduce its income taxes in a period of rising prices.

On the other hand, Lifo often charges against revenues the cost of goods not actually sold. It also may allow net income to be manipulated by changing the time at which additional purchases are made. Fifo and specific identification result in a more precise matching of historical cost with revenue, but specific identification can give rise to income manipulation and Fifo can give rise to "paper profits." The average cost method also allows manipulation of income. Only under Fifo is the manipulation of net income not possible.

Changing inventory methods.   A company generally is free to use the inventory method it believes best fits its individual circumstances. This freedom of choice of the company does not include changing inventory methods every year or so, especially if the goal is to report higher income. Such switching of methods would violate the accounting principle of consistency. Accounting information is more useful when it is gathered using the same methods, period after period.

The principle of consistency does not direct that a change in principles can never be made. If a company decides that a different acceptable method is now more appropriate, a change can be made, but such a change must be fully disclosed. Full disclosure usually is made in a footnote to the financial statements and consists of a full description of the change, the reasons why it was made, and, if possible, the effect of the change upon net income.

DEPARTURES FROM COST

As was mentioned earlier, historical cost should generally be used to value inventories and cost of goods sold. But there are circumstances in which departures from cost are justified. One of these times is when the utility or value of inventory items is less than the cost of those items. Such loss of utility may be evidenced by a decline in selling price of the goods.

Net realizable value

Damaged, obsolete, or shopworn goods should not be carried in inventory at more than net realizable value. *Net realizable value* is the estimated selling price of an item less all costs to complete and dispose of it. For example, assume an auto dealer has a demonstrator car on hand. The car was acquired at a cost of $8,000 and had an original sales price of $9,600. But because it has been used and it is now late in the model year, the car has an estimated selling price of only $8,100. It will sell for $8,100 if the dealer performs scheduled maintenance, including a tune-up, and repairs some paint damage. This work and a sales commission will cost $300. The net realizable value of the demonstrator is, then, $7,800 (selling price of $8,100 less costs of $300).

For inventory purposes, the cost of the auto would be written down from $8,000 to $7,800. The required journal entry is:

```
Loss Due to Decline in Market Value ....................................  200
     Inventory  ....................................................            200
     To write down inventory to net realizable value.
```

In this way, the $200 inventory reduction would be treated as an expense in the period in which the decline in utility occurred. If net realizable value exceeds cost, the item would continue to be carried at cost.

Lower of cost or market

Valuing inventory at the lower of cost or market (LCM) has long been accepted in accounting. The *lower-of-cost-or-market method* is an inventory pricing method that values inventory at the lower of its historical cost or its current market (replacement) cost. The basic assumption behind the method is that if the purchase price of an item has fallen, its selling price has also fallen or will fall. The term *market* generally refers to the replacement cost of an item in the quantity usually purchased. Cost refers to historical cost of the inventory determined under an inventory method: specific identification, Fifo, Lifo, or weighted-average cost.

Under LCM, inventory items are written down to market value when that value is less than cost of the item. For instance, if ending inventory has a cost of $40,000 and a market value of $45,000, this increase in value is not recognized. To do so would recognize revenue before the time of sale. On the other hand, if the market value of the inventory was $39,600, a $400 loss is recorded on the grounds that inventory has lost some of its revenue-generating ability and the loss needs to be recognized in the period that it occurred.

LCM applied. LCM may be applied to each inventory item, each inventory class, or total inventory. Illustration 9.9 shows an application of the

Illustration 9.9:   Application of lower-of-cost-or-market method

Item	Quantity	Unit cost	Unit market	Total cost	Total market	Lower of cost or market on item-by-item basis
1........	100 units	$10	$9.00	$1,000	$ 900	$ 900
2........	200 units	8	8.75	1,600	1,750	1,600
3........	500 units	5	5.00	2,500	2,500	2,500
				$5,100	$5,150	$5,000

method to individual items and total inventory. If LCM is applied on an item-by-item basis, ending inventory would be $5,000. The $5,000 ending inventory would be deducted from cost of goods available for sale on the income statement and would be reported in the current assets section of the balance sheet. If the LCM is applied on a total inventory basis, ending inventory would be $5,100, since total cost of $5,100 is lower than total market of $5,150.

Estimating inventory

A company using periodic inventory procedure may wish to estimate its inventory for any of the following reasons:

1. To obtain an inventory cost figure for use in monthly or quarterly financial statements without taking a physical inventory. The effort of taking a physical inventory is often very expensive and disrupts normal business operations; once a year is often enough.
2. To compare with physical inventories to determine whether shortages exist.
3. To determine the amount recoverable from an insurance company when inventory is destroyed by fire or stolen.

There are two recognized methods of estimating the cost of ending inventory: the gross margin method and the retail method.

Gross margin method. The *gross margin method* is a procedure for estimating inventory cost in which estimated cost of goods sold, determined by deducting estimated gross margin from sales, is deducted from cost of goods available for sale. Estimated gross margin is calculated using gross margin rates experienced in prior periods. The method is based on the assumption that there has been a fairly stable relationship between gross margin and sales in prior periods. This relationship is assumed to have continued into the current period. If conditions have changed, the gross margin method will not yield satisfactory results.

To illustrate the gross margin method of computing inventory, assume that the Field Company has for several years maintained a rate of gross margin on sales of 30 percent. The following data for 1984 are available: the January 1 inventory was $40,000; purchases of merchandise were $480,000; and sales of merchandise were $700,000. The inventory for December 31, 1984, can be estimated as follows:

Inventory, January 1, 1984		$ 40,000
Purchases		480,000
Cost of goods available for sale		$520,000
Less estimated cost of goods sold:		
Sales	$700,000	
Gross margin (30% of $700,000)	210,000	
Estimated cost of goods sold		490,000
Estimated inventory, December 31, 1984		$ 30,000

Ending inventory is estimated by deducting the estimated cost of goods sold from the actual cost of goods available for sale. If the gross margin rate is 30 percent, then cost of goods sold is equal to 70 percent of sales, or is equal to $1 - 0.30 = 0.70$. The significant figure in the calculation is the amount of estimated cost of goods sold rather than the amount of gross margin.

The gross margin method is not suitable for year-end statements because it is not precise enough. At year-end, a physical inventory must be taken and valued by use of one of the previously mentioned historical cost-based methods.

Retail inventory method. Another widely used method of estimating ending inventory is the retail inventory method. The *retail inventory method* is a procedure for estimating the cost of the ending inventory by applying a cost/price ratio to ending inventory stated at retail prices. The method is used in firms which mark or tag inventory items with selling prices. Inventories and goods sold are usually referred to in terms of these selling or retail prices. Even physical inventories are stated in retail terms when first compiled. These prices, of course, cannot be used for inventories and cost of goods sold until converted to cost using a cost-to-retail price ratio (or simply a cost/price ratio).

When the retail method is used, accounting records are still kept on a cost basis. Upon purchase, goods are immediately tagged for sale so that the firm knows the amount of goods available in the store at retail prices. A cost/price ratio is developed to indicate what proportion cost is to each sales dollar. The cost/price ratio is the complement of the gross margin rate.

Illustration 9.10 provides an example of the retail method for a firm in its first year in business.

Illustration 9.10: Inventory calculation using retail method

	Cost	Retail
Beginning inventory, January 1, 1984	$ –0–	$ –0–
Purchases, net	204,000	340,000
Cost of goods available for sale	$204,000	$340,000
Cost/retail price ratio: $204,000/340,000 = 60%		
Sales		280,000
Ending inventory at retail		$ 60,000
Times cost/retail price ratio		×60%
Ending inventory at cost, December 31, 1984	36,000	
Cost of goods sold	$168,000	

The cost amount for purchases was obtained from the accounting records; retail prices were tallied during the pricing of the goods for sale. The sales amount is obtained from the Sales account and is, of course, stated in retail (sales) prices. The difference between what was available for sale at retail prices and what was sold at retail prices (which, of course, is sales) equals what should be on hand (ending inventory) expressed in retail prices. The retail price of the ending inventory needs to be converted into cost for use in financial statements by application of the cost/price ratio. In the example, the cost/price ratio is 60 percent, which means that on the average, 60 cents of each sales dollar is cost of goods sold. Ending inventory at cost ($36,000) is estimated by multiplying the $60,000 ending inventory at retail times 60 percent. Once inventory has been estimated at cost ($36,000), it can be deducted from cost of goods available for sale ($204,000) to determine cost of goods sold ($168,000).

In 1985, the $36,000 and $60,000 amounts will appear on the schedule as beginning inventory at cost and retail, respectively. Purchases at cost and at retail will be added to determine goods available for sale at cost and at retail and from which 1985's cost/price ratio will be computed.

As an illustration of how the retail method can be used to detect inventory shortages, a physical inventory taken on December 31, 1984, may show only $56,000 of retail-priced goods in the store. Comparing this to the $60,000 of goods shown in Illustration 9.10 which should be on hand indicates a $4,000 inventory shortage at retail. The $4,000 will be converted to $2,400 of cost ($4,000 × 0.60) and reported as a Loss from Inventory Shortage in the income statement. Knowledge of such shortages may lead to management action to reduce or prevent them.

PERPETUAL INVENTORY PROCEDURE

Emphasis thus far in this chapter has been on periodic inventory procedure. Under periodic procedure, the Purchases account is debited when goods are acquired; other accounts are used for purchase-related items, and cost of goods sold is determined only at the end of the period as the difference between cost of goods available for sale and ending inventory. No records are kept of the cost of items as they are sold and no information is provided on possible inventory shortages. Any goods not in ending inventory are assumed to have been sold.

Under perpetual inventory procedure, there are no purchases and purchases related accounts. All entries involving merchandise purchased for sale to customers are entered in Merchandise Inventory. Since an entry is also made to reduce inventory for the cost of each item sold, Merchandise Inventory at the end of the period will show the cost of the goods that should be on hand. Comparison of this amount with the cost obtained by taking and pricing a physical inventory will reveal inventory shortages. Thus, perpetual inventory procedure is an important element in providing internal control over goods with high unit costs, such as autos, television sets, jewelry, and cameras.

Perpetual inventory cards

Perpetual inventory procedure can be applied manually or by use of computers. In either procedure, a card will be maintained for each item in inventory. As an example, Entertainment World has many different brands

Illustration 9.11: Perpetual inventory card (Fifo)

Item	TV-96874					Maximum	26			
Location						Minimum	6			

	Purchased			Sold			Balance		
1984 Date	**Units**	**Unit cost**	**Total**	**Units**	**Unit cost**	**Total**	**Units**	**Unit cost**	**Total**
July 1							8	$300	$2,400
5	10	$300	$3,000				18	300	5,400
7				12	$300	$3,600	6	300	1,800
12	10	315	3,150				6	300	1,800
							10	315	3,150
22				6	300	1,800			
				2	315	630	8	315	2,520
24	8	320	2,560				8	315	2,520
							8	320	2,560

of television sets in inventory. Illustration 9.11 shows the information on one particular brand and model of set carried in the store.

The card provides information on the maximum and minimum number of units the firm wishes to stock at any time, when and how many units were acquired and at what cost, and when and how many units were sold and what cost was assigned to cost of goods sold. The number of units on hand and their cost are readily available also.

The Fifo method is used by Entertainment World for this type of television set as can be determined from the calculation of the cost of the eight units sold on July 22. Prior to this sale, there were 16 units on hand: six with a unit cost of $300 and 10 with a unit cost of $315. Cost assigned to the units sold on the 22nd consists of the cost of the six oldest units and two of the more recently purchased units. Costs are being removed from inventory on a Fifo basis.

Illustration 9.12: Perpetual inventory card (weighted average)

	Purchased			Sold			Balance		
1984 Date	**Units**	**Unit cost**	**Total**	**Units**	**Unit cost**	**Total**	**Units**	**Unit cost**	**Total**
July 1							8	$300	$2,400
5	10	$300	$3,000				18	$300	$5,400
7				12	$300	$3,600	6	$300	$1,800
12	10	315	3,150				10	315	3,150
							16	309.375	$4,950*
22				8	309.375	2,475	8	$309.375	$2,475
24	8	320	2,560				8	320.000	2,560
							16	314.6875	$5,035†

* $4,950/16 = $309.375
† $5,035/16 = $314.6875

Illustration 9.12 shows the same information as in Illustration 9.9 except that weighted-average cost is used rather than Fifo. Note that a new weighted-average unit cost is computed after *each purchase* by dividing total cost of goods available for sale by total units available for sale. Thus, the unit cost after the purchase of July 12 is $309.375 ($4,950/16). The cost of the eight units sold on July 22 is $2,475 (8 × $309.375). A new weighted-average unit cost is computed after the purchase of July 24. The unit cost is referred to as a moving weighted average because it changes after each purchase.

Because the advantages of Lifo are maximized when it is applied on an annual basis, Lifo is not likely to be applied on a perpetual basis. If it is, special adjustments which are beyond the scope of this text must be made. For this reason the text does not illustrate the application of Lifo under perpetual procedure.

Journal entries under perpetual procedure

Part of the data in Illustration 9.12 are used to show the entries required under perpetual procedure. The purchase of 10 units on July 5 would be recorded as follows:

```
July 5   Merchandise Inventory ....................................... 3,000
             Accounts Payable ....................................... 3,000
         To record purchase on account.
```

The 10 sets purchased must also be recorded on the perpetual inventory card, as shown in Illustration 9.12. Merchandise acquisitions are best recorded at net invoice prices to avoid the problem of adjusting the gross invoice prices entered on all the inventory cards when purchase discounts are subsequently taken.

Assuming 12 sets were sold on July 12 at a price of $450, the following entries are required:

```
July 12  Accounts Receivable ..................................... 5,400
             Sales ................................................ 5,400
         To record 12 sets sold on account.

     12  Cost of Goods Sold ...................................... 3,600
             Merchandise Inventory ................................ 3,600
         To record cost of 12 sets sold.
```

Perpetual procedure requires an entry to merchandise inventory whenever goods are purchased, returned, sold, or otherwise adjusted, if inventory records are to reflect actual units on hand at all times. Thus, an entry is required to record cost of goods sold for each sale. Also, transportation costs incurred on goods purchased are debited to Merchandise Inventory.

At year-end, a physical inventory is taken and compared with perpetual records. If a shortage is discovered, an adjusting entry is required. The entry, assuming a $2,000 shortage is discovered, is:

```
Loss from Inventory Shortage ....................................... 2,000
    Merchandise Inventory .......................................... 2,000
  To record inventory shortage.
```

No other entries are required. The only inventory amount in the accounts is the properly stated ending inventory amount. There are no purchases and purchase related accounts to be closed, only cost of goods sold requires a closing entry.

NEW TERMS INTRODUCED IN CHAPTER

Fifo (first-in, first-out)
A method of pricing inventory under which the costs of the first goods acquired are the first costs charged to cost of goods sold when goods are actually sold.

Gross margin method
A procedure for estimating inventory cost in which estimated cost of goods sold, determined by deducting estimated gross margin from sales, is deducted from cost of goods available for sale. Estimated gross margin is calculated using gross margin rates of prior periods.

Inventory or "paper" profits
The increase in the cost to acquire a unit of inventory at time of sale over the unit's historical cost.

Lifo (last-in, first-out)
A method of pricing inventory under which the costs of the last goods acquired are the first costs charged to cost of goods sold when goods are actually sold.

Lower-of-cost-or-market method
An inventory pricing method that values inventory at the lower of its historical cost or its current (replacement) cost.

Net realizable value
Estimated selling price of an item less all costs to complete and dispose of it.

Retail inventory method
A procedure for estimating the cost of the ending inventory by applying a cost/price ratio to ending inventory stated in retail prices.

Specific identification
An inventory pricing method that attaches a known actual cost to an identifiable unit of product.

Weighted-average method
A method of pricing inventory under which the total number of units purchased plus those in beginning inventory is divided into total cost of goods available for sale to arrive at a weighted-average unit cost. Units in ending inventory are carried at this per unit cost. Under perpetual procedure a *moving* weighted-average unit cost is calculated.

DEMONSTRATION PROBLEM

Following are data related to the beginning inventory and purchases of a given item of product of the Van Company for the year 1984:

Inventory, January 1	5,000 @ $2.00
March 15	4,000 @ $2.10
May 10	7,000 @ $2.25
August 12	5,000 @ $2.40
November 20	3,000 @ $2.60
	24,000

During the year, 20,000 units were sold. Periodic inventory procedure is used.

Required:

Compute the ending inventory under each of the following methods:

a. Fifo.

b. Lifo.

c. Weighted average.

Solution to demonstration problem

The ending inventory consists of 4,000 units (24,000 − 20,000).

a. Ending inventory under Fifo:

Purchased	Units	Unit cost	Total cost
November 20	3,000	$2.60	$ 7,800
August 12	1,000	2.40	2,400
	4,000		$10,200

b. Ending inventory under Lifo:

	Units	Unit cost	Total cost
Inventory, January 1	4,000	$2.00	$ 8,000

c. Ending inventory under weighted average:

Purchased	Units	Unit cost	Total cost
Inventory, January 1	5,000	$2.00	$10,000
March 15	4,000	2.10	8,400
May 10	7,000	2.25	15,750
August 12	5,000	2.40	12,000
November 20	3,000	2.60	7,800
	24,000		$53,950

Weighted-average unit cost is $53,950 ÷ 24,000, or $2.25.
Ending inventory cost is $2.25 × 4,000 = $9,000.

QUESTIONS

1. Why is proper inventory valuation so important?

2. Why does an understated ending inventory understate net income for the period by the same amount?

3. Why does an error in ending inventory affect two accounting periods?

4. What cost elements are included in inventory? What practical problems are faced in including the costs of such elements?

5. What is the meaning of "to take a physical inventory?"

6. What are cost flows? What is meant by the physical flow of goods? Is there or should there be a relationship between cost flows and the flow of goods?

7. Indicate how a company can manipulate its net income if it uses Lifo. Is the same opportunity available under Fifo? Why or why not?

8. What are the main advantages from the use of Fifo? Of Lifo?

9. Which inventory method is the correct one? Can a company change inventory methods?

10. What is net realizable value and how is it used?

11. Why is it considered acceptable accounting practice to recognize a loss by writing down an item of merchandise in inventory to market, but unacceptable to recognize a gain by writing up an inventory item?

12. Under what conditions will the gross margin method of computing an inventory yield approximately correct amounts?

13. What are the main reasons for estimating ending inventory?

14. How can the retail method be used to estimate inventory?

15. When is it advisable to use perpetual inventory procedure? What problem is faced in accounting for purchase discounts under perpetual procedure? How is it best resolved?

EXERCISES

E-1. The Flint Company inventory records show:

	Units	Amount
Beginning inventory	2,000	@ $9.00 = $18,000
February 14	600	@ $8.40 = $ 5,040
March 18	1,600	@ $8.25 = $13,200
July 21	1,200	@ $8.70 = $10,440
September 27	1,200	@ $8.40 = $10,080
November 27	400	@ $8.85 = $ 3,540

The December 31 inventory was 2,800 units.

a. Present a short schedule showing the measurement of the ending inventory using the Fifo method.

b. Do the same using the Lifo method.

c. Repeat, using the weighted-average method.

E-2. The Tuber Company's inventory of a certain product was 12,000 units with a cost of $16 each on January 1, 1984. During 1984, numerous units of this product were purchased and sold. Also during 1984, the purchase price of this product fell steadily until at year-end it was $12. The inventory at year-end was 18,000 units. State which of the two methods of inventory measurement, Lifo or Fifo, would have resulted in the higher reported net income and explain briefly.

E-3. Following are inventory data for 1984 for the Newport Company:

1. January 1 inventory on hand, 400 units @ $5 = $2,000.
2. January sales were 80 units.
3. February sales totaled 120 units.
4. March 1, purchased 200 units @ $5.25.
5. Sales for March through August were 160 units.
6. September 1, purchased 40 units @ $5.75.
7. September through December sales were 180 units.

Prepare only the journal entries affecting inventory assuming use of periodic procedure. A physical inventory on December 31, 1984, showed 100 units on hand. Price the ending inventory at its weighted-average cost.

E-4. Your assistant has compiled the following data to assist you in determining the decline in inventory from cost to the lower of cost or market applied on an item-by-item basis:

Item	Quantity (units)	Unit cost	Unit market	Total cost	Total market
A	300	$24	$23	$7,200	$6,900
B	300	12	14	3,600	4,200
C	900	9	9	8,100	8,100
D	500	5	5.50	2,500	2,750

Determine the dollar amount of the ending inventory at lower of cost or market, determined on an item-by-item basis, and the amount of the decline from cost to lower of cost or market.

E–5. Use the data in Exercise E–4 above and compute the cost of the ending inventory using the lower-of-cost-or-market method applied to total inventory.

E–6. Benz Company follows the practice of taking a physical inventory at the end of each calendar-year accounting period to establish the ending inventory amount for financial statement purposes. Its financial statements for the past few years indicate a normal gross margin of 25 percent. On July 18, a fire destroyed the entire store building and contents. The records were in a fireproof vault and are intact. These records, through July 17, show:

Merchandise inventory, January 1	$ 300,000
Merchandise purchases	4,200,000
Purchase returns	60,000
Transportation-in	225,000
Sales	6,400,000
Sales returns	300,000

The company was fully covered by insurance and asks you to determine the amount of its claim for loss of merchandise.

E–7. Douglas Motor Company owns a Howard automobile that it has used as a demonstrator for eight months. The auto has a list or sticker price of $10,000 and cost Douglas $8,500. The auto is on hand at the end of the fiscal year, at which time it has an expected selling price of $9,000. Costs expected to be incurred to sell the auto include tune-up and maintenance costs of $200, advertising of $50, and a commission to the employee selling the auto of 5 percent of selling price. Compute the amount at which the auto should be carried in inventory.

E–8. Listed below are the purchases of Product X made by the Black Company in its first year of operation:

January 2	700 @ $1.85
March 31	600 @ $1.75
July 5	1,200 @ $1.90
November 1	900 @ $2.00

The ending inventory for the year consisted of 1,200 units.

a. Compute the cost of the ending inventory using each of the following methods: (1) Fifo, (2) Lifo, and (3) weighted average.

b. Which method would yield the highest amount of gross margin? Explain why it does.

E–9. A company purchased 1,000 units of a product at $10 and 2,000 units at $11. It sold all of these units at $15 each at a time when the current cost to replace the units sold was $11.50. Compute the amount of gross margin under Fifo that Lifo supporters would call inventory profits or "paper" profits.

E–10. Following are selected transactions of the Neal Company:

Transactions:

1. Purchased 100 units of merchandise at $100 each; terms, 2/10, n/30.
2. Paid the invoice in No. 1 within the discount period.

3. Sold 80 units at $160 each for cash.
4. Purchased 100 units at $150; terms, 2/10, n/30.
5. Paid the invoice in No. 4 within the discount period.
6. Sold 60 units at $230 each for cash.

Prepare journal entries for the six numbered items above. Assume goods acquired are recorded at net invoice prices, accounted for under perpetual procedure, and the Fifo inventory method is used.

E-11. Compute the cost of the goods sold in Exercise E–10 above, item No. 6, assuming perpetual procedure is used, with unit costs calculated under the moving weighted-average method. Round decimals to three places.

PROBLEMS, SERIES A

P9-1-A. Prospect Company reported net income of $238,400 for 1984, $247,600 for 1985, and $217,200 for 1986, using the incorrect inventory amounts shown for December 31, 1984, and 1985. The correct inventory amounts for those dates are also given. The correct December 31, 1986, inventory amount was used in calculating 1986 net income.

	Incorrect	*Correct*
December 31, 1984	$48,400	$56,800
December 31, 1985	56,000	46,800

Required:

Prepare a schedule that shows: (1) the reported net income for each year in one column, (2) the amount of correction needed for each year in a second column, and (3) the correct net income for each year in a third column.

P9-2-A. As of December 31, 1984, the financial records of the Burnham Company were examined for the years ended December 31, 1981, 1982, 1983, and 1984. With regard to the inventory, the examination disclosed the following:

1. December 31, 1981: Inventory was overstated $30,000.
2. December 31, 1982: Inventory was overstated $15,000.
3. December 31, 1983: Inventory was understated $33,000.
4. December 31, 1984: Inventory was correct.

The reported net income for each year was:

1981	$ 57,600
1982	81,600
1983	100,500
1984	126,900

Required:

(Assume that the errors were not discovered until the end of 1984, so no correcting entries have been made.)

a. What is the correct net income for each of the four years—1981–84?

b. What is (are) the error(s) in each December 31 balance sheet?

c. Comment on the implications of your corrected net income as contrasted with reported net income.

P9-3-A. The Technix Company sells home computers. It uses the specific identification method to account for its inventory. As of November 30, 1984, the company has 23 Orange III model home computers on hand which were acquired on the following dates and at the stated costs:

July 3 . . . . 5 @ $1,600
September 10 . . . . 10 @ $1,500
November 29 . . . . 8 @ $1,750

Technix sold 18 Orange III computers at $2,300 each in December. There were no purchases of this model in December.

Required:

　　a. Calculate gross margin on December sales of Orange III computers, assuming the company shipped those units that would maximize reported gross margin.

　　b. Repeat part (*a*) assuming the company shipped those units that would minimize reported gross margin for December.

　　c. In view of your answers to parts (*a*) and (*b*), what would be your reaction to an assertion that the specific identification method should not be considered an acceptable method for costing inventory?

P9–4–A. 　　The Beaver Company accounts for a certain product that it handles using Lifo and periodic inventory procedure. Data relative to this product for the year ended December 31, 1984, are:

Inventory January 1, 3,000 units @ $8

Purchases		**Sales**	
January 5	6,000 @ $10	January 10	4,000 @ $16
March 31	18,000 @ $12	April 2	15,000 @ $18
August 12	12,000 @ $15	August 22	16,000 @ $20
December 26 . .	6,000 @ $16	December 24 . .	3,000 @ $22

Required:

　　a. Compute the gross margin earned on sales of this product for 1984.

　　b. Repeat part (*a*) assuming that the December 26 purchase was made in January of 1985.

　　c. Recompute gross margin assuming that 10,000 rather than 6,000 units were purchased on December 26.

　　d. Solve parts (*a*), (*b*), and (*c*) again assuming use of the Fifo inventory method.

P9–5–A. 　　The purchases and sales of a certain product for the Outland Company for April 1984 are shown below. There was no inventory on April 1.

Purchases		**Sales**	
April 3	2,000 units @ $3.50	April 4	1,200 units
April 10	1,600 units @ $3.60	April 11	1,000
April 22	3,200 units @ $3.30	April 16	1,000
April 28	1,800 units @ $3.40	April 26	800
		April 30	1,200

Required:

　　a. Using periodic procedure, compute the ending inventory of the above product as of April 30 under each of the following methods: (1) Fifo, (2) Lifo, and (3) weighted average.

　　b. Give the journal entries to record the purchases and the cost of goods sold for the month under both Fifo and Lifo.

P9–6–A.   Listed below are the purchases and sales of a certain product made by the Paulsen Company during 1984 and 1985. The company had 15,000 units of this product on hand at January 1, 1984, with a cost of $2.50 per unit.

Purchases		Sales	
1984		**1984**	
February 20	3,000 @ $2.50	February 2	4,500 @ $3.50
April 18	7,500 @ $2.45	April 23 ..../...	6,000 @ $3.00
August 28	7,500 @ $2.40	September 3	6,000 @ $2.90
December 22	6,000 @ $2.42	December 24	5,250 @ $2.95
1985		**1985**	
January 26	4,500 @ $2.50	January 7	3,750 @ $3.00
March 6	7,500 @ $2.50	March 21	6,000 @ $3.10
August 12	4,500 @ $2.60	September 8	3,750 @ $3.10
November 15	6,000 @ $2.70	December 2	6,750 @ $3.25

The company uses periodic inventory procedure.

Required:

a.   Compute the cost of the ending inventory and the cost of goods sold for both years assuming the use of the Fifo method of inventory measurement.

b.   Repeat (a) above assuming the use of Lifo.

P9–7–A.   Given below are the inventory amounts under Fifo and Lifo for the Clark Company:

December 31	Fifo	Lifo
1983	$120,000	$ 98,000
1984	124,000	116,000
1985	138,000	136,000

The Clark Company has used the Fifo method of inventory measurement and reported net income of $330,000 in 1984 and $340,000 in 1985.

Required:

State the amount of net income that the company would have reported in 1984 and 1985 if it had used the Lifo method rather than Fifo.

P9–8–A.   The accountant for the Antoy Company prepared the following schedule of the company's inventory at December 31, 1984, and used the lower of the total cost or total market value in determining cost of goods sold.

Item	Quantity	Unit cost	Unit market	Total cost	Total market
Q	3,500	$3.00	$3.00		
R	2,000	2.50	2.40		
S	4,500	2.00	1.90		
T	4,000	1.75	1.80		

Required:

a.   State whether this is an acceptable method of inventory measurement and determine the amounts computed.

b.   Compute the amount of the ending inventory using the lower-of-cost-or-market method on an item-by-item basis.

    c. State the effect upon net income in 1984 if the method in (*b*) was used rather than the method in (*a*).

P9–9–A. As part of a loan agreement with a local bank, the York Company must present quarterly and cumulative income statements for the year 1984. The company uses periodic inventory procedure and marks its merchandise to sell at a price which will yield a gross margin of 30 percent. Selected data for the first six months of 1984 are as follows:

	First quarter	Second quarter
Sales	$155,000	$160,000
Purchases	100,000	115,000
Purchase returns and allowances	6,000	7,000
Purchase discounts	2,000	2,200
Sales returns and allowances	5,000	3,000
Transportation-in	5,000	5,200
Selling expenses	16,000	15,000
Administrative expenses	6,000	5,000

The cost of the physical inventory taken December 31, 1983, was $19,000.

Required:

    a. Indicate how the income statements may be prepared without taking a physical inventory at the end of each of the first two quarters of 1984.

    b. Prepare income statements for the first quarter, the second quarter, and the first six months of 1984.

P9–10–A. The following data pertain to the Small Department Store for the fiscal year ended June 30, 1984:

	Cost	Retail
Merchandise inventory, July 1, 1983	$ 50,000	$ 74,000
Purchases, net	625,000	826,000
Sales		860,000

Required:

    a. Use the retail method to compute the cost of the inventory on June 30, 1984.

    b. If a physical inventory shows goods on hand on June 30, 1984, with a retail price of $36,000, what is the estimated cost of the inventory shortage?

PROBLEMS, SERIES B

P9–1–B. Oakdale Company reported net income of $65,000 for 1984, $67,500 for 1985, and $72,500 for 1986, using the incorrect inventory amounts shown for December 31, 1984, and 1985. The correct inventory amounts are also shown for those dates. The correct December 31, 1976, inventory amount was used in calculating 1986 net income.

	Incorrect	Correct
December 31, 1984	$20,000	$22,500
December 31, 1985	19,000	17,500

Required:

    Prepare a schedule that shows: (1) the reported net income for each year in one column, (2) the amount of correction needed for each year in a second column, and (3) the correct net income for each year in a third column.

P9–2–B. An examination of the records of the Da-Lite Company on December 31, 1984, disclosed the following with regard to merchandise inventory for 1984 and prior years:

1. December 31, 1981: Inventory was understated $20,000.
2. December 31, 1982: Inventory was overstated $14,000.
3. December 31, 1983: Inventory was understated $12,000.
4. December 31, 1984: Inventory was correct.

The reported net income for each year was as follows:

1981	$117,000
1982	142,000
1983	153,000
1984	140,000

Required:

(Assume that the errors were not discovered until the end of 1984, so that no correcting entries have been made.)

a. What is the correct net income for each of the four years—1981–84?

b. What is (are) the errors in each December 31 balance sheet?

c. Comment on the implications of the corrected net income as contrasted with reported net income.

P9–3–B. Wind-Sail Company sells the Ultra-Light model wind surfer. All of the Ultra-Lights are identical, except for identifying serial numbers. Wind-Sail Company had three Ultra-Lights in its inventory on August 1, 1984, that cost $2,800 each. During the month, the company purchased five Ultra-Lights from a dealer going out of business at $2,600 each. On August 17, six units were purchased at $2,900; and on August 28, six units were purchased at $3,000 each.

Wind-Sail Company sold 13 Ultra-Lights in August at $4,000 each. The company uses the specific identification method of accounting for its sales and purchases of Ultra-Lights.

Required:

a. Compute the gross margin earned by the company in August if it shipped the units that would maximize gross margin and net income.

b. Repeat part (a) assuming the company shipped the units that would minimize gross margin and net income.

c. Do you think Wind-Sail Company should be permitted to use the specific identification method of accounting for Ultra-Lights in view of the manipulation possible as shown by your calculations in (a) and (b)?

P9–4–B. Hadley Company accounts for its inventory using the Lifo method under periodic procedure. Data on purchases, sales, and inventory for the year ended December 31, 1984, are:

Inventory, January 1, 4,000 units @ $5

Purchases:

January 7	10,000 units @ $6
July 7.............................	20,000 units @ $7
December 21	12,000 units @ $8

During 1984, 32,000 units were sold for $320,000, leaving an inventory on December 31, 1984, of 14,000 units.

Required:

a.   Compute the gross margin earned on sales during 1984.

b.   Compute the change in gross margin that would have resulted if the purchase of December 21 had been delayed until January 6, 1985.

c.   Recompute the gross margin that would have resulted if 18,000 units rather than 12,000 units had been purchased on December 21.

d.   Solve parts (a), (b), and (c) again assuming use of the Fifo inventory method.

P9–5–B.   Following are data for the Ivory Company for the year 1984:

Inventory, January 1	700 @ $2.60
Purchases:	
February 2	500 @ $2.50
April 5	1,000 @ $2.00
June 15	600 @ $1.75
September 30	700 @ $1.70
November 28	900 @ $2.25

During the year, 3,300 units were sold. Periodic inventory procedure is used.

Required:

a.   Compute the ending inventory as of December 31, 1984, under each of the following methods: (1) Fifo, (2) Lifo, and (3) weighted average.

b.   Give the journal entries to record the purchases for the year and necessary year-end entries to charge Income Summary with the cost of goods sold for the year under Fifo.

P9–6–B.   The Evans Company was organized on January 1, 1982. Selected data for 1982–84 are as follows:

Year ended December 31	Inventory		Annual data	
	Fifo	Lifo	Purchases	Sales
1982	$3,200	$2,400	$14,400	$16,200
1983	4,000	2,800	12,000	19,000
1984	6,600	4,000	14,800	16,400

Required:

a.   Compute the cost of goods sold and gross margin for each of the three years 1982–84, using the Fifo method of inventory measurement.

b.   Repeat part (a) assuming the use of Lifo.

P9–7–B.   The Pitcher Company determined its net income for the years 1983, 1984, and 1985 as $204,000, $196,200, and $201,900, respectively, using the Fifo method of inventory pricing. Inventories on the Fifo and Lifo bases were:

December 31	Fifo	Lifo
1982	$45,000	$42,000
1983	51,600	47,400
1984	50,400	46,800
1985	54,900	50,100

Required:

Compute the net income that would have been reported in 1983, 1984, and 1985 by the Pitcher Company had it used the Lifo method of inventory measurement.

P9–8–B. Given below are data on the ending inventory of the Raven Company on December 31, 1984:

Item	Quantity	Unit cost	Unit market
1	3,000	$2.00	$1.95
2	6,000	1.80	1.90
3	2,000	1.75	1.80
4	5,000	2.40	2.25
5	4,000	2.25	2.30
6	1,000	1.90	1.80

Required:

a. Compute the ending inventory applying the lower-of-cost-or-market method to the total inventory.

b. Repeat part (*a*) above; apply the method to the individual items.

P9–9–B. The sales and cost of goods sold for the Grunther Company for the past five years were as follows:

Year	Sales (net)	Cost of goods sold
1979	$1,040,100	$650,410
1980	1,124,400	703,125
1981	1,286,100	792,238
1982	1,230,900	781,211
1983	1,328,400	830,693

For the seven months ended July 31, 1984, the following information is available from the accounting records of the company:

Sales	$807,100
Purchases	478,000
Purchase returns	3,000
Sales returns	18,100
Inventory, January 1, 1984	98,750

Upon requesting a new supplier to extend credit to it, the Grunther Company was asked to present current financial statements. But the company does not wish to take a complete physical inventory as of July 31, 1984.

Required:

     a. Indicate how financial statements can be prepared without taking a complete physical inventory.

     b. From the data given, compute the estimated inventory as of July 31, 1984.

P9–10–B. The following data pertain to a certain department of the Dalton Department Store for the year ended December 31, 1984:

	Cost	Retail
Merchandise inventory, January 1, 1984 ...	$ 62,500	$ 80,000
Purchase, net	500,000	820,000
Sales		840,000

Required:

     a. Use the retail method to compute the cost of the inventory on December 31, 1984.

     b. If a physical inventory on December 31, 1984, shows goods on hand with a retail price of $55,000, what is the approximate cost of the inventory shortage?

BUSINESS DECISION PROBLEM 9–1

     The Maxwell Company, which began operations on January 2, 1984, sells a single product, Product X. Purchases for the year were:

January 2	1,000 at $4.00
February 15	1,600 at $4.00
April 8	2,000 at $4.15
June 6	800 at $4.25
August 19	1,600 at $4.30
October 5	1,200 at $4.50
November 22	800 at $4.80

     Periodic inventory procedure is used. On December 31, a physical inventory shows 1,600 units on hand.

     Mr. Maxwell is trying to decide which of the following inventory costing methods he should adopt for tax purposes: Fifo, Lifo, or weighted average. Since Mr. Maxwell is short of cash, he wants to minimize the amount of income taxes payable.

Required:

     In this case, which of the three inventory costing methods will minimize Mr. Maxwell's net income (and income taxes)? What will be the cost of goods sold and the cost of the ending inventory under this method?

BUSINESS DECISION PROBLEM 9–2

     Mary Thin owns and operates a sporting goods store. On February 2, 1984, the store suffered extensive fire damage and all of the inventory was destroyed. Ms. Thin uses periodic inventory procedure and has the following information in her accounting records, which were undamaged:

Inventory, January 1	$30,000
Purchases:	
January 8	12,000
January 20	18,000
January 30	24,000
Sales:	
During January	90,000
February 1 and 2	6,000

Ms. Thin also knows that her gross margin rate has been 40 percent for the past three years.

Ms. Thin's insurance company has offered to pay $21,000 to settle her inventory loss unless she can show that she suffered a greater loss.

Required:

Should Ms. Thin settle for $21,000? If not, how can she show that she suffered a greater loss? What is the estimated loss?

Chapter 10

Property, plant, and equipment

CHAPTER GOALS

After study of this chapter, you should be able to:

1. State the characteristics of plant assets.

2. Apply the general rule that plant asset acquisitions should be recorded at cost.

3. Compute plant asset depreciation under various methods and circumstances.

4. Cite and discuss the theoretical and practical advantages of the major depreciation methods.

5. Illustrate the reporting of plant assets and their related depreciation.

6. Distinguish between capital and revenue expenditures on plant assets.

7. Define and use correctly the new terms in the glossary.

Property, plant, and equipment is often referred to as *plant and equipment* or simply *plant assets.* Plant assets consist of land and manufactured or constructed assets, such as buildings, machinery, vehicles, and furniture. The tasks faced in accounting for plant assets include:

1. Identifying the types and amounts of expenditures which make up the acquisition cost of an asset.
2. Distinguishing between routine expenditures which must be expensed in the period in which they are incurred and expenditures which increase capacity or extend asset life which must be capitalized when incurred.
3. Allocating asset cost to the periods of its useful life through a process of depreciation.
4. Recognizing the gain or loss, if any, upon retirement or disposition of an asset.

These accounting tasks must be carried out correctly to bring about a proper matching of costs with the revenues generated by the asset. Because net income is affected, measurement of periodic expense associated with an asset is likely to be of concern to all financial statement users.

NATURE OF PLANT ASSETS

An asset must possess three attributes to be classified as a plant asset: (1) it must be tangible, that is, it must be capable of being seen and touched; (2) it must have a useful service life of more than one year; and (3) it must be used in business operations rather than held for resale to a customer.

Inventory is a tangible asset but not a plant asset because it is held for sale rather than use. A delivery truck may be classified by one firm (a dealership) as inventory because it is held for sale and by another firm (a retail appliance store) as a plant asset because it is being used rather than offered for sale. Land held for speculation or not yet put into service is a long-term investment rather than a plant asset because it is not being used by the business. Standby equipment that is used only in peak or emergency periods is classified as a plant asset because it is used in operations. Plant assets should include all long-lived tangible assets that are used to generate the principal revenues of the firm.

Plant assets as service potentials

A plant asset can be viewed as a collection of *service potentials* with such services being used up or consumed over a period of time. For example, a delivery truck may provide 100,000 miles of delivery service over several years. A new building may provide 40 years of shelter, while a machine may perform a certain operation on 400,000 parts. In each instance, purchase of the plant asset actually consists of the advance payment or prepayment for expected services. Plant asset costs are an *extreme form of prepaid expense;* and as was the case in short-term prepayments, the accounting task faced is to allocate the cost of these services to the periods benefitted.

INITIAL RECORDING OF PLANT ASSETS

Plant assets are recorded initially at cost. Cost is used because it is the best measure of the asset's fair value at acquisition and because it is objective and verifiable. This historical cost is the amount reported for the asset in subsequent periods. Usually no attempt is made to reflect changing market values for plant assets. Cost is measured as the amount of cash and/or cash equivalent given up to acquire a plant asset and place it in operating condition at its proper location. Thus, cost includes all normal, reasonable, and necessary expenditures to obtain the asset and get it ready for use.

Cost does not include losses, such as the cost of waste or inefficiency. For example, cost does not include fines or penalties from traffic violations or from failure to secure necessary permits to move heavy machinery on city streets. Also excluded from cost are expenditures incurred to repair damages suffered after purchase resulting from vandalism or improper handling of an asset. Plant asset cost *does* include repair and reconditioning costs of assets which were acquired in used or damaged condition.

Cost of a plant asset normally does not include interest charges incurred on a debt arising from *purchase* of the asset. Such charges are treated as expenses of the period. But an exception to this general rule exists. Interest charges incurred on funds borrowed to finance the *construction* of a major asset must be added to asset cost.[1] The asset's construction period must extend over one year. Thus, interest paid must be capitalized (recorded in an asset account) for construction projects for dams, buildings, ships, and similar major assets. Miscellaneous receipts during construction reduce the cost of the asset.

Land and land improvements

Cost of land includes the purchase price and a number of other costs. These other costs include: option cost, if any; real estate commissions; title search and title transfer fees; title insurance premiums; unpaid taxes (back taxes) assumed by the purchaser; cost of surveying, clearing, grading, and landscaping; and local assessments for sidewalks, streets, sewers, and water mains. Sometimes land purchased as a building site contains an old building that must be removed. In such cases, the entire purchase price should be debited to the Land account because the old building is not to be used. The Land account also should be debited for the cost of removing the old building, less any cash received from sale of salvaged materials. The Land account should be credited for an excess of sales price of salvaged materials over removal cost and for other miscellaneous receipts while the land is being readied for use.

Land purchased as a building site or location generally retains its ability to render services indefinitely. Land typically does not deteriorate gradually with use, except agricultural land which may lose its fertility or be subject

---

[1] FASB, "Capitalization of Interest Cost," *Statement of Financial Accounting Standards No. 34* (Stamford, Conn., 1979).

to erosion. In any event, land typically is not subject to depreciation. But *land improvements,* attachments to land, such as driveways, parking lots, fences, lighting systems, and sprinkler systems, have limited lives and are depreciable. Hence, the costs of land and land improvements should be recorded in separate accounts.

Buildings

When a building is purchased, its cost includes purchase price, repair and remodeling costs, unpaid taxes assumed by the purchaser, legal costs, and real estate brokerage commissions paid. When land and buildings are purchased together, total cost should be divided so that separate accounts may be established for land and for buildings. Once again, separation is needed in order to record proper depreciation charges on the building.

To illustrate, assume that Bonner Company purchased a farm on the outskirts of Lima, Ohio, as a factory site. The farm consisted of land and one building, which is to be remodeled for use. Total purchase price of the farm was $180,000, which must be allocated to the land and the building. A possible method of allocation is based on relative appraised values. If the land was appraised at $160,000, and the building at $40,000, the $180,000 purchase price would be allocated 80 percent to the land and 20 percent to the building as shown by this schedule:

	Appraised value	Percent of total appraised value	Total cost	Allocated cost
Land............	$160,000	80	$180,000	$144,000 (80% × $180,000)
Building	40,000	20	180,000	36,000 (20% × $180,000)
Total	$200,000	100		$180,000

The journal entry to record the purchase of the farm by Bonner would be:

Land	144,000	
Building...	36,000	
Cash		180,000
To record purchase of land and building.		

Instead of the situation just described, assume Bonner purchased the farm and intended to raze (tear down) the building and construct new facilities. In addition to the $180,000 purchase price, the company paid unpaid taxes from previous periods of $8,000 and attorney and legal fees of $1,200. The farm building was torn down at a cost of $13,000, but Bonner was able to salvage and sell for $3,000 several of the antique fixtures which were in the building. A new factory was constructed at a cost of $200,000; building permits and architects' fees totaled $15,000. Finally, the city assessed Bonner $6,000 for water mains, sewers, and street paving. These assessments will be paid by Bonner so the company can be provided city services, but Bonner will not own or repair the mains, sewers, or streets. These items are capitalized as part of land cost rather than land improvements because, since Bonner has no responsibility for them, they do not need to be depreciated. The costs of the land and building are computed as follows:

	Land	Building
Cost of factory site	$180,000	
Back taxes	8,000	
Attorney and legal fees	1,200	
Demolition costs	13,000	
Salvage value of scrap	(3,000)	
Factory construction		$200,000
Permits and fees		15,000
City assessments	6,000	
	$205,200	$215,000

Notice that all costs of purchasing the farm and razing the building are recorded in the Land account because the old building is not to be used. Bonner's real goal was to purchase the land, which was not available without taking the building also.

When a building is constructed, its cost is often more difficult to determine. But cost usually will include payments to contractors, labor and materials, architect's fees, building permits, salaries of officers supervising construction, and insurance, taxes, and interest during the construction period.

Machinery

When machinery is purchased, its cost includes the seller's *net* invoice price, regardless of whether the discount was taken, since the net price is the machine's cash price. Discounts not taken are best viewed as losses and are not capitalized as part of an asset's cost. Examples of other costs include sales taxes, transportation charges, insurance paid while the machine was in transit to its location, and installation costs. Installation costs could include cost of special foundations necessary to support the weight of the machine, testing and break-in costs, costs of accessories, and any other costs incurred to put the machine in operating condition. Cost does not include costs of removing and disposing of a replaced old machine that has been used in operations. Such costs are part of the gain or loss on disposal of the old machine, as is discussed further in the next chapter.

Self-constructed assets. If a company builds a machine for its own use, cost would include the cost of materials and labor directly traceable to construction of the machine. Cost would also include amounts paid for such items such as heat, light, power, and supplies used during construction. The amount to capitalize related to these indirect services would be determined by comparing utility and supply costs during the period of construction with the normal costs paid in a period when there was no construction. The increase in the bills would be recorded as part of the machine's cost. For example, assume a company normally incurred a $400 utility bill for the month of June. This year, a machine was also constructed during June and the company received a bill of $650 for June. The $250 increase would be recorded as part of the machine's cost.

To illustrate further, assume that Henkel Company needed a new die-casting machine and found that the purchase price from Silkin Company was $23,000, plus $1,000 freight costs. Henkel decided to build the machine rather than buy it. The company incurred costs to build the machine of materials, $4,000; labor, $13,000; and indirect services of heat, power, and supplies, $3,000. The machine should be recorded at $20,000 ($4,000 + $13,000 + $3,000) rather than $24,000, the price that would have been paid if the machine were purchased. The $20,000 is the cost of the resources given up to construct the machine. Also, to record the machine at $24,000 would require Henkel to recognize a gain on self-construction of assets. Accountants generally do not subscribe to the idea that a firm can earn revenue and net income by dealing with itself.

The general guidelines discussed and illustrated can be applied to other plant assets such as delivery, selling, and office equipment; fixtures; and furniture. The accounting is the same as presented above. Further illustration is not needed.

Noncash acquisitions

The cost to be recorded for a plant asset purchased for cash is easily determined. It is simply the agreed-upon cash price. More difficult problems are faced when plant assets are acquired in exchange for other noncash assets (shares of stock, a customer's note, or a tract of land) or by giving a note payable to the seller. Possible asset valuation bases are discussed below.

Fair market value. Accountants seek to record noncash exchange transactions at fair market value. Thus, *the noncash asset received is valued at its fair market value or the fair market value of what was given up, whichever is more clearly evident.* If 100 shares of General Motors stock with a total market value of $5,000 are exchanged for a used machine with no known market value, the machine is recorded at $5,000. If a machine with a market value of $4,500 is acquired in exchange for a tract of land having a cost of $4,000, the machine is recorded at $4,500 and a $500 gain on the land exchange is recognized. If a machine, which is offered for sale for $10,000 cash, is purchased by giving a noninterest-bearing note payable for $11,500, the machine is recorded as follows:

```
Machinery ...............................................  10,000
Discount on Notes Payable ...............................   1,500
    Notes Payable .......................................           11,500
    To record purchase of machine by giving a $11,500 note.
```

The machine is recorded at its fair market value, its cash price. The note is recorded at face value. The discount also is recorded, with the result that the net amount of the note and its discount is equal to the note's fair market value. The discount is amortized over the life of the note as interest expense.

Appraised value. Exchanges of items, neither of which has a market value, may be recorded at their appraised values as determined by a professional appraiser. Appraised values are an expert's opinion as to what an item's market price would be if the item were sold. Appraisals are often used to value works of art, rare books, and antiques.

Book value. Book value of an asset is its recorded cost less accumulated depreciation. Book value of an asset given up is an acceptable basis for measuring the value of the new asset received *only if* a better basis is not available. Book value of an old asset is usually not a valid indicator of the new asset's economic value.

Gifts of plant assets

Occasionally, a company will receive an asset without giving up anything for it. A common example is a gift by a city to a business of a tract of land on which to build a factory in order to attract industry to an area and provide jobs for local residents. Although such a gift costs the recipient nothing, the asset is usually recorded at its fair market value. The credit to record the gift in a sole proprietorship is to owner's capital. Gifts of plant assets are recorded at fair value because accounting seeks to provide information on all assets owned by the firm. Omitting some assets may make information provided misleading.

DEPRECIATION OF PLANT ASSETS

Every business records depreciation on all plant assets except land. Depreciation expense often is a significant factor in determining net income because its amount may be relatively large. Since most financial statement users are interested in a firm's net income, they are also likely to be interested in the amount and methods of computing a firm's depreciation expense.

Nature of depreciation

Depreciation is the amount of plant asset cost allocated to each period benefiting from the asset's use. Depreciation must be recorded on every plant asset except land because these assets will eventually wear out or become so inadequate or outmoded that they will be sold or discarded. Depreciation is recorded even when the current market value of a plant asset is greater than its original cost. Thus, depreciation is a *process of allocation, not valuation.*

Depreciation is a cost of operating a business. The use of a plant asset in business operations transforms a plant asset cost into an operating expense. Depreciation is often called a noncash expense because it does not require an outlay of cash when it is recorded. Rather, the cash was given up when the asset was acquired, not when that asset's cost is allocated to the periods of useful life of the asset. Plant asset costs are recovered from customers in the same manner that inventory costs are recovered by pricing goods sold or services rendered high enough to cover all expenses, including depreciation.

Recording depreciation

Summarized briefly below is what has been said about recording and reporting depreciation in Chapter 3. Depreciation is usually recorded by debiting a depreciation expense and crediting an accumulated depreciation account. Accumulated depreciation is a contra account to the asset account, which carries original cost. A contra account is used because depreciation is an estimate that is likely to be inexact. Also, more information is provided by showing both the asset's original cost and its accumulated depreciation than by showing only book value of an asset.

Depreciation expense is shown on the income statement and may be classified as a selling expense or administrative expense, depending upon the functional area in which the asset is used. For example, depreciation on delivery trucks would be classified as a selling expense, while depreciation on office machines would be an administrative expense. In yet other situations, manufacturing services are received and periodic depreciation cost is considered a cost of manufacturing goods for sale. In such a case, depreciation becomes an expense (as part of the cost of goods sold) when the goods are sold. Also, the depreciation on one plant asset may be considered one of the costs of another plant asset as, for example, when a truck is used in constructing a building.

Factors affecting depreciation

Computation of periodic depreciation is affected by three major items: cost, estimated salvage, and estimated life. Determination of plant asset cost, which is the most objectively determined item in the computation of depreciation, has already been discussed.

Estimated salvage value. *Salvage value* (also called *scrap* or *residual value*) is the amount of money expected to be recoverable, less disposal costs, on the date a plant asset is scrapped, sold, or traded in. The cost of an asset's service potential is acquisition cost less estimated salvage value and is the asset's *depreciable cost.* An asset's depreciable cost must be charged to operations through periodic depreciation entries.

When an asset has a relatively short life and there is an active market for used assets, salvage value may be accurately estimated. Automobiles and computers are types of assets for which salvage value can be estimated fairly well. Other assets may be unique and have no salvage value except proceeds from their sale as scrap metal. In yet other cases, the cost of demolishing an asset, such as a building, may equal the proceeds secured from sale of salvaged materials, resulting in a zero salvage value.

Estimated useful life.   Useful life is the period of time over which an asset is expected to provide services to the firm. The useful, service, or economic life of an asset may differ from its physical life. For example, a company may determine that costs can be minimized by trading in its autos after three years of use even though the autos could be driven for at least eight years. In this case, the company would charge off depreciable cost to depreciation expense over a useful life of three years rather than a physical life of eight. The fact that the autos will be traded after three rather than eight years will undoubtably affect the estimation of salvage value.

Estimates of useful life are likely to be influenced by three factors: (1) physical deterioration, (2) inadequacy, and (3) obsolescence. *Physical deterioration* results from use, wear and tear, and the action of the elements. No matter how carefully an asset is maintained, it will eventually wear out. An automobile may have to be replaced because its body rusted out. *Inadequacy* is the inability of a plant asset to produce enough products or provide enough services to meet current demands. For example, an airline cannot provide air service for 125 passengers on a flight serviced by a plane with a seating capacity of 90. *Obsolescence* is the decline in usefulness of an asset brought about by invention and technological progress. For example, the development of the xerographic process of reproduction of printed matter rendered almost all prior methods of duplication obsolete. Both inadequacy and obsolescence may bring about the discarding of an asset before it is worn out.

DEPRECIATION METHODS[2]

Many different methods of depreciation are used in the business world. Four of the most common are discussed and illustrated below. As is true for inventory methods, a company is normally free to adopt the method(s) of depreciation it believes most appropriate for its operations. The theoretical guideline is to use a method that reflects most closely the actual underlying economic circumstances. In other words, a company should attempt to allocate plant asset cost to periods in accordance with benefits received from the use of that asset. The measurement of benefits is often not possible as a practical matter. As a result, a depreciation method really must meet only one standard: it *must* allocate plant asset cost to periods in a systematic and rational manner. The methods discussed below meet this requirement. For illustrative purposes, all depreciation calculations assume the purchase on January 1, 1984, for $27,000 of a machine which has an estimated useful life of 10 years, or 50,000 units of output, and an estimated salvage value of $2,000.

Straight-line depreciation

The *straight-line depreciation* method has been the most widely used method by companies in the United States for many years because it is easily

[2] Because depreciation expense is an estimate, calculations should be rounded at least to the nearest dollar.

applied. The straight-line method charges an equal amount of plant asset cost to each period. The formula for calculating depreciation under the straight-line method is:

$$\frac{\text{Cost } - \text{ Estimated salvage value}}{\text{Number of accounting periods in estimated life}} = \text{Depreciation per period}$$

The annual depreciation charge for the $27,000 machine is $2,500 [($27,000 − $2,000)/10]. The schedule in Illustration 10.1 presents the annual depreciation entries, the cumulative balances in the accumulated depreciation account, and the book (or carrying) value of the asset.

Illustration 10.1: Depreciation schedule—straight-line method

End of year	Depreciation expense Dr.; accumulated depreciation Cr.	Total accumulated depreciation	Book value
			$27,000
1	$ 2,500	$ 2,500	24,500
2	2,500	5,000	22,000
3	2,500	7,500	19,500
4	2,500	10,000	17,000
5	2,500	12,500	14,500
6	2,500	15,000	12,000
7	2,500	17,500	9,500
8	2,500	20,000	7,000
9	2,500	22,500	4,500
10	2,500	25,000	2,000*
	$25,000		

* Estimated salvage value.

Use of the straight-line method seems appropriate where (1) time rather than obsolescence is the major factor limiting the asset's life and (2) relatively constant amounts of periodic services are received from the asset. Assets that may possess these features include pipelines, fencing, and storage tanks.

Units-of-production (output) method

The *units-of-production depreciation* method assigns an equal amount of depreciation to each unit of product produced or service rendered by an asset. If usage is the main factor leading to the demise of an asset, depreciation may be based on physical output. A constant charge per unit of output is computed and then multiplied by the number of units produced during the period to find depreciation expense for the period. The formula is:

$$\frac{\text{Cost } - \text{ Estimated salvage value}}{\text{Estimated units of production}} = \text{Depreciation per unit}$$

Depreciation per unit × Number of units produced = Depreciation per period

The depreciation charge for the $27,000 machine is $0.50 per unit

[($27,000 − $2,000)/50,000]. If the machine produced 1,000 units in 1984 and 2,500 units in 1985, depreciation expense would be $500 and $1,250, respectively. A partial schedule of depreciation for this machine is:

End of year	Depreciation expense Dr.; accumulated depreciation Cr.	Total accumulated depreciation	Book value
			$27,000
1	$ 500	$ 500	26,500
2	1,250	1,750	25,250

Accelerated depreciation methods

Accelerated depreciation methods record higher amounts of depreciation in the early years of an asset's life and lower amounts in the asset's later years. A firm might use this type of method for income tax purposes to have larger expense and, therefore, lower taxable income and lower income taxes to pay in the asset's early years. Thus, use of an accelerated depreciation method legally postpones payment of income taxes to later periods—an event preferred by most taxpayers. A business might choose an accelerated method of depreciation because (1) the value of the benefits received from an asset decline with age (office buildings), (2) the asset is of the high-technology type which is subject to rapid obsolescence (computers), or (3) repairs increase substantially in later years and depreciation and repairs together remain fairly constant over the asset's life (automobiles). The two most common accelerated methods of depreciation are the sum-of-the-years'-digits (SYD) method and the fixed-percentage-of-declining-balance methods.

Sum-of-the-years'-digits (SYD) method. The *sum-of-the-years'-digits (SYD)* method is applied as follows. The consecutive digits for each year of estimated life of an asset are added together and used as the denominator of a fraction. The number of years of life remaining at the beginning of the accounting period is the numerator of the fraction. This fraction is then multiplied times cost less estimated salvage to compute periodic depreciation. The formula is:

$$\frac{\text{Number of years remaining}}{\text{SYD}} \times (\text{Cost} - \text{Estimated salvage value}) = \text{Depreciation expense}$$

The formula for finding the SYD for any given number of periods is:

$$\text{SYD} = \frac{n(n + 1)}{2}$$

where n is the number of periods in the asset's life. Thus, SYD for an asset with a 10-year useful life is:

$$\text{SYD} = \frac{10(10 + 1)}{2} = 55$$

At the beginning of year 1 (1984) there were 10 years of life remaining. The ratio used to compute the first year's depreciation on the $27,000 asset is 10/55, and the depreciation is $4,545, as shown in the schedule below. Notice that the fraction gets smaller every year, resulting in a declining depreciation charge to successive years.

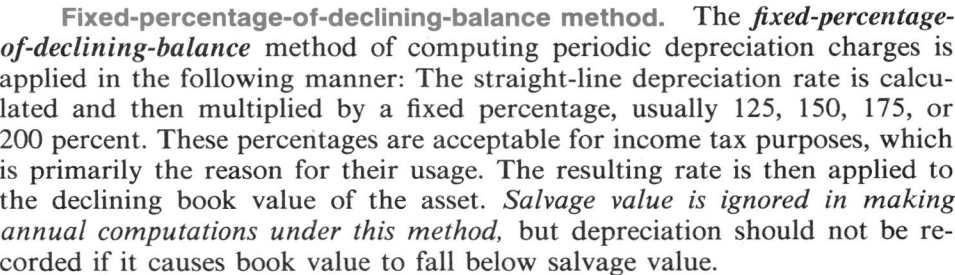

Depreciation
Year 1: $^{10}\!/_{55}$ ($27,000 − $2,000) ..... $ 4,545
Year 2: $^{9}\!/_{55}$ ($25,000) 4,091
Year 3: $^{8}\!/_{55}$ ($25,000) 3,636
Year 4: $^{7}\!/_{55}$ ($25,000) 3,182
Year 5: $^{6}\!/_{55}$ ($25,000) 2,727
Year 6: $^{5}\!/_{55}$ ($25,000) 2,273
Year 7: $^{4}\!/_{55}$ ($25,000) 1,818
Year 8: $^{3}\!/_{55}$ ($25,000) 1,364
Year 9: $^{2}\!/_{55}$ ($25,000) 909
Year 10: $^{1}\!/_{55}$ ($25,000) 455
    Total depreciation $25,000

Fixed-percentage-of-declining-balance method. The *fixed-percentage-of-declining-balance* method of computing periodic depreciation charges is applied in the following manner: The straight-line depreciation rate is calculated and then multiplied by a fixed percentage, usually 125, 150, 175, or 200 percent. These percentages are acceptable for income tax purposes, which is primarily the reason for their usage. The resulting rate is then applied to the declining book value of the asset. *Salvage value is ignored in making annual computations under this method,* but depreciation should not be recorded if it causes book value to fall below salvage value.

When 200 percent is used (the maximum acceptable for tax purposes), the depreciation method is called the *double-declining-balance (DDB) method.* The formula for DDB depreciation is:

Depreciation expense = (2 × Straight-line rate) (Cost − Accumulated depreciation)

The straight-line rate is calculated by dividing 100 percent by the number of years of useful life of the asset.

The calculations for the $27,000 machine using the DDB method are shown in Illustration 10.2. The straight-line rate is 10 percent (100 percent/10 years), which yields a DDB rate of 20 percent. Since in year 1 there is no accumulated depreciation, the calculation is based on cost. In each of the following years, the calculation is based on book value at the beginning of the year.

In the 10th year, depreciation could be increased to $1,624 if the asset is to be retired and its salvage value is still $2,000. If the asset is continued in service, depreciation could be recorded until the asset's book value is equal to its estimated salvage value.

Accelerated depreciation and taxes. Theoretical support exists for the accelerated depreciation methods. As mentioned, their use seems appropriate where the service-rendering or revenue-producing capacity of an asset declines over time or the asset is subject to a high rate of obsolescence.

Illustration 10.2 Double-declining-balance (DDB) depreciation method
schedule

End of year		Depreciation expense Dr.; accumulated depreciation Cr.	Total accumulated depreciation	Book value
				$27,000
1	(20% of $27,000)	$5,400	$ 5,400	$21,600
2	(20% of $21,600)	4,320	9,720	17,280
3	(20% of $17,280)	3,456	13,176	13,824
4	(20% of $13,284)	2,765	15,941	11,059
5	(20% of $11,059)	2,212	18,153	8,847
6	(20% of $8,847)	1,769	19,922	7,078
7	(20% of $7,078)	1,416	21,338	5,662
8	(20% of $5,662)	1,132	22,470	4,530
9	(20% of $4,530)	906	23,376	3,624
10	(20% of $3,624)	725*	24,101	2,899

* This amount could be $1,624 so as to reduce the book value to the estimated salvage value of $2,000.

The main reason for using an accelerated depreciation method for tax purposes is intensely practical—it reduces the amount of income taxes payable currently. Depreciation expense in the early years of an asset's life is increased to an amount greater than that computed using the straight-line method. Deduction of the larger amount of depreciation expense reduces taxable income and income taxes payable for the year. In general, the amount of the reduction is equal to the extra depreciation deducted multiplied by the appropriate tax rate. If, for example, accelerated depreciation for the year was $32,000 while straight-line depreciation was only $20,000 and the income tax rate was 40 percent, the reduction in income taxes payable for the year is $4,800—0.4 ($32,000 − $20,000). Note that the $4,800 reduction in income taxes payable for the year is not a permanent reduction in taxes. Rather, a postponement is involved. Increased income taxes will be paid in later years when smaller than straight-line amounts of depreciation are deducted. But, because firms prefer to pay taxes later rather than sooner, the use of accelerated depreciation methods is common among business firms, especially for tax purposes.

Partial year depreciation

When assets are acquired during an accounting period, depreciation for the period is normally calculated to the nearest full month. Thus, an asset purchased on or before the 15th day of the month is treated as if it had been purchased on the first of the month. An asset purchased after the 15th day of the month is treated as if it had been acquired on the first of the following month.

Straight-line method.   The calculations for partial year depreciation are quite easy for straight-line depreciation. The normal computation is made to find the 12-month charge, and this annual amount is multiplied by the fraction of the year for which depreciation should be recorded. For example, assume a machine was purchased on September 3, 1984, that cost $7,600 and has an estimated salvage value of $400 and an estimated life of five years. Annual straight-line depreciation is $1,440 ($7,600 − $400)/5 years. The machine will be used four months prior to the end of the accounting year, December 31, or one third of a year. The 1984 depreciation is $480 ($1,440/3).

Units-of-production method. No unusual computations are required to record depreciation for a partial period under the units-of-production method. The depreciation charge for the partial period is still computed by multiplying the depreciation charge per unit by the number of units produced. The charge for a partial period is likely to be less than for a full year because fewer units were produced.

Fixed-percentage method. Depreciation for a partial period and for subsequent full years is quite easy to find under the fixed-percentage-of-declining-balance method. For the partial period, simply multiply the fixed rate times the cost of the asset times the fraction for the partial period. For example, DDB depreciation on the $7,600 asset for 1984 is $1,013 ($7,600 × 0.4 × $\frac{1}{3}$). For subsequent years, the depreciation is computed using the normal procedure of multiplying the book value at the beginning of the period by the fixed rate. In this case, the 1985 depreciation would be $2,635 [($7,600 − $1,013) × 0.4].

SYD method. The computation of periodic depreciation is more complex when an asset is purchased during the year and the SYD method is used. The reason is that the 12 months for which depreciation is computed using the SYD fraction do not correspond with the 12 months for which the financial statements are being prepared. For example, the depreciation recorded in 1984 on the $7,600 asset is for the last four months of 1984, which is the first one third of the first year of the asset's life. The depreciation recorded is $800; the amount is computed as [($7,600 − $400) × $\frac{5}{15}$ × $\frac{1}{3}$]. In 1985, the depreciation recorded is $2,240, computed as follows:

For the first two thirds of the year:	($7,200 × $\frac{5}{15}$ × $\frac{2}{3}$) =	$1,600
For the last one third of the year:	($7,200 × $\frac{4}{15}$ × $\frac{1}{3}$) =	640
Total depreciation expense for 1985		$2,240

This form of computation of annual depreciation charges will continue throughout the asset's life.

Changes in estimates

After an asset has been depreciated down to its estimated salvage value, no more depreciation is recorded on that asset even if it continues to be used. But when asset lives or salvage values are found to be incorrect *before* the asset has been depreciated down to its estimated salvage value, revised depreciation charges need to be computed. The revised charges do not correct *past* depreciation taken; they merely compensate for the incorrect charges through changed expense amounts in the current and future periods. The new depreciation charge per period is computed by dividing net book value less salvage value by the estimated number of life periods remaining.

For example, assume that a machine cost $30,000, had an estimated salvage value of $2,000, and an estimated life of seven years. At the end of the fourth year, the balance in the machine's accumulated depreciation account is $16,000, which is four years of $4,000 annual depreciation. At the beginning of the fifth year, it is estimated that the asset will last five more years, with a revised salvage value of $1,000. The revised annual depreciation charge for the current and next four years is computed as follows:

Asset cost	$30,000
Less accumulated depreciation	16,000
Book value	$14,000
Less salvage value	1,000
Remaining depreciable amount	$13,000
Divided by years of life remaining	÷5
Straight-line depreciation per year	$ 2,600

Note that the adjustment procedure used does not correct past overstated depreciation and other misstated accounts. The overstatement will be offset by future understatement of depreciation. The many immaterial errors in estimating depreciation are routinely disposed of in this practical way.

CAPITAL AND REVENUE EXPENDITURES

Expenditures on plant assets often are made in periods subsequent to their acquisition. Such expenditures may be debited to (1) an asset account, (2) an accumulated depreciation account, or (3) an expense account.

Expenditures that are debited to an asset account or to an accumulated depreciation account often are called *capital expenditures.* Capital expenditures are major expenditures or expenditures that increase the amount of capital or long-term assets. Capital expenditures increase the book value of plant assets. On the other hand, expenditures immediately expensed are called *revenue expenditures* because they help to generate the current period's revenues rather than future periods' revenues.

Expenditures capitalized in asset accounts

Betterments or *improvements* to existing assets are capital expenditures. They are properly chargeable to asset accounts because they add to the service-rendering ability of the assets. Betterments or improvements increase the *quality* of services which can be obtained from an asset. For instance, installing an air conditioner in an auto that did not previously have one is a betterment. Betterments are added to the account set up for the asset they improve.

Expenditures capitalized as charges to accumulated depreciation

Occasionally expenditures are made on plant assets that will extend the *quantity* of services *beyond the original estimate* but do not improve the quality of services. Because they will benefit an increased number of future periods, these expenditures are properly capitalized rather than expensed. But because there is no visible, tangible addition to or improvement in the quality of services, they are often charged to the accumulated depreciation account. Such expenditures are viewed as canceling a part of the existing accumulated depreciation, and often are called *extraordinary repairs.*

To illustrate, assume that after operating a press for four years, a company spent $3,750 to recondition it. The effect of reconditioning is to increase the machine's life to a total of 14 years from an original estimate of 10 years. The journal entry to record the major repair is:

Accumulated Depreciation—Machinery	3,750	
Cash (or Accounts Payable)		3,750
Cost of reconditioning press.		

When it was acquired, the press cost $30,250. It had an estimated life of 10 years with no expected salvage value. At the end of the fourth year the balance in its accumulated depreciation account under the straight-line method is $12,100 [($30,250 ÷ 10) × 4]. After the $3,750 debit to the accumulated depreciation account, the balances in the asset account and its related accumulated depreciation account are as follows:

Cost of press	$30,250
Accumulated depreciation	8,350
Book value (end of four years)	$21,900

Book value of $21,900 is divided equally among the 10 remaining years in amounts of $2,190 per year under the straight-line method. The effect of the expenditure, then, is to increase the carrying amount of the asset by reducing its contra account, accumulated depreciation.

Expenditures for major repairs that do not extend the asset's life are also sometimes charged to accumulated depreciation and a revised depreciation expense calculated. The purpose is to avoid distortion of net income which might result if such expenditures were expensed in the year incurred. In this way, the cost of major repairs is spread over a number of years.

To illustrate, assume the same facts as in the above example except that the expenditure did not extend the life of the asset. Because of the size of the $3,750 expenditure, it was charged to accumulated depreciation. The $21,900 remaining book value would be spread over the remaining six years of life. Annual charges would be $3,650 ($21,900 ÷ 6) under the straight-line method.

Expenditures charged to expense

Recurring and/or minor expenditures that neither add to the quality of service-rendering abilities of the asset nor extend the quantity of services beyond the original estimate are treated as expenses. Thus, regular maintenance (lubricating a machine) and ordinary repairs (replacing a broken fan belt) are expensed immediately as revenue expenditures. For example, if the company above spends $190 to repair the press after using it for some time, that amount should be debited to Maintenance or Repairs Expense.

In many companies, any expenditure below an arbitrary minimum, such as $25, is charged to expense regardless of its service-rendering abilities. The reason for doing this is to avoid having to calculate or adjust depreciation for an asset with such a nominal cost.

Improper cost assignment

If a revenue expenditure is improperly capitalized during a period, asset costs are overstated, expenses are understated, and net income and owner's equity are overstated. During the rest of the asset's life, net income will be understated because of incorrect depreciation charges. If a capital expenditure is improperly charged to an expense account, the book value of the asset is understated. In addition, expenses are overstated for that period, and net income and owner's equity are understated. In the periods that follow, expenses will be understated and net income overstated because depreciation expense will be understated in those periods.

To illustrate, assume that on January 2, 1984, Ross Company purchased a machine for cash at an invoice price of $30,000. In addition, the company paid $500 of freight charges and $800 of installation costs. The invoice price was correctly debited to the Machinery account, but freight and installation costs were debited to Maintenance Expense. The machine has a useful life of 10 years. If this error is not discovered and corrected, net income for 1984 will be understated $1,170. The error may be explained as follows. The $1,300 overstatement of maintenance expense will cause net income to be understated $1,300. But the asset account has been understated, and hence depreciation has been based on too small a figure. Assuming the machine is being depreciated on a straight-line basis, the understatement of depreciation is $130 ($1,300/10 years), which results in an overstatement of income. Net income for 1984 is, therefore, understated by the net amount of $1,170 ($1,300 − $130). If the error is not corrected, depreciation for 1985–93 will be understated by $130 each year, and net income for 1985–93 will be overstated by $130 each year.

DEPRECIATION AND FINANCIAL REPORTING

APB Opinion No. 12 requires that the amount of depreciation expense for the period be separately disclosed in the body of the income statement or in the footnotes. The depreciation methods used must also be disclosed. Major classes of plant assets and their related accumulated depreciation also are to be reported. An acceptable presentation would read:

Property, plant, and equipment:

Land		$ 40,000
Building	$100,000	
Less: Accumulated depreciation	20,000	80,000
Store equipment	$ 12,000	
Less: Accumulated depreciation	2,000	10,000
Total property, plant, and equipment		$130,000

The presentation of cost less accumulated depreciation provides a financial statement reader with a better understanding of a company's plant assets than does the reporting of just book value (remaining undepreciated cost). For instance, reporting $100,000 of plant assets with $60,000 of accumulated depreciation says something quite different from $40,000 of new assets.

A misconception

Some financial statement readers mistakenly believe that the amount of accumulated depreciation represents funds available for replacing old plant assets with new assets. But accumulated depreciation shows simply what part of an asset's cost has been charged to expense. The credits could have been entered directly in the asset account. A contra account is used only as a means of having data on total original acquisition cost and accumulated depreciation readily available to meet reporting requirements. Cash is required to replace assets, and a firm's cash is accounted for in its Cash account.

Costs or market values in the balance sheet

Plant assets are reported in the balance sheet at original cost less accumulated depreciation. The going-concern concept is the justification for reporting remaining undepreciated costs rather than market values. Under the *going-concern* concept, the assumption is made that the firm will remain in business and will use its plant assets in operations rather than selling them. Market values are thus not considered relevant for use in the primary financial statements, although certain large companies are required to disclose information on current costs of plant assets and inventories (see Chapter 13).

Furthermore, the accounting requirement of realization does not allow the recording of market prices greater than cost before an asset is sold. It is also improper to record a loss by writing an asset down to a lower market value if the asset's remaining cost is expected to be recovered from future revenues.

NEW TERMS INTRODUCED IN CHAPTER 10

Accelerated depreciation methods
Record higher amounts of depreciation in the early years of an asset's life and lower amounts in later years.

Betterments (improvements)
Capital expenditures that are properly chargeable to asset accounts because they add to the service-rendering ability of the assets.

Capital expenditures
Expenditures that are debited to an asset account or to an accumulated depreciation account.

Depreciable cost
Acquisition cost less estimated salvage value.

Depreciation
The amount of plant asset cost allocated to each period benefitting from the plant asset's use. The straight-line depreciation method charges an equal amount of plant asset cost to each period. The units-of-production depreciation method assigns an equal amount of depreciation to each unit of product produced or service rendered by an asset. The sum-of-the-years'-digits (SYD) and the fixed-percentage-of-declining-balance depreciation methods assign decreasing amounts of depreciation to successive periods of time.

Extraordinary repairs
Expenditures that are viewed as canceling a part of the existing accumulated depreciation because they increase the quantity of services expected from an asset.

Inadequacy
The inability of a plant asset to produce enough products or provide enough services to meet current demands.

Land improvements
Attachments to land, such as driveways, parking lots, fences, lighting systems, and sprinkler systems, that have limited lives and are subject to depreciation.

Obsolescence
Decline in usefulness of an asset brought on by invention and technological progress.

Plant and equipment
A shorter title for property, plant, and equipment; also often called plant assets. Included are land and manufactured or constructed assets such as buildings, machinery, vehicles, and furniture.

Physical deterioration
Results from use, wear and tear, and the action of the elements.

Revenue expenditures
Expenditures (on a plant asset) that are immediately expensed.

Salvage value
The amount of money expected to be recoverable, less disposal costs, on the date a plant asset is scrapped, sold, or traded in. Also called scrap or residual value.

DEMONSTRATION PROBLEM

The McBride Company acquired a machine on January 2, 1984, at a total cost of $82,000. The machine was estimated to have a useful life of 10 years and a scrap value of $2,000. It was also estimated that the machine would produce one million units of product during its life. The machine produced 90,000 units in 1984 and 125,000 units in 1985.

Required:

Compute the amounts of depreciation to be recorded in 1984 and 1985 under each of the following:

 a.   Straight-line method.

 b.   Double-declining-balance method.

 c.   Sum-of-the-years'-digits method.

 d.   Units-of-production method.

 e.   Assume 30,000 units were produced in the first quarter of 1986. Compute depreciation for this quarter under each of the four methods.

Solution to demonstration problem

 a.   Straight-line method:

$$1984: (\$82{,}000 - \$2{,}000) \div 10 = \underline{\underline{\$8{,}000}}$$

$$1985: (\$82{,}000 - \$2{,}000) \div 10 = \underline{\underline{\$8{,}000}}$$

b. Double-declining-balance method:

   1984: $82,000 × 20% = $16,400
   1985: ($82,000 − $16,400) × 20% = $13,120

c. Sum-of-the-years'-digits method:

   1984: ($82,000 − $2,000) × $^{10}\!/_{55}$ = $14,545
   1985: ($82,000 − $2,000) × $^{9}\!/_{55}$ = $13,091

d. Units-of-production method:

   1984: [($82,000 − $2,000)/1,000,000] × 90,000 = $7,200
   1985: [($82,000 − $2,000)/1,000,000] × 125,000 = $10,000

e. Straight line: ($82,000 − $2,000) ÷ 10 × ¼ = $2,000.

   Double-declining-balance method: ($82,000 − $16,400 − $13,120)
   × 0.2 × ¼ = $2,624.
   Sum-of-the-years'-digits method: ($82,000 − $2,000) × $^{8}\!/_{55}$ × ¼ = $2,909.
   Units-of-production method: (30,000 × $0.08) = $2,400.

QUESTIONS

1. What is the main distinction between inventory and a plant asset?

2. Which of the following items are properly classifiable as plant assets on the balance sheet?

   a. Advertising to inform the public about new energy-saving programs at a manufacturing plant.
   b. A truck acquired by a manufacturing company to be used to deliver the company's products to wholesalers.
   c. An automobile acquired by an insurance company to be used by one of its salespersons.
   d. Adding machines acquired by an office supply company to be resold to customers.
   e. The cost of constructing and paving a driveway which has a useful life of 10 years.

3. In general terms, what does the cost of a plant asset include?

4. A friend, Sara Jones, tells you her car depreciated $2,500 last year. Explain whether her concept of depreciation is the same as the accountant's concept.

5. Why should periodic depreciation be recorded on all plant assets except land?

6. In any exchange of noncash assets, the accountant's task is that of finding the most appropriate valuation to assign to the assets received. What is the general rule for determining the most appropriate valuation in such a situation?

7. What does the term *accelerated depreciation* mean? Give an example showing how depreciation is accelerated.

8. Define the terms *inadequacy* and *obsolescence* as used in accounting for plant and equipment.

9. What three factors must be known in order to compute depreciation on a plant asset?

10. If a machine has an estimated useful life of nine years, what will be the total digits to use in calculating depreciation under the sum-of-the-year's-digits method?

11. What does the balance in the accumulated depreciation account represent? Can this balance be used to replace the related plant asset?

12. What is the justification for reporting plant assets on the balance sheet at undepreciated cost rather than market value?

13. Distinguish between *capital expenditures* and *revenue expenditures*.

14. For each of the following, state whether the expenditure made should be charged to an expense, an asset, or an accumulated depreciation account:

a. Cost of installing air-conditioning equipment in a leased building.

b. Biennial painting of an owned factory building.

c. Cost of replacing the roof on a 10-year-old building which was purchased new and has an estimated total life of 40 years.

d. Cost of rewinding the armature of an electric motor.

15. Classify each of the following as either a capital expenditure or a revenue expenditure:

a. Painting of office building at a cost of $400. The building is painted every year.

b. Addition of a new plant wing at a cost of $100,000.

c. Expansion of a paved parking lot at a cost of $60,000.

d. Replacement of a stairway with an escalator at a cost of $16,000.

e. Lubricating a machine at a cost of $200.

f. Replacing a broken fan belt at a cost of $150.

16. Provide a theoretical reason to support using an accelerated depreciation method; also, give a practical reason for its widespread use.

EXERCISES

E–1. Baker Company purchased for $200,000 cash a tract of land upon which it planned to erect a new warehouse. Baker paid legal fees related to the purchase of $2,500. Baker also agreed to assume responsibility for $8,000 of taxes on the property. It incurred $9,000 of cost to remove an old apartment building on the land.

Prepare a schedule showing the cost of the land acquired.

E–2. Husky Company purchased a heavy machine to be used in its factory for $100,000, less a 2 percent cash discount. The company paid a fine of $500 because an employee hauled the machine over city streets without securing the required permits. The machine was installed at a cost of $3,000, and testing costs of $1,000 were incurred to place the machine in operation.

Prepare a schedule showing the recorded cost of the machine.

E–3. Case Company paid $350,000 cash for real property consisting of a tract of land and two buildings. The company intended to raze the old factory building and remodel and use the old office building. To allocate the cost of the property acquired, the company had the property appraised. The appraised values were: land, $120,000; factory building, $120,000; and office building, $160,000. The factory building was demolished at a net cost of $16,000. The office building was remodeled at a cost of $32,000. The cost of a new identical office building was estimated to be $180,000.

Prepare a schedule showing the cost of the assets acquired.

E–4. The Harold Company purchased on March 1, 1984, some office equipment for $6,200 cash. Cash of $100 was paid for freight costs incurred. The furniture is being depreciated over four years under the straight-line method, assuming a salvage value of $300. The company employs a calendar-year accounting period and records depreciation for the full month in which the asset was acquired. On July 1, 1985, $40 was spent to refinish the furniture.

Prepare journal entries for the Harold Company to record all of the above data, including the annual depreciation adjustments through 1985.

E–5. On January 2, 1984, a new machine was acquired for $60,000. The machine has an estimated salvage value of $5,000 and an estimated useful life of 10 years. The machine is expected to produce a total of 500,000 units of product throughout its useful life. Compute depreciation for 1984 and 1985 using each of the following methods:

    a.   Straight line.
    b.   Units of production (assume 30,000 and 50,000 units were produced in 1984 and 1985, respectively).
    c.   Double-declining balance.
    d.   Sum-of-the-years' digits.

E–6. Arcane Company purchased a machine for $1,600 and incurred installation costs of $400. The estimated salvage value of the machine is $100.

Compute the annual depreciation charges for this machine under the double-declining-balance method assuming the machine has an estimated useful life of four years.

E–7.

The Hartwig Company acquired a delivery truck on January 2, 1984, for $33,500. The truck has an estimated salvage value of $1,500 and an estimated useful life of eight years. At the beginning of 1987, it is estimated that the truck has a remaining useful life of eight years.

Compute the depreciation charge for 1984 and 1987 using the straight-line method.

E–8. Assume that the truck described in Exercise E–7 was used 40 percent of the time in 1985 to haul materials used in the construction of a building by the Hartwig Company for its own use. In the remaining part of the time, the truck was used to deliver merchandise sold by Hartwig to its customers.

Prepare the journal entry to record straight-line depreciation on the truck for 1985.

E–9. Rem Company purchased a machine on July 1, 1984, for $30,000. The machine has an estimated useful life of five years with no expected salvage value.

Compute the depreciation expense for 1985 under (*a*) the sum-of-the years'-digits method and (*b*) the double-declining-balance method. The company's accounting year ends on December 31.

E–10. Rhode Company owns a machine which it acquired at a cost of $30,000. The company had the option of using either the straight-line or an accelerated depreciation method for tax purposes. For a given year, the straight-line depreciation would be $3,000, while under an accelerated method it would be $5,400. Assume the company is subject to a 40 percent income tax rate. Compute the reduction in income taxes payable for the year if the company chose the accelerated method rather than the straight-line method of computing periodic depreciation expense.

E–11. On January 2, 1984, a company purchased and placed in operation a new machine at a total cost of $12,000. Depreciation was recorded on the machine for 1984 and 1985 under the straight-line method using an estimated useful life of four years and no expected salvage value. Early in 1986, the machine was overhauled at a cost of $4,000. The total useful life of the machine was revised upward to a total of six years.

Compute the depreciation on the machine for 1986.

E–12. Boyne Company purchased a computer for $25,000 and placed it in operation on January 2, 1983. Depreciation was recorded for 1983 and 1984 using the straight-line method, a six-year life, and $1,000 of expected salvage value. The introduction of a new model of this computer caused the company in 1985 to revise its estimate of useful life to a total of four years and to reduce the estimated salvage value to zero.

Compute the revised depreciation for 1985.

E–13.   Arnold Company purchased a machine on January 3, 1984, at a cost of $20,000. Freight and installation charges of $4,000 were incurred and debited to Repairs Expense. Straight-line depreciation was recorded on the machine in 1984 and 1985 using an estimated life of 10 years and no expected salvage value.

Compute the amount of the error in net income for 1984 and 1985 and state whether net income is understated or overstated.

PROBLEMS, SERIES A

P10–1–A.   In seeking a site for its new home office building, Ball Company paid a local realtor $3,000 to find the appropriate location. Ball agreed to pay the owner of the site $50,000 cash, to assume responsibility for a $20,000 mortgage note on the property and $300 of accrued interest on the note, and to pay back taxes on the property of $800. Ball also paid legal fees of $400 and a $500 title insurance premium in acquiring the property. A local salvage company paid Ball $9,000 for a building that it moved from the property. Ball also paid the city $8,000 to extend water mains and sewer lines to the property.

Required:

Prepare a schedule showing the amount to be recorded as the carrying value of the land.

P10–2–A.   Carter Company purchased a machine for use in its operations that had a gross invoice price of $10,000 excluding sales tax. A 4 percent sales tax was levied on the sale, with the dealer granting a 2 percent sales discount when Carter paid cash for the machine. The company estimated the total cost of hauling the machine from the dealer's warehouse to the company's plant at $700, which does not include a fine of $200 for failure to secure the necessary permits to use city streets in transporting the machine. In delivering the machine to its plant, a Carter employee damaged the truck used to the extent of $450. The machine was also slightly damaged with repair costs amounting to $200.

Carter incurred installation costs of $4,000 that include the $500 cost of shoring up the floor under the machine. Testing costs amounted to $300. Safety guards were installed on the machine at a cost of $80, and the machine was placed in operation.

Required:

Prepare a schedule showing the computation of the amount at which the machine should be recorded in Carter's accounts.

P10–3–A.   Green Company planned to erect a new factory building and a new office building in Atlanta, Georgia. A report on a suitable site showed an appraised value of $300,000 for land and orchard and $200,000 for a building.

After considerable negotiation, the company and the owner reached the following agreement. Green Company was to pay $360,000 in cash, assume a $150,000 mortgage note on the property, assume the interest accrued on the mortgage note of $3,200, and assume unpaid property taxes of $22,000. Green Company paid $30,000 cash for brokerage and legal services in acquiring the property.

Shortly after acquisition of the property, Green Company sold the fruit on the trees for $4,400, remodeled the building into an office building at a cost of $64,000, and removed the trees from the land at a cost of $15,000. Construction of the factory building is to begin in a week.

Required:

Prepare schedules showing the proper valuation of the assets acquired by the Green Company.

P10–4–A.   Mohr Company acquired a heavy factory machine on July 1, 1984. The machine had an invoice price of $72,000, but the company received a 3 percent cash discount by paying the bill on the date of acquisition. An employee of Mohr Company hauled the machine down a city street without a permit. As a result, the company had to pay a $300 fine. Installation and testing costs totaled $7,160. The machine is estimated to have a $7,000 salvage value and a seven-year useful life.

Required:

a.   Prepare the journal entry to record the acquisition of the machine.

b.   Prepare the journal entry to record depreciation for 1984 under the double-declining-balance method.

c.   Assume that the straight-line depreciation method is being used and at the beginning of 1987 it is estimated the machine will last another six years. Prepare the journal entry to record depreciation for 1987.

P10–5–A.   Brown Company acquired equipment on January 2, 1984, at a cash cost of $128,000. Transportation charges amounted to $1,000, and installation and testing costs totaled $4,000. The equipment was damaged while being installed, and the cost of repairing the damage was $600.

The equipment was estimated to have a useful life of nine years and a salvage value of $5,000 at the end of its life. It was further estimated that the equipment would be used in the production of 640,000 units of product during its life. During 1984, 142,000 units of product were produced.

Required:

Compute the depreciation for the year ended December 31, 1984, if the company used—

a.   The straight-line method.

b.   The units-of-production method.

c.   The sum-of-the-years'-digits method.

d.   The double-declining-balance method.

P10–6–A.   Crest Company's fiscal year ends May 31. The company has its own fleet of delivery vehicles. Included are the following:

Description	Date acquired	Cost	Estimated life	Estimated salvage value
Sedan No. 3	June 1, 1983	$ 9,000	4 years	$2,200
Truck No. 2	June 1, 1979	12,000	100,000 miles	1,000
Truck No. 5	Jan. 1, 1985	28,000	150,000 miles	2,800
Trailer No. 8	Apr. 1, 1982	32,000	400,000 miles	–0–

Speedometer and other mileage records show:

	Total miles as of May 31		Mileage for year ended May 31, 1985
	1984	1985	
Sedan No. 3	15,000	28,000	13,000 miles
Truck No. 2	120,000	150,000	30,000 miles
Truck No. 5	–0–	20,000	20,000 miles
Trailer No. 8	50,000	75,000	25,000 miles

Required:

Set up schedules showing in full detail the amount of depreciation to be recorded for the year ended May 31, 1985, on each of the above assets. (Use the straight-line method for Sedan No. 3 and the units-of-production [number of miles driven] method for the other vehicles.) No revision of estimated life was made on any of the assets.

P10–7–A. Benson Company has the following entries in its Building account:

		Debits
1984		
May 5	Cost of land and building purchased	$500,000
5	Broker fees incident to purchase	30,000
1985		
Jan. 3	Contract price of new wing added to south end of building	210,000
15	Cost of new machinery, estimated life 10 years	400,000
June 10	Real estate taxes for six months ended 6/30/85	9,000
Aug. 10	Cost of landscaping and building parking lot for employees in back of building	12,400
Sept. 6	Replacement of windows broken in August	400
Oct. 10	Repairs due to regular usage	5,600

		Credits
1984		
Dec. 31	Transfer to Land account, as per allocation of purchase cost authorized in minutes of board of directors	80,000
1985		
Jan. 5	Proceeds from lease of second floor for six months ended 12/31/84	20,000

The original property was acquired on May 5, 1984. Benson Company immediately engaged a contractor to construct a new wing on the south end of the building. While the new wing was being constructed, the company leased the second floor as temporary warehouse space to Charles Company. During this period (July 1 to December 31, 1984), the company installed new machinery costing $400,000 on the first floor of the building. Regular operations began on January 2, 1985.

Required:

a. Compute the correct balance for the Building account as of December 31, 1985. The building is expected to last 40 years. The company employs a calendar-year accounting period.

b. Prepare the necessary journal entries to correct the records of Benson Company at December 31, 1985. No depreciation entries are required.

PROBLEMS, SERIES B

P10–1–B.   In seeking a site for its new factory, Hanson Company paid a local realtor $4,000 to find a suitable site. When found, Hanson agreed to pay the owner of the site $60,000 cash, to assume responsibility for a $20,000 mortgage note on the property and $400 of accrued interest on the note, and to pay back taxes on the property of $1,000. Hanson also paid legal fees of $500 and a $600 title insurance premium in acquiring the property. A local lumber yard paid Hanson $800 for some walnut trees that it removed from the property. Hanson also paid the city $7,000 to widen the street in front of the property and received $2,000 for a narrow strip of land deeded to the city in order to widen the street. Grading and leveling costs of $3,000 were also incurred by Hanson.

Required:
Prepare a schedule showing the amount to be recorded as the carrying value of the land.

P10–2–B.   Disc Company purchased a machine for use in its operations that had a gross invoice price of $20,000 excluding sales tax. A 4 percent sales tax was levied on the sale. The company paid freight costs of $500. Special electrical connections were run to the machine at a cost of $700, and a special reinforced base was built at a cost of $900 for the machine. The machine was dropped and damaged while being mounted on this base. Repairs cost $200. Raw materials with a cost of $50 were consumed in testing the machine. Safety guards were installed on the machine at a cost of $70, and the machine was placed in operation.

Required:
Prepare a schedule showing the computation of the amount at which the machine should be recorded in the Disc Company's accounts.

P10–3–B.   The Martin Company purchased two square miles of farm land from their owner under the following terms: $605,000 cash; liability assumed on mortgage note of $200,000; and interest accrued on mortgage note assumed, $8,000. The company paid $42,000 of legal and brokerage fees and also paid $2,000 for a title search on the property.
The company planned to use the land as a site for a new office building and a new factory. Clearing and leveling costs of $18,000 were paid. Crops on the land were sold for $4,600, and one of the houses on the property was sold for $12,000. The other buildings were razed at a cost of $9,000; sale of salvaged materials yielded cash proceeds of $8,500. Approximately 1 percent of the land acquired was deeded to the county for roads. The cost of excavating a basement for the office building amounted to $5,700. A bulldozer, undepreciated cost, $38,000, was stolen immediately after the land was cleared and leveled.

Required:
Prepare a schedule showing the amount at which the land should be carried on Martin Company's books.

P10–4–B.   Argonne Company purchased a used panel truck for $6,000 cash. The next day the truck was painted with the company's name and business lettered on it at a total cost of $310. The truck was then given a minor overhaul at a cost of $40, and new tires were mounted on the truck at a cost of $400, less a trade-in allowance of $50 for the old tires. The truck was placed in service on April 5, 1984, at which time it has an estimated useful life of five years and a salvage value of $700.

Required:

      a.   Prepare a schedule showing the cost to be recorded for the truck.

      b.   Prepare the journal entry needed to record depreciation as of the end of the calendar-year accounting period, December 31, 1984. Use the double-declining-balance method.

P10–5–B.   Jensen Company acquired a machine on July 1, 1984, at a cash cost of $24,000 and immediately spent $1,000 to install it. The machine was estimated to have a useful life of eight years and a scrap value of $5,000 at the end of this time. It was further estimated that the machine would produce 500,000 units of product during its life. In the first year, the machine produced 100,000 units.

Required:

      Prepare journal entries to record depreciation for the fiscal year ended June 30, 1985, if the company used—

      a.   The straight-line method.

      b.   The units-of-production method.

      c.   The sum-of-the-years'-digits method.

      d.   The double-declining-balance method.

P10–6–B.   The Edgar Company owns one auto and three trucks as follows:

Description	Date acquired	Cost	Estimated life	Estimated salvage value
Auto No. 1	July 1, 1982	$ 8,000	4 years	$2,000
Truck No. 1	July 1, 1983	20,000	5 years	2,000
Truck No. 3	Jan. 2, 1980	44,000	100,000 miles	4,000
Truck No. 4	Apr. 1, 1978	50,000	150,000 miles	–0–

      Other records of the company show that Auto No. 1 is being depreciated on a straight-line basis, Truck No. 1 is being depreciated using the double-declining-balance method, while the units-of-production (miles) method is used on Trucks No. 3 and No. 4. Speedometer readings for these two trucks show:

	Total miles as of December 31		Mileage for year ended December 31, 1984
	1983	1984	
Truck No. 3	65,000	82,000	17,000 miles
Truck No. 4	170,000	192,000	22,000 miles

Required:

      Prepare a schedule showing the computation of depreciation on each of the above assets for the year ended December 31, 1984. No revision of estimated life was made on any of the assets.

P10–7–B.   You are the new controller for Wilson Company which began operations on October 1, 1984, after a "start-up" period that ran from the middle of 1983. You are reviewing the accounts and find an account entitled "Fixed Assets" which contains the following items:

Cash paid to previous owner of land and old building	$ 80,000
Treasury bills given to construction company as partial payment	28,000
Legal and title search fees	1,000
Real estate commission	6,000
Cost of demolishing old building	7,000
Cost of leveling and grading	4,000
Architect's fee (90% building and 10% improvements)	15,000
Cost of excavating basement for new building	9,000
Cash paid to construction company for new building	120,000
Sprinkler system for lawn	13,000
Lighting system for parking lot	17,000
Paving of parking lot	25,000
Net invoice price of machinery	480,000
Freight cost incurred on machinery	21,000
Installation and testing of machinery	8,000
Landscaping	16,000
Repair damage done by vandals	3,000
Repair damage to building in installation of machinery	2,000
Medical bill paid for employee injured in installing machinery	1,500
Special assessment paid to city for water mains and sewer line	19,000
Account balance	$875,500

In addition to the above, you discover that cash receipts from sale of salvaged materials from old building of $500 were credited to Miscellaneous Revenues in 1984. The Treasury bills given to the construction company had a market value of $30,000 on the date transferred. Digging deeper, you find that the plant manager spent all of his time for the *first nine months* of 1984 supervising building construction (40 percent), installation of land improvements (10 percent), and installation of machinery (50 percent). The plant manager's nine-month salary of $45,000 was debited to Officers' Salaries Expense.

Required:

    a. Prepare a form containing a column for Item, Land, Land Improvements, Building, and Machinery. List the above items and sort them to the appropriate columns, omitting the items not properly includable as an element of asset cost. Show negative amounts in parentheses. Total your columns.

    b. Prepare one compound journal entry to reclassify and adjust the accounts and to eliminate the Fixed Assets account. Do not attempt to record depreciation for the partial year.

BUSINESS DECISION PROBLEM 10–1

    Roman Company has the following entries in its Building account:

			Debits
1984			
Jan.	2	Cost of land and old buildings purchased	$300,000
	2	Legal fees incident to purchase	4,000
	2	Fee for title search	500
	12	Cost of demolishing old buildings on land	8,000
June	16	Cost of insurance during construction of new building	2,000
July	30	Payment to contractor upon completion of new building	450,000
Aug.	5	Architect's fees for design of new building	20,000
Sept.	15	City assessment for sewers and sidewalks	7,000
Oct.	6	Cost of landscaping	4,000
Nov.	1	Cost of driveways and parking lots	25,000

		Credits
Jan. 15	Proceeds received upon sale of salvaged materials from old buildings	$ 2,000
Dec. 31	Depreciation for 1984 at 2½%	17,962.50

You are in charge of auditing the Roman Company's Building account. In addition to the entries in the account, you are given the following information:

1. The company began using the new building on September 1, 1984. The building is estimated to have a 40-year useful life and no salvage value.
2. The company began using the driveways and parking lots on November 1, 1984. The driveways and parking lots are estimated to have a 10-year useful life and no salvage value.
3. The straight-line depreciation method is used to depreciate all the company's plant assets.

Required:

    a. Prepare a schedule which shows separately the cost of land, buildings, and land improvements.

    b. Compute the amount of depreciation expense for 1984.

    c. What journal entries are required to correct the accounts at December 31, 1984? (Assume that Depreciation Expense, Buildings was debited for the entire amount of depreciation credited to the Buildings account. Also assume that closing entries have not been made.)

BUSINESS DECISION PROBLEM 10–2

    On July 1, 1985, Brody Company acquired new equipment costing $210,000. The equipment has a useful life of five years and an estimated salvage value of $10,000. It is estimated that the equipment will produce 4,000,000 units of product during its life. In the second half of 1985, the equipment produced 240,000 units of product.

Required:

    a. Compute the depreciation for the second half of 1985 using each of the following methods:

1. Straight line.
2. 175 percent declining balance.
3. Sum-of-the-years' digits.
4. Units of production.

    b. Describe the conditions in which each of the above four methods would seem most appropriate.

Chapter 11

Plant asset dispositions, natural resources, and intangible assets

CHAPTER GOALS

After study of this chapter, you should be able to:

1. Prepare entries to record the disposal of a plant asset.
2. Explain and illustrate how the accounting for trade-ins of plant assets differs for tax purposes and generally accepted accounting purposes.
3. Show how accounting records are used to control plant assets.
4. Determine the cost of natural resources; record depletion on such resources; and determine the cost of resources sold.
5. Prepare entries to account for the acquisition, amortization, and disposition of intangible assets.
6. Define and use correctly the new terms in the glossary.

Discussion in the preceding chapter focused on certain problems encountered in accounting for plant assets, such as determining asset cost, estimating depreciation, and distinguishing between capital and revenue expenditures. This chapter examines accounting for (1) plant asset dispositions, (2) natural resources, and (3) intangible assets.

DISPOSITION OF PLANT ASSETS

Plant assets eventually wear out, become inadequate or obsolete, and must be sold, retired, or traded in on new assets. Upon disposition of a plant asset, both the asset's cost and accumulated depreciation must be removed from the accounts.

Sale of plant assets

When a plant asset is sold, there may be a gain or loss on the sale. Gain or loss is determined by comparing the asset's book value (cost less accumulated depreciation) with its sales price. If sales price is greater than the asset's book value, there is a gain. If sales price is less than the asset's book value, there is a loss. Of course, if sales price is equal to the asset's book value, there is no gain or loss.

To illustrate accounting for the sale of a plant asset, assume equipment costing $30,000 with accumulated depreciation of $12,000 is sold for $20,000. A gain of $2,000 is realized as computed below:

Equipment cost	$30,000
Accumulated depreciation	12,000
Book value	$18,000
Sales price	20,000
Gain realized	$ 2,000

The journal entry to record the sale is:

Cash	20,000	
Accumulated Depreciation—Equipment	12,000	
Equipment		30,000
Gain on Disposal of Plant Assets		2,000
To record sale of equipment at a price greater than book value.		

If the equipment is sold for $16,500, a loss of $1,500 ($18,000 book value − $16,500 sales price) is realized, and the journal entry to record the sale is:

Cash	16,500	
Accumulated Depreciation—Equipment	12,000	
Loss on Disposal of Plant Assets	1,500	
Equipment		30,000
To record sale of equipment at a price less than book value.		

If the equipment is sold for $18,000, there is no gain or loss, and the journal entry to record the sale is:

```
Cash ...........................................................   18,000
Accumulated Depreciation—Equipment ...........................   12,000
    Equipment .................................................              30,000
```
To record sale of equipment at a price equal to book value.

Accounting for depreciation to date of disposition. When a plant asset is sold or otherwise disposed of, it is important to record the depreciation to the date of sale or disposition. For example, if an asset were sold on July 1 and depreciation was last recorded on December 31, depreciation for six months (January 1–June 30) should be recorded. If depreciation is not recorded for that period, operating expenses will be understated and the gain on the sale of the asset will be understated or the loss overstated.

To illustrate, assume that on August 1, 1985, Ray Company sold a machine for $1,500. The machine cost $12,000 and was being depreciated at the straight-line rate of 10 percent per year. As of December 31, 1984, after closing entries were made, the machine's accumulated depreciation account had a balance of $9,600. Before a gain or loss can be determined and an entry can be made to record the sale, the following entry must be made to record depreciation for the seven months ended July 31, 1985:

```
Depreciation Expense—Machinery .................................   700
    Accumulated Depreciation—Machinery .........................          700
```
To record depreciation for seven months ($12,000 $\times$ 0.10 $\times$ $\frac{7}{12}$).

The $200 loss on the sale is computed as shown below:

```
Machine cost ..............................   $12,000
Accumulated depreciation ($9,600 + $700) ....    10,300
Book value ...............................    $ 1,700
Sales price ..............................      1,500
Loss realized ............................    $   200
```

The journal entry to record the sale is:

```
Cash .........................................................    1,500
Accumulated Depreciation—Machinery ...........................   10,300
Loss on Disposal of Plant Assets .............................      200
    Machinery ................................................              12,000
```
To record sale of machinery at a price less than book value.

Retirement of plant assets without sale

When a plant asset is retired from productive service, the asset's cost and accumulated depreciation must be removed from the plant asset accounts. For example, Hayes Company would make the following journal entry when a fully depreciated machine that cost $15,000 and had no salvage value is retired:

```
Accumulated Depreciation—Machinery ...........................   15,000
    Machinery ................................................              15,000
```
To record the retirement of a fully depreciated machine.

Occasionally a plant asset is continued in use after it has been fully depreciated. In such a case, the asset's cost and accumulated depreciation should *not* be removed from the accounts until the asset is sold, traded, or retired from service. Of course, no more depreciation can be recorded on a fully depreciated asset because total depreciation expense may never exceed the asset's cost.

Sometimes a plant asset is retired from service or discarded before it is fully depreciated. If the asset is to be sold as scrap (even if not immediately), its cost and accumulated depreciation should be removed from those accounts, its estimated scrap value recorded in a Salvaged Materials account, and a gain or loss on disposal recognized. To illustrate, assume a machine with $7,000 original cost and $6,200 accumulated depreciation is retired. If the machine's scrap value is estimated at $375, the following entry is required:

Salvaged Materials	375	
Accumulated Depreciation—Machinery	6,200	
Loss on Disposal of Plant Assets	425	
Machinery		7,000
To record retirement of machinery.		

Destruction of plant assets

Plant assets are sometimes wrecked in accidents or destroyed by fire, flood, storm, or other causes. Losses are normally incurred in such situations. For example, assume that an uninsured building costing $40,000 with accumulated depreciation of $12,000 is completely destroyed by a fire. The journal entry is:

Fire Loss	28,000	
Accumulated Depreciation—Building	12,000	
Building		40,000
To record fire loss.		

If the building were insured, only the amount of the fire loss in excess of the amount to be recovered from the insurance company would be debited to the Fire Loss account. To illustrate, assume that in the example above, the building was partially insured and that $22,000 was recovered from the insurance company. The journal entry is:

Cash	22,000	
Fire Loss	6,000	
Accumulated Depreciation—Building	12,000	
Building		40,000
To record fire loss and amount recovered from insurance company.		

If the proceeds had not been received from the insurance company, the debit for $22,000 would have been to Receivable from Insurance Company.

Exchanges of dissimilar plant assets

Certain plant assets, such as automobiles, trucks, and office equipment, are often acquired by trading in an old asset. In such cases, a trade-in allowance is usually granted on the old asset and the balance of the price is paid in cash. The accountant must determine the amount at which the new asset is to be recorded and the gain or loss, if any, to be recognized on the exchange. Such transactions should be accounted for using the fair market value of the asset given up or the asset received, whichever is more clearly evident, and a gain or loss recorded.[1] Thus, the asset received would normally be recorded at either fair value (cash price) of the new asset or fair value of the asset given up plus cash paid. A loss would occur if fair value of the old asset is less than book value; a gain occurs if the old asset's fair value is greater than book value. The APB in 1973 continued this long-standing general valuation rule of accounting, but limited its applicability to exchanges of dissimilar assets, such as a machine for a truck. Thus, both gains and losses from exchanges of dissimilar assets are recognized for both accounting and tax purposes.

To illustrate such an exchange, assume that an old factory machine is exchanged for a new delivery truck. The machine cost $40,000 and had an accumulated depreciation balance of $33,000. The truck had a $50,000 cash price and was acquired by trading in the machine and paying $47,000 cash. A $4,000 loss is realized on the exchange, computed like this:

Machine cost	$40,000
Accumulated depreciation	33,000
Book value	$ 7,000
Trade-in allowance (fair value) ($50,000 − $47,000)	3,000
Loss realized	$ 4,000

Notice in this exchange the trade-in allowance is the difference between the cash price of the new asset and cash paid. The journal entry to record the exchange is:

Delivery Truck	50,000	
Accumulated Depreciation—Factory Machinery	33,000	
Loss on Disposal of Plant Assets	4,000	
Factory Machinery		40,000
Cash		47,000
To record loss on exchange of dissimilar plant assets.		

To illustrate recognition of a gain on exchange of dissimilar plant assets, assume fair market value of the above machine (the trade-in allowance) was $8,000 instead of $3,000 and that $42,000 was paid in cash. The gain would be $1,000 ($8,000 fair market value less $7,000 book value). The journal entry to record the exchange would be:

Delivery Truck	50,000	
Accumulated Depreciation—Factory Machinery	33,000	
Factory Machinery		40,000
Cash		42,000
Gain on Disposal of Plant Assets		1,000
To record gain on exchange of dissimilar plant assets.		

---

[1] APB, "Accounting for Nonmonetary Transactions," *APB Opinion No. 29* (New York: AICPA, May 1973), par. 16.

Exchanges of similar plant assets

When similar assets are exchanged, the general rule of recording the new asset at fair value of what was given up or at what was received is modified slightly. The new asset will be recorded at (1) the book value of the old asset plus the cash paid or (2) the fair value of the asset received, whichever is lower. Applying this rule to exchanges of similar assets means that *losses are recognized, but gains are not.*

To illustrate accounting for exchanges of similar plant assets, assume $47,000 cash and delivery truck No. 1, which cost $40,000 and had $33,000 accumulated depreciation, were exchanged for delivery truck No. 2. The new truck has a cash price (fair value) of $50,000. A loss of $4,000 is realized on the exchange.

Cost of delivery truck No. 1	$40,000
Accumulated depreciation	33,000
Book value	$ 7,000
Trade-in allowance ($50,000 − $47,000) . .	3,000
Loss on exchange of plant assets	$ 4,000

The journal entry to record the exchange is:

Delivery Trucks (cost of No. 2)	50,000	
Accumulated Depreciation—Delivery Trucks	33,000	
Loss on Disposal of Plant Assets	4,000	
Delivery Trucks (cost of No. 1)		40,000
Cash		47,000
To record loss on exchange of similar plant assets.		

Notice that exchanges of similar plant assets are recorded just like exchanges of dissimilar plant assets *provided* a *loss* occurs on the exchange.

In the preceding example, assume delivery truck No. 1 and $42,000 cash were given in exchange for delivery truck No. 2. A gain of $1,000 is indicated on the exchange:

Cost of delivery truck No. 1	$40,000
Accumulated depreciation	33,000
Book value	$ 7,000
Trade-in allowance ($50,000 − $42,000) . .	8,000
Gain indicated	$ 1,000

The journal entry to record the exchange is:

Delivery Trucks (cost of No. 2)	49,000	
Accumulated Depreciation—Delivery Trucks	33,000	
Delivery Trucks (cost of No. 1)		40,000
Cash		42,000
To record exchange of similar plant assets.		

Notice that a gain is *not* recognized on an exchange of similar assets. The new asset is recorded at book value of the old asset ($7,000) plus cash paid ($42,000). The gain is deducted from the cost of the new asset. Thus, the cost basis of the new delivery truck is equal to its cash price of $50,000 less the $1,000 gain. The $49,000 cost basis of the delivery truck is used in recording depreciation on the truck and in determining any gain or loss on its disposition.

Justification for not recognizing gains on exchanges of similar plant assets is that ". . . revenue should not be recognized merely because one productive asset is substituted for a similar productive asset but rather should be considered to flow from the production and sale of the goods or services to which the substituted productive asset is committed."[2] In effect, the gain on exchanges of similar plant assets is realized in the form of increased net income because of smaller depreciation charges on the newly acquired asset. In the preceding example, annual depreciation expense is less if it is based on the truck's $49,000 cost basis than if it is based on the truck's $50,000 cash price. Thus, future net income per year is larger.

When gains or losses are recognized on the disposal of plant assets, they should be reported on the income statement among operating expenses. If gains or losses are material (relatively large), they should be separately disclosed as such.

Tax rules and plant asset exchanges. The Internal Revenue Code does not allow recognition of *gains or losses* for tax purposes when similar productive assets are exchanged. For tax purposes, the cost basis of the new asset is book value of the old asset plus any additional cash paid. The additional cash outlay is called *boot.*

In comparing accounting and tax methods, accounting principles and income tax laws agree on the treatment of gains, but they disagree on the treatment of losses. Thus, the previous example involving a $4,000 loss on the exchange of delivery trucks must be recorded as follows for tax purposes:

Delivery Trucks (cost of No. 2) ($7,000 + $47,000)	54,000	
Accumulated Depreciation—Delivery Trucks	33,000	
Delivery Trucks (cost of No. 1)		40,000
Cash		47,000
To record exchange of similar plant assets using tax method.		

Because of differences between accounting principles and income tax laws, two sets of depreciation records must be kept if a *material loss* occurs on an exchange of similar plant assets. One set of records will be based on accounting valuation of the new asset (fair market value of the old asset plus cash paid) and will be used for determining net income for financial reporting purposes. The second set of records will record tax basis of the new asset (book value of old asset plus cash paid).

Under the accounting principle of materiality, two sets of records do not have to be kept if the loss on exchange is immaterial. In the case of an immaterial loss, the new asset can be recorded at book value of the old asset plus cash paid for both tax purposes and financial reporting purposes. For example, assume a company that earns approximately $1,000,000 per year suffers a $25 loss on an exchange of plant assets. In relation to $1,000,000,

---

[2] Ibid., par. 16.

$25 is immaterial. Thus, the company can record the newly acquired asset at the sum of book value of the old asset and cash paid.

Removal costs. Removal costs are costs incurred to dismantle and otherwise remove an old asset that has been used by the company. Such costs are deducted from salvage proceeds to determine net salvage value. If removal costs exceed salvage proceeds, they increase the loss or reduce the gain recognized on disposition of a plant asset. Such costs are not a cost of benefits expected from the new asset. Rather, removal costs are costs of benefits already received.

SUBSIDIARY PLANT ASSET RECORDS

Most business firms maintain formal records (ranging from handwritten to computer tapes) to ensure control over their plant assets. These records include an asset account and related accumulated depreciation account in the general ledger for each major class of depreciable plant and equipment—buildings, factory machinery, office equipment, delivery equipment, and store equipment. The general ledger account for office equipment contains entries for such items as typewriters, desks, adding machines, dictating equipment, chairs, and filing cabinets. A single general ledger account cannot maintain detailed information about each individual item of office equipment. Thus, many firms use subsidiary plant asset ledgers or records to maintain better control over plant and equipment.

A subsidiary ledger consisting of plant asset records usually is maintained for each major class of plant and equipment. Thus, there may be a subsidiary ledger for factory machinery, office equipment, and other such assets. Each subsidiary record will contain detailed information about a single item of property, such as a desk or a typewriter. Information should include the following: description of asset, identification or serial number, location of asset, date of acquisition, cost, estimated useful life, depreciation, accumulated depreciation, insurance coverage, repairs, and gain or loss on final disposition of the asset. The identification or serial number for each asset should be stenciled on or otherwise attached to the asset to enhance control over plant and equipment. A physical inventory should be taken periodically to determine whether all items shown in the accounting records actually exist, are where they should be, and are still being used. A company that does not use subsidiary records and identification numbers and take physical inventories may find it difficult to determine whether assets have been discarded or stolen.

The general ledger control account balance for each major class of plant and equipment should equal the total of the amounts shown on all the subsidiary records for that class of plant and equipment. Each time a plant asset is acquired, exchanged, or disposed of, an entry should be posted to both a general ledger control account and an appropriate subsidiary record.

Subsidiary plant asset records show total cost and accumulated depreciation to be written off upon disposition of plant assets. Such records provide supporting evidence for depreciation deductions and gains and losses reported on income tax returns and the income statement. These records can also be used as a basis for obtaining the proper amount of insurance coverage and for substantiating claims for losses sustained on insured plant assets.

Since subsidiary plant asset records are costly to maintain, most companies do not keep such records for assets that cost less than an established minimum of, say, $50 or $100. The materiality principle provides justification for immediately expensing plant assets which cost less than the minimum established amount.

NATURAL RESOURCES

Ore deposits, mineral deposits, oil reserves, gas deposits, and timber stands supplied by nature are known as *natural resources* or *wasting assets*. In their natural state, they represent inventories of raw materials which can be consumed or exhausted through extraction or removal of their physical properties. On the balance sheet, natural resources are classified as a separate group of noncurrent assets, within the property, plant, and equipment section, under such headings as "Timber stands" or "Oil reserves."

Natural resources typically are recorded at cost of acquisition plus exploration and development cost, and are reported on the balance sheet at total cost less accumulated depletion. Caution must be exercised in analyzing the financial condition of firms that own wasting assets because historical costs reported may be but a fraction of the current value of the natural resources.

Depletion

Depletion is the exhaustion of a natural resource. It results from the physical removal of a part of the resource. Depletion is recognized in a period as an estimate of the cost of the resource that was removed during the period. Depletion is recorded by debiting a depletion account and crediting an accumulated depletion account. This depletion cost is combined with other extraction, mining, or removal costs to determine total cost of the resource available. This total cost is then divided between cost of the natural resources which were sold and inventory of the natural resource still on hand. Thus, it is possible that all, some, or none of the depletion recognized in a period will be expensed in that period. The part not considered an expense will be part of the cost of a current asset—inventory.

Computing periodic depletion cost

Depletion charges usually are computed through use of a units-of-production method. Total cost is divided by the estimated number of units—tons, barrels, or board feet—*that can be economically extracted* from the property. This calculation provides a per-unit depletion cost. For example, assume that in 1984, $650,000 was paid for a tract of land containing an ore deposit. Incurrence of $100,000 of exploration costs indicated that approximately 900,000 tons of ore can be removed from the land, after which the land will be worth $50,000. Costs of $200,000 were incurred to develop the site, including the cost of running power lines and building roads. Total cost subject to depletion then is the net cost assignable to the natural resource plus the exploration and development costs. Upon the purchase of the property, a journal entry would be made to assign the purchase price to the two assets purchased—the natural resource and the land. The entry would be:

```
Land .............................................  50,000
Mineral Deposits ..................................  600,000
    Cash ..........................................              650,000
    To record purchase of land and mine.
```

After the purchase, all other costs mentioned above would be debited to the natural resource account, yielding a total cost for the resource of $900,000 ($600,000 + $100,000 + $200,000). The entry would be:

```
Mineral Deposits ($100,000 + $200,000) ............  300,000
    Cash ..........................................              300,000
    To record costs of exploration and development.
```

The unit (per-ton) depletion charge is $1 ($900,000/900,000 tons). If 100,000 tons are mined in 1984, the entry to record the depletion charge is:

```
Depletion of Mineral Deposits .....................  100,000
    Accumulated Depletion—Mineral Deposits ........              100,000
    To record depletion for 1984.
```

The Mineral Deposits account could have been credited directly instead of the accumulated depletion account. The depletion account contains the "in the ground" cost of the ore or natural resource mined. This cost is combined with other extractive or, in the case of oil deposits, lifting costs to determine the total cost of the ore mined. To illustrate, assume that in addition to the $100,000 depletion cost, mining labor costs totaled $300,000, and other mining costs, such as depreciation, property taxes, power, and supplies, totaled $80,000. If 80,000 tons were sold and 20,000 remained on hand at the end of the period, total cost of $480,000 would be allocated as follows:

```
Depletion cost ....................................  $100,000
Mining labor cost .................................   300,000
Other mining costs ................................    80,000
Total mining costs for 100,000 tons ($4.80 per ton) ...  $480,000
    Less: Ore inventory (20,000 tons at $4.80) .........    96,000
Cost of ore sold ..................................  $384,000
```

The average cost per ton to mine 100,000 tons was $4.80 ($480,000/100,000). The income statement would show cost of ore sold of $384,000. There would be no separate reporting of depletion expense because depletion is included in cost of ore sold. The balance sheet would show inventory of ore on hand (a current asset) at $96,000 ($4.80 × 20,000). The balance sheet would also report the cost less accumulated depletion of the natural resource as follows:

```
Mineral deposits ...............  $900,000
    Less: Accumulated depletion ...   100,000
                                     $800,000
```

Depreciation of plant assets on extractive industry property.   Depreciable plant assets erected on extractive industry property are depreciated in the same manner as other depreciable assets. If such assets will be abandoned when the natural resource is exhausted, they should be depreciated over the shorter of the (*a*) physical life of the asset or (*b*) life of the natural resource. In some cases periodic depreciation charges are computed using the units-of-production method.

To illustrate the computation of depreciation using a units-of-production method, assume a building costing $310,000 and having an estimated physical life of 20 years and an estimated salvage value of $10,000 is constructed at a mine site. The mine is estimated to contain 1,000,000 tons of ore and is expected to be completely exhausted within 10 years. During the first year of mine operations, 150,000 tons of ore are extracted. Since the life of the mine (10 years or 1,000,000 tons) is shorter than the life of the building (20 years), the building should be depreciated over the life of the mine. The depreciation charge is based on tons of ore rather than years because the mine's "life" could be longer or shorter than 10 years depending on how rapidly the ore is removed from the mine. Building depreciation for the first year is $45,000, computed as follows:

$$\text{Depreciation per unit} = \frac{\text{Cost} - \text{Estimated salvage value}}{\text{Total tons of ore in mine}}$$

$$\text{Depreciation per unit} = \frac{\$310,000 - \$10,000}{1,000,000} = \$0.30 \text{ per ton}$$

$$\text{Depreciation for year} = \text{Depreciation per unit} \times \text{Units extracted}$$

$$\text{Depreciation for year} = \$0.30 \times 150,000 \text{ tons} = \$45,000$$

Depreciation on the building would be included on the income statement as part of the cost of ore that was sold and would be carried as part of inventory cost for those tons of ore which were not sold during the period. Accumulated depreciation on the building would be reported on the balance sheet with the related asset account.

INTANGIBLE ASSETS

Intangible assets are items which have no physical characteristics but are of value because of the business advantages or exclusive privileges and rights they provide. Intangible assets generally arise from two sources: (1) exclusive privileges granted by governmental authority or by legal contract, such as patents, copyrights, franchises, trademarks and trade names, and leases; and (2) superior entrepreneurial capacity or management know-how and customer loyalty, which is called goodwill.

All intangible assets are nonphysical, but not all nonphysical assets are classified as intangibles. For example, accounts receivable and prepaid expenses are nonphysical, but they are classified as current assets. Thus, intangible assets are generally both nonphysical and noncurrent.

Acquisition of intangible assets

Intangible assets are recorded initially at cost as are most other assets. But a major difference exists for intangible assets in contrast with plant assets. Cost of acquisition of an intangible asset does not include cost of internal development or self-creation of the asset. *Only outright purchase costs are included.* For this reason, some companies have extremely valuable assets which may not even be recorded in their accounts. The reasons for proceeding in this manner can be studied by looking at the history of accounting for research and development costs.

Research and development costs are costs incurred in a planned search for new knowledge and in translating such knowledge in a manner that yields a new product or process. Prior to 1975, research and development costs were often capitalized as intangible assets when future benefits were expected from their incurrence. Since it was often difficult to determine the costs applicable to future benefits, many firms expensed all such costs as they were incurred. Other firms capitalized those costs which related to proven products and expensed the rest as incurred. As a result of these varied accounting practices, the Financial Accounting Standards Board in *Statement No. 2* in 1974 ruled that all research and development costs, other than those directly reimbursable by government agencies and others, must be expensed when incurred. Immediate expensing is justified on the grounds that (1) the amount of costs applicable to the future cannot be measured with any high degree of precision, (2) doubt exists as to whether any future benefits will be received, and (3) even if benefits are expected they cannot be measured. As a result of the ruling, research and development costs will no longer appear as intangible assets on the balance sheet.

The same line of reasoning is applied to other costs incurred to create internally generated intangible assets to prevent them from being capitalized and reported as intangible assets.

Amortization of intangible assets

Amortization is the term used to describe the systematic write-off to expense of the cost of an intangible asset. All intangible assets are subject to amortization. Amortization is similar to plant asset depreciation and natural resource depletion. It is that portion of intangible asset cost allocated to each year in the economic (useful) life of the asset. Generally, amortization is recorded by debiting Amortization Expense and crediting the intangible asset account. An Accumulated Amortization account could be used to record amortization, but in most cases, the information gained from such accounting or presentation would not be significant. This is due to the fact that intangibles do not normally account for as significant an amount of total asset dollars as do plant assets.

Intangibles should be amortized over the shorter of their economic or legal life. Economic life is considered because that is the period in which benefits are received from the asset. *APB Opinion No. 17* required that an intangible asset acquired after October 1, 1970, be amortized over a period not to exceed 40 years. Straight-line amortization must be used, unless another method of amortization (such as units-of-production) can be shown to be superior.

Patents

A *patent* is a right granted by a government which gives the owner of the patent the exclusive right to manufacture, sell, lease, or otherwise benefit from an invention. The real value of a patent lies in its ability to produce earnings. The legal life of a patent is 17 years. Protection under the patent starts at time of application for the patent and lasts for 17 years from the date it is granted.

A purchased patent should be recorded in the Patents account at cost. The Patents account should also be debited for the cost of successfully defended patent infringement suits and for the cost of any competing patents which were purchased in order to ensure revenue-generating capability of the purchased patent.

The cost of a purchased patent should be amortized over the shorter of 17 years (or remaining legal life) or its estimated useful life. If a patent cost $40,000 and has a useful life of 10 years, the journal entry to record periodic amortization is:

```
Patent Amortization Expense ........................................  4,000
    Patents ........................................................          4,000
    To record patent amortization.
```

If after a few years the patent becomes worthless, the unamortized balance in the Patents account should be charged to expense, and, if material in amount, it should be disclosed separately in the income statement.

Copyrights

A *copyright* gives its owner an exclusive right protecting writings, designs, and literary productions from being reproduced illegally. A copyright has a legal life equal to the life of the creator plus 50 years. Since most publications have a limited life, the cost of the copyright may appropriately be charged to expense over the life of the first edition published.

Franchises

A *franchise* is a contract between two parties which grants the franchisee certain rights and privileges ranging from name identification to complete monopoly of service. The two parties can both be private businesses such as an individual who wishes to open a hamburger restaurant and who purchases a McDonald's franchise; the two parties involved are the individual business and McDonald's. This franchise would allow the business to use the McDonald's logo, advertising, and provide many other benefits. On the other hand, a franchise may be granted between a government agency and a private company; an example would be a city which gave a franchise to a utility company, giving the utility exclusive right to provide service to a particular area.

A franchise also places certain restrictions on the company which purchased the franchise. These restrictions are generally related to rates or prices charged. The restrictions may also be in regard to product quality or from whom supplies and inventory items must be purchased.

If periodic payments to the grantor of the franchise are required, they should be debited to a Franchise Expense account. If a lump-sum payment is made to obtain the franchise, the cost should be recorded in an asset account entitled Franchise and amortized over the shorter of useful life of the franchise or 40 years.

Trademarks; trade names

A *trademark* is a symbol, design, or logo which is used in conjunction with a particular product or company. A *trade name* is a brand name under which a product is sold or a company does business. Many times these are extremely valuable to a company, but they may have been internally developed and therefore have no recorded cost. But if such items were purchased by a business, they would be recorded at cost and amortized over their economic life. A purchase might be made from an advertising company, and the cost could be material.

Leases

A *lease* is a contract to rent property. The owner of the property is the grantor of the lease and is called the *lessor.* The person or company obtaining rights to possess and use property is called the *lessee.* The rights granted under the lease are called a *leasehold.* The accounting for a lease depends upon whether it is a capital lease or an operating lease.

Capital leases. In concept, a *capital lease* is a lease that transfers to the lessee virtually all rewards and risks that accompany ownership of property. A lease is a capital lease if it, among other provisions, (1) transfers ownership of the leased property to the lessee at the end of the lease term, or (2) contains a bargain purchase option which permits the lessee to buy the property at a price significantly below fair value at the end of the lease term.

A capital lease is a means of financing property acquisitions and has the same economic impact as an installment purchase. Thus, the lessee in a capital lease must record the leased property as an asset and the lease obligation as a liability. The leased property is depreciated over the useful life to the lessee. A part of each lease payment is recorded as interest expense, with the balance viewed as a payment on the lease liability.

The proper accounting for capital leases for both lessees and lessors has been an extremely difficult problem. Further discussion of capital leases is left for an intermediate accounting text.

Operating leases. If a lease does not qualify as a capital lease, it is an *operating lease.* A one-year lease on an apartment or a week's rental of an automobile are examples of operating leases. Such leases make no attempt to transfer any of the rewards and risks of ownership to the lessee. As a result, there may be no recordable transaction when a lease is signed.

In other situations, the lease may call for an immediate cash payment that must be accounted for. Assume, for example, that the first and fifth years' $12,000 annual rent is paid when a lease is signed. The lessee would record the payment as follows:

```
Prepaid Rent..............................................  12,000
Leasehold ................................................  12,000
   Cash ...................................................          24,000
   To record first and fifth years' rent on five-year lease.
```

The Leasehold account is actually a long-term prepaid rent account. The accounting for a balance in such an account depends on the terms of the lease. In the example, the $12,000 in the Leasehold account will be charged to expense over the fifth year only. The balance in Prepaid Rent will be charged to expense in the first year. Thus, the entry for the first year, assuming lease year and fiscal year coincide, is:

```
Rent Expense .............................................  12,000
   Prepaid Rent ..........................................          12,000
   To record rent expense.
```

The entry in the fifth year is:

```
Rent Expense .............................................  12,000
   Leasehold .............................................          12,000
   To record rent expense.
```

The accounting for the second, third, and fourth years will be the same as for the first year: the rent will be set up in Prepaid Rent when paid in advance for the year and then expensed.

A lump-sum down payment may be paid upon signing of a lease which is not a specific period's rent. If so, the payment is debited to the Leasehold account and amortized over the life of the lease. The straight-line method is required unless another method can be shown to be superior. Assume the $12,000 rent for the fifth year in the example was, instead, a lump-sum down payment on the lease. An annual adjusting entry to amortize the $12,000 over five years is required. The entry would read:

```
Rent Expense .............................................  2,400
   Leasehold .............................................          2,400
   To amortize leasehold.
```

The annual rental expense is $14,400: $12,000 annual cash rent plus $2,400 amortization of leasehold ($12,000/5).

Periodic rent may be based on sales or usage rather than being a constant amount. For example, the rent for 1984 would be $20,000 if the lease called for rent equal to 5 percent of sales and sales were $400,000 in 1984.

Leasehold improvements

A *leasehold improvement* is any physical alteration to leased property from which benefits are expected beyond the current accounting period. If the lessee improves leased property, these leasehold improvements will usually become the property of the lessor after the lease has expired. Leasehold improvements are an asset of the lessee and should be debited to a Leasehold Improvements account. Leasehold improvements will be amortized to expense over the period of time benefited by the improvements. The amortization period for leasehold improvements should be the shorter of the life of the improvements or the life of the lease.

As an illustration, assume that on January 2, 1984, Wolf Company leases a building for 20 years under a nonrenewable lease at an annual rental of $20,000, payable on each December 31. Wolf immediately incurs a cost of $80,000 for improvements to the building, such as interior walls for office separation, ceiling fans, and recessed lighting. The improvements have an estimated life of 30 years. The $80,000 should be amortized over the 20-year lease period, since that is shorter than the life of the improvements, and Wolf will not be able to use the improvements beyond the life of the lease. If only annual financial statements are prepared, the following journal entry will properly record the rental expense for the year ended December 31, 1984:

Rent Expense (or Leasehold Improvement Expense)	4,000	
Leasehold Improvements		4,000
To record leasehold improvement amortization.		
Rent Expense	20,000	
Cash		20,000
To record annual rent.		

Thus, the total cost to rent the building each year includes the $20,000 cash rent plus the amortization of the leasehold improvements.

Although leaseholds are intangible assets, leaseholds and leasehold improvements are sometimes shown in the property, plant, and equipment section of the balance sheet.

Goodwill

Goodwill is best viewed as an intangible value attaching to an entity that results chiefly from its management's skill or know-how and a favorable reputation with customers. An entity's value may be greater than the total of the fair market values of its tangible and identifiable intangible assets. This greater value means that the company is able to generate an above-average rate of income on each dollar invested in the business. Thus, proof of the existence of goodwill for a company can be found *only* in its ability to generate superior earnings or income.

A Goodwill account will appear in the accounting records only if goodwill has been bought and paid for in cash or other property. Goodwill cannot be purchased by itself; an entire business or a part of a business must be purchased to obtain the accompanying intangible asset, goodwill.

To illustrate, assume that Foster Company purchased all of Hiser Company's assets for $600,000. Foster also agrees to assume responsibility for $300,000 of debts owed by Hiser. Goodwill is determined to be the difference between the amount paid for the business ($900,000) and the *fair market value* of the assets purchased. Notice that market value rather than book value is used to determine the amount of goodwill. The following shows the computation for the amount of goodwill purchased by Foster:

Cash paid		$600,000
Liabilities assumed		300,000
Total price paid		$900,000
Less fair market values of individually identifiable assets:		
Accounts receivable	$100,000	
Inventories	90,000	
Land	150,000	
Buildings	250,000	
Equipment	200,000	
Patents	35,000	825,000
Goodwill		$ 75,000

The $75,000 is the amount of goodwill to be recorded as an intangible asset on the books of Foster Company; all of the other assets will be recorded at fair market value, and the liabilities will be recorded at the amounts due. It is difficult to identify the specific reasons for the existence of goodwill in a company, but those reasons might include good reputation, customer loyalty, product design, and human resources. Since these are not individually quantifiable, they are all grouped together and referred to as goodwill.

Goodwill, like all other intangibles, must be amortized. There is no legal life for goodwill, and useful life is not validly estimable. For example, if the new owner made substantial changes in the method of doing business, goodwill which existed at purchase date could rapidly disappear. Therefore, current accounting practice requires the amortization of goodwill over a period not to exceed 40 years. This requirement is due to the fact that the value of purchased goodwill will eventually disappear. Other goodwill may be generated in its place, but the organization cannot book its internally created goodwill any more than it can record other internally generated intangible assets.

Reporting amortization

Amortization expense for most intangible assets discussed would appear among the operating expenses on the income statement. The account titles used are all of this type: "Amortization of Goodwill (or Patents, Copyrights, Franchises, Leaseholds) Expense." Periodic amortization of leaseholds and leasehold improvements is often reported as rent expense. The amortization of goodwill is an expense in determination of accounting income, but is not a deductible item in the determination of taxable income.

NEW TERMS INTRODUCED IN CHAPTER 11

Amortization
The term used to describe the systematic write-off to expense of the cost of an intangible asset.

Boot
The additional cash outlay made when one asset is traded for a similar asset.

Capital lease
A lease that transfers to the lessee virtually all of the rewards and risks that accompany ownership of property.

Copyright
Gives its owner an exclusive right protecting writings, designs, and literary productions from being illegally reproduced.

Depletion
The exhaustion of a natural resource; an estimate of the cost of the resource which was removed during the period.

Franchise
A contract between two parties which grants the franchisee certain rights and privileges ranging from name identification to complete monopoly of service.

Goodwill
An intangible value attaching to an entity which results chiefly from its management's skill or know-how and a favorable reputation with customers. The ability to generate an above-average rate of income on each dollar invested in a business.

Intangible assets
Items that have no physical characteristics but are of value because of the business advantages or exclusive privileges they provide.

Lease
A contract to rent property. Grantor of the lease is the *lessor;* the party obtaining the rights to possess and use property is the *lessee.*

Leasehold
The rights granted under a lease.

Leasehold improvement
Any physical alteration to leased property from which benefits are expected beyond the current accounting period.

Natural resources
Ore deposits, mineral deposits, oil reserves, gas deposits, and timber stands supplied by nature.

Operating lease
A lease that does not qualify as a capital lease.

Patent
A right granted by a government which gives its owner the exclusive right to manufacture, sell, lease, or otherwise benefit from an invention.

Research and development costs
Costs incurred in a planned search for new knowledge and in translating such knowledge in a manner that yields a new product or process.

Trademark
A symbol, design, or logo which is used in conjunction with a particular product or company.

Trade name
A brand name under which a product is sold or a company does business.

Wasting assets
See natural resources.

DEMONSTRATION PROBLEM

On January 2, 1981, the Hopper Company purchased a machine for $60,000 cash. The machine has an estimated useful life of six years and an estimated salvage value of $2,000. The double-declining-balance method of depreciation is being used.

Required:

a. Compute the book value of the machine as of July 1, 1984.

b. Assume the machine was disposed of on July 1, 1984. Prepare the journal entries to record the disposition of the machine under each of the following unrelated assumptions:

1. The machine was sold for $10,000 cash.
2. The machine was sold for $15,000 cash.

3. The machine and $60,000 cash were exchanged for a new machine that had a cash price of $65,000. Use the accounting method rather than the tax method.
4. The machine was completely destroyed by fire. Cash of $8,000 is expected to be recovered from the insurance company.

Solution to demonstration problem

a.

HOPPER COMPANY		
Schedule to Compute Book Value		
July 1, 1984		
Cost		$60,000
Less accumulated depreciation:		
Depreciation for 1981 ($60,000 × 33⅓%)	$20,000	
Depreciation for 1982 ($60,000 − $20,000) × 33⅓%	13,333	
Depreciation for 1983 ($60,000 − $33,333) × 33⅓%	8,889	
Depreciation for first half of 1984 ($60,000 − $42,222) × 33⅓% × ½ . .	2,963	45,185
Book value		$14,815

b.

1.
Cash	10,000	
Accumulated Depreciation—Machinery	45,185	
Loss on Disposal of Plant Assets	4,815	
Machinery		60,000

To record sale of machinery at a loss.

2.
Cash	15,000	
Accumulated Depreciation—Machinery	45,185	
Machinery		60,000
Gain on Disposal of Plant Assets		185

To record sale of machinery at a gain.

3.
Machinery (New)	65,000	
Accumulated Depreciation—Machinery	45,185	
Loss on Disposal of Plant Assets	9,815	
Machinery (Old)		60,000
Cash		60,000

To record exchange of machines.

4.
Receivable from Insurance Company	8,000	
Accumulated Depreciation—Machinery	45,185	
Fire Loss	6,815	
Machinery		60,000

To record loss of machinery.

QUESTIONS

1. When depreciable plant assets are sold for cash, how is the gain or loss measured?

2. A plant asset that cost $15,000 and has a related accumulation depreciation account balance of $15,000 is still being used in business operations. Would it be appropriate to continue recording depreciation on this asset? Explain. When should the asset's cost and accumulated depreciation be removed from the accounting records?

3. A piece of factory equipment and $10,000 cash were exchanged for a delivery truck. How should the cost basis of the delivery truck be measured?

4. A plant asset was exchanged for a new asset of a similar type. How should the cost basis of the new asset be measured under generally accepted accounting principles?

5. A plant asset was exchanged for an asset of a similar type. What is the cost basis of the new asset for tax purposes?

6. How do subsidiary records provide control over a company's plant assets?

7. What advantages can accrue to a company that maintains subsidiary plant asset records?

8. *a.* Distinguish between depreciation, depletion, and amortization. Name two assets which are subject to depreciation; to depletion; and to amortization.

    b. Distinguish between tangible and intangible assets and classify the above-named assets accordingly.

9. A building with an estimated physical life of 40 years was constructed at the site of a coal mine. The coal mine is expected to be completely exhausted within 20 years. Over what length of time should the building be depreciated, assuming the building will be abandoned after all the coal has been extracted?

10. What are the characteristics of intangible assets? Give an example of an asset which has no physical existence but is not classified as an intangible asset.

11. Over what length of time should intangible assets be amortized?

12. You note that a certain store seems to have a steady stream of regular customers, a favorable location, courteous employees, high-quality merchandise, and a reputation for fairness in dealing with customers, employees, and suppliers. Does it follow automatically that this business has goodwill? Explain.

13. What is the difference between a leasehold (under an operating lease contract) and a leasehold improvement? Is there any difference in accounting procedures applicable to each?

14. Brush Company leased a tract of land for 40 years at an agreed annual rental of $10,000. The effective date of the lease was July 1, 1984. During the last six months of 1984, Brush constructed a building on the land at a cost of $250,000. The building was placed in operation on January 2, 1985, at which time it was estimated to have a physical life of 50 years. Over what period of time should the building be depreciated? Why?

15. What reasons justify the immediate expensing of most research and development costs?

16. What is a capital lease? How does a person recognize one when it is encountered?

17. Why are intangible assets amortized over their economic rather than their legal life?

18. Describe the typical accounting for a patent.

EXERCISES

E–1.   Plant equipment originally costing $36,000 on which $24,000 of depreciation has been accumulated was sold for $9,000.

    a. Prepare the journal entry to record the sale.
    b. Prepare the entry to record the sale of the equipment if $100 of removal costs were incurred to allow the equipment to be moved.

E–2.   A machine costing $8,000 on which $6,000 of depreciation has been accumulated was completely destroyed by fire. What journal entry should be made to record the machine's destruction and the resulting fire loss under each of the following unrelated assumptions:

a. The machine was *not* insured.

b. The machine was insured; and it is estimated that $1,500 will be recovered from the insurance company.

E–3. King Company owned an automobile acquired on July 1, 1982, at a cash cost of $5,200; at that time, it was estimated to have a life of four years and a $400 salvage value. Depreciation has been recorded through June 30, 1985, on a straight-line basis. On July 1, 1985, the auto was traded for a new auto. The old auto had a fair value of $1,000. Cash of $4,600 was paid. Prepare the journal entry to record the trade-in under generally accepted accounting principles.

E–4. Equipment costing $22,000, on which $15,000 of accumulated depreciation had been recorded, was disposed of on January 2, 1984. What journal entries are required to record the equipment's disposition under each of the following unrelated assumptions?

a. The equipment was sold for $9,000 cash.

b. The equipment was sold for $5,800 cash.

c. The equipment was retired from service and hauled to the junkyard. No material was salvaged.

d. The equipment was exchanged for similar equipment having a cash price of $30,000. A trade-in allowance of $10,000 was received, and the balance was paid in cash.

e. The equipment was exchanged for similar equipment having a cash price of $30,000. A trade-in allowance of $5,000 was received, and the balance was paid in cash. (Record this transaction twice: first, for tax purposes; and, second, for financial reporting purposes.)

E–5. On August 31, 1984, Bing Company sold a truck for $2,300 cash. The truck was acquired on July 1, 1981, at a cost of $5,800. Depreciation of $3,000 on the truck has been recorded through December 31, 1983, using the straight-line method, a four-year expected life, and an expected salvage value of $1,000. Prepare the journal entries to update the depreciation on the truck on August 31, 1984, and to record the sale of the truck.

E–6. Bell Company paid $1 million for the right to extract all of the mineral-bearing ore that can be economically extracted, estimated at five million tons, from a certain tract of land. During the first year, Bell Company extracted 500,000 tons of the ore and sold 400,000 tons. What part of the $1,000,000 should be charged to expense during the first year?

E–7. Herman Company purchased a patent on January 1, 1968, at a total cost of $68,000. In January 1979 the company successfully defended an infringement suit. The legal fees amounted to $15,000. What will be the amount of patent cost amortized in 1984? (The useful life of the patent is the same as its legal life—17 years.)

E–8. Preston Company leased the first three floors in a building under an operating lease contract for a 10-year period beginning January 1, 1984. The company paid $80,000 in cash (not representing a specific period's rent) and agreed to make annual payments equal to 1 percent of the first $500,000 of sales and one half of 1 percent of all sales over $500,000. Sales for 1984 amounted to $1,500,000. Payment of the annual amount will be made on January 12, 1985. Prepare journal entries to record the cash payment of January 1, 1984, and the proper expense to be recognized for the use of the space in the leased building for 1984.

E-9.   Joe Gordon paid Hungry Hank's Hamburgers $20,000 for a perpetual right to operate a fast-food restaurant in Gordonville under the Hungry Hank's name. Joe also agreed to pay an operating fee of one half of 1 percent of sales for advertising and other services rendered by Hungry Hank's. Joe began operations on January 2, 1984. Sales for 1984 amounted to $200,000. Give the entries needed to record the payment of the $20,000 and to record expenses incurred relating to the right to use the Hungry Hank's name.

PROBLEMS, SERIES A

P11-1-A.   On July 31, 1984, Roberts Company sold a truck for $3,700 cash. The truck was acquired on July 1, 1981, at a cost of $11,600; depreciation has been recorded on the truck through December 31, 1983, using the straight-line method, a four-year useful life, and $2,000 of expected salvage value.

Required:

      Prepare all entries needed for the above information for the year 1984.

P11-2-A.   Blake Company traded an auto that cost $6,000 and on which $5,000 of depreciation has been recorded for a new auto with a "sticker price" of $11,500. The company received a trade-in allowance for the old auto of $1,500 and paid the balance in cash. The old auto had a fair value of $700.

Required:

      a.   Record the exchange of the autos applying generally accepted accounting principles. (Hint: The sticker price is not necessarily the cash price.)

      b.   Record the exchange, applying federal income tax regulations.

P11-3-A.   On January 2, 1982, the Brummet Company purchased a delivery truck for $21,000 cash. The truck has an estimated useful life of six years and an estimated salvage value of $1,000. The double-declining-balance method of depreciation is being used.

Required:

      a.   Prepare a schedule which shows how the truck's book value on January 1, 1985, would be computed.

      b.   Assume the truck is to be disposed of on July 1, 1985. What journal entry is required to record depreciation for the six months ended June 30, 1985?

      c.   Prepare the journal entries to record the disposition of the truck under each of the following unrelated assumptions:

1.   The truck was sold for $3,000 cash.
2.   The truck was sold for $7,000 cash.
3.   The truck was retired from service, and it is expected that $1,500 will be received from the sale of salvaged materials.
4.   The truck and $20,000 cash were exchanged for office equipment which had a cash price of $28,000.
5.   The truck and $22,000 cash were exchanged for a new delivery truck which had a cash price of $30,000.
6.   The truck was completely destroyed in an accident. Cash of $2,800 is expected to be recovered from the insurance company.

P11-4-A.   Raines Moving Company purchased a new moving van on October 1, 1984. The cash price of the new van was $22,000, and the company received a trade-in allowance of $4,000 for a 1982 model. The balance was paid in cash. The 1982 model had been acquired on October 1, 1982, at a cost of $18,000. Depreciation had been recorded through December 31, 1983, on a double-declining-balance basis, with three years of useful life expected. At the time of trade, the 1982 van had a cash value of $4,000.

Required:

Present journal entries to record the exchange of the moving vans using the method required by generally accepted accounting principles.

P11–5–A. On January 1, 1984, Weston Company had the following balances in its plant asset and accumulated depreciation accounts:

	Asset	Accumulated depreciation
Land . . . ./.	$ 40,000	
Leasehold	50,000	
Buildings	219,600	$18,375
Equipment	192,000	89,100
Trucks	28,800	14,025

Additional data:

1. The leasehold covers a plot of ground leased on January 1, 1980, for a period of 20 years.
2. Building No. 1 is on the owned land and was completed on July 1, 1983, at a cost of $126,000. Its life is set at 40 years. Building No. 2 is on leased land and was completed on July 1, 1980, at a cost of $93,600. Its life is also set at 40 years.
3. Equipment is depreciated at 12.5 percent per year.
4. Truck A, purchased on January 1, 1982, at a cost of $9,600, had an expected life of 2½ years and a scrap value of $600. Truck B, purchased on July 1, 1982, at a cost of $8,400, had an expected life of two years and a scrap value of $1,400. Truck C, purchased on July 1, 1983, at a cost of $10,800, had an expected life of three years and a scrap value of $1,350.

The following events occurred in 1984:

Transactions:

Jan. 2 Rent for 1984 on leased land was paid, $5,600.

Apr. 1 Truck B was traded in on Truck D. Cash price of the new truck was $9,600. A trade-in allowance of $1,800 was granted ($1,800 was also the cash value of Truck B). The balance was paid in cash. Truck D has an expected life of 2½ years and a scrap value of $600. (Do not use tax method.)

1 Truck A was sold for $1,800 cash.

Required:

Prepare journal entries to record the 1984 transactions and the necessary December 31, 1984, adjusting entries, assuming a calendar-year accounting period. Use the straight-line depreciation method.

P11–6–A. King Mining Company, on January 2, 1984, acquired ore deposits at a cash cost of $1,985,000. Exploration and development costs amounted to $200,000. The residual value of the land is expected to be $400,000. The ore deposits contain an estimated three million tons. Present technology will allow the economical extraction of only 85 percent of the total deposit. Machinery, equipment, and temporary sheds were installed at a cost of $306,000. These assets will have no further value to the company when the ore body is exhausted; they have a physical life of 12 years. In 1984, 350,000 tons of ore were extracted. The company expects the mine to be exhausted in 10 years, with sharp variations in annual production.

Required:

a. Compute the depletion charge for 1984.

b. Compute the depreciation charge for 1984 under the following methods: (1) double-declining-balance and (2) units-of-production.

c. Which depreciation method do you believe to be most appropriate in the circumstances cited?

d. If all other mining costs, except depletion, amounted to $1,400,000, what was the average cost per ton mined in 1984?

P11–7–A.   Weer Company spent $83,300 to purchase a patent on January 2, 1984. It is assumed that the patent will be useful during its full legal life. In January 1985, the company successfully defended an infringement suit at a cost of $16,000. Also in January 1985, the company paid $24,000 to obtain patents that could, if used by competitors, make the earlier Weer patents useless. The purchased patents will never be used.

Required:

Give the entries to record the information relative to the patents in 1984 and 1985.

P11–8–A.   Following are selected transactions and other data relating to the White Company for the year ended December 31, 1984.

Required:

For each of the situations described below, prepare only the journal entries to record the expense applicable to 1984.

a. Rented the second floor of a building for five years on January 2, 1984, and paid the first and last year's rent of $5,000 for each year in advance.

b. In 1983, incurred legal fees of $15,000 in applying for a patent and paid a bonus of $5,000 to an employee who conceived of a device which substantially reduced the cost of manufacturing one of the company's products. The patent on the device has a market value of $150,000 and is expected to be useful for 10 years.

c. In 1983, the company entered into a 10-year operating lease on several floors of a building, paying $10,000 in cash immediately and agreeing to pay $5,000 at the end of each of the 10 years of life in the lease. It then incurred costs of $20,000 to install partitions, shelving, and fixtures. These items would normally last 25 years.

d. The company spent $6,000 promoting a trademark in a manner that it believed enhanced its value considerably. The trademark has an indefinite life.

e. Incurred costs of $50,000 in 1983 and of $65,000 in 1984 on research and development of new products that are expected to enhance the company's revenues for at least five years.

f. Paid $50,000 to the author of a book that the company published on July 2, 1984. Sales of the book are expected to be made over a two-year period from that date.

PROBLEMS, SERIES B

P11–1–B.   On October 1, 1982, Williams Company purchased an electronic typewriter for $4,700 cash. The typewriter has a useful life of five years, an expected salvage value of $200, and is being depreciated under the sum-of-the-years'-digits method. The company spent $120 to clean and adjust the typewriter on February 2, 1985, and sold the typewriter on August 1, 1985, for $1,000.

Required:

Prepare journal entries to record the above data for 1985, assuming Williams Company has a calendar-year accounting period.

11–2–B. Keys, Inc., purchased a new 1985 model automobile on December 29, 1985. The "sticker price" on the new auto was $13,000, from which Keys received a trade-in allowance of $2,000 for a 1982 model traded-in. The 1982 model had been acquired on September 1, 1982, at a cost of $9,600. Depreciation has been recorded on the 1982 model through December 31, 1984, using the double-declining-balance method and an expected four-year useful life. At the time of the exchange, the 1982 model auto had a cash (fair) value of $2,600.

Required:

a. Record depreciation expense for 1985.

b. Prepare the journal entries needed to record the exchange of autos using the method required under generally accepted accounting principles. (Hint: The sticker price is not necessarily the cash price.)

P11–3–B. On January 2, 1982, a company purchased a truck for $24,000 cash. The truck has an estimated useful life of six years and an expected salvage value of $3,000. Depreciation on the truck was computed using the sum-of-the-years'-digits method.

Required:

a. Prepare a schedule showing the computation of the book value of the truck on December 31, 1984.

b. Prepare the journal entry to record depreciation for the six months ended June 30, 1985.

c. Prepare journal entries to record the disposal of the truck on June 30, 1985, under each of the following unrelated assumptions:

1. The truck was sold for $2,000 cash.
2. The truck was sold for $8,000 cash.
3. The truck was scrapped. Used parts valued at $3,700 were salvaged.
4. The truck (which has a fair value of $6,000) and $18,000 of cash were exchanged for a used back hoe which did not have a known market value.
5. The truck and $20,000 cash were exchanged for another truck which had a cash price of $28,500.
6. The truck was stolen on July 1, and insurance proceeds of $4,200 were received.

P11–4–B. Hanson Company purchased a new model II computer on October 1, 1984. The cash price of the new computer was $20,800, and Hanson received a trade-in allowance for a model I computer of $9,000. The old computer was acquired on September 1, 1982, at a cost of $19,200. Depreciation had been recorded through December 31, 1983, on a straight-line basis, with an estimated useful life of four years and $3,200 of expected salvage value. At the date of the trade, the model I computer had a fair value of $9,000.

Required:

a. Prepare the entries needed to record the exchange using the income tax method.

b. Repeat part (*a*) applying generally accepted accounting principles.

P11–5–B. On July 1, 1984, Pearl Company had the following balances in its plant asset and accumulated depreciation accounts:

	Asset	Accumulated depreciation
Land	$200,000	
Leasehold	75,000	
Buildings	938,000	$129,250
Equipment	408,000	130,000
Trucks	71,000	21,325

Additional data:

1. The leasehold covers a plot of ground leased on July 1, 1979, for a period of 25 years under an operating lease.
2. The office building is on the leased land and was completed on July 1, 1980, at a cost of $288,000. Its physical life is set at 40 years. The factory building is on the owned land and was completed on July 1, 1979, at a cost of $650,000. Its life is also set at 40 years.
3. Equipment is depreciated at 6⅔ percent per year.
4. The company owns three trucks—A, B, and C. Truck A, purchased on July 1, 1982, at a cost of $16,000, had an expected life of three years and a scrap value of $1,000. Truck B, purchased on January 2, 1983, at a cost of $25,000, had an expected life of four years and a scrap value of $2,000. Truck C, purchased on January 2, 1984, at a cost of $30,000, had an expected life of five years and a scrap value of $3,000.

The following events occurred in the fiscal year ended June 30, 1985:

Transactions:

1984
July 1   Rent for July 1, 1984–June 30, 1985, on leased land was paid, $9,500.
Oct. 1   Truck A was traded in on Truck D. Cash price of the new truck was $32,000. Cash of $27,000 was paid. Truck D has an expected life of four years and a scrap value of $1,750.

1985
Feb. 2   Truck B was sold for $14,000 cash.
June 1   Truck C was completely demolished in an accident. The truck was not insured.

Required:

Prepare journal entries to record the above transactions and the necessary June 30, 1985, adjusting entries. Use the straight-line depreciation method.

P11–6–B.   Teller Company acquired a mine for $4,500,000. The mine contained an estimated 9 million tons of ore. It was also estimated that the land would have a value of $400,000 when the mine was exhausted and that only eight million tons of ore could be economically extracted. A building was erected on the property at a cost of $600,000. The building had an estimated useful life of 35 years and no scrap value. Specialized mining equipment was installed at a cost of $825,000. This equipment had an estimated useful life of seven years and an estimated $21,000 salvage value. The company began operating on July 1, 1984. During the fiscal year ended June 30, 1985, 800,000 tons of ore were extracted. The company decided to use the units-of-production method to record depreciation on the building and the sum-of-the-years'-digits method to record depreciation on the equipment.

Required:

Prepare journal entries to record the depletion and depreciation charges for the fiscal year ended June 30, 1985. Show calculations.

P11–7–B.   Hacker Company purchased a patent for $60,000 on January 2, 1984. The patent was estimated to have a useful life of 10 years. The $60,000 cost was properly charged to an asset account and amortized in 1984. On July 1, 1985, the company incurred legal and court costs of $18,000 in a successful defense of the patent in an infringement suit.

Required:

      a. Compute the patent amortization cost for 1984 and give the entry to record it.

      b. Compute the patent amortization cost for 1985 and give the entry to record it.

P11–8–B.   Given below are selected transactions and other data for Green Company.

Required:

      Prepare journal entries to record *only* the effects upon 1984 of the data below. If any of the unrelated items given below would not require an entry in 1984, state so.

      a. The company purchased a patent in January of 1981 for $30,000 and began amortizing it over 10 years. In 1983, the company defended the patent in an infringement suit at a cost of $8,000.

      b. Research and development costs incurred in 1983 of $9,000 were expected to provide benefits over the three succeeding years.

      c. On January 2, 1984, the company rented space in a warehouse for five years at an annual rental of $2,000. The first and last years' rent was paid in advance.

      d. A total of $20,000 was spent uniformly throughout 1984 by the company in promoting its lesser known trademark, which is expected to have an indefinite life.

      e. In January of 1982, the company purchased all of the assets and assumed all of the liabilities of another company, paying $40,000 more than the fair market value of all identifiable assets acquired, less the liabilities assumed. The company expects the benefits for which it paid the $40,000 to last 10 years.

BUSINESS DECISION PROBLEM 11–1

      Laborteaux Company acquired machine A for $50,000 on January 2, 1982. Machine A had an estimated useful life of four years and no salvage value. The machine was depreciated on the double-declining-balance basis. On January 2, 1984, machine A was exchanged for machine B. Machine B had a cash price of $60,000. In addition to machine A, cash of $50,000 was given up in the exchange. The company recorded the exchange in accordance with income tax regulations but failed to record the exchange in accordance with generally accepted accounting principles. Machine B has an estimated useful life of five years and no salvage value. The machine is being depreciated under the straight-line method.

Required:

      a. What journal entry did the Laborteaux Company make when it recorded the exchange of machines? (Show computations.)

      b. What journal entry should the Laborteaux Company have made to record the exchange of machines in accordance with generally accepted accounting principles?

      c. Assume the error is discovered on December 31, 1985, before adjusting journal entries have been made. What journal entries should be made to correct the accounting records? What adjusting journal entry should be made to record depreciation for 1985? (Ignore income taxes.)

      d. What effect did the error have on reported net income for 1984? (Ignore income taxes.)

      e. How should machine B be reported on the December 31, 1985, balance sheet?

BUSINESS DECISION PROBLEM 11–2

John Briarwood is trying to decide whether to buy Company A or Company B. Both Company A and Company B have assets with the following book values and fair market values:

	Book value	Fair market value
Accounts receivable ..	$100,000	$100,000
Inventories	300,000	500,000
Land	250,000	450,000
Buildings	300,000	700,000
Equipment..........	120,000	200,000
Patents	80,000	100,000

Liabilities which would be assumed include accounts payable, $200,000, and notes payable, $50,000.

The only difference between Company A and Company B is that Company A has net income which is about average for the industry while Company B has net income which is greatly above average for the industry.

Required:

a. Assume Briarwood can buy Company A for $1,800,000 or can buy Company B for $2,300,000. Prepare the journal entry to record the acquisition assuming Briarwood bought (1) Company A or (2) Company B. What accounts for the difference between the purchase price of the two companies?

b. Assume Briarwood can buy either company for $1,800,000. Which company would you advise Briarwood to buy? Why?

Chapter 12

Payroll accounting

CHAPTER GOALS

After study of this chapter, you should be able to:

1. Describe the essential internal control features for payrolls.
2. Prepare and record a payroll.
3. Illustrate the use of a payroll checking account.
4. Prepare an employee's earnings record.
5. Prepare entries to record employer's payroll taxes and vacation pay.
6. Define and use correctly the new terms in the glossary.

Payroll accounting is a very important function in most business firms because payroll cost is often the largest expense incurred. Furthermore, federal and state laws require employers to maintain payroll records showing the amount each employee has earned and the various payroll deductions taken during the period. This information must be filed regularly with certain federal and state agencies.

This chapter discusses the objectives of payroll accounting and the methods of achieving these objectives. Computations of gross and net earnings and the major documents and forms used in payroll accounting are explained.

OBJECTIVES OF PAYROLL ACCOUNTING

In general, the objectives of payroll accounting are to process data such as hours worked, pay rates, and payroll deductions so that the firm can:

1. Provide accurate paychecks to employees.
2. Produce necessary employee and employer records, withholding statements, and reports to governmental agencies.
3. Protect against fraud in payroll transactions.
4. Control salary and wage expense.

INTERNAL CONTROL OVER PAYROLL

In a small business, adequate internal control over payroll transactions may be provided by the owner-manager, who may actually compute and prepare the payroll. In larger companies, internal control is obtained through application of the general principles of internal control and the more specific guides to control over cash disbursements provided in Chapters 6 and 7. Separation of duties is a crucial aspect of payroll internal control. Ideally, timekeeping, payroll preparation, payroll record keeping, and payroll distribution functions should be performed by different persons.

An accurate method must be used to record the time each employee works if compensation is based on hours worked. In a small firm, the owner may simply make notations in a notebook when employees report to and leave work. In a larger firm, a time clock is often used for hourly employees. Each day when employees report to work, every employee inserts a *timecard* into the time clock. The time clock prints the date and the time on the card. The same procedure is used when employees leave work. Safeguards must be set up to ensure that no employee punches in or out for another employee.

Prior to payroll preparation, timecards are collected by the payroll department. Verified pay rates and hours are used to compute gross pay. Legally required and authorized deductions are subtracted from gross pay, individual payroll records are updated, and payroll checks are prepared.

The checks are sent to the treasurer's office for signature. Supporting documents may accompany the checks. Each check should be delivered to the employee in person or deposited directly by the employer into the employee's bank account.

Payroll fraud

Whenever cash is disbursed, the potential for fraud exists. Some of the techniques used successfully in the past to defraud employers are listed below.

1. A payroll department employee pays another employee more than that employee has actually earned and then the payroll employee receives a kickback of part of the overpayment.
2. A payroll department employee makes out a payroll check payable to a former or fictitious employee and cashes the check.
3. A payroll department employee prepares and cashes duplicate payroll checks.

Because of these and other schemes, great care must be exercised to ensure payroll accuracy. Separation of duties will help provide the required accuracy. When separation exists, it is difficult to arrange and cover up fraudulent transactions. One employee's work serves as a check upon another's. For example, if a payroll department employee falsifies the hours worked by a plant employee in an attempt to overpay that employee, the changed hours will not agree with the timecard record. Collusion by two payroll department employees will be required to commit such a fraud unless the same employee has access to timecards, other payroll records, and payroll checks.

Maintenance of accurate employment and payroll records also is crucial. The payroll department must be informed of hirings and terminations as soon as possible. Current copies of documents authorizing payroll deductions should be on hand. Payroll fraud may be reduced by the detailed records that must be kept for each employee to meet federal and state agency reporting requirements. Firms must be alert to the possibility of payroll fraud and take steps to prevent it.

GROSS EARNINGS OF EMPLOYEES

Although the terms often are used interchangeably, wages differ from salaries. The term *wages* generally refers to gross earnings of an employee who is paid by the hour for only the actual hours worked. The term *salaries,* on the other hand, usually refers to gross earnings of an employee who is paid a flat amount per week or month regardless of the number of hours worked in a period.

Computing gross earnings

Payroll preparation begins with the computation of gross earnings of each of a firm's employees. *Gross earnings* is total pay or total compensation of an employee, including regular pay and overtime premium. In most instances, computation of gross earnings is a simple calculation, such as multiplying number of hours worked by the hourly wage rate for the employee—40 hours times $10 per hour gives gross earnings of $400 for the week. Or, an annual salary of $36,000 is divided by 12 months to determine monthly gross earnings of $3,000. But some complexities are faced in calculating gross earnings.

The *Wages and Hours Law* (also called the *Fair Labor Standards Act*) requires that most employees be paid a minimum of 1½ times their normal rate for hours worked in excess of 40 per week and that at least the minimum wage be paid to employees. The *minimum wage* rate is set by the federal government and changes frequently. Some union contracts also call for premium pay rates for certain hours worked, such as double time for work on Sunday. Detailed time records must be maintained to ensure that legal and contractual requirements are being met. In the absence of valid records, assessments for overtime pay may later be made against the employer. Executive, administrative, and professional employees are exempt from both the minimum wage and overtime pay provisions.

Following are three situations involving computing employee earnings. Computations are made for gross pay, including overtime premiums.

1. Mary Kennedy's basic wage rate is $6 per hour. Her overtime premium, then, is one half of $6, or $3 per hour. Mary's gross pay for a week in which she worked 48 hours is $312. The $312 is computed as (48 × $6) + (8 × $3), or ($288 + $24) = $312.
2. Grace Early's $13,000 annual salary is paid over 52 weeks at a guaranteed weekly minimum of $250, (40 × $6.25 per hour), even though she often works only 37.5 hours a week. She is entitled to overtime pay for hours worked in excess of 40 per week. Her gross earnings for working 42 hours in a week are $268.75, $250 + (2 × 1.5 × $6.25).
3. Dan Brown is paid $0.50 for each unit of product machined. In the current week, he worked 44 hours and completed 924 units. His gross pay before overtime premium is $462, (924 × $0.50). The $462 is divided by 44 hours to get $10.50 as his regular hourly rate for the week. Therefore, Dan's overtime premium is $5.25 per hour, and his total overtime pay is $21 (4 × $5.25). His gross earnings for the week are $462 + $21, or $483.

PAYROLL TAXES AND DEDUCTIONS

Deductions from gross earnings commonly include withholdings for federal and state income taxes, FICA (social security) taxes, and a number of other items.

Federal income tax

Wage earners in the United States are under a pay-as-you-go federal income tax system. This means that most employees must pay federal income taxes on wages as they are earned during the year. Income tax is withheld by the employer when the employee's earnings are paid. These taxes are remitted periodically to a depository bank or to the Internal Revenue Service (IRS).

The amount of income tax withheld from each employee's pay depends

Illustration 12.1: Employee's Withholding Allowance Certificate (Form W-4)

Form **W-4** (Rev. January 1982)	Department of the Treasury—Internal Revenue Service **Employee's Withholding Allowance Certificate**	OMB No. 1545–0010 Expires 4–30–83

1 Type or print your full name
    Ronald Mark Kyle

2 Your social security number
    107 24 4260

Home address (number and street or rural route)
    52 Allendale Road

City or town, State, and ZIP code
    Dunwoody, Georgia 30338

3 Marital Status

☐ Single   ☒ Married
☐ Married, but withhold at higher Single rate

Note: If married, but legally separated, or spouse is a nonresident alien, check the Single box.

4 Total number of allowances you are claiming (from line F of the worksheet on page 2)   4

5 Additional amount, if any, you want deducted from each pay . . . . $

6 I claim exemption from withholding because (see instructions and check boxes below that apply):
  a ☐ Last year I did not owe any Federal income tax and had a right to a full refund of **ALL** income tax withheld, **AND**
  b ☐ This year I do not expect to owe any Federal income tax and expect to have a right to a full refund of **ALL**
      income tax withheld. If both a and b apply, enter "EXEMPT" here . . . . ▶
  c If you entered "EXEMPT" on line 6b, are you a full-time student? . . . . ☐ Yes ☐ No

Under the penalties of perjury, I certify that I am entitled to the number of withholding allowances claimed on this certificate, or if claiming exemption from withholding, that I am entitled to claim the exempt status.

Employee's signature ▶ *Ronald Mark Kyle*   Date ▶   January 1,   19 82

7 Employer's name and address (including ZIP code) (FOR EMPLOYER'S USE ONLY)
    Beacham-Moorhead Ace Hardware
    7360 Roswell Road
    Atlanta, Georgia 30328

8 Office code

9 Employer identification number
    14 162184

on the amount of earnings, frequency of the payroll period, and the number of *withholding allowances* claimed by the employee. Withholding allowances are claimed by the employee on an *Employee's Withholding Allowance Certificate (Form W-4)* filed with the employer. Ronald Kyle in the W-4 shown in Illustration 12.1 claims four withholding allowances, which usually means that he will claim four exemptions on his federal income tax return—one for himself, one for his wife, and one each for each of their two children. An *exemption* is a fixed amount ($1,000 in 1982) of income that is not subject to taxation.

If Kyle's gross pay for a week was $400, the amount of income tax withheld can be found on an IRS-provided *wage bracket withholding table* such as the one shown in Illustration 12.2. Both wages and withholding allowances claimed must be known to use the table. On the line labeled "$400—but less than $410" and in the column headed "4," the amount $49.40 is shown. This amount is the income tax to be withheld from Kyle's wages for this pay period.

Different tables are prepared for use with biweekly or monthly payroll periods and for single taxpayers. Note that the amount of income taxes withheld changes with the number of withholding allowances claimed. The table amounts are changed to reflect changes in federal income tax laws.

On or before January 31, after the end of each calendar year, an employer must furnish each employee with a four-copy *Wage and Tax Statement (Form W-2)* as shown in Illustration 12.3. This form provides wage and tax data needed to prepare the employee's personal federal and state income tax returns. One copy is sent by the employer to the Social Security Administration, which then transmits data contained on the form to the Internal Revenue Service. The other three copies of the W-2 are given to the employee. Of these, one

Illustration 12:2: Wage bracket withholding table

MARRIED Persons — WEEKLY Payroll Period

And the wages are—		And the number of withholding allowances claimed is—										
At least	But less than	0	1	2	3	4	5	6	7	8	9	10
		The amount of income tax to be withheld shall be—										
$310	$320	$46.20	$41.40	$37.50	$33.70	$29.80	$26.00	$22.50	$19.50	$16.40	$13.40	$10.70
320	330	48.70	43.80	39.50	35.70	31.80	28.00	24.10	21.10	18.00	14.90	12.10
330	340	51.20	46.30	41.50	37.70	33.80	30.00	26.10	22.70	19.60	16.50	13.50
340	350	53.70	48.80	44.00	39.70	35.80	32.00	28.10	24.30	21.20	18.10	15.00
350	360	56.20	51.30	46.50	41.70	37.80	34.00	30.10	26.30	22.80	19.70	16.60
360	370	58.70	53.80	49.00	44.20	39.80	36.00	32.10	28.30	24.40	21.30	18.20
370	380	61.20	56.30	51.50	46.70	41.90	38.00	34.10	30.30	26.40	22.90	19.80
380	390	63.70	58.80	54.00	49.20	44.40	40.00	36.10	32.30	28.40	24.60	21.40
390	400	66.20	61.30	56.50	51.70	46.90	42.10	38.10	34.30	30.40	26.60	23.00
400	410	68.70	63.80	59.00	54.20	49.40	44.60	40.10	36.30	32.40	28.60	24.80
410	420	71.20	66.30	61.50	56.70	51.90	47.10	42.30	38.30	34.40	30.60	26.80
420	430	73.70	68.80	64.00	59.20	54.40	49.60	44.80	40.30	36.40	32.60	28.80
430	440	76.20	71.30	66.50	61.70	56.90	52.10	47.30	42.50	38.40	34.60	30.80
440	450	78.70	73.80	69.00	64.20	59.40	54.60	49.80	45.00	40.40	36.60	32.80
450	460	81.60	76.30	71.50	66.70	61.90	57.10	52.30	47.50	42.70	38.60	34.80
460	470	84.70	78.80	74.00	69.20	64.40	59.60	54.80	50.00	45.20	40.60	36.80
470	480	87.80	81.90	76.50	71.70	66.90	62.10	57.30	52.50	47.70	42.90	38.80
480	490	90.90	85.00	79.00	74.20	69.40	64.60	59.80	55.00	50.20	45.40	40.80
490	500	94.00	88.10	82.10	76.70	71.90	67.10	62.30	57.50	52.70	47.90	43.10
500	510	97.10	91.20	85.20	79.20	74.40	69.60	64.80	60.00	55.20	50.40	45.60
510	520	100.20	94.30	88.30	82.30	76.90	72.10	67.30	62.50	57.70	52.90	48.10
520	530	103.30	97.40	91.40	85.40	79.50	74.60	69.80	65.00	60.20	55.40	50.60
530	540	106.40	100.50	94.50	88.50	82.60	77.10	72.30	67.50	62.70	57.90	53.10
540	550	109.50	103.60	97.60	91.60	85.70	79.70	74.80	70.00	65.20	60.40	55.60
550	560	112.60	106.70	100.70	94.70	88.80	82.80	77.30	72.50	67.70	62.90	58.10

Illustration 12.3: Wage and Tax Statement (Form W-2)

1 Control number 22222		For Official Use Only	
2 Employer's name, address, and ZIP code	3 Employer's identification number 14 162184		4 Employer's State number 33048
Beacham-Moorhead Ace Hardware 7360 Roswell Road Atlanta, Georgia 30328	5 Stat. employee ☐ Deceased ☐ Pension plan ☐ Legal rep. ☐ 942 emp. ☐ Sub-total ☐ Correction ☐ Void ☐		
	6 *		7 Advance EIC payment
8 Employee's social security number 107 24 4260	9 Federal income tax withheld $2,186.60	10 Wages, tips, other compensation $19,802.30	11 FICA tax withheld $1,316.85
12 Employee's name (first, middle, last) Ronald Mark Kyle	13 FICA wages $19,802.30		14 FICA tips
52 Allendale Road Dunwoody, Georgia 30338	16 Employer's use		
	17 State income tax $261.39	18 State wages, tips, etc. $19,802.30	19 Name of State Georgia
15 Employee's address and ZIP code	20 Local income tax	21 Local wages, tips, etc.	22 Name of locality

Form **W-2 Wage and Tax Statement 1981** ▼   Copy A For Social Security Administration   Department of the Treasury
* See Instructions for Forms W-2 and W-2P   Internal Revenue Service

copy is filed with the employee's federal income tax return, one is filed with the state income tax return, if any, and one is retained by the employee. The IRS uses data from the form in determining if the employee has filed a proper income tax return.

FICA (social security) taxes

The *FICA (social security) tax* was created by passage of the Federal Insurance Contributions Act in 1935. Persons who are currently working in jobs covered by the act must pay a certain percentage of their earnings (up to a maximum amount) into special trust funds. Employee contributions are matched by equal payments by employers. Money paid into the trust is used to finance retirement benefits and medical benefits (medicare) paid to persons and their families who are currently retired or disabled and who qualify for such benefits under the act. Full retirement benefits are available to workers who reach age 65; reduced benefits can be applied for at age 62. Additional voluntary medical insurance is available to persons age 65 and over.

The amount of FICA withholding for each employee for the year 1982 was 6.7 percent of the first $32,400 of wages. The rates and bases tentatively scheduled to go into effect for 1982–89 are shown in Illustration 12.4. As of this writing, a national commission has been considering recommending further significant changes in the base, rate, and/or benefits to make the social security fund financially sound.

Illustration 12.4:   FICA (social security) rates and bases

Year	Rate	Base
1982 . . .	6.70	$32,400
1983 . . .	6.70	35,700*
1984 . . .	6.70	38,700*
1985 . . .	7.05	42,600*
1986 . . .	7.15	46,200*
1987 . . .	7.15	49,800*
1988 . . .	7.15	53,400*
1989 . . .	7.15	56,700*

* These amounts are estimates since the actual increases will depend on the percentage increase in the average covered wage in the preceding calendar year. Congress may, of course, revise these at any time it chooses.

Other payroll deductions

Deductions, other than those for taxes, may be made from an employee's gross earnings. Some union contracts require the company to deduct union dues from gross pay as a convenience to employees and the union. Remittances are then made by the employer to the union.

Medical insurance and life insurance premiums may be deducted from gross pay. This is especially true when group insurance plans are in effect. The amounts deducted are paid directly to the insurance companies. Employees may also authorize payroll deductions for loan repayments to, or savings in, the employees' credit union. Pledges to charities such as the United Way Fund are often paid through payroll deductions.

Other deductions may also be made. For instance, deductions may be made for pension or retirement plans, where the employee is obligated to pay at least a portion of the cost. Other deductions might include those to pay for merchandise purchased by the employee from the employer or to accumulate funds to purchase U.S. Savings Bonds.

EMPLOYEE EARNINGS RECORD

Various federal laws affect employee payroll deductions and payroll taxes levied on the employer. These laws require that adequate payroll records be maintained by the employer for each employee. For this reason, employers maintain an *employee earnings record* for each employee showing information such as name, social security number, address, phone number, date employed, date of birth, marital status, number of withholding allowances claimed, pay rate, and present job within the company. For each pay period, the record also shows the number of hours worked, gross pay, deductions, and net pay. Cumulative gross pay during the year is included to indicate when the maximum amounts have been reached for FICA tax withholdings and unemployment taxes (which will be discussed later in the chapter). Illustration 12.5 shows an example of an employee earnings record.

PAYROLL JOURNAL

A *payroll journal* (Illustration 12.6) may be used to reduce the work involved in recording payroll. A payroll journal will contain a debit column for each category of salary expense, such as sales, delivery, and office. Credit columns will be included for withholdings made for various taxes and other deductions and Salaries Payable. These amounts all represent liabilities which must be paid either to agencies on the employees' behalf or to the employees. Except for items entered in the Other column, the payroll journal is posted by column totals only. Notice that a Check No. column is included to show which check was used to pay the Salaries Payable liability amounts.

Some companies maintain a payroll journal only as a memorandum record, which means no postings are made from it. In these firms, the entry for payroll would have to be made in the general journal. The entry made for the column totals shown in Illustration 12.6 would be as follows:

1982			
Mar. 27	Sales Salaries Expense	1,780.00	
	Delivery Salaries Expense	300.00	
	Office Salaries Expense	320.00	
	Employees' Federal Income Taxes Payable		327.20
	FICA Taxes Payable		160.80
	Employees' State Income Taxes Payable		42.53
	Employees' Medical Insurance Premiums Payable		90.00
	Salaries Payable		1,779.47
	To record the payroll for the week ending March 27.		

All accounts credited in the March 27 entry are current liabilities and will be reported on the balance sheet if not paid prior to the preparation of

Illustration 12.5: Employee earnings record

Name Ronald Mark Kyle
Address 52 Allendale Road
Dunwoody, Georgia 30338
Date of birth July 14, 1946
Date employed March 12, 1966

Social Security No. 107 24 4260
Sex: Male (x) Female ( )
Single ( ) Married (x)
Withholding allowances 4
Date terminated

Employee No. 6
Position Sales
Hourly pay rate $10.00
Spouse Barbara
Telephone No. 394-1776

1982 Period Ended	Total Hours	Earnings			Deductions					Payment		Cumulative Gross Earnings
		Regular	Overtime	Gross	Federal Income Tax	FICA Tax	State Income Tax	Medical Insurance	Other	Net Pay	Check No.	
Jan. 2	40	400.00		400.00	49.40	26.80	5.30	20.00		298.50	570	400.00
9	40	400.00		400.00	49.40	26.80	5.30	20.00		298.50	576	800.00
16	42	400.00	30.00	430.00	56.90	28.81	5.70	20.00		318.59	582	1,230.00

Illustration 12.6: Payroll journal

PAYROLL JOURNAL

Date Week Ended	Employee	Sales Salaries Expense	Delivery Salaries Expense	Office Salaries Expense	Deductions				Salaries Payable (Net Pay)	Check No.
					Federal Income Taxes Payable	FICA Taxes Payable	State Income Taxes Payable	Medical Insurance Premiums Payable		
Mar. 27	Ronald Kyle	400.00			49.40	26.80	5.30	20.00	298.50	642
	Rick Larson		300.00		35.50	20.10	3.01	10.00	231.39	643
	Lou Mason	500.00			74.40	33.50	12.25	20.00	359.85	644
	Arthur Niles	480.00			74.20	32.16	9.70	15.00	348.94	645
	Sally Wallen	400.00			54.20	26.80	6.85	15.00	297.15	646
	Betty Yates			320.00	39.50	21.44	5.42	10.00	243.64	647
		1,780.00	300.00	320.00	327.20	160.80	42.53	90.00	1,779.47	

financial statements. When the payroll is actually paid, the payment will be recorded in the cash disbursements journal as a debit to Salaries Payable and a credit to Cash of $1,779.47.

PAYROLL CHECKING ACCOUNT

The use of a *payroll checking account* is very common among firms with many employees who are paid by check. In general, a payroll checking account is used as follows. Before each payday, the payroll is prepared and recorded in a routine manner. One check is drawn on the firm's regular checking account for the net payroll amount. This check is recorded in the check register or cash disbursements journal and deposited in the payroll checking account.

Payroll checks are drawn on the payroll account and issued to employees. A payroll check register could be used to record the payroll checks. Some firms prefer merely to list the check numbers in the payroll journal (as was shown in Illustration 12.6). When the payroll checks are cashed by the employees, the payroll checking account is reduced to a zero balance or to an amount (such as $1,000) which was deposited when the account was originally opened. This balance would be available to cover payroll checks which might be issued between regular payroll dates for advances to employees or for employee termination pay. No formal journal entry is required when a payroll check is issued as a payroll advance (essentially a loan) or to pay termination pay. The advance will be deducted from the employee's net pay in the next payroll. The termination pay will be included as part of the earnings recorded in the next payroll.

As an illustration, the above procedures are applied to the payroll for the week ending on March 27 in Illustration 12.6. Payroll checks are issued on March 31.

Step 1. On March 29, the payroll for the week ending March 27 is prepared as shown in Illustration 12.6. Column totals are posted to the accounts represented in the column headings.

Step 2. On March 30, a check for $1,779.47 is drawn and recorded as a debit to Salaries Payable and a credit to Cash in the check register.

Step 3. No formal journal entry is required when the check is deposited in the payroll checking account.

Step 4. On March 31, payroll checks are issued. No formal entries are required. The payroll liability was debited for the check drawn and deposited in the payroll checking account. The individual paychecks could be recorded in a payroll check register. Alternatively, the payroll journal in Illustration 12.6 could serve as a check register.

The payroll for the week has been properly prepared, recorded, and paid with the completion of the above four steps. To complete the illustration, assume a payroll check is drawn on April 1 loaning Lou Mason $200. No formal entry is required. The $200 will be deducted in computing Mason's net pay in the next regular payroll.

The use of a payroll account has several advantages:

Illustration 12.7: Payroll check

Employee	Hours Worked	Rate per Hour	Regular Earnings	Extra for Overtime	Gross Earnings	Fed. Inc. Tax W/H	Soc. Sec. Tax	State Inc. Tax W/H	Hosp. Ins.	Net Pay
Ronald Mark Kyle	40	10.00	400.00		400.00	49.40	26.80	5.30	20.00	298.50

Retain this stub for your records – Detach before cashing check

ACE HARDWARE

BEACHAM-MOORHEAD ACE HARDWARE
7360 ROSWELL RD.
ATLANTA, GEORGIA 30328

335

March 30, 19 82   64-1240 / 611

PAY TO THE ORDER OF Ronald Mark Kyle $ 298.50

Two hundred ninety-eight and 50/100 -- DOLLARS

The CITIZENS and SOUTHERN BANK
NORTH SPRINGS OFFICE
ATLANTA, GEORGIA

George C. Beacham

FOR_____

⑈000335⑈ ⑆0611⑈1240⑆ 038 82 131⑈

1. A distinctive payroll check form may be used, with spaces provided on an attachment for gross earnings, various payroll deductions, and net cash paid. See Illustration 12.7.
2. Payroll checks, identifiable as such, are easily cashed by employees.
3. The work of reconciling the bank balances may be divided among employees. One check is drawn on the general bank account. The hundreds or thousands of payroll checks issued each payday are drawn on the payroll bank account. Occasionally, payroll checks are lost or negotiated many times before clearing the bank. Including these items in the payroll reconciliation simplifies the reconciliation of the general Cash account.
4. Only one authorization is prepared, calling for one check drawn on the general bank account; therefore, payroll checks are issued without separately prepared and signed authorizations.
5. Individual payroll checks need not be entered in the regular cash disbursements record; payroll check numbers are inserted in the payroll journal, and repetition of the entering of checks is avoided.

EMPLOYER PAYROLL TAXES

An employer is generally obligated to pay three taxes levied upon payrolls: FICA (social security) taxes and federal and state unemployment taxes.

FICA (social security) taxes

An employer is required to match the amount of FICA tax withheld from each employee's pay. Thus, total FICA tax in 1982 amounted to 13.4 percent of the first $32,400 of each employee's earnings; half was paid by the employee and half by the employer.

Federal unemployment tax

The Federal Unemployment Tax Act (FUTA) provides for a *federal unemployment tax* on employers based on employee salaries and wages. The tax helps finance a cooperative federal-state system of unemployment compensation. Unemployment benefits are paid to qualified unemployed persons by each of the states and territorial governments. State unemployment laws vary only in minor respects; the Federal Unemployment Tax Act sets forth certain minimum standards that must be met by each state.

The federal unemployment tax rate generally has varied between 3 and 3.5 percent. In 1983 and 1984, the rate is 3.5 percent of the first $7,000 of wages paid to each employee. This rate will be used for illustrative purposes. The Federal Unemployment Tax Act provides that in 1983 and 1984 employers may have a maximum credit of 2.7 percent against their federal unemployment tax for amounts which were paid to the state. This, in effect, makes the federal unemployment tax rate 0.8 percent (3.5 percent − 2.7 percent) on the first $7,000 of individual employee wages. Effective January 1, 1985, the rate will increase to 6.2 percent and the state credit will be increased to 5.4 percent.

State unemployment tax

The *state unemployment tax* generally is 2.7 percent of the first $7,000 of earnings per employee in 1983 and 1984. This rate and base will be used for illustrative purposes in the text. A *merit rate* can be gained by employers to reduce the state rate to as little as 0.5 percent in some states and even to zero in other states. A reduced rate is earned by employers with low turnover and few layoffs. Employers with lower merit rates can still deduct a credit of 2.7 percent on its federal unemployment tax rate.

Employer payroll taxes are usually recorded at the same time as the payroll to which they relate. For example, the employer's payroll taxes at 1983 rates on the March 27 payroll in Illustration 12.6 are recorded as follows:

```
Mar. 27  Payroll Taxes Expense ..................................  244.80
             FICA Taxes Payable ...............................            160.80
             State Unemployment Taxes Payable ...................             64.80
             Federal Unemployment Taxes Payable .................             19.20
         To record employer's payroll taxes.
```

Payroll Taxes Expense is debited for the total of the employer's three payroll taxes. The credit to FICA Taxes Payable is equal to the amount deducted from the employees' gross pay. Both the employer's and employees' FICA taxes can be credited to the same liability account, since both are payable at the same time to the same agency. The credits to the state and federal unemployment accounts are for 2.7 and 0.8 percent, respectively, of the $2,400 of gross pay for this payroll period. It was assumed that no employee had been paid more than $7,000 in the current year. Any earnings in excess of $7,000 would have been excluded from the computation, since unemployment taxes are levied only on the first $7,000 of annual income per employee.

REMITTING WITHHOLDING, TAXES, AND DEDUCTIONS

Within one month after the end of each calendar quarter, an employer must file an *Employer's Quarterly Federal Tax Return (Form 941)* with the Internal Revenue Service. This form reports the amount of FICA and income taxes withheld for each quarter. The employer reports (1) total wages subject to withholding, (2) federal income taxes withheld, (3) total wages subject to FICA tax, (4) amount of FICA taxes due (from both employer and employees), and (5) combined amount of income tax withheld and FICA taxes due. A similar form is required by states with state income tax laws.

Taxes withheld

For remittance purposes, federal income taxes withheld and both the employees' and employer's FICA taxes are combined. Generally, employers are required to deposit such taxes in a Federal Reserve Bank or an authorized commercial bank called a *federal depository bank*. When deposited, these amounts are credited to the Internal Revenue Service. Deposit requirements are quite detailed and depend upon the amount of taxes collected relative to the time elapsed since the last deposit. The more dollars of taxes which are collected, the more rapidly deposits must be made.

Taxes properly deposited are considered paid. The entry to record the deposit of $1,150 of federal income taxes withheld and $925 of FICA taxes is:

Employees' Federal Income Taxes Payable	1,150	
FICA Taxes Payable	925	
Cash		2,075
To record deposit of taxes withheld and employer FICA taxes.		

State and city income taxes must be withheld by employers in most states and in many cities. The procedures for withholding and the required remittances are usually modeled after federal income tax regulations. The entry to record payment of these taxes debits Employees' State (City) Income Taxes Payable and credits Cash.

Unemployment taxes

The amount of federal unemployment taxes to be deposited is determined quarterly. Upon reaching a certain amount, these taxes must be deposited in a federal depository bank. The entry to record the deposit of $125 of federal unemployment taxes is:

Federal Unemployment Taxes Payable	125	
Cash		125
To record deposit of federal unemployment taxes.		

Remittance requirements for state unemployment taxes vary from state to state. Quarterly reports and payments are usually required by the end of the month following the quarter. The entry to record the payment is a debit to State Unemployment Taxes Payable and a credit to Cash.

Illustration 12.8: Summary of payroll taxes

Tax	Paid by	Rate
FICA (social security)	Both employer and employee pay at current rate	6.70% of first $32,400 each employee earns annually*
Income tax	Employee	Varies with earnings and exemptions
State unemployment	Employer (usually)	2.7% of first $7,000 each employee earns annually†
Federal unemployment	Employer	0.8% of first $7,000 each employee earns annually‡

* This rate and base are for 1982. The base is expected to be $35,700 in 1983.
† Some states have a higher rate and/or base than this. Also, most states allow a reduction from the basic rate to firms with low labor turnover.
‡ The federal rate varies, but in this text it is assumed to be 3.5 percent. An allowance of 2.7 percent is granted for amounts paid to the state, thus reducing the effective rate to 0.8 percent.

Other payroll deductions

The remittance of other types of payroll deductions varies based on the agency or organization to which payment is to be made. Monthly payment is likely for union dues, medical insurance premiums, charitable contributions, and pension contributions.

A summary of the various payroll taxes appears in Illustration 12.8.

END OF PERIOD ACCRUALS

Adjusting entries are likely to be needed at year-end to accrue wages and employer's payroll taxes and vacation pay.

Wages and payroll taxes

The matching principle requires that accrued wages and employer payroll taxes on these wages be recorded at the end of the period. To illustrate, assume the Beacham Hardware Company accrues the following salaries and payroll taxes on December 31, 1984: sales salaries, $850; delivery salaries, $150; office salaries, $200; and payroll tax expense, $80.40. The required entries are:

Dec. 31	Sales Salaries Expense		850.00	
	Delivery Salaries Expense		150.00	
	Office Salaries Expense		200.00	
	Salaries Payable			1,200.00
	To accrue salaries.			
31	Payroll Taxes Expense		80.40	
	FICA Taxes Payable			80.40
	To accrue payroll taxes.			

Notice in the first entry, credits are not entered in separate liability accounts for payroll deductions. These deductions will be recorded when the payroll is paid since they are not withheld from the employees until the payroll is paid. The second entry records the employer's FICA taxes on $1,200 of salaries. The assumption was made that no employee had reached the maximum FICA limit; and, therefore, all accrued salaries were subject to FICA taxation. Accrued federal and state unemployment taxes were not included in the example. It was assumed that by year-end, all employees' earnings had surpassed the $7,000 maximum amount subject to taxation.

Some firms do not accrue employer's payroll taxes at year-end. The following reasons are given for this violation of the matching principle: (1) there is no legal liability for such taxes until the wages are paid, (2) such taxes do not vary much in amount from year to year, and (3) the amounts of such taxes are likely to be immaterial. A policy of not accruing payroll taxes is acceptable under these circumstances.

Vacation pay

Most employees in this country are entitled to annual vacations of from one to four weeks at full regular pay. The compensation received while on vacation is called *vacation pay*. Thus, the employer annually pays an employee for 52 weeks, but receives services for a lesser number of weeks.

A question immediately arises on how to account for this vacation pay. Should it be expensed when paid or should it be accrued over the period in which the employee works to earn the vacation? *FASB Statement No. 43*, "Accounting for Compensated Absences," requires the accrual of a liability for vacation pay if the following conditions are met:

1. The employer is obligated to pay as a result of services already received.
2. The employee's right to vacation pay does not depend upon continued performance of services.
3. It is probable the vacation pay will be paid.
4. The amount of vacation pay can be reasonably estimated.

Assume the Sun Company estimates that out of every 20 workdays employees will earn one day of vacation pay. As a result, vacation pay is to be accrued at a rate of 5 percent (1 day/20 days) of gross pay. The entry to accrue vacation pay on a $2,400 payroll is:

```
Vacation Pay Expense ($2,400 × 0.05) ........................   120.00
     Estimated Vacation Pay Payable ............................           120.00
   To accrue vacation pay.
```

Accruing vacation pay in this manner records the expense over the period in which it was earned rather than when it was paid, which results in better matching of expenses and revenues. A liability is also recorded for the vacation pay currently owed by the employer to the employees. Often employees must forfeit vacation pay earned if they leave the company before some minimum length of time, such as one year. If turnover of these employees is expected, the amount of the entry to accrue vacation pay should be reduced accordingly.

When vacation pay is paid, the estimated liability account is debited and various accounts are credited for taxes, other deductions, and cash payment. For example, an employee earning $500 per week is to be paid for three weeks' vacation. A payroll check is drawn for the net pay due and entered in the payroll journal. Using assumed deductions, the entry in general journal form would be:

Estimated Vacation Pay Payable	1,500.00	
Employees' Federal Income Taxes Payable		223.20
FICA Taxes Payable.......................................		100.50
Employees' Medical Insurance Premiums Payable		60.00
Salaries Payable (Cash)		1,116.30
To record payment of vacation pay.		

MORE EFFICIENT METHODS FOR PAYROLL ACCOUNTING

The payroll procedures described in this chapter are used effectively by many small businesses. In larger companies where there are many employees, a more efficient method is desirable.

One possibility for medium-sized businesses is to use what is called a *pegboard system of payroll accounting.* Such a system aligns the payroll check, the individual earnings record, and the payroll journal in such a way that all three are completed with one writing. Instead of having to record gross pay, deductions, and net pay three different times for each employee it is done only once. Of course, the forms must be designed so as to be completely compatible. Use of such a system can reduce clerical time dramatically.

Other methods for increasing efficiency are by utilizing a payroll machine to serve the same function as the pegboard system or to utilize a computer. As payrolls grow, the speed and efficiency of the computer make its use a virtual necessity. Many firms, including banks, offer computerized payroll processing services.

NEW TERMS INTRODUCED IN CHAPTER 12

Deductions from gross earnings
Required payroll deductions, such as federal and state income taxes withheld, FICA taxes withheld, and other deductions, such as medical insurance premiums and union dues.

Employee earnings record
A record maintained by an employer for each employee showing details such as hours worked, pay rate, gross earnings, payroll deductions, net pay, and personal biographical data (Illustration 12.5).

Employee Withholding Allowance Certificate (Form W-4)
The form on which an employee indicates the number of withholding allowances to be used in calculating federal (and state) income taxes to be withheld (Illustration 12.1).

Employer's Quarterly Federal Tax Return (Form 941)
A form used to report income and FICA taxes withheld and deposits of such taxes, if any.

Exemption
A fixed amount ($1,000 in 1982) of income not subject to federal income taxation.

Federal depository bank
A bank authorized to accept deposits of taxes by employers for credit to the Internal Revenue Service.

Federal (state) income taxes withheld
The amount of federal (state) income taxes deducted from employee earnings by the employer and remitted to the appropriate governmental agency under the pay-as-you-go system of government financing.

Federal unemployment tax
A tax of 3.5 percent levied upon the first $7,000 of wages paid per employee to help finance the joint federal-state system of unemployment compensation. A credit of up to 2.7 percent may be taken for amounts paid to a state unemployment fund, thus reducing the rate to 0.8 percent.

FICA (social security) tax
The amount deducted from an employee's wages and paid into a special fund used to pay retirement and other benefits. In 1982, the tax rate was 6.7 percent of the first $32,400 of wages paid each employee. The employer pays a like amount.

Gross earnings
Total pay or compensation of an employee, including regular pay and overtime premium.

Merit rate
A reduction in the state unemployment tax rate below 2.7 percent as a reward for low turnover and few layoffs.

Minimum wage
Lowest hourly compensation an employer can pay an employee as required by the Wages and Hours Law.

Payroll checking account
A separate checking account used only for payroll checks. Each payday an amount is transferred from the general Cash account to cover the amount of the payroll checks. One of the purposes is to keep the "clutter" of outstanding payroll checks from making more complex the reconciliation of the general Cash account.

Payroll journal
A formal record showing the details of each payroll including for each employee the gross pay, deductions, net pay, and check number. It may be used as a book of original entry (in which case postings to accounts would be made from it), or it may be only a memorandum record.

Pegboard system of payroll accounting
A system which aligns the payroll check, the indi-
vidual earnings record, and the payroll journal in such a way that all three are completed simultaneously (with one writing).

Social security tax
See FICA tax.

State unemployment tax
A tax of 2.7 percent (typically) on the first $7,000 of earnings per employee per year to finance unemployment benefits. A **merit rate** for low labor turnover may reduce the rate to less than 2.7 percent.

Withholding allowances
A means of adjusting income taxes withheld from employee periodic earnings for exemptions that will be claimed on the income tax return.

Timecard
A form used to show the time an employee reports to and leaves work.

Vacation pay
Compensation earned by employees in the periods worked prior to a period of absence from work; such compensation is paid to employees while on vacation.

Wage and Tax Statement (Form W-2)
A form which the employer must furnish to each employee after the end of the year showing gross wages, amounts withheld, and net pay. It is used by the employee in preparing his or her personal federal income tax return (Illustration 12.2).

Wage bracket withholding table
A table supplied by the IRS which shows the amount of income tax to be withheld given the wage and number of withholding allowances claimed (Illustration 12.3).

Wages and Hours Law (Fair Labor Standards Act)
Requires that employees engaged in interstate commerce be paid at least 1½ times their normal rate for hours worked in excess of 40 hours per week. It also requires that at least the minimum wage be paid.

DEMONSTRATION PROBLEM

The Fargo Company employs four persons (all are married) and pays them weekly salaries as shown below. The number of exemptions and weekly deductions for medical insurance for each employee are also given.

	Weekly salary	Withholding allowances	Medical insurance	Position
Robbin Lucia	$375	3	15	Salesperson
Jo Ann Morgan	400	2	15	Salesperson
Robert Pearson	390	4	20	Salesperson
John Travis	310	2	15	Office manager

Each employee has 5 percent withheld for state income tax and 8 percent withheld for the retirement plan. Use the wage bracket withholding table in Illustration 12.2 to determine the federal income taxes to be withheld.

Required:

a. Prepare the payroll journal for the week ending January 8, 1983, using headings which will accomplish the purpose. (The check numbers used are 604–7.) Use 7 percent rate for FICA taxes.

b. Assuming that the payroll journal is a memorandum record only, prepare the general journal entry to record the payroll.

c. Prepare the entry to transfer funds from general cash to the special payroll checking account.

d. Prepare the entry to record the employer's payroll taxes using 7 percent for FICA taxes and other rates given in this chapter. (In actual practice, this often is done only at the end of the month.)

e. Prepare the entry to record payment on January 14 of the federal income taxes and FICA taxes due to be paid to the federal government. (In actual practice, payment often is made at various times, depending on the amounts involved.)

Solution to demonstration problem

a.

PAYROLL JOURNAL

Date Week Ended	Employee	Office Salaries Expense	Sales Salaries Expense	Deductions					Salaries Payable (Net Pay)	Check No.
				Federal Income Taxes Payable	FICA Taxes Payable	State Income Taxes Payable	Medical Insurance Premiums Payable	Retirement Plan		
1983 Jan. 8	Robbin Lucia		375.00	46.70	26.25	18.75	15.00	30.00	238.30	604
	Jo Ann Morgan		400.00	59.00	28.00	20.00	15.00	32.00	246.00	605
	Robert Pearson		390.00	46.90	27.30	19.50	20.00	31.20	245.10	606
	John Travis	310.00		37.50	21.70	15.50	15.00	24.80	195.50	607
		310.00	1,165.00	190.10	103.25	73.75	65.00	118.00	924.90	

b.

```
1983
Jan.  8   Office Salaries Expense ..............................      310.00
          Sales Salaries Expense ..............................    1,165.00
                Employees' Federal Income Taxes Payable ..........              190.10
                FICA Taxes Payable ...............................              103.25
                Employees' State Income Taxes Payable ............               73.75
                Employees' Medical Insurance Premiums Payable ......             65.00
                Employees' Retirement Plan Premiums Payable ........            118.00
                Salaries Payable .................................              924.90
          To record the payroll for the week ending January 8.
```

c.

```
1983
Jan.  8   Salaries Payable ...................................      924.90
                Cash .........................................              924.90
          To record the transfer of funds to cover the January 8 payroll.
```

d.

```
1983
Jan.  8   Payroll Taxes Expense ..............................      154.88
                FICA Taxes Payable ...........................              103.25
                State Unemployment Taxes Payable .................           39.83
                Federal Unemployment Taxes Payable ..............            11.80
          To record payroll taxes on the January 8 payroll.
```

e.

```
1983
Jan. 14   Employees' Federal Income Taxes Payable ..............      190.10
          FICA Taxes Payable..................................      206.50
                Cash .........................................              396.60
          To record payment of federal income tax withheld and FICA
          taxes payable from the January 8 payroll.
```

QUESTIONS

1. Describe some of the purposes of a payroll accounting system.

2. List the various functions regarding payroll and give a method for establishing internal control over these functions.

3. What requirements does the Wages and Hours Law place on employers? Why should accurate records be maintained as to hours worked by employees?

4. List the possible deductions from gross pay which are common.

5. What is the purpose of the Employee's Withholding Allowance Certificate (Form W-4)?

6. What purposes does the Wage and Tax Statement (Form W-2) serve?

7. Against which parties are FICA taxes levied and in what amounts?

8. What is the purpose of the Employer's Quarterly Federal Tax Return (Form 941)?

9. What are the federal and state rates for unemployment tax? What is a merit rate and what effect does it have on the credit granted by the federal government for amounts paid to the state?

10. Why should an employer maintain an earnings record for each employee?

11. Under what conditions would the use of a special payroll checking account be desirable? How does such an account operate?

12. What are the arguments for and against accruing employer's payroll taxes at the end of the accounting period?

13. Under what conditions should an employer accrue a liability for future vacation pay earned by employees in the current accounting period?

EXERCISES

E–1. The Gomez Company employs four persons, each of whom is married, whose weekly wages and withholding allowances are:

	Wages	Withholding allowances
John Sampson	$350	5
Thomas McPherson	520	3
John Lauber	310	4
Robert Conrad	410	2

Using Illustration 12.2, determine the correct amount to withhold for federal income taxes per week for each employee.

E–2. Using the data in Exercise E–1, calculate in which one of the weekly payroll periods the Gomez Company can stop recording state and federal unemployment taxes for each one of the employees. Also, compute the annual amount of such taxes the company will incur on the wages paid to these employees assuming the same weekly wages were earned by each employee in each week.

E–3. Using the data in Exercise E–1 and the rate and base for 1983, compute the amount of FICA taxes the employer will withhold from each employee for the entire year, assuming the same weekly wage was paid each week. Also, calculate the employer's FICA tax expense for the year.

E–4. The gross payroll for salaries of the Mateer Corporation is $1,600. Federal income taxes withheld amount to $325. The employees' FICA taxes withheld amount to $112. Give the entry to record the payroll at the time of payment, assuming no prior recording of salaries.

E–5. Rubin Company is trying to decide whether to hire four workers at $40,000 each per year, or 16 workers on a part-time basis at $10,000 each per year. Using the rates given in the chapter for 1983, calculate the difference in the employer's payroll tax expense for a year under the two alternatives.

E–6. The D. Williams Company operates in a state that has a 2.7 percent unemployment tax rate. Due to a record of stable employment, the company has earned a merit rate of 2.1 percent. Total wages on which it incurred federal and state unemployment taxes for March were $12,000. Prepare the entry to record federal and state unemployment taxes for the month.

E–7. At the end of December 1983, the M. Harris Company had accrued wages of $1,000 ($500 for sales salaries, $300 for office salaries, and $200 for maintenance wages). The company accrues payroll taxes on accrued salaries and wages. Assume that no employee has earnings over $30,000 (including the above accrued wages) and that unemployment taxes accrue only on the maintenance wages. Prepare the necessary adjusting entries to accrue wages and payroll taxes.

E–8.   Bob Barnes worked 44 hours last week, 4 of which are considered overtime hours. His pay rate for regular hours is $8 per hour. His weekly pay is subject to federal income tax withholding and to FICA tax withholding at a rate of 6.7 percent. Bob is married and claims three withholding allowances. Calculate Bob's gross pay, payroll deductions, and net pay, using Illustration 12.2 to compute federal income taxes withheld.

E–9.   Adams Company estimated its accrued vacation pay liability at the end of the year at $3,500. Bob Barnes (Exercise E–8) took one week of vacation in the following year for which he was paid one week's regular earnings of 40 hours at $8 per hour. Give the entry for the vacation pay accrual. Also, give the entry to record the payment of a week's vacation pay to Bob Barnes.

PROBLEMS, SERIES A

P12–1–A.   The following data are available for use in computing the net pay of the employees for a certain week:

1. Amy is guaranteed a minimum weekly salary of $400 plus overtime for hours worked in excess of 40 per week. She is married and claims three withholding allowances. She worked 46 hours in the week, including 6 hours of overtime.
2. Bob is paid $12 per hour, is married, and claims two withholding allowances. He worked 42 hours during the week, including 2 hours of overtime.
3. Carl is paid $2 for each unit completed. He is married and claims four withholding allowances. During the week, he completed 220 units while working 44 hours.

         The gross pay of each of these employees is subject to federal income tax withholding (use Illustration 12.2), FICA tax withholding at the rate of 6.7 percent, and withholding for union dues of $2 per week.

Required:

         a. Compute the regular pay, the overtime premium, if any, and the net pay for each of the above employees.

         b. Prepare journal entries to record the payroll and the employer's payroll taxes, using rates of 2.7 percent and 0.8 percent for state and federal unemployment taxes.

P12–2–A.   The Smith Company has an annual payroll of $680,000. There are 10 employees who earned $38,000 each and 40 part-time employees, each of whom earned an equal share of the remaining payroll.

Required:

         a. What are the total employee and employer portions of the FICA tax for the year? (Use a 6.7 percent rate and $35,700 maximum base.)

         b. What are the amounts of federal and state unemployment tax per year assuming that the federal rate is 0.8 percent and the state rate is 2.7 percent for this company?

         c. What is the total expense incurred by the employer for these items?

         d. Compute the company's total payroll tax expense assuming it has earned a merit rate of 2.1 percent from the state.

P12–3–A.   First Company uses a payroll checking account, with a $1,000 balance. This balance is used for payroll advances and to pay employees whose services are terminated between payroll payment dates. Following are selected transactions of the First Company during 1983:

Transactions:

June 15   Payroll department determines that the payroll and payroll deductions for the first half of the month of June are:

Office salaries	$25,000
Sales salaries and commissions	41,000
Sales office salaries	20,000
	$86,000

Payroll deductions:		
Federal income taxes withheld	$11,000	
FICA taxes withheld	2,000	
Community Fund contributions withheld	3,000	16,000
Net payroll		$70,000

17   A check in the amount of the net payroll is drawn on the general checking account and deposited in the payroll checking account.

20   Payroll checks are issued.

24   One employee's services are terminated. The salary of this office employee for the partial period is $300, and the only deduction is for $45 of income taxes to be withheld. A payroll check is issued.

Required:

    a.   Assume that a payroll journal was prepared for the June 15 payroll and prepare entries in general journal form for those transactions on June 15, 17, 20, and 24 that require formal journal entries. For those dates that do not require a formal entry, state the accounting actions that would be taken.

    b.   Assume that the federal income taxes withheld and the FICA taxes owed are deposited on June 23 in a federal depository bank. Prepare the required entry to record the employer's FICA taxes and then prepare the entry for the depositing of the taxes.

P12–4–A.   The Tasty Bakery employs five persons. Their names, weekly wages, number of withholding allowances claimed, and medical insurance premiums withheld are:

Employee	Weekly wage	No. of withholding allowances	Medical insurance premiums	Position
Marge Authier	$540	3	$15	Office manager
Alice Cummings	310	2	10	Bakery
Becky Hooten	400	2	10	Bakery
Betty McDowell	460	3	15	Bakery
Louetta Nowlin	310	3	15	Office clerk

Required:

    a.   Prepare a payroll journal with the following headings: Date Week Ended, Employee, Office Salaries Expense, Bakery Salaries Expense, Federal Income Taxes Payable, FICA Taxes Payable, State Income Taxes Payable, Medical Insurance Premiums Payable, Salaries Payable, and Check No.

    b.   Assuming each employee is married, that the state income tax rate is 5 percent, and that the FICA tax rate is 7 percent, enter the payroll for the week ended March 12 in the payroll journal. Use Illustration 12.2 for federal income taxes withheld.

    c.   Prepare the journal entry to record the transfer of funds to the payroll checking account on March 16. Checks with numbers 210–214 are issued today.

    d.   Prepare the journal entry to record the employer's social security and unemployment taxes. Marge Authier is the only employee who has earned more than $7,000 prior to this payroll. Use 1983 rates for unemployment taxes.

     e. Using T-accounts, post the totals of the payroll journal and the entries made in (*c*) and (*d*).

P12–5–A.   ***Part I.***   The Sundell Company operates an indoor tennis complex. At the end of 1984, the company has accrued wages of $18,000 ($9,000 for professional tennis staff, $5,000 for administrative staff, and $4,000 for maintenance personnel). Of these wages, $12,000 are subject to FICA taxes and $5,000 are subject to employment taxes.

Required:

    a. Describe two alternative ways in which the company can prepare the adjusting entry. Explain why these alternatives exist.

    b. Prepare the adjusting entries under the two alternatives. (Use a 7 percent rate for social security tax.)

    Part II.   On December 31, 1984, Downey Company estimates that its hourly employees have earned an average of one week of paid vacation. The company has 20 employees who each have weekly regular gross earnings of $400. Downey also estimates that 5 percent of the employees will leave before they have been with the company a full year, thus forfeiting their vacation benefits.

    Assume that in 1985, a payroll check in the amount of $315 is issued to an employee as payment of $420 of vacation pay. Withholdings were: FICA taxes, $29.40; and federal income taxes, $75.60.

Required:

    a. Prepare an adjusting entry to accrue Downey's annual vacation pay expense at the end of 1984.

    b. Prepare in general journal form the entry to record the issuance of the $315 check.

PROBLEMS, SERIES B

P12–1–B.   The following data are available for use in preparing the payroll for a certain week:

1. Dave is guaranteed a weekly salary of $320 plus overtime for hours worked in excess of 40 per week. He is married, but claims no withholding allowances. He worked 48 hours during the week.
2. Edie is paid $7.50 per hour. She is married and claims three withholding allowances. She worked 48 hours this week, including 8 hours of overtime.
3. Fred is paid $0.10 per unit completed. He is married and claims two withholding allowances. He worked 43 hours this week and completed 4,386 units.

Required:

    a. Compute the regular pay, the overtime premium, and the net pay for each of the above employees.

    b. Prepare the journal entry to record the payroll, including the withholdings for federal income taxes (Illustration 12.2), FICA taxes at a rate of 6.7 percent, $20 contributed by Edie to United Way, and $40 to repay a payroll advance given to Fred and recorded in Loans to Employees. Also prepare the journal entry to record the employer's state and federal unemployment taxes at the typical rates of 2.7 percent and 0.8 percent.

P12–2–B.

Required:

    a. The Daly Company has 36 employees and a payroll of $451,600: 8 employees earned $40,000 each, and 28 employees each earned an equal share of the remaining payroll. What is the 1983 FICA tax (1) for the employees and (2) for the employer? (Use a 6.7 percent rate and $35,700 maximum base.)

    b. What is the amount of the federal and state unemployment tax per year assuming a federal rate of 0.8 percent and a state rate of 2.7 percent for this employer?

    c. Which of the preceding items would constitute expenses on the records of the Daly Company?

    d. Compute the company's 1983 payroll tax expense assuming it has earned a merit rate from the state of 1.6 percent.

P12–3–B. West Company employs a special checking account upon which its payroll checks are drawn. Employees are paid on the 5th and the 20th of each month for the salaries earned in the preceding half-month. The following transactions occur in December:

Transactions:

1. A check for $1,000 is drawn and deposited in the payroll checking account to cover advances to employees and checks issued to employees whose services are terminated.
2. The payroll for the last half of November consists of the following:

Gross wages of employees		$26,200
Less: Income taxes withheld	$3,500	
FICA taxes withheld	400	3,900
Net payroll		$22,300

3. On December 4, a check is drawn in the amount of the net payroll and deposited in the payroll checking account.
4. Payroll checks aggregating the amount of the net payroll are issued to employees.
5. A payroll check in the amount of $40 is issued to John Jackson as an advance on the wages he will be receiving on December 20.
6. The federal income taxes withheld and the FICA taxes of both the employees and the employer are deposited in a federal depository bank.

Required:

    Assume that the company uses a payroll journal to record its payroll. Prepare in general journal form the entries needed for the six numbered items above. Assume in No. 2 that an entry is to be made for the employer's FICA taxes and that the company is not subject to further unemployment taxation. Where no formal entry is needed, describe the accounting action that would be taken.

P12–4–B. The Bently Company employs six persons in operations. Garcha and Harbaugh are office employees, the rest are store employees. The names of the employees, their weekly wages, and withholding allowances claimed (each is married) are:

Employee	Weekly wage	Withholding allowances
Bikram Garcha	$550	4
Norman Harbaugh	450	2
Fred Massey	400	3
Becky Rogers	400	3
Marc Schaefer	450	2
Paula Stephan	320	5

State income taxes are withheld at a 5 percent of gross pay rate.

Required:

   a. Prepare a payroll journal with columns headed: Date Week Ended, Employee, Office Salaries Expense, Store Salaries Expense, Federal Income Taxes Payable, FICA Taxes Payable, State Income Taxes Payable, Salaries Payable, and Check No.

   b. Using the withholding table in Illustration 12.2 and assuming FICA taxes are levied at a 7 percent rate, enter the payroll data for the week ended March 12 in the payroll journal.

   c. Assuming the payroll journal is used only as a memorandum record, prepare the journal entry to record the payroll.

   d. Prepare the entry to record the employer's payroll taxes assuming that only the wages of Garcha exceeded $7,000 before this payroll. No employee's wages reached $7,000 as a result of this payroll. Use 1983 unemployment tax rates.

   e. Prepare the entry to record the transfer of funds to the payroll checking account on March 14. Payroll checks numbered 405–10 were issued today.

P12–5–B.   ***Part I.***   At the end of 1984, the Thornton Company had $30,000 of accrued wages ($15,000 sales salaries, $9,000 delivery wages, and $6,000 office salaries). Of this total, $25,000 are subject to social security tax and $8,000 are subject to unemployment taxes.

Required:

   a. Describe the two alternatives the company may follow in making adjusting entries and explain why these alternatives exist.

   b. Prepare the adjusting entry(ies) under the two alternatives, using a 7 percent rate for social security taxes.

   Part II.   On December 31, 1984, Barlow Company estimated that its hourly employees earned an average of two weeks of paid vacation for the 50 weeks worked. The company has 40 employees earning average weekly regular gross earnings of $500. Barlow also estimates that 6 percent of the employees will leave before they have been with the company a full year, thus forfeiting their vacation benefits.

   On June 1, 1985, a payroll check for $430 is issued to an employee as payment of $520 of vacation pay. Withholdings were: FICA taxes, $36.40; and federal income taxes, $53.60.

Required:

   a. Prepare an adjusting entry to accrue Barlow's annual vacation pay expense at the end of 1984.

   b. Prepare in general journal form the entry to record the issuance of the $430 check.

BUSINESS DECISION PROBLEM 12–1

   Peter Cote operates a fine restaurant and employs 15 employees. He is interested in food preparation, supervision of waiters, and customer relations. He has little aptitude for record keeping. As a result, he hired Michael Robbins to do all of the paper work for the business. This includes preparing the payroll, keeping payroll records, signing the payroll checks, distributing the payroll checks, and reconciling the bank account. The payroll checks are written on the general Cash account rather than a special payroll checking account.

Business seems to be good, but the cash position keeps getting tighter. Wages expense seems to be somewhat higher than Mr. Cote believes it should be. Mr. Robbins assures Mr. Cote that all is well regarding payroll. Mr. Cote suspects that something is wrong regarding the payroll function.

Required:

a. What could be wrong?

b. What would you recommend to Mr. Cote to correct the situation?

BUSINESS DECISION PROBLEM 12–2

For a number of years Rogers Company has provided steady, full-time jobs for 200 employees. Its employees currently are paid $12 per hour, and each earns over $7,000 per year. The employee's gross pay is subject to federal unemployment taxes at a 0.8 percent rate, and to state unemployment taxes at a merit rate of 0.5 percent.

The company has received an order for a customized version of one of its products. The order appears to be quite profitable and seems likely to be repeated for a number of years. Two alternative ways exist to fill the order:

1. Regular employees can work overtime at a pay rate 1½ times their regular rate. It is estimated that 100 employees would work eight hours a day for five consecutive Saturdays to fill the order.

2. Twenty persons could be hired to work six 40-hour weeks at $10 per hour. Because they are less skilled, these temporary employees will need more time than regular employees to fill the order.

All wages in either case will be subject to FICA taxes at a 7 percent rate. If new employees are hired for the job and then laid off, the company will lose its merit rating for state unemployment taxes. Use 1983 unemployment tax rates.

Required:

State which alternative should be used by the company to fill the order. Explain how you arrived at your decision.

Part Four

Accounting theory and partnerships

Chapter 13
Accounting theory; inflation accounting

Chapter 14
Partnership accounting

Chapter 13

Accounting theory;
inflation accounting

CHAPTER GOALS

After study of this chapter, you should be able to:

1. Discuss the basic assumptions, principles, and modifying conventions of accounting.
2. Describe how inflation affects information presented in conventional financial statements.
3. Apply the two basic approaches to income statement adjustment under inflationary conditions.
4. Discuss how constant dollar and current cost information may be significant to users of financial statements.
5. Describe the Conceptual Framework Project of the Financial Accounting Standard Board (covered in the Appendix).
6. Define and use correctly the new terms in the glossary.

The preceding chapters have discussed and illustrated the accounting cycle. Only brief mention has been made of the theory underlying the procedures which have been used. *Accounting theory* is a "set of basic concepts and assumptions and related principles that explain and guide the accountant's actions in identifying, measuring, and communicating economic information."[1] The first part of this chapter discusses the theory which underlies the preparation of financial statements. The second part of the chapter discusses the important topic of inflation accounting.

UNDERLYING ASSUMPTIONS OR CONCEPTS

The underlying assumptions or basic concepts of accounting mentioned in Chapter 1 are discussed more fully in this chapter. Other concepts are also introduced, discussed, and illustrated.

Entity

An *entity* is a specific unit, such as a business, for which accounting information is gathered. An entity has an existence apart from its owners, creditors, employees, and other interested parties. For a single proprietorship, the business, not the individual, is the accounting entity. Financial statements must identify the entity for which they are prepared; and their content must be limited to reporting the activities, resources, and obligations of that entity.

Going concern (continuity)

The *going-concern* (*continuity*) assumption states that an entity will continue to operate indefinitely unless there is evidence that the entity will terminate. An entity is terminated by ceasing business operations and selling off the assets. The process of termination is called *liquidation.* If liquidation appears likely, the going-concern assumption can no longer be used.

The going-concern assumption often is used to justify the use of costs, rather than market values, in measuring assets. Market values are thought to be of little or no significance to an entity that intends to use rather than sell its assets. On the other hand, if an entity is to be liquidated, market values should be used to report assets.

The going-concern assumption permits the accountant to record certain items as assets. For example, printed advertising matter may be on hand to be used to promote a special sale next month and may have little, if any, value to anyone but its owner. Prepaid advertising is recorded as an asset because its owner is expected to continue operating long enough to benefit from it.

---

[1] American Accounting Association, *A Statement of Basic Accounting Theory* (Sarasota, Fla., 1966), pp. 1–2.

Money measurement

Accounting measurements normally will be expressed in money terms. *Money measurement* means quantification in terms of a monetary unit of measurement, such as the dollar, instead of quantification in terms of physical or other units of measurement—feet, inches, grams, and so on. The unit of measure (the dollar in the United States) is identified in the financial statements.

The monetary unit, the dollar, also provides accountants with a common unit of measure in reporting upon economic activity. Without using the monetary unit, it would be impossible to add buildings, equipment, and inventory on a balance sheet. Even if prepared, such a statement would probably be of little value to anyone.

Stable dollar. The *stable dollar* assumption is that fluctuations in the value of the dollar are insignificant and may, therefore, be ignored. Use of the stable dollar assumption means that a portion of the cost of a building acquired in 1954 is deducted as depreciation, without adjustment for change in the value of the dollar, from revenues earned in 1984 in arriving at the net income for 1984. The 1954 and 1984 dollars are treated as equal units of measure, even though substantial price inflation has occurred over the 30-year period. The inflation rate experienced since 1970 has created interest in the problem of adjusting financial statements for changes in the general price level. Inflation accounting will be discussed in more detail later in this chapter.

Periodicity (time periods)

The *periodicity* (*time periods*) assumption is that an entity's life can be subdivided into time periods for purposes of reporting on its economic activities. Accountants subdivide the life of an entity into periods and prepare reports on the activities of those periods to provide useful and timely financial information to investors and creditors. The reports cover relatively short periods of time. The time periods usually are of equal length so that valid comparisons can be made of a company's performance from period to period. The length of the period must be stated in the financial statements.

Accrual basis. Financial statements better reflect the financial status and operations of a firm when prepared under the accrual basis of accounting. Under the accrual basis, revenues are recorded when services are rendered or products are sold and delivered. Expenses are recorded as incurred.

Approximation and judgment. Many accounting measurements are estimates. To provide periodic financial information, estimates must often be made of such things as expected uncollectible accounts and useful lives of depreciable assets. Uncertainty about future events prevents precise measurement and makes estimates necessary. Estimates are often reasonably accurate because they are made by an informed accountant. The need to exercise judgment prevents accountants from stating a set of inflexible rules, such as depreciate all trucks over three years regardless of their useful lives.

General purpose financial statements

Results of the financial accounting process are presented in general purpose financial statements. General purpose financial statements are presented to external parties and top-level internal managers. The statements try to meet the common needs of these and other users. Special purpose financial information can be developed from accounting records. For example, some information needed by management to decide whether to purchase a new computer can be obtained from the accounting records rather than the financial statements.

Substance over form

In some instances, the economic substance of a transaction may conflict with its legal form. A contract which is legally a lease may, in fact, be equivalent to a purchase. For example, a company may have a three-year contract to lease (rent) an auto at a stated monthly rental fee. At the end of the lease period, upon the payment of a nominal sum (say, $1), the company will receive title to the auto. The economic substance of this transaction is to purchase rather than lease the auto. The accountant should always record the economic substance of a transaction rather than be guided by the legal form of the transaction.

Consistency

Consistency generally requires a company to use the same accounting principles and reporting practices through time; this concept bars indiscriminate switching of principles or methods, such as changing depreciation methods every year. Consistency does not bar a change in principles if the information needs of users are better served by the change. When a change in principles is made, disclosure of the change, reasons for the change, and its effect on net income, if significant, are required.

Other assumptions or concepts

The *transactions approach* is used in financial accounting. Under the transactions approach, every transaction has a *dual* effect upon each party engaging in it. This assumption gives rise to the double-entry form of accounting.

Also, financial statements are *fundamentally related* and articulate (interact) with each other. For example, the amount of net income is carried from the income statement to complete the statement of owner's equity. The ending balance on the statement of owner's equity is carried to the balance sheet to bring total assets and total equities into balance.

MEASUREMENT IN ACCOUNTING

Accounting is often defined as a measurement process. The accountant seeks to measure the assets, liabilities, and owner's equity of an accounting entity. Changes which occur in assets, liabilities, and owner's equity are also measured and the effects of these changes are assigned to particular time periods to find net income of the accounting entity.

Measuring assets

Cash is measured at its specified amount. Claims to cash, such as notes and accounts receivable, are measured at their expected cash inflows, taking into consideration possible uncollectibles. Inventories, prepaid expenses, plant assets, and intangibles are measured at their costs at time of acquisition.

Measuring liabilities

Liabilities are measured in terms of the cash that will be paid or the value of services that will be performed to satisfy the liabilities.

Measuring changes in assets and liabilities

Some changes in assets and liabilities are easily measured by the accountant. Such changes include the exchange of one asset for another of equal value, acquisition of an asset on credit, and payment of a liability. Other changes in assets and liabilities are more difficult to measure because they affect net income and owner's equity. The accountant must determine when a change has taken place and the amount of the change. These decisions involve matching revenues and expenses and are guided by the principles discussed below.

THE MAJOR PRINCIPLES

Generally accepted accounting principles are presented and discussed below. The effects of these principles have been mentioned previously; the purpose here is to expand the coverage.

The exchange price (or cost) principle

The *exchange price* (*or cost*) *principle* is that transfers of resources are recorded at prices agreed upon by the parties to the exchange at the time of exchange. Thus, for any firm, this exchange price principle determines (1) what goes into the accounting system—transaction data; (2) when it is recorded—at the time of exchange; and (3) the amounts—exchange prices— at which assets, liabilities, owner's equity, revenues, and expenses are recorded. As applied to certain assets, this principle is often called the *cost principle,* meaning that initially assets are recorded at historical cost. *Historical cost* is the amount paid or fair value of liability incurred or other resource surrendered to acquire an asset. Terminology such as exchange price principle is preferred to cost principle because it seems inappropriate to refer to liabilities, owner's equity, and assets such as cash and accounts receivable as being measured in terms of cost.

The matching principle

Using the *matching principle,* net income of a period is determined by associating or relating revenues earned in a period with expenses incurred to generate the revenues. The logic underlying this principle is that whenever economic resources are used, someone will want to know what was accomplished and at what cost. Every evaluation of economic activity will involve matching benefit with sacrifice. The application of the matching principle is discussed and illustrated below.

Revenue recognition

Revenue is the inflow of assets from the sale of goods and services to customers. It is measured by the amount of cash expected to be received from the customer. A question arises as to when this revenue should be recorded (credited to a revenue account). The general answer given by the *revenue recognition principle* is that the revenue should be *earned* and *realized* before it is recognized (recorded).

The earning of revenue. All activities undertaken by a firm to create revenues are part of the earning process. The actual receipt of cash from a customer may have been preceded by many activities including (1) placing advertisements, (2) calling on the customer several times, (3) submitting samples, (4) acquiring or manufacturing goods, and (5) delivering goods. Costs were incurred for these activities. Revenue actually was being earned by these activities, even though in most instances accountants do not recognize revenue until time of sale because of the requirement that revenue be substantially earned before it is recognized (recorded). This requirement is referred to as the *earning principle.*

The realization of revenue. Under the *realization principle,* revenue is recognized only after the seller acquires the right to receive payment from the buyer. The seller acquires the right to receive payment from the buyer at time of sale for merchandise transactions and when services have been performed in service transactions. Legally, a sale of merchandise occurs when title to the goods passes to the buyer. As a practical matter, accountants generally record revenue when goods are delivered.

The advantages of recognizing revenue at time of sale are that (1) delivery of goods is an observable event; (2) revenue is measurable; (3) risk of loss due to price decline or destruction of the goods has passed to the buyer; (4) revenue has been earned, or substantially so; and (5) because the revenue has been earned, expenses and net income can be determined. As discussed below, the disadvantage of recognizing revenue at time of sale is that the revenue might not be recorded in the period in which most of the activity creating it occurred.

Exceptions to the realization principle

The following examples illustrate instances in which practical considerations may cause accountants to vary the point of revenue recognition from point of sale. These examples illustrate the effect that the business environment has on the development of accounting principles and standards.

Cash collection as point of revenue recognition. Some small firms record revenues and expenses at the time of cash collection and payment. This procedure is known as the *cash basis* of accounting. The cash basis is acceptable primarily in service enterprises which do not have substantial credit transactions or inventories.

Installment basis of revenue recognition. When the selling price of goods sold is to be collected in installments (such as monthly or annually) and considerable doubt exists as to collectibility, the installment basis of accounting may be used. Such sales are made in spite of the doubtful collectibility because the margin of profit is high and the goods can be repossessed if the payments are not received. The *installment basis* is a revenue recognition procedure in which the gross margin on an installment sale is recognized in proportion to the cash collected on the receivable. In other words, under the installment basis, gross margin on a sale (selling price of a good minus its cost) is recognized as cash is collected from customers. For example, assume the following facts concerning a stereo set:

Date of sale	Selling price	Cost	Gross margin (Selling price − Cost)	Gross margin percentage (Gross margin ÷ Selling price)
October 1, 1984	$500	$300	($500 − $300) = $200	($200 ÷ $500) = 40 percent

Ten equal monthly installment payments of $50 each are required to pay for the set (10 × $50 = $500). If three monthly payments are received in 1984, the total amount of cash received in 1984 is $150 (3 × $50). The total gross margin to recognize or record in 1984 is computed as cash received times gross margin percentage, or $150 × 0.40 = $60.

The other installments are collected when due so that a total of $350 is received in 1985. The total gross margin to recognize in 1985 is $140 ($350 × 0.40). In summary, the total receipts and gross margin recognized in the two years are as follows:

	Total amount of cash received	Gross margin recognized
1984	$150	$ 60
1985	350	140
Total	$500	$200

The installment basis of revenue recognition is accepted for tax purposes. But for accounting purposes, since the installment basis delays revenue recognition beyond the time of sale, it is acceptable only when considerable doubt exists as to collectibility of the installments.

Revenue recognition on long-term construction projects. Revenue from a long-term construction project can be recognized under two different methods: (1) the completed-contract method or (2) the percentage-of-completion method. The *completed-contract method* is a method of recognizing revenue on long-term projects in which no revenue is recognized until the period in which the project is completed. At that point, all revenue is recognized even though the contract may have required three years to complete. Thus, the *completed-contract method recognizes revenues at the point of sale.* Costs incurred on the project are carried forward in an inventory account (Construction in Process) and are charged to expense in the period in which the revenue is recognized.

Some accountants argue that it is unreasonable to wait so long to recognize any revenue. Revenue-producing activities have been performed during each year of construction, and revenue should be recognized even if estimates are needed. The *percentage-of-completion method* is a method of recognizing revenue based on the estimated stage of completion of a long-term project. The stage of completion is measured by comparing actual costs incurred in a period with the total estimated costs to be incurred on the project. To illustrate, assume that a firm has a contract to build a dam for $44 million that has an estimated construction cost of $40 million, as shown:

Sales price of dam	Estimated costs to construct dam	Estimated gross margin (Sales price — Estimated costs)
$44 million	$40 million	($44 million — $40 million) = $4 million

By the end of the first year (1984), the company had incurred *actual* construction costs of $30 million. The $30 million of construction costs are 75 percent of total estimated construction costs ($30 million ÷ $40 million = 75 percent). Under the percentage-of-completion method, the 75 percent figure would be used to *assign* revenue to the first year. In 1985, another $4 million of construction costs are incurred. The amount of revenue to assign to each year is determined as follows:

Year	Ratio of actual construction costs to total estimated construction costs	×	Agreed price of dam	=	Amount of revenue to recognize
1984	($30 million ÷ $40 million) = 75 percent	×	$44 million	=	$33 million
1985	($4 million ÷ $40 million) = 10 percent	×	$44 million	×	$4.4 million

The amount of gross margin in 1984 is equal to revenue of $33 million minus construction costs of $30 million. Thus, $3 million of gross margin is recognized in 1984. Gross margin in 1985 would be $0.4 million or $400,000 computed as $4.4 million of revenues minus construction costs of $4 million. Period costs, such as general and administrative expenses, would be deducted from gross margin to determine net income. For instance, assuming general and administrative expenses were $100,000 in 1985, net income would be $300,000 ($400,000 − $100,000).

Revenue recognition at completion of production. Recognizing revenue at the time of completion of production or extraction is called the *production basis*. The production basis is considered acceptable procedure for many farm products such as wheat, corn, and soybeans and for certain precious metals (gold). The reasons advanced to justify recognizing revenue prior to sale for these products include the homogeneous nature of the products, the fact that the products can usually be sold at their market prices, and the difficulties sometimes encountered in determining unit production costs.

Recognizing revenue upon completion of production or extraction is accomplished by debiting inventory (an asset) and crediting a revenue account for the expected selling price of the goods. All costs incurred in the period can then be treated as expenses. For example, assume that 1,000 ounces of gold are mined at a time its market price is $400 per ounce. The entry to record the extraction of 1,000 ounces of gold would be:

```
Inventory of Gold ..............................................  400,000
    Revenue from Extraction of Gold ..........................             400,000
    To record extraction of 1,000 ounces of gold. Selling price is $400
    per ounce.
```

If expenses in producing the gold were $300,000, net income on the gold mined would be $100,000.

Expense and loss recognition

An *expense* is the outflow or using up of assets in the generation of revenue. An expense is incurred *voluntarily* to produce revenue. For instance, the cost of a television set delivered by a dealer to a customer in exchange for cash can readily be thought of as an asset expiration to produce revenue. Similarly, the cost of services such as labor can be thought of as expiring in the production of revenue.

Losses are also asset expirations, but they are *involuntary* and do not create revenue. Fire losses are an example. The cost of an uninsured building which was destroyed in a fire is a loss suffered involuntarily with no revenue being produced.

The measurement of expense. Most assets used in operating a business are measured in terms of historical costs. Therefore, expenses resulting from expired assets are measured in terms of the historical costs of those assets. Other expenses are paid for currently and are measured in terms of their current costs.

The timing of expense recognition. The matching principle implies that a relationship exists between expenses and revenues. For certain expenses, the relationship is easily seen, as in the case of goods delivered to customers. When a direct relationship cannot be seen, the costs of assets with limited lives may be charged to expense in the periods benefited on a systematic and rational allocation basis. Depreciation of plant assets is an example. In other instances, the relationship between expense and revenue can only be assumed to exist, as in the case of a contribution to the local community fund. Consequently, the timing of expense recognition is guided by the concepts of product costs and period costs.

Product costs are costs incurred in the acquisition or manufacture of goods. Included as product costs for purchased goods are invoice, freight, and insurance-in-transit costs. For manufacturing firms, product costs include all costs of materials, labor, and factory operations necessary to produce goods. Product costs are assumed to attach to the goods purchased or produced and are carried in inventory accounts as long as the goods are on hand. Product costs are charged to expense when the goods are sold. The result is a precise matching of cost of goods sold expense and its related revenue.

Period costs are costs that cannot be traced to specific revenue and that are, as a result, expensed in the period in which incurred. Selling and administrative costs are examples of period costs.

MODIFYING CONVENTIONS

In certain instances accounting principles might not be strictly applied because of modifying conventions. *Modifying conventions* are customs emerging from accounting practice that alter results that would be obtained from a strict application of accounting principles. Two such modifying conventions are materiality and conservatism.

Materiality. *Materiality* is a modifying convention which allows the accountant to deal with immaterial (unimportant) items in a theoretically incorrect, expedient manner. Small dollar amount items often do not make a difference in a decision and are considered to be *immaterial* to the decision. Large dollar amount items usually do make a difference in a decision and are considered to be *material* (important) to the decision. The accountant records all material items in a theoretically correct way. *Immaterial items may be recorded in a theoretically incorrect way simply because it is more convenient and less expensive to do so.* For example, the purchase of a wastebasket may be debited to an expense account rather than an asset account even though the wastebasket has an expected useful life of 30 years. It simply is not worth the expense of recording depreciation expense on such a small item over its life.

There is more to materiality than relative size of dollar amounts. The very nature of the item may make it material. For example, it may be quite significant to know that a firm is paying bribes or making illegal political contributions, even if the dollar amounts of such items are relatively small.

Conservatism.   *Conservatism* means being cautious or prudent and making sure that any errors in estimates tend to understate rather than overstate net assets and net income. Conservatism is the accountant's response to the uncertainty faced in the environment in which accounting is practiced. Many accounting measurements are estimates and involve the exercise of judgment. In such cases, conservatism tells the accountant "to play it safe." Playing it safe usually involves trying to avoid overstating net assets or net income.

Conservatism may be applied differently in various firms, causing decreased comparability among their financial statements. Conservative reporting may cause investors to act in a manner not in their best interest. Investors may, for example, dispose of their interest in a firm because earnings of the firm did not meet investors' expectations. Yet this failure of earnings to reach expectations may have been due solely to a conservative measurement of inventories. Thus, a fine line exists between conservative and incorrect accounting.

The conceptual framework project

The Appendix to this chapter discusses the Conceptual Framework Project of the Financial Accounting Standards Board. The Conceptual Framework Project is designed to resolve some disagreements as to the proper theoretical foundation for accounting. The project is underway as of this writing. The initial results of the project which pertain to the content of this text are presented in the Appendix.

INFLATION—A SERIOUS REPORTING PROBLEM

Many users have begun to question the adequacy of financial statement information. This questioning has arisen largely from the fact that in the past no attempt was made to include the impact of inflation upon the results of operations and financial position of the reporting company. One of the most serious problems ever faced by accountants—how to account for and report financial data in periods of inflation—is now discussed.

In response to some criticisms of historical cost accounting, accountants have recently used various alternatives to deal with the problem of inflation.

A *period of inflation* is a time during which prices in general are rising, while a *period of deflation* is when prices in general are falling. Only in periods of high inflation has the historical cost approach to recording accounting data been severely criticized. During times of inflation, the historical cost approach often reports income when the economic value of the owner's investment has not even been maintained.

There are two widely recommended accounting approaches to the problem of inflation. One is general price-level adjusted accounting, also known as constant dollar accounting. This approach shows financial statement historical cost figures as adjusted for changes in the general price level. The other approach is current cost accounting. The current cost approach shows the current cost or value of items in the financial statements.

The nature and measurement of inflation

In a period of inflation, the "real value" of the dollar—its ability to purchase goods and services—is falling. In a period of deflation, the real value of the dollar is rising.

Changes in the general level of prices are measured by means of a general price index such as the consumer price index (CPI). A *price index* is a weighted average of prices for various goods and services. A base year is chosen and assigned a value of 100 for comparative purposes. If the index stands at 108 a year later, this means that prices in general rose 8 percent during the year. An index of 200 would mean that prices on the average have doubled. Prices of individual types of items may change at different rates and may, in some cases, actually decline. For example, the CPI shows that prices for a "basket" of selected consumer goods doubled in the decade of the 1970s. But during that same decade, gasoline prices quadrupled, while the price of electronic handheld calculators declined very sharply.

The real value or purchasing power of the dollar relative to that of the base year is shown by the reciprocal of the price index. The ratio is merely inverted. For example, if the index for 1984 is 200 and for 1974 is 100, the price index is 200/100, meaning that prices have doubled since 1974. Alternatively, the reciprocal of the price index is 100/200, meaning that the value of the dollar in 1984 has dropped to one half or 50 percent of its purchasing power in 1974.

It is said that financial reports are inadequate in periods of inflation because accounting measurements consist largely of dollars of historical cost. *Historical cost accounting* measures accounting transactions in terms of the actual dollars expended or received. Such a measurement system has worked well in periods of stable prices. But the system does not work well when the dollar, in terms of its purchasing power, is a sharply changing unit of measure.

To illustrate, assume that a tract of land was purchased for $2,000 and held several years before being sold for $2,500. While the land was held, a general price index rose from 100 to 140. Historical cost accounting would report recovery of the $2,000 cost and income from gain on sale of land of

$500. Measured in terms of dollars of constant purchasing power, a far different result is obtained. To get back the purchasing power originally invested in the land, the land would have to be sold for $2,800 ($2,000 × 140/100). Since only $2,500 was received, no income has been earned because cost has not been recovered. In fact, a loss of $300 of current purchasing power was incurred.

Consequences of ignoring effects of inflation

As shown in the example above, transactions and, therefore, financial statements that have not been adjusted for the effects of inflation may yield misleading information. Such information may make comparisons of firms difficult. Suppose Company A acquired a tract of land for $100,000 several years ago. Now Company B acquires a virtually identical tract of land for $150,000, paying the higher price because prices in general have risen 50 percent since Company A bought its land. Immediately, both companies sell their land for $150,000 each. Company A would appear to have the more efficient management because it was able to earn $50,000 on the sale of the land, while Company B earned $0. In reality, the two companies are in the same position relative to the sale of the land because they have the same number of dollars of current purchasing power. The financial statement difference is caused by recording the land at its historical cost.

As another example, assume the above land was instead a depreciable asset. Company A and Company B earn exactly the same number of dollars of revenues and incur, except for depreciation, exactly the same number of dollars of expenses. If both companies had assumed a 10-year useful life on the asset and apply straight-line depreciation, Company A will have a larger net income than Company B simply due to the fact that the historical cost of its depreciable asset and, therefore, its recorded depreciation expense is lower than for Company B.

Failure to adjust for the impact of inflation may lead to conclusions that are not valid. A five-year summary of sales may show that sales dollars have increased 50 percent over the period. If sales prices have increased 60 percent over the five years, physical sales volume has actually declined.

There are many other consequences that flow from a failure to adjust financial reports for the effects of inflation. Companies are paying taxes on "income" when in reality, costs may not have been covered. Also, financial reports that fail to reflect the impact of inflation may be misleading to individual decision makers, causing them to make decisions that are not in their best interests.

Accounting responses to inflation

Because there are two types of price changes—general and specific—there are two recommended approaches to accounting for changing prices. These are:

1. Change the unit of measure from the nominal dollar to a dollar of constant purchasing power; this approach is referred to as *constant dollar accounting.*
2. Change the unit of measure from historical cost to current cost or value; this approach is called *current cost accounting.*

An example of these two approaches is necessary before turning to a more detailed illustration. Assume the following facts regarding the purchase and resale of 1,000 units of a product:

Date	Transaction	Amount	Price-level index
January 1, 1984	Purchased 1,000 units	$3,000	100
December 31, 1984	Sold 1,000 units	5,000	120

The current cost of the units on December 31, 1984, was $3,900. The company incurred $800 of expenses to sell the units.

Under conventional (historical cost) accounting, net income from continuing operations for 1984 would be:

Sales		$5,000
Cost of goods sold	$3,000	
Other expenses	800	3,800
Net income from continuing operations		$1,200

The $1,200 of income results from deducting the historical cost of the goods sold as well as the other expenses from sales revenue. The company appears to be better off after the transactions because it has not only recovered the original dollar investment in the goods, together with the expenses incurred, but has an additional $1,200. No attention is paid to the fact that the dollars recovered do not have the same purchasing power as those originally invested. The fact that current replacement cost of the goods sold exceeds their historical cost by $900 ($3,900 − $3,000) also is ignored.

What would a statement reporting on the company's net income from

Illustration 13.1: **Alternative reporting approaches—statement of net income from continuing operations**

Statement of Net Income from Continuing Operations						
		Historical cost accounting		**Constant dollar accounting**		**Current cost accounting**
Sales		$5,000		$5,000		$5,000
Cost of goods sold	$3,000		$3,600		$3,900	
Other expenses	800		800		800	
Total expenses		$3,800		$4,400		$4,700
Net income from continuing operations		$1,200		$ 600		$ 300

continuing operations for 1984 contain under the alternative approaches given above? The possible reports are shown in Illustration 13.1.

Constant dollar accounting.   In the column headed "Constant dollar accounting," cost of goods sold is restated into end-of-1984 dollars by use of a ratio of the current price index to the old price index: $3,000 × 120/ 100 = $3,600. The $3,600 is the amount of purchasing power invested in the goods expressed in the end-of-1984 dollars. Thus, the $3,600 is restated into the same dollars in which the sales revenue is expressed. The $800 of other expenses are assumed to be selling expenses incurred at point of sale (such as sales commissions), and are already stated in end-of-1984 dollars. All dollar amounts are now expressed in comparable terms—end-of-1984 dollars. The company is better off because it has increased its purchasing power by $600. Under constant dollar accounting, income means increased ability to acquire goods and services.

Current cost accounting.   The *current cost* of an asset is the amount that would have to be paid currently to acquire the asset. In the column headed "Current cost accounting," net income from continuing operations is computed by deducting the current cost of replacing the goods sold, together with other expenses, from current revenues. No adjustments are made for *general* price-level changes. Calculating net income from continuing operations in this manner is supported on the grounds that the sale of an inventory item leads directly to a further action—replenishment of the inventory—if the firm is to remain a going concern. A better picture of a firm's ability to compete in its markets may also be provided by comparing current revenues with current costs rather than with outdated historical costs. An argument can be made that the $300 represents "disposable" income. Only $300 or less can be distributed to owners without reducing the scale of operations.

Choosing the correct method.   With two different methods of adjusting for inflation available, the question of which is the correct method arises. There is no direct answer possible. Each method is correct if one accepts the definitions of cost and income implicit in the method. A much more important question is: Which method is more useful to users of the financial reports? The answer to this question is of considerable concern to many people, including members of the FASB and the staff of the SEC. But, as of this writing, the question remains unanswered.

CONSTANT DOLLAR ACCOUNTING

As already discussed briefly, historical dollar amounts in an income statement may be converted or restated into a number of constant dollars which have an equivalent amount of purchasing power. When adjusted for inflation, conventional financial statements are called constant dollar or general price-level adjusted financial statements.

In the past, inflation adjusted statements generally have been recommended, not required, as supplementary information to conventional financial statements. In 1979, the FASB issued a standard that *requires* certain large, publicly held corporations to present certain supplementary information about the effects of inflation.[2]

Presented below is an example of how the income statement can be adjusted for changes in the general price level. Knowing how this is done will lead to a better understanding of the FASB requirements. To serve as a basis for illustration, the income statement of the Carol Company is presented in Illustration 13.2.

Illustration 13.2: Income statement—historical cost basis

CAROL COMPANY
Income Statement
For the Year Ended December 31, 1984

Sales		$200,000
Cost of goods sold:		
Inventory, December 31, 1983	$ 20,000	
Purchases	160,000	
Goods available for sale	$180,000	
Inventory, December 31, 1984	40,000	140,000
Gross margin		$ 60,000
Depreciation	$ 4,000	
Other expenses	46,000	50,000
Net income		$ 10,000

To convert historical dollars into constant end-of-year dollars, the formula is:

$$\text{Historical dollars} \times \frac{\text{Price index at end of current period}}{\text{Price index at date of historical transaction}} = \text{Constant dollars}$$

In order to convert the income statement of the Carol Company, certain assumptions must be made or information provided. These data are as follows.

1. The general price-level index stood at 100 on December 31, 1983, and at 108 on December 31, 1984.
2. Sales, purchases, other expenses, and taxes were incurred uniformly throughout the year. This means that on the average, these items were incurred when the price index was 104.
3. Inventories are costed on a Fifo basis. The beginning inventory was acquired when the price index was 98 and the ending inventory was acquired when the index stood at 106.
4. The price index was 54 when the plant assets were acquired.

---

[2] FASB "Financial Reporting and Changing Prices," *Statement of Financial Accounting Standards No. 33* (Stamford, Conn., 1979). Copyright © by Financial Accounting Standards Board, High Ridge Park, Stamford, Connecticut 06905, U.S.A. Quoted (or excerpted) with permission. Copies of the complete document are available from the FASB.

The following procedures were applied in the conversion of the Carol Company income statement. First, all items incurred uniformly throughout the year are converted by multiplying their historical amounts by a ratio of 108/104. Beginning inventory is converted using a ratio of 108/98, while ending inventory is converted to constant dollars by multiplying by 108/106. Since depreciation is calculated on the historical costs of the related assets which were acquired when the index stood at 54, depreciation expense is converted using a ratio of 108/54. Illustration 13.3 shows the restated income statement for the Carol Company.

Illustration 13.3: Income statement—constant dollar basis (end-of-year dollars)

CAROL COMPANY
Restated Income for the Year Ended December 31, 1984
(in constant end-of-year 1984 dollars)

	Historical dollars		Conversion ratio		Constant dollars
Sales	$200,000	×	108/104	=	$207,692
Cost of goods sold:					
Inventory, December 31, 1983	$ 20,000	×	108/98	=	$ 22,041
Purchases	160,000	×	108/104	=	166,154
Goods available for sale	$180,000				$188,195
Inventory, December 31, 1984	40,000	×	108/106	=	40,755
Cost of goods sold	$140,000				$147,440
Gross margin	$ 60,000				$ 60,252
Depreciation	$ 4,000	×	108/54	=	$ 8,000
Other expenses	46,000	×	108/104	=	47,769
Total expenses	$ 50,000				$ 55,769
Net income from continuing operations	$ 10,000				$ 4,483
Purchasing power gain on monetary items					2,625
Net income	$ 10,000				$ 7,108

Purchasing power gains and losses. Purchasing power gains and losses result from holding monetary assets and liabilities during inflation or deflation. *Monetary items* are cash and other assets and liabilities that represent fixed claims to cash, such as accounts and notes receivable and payable. *Nonmonetary items* include all items on the balance sheet other than monetary items. A *purchasing power gain* results from holding monetary liabilities during inflation or monetary assets during deflation. A *purchasing power loss* results from holding monetary assets during inflation or monetary liabilities during deflation.

Assume that Bill Allen holds $1,000 of cash during a year in which prices in general rose 25 percent. Even though Bill still has his $1,000 at year-end, he has less purchasing power than he did at the beginning of the year. Bill needs to have $1,250 ($1,000 × 125/100) at year-end to be as well off as he was at the start of the year. Therefore, during the year, Bill has sustained a purchasing power loss of $250.

Conversely, a gain results from being in debt during inflation. Assume that Kathy Rice owes $600 during a year in which prices rise 40 percent. The original debt has a year-end purchasing power equivalent of $840 ($600 × 140/100). Kathy can satisfy the debt by paying $600 currently. Thus, she has experienced a purchasing power gain of $240.

If Carol Company, in Illustration 13.2, experienced a purchasing power gain of $2,625 during 1984, this amount would be added to net income from continuing operations on the restated income statement. This gives a net income on a constant dollar basis of $7,108, which is nearly 30 percent less than the net income shown on the conventional (historical cost) income statement.

Constant dollar accounting—pro and con

The advantages of constant dollar accounting include the following:

1. Measurement of the impact of inflation upon a company is objective because adjustments are based on historical cost.
2. Comparability of the financial statements between firms is improved because of the use of the same procedures and the same index numbers.
3. There is greater comparability of the financial statements of a single company through time since effects of price-level changes are removed.

The disadvantages of constant dollar accounting include:

1. Benefits resulting from the use of such statements have not been shown to be in excess of the cost of preparing these statements.
2. The assumption that the impact of inflation affects all firms equally is not true.
3. Only one deficiency—the changing value of the measuring unit—is corrected; the effects of specific price changes are ignored. This is undoubtedly the most significant limitation to constant dollar accounting.

CURRENT COST ACCOUNTING

An income statement for Carol Company on a current cost basis will now be discussed. Management has determined that the current value (cost) of cost of goods sold was $146,000 and current cost of the plant assets was $160,000 on December 31, 1983, and $180,000 on December 31, 1984. There were no additions or retirements of plant assets in 1984. Carol Company depreciates its plant assets over a 20-year life, or an annual rate of 5 percent on a straight-line basis.

Current cost depreciation for 1984 can be computed by multiplying the average current cost of the plant assets for the year times the annual depreciation rate of 5 percent. The amount is:

$$\frac{\$160,000 \ + \ \$180,000}{2} \times 5 \text{ percent} = \$8,500$$

The $146,000 current cost of goods sold and $8,500 current cost depreciation are shown in an income statement prepared under current cost accounting. There is no need to adjust sales or other expenses since they are already expressed at current cost for the year.

Illustration 13.4 shows the amounts which would be reported in the two income statements shown for the Carol Company thus far, plus the amounts which would be shown under the current cost basis.

Illustration 13.4: Inflation impact disclosures

CAROL COMPANY
Statement of Income from Continuing Operations Adjusted for Changing Prices
For the Year Ended December 31, 1984

	Historical cost	Constant dollar (end-of-year dollars)	Current cost
Sales	$200,000	$207,692	$200,000
Cost of goods sold	$140,000	$147,440	$146,000
Depreciation expense	4,000	8,000	8,500
Other expenses	46,000	47,769	46,000
Total	$190,000	$203,209	$200,500
Net income (loss) from continuing operations	$ 10,000	$ 4,483	$ (500)
Purchasing power gain on monetary items		$ 2,625	

Current cost accounting—pro and con

The advantages of current cost accounting include:

1. Specific current costs incurred by a firm are shown instead of costs adjusted for general price-level changes.
2. Current costs, rather than costs based on historical costs, are deducted from current revenue to calculate net income.
3. If owner withdrawals are limited to an amount equal to or less than current cost income from continuing operations, the economic capital of the firm is maintained.

The disadvantages of current cost include:

1. Current costs are subjective.
2. Current costs may be difficult and costly to determine.

THE FASB REQUIREMENTS

FASB Statement No. 33 calls for disclosure by companies in their annual reports of the impact of general inflation and of specific price changes upon earnings and other selected items. The statement does not require full, completely adjusted financial statements, nor does it affect the way in which the basic (primary) financial statements are prepared, since all required disclosures are to be reported only as supplementary information. The statement applies only to publicly held companies with total assets in excess of $1 billion (after deducting accumulated depreciation) or to those having $125 million (before deducting accumulated depreciation) of inventories and property, plant, and equipment. Thus, about 1,200 to 1,400 large, publicly held companies are directly affected. The FASB also *encourages all* companies to report the effects of inflation by applying the methods described in *FASB Statement No. 33.*

For fiscal years ended on or after December 25, 1979, affected companies are to report as supplementary information:

a. Net income on a constant dollar basis (historical cost adjusted for the effects of general inflation).
b. Net income on a current cost basis.
c. Purchasing power gain or loss on monetary items.[3]

Other disclosure requirements including a five-year summary of selected financial data are discussed in more advanced texts on accounting. An example of how an actual company reports inflation data can be seen in Appendix B at the end of the text.

Uncertainty over whether constant dollar information or current cost information is preferable caused the FASB to require both types. This uncertainty was shown in responses to the exposure draft of the new standard. Some knowledgeable persons preferred constant dollar information, while others preferred current-cost information. The FASB foresees a period of experimentation with the new disclosures and has promised to review the standard in five years from its publication date. Experience in using and compiling the newly required information is expected to provide needed answers to a number of questions.

APPENDIX: THE CONCEPTUAL FRAMEWORK PROJECT

The exact nature of the basic concepts and related principles comprising accounting theory has been debated for years. The debate continues today even though numerous references can be found to "generally accepted accounting principles" (GAAP). To date, all attempts to present a concise statement of GAAP have received only limited acceptance.

This limited success has led many accountants to suggest the starting point is to seek agreement on the objectives of financial accounting and reporting. The belief is that if one (1) carefully studies the environment, (2) knows what objectives are sought, (3) can identify certain qualitative traits of accounting information, and (4) can define the basic elements of financial statements, one can discover the principles and standards that will lead to the attainment of the stated objectives. The FASB has taken the first three steps in the above approach in "Objectives of Financial Reporting by Business Enterprises"

---

[3] *FASB Statement No. 33,* pars. 29–35.

and in "Qualitative Characteristics of Accounting Information."[4] The fourth step is represented by "Elements of Financial Statements of Business Enterprises."[5]

OBJECTIVES OF FINANCIAL REPORTING

Financial reporting objectives are the broad overriding goals sought by engaging in financial reporting. Objectives provide informed investors and creditors with information useful in making rational investment and credit decisions. According to the FASB, the first objective of financial reporting is to:

> . . . provide information that is useful to present and potential investors and creditors and other users in making rational investment, credit, and similar decisions. The information should be comprehensible to those who have a reasonable understanding of business and economic activities and are willing to study the information with reasonable diligence.[6]

The term *other users* is interpreted broadly and includes employees, security analysts, brokers, and lawyers. Financial reporting should provide information to all who are willing to learn to use it properly. Although the Board's objectives are stated in terms of the corporate form of business organization, they apply equally well to single proprietorships and partnerships.

The second objective of financial reporting is to:

> . . . provide information to help present and potential investors and creditors and other users in assessing the amounts, timing, and uncertainty of prospective cash receipts from dividends [owner withdrawals] or interest and the proceeds from the sale, redemption, or maturity of securities or loans. Since investors' and creditors' cash flows are related to enterprise cash flows, financial reporting should provide information to help investors, creditors, and others assess the amounts, timing, and uncertainty of prospective net cash inflows to the related enterprise.[7]

This objective ties the cash flows of investors (owners) and creditors to the cash flows of the enterprise, a tie-in that appears entirely logical. Enterprise cash inflows are the source of cash for dividends (owner withdrawals), interest, and redemption of maturing debt.

Third, financial reporting should:

---

[4] FASB, "Objectives of Financial Reporting by Business Enterprises," *Statement of Financial Accounting Concepts No. 1* (Stamford, Conn., 1978). FASB, "Qualitative Characteristics of Accounting Information," *Statement of Financial Accounting Concepts No. 2* (Stamford, Conn., 1980). Copyright © by the Financial Accounting Standards Board, High Ridge Park, Stamford, Connecticut 06905, U.S.A. Quoted (or excerpted) with permission. Copies of the complete document are available from the FASB.

[5] FASB, "Elements of Financial Statements of Business Enterprises," *Statement of Financial Accounting Concepts No. 3* (Stamford, Conn., 1980). Copyright © by the Financial Accounting Standards Board, High Ridge Park, Stamford, Connecticut 06905, U.S.A. Quoted (or excerpted) with permission. Copies of the complete document are available from the FASB.

[6] FASB, "Objectives of Financial Reporting by Business Enterprises," p. viii.

[7] Ibid.

. . . provide information about the economic resources of an enterprise, the claims to those resources (obligations of the enterprise to transfer resources to other entities and owners' equity), and the effects of transactions, events, and circumstances that change its resources and claims to those resources.[8]

A number of conclusions can be drawn from the three objectives and from a study of the environment in which financial reporting is carried out. Financial reporting should provide information about an enterprise's past performance because such information is used as a basis for prediction of future enterprise performance. Financial reporting should focus upon earnings and its components, despite the emphasis in the objectives upon cash flows. Earnings computed under the accrual basis provide a better indicator of ability to generate favorable cash flows than do statements prepared under the cash basis. Financial reporting does not seek to measure the value of a business, but to provide information that may be useful for doing so. Financial reporting does not seek to evaluate management's performance, predict earnings, assess risk, or estimate earning power, but should provide information to persons who wish to do so.

These conclusions are some of those reached in *Statement of Financial Accounting Concepts No. 1.* As the Board says, these statements "are intended to establish the objectives and concepts that the Financial Accounting Standards Board will use in developing standards of financial accounting and reporting."[9] How successful the Board will be in the approach adopted remains to be seen. But it appears likely that the obstacle of conflicting objectives barring success in previous efforts to specify accounting principles has been removed.

QUALITATIVE CHARACTERISTICS

Qualitative characteristics are those characteristics which accounting information should possess to be useful in decision making. This is a difficult criterion to apply. The usefulness of accounting information in a given instance depends not only upon information characteristics but also upon the capabilities of the decision makers and their professional advisers, if any. Accountants cannot specify who the decision makers are, their characteristics, the decisions to be made, or the methods chosen to make the decisions; therefore attention is directed to characteristics of accounting information. The FASB's graphic summarization of the problems faced is presented in Illustration 13.5.[10]

Relevance

For information to have *relevance,* it must be pertinent to or bear upon a decision. The information must "make a difference" to someone who does not already have the information. Relevant information is capable of making

[8] Ibid.

[9] Ibid., p. i.

[10] FASB, "Qualitative Characteristics of Accounting Information," p. 15.

Illustration 13.5:   A hierarchy of accounting qualities

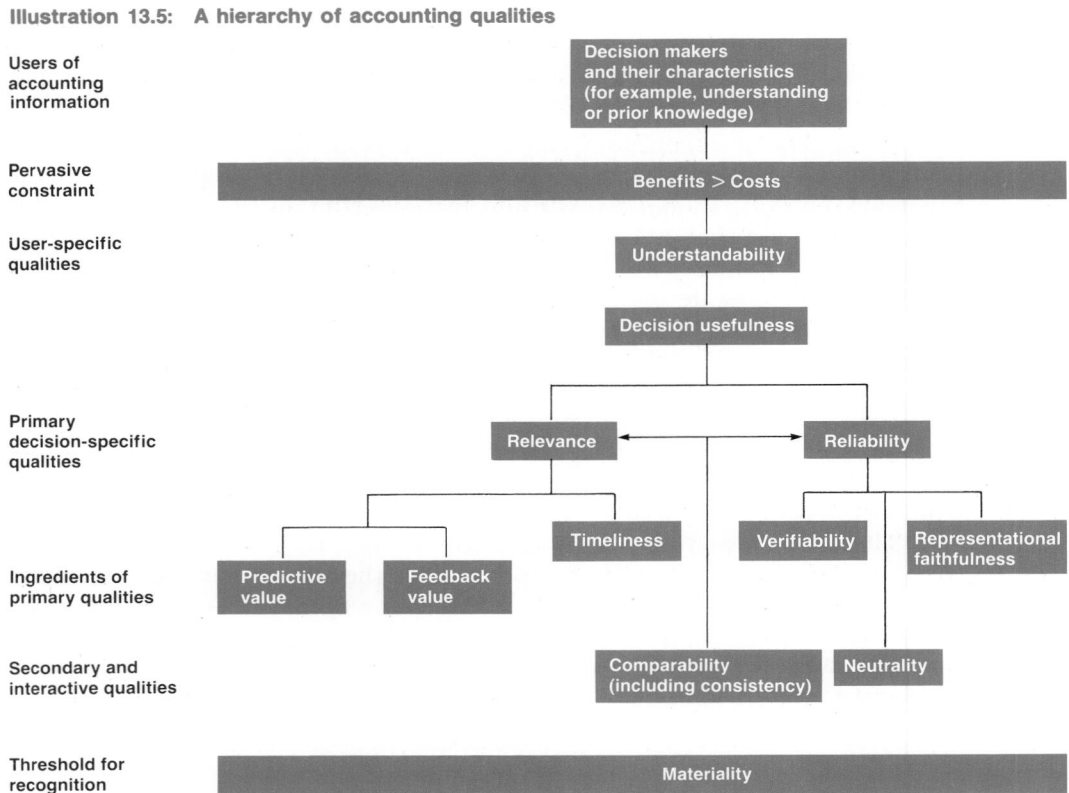

a difference in a decision either by affecting user predictions of outcomes of past, present, or future events or by confirming or correcting expectations. Note that information need not be a prediction to be useful in developing, confirming, or altering expectations. Expectations are commonly based upon the present or past. For example, any attempt to predict future earnings of a firm would quite likely start with a review of present and past earnings. Also, information that merely confirms prior expectations may be less useful, but is still relevant since it reduces uncertainty.

Some types of accounting information are under attack today because of an alleged lack of relevance. For example, it is argued that the fact that a tract of land cost its owner $1 million over 40 years ago and is reported in the current balance sheet at that amount is irrelevant (except for possible tax implications) to users for decision making today. Such attacks have encouraged research into the types of information that are relevant to users. The attacks have also brought forth suggestions that a different valuation basis, such as current cost, be used in reporting such assets.

Predictive value and feedback value.   Because actions taken now can affect only future events, information is obviously relevant when it possesses *predictive value* or improves users' abilities to predict outcomes of events.

Information that reveals the relative success of users in predicting outcomes possesses *feedback value*. Because feedback reports on past activities, it can make a difference in decision making by (1) reducing uncertainty in a situation, (2) refuting or confirming prior expectations, and (3) providing a basis for further predictions. For example, a report on the first quarter's earnings of a firm reduces the uncertainty surrounding the amount of such earnings, confirms or refutes the predicted amount of such earnings, and provides a possible basis for one to predict earnings for the full year. With regard to the latter item, accounting information may possess predictive value, but it does not consist of predictions. Making predictions is a function performed by the decision maker, not the accountant.

Timeliness. *Timeliness* requires that accounting information be provided at a time when it may be considered in reaching a decision. Utility of information decreases with age. It is much more useful to know what the net income for 1982 was in early 1983 than to receive this information a year later. If information is to be of any value in decision making, it must be available *before* the decision is made. If not, the information is useless. In determining what constitutes timely information, consideration must be given to the other qualitative characteristics and to the cost of gathering information. For example, a timely estimated amount for uncollectible accounts may be more valuable than a later, verified actual amount. Timeliness alone cannot make information relevant, but otherwise relevant information might be rendered irrelevant by a lack of timeliness.

Reliability

In addition to being relevant, information must be reliable to be useful. Information has *reliability* when it faithfully depicts for users what it purports to represent. Thus, accounting information is reliable if users can depend upon it to reflect the underlying economic activities of the organization. The reliability of information depends upon its representational faithfulness, verifiability, and neutrality.

Representational faithfulness. Insight into this quality may be gained by considering a map. A map possesses representational faithfulness when it shows roads and bridges (among other things) where roads and bridges actually exist. There is correspondence between what is shown on the map and what is present physically. Similarly, there is *representational faithfulness* when accounting statements on economic activity correspond to the actual underlying activity. An accounting measurement may show what it is designed to show and still not be useful if that which it measures is irrelevant. Recall the example of the tract of land acquired over 40 years ago. The historical cost information may be irrelevant to the informed, but to uninformed persons who believe that accounting statements show values or the current worth of a business, there exists representational failure. The reasonably informed user, for whom accounting reports are designed, understands that assets typically are reported at historical cost and that accounting information is based upon numerous estimates, approximations, allocations, and the application of judgment.

Effects of bias. Accounting measurements are biased if they are consistently too high or too low. Bias in accounting measurements may exist due to the choice of measurement method or to bias introduced either deliberately or through lack of skill by the measurer. These two types of bias are discussed below.

Completeness. To be free from bias, information must be sufficiently complete to ensure that it validly represents the underlying events and conditions. *Completeness* means that it must fully disclose all significant information in a way that aids understanding and does not mislead. Relevance of information also may be reduced if information that would make a difference to a user is omitted. Currently, full disclosure generally requires presentation of a balance sheet, an income statement, a statement of changes in financial position, and necessary footnotes and supporting schedules. Such statements are to be complete, with items properly classified and segregated (such as reporting sales revenue separately from other revenues). Required disclosures may be made in (1) the body of the financial statements, (2) in the notes to such statements, (3) in special communications, and (4) in the president's letter or in other management reports in the annual report.

Another aspect of completeness is that full disclosure must be made of all changes in accounting principles and their effects.[11] Also disclosure should be made of unusual activities (loans to officers), changes in expectations (losses on inventory), depreciation expense for the period, long-term obligations entered into that are not recorded by the accountant (a 20-year lease on a building), new arrangements with certain groups (pension and profit-sharing plans for employees), significant events that occur after the date of the statements (loss of a major customer), and accounting policies (major principles and their manner of application) followed in preparing the financial statements.[12] Because of its emphasis upon disclosure, this aspect of reliability is often called the full-disclosure principle.

Verifiability. Financial information has *verifiability* when it can be substantially duplicated by independent measurers using the same measurement methods. Verifiability is directed toward eliminating measurer bias, rather than measurement method bias. The requirement that financial information be based upon objective evidence is based upon demonstrated needs of users for reliable, unbiased financial information. Unbiased information is needed especially when parties with opposing interests (credit seekers and credit grantors) rely upon the same information. Reliability of information is enhanced if it is verifiable.

---

[11] APB, "Accounting Changes," *APB Opinion No. 20* (New York: AICPA, July 1971).

[12] APB, "Disclosure of Accounting Policies," *APB Opinion No. 22* (New York: AICPA, April 1971).

Financial information will never be free of subjective opinion and judgment. It will always possess varying degrees of verifiability. Some measurements can be supported by canceled checks and invoices. Others, such as periodic depreciation charges, can never be verified because of their very nature. Thus, financial information in many instances is verifiable only in that it represents a consensus as to what would be reported if the same procedures had been followed by other accountants.

Neutrality. *Neutrality* in accounting information means that the information should be free of measurement method bias. The primary concern should be the relevance and reliability of the information that result from application of the principle, not the effect that the principle may have on a particular interest. "To be neutral, accounting information must report economic activity as faithfully as possible, without coloring the image it communicates for the purpose of influencing behavior in *some particular direction.*"[13] Accounting standards should not be developed and used like certain tax regulations which seek deliberately to foster or restrain certain types of activity. Verification seeks to eliminate measurer bias; neutrality seeks to eliminate measurement method bias.

Comparability (and consistency)

When *comparability* in financial information exists, reported differences and similarities in information are real and not the result of differing accounting treatments. Comparable information will reveal relative strengths and weaknesses in a single company through time and between two or more companies at the same point in time.

Consistency leads to comparability of financial information for a single company through time. Comparability between companies is more difficult to achieve because the same activities may be accounted for in different ways. For example, B may use one method of depreciation, while C accounts for an identical asset in similar circumstances using another method. A high degree of intercompany comparability in accounting information will not exist unless the same activities are required to be accounted for in the same manner across companies and through time.

Pervasive constraints

As Illustration 13.5 shows, there are two pervasive constraints faced in providing useful information. First, benefits secured from the information must be greater than the cost of providing that information. Second, only material items need be disclosed and accounted for strictly in accordance with generally accepted accounting principles (GAAP).

---

[13] FASB, "Qualitative Characteristics of Accounting Information," par. 100.

Cost/benefit analysis. Accounting information is a commodity and, like all commodities, is desired only if it provides benefits greater than its cost. But, unlike most commodities, accounting information has no direct cost to users, since all costs are borne by the provider of the information. This fact has led users and authoritative organizations to demand ever greater amounts of financial information, which have often been answered with claims that the information desired costs more than it is worth. Such a contention was encountered frequently when the FASB proposed requiring disclosure of the impact of inflation upon financial statements. Complicating the issue is the fact that there is no agreed-upon method of measuring benefits of information and that even measurement of cost cannot be carried out without some disagreement. Yet, in the development of accounting standards, an attempt must be made to ensure that the benefits of required disclosures exceed the cost of providing the disclosures.

Materiality. As discussed earlier in the chapter, the basic idea inherent in materiality is simply that one need be concerned only with significant items; insignificant ones can be ignored. Materiality has been defined by the FASB as "the magnitude of an omission or misstatement of accounting information that, in the light of surrounding circumstances, makes it probable that the judgment of a reasonable person relying on the information would have been changed or influenced by the omission or misstatement."[14] The term *magnitude* in this definition suggests that the materiality of an item may be assessed by looking at its *relative* size. A $10,000 error in an expense in a firm with earnings of $30,000 would seem to be material. The same error in a firm earning $30,000,000 may not be material.

THE BASIC ELEMENTS OF FINANCIAL STATEMENTS

Having discussed objectives of financial reporting and qualitative characteristics of accounting information, basic elements of financial statements will be considered. A most important task in developing a conceptual framework for any discipline is that of identifying and defining its basic elements. The following definitions by the FASB are likely to have a major impact upon financial accounting. Most of the terms were defined earlier in this text in a less precise way to convey a general understanding of the terms. The more technical definitions are as follows (these items are not repeated in the glossary):

Assets are probable future economic benefits obtained or controlled by a particular entity as a result of past transactions or events affecting the enterprise.

Liabilities are probable future sacrifices of economic benefits arising from present obligations of a particular entity to transfer assets or provide services to other entities in the future as a result of past transactions or events.

Equity is the residual interest in the assets of an entity that remains after deducting its liabilities. In a business enterprise, the equity is the ownership interest.

---

[14] Ibid., p. xv.

Comprehensive income is the change in equity (net assets) of an entity during a period from transactions and other events and circumstances from nonowner sources. It includes all changes in equity during a period except those resulting from investments by owners and distributions to owners.

Revenues are inflows or other enhancements of assets of an entity or settlements of its liabilities (or a combination of both) during a period from delivering or producing goods, rendering services, or other activities that constitute the entity's ongoing major or central operations.

Expenses are outflows or other using up of assets or incurrences of liabilities (or a combination of both) during a period from delivering or producing goods, rendering services, or carrying out other activities that constitute the entity's ongoing major or central operations.

Gains are increases in equity (net assets) from peripheral or incidental transactions of an entity and from all other transactions and other events and circumstances affecting the entity during a period except those that result from revenues or investments by owners.

Losses are decreases in equity (net assets) from peripheral or incidental transactions of an entity and from all other transactions and other events and circumstances affecting the entity during a period except those that result from expenses or distributions to owners.

Investments by owners in the entity are increases in net assets of a particular enterprise resulting from transfers to it from other entities of something of value to obtain or increase ownership interests (or equity) in it. Assets are most commonly received as investments by owners, but that which is received may also include services or satisfaction or conversion of liabilities of the enterprise.

Distributions by the entity to owners are decreases in net assets of a particular enterprise resulting from transferring assets, rendering services, or incurring liabilities by the enterprise to owners. Distributions to owners decrease ownership interests (or equity) in an enterprise.[15]

Note that the requirement that assets and liabilities be based upon past transactions normally rules out the recording of contracts that are mutual promises to do something, such as entering into an employment contract with an officer. On a similar basis, the accountant refuses to record an asset and a liability when a contract is signed whereby the entity agrees to purchase a certain number of units of a product over a coming period of time.

NEW TERMS INTRODUCED IN CHAPTER 13

Accounting theory
A set of basic concepts and assumptions and related principles that explain and guide the accountant's actions in identifying, measuring, and communicating ecnomic information.

Comparability
A qualitative characteristic of accounting information; when information is comparable, it reveals differences and similarities that are real and not the result of differing accounting treatments.

Completed-contract method
A method of recognizing revenue on long-term projects in which no revenue is recognized until the period in which the project is completed; similar to recognizing revenue upon the completion of a sale.

---

[15] FASB, "Elements of Financial Statements of Business Enterprises."

Completeness
A qualitative characteristic of accounting information; requires disclosure of all significant information in a way that aids understanding and does not mislead; sometimes called the full-disclosure principle.

Conservatism
Being cautious or prudent and making sure that any errors in estimates tend to understate rather than overstate net assets and net income.

Consistency
Requires a company to use the same accounting principles and reporting practices through time.

Constant dollar accounting
A system of accounting that changes the unit of measure from the nominal dollar to a dollar of constant purchasing power.

Cost principle
See exchange price principle.

Current cost
The amount that would have to be paid currently to acquire an asset.

Current cost accounting
A system of accounting that changes the unit of measure from historical cost to current cost or value.

Deflation (period of)
Exists when prices in general are falling.

Earning principle
The requirement that revenue be substantially earned before it is recognized (recorded).

Entity
The specific unit, such as a business, for which accounting information is gathered. Entities have a separate existence from owners, creditors, managers, employees, and other interested parties.

Exchange price (or cost) principle
Transfers of resources are recorded at prices agreed upon by the parties to the exchange at the time of the exchange.

Feedback value
A qualitative characteristic that information has when it reveals the relative success of users in predicting outcomes.

Financial reporting objectives
The broad overriding goals sought by engaging in financial reporting; providing informed investors and creditors with information useful in making rational investment and credit decisions.

Going concern (continuity) assumption
The assumption that an entity will continue to operate indefinitely unless there is evidence that the entity will terminate.

Historical cost
The amount paid or fair value of liability incurred or other resource surrendered to acquire an asset.

Historical cost accounting
Conventional accounting in which accounting measurements are in terms of the actual dollars expended or received.

Inflation (period of)
Exists when prices in general are rising.

Installment basis
A revenue recognition procedure in which the gross margin on an installment sale is recognized in proportion to the cash collected on the receivable.

Liquidation
Terminating a business by ceasing business operations and selling off the assets.

Losses
Are asset expirations which are involuntary and do not create revenue.

Matching principle
The principle that net income of a period can be determined by associating or relating revenues earned in a period with expenses incurred to generate the revenues.

Materiality
A modifying convention which allows the accountant to deal with immaterial (unimportant) items in a theoretically incorrect, expedient manner; also a qualitative characteristic specifying that financial accounting report only information significant enough to influence decisions or evaluations.

Modifying conventions
Customs emerging from accounting practice that alter results that would be obtained from a strict application of accounting principles; conservatism is an example.

Monetary items
Are cash and other assets and liabilities that represent fixed claims to cash, such as accounts and notes receivable and payable.

Money measurement
Quantification in terms of a monetary unit of measurement, such as the dollar, instead of quantification in terms of physical or other units of measurement—feet, inches, grams, and so on.

Neutrality
A qualitative characteristic that requires accounting information to be free of measurement method bias.

Nonmonetary items
All items on the balance sheet other than monetary items; examples are inventories, plant assets, capital stock, and owner's equity.

Percentage-of-completion method
A method of recognizing revenue based on the estimated stage of completion of a long-term project. The stage of completion is measured by comparing actual costs incurred in a period with total estimated costs to be incurred in all periods.

Period costs
Costs that cannot be traced to specific revenue and that are, as a result, expensed in the period in which incurred.

Periodicity (time periods)
An assumption of the accountant that an entity's life can be subdivided into time periods for purposes of reporting on its economic activities.

Predictive value
A qualitative characteristic that information has when it improves users' abilities to predict outcomes of events.

Price index
A weighted average of prices for various goods and services. A base year is chosen and assigned a value of 100 for comparative purpose.

Product costs
Costs incurred in the acquisition or manufacture of goods. Product costs are accounted for as if they were attached to the goods, with the result that they are charged to expense when the goods are sold.

Production basis
A method of revenue recognition used in limited circumstances which recognizes revenue at the time of completion of production or extraction.

Purchasing power gain
The gain that results from holding monetary liabilities during inflation or monetary assets during deflation.

Purchasing power loss
The loss that results from holding monetary assets during inflation or monetary liabilities during deflation.

Qualitative characteristics
Characteristics which accounting information should possess to be useful.

Realization principle
A principle which directs that revenue is recognized only after the seller acquires the right to receive payment from the buyer.

Relevance
A qualitative characteristic requiring that information be pertinent to or bear upon a decision.

Reliability
A qualitative characteristic requiring that information faithfully depict for users what it purports to represent.

Representational faithfulness
A qualitative characteristic requiring that accounting statements on economic activity correspond to the actual underlying activity.

Revenue recognition principle
That revenue should be earned and realized before it is recognized (recorded).

Stable dollar
An assumption that fluctuations in the value of the dollar are insignificant and may, therefore, be ignored.

Timeliness
A qualitative characteristic requiring that accounting information be provided at a time when it may be considered in reaching a decision.

Verifiability
A qualitative characteristic of accounting information; information is verifiable when it can be substantially duplicated by independent measurers using the same measurement methods.

DEMONSTRATION PROBLEM 13–1

For each of the transactions or circumstances described below and the entries made, state which, if any, of the assumptions or concepts, principles, or modifying conventions of accounting were violated. If any were violated, give the entry to correct the improper accounting assuming the books have not been closed.

During the year, the Dorsey Company—

Transactions:

1. Had its buildings appraised. They were found to have a market value of $410,000, although their book value was only $380,000. The accountant debited the Buildings and Accumulated Depreciation—Buildings accounts for $15,000 each and credited R. Dorsey, Capital. No separate mention was made of this action in the financial statements.
2. Purchased a number of new electric pencil sharpeners for its offices at a total cost of $60. These were recorded as assets and are being depreciated over five years.
3. Produced a number of agricultural products at a cost of $26,000. These costs were charged to expense when the products were harvested. The products were set up in inventory at their net market value of $35,000, and the Farm Revenues Earned account was credited for $35,000.

Solution to demonstration problem 13–1

1. The realization principle and the modifying convention of conservatism may have been violated. Such write-ups simply are not looked upon with favor in accounting. To correct the situation, the entry made needs to be reversed:

R. Dorsey, Capital	30,000	
Buildings		15,000
Accumulated Depreciation—Buildings		15,000

2. Theoretically, there were no violations unless there is one relating to the cost of compiling insignificant information. As a practical matter, the $60 could have been expensed on materiality grounds.

3. There were no violations. The procedures followed are considered acceptable for farm products that are interchangeable and readily marketable. No correcting entry is needed, provided due allowance has been made for the costs to be incurred in delivering the products to the market.

DEMONSTRATION PROBLEM 13–2

Duncan Book Company's financial statements included the following partial income statement:

```
                  DUNCAN BOOK COMPANY
                  Partial Income Statement
            For the Year Ended December 31, 1984

Sales .............................              $250,000
Cost of goods sold  ...............   $180,000
Depreciation ......................      3,000
Other expenses ....................     15,000    198,000
Income from continuing operations .......        $ 52,000
```

Sales were made uniformly throughout the year. The cost of goods sold consisted of books acquired when the general price index stood at 105. This same index ended the year at 120 and averaged 110 for the year. The current cost of the goods sold was $200,000.

The $3,000 depreciation reported is on a delivery truck that cost $12,000 when the general price index stood at 100. The truck has a current cost of $14,000 at the beginning of 1984 and a current cost of $16,000 at the end of 1984. The other expenses were incurred uniformly throughout the year, were paid in cash, and are substantially equal to their current cost at time of incurrence.

Required:

a.   Prepare a statement showing constant dollar income from continuing operations in December 31, 1984, dollars for the year then ended.

b.   Prepare a statement showing current cost income from continuing operations for the year ended December 31, 1984.

Solution to demonstration problem 13–2

a.

DUNCAN BOOK COMPANY
Statement of Constant Dollar Income from Continuing Operations
In End-of-Year Dollars
For the Year Ended December 31, 1984

Sales ($250,000 × 120/110)		$272,727
Cost of goods ($180,000 × 120/105)	$205,714	
Depreciation ($3,000 × 120/100)	3,600	
Other expenses ($15,000 × 120/110)	16,364	225,678
Income from continuing operations		$ 47,049

---

b.

DUNCAN BOOK COMPANY
Statement of Current Cost Income from Continuing Operations
For the Year Ended December 31, 1984

Sales		$250,000
Cost of goods sold	$200,000	
Depreciation ($14,000 + $16,000)/2 × 0.25	3,750	
Other expenses	15,000	218,750
Income from continuing operations		$ 31,250

QUESTIONS

1.   Name the assumptions underlying generally accepted accounting principles. Comment on the validity in recent years of the stable unit of measurement assumption.

2.   Why does the accountant assume the existence of an entity?

3.   When is the going-concern assumption not to be used?

4.   What is meant by the term *accrual basis of accounting?* What is its alternative?

5.   What does it mean to say that accountants record substance rather than form?

6.   If a company changes an accounting principle because the change better meets the information needs of users, what disclosures must be made?

7. What is the exchange price (or cost) principle? What is the significance of adhering to this principle?

8. What two requirements generally must be met before revenue will be recognized in a period?

9. Under what circumstances, if any, is the receipt of cash an acceptable time to recognize revenue?

10. What two methods may be used in recognizing revenues on long-term construction contracts?

11. Define expense. What principles guide the recognition of expense?

12. How does an expense differ from a loss?

13. What is meant by the accounting term *conservatism?* How does it affect the amounts reported in the financial statements?

14. Does materiality relate only to relative size of dollar amounts?

15. How might it be argued that a tax supposedly upon earnings or income is really a tax upon capital?

16. What are the two basic approaches that might be used to reveal the impact of inflation upon financial statements?

17. Explain what the significance is of the dollar amount attaching to an asset under constant dollar accounting.

18. If an index of the general level of prices rose 15 percent in a period, what is the effect upon the value or real worth of the dollar?

19. How is the dollar amount attaching to land adjusted under constant dollar accounting?

20. Explain the typical adjustment of sales and most expenses under constant dollar accounting.

21. Identify whether each of the following items is a monetary or nonmonetary item.

a. Cash.
b. Equipment.
c. Notes receivable.
d. Merchandise inventory.
e. Accounts receivable.
f. Patents.
g. Common stock.
h. Land.
i. Accounts payable.
j. Buildings.

22. What are purchasing power gains and losses? When do purchasing power gains occur? When do purchasing power losses occur?

23. In the supplementary disclosures required by the FASB, what basis of accounting measurement is to be applied?

24. What is the major deficiency in constant dollar accounting?

25. (Based on the Appendix) Identify the three major parts of the conceptual framework project that are included in the text.

26. (Based on the Appendix) In general, what are the qualitative characteristics? Which are the primary qualitative characteristics?

EXERCISES

E-1. Match the items in Column A with the proper descriptions in Column B.

Column A

1. Going concern (continuity).
2. Consistency.
3. Disclosure.
4. Periodicity.
5. Conservatism.
6. Stable dollar.
7. Matching.
8. Materiality.
9. Exchange prices.
10. Entity.

Column B

a. An assumption relied on in the preparation of the primary financial statements that would be unreasonable when the inflation rate is high.

b. Concerned with relative dollar amounts.

c. The usual basis for the recording of assets.

d. Required if the accounting treatment differs from that previously accorded a particular item.

e. An assumption that would be unreasonable to use in reporting on a firm that had become insolvent.

f. None of these.

g. Requires a company to use the same accounting procedures and practice through time.

h. An assumption that the life of an entity can be subdivided into time periods for purposes of reporting.

i. Discourages undue optimism in measuring and reporting net assets and net income.

j. Requires separation of personal from business activity in the recording and reporting processes.

E–2. Royce Company sells its products on an installment sales basis. Data for 1983 and 1984 are as follows:

	1983	1984
Installment sales	$100,000	$120,000
Cost of goods sold on installment	70,000	90,000
Other expenses	15,000	20,000
Cash collected from 1983 sales	60,000	30,000
Cash collected from 1984 sales		80,000

a. Compute the net income for 1984 assuming use of the accrual (sales) basis of revenue recognition.

b. Compute the net income for 1984 assuming use of the installment method of recognizing gross margin.

E–3. A firm has a contract to build a ship at a price of $100 million and an estimated cost of $80 million. In 1984, costs of $20 million were incurred. Under the percentage-of-completion method how much revenue would be recognized in 1984?

E–4. A company follows a practice of expensing the premium on its fire insurance policy when it is paid. In 1984, it charged to expense the $720 premium paid on a three-year policy covering the period July 1, 1984, to June 30, 1987. In 1981, a premium of $660 was charged to expense on the same policy for the period July 1, 1981, to June 30, 1984.

a. State the principle of accounting that was violated by this practice.

b. Compute the effects of this violation on the financial statements for the calendar year 1984.

c. State the basis upon which the company's practice might be justified.

E–5. Holland Company produces a product at a cost of $10 per unit which it sells for $15. The company has been very successful and is able to sell all of the units that it can produce. During 1984, the company manufactured 50,000 units, but because of a transportation strike, it was able to sell and deliver only 40,000 units.

a. Compute the gross margin for 1984 following generally accepted accounting principles. The cost of the units sold should be entitled "cost of goods sold" and treated as an expense.

b. Compute the gross margin for 1984 assuming that the realization principle is ignored and that revenue is recognized as production is completed.

E-6.   Assume the following facts regarding the purchase and sale of 100 units of a product:

Date	Transaction	Amount	Price-level index
January 1, 1984	Purchased 100 units	$ 6,000	100
December 31, 1984	Sold 100 units	10,000	110

The company incurred $1,200 of expenses to sell the units. The replacement cost of the units on December 31, 1984, was $7,000. Prepare a schedule showing net income from continuing operations under historical cost accounting, constant dollar accounting, and current cost accounting.

E–7.   The cost of goods sold section of the conventional (historical cost) income statement for the Russell Company was:

Cost of goods sold:
Inventory, December 31, 1983	$10,000
Purchases	30,000
Goods available for sale	$40,000
Inventory, December 31, 1984	5,000
Cost of goods sold	$35,000

The general price level index was 100 on December 31, 1983, and 110 on December 31, 1984. The Fifo inventories were acquired when the index stood at 96 for the beginning inventory and 108 for the ending inventory. Purchases were incurred uniformly throughout the year. Convert the cost of goods sold section of the income statement to end-of-year constant dollar amounts.

E–8   C Company's plant assets at December 31, 1983, had a historical cost of $100,000 and accumulated depreciation of $40,000 (10 percent annual depreciation rate). There were no additions or retirements in 1984. The current cost of the plant assets on December 31, 1983, was $130,000 and on December 31, 1984, was $150,000. Compute the current cost depreciation for 1984.

E–9.   In each of the situations given, determine the amount of purchasing power gain or loss.

a.   You hold cash of $20,000 during a year in which prices in general rose 10 percent.

b.   You are in debt $10,000 during a year in which prices in general rose 8 percent.

PROBLEMS, SERIES A

13–1–A.   Video, Inc., sells a video recorder under terms calling for a small down payment and monthly payments spread over three years. Following are data for the first three years of the company's operations:

	1982	1983	1984
Sales	$200,000	$300,000	$400,000
Cost of video sets sold	140,000	180,000	200,000
Gross margin	$ 60,000	$120,000	$200,000
Gross margin as a percentage of sales	30%	40%	50%
Cash collected in 1984			
From 1982 sales			$ 60,000
From 1983 sales			80,000
From 1984 sales			130,000

General and selling expenses amounted to $120,000 in 1984.

Required:

   a.   Compute the net income for 1984 assuming that revenues are recognized at the time of sale.

   b.   Compute the net income for 1984 using the installment method of accounting for sales and gross margin.

13–2–A.   The following data relate to the Unger Construction Company's long-term construction projects for the year 1984:

	Completed project	Incomplete projects
Contract price	$4,500,000	$24,000,000
Costs incurred prior to 1984	–0–	4,000,000
Costs incurred in 1984	3,700,000	8,000,000
Estimated costs to complete (at 12/31/84) ...	–0–	8,000,000

General and administrative expenses incurred in 1984 amounted to $500,000, none of which is to be considered a construction cost.

Required:

   a.   Compute net income for 1984 under the completed-contract method.

   b.   Compute net income for 1984 using the percentage-of-completion method.

P13–3–A.   For each of the numbered items listed below, state the letter or letters of the principles, assumptions, or concepts used to justify the accounting procedure followed:

   A—Entity.
   B—Conservatism.
   C—Earning principle of revenue recognition.
   D—Going concern (continuity).
   E—Exchange price principle.
   F—Matching principle.
   G—Period cost (or principle of immediate recognition of expense).
   H—Realization principle.
   I—Stable dollar assumption.

1. The estimated liability for federal income taxes was increased by $5,000 over the amount reported on the tax return to cover possible differences found by the Internal Revenue Service in determining the amount of income taxes payable.
2. A truck purchased in January was reported at 80 percent of its cost even though its market value at year-end was only 70 percent of its cost.
3. The collection of $10,000 of cash for services to be performed next year was reported as a current liability.
4. The president's salary was treated as an expense of the year even though he spent most of his time planning the next two years' activities.
5. No entry was made to record that the company received an offer of $100,000 for land carried in its accounts at $60,000.
6. A stock of printed stationery, checks, and invoices with a cost of $2,000 was treated as a current asset at year-end even though it had no value to others.
7. A tract of land acquired for $35,000 was recorded at that price even though it was appraised at $40,000 and the company would have been willing to pay that amount if pushed.
8. Paid and charged to expense the $1,500 paid to Mike Kruger for rent of a truck owned by him. Mike Kruger is owner of the company.
9. Recorded the $12,000 of interest collected on $100,000 of 12 percent bonds as interest revenue even though the general level of prices increased 16 percent during the year.

P13–4–A.   A partial income statement for the X Company for the year ended December 31, 1984, in terms of historical dollars is as follows:

X COMPANY
Partial Income Statement
For the Year Ended December 31, 1984

Sales		$110,000
Cost of goods sold	$63,000	
Depreciation	6,000	
Other expenses	12,100	81,100
Net income from continuing operations		$ 28,900

The sales were made uniformly throughout the year. The cost of goods sold consisted of goods acquired when the general price index stood at 105. This same index ended the year at 120 and averaged 110 for the year. The current cost of the goods sold was $75,000.

The $6,000 of depreciation reported is on a machine that cost $30,000 when the general price index stood at 90. The machine had a current cost of $50,000 at the beginning of 1984 and a current cost of $60,000 at the end of 1984.

The other expenses were incurred uniformly throughout the year, were paid in cash, and are substantially equal to their current cost at time of incurrence.

Required:

a. Prepare a statement showing net income from continuing operations in constant end-of-year 1984 dollars.

b. Prepare a statement showing current cost net income from continuing operations for the year ended December 31, 1984.

P13–5–A.   Barton Company began business on January 2, 1984, with $80,000 of inventory and $60,000 of equipment. An index of the general level of prices stood at 100 on January 2, 1984. This index rose uniformly throughout the year, averaging 125 for the year, and ending at 150. Barton's income statement for the year in historical dollars is given below.

```
                    BARTON COMPANY
                    Income Statement
         For the Year Ended December 31, 1984

Sales ................            $100,000
Cost of goods sold .....            50,000
Gross margin ..........           $ 50,000
Depreciation ..........  $10,000
Other expenses ........   20,000   30,000
Net income ............           $ 20,000
```

In 1984, Barton sold goods out of the beginning inventory with a cost of $50,000 for cash of $100,000. Expenses in the amount of $20,000 were incurred uniformly throughout the year and were paid in cash. No new equipment was purchased during the year.

Required:

Prepare an income statement for 1984 with all amounts expressed in constant end-of-year 1984 dollars. The purchasing power loss on net monetary items was $1,000.

P13–6–A. The following is a partial income statement for Davis Shoes for the year ended December 31, 1984:

```
                       DAVIS SHOES
                 Partial Income Statement
         For the Year Ended December 31, 1984

Sales ..........................            $420,000
Cost of goods sold ............  $270,400
Depreciation ..................    16,000
Other expenses ................    84,000   370,400
Net income from continuing operations .....  $ 49,600
```

Sales were made uniformly throughout the year. Other expenses were also incurred rather uniformly throughout the year and largely on a cash basis. Thus, their historical cost is substantially equal to their current cost. The depreciation reported relates to a machine acquired at a cost of $160,000 which is being depreciated over a 10-year life on a straight-line basis.

The current cost of the goods sold was $300,000 at the time of sale. The current (gross) cost of the machine was $260,000 at the beginning of 1984 and $300,000 at the end of the year. An index of the general level of prices stood at 80 when the machine was acquired, at 100 at the beginning of 1984, averaged 105 for 1984, and ended the year at 110. The index stood at 104 when the goods sold were acquired.

Required:

a. Prepare a statement showing constant dollar net income from continuing operations in end-of-year dollars for the year ended December 31, 1984.

b. Prepare a statement showing current cost net income from continuing operations for the year ended December 31, 1984.

PROBLEMS, SERIES B

P13–1–B.   The Smooth Real Estate Sales Company sells lots in its development in Flash Flood Canyon under terms calling for small cash down payments with monthly installment payments spread over a few years. Following are data on the company's operations for its first three years:

	1982	1983	1984
Gross margin rate	45%	48%	50%
Cash collected in 1984 from sales of lots made in	$80,000	$100,000	$120,000

The total selling price of the lots sold in 1984 was $400,000, while general and administrative expenses (which are not included in the costs used to determine gross margin) were $100,000.

Required:

   a.   Compute the net income for 1984 assuming revenue is recognized upon the sale of a lot.

   b.   Compute net income for 1984 assuming use of the installment method of accounting for sales and gross margin.

P13–2–B.   Given below are the contract prices and costs relating to all of the Bird Company's long-term construction contracts (in millions of dollars):

	Contract price	Costs incurred Prior to 1984	Costs incurred In 1984	Costs yet to be incurred
On contracts completed in 1984	$16.0	–0–	$14.0	–0–
On incomplete contracts	48.0	$8.0	16.0	$16.0

General and administrative expenses for 1984 amounted to $600,000.

Required:

   a.   Compute net income for 1984 using the completed-contract method.

   b.   Compute net income for 1984 using the percentage-of-completion method. Assume that the general and administrative expenses are not to be treated as a part of the construction cost of the contracts.

P13–3–B.   In each of the circumstances described below, the accounting practices followed may be questioned. You are to indicate whether you agree or disagree with the accounting employed and to state the assumptions, concepts, or principles on which you would rely to justify your position.

1. The cost of certain improvements to leased property having a life of five years was charged to expense because they would revert to the lessor when the lease expires in three years.
2. The salaries paid to the top officers of the company were charged to expense in the period in which they were incurred, even though the officers spent over half of their time planning next year's activities.
3. A company spent over $4 million in developing a new product and then spent an additional $4.5 million promoting it. All of these costs were incurred and charged to expense this year even though future years would also benefit.

4. No entry was made to record the belief that the market value of the land owned (carried in the accounts at $58,000) increased.

5. No entry was made to record the fact that costs of $50,000 were expected to be incurred in fulfilling warranty provisions on products sold this year. The revenue from products sold was recognized this year.

6. The acquisition of a tract of land was recorded at the price paid for it of $108,000, even though the company would have been willing to pay $125,000.

7. A truck acquired at the beginning of the year was reported at year-end at 80 percent of its acquisition price, even though its market value then was only 65 percent of its original acquisition price.

P13–4–B.   A partial income statement for the Reed Company for the year ended December 31, 1984 in terms of historical dollars is given below:

REED COMPANY
Partial Income Statement
For the Year Ended December 31, 1984

Sales		$210,000
Cost of goods sold	$135,200	
Depreciation	8,000	
Other expenses	42,000	185,200
Net income from continuing operations		$ 24,800

The sales were made rather uniformly throughout the year. Other expenses were also incurred rather uniformly throughout the year and largely on a cash basis. Thus, their historical cost is substantially equal to their current cost. The depreciation reported relates to a machine acquired at a cost of $80,000 which is being depreciated over a 10-year life on a straight-line basis.

The current cost of the goods sold was $150,000 at the time of their sale. The current cost (gross) of the machine was $130,000 at the beginning of 1984 and $150,000 at the end of the year. An index of the general level of prices stood at 80 when the machine was acquired, at 100 at the beginning of 1984, averaged 105 for 1984, and ended the year at 110. This same index stood at 104 when the goods sold were acquired.

Required:

   a.   Prepare a statement showing constant dollar net income from continuing operations in constant end-of-year 1984 dollars for the year ended on that date.

   b.   Prepare a statement showing current cost net income from continuing operations for the year ended December 31, 1984.

P13–5–B.   Morton Company was organized on December 31, 1983. It immediately paid a year's rent of $24,000 on a building in advance, purchased $12,000 of supplies, and purchased $40,000 of cleaning equipment. It began operations on January 1, 1984.

During 1984, services were rendered for customers and other expenses were incurred uniformly throughout the year. An index of the general level of prices stood at 80 at the beginning of the year, averaged 100 for the year, and ended the year at 120. The income statement for the year is as follows:

```
                        MORTON COMPANY
                        Income Statement
              For the Year Ended December 31, 1984

    Service revenue . . . . . . . . .          $100,000
    Supplies expense . . . . . . . .   $ 8,000
    Rent expense . . . . . . . . . . .   24,000
    Depreciation expense . . . . .       10,000
    Other expenses  . . . . . . . . .    40,000      82,000
    Net income . . . . . . . . . . . .             $ 18,000
```

Required:

Prepare a schedule converting the income statement for 1984 into constant end-of-year 1984 dollars. The purchasing power loss on net monetary items was $14,000.

P13–6–B.   The following is a partial income statement for the Jackson Corporation for the year ended June 30, 1985.

```
                     JACKSON CORPORATION
                    Partial Income Statement
              For the Year Ended June 30, 1985

    Sales . . . . . . . . . . . . . . . . .          $220,000
    Cost of goods sold  . . . . .   $126,000
    Depreciation . . . . . . . . . .   12,000
    Other expenses  . . . . . . . .   24,200      162,200
    Net income . . . . . . . . . . .              $ 57,800
```

Sales were made uniformly throughout the year, while cost of goods sold consisted of goods acquired when the general price index stood at 105. This index was 120 on June 30, 1985, and had averaged 110 for the preceding 12 months. The current cost of the goods sold was $145,000.

The depreciation reported is on a machine which cost $60,000 when the general price index stood at 90. The machine had a current cost of $100,000 on June 30, 1984, and on June 30, 1985, the current cost was $120,000. All other expenses were incurred uniformly throughout the year, were paid in cash, and were basically equal to their current cost at time of incurrence.

Required:

a.   Prepare a statement showing constant dollar net income from continuing operations in end-of-year dollars for the year ended June 30, 1985.

b.   Prepare a current cost statement of net income from continuing operations for the year ended June 30, 1985.

BUSINESS DECISION PROBLEM

Brinkmann Company was organized on December 31, 1983. It immediately paid a year's rent of $54,000 on a building in advance, purchased $27,000 of supplies, and purchased $90,000 of cleaning equipment. It began operations on January 1, 1984.

Revenues were earned and expenses were incurred evenly throughout 1984. An index of the general level of prices was 95 at the beginning of the year, averaged 110 for the year, and rose to 125 at year-end. The conventional income statement for the year is as follows:

```
                        BRINKMANN COMPANY
                         Income Statement
                 For the Year Ended December 31, 1984

Services revenue . . . . . . . . .              $225,000
Supplies expense . . . . . . . .      $18,000
Rent expense . . . . . . . . . . .     54,000
Depreciation expense . . . . .         22,500
Other expenses . . . . . . . . .       90,000     184,500
Net income . . . . . . . . . . . . .             $  40,500
```

Required:

    a.   Prepare a schedule converting the income statement into constant December 31, 1984, dollars. The purchasing power gain on net monetary items was $21,251.

    b.   Assuming you are evaluating this company, what would you conclude about its earnings performance?

Chapter 14

Partnership accounting

CHAPTER GOALS

After study of this chapter, you should be able to:

1. Describe the partnership form of organization, citing its advantages and disadvantages.
2. Record the formation of a partnership.
3. Apply the provisions of a partnership agreement to distribute net income or net loss to the partners.
4. Prepare financial statements for a partnership.
5. Journalize the admission of a partner to or the withdrawal of a partner from a partnership.
6. Record the liquidation of a partnership.
7. Define and use correctly the new terms in the glossary.

There are three common forms of business organizations in the United States: single proprietorships, partnerships, and corporations. Single proprietorships have been used for illustrative purposes up to this point. Single proprietorships and partnerships are more numerous than corporations, but corporations hold more assets and generate substantially more revenues than unincorporated businesses.

This chapter presents the features of and accounting for a partnership, while Chapter 15 will begin a discussion of corporations. The major difference between a sole proprietorship and a partnership is the number of owners. The *Uniform Partnership Act* defines a *partnership* as "an association of two or more persons to carry on as co-owners a business for profit."

THE PARTNERSHIP AGREEMENT

A partnership is based on a *partnership agreement* or contract known as the *articles of copartnership*. This contract serves as a basis for the formation, operation, and liquidation of a partnership and should be in writing in order to avoid any misunderstandings or disagreements. Among many points, the partnership agreement should specify the nature of the business, the capital contributions and duties of each partner, and the rights of each partner in the event of dissolution of the partnership. Another important item which should be carefully stated in the partnership agreement is the manner in which income and loss are to be divided among the partners.

When a partnership agreement is originally drawn up, it is difficult to anticipate all future events. If an issue arises that is not covered by the agreement, the provisions of the Uniform Partnership Act govern in those states which have adopted this act. Otherwise, common law as found in prior court decisions will determine the outcome of the disputed issue.

The Uniform Partnership Act has 45 sections presented in eight major parts. Three of these major parts pertain to:

1. Relations of partners to persons dealing with the partnership.
2. Relations of partners to one another.
3. Dissolution and winding up of a partnership.

Attention will be drawn to some of the sections in the discussion that follows.

CHARACTERISTICS OF A PARTNERSHIP

A partnership has several unique features that distinguish it from a corporation. These features include voluntary association, mutual agency, limited life, and unlimited liability. Each of these is discussed below.

Voluntary association

Any person who has the right to enter into contracts may enter into a partnership with other persons. But a person may not be forced into a partnership against that person's will. Each partner is an owner and member of management, and, unless otherwise specified in the partnership agreement, each has an equal voice or vote in the partnership's activities.

Mutual agency

Each partner is an *agent* of the partnership. The *mutual agency* of partners means each partner has the power to bind the remaining partners to any contract within the apparent scope of the partnership's business. For example, a partner could bind a partnership composed of physicians to a contract for medical supplies, but not to a contract to deliver an airplane. The individual partners must act in the best interests of the partnership and not their own personal interests when dealing in business matters.

Limited life

A partnership can be terminated at any time since it is a voluntary association. The *termination* (*dissolution*) of a partnership may be caused by the withdrawal, retirement, insanity, death, or bankruptcy of any one of the partners. Thus, a partnership is said to have a limited life. If any of the events leading to dissolution occurs, the remaining partners may continue the business; but a new partnership entity is created. A partnership may also end because the period for which it was formed has expired, or the specific purpose for which it was organized has been achieved.

Unlimited liability

Each partner may be held liable for all debts of the partnership—a potential peril known as *unlimited liability* of each partner. If the partnership cannot pay its debts, creditors may satisfy their claims by attaching (seizing) a partner's personal assets. Each partner's personal creditors have first claim on that partner's personal assets. Any remaining personal assets may be used to satisfy partnership creditors. For example, assume partner A has $10,000 of personal assets and $8,000 of personal liabilities. The partnership is now unable to pay its creditors; these creditors could require partner A to pay the $2,000 excess of personal assets over personal debts to satisfy creditor claims. The partnership creditors do not have to divide the debts among all partners; the creditors can seize the assets of only one partner to satisfy their claims. A partner who pays all of the partnership's debts acquires the right to be reimbursed by the other partners for their shares of the debts. This unlimited liability feature may discourage some individuals from investing in partnerships.

ADVANTAGES OF A PARTNERSHIP

A partnership is sufficiently flexible to permit reasonable accumulations of capital and talent. Partnerships are formed when (1) business capital requirements exceed the amount that may be raised by a single proprietor, (2) a single proprietor desires to obtain a variety of talent or knowledge of other persons who will also share in the risks and rewards of ownership, or (3) a single proprietor seeks to induce an employee to stay with the business by making that employee a partner.

A partnership is easier and less expensive to organize than a corporation. It is not required to observe as many laws and regulations as a corporation, nor is it subject to separate income taxation as is a corporation. Each partner reports his or her share of partnership income to the Internal Revenue Service and is taxed individually.

DISADVANTAGES OF A PARTNERSHIP

Perhaps the greatest disadvantage of a partnership lies in the unlimited liability feature or the fact that each partner may be held liable for all partnership debts. In general, a corporation's stockholders are not liable for the corporation's debts. Stockholder losses usually cannot exceed the amount invested.

Another disadvantage is the feature of mutual agency. Since one partner may bind the partnership to a contract, a partner who fails to exercise good judgment can cause the loss of partnership assets and, possibly, the loss of personal assets of the other partners.

As a functioning organization, the partnership generally becomes unwieldy when there are many partners. And, by virtue of the limited life feature, a partnership is subject to possible discontinuance due to many uncontrollable circumstances, such as the death of a partner.

Because partners are co-owners of a partnership's net assets, the transfer of ownership from one partner to another person may be difficult to accomplish. Upon the withdrawal of a partner from the partnership, the remaining partners will either have to purchase the withdrawing partner's interest or approve of the person to whom that interest is sold. Since a partnership is a voluntary association of persons, the remaining partners do not have to accept the buyer of an interest in a partnership as a partner. If a buyer acceptable as a partner cannot be found, the partners may have to terminate the partnership.

To summarize, some of the unique characteristics of partnerships are also the potential disadvantages of that form of business organization.

UNIQUE FEATURES IN PARTNERSHIP ACCOUNTING

The need for adequate accounting records is greater in a partnership than in a single proprietorship because of the division of interests that exists and because of the complications that arise in the treatment of such matters as partners' drawings and the division of income.

The partners' capital accounts

A capital account is maintained for each partner. The total in the partner's capital account after closing represents the partner's equity. Each partner's capital account is:

1. Credited with the original investment.
2. Credited with subsequent investments.
3. Credited (debited) with the agreed-upon share of net income (loss).
4. Debited with permanent capital reductions.
5. Debited with the balance of the partner's drawing account at the end of each fiscal period.

To illustrate the use of the capital accounts, assume that James Law and Todd Hart, who have been in business as single proprietors, form a partnership. The formation of the partnership creates a new accounting entity. Since assets of a business should be accounted for at fair market value when they are acquired, the assets contributed by each partner will be recorded at their current market values; these amounts may differ from what appeared on the separate accounting records of the individual proprietorships. Assets contributed, liabilities assumed, and their values are shown below:

Law		Hart	
Cash	$ 5,600	Cash	$ 6,600
Accounts receivable	6,800	Merchandise	3,400
Merchandise	12,000	Land	8,000
Delivery equipment	3,000	Building	20,000
Accounts payable	(3,200)	Accounts payable	(2,200)

The journal entries on January 1, 1984, to record the investment of each partner are as follows:

Cash	5,600	
Accounts Receivable	6,800	
Merchandise Inventory	12,000	
Delivery Equipment	3,000	
Accounts Payable		3,200
James Law, Capital		24,200
To record the investment of Law in the partnership of Law and Hart.		

Cash	6,600	
Merchandise Inventory	3,400	
Land	8,000	
Building	20,000	
Accounts Payable		2,200
Todd Hart, Capital		35,800
To record the investment of Hart in the partnership of Law and Hart.		

On August 1, 1984, the partners made the following additional investments which were credited to their capital accounts:

Cash	5,800	
James Law, Capital		2,400
Todd Hart, Capital		3,400
To record additional cash investments.		

On December 31, 1984, before closing the books, the capital accounts of the partners will appear as follows:

James Law, Capital

Date		Explanation	Post. Ref.	Debit	Credit	Balance
1984						
Jan.	1	Original investment			24,200	24,200
Aug.	1	Additional cash investment			2,400	26,600

Todd Hart, Capital

Date		Explanation	Post. Ref.	Debit	Credit	Balance
1984						
Jan.	1	Original investment			35,800	35,800
Aug.	1	Additional cash investment			3,400	39,200

The partners' drawing accounts

A drawing account is maintained for each partner. During an accounting period, any partner may withdraw cash or merchandise for personal use. The partnership agreement should specify whether withdrawals of merchandise are priced at cost or at selling price. Withdrawals of merchandise are charged to the drawing accounts of partners making such withdrawals and credited either to Purchases (if priced at cost) or Sales (if priced at selling price). Generally, drawings are made against income of the current year.

As a rule, partners cannot withdraw any part of their original investment without the consent of all partners. Whether partners may withdraw against subsequent additions to their capital accounts depends upon the partnership agreement. Withdrawals of investments should be debited directly to the capital account rather than the drawing account. Drawings are considered to be normal withdrawals rather than withdrawals of investment unless stated otherwise.

To illustrate drawing accounts, assume that Hart and Law made withdrawals as indicated below:

James Law, Drawing

Date		Explanation	Post. Ref.	Debit	Credit	Balance
1984						
Feb.	7	Cash		1,600		1,600
Apr.	8	Merchandise (at cost)		1,700		3,300
July	31	Cash		1,750		5,050
Dec.	1	Cash		1,650		6,700

Todd Hart, Drawing						
Date		Explanation	Post Ref.	Debit	Credit	Balance
1984						
Mar.	1	Cash		1,900		1,900
June	7	Cash		1,700		3,600
Sept.	18	Cash		2,000		5,600
Dec.	4	Merchandise (at cost)		1,600		7,200

End-of-period entries

At the end of the fiscal period, adjusting entries are made and all expense and revenue accounts are closed to Income Summary in the same manner as was illustrated for a single proprietorship. The Income Summary account is then closed to the partners' capital accounts; the amount of net income or loss assigned to each partner is based on methods outlined in the partnership agreement. Each partner's drawing account is then closed to that partner's capital account.

To illustrate, assume that the net income of the partnership of Law and Hart for the year ended December 31, 1984, is $30,000 and that the partners divide the income equally. The journal entry to close the net income to the capital accounts is:

```
Income Summary ...........................................  30,000
      James Law, Capital .......................................        15,000
      Todd Hart, Capital .......................................        15,000
   To close the net income to the capital accounts.
```

Another step is to close the balance of the drawing accounts to tne capital accounts by the following journal entries:

```
James Law, Capital .........................................   6,700
      James Law, Drawing ......................................          6,700
   To close the December 31, 1984, drawing account balance.

Todd Hart, Capital .........................................   7,200
      Todd Hart, Drawing ......................................          7,200
   To close the December 31, 1984, drawing account balance.
```

After the entries are posted, the drawing accounts and the capital accounts of Law and Hart appear as follows:

James Law, Drawing

Date		Explanation	Post. Ref.	Debit	Credit	Balance
1984						
Feb.	7	Cash		1,600		1,600
Apr.	8	Merchandise (at cost)		1,700		3,300
July	31	Cash		1,750		5,050
Dec.	1	Cash		1,650		6,700
	31	To capital			6,700	–0–

James Law, Capital

Date		Explanation	Post. Ref.	Debit	Credit	Balance
1984						
Jan.	1	Original investment			24,200	24,200
Aug.	1	Additional cash investment			2,400	26,600
Dec.	31	Net income			15,000	41,600
	31	From drawing		6,700		34,900

Todd Hart, Drawing

Date		Explanation	Post. Ref.	Debit	Credit	Balance
1984						
Mar.	1	Cash		1,900		1,900
June	7	Cash		1,700		3,600
Sept.	18	Cash		2,000		5,600
Dec.	4	Merchandise (at cost)		1,600		7,200
	31	To capital			7,200	–0–

Todd Hart, Capital

Date		Explanation	Post. Ref.	Debit	Credit	Balance
1984						
Jan.	1	Original investment			35,800	35,800
Aug.	1	Additional cash investment			3,400	39,200
Dec.	31	Net income			15,000	54,200
	31	From drawing		7,200		47,000

DIVISION OF PARTNERSHIP INCOME OR LOSS

Partnership income and losses are divided in accordance with provisions in the partnership agreements. The agreed-upon way that a partnership's income or losses are to be shared is called the *income and loss ratio* (*profit and loss ratio* or *earnings and loss ratio.*) If the agreement is silent with respect to the division of income, income is divided equally among the partners. If the agreement is silent as to loss distribution, losses are divided in the same manner as income. A properly drawn partnership agreement will specify the means by which income and losses are to be distributed to the partners. Distribution may be based on many factors.

If each of the partners invests an equal amount of assets, has approximately equal ability, devotes the same amount of time to the business, and has the same wealth at risk, then net income and net losses should probably be divided equally. If variations in the foregoing factors exist between partners, a method of income or loss distribution should be provided to reflect such differences. For example, a partner who manages the business all week long may be allocated a *salary* out of net income prior to an equal distribution of the remainder to all partners. This "salary" is part of the income sharing agreement and is *not* an expense of the partnership in the determination of net income.

For example, assume net income of the A&B partnership is $50,000. Partner A manages the store during the week, and both partners share the work load equally on the weekends. The partnership agreement states that in sharing income and loss, A is to be given credit for a salary of $10,000 and the remaining net income is to be shared equally by the two partners. When the Income Summary account is closed, A's capital account will be credited with $30,000 and B's capital account will be credited with $20,000, as shown:

	A	B	Both	Net income to be distributed
Net income				$50,000
Salary to A	$10,000		$10,000	40,000
Remainder equally	20,000	$20,000	40,000	–0–
Total	$30,000	$20,000	–0–	

As another illustration, one partner may invest a larger amount of capital than another partner. In this case, the partner with the larger capital investment may insist that *interest* be allowed on capital balances in the division of income, with the remainder divided equally between the partners. This *interest* would simply be a means of equitable compensation to the partner with the larger investment. As in the salary example, this interest factor is *not* an expense in income determination.

Common methods of dividing income are as follows:

1. In a set ratio such as:
   a. Equally.
   b. In an agreed ratio other than equal.
   c. In the ratio of the partners' capital account balances at the beginning of the fiscal period.
   d. In the ratio of the average capital investment.

2. By allowing interest on the capital investments, or salaries, or both, and dividing the remaining net income in an agreed ratio.

Assume that Rogers and Morgan form a partnership. Rogers' initial capital investment is $75,000; Morgan's is $25,000. The partners have agreed that Rogers will devote only half time to partnership business, whereas Morgan will devote full time.

Under these circumstances, the most equitable method of dividing income and losses is to allow salaries for time devoted to the business, interest on the capital investments, and then divide the remaining net income equally. This method adjusts for differences in capital and the time contributed by the partners. The equal division of the remaining income also seems equitable, since the partners share equally in the management decisions and are equally competent in operating a business of this kind. If one of the partners brings special talents to the firm, the division of partnership income should take this fact into account.

Illustrations of distributions of partnership income

The illustrations which follow are based on these data about the partnership of Anders and Budd: net income for the year ended December 31, 1984, was $60,000. During 1984, Anders' drawings were $14,000 and Budd's drawings were $22,000. The capital account balances of the partners on December 31, 1984, before closing were Anders, $85,000, and Budd, $134,000.

Case 1. Income divided in a set ratio.   A. Net income is to be divided equally. In this instance, the income and loss ratio is 1 to 1, or 50 percent and 50 percent. The capital accounts of Anders and Budd would each be credited with $30,000 of net income.

B.   Net income is to be divided 60 percent to Anders and 40 percent to Budd. Such an income and loss sharing ratio may reflect an attempt to take factors such as ability or special talent into consideration. In this case, Anders would be credited with $36,000 and Budd with $24,000. The journal entry to close Income Summary would read:

Income Summary	60,000	
Anders, Capital		36,000
Budd, Capital		24,000

To record distribution of net income to partners.

C.   Net income is to be divided in the ratio of beginning capital balances. Anders' beginning capital balance was $40,000, and Budd's was $80,000. Total capital of the partnership at the beginning of the year was $120,000. Anders had one third ($40,000/$120,000) of the total capital and Budd two thirds ($80,000/$120,000). Income is allocated $20,000 (one third of $60,000) to Anders and $40,000 (two thirds of $60,000) to Budd.

D.   Net income is to be divided in the ratio of average capital investment. If income distribution is to be based on average capital balance, details must be provided showing the timing of the investment by each partner. Illustration

Illustration 14.1: Computation of average capital

Anders, capital

Date	Debits	Credits	Balance	Months unchanged	Month-dollars (weighted equivalent)
Jan. 1			$40,000	6	$240,000
July 1		$15,000	55,000	5	275,000
Dec. 1		30,000	85,000	1	85,000
				12	$600,000

Average capital of Anders: $600,000 ÷ 12 = $50,000.

Budd, capital

Date	Debits	Credits	Balance	Months unchanged	Month-dollars (weighted equivalent)
Jan. 1			$ 80,000	7	$ 560,000
Aug. 1		$ 4,000	84,000	3	252,000
Nov. 1		50,000	134,000	2	268,000
				12	$1,080,000

Average capital of Budd: $1,080,000 ÷ 12 = $90,000.

14.1 contains such data on Anders' and Budd's capital balances. The "month-dollars" amount in each case is found by multiplying the balance times the months unchanged. The average capital is found by dividing the total month-dollars by 12.

The ratio of average capital investment is computed by dividing each partner's average capital by the total average capital of $140,000 ($50,000 for Anders and $90,000 for Budd). Thus, Anders is credited with $21,428 ($50,000/$140,000 × $60,000) of net income; Budd is credited with $38,572 ($90,000/$140,000 × $60,000).

Case 2. Interest and/or salary allowances with remainder in set ratio. Interest and salary allocations may be specified in the partnership agreement to compensate partners for differences in investment, time spent with the business, and other factors.

A.   Continuing the example of Anders and Budd, assume that the partners are to be allowed 6 percent interest on their beginning capital balances. January 1 capital balances were: Anders, $40,000; and Budd, $80,000. Salaries allowed are: Anders, $16,000; and Budd, $10,000. The $60,000 income for the current year is distributed as follows:

	Anders	Budd	Both	Income to be distributed
Net income				$60,000
Interest	$ 2,400	$ 4,800	$ 7,200	52,800
Salary	16,000	10,000	26,000	26,800
Remainder	13,400	13,400	26,800	–0–
Distribution	$31,800	$28,200	$60,000	

The entry to divide net income is:

Income Summary	60,000	
Anders, Capital		31,800
Budd, Capital		28,200
To divide net income for the year between the partners.		

B. Even if the allowances for salaries or interest exceed net income, or if there is a net loss for the period, the partners still are given credit for their full amounts of interest and salary. For example, if in the situation above, there was a net loss of $20,000 instead of net income of $60,000 for the year, the division would be as follows:

	Anders	Budd	Both	Income to be distributed
Net loss				$(20,000)
Interest	$ 2,400	$ 4,800	$ 7,200	(27,200)
Salary	16,000	10,000	26,000	(53,200)
Remainder	(26,600)	(26,600)	(53,200)	–0–
Distribution	$ (8,200)	$(11,800)	$(20,000)	

The entry to divide the net loss would be:

Anders, Capital	8,200	
Budd, Capital	11,800	
Income Summary		20,000
To divide the net loss between the partners.		

C. The sharing of income may result in a credit to one partner's capital account and a debit in another partner's capital account. As a final example, assume that Anders and Budd earned $3,200 of net income for a year. The $3,200 would be shared as follows:

	Anders	Budd	Both	Income to be distributed
Net income				$ 3,200
Interest	$ 2,400	$ 4,800	$ 7,200	(4,000)
Salary	16,000	10,000	26,000	(30,000)
Remainder	(15,000)	(15,000)	(30,000)	–0–
	$ 3,400	$ (200)	$ 3,200	

The entry to close the Income Summary account would be:

Income Summary	3,200	
Budd, Capital	200	
Anders, Capital		3,400

To divide net income for the year between the partners.

Partnership agreement governs. Up to this point, some factors that partners might consider when drawing up the income sharing provisions in the partnership agreement have been indicated. Application of some of the more common provisions has also been illustrated. But income may be shared in any manner the partners decide. Once the partners agree on how income is to be shared, the accountant's task is simply to apply the agreed-upon provisions as literally as possible.

FINANCIAL STATEMENTS OF A PARTNERSHIP

Since a partnership is very similar to a single proprietorship, the accounting and financial reporting for these forms of organization are basically the same. The major difference lies in the additional capital accounts needed in a partnership and the distribution of income or loss to these accounts.

Partnership income statement

A partnership's income statement may differ slightly from that of a single proprietorship. Because partners are co-owners of the business, the income statement may contain a schedule showing the distribution of the period's net income or net loss to each partner. Illustration 14.2 shows this feature for Anders and Budd.

Partnership balance sheet

The only distinctive feature of a partnership balance sheet is the presentation of the capital accounts in the owners' equity section. Instead of a single capital account, the owners' equity section contains a separate capital account for each partner unless there are many partners. If so, the balance sheet may show only a single item and amount called "Partners' capital." Each partner's name and capital balance would be reported in a supporting schedule.

Illustration 14.2: Partnership income statement

```
                    ANDERS AND BUDD
                    Income Statement
              For Year Ended December 31, 1984

Sales......................................................   $600,000
Cost of goods sold ........................................    360,400
Gross margin ..............................................   $239,600
Operating expenses:
  Selling..................................  $100,000
  Administrative...........................    80,000        180,000
      Net operating income ................................  $ 59,600
Nonoperating revenue: Interest ............................       400
Net income ................................................  $ 60,000
```

```
                    Distribution of Net Income

                            Anders      Budd       Total
         Interest ........  $ 2,400   $ 4,800    $ 7,200
         Salary ..........   16,000    10,000     26,000
         Remainder equally   13,400    13,400     26,800
         Net income ......  $31,800   $28,200    $60,000
```

Statement of partners' capital

At the close of each period, a *statement of partners' capital* is prepared. This statement summarizes the effects of transactions on the capital of each partner and in total for all partners for the period. It is prepared from data in the capital accounts in the general ledger. The statement serves the same purpose as the statement of owner's capital in a single proprietorship.

The statement of partners' capital presents details not readily shown on the balance sheet. The balance sheet contains only the final balance of each partner's capital account when it is accompanied by a statement of partners' capital.

Illustration 14.3: Statement of partners' capital

```
                          ANDERS AND BUDD
                   Statement of Partners' Capital
              For the Year Ended December 31, 1984

                                        Anders      Budd       Total
Balance January 1, 1984 .............  $ 40,000   $ 80,000   $120,000
  Add: Additional investments .......    45,000     54,000     99,000
Capital account balances, December 31, 1984,
  before drawing charges ............  $ 85,000   $134,000   $219,000
  Deduct: Drawings ..................    14,000     22,000     36,000
Capital account balances before 1984
  income distribution ...............  $ 71,000   $112,000   $183,000
Net income per income statement......    31,800     28,200     60,000
Capital account balances, December 31, 1984 ...  $102,800  $140,200   $243,000
```

The statement of partners' capital for Anders and Budd is presented in Illustration 14.3. The information on additional investment was given in Illustration 14.1, page 502, and information on drawings was given on page 501. The statement could show net income added to the beginning capital balances before drawings are deducted, instead of after; either format is correct.

CHANGES IN PARTNERSHIP PERSONNEL

Legally, a partnership is terminated when a new partner is admitted or an existing partner withdraws or retires. In most cases, the old partnership is succeeded immediately by a new partnership. The new partnership differs from the old one only to the extent of the change in partners. In these cases, the "termination" is technical only, and business operations and the accounting for them continue without pause. A technical termination of a partnership differs substantially from liquidation of a partnership, as is discussed later.

Admission of a new partner

A new partner can gain admission to a partnership in either of two ways: purchase of an interest from one or more existing partners, or by investment of assets in the partnership.

Purchase of an interest. When a new partner purchases an interest directly from an existing partner, the partnership's assets and liabilities remain unchanged. The exchange of cash and other assets for the equity interest is a personal transaction between two individuals, occurring outside the partnership accounting entity. The entry on the partnership's books simply transfers a portion of the partnership capital from an existing partner to a new partner.

To illustrate, assume that Smith and Jones are partners with capital account balances of $15,000 and $13,000, respectively. Farr purchases an $8,000 interest in the partnership capital from Jones. The journal entry on the partnership's books is:

```
Jones, Capital . . . . . . . . . . . . . . . . . . . . . . . . . . . . . . . . . . . . . . . . . . . . . . . .   8,000
     Farr, Capital  . . . . . . . . . . . . . . . . . . . . . . . . . . . . . . . . . . . . . . . . . . . .            8,000
     To transfer $8,000 of Jones's interest in the partnership assets to Farr.
```

The price that Farr paid Jones might be more or less than $8,000, but this difference is not reflected on the books of the partnership. The journal entry merely shows the book value of the interest that is purchased and sold.

Investment in the partnership. When a new partner acquires an interest in a partnership by investing assets in the business, both partnership assets and total owners' equity increase. In this case, the assets given up by the new partner become the property of the partnership.

To illustrate, assume that the partnership of Crowe and Lang has the following assets and equities:

Assets		Equities	
Cash	$15,000	Crowe, capital	$35,000
Other assets	55,000	Lang, capital	35,000
Total assets	$70,000	Total equities	$70,000

Crowe and Lang agree to admit Potter as a partner with a one-half interest in the partnership upon Potter's investment of $70,000 cash. The entry to record Potter's investment is:

```
Cash ....................................................... 70,000
      Potter, Capital ........................................         70,000
   To record Potter's investment of $70,000 cash.
```

After the above entry is posted, the partnership has the following assets and equities:

Assets		Equities	
Cash	$ 85,000	Crowe, capital	$ 35,000
Other assets	55,000	Lang, capital	35,000
		Potter, capital	70,000
Total assets	$140,000	Total equities	$140,000

The one-half interest in the equity of the partnership credited to Potter does not carry with it the right to receive one half of the future income or loss of the partnership. Income and loss distribution is a separate matter upon which the three partners must agree. If the new partnership agreement does not specify how income and losses are to be shared, the law assumes that the new partners intend to share income and losses equally; in this case, each would receive one third of income or loss.

Bonus to the old partners. If an existing partnership consistently earns above-average income, the existing partners may require a new partner to pay a bonus for admission to the partnership. For example, Marsh and Will operate a partnership which has had above-average net income for the last 10 years. The partners share income and losses in a ratio of 2:1—that is, Marsh receives two thirds and Will receives one third. The partners' capital account balances show $55,000 for Marsh and $75,000 for Will. Marsh and Will agree to admit Gray as a partner with a one-fourth interest in both capital and income in exchange for $50,000. Gray's equity in the partnership is $45,000, computed as follows:

```
Equities of old partners ($55,000 + $75,000) ....... $130,000
Investment of new partner ......................      50,000
      Total equities of new partnership ............ $180,000
Gray's one-fourth equity ($180,000 × ¼) ......... $ 45,000
```

The entry to record Gray's investment in the partnership is:

Cash	50,000	
Gray, Capital		45,000
Marsh, Capital		3,333
Will, Capital		1,667

To record Gray's investment in partnership.

Notice that Gray paid $50,000 for an equity of only $45,000. The $5,000 difference is a bonus to the old partners which they share in their income and loss ratio.

Bonus to the new partner. Sometimes an incoming partner may be able to provide cash which is desperately needed, or may have extraordinary abilities or business contacts which can help increase the partnership's income. In such cases, the existing partners may be willing to give the new partner a bonus—that is, an equity in the partnership greater than the new partner's investment. For example, assume Bentz and Hahn are partners with capital balances of $100,000 and $60,000, respectively. They share income and losses in a 3:2 ratio. The partnership desperately needs cash, and the partners are willing to give Kirby a one-fourth equity interest in the firm for an investment of $40,000 cash. Kirby agrees, invests $40,000, and receives an equity interest computed as follows:

Equities of old partners ($100,000 + $60,000)	$160,000
Investment of new partner	40,000
Total equities of new partnership	$200,000
Kirby's one-fourth interest ($200,000 × ¼)	$ 50,000

The entry to record Kirby's investment in the partnership is:

Cash	40,000	
Bentz, Capital	6,000	
Hahn, Capital	4,000	
Kirby, Capital		50,000

To record Kirby's investment in the partnership.

Notice that the $10,000 bonus is contributed by the old partners in their income and loss sharing ratio. After Kirby is admitted to the firm, the partners should agree on new income sharing provisions.

There are alternative methods that could be used to record the admission of a new partner, but these will be left for an advanced text. Considered next are changes in firm ownership brought about by the retirement or withdrawal of a partner.

Retirement of a partner

A partnership agreement should contain provisions that describe the procedures to be followed when a partner retires. The procedures followed should indicate how to compute the price to be paid by the firm for the retiring partner's equity interest.

Typically, an audit of the accounts is required to ensure their accuracy. Also, the fair market values of the assets must be determined. If asset values are restated, gains and losses from revaluation will be reflected in the partners' capital accounts. One reason for revaluation is that after the withdrawal by a partner, a new entity is created which should record its assets at fair value at time of formation. Secondly, the withdrawing partner will be credited and charged for a share of unrecorded gains and losses. Such unrecorded gains and losses must be considered in computing the retiring partner's share of the firm's net assets at the time of withdrawal. The retiring partner typically is paid an amount equal to the adjusted balance in that partner's capital account. But in some cases, assets revaluations are not recorded and the retiring partner is paid an amount that differs from that partner's capital account balance. Three cases to illustrate the accounting for the retirement of a partner are presented.

Case 1. Retiring partner receives adjusted book value of equity. Assume that Snow, South, and Stone are partners sharing income and loss in a 3:1:1 ratio. Stone retires when the partnership book's show:

Assets			Equities	
Cash		$ 30,000	Snow, capital	$ 50,000
Accounts receivable		10,000	South, capital	30,000
Merchandise inventory		40,000	Stone, capital	20,000
Plant and equipment	$50,000			
Less: Accumulated depreciation	30,000	20,000		
Total assets		$100,000	Total equities	$100,000

The partnership books are audited. Certain accounts receivable, recorded at $500, are deemed worthless and are written off. Merchandise inventory is revalued at $45,500, and plant and equipment are revalued at $54,000 with $32,000 accumulated depreciation. The journal entries to record this information are:

Snow, Capital	300	
South, Capital	100	
Stone, Capital	100	
Accounts Receivable		500
To write off worthless accounts.		
Merchandise Inventory	5,500	
Snow, Capital		3,300
South, Capital		1,100
Stone, Capital		1,100
To revalue inventory.		
Plant and Equipment	4,000	
Accumulated Depreciation		2,000
Snow, Capital		1,200
South, Capital		400
Stone, Capital		400
To revalue plant and equipment.		

The gains and losses from asset revaluations eventually would have been realized and reflected in net income. Thus, gains and losses should be shared by the partners in their income and loss ratio.

After the above entries have been posted, the partnership's assets and equities are:

Assets			Equities	
Cash		$ 30,000	Snow, capital	$ 54,200
Accounts receivable		9,500	South, capital	31,400
Merchandise inventory		45,500	Stone, capital	21,400
Plant and equipment	$54,000			
Less: Accumulated depreciation	32,000	22,000		
Total assets		$107,000	Total equities	$107,000

With assets revalued and capital accounts adjusted, Stone has a $21,400 interest in partnership net assets. Assuming Stone is paid cash, the entry to record Stone's retirement is:

Stone, Capital	21,400	
Cash		21,400
To record Stone's withdrawal from the firm.		

Stone could have received any combination of assets totaling $21,400 to which the partners agreed. Or Stone could have accepted a note payable by the new partnership of Snow and South. Snow and South must now agree upon a new income and loss sharing provision.

Case 2. Retiring partner receives more than the book value of equity.

Sometimes the partners may not revalue assets and adjust the accounts when a partner withdraws. In such cases, the partners may agree that the assets are undervalued and that the withdrawing partner should receive assets worth more than the book value of that partner's equity. At other times, the remaining partners may be so anxious for the partner to withdraw that they are willing to give up assets worth more than the book value of that partner's equity. In both cases, the withdrawing partner, in effect, withdraws assets equal to the book value of that partner's own equity plus part of the book value of the remaining partners' equities.

To illustrate, assume that North, East, and West are partners who share income and losses in a 3:2:1 ratio. East withdraws from the partnership at a time when it has the following assets and equities:

Assets		Equities	
Cash	$30,000	North, capital	$50,000
Merchandise inventory	40,000	East, capital	25,000
Equipment, net	20,000	West, capital	15,000
Total assets	$90,000	Total equities	$90,000

The partners agree that assets are undervalued by $3,000, but they do not wish to adjust the accounts to current market values. If the accounts had been revalued, East's capital account would have been increased by $1,000, or two sixths of the $3,000 adjustment. East is therefore allowed to withdraw $26,000 cash from the partnership for his equity interest. The entry to record East's withdrawal is:

East, Capital	25,000	
North, Capital	750	
West, Capital	250	
Cash		26,000
To record East's withdrawal.		

East withdrew $1,000 more than the book value of his equity. This excess amount is charged to North's and West's capital accounts on the basis of their income and loss ratio of 3:1 (¾ × $1,000 = $750 to North and ¼ × $1,000 = $250 to West).

Case 3: Retiring partner receives less than the book value of equity. Sometimes the partners may agree that the assets are overvalued but that they do not want to adjust the accounts. In such cases, the partners may also agree that the withdrawing partner should receive assets worth less than the book value of that partner's equity. At other times, a partner who is very anxious to withdraw from a partnership may be willing to accept assets worth less than the book value of that partner's equity. The undrawn equity is divided between the remaining partners in their income and loss ratio, and credited to their capital accounts.

To illustrate, assume that Alda, Fonda, and Moore are partners who share earnings and losses in an 8:7:5 (40 percent, 35 percent, 25 percent) ratio. The partnership's assets and equities are as follows:

Assets		Equities	
Cash	$21,000	Alda, capital	$25,000
Merchandise inventory	24,000	Fonda, capital	22,000
Plant and equipment, net	20,000	Moore, capital	18,000
Total assets	$65,000	Total equities	$65,000

Moore is very anxious to withdraw from the partnership and is willing to accept $16,000 in settlement of her equity. Alda and Fonda agree to the settlement. The entry to record Moore's withdrawal is:

Moore, Capital	18,000	
Cash		16,000
Alda, Capital		1,067
Fonda, Capital		933
To record Moore's withdrawal.		

Moore withdrew $2,000 less than the book value of her equity. The undrawn $2,000 is credited to the capital accounts of Alda and Fonda in their income and loss sharing ratio of 8:7; that is, 8/15 × $2,000 and 7/15 × $2,000.

The above illustrations all involved technical terminations or dissolutions of partnerships. One partnership was legally terminated and succeeded by another partnership which carried on substantially the same business operations.

Attention is next turned to circumstances where business operations cease and the partnership is legally terminated.

LIQUIDATION OF A PARTNERSHIP

The *liquidation* of a partnership involves an end to business operations, sale of the assets for cash, payment of cash to creditors and partners, and legal termination of the partnership.

Partnerships may be liquidated for a number of reasons including:

1. The objective sought in forming the partnership has been achieved.
2. The time period for which the partnership was formed has expired.
3. Newly enacted legislation has made the partnership's activities illegal.
4. The partnership or one of its partners is bankrupt.

Liquidation may take place rapidly, or over an extended period. If liquidation is rapid, a single cash distribution may be made to the partners after all assets are sold and the liabilities paid. If liquidation is prolonged, more than one cash distribution may be made to the partners. Only those liquidations that involve a single payment to partners are discussed below.

Partnership liquidations illustrated

In the following illustrations it is assumed that all assets were sold, all liabilities paid, and that a single distribution was made to partners to liquidate their capital accounts.

The partnership of Ring, Scott, and Terry is liquidated on August 1, 1984. The income and loss ratio is: Ring, 40 percent; Scott, 35 percent; and Terry, 25 percent. Business operations are discontinued on August 1, 1984. Immediately preceding liquidation, the trial balance of the firm, in condensed form, is as shown in Illustration 14.4. Three cases are presented below.

Illustration 14.4: Condensed trial balance

	Debits	Credits
RING, SCOTT, AND TERRY Trial Balance August 1, 1984		
Assets	$100,000	
Liabilities . . .		$ 10,000
Ring, capital		30,000
Scott, capital		30,000
Terry, capital		30,000
	$100,000	$100,000

Case 1: Assets sold at a gain.   The assets are sold for $105,000, and the $5,000 gain on the sale is distributed to the partners in their income and loss ratio. The liabilities are paid in full. The remaining cash is distributed to the partners in accordance with the balances of their capital accounts, not in the income and loss ratio.

The journal entries to record the foregoing facts and the liquidation of the partnership on August 1, 1984, are as follows:

```
Cash ...................................................    105,000
    Assets ...............................................               100,000
    Gain on Sale of Assets ...............................                 5,000
    To record the sale of the assets.

Gain on Sale of Assets ....................................      5,000
    Ring, Capital ($5,000  ×  0.40) ......................                 2,000
    Scott, Capital ($5,000  ×  0.35) .....................                 1,750
    Terry, Capital ($5,000  ×  0.25) .....................                 1,250
    To distribute the gain on the sale of the assets.

Liabilities ..............................................     10,000
    Cash .................................................                10,000
    To record the settlement of partnership liabilities.
```

After the above entries are posted, the partners' capital accounts show:

Ring, Capital		Scott, Capital		Terry, Capital	
Beg. bal.	30,000	Beg. bal.	30,000	Beg. bal.	30,000
Gain from sale of assets	2,000	Gain from sale of assets	1,750	Gain from sale of assets	1,250
End. bal.	32,000	End. bal.	31,750	End. bal.	31,250

The entry to record the cash distributed to partners is:

```
Ring, Capital .............................................     32,000
Scott, Capital ............................................     31,750
Terry, Capital ............................................     31,250
    Cash .................................................                95,000
    To distribute the remaining cash to the partners in accordance with
    the balances of their capital accounts.
```

Case 2.   Assets sold at a loss.   The assets of Ring, Scott, and Terry are sold for $80,000, and the $20,000 loss on the sale is distributed to the partners in the income and loss ratio. The liabilities are paid in full. The remaining cash is distributed to the partners in accordance with the balances of their capital accounts.

The journal entries are:

```
Cash ......................................................     80,000
Loss on Sale of Assets ....................................     20,000
    Assets ...............................................               100,000
    To record the sale of the assets.
```

Ring, Capital (40 percent)	8,000	
Scott, Capital (35 percent)	7,000	
Terry, Capital (25 percent)	5,000	
Loss on Sale of Assets		20,000

To distribute the loss on the sale of the assets.

| Liabilities | 10,000 | |
| Cash | | 10,000 |

To record the settlement of the liabilities of the firm.

After the above entries have been posted, the accounts show Cash, $70,000; Ring, Capital, $22,000; Scott, Capital, $23,000; and Terry, Capital, $25,000. The entry to record the cash distributed to partners is:

Ring, Capital	22,000	
Scott, Capital	23,000	
Terry, Capital	25,000	
Cash		70,000

To record the distribution of the cash to the partners.

Case 3: Assets sold at a loss when one partner's share of the loss is greater than the balance of that partner's capital account. In Case 2, the loss charged to the capital account of each partner is smaller than that partner's capital account balance. But it is possible that a partner's portion of the loss may be greater than that partner's capital account balance. When a loss is charged to a partner and a debit balance is created in that partner's capital account, the debit balance represents an amount owed by that partner to the other partners. The cash available for distribution will be insufficient to pay the other partners in full until the partner with the debit balance pays in the amount of the debit balance. If the partner with the debit balance is unable to pay the amount owed, the remaining partners must bear this loss in the income and loss ratio existing between them.

To illustrate, assume that the assets of Ring, Scott, and Terry were sold for only $20,200. Entries to record the foregoing facts and the liquidation follow:

Cash	20,200	
Loss on Sale of Assets	79,800	
Assets		100,000

To record the sale of the assets.

Ring, Capital (40 percent)	31,920	
Scott, Capital (35 percent)	27,930	
Terry, Capital (25 percent)	19,950	
Loss on Sale of Assets		79,800

To distribute the loss on the sale of the assets.

| Liabilities | 10,000 | |
| Cash | | 10,000 |

To record the settlement of the liabilities of the partnership.

At this stage of the liquidation, the accounts of the partnership have the following balances:

Cash	Ring, Capital	Scott, Capital	Terry, Capital
10,200	1,920	2,070	10,050

Only $10,200 of cash is available for distribution to Scott and Terry, while the combined balance of their capital accounts is $12,120. To pay Scott and Terry the amounts owed, the firm needs $1,920 more cash, which is the amount owed the firm by Ring, and which Ring is unable to pay. The $1,920 is thus a loss that must be shared by Scott and Terry in their income and loss sharing ratio. Omitting Ring, Scott and Terry share losses in a 35:25 ratio. Thus, Scott's share of the loss is $1,120 (35/60 × $1,920) and Terry's share is $800 (25/60 × $1,920).

The debit balance in Ring's capital account is closed and the loss absorbed by Scott and Terry as shown in the following entry:

Scott, Capital	1,120	
Terry, Capital	800	
Ring, Capital		1,920
To charge Scott and Terry with Ring's capital deficiency.		

The only accounts left on the books now are the Cash account and Scott's and Terry's capital accounts. The remaining cash is distributed to Scott and Terry in the amounts now shown in their capital accounts:

Scott, Capital	950	
Terry, Capital	9,250	
Cash		10,200
To record final cash distribution to partners.		

With this entry, all accounts of the partnership now have a zero balance and the partnership is ended. Scott and Terry do have the legal right to collect the $1,920 Ring owes them. But the firm is now liquidated; no further entries will be made on its books.

Alternatively, if Ring paid the $1,920 owed the firm prior to closing of the accounts, the following entries would be needed:

Cash	1,920	
Ring, Capital		1,920
To record payment of capital deficiency by Ring.		

Scott, Capital	2,070	
Terry, Capital	10,050	
Cash		12,120
To distribute cash to partners in liquidation.		

Notice that Ring does not receive any cash in the final settlement. He had to pay cash to the firm to reduce his capital account to a zero balance.

The analysis of a partnership liquidation, assuming Ring pays the amount owed to the partnership, may be aided by the preparation of a liquidation work sheet as shown in Illustration 14.5.

Illustration 14.5:   Liquidation work sheet

	Ring	Scott	Terry	Total
Income and loss ratio	**40 percent**	**35 percent**	**25 percent**	**100 percent**
Capital account balance	$30,000	$30,000	$30,000	$90,000
Apportionment of loss on sale of assets	31,920	27,930	19,950	79,800
Capital balances after loss apportionment	$ (1,920)	$ 2,070	$10,050	$10,200
Ring's contribution	1,920			1,920
Capital account balances	–0–	$ 2,070	$10,050	$12,120
Liquidating distribution		(2,070)	(10,050)	(12,120)
Balance	–0–	–0–	–0–	–0–

Note: ( ) = debit.

NEW TERMS INTRODUCED IN CHAPTER 14

Agent
One who has the authority to act for another (the partnership) or in the place of another. See mutual agency.

Articles of copartnership
See partnership agreement.

Income and loss ratio
The agreed-upon way that a partnership's income or losses are shared. Often called the *profit and loss ratio* or the *earnings and loss ratio*.

Interest (on capital invested)
A means often used in the sharing of income to give weight to the relative amounts of capital invested by the partners. The interest is sometimes based on the beginning-of-year balances in the capital accounts and sometimes on the average balances in the capital accounts. The interest is *not* an expense to be deducted in arriving at net income.

Liquidation (of a partnership)
Involves an end to business operations, sale of assets for cash, distribution of cash to creditors and partners, and legal termination of the partnership.

Mutual agency
The power possessed by a partner to bind a partnership to any contract within the apparent scope of the partnership's business.

Partnership
An association of two or more persons to carry on a business as co-owners for profit. Often referred to as a firm, such as a law firm.

Partnership agreement
Also known as articles of copartnership (when in written form); the conditions or provisions accepted by all of the partners to serve as the basis for the formation, operation, and liquidation of the partnership.

Salary (granted to partners)
A means often used in the sharing of income to reward certain partners for spending more time than other partners in running the affairs of the business. The salary is *not* an expense of the partnership in determining net income.

Statement of partners' capital
A financial statement which summarizes the transactions affecting the capital balance of each partner and in total for all partners.

Termination
The legal *dissolution* of a partnership brought on by a change in partners.

Uniform Partnership Act
A written law adopted in all states which provides the general framework of law relating to the formation, operation, and termination of a partnership.

Unlimited liability
A characteristic of partnerships under which owners are liable for more than merely the amounts invested in the business, since their personal assets may also be taken to satisfy the claims of business creditors.

DEMONSTRATION PROBLEM

The Cox and Long partnership had the following income and loss sharing agreement:

1. Cox receives an annual salary of $12,000.
2. Cox and Long each receive interest at 10 percent on their capital balances at the beginning of the year.
3. The remainder is divided by Cox and Long in a 2:1 ratio.

On January 1, 1984, the partners' capital account balances were Cox, $30,000, and Long, $40,000. On December 31, 1984, the partners' drawing account balances were Cox, $10,000, and Long, $8,000. Net income for the year ended December 31, 1984, was $20,000.

Required:

a. Prepare a schedule showing the distribution of net income to the partners.

b. Prepare journal entries to close the Income Summary account and the drawing accounts.

c. Assume that on January 1, 1985, Cox and Long admit Neil to a 25 percent interest in capital for an investment of $32,000 cash. Prepare the entry to admit Neil using the bonus method.

Solution to demonstration problem

a.

	Cox	Long	Both	Amount to be distributed
Net income				$20,000
Salaries	$12,000	$ –0–	$12,000	8,000
Interest:				
Cox (10% of $30,000) . . .	3,000			
Long (10% of $40,000) . .		4,000	7,000	1,000
Remainder (2:1)	667	333	1,000	–0–
Distribution	$15,667	$4,333	$20,000	

b.

1981
Dec. 31 Income Summary 20,000
         Cox, Capital   15,667
         Long, Capital   4,333
    To distribute balance in Income Summary.

    31 Cox, Capital 10,000
        Long, Capital 8,000
         Cox, Drawing   10,000
         Long, Drawing   8,000
    To close drawing accounts.

c.

Cash 32,000		
Neil, Capital		26,000
Cox, Capital		4,000
Long, Capital		2,000

    To record admission of Neil to the firm.

Computations are:

Capital on January 1, 1984: $30,000 + $40,000 = ...	$ 70,000
Net income for 1984	20,000
Drawings in 1984	(18,000)
Total capital, January 1, 1985	$ 72,000
Capital contributed by Neil........................	32,000
Total capital after admission of Neil	$104,000
Neil's share (25%)	$ 26,000

QUESTIONS

1. Jim Black currently is operating a small machine shop. He is considering forming a partnership with an employee, Fred Brown, whom he considers an excellent worker and supervisor and with whom it is easy to associate. Prepare a brief list of the advantages and disadvantages to Black of the potential partnership.

2. Many matters usually are covered in the typical partnership agreement. Some of them are of little significance to the accountant, while others are quite crucial. What are some of the crucial provisions as far as the accountant is concerned?

3. Jones and Smith are partners in a local grocery store. Both take home sufficient merchandise to feed their families. Would you suggest that the merchandise taken home be recorded at selling price or cost? Why?

4. Can you think of a set of circumstances in which you might be willing to enter into a partnership with another person, do all of the work needed to run the business, provide all of the capital, and yet be willing to allow the other person a substantial share of the net income?

5. Why should a partnership agreement be quite specific regarding the treatment of withdrawals by partners insofar as the sharing of income and losses is concerned?

6. What are three reasons for the formation of partnerships?

7. What is a statement of partners' capital?

8. Describe two different ways in which a new partner can be admitted to a partnership.

9. Why might a newly admitted partner's capital account balance differ from the amount actually invested?

10. Why might a withdrawing partner receive assets worth more or less than the book value of his or her equity?

11. What procedures are followed in liquidating a partnership?

12. What are three acts or conditions that will lead to the liquidation of a partnership?

EXERCISES

E-1. Blue, Lilac, and Aqua are partners. In 1984, net income of their partnership is $180,000. How much will be credited to each partner in the income distribution if:

    a. Nothing is said in the partnership agreement concerning the division of income?

    b. The income and loss sharing ratio is 50:30:20, respectively?

E–2.   Give the entries to record the division of income in (*b*) of Exercise E–1. Also give the entries to record the closing of the drawing accounts assuming drawings were $30,000, $40,000, and $20,000, respectively.

E–3.   Given an income and loss ratio of 5:3:2, how would the three partners in Exercise E–1 share a loss of $90,000? Give the journal entry.

E–4.   Partner A was credited with a salary of $24,000 and interest of $12,000 on her capital account and was charged with $2,000 as her share of the balance in the Income Summary account after taking partners' salaries and interest on partners' capital balances into account. She withdrew $28,000 during the year. What amount will she report to the Internal Revenue Service as her share of the partnership's income?

E–5.   The capital account balances of A and B stood at $20,000 and $75,000 throughout the entire year. A withdrew $8,000 and B withdrew $12,000, and these drawings were normal withdrawals rather than withdrawals of investment.

     Net income for the year was $20,000. If salaries are to be allowed A and B in the amounts of $8,000 and $7,000 and the balance of the income is distributed equally, what will be each partner's total share of the income for the year?

E–6.   Given the following capital account, compute the average capital investment for the year:

Carson, Capital

Mar. 1	9,000	Jan. 1	48,000
Aug. 1	2,000	May 1	24,000
Dec. 1	5,000	June 1	3,000

E–7.   E and F are partners. They agree that each partner can withdraw $1,000 in cash at the end of each month, with such withdrawals debited to each partner's drawing account. In sharing income, 10 percent interest is to be allowed on average capital investment taking into consideration withdrawals in excess of the allowed $1,000 per month. Each partner is to be credited with a salary of $12,000 per year. The remainder of the income or loss is to be shared equally by E and F.

     E's capital account at January 1 was $100,000. She withdrew $5,000 on July 1, in addition to the allowed $1,000 monthly cash withdrawals.

     F's capital account balance at January 1 was $150,000. She withdrew $8,000 on April 1 and $12,000 on October 1. She also withdrew the allowed $1,000 cash per month.

     Prepare a short schedule showing the distribution of $75,000 net income for the current year.

E–8.   L, M, and N are partners with capital account balances of $90,000, $110,000, and $80,000, respectively. G now acquires one third of L's interest and one half of N's interest for $63,000. Prepare the entry to record G's acquisition of an interest in the partnership.

E–9.   Colt, Jeep, and Ram are partners with capital account balances of $20,000, $30,000 and $50,000, respectively. The partners agree to admit Scamp to a one-fourth interest in both capital and income for a $20,000 cash investment in the partnership. Determine Scamp's equity in the new partnership, and prepare the journal entry to record the admission of Scamp. (Assume that the original partners shared income and losses in the ratio of 3:3:4.)

4/9 3/9 2/9

E-10.   A, B, and C are partners with capital account balances of $150,000, $100,000, and $75,000, respectively. They share income and losses in a 4:3:2 ratio. B decides to withdraw. The partnership revalues its assets from $325,000 to $370,000. B then receives cash equal to the recorded amount of his equity after assets have been adjusted to current market value. These adjustments involved an increase in inventory of $25,000 and an increase in plant and equipment of $20,000. Prepare journal entries to adjust the partnership accounts and to record the withdrawal of B.

E-11.   Smith, Jones, and Jackson are partners with capital balances of $30,000, $20,000, and $10,000, respectively. They share income and losses in a 5:2:2 ratio. Jackson withdraws and is paid $13,500 for his equity interest by the partnership. Give the journal entry to record the withdrawal of Jackson using the bonus method.

E-12.   Law, Hamlin, and Frazier are partners with capital accounts of $35,000, $60,000, and $45,000, respectively. They share income and losses in a 2:3:4 ratio. Although she believes the assets of the partnership are fairly valued, Frazier is so anxious to retire that she accepts $40,000 cash as payment in full for her equity. Prepare the journal entry to record Frazier's withdrawal.

E-13.   X, Y, and Z are partners with capital balances of $286,000, $130,000, and $100,000, respectively. They share income and losses in a 4:4:2 ratio. Total net assets (assets − liabilities) are $516,000, consisting of $616,000 of noncash assets and $100,000 of liabilities. The partnership is liquidated by selling the assets for $520,000, paying the liabilities, and distributing cash to the partners. Prepare the necessary journal entries.

E-14.   The liability and capital accounts of the firm of Black and Blue are as follow:

Accounts payable	$ 30,000
Black, capital	45,000
Blue, capital	90,000
Total	$165,000

All of the firm's assets (all noncash) are sold for $147,000, and that amount of cash is on hand even though the entry to record sale of the assets has not been recorded. Income and losses are shared 3:2 to Black and Blue. Prepare entries to record sale of the assets, distribution of the loss, and payment of the $147,000 to creditors and the partners.

E-15.   The trial balance of the T-V partnership is as follows:

	Debits	Credits
Assets	$200,000	
Accounts payable		$ 20,000
T, capital		120,000
V, capital		60,000
	$200,000	$200,000

The partners decide to liquidate. The assets are sold for $90,000, and the cash is paid out. Prepare the necessary journal entries, assuming an equal sharing of income and losses.

E-16.   Alice, May, and Jean are partners. Certain data for their firm are:

	Alice	May	Jean	Total
Capital balances prior to entering effects of 1984 operations	$147,000	$41,000	$97,000	$285,000
Loss for year ended December 31, 1984 ..				30,000
Income and loss ratio	20%	50%	30%	100%

The partners decide to liquidate. There are no liabilities. All of the assets are noncash assets and are sold for $150,000 cash.

    a.   Prepare the journal entry to close the 1984 loss.

    b.   Prepare journal entries for the sale of the assets and the distribution of cash to partners. Each partner had invested all of her personal assets in the firm prior to liquidation and will not be able to pay any deficiency in her capital account.

PROBLEMS, SERIES A

P14–1–A.   Darryl Jones and Ernest Hiller, who have been in business as sole proprietors, decided to combine all of their business assets and liabilities in a new partnership in which they will share income and losses equally. Balance sheets of the two individuals on the date of the formation of the partnership were as shown:

DARRYL JONES
Balance Sheet
September 4, 1984

Assets

Cash	$ 4,000
Accounts receivable (net)	15,000
Inventory	9,000
Equipment (net)	20,000
Total assets	$48,000

Liabilities and Owner's Equity

Accounts payable	$23,000
Darryl Jones, capital	25,000
Total liabilities and owner's equity	$48,000

ERNEST HILLER
Balance Sheet
September 4, 1984

Assets

Cash	$14,000
Accounts receivable (net)	17,000
Inventory	20,000
Total assets	$51,000

Liabilities and Owner's Equity

Accounts payable	$22,000
Ernest Hiller, capital	29,000
Total liabilities and owner's equity	$51,000

An appraisal of the assets showed market values for the assets of Jones as follows: accounts receivable, $14,000; inventory, $12,000; and equipment, $15,000. A similar appraisal placed the following market values upon Hiller's assets: accounts receivable, $17,000; and inventory, $13,000.

Required:

Prepare journal entries to record the capital contributions of Jones and Hiller to their newly formed partnership.

P14–2–A. An analysis of the capital accounts for 1984 of White and Stevens, partners, showed:

White

Jan. 1	Balance	$90,000
June 1	Capital withdrawal	15,000
Nov. 1	Additional investment . .	22,500

Stevens

Jan. 1	Balance	$15,000
July 1	Additional investment . .	30,000

The balance in the Income Summary account showed net income of $45,000 for 1984.

Required:

Prepare a schedule showing the distribution of the net income under each of the following assumptions with regard to income distribution. Also prepare the entries to distribute the income and to close the drawing accounts. (Note: In each instance assume drawings were equal to salaries allowed for each partner.)

a. White and Stevens are allowed annual salaries of $12,000 and $15,000; 8 percent interest is allowed on average capital balances; and the balance of the income is shared equally.

b. Equal annual salaries of $18,000 are allowed to each partner; interest at 10 percent is allowed on capital balances at the beginning of the year; and the balance is shared in a 3:2 ratio between White and Stevens.

P14–3–A. The B and D partnership agreement stated the following relative to the sharing of income and losses: (1) B is to be allowed interest at 10 percent on her capital account balance as of the beginning of the year; (2) D is to be allowed a salary of $1,800 per month; and any remaining balance of income or loss is to be shared equally. The net income for 1984 was $54,000.

Required:

a. Assuming that B's and D's capital account balances on January 1, 1984, were $180,000 and $45,000, respectively, prepare a schedule showing the distribution of net income and the entry required to record it.

b. Prepare the entry needed to close the drawing accounts of the partners, which had the following balances (before closing) on December 31, 1984: B, zero; and D, $21,600.

c. Present a schedule showing the changes occurring in 1984 in the capital account of each partner.

P14–4–A. The capital account balances (unchanged during the year) on December 31, 1984, for N and I, partners, are $240,000 for N and $120,000 for I. N withdrew $24,000 and I withdrew $60,000 during the year, with all withdrawals charged to the respective drawing accounts. Net loss for the year amounted to $24,000.

Required:

Prepare schedules showing the distribution of income to each partner for the year 1984 under each of the following assumed provisions in the partnership agreement relating to the sharing of income:

a. Salaries are allowed of $18,000 and $45,000 to N and I; remaining income is divided according to capital account balances at the beginning of the year.

b. Salaries are allowed of $12,000 and $20,000; interest is allowed on capital account balances at the beginning of the year at 10 percent; no further provisions relating to income sharing are included in the partnership agreement.

P14–5–A. Mike and John are partners in a retail hardware store. Their partnership agreement calls for salaries to Mike and John of $12,000 and $24,000, and interest at 10 percent on average capital for the year. Any remaining balance is to be shared equally.

During 1984, each partner drew his allowed salary; there were no withdrawals in excess of allowed salaries. The capital accounts of the two partners remained unchanged during the year at $60,000 for Mike and $90,000 for John.

Required:

Present schedules showing the distribution of net income assuming that the income statement for 1984 showed:

a. $72,000 of net income.

b. $30,000 of net income.

c. A loss of $12,000.

P14–6–A. Poole and Rankin are partners operating a retail store having a fiscal year ending on June 30. Their partnership agreement calls for annual salaries of $12,000 to Poole and $16,000 to Rankin, interest at 8 percent on average capital account balances throughout the year, and the balance of the income to be shared equally. Their June 30, 1984, trial balance follows:

	Debits	Credits
Cash	$ 40,400	
Accounts receivable	64,000	
Inventory, July 1, 1983	28,800	
Accounts payable		$ 40,800
Notes payable		20,000
Poole, capital		28,000
Rankin, capital		20,000
Poole, drawing	8,000	
Rankin, drawing	10,000	
Sales		428,000
Purchases	272,000	
Purchase returns		4,000
Employee salaries and wages	12,000	
Rent expense	52,000	
Delivery expense	16,800	
Store expense	36,800	
	$540,800	$540,800

The $20,000 note payable is a 120-day note dated April 1, 1984, and calls for interest at 10 percent per year. The inventory at June 30, 1984, is $33,200. The only change in the capital accounts during the year was an additional $8,000 investment by Poole on January 1.

Required:

You are to prepare the following for the partnership:

a. The necessary adjusting and closing entries.

b. An income statement for the year ended June 30, 1984.

c. A statement of partners' capital for the year ended June 30, 1984.

d. A balance sheet for June 30, 1984.

P14–7–A. Able, Robin, and Watts are partners who share income and losses in a 3:2:1 ratio. They decided to admit Andy to the partnership at a time when their capital account balances were:

Able, capital	$60,000
Robin, capital	30,000
Watts, capital	30,000

Required:

Prepare journal entries to record Andy's admission to the partnership under each of the following unrelated conditions:

a. Andy acquired 40 percent of Robin's interest for $18,000.

b. Andy acquired all of Watt's interest for $27,000 cash.

c. Andy invested $100,000 in the firm for a one-half interest in capital.

d. Andy was admitted to a one-fifth interest in capital for an investment of $20,000 because the old partnership was badly in need of cash to pay a maturing debt.

P14–8–A. A and B are partners with capital account balances of $66,000 and $36,000, respectively. Income and losses are shared in a 3:2 ratio.

Required:

Prepare the journal entries to record the admission of C to the partnership in each of the following independent situations.

a. C paid B personally $20,000 for one half of B's interest.

b. C invested sufficient cash in the firm to acquire a one-fourth interest in capital of the new firm.

c. C invested $38,000 for a one-fifth interest in capital (use the bonus method).

d. C invested $26,000 for a one-fourth interest (use the bonus method).

P14–9–A. On December 31, Joe Dodd, a member of the firm of Dodd and Ebel, decided to retire. The partners have shared income and losses equally. On this date their capital account credit balances were:

Joe Dodd	$90,000
Pat Dodd	60,000
Fred Ebel	60,000

Required:

Prepare entries to record the withdrawal of Joe Dodd under each of the following assumptions. All payments are to be in cash and assets are not to be revalued.

a. Joe Dodd was paid $90,000.

b. Joe Dodd was paid $96,000.

c. Joe Dodd was paid $80,000.

P14–10–A. Donald, John, and Charles are partners in the DJC Company. Ledger account balances on January 1, 1984, are:

Cash	$ 7,000	
Accounts receivable	12,000	
Allowance for doubtful accounts		$ 1,000
Merchandise inventory	25,000	
Equipment	6,000	
Accumulated depreciation		2,000
Accounts payable		8,000
Donald, capital		20,000
John, capital		15,000
Charles, capital		4,000
	$50,000	$50,000

The partners share income and losses in a 5:3:2 ratio.

Required:

Assume that Charles retires from the firm and receives a check for $5,000. Prepare entries to record Charles' retirement assuming:

a. The assets were not revalued.

b. Inventory was revalued at $31,000 and equipment was revalued at $3,000.

P14–11–A. Use the data in Problem P14–10–A above but ignore the revaluation of assets in part (b). Assume that the partners decided to liquidate. All of the noncash assets were sold for $15,000. After the assets were sold, the liabilities were paid, the remaining cash distributed to the partners, and the books were closed.

Required:

Prepare journal entries to record liquidation of the partnership. Assume that none of the partners has other assets to cover possible debit balances in his capital account.

P14–12–A. Given below is the balance sheet of the XYZ Partnership on April 30, 1984—the date the partners decided to liquide their firm.

XYZ PARTNERSHIP
Balance Sheet
April 30, 1984

Assets

Cash	$ 5,000
Accounts receivable	10,000
Merchandise inventory	25,000
Plant and equipment	50,000
Total assets	$90,000

Liabilities and Owners' Equity

Accounts payable	$47,500
X, capital	17,500
Y, capital	12,500
Z, capital	12,500
Total liabilities and owners' equity	$90,000

On May 1, the noncash assets were sold for $44,500. X, Y, and Z share income and losses in a 5:3:2 ratio.

Required:

Prepare all necessary journal entries to record the sale of the assets and the distribution of cash to creditors and partners. Assume that any partners who had debit balances in their capital accounts after loss distributions immediately paid cash to the firm equal to the debit balances.

PROBLEMS, SERIES B

P14–1–B.   Aaron Griffins and Douglas Sawyer decided to form a partnership by combining their business assets and liabilities (from their sole proprietorships). Income and losses will be shared in a 2:3 ratio to Griffins and Sawyer, respectively. Balance sheets on November 23, 1984, the date the partnership was formed were:

AARON GRIFFINS
Balance Sheet
November 23, 1984

Assets

Cash	$ 8,000
Accounts receivable (net)	23,000
Inventory	34,000
Total assets	$65,000

Liabilities and Owner's Equity

Accounts payable	$22,000
Notes payable	18,000
Aaron Griffins, capital	25,000
Total liabilities and owner's equity	$65,000

DOUGLAS SAWYER
Balance Sheet
November 23, 1984

Assets

Cash	$ 2,000
Accounts receivable (net)	24,000
Inventory	47,000
Equipment (net)	15,000
Total assets	$88,000

Liabilities and Owner's Equity

Accounts payable	$48,000
Douglas Sawyer, capital	40,000
Total liabilities and owner's equity	$88,000

Current market values for Griffins' assets were: accounts receivable, $23,000; and inventory, $40,000. For Sawyer, market values were: accounts receivable, $19,500; inventory, $25,000; and equipment, $18,000.

Required:

Prepare journal entries to record the capital contributions by Griffins and Sawyer upon the formation of their partnership.

P14–2–B. An analysis of Wright's capital account for the year 1984 showed a beginning balance of $45,000, a capital withdrawal on June 1 of $15,000, and an additional investment on November 1 of $7,500. A similar analysis of partner Smith's capital account showed a beginning balance of $7,500 and an additional investment on July 1 of $30,000. The balance in the Income Summary account showed net income for the year of $33,000.

Required:

Prepare a sechdule and the required journal entry to record the distribution of the net income to the partners under each of the following independent assumptions:

a. Wright and Smith are allowed annual salaries of $12,000 and $15,000; 8 percent interest on average capital balance is to be credited to each partner, and the balance of income and losses is to be shared equally.

b. Equal annual salaries of $15,000 and interest at 6 percent on beginning capital balance are allowed each partner, and the remaining balance is shared in a 2:1 ratio to Wright and Smith.

P14–3–B. The balances in the capital accounts of P and S at June 30, 1984, were $240,000 and $120,000. These balances were unchanged during the year. P drew $32,000 during the year, and S drew $36,000. Net income for the year was $160,000.

Required:

Compute the income to be distributed to each partner at the end of the year under each of the following independent conditions:

a. Salaries allowed are $24,000 and $40,000 to P and S; remaining income is to be divided in the ratio of the beginning of the year capital account balances.

b. Salaries allowed are $76,000 and $64,000 to P and S; interest at 10 percent is allowed on capital account balances at the beginning of the year; there were no other provisions relating to the sharing of income and losses in the partnership agreement.

c. Assuming that income is shared as in (*a*) above, prepare a statement of partners' capital for the year.

d. Using the data in (*c*), prepare entries to distribute the income and to close the drawing accounts.

P14–4–B. Tall and Short formed a partnership on March 1, 1984, by investing $60,000 and $96,000, respectively. Tall and Short invested additional capital of $24,000 and $36,000 on July 1. At that time, the partners agreed that, in dividing net income, interest at 10 percent would be allowed on average capital account balances for the period. On September 1, Tall invested another $116,000 and Short invested another $88,000. The partnership agreement also allowed monthly drawings of $3,600 for Tall and $4,800 for Short. Both partners withdrew the allowed amounts. Nothing further was said about the sharing of income and losses. Net income for the year ended February 28, 1985, was $160,000.

Required:

Prepare a schedule showing the distribution of income for the year ended February 28, 1985, assuming that:

a. The allowed monthly drawings were salaries and are used in determining the distribution of income.

b. The allowed monthly drawings were normal drawings (not salaries) and are not to be used in determining the distribution of income.

P14–5–B.   Jane and John, as partners, have agreed to the following distribution of net income:

1. Salaries of $12,000 and $9,000 to Jane and John.
2. A bonus to Jane of 25 percent of net income in excess of salaries.
3. The remainder equally.

Net income for 1983 and 1984 was $45,000 and $15,000, respectively, and in 1985 there was a net loss of $7,500.

Required:

Prepare schedules showing the distribution of the income and losses to the partners for each of the years 1983, 1984, and 1985.

P14–6–B.

BLUE AND GRAY
Trial Balance
December 31, 1984

	Debits	Credits
Cash	$ 20,500	
Accounts receivable	30,000	
Allowance for doubtful accounts		$ 500
Inventory	18,500	
Equipment	35,000	
Accumulated depreciation—equipment		8,500
Unexpired insurance	455	
Accounts payable		25,500
Blue, capital		18,500
Gray, capital		36,500
Blue, drawing	500	
Gray, drawing	6,000	
Sales		275,000
Purchases	220,000	
Selling expenses	20,000	
Administrative expenses	16,500	
Other revenue		2,955
	$367,455	$367,455

The articles of copartnership for Blue and Gray provide for the distribution of income and losses in the following manner:

1. Each partner is allowed 6 percent interest per year on his capital investment as of the beginning of the year.
2. Blue is allowed a salary of $15,000 and Gray a salary of $18,000 per year as a distribution of income.
3. The remaining income and losses are divided equally.

Your analysis of the books and records discloses the following data that require your consideration: the ending inventory is $15,500; 1 percent of sales is to be added to the allowance for doubtful accounts; and depreciation on the equipment should be recorded at 10 percent of cost. Blue's capital account includes a credit for $2,000 invested on July 15 of the current year. Unexpired insurance at December 31, 1984, is $40.

Required:

You are to prepare the following for the partnership:

a. Adjusting and closing journal entries.

b. An income statement for the year.

c. A statement of partners' capital for the year.

d. A balance sheet for December 31, 1984.

P14–7–B. Frank and Lloyd are partners who share income and losses in a 3:2 ratio. They decided to admit Ann as a new partner at a time when their capital account balances were $240,000 for Frank and $120,000 for Lloyd.

Required:

Prepare journal entries to record Ann's admission to the firm in each of the following unrelated situations:

a. Ann acquired one half of Frank's interest for $125,000 cash paid to Frank personally.

b. Ann acquired one fifth of Frank's equity for $50,000 cash and one fourth of Lloyd's equity for $31,000 cash. Both amounts were paid to the partners personally.

c. Ann invested $90,000 for a 20 percent interest in capital.

d. Ann invested $60,000 and was granted a 15 percent interest in capital because the old partnership was badly in need of cash to pay maturing debts.

e. Ann invested $210,000 for a one-third interest in capital; her admission was recorded using the bonus method.

P14–8–B. A and B are partners who have capital account balances of $40,000 and $20,000 and who share income and losses in a 3:2 ratio. They negotiated the admission of C to their firm.

Required:

Prepare journal entries to record C's admission to the firm under each of the following assumed amounts invested:

a. C invested $36,000 cash and received a one-third interest in the capital of the new firm. The bonus method is used to record C's admission.

b. C invested $27,000 for a one-third interest in capital. C was granted a bonus upon joining the firm.

c. C invested sufficient cash to secure exactly a 40 percent interest in the new firm.

P14–9–B. On July 31, 1984, Jack Nelson, a member of the firm of Nelson and Hardman, decided to retire. The partners have shared income and losses equally. On this date, their capital balances were: Jack Nelson, $80,000; Jill Nelson, $100,000; and Harold Hardman, $60,000.

Required:

Prepare entries to record the withdrawal of Jack Nelson under each of the following assumptions. All payments were made in cash, and the assets were not to be revalued since they are recorded in accordance with generally accepted accounting principles.

     a.   Jack Nelson was paid $80,000.

     b.   Jack Nelson was paid $84,000.

     c.   Jack Nelson was paid $74,000.

P14–10–B.   J, K, and P are partners who share income and losses in a 3:2:1 ratio. On December 31, 1984, J decided to retire. At that time, the partners' capital account balances were:

J, capital	$40,000
K, capital	35,000
P, capital	60,000

Required:

     Prepare entries to record the retirement of J in each of the following unrelated situations:

     a.   The partners agreed that inventory was undervalued by $18,000 and that the books should be adjusted to reflect market values. After the books were adjusted, J received cash equal to the balance in his capital account.

     b.   The partners agreed that inventory was undervalued on the books by $18,000, but the books should *not* be adjusted to reflect market values. J was paid cash equal to the balance that would have been shown in his capital account if the increase to market value had been recorded.

     c.   The partners agreed that the amount shown for inventory was $12,000 more than its current market value, but the inventory was *not* to be adjusted to reflect market values. J was paid cash equal to the balance that would have been in his capital account if the books had been adjusted.

P14–11–B.   The PQR partnership was liquidated on January 2, 1984. Before any of the firm's $390,000 of assets (all noncash) were sold, the liabilities and capital account credit balances were:

Accounts payable	$200,000
P, capital	20,000
Q, capital	80,000
R, capital	90,000

     The assets were sold for $270,000.

Required:

     Prepare the journal entries to record the sale of the assets (credit an Assets account) and the distribution of the cash to creditors and partners. Assume that all available assets of each partner had been invested in the firm prior to liquidation.

P14–12–B.   The partners of the WWV Company decided to liquidate because of demands of creditors for payment of amounts owed. On March 31, 1984, balance sheet data for the firm were:

Cash	$ 30,000
Accounts receivable	65,000
Merchandise inventory	90,000
Plant and equipment	265,000
	$450,000

Accounts payable	$165,000
Winkler, capital	75,000
Wright, capital	90,000
Virma, capital	120,000
	$450,000

The noncash assets were sold on April 1, 1984, for $180,000. The partners share income and losses in a 50:25:25 ratio.

Required:

Prepare journal entries to record the sale of the assets and the distribution of cash to creditors and partners. Assume that partners developing debit balances in their capital accounts are not able to pay them from other assets.

BUSINESS DECISION PROBLEM 14–1

Joe Franklin and Bob Cummings have owned and operated a men's clothing store as a partnership. Their capital account balances as of December 31, 1984, were: Franklin, $160,000; and Cummings, $54,000. Income and losses are shared equally after allowing salaries of $16,000 to Franklin and $14,000 to Cummings. Applying these provisions to the net income of $60,000 in 1984 resulted in a distribution of $31,000 to Franklin and $29,000 to Cummings. Franklin considers this sharing to be quite unfair. He notes that he devotes full time to the store, while Cummings has other interests that occupy about half of his time. Franklin also notes that his equity was substantially more than Cummings' in the partnership because he has not drawn all of his income. He proposes that the partnership agreement be changed to call for salaries of $20,000 and $10,000 to himself and to Cummings, that interest at 10 percent per year be allowed on beginning of the year capital account balances, and that any remaining income be shared equally.

Cummings agrees that some modification seems necessary because of changed circumstances. But before agreeing to Franklin's proposed changes, he wants to know the effects of such changes.

Required:

Assume that the capital account balances as of January 1, 1984, were Franklin $140,000, and Cummings, $50,000.

a. Prepare a schedule showing how the income for 1984 would have been shared if Franklin's suggested provisions had been in effect for the year.

b. Prepare a schedule showing how much each partner's share of the 1984 income would have increased or decreased if Franklin's proposed revisions of the partnership agreement had been in effect for 1984.

c. Is Cummings more or less likely to accept Franklin's proposals if future net income is substantially greater or less than $60,000 per year?

BUSINESS DECISION PROBLEM 14–2

Roy Baker and Lee Boland are partners sharing income and losses equally in a business that has been very successful for all 25 years of its existence. The partners have been studying what they consider a very tempting offer to buy their business, thus allowing the partners to retire. Shortly after receiving this offer, Baker was hospitalized as a result of an auto accident. The partners agreed that they should sell, and Boland was authorized to negotiate the sale of the business.

Some time later, Boland appeared at the hospital and gave Baker a check for $80,000 as his share of the cash available to the partners upon liquidation of the partnership. He also gave Baker a balance sheet for the partnership as of the day before the date of the sale. Summarized, this balance sheet showed:

Cash	$ 10,000
Other assets	130,000
Total	$140,000
Liabilities	30,000
Baker, capital	60,000
Boland, capital	50,000
Total	$140,000

Boland explained that he had sold all of the other assets and the firm name for $180,000—a price he considered excellent. Baker agreed the price was excellent, but was unsure about whether the check Boland gave him was in the correct amount.

Required:

a. Show the computations Boland made to arrive at an $80,000 check for Baker.

b. Is $80,000 the correct amount? If not, compute the correct amount.

Part Five

Corporations

Chapter 15
Corporations: Formation, administration, and classes of capital stock

Chapter 16
Corporations: Paid-in capital, retained earnings, dividends, and treasury stock

Chapter 17
Bonds payable; bond and stock investments

Chapter 18
Corporations: Consolidated financial statements

Chapter 15

Corporations: Formation, administration, and classes of capital stock

CHAPTER GOALS

After study of this chapter, you should be able to:

1. State the advantages and disadvantages of a corporation.
2. List the various kinds of stock and describe the differences between them.
3. Record transactions involving stock with par value, with stated value, or without par or stated value, issued for cash, property, or services.
4. Present in proper form the stockholders' equity section of a balance sheet.
5. List values commonly associated with capital stock and give their definitions.
6. Determine book values of both preferred and common stock.
7. Define and use correctly the new terms in the glossary.

Although fewer in number than single proprietorships and partnerships, corporations possess the bulk of our business capital and currently supply us with most of our goods and services. This chapter discusses the corporate form of business organization, its administration, and some of the unique situations encountered in accounting for and reporting on the different classes of stock.

THE CORPORATION

A *corporation* is an entity recognized by law as possessing an existence separate and distinct from its owners; that is, it is a separate legal entity. A corporation is an artificial, invisible, intangible being or person created by law. A corporation is endowed with many of the rights and obligations possessed by a natural person. A corporation can, for example, enter into contracts in its own name; buy, sell, or hold real or personal property; borrow money; hire and fire employees; and sue and be sued.

Corporations have proved to be remarkably well-suited vehicles for obtaining the huge amounts of capital necessary for large-scale mass production. Corporations acquire their capital by issuing shares of stock, which are the units into which the ownership of a corporation is divided. Investors buy shares of stock in a corporation principally for two reasons. Investors expect the value of their shares to increase over time so that the stock may be sold in the future at a profit. Also, while investors hold stock, they expect the corporation to pay them dividends, usually in cash, in return for using their money. The various kinds of dividends and their accounting treatment are discussed in Chapter 16.

Advantages of a corporation

There are many advantages of a corporation as compared to other forms of business organization. The major advantages of a corporation over a single proprietorship are sharing of responsibilities and risk, and a broader base of investment and talent. These are the same advantages a partnership has over a single proprietorship. The discussion of advantages here will relate to the more comparable forms of business: the partnership and corporation.

1. *Easy transfer of ownership.* In a partnership, one partner could not transfer ownership in the business very easily due to the fact that the other partners might not want the new person involved in the business. In a corporation, stock is generally traded on a stock exchange between unknown parties; one owner cannot usually dictate to whom shares can or cannot be sold by another owner.
2. *Limited liability.* Each partner in a partnership is personally responsible for all the debts of the business. In a corporation, the stockholders are not personally responsible for the corporation's debts; the maximum that a stockholder can lose is the amount of his or her investment.
3. *Continuous existence of the entity.* In a partnership, many circumstances

can cause the termination of the business entity. These same circumstances have no effect on a corporation because it is a legal entity separate and distinct from the owners.

4. *Professional management.* Generally, the partners in a business are also the managers of that business. The partners may or may not have the necessary expertise to manage a business. In a corporation, most of the owners do not participate in the day-to-day operations and management of the entity. Usually, professionals are hired to run the business on a daily basis.

5. *Separation of owners and entity.* Since the corporation is considered a separate legal entity, the owners do not have the power to bind the corporation to business contracts. This eliminates the potential problem of mutual agency between partners. One owner cannot jeopardize other owners through poor decision making.

Disadvantages of the corporation

The corporate form of organization is not without its disadvantages.

These include the following:

1. *Double taxation.* Because a corporation is a separate legal entity, its net income is subject to taxation twice. The corporation pays a tax on its income, and stockholders pay a tax on corporate income received as dividends.

2. *Government regulation.* Because corporations are created by law, they are subject to greater regulation and control than the sole proprietorship or partnership.

3. *Entrenched inefficient management.* A corporation may be burdened with an inefficient management that remains in control because it can use corporate funds to solicit the needed stockholder votes.

4. *Limited ability to raise creditor capital.* The limited liability of stockholders makes a corporation an attractive means for accumulating stockholder capital. At the same time, this limited liability feature limits the amount of creditor capital a corporation can amass *because creditors cannot look to the personal assets of stockholders for satisfaction of the debts* of a corporation if the corporation cannot pay. Thus, beyond a certain point, creditors will not lend some corporations money without the personal guarantee of a shareholder to repay the loan if the corporation does not.

Incorporating

Corporations are chartered by the state. Each state has a corporation act which permits the formation of corporations by qualified persons. *Incorporators* are persons seeking to bring a corporation into existence. Most state corporation laws require a minimum of three incorporators, each of whom must be a *natural person* of legal age, and a majority of whom must be citizens of the United States.

The laws of each state view a corporation organized in that state as a *domestic corporation,* and a corporation organized in any other state as a *foreign corporation.* If a corporation intends to conduct business solely within one state, it normally seeks incorporation in that state because most state laws are not as severe for domestic corporations as for foreign corporations. Corporations conducting interstate business usually incorporate in the state which has laws most advangageous to the corporation being formed. Important considerations in choosing a state are the powers granted to the corporation, the taxes levied, and the reports required.

Articles of incorporation

A *corporate charter* is a contract between the state and the incorporators of a corporation and their successors granting the corporation its legal existence. The application for the corporation's charter is called the *articles of incorporation.* After the information requested in the application form is supplied, the articles are filed with the proper office of the state of incorporation. Upon approval by that office (frequently that of the secretary of state), the charter is granted and the corporation is created. Different states require different information in the articles of incorporation. The following list is representative of the information that normally must be supplied: (1) name of corporation; (2) location of principal office; (3) purposes of business; (4) number of shares of stock authorized, class or classes of shares, and voting and dividend rights of each class of shares; (5) value of assets paid in by the original *subscribers* (persons who contract to acquire shares); and (6) limitations on authority of the management and owners of the corporation.

Bylaws

As soon as the charter is obtained, the corporation is authorized to operate its business. The incorporators call the first meeting of the stockholders. Two of the purposes of this meeting are to elect a board of directors and to adopt the bylaws of the corporation.

The *bylaws* are a set of rules or regulations that are adopted by the board of directors of a corporation to govern the conduct of corporate affairs. The bylaws must be in agreement with the laws of the state and the policies and purposes in the corporate charter. The bylaws contain, along with other information, provisions for the following: (1) the place, date, and manner of calling the annual stockholders' meeting; (2) the number of directors and the method for electing them; (3) the duties and powers of the directors; and (4) the method for selecting officers of the corporation.

Organization costs

Organization costs are costs of organizing a corporation, such as state incorporation fees and legal fees applicable to incorporation. These costs should be debited to an account called Organization Costs. Organization costs are carried as an asset since they yield benefits over the life of the corporation; if the fees had not been paid, there would be no corporate entity. The account is classified on the balance sheet as an intangible asset and amortized over a period not to exceed 40 years. Most organization costs are written off fairly rapidly because they are small in amount and a rapid amortization is allowed for tax purposes.

Directing the corporation

The corporation is managed through the delegation of authority in a line from the stockholders to the directors to the officers, as shown in the organization chart in Illustration 15.1. For any given organization, the lower level of the chart could differ from that shown. The stockholders elect the board of directors. The board of directors formulates the broad policies of the company and selects the principal officers, who execute the policies.

Stockholders. Stockholders, as such, do not have the right to participate actively in the management of the business, unless they serve as directors and/or officers. But stockholders do have certain basic rights; these include the right to (1) dispose of their shares, (2) buy additional newly issued shares in a proportion equal to the percentage of shares already owned (called the *preemptive right*), (3) share in dividends when declared, (4) share in assets in liquidation, and (5) participate in management indirectly by voting their shares of stock.

An example of the operation of the preemptive right may be helpful. Assume Joe Thornton now owns 10 percent of the outstanding shares of Corporation X. Corporation X now decides to issue 1,000 additional shares of stock. Joe Thornton has the right to buy 100 (10 percent) of the new shares should he decide to do so. If he does not wish to exercise his preemptive right, the shares may be sold to others.

Normally, stockholders' meetings are held annually. At these meetings,

Illustration 15.1: Typical corporation's organization chart

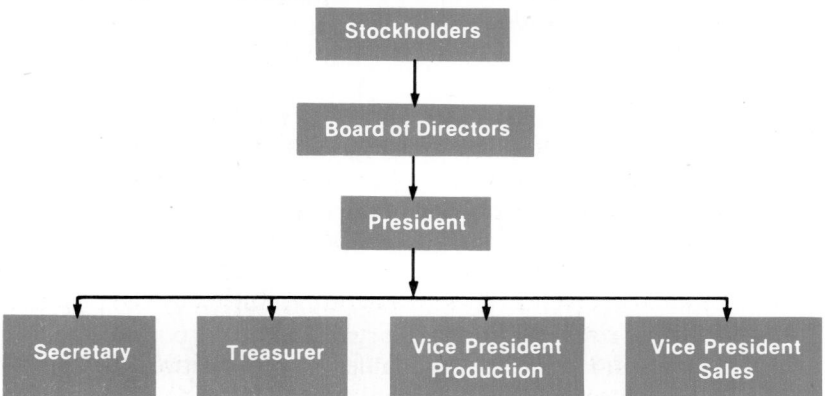

each stockholder is entitled to one vote for each share of voting stock held. Stockholders who do not personally attend the stockholders' meeting may vote by proxy. A *proxy* is a legal document that is signed by the stockholder and gives another person the authority to vote the stockholder's shares at a stockholders' meeting. At the annual meeting, stockholders indirectly share in management by voting on such questions as changing the charter, increasing capital stock issues, approving pension plans, selecting the independent auditor, and related matters.

Board of directors. The *board of directors* is elected by the stockholders and is primarily responsible for formulating broad policies for the corporation. The board appoints administrative officers and delegates to them the execution of the policies established by the board. The board also has more specific duties including (1) authorizing contracts, (2) declaring dividends, (3) establishing executive salaries, and (4) granting authorization to borrow money. The decisions of the board are recorded in the minutes of its meetings. These minutes are an important source of information to the independent auditor, since they may serve as notice to record transactions (such as a dividend declaration) or to recognize that certain transactions may be taking place in the near future (such as a large loan).

Corporate officers. Officers of a corporation usually are specified in the corporation's bylaws. Officers usually include: president, vice presidents, secretary, and treasurer.

The president is the chief executive officer of the corporation. He is empowered by the bylaws to appoint all necessary employees except those appointed by the board of directors.

A company will generally have more than one vice president. Each vice president is usually responsible for one particular corporate operation, such as sales, engineering, production, or finance. The corporate secretary is responsible for maintaining the official records of the company and records the proceedings of meetings of stockholders and directors. The treasurer is accountable for corporate funds and may be charged with the general supervision of the accounting function within the company.

DOCUMENTS, BOOKS, AND RECORDS RELATING TO CAPITAL STOCK

Millions of shares of corporate capital stock are traded every business day on organized stock exchanges such as the New York Stock Exchange, the American Stock Exchange, and in the over-the-counter market. These sales (or "trades") seldom involve the corporation issuing the stock as a party to the exchange, but rather are made by existing stockholders to other individual or institutional investors. These trades are followed by the physical transfer of the stock certificates.

A *stock certificate* is a printed or engraved document serving as evidence of ownership of a certain number of shares of capital stock. When a stockholder sells shares of stock, the stockholder signs over the stock certificate to the new owner who presents it to the issuing corporation. The certificate is canceled and attached to its corresponding stub in the stock certificate book, and a new certificate is prepared for the new owner. The number of shares of stock outstanding at any time can be determined by summing the shares shown on the open stubs (stubs without certificates attached).

Stockholders' ledger

Among the more important records maintained by a corporation is the stockholders' ledger. The *stockholders' ledger* contains a group of subsidiary accounts showing the number of shares of stock currently held by each stockholder. Because it contains an account for each stockholder, in a large corporation this ledger may have more than a million individual accounts. Each stockholder's account shows the number of shares owned, their certificate numbers, and the dates on which shares were acquired or sold. Entries are made in terms of the number of shares rather than in dollars.

The stockholders' ledger contains the same information as the stock certificate book but summarizes it alphabetically by stockholder, since a stockholder may own a dozen or more certificates. This summary enables a corporation to determine the number of shares a stockholder is entitled to vote at a stockholders' meeting, and to limit dividend checks to one per stockholder rather than one per stock certificate.

Many large corporations with actively traded shares turn the task of maintaining reliable stock records over to an outside stock transfer agent and a stock registrar. The *stock transfer agent,* usually a bank or trust company, is employed by a corporation to transfer stock between buyers and sellers. The stock transfer agent cancels the certificates covering shares sold, issues new stock certificates, and makes appropriate entries in the stockholder's ledger. New certificates are sent to the *stock registrar,* typically another bank, which maintains separate records of the shares outstanding. This control system makes it highly unlikely that a corporation employee can issue stock certificates fraudulently and steal the proceeds.

The minutes book

The *minutes book,* kept by the secretary of the corporation, is a record book in which actions taken at stockholders' and board of directors' meetings are recorded. The minutes book is the written authorization for many actions taken by corporate officers. All actions taken by the board of directors and the stockholders must be in accordance with the provisions contained in the charter and in the bylaws. The minutes books contains a variety of data, including the following:

1. A copy of the corporate charter.
2. A copy of the bylaws.
3. Dividends declared by the board of directors.

4. Authorization for the acquisition of major assets.
5. Authorization for borrowing.
6. Authorization for increases or decreases in capital stock.
7. Authorization for pension plans.

CAPITAL STOCK AUTHORIZED

Capital stock authorized is the number of shares of stock that a corporation is entitled to issue as designated in its charter. The corporate charter states the number of shares and the par value, if any, per share of each class of stock that the corporation is permitted to issue. The corporation might not issue all of its authorized stock immediately. It might hold some for issuance in the future when additional capital is needed. If all authorized stock has been issued and more capital is needed, the consent of the state of incorporation will be required to increase the number of authorized shares.

CAPITAL STOCK OUTSTANDING

Capital stock outstanding is the number of shares of stock that have been authorized and issued and which are currently held by stockholders. The total ownership of a corporation rests with the holders of the outstanding shares of stock—that is, the shares authorized, issued, and currently held by stockholders. If, for example, a corporation is authorized to issue 10,000 shares of capital stock but has issued only 8,000 shares, the holders of the 8,000 shares own 100 percent of the corporation.

Each outstanding share of stock of a given class is identical to any other outstanding share of that class with respect to the rights and privileges possessed. Shares authorized but not yet issued are referred to as unissued shares (there are 2,000 unissued shares in the above example). No rights or privileges attach to these shares until they are issued; they are not, for example, entitled to dividends, nor can they be voted at stockholders' meetings.

There is a difference between outstanding stock and issued stock. Issued stock includes shares which have been sold at some point in time, while outstanding shares are those shares which are currently held by stockholders. All outstanding stock is issued stock, but the reverse is not necessarily true. The difference is due to shares, called treasury stock, which have been returned to the corporation by stockholders. Treasury stock will be discussed in Chapter 16.

PAR VALUE AND NO PAR VALUE CAPITAL STOCK

Par value stock

Many times par value stock is issued. *Par value* is an arbitrary amount assigned to each share of a given class of stock and printed on the stock certificate. Par value per share is no indication of the amount for which the stock will sell. Par value is the amount per share that is credited to the capital stock account for each share issued. Also, the total par value of all issued stock constitutes the legal capital of the corporation. The concept of legal capital exists to help protect creditors from losses. *Legal capital* (*stated capital*) is an amount prescribed by law below which a corporation may not reduce stockholders' equity through declaration of dividends or other payments to stockholders. Legal capital does not guarantee that a company will be able to pay its debts, but it does serve to keep a company from compensating owners to the detriment of the creditors.

No par value stock

Laws permitting the issuance of shares of *stock without par value* (sometimes referred to as no par value stock) were first enacted in New York in 1912. Similar, but not uniform, legislation has since been passed in many states.

A corporation might issue capital stock without par value for various reasons, two of which are to avoid confusion and for legal reasons. The use of a par value may confuse some investors because it does not conform to market value. When there is no par value, this source of confusion is avoided.

A second reason is related to state laws regarding the original issue price per share. A *discount on capital stock* is the amount by which the par value of shares issued exceeds their issue price. Thus, if stock with a par value of $100 is issued at $80, the discount is $20. Some states will not permit the original issuance of stock at a discount. Other states allow its issuance but hold the purchasers responsible for the discount amount in the event of failure of the corporation. Thus, these stock purchasers are contingently liable to creditors for the difference between par value and issue price. Although this liability is seldom paid, issuance of no par stock avoids such a possibility.

No par value stock with a stated value

The board of directors of a corporation issuing stock without par value may assign a stated value to each share of capital stock. *Stated value* is an arbitrary amount assigned by the board of directors to each share of a given class of no par value stock. This stated value, like par value, may be set at any amount by the board, although some state statutes specify a minimum amount such as $5 per share. Stated value may be established either before or after the shares are issued, if not specified by applicable state law.

OTHER VALUES COMMONLY ASSOCIATED WITH CAPITAL STOCK

Market value

Market value is the price at which shares of capital stock are bought and sold by investors in the open market. Market price is affected directly by all the factors that influence general economic conditions, investors' expectations concerning the corporation, the money market, and the corporation's earnings. It is the value of greatest interest to most investors, assuming dissolution of the corporation or redemption of the stock involved is not expected.

Liquidation value

Liquidation value is the amount a stockholder will receive if a corporation discontinues operations and liquidates by selling its assets, paying its liabilities, and distributing the remaining cash among the stockholders. Since the assets might be sold for more or less than the amounts at which they are recorded in the corporation's accounts, liquidation value may be more or less than book value, which is discussed below. If only one class of capital stock is outstanding, each stockholder will receive, per share, the amount obtained by dividing the remaining cash by the number of shares of stock outstanding. If two or more classes of stock are outstanding, liquidation values depend on the rights of the various classes.

Redemption value

Certain capital stock may be issued with the stipulation that the corporation has the right to redeem it. *Redemption value* is the price per share at which a corporation may call its capital stock for retirement.

Book value

Book value per share is the amount per share that each stockholder would receive if the corporation were liquidated without incurring any further expenses and if assets were sold and liabilities liquidated at their recorded amounts. A later section discusses book value in greater detail.

CLASSES OF CAPITAL STOCK

Two classes of capital stock—preferred and common—may be issued by a corporation.

Common stock

If only one class of stock is issued, it is known as *common stock*. The rights of the stockholder are enjoyed equally by all the holders of shares. *Common stock* is usually referred to as the *residual equity* in the corporation. This means that all other claims against the corporation rank ahead of the claims of the common stockholder.

Preferred stock

A corporation may also issue *preferred stock*. *Preferred stock* is capital stock which carries certain privileges not carried by common stock. Further, different classes of preferred stock may exist, each with slightly different characteristics.

Corporations generally issue preferred stock for one of the following reasons: (1) Capital may be attracted from investors with differing investment objectives. (2) Since preferred stocks may have no voting rights, their issuance does not dilute the common stockholders' control of the corporation. (3) Unlike common stock, which has no set maximum or minimum dividend, the dividend return on preferred stocks is usually stated at an amount per share or as a percentage of par value. Therefore, the amount of the dividend per share is fixed.

TYPES OF PREFERRED STOCK

When a corporation issues both preferred and common stock, the preferred stock may be:

1. Preferred as to dividends. If it is, it may be:
   a. Cumulative or noncumulative.
   b. Participating or nonparticipating.
2. Preferred as to assets in the event of liquidation.
3. Convertible or nonconvertible.
4. Callable.

Stock preferred as to dividends

Stock preferred as to dividends means that the preferred stockholders are entitled to a specified dividend per share before any dividend on common stock is paid. A *dividend* is a distribution of assets (usually cash) that represents a withdrawal of earnings by the owners. Dividends are similar in nature to withdrawals by sole proprietors and partners. A *dividend on preferred stock* is the amount paid to preferred stockholders as a return for the use of their money. The required preferred dividend may be stated as a specific dollar amount per share per year, such as $4.40, or as a percentage of the par value of the preferred stock, such as 8 percent of par value. Dividends on preferred stock usually are paid quarterly. A dividend—in full or in part— can be paid on the preferred stock only if it is declared by the board of directors, and in some states, only if the corporation has retained earnings at least equal in dollar amount to the dividend declared.

Cumulative preferred stock. *Cumulative preferred stock* is preferred stock for which the right to receive a basic dividend, usually each quarter, accumulates if not paid. Unpaid cumulative preferred dividends must be paid before any dividends can be paid on the common stock. For example, assume a company has cumulative, 10 percent preferred stock outstanding of $100,000, common stock outstanding of $100,000, and retained earnings of $30,000. No dividends have been paid for two years. The preferred stockholders are entitled to dividends of $20,000 before any dividends can be paid to the common stockholders.

Dividends in arrears are cumulative unpaid dividends, including the passed quarterly dividends for the current year. Dividends in arrears are never shown as a liability of the corporation since they are not a legal liability until declared by the board of directors. But, since the amount of dividends in arrears may influence the decisions of users of a corporation's financial statements, such dividends should be, and usually are, disclosed in a footnote. An appropriate footnote might read: "Dividends in the amount of $20,000, representing two years' dividends on the company's 10 percent, cumulative preferred stock, were in arrears as of December 31, 1984."

Noncumulative preferred stock. *Noncumulative preferred stock* is preferred stock on which the right to receive a dividend expires if the dividend is not declared. Where noncumulative preferred stock is outstanding, a dividend omitted or not paid in any one year need not be paid in any future year. Because omitted dividends are usually lost forever, noncumulative preferred stocks hold little attraction for investors and rarely are issued.

Participating preferred stock. *Participating preferred stock* is preferred stock that is entitled to receive dividends above the stated preference rate under certain conditions which are specified in the preferred stock contract. For example, assume that the preferred stock contract states that when the total dividend distributed to stockholders in a given year exceeds $8 per share to preferred shareholders and $8 per share to common shareholders, the remaining amount will be distributed in an equal amount per share to all stockholders. If there are 2,000 shares of preferred stock and 4,000 shares of common stock outstanding, a distribution of $108,000 would be shared as follows:

			Preferred	Common
1.	Preferred stockholders are paid their dividend (2,000 shares × $8)		$16,000	
2.	Common stockholders are paid an amount equal to the preferred dividend per share (4,000 × $8)			$32,000
3.	The remainder is divided so as to pay the same amount per share.			

	Shares	Ratio		
Preferred	2,000	(²⁄₆ × $60,000)	20,000	
Common	4,000	(⁴⁄₆ × $60,000)		40,000
Total	6,000			
Total dividend			$36,000	$72,000

The preferred stockholders receive the first $16,000 of dividends. The common stockholders receive the next $32,000 of dividends. Any dividends over $48,000 per year are paid in an equal amount per share. In years when dividends are not sufficient to pay at least $48,000 of dividends, the distribution would be as follows:

Amount of dividends to be paid	Split between	
	Preferred	Common
$ 8,000	$ 8,000	$ –0–
16,000	16,000	–0–
24,000	16,000	8,000
32,000	16,000	16,000
40,000	16,000	24,000

Participating preferred stock is quite rare. Most preferred stock is nonparticipating. *Nonparticipating preferred stock* is preferred stock that is entitled to its cumulative stated dividend only, regardless of the size of the dividend on common stock.

Stock preferred as to assets

Most preferred stocks are preferred as to assets in the event of dissolution and liquidation of the corporation. *Stock preferred as to assets* means that in liquidation the preferred stockholders are entitled to receive the par value (or a larger stipulated liquidation value) per share before any assets may be distributed to common stockholders. If there are cumulative preferred dividends in arrears at liquidation, they usually are payable even if there are not enough accumulated earnings to cover the dividends. Also, the cumulative dividend for the current year is payable. Stock may be preferred as to assets, dividends, or both.

Convertible preferred stock

Convertible preferred stock is preferred stock that is convertible into common stock of the issuing corporation. Holders of convertible preferred stock may exchange it, at their option, for shares of common stock of the same corporation at a conversion ratio stated in the preferred stock contract.

Preferred stock is issued by a company for two main reasons: (1) to avoid the use of bonds which have fixed interest charges that must be paid regardless of the amount of net income, and (2) to avoid issuing so many additional shares of common stock that earnings per share will be less in the current year than in prior years.

Investors find convertible preferred stock attractive because of the greater probability that the dividends on the preferred stock will be paid (as compared to dividends on common shares) and because the conversion privilege may be the source of substantial price appreciation. The second advantage is especially attractive to those institutional investors prohibited by law or by established policy from owning common stocks.

To illustrate this latter attraction, assume that the Olsen Company issued 1,000 shares of 6 percent, $100 par value convertible preferred stock at $100 per share. The stock is convertible at any time into four shares of Olsen $10 par value common stock, which has a current market value of $20 per share. In the next several years, the company reports sharply increased net income and increases the dividend on the common stock from $1 to $2 per share. Assume that the common stock now sells at $40 per share. The preferred stockholders can convert each share of preferred stock into four shares of common stock and increase the annual dividend they receive from $6 to $8. Or they can sell their preferred stock at a substantial gain, since it will sell in the market at approximately $160 per share, the market value of the four shares of common stock into which it is convertible. Or the holders may continue to hold their preferred shares in the expectation of realizing an even larger gain at a later date.

Callable preferred stock

An issuing corporation may force conversion of convertible preferred stock by calling the preferred stock for redemption. Virtually all preferred stocks, convertible or nonconvertible, are *callable* at the option of the issuing corporation. *Callable preferred stock* means that the holders of nonconvertible preferred stock must surrender it to the company when requested to do so. Holders of convertible preferred stock may either surrender it or convert it into common shares. The preferred shares are usually callable at par value plus a small premium (the call premium) of 3 or 4 percent of the par value of the stock. A *call premium* is the difference between the amount at which a corporation may call its preferred stock for redemption and the par value of the stock. If the stock is surrendered, the former holder receives par value, plus the call premium, plus any dividends in arrears and a prorated portion of the current period's dividend. If the market value of the common shares is higher than the amount that would be received in redemption, the holder would be foolish not to convert the preferred shares into common shares.

A corporation might call its preferred stock for many reasons: (1) the outstanding preferred stock may require, for example, a 12 percent annual dividend at a time when capital to retire the stock can be secured by issuing a new 8 percent preferred stock; (2) the issuing company may have been sufficiently profitable to enable it to retire the preferred stock out of earnings; and (3) the company may wish to force conversion of a convertible preferred stock because the cash dividend on the equivalent common shares will be less than the dividend on the preferred shares.

BALANCE SHEET PRESENTATION OF STOCK

The stockholders' equity section of a corporation's balance sheet contains two main elements: paid-in capital and retained earnings. *Paid-in capital* is that part of stockholders' equity which results from cash or other assets invested by owners. *Retained earnings* is that part of stockholders' equity resulting from earnings. The Retained Earnings account is increased (decreased) *periodically* by the amount of net income (loss) earned. Retained Earnings is *decreased* principally by *dividends* declared and paid to stockholders. Since Retained Earnings is a capital account and represents accumulated *earnings,* it normally has a *credit* balance. Retained Earnings is discussed in Chapter 16.

The illustration below shows the proper financial reporting for preferred and common stock. Assume that a corporation is authorized to issue 10,000 shares of $100 par value, 6 percent, cumulative, convertible preferred stock, all of which have been issued and are outstanding; and 200,000 shares of $10 par value common stock, of which 80,000 shares are issued and outstanding. The stockholders' equity section of the balance sheet (assuming $450,000 of retained earnings) is:

Paid-in capital:		
Preferred stock, $100 par value, 6 percent, cumulative, convertible; authorized, issued, and outstanding, 10,000 shares	$1,000,000	
Common stock, $10 par value; authorized, 200,000 shares; issued and outstanding, 80,000 shares	800,000	$1,800,000
Retained earnings		450,000
Total stockholders' equity		$2,250,000

A footnote to the balance sheet states the rate at which the preferred stock is convertible into common stock. Alternatively, the information could be disclosed in a parenthetical note within the description of preferred stock.

STOCK ISSUANCES FOR CASH

Capital stock with par value

Each share of capital stock (common or perferred) is either with par value or without par value, depending on the terms of the corporation's charter. The par value, if any, is stated in the charter and printed on the stock certificates issued. Par value may be of any amount—1 cent, 10 cents, $16\frac{2}{3}$ cents, $1, $5, or $100. Low par values, $10 or less, are common in our economy.

Par value per share does not indicate the amount of *stockholders' equity* per share (called book value per share) that is recorded in the corporation's accounting records. Stockholders' equity consists of paid-in capital and retained earnings. The retained earnings may be either positive or negative. In addition, as previously mentioned, par value does not give any clue to the stock's market value. Shares with a par value of $5 have sold in the market for well over $600, and many $100 par value preferred stocks have sold for considerably less than par. Par value is not even a reliable indicator of the price at which shares can be issued. Even in new corporations, shares are often issued at prices well in excess of par value and may even be issued for less than par value if state laws permit.

To illustrate the issuance of stock for cash, assume that 200 shares of an authorized 1,000 shares of $100 par value common stock are issued for $23,000 cash. The following entry would be made:

Cash	23,000	
Common Stock		20,000
Paid-In Capital in Excess of Par Value—Common		3,000
To record the issuance of 200 shares of stock for cash.		

Notice that the credit to the Common Stock account is at par value ($100) times the number of shares issued. The excess over par value ($3,000) is credited to Paid-In Capital in Excess of Par Value, and is part of the paid-in capital contributed by the stockholders. Thus, *paid-in capital in excess of par (or stated) value* represents capital contributed to a corporation in addition to that assigned to the shares issued and recorded in capital stock accounts.

The paid-in capital section of the balance sheet would appear as follows:

Common stock, par value, $100; 1,000 shares	
authorized; 200 shares issued and outstanding	$20,000
Paid-in capital in excess of par value—Common	3,000
Total paid-in capital	$23,000

Capital stock without par value

When shares without par value but with stated value are issued, the shares are carried in the capital stock account at a uniform amount per share—the stated value. Any amounts received in excess of the stated value per share represent a part of the capital of the corporation and should be credited to Paid-in Capital in Excess of Stated Value. The stated or legal capital of a corporation issuing shares with a stated value is generally equal to the aggregate of the stated value of the shares issued.

As an illustration, assume that the DeWitt Corporation, which is authorized to issue 10,000 shares of capital stock without par value, assigns a stated value of $20 per share to its stock. The 10,000 authorized shares are issued for cash at $22 per share. The entry would be as follows:

Cash	220,000	
Common Stock		200,000
Paid-In Capital in Excess of Stated Value—Common		20,000
To record issuance of 10,000 shares for cash.		

The paid-in capital section of the balance sheet would appear as follows:

Common stock without par value, stated value, $20;	
10,000 shares authorized, issued, and outstanding ...	$200,000
Paid-in capital in excess of stated value—Common	20,000
Total paid-in capital	$220,000

The $20,000 received over and above the stated value of $200,000 is carried permanently as paid-in capital because it is a part of the capital originally contributed by the stockholders. But the legal capital of the DeWitt Corporation is $200,000.

Shares without par value or stated value

If a corporation issues shares without par value or stated value, the entire amount received is credited to the capital stock account. For instance, consider the above illustration of the DeWitt Corporation involving the issuance of stock without par value. If no stated value had been set, the entry would have been as follows:

```
Cash ..........................................................  220,000
    Common Stock  .........................................              220,000
        To record issuance of 10,000 shares for cash.
```

Because shares may be issued at different times and at differing amounts, the credit to the capital stock account is not at a uniform amount per share, in contrast to par value shares or shares with a stated value. In some states, the entire amount received for shares without par or stated value is the amount of legal capital.

The paid-in capital section of the company's balance sheet would be as follows:

```
Common stock without par or stated value; 10,000
    shares authorized, issued, and outstanding  ........  $220,000
        Total paid-in capital .......................  $220,000
```

The actual capital contributed by stockholders is $220,000. In some states, the legal capital is also $220,000.

Some general guides to the concept of legal capital have been presented. In actual situations, the legal capital of a corporation is governed by the laws of the state of incorporation. These laws vary considerably among states.

RECORDING CAPITAL STOCK ISSUES BY SUBSCRIPTION

Stock is often issued through subscriptions. A *subscription* is a contract to acquire a certain number of shares of stock at a specified price, with payment to be made at a specified date or dates. A *subscriber* is a person contracting to acquire the shares. The steps in recording the issuance of capital stock by subscription are as follows:

1. Receipt of subscriptions for the issuance of the capital stock.
2. Collection of the subscriptions.
3. Issuance of the stock certificates.

In most states, authorized stock becomes legally (but not actually) issued at the time a subscription is accepted. A bona fide subscription contract may be regarded as an asset of the corporation. Thus, the subscriber is a stockholder. The subscriber's legal status as a stockholder is not dependent on the issuance of the stock certificate. Nevertheless, for accounting purposes capital stock is not recorded as issued until the stock certificate is delivered to the stockholder.

The authorization of a stock issue does not create an asset or a capital item; it merely establishes the possibility of obtaining assets through the issuance of the stock. Therefore, the authorization to issue stock is not a transaction to be recorded by journal entry. But the authorization is noted as a memorandum in the ledger (and often in the general journal) to avoid issuing shares in excess of the number authorized.

The stock subscribed account

A *stock certificate* is a printed or engraved document serving as evidence of ownership of a certain number of shares of stock. When stock certificates are not issued until a subscriber has paid in full, a separate account must be maintained to show the amount of stock subscribed but not yet outstanding. This is accomplished by setting up a Common (or Preferred) Stock Subscribed account. *Subscribed stock* is stock for which subscriptions have been received, but for which stock certificates have not been issued.

Issuance by subscription of par value stock

The following examples illustrate the conventional method for recording the issuance by subscription of par value stock. The method follows the practice indicated in accounting for shares with stated value, where it was assumed that the shares were issued when subscriptions were fully paid. The examples differ from each other in the degree of completion of the various steps of subscription of stock, collection of cash, and issuance of certificates. The data used concern the Lake Company, organized as a corporation with an authorized capital stock of 5,000 shares with a par value of $100 each. Authorization is noted in memorandum form in the general journal and in the Common Stock account.

If all capital stock is subscribed at par the entry is:

Subscriptions Receivable—Common	500,000	
Common Stock Subscribed		500,000
To record subscriptions to 5,000 shares at par.		

For a 20 percent cash collection of the subscriptions, the entry is:

Cash	100,000	
Subscriptions Receivable—Common		100,000
To record partial collection of the subscriptions.		

When subscriptions are collected in full, certificates are issued and the following entries are prepared:

Cash	400,000	
Subscriptions Receivable—Common		400,000
To record collection of the remaining subscriptions.		

Common Stock Subscribed	500,000	
Common Stock		500,000
Certificates issued for 5,000 shares paid in full.		

If the stock had been subscribed at a $100,000 premium (the amount in excess of par value), the entry would have been:

```
Subscriptions Receivable—Common ...........................   600,000
     Common Stock Subscribed ................................              500,000
     Paid-In Capital in Excess of Par Value—Common ..............          100,000
     To record subscriptions to 5,000 shares of common stock
     per share.
```

If preferred stock were involved, the entries would be the same except that the corresponding preferred stock account titles would be used.

Issuance by subscription of no par value stock

To illustrate, assume the Grayson Corporation was authorized to issue 100,000 shares of common stock without par value. On January 2, 1984, the corporation received subscriptions for 20,000 shares at $21 per share. The subscriptions were collected on January 10, 1984. The journal entries would be as follows:

January 2, 1984

On this day, the corporation was authorized to issue 100,000 shares of common stock without par value.

```
1984
Jan.  2  Subscriptions Receivable—Common .....................   420,000
             Common Stock Subscribed ........................              420,000
             To record subscriptions to 20,000 shares of common stock
             without par or stated value at $21 per share.

      10  Cash ...............................................   420,000
             Subscriptions Receivable—Common .................              420,000
             To record the collection of subscriptions in full.

      10  Common Stock Subscribed ...........................   420,000
             Common Stock ...................................              420,000
             To record issuance of stock certificates for 20,000 shares.
```

Note that the subscriptions received on January 2 were at $21 per share. On January 15, the board of directors of the corporation decided to assign a stated value of $20 to each share. This means that the board wished to credit the appropriate capital stock account at the uniform amount of $20 per share. Any amount received in the future or in the past in excess of $20 per share ($1 in this case) would be credited to a capital account called Paid-In Capital in Excess of Stated Value. This account represents a portion of the capital contributed by the stockholders. Thus, the Common Stock account needs to be changed for the January 10th entry in which shares were recorded in that account at $21 per share. The necessary entry is:

```
Jan. 15  Common Stock .......................................   20,000
             Paid-in Capital in Excess of Stated Value—Common .......         20,000
             To reduce the balance in the common stock account to $20
             per share outstanding.
```

To continue the Grayson Corporation illustration, assume that on January 15, 1984, subscriptions were received for 30,000 shares at $22 per share, and 80 percent of each of the subscriptions was collected on January 25, 1984. Certificates for these shares are to be issued when the subscriptions are collected in full.

The journal entries needed to record the new subscription on January 15 and the collection of part of the subscription on January 25 are:

```
1984
Jan. 15  Subscriptions Receivable—Common .....................  660,000
              Common Stock Subscribed  .......................               600,000
              Paid-In Capital in Excess of Stated Value—Common .....         60,000
         Subscriptions received for 30,000 shares of stock without par
         value at $22 per share. The stated value is $20 per share.

     25  Cash .................................................  528,000
              Subscriptions Receivable—Common .................               528,000
         Received 80 percent on each of the subscriptions of January
         15, 1984.
```

The $600,000 balance in the Common Stock Subscribed account on January 25, 1984, represents the stated value of stock subscribed but not yet issued to subscribers.

Balance sheet presentation of subscriptions receivable and stock subscribed

Illustration 15.2 is a balance sheet prepared from the accounts presented above.

Two accounts, Subscriptions Receivable—Common (or Preferred) and Common (or Preferred) Stock Subscribed, must be shown on any balance sheet prepared before the full amounts owed by subscribers are collected and the stock certificates issued.

The Common Stock Subscribed account should be regarded as a temporary capital stock account. The balance of this account represents the par or stated value of shares subscribed but not yet issued. For stock with no par or stated value, the balance represents the subscription price of shares

Illustration 15.2: Balance Sheet

THE GRAYSON CORPORATION
Balance Sheet
January 25, 1984

Assets

Current assets:

Cash	$ 948,000
Subscriptions receivable—common	132,000
Total assets	$1,080,000

Stockholders' Equity

Paid-in capital:

Common stock without par value, stated value, $20 per share; 100,000 shares authorized:		
Issued and outstanding, 20,000 shares	$400,000	
Subscribed but not issued, 30,000 shares (see subscriptions receivable)	600,000	$1,000,000
Paid-in capital in excess of stated value—common		80,000
Total stockholders' equity		$1,080,000

subscribed but not yet issued. The balance of the Common Stock Subscribed account should be presented immediately below the Common Stock account. The two account balances should be totaled, and to this amount should be added the balance, if any, of the Paid-In Capital in Excess of Stated (or Par) Value—Common account.

The reference in Illustration 15.2 to subscriptions receivable (following the caption "Subscribed but not issued, 30,000 shares") informs the reader that $132,000 remains to be paid in before the 30,000 subscribed shares will be issued.

Subscriptions receivable normally will be collected within a matter of days or weeks. Subscriptions receivable are, therefore, properly classified as a current asset in the balance sheet, although the account should be displayed separately and not included in the total of trade accounts receivable. In some instances, the subscriptions will not be collected within the coming operating cycle. The account Subscriptions Receivable is then properly classifiable as a noncurrent asset and preferably shown under the caption "Other assets" near the bottom of the assets section of the balance sheet.

Balance sheet presentation of paid-in capital in excess of par (or stated) value—common or preferred

As already noted, amounts received in excess of the par or stated value of shares issued should be credited to an account called Paid-In Capital in Excess of Par (or Stated) Value—Common (or Preferred). The amounts received in excess of par or stated value should be carried in separate accounts for each class of stock issued and reported in the balance sheet as follows:

Paid-in capital:			
Preferred stock—$100 par value, 6% cumulative;			
1,000 shares authorized, issued, and outstanding	$100,000		
Common stock—without par value, stated value			
$5; 100,000 shares authorized, 80,000			
shares issued and outstanding	400,000	$500,000	
Paid-in capital in excess of par or stated value:			
From preferred stock issuances	$ 5,000		
From common stock issuances	20,000	25,000	$525,000
Retained earnings			200,000
Total stockholders' equity			$725,000

Defaulted subscriptions

A *defaulted subscription* is a contract to acquire stock on which a required installment payment has not been made. It is possible that subscribers may be unable or unwilling to fulfill their subscription contracts. Since these contracts often call for an immediate initial cash payment, with the balance payable in periodic installments, the defaulting subscriber may have paid part of the total subscription price. State incorporation laws generally govern the disposition of the amount paid in and the balance of the contract. Three usual courses of action are: (1) the subscriber may receive as many shares as have been paid for in full, with the balance of the contract being canceled; (2) the amount paid in may be refunded (often after deducting any expenses and losses incurred in selling the shares to another party); or (3) the amount paid in may be declared forfeited to the corporation. In the third case, the amount retained should be credited to a Paid-In Capital from Defaulted Subscriptions account to indicate the source of the capital.

CAPITAL STOCK ISSUED FOR PROPERTY OR SERVICES

When capital stock is issued for property or services, the dollar amount of the exchange must be determined. In general, accountants seek to measure the economic significance of such exchanges by recording them at the fair value of the property or services received or of the stock issued, whichever is more clearly evident.

As an example, assume the owners of a tract of land deed it to a corporation in exchange for 1,000 shares of $12 par value common stock. The stock, at the time of the exchange, has a value of $14,000. The required entry is:

Land	14,000	
Common Stock		12,000
Paid-In Capital in Excess of Par Value—Common		2,000
To record the receipt of land for capital stock.		

Now, assume 100 shares of common stock with a par value of $40 per share are issued in exchange for legal services received in organizing a corporation. The attorney previously agreed to a price of $5,000 for these services but decided to accept stock in lieu of cash. In this example, the correct entry is:

Organization Costs	5,000	
Common Stock		4,000
Paid-In Capital in Excess of Par Value—Common		1,000
To record the receipt of legal services for capital stock.		

The services should be valued at the price previously agreed on and charged to an asset account because these services will benefit the corporation indefinitely. The amount by which the value of the services received exceeds the par value of the shares issued is properly credited to a Paid-In Capital in Excess of Par Value—Common account.

BOOK VALUE

The *book value* of all of a corporation's outstanding shares is the total of the recorded net asset values of the corporation—that is, total assets minus liabilities. Quite simply, the amount of net assets is equal to total stockholders' equity. When only common stock is outstanding, *book value per share* is computed by dividing stockholders' equity by the number of shares outstanding plus shares subscribed but not yet issued, if any.

Assume the stockholders' equity of a corporation is as follows:

Common stock without par value, stated value $10; authorized,
   20,000 shares; issued and outstanding, 15,000 shares $150,000
Paid-in capital in excess of stated value 10,000 $160,000
Retained earnings 50,000
      Total stockholders' equity $210,000

The book value per share of the stock is determined as follows:

Total stockholders' equity $210,000
Total shares outstanding .... ÷ 15,000
Book value per share .... $ 14

When two or more classes of capital stock are outstanding, the computation of book value per share is more complex. The usual approach is to assume that assets and liabilities would be liquidated at book value. This means the corporation would have cash equal to its stockholders' equity to distribute to its stockholders. The amount of cash that would be distributed for each share of stock then depends upon the rights of the preferred stockholders. Preferred stockholders typically are entitled to a specified liquidation value per share, plus cumulative dividends in arrears, if any, since most preferred stocks are preferred as to assets and are cumulative. In each case, the specific provisions in the preferred stock contract will govern.

To illustrate, the Celoron Company's stockholders' equity is as follows:

Preferred stock, $100 par value, 5,000 shares .... $ 500,000
Common stock, $10 par value, 200,000 shares 2,000,000
Paid-in capital in excess of par value—common 200,000
Retained earnings 400,000
      Total stockholders' equity $3,100,000

The preferred stock is 6 percent, cumulative, and nonparticipating. It is preferred as to dividends and as to assets in liquidation to the extent of the liquidation value of $100 per share, plus any cumulative dividends on the preferred stock. Dividends for the last four years are unpaid. Book values of each class of stock are as follows:

		Total	Per share
Total stockholders' equity.........................		$3,100,000	
Book value of preferred stock (5,000 shares):			
Liquidation value (5,000 × $100)	$500,000		
Dividends (four years at $30,000)	120,000	620,000	$124.00
Book value of common stock (200,000 shares)		$2,480,000	12.40

Assume now the features attached to the preferred stock in the above example are the same except that the preferred stockholders have the right to receive $103 per share in liquidation. The book values of each class of stock would be:

		Total	Per share
Total stockholders' equity		$3,100,000	
Book value of preferred stock (5,000 shares):			
Liquidation value (5,000 × $103)	$515,000		
Dividends (four years at $30,000)	120,000	635,000	$127.00
Book value of common stock (200,000 shares)		$2,465,000	12.33

It is important not to attach too much significance to book value. The shares of many corporations are traded regularly at market prices different from their book values.

NEW TERMS INTRODUCED IN CHAPTER 15

Articles of incorporation
The application for the corporation's charter.

Board of directors
Elected by the stockholders and is primarily responsible for formulating broad policies for the corporation. The board also authorizes contracts, declares dividends, establishes executive salaries, and grants authorization to borrow money.

Book value per share
Stockholders' equity per share; computed as the amount per share each stockholder would receive if the corporation were liquidated without incurring any further expense and if assets were sold and liabilities liquidated at their recorded amounts.

Bylaws
A set of rules or regulations that is adopted by the board of directors of a corporation to govern the conduct of corporate affairs. The bylaws must be in agreement with the laws of the state and the policies and purposes in the corporate charter.

Call premium (on preferred stock)
The difference between the amount at which a corporation may call its preferred stock for redemption and the par value of the stock.

Callable preferred stock
Must be surrendered to the company when the holder is requested to do so. But if the stock is convertible, it may be converted into common shares when called.

Capital stock authorized
The number of shares of stock that a corporation is entitled to issue as designated in its charter.

Capital stock outstanding
The number of shares of stock that have been authorized and issued and which are currently held by stockholders.

Charter, corporate
The contract between the state and the incorporators of a corporation or their successors granting the corporation its legal existence.

Common stock
Shares of stock representing the residual equity in the corporation. If only one class of stock is issued, it is known as common stock. All other claims rank ahead of common stockholders' claims.

Convertible preferred stock
Preferred stock that is convertible into common stock of the issuing corporation.

Corporation
An entity recognized by law as possessing an existence separate from its owners; that is, it is a separate legal entity. It is granted many of the rights and placed under many of the obligations of a natural person. In the eyes of the law of a given state, all corporations organized under the laws of that state are domestic corporations; all other are foreign.

Cumulative preferred stock
Preferred stock for which the right to receive a basic dividend accumulates if not paid; dividends in arrears must be paid before any dividends can be paid on the common stock.

Defaulted subscription
A contract to acquire stock on which a required installment payment has not been made.

Discount on capital stock
The amount by which the par value of shares issued exceeds their issue price. The original issuance of shares at a discount is illegal in most states.

Dividend
A distribution of assets (usually cash) that represents a withdrawal of earnings by the owners. Dividends are similar in nature to withdrawals by sole proprietors and partners.

Dividend on preferred stock
The amount paid to preferred stockholders as a return for the use of their money; usually a fixed or stated amount expressed in dollars per share or as a percentage of par value per share.

Dividends in arrears
Cumulative unpaid dividends, including passed quarterly dividends for the current year.

Domestic corporation
See corporation.

Foreign corporation
See corporation.

Incorporators
Persons seeking to bring a corporation into existence.

Legal capital (stated capital)
An amount prescribed by law (often par value or stated value of shares outstanding) below which a corporation may not reduce stockholders' equity through the declaration of dividends or other payments to stockholders.

Liquidation value
The amount a stockholder will receive if a corporation discontinues operations and liquidates by selling its assets, paying its liabilities, and distributing the remaining cash among the stockholders.

Market value
At a given time is the price at which shares of stock are bought and sold in the open market.

Minutes book
The record book in which actions taken at stockholders' and board of directors' meetings are recorded.

Noncumulative preferred stock
Preferred stock on which the right to receive a dividend expires if the dividend is not declared.

Nonparticipating preferred stock
Preferred stock that is entitled to its stated cumulative dividend only, regardless of the size of the dividend paid on common stock.

Organization costs
Costs of organizing a corporation, such as incorporation fees and legal fees.

Paid-in capital
That amount of stockholders' equity resulting from cash or other assets invested by owners.

Paid-in capital in excess of par (or stated) value—common or preferred
Capital contributed to a corporation in addition to that assigned to the shares issued and recorded in capital stock accounts.

Participating preferred stock
Preferred stock that is entitled to receive dividends above the stated preference rate under certain conditions specified in the preferred stock contract.

Par value
An arbitrary amount assigned to each share of a given class of stock and printed on the stock certificate.

Preemptive right
The right of stockholders to buy additional shares in a proportion equal to the percentage of shares already owned.

Preferred stock
Capital stock which carries certain privileges or rights not carried by common stock. Preferred stock may be preferred as to dividends, preferred as to assets, or preferred as to both dividends and assets. Preferred stock may be cumulative or noncumulative and participating or nonparticipating.

Proxy
A legal document that is signed by the stockholder and gives another person the authority to vote the stockholder's shares at a stockholders' meeting.

Redemption value
The price per share at which a corporation may call its capital stock for retirement.

Retained earnings
That part of stockholders' equity resulting from earnings; the account in which the results of corporate activity are reflected and to which dividends are charged.

Stated value
An arbitrary amount assigned by the board of directors to each share of a given class of no par value stock.

Stock certificate
A printed or engraved document serving as evidence of ownership of a certain number of shares of capital stock.

Stock preferred as to assets

Means that in liquidation the preferred stockholders are entitled to receive the par value (or a larger stipulated liquidation value) per share before any assets may be distributed to common stockholders.

Stock preferred as to dividends

Means that the preferred stockholders are entitled to receive a specified dividend per share before any dividend on common stock is paid.

Stock registrar

Typically a bank which maintains records of the shares outstanding for a company.

Stock transfer agent

Typically a bank or trust company employed by a corporation to transfer stock between buyers and sellers.

Stock without par value (no par value stock)

Capital stock without par value, to which a stated value may or may not be assigned.

Stockholders' ledger

Contains a group of subsidiary accounts showing the number of shares of stock currently held by each stockholder.

Subscribed stock

Stock for which subscriptions have been received, but for which stock certificates have not been issued.

Subscriber

A person who contracts to acquire shares, usually in an original issuance of stock by a corporation.

Subscription

A contract to acquire a certain number of shares of stock, at a specified price, with payment to be made at a specified date or dates.

DEMONSTRATION PROBLEM 15–1

The Dey Company has paid all required preferred dividends through December 31, 1979. Its outstanding stock consists of 10,000 shares of $100 par value common stock and 4,000 shares of 6 percent, $100 par value preferred stock. During five successive years, the company's dividend declarations were as follows:

1980	$140,000
1981	84,000
1982	12,000
1983	24,000
1984	108,000

Required:

Compute the amount of dividends which would have been paid to each class of stock in each of the last five years assuming the preferred stock is:

a. Cumulative and nonparticipating.

b. Noncumulative and nonparticipating.

Solution to demonstration problem 15–1

DEY COMPANY

		Assumptions	
Year	**Dividends to**	**(a)**	**(b)**
1980	Preferred	$ 24,000	$ 24,000
	Common	116,000	116,000
1981	Preferred	24,000	24,000
	Common	60,000	60,000
1982	Preferred	12,000	12,000
	Common	–0–	–0–
1983	Preferred	24,000	24,000
	Common	–0–	–0–
1984	Preferred	36,000	24,000
	Common	72,000	84,000

DEMONSTRATION PROBLEM 15–2

The Pinto Company has been authorized to issue 100,000 shares of $10 par value common stock and 1,000 shares of 14 percent, cumulative, nonparticipating preferred stock with a par value of $20.

Required:

Prepare the entries for the following transactions.

a. 50,000 shares of common stock are subscribed at $40 per share, with a down payment of 50 percent of the issue price.

b. 750 shares of preferred stock are issued for cash at $30 per share.

c. 1,000 shares of common stock are issued in exchange for legal services received in the incorporation process. The fair market value of the legal services is $15,000.

d. The balance of the stock subscriptions is paid, and the stock is issued.

Solution to demonstration problem 15–2

a. Cash 1,000,000
    Subscriptions Receivable—Common 1,000,000
        Common Stock Subscribed   500,000
        Paid-In Capital in Excess of Par Value—Common   1,500,000
    To record subscriptions to 50,000 shares at $40 per share,
    with 50 percent down payment.

b. Cash 22,500
        Preferred Stock   15,000
        Paid-In Capital in Excess of Par Value—Preferred   7,500
    To record the issuance of 750 shares for cash, at $30 per
    share.

c. Organization Costs 15,000
        Common Stock   10,000
        Paid-In Capital in Excess of Par Value—Common   5,000
    To record issuance of 1,000 shares in exchange for legal
    services.

d. Cash 1,000,000
        Subscriptions Receivable—Common   1,000,000
    To record collection of balance due on subscriptions.

    Common Stock Subscribed............................. 500,000
        Common Stock   500,000
    To record issuance of certificates for 50,000 shares, fully paid.

QUESTIONS

1. Cite the major advantages of the corporate form of business organization and indicate why each is considered an advantage.

2. What is meant by the allegation that corporation earnings are subject to double taxation? Cite several other disadvantages of the corporate form of organization.

3. Why is the title Organization Expense not a good one for the account which records the costs of organizing a corporation? Could you justify leaving the balance of an Organization Costs account intact throughout the life of a corporation?

4. What are the basic rights associated with a share of capital stock if there is only one class of stock outstanding?

5. Explain the purpose of (a) the stockholders' ledger, (b) the minutes book, (c) the stock transfer agent, and (d) the stock registrar.

6. Explain the terms *liquidation value* and *redemption value*. To what class of stock do they usually apply?

7. What is the meaning of the terms *stock preferred as to dividends* and *stock preferred as to assets?*

8. With reference to preferred stock, what is the meaning of the terms (a) *cumulative* and *noncumulative* and (b) *participating* and *nonparticipating.*

9. A corporation has outstanding 1,000 shares of 8 percent, $100 par value, cumulative, preferred stock. Dividends on this stock have not been declared for three years. Is the corporation liable to its preferred stockholders for these dividends? How should they be shown in the balance sheet, if at all?

10. Explain why a corporation might issue a preferred stock that is both convertible into common stock and callable.

11. What are the differences between par value stock and stock with no par value?

12. Corporate capital stock is seldom, if ever, issued for less than par value. Give two reasons why this is true.

13. Explain the nature of the Subscriptions Receivable account. How should it be classified in the balance sheet? On what occasions is it debited or credited?

14. What is the general approach of the accountant in seeking the dollar amount at which to record the issuance of capital stock for services or property other than cash?

15. Explain the nature of the account entitled Paid-In Capital in Excess of Par Value. Under what circumstances is an entry recorded in this account?

16. Assuming there is no preferred stock outstanding, how can the book value per share of common stock be determined? Of what significance is it? What is its relationship to market value per share?

EXERCISES

E–1.   Walsh Corporation has outstanding 1,000 shares of noncumulative, nonparticipating preferred stock and 2,000 shares of common stock. The preferred stock is entitled to an annual dividend of $5 per share before dividends are declared on common stock. What are the total dividends received by preferred stockholders and common stockholders if Walsh Corporation distributes $14,000 in dividends in 1984?

E–2.   Betty Corporation has outstanding 2,000 shares of cumulative, nonparticipating preferred stock and 6,000 shares of common stock. The preferred stock is entitled to an annual dividend of $5 per share before dividends are declared on common stock. No preferred dividends were paid for the last two years. What are the total dividends received by preferred stockholders and common stockholders if Betty Corporation distributes $60,000 in dividends?

E–3.   The preferred stock contract of Able Corporation specifies that the preferred shares will participate on an equal amount per share basis with the common shares after $4 per share has been distributed per share of preferred stock and common stock. There are 1,000 shares of preferred stock outstanding and 9,000 shares of common stock outstanding. Determine the dividends that will be paid to each class for the following years:

	Total dividend to be distributed
1984	$ 4,000
1985	20,000
1986	40,000
1987	50,000
1988	60,000

E–4.   Pool Company issued 10,000 shares of common stock for $75,000 cash. The common stock has a par value of $5 per share. Give the journal entry for the stock issuance.

E–5.   McComb Company issued 20,000 shares of $10 par value common stock for $340,000. What is the journal entry for this transaction? What would the journal entry be if the common stock had no par value?

E–6.   Trueblood Company has 100,000 shares authorized and 20,000 shares outstanding of $100 par value common stock. On February 20, 1984, the company received subscriptions for 15,000 shares at $200 per share. What would the journal entry be on February 20, 1984?

E–7.   One hundred shares of $100 par value common stock are issued to the promoters of a corporation in exchange for land (which cost the promoters $13,000 one year ago) needed by the corporation for use as a plant site. Experienced appraisers recently estimated the value of the land to be $15,000. What journal entry would be appropriate to record the acquisition of the land?

E–8.   Delcore Corporation owes a trade creditor $15,000 on open account which it does not have sufficient cash to pay. The trade creditor suggests that Delcore Corporation issue to him 750 shares of the company's $10 par value common stock, which is currently selling on the market at $20. Present the entry or entries that should be made on Delcore Corporation's books.

E–9.   Why would a law firm ever consider accepting stock having a par value of $10,000 as payment in full of a bill for legal services rendered of $15,000? If such a transaction could occur, give the journal entry on the issuing company's books to record it.

E–10.   The stockholders' equity section of the Denver Company's balance sheet is as follows:

Paid-in capital:

Common stock without par value. $5 stated value; authorized 100,000 shares; issued and outstanding, 40,000 shares	$200,000
Subscribed but not issued, 30,000 shares	150,000
Paid-in capital in excess of stated value	190,000
Paid-in capital	$540,000
Retained earnings	60,000
	$600,000

The 30,000 shares of subscribed but not issued stock were subscribed at $10 per share. Compute the average price at which the 40,000 issued shares of common stock were sold. Compute the book value per share of common stock.

PROBLEMS, SERIES A

P15–1–A. Hall, Inc., was authorized to issue 3,000 shares of $2.50 cumulative preferred stock, par value $50, and 30,000 shares of common stock, par value $25.

HALL, INC.
Post-Closing Account Balances
December 31, 1984

Paid-in capital in excess of par value—preferred	$ 7,500
Accounts payable	45,000
Inventory	150,000
Unexpired insurance	4,500
Organization costs	75,000
Common stock subscribed, 2,000 shares	50,000
Subscriptions receivable—common	60,000
Buildings and equipment	180,000
Notes payable, due June 30, 1985	22,500
Cash	90,000
Accumulated depreciation	30,000
Preferred stock, $50 par value; 3,000 shares authorized, issued and outstanding	150,000
Paid-in capital in excess of par value—common	18,000
Common stock, $25 par value; 30,000 shares authorized; issued and outstanding 8,000 shares	200,000
Accounts receivable	152,000
Retained earnings	?

Required:

From the above list of account balances, prepare the December 31, 1984, balance sheet in good form.

P15–2–A. The outstanding capital stock of the Miller Corporation consisted of 3,000 shares of $6 preferred stock, $100 par value, and 30,000 shares of no-par-value common stock with a stated value of $100. The preferred was issued at $103, the common at $120 per share. On January 1, 1980, the retained earnings of the company were $100,000. During the succeeding five years, net income was as follows:

1980	$192,000
1981	128,000
1982	12,000
1983	40,000
1984	160,000

No dividends were in arrears as of January 1, 1980, and during the five years 1980–84, the board of directors declared dividends in each year equal to net income of the year.

Required:

Prepare a schedule showing the dividends declared each year on each class of stock assuming the preferred stock is:

    a. Cumulative and nonparticipating.

    b. Noncumulative and nonparticipating.

P15–3–A. On December 27, 1983, the Jason Company was authorized to issue 250,000 shares of $2 par value common stock. It then completed the following transactions:

Transactions:

1984

Jan. 14   Issued 45,000 shares of common stock at $2.25 per share for cash.
     29   Gave the promoters of the corporation 25,000 shares of common stock for their services in organizing the company. The board of directors valued these services at $65,000.

Feb. 19   Exchanged 50,000 shares of common stock for the following assets at fair market values:

Land	$15,000
Building	70,000
Machinery	62,000

Required:

    a.   Prepare general journal entries to record the transactions.

    b.   Prepare the balance sheet of the company as of March 1, 1984.

P15–4–A.   In the corporate charter which it received on May 1, 1984, the Smith Company was authorized to issue 15,000 shares of common stock. The company issued 1,000 shares immediately to two of the promoters for $30 per share, cash.

     On May 2, the company issued 100 shares of stock and paid $1,000 cash to a lawyer for legal services rendered in organizing the corporation and billed at $3,000.

     On July 3, subscriptions, accompanied by a 10 percent down payment, were received from the general public for 6,000 shares at $20 per share.

     On July 5, the company issued 1,000 shares to the principal promoter of the corporation in exchange for a patent. Another 200 shares were issued to this same person for costs incurred and services rendered in bringing the corporation into existence.

Required:

    a.   Prepare a balance sheet for the Smith Company as of July 5, 1984, assuming the authorized stock had a par value of $20 per share. (It may be helpful to set up T-accounts to post the transactions first.)

    b.   Prepare the stockholders' equity section of the July 5 balance sheet assuming the stock authorized had no par value but had a $10 per share stated value.

    c.   Repeat (*b*) assuming the stock authorized had neither par nor stated value.

P15–5–A.   In the charter granted January 2, 1984, the Jones Corporation was authorized to issue 2,000 shares of common stock without par value. The stock is to be issued under subscription agreements that call for immediate payment of one half of each subscription, with the remainder due on the first day of the following month.

     On January 5, subscriptions for 600 shares at $50 per share were received, and on May 1 an additional 400 shares were subscribed at $60 per share. All subscriptions were collected in accordance with the agreements.

Required:

    a.   Prepare the entries to record all the transactions of January through May 1984, assuming no stock was issued until the subscriptions were paid in full.

    b.   Prepare the May 31, 1984, balance sheet assuming there were no transactions other than those described above.

P15–6–A.   The Sellers Company was authorized on September 1, 1984, to issue 50,000 shares of common stock without par value. On this date, subscriptions for 25,000 shares were received from the public at $4 per share, with cash payment in full accompanying the subscriptions. Subsequent transactions were as follows:

Transactions:

Sept. 2   2,000 shares were issued to the three promoters for legal fees, accounting services, printing costs, state incorporation fees, and other costs incurred in promoting the corporation.

      5   Certificates covering the shares subscribed on September 1 were issued, as per stock transfer agent's report.

      8   Subscriptions for an additional 10,000 shares were received at $4.50 per share.

      9   4,000 shares were issued to one of the promoters for certain patents which the promoter held and believed were worth $20,000.

Oct. 1   The subscriptions of September 8 were collected in full.

      5   Certificates covering the subscriptions of September 8 were issued.

      9   The board of directors established a stated value of $2 per share on the common stock.

Required:

    a.   Prepare journal entries for all of the above transactions starting with September 1.

    b.   Prepare the October 9, 1984, balance sheet assuming there were no transactions other than those given above.

P15–7–A.   Bell Company, on May 1, 1984, received a charter which authorized it to issue:

1.   4,000 shares of preferred stock without par value to which a stated value of $3 per share was assigned. The stock was entitled to a cumulative dividend of $2.40, convertible into two shares of common stock, callable at $52, and entitled to $50 per share in liquidation.
2.   1,500 shares of $100 par value, $5 cumulative preferred stock which is callable at $105 and entitled to $103 in liquidation.
3.   60,000 shares of common stock without par value to which a stated value of $10 was assigned.

Transactions:

May 1   All of the $2.40 convertible preferred was subscribed and issued at $51 per share, cash.

      2   All of the $5 cumulative preferred was exchanged for inventory, land, and buildings valued at $32,000, $40,000, and $85,000, respectively.

      2   Subscriptions were received for 50,000 shares of common at $20 per share, with 10 percent of the subscription price paid immediately in cash.

      3   Cash of $3,000 was paid to reimburse promoters for costs incurred for accounting, legal, and printing services. In addition, 1,000 shares of common stock were issued to the promoters for their services.

    31   All of the subscriptions to the common stock were collected and the shares issued.

Required:

    a.   Prepare journal entries for the above transactions.

    b.   Assume that retained earnings were $50,000. Prepare the stockholders' equity section of the May 31, 1984, balance sheet.

P15–8–A.   On January 2, 1983, the date the Brass Company received its charter, it issued all of its authorized 3,000 shares of preferred stock without par value at $104 and all of its 12,000 authorized shares of common stock without par value at $40 per share. The preferred stock has a stated value of $5 per share, is entitled to a basic cumulative preference dividend of $6 per share, is callable at $106 beginning in 1985, and is entitled to $100 per share plus cumulative dividends in the event of liquidation. The common stock has a stated value of $1 per share.

    On December 31, 1984, the end of the second year of operations, retained earnings were $60,000. No dividends had been declared or paid on either class of stock.

Required:

    a.   Prepare the stockholders' equity section of the Brass Company's December 31, 1984, balance sheet.

> *b.* Compute the book value of each class of stock assuming the preferred stock is nonparticipating.
>
> *c.* If $70,000 of dividends were declared as of December 31, 1984, compute the amount paid to each class of stock assuming the preferred stock is nonparticipating.

P15–9–A. The common stock of Bike Corporation is selling on a stock exchange for $25 per share. The stockholders' equity of the corporation at December 31, 1984, is as follows:

Stockholders' Equity

Preferred stock, 9% cumulative and nonparticipating, $100 par value, 1,000 shares authorized and outstanding	$100,000
Common stock, $20 par value, 30,000 shares authorized and outstanding	600,000
Retained earnings	98,500
Total stockholders' equity	$798,500

Assume that in a liquidation the preferred stock has the right to the return of par value plus cumulative unpaid dividends.

Required:

> *a.* What is the total market value of all of the corporation's common stock?
>
> *b.* If there were no dividends in arrears as of January 1, 1984, what are the book values of the preferred stock and the common stock?
>
> *c.* If two years' dividends were in arrears as of January 1, 1984, on the preferred stock, what are the book values of the preferred stock and common stock?

P15–10–A. Bishop Corporation has an agreement with each of its 15 preferred and 30 common stockholders that in the event of the death of a stockholder, it will purchase at book value from the stockholder's estate or heirs the shares of Bishop Corporation stock held by the deceased at the time of death. The book value is to be computed in accordance with generally accepted accounting principles.

Following is the stockholders' equity section of the Bishop Corporation's December 31, 1984, balance sheet:

$5 preferred stock without par value, $10 stated value; 3,000 shares authorized, issued, and outstanding	$ 30,000
Common stock, $20 par value, 60,000 shares authorized, issued, and outstanding	1,200,000
Paid-in capital in excess of stated value—preferred	300,000
Paid-in capital in excess of par value—common	60,000
Retained earnings	600,000
	$2,190,000

The preferred stock is cumulative and entitled to $100 per share plus cumulative dividends in liquidation. No dividends have been paid for 1½ years.

A stockholder, owner of 100 shares of preferred stock and 1,000 shares of common stock, died on December 31, 1984. You have been employed by the stockholder's widow to compute the book value of each class of stock and to determine the price to be paid for the stock held by her late husband.

Required:

Prepare a schedule showing the computation of the amount to be paid for the deceased stockholder's preferred and common stock.

PROBLEMS, SERIES B

P15–1–B. The Wayside Company was authorized to issue 2,000 shares of preferred stock, par value $100, and 10,000 shares of common stock, par value $40.

WAYSIDE COMPANY
Post-Closing Account Balances
December 31, 1984

Organization costs	$ 80,000
Inventory	48,000
Common stock subscribed, 4,000 shares	160,000
Buildings	200,000
Accumulated depreciation—buildings	40,000
Cash	172,000
Accounts payable	12,000
Preferred stock, $100 par; 2,000 shares authorized, issued, and outstanding	200,000
Accounts receivable	220,000
Common stock, $40 par; 10,000 shares authorized, 6,000 shares issued and outstanding	240,000
Paid-in capital in excess of par—common	28,000
Notes payable (due June 30, 1985)	50,000
Unexpired insurance	13,000
Subscriptions receivable—common	38,400
Paid-in capital in excess of par—preferred	10,000
Retained earnings	?

Required:

From the above list of accounts and balances, present in good form the December 31, 1984, balance sheet.

P15–2–B. On January 1, 1980, the retained earnings of the Taffy Company were $90,000. Net income for the succeeding five years was as follows:

1980	$60,000
1981	45,000
1982	1,000
1983	10,000
1984	55,000

The outstanding capital stock of the corporation consisted of 2,000 shares of $4 preferred stock with a par value of $100 per share and 8,000 shares of common stock without par value having a stated value of $50 per share. No dividends were in arrears as of January 1, 1980.

Required:

Prepare schedules showing how the net income for the above five years was distributed to the two classes of stock if, in each of the years, the entire current net income was distributed as dividends and the preferred stock was:

    a. Cumulative and nonparticipating.

    b. Noncumulative and nonparticipating.

P15–3–B. The C. D. Allan Company had the following stockholders' equity and related accounts on January 1, 1984:

Subscriptions receivable, preferred stock	$ 10,000
Preferred stock, 8%, $10 par, 20,000 shares	
authorized, 10,000 shares issued	100,000
Preferred stock subscribed (2,500 shares)	25,000
Common stock, $100 par, 10,000 shares	
authorized, 7,500 shares issued	750,000
Paid-in capital in excess of par value—common	75,000
Retained earnings	250,000

The following transactions occurred during 1984:

Transactions:

Jan. 10   Received the balance due on preferred stock subscribed; issued stock certificates.
Mar. 1   Subscriptions were received for 5,000 shares of preferred stock at $12; 50 percent of the subscription price was paid in cash.
Aug. 3   Issued 2,000 shares of common stock for cash, at $115.

Required:

a.   Prepare journal entries for the transactions which occurred in 1984.

b.   Prepare the stockholders' equity section of the balance sheet as of August 3, 1984.

P15–4–B.   On July 3, 1984, the Pudding Company was authorized to issue 15,000 shares of common stock, and 3,000 shares were issued immediately to the promoters of the company for cash at $20 per share. Another 300 shares were issued to the promoters for services rendered in organizing the company.

On July 5, 1984, legal and printing costs of $750 were paid. These costs related to securing the corporate charter and the stock certificates.

On July 10, subscriptions were received from the general public for 4,500 shares at $18 per share, with one half of the subscription price paid in cash immediately. The balance is due August 10, 1984.

Required:

a.   Prepare the balance sheet of the Pudding Company as of the close of July 10, 1984, assuming the authorized stock has a $10 par value. (It may be helpful to set up T-accounts to post the transactions first.)

b.   Repeat (a) assuming the stock is without par value but is to have a $15 stated value.

c.   Repeat (a) assuming the stock is without par or stated value.

P15–5–B.   On July 1, 1984, the Jason Company was authorized to issue 20,000 shares of $25 par value common stock. On July 7, subscriptions for 1,500 shares at $30 per share were received. The subscription contract required a 10 percent immediate payment, with the remainder due on July 31. No stock certificates were to be issued until the subscriptions were paid in full.

Required:

a.   Prepare the entries to record all transactions during July 1984. Subscriptions were collected when due.

b.   Prepare the July 1984 entries assuming the stock is without par value.

c.   Prepare the entry for July 7, 1984, if the subscriptions for the stock without par value were accompanied by cash payment in full and the stock was issued.

P15–6–B.   On July 1, 1984, the Dale Corporation received authorization to issue 40,000 shares of common stock without par value. On that date, subscriptions were received from the general public for 7,000 shares at $60 per share. Also, on the same date, 1,000 shares were issued to Mr. Dale and his sons for services rendered and costs incurred in organizing the corporation. The following transactions occurred during the remainder of the month of July.

Transactions:

July   10   Received subscriptions for another 3,000 shares at $64 per share and collected one third of each of the July 1 subscriptions for 7,000 shares.
       11   Issued 2,000 shares in exchange for a tract of land.
       20   Collected the balance of each of the July 1 subscriptions and issued the shares. Also, collected one half of each of the July 10 subscriptions.
       30   Collected the balance of each of the July 10 subscriptions and issued the shares.
Sept.   1   The board of directors decided to place a stated value of $25 per share on the common stock.

Required:

   a.   Prepare journal entries to record all of the July transactions and the entry needed on September 1.

   b.   Prepare journal entries to record all of the July transactions assuming that the stock issued was $50 par value stock.

P15–7–B.   The Sail Company received its charter on April 1, 1984, authorizing it to issue 5,000 shares of $100 par value, $4 cumulative, convertible preferred stock; 10,000 shares of $1.50 cumulative preferred stock without par value having a stated value of $5 per share and a liquidation value of $25 per share; and 100,000 shares of common stock without par or stated value.

      On April 2, promoters of the corporation acquired 50,000 shares of the common stock for cash at $10 per share, and 200 shares were issued to an attorney for services rendered in organizing the corporation. On April 3, the company issued all of its authorized shares of $4 convertible preferred stock for land valued at $200,000 and a building valued at $600,000. The property was subject to a mortgage of $300,000.

      On April 4, subscriptions for 5,000 shares of the $1.50 preferred stock were received at $26 per share, with one half of the subscription price paid in cash. On April 8, the remaining 5,000 shares of $1.50 preferred stock were issued to an inventor for a patent. A subscription for 1,000 shares of common stock at $10 per share was also received, with a cash payment of $1,000 accompanying the subscription.

      On April 25, the balance due on the April 4 subscriptions was collected and the shares issued. By April 30, the subscriber to 1,000 shares of common stock had failed to pay the balance of her subscription, which she had agreed to pay in 10 days. Shares were issued for her down payment, and the balance of the contract was canceled.

Required:

   a.   Prepare general journal entries for the above transactions.

   b.   Prepare the stockholders' equity section of the April 30, 1984, balance sheet. Assume a deficit of $10,000.

   c.   Assume that each share of the $4 convertible preferred stock was convertible into six shares of common stock and that all of the preferred was converted on September 1, 1987. Give the required journal entry.

P15–8–B.   The McCall Company issued all of its 2,500 shares of authorized preferred stock on July 1, 1982, at $103 per share. The preferred stock is without par value, has a stated value of $5 per share, is entitled to a cumulative basic preference dividend of $6 per share, is callable at $105 beginning in 1988, and is entitled to $100 per share in liquidation plus cumulative dividends. McCall also issued its 5,000 authorized shares of common stock without par value but with a $10 stated value on this date at $50 per share.

    On June 30, 1984, the end of its second fiscal year of operations, the company's retained earnings amounted to $80,000. No dividends have been declared or paid on either class of stock since the date of issue.

Required:

    a.   Prepare the stockholders' equity section of the McCall Company's June 30, 1984, balance sheet.

    b.   Compute the book value in total and per share of each class of stock as of June 30, 1984, assuming the preferred stock is nonparticipating.

    c.   If $55,000 of dividends are to be declared as of June 30, 1984, compute the amount payable to each class of stock assuming the preferred stock is nonparticipating.

P15–9–B.   The stockholders' equity sections from three different corporations' balance sheets follow:

1. Stockholders' equity:

Preferred stock, 7% cumulative and nonparticipating, $50 par value, 500 shares authorized and outstanding	$ 25,000
Common stock, $10 par value, 10,000 shares authorized and outstanding	100,000
Retained earnings	88,000
Total stockholders' equity	$ 213,000

2. Stockholders' equity:

Preferred stock, 6% cumulative and nonparticipating, $17 par value, 10,000 shares authorized and outstanding	$ 170,000
Common stock, $50 par value, 30,000 shares authorized and outstanding	1,500,000
Retained earnings	15,000
Total stockholders' equity	$1,685,000

(The current year's dividends have not been paid.)

3. Stockholders' equity:

Preferred stock, 7% cumulative and nonparticipating, $100 par value, 10,000 shares authorized and outstanding	$1,000,000
Common stock, $50 par value, 50,000 shares authorized and outstanding	2,500,000
Deficit	(390,000)
Total stockholders' equity	$3,110,000

(Dividends have not been paid for 2 previous years or the current year.)

Required:

    Compute the book values per share of the preferred and common stock of each corporation assuming that in a liquidation the preferred stock receives par value plus dividends in arrears.

P15–10–B.   Lakeside, Inc., is a corporation in which all of the outstanding preferred and common stock is held by four Lakeside brothers. The brothers have an agreement stating that the remaining brothers will, upon the death of a brother, purchase from his estate at book value, his holdings of stock in the company.

The stockholders' equity accounts of the company on June 30, 1984, the date of the death of William Lakeside, show:

Preferred stock, 6%; $100 par value; $100 liquidation value;	
4,000 shares authorized, issued, and outstanding	$ 400,000
Paid-in capital in excess of par—preferred	20,000
Common stock without par value, $5 stated value,	
60,000 shares authorized, issued, and outstanding	300,000
Paid-in capital in excess of par—common	300,000
Retained earnings	40,000
	$1,060,000

No dividends have been paid on the preferred stock, which is cumulative and nonparticipating, in the last six months. William Lakeside held, at the time of his death, 2,000 shares of preferred stock and 10,000 shares of common stock of the company.

Required:

a.   Compute the book value of the preferred stock.

b.   Compute the book value of the common stock.

c.   Compute the amount the remaining brothers must pay to the estate of William Lakeside for the preferred and common stock which he held at the time of his death.

BUSINESS DECISION PROBLEM 15–1

Southern Company and Northern Company are two companies that have extremely stable net income of $6,000,000 and $4,000,000, respectively. Both companies distribute all their net income as dividends each year. Southern Company has 100,000 shares of $100 par value, 6 percent preferred stock and 500,000 shares of $10 par value common stock outstanding. Northern Company has 50,000 shares of $50 par value, 8 percent preferred stock and 400,000 shares of $5 par value common stock outstanding. Both preferred stocks are cumulative and nonparticipating.

Required:

a.   Compute the annual dividend per share of preferred stock and per share of common stock for each company.

b.   Based solely upon the above information, which common stock would you predict to have the higher market price per share? Why?

BUSINESS DECISION PROBLEM 15–2

Robert Douglas recently inherited $40,000 cash that he wishes to invest in one of the following securities: common stock of the Duffy Corporation or common stock of the Gaylord Corporation. Both corporations manufacture the same types of products and have been in existence for five years. The stockholders' equity sections of the two corporations' latest balance sheets are shown below:

DUFFY CORPORATION

Common stock, $10 par value, 30,000 shares authorized,
   issued, and outstanding $300,000
Retained earnings 300,000
      Total stockholders' equity $600,000

GAYLORD CORPORATION

Preferred stock, $100 par value, 8% cumulative and
   nonparticipating, 2,000 shares authorized, issued,
   and outstanding $200,000
Common stock, $10 par value, 40,000 shares authorized,
   issued, and outstanding 400,000
Retained earnings 30,000
      Total stockholders' equity $630,000

The Duffy Corporation has paid a cash dividend of $0.50 per share each year since its creation; its common stock is currently selling for $50 per share. The Gaylord Corporation's common stock is currently selling for $40 per share. The current year's dividend and three prior years' dividends on the preferred stock are in arrears. The preferred stock has a liquidation value of $100 per share.

Required:

    a. What is the book value per share of the Duffy Corporation common stock and the Gaylord Corporation common stock? Is book value the major determinant of market value of the stock?

    b. Based solely upon the above information, which investment would you recommend? Why?

Chapter 16

Corporations: Paid-in capital, retained earnings, dividends, and treasury stock

CHAPTER GOALS

After study of this chapter, you should be able to:

1. Identity the different sources of paid-in capital and describe how they would be presented in a balance sheet.

2. Give journal entries for a retained earnings appropriation, a cash dividend, a large or small stock dividend, a stock split, and the acquisition and reissuance of treasury stock.

3. Define extraordinary items and prior period adjustments and show their proper presentation in the financial statements.

4. Describe the proper treatment of various accounting changes.

5. Define and use correctly the new terms in the chapter glossary.

The preceding chapter dealt with paid-in capital resulting from issuing shares of stock for cash, other property, or services. Attention is now directed to other sources of paid-in capital and other matters affecting stockholders' equity.

PAID-IN (OR CONTRIBUTED) CAPITAL

The term *paid-in capital,* or *contributed capital,* is applied to all of the contributed capital of a corporation, including that carried in the capital stock accounts. No single account entitled Paid-In Capital is maintained in the ledger. Instead, a separate account is established for each source of capital. Each of these accounts could carry the words *paid-in capital* in the account title. For example, the Common Stock and the Preferred Stock accounts could quite properly be titled Paid-In Capital—Common Stock and Paid-In Capital—Preferred Stock, since both accounts record capital contributions made by stockholders. The shorter titles are used in this text because of their widespread acceptance in practice.

Illustration 16.1 summarizes several sources of stockholders' equity and gives examples of titles for the general ledger accounts used to record increases and decreases in capital from each of these sources.

Illustration 16.1: Sources of stockholders' equity

Source of stockholders' equity	Illustrative general ledger account titles
I. Capital contributed	
A. For, or assigned to, shares:	
1. To the extent of par or stated value or the amount received for shares without par or stated value.	Common Stock 5 Percent Preferred Stock
2. In addition to par or stated value:	
a. In excess of par.	Paid-In Capital in Excess of Par Value—Common (Preferred)
b. In excess of stated value.	Paid-In Capital in Excess of Stated Value—Common (Preferred)
c. Resulting from reduction in par or stated value of shares.	Paid-In Capital—Recapitalization
d. Resulting from reissue of treasury stock at a price above its acquisition price.	Paid-In Capital—Common (Preferred) Treasury Stock Transactions
B. Other than for shares, whether from shareholders or from others.	Paid-In Capital—Donations
II. Capital accumulated by retention of earnings.	Retained Earnings or Retained Income

The stockholders' equity section of the balance sheet should show the different sources of the corporation's paid-in capital. Such a presentation provides important information. For example, assume a corporation has issued both preferred and common stock. The stock was issued at various times and in various amounts. Assume now that total paid-in capital in excess of

577

par is $25,000 for preferred stock and $15,000 for common stock. If only one premium account for all classes of stock (Paid-In Capital in Excess of Par) were established, it would be impossible to determine whether the capital came from preferred stock or from common stock. But if separate accounts for premiums are maintained, a proper accounting for the retirement of all or part of the outstanding preferred stock is possible without extensive review of prior years' records.

The accounts shown opposite the sources listed under 1A in Illustration 16.1 represent amounts paid in by either past or present stockholders of the corporation. The capital contributions represented by the Paid-In Capital—Donations account (IB) may have come from either stockholders or other donors, such as a chamber of commerce which has donated a plant site as a means of attracting industry to the community. Regardless of the specific source, paid-in capital is regarded as the relatively permanent portion of stockholders' equity. On the other hand, retained earnings (II)—typically the source of dividend distributions—is regarded as the relatively temporary portion of corporate capital.

Paid-in capital—recapitalization

A corporation may find it necessary to change its capitalization. For example, a company having 5,000 shares of common stock with a par value of $100 may find that it cannot issue additional shares at $100 because the shares will not sell at that price. To avoid issuing shares at a discount, the company may decide to reduce the par value of its stock to $80. The entry to record the exchange of all the $100 shares for the new $80 shares would be:

Common Stock—$100 Par Value	500,000	
Common Stock—$80 Par Value		400,000
Paid-In Capital—Recapitalization		100,000

To record the exchange of 5,000 new $80 par value common shares for 5,000 old $100 par value common shares.

The *Paid-In Capital—Recapitalization account* contains the amount of capital removed from the capital stock account when the par or stated value of the outstanding shares is reduced.

The process of reducing the par or stated value of outstanding shares is called *recapitalization.*

Paid-in capital—treasury stock transactions

Another source of capital may be treasury stock transactions. *Treasury stock* is the corporation's own stock, either preferred or common, which has been issued and reacquired by the issuing corporation. It has not been canceled and is legally available for reissuance. If a corporation reacquires shares of its own outstanding capital stock at one price and later reissues them at a higher price, corporate capital is increased by the difference between the two prices. If the reissue price is less than acquisition cost, corporate capital is decreased. Treasury stock transactions are treated at length later in this chapter.

Paid-in capital—donations

Donated capital increases stockholders' equity and results from donation of assets to the corporation. Occasionally a corporation receives gifts of assets— a gift of land from the chamber of commerce is an example. Donated gifts increase corporate capital but not through earnings or transactions involving capital stock. The entry to record the gift of a $5,000 land site is a debit to Land and a credit to Paid-In Capital—Donations, regardless of the identity of the donor. The entry should be made in the amount of the fair market value of the gift when received.

RETAINED EARNINGS

The stockholders' equity or interest in a corporation generally consists of two elements: (1) paid-in (or contributed) capital and (2) retained earnings. *Retained earnings* is that part of stockholders' equity resulting from earnings. As such, it indicates the source of certain assets received but not distributed to stockholders as dividends. Thus, both paid-in capital and retained earnings are sources of assets received by the corporation—actual investment by the stockholders and investment by the stockholders through earnings not yet withdrawn. The balance in the Retained Earnings account is viewed as the net income of the corporation from the date of incorporation to the present less the sum of dividends declared during the same period. Income increases the Retained Earnings and dividends decrease Retained Earnings in any given year. Thus, the balance in Retained Earnings represents the accumulated income not distributed to stockholders. Occasionally other debits and credits are made to the Retained Earnings account. Some of those entries will be discussed later in the chapter.

When the Retained Earnings account has a debit balance, a *deficit* exists. A deficit is shown as retained earnings with a negative amount in the stockholders' equity section of the balance sheet. The title of the general ledger account need not be changed even though it contains a debit balance.

The net income or loss of a corporation, as shown in the income statement, is transferred to the Retained Earnings account during the closing process at the end of the accounting period. The Retained Earnings account is credited for the amount of net income (or debited for the amount of net loss), and the Income Summary account is closed by a corresponding debit (or credit) entry.

Since dividends reduce the capital accumulated through retention of earnings, they are debited to Retained Earnings.

PAID-IN CAPITAL AND RETAINED EARNINGS IN THE BALANCE SHEET

The following stockholders' equity section of a balance sheet illustrates the presentation of the various sources of capital:

Stockholders' equity:
  Paid-in capital:
    Preferred stock, 6% $100 par value; authorized, issued, and

outstanding, 4,000 shares	$ 400,000	
Common stock, no-par value, $5 stated value, authorized, issued, and outstanding, 200,000 shares	1,000,000	$1,400,000
Paid-in capital—		
From preferred stock issuances	$ 40,000	
From recapitalization of common stock	1,000,000	
From donations	10,000	1,050,000
Total paid-in capital		$2,450,000
Retained earnings		500,000
Total stockholders' equity........................		$2,950,000

In highly condensed, published balance sheets, the details regarding the sources of the paid-in capital in excess of par or stated value are often omitted and replaced by a single item, such as:

Paid-in capital in excess of par or stated value . . $1,050,000

RETAINED EARNINGS APPROPRIATIONS

The amount of retained earnings that may be paid out as cash dividends may be less than total retained earnings for several reasons, contractual or voluntary. For example, a loan agreement may state that $100,000 of retained earnings are not available for cash dividends until the loan is repaid. Or the board of directors may decide that the assets brought in by the earning of net income are to be used for plant expansion rather than cash dividends. Such voluntary or contractual restrictions or limitations on retained earnings are called *retained earnings appropriations* and may be formally recorded by transferring amounts from Retained Earnings to accounts such as "Appropriation for Loan Agreement" or "Retained Earnings Appropriated for Plant Expansion." Retained earnings appropriations are often referred to as retained earnings reserves. Appropriations may be made for pending litigation, for debt retirement, for contingencies in general, and for other purposes.

Such appropriations do *not* reduce total retained earnings. Their purpose is merely to disclose to balance sheet readers that a portion of retained earnings is not available for cash dividends. Recording retained earnings appropriations does *not* involve the setting aside of cash for the indicated purpose. The establishment of a separate fund would require a specific directive from the board of directors. Such funds are quite rare. Thus, the only entry required to record the appropriation of $25,000 of retained earnings to fulfill the provisions in a loan agreement is:

Retained Earnings	25,000	
Appropriation per Loan Agreement		25,000
To record restriction on retained earnings.		

When the retained earnings appropriation has served its purpose of restricting dividends and the loan has been repaid, the board of directors may decide to return the appropriation intact to Retained Earnings. The entry is simply a debit to the Appropriation per Loan Agreement account and a credit to Retained Earnings. No actual cash has been involved in the appropriation transaction.

Retained earnings appropriations in the balance sheet

In the balance sheet, retained earnings appropriations should be shown in the stockholders' equity section as follows:

Stockholders' equity:		
Paid-in capital:		
Preferred stock, $50 par; 500 shares authorized, issued, and		
outstanding	$25,000	
Common stock, $5 par; 10,000 shares authorized, issued,		
and outstanding	50,000	
Total paid-in capital		$ 75,000
Retained earnings:		
Appropriated:		
Per loan agreement	$25,000	
Free and unappropriated	20,000	
Total retained earnings		45,000
Total stockholders' equity		$120,000

Note that a retained earnings appropriation does not reduce stockholders' equity; it merely earmarks (restricts) a portion of that equity for a specific reason.

The formal recording and reporting of retained earnings appropriations is decreasing and is being replaced by footnote explanations such as the following:

Note 7. Retained earnings restrictions. According to provisions in the loan agreement, retained earnings available for dividends are limited to $20,000.

THE STATEMENT OF RETAINED EARNINGS

Most corporations include four financial statements in their annual reports to stockholders: a balance sheet, an income statement, a statement of retained earnings, and a statement of changes in financial position (to be discussed in Chapter 19). A *statement of retained earnings* is a formal statement showing the items causing changes in retained earnings during a stated period of time. These changes usually consist of the addition of net income (or deduction of net loss) and the deduction of dividends and appropriations. A typical statement of retained earnings is shown in Illustration 16.2.

Illustration 16.2:   Statement of retained earnings

WARD CORPORATION
Statement of Retained Earnings
For Year Ended December 31, 1984

Unappropriated retained earnings:		
January 1, 1984 balance		$180,000
Add: Net income		80,000
		$260,000
Less: Dividends	$25,000	
Appropriation for plant expansion	25,000	50,000
Unappropriated retained earnings, December 31, 1984		$210,000
Appropriated retained earnings:		
Appropriation for plant expansion, January 1, 1984 balance	$25,000	
Add: Increase in 1984	25,000	50,000
Appropriation for contract obligation, January 1, 1984 balance		25,000
Appropriated retained earnings, December 31, 1984		75,000
Total retained earnings, December 31, 1984		$285,000

DIVIDENDS

Dividends are *distributions of earnings by a corporation to its stockholders.* The normal dividend is a cash dividend, but additional shares of the corporation's own capital stock may also be distributed as dividends.

Since dividends are the means whereby the owners of a corporation share in the earnings of the corporation, they usually are charged against retained earnings. They must be declared by the board of directors and recorded in the minutes book. The significant dates concerning dividends are the date of *declaration,* the date of *record,* and the date of *payment.* For example, the board of directors of the Allan Corporation may declare on May 5, 1984, a cash dividend of $1.25 per share to stockholders of record on July 1, 1984, payable on July 10. The **date of declaration** is the date the board takes action in the form of a motion that dividends be paid. This action creates the liability for dividends payable. The **date of record** is the date established by the board to determine who will receive the dividends. The stockholders on the date of record are determined from the corporation's records (a subsidiary stockholders' ledger). The **date of payment** is the date of actual payment of the dividend. Since a financial transaction occurs on the date of declaration (a liability is incurred) and on the date of payment (cash is paid), journal entries will be required on these dates. No journal entry is required on the date of record.

Cash dividends

Cash dividends are a cash distribution of earnings by a corporation to its stockholders. To illustrate the entries for cash dividends, consider the following example. On January 21, 1984, a corporation's board of directors declares a 2 percent quarterly cash dividend on $100,000 (one fourth of the annual dividend on 1,000 shares of $100 par value, 8 percent preferred stock). The dividend will be paid on March 1, 1984, to stockholders of record on February 5, 1984. The entries at the declaration and payment dates are as follows:

Jan. 21	Retained Earnings	2,000	
	Dividends Payable		2,000
	Dividends declared: 2 percent on $100,000 of outstanding preferred stock, payable March 1, 1984, to stockholders of record on February 5, 1984.		

Mar. 1	Dividends Payable	2,000	
	Cash		2,000
	Paid the dividend declared on January 21, 1984.		

No entry is made on the date of record.

When a cash dividend is declared, some companies debit a Dividends account instead of Retained Earnings. The Dividends account is then closed to Retained Earnings at the end of the fiscal year. Both methods are acceptable.

Once a cash dividend is declared and notice of the dividend is given to stockholders, it cannot be rescinded unless all stockholders agree to such action. A legally declared cash dividend is a current liability of the corporation, so Dividends Payable will be presented as a current liability on the balance sheet.

Stock dividends

A corporation may declare a *stock dividend* which is a dividend that is payable in additional shares of the declaring corporation capital stock. Stock dividend declarations usually call for the distribution of additional shares of the same class of stock as that held by the stockholders—for example, additional common stock to common stockholders. The usual accounting for a stock dividend distribution is to transfer a sum from retained earnings to permanent paid-in capital. The amount transferred for stock dividends is usually the fair market value of the distributed shares. Most states permit the use of retained earnings or paid-in capital from any source (other than amounts already credited to capital stock) for stock dividends. But in most circumstances Retained Earnings will be debited for the declaration of a stock dividend.

Stock dividends have no effect on the total amount of stockholders' equity. They merely decrease retained earnings and increase paid-in capital by an equal amount. Immediately after the declaration and distribution of a stock dividend, each share of similar stock has a lower book value per share. This is because more shares are outstanding with no increase in total stockholders' equity.

Stock dividends do not affect the individual stockholder's percentage of ownership in the corporation. For example, if a stockholder owns 1,000 shares in a corporation having 100,000 shares of stock outstanding, that stockholder owns 1 percent of the outstanding shares. After a 10 percent stock dividend, the stockholder will still own 1 percent of the outstanding shares—1,100 of 110,000 outstanding.

Reasons for declaring a stock dividend include:

1. Retained earnings may have become large relative to total stockholders' equity, or the corporation may simply desire a larger permanent capitalization.
2. The market price of the stock may have risen above a desirable trading range. A stock dividend will generally reduce the per share market value of the company's stock.
3. The corporation may wish to have more stockholders and expects to increase their number by increasing the number of shares outstanding.
4. Stock dividends may be used to silence stockholders' demands for dividends from a corporation which does not have sufficient cash to pay cash dividends.

Recording stock dividends

Small stock dividends. A stock dividend of less than 20 to 25 percent of the previously outstanding shares is assumed to have little effect on the market value of the shares. Thus, the dividend should be accounted for at the present market value of the outstanding shares.

Assume a corporation is authorized to issue 20,000 shares of $100 par value common stock, of which 8,000 shares are outstanding. Its board of directors now declares a 10 percent stock dividend (800 shares). The market price of the stock is $125 per share immediately before the stock dividend is announced. Since distributions of less than 20 to 25 percent of the previously outstanding shares are to be accounted for at market value, the entry for the declaration of the dividend is as follows (assuming the dividend was declared on August 10, 1984):

Aug. 10	Retained Earnings	100,000	
	Stock Dividend Distributable—Common		80,000
	Paid-In Capital—Stock Dividend		20,000
	To record the declaration of a 10 percent stock dividend; shares to be distributed on September 20, 1984, to stockholders of record on August 31, 1984.		

The entry to record the issuance of the shares is as follows:

Sept. 20	Stock Dividend Distributable—Common	80,000	
	Common Stock		80,000
	To record distribution of 800 shares of common stock as authorized in stock dividend declared on August 10, 1984.		

The *Stock Dividend Distributable—Common account* is a stockholders' equity account which is credited for the par or stated value of the shares distributable when recording the declaration of a stock dividend. Since a stock dividend distributable (payable) is not payable with assets, it is not a liability. If a balance sheet is prepared between the date of declaration of the 10 percent dividend and the date of issuance of the shares, the proper statement presentation of the effects of the stock dividend is as follows:

Stockholders' equity:
  Paid-in capital:
    Common stock, $100 par value; authorized, 20,000 shares;
      issued and outstanding, 8,000 shares $800,000
    Stock dividend distributable on September 20, 1984,
      800 shares at par value 80,000
    Total par value of shares issued and to be issued $880,000
    From capitalization of retained earnings through declaration
      of stock dividend 20,000
        Total paid-in capital .... $ 900,000
  Retained earnings 150,000
        Total stockholders' equity $1,050,000

Alternatively, suppose that the market price is $125 per share on the date of declaration, and that the common stock is without par value but has a stated value of $50 per share. In this case, the entry to record the declaration of the stock dividend would be:

Retained Earnings 100,000
    Stock Dividend Distributable—Common 40,000
    Paid-In Capital—Stock Dividend 60,000
  To record the declaration of a stock dividend.

The entry to record the issuance of the stock dividend is:

Stock Dividend Distributable—Common 40,000
    Common Stock 40,000
  To record the issuance of the stock dividend.

Large stock dividends. Stock dividends of over 20 to 25 percent of the previously outstanding shares are considered to be large stock dividends. Since one purpose of a large stock dividend is to reduce the market value of the stock, the old market value of the stock should not be used in the entry. Such dividends are accounted for at their *par* or *stated* value rather than at their fair market value. Stocks without par or stated value are accounted for at the amounts established by the laws of the state of incorporation or by the board of directors.

To illustrate the treatment of a stock dividend of over 20 to 25 percent, assume X Corporation has authorized capital of 10,000 shares of $10 par value common stock and has 5,000 shares issued and outstanding. X Corporation declares a 30 percent stock dividend (1,500 shares) on September 20, 1984, to be issued on October 15, 1984. The required entries are:

Sept. 20 Retained Earnings 15,000
              Stock Dividend Distributable 15,000
          To declare a 30 percent stock dividend.

Oct. 15 Stock Dividend Distributable 15,000
              Common Stock 15,000
          To issue the 30 percent stock dividend.

Note that in contrast to the small stock dividend that was accounted for at market value, the 30 percent stock dividend was accounted for at par value (1,500 shares $\times$ \$10 = \$15,000). Because of the differences in accounting for large and small stock dividends, the relative size of the stock dividend must be determined before making any journal entries.

Stock splits

A *stock split,* as used in *Accounting Research Bulletin No. 43,* is a distribution of additional shares of the issuing corporation's stock for which the corporation receives no assets and for the purpose of causing a large reduction in the market price per share of the outstanding stock. The usual stock split is one in which the number of shares outstanding is increased with a corresponding reduction in the par value per share. A two-for-one split doubles the shares outstanding, a three-for-one split triples the shares, and so on. The par value per share is usually reduced so that the total dollar amount credited to common stock remains the same. For instance, in a two-for-one split, the par value per share is usually halved.

The entry to record a stock split depends on the particular circumstances. Usually, only the number of shares outstanding and the par or stated value need to be changed in the records. Thus, a two-for-one stock split in which the par value of the shares is decreased from \$20 to \$10 would be recorded as follows:

```
Common Stock—$20 par value ................................    100,000
    Common Stock—$10 par value ...........................               100,000
    To record a two-for-one stock split. 5,000 shares of $20 par value
    common stock were replaced by 10,000 shares of $10 par value com-
    mon stock.
```

Legality of dividends

State corporate laws differ in their provisions regarding the legality of a dividend. The legal or stated capital of a corporation is established by state law as that portion of the stockholders' equity that must be maintained intact, unimpaired by dividend declarations or other distributions to stockholders. The legal capital often is established at an amount equal to the par or stated value of the shares issued or at an amount equal to a minimum price per share issued. The objective of the statutes in prohibiting the impairment of legal capital by the declaration of dividends is to protect the creditors of the corporation, whose claims are superior to those of stockholders.

The board of directors of a corporation possesses sole power to declare dividends. The *legality* of a dividend generally depends upon the amount of retained earnings available for dividends—not upon the net income of any one period or the size of the cash balance. But in some states, dividends may be declared from current earnings even though there is an accumulated deficit. The *financial advisability* of declaring a dividend depends on the working capital position of the corporation. Dividends may be paid in periods in which losses are incurred, provided retained earnings and the working capital position justify the dividend.

Liquidating dividends

Dividends are normally reductions of retained earnings since they are distributions of earnings. Dividends which are a distribution of contributed capital are called *liquidating dividends.* Dividends from permanent paid-in capital are unusual. If permanent paid-in capital is being distributed, such dividends reduce the "permanent" portion of the stockholders' equity. The corporation should disclose to its stockholders the source of those dividends which are not distributions of earnings. The legality of such dividends depends on the precise source of the capital and on the laws of the state of incorporation.

TREASURY STOCK

Treasury stock is the corporation's own capital stock, which has been issued and reacquired by the issuing corporation. It has not been canceled and is legally available for reissuance. Treasury stock is not termed *unissued stock;* unissued stock is the difference between the number of shares authorized and the number of shares which have been sold (issued) at some point in time.

When a corporation reacquires its own capital stock as treasury stock, the purpose of the acquisition may be (1) to cancel and retire the stock, (2) to reissue it later at a higher price, (3) to reduce the number of shares outstanding and thereby increase earnings per share, or (4) to use the stock for issuance to employees. If the intent of acquisition is cancellation and retirement, the treasury shares exist as such simply because they have not yet been retired and canceled by formal reduction of the authorized capital.

Most state corporate laws consider treasury stock as issued but not outstanding for dividend or voting purposes, since the shares are no longer in the possession of stockholders. But treasury shares usually are considered to be outstanding for purposes of determining legal capital. Thus, the legal capital would include outstanding shares plus those held in the treasury. In states that consider treasury stock part of legal capital, the cost of treasury stock may not exceed the amount of retained earnings at the date the shares are reacquired. The purpose is to protect creditors by preventing the corporation from using funds to purchase stock instead of paying its debts when the corporation is in financial difficulty. Thus, if a corporation is subject to such a law (as is assumed in this text), the retained earnings available for dividends are limited to the amount in excess of the cost of the treasury shares on hand.

Treasury stock may be reissued without violating the preemptive right provisions of state laws; that is, they do not need to be offered to the current stockholders on a prorata basis. As previously explained, if additional *authorized* but *unissued* shares are to be issued after the date of original issue, the additional authorized and unissued shares must, in most states, be offered first to existing stockholders. The requirement to offer the stock on a prorata basis does not apply to treasury stock.

Acquisition and reissuance of treasury stock

When treasury stock is acquired, the stock is recorded at cost in a debit balance stockholders' equity account called Treasury Stock. Reissuances are credited to the Treasury Stock account at the cost of acquisition. The excess of the reissue price over cost is credited to *Paid-In Capital—Treasury Stock Transactions* because it represents additional paid-in capital. This account is credited when treasury stock is reissued for more than its cost and usually is debited when shares are reissued at less than their cost.

For example, the Hillside Corporation, whose stockholders' equity consists solely of common stock and retained earnings, reacquires 100 shares of its outstanding common stock for $55 each and two months later reissues 30 shares for $58 each. The entries are:

```
Treasury Stock—Common (100  ×  $55) .........................     5,500
    Cash ...........................................................            5,500
    Acquired 100 shares of treasury stock at $55.

Cash (30  ×  $58) ...........................................     1,740
    Treasury Stock—Common (30  ×  $55) ......................            1,650
    Paid-In Capital—Common Treasury Stock Transactions ..........               90
    Reissued 30 shares of treasury stock at $58; cost $55 per share.
```

If the reissue price of subsequent shares is less than the acquisition price, the difference is debited to Paid-In Capital—Common Treasury Stock Transactions. But that account is not permitted to develop a debit balance. By definition, no paid-in capital account can have a debit balance. If the Hillside Corporation reissues an additional 20 shares at $52 per share, the entry is:

```
Cash (20  ×  $52) ...........................................     1,040
Paid-In Capital—Common Treasury Stock Transactions ..............        60
    Treasury Stock—Common (20  ×  $55) ......................            1,100
    Reissued 20 shares of treasury stock at $52; cost $55 per share.
```

At this point, the credit balance in the Paid-In Capital—Common Treasury Stock Transactions account is $30. If the remaining 50 shares are reissued for $53 per share, the entry is:

```
Cash (50  ×  $53) ...........................................     2,650
Paid-In Capital—Common Treasury Stock Transactions ..............        30
Retained Earnings ...........................................             70
    Treasury Stock—Common (50  ×  $55) ......................            2,750
    Reissued 50 shares of treasury stock at $53; cost $55 per share.
```

Note that the Paid-In Capital—Common Treasury Stock Transactions account balance has been exhausted. The remaining $70 of the excess of cost over reissue price is regarded as a special distribution to the stockholders involved and is charged to the Retained Earnings account.

When stockholders *donate* stock to a corporation, the treatment is slightly different. Since donated treasury shares have no cost, only a memo entry is made when they are received. The only formal entry required is to debit Cash and credit the Paid-In Capital—Donations account when the stock is reissued.

Treasury stock in the balance sheet

When treasury stock is held on a balance sheet date, it customarily is shown in that statement at cost, as a deduction from the sum of total paid-in capital and retained earnings, as follows:

Stockholders' equity:	
Paid-in capital:	
Common stock, authorized and issued, 20,000 shares, of which 2,000 shares are in the treasury	$200,000
Retained earnings (including $22,000 restricted by acquisition of treasury stock)	80,000
Total paid-in capital and retained earnings	$280,000
Less: Treasury stock at cost, 2,000 shares	22,000
Total stockholders' equity	$258,000

Stockholders' equity in the balance sheet

Much of what has been discussed so far in Chapters 15 and 16 can be summarized through presentation of the stockholders' equity section of the balance sheet of a hypothetical corporation (Illustration 16.3). This partial balance sheet shows (1) the amount of capital assigned to shares outstanding; (2) the capital contributed for outstanding shares in addition to that assigned

Illustration 16.3:   Stockholders' equity section of the balance sheet

HYPOTHETICAL CORPORATION
Partial Balance Sheet
December 31, 1984

Stockholders' equity:			
Paid-in capital:			
Preferred stock, 8%, $100 par value; 2,000 shares authorized, issued, and outstanding			$ 200,000
Common stock, $10 par value; authorized, 100,000 shares, issued, 80,000 shares of which 1,000 are held in the treasury		$800,000	
Stock dividend distributable on common stock on January 15, 1985, 7,900 shares		79,000	879,000
Paid-in capital—			
From common stock issuances		$ 40,000	
From capitalization of retained earnings through stock dividends		60,000	
From treasury stock transactions		30,000	
From donations		50,000	180,000
Total paid-in capital			$1,259,000
Retained earnings:			
Appropriated:			
For loan agreement		$250,000	
Unappropriated (restricted to the extent of $20,000, the cost of treasury shares held)		150,000	400,000
			$1,659,000
Less: Treasury stock, common, 1,000 shares at cost			20,000
Total stockholders' equity			$1,639,000

to the shares; (3) other forms of paid-in capital; and (4) retained earnings, appropriated and unappropriated.

NET INCOME INCLUSIONS AND EXCLUSIONS

Accounting has long faced the problem of what to include in the net income reported for a period. Should net income include only the revenues and expenses related to normal operations? Or should it include unusual, nonrecurring gains and losses? And further, should the net income for 1984, for example, include an item that can be clearly associated with a prior year, such as additional federal income taxes for 1980? Or should such items, including corrections of errors, be carried directly to retained earnings?

APB Opinion No. 9 (December 1966) sought to provide answers to these questions. It directed that unusual or nonrecurring items that have an earnings or loss effect be classified as extraordinary items (reported in the income statement) or as prior period adjustments (reported in the statement of retained earnings). Extraordinary items were to be reported separately after net income from regular continuing activities.

Extraordinary items

Abuses in the financial reporting of gains and losses as extraordinary items led to the issuance of *APB Opinion No. 30* (September 1973). This Opinion, redefines *extraordinary items* as those that are unusual in nature *and* that occur infrequently. Note that both conditions must be met—unusual nature and infrequent occurrence. Whether an item is unusual and infrequent is to be determined in light of the environment in which the firm operates. Examples include gains or losses that are the direct result of a major casualty (a flood), a confiscation of property by a foreign government, or a prohibition under a newly enacted law. Such items are to be included in the determination of periodic net income, but disclosed separately (net of their tax effects, if any) in the income statement. *FASB Statement No. 4* further directs that gains and losses from the voluntary early *extinguishment* of debt are extraordinary items. Income before extraordinary items must be reported and then income after extraordinary items, as shown in Illustration 16.4. *Income before extraordinary items* is income from operations less applicable income taxes.

Gains or losses related to ordinary business activities are not extraordinary items regardless of their size. For example, material write-downs of uncollectible receivables, obsolete inventories, and intangible assets are not extraordinary items. But such items may be separately disclosed as part of net income from continuing activities.

Accounting changes

A company's reported net income and financial position can be altered materially by changes in accounting methods. *Accounting changes* are changes in accounting data caused by accounting errors, mistakes, estimates, and

Illustration 16.4:   Income statement

ANSON COMPANY
Income Statement
For the Year Ended December 31, 1984

Net sales		$41,000,000
Other revenues		2,250,000
Total revenue		$43,250,000
Cost of goods sold	$22,000,000	
Administrative, selling, and general expenses	12,000,000	34,000,000
Net income before income taxes		$ 9,250,000
Federal income taxes (50%)		4,625,000
Net income before extraordinary item and the cumulative effect of an accounting change		$ 4,625,000
Extraordinary item:		
Gain on retirement of debt	$ 40,000	
Less: Tax effect	20,000	20,000
		$ 4,645,000
Cumulative effect on prior years' earnings of changing to a different depreciation method (net of 50% tax)		20,000
Net income		$ 4,665,000
Earnings per share of common stock:		
Net income before extraordinary item and the cumulative effect of an accounting change		$4.625
Extraordinary item		0.020
Cumulative effect on prior years' earnings of changing to a different depreciation method		0.020
Net income		$4.665

changes in principles. A change in inventory valuation method (for example, from Fifo to Lifo) or a change in depreciation method (for example, from accelerated to straight line) are examples of accounting changes. According to *APB Opinion No. 20,* a company should consistently apply the same accounting methods from one period to another. But a change may be made if the newly adopted method is preferable and if the change is adequately disclosed in the financial statements. In the period in which an accounting change is made, the nature of the change, its justification, and its effect on net income must be disclosed in the financial statements. Also, the cumulative effect of the change on prior years' earnings (net of tax) must be shown in the income statement for the year of change (Illustration 16.4).

Prior period adjustments

Prior period adjustments are a special kind of accounting change and require different treatment. According to *FASB Statement No. 16, prior period adjustments* consist almost entirely of corrections of errors in previously published financial statements. Normal, recurring corrections and adjustments, which follow inevitably from the use of estimates in accounting practice, are not to be treated as prior period adjustments. But corrections of errors which may have been caused by the improper use of an accounting principle or by mathematical mistakes are considered to be prior period adjustments. For example, suppose that land purchased in 1983 at a total cost of $200,000 was recorded in an expense account instead of in the Land account. Discovery of the error in 1984, after publication of the 1983 financial statements, would require a prior period adjustment. The adjustment would be recorded directly in the Retained Earnings account. Assuming the error had resulted in a $100,000 underpayment of taxes in 1983, the entry to correct the error would be:

Land	200,000	
Federal Income Taxes Payable.............................		100,000
Retained Earnings		100,000
To correct an accounting error expensing land.		

Prior period adjustments are not reported in the income statement but are shown in the financial statements as adjustments to the opening balance of retained earnings in the statement of retained earnings (Illustration 16.5).

Illustration 16.5:   Statement of retained earnings

ANSON COMPANY
Statement of Retained Earnings
For the Year Ended December 31, 1984

Retained earnings, January 1, 1984	$5,000,000
Prior period adjustment:	
Correction of error of expensing land (net of tax effect of $100,000)	100,000
Adjusted retained earnings, January 1, 1984	$5,100,000
Add: Net income	4,665,000
	$9,765,000
Less: Dividends	500,000
Retained earnings, December 31, 1984	$9,265,000

Accounting for tax effects

Most extraordinary items, accounting changes, and prior period adjustments will affect the amount of income taxes payable. A question then arises as to how to report the impact on taxes payable. *APB Opinion No. 9* recommends that extraordinary items and prior period adjustments be reported *net of their tax effects,* as shown in Illustrations 16.4 and 16.5. *Net-of-tax effect* means that items are shown at the dollar amounts remaining after deducting the effects on such items of the income taxes payable currently. The total effect of an extraordinary item, prior period adjustment or accounting change is shown in one place, and net income before extraordinary items represents the results of transactions (including income taxes) which are normal for the business and may be expected to recur. The tax effect of an item may be shown separately, as it is for the gain on retirement of debt in Illustration 16.4. Alternatively, it may be mentioned parenthetically with only the net amount shown (see correction of error illustrated in 16.5).

Summary of illustrative financial statements

The reporting of items such as those discussed above is shown in Illustrations 16.4 and 16.5. The financial statements assume the following:

a. Anson Company had a taxable gain in 1984 of $40,000 from retirement of debt (extraordinary item).
b. The company changed depreciation methods in 1984 (accounting change), and the cumulative effect of the change was $40,000.
c. In 1984, it was discovered that the $200,000 cost of land acquired in 1983 had been expensed for both financial accounting and tax purposes. A prior period adjustment was made in 1984.
d. Anson Company has 1,000,000 shares of common stock outstanding.
e. The current tax rate is 50 percent.

Note especially the following in Illustrations 16.4 and 16.5:

1. Net income of $4,625,000 before extraordinary item and the cumulative effect of an accounting change is more representative of the continuing earning power of the firm than is the final net income figure.
2. The gain on retirement of debt is reported at its actual impact upon the company—that is, net of its tax effect.
3. Earnings per share are reported both before and after the extraordinary item and the cumulative effect of an accounting change.
4. The correction of the $200,000 error adds only $100,000 to retained earnings. This is because the mistake was included in the 1983 tax return and taxes were therefore underpaid by $100,000. In 1984 the $100,000 of taxes would have to be paid.

EARNINGS PER SHARE

One final item needs to be discussed regarding corporations and income statement presentations, and that is earnings per share. A major item of interest to investors and potential investors is how much a company earned during the current year, both in total and for each share of stock outstanding. Earnings per share is calculated only for the residual or common shares of ownership. *Earnings per share* is earnings to the common stockholders on a per share basis, computed as net income available to common stockholders divided by the number of common shares outstanding. Income available to common stockholders is net income less any dividends on preferred stock.

Earnings per share (EPS) is usually calculated and presented for each major category on the face of the income statement. In other words, an EPS calculation is made for ordinary income after taxes, extraordinary items, and accounting changes. Notice in Illustration 16.4 the earnings per share amounts are reported at the bottom of the illustration.

Stockholders can compare the earnings per share of two companies more easily than total dollars of earnings. EPS is very useful in making decisions about the price to pay for stock and the return on that investment. Also, earnings per share is related to market price per share of stock in that if EPS increases, generally market price per share also increases.

NEW TERMS INTRODUCED IN CHAPTER 16

Accounting changes
Changes in accounting data caused by accounting errors (for example, expensing an asset), mistaken estimates (for example, in depreciation), and changes in principles (for example, from Fifo to Lifo).

Appropriations (retained earnings)
Voluntary or contractual restrictions on retained earnings which reduce the amount of dividends which may be declared.

Cash dividend
See Dividend (cash).

Contributed capital
All capital paid into a corporation, including that carried in capital stock accounts.

Date of declaration (of dividends)
The date the board of directors takes action in the form of a motion that dividends be paid.

Date of payment (of dividends)
The date of actual payment of a dividend, or issuance of additional shares in the case of a stock dividend.

Date of record (of dividends)
The date established by the board to determine who will receive a dividend.

Deficit
A debit balance in the Retained Earnings account.

Dividend (cash)
A cash distribution of earnings by a corporation to its stockholders.

Dividend (stock)
See Stock dividend.

Donated capital
Increases stockholders' equity and results from donation of assets to the corporation.

Earnings per share
Earnings to the common stockholders on a per share basis, computed as net income available to common stockholders divided by the number of common shares outstanding.

Extraordinary items
Items that are unusual in nature and that occur infrequently; reported in the income statement net of tax effects, if any.

Income before extraordinary items
Income from operations less applicable income taxes (federal and state, if any).

Liquidating dividends
Dividends which are a return of contributed capital, not a distribution chargeable to retained earnings.

Net-of-tax effect
Used for extraordinary items, prior period adjustments, and accounting changes whereby items are shown at the dollar amounts remaining after deducting the effects on such items of the income taxes (federal and state, if any) payable currently.

Paid-in capital
All of the contributed capital of a corporation, including that carried in capital stock accounts. When the words *paid-in capital* are included in the account title, the account contains capital contributed in addition to that assigned to the shares issued and recorded in the capital stock accounts.

Paid-In Capital—Recapitalization
The amount of capital removed from the capital stock account when the par or stated value of the outstanding shares is reduced.

Paid-In Capital—Treasury Stock Transactions
The title of the account credited when treasury stock is reissued for more than its cost; this account is also debited, to the extent of its balance for deficiencies when such shares are reissued at less than cost.

Prior period adjustments
Consist almost entirely of corrections of errors in previously published financial statements. Prior period adjustments are reported in the statement of retained earnings net of their tax effects, if any.

Recapitalization
The process of reducing the total par or stated value of outstanding shares.

Retained earnings
That part of stockholders' equity resulting from earnings; the account to which the results of corporate activity, including prior period adjustments, are carried and to which dividends and certain items resulting from capital transactions are charged.

Retained earnings appropriations
See Appropriations (retained earnings).

Statement of retained earnings
A formal statement showing the items causing changes in retained earnings during a stated period of time.

Stock dividend
A dividend that is payable in additional shares of the declaring corporation's capital stock.

Stock Dividend Distributable—Common account
The stockholders' equity account which is credited for the par or stated value of the shares distributable when recording the declaration of a stock dividend.

Stock split
As used in *Accounting Research Bulletin No. 43,*

a distribution of additional shares of the issuing corporation's stock for which the corporation receives no assets and for the purpose of causing a large reduction in the market price per share of the outstanding stock.

Treasury stock
Shares of capital stock issued and reacquired by the issuing corporation; they have not been formally canceled and are available for reissuance.

DEMONSTRATION PROBLEM

Following are selected transactions of the Morgan Company:

Transactions:

1. The company acquired 200 shares of its own $100 par value common stock, previously issued at a premium of 5 percent, for $20,600 cash.
2. Fifty of the treasury shares are reissued at $110 per share, cash.
3. Seventy of the treasury shares are reissued at $95 per share, cash.
4. Stockholders of the corporation donated 100 shares of their common stock to the company.
5. The 100 shares of treasury stock received by donation are reissued for $9,000.

Required:

Prepare the necessary journal entries to record the above transactions.

Solution to demonstration problem

1.	Treasury Stock	20,600	
	Cash		20,600
	Acquired 200 shares at $20,600 ($103 per share).		
2.	Cash	5,500	
	Treasury Stock (50 × $103 per share)		5,150
	Paid-In Capital—Treasury Stock Transactions		350
	Reissued 50 shares at $110 per share; cost is $5,150.		
3.	Cash	6,650	
	Paid-In Capital—Treasury Stock Transactions	350	
	Retained Earnings	210	
	Treasury Stock (70 × $103 per share)		7,210
	Reissued 70 shares at $95 per share; cost is $7,210.		
4.	Stockholders donated 100 shares of common stock to the company.		
5.	Cash	9,000	
	Paid-In Capital—Donations		9,000
	Reissued donated shares at $90 per share.		

QUESTIONS

1. What are the two main elements of the stockholders' equity in a corporation? Explain the difference between them.

2. Name several sources of paid-in capital. Would it suffice to maintain one account called Paid-In Capital for all sources of paid-in capital? Why or why not?

3. What is the purpose of a retained earnings appropriation?

4. What is the effect of each of the following on the total stockholders' equity of a corporation? (*a*) declaration of a cash dividend, (*b*) payment of a cash dividend already declared, (*c*) declaration of a stock dividend, and (*d*) issuance of a stock dividend already declared?

5. The following dates are associated with a cash dividend of $50,000: July 15, July 31, and August 15. Identify each of the three dates and give the journal entry required on each, if any.

6. How should a declared but unpaid cash dividend be shown on the balance sheet? A declared but unissued stock dividend?

7. On May 10, Power sold his capital stock in the Tanner Corporation directly to Bright for $10,000, endorsing his stock certificate and giving it to Bright. Bright placed the stock certificate in her safe. On May 8, the board of directors of the Tanner Corporation declared a dividend, payable on June 5 to stockholders of record on May 17. On May 30, Bright sent the certificate to the transfer agent of the Tanner Corporation for transfer. Who received the dividend? Why?

8. What are liquidating dividends?

9. Does accounting for treasury stock resemble accounting for an asset? Is treasury stock an asset? If not, where is it properly shown in a balance sheet?

10. What are some possible reasons for a corporation to acquire its own capital stock as treasury stock?

11. What are extraordinary items? Where and how are they reported?

12. What are prior period adjustments? Where and how are they reported?

13. Name two types of accounting changes. How are accounting changes reported?

14. Why are stockholders and potential investors interested in the amount of a corporation's earnings per share? What does the earnings per share amount reveal which total earnings does not?

EXERCISES

E–1.   The trial balance of the Marcus Corporation at December 31, 1984, has the following account balances:

Allowance for doubtful accounts	$ 12,000
Common stock, no par value; 200,000 shares authorized, issued, and outstanding; stated value of $10 per share	2,000,000
Notes payable, 12% due May 1, 1985	250,000
Retained earnings, unappropriated	1,250,000
Dividends payable in cash, declared December 15, on preferred stock	6,000
Appropriation for contingencies	240,000
Preferred stock, 6%, par value $100; 2,000 shares authorized, issued, and outstanding	200,000
Paid-in capital in excess of stated value— common stock	150,000
Paid-in capital in excess of par value— preferred stock	20,000

Required:
        Present in good form the stockholders' equity section of the balance sheet.

E–2.   The balance sheet of Day Company contains the following:

Appropriation for contingencies ... $150,000

    a. Give the journal entry made to create this account.

    b. Explain the reason for its existence and its manner of presentation in the balance sheet.

E–3. Baker Company has authorized and outstanding 5,000 shares of $100 par value common stock. On February 1, 1984, the board of directors declared a dividend of $3 per share payable on March 15, 1984, to stockholders of record on March 1, 1984. Give the necessary journal entries.

E–4. Allstar Corporation's stockholders' equity consists of 30,000 authorized shares of $10 par value common stock, of which 15,000 shares have been issued at par, and retained earnings of $300,000. The company now splits its stock, two for one, by changing the par value of the old shares and issuing new $5 par shares.

    a. Give the required journal entry.

    b. Suppose instead that the company declared and later issued a 10 percent stock dividend. Give the required journal entries, assuming that the market value on the date of declaration is $12.50 per share.

E–5. The stockholders' equity section of Hill Company's balance sheet on December 31, 1984, shows 100,000 shares of authorized and issued $10 stated value common stock, of which 9,000 shares are held in the treasury. On this date, the board of directors declares a cash dividend of $1 per share payable on January 21, 1985, to stockholders of record on January 10. Give dated journal entries for the above.

E–6. Eddy Company has outstanding 75,000 shares of common stock without par or stated value which were issued at an average price of $10 per share, and retained earnings of $400,000. The current market price of the common stock is $15 per share. Total authorized stock consists of 500,000 shares.

    a. Give the required entry to record the declaration of a 10 percent stock dividend.

    b. If, alternatively, the company declared a 30 percent stock dividend, what additional information would you need before making a journal entry to record the dividend?

E–7. Brown Company has outstanding 50,000 shares of $10 stated value common stock, all issued at $12 per share, and retained earnings of $400,000. The company now acquires 2,000 shares of its stock for cash at book value from the widow of a deceased stockholder.

    a. Give the entry to record the acquisition of the stock.

    b. Give the entry to record the subsequent reissuance of this stock at $25 per share.

    c. Give the entry required if the stock is reissued at $15 per share and there have been no prior treasury stock transactions.

E–8. Baker Company received 200 shares of its $10 stated value common stock on December 1, 1984, as a donation from a stockholder. On December 15, 1984, it reissued the stock for $3,000 cash. Give the journal entry or entries necessary for these transactions.

E–9. Jay Company has revenues of $40 million, expenses of $32 million, a tax-deductible earthquake loss (its first such loss) of $2 million, a tax-deductible downward adjustment of $3 million resulting from renegotiation of a contract completed two years ago, and an income tax rate of 50 percent. The beginning retained earnings were $15 million, and a dividend of $1,000,000 was declared.

      a.   Prepare an income statement for the year.

      b.   Prepare a statement of retained earnings for the year.

E–10.   The Cliff Company had retained earnings of $35,000 as of January 1, 1984. In 1984, Cliff Company had sales of $100,000, cost of goods sold of $60,000, and other operating expenses, excluding taxes, of $20,000. In 1984, Cliff Company discovered that it had, in error, depreciated land over the last three years resulting in a balance in the accumulated depreciation account of $20,000. The tax rate for Cliff Company is 50 percent.

      a.   Give the correcting journal entry needed.

      b.   Present in proper form a statement of retained earnings for the year ended December 31, 1984.

E–11.   The following information relates to the H. S. Odom Corporation for the year ended December 31, 1984:

Common stock outstanding	75,000 shares
Net income before extraordinary items . . .	$476,000
Extraordinary gain	45,000

Calculate earnings per share for the year ended December 31, 1984. Present the information in the same format as would be presented in the corporation's income statement.

E–12.   The Hart Company had common stock outstanding of 200,000 and 215,000 shares at December 31, 1984 and 1985, respectively. Net income for the above years is as follows:

December 31, 1984	$575,000
December 31, 1985	600,000

      a.   Calculate earnings per share for the years ended December 31, 1984, and 1985.

      b.   What might the resulting figures tell a potential investor or stockholder?

PROBLEMS, SERIES A

P–16–1–A.   Following are selected data and accounts of Job, Inc., at May 31, 1984:

Estimated liability for product warranties	$	8,000
Paid-in capital in excess of par value—preferred		7,000
Retained earnings, unappropriated		120,000
Allowance for doubtful accounts		40,000
Common stock without par value, stated value $50; 20,000 shares		
authorized, issued, and outstanding		1,000,000
Appropriation for retirement of bonds		150,000
Dividends payable (cash)		6,000
Paid-in capital in excess of stated value—common		40,000
17% notes payable, due April 1, 1990		600,000
Preferred stock: 7%, par value $100; 2,000 shares		
authorized, issued, and outstanding		200,000
Paid-in capital—donations		30,000

Required:

       Present the stockholders' equity section of the company's balance sheet as of May 31, 1984.

P16–2–A.   The bookkeeper of J. C. Cranton Company has prepared the following statement of stockholders' equity for the year ended December 31, 1984:

Stockholders' equity:	
Preferred stock, 6% cumulative (8,000) shares	$ 209,000
Common stock (50,000 shares)	595,000
Retained earnings	341,000
Total stockholders' equity	$1,145,000

The authorized stock consists of 12,000 shares of preferred stock with a $25 par value and 75,000 shares of common stock, $10 par value. The preferred stock was issued on two occasions; first, 5,000 shares at par; and second, 3,000 shares at $28 per share. The 50,000 shares of common stock were issued at $13 per share. Five thousand shares of treasury common stock were reacquired for $55,000; the bookkeeper deducted the cost of the treasury stock from the Common Stock account.

Required:

Prepare the correct stockholders' equity section of the balance sheet at December 31, 1984.

P16–3–A. The stockholders' equity of the P. F. Hodge Company at January 1, 1984, is as follows:

Common stock, stated value $10, 100,000 shares	
authorized, 60,000 shares issued	$600,000
Paid-in capital in excess of stated value	125,000
Appropriation per loan agreement	47,000
Unappropriated retained earnings	265,000
Treasury stock (3,000 shares at cost)	(45,000)

During 1984, the following transactions occurred (in the order listed):

Transactions:

1. 10,000 shares of stock were issued for $230,000.
2. A 4 percent stock dividend was declared when the market price was $28 per share.
3. Sold 1,000 shares of treasury stock for $27,000.
4. Issued stock certificates for the stock dividend declared in transaction 2.
5. Bought 2,000 shares of treasury stock for $42,000.
6. The appropriation per loan agreement was increased by $27,000.

Required:

Prepare journal entries as necessary for the above transactions.

P16–4–A. Following are selected transactions of the Bond Corporation:

Transactions:

1979

Dec. 31 The board of directors authorized appropriation of $100,000 of retained earnings to provide for the future acquisition of a new plant site and the construction of a new building. (On the last day of the six preceding years, the same action was taken. You need not make entries for these six years.)

1982

Jan. 2 Purchased a new plant site for cash, $200,000.

Mar. 29 Entered into a contract for construction of a new building, payment to be made within 30 days following completion.

1984

Feb. 10 Following final inspection and approval of the new building, the Dome Construction Company was paid in full, $1,000,000.

Mar. 10 The board of directors authorized release of the retained earnings appropriated for the plant site and building.

Apr. 2 A 5 percent stock dividend on the 100,000 shares of $100 par value common stock outstanding was declared. The market price on this date was $110 per share.

Required:

Prepare journal entries for all of the above transactions.

P16–5–A.   Following are selected data and accounts of the May Corporation at December 31, 1984:

Net income for the year	$320,000
Dividends declared on preferred stock	45,000
Retained earnings appropriated for future plant expansion during the year	150,000
Dividends received on May Corporation's investments in stock of XYZ Corporation	20,000
Dividends paid on common stock	35,000
Excess over stated value received for shares of common stock issued during the year	70,000
Dividends declared on common stock	40,000
Retained earnings, January 1, unappropriated	450,000
Directors ordered that the balance in the "Appropriation for bond sinking fund," related to a bond issue retired on March 31, 1984, be returned to unappropriated retained earnings	300,000

Required:

Prepare a statement of retained earnings for the year December 31, 1984.

P16–6–A.   The only stockholders' equity items of the Cold Company at June 30, 1984, are:

Common stock, $50 par value, 3,000 shares authorized, 2,000 shares issued and outstanding	$100,000
Paid-in capital in excess of par value	40,000
Retained earnings	40,000
Total stockholders' equity	$180,000

On August 4, a 4 percent cash dividend was declared, payable on September 3. On November 16, a 10 percent stock dividend was declared. The shares were issued on December 1. The market value of the common stock on November 16 was $60 per share and on December 1, $42. Net income for the six months ended December 31, 1984, was $5,000.

Required:

Prepare journal entries for the above transactions.

P16–7–A.   The stockholders' equity of the Cowboy Company on December 31, 1984, consisted of 1,000 authorized and outstanding shares of $7 cumulative preferred stock, stated value $20 per share, which were originally issued at $105 per share; 100,000 shares authorized and outstanding of $15 stated value common stock, which were originally issued at $15; and retained earnings of $100,000. Following are selected transactions and other data relating to 1984:

Transactions:

1. The company acquired 2,000 shares of its common stock at $30.
2. One thousand of the treasury shares were reissued at $26.
3. Stockholders donated 1,000 shares of common stock to the company. These shares were immediately reissued at $12 to provide working capital.
4. The first quarter's dividend of $1.75 per share was declared and paid on the preferred stock. No other dividends were declared or paid during 1984.

The company suffered a net loss of $20,000 for the year 1984.

Required:

    a. Prepare journal entries for the numbered transactions above.

    b. Prepare the stockholders' equity section of the December 31, 1984, balance sheet.

P16–8–A.   The stockholders' equity section of the Bat Company's October 31, 1983, balance sheet was:

Stockholders' equity:
  Paid-in capital:
    Preferred stock: $100 par value, 6%; 1,000 shares
      authorized, 350 shares issued and outstanding ...... $ 35,000
    Common stock: $10 par value; 100,000 shares
      authorized, 40,000 shares issued and outstanding ...   400,000
    Paid-in capital from donation of plant site   25,000
        Total paid-in capital $460,000
  Retained earnings:
    Appropriated:
      Appropriation for contingencies $20,000
      Unappropriated   55,500
        Total retained earnings   75,500
        Total stockholders' equity $535,500

During the ensuing fiscal year, the following transactions were entered into by the Bat Company:

Transaction:

1. Appropriation of $20,000 of retained earnings had been authorized in October 1983 because of the likelihood of an unfavorable court decision in a pending lawsuit. The suit was brought by a customer seeking damages for the company's alleged breach of a contract to supply the customer with certain products at stated prices in 1982. The suit was concluded on March 6, 1984, with a court order directing the company to pay $17,500 in damages. These damages were deductible in determining income tax liability (the tax rate was 50 percent). The board ordered the damages paid and the appropriation closed.
2. The company acquired 1,000 shares of its own common stock at $15 in May 1984. On June 30, it reissued 500 of these shares at $12.
3. Dividends declared and paid during the year were 6 percent on preferred stock, and 30 cents per share on common stock. Both dividends were declared on September 1 and paid on September 30, 1984.

The company had net income after income taxes for the year of $19,000, excluding the loss on the lawsuit and the related tax effects.

Required:

    a. Prepare general journal entries for the numbered transactions above.

    b. Prepare a statement of retained earnings for the year ended October 31, 1984.

    c. Prepare the stockholders' equity section of the October 31, 1984, balance sheet.

P16–9–A.   Selected accounts and other data for the Lamp Company for 1984 are:

Common stock—$10 par value	$1,000,000
Sales, net	4,000,000
Selling and administrative expenses	800,000
Cash dividends declared and paid	300,000
Cost of goods sold	2,000,000
Gain on sale of securities	350,000
Depreciation expense	300,000
Interest revenue	50,000

Loss on write-down of obsolete inventory	100,000
Retained earnings (as of 12/31/83)	5,000,000
Earthquake loss	240,000
Cumulative negative effect on prior years' earnings of changing from straight-line to an accelerated method of computing depreciation	160,000

The applicable federal income tax rate is 50 percent. All of the items of expense, revenue, and loss are includable in the computation of the amount of income taxes payable. The gain on sale of securities is a common item for the company, while the earthquake loss resulted from the first earthquake experienced at the company's location. In addition, the company discovered that in 1983 it had erroneously charged to expense the $400,000 cost of a tract of land purchased that year and had made the same error on its tax return for 1983.

Required:

    a.   Prepare an income statement for the year ended December 31, 1984.

    b.   Prepare a statement of retained earnings for the year ended December 31, 1984.

PROBLEMS, SERIES B

P16–1–B.   The trial balance of the Plant Corporation at December 31, 1984, contains the following selected account balances:

Notes payable, 17%, due May 1, 1986	$2,000,000
Allowance for doubtful accounts	30,000
Common stock without par value, $10 stated value, 300,000 shares authorized, issued, and outstanding	3,000,000
Retained earnings, unappropriated	250,000
Dividends payable in cash declared December 15 on preferred stock	7,000
Appropriation for pending litigation	300,000
Preferred stock, $100 par value, 6%, 3,000 shares authorized, issued, and outstanding	300,000
Paid-in capital from donation of plant site	200,000
Paid-in capital in excess of par value—preferred	5,000

Required:

    Present in good form the stockholders' equity section of the balance sheet.

P16–2–B.   The retained earnings of the Castleberry Company include the following accounts:

Appropriation for contingencies	$ 60,000
Appropriation for plant expansion	112,000
Retained earnings, unappropriated	200,000

During the month of October 1984, the company took action to:

1. Increase the appropriation for contingencies by $18,000.
2. Decrease the appropriation for plant expansion by $47,000.
3. Establish an appropriation for bonded indebtedness, with an annual increase of $15,000.
4. Declare a cash dividend of $45,000.

Required:

    Prepare the general journal entries to record the transactions of the Castleberry Company.

P16–3–B.   Using the information given in Problem P16–2–B, prepare a statement of retained earnings for the Castleberry Company for the period ended October 31, 1984.

P16–4–B. Following are selected transactions of the Door Corporation:

Transactions:

1979
Dec. 31 By action of the board of directors, $30,000 of retained earnings was appropriated to provide for future expansion of the company's main building. (On the last day of each of the four succeeding years, the same action was taken. You need not make entries for these years.)

1984
Jan. 3 Obtained, at a cost of $300, a building permit to construct a new wing on the main plant building.

July 30 Paid $120,000 to the Able Construction Company for completion of the new wing.

Aug. 4 The board of directors authorized the release of the sum appropriated for expansion of the plant building.

4 The board of directors declared a 10 percent common stock dividend on the 25,000 shares of $40 par value common stock outstanding. The market price on this date was $44 per share.

Required:

Prepare journal entries to record all of the above transactions.

P16–5–B. The following information relates to the Bulldog Corporation for the year 1984.

Net income for the year	$ 500,000
Dividends declared on common stock	70,000
Dividends paid on common stock during 1984	60,000
Dividends declared on preferred stock	40,000
Dividends received on investments	5,000
Retained earnings, January 1, unappropriated	1,500,000
Appropriation for retirement of bonds	200,000
Premium received on shares of preferred stock issued during the year	6,000
Balance in "Appropriation for possible loss of a lawsuit," no longer needed on December 31 because of favorable court decision, is (at directors' orders) returned to unappropriated retained earnings	250,000

Required:

Prepare a statement of retained earnings for the year ended December 31, 1984.

P16–6–B. The stockholders' equity section of the Joy Company's December 31, 1983, balance sheet is:

Stockholders' equity:
  Paid-In capital:

Capital stock—common, $20 par value; authorized, 2,000 shares, issued and outstanding, 1,000 shares	$20,000	
Paid-in capital in excess of par value	1,000	
Total paid-in capital	$21,000	
Retained earnings	8,000	
Total stockholders' equity	$29,000	

On July 15, 1984, the board of directors declared a cash dividend of $2 per share, which was paid on August 1, 1984. On December 1, 1984, the board declared a stock dividend of 10 percent and the shares were issued on December 15, 1984. Market value of the stock was $24 on December 1 and $28 on December 15. Net income for the year 1984 was $4,700.

Required:

Prepare journal entries for the above dividend transactions.

P16–7–B.   The stockholders' equity of the Island Company as of December 31, 1983, consisted of 20,000 shares of authorized and outstanding $10 par value common stock, paid-in capital in excess of par of $60,000, and retained earnings of $100,000. Following are selected transactions for 1984:

Transactions:

May   1   Acquired 3,000 shares of its own common stock at $25 per share.
June 1   Reissued 500 shares at $30.
      30 Reissued 700 shares at $23.
Oct. 1   Declared a cash dividend of $1 per share.
      31 Paid the cash dividend declared on October 1.

Net income for the year was $20,000. No other transactions affecting retained earnings occurred during the year.

Required:

    a.   Prepare general journal entries for the above transactions.

    b.   Prepare the stockholders' equity section of the December 31, 1984, balance sheet.

P16–8–B.   The stockholders' equity section of Ray Company's December 31, 1983, balance sheet was:

Stockholders' equity:
  Paid-in capital:

Preferred stock: $100 par value, 5%; authorized 5,000 shares, issued and outstanding, 2,500 shares	$250,000
Common stock without par or stated value; authorized, 50,000 shares, issued, 25,000 shares of which 500 are held in treasury	375,000
Paid-in capital in excess of par—preferred	5,000
Total paid-in capital	$630,000

Retained earnings:
  Appropriated:

For plant expansion	$ 25,000	
Unappropriated (restricted as to dividends to the extent of $10,000, the cost of the treasury stock held)	210,000	
Total retained earnings		235,000
Total		$865,000
Less: Treasury stock, common at cost (500 shares)		10,000
Total stockholders' equity		$855,000

Following are selected transactions which occurred in 1984.

Transactions:

Jan. 13   Subscriptions are received for 550 shares of previously unissued common stock at $22.
Feb. 4   A plot of land is accepted as payment in full for 500 shares of common, and the stock is issued. Closing market price on this date of the common stock is $21 per share.
Mar. 24   All of the treasury stock is reissued at $24.50 per share.
June 22   All stock subscriptions are collected in full, and the shares issued.
     23   The regular semiannual dividend on the preferred stock is declared.
     30   The preferred dividend is paid.
July 3   A 10 percent stock dividend is declared on the common stock. Market price on this date is $25.
     18   The stock dividend shares are issued.
Oct. 4   The company acquires 105 shares of its common stock at $24.
Dec. 18   The regular semiannual dividend on the preferred stock and a $0.40 per share dividend on the common stock are declared.
     31   Both dividends are paid.
     31   An additional appropriation of retained earnings of $5,000 for plant expansion is authorized.

Required:

     a.   Prepare journal entries to record the 1984 transactions.

     b.   Prepare a statement of retained earnings for the year 1984. The net income for the year was $43,125.

     c.   Prepare the stockholders' equity section of the December 31, 1984, balance sheet.

P16–9–B.   Selected data and accounts of the Pool Company for the year ended December 31, 1984, are:

Sales, net.	$1,000,000
Interest expense	90,000
Cash dividends on common stock	150,000
Selling and administrative expense	245,000
Cash dividends on preferred stock	70,000
Rent revenue	400,000
Cost of goods sold	650,000
Flood loss (has never occurred before)	200,000
Interest revenue.	90,000
Other revenue	150,000
Depreciation and maintenance on rental equipment . . .	270,000
Stock dividend on common stock	300,000
Litigation loss.	400,000
Cumulative positive effect on prior years' earnings of changing to a different depreciation method	80,000

The applicable federal income tax rate is 50 percent. All above items of expense, revenue, and loss are includable in the computation of taxable income. The litigation loss resulted from a court award of damages for patent infringement on a product the company produced and sold in 1980 and 1981, and which was discontinued in 1981. Retained earnings as of January 1, 1984, were $5,600,000.

Required:

     Prepare an income statement and a statement of retained earnings for 1984.

BUSINESS DECISION PROBLEM 16–1

     The stockholders' equity section of the Clay Corporation's balance sheet for June 30, 1984, is shown below:

Stockholders' equity:	
Paid-in capital:	
Common stock—$10 par value; authorized 200,000 shares,	
issued and outstanding 80,000 shares	$ 800,000
Paid-in capital in excess of par value	400,000
Total paid-in capital	$1,200,000
Retained earnings	500,000
Total stockholders' equity	$1,700,000

     On July 1, 1984, the corporation's directors declared a 10 percent stock dividend distributable on August 2 to stockholders of record on July 16. On November 1, 1984, the directors voted a $1 per share annual cash dividend payable on December 2 to stockholders of record on November 16. For four years prior to 1984, the corporation had paid an annual cash dividend of $1.05.

     Bob Jones owns 8,000 shares of Clay Corporation's common stock, which he purchased five years ago. The market value of his stock was $20 per share on July 1, 1984, and $18.18 per share on July 16, 1984.

Required:

a. What amount of cash dividends will Jones receive in 1984? How does this amount differ from the amount of cash dividends Jones received in the previous four years?

b. For what logical reason did the price of the stock drop from $20.00 to $18.18 on July 16, 1984?

c. Is Jones better off as a result of the stock dividend and the $1 cash dividend than he would have been if he had just received the $1.05 dividend? Why?

BUSINESS DECISION PROBLEM 16–2

Shown below are some journal entries made by the bookkeeper for the Plant Corporation:

1. Retained earnings   1,500
       Reserve for Doubtful Accounts   1,500
   To record bad debts expense.

2. Retained Earnings   6,000
       Reserve for Depreciation   6,000
   To record depreciation expense.

3. Retained Earnings   15,000
       Reserve for Plant Expansion   15,000
   To record retained earnings appropriation.

4. Retained Earnings   1,000
       Stock Dividend Distributable   1,000
   To record 10 percent stock dividend declaration (100 shares to be distributed—$10 par value, $15 market value).

5. Stock Dividend Distributable   1,000
       Common Stock   1,000
   To record distribution of stock dividend.

6. Treasury Stock   4,000
       Cash   4,000
   To record acquisition of 200 $10 par value common shares at $20 per share.

7. Cash   2,200
       Treasury Stock   2,200
   To record sale of 100 treasury shares at $22 per share.

8. Cash   850
       Treasury Stock   850
   To record sale of 50 treasury shares at $17 per share.

9. Common Stock   2,000
       Dividends Payable   2,000
   To record declaration of cash dividend.

10. Dividends Payable   2,000
        Cash   2,000
    To record payment of cash dividend.

Required:

Analyze the above journal entries in connection with their explanations and decide whether each is correct or incorrect. The explanations are all correct. If a journal entry is incorrect, prepare the journal entry that should have been made.

BUSINESS DECISION PROBLEM 16–3

An income statement and statement of retained earnings for the year ended December 31, 1984, for the Smith Company are presented below:

SMITH COMPANY
Income Statement
For the Year Ended December 31, 1984

Sales		$260,000
Cost and expenses:		
Costs of goods sold	$70,000	
Selling expenses	40,000	
Depreciation expense	3,000	
Loss on early retirement of debt	10,000	123,000
Net income before income taxes		$137,000
Federal income taxes		68,500
Net income before extraordinary items		$ 68,500
Extraordinary items:		
Gain on sale of equipment (net of tax effect of $30,000)	$30,000	
Write-down of obsolete inventory (net of tax effect of $40,000) . .	(40,000)	10,000
Net income		$ 58,500

SMITH COMPANY
Statement of Retained Earnings
For the Year Ended December 31, 1984

Retained earnings, January 1, 1984		$290,000
Add: Net income		58,500
		$348,500
Less:		
Dividends	$32,000	
General and administrative expenses incurred during		
a strike (net of tax effect of $10,000)	10,000	
Earthquake loss (net of tax effect of $40,000)	40,000	82,000
Retained earnings, December 31, 1984		$266,500

Several stockholders of the Smith Company have complained that the above statements are not prepared in accordance with generally accepted accounting principles. As a result, the stockholders cannot compare the financial statements of the Smith Company with those of other companies.

Required:

a. Are the above statements prepared in accordance with generally accepted accounting principles? If not, why not?

b. If your response to part (*a*) was negative, prepare the income statement and the statement of retained earnings in accordance with generally accepted accounting principles.

Chapter 17

Bonds payable; bond and stock investments

CHAPTER GOALS

After study of this chapter, you should be able to:

1. Describe the features of bonds and tell how bonds differ from shares of stock.
2. List the advantages and disadvantages of financing with long-term debt and prepare examples showing how financial leverage is employed.
3. Explain how interest rates affect bond prices and what causes a bond to sell at a premium or discount.
4. Apply the concepts of present value to compute the price of a bond.
5. Prepare journal entries to account for bonds payable.
6. Prepare journal entries to account for bond and stock investments.
7. Define and use correctly the terms in the glossary.

Previous chapters discussed how corporations obtain cash from profitable operations, short-term credit or borrowing, or stock issuances. Corporations may also raise cash by long-term borrowing, issuing either bonds or notes. The first part of this chapter will discuss long-term debt of a corporation.

Corporations may have cash available for investment purposes, rather than having the need to borrow. A corporation may invest on either a short-term or long-term basis. A company may invest in the stocks or bonds issued by other corporations which are regularly traded on national exchanges and offer a rate of return that may be substantially greater than on a savings account. The second part of the chapter will discuss such corporate investments.

BONDS

A *bond* is a long-term debt owed by its issuer. Physical evidence of the debt lies in a negotiable *bond certificate.* Long-term notes usually mature in 10 years or less, while bond maturities often run for 20 years or more. A bond derives its value primarily from two promises made by the borrower to the lender, or bondholder. The borrower promises to pay (1) the *face value* or *principal amount* of the bond on a specific maturity date in the future; and (2) periodic interest at a specified rate on face value at stated dates, usually semiannually, until maturity date.

A bond issue generally consists of numerous $1,000 bonds, rather than one very large bond. For example, a company seeking to borrow $100,000 would issue one hundred $1,000 bonds, rather than one $100,000 bond. Investors with less cash to invest are able to purchase the bonds.

Comparison with stock

A bond differs from a share of stock in several ways. A bond is a debt or liability of the issuer, while a share of stock is a unit of ownership. A bond has a maturity date when it must be paid, while a share of stock does not mature. Stock may remain outstanding until the company decides to retire it. Most bonds require stated periodic interest payments by the company. Dividends to stockholders are payable only when declared; even preferred dividends may be passed in a particular period if the board of directors so decides. Lastly, bond interest is deductible by the issuer in computing both net income and taxable income. Dividends are not deductible in either computation.

Issuance

A company seeking to borrow millions of dollars generally will not be able to borrow from a single lender. In such an instance, the company will sell (float) a bond issue in a public offering to secure the funds needed. Usually a bond issue is sold through an investment firm or banker, called an *underwriter.* The underwriter performs many tasks for the issuer, such as advertising and selling the bonds, securing legal opinions, and delivering the bonds. The underwriter often guarantees the issuer a fixed price for the bonds, expecting to earn income by selling the bonds for more than the guaranteed price.

When bonds are sold in a public offering, many investors are involved. Rather than deal with each bondholder individually, the issuing corporation appoints a trustee to represent the bondholders. The *trustee* usually is a bank or trust company. The main duty of the trustee is to see that the borrower fulfills the provisions of the bond indenture. A *bond indenture* is the contract or loan agreement under which the bonds are issued. The indenture deals with matters such as the interest rate, maturity amount and date, possible restrictions on dividends, repayment plans, and call or conversion privileges relating to the debt. If bond indenture provisions are not adhered to, the issuer is said to be in default. The trustee is expected to take action to force the issuer to comply with the indenture.

Characteristics of bonds

All bonds have two common characteristics: they promise to pay cash and they come due or mature. In all other respects, bonds may differ. For example, bonds may be secured or unsecured bonds, registered or bearer bonds, or term or serial bonds. Certain features are matters of legal necessity, such as the way interest is paid and ownership is transferred. Such differences may not affect the issue price of the bonds. Other features included, such as convertibility, are designed to make the bonds more attractive to investors. These added features are called "sweeteners."

Secured bonds. A *secured bond* is a bond for which specific property has been pledged to ensure its payment. Secured bonds often are mortgage bonds because they are backed by a mortgage on real property. A *mortgage* is a legal claim on a specific property which gives the bondholder the right to sell the pledged property if the company fails to make required payments.

Unsecured bonds. An *unsecured bond* is called a *debenture bond* or simply a *debenture*. A debenture is a bond backed only by the general credit worthiness of the issuer, not by a lien on any specific property. A financially sound company will be able to issue debentures more easily than a company experiencing financial difficulty.

Registered bonds. A bond is a *registered bond* when its owner's name appears on the bond certificate and in the record of bond owners kept by the issuer or its agent, the registrar. Bonds may be registered as to principal or as to both principal and interest. If a bond is registered as to both, interest on the bond is paid by check. Ownership of registered bonds is transferred by endorsing the bond and registering it in the new owner's name. Registered bonds are easily replaced if lost or stolen. Most bonds in our economy are registered as to principal only.

Bearer bonds. A *bearer bond* is an unregistered bond. It is assumed to be the property of its holder or bearer; ownership is transferred by physical delivery of the bond.

Coupon bonds. A *coupon bond* is a bond not registered as to interest. A coupon bond carries detachable coupons for the interest it pays. At the end of each interest period, the coupon for the period is clipped and given to a stated party, usually a bank, for collection.

Term bonds and serial bonds. A *term bond* is a bond that matures on the same date as all other bonds in a given bond issue. *Serial bonds* are bonds that mature in installments through time. Both types of bonds are discussed later in the chapter.

Callable bonds. A *callable bond* contains a provision which gives the issuer the right to call (buy back) the bond before its maturity date. The provision is very similar to the call provision in some preferred stocks. A company will exercise this right if outstanding bonds bear interest at a much higher rate than the company would have to pay if it issued similar bonds now. The exercise of the call provision normally requires the payment of a *call premium* of about $30 to $70 per $1,000 bond.

Convertible bonds. A *convertible bond* is a bond that may be exchanged, at the holder's option, for shares of stock of the issuing corporation. A convertible bond has a stipulated conversion rate of some number of shares for each $1,000 bond. Any type of bond may be convertible. But this feature usually is added to rather risky debenture bonds to make them more attractive to investors.

Bonds with stock warrants. A *stock warrant* allows the holder to purchase shares of common stock at a fixed price for some stated period of time. Warrants issued with long-term debt may be detachable or nondetachable. Debt with nondetachable warrants is virtually the same as convertible debt; the holder must surrender the bond in order to acquire the common stock. Detachable warrants allow holders to maintain their creditor position and still purchase shares of stock through exercise of the warrants.

Advantages of issuing debt

Several advantages come from financing with long-term debt. Current stockholders need not dilute or surrender their control of the firm if needed funds can be obtained through borrowing rather than issuing more shares of stock. It also may be less expensive to issue debt than additional stock. But probably most important, the use of debt may increase the earnings of stockholders through favorable financial leverage.

Favorable financial leverage. A firm has *favorable financial leverage* when borrowed funds are used to increase earnings per share of common stock. Increased earnings per share usually result from earning a higher rate of return than the rate of interest paid for the borrowed money. For example, suppose that you borrowed money at 10 percent and used the money in your firm where it earned 15 percent. The 5 percent difference increased your earnings. You have favorable financial leverage.

A more complex example of financial leverage is provided in Illustration 17.1. The two companies in the illustration are identical in every respect except in the way they are financed. Company A used only capital stock, while Company B used equal amounts of 10 percent bonds and capital stock. Both companies used $20,000,000 of assets and both earned $4,000,000 of income from operations, which yielded an identical 20 percent rate of operating income to assets employed. Yet B's stockholders fared far better than A's. The ratio of net income to stockholders' equity is 18 percent for B while it is only 12 percent for A. The 6 percent difference can be explained as follows:

Operating income earned on $10,000,000 debt (20%)	$2,000,000
Interest paid on the debt (10%)	1,000,000
Net increase in income before taxes due to debt	$1,000,000
Less income taxes (40%)	400,000
Net increase in income due to debt financing	$ 600,000

Net increase in income due to debt financing as a percentage of stockholders' equity, $600,000/$10,000,000 = 6%.

Illustration 17.1: Favorable financial leverage

COMPANIES A AND B CONDENSED STATEMENTS
Balance Sheets
January 1, 1984

	Company A	Company B
Total assets	$20,000,000	$20,000,000
Bonds payable, 10%		$10,000,000
Stockholders' equity (capital stock)	$20,000,000	10,000,000
Total equities	$20,000,000	$20,000,000

Income Statements
Year Ended December 31, 1984

	Company A	Company B
Net income from operations	$ 4,000,000	$ 4,000,000
Interest expense		1,000,000
Net income before income taxes	$ 4,000,000	$ 3,000,000
Income taxes (40%)	1,600,000	1,200,000
Net income	$ 2,400,000	$ 1,800,000
Number of common shares outstanding	2,000,000	1,000,000
Earnings per share	$1.20	$1.80
Rate of return on assets employed (both companies:		
$4,000,000/$20,000,000)	20%	20%
Rate of return on stockholders' equity:		
Company A ($2,400,000/$20,000,000)	12%	
Company B ($1,800,000/$10,000,000)		18%

Because interest expense is tax deductible, the fixed interest cost of borrowed funds is reduced and the effects of leveraging magnified. The net aftertax cost to Company B of the borrowed money is 6 percent: 10 percent − (0.4 × 10 percent) = 6 percent. The net aftertax interest cost of the $10,000,000 debt then is $600,000. The net aftertax income earned with the borrowed funds is $1,200,000 ($10,000,000 × 0.2) − ($2,000,000 × 0.4), for a net gain to stockholders from leveraging of $600,000.

If both companies issued their stock at the beginning of 1984 at $10 per share, B's $1.80 earnings per share are 50 percent greater than A's $1.20 per share. This difference probably would cause B's shares to sell at a substantially higher market price than A's shares. B's larger earnings per share would also allow a larger dividend on B's shares.

Company B, in the above illustration, is employing financial leverage, or is said to be *trading on the equity*. It is using its stockholders' equity as a basis for securing funds on which a fixed return is paid. It expects to earn more from the use of such funds than their fixed aftertax cost and, in this way, increase the rate of return on stockholders' equity and earnings per share.

Disadvantages in issuing debt

Several disadvantages accompany the use of debt financing. The borrower now has a fixed interest payment that must be met each period to avoid default. Use of debt reduces a company's ability to sustain a major loss. Suppose that both Company A and Company B sustain losses of $11,000,000. Company A will have $9,000,000 of stockholders' equity and can continue operations with a chance of recovery. Company B, on the other hand, would have negative stockholders' equity of $1,000,000, and the bondholders could force the company to liquidate if B could not make interest payments as they came due.

A company may experience unfavorable financial leverage if debt financing is used and income from operations falls below a certain level. *Unfavorable financial leverage* results when the cost of borrowed funds exceeds the revenue they generate; it is the opposite of favorable financial leverage. In the above example, if income from operations fell to $1,000,000, the rates of return upon stockholders' equity would be 3 percent for A and zero for B. (You may want to prove this to yourself. Repeat the example in Illustration 17.1, except start the income statement with $1,000,000 of net income from operations.) Finally, loan agreements often require the maintenance of a certain amount of working capital and place limitations on dividends and additional borrowings. Requirements like these may prevent a company from acting in a manner most beneficial to its stockholders.

Accounting for bonds

When a company issues bonds, it incurs a long-term liability on which periodic interest payments must be made, usually twice a year. If interest dates fall on other than balance sheet dates, interest will need to be accrued in the proper periods. The following example illustrates the accounting for bonds issued at face value:

On December 31, 1984, Valley Company, with an accounting year ending on December 31, issued $100,000 face value of 10-year, 12 percent bonds for cash of $100,000. The bonds are dated December 31, 1984, call for semiannual interest payments on June 30 and December 31, and mature on December 31, 1994. Valley Company made all required cash payments when due. The entries for the 10 years are summarized below.

On December 31, 1984, the date of issuance:

Dec 31	Cash	....	100,000	
	Bonds Payable	....		100,000
	To record bonds issued at face value.			

On each June 30 and December 31 for 10 years, beginning June 30, 1985:

June 30 and Dec 31	Bond Interest Expense ($100,000 $\times$ 0.12 $\times$ $\frac{1}{2}$)	....	6,000	
	Cash	....		6,000
	To record periodic interest payment.			

On December 31, 1994, the maturity date:

Dec 31	Bonds Payable	....	100,000	
	Cash	....		100,000
	To record bond redemption.			

Note that no adjusting entries are needed when an interest payment date falls on the last day of the accounting period. The income statement for each of the 10 years 1985–94 would show Bond Interest Expense of $12,000; the balance sheet at the end of each of the years 1984–92 would report Bonds payable of $100,000 in long-term liabilities. At the end of 1993, the bonds would be reclassified as a current liability because they will be paid within the next year.

But the real world is seldom so uncomplicated. For example, Valley's fiscal year may end on October 31. If so, the June 30 entry remains unchanged, but an adjusting entry is needed on October 31 to accrue interest for the four months, July through October. That entry would read:

Oct 31	Bond Interest Expense ($100,000 $\times$ 0.12 $\times$ $\frac{4}{12}$)	....	4,000	
	Accrued Bond Interest Payable	....		4,000
	To accrue four months' interest expense.			

The December 31 entry would then read:

Dec 31	Bond Interest Expense ($100,000 $\times$ 0.12 $\times$ $\frac{2}{12}$)	....	2,000	
	Accrued Bond Interest Payable	....	4,000	
	Cash	....		6,000
	To record semiannual interest payment			

Each year similar entries would be made for the semiannual payments and the year-end accrual. The $4,000 Accrued Bond Interest Payable would be reported as a current liability on the October 31 balance sheet for each year.

Bonds issued at face value between interest dates. Bonds are not always issued on the date they start to bear interest. An issue might be delayed for several reasons. One reason might be because lower interest rates are anticipated. But interest does start to accrue from the most recent interest date, whether the bonds have been physically issued or not. Investors purchasing such bonds after they began to accrue interest are required to pay for the accrued interest because the issuer of the bonds is required to pay investors a full six months' interest at each interest date. The bonds are reported to be selling at a stated price "plus accrued interest."

Suppose Valley Company issued its bonds on April 30, 1985, instead of on December 31, 1984. The entry required is:

```
Apr. 30   Cash ..........................................    104,000
              Bonds Payable ...................................              100,000
              Accrued Bond Interest Payable
              ($100,000  ×  0.12  ×  4/12) ........................              4,000
          To record bonds issued at face value plus accrued interest.
```

This entry records the cash received for the accrued interest as a liability. The entry required on June 30, 1985, when the full six months' interest is paid is:

```
June 30   Bond Interest Expense ...................................    2,000
          Accrued Bond Interest Payable ...........................    4,000
              Cash ..............................................              6,000
          To record bond interest payment.
```

This entry records $2,000 interest expense on the $100,000 of bonds that were outstanding for two months. The $4,000 is the amount previously collected from the bondholders on April 30 as accrued interest and is now being returned to them.

Bond prices and interest rates

The price of a bond issue sold to investors often differs from its face value. A difference between face value and price will exist whenever the market rate of interest differs from the contract rate of interest on the bonds. The *contract rate of interest* is stated in the bond indenture and printed on the face of each bond and is also called the *stated, coupon,* or *nominal rate.* The contract rate is used to determine the actual amount of cash that will be paid each interest period. The *market interest rate,* also called the *effective interest* or *yield rate,* is the minimum rate of interest investors are willing to accept on bonds of a particular risk category. The market rate fluctuates from day to day, responding to the supply of and demand for money.

Contract and market rates of interest are likely to differ. The contract rate must be set before the bonds are actually sold to allow time for such things as printing the bonds. By the time the bonds are sold and the market rate becomes known, the contract rate could be higher or lower than the market rate. *If the contract rate is higher than the market rate, the bonds will sell for more than face value.* Investors will be attracted to bonds offering a contract rate greater than the market rate for such bonds and will bid up their price. *If the contract rate is lower than the market rate, the bonds will sell for less than face value.* Investors will not be interested in bonds bearing a contract rate less than the market rate until their price falls. The amount a bond sells for above face value is called a *premium;* if sold for less than face value, the reduction is called a *discount.*

The effect of selling a bond at a premium or discount is to change the nominal rate of interest on the bond to the market rate. To illustrate using a short-term note: Assume that you paid the McNeil Company $9,800 for its $10,000, 10 percent note which matures in one year. The contract interest rate is 10 percent. But, if McNeil pays the note at maturity, the effective rate of interest in the transaction is about 12.2 percent. Your actual interest earned is $1,200—the difference between the amount collected at the end of one year, $11,000 (principal plus interest), and the amount invested, $9,800. The effective rate of interest is 12.2 percent ($1,200/ $9,800) per annum, simple interest.

Computing bond prices

Computing long-term bond prices is a more complex process than finding the effective rate of interest on a one-year note at simple interest. The process involves finding present values using compound interest. The concept of present value is explained in the Appendix to this chapter. If you do not understand the present value concept, you should read the Appendix before continuing.

To compute the price investors will pay for a given bond issue, compute the present value of the bonds. Present value is computed by discounting promised cash flows in the bonds—principal and interest—using the market or effective interest rate. Market rate is used because the bonds must yield at least this rate or investors will invest in alternative investments that do. The life of the bonds is stated in terms of interest periods, which indicate how frequently interest is compounded. The interest rate used is the effective rate *per interest period,* which often is found by dividing the annual rate by the number of times interest is paid per year.

Bonds issued at face value.   Specific steps involved in computing the price of a bond are illustrated by an example. Assume $100,000 face value of 12 percent bonds are issued by Carr Company to yield 12 percent. The bonds are dated and issued on July 1, 1984; call for semiannual interest payments; and mature on July 1, 1987. The bonds will sell at face value because they offer 12 percent and investors seek 12 percent. There is no reason to offer a premium or demand a discount. One way to prove the bonds would be sold at face value is by showing that their present value is $100,000:

	Present value factor	Present value
Principal of $100,000 due in six periods multiplied by present value factor from Table 3, Appendix C (end of text)	$100,000 × 0.70496 =	$ 70,496
Interest of $6,000 due at end of each of six periods multiplied by present value factor from Table 4, Appendix C (end of text)	$6,000 × 4.91732 =	29,504
Total price (present value)		$100,000

The schedule shows that if investors seek an effective rate of 6 percent per six-month period, they should pay $100,000 for these bonds. When the bonds are sold on July 1, 1984, the entry required debits Cash and credits Bonds Payable for $100,000.

Bonds issued at a discount. Assume the Carr Company bonds are sold to yield the market rate of 14 percent—actually 7 percent per semiannual period. The present value and selling price of the bonds is computed as follows:

	Present value factor	Present value
Principal of $100,000 due in six periods multiplied by present value factor from Table 3, Appendix C (end of text)	$100,000 × 0.66634 =	$66,634
Interest of $6,000 due at end of each of six periods multiplied by present value factor from Table 4, Appendix C (end of text) ..../..............	$6,000 × 4.76654 =	28,599
Total price (present value)		$95,233

Note that in computing present value of the bonds, the actual cash interest payments that will be made were used. The amount of cash flow does not change with changes in the market interest rate. Also, the market rate per semiannual period—7 percent—was used in finding interest factors in the tables. The journal entry to record issuance of the bonds is:

```
1984
July 1  Cash ..........................................    95,233
          Discount on Bonds Payable ............................    4,767
             Bonds Payable ....................................           100,000
          To record bonds issued at a discount.
```

Note in recording the bond issue, Bonds Payable is credited for the face value of the debt. The difference between face value and price received is debited to a contra account to Bonds Payable. Bonds Payable and the Discount on Bonds Payable are reported in the balance sheet like this:

```
Long-term liabilities:
   Bonds payable, 12%, due July 1, 1987  .....   $100,000
      Less: Unamortized discount  ............      4,767    $95,233
```

The $95,233 is called the *carrying value* or *net liability* of the bonds. Unamortized discount is discussed below.

Bonds issued at a premium. Assume that Carr Company issued the $100,000 face value of 12 percent bonds to yield 10 percent. The bonds would sell at a premium calculated as follows:

	Present value factor	Present value
Principal of $100,000 due in six periods multiplied by present value factor from Table 3, Appendix C (end of text)	$100,000 × 0.74622 =	$ 74,622
Interest of $6,000 due at end of each of six periods multiplied by present value factor from Table 4, Appendix C (end of text)	$6,000 × 5.07569 =	30,454
Total price (present value)		$105,076

The journal entry to record the issuance of the bonds is:

```
1984
July 1  Cash ................................................ 105,076
            Bonds Payable .....................................          100,000
            Premium on Bonds Payable .........................            5,076
        To record bonds issued at a premium.
```

Carrying value of these bonds at issuance is $105,076 consisting of face value of $100,000 and premium of $5,076. Premium is shown on the balance sheet as an addition to face value, usually described as unamortized premium.

Discount/premium amortization

When bonds are issued at a premium or discount, total actual interest expense on the bonds differs from total interest paid periodically in cash. A discount increases and a premium decreases the cash interest to actual interest. For example, if $100,000 face value of Carr Company bonds were issued for $95,233, the total interest cost of borrowing would be $40,767: $36,000 (six payments of $6,000) plus discount of $4,767. The $4,767 discount must be allocated or charged to the six periods that benefit from the use of borrowed money. *APB Opinion No. 21* recommends an amortization procedure called the *effective interest rate method,* or, simply, the *interest method.*

Under the interest method, *interest expense for any interest period is equal to the effective (market) rate of interest at date of issuance times the carrying value of the bonds at the beginning of that interest period.* Using the Carr Company example of $100,000 face value of 12 percent bonds sold to yield 14 percent, the carrying value at the beginning of the first interest period is the selling price of $95,233. The interest expense for the first semiannual period would be recorded in this way:

```
1985
Jan. 1  Bond Interest Expense ($95,233 × 0.14 × ½) ...........   6,666
             Cash ($100,000 × 0.12 × ½) ....................            6,000
             Discount on Bonds Payable ........................            666
        To record discount amortization and interest payment.
```

Note that interest expense is calculated using the effective interest rate. The cash payment is calculated using the contract rate. The discount amortized for the period is the difference between the two amounts.

After the above entry, carrying value of the bonds is $95,899. The balance in the discount account was reduced by $666 to $4,101. Assuming a fiscal year ending on June 30, the entry to accrue six month's interest at fiscal year-end is:

```
1985
June 30  Bond Interest Expense ($95,899 × 0.14 × ½) ..........   6,713
              Accrued Bond Interest Payable .....................           6,000
              Discount on Bonds Payable .........................            713
         To accrue six months' interest and discount amortization.
```

If the Carr Company bonds had been issued to yield 10 percent, the premium would be $5,076. But interest expense would be calculated in the same manner as for bonds sold at a discount. The entry would differ somewhat, showing a debit to the premium account. The entries for the first two interest periods are:

```
1985
Jan.  1  Bond Interest Expense ($105,076 × 0.10 × ½) .........   5,254
         Premium on Bonds Payable ...........................     746
              Cash .........................................            6,000
         To record interest payment and premium amortization.
```

```
1985
June 30  Bond Interest Expense ($104,330 × 0.10 × ½) .........   5,216
         Premium on Bonds Payable ...........................     784
              Accrued Bond Interest Payable .....................          6,000
         To accrue six months' interest expense and premium amorti-
         zation.
```

Discount and premium amortization schedules.   A discount amortization schedule (Illustration 17.2) and a premium amortization schedule (Illustration 17.3) can be prepared to aid in preparing entries for interest expense. Companies usually prepare such schedules when bonds are first issued, often using standard computer programs. The schedules are then referred to whenever journal entries for interest are to be made. Note that, in each period, the amount of interest expense changes; expense gets smaller when a premium is involved and larger when a discount is involved. The reason is the carrying value to which a constant interest rate is applied changes each interest payment date. With a premium, carrying value decreases; with a discount, it increases. But cash is always a constant amount determined by multiplying face value by the contract rate per interest period.

Note that interest expense in Illustration 17.2 of $40,767 agrees with the earlier computation of total interest expense. In Illustration 17.3, total

Illustration 17.2:   Discount amortization schedule

(A) Interest payment date	(B) Interest Expense debit (E × 0.14 × ½)	(C) Cash credit ($100,000 × 0.12 × ½)	(D) Discount on Bonds Payable credit (B − C)	(E) Carrying value of Bonds Payable (E + D)
Issue price				$ 95,233
1/1/85	$ 6,666	$ 6,000	$ 666	95,899
7/1/85	6,713	6,000	713	96,612
1/1/86	6,763	6,000	763	97,375
7/1/86	6,816	6,000	816	98,191
1/1/87	6,873	6,000	873	99,064
7/1/87	6,936*	6,000	936	100,000
	$40,767	$36,000	$4,767	

* Includes rounding difference.

interest expense is shown as $30,924, which is equal to $36,000 (six $6,000 payments) *less* the $5,076 premium. In both illustrations, carrying value of the bonds has been reduced to face value at the maturity date.

Adjusting entry for partial period.   Illustration 17.3 can be used to obtain amounts needed if interest must be accrued for a partial period. Assume the fiscal year of the bond issuer ends on August 31. The adjusting entry needed on August 31, 1984, is:

Aug. 31   Bond Interest Expense ($5,254 × $\frac{2}{6}$) 1,751
          Premium on Bonds Payable ($746 × $\frac{2}{6}$) 249
               Accrued Bond Interest Payable ($6,000 × $\frac{2}{6}$) 2,000
          To record two months' accrued interest.

The entry records interest for two months, July and August, of the six-month interest period ending on January 1, 1985. The first line of Illustration 17.3 shows the interest expense and premium amortization for the six months. The above entry thus records two sixths (or one third) of the amounts

Illustration 17.3:   Premium amortization schedule

(A) Interest payment date	(B) Interest Expense debit (E × 0.10 × ½)	(C) Cash credit ($100,000 × 0.12 × ½)	(D) Premium on Bonds Payable debit (C − B)	(E) Carrying value of Bonds Payable (E − D)
Issue price				$105,076
1/1/85	$ 5,254	$ 6,000	$ 746	104,330
7/1/85	5,216	6,000	784	103,546
1/1/86	5,177	6,000	823	102,723
7/1/86	5,136	6,000	864	101,859
1/1/87	5,093	6,000	907	100,952
7/1/87	5,048	6,000	952	100,000
	$30,924	$36,000	$5,076	

for this six-month period. The remaining four months' interest is recorded when the first payment is made on January 1, 1985. That entry reads:

```
Jan.  1  Accrued Bond Interest Payable .........................    2,000
         Bond Interest Expense ($5,254 × ⁴⁄₆) ..................    3,503
         Premium on Bonds Payable ($746 × ⁴⁄₆) ...............      497
             Cash ........................................                    6,000
             To record interest expense and interest payment.
```

Similar entries for August 31 and January 1 will be made in the remaining years in the life of the bonds. But the amounts will differ because the interest method of accounting for bond interest is being used.

The straight-line method. When applied to bond discount or premium, the *straight-line method of amortization* is a procedure that allocates an equal amount of discount or premium to each period in the life of a bond. The amount is calculated by dividing discount or premium by the total number of interest periods from date of issuance to maturity date. For example, if the $100,000 face value of Carr Company bonds were sold for $95,233, the $4,767 discount would be charged to interest expense at a rate of $795 ($4,767/6) per interest period. Interest expense for each period then would be $6,795. The entry to record the expense would have the same form as under the interest method.

The $5,076 premium on the $100,000 face value of bonds sold for $105,076 would be amortized at a rate of $846 ($5,076/6) per period. The entry for the first period's expense on bonds sold at a premium reads:

```
Jan. 1  Bond Interest Expense ...............................    5,154
        Premium on Bonds Payable ...........................      846
            Cash ..........................................                  6,000
            To record interest payment and premium amortization.
```

Interest expense is recorded at a *constant amount* under the straight-line method and at a *constant rate* under the interest method. Since the interest method is theoretically correct, *APB Opinion No. 21* states that the straight-line method may be used only when it does not differ materially from the interest method. In many cases, differences will not be material. In the premium example above, the difference in the first period's interest expense is only $100 ($5,254 − $5,154), and may not be material.

Redeeming bonds payable

Bonds may be paid at maturity, purchased in the market and retired, or called. Each of these actions is referred to as redemption of bonds or as extinguishment of debt. If bonds are paid at maturity, any related discount or premium would have been amortized. The only entry required would debit Bonds Payable and credit Cash. More typical redemptions are discussed below.

An issuer may redeem some or all of its outstanding bonds before maturity date by calling them. Or bonds may be purchased in the market and retired. In either case, the accounting is the same. Assume that on January 1, 1986,

$10,000 face value of the bonds in Illustration 17.3 are called (or else purchased in the market) at 103. Bond prices usually are quoted as percentages—the 103 means 103 percent of face value. For a $1,000 bond, the price is $1,030. A quote of 99.5 means a price of $995 for a $1,000 bond. In both cases, accrued interest, if any, will be added to the price. Assume that coupons for the interest due on this date have been detached so there is no accrued interest. A look at the last column on the line dated 1/1/86 in Illustration 17.3 reveals that the carrying value of the bonds is $102,723, which consists of Bonds Payable of $100,000 and Premium on Bonds Payable of $2,723. Since 10 percent of the bond issue is redeemed, 10 percent must be removed from each of these two accounts. A loss is incurred for the excess of the price paid for the bonds, $10,300, over their carrying value, $10,272. The required entry reads:

Bonds Payable	10,000	
Premium on Bonds Payable	272	
Loss on Bond Redemption	28	
Cash		10,300
To record bonds redeemed.		

According to *FASB Statement No. 4*, gains and losses from *voluntary early* retirement of bonds are extraordinary items, if material. Such gains and losses are reported in the income statement, net of their tax effects, as described in Chapter 16.

Serial bonds

To avoid the burden of redeeming an entire bond issue at one time, serial bonds may be issued. *Serial* bonds are bonds that mature in installments. To illustrate: On July 1, 1979, Jasper Company issued $100,000 face value of 12 percent serial bonds at 100. Interest is payable on January 1 and July 1. The bonds mature in $20,000 annual installments starting on July 1, 1984. Jasper Company has a calendar accounting year. Entries required for 1984 for interest expense and maturing debt are:

1984			
July 1	Bond Interest Expense ($100,000 × 0.12 × ½)	6,000	
	Cash		6,000
	To record interest payment.		
1	Serial Bonds Payable	20,000	
	Cash		20,000
	To record retirement of serial debt.		
Dec. 31	Bond Interest Expense ($80,000 × 0.12 × ½)	4,800	
	Accrued Bond Interest Payable		4,800
	To accrue semiannual interest expense.		

Note that interest expense for the last six months of 1984 is calculated only on the remaining outstanding debt ($100,000 original issue less $20,000 installment). Each year after the serial installment is retired, interest expense decreases proportionately. The $20,000 installment maturing next year is reported as a current liability in the year-end balance sheet. The remaining debt is a long-term liability.

Bond redemption or sinking funds

Investors in bonds typically are concerned about the safety of their investments. To reduce risk of default at maturity date, provisions in modern bond indentures often require periodic payments be made to a *bond redemption fund,* often called a *sinking fund.* Such payments are to be used by the fund trustee (usually a bank) to redeem a stated amount of bonds annually and to pay accrued interest on those bonds. The trustee determines by lot the bonds that are to be called. The cash deposited with the trustee can be used *only* to redeem issuer's bonds and pay accrued interest on bonds redeemed. This restriction differs from the earlier practice of investing cash received in a portfolio of securities. These securities were subsequently sold, with the proceeds used to retire all bonds on their maturity date.

To illustrate, assume Hand Company has 12 percent, semiannual coupon bonds outstanding that were issued at face value. The bond indenture requires the company to pay a trustee the sum of $53,000 on each September 30. The trustee is to use the funds to call $50,000 of Hand's bonds and to pay $3,000 accrued interest on bonds called. The entry for the payment to the trustee reads:

```
Sept. 30   Sinking Fund ........................................   53,000
               Cash .........................................              53,000
           To record payment to trustee of required deposit.
```

The trustee calls $50,000 of bonds, pays for the bonds and accrued interest, and notifies the company. The trustee also bills the company for its fee and expenses incurred of $325. Assuming the accrued interest has been recorded, the entries are:

```
Oct.   1   Bonds Payable .....................................   50,000
           Accrued Bond Interest Payable ........................    3,000
               Sinking Fund ..............................              53,000
           To record bond redemption and interest paid by trustee.

           Sinking Fund Expenses................................      325
               Cash .........................................                 325
           To record trustee fee and expenses.
```

The $50,000 of bonds that must be retired each year usually is described as "Current maturity of long-term debt" and reported as a current liability.

Convertible bonds

A company may add to the attractiveness of its bonds by making them *convertible,* at the bondholder's option, into shares of the issuer's common stock. Bond conversions are accounted for by treating the carrying value of bonds surrendered as the capital contributed for shares issued.

Suppose a company has $10,000 face value of bonds outstanding. Each

$1,000 bond is convertible into 50 shares of the issuer's $10 par value common stock. On May 1, when the carrying value of the bonds was $9,800, all of the bonds were presented for conversion. The entry required is:

May 1 Bonds Payable	10,000	
Discount on Bonds Payable		200
Common Stock		5,000
Paid-In Capital in Excess of Par Value—Common		4,800
To record bonds converted into common stock.		

Long-term mortgage notes payable

Sometimes companies give their own notes to finance plant asset acquisitions. Such notes usually are long-term liabilities and are secured by a mortgage on the property acquired. Most family homes are purchased in this way.

Assume that a company acquired a building by giving a $100,000, 16 percent, 20-year mortgage note payable. The note calls for equal monthly payments, exclusive of real estate taxes and insurance. In the early stages, a very large portion of the monthly payment is for interest and only a limited amount is for reducing principal. There are mortgage payment schedule books which indicate that the monthly payment for principal and interest is $1,391.26. Here is how the first two month's and the last month's payments are applied:

Date of purchase	Monthly payment	Interest	Principal	Principal balance
				$100,000.00
First month	$1,391.26	$1,333.33	$ 57.93	99,942.07
Second month	1,391.26	1,332.56	58.70	99,883.37
240th month	1,391.26	18.31	1,372.95	–0–

Notice that interest is calculated on the latest principal balance. For instance, when the first $1,391.26 payment is made, interest for the month is calculated as follows:

$$\$100,000 \times 0.16 \times \tfrac{1}{12} = \$1,333.33$$

The excess of the first payment over interest is applied against principal ($57.93 in the first payment above). Thus, the principal balance decreases slowly (but more rapidly each month), so that the last payment at the end of 20 years pays interest of $18.31 on the remaining principal balance of $1,372.95 and reduces the principal balance to zero.

BOND INVESTMENTS

Bonds may be purchased as either short-term or long-term investments. Short-term investments in bonds are generally made to earn income on what might otherwise be idle cash. Such investments may yield a higher return than available alternatives. Long-term investments in bonds usually are made for reasons other than a return on idle cash. A company may invest on a long-term basis in another company to guarantee needed raw materials. Or one company could be a dealer or distributor of the other company's products. In any event, the most common reason is establishment of a long-term relationship between two companies. If short-term bond investments are marketable and are considered a temporary use of cash available for operations, they are reported as current assets. All other bond investments are long-term and are reported in the Investments section in the balance sheet below current assets, whether marketable or not.

Short-term bond investments

Short-term bond investments are recorded at cost, which includes price paid for the bonds and often includes a broker's commission. If bonds are purchased between interest dates, investors pay for accrued interest and collect the amount paid later when the semiannual interest is received. Premiums and discounts on short-term investments are *not amortized because the length of time the bonds will be held is not known.*

To illustrate: On June 1, 1984, Bay Company purchased $10,000 face value of Ace Company 12 percent bonds at 102, plus $100 of accrued interest from May 1, and a $70 broker's commission. The entry required is:

```
June  1  Temporary Investments ($10,200 + $70) ...............   10,270
          Accrued Bond Interest Receivable ($10,000 × 0.12 × ¹⁄₁₂)      100
            Cash ........................................               10,370
            To record bonds purchased.
```

On October 1, 1984, Bay sold the Ace bonds at 103.5, plus accrued interest of $500, and less a $70 broker's commission. To compute gain or loss on the sale, the broker's commission is deducted from selling price to get net proceeds to the seller. The gain or loss is the difference between net proceeds and cost. In this example, the gain is $10, ($10,350 − $70) − ($10,270). Note that accrued interest does not affect the amount of gain or loss because it is paid for by the purchaser. The entry to record the sale is:

```
Oct.  1  Cash ($10,350 + $500 − $70) ......................   10,780
            Temporary Investments ............................          10,270
            Accrued Bond Interest Receivable (from above entry) ....       100
            Interest Revenue ($10,000 × 0.12 × ⁴⁄₁₂) ...........          400
            Gain on Sale of Temporary Investments ..............           10
            To record sale of temporary investments.
```

The purchaser will receive the semiannual interest check from Ace Company to cover the $500 of accrued interest paid to Bay Company. Bay records only $400 of the $500 of interest received as interest revenue, since it held the bonds for only four months.

Long-term bond investments

Long-term investments in bonds also are recorded in a single account at cost which includes any premium or discount. Although not set up in a separate account as it is for the issuing company, premium or discount on long-term bond investments is amortized.

Bonds purchased at a discount. For example, assume that on July 1, 1984, Mann Company purchased $100,000 face value of 12 percent bonds for $95,233, a price that yields 14 percent. These bonds are the bonds described in Illustration 17.2. The entry to record the purchase is:

```
Bond Investments .........................................  95,233
    Cash ...................................................           95,233
    To record bonds purchased at a discount.
```

If a broker's commission was paid to acquire the bonds, it would be added to the Bond Investments account.

Since Mann intends to hold the bonds to maturity, discount is amortized over remaining life of the bonds, using the interest method. Interest revenue and discount amortization on the bonds purchased by Mann are computed the same way issuer's expense and amortization are computed: multiply bond price by the effective rate per period. The first period's interest revenue is $6,666 ($95,233 × 0.14 × ½). Discount amortized is $666 ($6,666 − $6,000). If Mann has a calendar accounting year, the required adjusting entry is:

```
Dec. 31  Accrued Bond Interest Receivable ......................  6,000
         Bond Investments ....................................     666
             Interest Revenue ................................           6,666
         To record accrued interest revenue.
```

Note in the entry, the amount added to the Bond Investments account is equal to discount amortized on issuer's books. Discount is amortized even though it is not set up in a separate account on the investor's books. The original discount is $4,767, and this amount must be included in interest revenue on Mann's books during the life of the bonds. Illustration 17.4 shows

Illustration 17.4: Discount amortization schedule

(A)	(B)	(C)	(D)	(E)
	Cash debit	Interest Rev-	Bond Invest-	Carrying value of Bond
Interest date	($100,000 × 0.12 × ½)	enue credit (E × 0.14 × ½)	ments debit (C − B)	Investments (E + D)
Purchase price				$ 95,233
1/1/85	$ 6,000	$ 6,666	$ 666	95,899
7/1/85	6,000	6,713	713	96,612
1/1/86	6,000	6,763	763	97,375
7/1/86	6,000	6,816	816	98,191
1/1/87	6,000	6,873	873	99,064
7/1/87	6,000	6,936*	936	100,000
	$36,000	$40,767	$4,767	

* Includes rounding difference.

how the $4,767 is added to periodic interest revenue and to Bond Investments. The debits gradually increase the Bond Investments account balance to face value at maturity date.

Mann's December 31, 1984, balance sheet would show Accrued Bond Interest Receivable of $6,000, and Bond Investments of $95,899. If Mann's fiscal year ended on November 30, the adjusting entry on that date would be the same as the December 31 entry, except all amounts would be five sixths of the December 31 amounts.

If the straight-line method is used, discount amortization would be $795 ($4,767/6) per period and interest revenue would be $6,795 ($6,000 + $795).

Bonds purchased at a premium. To illustrate accounting for bonds purchased at a premium, assume Ladd Company paid $105,076 for $100,000 face value of 12 percent bonds, a price that yields 10 percent. These are the bonds in Illustration 17.3. The entry to record the purchase would debit Bond Investments and credit Cash for $105,076.

Here again, interest revenue for the first interest period can be computed by multiplying purchase price by the effective rate: $105,076 \times 0.10 \times \frac{1}{2} = $5,254. The entry to record the $5,254 is:

Cash	6,000	
Bond Investments		746
Interest Revenue		5,254
To record interest revenue collected.		

The premium is amortized by crediting the Bond Investments account. If bonds are held to maturity, the balance in the Bond Investments account would be gradually decreased to maturity value of $100,000 (Illustration 17.5). Interest revenue for the second six months can be read from Illustration 17.5. Or it can be computed: ($105,076 − $746) \times 0.10 \times \frac{1}{2} = $5,216. If the straight-line method were used, the periodic amortization of premium would be $846 ($5,076/6). Interest revenue would be a constant semiannual $5,154 ($6,000 − $846).

Illustration 17.5: **Premium amortization schedule**

(A) Interest date	(B) Cash debit ($100,000 × 0.12 × ½)	(C) Interest Rev- enue credit (E × 0.10 × ½)	(D) Bond Invest- ments credit (B − C)	(E) Carrying value of Bond Investments (E − D)
Purchase price				$105,076
1/1/85	$ 6,000	$ 5,254	$ 746	104,330
7/1/85	6,000	5,216	784	103,546
1/1/86	6,000	5,177	823	102,723
7/1/86	6,000	5,136	864	101,859
1/1/87	6,000	5,093	907	100,952
7/1/87	6,000	5,048	952	100,000
	$36,000	$30,924	$5,076	

Sale of bond investments

When bond investments are sold, a gain or loss usually must be recorded. Gain or loss is computed as the difference between the price received and the carrying value of the bonds on the date sold. Suppose that on July 1, 1986, when their carrying value was $101,859 (Illustration 17.5), the Ladd Company sold all of its bonds for $102,500, less a $500 broker's commission. The required entry is:

Cash	102,000	
Bond Investments		101,859
Gain on Sale of Bond Investments		141
To record sale of bond investments.		

There was no accrued interest because the sale occurred on an interest payment date. The gain is reported in the income statement, but not as an extraordinary item.

Valuation of bond investments

Short-term bond investments are carried and reported at cost. Long-term bond investments are carried and reported at amortized cost. Amortized cost is equal to acquisition cost less premium amortized or plus discount amortized. An exception exists when a substantial, permanent decline occurs. Bond investments are then written down by debiting an account called Loss on Market Decline of Bond Investments and crediting Bond Investments.

Once bond investments have been written down, traditional accounting conservatism dictates they may not be written up, not even to their original cost, if market price recovers. The written down amount serves as the basis for computing gain or loss when the bonds are sold.

STOCK INVESTMENTS

As in the case of bond investments, a company may invest in the stocks of other companies for both short-term and long-term purposes. Stock may be acquired for the return that can be earned on a temporary investment of cash available for operations. If readily marketable, such stock is a current asset.

Stock may be held for long-term purposes such as establishing a closer business relationship with a supplier or a customer. In such instances, the stock, whether readily marketable or not, will be classified as an investment on the balance sheet. How a given stock investment is classified is determined largely by management intent.

Accounting for stock investments

There are two methods of accounting for long-term stock investments: the cost and the equity methods. The cost method is discussed in this chapter, and the equity method is discussed in the next chapter. The cost method is used when the investing company owns 20 percent or less of the outstanding stock of the other company. It is also used to account for short-term investments in stock. The discussion below applies to both short-term and long-term stock investments.

Recording stock acquisitions. Stock investments are recorded at cost—the cash paid in most instances. Most stocks are purchased from other investors (not the issuing company) through brokers who execute "trades" in an organized market, such as the New York Stock Exchange. Thus, cost will usually consist of the price paid for the shares, plus a broker's commission.

For example, assume that Brewer Corporation purchased 1,000 shares of Cowen Company's $10 par value common stock at 14⅛, plus a $175 broker's commission. The entry needed by Brewer is:

```
Stock Investments (or Noncurrent Marketable Equity Securities) . . . . . . .    14,300
    Cash . . . . . . . . . . . . . . . . . . . . . . . . . . . . . . . . . . . . . . . . . . . . . . . . . . . . .             14,300
    Purchased 1,000 shares of Cowen Company common stock at 14⅛, plus commission.
```

Note that the par value of Cowen's stock is not recorded in one account and remaining cost in another. Par value of shares owned is of little significance, if any, to investors. Note also the way stock prices are quoted: in dollars and fractions of a dollar. Thus, 14⅛ means $14.125 per share.

Accounting for cash dividends received. Investments in bonds yield interest; investments in stock yield dividends. As a general rule, cash dividends are debited to Cash and credited to Dividend Revenue when received by the investor. The only exception to this general rule is when a dividend is declared in one accounting period that is payable in the next. Assume that Cowen Company declared a $1 per share cash dividend on December 1, 1984, to stockholders of record as of December 20, payable on January 15, 1985. The following entry should be made in 1984:

```
Dividends Receivable . . . . . . . . . . . . . . . . . . . . . . . . . . . . . . . . . . . . . . .     1,000
    Dividend Revenue . . . . . . . . . . . . . . . . . . . . . . . . . . . . . . . . . . . . . . .               1,000
    To record $1 per share cash dividend on Cowen common stock, pay-
    able January 15, 1985.
```

When the dividend is collected on January 15, Cash is debited and Dividends Receivable is credited.

Stock dividends and stock splits. An investor does not recognize income upon receipt of a stock dividend. The investing company notes receipt of the dividend shares and reduces its cost per share. For example, if Cowen Company distributes a 10 percent stock dividend in February 1985, Brewer Corporation would then hold 1,100 shares at a cost per share of $13 ($14,300/1,100 shares). Similarly, when a corporation declares a stock split, the investor would note the shares received and the reduction in the per share cost.

Sale of stock investments. When shares are sold, the gain or loss on the sale is the difference between the net proceeds received and the carrying

value, usually cost, of the shares sold. Assume, for example, that on May 1,
Brewer sold 500 of the Cowen shares at 17, less a $200 broker's commission.
The entry needed is:

```
May  1  Cash [(500 × $17) − $200] .........................  8,300
            Stock Investments (500 × $13) ..................          6,500
            Gain on Sale of Stock Investments .................         1,800
        To record sale of 500 shares of Cowen common stock.
```

Valuation of stock investments

Stock which does not have a market value is carried at cost, unless it has suffered a permanent decline in value. In this case, the stock is written down to the lower value.

FASB Statement No. 12 (1975) governs valuation of stock carried at cost which also has a market value. The statement requires use of the lower-of-cost-or-market (LCM) method of accounting for *marketable equity securities* which are readily salable common and preferred stocks of other companies. LCM is applied independently to the current and noncurrent investment accounts. The write-down to market is made through use of a valuation account called Allowance for Market Decline of Current (Noncurrent) Marketable Equity Securities, rather than a direct credit to the investment account. The valuation account is used because the LCM valuation is based upon the total portfolio of securities, rather than the individual securities held.

For example, Hanson Company has the securities shown in Illustration 17.6 in its stock portfolio.

Applying the LCM method would require that the portfolio be written down $1,000—from $20,000 to $19,000. Note that the increases in the market value of the A and B shares offset $3,000 of the $4,000 decrease in market value of the C shares, leaving only the net decrease of $1,000 to be accounted for.

Current marketable equity securities. If the portfolio in Illustration 17.6 is a short-term portfolio, the journal entry required at the end of 1984 then is:

```
Dec. 31  Net Unrealized Loss on Current Marketable
             Equity Securities ..................................  1,000
             Allowance for Market Decline of Current Marketable
                 Equity Securities ................................         1,000
         To record unrealized loss from market decline of current
         marketable equity securities
```

Illustration 17.6: Stock portfolio

Company	No. of shares	Cost per share	Market price per share	Total cost	Total market
A	200	$35	$40	$ 7,000	$ 8,000
B	400	10	15	4,000	6,000
C	100	90	50	9,000	5,000
				$20,000	$19,000

630

Chapter 17

The net loss is called unrealized because the securities have not been sold. It is reported in the income statement. The credit in the above entry is to a contra account somewhat similar to the Allowance for Doubtful Accounts. The securities and the contra account are reported in the balance sheet like this:

Current assets:
Marketable equity securities (cost $20,000, less allowance for market decline
of $1,000) 19,000

Assume that in 1985 Hanson sold the B shares for $6,000. The entry for the sale is:

Cash 6,000
   Current Marketable Equity Securities 4,000
   Realized Gain on Sale of Securities 2,000
To record sale of securities.

Note that gain on sale of B stock is calculated without reference to the balance in the allowance. The credit to the allowance does not change the carrying value of any individual security. So realized gains and losses are calculated by comparison of net proceeds from the sale with the actual cost of the securities sold.

At the end of 1985, Hanson Company would again determine the cost and market value of its portfolio. Assume that total cost is $16,000 (the cost of the A and the C shares). Total market value is $15,600. Thus, an allowance of only $400 is needed to state the portfolio at lower of cost or market. Since the allowance has a $1,000 balance, the following entry reduces it from $1,000 to $400:

Dec. 31   Allowance for Market Decline of Current Marketable Equity
        Securities 600
          Recovery of Market Value of Current Marketable Equity
            Securities 600
        To record gain from recovery of market value of current mar-
        ketable equity securities.

The account credited is an unrealized gain and is reported in the income statement. The securities and the allowance are shown in the 1985 balance sheet like this:

Current assets:
Marketable equity securities (cost $16,000, less allowance for market decline
of $400) $15,600

Noncurrent marketable equity securities.   Assume a portfolio of noncurrent marketable equity securities has a cost of $32,000 and a current market value of $31,000. The loss is considered "temporary." The required entry is:

Dec. 31   Net Unrealized Loss on Noncurrent Marketable Equity
        Securities 1,000
          Allowance for Market Decline of Noncurrent Equity
            Securities 1,000
        To record unrealized loss from market decline of noncur-
        rent equity securities.

Both of the above accounts would appear in the balance sheet as follows:

Investments:
Noncurrent marketable equity securities (cost $32,000, less
   allowance for market decline, $1,000) .... $ 31,000

Stockholders' equity:
  Capital stock .... $ xxx,xxx
  Additional paid-in capital ....   x,xxx
     Total paid-in capital .... $ xxx,xxx
  Less: Unrealized loss on noncurrent marketable equity securities   1,000
                                          $ xxx,xxx
  Retained earnings ....   xx,xxx
     Total stockholders' equity .... $ xxx,xxx

Alternatively, the unrealized loss could be reported as a deduction from total stockholders' equity. It is *not* included in the determination of net income because it is viewed as temporary. Losses on current securities are included in net income because, being related to a current asset, they are more likely to be actually realized.

Later recoveries of market value up to original cost of $32,000 are debited to the allowance and credited to the unrealized loss account. Thus, if the market value of the noncurrent portfolio increases by $1,700, the adjusting entry needed is:

Dec. 31 Allowance for Market Decline of Noncurrent Marketable
          Equity Securities   1,000
            Net Unrealized Loss on Noncurrent Marketable Equity
              Securities   1,000
            To record recovery of market value of noncurrent market-
            able equity securities.

Only $1,000 of the $1,700 increase in market value may be recorded. To record the $1,700 would value the securities at more than cost.

If a loss on an individual noncurrent security is determined to be "permanent," it is recorded as a realized loss and deducted in determining net income. The entry to record a permanent loss of $1,400 reads:

Dec. 31 Realized Loss on Noncurrent Marketable Equity
          Securities   1,400
            Noncurrent Marketable Equity Securities   1,400
            To record loss in value of noncurrent marketable equity secu-
            rities.

No part of the $1,400 loss is subject to reversal if market price of the stock recovers. *The stock's reduced value is now its "cost," and values in excess of cost are not recorded until a sale occurs.*

APPENDIX: FUTURE WORTH AND PRESENT VALUE

The concepts of interest, future worth, and present value are widely applied in business decision making. Accountants may be better able to account properly for business activity if they understand how the concepts of interest, future worth, and present value influence this activity.

INTEREST

As a general definition, interest is the *time value of money.* More specifically, it is the cost incurred from borrowing money or the revenue earned from lending money. The cost or revenue typically is measured by comparing the amount loaned with the amount repaid. Thus, if $100 is borrowed and $110 is repaid one year later, the interest cost (revenue) is $10 and the interest rate is 10 percent per annum ($10/$100). But there is more to the concept of interest than the amount that is recorded as interest revenue or interest expense. The foregone opportunity to earn interest must be considered. If you have money and earn no interest on it, you have a cost in the sense of a revenue foregone.

The concept of the time value of money stems from the logical preference for a dollar today rather than a dollar at any future date. Most individuals would prefer having a dollar today rather than at some future date because: (1) the risk exists that the future dollar will never be received; and (2) if the dollar is on hand now it can be invested, resulting in an increase in total dollars possessed at that future date.

Most business decisions involve a comparison of cash flows in and out of the firm. To be useful in decision making, such comparisons must be in terms of dollars of the same point in time, or "vintage." That is, the dollars held now must be accumulated or rolled forward or future dollars must be discounted or brought back to today before comparisons are valid. Such comparisons involve future worth and present value concepts.

FUTURE WORTH

The *future worth* or *value* of any investment is the amount to which a sum of money invested today will grow in a stated time period at a specified interest rate. The interest involved may be simple interest or compound interest. *Simple interest* is interest on principal only. For example, $1,000 invested today for two years at 12 percent simple interest will grow to $1,240 since interest is $120 per year. The principal of $1,000, plus 2 × $120, is equal to $1,240. *Compound interest* is interest on principal and on interest of prior periods. For example, $1,000 invested for two years at 12 percent compounded annually will grow to $1,254.40. Interest for the first year is $120 ($1,000 × 0.12). For the second year, interest is earned on the principal plus the interest of the previous year, $120. Thus, the interest for the second year is $134.40 ($1,120 × 0.12). Future value at the end of year 2 is $1,254.40. The $1,254.40 is found by adding the second year's interest ($134.40) to the value at the beginning of the second year ($1,120). These computations of future worth may be portrayed graphically (see Illustration 17.7).

Illustration 17.7 shows the growth of $1,000 to $1,254.40 when the inter-

Illustration 17.7

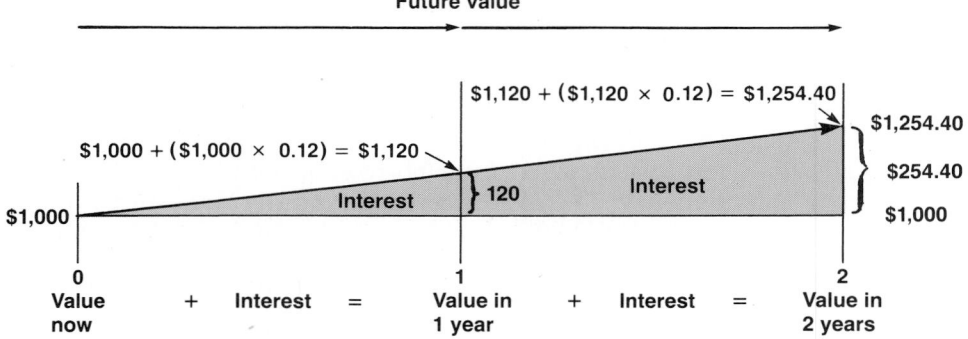

est rate is 12 percent compounded annually. The effect of compounding is $14.40—the interest in the second year that was based on the interest computed for the first year, or $120 × 0.12 = $14.40.

The task of computing the future worth to which any invested amount will grow at a given rate for a stated period is aided by the use of interest tables. An example is Table 1 in Appendix C at the end of this text. To use the Appendix C tables, first determine the number of compounding periods involved. The compounding period tells how frequently interest is computed and added to the base upon which future interest calculations will be based. A compounding period may be any length of time, such as a day, a month, a quarter, a half-year, or a year, but normally not more than a year. The number of compounding periods is equal to the number of years in the life of the investment times the number of compoundings in a year. Five years compounded annually is five periods, five years compounded quarterly is 20 periods, and so on.

Next, determine the interest rate per compounding period. Interest rates are usually quoted in annual terms. In fact, federal law requires statement of the interest rate in annual terms in certain situations. Divide the annual rate by the number of compounding periods per year to get the proper rate per period. Only with an annual compounding will the annual rate be the rate per period. All other cases involve a lower rate. For example, the rate per period will be 1 percent if the annual rate is 12 percent, compounded monthly.

To use the table in a given situation, find the number of periods involved in the Period column. Move across the table to the right, stopping in the column headed by the interest rate per period, which yields a number called a factor. The factor shows the amount to which an investment of $1 will grow for the periods and the rate involved. To compute future worth of the investment, multiply the number of dollars in the given situation by this factor. For example, suppose your parents tell you that they will invest $8,000 at 12 percent for four years and give you the amount to which this investment will grow if you graduate from college in four years. How much will you receive at the end of four years if the interest rate is 12 percent compounded annually? How much will you receive if the interest rate is 12 percent compounded quarterly?

In Appendix C, Table 1, in the 4 period row in the 12 percent column, you find the factor 1.57352. Multiply the factor by $8,000 to get $12,588.16 as the answer to the first question. Then look for 16 in the Period column and under 3 percent for the needed factor to answer the second question. The factor is 1.60471, and the value of your investment is $12,837.68. The more frequent compounding would add $249.52 ($12,837.68 − $12,588.16) to the value of your investment. The reason for this difference in amounts is that 12 percent compounded quarterly is a higher rate than 12 percent compounded annually.

PRESENT VALUE

Present value is the current worth of a future cash receipt and is essentially the reverse of future worth. In future worth, a sum of money is possessed now and its future worth must be calculated. In present value, rights to future cash receipts are possessed now and their current worth is to be calculated. Future cash receipts are discounted to find their present value. To discount future receipts is to deduct interest from them. If the proper interest rate is used, it should not matter to you whether you have cash in an amount equal to present value or have the rights to the larger amount of future receipts.

Assume that you have the right to receive $1,000 in one year. If the appropriate interest rate is 12 percent compounded annually, what is the present value of this $1,000 future cash receipt? You know that the present value is less than $1,000 because $1,000 due in one year is not worth $1,000 today. You also know that the $1,000 due in one year is equal to some amount, P, plus interest on P at 12 percent for one year. In other words, $P + 0.12P = \$1,000$, and $1.12P = \$1,000$. Dividing $1,000 by 1.12, you get $892.86. If the $1,000 was due in two years, you would find its present value by dividing $892.86 by 1.12 which equals $797.20. Portrayed graphically, present value looks very much like future worth, except for the direction of the arrows (Illustration 17.8).

Appendix C, Table 3, contains present value factors for a number of periods and interest rates. Table 3 is used in the same manner as Table 1. For example, the present value of $1,000 due in four years at 16 percent compounded annually is $552.29, computed as $1,000 × 0.55229. The 0.55229 is the present value factor found in the 4 period row in the 16 percent column.

As another example, suppose that you wish to have $4,000 in three years to pay for a vacation in Europe. If your investment will earn at a 20 percent rate compounded quarterly, how much should you invest now? To find the amount, you would use the present value factor found in Appendix C, Table 3, 12 period row, 5 percent column. This factor is 0.55684, which means that an investment of about 55½ cents today would grow to $1 in 12 periods at 5 percent per period. To have $4,000 at the end of three years, you must invest 4,000 times this factor, or $2,227.36.

Illustration 17.8

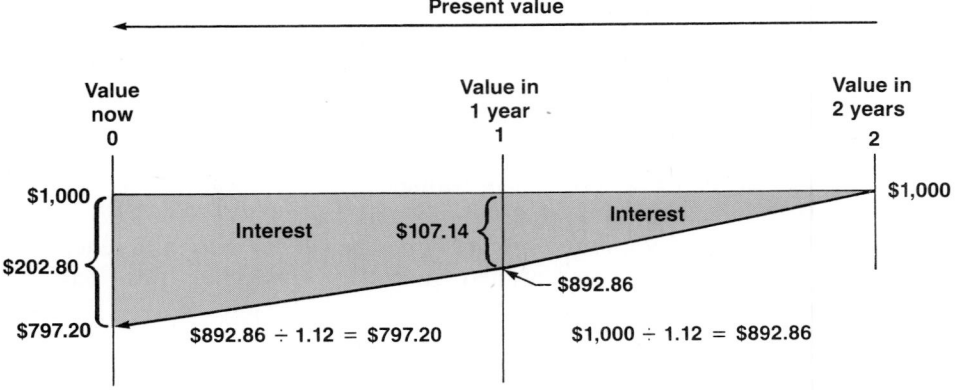

Present value of an annuity

An *annuity* may be defined as a series of equal cash flows (often called rents) spaced equally in time. The semiannual interest payments on a bond form a frequently encountered annuity. The approach to valuing an annuity can be illustrated by finding the present value, at 6 percent per semiannual period, of an annuity calling for the payment of $100 at the end of each of the next three semiannual periods. It would be possible, by use of Appendix C, Table 3, to find the present value of each of the $100 payments as follows:

```
Present value of $100 due in:
  1 period  is 0.94340 × $100 = $ 94.34
  2 periods is 0.89000 × $100 =   89.00
  3 periods is 0.83962 × $100 =   83.96
    Total present value . . . . . . . . . . $267.30
```

Such a procedure could become quite tedious if the annuity consisted of 50 to 100 or more payments. Fortunately, tables are also available showing the present values of an annuity of $1 per period for varying interest rates and periods. See Appendix C, Table 4. A single figure or factor can be obtained from the table which represents the present value of an annuity of $1 per period for three (semiannual) periods at 6 percent per (semiannual) period. The figure is 2.67301, and when multiplied by $100, the number of dollars in each payment, yields the present value of the annuity as $267.30. The present value of an annuity can be presented graphically (Illustration 17.9).

Illustration 17.9 shows that to find the present value of the three $100 cash flows, multiply the $100 by a present value of an annuity factor, 2.67301. The 2.67301 is equal to the sum of the present value factors for $1 due in one period, $1 in two periods, and $1 in three periods. Present value factors, such as the 2.67301, can be found in Appendix C, Table 4, for varying periods and interest rates.

Illustration 17.9

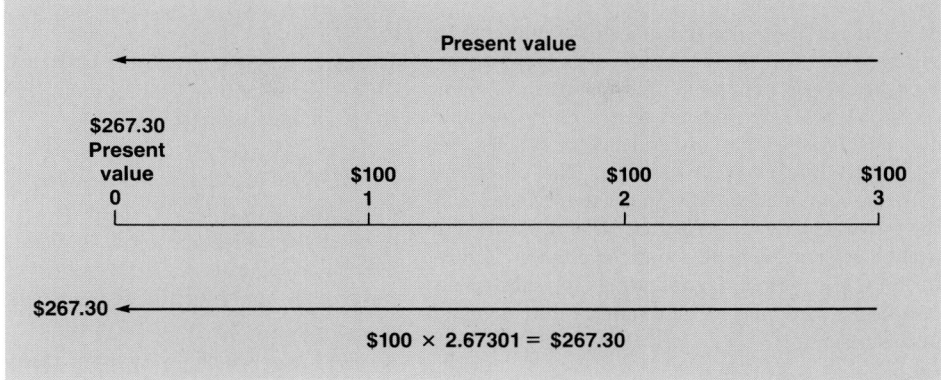

Suppose you won a prize in a lottery that awarded you your choice of $10,000 at the end of each of the next five years, or $35,000 cash immediately. You believe you can earn interest on invested cash at 15 percent per annum. Which option should you choose? To answer the question you should compute the present value of an annuity of $10,000 per period for five years at 15 percent. The present value is $33,521.60, ($10,000 × 3.35216). You should accept the immediate payment of $35,000; since it is the larger present value.

NEW TERMS INTRODUCED IN CHAPTER 17

Annuity
A series of equal cash flows spaced equally in time.

Bearer bond
An unregistered bond, ownership of which transfers by physical delivery.

Bond
A long-term debt owed by its issuer. A **bond certificate** is a negotiable instrument and is the formal, physical evidence of the debt owed.

Bond indenture
The contract or loan agreement under which bonds are issued.

Bond redemption (sinking) fund
A fund used to bring about gradual redemption of a bond issue.

Call premium
The price paid in excess of face value which the issuer of bonds may be required to pay to redeem (call) bonds before their maturity date.

Callable bond
A bond that can be redeemed at the issuer's option prior to maturity date.

Carrying value (of bonds)
The face value of bonds plus unamortized premium or less unamortized discount, if any. Sometimes referred to as **net liability** on the bonds when used for bonds payable.

Compound interest
Interest calculated on the principal plus interest earned in prior periods.

Contract rate of interest
The interest rate printed on the bond certificates and specified in the bond indenture; also called the **stated, coupon,** or **nominal rate.**

Convertible bond
A bond that may be exchanged, at the holder's option, for shares of the issuer's stock.

Coupon bond
A bond not registered as to interest; a bond that carries coupons that are to be clipped and presented for payment of interest due.

Debenture bond
An unsecured bond backed only by the general credit worthiness of its issuer.

Discount (on bonds)
Excess of face value over issue or selling price.

Effective interest rate method (interest method)
A procedure for calculating periodic interest expense (or revenue) in which the first period's interest is computed by multiplying the carrying value of bonds payable (bond investments) by the effective or market rate at the issue date. The difference between computed interest expense (revenue) and the interest paid (received), based on nominal rate times face value, is the discount or premium amortized for the period. Computations for subsequent periods are based on carrying value at the beginning of the period.

Effective interest rate
The interest rate that an investor will earn on a bond investment by paying a specified price for it and the rate of expense a borrower will incur by issuing bonds at that price. Also called **market rate** or **yield rate.**

Face value
Principal amount or maturity amount or value.

Favorable financial leverage
An increase in earnings per share and rate of return on owners' equity resulting from earning a higher rate of return on borrowed funds than the fixed cost of such funds. **Unfavorable financial leverage** results when the cost of borrowed funds exceeds the income they generate, resulting in decreased income to owners.

Future worth or **value**
The amount to which a sum of money invested today will grow in a stated time period at a specified interest rate.

Interest method
See effective interest rate method.

Market interest rate
See effective interest rate.

Marketable equity securities
Readily salable common and preferred stocks of other companies. Classified as current assets if an investment of cash available for current operations; otherwise classified as a long-term (noncurrent) investment.

Mortgage
A legal claim (lien) on a specific property which gives the holder the right to sell the pledged property if its owner fails to make required payments.

A bond secured by a mortgage is called a **mortgage bond.**

Present value
The current worth of a future cash receipt(s); present value is computed by discounting future receipts at a stipulated interest rate.

Premium (on bonds)
Excess of selling or issue price over face value.

Registered bond
A bond for which the owner's name appears on the bond certificate and in the record of bond owners kept by the issuer or its agent, the registrar.

Secured bond
A bond for which specific property has been pledged to ensure its payment.

Serial bonds
Bonds that mature in installments through time.

Simple interest
Interest on principal only.

Stock warrant
A right to purchase shares of the issuer's stock at a stated price for a stated time period.

Straight-line method of amortization
A procedure that, when applied to bond discount or premium, allocates an equal amount of discount or premium to each period in the life of a bond.

Term bond
A bond that matures on the same date as all other bonds in a given bond issue.

Trading on the equity
See favorable financial leverage.

Trustee
Usually a bank or trust company appointed to represent the bondholders in a bond issue and to enforce the provisions of the bond indenture against the issuer.

Underwriter
An investment firm that performs many tasks for the bond issuer in issuing bonds; may also guarantee issuer a fixed price for the bonds.

Unfavorable financial leverage
Results when the cost of borrowed funds exceeds the revenue they generate; it is the reverse of **favorable financial leverage.**

Unsecured bond
A **debenture bond** or, simply, a **debenture.**

DEMONSTRATION PROBLEM 17–1

Following are selected transactions and other data for the Shane Company for 1984:

Transactions:

Mar. 21   Purchased 600 shares of Tay Company common stock at $32.50 per share, plus a $300 broker's commission. Also purchased 100 shares of Raynor Company common stock at $150 per share, plus a $250 broker's commission. Both investments are expected to be temporary.

June   2   Received cash dividends of $2 per share on the Raynor common shares and $1 per share on the Tay common shares.

Aug. 12   Received shares representing a 100 percent stock dividend on the Raynor shares.

     30   Sold 100 shares of Raynor common stock at $80 per share, less a $240 broker's commission.

Sept. 15   Received shares representing a 10 percent stock dividend on the Tay common stock. Market price today was $35 per share.

Nov. 30   Issued $100,000 face value of 8 percent, 10-year bonds. Bonds mature on November 30, 1994, call for semiannual interest payments, and were issued for cash of $87,538, a price that yields an effective rate of 10 percent.

Dec. 31   Per share market values for the two investments in common stock are: Tay, $30.50; and Raynor, $71. Both investments are considered temporary.

Required:

Prepare journal entries to record the above transactions and the necessary adjustments for a December 31 closing. Use the interest method on the bonds.

Solution to demonstration problem 17–1

SHANE COMPANY
GENERAL JOURNAL

1984

Mar. 21   Current Marketable Equity Securities   35,050

          Cash   35,050

          To record purchase of 600 shares of Tay common stock for $19,800 and 100 shares of Raynor common stock for $15,250.

June 2   Cash   800

          Dividend Revenue   800

          To record cash dividends: $600 Tay, and $200 Raynor.

Aug. 12   Received 100 shares of Raynor common stock as a 100 percent stock dividend.

30   Cash   7,760

          Current Marketable Equity Securities   7,625

          Gain on Sale of Current Marketable Equity Securities   135

          To record sale of current marketable equity securities. Proceeds = $8,000 − $240; cost = $15,250/2.

Sept. 15   Received 60 shares of Tay common stock as a 10 percent stock dividend.

Nov. 30   Cash   87,538

        Discount on Bonds Payable   12,462

          Bonds Payable   100,000

          Issued $100,000 face value of bonds at a discount.

Dec. 31   Net Unrealized Loss on Current Marketable Equity Securities .   195

          Allowance for Market Decline of Current Marketable Equity

              Securities   195

          To write current marketable equity securities down to market value:

	Cost	Market
Tay common stock	19,800	$20,130*
Raynor common stock	7,625	7,100†
Total	$27,425	$27,230

          *$30.50 × 660 shares = $20,130.

          †$71.00 × 100 shares = $ 7,100.

31   Bond Interest Expense ($87,538 × 0.10 × $\frac{1}{12}$)   729

          Discount on Bonds Payable   62

          Accrued Bond Interest Payable ($100,000 × 0.08 × $\frac{1}{12}$)   667

          To accrue interest expenses.

DEMONSTRATION PROBLEM 17–2

On November 30, 1984, Martin Company purchased $10,000 face value of the bonds issued by Shane Company (Demonstration Problem 17–1) at a price to yield 10 percent. The bonds are considered a long-term investment by Martin Company which has a fiscal year ending on June 30.

Required:

Prepare journal entries to record the investment in the Shane bonds, the interest collected on May 31, 1985, and to adjust the accounts on June 30, 1985. Use the effective interest method.

Solution to demonstration problem 17–2

MARTIN COMPANY

GENERAL JOURNAL

1984			
Nov. 30	Bond Investments ($87,538 × 0.1)	8,754	
	Cash		8,754
	To record purchase of $10,000 face value of bonds.		
1985			
May 31	Cash ($10,000 × 0.08 × ½)	400	
	Bond Investments	38	
	Interest Revenue ($8,754 × 0.10 × ½)		438
	To record semiannual interest revenue.		
June 30	Accrued Interest Receivable ($10,000 × 0.08 × $\frac{1}{12}$)	67	
	Bond Investments	6	
	Interest Revenue [($8,754 + $38) × 0.10 × $\frac{1}{12}$]		73
	To accrue one month's interest revenue		

QUESTIONS

1. What is meant by the term *trading on the equity*?

2. What are the advantages of obtaining long-term funds by the issuance of bonds rather than additional shares of capital stock? What are the disadvantages?

3. What is a bond indenture? What parties are usually associated with it? Explain why.

4. Explain what is meant by the term *coupon, callable, convertible debenture.*

5. When bonds are issued between interest dates, why is it appropriate that the issuing corporation should receive cash equal to the amount of accrued interest in addition to the issue price of the bonds?

6. Why might it be more accurate to describe a sinking fund as a bond redemption fund?

7. Indicate how each of the following terms should be classified in a balance sheet on December 31, 1984.

a. Cash balance in a sinking fund.
b. Accrued interest on bonds payable.
c. Debenture bonds payable due in 1994.
d. Premium on bonds payable.
e. First-mortgage bonds payable, due July 1, 1985.
f. Discount on bonds payable.
g. First National Bank—Interest account.
h. Convertible bonds payable due in 1987.

8. Why would an investor whose intent is to hold bonds to maturity pay more for the bonds than their face value?

9. Explain the main problem encountered in classifying marketable securities in the balance sheet.

10. Describe the valuation bases used for marketable equity securities.

11. Explain briefly the accounting for stock dividends and stock splits from the investor's point of view.

12. Why is the effective interest rate method of computing periodic interest expense consid- ered theoretically preferable to the straight-line method?

EXERCISES

E–1.   Interest on Martin Corporation's coupon bonds is paid by a trustee, the Third National Bank. Assuming the semiannual interest amounts to $25,000 and all coupons are cashed, prepare the entries to record the deposit of cash for interest with the trustee, the accrual of the interest, and the cashing of the coupons.

E–2.   On July 1, 1984, the Bailey Company issued $100,000 face value of 10-year, 18 percent bonds, dated June 1, 1984, at 100, plus accrued interest. Bailey's fiscal year ends on Sept. 30. Prepare journal entries to record the issuance of these bonds, the accrual of interest at Sept. 30, and the payment of the first semi-annual interest coupon.

E–3.   Wonder Company, with a fiscal year ending on December 31, bought $10,000 face value of the bonds in Exercise E–2. Prepare entries to record the purchase and the receipt of the first six month's interest.

E–4.   On December 31, 1983, Thayer Company issued $200,000 face value of 10-year, 8 percent bonds for cash of $151,862. Assume that this price yields 11 percent. The bonds pay interest semiannually and mature December 31, 1993.

  a.   State which was higher: the effective rate of interest or the nominal rate.
  b.   Compute the bond interest expense for the first six months of 1984 using the interest method.

E–5.   Baxter Company purchased $40,000 of the bonds issued by Thayer Company (Exercise E–4) as a long-term investment. Prepare a journal entry to record the investment. Prepare the entry to record the interest revenue earned on the bonds in the first six months of 1984 using the interest method.

E–6.   Compute the annual interest expense on the bonds in Exercise E–4 and the interest revenue on the bonds in Exercise E–5 assuming the bond discount is amortized under the straight-line method.

E–7.   After recording the payment of the interest coupon due on July 1, 1985, the accounts of the Theis Company showed Bonds Payable of $200,000 and Premium on Bonds Payable of $7,048. The $200,000 face value of five-year, 12 percent bonds, interest payable semiannually on January 1 and July 1, were originally issued to yield 10 percent. Prepare the entry to accrue interest on December 31, 1985. Use the interest method.

E–8.   On April 30, 1985, the end of its fiscal year, Dell Company prepared an adjusting entry to record $4,444 of accrued interest revenue earned on $100,000 face value of 12 percent bonds that were purchased on January 1, 1985, to yield 14 percent. The bonds are dated January 1, 1985, and call for semiannual interest payments on July 1 and January 1. Prepare the entry to record the interest revenue, the discount amortization, and the collection of interest on July 1, 1985.

E–9.   On June 30, 1985 (a semiannual interest payment date), Duke Company redeemed all of its $100,000 face value of 10 percent bonds outstanding by calling them at 105.

The bonds were originally issued on June 30, 1981, at 100. Prepare entries to record the payment of the interest and the redemption of the bonds on June 30, 1985.

E–10.   After interest was paid on September 30, 1985, $10,000 face value of the Burns Company's $100,000 face value of outstanding bonds were converted into 2,000 shares of the company's $2 par value common stock. Prepare the entry to record the conversion assuming the bonds were issued at 100.

E–11.   The Wixon Company, pursuant to provisions of its bond indenture, acquired $20,000 of its outstanding bonds on the open market at 97 plus accrued interest. These bonds were originally issued at face value and carry a 6 percent interest rate payable semiannually. The acquisition was made on September 1, 1984, and the bonds are dated December 1, 1973. Prepare the entries required to record the acquisition and the accrual of the interest to the acquisition date on the bonds acquired.

E–12.   The K Company is required to make a deposit of $40,000 plus accrued interest of $1,200 on April 30, 1983, to the trustee of its sinking fund so that the trustee can redeem $40,000 of K's bonds on May 1, 1983. Prepare the entries required on April 30 to record the interest accrual and sinking fund deposit and the entries on May 1 to record the bond retirement, payment of interest, and payment of trustee expenses assuming the latter amount to be $125. (The bonds were issued at 100.)

E–13.   Wells Company purchased 100 shares of Tinker Company stock at a total cost of $1,050 on July 1, 1984. At the end of the accounting year (December 31, 1984), the market value for these shares was $950. By December 31, 1985, the market value had risen to $1,100. This is the only marketable equity security that Wells Company owns. The company classifies the securities as current assets. Give the entries which would be necessary at the date of purchase and at December 31, 1984, and 1985.

E–14.   Bentley Company purchased on July 1, 1984, 100 shares of Pool Company capital stock at $47 per share plus a commission of $50. On July 15, a 10 percent stock dividend was received. Bentley received a cash dividend of 50 cents per share on August 12, 1984. On November 1, Bentley sold all of the above shares for $58 per share, less a commission of $55. Prepare entries to record all of the above transactions in Bentley Company's accounts.

E–15.   The Delex Company has marketable equity securities which have a market value at year end that is $800 below their cost. Give the required entry if—

   a.   The securities are current assets.
   b.   The securities are noncurrent assets and the loss is considered to be temporary.
   c.   The securities are noncurrent assets and the loss is considered to be permanent.
   d.   State where each of the accounts debited in (a), (b), and (c) would be reported.

E–16.   On July 1, 1984, Toy Company purchased as a temporary investment $20,000 face value of Rome Company's 12 percent bonds at 101, plus $400 of accrued interest from May 1, and a $140 broker's commission.
   On October 1, 1984, Toy sold the Rome bonds at 102.5, plus accrued interest of $1,000, and less a $140 broker's commission.
   Prepare journal entries on Toy Company's books to record the purchase and sale of the Rome Company bonds.

E–17. (Based on the Appendix)

Conceptually, what is the present worth of a lump-sum payment of $10,000 due in five years? If the going market rate of interest on investments of this type is 10 percent per year and the present value of $1 due in five years at 10 percent is 0.62092, what is its specific worth?

E–18. (Based on the Appendix)

Conceptually, what is the present worth of a series of semiannual payments of $1,000 due at the end of each six months of the next five years? If the going market rate of interest on investments of this type is 10 percent per year and the present value of an annuity of $1 for 10 periods at 5 percent is 7.72173, what is its specific worth?

PROBLEMS, SERIES A

P17–1–A.   Baker Company is seeking to issue $100,000 face value of 10 percent, 15-year bonds. The bonds are dated June 30, 1984; call for semiannual interest payments; and mature on June 30, 1999.

Required:

a.   Compute the price investors should offer if they seek a yield of 8 percent on these bonds. Also, compute the first six months' interest assuming the bonds are issued at this price. Use the interest method.

b.   Repeat part (*a*) assuming investors seek a yield of 12 percent.

P17–2–A.   On July 1, 1984, Remy Corporation issued $100,000 face value of 10 percent, 10-year bonds. The bonds call for semiannual interest payments and mature on July 1, 1994. Remy received cash of $88,530, a price that yields 12 percent.

On September 30, 1984, Remy also borrowed $50,000 on a 10-year mortgage note that called for 40 equal quarterly payments of $2,261. The note bears interest at 12 percent per year.

Required:

Assume that Remy's fiscal year ends on March 31. Prepare entries to record the bond interest expense on January 1, 1985, and the adjustment needed on March 31, 1985, using the interest method. Also, prepare entries to record the first two quarterly payments on the mortgage note.

P17–3–A.   On June 1, 1984, Ackerman Corporation issued $900,000 of 10-year, 16 percent bonds dated April 1, 1984, at 100. Interest on the bonds is payable semiannually upon presentation of the appropriate coupon. All of the bonds are of $1,000 denomination. The company's accounting period ends on June 30, with semiannual statements prepared on December 31 and June 30.

All of the first coupons on the bonds are presented to the company's bank and paid by October 2, 1984. All but two of the second coupons on the bonds are similarly received and paid on April 1, 1985.

Required:

a.   Prepare all necessary journal entries for the above transactions through April 1, 1985, including the adjusting entry needed at June 30, 1984.

b.   Allen Company purchased $300,000 of Ackerman Corporation's bonds on June 1, 1984, as a long-term investment. The company prepares financial statements on September 30. Prepare all journal entries for Allen Company relating to the bonds through September 30, 1984.

P17–4–A. Prior Company issued $100,000 face value of 15 percent, 20-year bonds on October 1, 1984. The bonds are dated October 1, 1984, call for semiannual interest payments on April 1 and October 1, and are issued to yield 16 percent (8 percent per period).

Required:

    a. Compute the amount received for the bonds.

    b. Prepare an amortization schedule similar to that shown in Illustration 17.2. Enter data in the schedule for only the first two interest periods. Use the interest method.

    c. Prepare journal entries to record issuance of the bonds, the first six months' interest expense on the bonds, and the adjustment needed on May 31, 1985, assuming Prior's fiscal year ends on that date.

P17–5–A. Hind Company purchased $40,000 face value of the Prior Company bonds (Problem P17–4–A) when they were issued on October 1, 1984, as a long-term investment.

Required:

    a. Prepare entries to record purchase of the bonds, receipt of the first six months' interest, and the adjustment needed on June 30, 1985, assuming a fiscal year ended on that date. Use the interest method.

    b. Assume that the Hind Company sold all of these bonds on October 1, 1994, for cash of $39,800, after detaching the interest coupon due on this date. The bonds have a carrying value, properly adjusted to date, of $38,054. Prepare the journal entry to record the sale.

P17–6–A. Stanton Company issued $100,000 face value of 18 percent, 20-year bonds on October 1, 1984. The bonds are dated October 1, 1984, call for semiannual interest payments on April 1 and October 1, and are issued to yield 16 percent (8 percent per period).

Required:

    a. Compute the amount received for the bonds.

    b. Prepare an amortization schedule similar to that shown in Illustration 17.3. Enter data in the schedule for only the first two interest periods. Use the interest method.

    c. Prepare entries to record the issuance of the bonds, the first six months' interest on the bonds, and the adjustment needed on June 30, 1985, assuming Stanton's fiscal year ends on that date.

P17–7–A. Orchard Corporation purchased $30,000 face value of the Stanton bonds (Problem P17–6–A) when they were issued on October 1, 1984, as a long-term investment.

Required:

    a. Prepare journal entries to record the purchase of the bonds, the receipt of the first six months' interest, and the adjustment needed on June 30, 1985, assuming a fiscal year ending on that date. Use the interest method.

    b. Assume that on October 1, 1994, Stanton called all of the bonds at 105. Orchard received a check for $34,200, including $2,700 as payment of the semiannual interest due on this date. Prepare the entry to record the receipt of the $34,200. The properly adjusted carrying value of the bonds on this date was $32,959.

P17–8–A.   Wilkerson Company issued $200,000 of 16 percent serial bonds on July 1, 1984, at face value. The bonds are dated July 1, 1984; call for semiannual interest payments on July 1 and January 1; and mature at the rate of $40,000 per year, with the first maturity falling on July 1, 1989. The company's accounting period ends on September 30.

Required:

Prepare journal entries to record the interest payment of July 1, 1989; the maturing of $40,000 of bonds on July 1, 1989; and the adjusting entry needed on September 30, 1989. Also, show how the bonds will be presented in the company's balance sheet for September 30, 1989.

P17–9–A.   On September 1, 1984, Landry Company purchased the following securities as long-term investments:

1. One thousand shares of Hi-Flyer Company capital stock at $61 plus broker's commission of $400.
2. Five hundred shares of Turkey Company capital stock at $98 plus broker's commission of $350.

Cash dividends of $1.25 per share on the Hi-Flyer capital stock and $1 per share on the Turkey capital stock were received on December 7 and December 10, respectively.

Market prices at December 31, 1984, are Hi-Flyer stock, $64; and Turkey stock, $91.

Required:

a.   Prepare journal entries to record the above transactions.

b.   Prepare the necessary adjusting entry(ies) at December 31, 1984, to adjust the carrying values assuming that market price changes are believed to be permanent.

c.   Repeat part (b), assuming the changes in market prices are expected to be temporary.

P17–10–A.   Muddy Waters, Inc., purchased on July 2, 1983, 100 shares of East Company $50 par value common stock at $80 per share, plus a commission of $60. A 20 percent stock dividend was received on December 15, 1984.

On July 15, 1985, a cash dividend of $1 per share was received. On September 15, 1985, the East Company split its $50 par value common shares two for one.

On November 2, 1985, Waters sold 100 shares of East common stock at $50, less commissions and taxes of $40.

Required:

a.   Prepare journal entries to record all of the above 1985 transactions.

b.   How would you recommend that the remaining shares be classified in the December 31, 1985, balance sheet if still held at that date?

c.   Assume the shares were considered current assets at the end of 1983, at which time their market value was $78 per share. At the end of 1984, the shares had a market value of 65¾. Prepare any necessary adjusting entries for the end of 1983 and 1984.

PROBLEMS, SERIES B

P17–1–B.   Barton Company is seeking to issue $100,000 face value of 10 percent, 20-year bonds. The bonds are dated June 30, 1984, call for semiannual interest payments, and mature on June 30, 2004.

Required:

   a.   Compute the price investors should offer if they seek a yield of 8 percent on these bonds. Also, compute the first six months' interest assuming the bonds are issued at that price. Use the interest method.

   b.   Repeat part (a) assuming investors seek a yield of 12 percent.

P17–2–B.   On July 1, 1984, Barry Corporation issued $100,000 face value of 8 percent, 10-year bonds. The bonds call for semiannual interest payments and mature on July 1, 1994. Barry received cash of $87,538, a price that yields 10 percent.

   On September 30, 1984, Barry also borrowed $50,000 on a 10-year mortgage note that called for 40 equal quarterly payments of $1,992. The note bears interest at 10 percent per year.

Required:

   Assume that Barry's fiscal year ends on March 31. Prepare entries to record the bond interest expense on January 1, 1985, and the adjustment needed on March 31, 1985, using the interest method. Also, prepare entries to record the first two quarterly payments on the mortgage note.

P17–3–B.   On December 1, 1984, Brooks Company issued $500,000 of 10-year, 18 percent bonds dated July 1, 1984, at 100. Interest on the bonds is payable semiannually on July 1 and January 1. All of the bonds are registered. The company's accounting period ends on March 31. Quarterly financial statements are prepared.

   The company deposits a sum of money sufficient to pay the semiannual interest on the bonds in a special checking account in the First National Bank and draws interest payment checks upon this account. The deposit is made the day before the checks are drawn.

Required:

   a.   Prepare journal entries to record the issuance of the bonds; the December 31 adjusting entry; the January 1, 1985, interest payment; and the adjusting entry needed on March 31, 1985.

   b.   The Brown Corporation bought $100,000 of the Brooks Company bonds on December 1, 1984, as a long-term investment. The company's year end is December 31. Prepare all journal entries for Brown Corporation for these bonds through December 31, 1984.

P17–4–B.   Johnson Company issued $100,000 face value of 16 percent, 20-year bonds on July 1, 1984. The bonds are dated July 1, 1984, call for semiannual interest payments on July 1 and January 1, and were issued to yield 12 percent (6 percent per period).

Required:

   a.   Compute the amount received for the bonds.

   b.   Prepare an amortization schedule similar to that shown in Illustration 17.3. Enter data in the schedule for only the first two interest periods. Use the interest method.

c. Prepare journal entries to record issuance of the bonds, the first six months' interest expense on the bonds, and the adjustment needed on May 31, 1985, assuming Johnson's fiscal year ends on that date.

P17–5–B.　　Hanes Company purchased $40,000 face value of the Johnson Company bonds (Problem P17–4–B) when they were issued on July 1, 1984, as a long-term investment.

Required:

a. Prepare entries to record purchase of the bonds, receipt of the first six months' interest, and the adjustment needed on June 30, 1985, assuming a fiscal year ended on that date. Use the interest method.

b. Assume that the Hanes Company sold all of these bonds on July 1, 1994, for cash of $48,000 after detaching the interest coupon due on this date. The bonds have a carrying value, properly adjusted to date, of $49,176. Prepare the journal entry to record the sale.

P17–6–B.　　Boston Company issued $100,000 face value of 10 percent, 20-year bonds on July 1, 1984. The bonds are dated July 1, 1984, call for semiannual interest payments on July 1 and January 1, and are issued to yield 12 percent (6 percent per period).

Required:

a. Compute the amount received for the bonds.

b. Prepare an amortization schedule similar to that shown in Illustration 17.2. Enter data in the schedule for only the first two interest periods. Use the interest method.

c. Prepare entries to record the issuance of the bonds, the first six months' interest on the bonds, and the adjustment needed on June 30, 1985, assuming Boston's fiscal year ends on that date.

P17–7–B.　　Tarwell Corporation purchased $20,000 face value of the Boston bonds (Problem P17–6–B) when they were issued on July 1, 1984, as a long-term investment.

Required:

a. Prepare journal entries to record the purchase of the bonds, the receipt of the first six months' interest, and the adjustment needed on June 30, 1985, assuming a fiscal year ending on that date. Use the interest method.

b. Assume that on July 1, 1994, Boston called all of the bonds at 105. Tarwell received a check for $22,000 including $1,000 as payment of the semiannual interest coupons due on this date. Prepare the entry to record the receipt of the $22,000. The properly adjusted carrying value of the bonds on this date was $17,706.

P17–8–B.　　Knobloch Company issued $200,000 of 18 percent bonds on July 1, 1984, at face value. The bonds are dated July 1, 1984, call for semiannual interest payments on July 1 and January 1; and mature at the rate of $20,000 per year on July 1, beginning in 1989. The company's accounting period ends on September 30.

Required:

a. Prepare journal entries to record the interest expense and payment for the six months ending July 1, 1989; the maturing of the bonds on July 1, 1989; and the adjusting entries needed on September 30, 1989.

b. Show how the bonds will be presented in the company's balance sheet for September 30, 1989.

P17–9–B.   The Bruns Company acquired on July 15, 1984, 200 shares of Reetz Company $100 par value capital stock at $97 per share plus a broker's commission of $120. On August 1, 1984, Bruns Company received a cash dividend of 60 cents per share. On November 3, 1984, it sold 100 of these shares at $105 per share less a broker's commission of $80. On December 1, 1984, the Reetz Company issued shares comprising a 100 percent stock dividend declared on its capital stock on November 18.

On December 31, 1984, the end of the calendar-year accounting period, the market quotation for Reetz's common stock was $46 per share. The decline was considered to be permanent.

Required:

a. Prepare journal entries to record all of the above data assuming the securities are considered temporary investments and are to be valued at the lower of cost or market.

b. If the remaining shares are to be held for affiliation purposes—Reetz Company has become a major customer—indicate how they should be shown in the balance sheet.

P17–10–B.   The Bryan Company purchased the following common stocks at per share prices that included commissions on October 27, 1983:

300 shares of Aye Company common stock @ $60	$18,000
500 shares of Bee Company common stock @ $40	$20,000
800 shares of Cey Company common stock @ $20	$16,000
	$54,000

On December 31, 1983, the market prices per share of the above common stocks were Aye, $62; Bee, $38; and Cey, $15.

Summarized, the cash dividends per share received in 1984 were Aye, $2; Bee, $1; and Cey, $0.75. Also, a 100 percent stock dividend (300 shares) was received on the Aye Company common stock after the cash dividend was paid.

On December 31, 1984, the per share market prices were Aye, $34; Bee, $32; and Cey, $20.

All of the changes in market prices given above are considered temporary.

Required:

a. Prepare journal entries for all of the above, including calendar year-end adjusting entries, assuming the shares of common stock acquired are considered short-term investments.

b. If the securities acquired were considered long-term investments, how would the entries made in (*a*) differ?

c. For both parts (*a*) and (*b*), give the descriptions (titles) and the dollar amounts of the items that would appear in the income statements for 1983 and 1984.

BUSINESS DECISION PROBLEM 17–1

A company is trying to decide whether to invest $2,000,000 on plant expansion and $1,000,000 to finance a related increase in inventories and accounts receivable. The $3,000,000 expansion is expected to increase business volume substantially. Profit forecasts indicate that net income from operations will rise from $1,600,000 to $2,200,000. The income tax rate will be about 40 percent. Net income last year was $915,000. Interest expense on debt now outstanding is $70,000 per year. There are 200,000 shares of common stock currently outstanding.

The $3,000,000 needed can be obtained in two alternative ways:

1. Finance entirely by issuing additional shares of common stock at an expected issue price of $75 per share.
2. Finance two thirds with bonds, one third with additional stock. The bonds would have a 20-year life, bear interest at 10 percent, and would sell at face value. The issue price of the stock would be $80 per share.

Required:

Should the investment be made? If so, which financing plan would you recommend? (Hint: Calculate earnings per share for last year and for future years under each of the alternatives.)

BUSINESS DECISION PROBLEM 17–2

Part 1. You are an investor in stocks and bonds of various companies. An account executive of a brokerage firm has brought the following bonds to your attention:

1. X Company bonds—remaining life 12 years, interest rate 6 percent, payable semiannually. Price: $640 per $1,000 bond.
2. Q Company bonds—remaining life, 13 years, interest rate 15 percent, payable semiannually. Price: $1,180 per $1,000 bond.

From a study of available alternatives, you reach the conclusion that either of these bonds would be a suitable investment if the yield were 12 percent.

Required:

In which of the above bonds should you invest, if either? Explain.

Part 2. You are the CPA engaged to audit the records of the Brown Company. You find that your client has a portfolio of marketable equity securities that have a market value (in total) that is $50,000 less than the total cost of the portfolio. You ask the vice president for finance if the client expects to sell these securities in the coming year. He answers that he doesn't know. The securities will be sold if additional cash is needed to finance operations. When you ask for a cash forecast, you are told that one has been prepared that covers the next year. It shows no need to sell the marketable securities.

Required:

How would you recommend that the client's portfolio of marketable securities be classified in the balance sheet? Why? Does it really make any difference whether the securities are classified as current or noncurrent? Explain.

Chapter 18

Corporations: Consolidated financial statements

CHAPTER GOALS

After study of this chapter, you should be able to:

1. Describe the nature of parent and subsidiary corporations.
2. Distinguish between the cost and equity methods of accounting for stock investments by the parent.
3. Prepare consolidated financial statements through the use of a consolidated statement work sheet.
4. Identify the difference between purchase accounting and pooling of interests accounting.
5. Describe the uses and limitations of consolidated financial statements.
6. Define and use correctly the new terms in the glossary.

Many companies have expanded in recent years by purchasing all or a part of another company. The purpose of such acquisitions ranges from seeking to ensure a source of raw materials (such as oil), enter a new industry, or receive income on the investment. Thus, a corporation might own a majority (more than 50 percent) of the outstanding voting common stock of a second corporation. In such cases, both corporations exist as separate legal entities. The corporation which owns more than 50 percent of the outstanding voting common stock of another corporation is referred to as the *parent company.* The corporation acquired and controlled by the parent company is known as the *subsidiary company.*

A parent company and its subsidiaries each maintains its own accounting records and prepares its own financial statements. But, since the parent and its subsidiaries are *controlled* by a central management and are related to each other, the parent company usually is *required* to prepare one set of financial statements as if the parent and its subsidiaries taken together were a single enterprise. The term *consolidated statements* refers to financial statements that result from combining the parent's financial statement amounts with those of its subsidiaries. Preparation of consolidated statements is discussed in this chapter. Consolidated statements *must be prepared* when (1) one company owns a majority (more than 50 percent) of the outstanding voting common stock of another company, and (2) the two companies are not in markedly dissimilar businesses, such as a bank and a manufacturer.

Eliminations

Financial transactions involving a parent and one of its subsidiaries or between two of the subsidiaries are called *intercompany transactions.* In preparing consolidated financial statements, intercompany transactions must be eliminated by making elimination entries. *Elimination entries* are made on a consolidated statement work sheet and are necessary to remove certain intercompany items and transactions. Elimination entries allow the presentation of all account balances as if the parent and its subsidiaries were a single economic enterprise. *Elimination entries are made only on a consolidated statement work sheet, not in the accounting records of the parent or subsidiaries.* After elimination entries are prepared, the amounts remaining for each account on the work sheet are totaled and used to prepare the consolidated financial statements.

One elimination entry offsets the parent company's subsidiary investment account against the stockholders' equity accounts of the subsidiary. Assume Y Company organized the Z Company, receiving all of Z Company's $100,000 par value common stock for $100,000 cash. The parent records the following entry on its books:

Investment in Z Company	100,000	
Cash		100,000
To record an investment in Z Company. Purchased 100 percent of Z Company stock.		

The subsidiary records the entry as follows on its books:

Cash 100,000
    Common Stock 100,000
    To record the issuance of all of the common stock to Y Company.

When the consolidated balance sheet is prepared, the required elimination on the work sheet is:

Common Stock—Z Company 100,000
    Investment in Z Company 100,000

This elimination is required because the parent company's investment in the stock of the subsidiary actually represents an equity in the net assets of the subsidiary. Unless the investment is eliminated, the same resources will appear twice on the consolidated balance sheet: First as the investment account and second as the assets of the subsidiary. The elimination of Z's common stock is necessary to avoid double counting stockholders' equity. Viewing the two companies as if they were one, the Z Company common stock is really not outstanding; it is held within the consolidated group.

Intercompany receivables and payables (due from and owed to companies in the consolidated group) are items which also must be eliminated during the preparation of consolidated statements. For example, assume a parent company owes a subsidiary $5,000 as evidenced by a $5,000 note receivable on the subsidiary's books and a $5,000 note payable on the parent's books. These balances would be eliminated by offsetting the note receivable against the note payable. No debt is owed to, or due from, any entity outside the consolidated enterprise. Since consolidated statements present financial data as though the companies were a single entity, no amount can be owed to or receivable from itself. Similarly, other intercompany balances would be eliminated when consolidated statements are prepared.

CONSOLIDATED BALANCE SHEET AT TIME OF ACQUISITION

Acquisition of subsidiary at book value

To combine assets and liabilities of a parent company and its subsidiaries, a consolidated statement work sheet similar to the one shown in Illustration 18.1 is prepared. A *consolidated statement work sheet* is an informal statement on which elimination entries are made for the purpose of showing account balances as if the parent and its subsidiaries were a single economic enterprise. The first two columns of the work sheet show assets, liabilities, and stockholders' equity of the parent and subsidiary as they appear on each corporation's individual balance sheet. The pair of columns labeled Eliminations allows intercompany items to be offset and consequently eliminated from the consolidated statement. The final column shows the amounts that will appear on the consolidated balance sheet.

This particular work sheet (Illustration 18.1) was prepared to consolidate the accounts of P Company and its subsidiary, S Company, on January 1,

Illustration 18.1: Work sheet for consolidated sheet

P COMPANY AND SUBSIDIARY S COMPANY
Work Sheet for Consolidated Balance Sheet
January 1, 1984 (date of acquisition)

	P Company	S Company	Eliminations Debit	Eliminations Credit	Consolidated Amounts
Assets					
Cash	26,000	12,000			38,000
Notes receivable	5,000			(b) 5,000	
Accounts receivable, net	24,000	15,000			39,000
Inventory	35,000	30,000			65,000
Investment in S Company	106,000			(a) 106,000	
Equipment, net	41,000	15,000			56,000
Buildings, net	65,000	35,000			100,000
Land	20,000	10,000			30,000
	322,000	117,000			328,000
Liabilities and Stockholders' Equity					
Accounts payable	18,000	6,000			24,000
Notes payable		5,000	(b) 5,000		
Common stock	250,000	100,000	(a) 100,000		250,000
Retained earnings	54,000	6,000	(a) 6,000		54,000
	322,000	117,000	111,000	111,000	328,000

1984. P Company acquired S Company on January 1, 1984, by purchasing all of its outstanding voting common stock for $106,000 cash, which was the *book value* of the stock. Book value is equal to stockholders' equity, or net assets. Thus, common stock ($100,000) plus retained earnings ($6,000) equals $106,000. When P Company acquired the S Company stock, P Company made the following entry:

Investment in S Company 106,000
   Cash 106,000
   To record investment in S Company.

Two elimination entries are required in this example. The investment appears as an asset on P Company's balance sheet. By buying the subsidiary's stock, the parent acquired a 100 percent equity or ownership interest in the subsidiary's net assets. Thus, if both the investment account and the subsidiary's assets appear on the consolidated balance sheet, the same resources will be counted twice. The Common Stock and Retained Earnings accounts of the subsidiary also represent an equity interest in the subsidiary's assets. Therefore, P's investment in S Company must be offset against S Company's stockholders' equity accounts so that the subsidiary's assets and the ownership interest in these assets appear only once on the consolidated statement. This elimination is accomplished by entry (*a*) on the work sheet. The entry debits S Company's Common Stock for $100,000 and Retained Earnings for $6,000 and credits Investment in S Company for $106,000. In journal entry form the elimination entry is:

```
Common Stock ..........................................    100,000
Retained Earnings ......................................      6,000
    Investment in S Company ...............................            106,000
    To eliminate original investment account and subsidiary stockholders'
    equity.
```

Entry (*b*) is required to eliminate the effect of an intercompany transaction (intercompany debt in this case). On the date it acquired S Company, P Company loaned S Company $5,000. The loan is recorded as a $5,000 note receivable on P's books and a $5,000 note payable on S's books. If the elimination entry is not made on the work sheet, the consolidated balance sheet will show $5,000 owed to the consolidated enterprise *by itself.* From the viewpoint of the consolidated entity, neither an asset nor a liability exists. Therefore, entry (*b*) is made on the work sheet to eliminate both the asset and liability. The entry debits Notes Payable and credits Notes Receivable for $5,000. In journal entry form, entry (*b*) is:

```
Notes Payable ..........................................      5,000
    Notes Receivable .......................................              5,000
    To eliminate intercompany debt.
```

In making elimination entries, it is important to understand that *the entries are made only on the consolidated statement work sheet; no elimination entries are made in the accounting records of either P Company or S Company.*

Acquisition of subsidiary at a cost above or below book value

In the previous illustration, P Company acquired 100 percent of S Company at a cost equal to book value. In some cases, subsidiaries may be acquired at a cost greater than or less than book value. For example, assume P Company purchases 100 percent of S Company's outstanding voting common stock for $125,000. The book value of this stock is $106,000. Cost exceeds book value by $19,000. P Company's management may have paid more than book value because it believed: (1) the subsidiary's earnings prospects justify paying a price greater than book value, or (2) the total fair value of the subsidiary's assets exceeds their total book value.

According to the Accounting Principles Board (*APB Opinion No. 16*), in cases where cost exceeds book value because of expected above-average earnings, the excess should be labeled goodwill on the consolidated balance sheet. *Goodwill* is an intangible value attaching to a business primarily due to above-average earnings prospects. On the other hand, if the excess is attributable to the belief that assets of the subsidiary are undervalued, then the asset values should be increased to the extent of the excess.[1] In Illustration 18.2,

---

[1] *APB Accounting Principles* (Chicago: Commerce Clearing House, Inc., 1973), vol. II, p. 6655.

Illustration 18.2: Work sheet for consolidated balance sheet

P COMPANY AND SUBSIDIARY S COMPANY
Work Sheet for Consolidated Balance Sheet
January 1, 1984 (date of acquisition)

	P Company	S Company	Eliminations Debit	Eliminations Credit	Consolidated Amounts
Assets					
Cash	7,000	12,000			19,000
Notes receivable	5,000			(b) 5,000	
Accounts receivable, net	24,000	15,000			39,000
Inventory	35,000	30,000			65,000
Investment in S Company	125,000			(a) 125,000	
Equipment, net	41,000	15,000			56,000
Buildings, net	65,000	35,000			100,000
Land	20,000	10,000	(a) 4,000		34,000
Goodwill			(a) 15,000		15,000
	322,000	117,000			328,000
Liabilities and Stockholders' Equity					
Accounts payable	18,000	6,000			24,000
Notes payable		5,000	(b) 5,000		
Common stock	250,000	100,000	(a) 100,000		250,000
Retained earnings	54,000	6,000	(a) 6,000		54,000
	322,000	117,000	130,000	130,000	328,000

it is assumed that $15,000 of the excess of cost over book value is attributable to expected above-average earnings, and the remaining $4,000 is due to the undervaluation of land. As a result, $4,000 of the $19,000 excess is added to Land, and the other $15,000 is identified as goodwill on the work sheet and on the balance sheet (Illustration 18.3).

The goodwill is established as part of the first elimination entry. Elimination entry (a) in Illustration 18.2 involves debits to the subsidiary's common stock for $100,000 and retained earnings for $6,000 and a credit to the parent's investment account for $125,000. Land is debited for $4,000, and Goodwill is debited for $15,000. In journal entry form, entry (a) is:

```
Common Stock ..............................................  100,000
Retained Earnings .........................................    6,000
Land ......................................................    4,000
Goodwill ..................................................   15,000
    Investment in S Company ...............................            125,000
    To eliminate original investment and subsidiary stockholders' equity
    and to establish the increased value of land and the goodwill.
```

Illustration 18.3:   Consolidated balance sheet

P COMPANY AND SUBSIDIARY S COMPANY
Consolidated Balance Sheet
January 1, 1984

Assets

Current assets:

Cash	$ 19,000	
Accounts receivable, net	39,000	
Inventory	65,000	
Total current assets		$123,000

Property, plant, and equipment:

Equipment, net	$ 56,000	
Buildings, net	100,000	
Land	34,000	
Total property, plant, and equipment		190,000
Goodwill		15,000
Total assets		$328,000

Liabilities and Stockholders' Equity

Current liabilities:

Accounts payable		$ 24,000

Stockholders' equity:

Common stock	$250,000	
Retained earnings	54,000	
Total stockholders' equity		304,000
Total liabilities and stockholders' equity		$328,000

Entry (*b*) is the same as elimination entry (*b*) in Illustration 18.1. Entry (*b*) eliminates the intercompany loan by debiting Notes Payable and crediting Notes Receivable for $5,000. After these elimination entries are made, the remaining amounts are combined and extended to the column labeled "Consolidated Amounts." The amounts in this column are then used to prepare the consolidated balance sheet shown in Illustration 18.3. Notice that the $15,000 debit to Goodwill is carried to the Consolidated Amounts column. The $15,000 goodwill appears as an asset in the consolidated balance sheet.

Under some circumstances, a parent company may pay less than book value of the subsidiary's net assets. In such cases, it is highly unlikely that a "bargain" purchase has been made. The most logical explanation for the price paid is that some of the subsidiary's assets are overvalued. The Accounting Principles Board requires that the excess of book value over cost be used to reduce proportionately the value of the noncurrent assets acquired.[2]

Acquisition of less than 100 percent of subsidiary

Sometimes a parent company acquires less than 100 percent of the outstanding voting common stock of a subsidiary. For example, assume P Company acquires 80 percent of S Company's outstanding voting common stock.

---

[2] Ibid., p. 6655.

P Company is the majority stockholder, but minority stockholders exist who own 20 percent of the stock. The claim or interest of the stockholders who own less than 50 percent of a subsidiary's outstanding voting common stock (minority stockholders) is called the *minority interest.* Minority stockholders have an interest in the subsidiary's net assets and share subsidiary earnings with the parent company.

Illustration 18.4 shows the elimination entries that are required when P Company purchases 80 percent of S Company's stock for $90,000. The book value of the stock acquired by P Company is $84,800 (80 percent of $106,000). The excess of cost ($90,000) over book value ($84,800) amounts to $5,200, which can be attributed to S Company's above-average earnings prospects.

The first elimination entry (*a*) eliminates S Company's stockholders' equity by debiting Common Stock for $100,000 and Retained Earnings for $6,000. Minority interest is established by crediting a Minority Interest account for $21,200 (20 percent of $106,000). The investment account is eliminated by crediting Investment in S Company for $90,000. The debit required to

Illustration 18.4: Work sheet for consolidated balance sheet

P COMPANY AND SUBSIDIARY S COMPANY
Work Sheet for Consolidated Balance Sheet
January 1, 1984 (date of acquisition)

	P Company	S Company	Eliminations Debit	Eliminations Credit	Consolidated Amounts
Assets					
Cash	42,000	12,000			54,000
Notes receivable	5,000			(*b*) 5,000	
Accounts receivable, net	24,000	15,000			39,000
Inventory	35,000	30,000			65,000
Investment in S Company	90,000			(*a*) 90,000	
Equipment, net	41,000	15,000			56,000
Buildings, net	65,000	35,000			100,000
Land	20,000	10,000			30,000
Goodwill			(*a*) 5,200		5,200
	322,000	117,000			349,200
Liabilities and Stockholders' Equity					
Accounts payable	18,000	6,000			24,000
Notes payable		5,000	(*b*) 5,000		
Common stock	250,000	100,000	(*a*) 100,000		250,000
Retained earnings	54,000	6,000	(*a*) 6,000		54,000
Minority interest				(*a*) 21,200	21,200
	322,000	117,000	116,200	116,200	349,200

Illustration 18.5:   Consolidated balance sheet

P COMPANY AND SUBSIDIARY S COMPANY
Consolidated Balance Sheet
January 1, 1984

Assets

Current assets:

Cash	$ 54,000	
Accounts receivable, net	39,000	
Inventory	65,000	
Total current assets		$158,000

Property, plant, and equipment:

Equipment, net	$ 56,000	
Buildings, net	100,000	
Land	30,000	
Total property, plant, and equipment		186,000
Goodwill		5,200
Total assets		$349,200

Liabilities and Stockholders' Equity

Liabilities:

Accounts payable		$ 24,000
Minority interest		21,200

Stockholders' equity:

Common stock	$250,000	
Retained earnings	54,000	
Total stockholders' equity		304,000
Total liabilities and stockholders' equity		$349,200

make the debits equal the credits is $5,200. The $5,200 is debited to Goodwill. In journal entry form, entry (*a*) is:

Common Stock	100,000	
Retained Earnings	6,000	
Goodwill	5,200	
Investment in S Company		90,000
Minority Interest		21,200

To eliminate original investment and subsidiary's stockholders' equity and to establish the minority interest and goodwill.

On the consolidated balance sheet (Illustration 18.5), minority interest appears between the liabilities and stockholders' equity sections. Actually, there is some disagreement among accountants as to whether minority interest is a liability or part of stockholders' equity.

The second elimination entry (*b*) is the same as in preceding illustrations. The entry eliminates intercompany debt by debiting Notes Payable and crediting Notes Receivable for $5,000.

ACCOUNTING FOR EARNINGS, LOSSES, AND DIVIDENDS OF A SUBSIDIARY

If a subsidiary is operating profitably, its net assets and retained earnings increase. When the subsidiary pays dividends, both the parent company and minority stockholders share in the distribution. All transactions of the subsidiary are recorded in the accounting records of the subsidiary in a normal manner.

Two different methods can be used by an investor to account for investments in common stock; they are the *cost* and *equity methods.* The Accounting Principles Board has identified the circumstances under which each method can be used. The *general rules* for determining the appropriate method of accounting are summarized below.

Percent of outstanding voting common stock of investee owned by investor	Method of accounting required by Accounting Principles Board in most cases
Less than 20%	Cost
20%–50%	Equity
More than 50%:	
Consolidated subsidiary	Cost or equity
Nonconsolidated subsidiary	Equity

According to the table, a parent company can use either the cost or equity method of accounting for its investment in a consolidated subsidiary. This is because the investment account is eliminated during the consolidation process and, therefore, the results are identical after consolidation.

Cost method

Under the *cost method,* the investor company records its investment at cost (price paid at acquisition) and does not adjust the investment account balance subsequently. Dividends received from the investee are recorded by debiting Cash and crediting Dividend Revenue. Thus, the investment account balance rarely changes under the cost method.

Equity method

Under the *equity method,* the parent or investor company initially records its investment at cost. The investment account is then adjusted periodically for the investor company's share of the investee's earnings, losses, and dividends as they are reported by the investee. The investor company's share of the investee's earnings is debited to the investment account and credited to an account labeled Earnings of X (Investee) Company.

For example, assume the subsidiary S Company mentioned in the preceding illustrations earned $20,000 during 1984. P Company owns 80 percent of S Company. P Company would record its share of S Company's earnings in the following manner:

Investment in S Company	16,000	
Earnings of S Company		16,000
To record 80 percent of subsidiary's earnings.		

The $16,000 debit to the investment account *increases the parent's equity in the subsidiary company.* The Earnings of S Company account will be closed at the end of the period to Income Summary, which then is closed to P Company's Retained Earnings.

If an investee incurs a loss, the investor company debits a loss account and credits the investment account for the investor's share of the loss. For example, assume S Company incurs a loss of $10,000 in 1985. Since P Company still owns 80 percent of S Company, P Company records its share of the loss as follows:

Loss of S Company	8,000	
Investment in S Company		8,000
To record 80 percent of subsidiary's loss.		

The $8,000 debit is closed first to Income Summary, which then is closed to Retained Earnings; the $8,000 *credit reduces P Company's equity in the subsidiary.*

When an investee declares and pays a dividend, the assets and retained earnings of the investee are reduced by the dividend payment amount. When the investor company receives its share of the dividends, it debits the asset received (Cash, in this case) and credits the investment account. For instance, assume S Company declares a cash dividend of $8,000 in 1984. P Company's share of the dividend amounts to $6,400 and is recorded as follows:

Cash	6,400	
Investment in S Company		6,400
To record dividend received from subsidiary.		

The receipt of the dividend *reduces the investor's equity in the investee* as shown by the credit to the investment account.

As noted earlier, a company may purchase all or part of another firm at more than book value and create goodwill on the consolidated balance sheet. The Accounting Principles Board in *APB Opinion No. 17* requires that all goodwill be amortized over a period not to exceed 40 years. This amortization is necessary under the equity method, but will be left to a more advanced text.

CONSOLIDATED FINANCIAL STATEMENTS AT A DATE AFTER ACQUISITION

Under the equity method, the investment account on the investor company's books increases and decreases as the investor records its share of the earnings, losses, and dividends reported by the investee. Thus, the balance in the investment account differs after acquisition from its balance on the date of acquisition. Therefore, the amounts eliminated on the consolidated statement work sheet will differ from year to year. As an illustration, assume the following facts:

1. P Company acquired 100 percent of the outstanding voting common stock of S Company on January 1, 1984. P Company paid $121,000 for stock-

holders' equity totaling $106,000. The excess of cost over book value is attributable to (1) an undervaluation of land amounting to $4,000 and (2) the remainder to S Company's above-average earnings prospects.

2. During 1984, S Company earned $20,000 from operations.
3. On December 31, 1984, S Company paid a cash dividend of $8,000.
4. S Company owes P Company $5,000 on a note.
5. Including its share (100 percent) of S Company's earnings, P Company earned $31,000 during 1984.
6. P Company paid a cash dividend of $10,000 during December 1984.
7. P Company uses the equity method of accounting for its investment in S Company.

The financial statements for the two companies are given in the first two columns of the work sheet for consolidated financial statements for December 31, 1984, Illustration 18.6.

In Illustration 18.6, notice that P Company has a balance of $20,000 in its Earnings of S Company account and a balance of $133,000 in its Investment in S Company account. The balances are the result of the following journal entries made by P Company in 1984:

1.	Investment in S Company	121,000	
	Cash		121,000
	To record 100 percent investment in subsidiary.		
2.	Investment in S Company	20,000	
	Earnings of S Company		20,000
	To record earnings of subsidiary.		
3.	Cash	8,000	
	Investment in S Company		8,000
	To record dividends received from subsidiary.		

The elimination entries on the work sheet in Illustration 18.6 are explained below.

Entry (a): During the year, S Company earned $20,000. P Company increased its investment account balance by $20,000. The first entry (a) on the work sheet eliminates the subsidiary's earnings from the investment account and Earnings of S Company ($20,000). This first entry reverses the entries made on the books of P Company to recognize the parent's share of the subsidiary's earnings (entry 2 above).

Entry (b): When S Company paid its cash dividend, P Company debited Cash and credited the investment account for $8,000 (entry 3 above). The second entry (b) restores the investment account to its balance before the dividends from S were deducted. That is, P's investment account is debited and S's dividends account is credited for $8,000. On a consolidated basis, a company cannot pay a dividend to itself.

Entry (c): This entry eliminates the original investment account balance ($121,000) and the subsidiary's stockholders' equity accounts as of the date of acquisition (retained earnings of $6,000 and common

Illustration 18.6:   Work sheet for consolidated financial statements

P COMPANY AND SUBSIDIARY S COMPANY
Work Sheet for Consolidated Financial Statements
December 31, 1984

	P Company	S Company	Eliminations Debit	Eliminations Credit	Consolidated Amounts
Income Statement					
Revenue from sales	397,000	303,000			700,000
Earnings of S Company	20,000		(a) 20,000		
Cost of goods sold	(250,000)	(180,000)			(430,000)
Expenses (excluding deprecia-					
tion and taxes)	(100,000)	(80,000)			(180,000)
Depreciation expense	(7,400)	(5,000)			(12,400)
Income tax expense	(28,600)	(18,000)			(46,600)
Net income—carried forward	31,000	20,000			31,000
Statement of Retained Earnings					
Retained earnings—January 1:					
P Company	54,000				54,000
S Company		6,000	(c) 6,000		
Net income—brought forward	31,000	20,000			31,000
	85,000	26,000			85,000
Dividends:					
P Company	(10,000)				(10,000)
S Company		(8,000)		(b) 8,000	
Retained earnings—December					
31—carried forward	75,000	18,000			75,000

stock of $100,000). The entry also establishes goodwill of $11,000 and increases land by $4,000.

After the first three elimination entries have been made, the investment account contains a zero balance from the viewpoint of the consolidated entity.

Entry (d):   This entry eliminates the intercompany debt of $5,000.

After the eliminations have been made, the corresponding amounts are added together and placed in the Consolidated Amounts column. The net income row in the Income Statement section is carried forward to the net income row in the Statement of Retained Earnings section. Likewise, the ending retained earnings row in the Statement of Retained Earnings section is carried forward to the retained earnings row in the Balance Sheet section. The final work sheet column is then used to prepare the consolidated income statement (Illustration 18.7), consolidated statement of retained earnings (Illustration 18.8), and consolidated balance sheet (Illustration 18.9). As stated earlier, amortization of goodwill is ignored in the illustration.

Balance Sheet							
Assets							
Cash	38,000	16,000					54,000
Notes receivable	5,000				(d)	5,000	
Accounts receivable, net	25,000	18,000					43,000
Inventory	40,000	36,000					76,000
Investment in S Company	133,000		(b)	8,000	(c)	121,000	
					(a)	20,000	
Equipment, net	36,900	12,000					48,900
Buildings, net	61,700	33,000					94,700
Land	20,000	10,000	(c)	4,000			34,000
Goodwill			(c)	11,000			11,000
	359,600	125,000					361,600
Liabilities and Stockholders' Equity							
Accounts payable	19,600	2,000					21,600
Notes payable	15,000	5,000	(d)	5,000			15,000
Common stock	250,000	100,000	(c)	100,000			250,000
Retained earnings—brought forward	75,000	18,000					75,000
	359,600	125,000		154,000		154,000	361,600

PURCHASE VERSUS POOLING OF INTERESTS

In the illustrations in this chapter, it has been assumed that the parent company acquired the subsidiary's common stock in exchange for cash; such a business combination is classified as a *purchase*. A purchase would also result if the acquiring company used assets other than cash in the acquisition. When assets other than cash are used, the cost of the acquired company's

Illustration 18.7: Consolidated income statement

P COMPANY AND SUBSIDIARY S COMPANY
Consolidated Income Statement
For the Year Ended December 31, 1984

Revenue from sales		$700,000
Cost of goods sold		430,000
Gross margin		$270,000
Expenses (excluding depreciation and taxes)	$180,000	
Depreciation expense	12,400	
Income tax expense	46,600	239,000
Net income		$ 31,000

Illustration 18.8:   Consolidated statement of retained earnings

P COMPANY AND SUBSIDIARY S COMPANY Consolidated Statement of Retained Earnings For the Year Ended December 31, 1984	
Retained earnings, January 1, 1984	$54,000
Net income	31,000
	$85,000
Dividends	10,000
Retained earnings, December 31, 1984	$75,000

stock is fair market value of the assets given up or of the stock received, whichever can be more clearly and objectively determined.

In some cases, one company issues common stock in exchange for the common stock of another company. In such cases, the stockholders of both companies maintain an ownership interest in the combined company. Such a business combination involving the issuance of common stock in exchange for common stock is classified as a *pooling of interests* if it meets all the criteria cited in *APB Opinion No. 16.* If a combination resulting from an

Illustration 18.9:   Consolidated balance sheet

P COMPANY AND SUBSIDIARY S COMPANY Consolidated Balance Sheet December 31, 1984		
Assets		
Current assets:		
Cash	$ 54,000	
Accounts receivable, net	43,000	
Inventory	76,000	
Total current assets		$173,000
Property, plant, and equipment:		
Equipment, net	$ 48,900	
Buildings, net	94,700	
Land	34,000	
Total property, plant, and equipment		177,600
Goodwill		11,000
Total assets		$361,600
Liabilities and Stockholders' Equity		
Current liabilities:		
Accounts payable	$ 21,600	
Notes payable	15,000	
Total liabilities		$ 36,600
Stockholders' equity:		
Common stock	$250,000	
Retained earnings	75,000	
Total stockholders' equity		325,000
Total liabilities and stockholders' equity		$361,600

exchange of stock does not qualify as a pooling of interests, it must be recorded as a purchase.

Given the circumstances surrounding a particular business combination, only one of the two methods—purchase or pooling of interests—is appropriate. It should be emphasized that the purchase and pooling of interest methods are *not* alternatives that can be applied to the same situation. *APB Opinion No. 16* specifies 12 conditions that must be met before a business combination can be classified as a pooling of interests. To illustrate, two of the conditions are that (1) the combination be effected in one transaction or be completed within one year in accordance with a specific plan, and (2) one corporation issue only its common stock for 90 percent or more of the voting common stock of another company. If *all 12 conditions are met, the resulting business combination must be accounted for as a pooling of interests. Otherwise, the purchase method must be used to account for the combination.*

When the pooling of interests method is used, the parent company's investment is recorded at the *book balue of the subsidiary's net assets* (assets minus liabilities). Since the investment is recorded at the book value of the subsidiary's net assets, there can be no goodwill or changes in asset valuations from consolidation. The subsidiary's retained earnings at date of acquisition become a part of the consolidated retained earnings, whereas under the purchase method they do not. Also, under the pooling of interests method, all subsidiary earnings for the year of acquisition are included in the consolidated earnings in the year of acquisition. But under the purchase method only that portion of the subsidiary's earnings which arises after the date of acquisition is included in consolidated net income.

From the above discussion, it should be apparent that significant differences will exist between financial statement amounts under the two different methods of accounting for a business combination. For instance, under the purchase method, any excess of cost over book value either must be used to increase the value of any assets that are undervalued or must be recognized as goodwill from consolidation. Thus, either more depreciation or more amortization will be recorded under the purchase method than under the pooling of interests method when cost exceeds book value. The result is that, when cost exceeds book value, consolidated net income is smaller under the purchase method than under the pooling of interests method.

USES AND LIMITATIONS OF CONSOLIDATED STATEMENTS

Consolidated statements are of primary importance to stockholders, managers, and directors of the parent company. The parent company benefits from the earnings, asset increases, and other financial strengths of the subsidiary. Likewise, the parent company suffers from a subsidiary's losses.

On the other hand, consolidated statements are of very limited use to the creditors and minority stockholders of the subsidiary. The subsidiary's creditors have a claim against the subsidiary alone; they cannot look to the parent company for payment. Minority stockholders in the subsidiary do not benefit or suffer from the parent company's operations. They benefit only from the subsidiary's earnings, asset increases, and financial strengths; they suffer only from the subsidiary's losses and financial weaknesses. Therefore, the subsidiary's creditors and minority stockholders are more interested in the subsidiary's individual financial statements than in the consolidated statements.

Appendixes A and B at the back of the text contain information relevant to this chapter. Appendix A covers international accounting, and Appendix B shows consolidated financial statements for an actual corporation.

NEW TERMS INTRODUCED IN CHAPTER 18

Consolidated statement work sheet
An informal statement on which elimination entries are made for the purpose of showing account balances as if the parent and its subsidiaries were a single economic enterprise.

Consolidated statements
The financial statements that result from combining the parent's financial statement amounts with those of its subsidiaries (after certain eliminations have been made). The consolidated statements reflect the financial position and results of operations of a single economic enterprise.

Cost method
A method of accounting for stock investments in which the investor company records its investment at cost (price paid at acquisition) and does not adjust the investment account balance subsequently. Dividends received from the investee are credited to a Dividend Revenue account.

Elimination entries
Entries made on a consolidated statement work sheet to remove certain intercompany items and transactions. Elimination entries allow the presentation of all account balances as if the parent and its subsidiaries were a single economic enterprise.

Equity method
A method of accounting for stock investments where the investment is initially recorded at cost. The investment account is then adjusted periodically for the investor company's share of the investee's earnings, losses, and dividends as they are reported by the investee.

Goodwill
An intangible value attaching to a business primarily due to above-average earnings prospects.

Intercompany transactions
Financial transactions involving a parent and one of its subsidiaries or between two of the subsidiaries.

Minority interest
The claim or interest of the stockholders who own less than 50 percent of a subsidiary's outstanding voting common stock. The minority stockholders have an interest in the subsidiary's net assets and share the subsidiary's earnings with the parent company.

Parent company
A corporation which owns more than 50 percent of the outstanding voting common stock of another corporation.

Pooling of interests
A business combination which meets certain criteria specified in *APB Opinion No. 16,* including the issuance of common stock in exchange for common stock.

Purchase
A business combination in which the acquiring company usually issues cash or other assets.

Subsidiary company
A corporation acquired and controlled by a parent corporation, with control established by ownership of more than 50 percent of the subsidiary's outstanding voting common stock.

DEMONSTRATION PROBLEM

The Stiller Company acquired all of the outstanding voting common stock of Meara Company on January 2, 1984, for $200,000 cash. On the date of acquisition, the balance sheets for the two companies were as follows:

	Stiller Company	Meara Company
Assets		
Cash	$ 50,000	$ 20,000
Accounts receivable	60,000	25,000
Notes receivable	10,000	5,000
Inventory	75,000	50,000
Investment in Meara Company	200,000	—
Plant and equipment, net	202,000	130,000
Total assets	$597,000	$230,000
Liabilities and Stockholders' Equity		
Accounts payable	$ 50,000	$ 30,000
Notes payable	15,000	10,000
Common stock—$5 par	350,000	100,000
Retained earnings	182,000	90,000
Total liabilities and stockholders' equity	$597,000	$230,000

Also on January 2, 1984, Meara Company borrowed $10,000 from Stiller Company by giving a note. The excess of cost over book value is attributable to Meara Company's above-average earnings prospects.

Required:

Prepare a work sheet for a consolidated balance sheet on the date of acquisiton.

Solution to demonstration problem

STILLER COMPANY AND SUBSIDIARY MEARA COMPANY
Work Sheet for Consolidated Balance Sheet
January 2, 1984 (date of acquisition)

	Stiller Company	Meara Company	Eliminations Debit	Eliminations Credit	Consolidated Amounts
Assets					
Cash	50,000	20,000			70,000
Accounts receivable	60,000	25,000			85,000
Notes receivable	10,000	5,000		(b) 10,000	5,000
Inventory	75,000	50,000			125,000
Investment in Meara Co.	200,000			(a) 200,000	
Plant and equipment, net	202,000	130,000			332,000
Goodwill			(a) 10,000		10,000
	597,000	230,000			627,000
Liabilities and Stockholders' Equity					
Accounts payable	50,000	30,000			80,000
Notes payable	15,000	10,000	(b) 10,000		15,000
Common stock—$5 par	350,000	100,000	(a) 100,000		350,000
Retained earnings	182,000	90,000	(a) 90,000		182,000
	597,000	230,000	210,000	210,000	627,000

QUESTIONS

1. What is the purpose of preparing consolidated financial statements?

2. Under what circumstances must consolidated financial statements be prepared?

3. Why is it necessary to make elimination entries on the consolidated statement work sheet? Are these elimination entries also posted to the accounts of the parent and subsidiary? Why or why not?

4. Why might a corporation pay an amount in excess of the book value for a subsidiary's stock? Why might it pay an amount less than the book value of the subsidiary's stock?

5. The item "Minority interest" often appears as one amount in the consolidated balance sheet. What does this item represent?

6. How do a subsidiary's earnings, losses, and dividends affect the investment account of the parent when the equity method of accounting is used?

7. When must each of the following methods be used to account for a business combination?
a. Purchase.
b. Pooling of interests

8. List three differences that exist between the purchase and pooling of interests methods of accounting for business combinations.

9. Why are consolidated financial statements of limited usefulness to the creditors and minority stockholders of a subsidiary?

EXERCISES

E-1.   On February 1, 1984, the Jernigan Company acquired 100 percent of the outstanding voting common stock of the Nunnelley Company for $500,000 cash. The stockholders' equity of the Nunnelley Company consisted of common stock, $400,000, and retained earnings, $100,000. Prepare (a) the entry to record the investment in Nunnelley Company and (b) the elimination entry that would be made on the consolidated statement work sheet for a balance sheet as of the date of acquisition.

E-2.   The Thompson Corporation acquired, for cash, 80 percent of the outstanding voting common stock of Story Company. On the date of its acquisition, the Story Company's stockholders' equity consisted of common stock, $350,000, and retained earnings, $130,000. The cost of the investment exceeded book value by $18,000 attributable to above-average earnings prospects. Prepare (a) the entry to record the investment in Story Company and (b) the entry to eliminate the investment for purposes of preparing consolidated financial statements as of the date of acquisition.

E-3.   On January 1, 1984, Company X acquired 85 percent of the outstanding voting common stock of Company Z. On that date, Company Z's stockholders' equity consisted of:

Common stock, $20 par; 15,000 shares authorized, issued, and outstanding	$300,000
Retained earnings	75,000
Total stockholders' equity	$375,000

Compute the difference between cost and book value in each of the following cases:

    a. Company X pays $318,750 cash for its interest in Z.
    b. Company X pays $375,000 cash for its interest in Z.
    c. Company X pays $290,000 cash for its interest in Z.

E-4.   Company A purchased 90 percent of Company B's outstanding voting common stock on January 2, 1984. Company A paid $310,000 for an equity of $270,000—$180,000, common stock, and $90,000, retained earnings. The difference was due to undervalued land owned by B. Company B earned $36,000 during 1984 and paid cash dividends of $12,000.

    a. Compute the balance in the investment account on December 31, 1984.
    b. Compute the amount of the minority interest on (1) January 2, 1984, and (2) December 31, 1984.

E-5.   The Armstrong Company owns 75 percent of the Evans Company's outstanding common stock and uses the equity method of accounting. The Evans Company reported net income of $78,000 for 1984. On December 31, 1984, the Evans Company paid a cash dividend of $21,000. In 1985, the Evans Company incurred a net loss of $15,000. Prepare entries to reflect these events on Armstrong Company's books.

E-6.   On January 1, 1984, the stockholders' equity section of the David Company's balance sheet was as follows:

Stockholders' equity:
Paid-in capital:
Common stock—$15 par value: authorized, 100,000 shares; issued
    and outstanding, 75,000 shares $1,125,000
Paid-in capital in excess of par value 187,500
    Total paid-in capital $1,312,500
Retained earnings 112,500
    Total stockholders' equity $1,425,000

Ninety percent of David Company's outstanding voting common stock was acquired by Jeff Company on January 1, 1984, for $1,252,500. Compute (a) the book value of the investment, (b) the difference between cost and book value, and (c) the minority interest.

PROBLEMS, SERIES A

P18–1–A. Tiger Company acquired 90 percent of the outstanding voting common stock of Bald Eagle Company on January 1, 1984, for $450,000 cash. Tiger Company uses the equity method. During 1984, Bald Eagle reported $90,000 of net income and paid $30,000 in cash dividends. The stockholders' equity section of the December 31, 1983, balance sheet for Bald Eagle was as follows:

Stockholders' equity:
Common stock—$5 par $400,000
Retained earnings 100,000
    Total stockholders' equity $500,000

Required:

    a. Prepare general journal entries to record the investment and the effect of Bald Eagle's earnings and dividends on Tiger Company's accounts.

    b. Prepare the elimination entry that would be made on the consolidated statement work sheet for a balance sheet as of the date of acquisition.

P18–2–A. Mountain Company acquired 68 percent of the outstanding voting common stock of Springs Company for $1,020,000 on January 1, 1983. The investment is accounted for under the equity method. During the years 1983–85, Springs Company reported the following:

	Net income (loss)	Dividends paid
1983	$173,200	$103,800
1984	44,400	26,600
1985	(2,800)	6,650

Required:

    a. Prepare general journal entries to record the investment and the effect of the subsidiary's earnings, losses, and dividends on Mountain Company's accounts.

    b. Compute the investment account balance on December 31, 1985.

P18–3–A. The Land Company acquired all of the outstanding voting common stock of the Bailey Company on January 3, 1984, for $126,000. On the date of acquisition, the balance sheets for the two companies were as follows:

	Land Company	Bailey Company
Assets		
Cash	$ 21,000	$ 18,000
Accounts receivable	40,500	37,500
Notes receivable	22,500	6,000
Inventory	58,500	27,000
Investment in Bailey Company	126,000	
Equipment, net	108,000	49,500
Total assets	$376,500	$138,000
Liabilities and Stockholders' Equity		
Accounts payable	$ 39,000	$ 12,000
Common stock—$10 par	180,000	87,000
Retained earnings	157,500	39,000
Total liabilities and stockholders' equity	$376,500	$138,000

Required:

Prepare a work sheet for a consolidated balance sheet on the date of acquisition.

P18–4–A. The Horizon Company acquired all of the outstanding voting common stock of the Sunset Company on January 1, 1984, for $240,000. On the date of acquisition, the balance sheets for the two companies were as follows:

	Horizon Company	Sunset Company
Assets		
Cash	$ 50,000	$ 15,000
Accounts receivable	24,000	20,000
Notes receivable	10,000	6,000
Inventory	76,000	48,000
Investment in Sunset Company	240,000	
Equipment, net	68,000	41,000
Buildings, net	185,000	92,000
Land	78,000	25,000
Total assets	$731,000	$247,000
Liabilities and Stockholders' Equity		
Accounts payable	$ 44,000	$ 20,000
Notes payable	12,000	14,000
Common stock—$20 par	530,000	198,000
Retained earnings	145,000	15,000
Total liabilities and stockholders' equity	$731,000	$247,000

The management of Horizon Company thinks that the Sunset Company's land is undervalued by $9,000. The remainder of the excess of cost over book value is due to superior earnings potential.

On the date of acquisition, Sunset Company borrowed $10,000 from Horizon Company by giving a note.

Required:

a. Prepare a work sheet for a consolidated balance sheet on the date of acquisition.

b. Prepare a consolidated balance sheet for January 1, 1984.

P18–5–A. Refer back to Problem P18–4–A. Horizon Company uses the equity method. Assume the following are the adjusted trial balances for the Horizon Company and the Sunset Company on December 31, 1984:

	Horizon Company	Sunset Company
Cash	$ 48,000	$ 20,238
Accounts receivable	30,752	23,000
Notes receivable	19,000	5,000
Inventory, December 31	85,000	56,000
Investment in Sunset Company	251,075	
Equipment, net	63,750	38,437
Buildings, net	175,750	87,400
Land	78,000	25,000
Cost of goods sold	448,000	120,000
Expenses (excluding depreciation and taxes)	120,000	45,000
Depreciation expense	13,500	7,163
Income tax expense	31,648	6,862
Dividends	26,500	9,900
Total debits	$1,390,975	$444,000
Accounts payable	$ 40,000	$ 21,000
Notes payable	15,000	10,000
Common stock—$20 par	530,000	198,000
Retained earnings	145,000	15,000
Revenue from sales	640,000	200,000
Earnings of Sunset Company	20,975	
Total credits	$1,390,975	$444,000

There is no intercompany debt at the end of the year.

Required:

       Prepare a work sheet for consolidated financial statements on December 31, 1984. (At the beginning of 1984, the equipment and buildings had remaining lives of 16 and 20 years, respectively.)

P18–6–A.   Using the work sheet prepared for Problem P18–5–A, prepare the following items:

      a.   Consolidated income statement for the year ended December 31, 1984.

      b.   Consolidated statement of retained earnings for the year ended December 31, 1984.

      c.   Consolidated balance sheet for December 31, 1984.

PROBLEMS, SERIES B

P18–1–B.   On January 1, 1984, Nash Company acquired 80 percent of the outstanding voting common stock of the Foshee Company for $240,000 cash. Nash Company uses the equity method. During 1984, Foshee reported $40,000 of net income and paid $20,000 in dividends. The stockholders' equity section of the December 31, 1983, balance sheet for Foshee was as follows:

Stockholders' equity:
Common stock—$5 par	$250,000
Retained earnings	50,000
Total stockholders' equity	$300,000

Required:

    a. Prepare general journal entries to record the investment and the effect on Foshee's earnings and dividends on Nash Company's accounts.

    b. Prepare the elimination entry that would be made on the consolidated statement work sheet for a balance sheet as of the date of acquisition.

P18–2–B. Douglas Company acquired 75 percent of the outstanding voting common stock of John Company for $344,000 cash on January 1, 1983. The investment is accounted for under the equity method. During 1983, 1984, and 1985, John Company reported the following:

	Net income (loss)	Dividends paid
1983	$ 85,200	$69,200
1984	(10,800)	–0–
1985	25,800	17,200

Required:

    a. Prepare general journal entries to record the investment and the effect of the subsidiary's earnings, losses, and dividends on Douglas Company's accounts.

    b. Compute the balance in the investment account on December 31, 1985.

P18–3–B. The Magnolia Company acquired 100 percent of the outstanding voting common stock of the College Company on January 1, 1984, for $76,000 cash. On the date of acquisition, the balance sheets for the two companies were as follows:

	Magnolia Company	College Company
Assets		
Cash	$ 6,000	$14,000
Accounts receivable	14,000	18,000
Notes receivable	10,000	6,000
Inventory	25,000	15,000
Investment in College Company	76,000	
Equipment, net..	22,000	28,000
Total assets	$153,000	$81,000
Liabilities and Stockholders' Equity		
Accounts payable	$ 16,000	$ 5,000
Notes payable	12,000	
Common stock—$20 par	100,000	60,000
Retained earnings	25,000	16,000
Total liabilities and stockholders' equity....................	$153,000	$81,000

Also on January 1, 1984, Magnolia Company borrowed $6,000 from College Company by giving a note.

Required:

    Prepare a work sheet for a consolidated balance sheet as of the date of acquisition.

P18–4–B. The Cleermont Company acquired 100 percent of the outstanding voting common stock of the Ballard Company on January 2, 1984, for $300,000 cash. On the date of acquisition, the balance sheets for the two companies were as follows:

	Cleermont Company	Ballard Company
Assets		
Cash	$ 35,000	$ 20,000
Accounts receivable	26,000	16,000
Notes receivable	40,000	10,000
Inventory	55,000	26,000
Investment in Ballard Company	300,000	
Equipment, net	72,000	50,000
Buildings, net	210,000	110,000
Land	85,000	45,000
Total assets	$823,000	$277,000
Liabilities and Stockholders' Equity		
Accounts payable	$ 13,000	$ 15,000
Notes payable	10,000	12,000
Common stock—$10 par	600,000	200,000
Retained earnings	200,000	50,000
Total liabilities and stockholders' equity	$823,000	$277,000

The excess of cost over book value is attributable to the above-average earnings prospects of Ballard Company. On the date of acquisition, Ballard Company borrowed $8,000 from Cleermont Company by giving a note.

Required:

a. Prepare a work sheet for a consolidated balance sheet as of the date of acquisition.

b. Prepare a consolidated balance sheet for January 2, 1984.

P18–5–B.   Refer back to Problem P18–4–B. Cleermont Company uses the equity method. Assume the following are the adjusted trial balances for the Cleermont Company and the Ballard Company on December 31, 1984:

	Cleermont Company	Ballard Company
Cash	$ 39,000	$ 35,000
Accounts receivable	42,000	20,000
Notes receivable	35,000	5,000
Inventory, December 31	55,000	31,900
Investment in Ballard Company	310,000	
Equipment, net	68,400	47,500
Buildings, net	201,600	105,600
Land	85,000	45,000
Cost of goods sold	200,000	70,000
Expenses (excluding depreciation and taxes)	80,000	30,100
Depreciation expense	12,000	6,900
Income tax expense	65,000	21,000
Dividends	60,000	12,000
Total debits	$1,253,000	$430,000
Accounts payable	$ 15,000	$ 20,000
Notes payable	16,000	10,000
Common stock—$10 par	600,000	200,000
Retained earnings—January 1	200,000	50,000
Revenue from sales	400,000	150,000
Earnings of Ballard Company	22,000	
Total credits	$1,253,000	$430,000

There is no intercompany debt at the end of the year.

Required:

Prepare a work sheet for consolidated financial statements on December 31, 1984.

P18–6–B.

Required:

Using the work sheet prepared for Problem P18–5–B, prepare the following items:

a. Consolidated income statement for the year ended December 31, 1984.

b. Consolidated statement of retained earnings for the year ended December 31, 1984.

c. Consolidated balance sheet for December 31, 1984.

BUSINESS DECISION PROBLEM

On January 2, 1984, Peeler Company acquired 60 percent of the voting common stock of Fixx Corporation for $200,000 cash. The excess of cost over book value was due to above-average earnings prospects. Peeler and Fixx are engaged in similar lines of business. Peeler has hired you to help it prepare consolidated financial statements. Peeler has already collected the following information for both companies as of January 2, 1984:

	Peeler Company	Fixx Corporation
Assets		
Cash	$ 20,000	$ 15,000
Accounts receivable	30,000	35,000
Inventories	80,000	60,000
Investment in Fixx Corporation	200,000	
Plant and equipment, net	260,000	205,000
Total assets	$590,000	$315,000
Liabilities and Stockholders' Equity		
Accounts payable	$ 40,000	$ 15,000
Common stock—$20 par	400,000	200,000
Retained earnings	150,000	100,000
Total liabilities and stockholders' equity	$590,000	$315,000

Required:

a. Peeler believes that consolidated financial statements can be prepared simply by adding together the amounts in the two individual columns. Is Peeler correct? If not, why not?

b. Prepare a consolidated balance sheet for the date of acquisition.

Part Six

Analysis of financial statements

Chapter 19
Statement of changes in financial position

Chapter 20
Analysis and interpretation of financial statements

Chapter 19

Statement of changes in financial position

CHAPTER GOALS

After study of this chapter, you should be able to:

1. List the major sources and uses of funds.
2. Explain why net income for a period is not equal to cash or working capital provided by operations.
3. Prepare a statement of changes in financial position and the related statement of changes in working capital.
4. Prepare a cash basis statement of changes in financial position.
5. Prepare a working paper for a statement of changes in financial position.
6. Define and use correctly the new terms in the glossary.

A firm's income statement and balance sheet often do not provide answers to all the questions raised by users of financial statements. Questions such as the following are not answered by reviewing either or both the income statement or the balance sheet. How much working capital or cash was generated by operations? Why is such a profitable firm only able to pay such meager dividends? How much was spent for new plant and equipment, and where did the company get the funds for the expenditures? How was the company able to pay a dividend when it incurred a net loss for the year?

The statement that provides information to answer these types of questions is called the *statement of changes in financial position.* This statement reports the flows of funds into and out of a business in an accounting period and often is called a *funds statement.* The APB requires that a statement of changes in financial position be presented for each period for which an income statement and a balance sheet are presented.[1] This chapter defines several concepts of funds and illustrates the procedures used to prepare a statement of changes in financial position.

THE CONCEPT OF FUNDS

The term *funds* needs to be defined before changes in financial position can be measured. *Funds* are often defined as working capital or cash. Both definitions are acceptable bases on which to prepare a statement of changes in financial position.

Funds defined as working capital

Funds have typically been defined as working capital. *Working capital is equal to current assets minus current liabilities. Using the working capital definition of funds, any transaction that increases or decreases working capital is included in the statement of changes.* The borrowing of cash by the use of long-term bonds would be included because the transaction increases total current assets, thus increasing working capital. The purchase of a plant asset on a short-term credit basis would be included because it reduces working capital by increasing total current liabilities. Defining funds as working capital also permits exclusion of many routine transactions. Examples are collection of an account receivable or payment of an account payable. The first transaction merely substitutes one current asset (cash) for another (accounts receivable). The second transaction reduces a current asset (cash) and reduces a current liability (accounts payable). Both transactions change the *composition* of working capital, but not its *amount.*

Funds defined as cash

When funds are defined as cash, any transaction that increases or decreases cash is included in the statement of changes in financial position. Many exam-

---

[1] APB, "Reporting Changes in Financial Position, *APB Opinion No. 19* (New York: AICPA, 1971), par. 7.

ples can be given, including transactions involving cash received from collections of accounts receivable and from sale of plant assets, as well as cash payments to retire long-term or short-term debt. When the cash basis of funds is strictly applied, only transactions that affect cash are reported.

Other significant financing and investing activities. Strict adherence to the cash or the working capital concept of funds could lead to the omission of significant transactions from the statement of changes in financial position. For example, a firm might double its assets by issuing common stock for some land and buildings. Since this transaction did not change the amount of working capital (no current asset or current liability was affected) nor did it change the amount of cash, it would not appear on the statement of changes if either of the above concepts of funds was strictly applied. But in developing the principles underlying the presentation of changes, *APB Opinion No. 19* requires a firm to report all significant financing and investing activities, regardless of whether cash or working capital is used to measure basic fund flows. Because the above transaction is a significant investing and financing event, it would be reported on the statement of changes.

Major sources and uses of funds

No matter how the term *funds* is defined, there are some basic sources and uses of funds in a business. A source of funds is a transaction that brings cash or working capital into the business, while a use of funds is a transaction that removes cash or working capital from the business. The major source of funds in a firm is operations. Sales create inflows of funds, while expenses cause outflows. In general, then, net income produces a positive flow of funds, while a net loss drains funds out of a firm in a negative flow. The major sources and uses of funds are portrayed graphically in Illustration 19.1.

Illustration 19.1: Sources and uses of funds

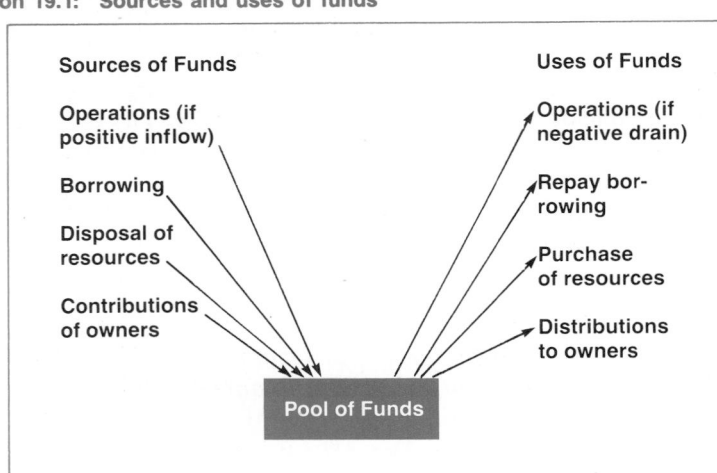

Funds from operations

The amount of funds provided by operations differs from net income because certain items which are included in determining net income do not affect either cash or working capital. The most common example is depreciation expense. The journal entry to record depreciation requires a debit to an expense account and a credit to an accumulated depreciation account. Neither account is a cash or working capital account, which suggests that the transaction has no effect on funds. But depreciation was deducted in arriving at net income. As a result, net income understates funds from operations. If net income is used as a starting point in measuring funds from operations, depreciation expense must be added back to net income.

Consider the following example. Company A had net income for the year of $20,000 after deducting depreciation of $10,000. Company B had a net loss for the year of $4,000 after deducting $10,000 of depreciation. Although A earned income and B experienced a loss, both companies have a positive funds flow from operations as shown below:

	Company A	Company B
Net income (loss)	$20,000	$ (4,000)
Add depreciation expense (which did not require use of funds)	10,000	10,000
Positive funds flow from operations	$30,000	$ 6,000

Only if B's loss had exceeded $10,000 would there have been a negative flow of funds from operations for the company.

There are other expenses and losses which are added back to net income because they do not reduce the amount of funds which flow into the company. These items include depletion expense, amortization of intangible assets such as patents and goodwill, amortization of discount on bonds payable, and losses from disposals of noncurrent assets. These addbacks are often called *nonworking capital (nonfund) charges or expenses.*

To illustrate why bond discount amortization is added back to net income, consider the following journal entry which would be recorded to amortize that discount.

Interest Expense	400	
Interest Payable		370
Discount on Bonds Payable		30

To record interest expense and amortize bond discount.

The debit to interest expense reduces net income by $400, but the effect on working capital or funds is only $370, the amount credited to the current liability account, Interest Payable. Therefore, the deduction from net income for interest expense was $30 larger than the actual effect on working capital. The $30 is the amount of bond discount amortization that must be added back to net income.

To illustrate the addback of the losses from disposals of noncurrent assets, assume that Quick Company sold a piece of equipment for $6,000. The equipment had cost $10,000 and had accumulated depreciation of $3,000. The journal entry to record the sale is:

Cash	6,000	
Accumulated Depreciation	3,000	
Loss on Sale of Equipment	1,000	
Equipment		10,000
To record disposal of equipment at a loss.		

The only "funds" account in the above journal entry is Cash. The $6,000 inflow from the sale of the equipment will be shown on the funds statement as a source of funds. The loss amount does not reduce working capital and is added back in converting net income to funds from operations.

There are also items called *nonworking capital (nonfund) credits or revenues* that must be deducted from net income in order to compute funds provided by operations. Such items include amortization of bond premiums, gains from disposals of noncurrent assets, earnings from investments carried under the equity method, and amortization of discounts on bond investments. In regard to the latter, the journal entry to record interest earned on bond investments purchased at a discount is as follows:

Cash (Interest Receivable)	780	
Bond Investments	20	
Interest Revenue		800
To record interest earned on bond investments and amortize the bond discount.		

The funds effect is the $780, but $800 was included in net income. So the $20 investment discount needs to be deducted from net income to show the actual funds effect. The $20 is a nonfund producing revenue item.

The next section of the chapter covers the various procedures used to prepare the statement of changes in financial position on a working capital basis. Then, the statement of changes in financial position focusing on cash flows is presented.

STATEMENT OF CHANGES IN FINANCIAL POSITION—
WORKING CAPITAL BASIS

The financial statements and additional data for the Welby Company, Illustration 19.2, will be used to prepare the company's statement of changes in financial position on a working capital basis. To prepare the statement, the change in working capital is first determined, and then all of the noncurrent accounts are analyzed for changes that affected working capital.

Determining the change in working capital

Opinion No. 19 states that a separate *statement of changes in working capital* should accompany the statement of changes in financial position. Such

Illustration 19.2: Financial statements and other data

WELBY COMPANY
Balance Sheets

	December 31	
	1984	1983
Assets		
Cash	$ 21,000	$ 10,000
Accounts receivable	30,000	20,000
Inventory	26,000	30,000
Plant assets	70,000	50,000
Accumulated depreciation	(10,000)	(5,000)
Total assets	$137,000	$105,000
Liabilities and Stockholders' Equity		
Accounts payable	$ 10,000	$ 15,000
Accrued liabilities	2,000	0
Common stock ($10 par value)	90,000	60,000
Retained earnings	35,000	30,000
Total liabilities and stockholder's equity	$137,000	$105,000

WELBY COMPANY
Income Statement
For the Year Ended December 31, 1984

Sales		$140,000
Cost of goods sold		100,000
Gross margin		$ 40,000
Operating expenses and taxes	$ 25,000	
Depreciation	5,000	30,000
Net income		$ 10,000

Additional data:
1. Plant assets purchased for cash during 1984, $20,000.
2. Common stock with a par value of $30,000 was issued at par for cash.
3. Cash dividends declared in 1984, $5,000.

a statement is presented in Illustration 19.3. Alternatively, a *schedule of changes in working capital components* may be presented immediately under the statement of changes in financial position, as in Illustration 19.4. This form will be used in the problems at the end of the chapter.

In Illustration 19.3, note that changes in current assets cause working capital to change in the same direction, while changes in current liabilities cause working capital to change in the opposite direction. Thus, both the $10,000 increase in accounts receivable and the $5,000 decrease in accounts payable increased working capital. The $4,000 decrease in inventory and the $2,000 increase in accrued liabilities decreased working capital. The schedule shows that Welby's working capital increased $20,000 during the year. The $20,000 increase in working capital is what must be explained by analyzing the noncurrent accounts. The statement of changes in financial position reports the causes of the change in working capital.

Illustration 19.3:   Statement of changes in working capital

WELBY COMPANY
Statement of Changes in Working Capital
For the Year Ended December 31, 1984

	December 31		Working capital	
	1984	**1983**	**Increase**	**Decrease**
Current assets:				
Cash	$21,000	$10,000	$11,000	
Accounts receivable	30,000	20,000	10,000	
Inventory	26,000	30,000		$ 4,000
Total current assets	$77,000	$60,000		
Current liabilities:				
Accounts payable	$10,000	$15,000	5,000	
Accrued liabilities	2,000	–0–		2,000
Total current liabilities	$12,000	$15,000		
Working capital	$65,000	$45,000		
Increase in working capital				20,000
			$26,000	$26,000

Illustration 19.4:   Statement of changes in financial position—working capital basis

WELBY COMPANY
Statement of Changes in Financial Position—Working Capital Basis
For the Year Ended December 31, 1984

Financial resources provided:		
Working capital from operations:		
Net income		$10,000
Add nonworking capital expenses:		
Depreciation		5,000
Working capital from operations		$15,000
Issuance of common stock		30,000
Total financial resources provided		$45,000
Financial resources applied:		
Purchase plant assets	$20,000	
Dividends	5,000	
Total financial resources applied		25,000
Increase in working capital		$20,000
Schedule of changes in working capital		
components:		
Increase (decrease) in current assets:		
Cash		$11,000
Accounts receivable		10,000
Inventory		(4,000)
		$17,000
Increase (decrease) in current liabilities:		
Accounts payable	$ (5,000)	
Accrued liabilities	2,000	3,000
Increase in working capital		$20,000

Analyzing the noncurrent accounts

At first, it may seem quite unusual to seek causes of the change in working capital by looking at the noncurrent (nonworking capital) accounts. But bear in mind that a transaction which is recorded *solely* in two working capital accounts can never increase or decrease working capital. Consider the effects upon working capital of collections of receivables, purchases of merchandise, and payment of accounts payable. These transactions change the *composition* of working capital, but not its *amount.* The noncurrent accounts must be analyzed for transactions affecting the amount of working capital. In this case, there are four noncurrent accounts to analyze: Plant Assets, Accumulated Depreciation, Common Stock, and Retained Earnings.

1. Because of the importance of working capital provided by operations, the analysis of the noncurrent accounts begins by reviewing the Retained Earnings account. Retained Earnings is the account to which net income or loss for the period was closed. The $5,000 increase in this account consists of $10,000 of net income less $5,000 of dividends. The net income amount can be found in the income statement. Both net income and dividends must be entered on the statement of changes in financial position in Illustration 19.4. The $5,000 of dividends reduced working capital when they were declared and credited to a current liability account, Dividends Payable. The declaration of dividends is a *use of working capital,* and is shown under *financial resources applied.* The $10,000 net income is used as the starting figure in determining working capital from operations. Net income of $10,000 is entered on the statement in the financial resources provided section under "Working capital from operations."
2. The plant assets account increased by $20,000 during the year. The additional data indicate that $20,000 of plant assets were purchased during the period. A purchase of plant assets is a use of funds and is entered under "Financial resources applied."
3. The $5,000 increase in the accumulated depreciation account equals the amount of depreciation expense for the period. Because depreciation does not affect or use up working capital, it must be added back to net income to convert net income to working capital from operations. *Working capital from operations* could be measured *directly* by deducting only those expenses that affect working capital from sales. For the Welby Company, the computation would be: $140,000 - $100,000 - $25,000 = $15,000. But, in actual practice, the indirect or addback method is used almost exclusively. The *indirect or addback method* is a way of determining working capital from operations that starts with net income and adjusts for expenses and revenues that do not affect working capital. Two reasons for this preference are: (*a*) the details of the income statement need not be repeated, and (*b*) the addback method's use of net income ties in directly to the income statement.
4. The $30,000 increase in common stock resulted from the issuance of stock at par, as disclosed in the additional data. The $30,000 is entered as a source of working capital under *Financial resources provided.*

The analysis of the noncurrent accounts is now complete. Note that the current accounts were not dealt with except to find the net change in working capital which is reported as the final item in the statement of changes in financial position.

The completed statement of changes in financial position and schedule of changes in working capital components are shown in Illustration 19.4. The headings "Sources of working capital" and "Uses of working capital" could have been used instead of the all-inclusive headings of *Financial resources provided* and *Financial resources applied*. The latter headings seem appropriate because of the APB requirement of reporting all significant investing and financing activities.

STATEMENT OF CHANGES IN FINANCIAL POSITION— CASH BASIS

Having presented a simple illustration showing the preparation of a statement of changes in financial position that focused on working capital, a statement of changes on a cash basis will be illustrated. Such a statement deals primarily with reporting the sources and uses of cash and is often referred to simply as a *cash flow statement.*

A cash basis statement of changes in financial position differs from one focusing on working capital primarily in the funds from operations section. A cash basis statement reports both cash and working capital from operations. *Cash flow from operations* is the net amount of cash received or disbursed on items which normally appear on the income statement. It is obtained by converting accrual basis net income to a cash basis amount.

Cash provided by operations

There are two steps in converting net income to cash basis income. First, convert net income to working capital from operations by adding back or deducting from net income those items that did not use up or provide working capital. Second, convert working capital from operations to cash from operations by including the changes that occurred in current accounts other than cash. Applying these two steps to the Welby Company financial statements and other data in Illustration 19.2 yields the following schedule:

Net income		$10,000
Add expenses not reducing working capital—depreciation		5,000
Working capital from operations		$15,000
Effects of changes in components of operating working capital on cash:		
Increase in accounts receivable	$(10,000)	
Decrease in inventory	4,000	
Decrease in accounts payable	(5,000)	
Increase in accrued liabilities	2,000	(9,000)
Cash provided by operations		$ 6,000

The $10,000 increase in accounts receivable is deducted from accrual basis net income to convert it to cash basis income. If accounts receivable increased in a period, sales to customers exceeded collections from customers. Accrual basis sales revenue is greater than cash basis sales revenue, and net income needs to be reduced by $10,000.

To clarify the effect of the inventory change upon the conversion, assume that all purchases are for cash. Cost of goods sold on a cash basis is the amount paid for merchandise during the period. Purchases would be $96,000, computed as follows:

Ending inventory	$ 26,000
+Cost of goods sold	100,000
Cost of goods available for sale	$126,000
−Beginning inventory	30,000
Purchases	$ 96,000

If all purchases are for cash, cost of goods sold under cash basis is $96,000, which is $4,000 less than the $100,000 accrual basis amount. Thus, $4,000 must be added to accrual basis net income to convert it to cash basis.

But, because accounts payable changed, purchases were on account. Accounts payable decreased during the year, so suppliers were paid more in cash during the year than was purchased from them. Thus, expenses on a cash basis were $5,000 greater than on an accrual basis. So, $5,000 is deducted from accrual basis net income to convert it to cash basis.

Alternatively, since cost of goods sold on a cash basis is the amount of cash paid for goods during the period, the following calculation could have been made rather than the two preceding computations:

Accounts payable, January 1	$ 15,000
Purchases (from prior schedule)	96,000
Total	$111,000
Accounts payable, December 31	10,000
Cash paid to suppliers during the year	$101,000

Cash basis cost of goods sold is $101,000, or $1,000 more than the accrual basis amount. Net income on a cash basis is, then, $1,000 less than the accrual basis amount. The $1,000 deduction agrees with the net amount of the individual analyses: $5,000 deducted for the decrease in accounts payable, and $4,000 added for the decrease in inventory nets out to a $1,000 deduction.

Accrued liabilities would be handled in a manner similar to accounts payable. Prepaid expenses would be treated the same as accounts receivable or inventory. These conversion procedures can be summarized as follows:

For changes in these working capital items:	Make these adjustments to convert accrual basis net income to cash basis net income:	
	Add	**Deduct**
Accounts receivable	Decrease	Increase
Inventory	Decrease	Increase
Prepaid expenses	Decrease	Increase
Accounts payable	Increase	Decrease
Accrued liabilities	Increase	Decrease

Notice in the above summary that in converting from accrual to cash basis, all changes in current assets accounts are handled in a similar manner. All changes in current liability accounts are also handled in a similar manner, but that manner is exactly the opposite from the handling of the current asset changes.

The complete adjustment or conversion procedure used in the following comprehensive example is summarized below:

Accrual basis net income
+ Expenses and losses not reducing working capital
− Revenues and gains not producing working capital
= Working capital from operations
+ or − Changes in working capital accounts related to operations
= Cash from operations

Cash basis statement preparation

The complete statement of changes in financial position on a cash basis is presented in Illustration 19.5. A comparison of this statement with the one in Illustration 19.4 shows that the two statements are virtually identical, except for the section "Effects of changes in components of operating working

Illustration 19.5: Statement of changes in financial position—cash basis

WELBY COMPANY
Statement of Changes in Financial Position—Cash Basis
For the Year Ended December 31, 1984

Financial resources provided:		
Cash from operations:		
Net income		$10,000
Add nonworking capital expenses:		
Depreciation		5,000
Working capital from operations		$15,000
Effects of changes in components of operating working capital on cash:		
Increase in accounts receivable	$(10,000)	
Decrease in inventory	4,000	
Decrease in accounts payable	(5,000)	
Increase in accrued liabilities	$ 2,000	(9,000)
Cash provided by operations		$ 6,000
Issuance of common stock		30,000
Total financial resources provided		$36,000
Financial resources applied:		
Purchase plant assets	$20,000	
Dividends	5,000	
Total financial resources applied		25,000
Increase in Cash		$11,000
Cash, December 31, 1983		10,000
Cash, December 31, 1984		$21,000

capital on cash" in the cash basis statement in Illustration 19.5. There are two reasons for this similarity:

1. Most sources and uses of funds involve cash receipts and disbursements and would be reported in the same way whether cash or working capital was the focus of attention.
2. The cash basis statement was prepared by focusing on working capital first and then making the adjustments necessary to convert working capital from operations to cash from operations.

A COMPREHENSIVE ILLUSTRATION

Presented and discussed below is a more complete example of the procedures followed to prepare a cash basis statement of changes in financial position. A working paper (shown later in Illustration 19.8) is used to aid in preparing the statement. The use of a working paper to prepare a working capital basis statement of changes in financial position is shown in the solution to the demonstration problem. The working paper in Illustration 19.8 could, with only minor revision, be adapted to a working capital focus.

The basic data for the example are found in Illustration 19.6 and Illustration 19.7, which present the income statement and comparative balance sheets of The United States Corporation. Assume the following information about the noncurrent accounts is available:

1. There were no purchases of investments during the year. Investments with an $8,000 cost were sold for $9,700.
2. Land and buildings valued at $65,000 ($45,000 for the buildings and $20,000 for the land) were acquired, subject to a mortgage note of $35,000.
3. During the year, the corporation disposed of equipment which had an original cost of $20,000 and accumulated depreciation of $16,500. The equipment was sold for $2,600.
4. The common stock was sold for cash.

The working paper in Illustration 19.8 for The United States Corporation is used to analyze the transactions and prepare the statement of changes in financial position. The discussion which follows will describe the items and trace their effects in the entries made on the working paper.

The steps in preparing the working paper are as follow:

1. Enter the account balances of all balance sheet accounts at the beginning of the period in the first column and at the end of the period in the fourth column. Notice the debit items are listed first, followed by the credit items.
2. Total the debits and the credits in the first and fourth columns to determine that debits equal credits in each column.
3. Write "Financial resources provided" immediately below the total of the credit items. Skip sufficient lines on which to record all sources of funds. Then write "Financial resources applied."
4. Analyzing entries are entered in the second and third columns. The entries,

Illustration 19.6: Statement of income and retained earnings

THE UNITED STATES CORPORATION
Statement of Income and Retained Earnings
For the Year Ended December 31, 1984

Net sales		$1,464,200
Cost of goods sold		871,150
Gross margin		$ 593,050
Operating expenses:		
Salaries	$215,000	
Depreciation expense ($3,250, buildings; $31,050, equipment)	34,300	
Supplies	7,320	
Advertising	90,000	
Taxes, payroll and other	26,000	
General administrative expenses	123,780	
Total operating expenses		496,400
Net income from operations		$ 96,650
Other revenue:		
Interest earned	$ 1,950	
Gain on sale of long-term investments	1,700	3,650
		$ 100,300
Other expenses:		
Interest expense	$ 3,800	
Loss on sale of equipment	900	4,700
Net income before federal income taxes		$ 95,600
Deduct: Federal income taxes		45,250
Net income to retained earnings		$ 50,350
Retained earnings, January 1		84,100
		$ 134,450
Deduct: Dividends declared		18,000
Retained earnings, December 31		$ 116,450

which may be made in any order, serve two functions: (*a*) they explain the change in each account and (*b*) they record the sources and uses of funds. These entries will be discussed individually.

5. Total the debits and credits in the second and third columns. There will be one pair of totals for the balance sheet items and another pair for the sources and uses of funds. The bottom portion of the working paper is used to prepare the formal statement of changes in financial position.

Completing the working paper

The working paper in Illustration 19.8 is completed by analyzing the change in each noncash balance sheet account. Changes in cash can be explained by changes in the noncash balance sheet accounts because every change in cash was accompanied by a change in a noncash balance sheet account. After entries have been properly made to analyze all changes in noncash balance sheet accounts, the working paper will show all sources and uses of cash. The explanations below are keyed to the entries on the working paper by numbers.

Illustration 19.7: Comparative balance sheet

THE UNITED STATES CORPORATION
Comparative Balance Sheet
December 31, 1983, and 1984

	1984	1983	Increase decrease*
Assets			
Current assets:			
Cash	$ 46,300	$ 40,900	$ 5,400
Accounts receivable (net)	112,160	101,000	11,160
Marketable securities	3,000	–0–	3,000
Inventories	127,600	115,300	12,300
Prepaid expenses	3,100	4,700	1,600*
Total current assets	$292,160	$261,900	$30,260
Investments	$ 17,000	$ 25,000	$ 8,000*
Property, plant, and equipment:			
Land	$100,000	$ 80,000	$20,000
Buildings	175,000	130,000	45,000
Accumulated depreciation—buildings	(29,750)	(26,500)	(3,250)
Equipment	198,000	175,000	23,000
Accumulated depreciation—equipment	(57,650)	(43,100)	(14,550)
Total property, plant, and equipment	$385,600	$315,400	$70,200
Total assets	$694,760	$602,300	$92,460
Liabilities and Stockholders' Equity			
Current liabilities:			
Accounts payable	$ 82,420	$ 78,870	$ 3,550
Accrued liabilities	9,890	12,230	2,340*
Estimated federal income tax liability	12,000	14,100	2,100*
Dividends payable	9,000	8,000	1,000
Total current liabilities	$113,310	$113,200	$ 110
Long-term liabilities:			
Mortgage note payable, 10% (on land and buildings)	$ 35,000	$ –0–	$35,000
Bonds payable, 8%, due 1986	40,000	40,000	–0–
Total long-term liabilities	$ 75,000	$ 40,000	$35,000
Total liabilities	$188,310	$153,200	$35,110
Stockholders' equity:			
Common stock, stated value, $50 per share	$390,000	$365,000	$25,000
Retained earnings	116,450	84,100	32,350
Total stockholders' equity	$506,450	$449,100	$57,350
Total liabilities and stockholders' equity	$694,760	$602,300	$92,460

Entry 1. The beginning and ending cash balances are compared to determine the change for the year, which is a $5,400 increase. An entry is made on the working paper debiting Cash for $5,400 and crediting Increase in Cash for the Year under "Financial resources applied." This entry indicates that of the cash flowing into the company during the year, $5,400 was used to increase the Cash balance. The entry also sets out the change in cash

Illustration 19.8

UNITED STATES CORPORATION
Working Paper for Statement of Changes in Financial Position—Cash Basis
For the Year Ended, December 31, 1984

	Account Balances 12/31/83	Analysis of Transactions for 1984		Account Balances 12/31/84
		Debit	Credit	
Debits				
Cash	40,900	(1) 5,400		46,300
Accounts receivable	101,000	(10) 11,160		112,160
Marketable securities	–0–	(16) 3,000		3,000
Inventories	115,300	(11) 12,300		127,600
Prepaid expenses	4,700		(12) 1,600	3,100
Investments	25,000		(2) 8,000	17,000
Land	80,000	(3) 20,000		100,000
Buildings	130,000	(3) 45,000		175,000
Equipment	175,000	(5) 43,000	(4) 20,000	198,000
Totals	671,900			782,160
Credits				
Accumulated depreciation—buildings	26,500		(6) 3,250	29,750
Accumulated depreciation—equipment	43,100	(4) 16,500	(6) 31,050	57,650
Accounts payable	78,870		(13) 3,550	82,420
Accrued liabilities	12,230	(14) 2,340		9,890
Federal income tax liability	14,100	(15) 2,100		12,000
Dividends payable	8,000	(17) 17,000	(9) 18,000	9,000
Mortgage note payable	–0–		(3) 35,000	35,000
Bonds payable	40,000			40,000
Common stock	365,000		(7) 25,000	390,000
Retained earnings	84,100	(9) 18,000	(8) 50,350	116,450
Totals	671,900	195,800	195,800	782,160

that the statement seeks to explain. No further attention need be paid to cash in completing the working paper.

Attention is now directed toward changes in other balance sheet accounts. These accounts can be dealt with in any order. But, in order to group certain items, the noncurrent accounts are analyzed first.

Entry 2. Investments is the first noncurrent account. The additional

Illustration 19.8 (concluded)

	Account Balances 12/31/83	Analysis of Transactions for 1984		Account Balances 12/31/84
		Debit	Credit	
Financial resources provided:				
By operations:				
Net income		(8) 50,350		
Depreciation—buildings		(6) 3,250		
Depreciation—equipment		(6) 31,050		
Loss on sale of equipment		(4) 900		
Gain on sale of investments			(2) 1,700	
Increase in accounts receivable			(10) 11,160	
Increase in inventories			(11) 12,300	
Decrease in prepaid expenses		(12) 1,600		
Increase in accounts payable		(13) 3,550		
Decrease in accrued liabilities			(14) 2,340	
Decrease in federal income tax				
liability			(15) 2,100	
Other sources:				
Sale of investments		(2) 9,700		
Assumption of mortgage note		(3) 35,000		
Sale of equipment		(4) 2,600		
Issuance of common stock		(7) 25,000		
Financial resources applied:				
Purchase of marketable securities			(16) 3,000	
Acquisition of land and buildings			(3) 65,000	
Acquisition of equipment			(5) 43,000	
Payment of cash dividends			(17) 17,000	
Increase in cash for year			(1) 5,400	
Totals		163,000	163,000	

information discloses that investments were sold at a gain which was recorded in the following manner:

Cash	9,700	
Investments		8,000
Gain on Sale of Investments		1,700

Since cash changes and their causes are the focus of the working paper, the following entry is made on the working paper to show the source of cash.

Sale of Investments	9,700	
Investments		8,000
Gain on sale of investments		1,700

The working paper now shows $9,700 cash provided by sale of investments and a $1,700 reduction in cash provided by operations. The gain on sale of investments is removed from cash provided by operations and included as part of the cash provided by sale of investments. If the $9,700 cash received from the sale is reported and the gain is not removed from cash provided by operations, the $1,700 gain is shown or counted twice. Note that the working paper entry is identical to the original journal entry for the sale, except for the $9,700 debit. Instead of debiting Cash, a properly described source of cash is debited. The sources and uses of cash are shown in the lower section of the working paper. The $8,000 credit accounts fully for the decrease in the Investments account.

Entry 3. The changes in the Land and Buildings accounts resulted from the following entry:

Land	20,000	
Buildings	45,000	
Cash		30,000
Mortgage Note Payable		35,000

The transaction requires two entries on the working paper. First, Land and Buildings are debited for $20,000 and $45,000, respectively, and a cash applied item described as "Acquisition of Land and Buildings" is credited for $65,000. Second, a source of cash called "Assumption of Mortgage Note" is debited and Mortgage Note Payable is credited for $35,000. In other words, the transaction is treated as if the mortgage note was issued for cash and then $65,000 cash had been spent to acquire land and buildings. This transaction is an example of a significant financing and investing activity that must be included on the statement even though it did not affect funds.

Entry 4. The Equipment account shows a net increase of $23,000 resulting from two transactions: a $43,000 purchase and a $20,000 retirement. The net change in the account must be analyzed to show both cash applied and cash provided. The amount shown under "Other sources" from sale of equipment is the amount received for the equipment. These data were included in the additional information given. The computation can be summarized as follows:

Cost of equipment sold	$20,000
Less: Accumulated depreciation	16,500
Book value of equipment sold	$ 3,500
Less: Loss on sale	900
Cash received	$ 2,600

The complete working paper entry for sale of equipment is:

Sale of Equipment	2,600	
Accumulated Depreciation—Equipment	16,500	
Loss on Sale of Equipment	900	
Equipment		20,000

This entry records cash provided by sale of equipment and explains part of the changes in Equipment and Accumulated Depreciation—Equipment. The loss is added back to net income as a noncash deduction in arriving at net income. The loss has exactly the same effect as depreciation, or the write-off of any noncash asset.

Entry 5. This entry debits the Equipment account and credits Acquisition of Equipment for the $43,000 cash spent to acquire new equipment.

Entry 6. This entry adds $3,250 building depreciation and $31,050 equipment depreciation back to net income and credits the respective accumulated depreciation accounts. The $31,050 credit to the accumulated depreciation account for equipment less the $16,500 debit to this account in Entry 4 explain fully the increase in this account from $43,100 to $57,650.

Entry 7. This entry shows the $25,000 cash received from sale of common stock as an "Other source" of cash. The entry also explains completely the change in the Common Stock account. If stock had been sold for more than its stated value of $50 per share, the excess would be recorded in a separate Paid-In Capital in Excess of Stated Value account. But only the total amount of cash received from the issuance would have been reported on the statement of changes in financial position as a single figure because only the total amount received is significant.

Entry 8. The statement of retained earnings and the income statement reveal that net income for 1984 was $50,350. Entry 8 records the $50,350 as the starting point in measuring cash from operations and credits Retained Earnings as a partial explanation of the change in that account.

Entry 9. This entry debits Retained Earnings and credits Dividends Payable for the $18,000 of dividends declared. The entry also completes the explanation of the change in Retained Earnings ($84,100 + $50,350 − $18,000 = $116,450).

In regard to this entry, the credit was made to Dividends Payable for the $18,000 of dividends declared rather than to a financial resources applied item because the statement of changes is focusing on cash. The amount of dividends declared would be reported on the statement of changes if the statement were prepared under a working capital basis. To find the amount of dividends *paid,* the change in the Dividends Payable account must be included in the analysis, which is done in entry 17 below.

If Retained Earnings had changed for reasons other than net income or cash dividends, the causes of the changes must be determined in order to decide whether they should be reported in the statement of changes in financial position. Transactions such as stock dividends and stock splits would not be reported because they lack significance from an analytical viewpoint and because these items never affect cash or working capital. But an entry must be made on the working paper to explain the changes caused by a stock dividend or split, even if cash was not affected. All changes in all noncash accounts must be explained to show that a change affecting cash was not overlooked.

The next task is to analyze changes in current accounts other than Cash. Most of these accounts are closely related to operations, and their changes are included in converting net income to cash from operations. The changes in the current accounts are analyzed in the manner previously discussed (see pages 688–90).

Entry 10. The $11,160 increase in accounts receivable must be deducted from net income when converting it to cash from operations. If accounts receivable increased, sales to customers exceeded cash received from customers. Accrual basis revenue and net income are larger than revenue (receipts) and net income on a cash basis. To convert net income to cash basis, the $11,160 must be deducted.

The working paper technique used makes the recording of these effects almost mechanical. Accounts Receivable must be debited for $11,160 to increase it from $101,000 to $112,160. If Accounts Receivable is debited, a credit must be entered for an item that can be entitled "Increase in Accounts Receivable." The increase is a deduction from net income in converting it to cash from operations.

Entry 11 is virtually a duplicate of entry 10, except that it involves inventories rather than receivables.

Entry 12 is similar to the above two entries, except that it is reversed because prepaid expenses decreased.

Entry 13 records the effect of an increase in accounts payable on net income in converting it to cash from operations.

Entries 14 and *15* record the effects of decreases in two other current liability accounts in converting net income to cash from operations.

Entry 16. The increase in marketable securities results from a purchase of such investments. The purchase of marketable securities is not related to net income in any way. Thus, the increase in this account is treated as an application of cash rather than an adjustment of net income. Marketable Securities is debited and a credit entered for the purchase in the cash applied section of the working paper.

Entry 17. This entry records the amount of dividends that were paid during the period. Entry 9 recorded $18,000 of dividends declared in the Dividends Payable account, which increased its balance to $26,000 ($8,000 + $18,000). But the liability for dividends was only $9,000 at the end of the period. So $17,000 of cash must have been paid to stockholders as dividends. Thus, entry 17 debits Dividends Payable and credits financial resources applied to Payment of Cash Dividends.

The analysis of the noncash accounts is now complete. To be sure that a change has not been overlooked, the debits and credits in the middle two columns opposite the 1983 balances are added to or subtracted from those balances, line by line. If the working paper has been properly prepared, the results will be the 1984 balances listed in the fourth column. For example, the $43,000 debit is added to the beginning balance for Equipment, and the $20,000 credit deducted to get an ending balance of $198,000. Next, the debits and credits for the balance sheet account entries and for the funds statement items are added to make sure that they are equal in both sections. Note that entries made in the working paper are used only to derive cash flows into and out of the firm. These entries are not entered in the firm's accounting system because the transactions which caused the fund flows have already been recorded.

The formal statement

The data in the lower section of the working paper are now used to prepare the formal statement of changes in financial position shown in Illustration 19.9. A standard format has not been prescribed for this statement. Both

Illustration 19.9:   Statement of changes in financial position—cash basis

THE UNITED STATES CORPORATION		
Statement of Changes in Financial Position—Cash Basis		
For the Year Ended December 31, 1984		
Financial resources provided:		
By operations:		
Net income		$ 50,350
Add: Charges not requiring outlay of funds:		
Depreciation—building	$ 3,250	
Depreciation—equipment	31,050	
Loss on sale of equipment	900	35,200
		$ 85,550
Deduct: Credits not providing funds:		
Gain on sale of investments		1,700
Working capital provided by operations		$ 83,850
Effect of change in components of operating working capital on cash:		
Increase in accounts receivable	$(11,160)	
Increase in inventories	(12,300)	
Decrease in prepaid expenses	1,600	
Increase in accounts payable	3,550	
Decrease in accrued liabilities	(2,340)	
Decrease in federal income tax liability	(2,100)	(22,750)
Cash provided from operations		$ 61,100
Other resources provided:		
Sale of investments	$ 9,700	
Sale of equipment	2,600	
Issuance of common stock	25,000	
Assumption of mortgage note	35,000	72,300
Total financial resources provided		$133,400
Financial resources applied:		
Purchase of marketable securities	$ 3,000	
Acquisition of land and building	65,000	
Acquisition of equipment	43,000	
Payment of cash dividends	17,000	
Total financial resources applied		128,000
Increase in cash for the year		$ 5,400
Cash: Beginning of year		40,900
Cash: End of year		$ 46,300

the APB and the FASB have recommended experimentation using alternative forms.

Several features of Illustration 19.9 should be noted. Its two sections are headed "Financial resources provided" and "Financial resources applied" reflecting the reporting of all significant financing and investing activities as required by *Opinion No. 19*. The headings are appropriate since an exchange involving assumption of liability on a mortgage note for land and buildings is reported. Note that the statement reports both working capital and cash provided by operations.

Losses on the working paper

If a firm incurs a net loss for a period, the entry on the working paper debits Retained Earnings and credits Net Loss under Financial Resources Provided by Operations. Then the net loss is adjusted for the nonfund items. After these adjustments, the firm may have funds provided by or applied to operations. If funds were applied to operations, all data relative to the net loss and its adjustments will be shown in the "Resources applied" section of the formal statement of changes in financial position.

Working paper for statement of changes on a working capital basis

Entries 2 through 9 shown above for a statement of changes prepared under the cash basis analyze noncurrent account changes which had a cash effect. Since cash is an element of working capital, the same entries, with one exception, would be made in preparing a statement of changes focusing on working capital. The exception is entry 9 which under a working capital focus would be entered on the working paper as a debit to Retained Earnings and a credit to Working Capital Applied to Dividends. (For a comprehensive illustration of this working paper technique, see the solution to the demonstration problem.)

The first line of a working paper for a statement of changes focusing on working capital for The United States Corporation would show $148,700 of working capital at the end of 1983 and $178,850 at the end of 1984. Entry 1 would debit Working Capital for $30,150 and credit Increase in Working Capital on the last line of the working paper. This single working capital amount would be substituted for the nine current asset and current liability accounts listed on the working paper for a cash basis statement of changes.

Also, note in The United States Corporation illustration that entries for net income and nonworking capital charges and credits are grouped to make it easy to compute working capital from operations. This amount is $83,850 which was computed by totaling the first five items in the lower section of the working paper in Illustration 19.8.

USES OF THE STATEMENT OF CHANGES
IN FINANCIAL POSITION

The statement of changes in financial position summarizes the financing and investing activities of a firm for a period. It reports upon past management decisions regarding such matters as issuance of capital stock or sale of long-term bonds. The statement directly reports information that is otherwise obtainable only in bits and pieces from the balance sheets and statements of income and retained earnings. Included in the statement is information on cash or working capital flows which are vital to a firm's financial health. Such information is useful to management and all other interested parties, especially creditors and investors.

Management uses

Management can use the statement of changes to determine why there are cash or working capital shortages if the company has been experiencing problems in these areas. Management may, after study of the information, change its dividend policy to conserve funds. Or the statement may show a flow of funds from operations large enough to finance all projected capital needs internally rather than through borrowings or stock issues. Since the statement presents all significant financing and investing activities, management can see the effects of its past major policy decisions in quantitative form by reviewing the statement of changes.

Creditor and investor uses

Information on the statement of changes in financial position may provide creditors and investors with valuable clues to:

1. The extent to which internally generated funds cover projected capital needs.
2. The likelihood of the company paying or increasing future dividends.
3. Management's preferences toward financing and investing.
4. The firm's ability to make principal and interest payments on its debt.
5. Whether, in the light of available resources, a planned expansion is feasible.

WORKING CAPITAL OR CASH FLOWS

In the past, statements of changes in financial position have generally focused on working capital flows. Such statements were prepared for several reasons. Information was needed about the flows of liquid assets (working capital) through a firm; such flows are the life-blood of a business. Constant changes in accounting principles yielded net income amounts that often were not good measures of such liquid assets flows from operations. Attention focused on working capital rather than cash because little significance was attached to the composition of working capital. Working capital turned over quickly enough so that, if not now in cash form, it would be shortly.

The shift toward cash flows

Recent events suggest that in the coming years statements of changes in financial position will focus increasingly upon cash flows. In the recent periods of high rates of inflation and depressed economic conditions, many firms experienced severe cash flow, not working capital, problems. The FASB noted the importance of cash flows in the Conceptual Framework Project, and made the statement "that the reporting of meaningful components of cash flows is generally more useful than reporting changes in working capital."[2] Shortly after publication of this statement, the Financial Executives Institute recommended that its members adopt the cash basis in preparing a statement of changes in financial position.[3] Approximately 95 percent of the companies with securities traded on the New York Stock Exchange and the American Stock Exchange are represented in the Financial Executives Institute.

The shifting of attention from working capital flows to cash flows also is supported by developments in modern finance. The investment decision is seen more clearly as one in which cash outlays are compared with expected cash returns, appropriately discounted for time and risk. Management, investors, and creditors are all alike in that each invests cash to get future cash returns. Thus, information is needed to enable users to make predictions of the amounts, timing, and uncertainty surrounding expected cash receipts. Information also is needed to provide feedback on prior assessments of cash flow.

Information on prior cash flows provides a better basis for making predictions of cash flows than does information on past working capital flows. This statement is true because it has been shown that past cash flows often differed sharply from working capital flows. For example, a rapidly expanding business will most likely find that it is increasing its working capital by expanding inventories and accounts receivable, yet never seeming to have enough cash to meet current bills. Cash flow analysis is required to reveal such problems.

[2] FASB, "Reporting Income, Cash Flows, and Financial Position of Business Enterprises," *Proposed Statement of Financial Accounting Concepts,* Exposure Draft (Stamford, Conn., 1981), p. xi.

[3] Financial Executives Institute, *Alert,* December 14, 1981.

NEW TERMS INTRODUCED IN CHAPTER 19

Cash flow from operations
The net amount of cash received or disbursed for a given period on items that normally appear on the income statement. Usually obtained by converting accrual basis net income to a cash basis amount.

Cash flow statement
Another title for a statement of changes in financial position prepared under cash basis; sometimes used as a title for a statement or schedule showing cash flows into and out of a business, together with beginning and ending cash balances.

Financial resources applied
The most all-inclusive title used to describe the uses made of a firm's resources in a period. In certain instances, the more restrictive titles of working capital applied or cash applied may be substituted.

Financial resources provided
The most all-inclusive title used to describe the sources of the resources flowing into a firm in a period. In certain instances, the more restrictive titles of sources of working capital or sources of cash may be appropriate.

Funds
Broadly, the financial resources of a firm; often defined as working capital or cash.

Indirect method
A way of determining cash or working capital from operations that starts with net income and adjusts for expenses and revenues that do not affect cash or working capital. Also called the *addback* method.

Nonworking capital (nonfund) charges or expenses
Expenses and losses deducted in arriving at net income that do not reduce working capital; examples are depreciation, depletion, and amortization of patents and goodwill.

Nonworking capital (nonfund) credits or revenues
Revenues included in arriving at net income that do not provide working capital; an example is discount amortized and included in interest revenue earned on bond investments purchased at a discount.

Statement of changes in financial positon
A statement that reports the flows of cash or working capital into and out of a business in a given time period; will also show significant financing and investing activities that do not involve cash or working capital flows.

Statement of changes in working capital
A statement listing all current assets and current liabilities, their beginning and ending balances, and the changes in these balances summarized into a single amount—the net change in working capital. The **schedule of changes in working capital components** shows only the change in each working capital item summarized into a single amount.

Working capital
A possible definition of funds; the excess of current assets over current liabilities.

Working capital from operations
Working capital generated by the regular operations of a business; usually computed as net income plus nonworking capital expenses deducted in arriving at net income, minus nonworking capital revenues included, and less certain gains which are included in the total proceeds received from sale of a noncash or nonworking capital asset.

DEMONSTRATION PROBLEM

Given below are comparative balance sheets of the Dells Corporation as of June 30, 1983, and June 30, 1984. Also given are the income statement for the year ended June 30, 1984, and certain additional data.

DELLS CORPORATION
Comparative Balance Sheet
June 30, 1983, and 1984

	1984	1983	Increase decrease*
Assets			
Current Assets:			
Cash	$ 30,000	$ 80,000	$ 50,000*
Accounts receivable	160,000	100,000	60,000
Inventory	100,000	70,000	30,000
Prepaid rent	20,000	10,000	10,000
Total current assets	$310,000	$260,000	$ 50,000
Property, plant, and equipment:			
Equipment	$400,000	$200,000	$200,000
Accumulated depreciation	(60,000)	(50,000)	(10,000)
Total property, plant, and equipment	$340,000	$150,000	$190,000
Total assets	$650,000	$410,000	$240,000
Liabilities and Stockholders' Equity			
Current liabilities:			
Accounts payable	$ 50,000	$ 40,000	$ 10,000
Notes payable—bank	–0–	50,000	50,000*
Accrued salaries	10,000	20,000	10,000*
Federal income tax payable	30,000	20,000	10,000
Total current liabilities	$ 90,000	$130,000	$ 40,000*
Stockholders' equity:			
Common stock, $10 par	$300,000	$100,000	$200,000
Capital in excess of par	50,000	–0–	50,000
Retained earnings	210,000	180,000	30,000
Total stockholders' equity	$560,000	$280,000	$280,000
Total liabilities and stockholders' equity	$650,000	$410,000	$240,000

DELLS CORPORATION
Statement of Income and Retained Earnings
For the Year Ended June 30, 1984

Sales		$1,000,000
Cost of goods sold	$600,000	
Salaries and wages	200,000	
Rent	40,000	
Depreciation	20,000	
Interest	3,000	
Loss on sale of equipment	7,000	870,000
Net income before federal income taxes		$ 130,000
Federal income taxes		60,000
Net income		$ 70,000
Retained earnings, July 1, 1983		$ 180,000
		$ 250,000
Dividends		40,000
Retained earnings, June 30, 1984		$ 210,000

Additional data

1. Equipment with a cost of $20,000, on which $10,000 of depreciation had been recorded, was sold for cash.
2. Additional borrowings from the bank during the year amounted to $30,000.
3. Stock was issued for cash.

Required:

Using the data given for the Dells Corporation, prepare a statement of changes in financial position—working capital basis after preparing a working paper similar to Illustration 19.8. The working papers for this type of statement were not illustrated but can easily be prepared with only minor changes from Illustration 19.8. The changes needed are: find the net working capital on June 30, 1983, and on June 30, 1984; on the first line of the working papers, change the item named from Cash to Working capital and enter the working capital amounts computed as entry (1) on the working papers; insert a debit for the increase in working capital on the first line and insert a credit on the last line in the lower section of the working paper describing the item as increase in working capital. Entries 2–8 in Illustration 19.8 are illustrative of the entries required here.

Solution to demonstration problem

DELLS CORPORATION
Working Paper for Statement of Changes in Financial Position
For the Year Ended June 30, 1984

	Account Balances 6/30/83	Analysis of Transactions for Fiscal Year		Account Balances 6/30/84
		Debit	Credit	
Debits				
Working capital	130,000	(1) 90,000		220,000
Equipment	200,000	(5) 220,000	(4) 20,000	400,000
Totals	330,000			620,000
Credits				
Accumulated depreciation	50,000	(4) 10,000	(3) 20,000	60,000
Common stock	100,000		(6) 200,000	300,000
Capital in excess of par	–0–		(6) 50,000	50,000
Retained earnings	180,000	(7) 40,000	(2) 70,000	210,000
Totals	330,000	360,000	360,000	620,000
Financial resources provided:				
By operations:				
Net income		(2) 70,000		
Add: Depreciation		(3) 20,000		
Loss on sale of equipment		(4) 7,000		
Other sources:				
Sale of equipment		(4) 3,000		
Sale of common stock		(6) 250,000		
Financial resources applied:				
Purchase of equipment			(5) 220,000	
Declaration of cash dividends			(7) 40,000	
Increase in working capital				
during year			(1) 90,000	
Totals		350,000	350,000	

DELLS CORPORATION
Statement of Changes in Financial Position—Working Capital Basis
For the Year Ended June 30, 1984

Financial resources provided:

By operations:

Net income		$ 70,000
Add: Depreciation	$20,000	
Loss on sale of equipment	7,000	27,000
Working capital provided by operations		$ 97,000

Other sources of working capital:

Sale of equipment	3,000
Sale of common stock	250,000
Total working capital provided	$350,000

Financial resources applied:

Purchase of equipment	$220,000	
Declaration of cash dividends	40,000	
Total working capital applied		$260,000
Increase in working capital		$ 90,000

Schedule of changes in working capital components:

Increases (decreases) in current assets:

Cash	$ (50,000)	
Accounts receivable	60,000	
Inventory	30,000	
Prepaid rent	10,000	$ 50,000

Increases (decreases) in current liabilities:

Accounts payable	$ 10,000	
Notes payable—bank	(50,000)	
Accrued salaries	(10,000)	
Federal income tax payable	10,000	40,000
Increase in working capital		$ 90,000

QUESTIONS

1. The term *funds* is used in many different ways in accounting. Indicate several of these uses other than those given in this chapter. What are the concepts of funds as the term is used in a statement of changes in financial position?

2. If the net income for a given period is $25,000, does this mean that there is an increase of cash of the same amount? Why or why not?

3. Explain the difference between the direct and indirect methods for computing working capital from operations.

4. What are the major sources of funds in a business? What are the major uses of funds? What use of funds might be called involuntary?

5. Does the declaration or payment of dividends affect working capital? Why?

6. Why might a company have a positive inflow of cash from operations even though operating at a net loss?

7. What are nonfund (nonworking capital or noncash) expenses? Of what significance are they?

8. Describe the treatment of a gain on the sale of equipment in preparing a statement of changes in financial position.

9. Why might an analysis of working capital flow be unsuitable for short-run planning?

10. Why is it unlikely that cash flow from operations will be equal to net income for the same period?

11. In what respects does cash flow analysis differ from working capital flow analysis?

12. In the preparation of a funds statement under the working capital basis, why are the noncurrent accounts analyzed rather than the current accounts?

13. Depreciation is often referred to as a source of funds. Is it a source of funds? Explain.

14. Give two reasons why analysts seem to prefer cash flow statements to statements that report working capital flows?

EXERCISES

E–1. Indicate how the following data should be reported in a statement of changes in financial position (working capital basis). A company purchased land valued at $20,000 and a building valued at $40,000 by payment of $10,000 by check, signing a $15,000 interest-bearing note due in six months, and assuming a $35,000 mortgage on the property.

E–2. A company sold for $5,000 equipment having an original cost of $7,000 and on which $4,000 of depreciation had been recorded. The gain was included in net income. How should these data be shown in the statement of changes in financial position and why?

E–3. The following data are from the Automobile and the Accumulated Depreciation—Automobile accounts of a certain company:

Automobile

Date			Debit	Credit	Balance
1984					
Jan.	1	Balance brought forward			$4,000
July	1	Traded for new auto		$4,000	–0–
		New auto	$4,400		4,400

Accumulated Depreciation—Automobile

Jan.	1	Balance brought forward			$3,000
July	1	One-half year's depreciation		500	3,500
		Auto traded	$3,500		–0–
Dec. 31		One-half year's depreciation		550	550

The old auto was traded for a new one with the difference in values paid in cash. The income statement for the year shows a loss on the exchange of autos of $300.

Indicate the dollar amounts, the descriptions of these amounts, and their exact locations in a statement of changes in financial position (working capital basis).

E–4. Following are balance sheet data for the Badger Corporation:

	December 31, 1984	December 31, 1983
Cash	$ 47,000	$ 26,000
Accounts receivable	141,000	134,000
Inventory	83,000	102,000
Prepaid expenses	9,000	11,000
Plant assets (net of accumulated depreciation)	235,000	230,000
Accounts payable	122,000	127,000
Accrued expenses payable	40,000	41,000
Capital stock	300,000	300,000
Retained earnings	53,000	35,000

Required:

Calculate the change in working capital for the year 1984.

E-5. Refer to the information in Exercise E-4. Assume that the depreciation recorded in 1984 was $15,000. Compute the cash applied to purchase of plant assets assuming no assets were sold or scrapped in 1984.

E-6. Given that net income for the year was $20,000, patent amortization was $500, loss on sale of patents was $1,000, depreciation was $2,000, gain on sale of equipment was $600, and accumulated depreciation on equipment was $10,000. Compute working capital from operations.

E-7. Use the data in Exercise E-4. Assume that net income for 1984 was $24,000, that depreciation was $15,000, and that dividends declared and paid were $6,000. Prepare a statement of changes in financial position using the working capital basis.

E-8. A company's financial statements for a given year show sales of $500,000, net income of $50,000, accounts receivable on January 1 of $44,000 and $47,000 on December 31. Compute the effect of the above information on net income as a measure of cash from operations.

E-9. The income statement of a company shows cost of goods sold of $350,000 and net income of $50,000; inventory on January 1 was $51,000 and on December 31 was $63,000; accounts payable for merchandise purchases were $38,000 on January 1 and $42,000 on December 31. Compute the effects of the above information on net income as a measure of cash from operations.

E-10. The operating expenses and taxes (including $10,000 of depreciation) of a company for a given year were $100,000. Net income was $50,000. Prepaid Insurance decreased from $3,000 to $2,000 during the year, while Accrued Wages increased from $4,000 to $6,000 during the year. Compute the effects of the above on net income as a measure of cash from operations.

E-11. Assume that the data in Exercises E-8, E-9, and E-10 above are for the same company. Prepare the section of the statement of changes in financial position showing conversion of net income to cash from operations. Show both working capital and cash from operations.

E-12. Dividends payable increased by $3,000 during the year in which total dividends declared were $60,000. What amount of dividends appears in the statement of changes in financial position under the working capital basis? What amount appears in the same statement prepared under the cash basis?

E-13. Refer to the data in Exercises E-4 and E-7. Prepare a statement of changes in financial position under the cash basis.

PROBLEMS, SERIES A

P19–1–A.

WIN CORPORATION
Comparative Balance Sheets

	December 31	
	1984	*1983*
Assets		
Cash	$ 30,000	$ 40,000
Accounts receivable (net)	112,000	80,000
Inventory	200,000	160,000
Equipment	550,000	420,000
Accumulated depreciation	(160,000)	(140,000)
Investments	100,000	20,000
Total assets	$832,000	$580,000
Liabilities and Stockholders' Equity		
Accounts payable	$ 29,000	$ 25,000
Accrued liabilities	3,000	5,000
Capital stock—common—$10 par	500,000	400,000
Capital in excess of par	200,000	100,000
Retained earnings	100,000	50,000
Total liabilities and stockholders' equity	$832,000	$580,000

Additional data:

1. Net income was $90,000 for the year.
2. Fully depreciated equipment costing $20,000 was sold for $5,000 and equipment costing $150,000 was purchased for cash.
3. Depreciation expense for the year was $40,000.
4. Investments were purchased, $80,000.
5. An additional 10,000 shares of common stock were issued for cash at $20 per share.
6. Cash dividends of $40,000 were declared.

Required:

Prepare a statement of changes in financial position (working capital basis) including a schedule of changes in components.

P19–2–A.

Required:

Using the information in Problem P19–1–A, prepare a statement of changes in financial position using the cash basis.

P19–3–A.

ZANE CORPORATION
Comparative Balance Sheets

	June 30	
	1984	*1983*
Assets		
Current assets	$ 305,000	$235,000
Investment in stock of affiliated company	180,000	150,000
Buildings	380,000	280,000
Accumulated depreciation—buildings	(60,000)	(50,000)
Equipment	490,000	400,000
Accumulated depreciation—equipment	(150,000)	(120,000)
Total assets	$1,145,000	$895,000
Liabilities and Stockholders' Equity		
Current liabilities	$ 160,000	$120,000
Five-year note payable	100,000	–0–
Capital stock, par $100	800,000	700,000
Retained earnings	85,000	75,000
Total liabilities and stockholders' equity	$1,145,000	$895,000

Additional data:

1. Net income for year ended June 30, 1984, was $50,000.
2. Dividends declared, $40,000.
3. Stock was issued at par for cash.
4. No equipment or building retirements occurred during the year.
5. The five-year note was issued to pay for a building erected on land leased by the company.
6. Additional shares of stock of the affiliated company were acquired for cash.
7. Equipment was also purchased for cash.

Required:

      Prepare a statement of changes in financial position using the working capital basis. Try to do so without preparing a working paper so that your conceptual understanding of the statement might be strengthened.

P19–4–A.   Assume that the current assets and current liabilities in Problem P19–3–A consisted of the following:

	June 30, 1984	June 30, 1983
Cash	$ 50,000	$ 40,000
Accounts receivable	160,000	80,000
Inventory	80,000	90,000
Prepaid expenses	15,000	25,000
Total current assets	$305,000	$235,000
Accounts payable	$140,000	$ 90,000
Accrued liabilities	20,000	30,000
Total current liabilities	$160,000	$120,000

Required:

    a. Use the data in Problem P19–3–A and the above data and prepare a working paper for a statement of changes in financial position under the cash basis.

b. Prepare the formal statement of changes in financial position under the cash basis for Zane Corporation for the year ended June 30, 1984.

P19–5–A.

PALMER CORPORATION
Comparative Balance Sheets

	December 31	
	1984	*1983*
Assets		
Cash	$ 15,000	$ 20,000
Accounts receivable	127,000	98,000
Inventories	122,000	112,000
Unexpired insurance	3,000	4,000
Total current assets	$267,000	$234,000
Land	50,000	30,000
Buildings	200,000	100,000
Accumulated depreciations—buildings	(25,000)	(20,000)
Equipment	230,000	215,000
Accumulated depreciation—equipment	(125,000)	(100,000)
Total assets	$597,000	$459,000
Liabilities and Stockholders' Equity		
Accounts payable	$ 82,000	$ 80,000
Dividends payable	12,000	10,000
Federal income taxes payable	36,000	30,000
Accrued salaries and wages payable	4,000	3,000
Accrued expenses payable	6,000	4,000
Total current liabilities	$140,000	$127,000
Bonds payable—9%	100,000	100,000
Total liabilities	$240,000	$227,000
Capital stock—common	300,000	200,000
Capital in excess of par	15,000	–0–
Retained earnings	42,000	32,000
Total liabilities and stockholders' equity	$597,000	$459,000

PALMER CORPORATION
Income Statement and Statement of Retained Earnings
For Year Ended December 31, 1984

Sales (net)		$900,000
Cost of goods sold		600,000
Gross margin		$300,000
Salaries and wages	$150,000	
Depreciation	37,000	
Insurance	2,000	
Other expenses (including interest)	50,000	
Loss on sale of equipment	1,000	240,000
Net income before federal income taxes		$ 60,000
Federal income taxes		26,000
Net income		$ 34,000
Retained earnings, December 31, 1983		32,000
		$ 66,000
Less: Dividends		24,000
Retained earnings, December 31, 1984		$ 42,000

Additional data:

1. Equipment having an original cost of $10,000 and on which $7,000 of depreciation was recorded was sold at a loss of $1,000. Equipment additions were for cash.
2. All of the additional capital stock issued during the year, plus $5,000 of cash, was exchanged for land and a building.

Required:

   a.   Prepare a working paper similar to the one used to solve the demonstration problem. Use the working capital basis.

   b.   Prepare a statement of changes in financial position using the working capital basis.

P19–6–A.   Use the data in Problem P19–5–A. Assume that the accounts payable are for merchandise purchases only and that the accrued expenses payable are for accrued expenses included in the "other expenses" in the income statement.

Required:

   a.   Prepare a working paper for a statement of changes in financial position using the cash basis.

   b.   Prepare the formal statement of changes in financial position using the cash basis.

PROBLEMS, SERIES B

P19-1-B. Following are comparative ledger balance data and a statement of retained earnings for the year ended May 31, 1984, for Astro Company (000 omitted):

	May 31	
	1984	*1983*
Debits		
Cash	$ 63	$ 56
Marketable securities	30	24
Accounts receivable, net	126	144
Inventories	120	100
Investment in subsidiary	95	80
Land	70	50
Buildings and equipment	433	380
Patents	11	16
Total	$948	$850
Credits		
Accounts payable	$ 90	$ 64
Taxes payable	16	12
Accumulated depreciation	78	60
Bonds payable	200	200
Common stock, $100 par	400	400
Retained earnings	164	114
Total	$948	$850

Statement of Retained Earnings	
Balance, May 31, 1983	$114
Net income	100
	$214
Dividends declared	50
Balance, May 31, 1984	$164

Additional data:

1. Additional shares of stock of the subsidiary company were acquired for cash.
2. A tract of land adjacent to land owned was purchased during the year.
3. Depreciation of $30,000 and patent amortization of $5,000 were charged to expense during the year.
4. New equipment with a cost of $65,000 was purchased during the year, while fully depreciated equipment with a cost of $12,000 was scrapped and discarded.

Required:

Prepare a statement of changes in financial position using the working capital basis, and include a comparative schedule of changes in working capital components. Try to do so without preparing a working paper so that your conceptual understanding of the statement may be strengthened.

P19-2-B. Use the data for Problem P19-1-B.

Required:

Prepare a statement of changes in financial position under the cash basis. Account for the increase in marketable securities as an application of cash, not as an element of working capital related to operations for which net income is adjusted.

P19–3–B.   The income statement for the Miles Company for the year ended December 31, 1984, shows:

Net sales		$640,000
Cost of goods sold	$375,000	
Operating expenses	100,000	
Major repairs	50,000	
Interest expense	15,000	
Loss on sale of equipment ...	8,000	548,000
Net income before taxes		$ 92,000
Federal income taxes		48,000
Net income		$ 44,000

A comparative balance sheet for the company shows:

	December 31	
	1984	**1983**
Assets		
Cash	$ 48,000	$ 40,000
Accounts receivable, net	97,000	76,000
Inventories	210,000	180,000
Prepaid expenses	16,000	6,000
Total current assets	$371,000	$302,000
Buildings	100,000	100,000
Accumulated depreciation—buildings	(55,000)	(50,000)
Equipment	185,000	130,000
Accumulated depreciation—equipment	(63,000)	(60,000)
Total assets	$538,000	$422,000
Liabilities and Stockholders' Equity		
Accounts payable	$ 47,000	$ 75,000
Accrued expenses payable	16,500	14,500
Federal income taxes payable	48,000	45,000
Dividends payable	9,500	7,500
Total current liabilities	$121,000	$142,000
Bonds payable (15%)	100,000	100,000
Total liabilities	$221,000	$242,000
Capital stock—par $100	$250,000	$150,000
Capital in excess of par	25,000	–0–
Retained earnings	42,000	30,000
Total stockholders' equity	$317,000	$180,000
Total liabilities and stockholders' equity ...	$538,000	$422,000

Additional data:

1. Capital stock was issued for cash.
2. Accrued expenses payable relate solely to operating expenses.
3. The depreciation on equipment for the year amounted to $15,000. The equipment sold had an original cost of $30,000.
4. Dividends declared during the year totaled $32,000.
5. Accounts payable arose solely from purchases of merchandise.

Required:

   a.   Prepare a working paper for a statement of changes in financial position under the working capital basis. See the solution to the demonstration problem.

   b.   Prepare a formal statement of changes in financial position under the working capital basis.

P19–4–B.   Use the data for Problem P19–3–B.

Required:

    a. Prepare a working paper for a statement of changes in financial position under the cash basis.

    b. Prepare the formal statement of changes in financial position under the cash basis.

P19–5–B.   Given below are comparative balance sheet account balances and other data of the Bell Corporation (000 omitted):

	June 30	
	1984	1983
Debit balances		
Cash	$ 124	$ 68
Accounts receivable	385	222
Inventories	420	436
Unexpired insurance	2	3
Land	160	180
Buildings	1,120	620
Machinery and tools	440	240
Discount on bonds payable	4	5
	$2,655	$1,774
Credit balances		
Accumulated depreciation	$ 415	$ 262
Accounts payable	65	90
Accrued liabilities	44	6
Bank loans (90-day)	29	34
Mortgage bonds payable	200	100
Common stock, $100 par	900	300
Capital in excess of par	30	0
Retained earnings	972	982
	$2,655	$1,774

Additional data:

1. Net income for the year was $40,000.
2. Discount on bonds payable amortized was $1,000.
3. Depreciation for the year was $183,000.
4. Dividends declared and paid were $50,000.
5. Additional common stock was issued at $105 per share.
6. The mortgage bonds were issued at face value as partial payment for a building valued at $500,000. Machinery and tools were purchased for $230,000.
7. There was a gain of $4,000 on the sale of land.
8. Fully depreciated machinery with a cost of $30,000 was scrapped and written off.

Required:

    a. Prepare a working paper for a statement of changes in financial position under the working capital basis. See the solution to the demonstration problem.

    b. Prepare the formal statement of changes in financial position under the working capital basis.

P19–6–B.   Use the data in Problem P19–5–B. Assume that the bank loans do not relate directly to operations and the reduction in the loans is to be treated as an application of cash, not as an adjustment to net income in deriving cash flow from operations.

Required:

    a. Prepare a working paper for a statement of changes in financial position under the cash basis.

    b. Prepare the formal statement of changes in financial position under the cash basis.

BUSINESS DECISION PROBLEM 19–1

Following are comparative ledger balances for the Clayton Company:

	December 31	
	1984	**1983**
Debit balances		
Cash	$ 40,000	$ 25,000
Accounts receivable	40,000	30,000
Inventory	60,000	35,000
Land................................	45,000	40,000
Building	60,000	60,000
Equipment	190,000	150,000
Goodwill	80,000	100,000
Total	$515,000	$440,000

	December 31	
	1984	**1983**
Credit balances		
Accumulated depreciation—building	20,000	18,000
Accumulated depreciation—equipment	35,000	32,000
Accounts payable	50,000	30,000
Accrued liabilities	20,000	15,000
Capital stock	210,000	200,000
Paid-in capital—stock dividends	50,000	45,000
Paid-in capital—land donation	10,000	–0–
Retained earnings	120,000	100,000
Total	$515,000	$440,000

An analysis of the Retained Earnings account for the year reveals the following:

Balance, December 31, 1983 ..		$100,000
Add:		
Net income for the year ...		65,000
		$165,000
Less:		
Cash dividends	$30,000	
Stock dividends	15,000	45,000
Balance, December 31, 1984 ..		$120,000

Additional data:

    Equipment with a cost of $20,000 on which $18,000 of depreciation had been accumulated was sold during the year at a loss of $1,000. Included in net income is a gain on the sale of land of $6,000.

    The president of the Clayton Company has set two goals for 1985: (1) increase working capital by $40,000 and (2) increase cash dividends to $60,000. The company's activities in 1985 are expected to be quite similar to those of 1984.

Required:

Prepare a schedule showing working capital and cash provided by operations for 1984. Does it appear that the company can meet its president's goals for 1985? Explain.

BUSINESS DECISION PROBLEM 19–2

Hi Fli, Inc., is a video games and supplies center, owned and operated by Bobby Powers. During 1984, the company replaced $36,000 of the center's fully depreciated equipment with new equipment costing $46,000. Although a midyear dividend of $10,000 was paid, Bobby found it necessary to borrow $10,000 from his bank on a 180-day note. He feels further borrowing may be needed since the cash account is dangerously low at year-end.

Given below are the income statement and a funds statement, as Bobby's accountant calls it, for 1984.

HI FLI, INC.
Income Statement
For Year Ended December 31, 1984

Sales		$400,000
Cost of goods sold	$280,000	
Operating expenses and taxes	99,400	379,400
Net income		$ 20,600

HI FLI, INC.
Funds Statement
For Year Ended December 31, 1984

Funds provided:		
From operations:		
Net income		$20,600
Depreciation		10,000
Total funds from operations		$30,600
Mortgage note issued		32,000
Total funds provided		$62,600
Funds applied:		
New equipment	$46,000	
Dividends	10,000	56,000
Increase in funds		$ 6,600

Bobby is very concerned about what he sees in the above statements and how it relates to what he knows has actually happened. He turns to you for help. Specifically, he wants to know why the funds statement shows an increase in funds when he knows the cash balance decreased from $22,000 to $3,000 during the year. Also, why is depreciation shown as providing funds while the bank loan is not reported in the funds statement.

You believe that you can answer Bobby's questions. You ask for and receive the following condensed balance sheet data:

	December 31, 1984	December 31, 1983
Current assets:		
Cash	$ 3,000	$ 22,000
Accounts receivable	35,600	26,400
Merchandise inventory	57,000	35,000
Prepaid expenses	1,400	600
Total current assets	$ 97,000	$ 84,000
Equipment	80,000	70,000
Accumulated depreciation	(22,000)	(48,000)
Total assets	$155,000	$106,000
Current liabilities:		
Accounts payable	$ 17,400	$ 20,000
Notes payable	10,000	–0–
Accrued liabilities	1,200	2,200
Total current liabilities	$ 28,600	$ 22,200
Mortgage note payable...........................	32,000	–0–
Common stock	80,000	80,000
Retained earnings	14,400	3,800
Total liabilities and stockholders' equity	$155,000	$106,000

Required:

Prepare a statement that will show more clearly why the Hi Fli, Inc., center is having such a difficult time keeping sufficient cash on hand. Also, answer Bobby's questions.

Chapter 20

Analysis and interpretation of financial statements

CHAPTER GOALS

After study of this chapter, you should be able to:

1. Explain how comparative financial statements may be used to analyze and appraise the financial position of a firm and the results of its operations.

2. Calculate the amount of change in financial statement items for successive periods in dollars and percentages (horizontal and trend analysis).

3. Prepare common-size financial statements (vertical analysis).

4. Perform ratio analysis using the widely applied financial ratios and explain what each ratio seeks to show or measure.

5. Define and use correctly the new terms in the glossary.

This chapter presents some common methods used to analyze and interpret data in financial statements. A firm's financial statements may be analyzed by investors and creditors as an aid in deciding whether to invest in, or extend credit to, the company.

Management conducts its own analysis in seeking to evaluate, plan, and control its operations as they are carried out by subordinates and operating divisions. Such an analysis may lead to changes in operating policies with respect to items such as credit granting, product pricing, and number of products and amounts of each maintained in inventory. Much of management's analysis relates to parts of the company rather than to the company as a whole. And further, management's analysis is more likely to involve a comparison of actual with budgeted results or position (discussed in Chapter 25). For these reasons, discussion and illustration of financial statement analysis will be in the context of those outside the firm, such as investors and creditors, relying primarily upon the company's annual report for their information about a firm.

OBJECTIVES OF FINANCIAL STATEMENT ANALYSIS

Financial statement analysis consists of applying analytical tools and techniques to financial statements and other relevant data to obtain useful information. Financial statement analysis draws attention to significant relationships and trends. The information obtained is useful in *assessing past performance* and *current financial position,* which are the results or consequences of prior decisions. But the information is most useful for *making predictions* that may have a direct effect upon decisions made by many users of financial statements.

Information needed by outside users of financial statements often relates to a firm's profitability or liquidity or both. For example, a person considering purchase of shares of a firm's common stock may wish to predict future dividends and changes in the market price of the shares. Since both dividends and price changes are likely to be influenced by earnings, the investor may seek to predict earnings. The firm's past earnings record is the logical starting point in predicting future earnings.

On the other hand, a bank asked to extend a 90-day loan would be interested in a firm's projected short-term liquidity. Here again, the predicted ability to repay the loan is likely to be based, at least partially, upon proven past ability to pay off debts.

FINANCIAL STATEMENT ANALYSIS

Several types of analysis may be performed on a company's financial statements. Comparisons or relationships are almost always helpful since they enhance the utility of accounting information. For example, little useful information is conveyed by a statement that a firm's net income was $100,000 last year. Some utility is added if it is known that the prior year's net income was $25,000. Even more information is available if the amounts of sales and assets of a firm are known. Such comparisons or relationships may be expressed as:

1. Absolute increases and decreases for an item from one period to the next.
2. Percentage increases and decreases for an item from one period to the next.
3. Trend percentages.
4. Percentages of single items to an aggregate total.
5. Ratios.

Items 1 and 2 make use of comparative financial statements. Comparative financial statements present the same firm's financial statements for two or more successive periods in side-by-side columns. The calculation of dollar or percentage changes in the statement items or totals is known as *horizontal analysis*. This type of review helps detect changes in a firm's performance and highlights trends.

Trend percentages (item 3) are very similar to horizontal analysis except that a base year is selected and comparisons are made to the base year. Trend percentages are useful for comparing financial statements over several years because they disclose changes and trends occurring through time.

Information may also be gained by analyzing a financial statement of a firm for a single year to understand its composition. *Vertical analysis* (item 4) consists of the study of a single financial statement by expressing each item on the statement as a percentage of a significant total. Vertical analysis is especially useful in analyzing income statement data such as the percentage of cost of goods sold to sales or the gross margin on sales. When financial statements are presented showing only percentages and no absolute amounts, they are called *common-size statements*.

Ratios (item 5) are expressions of logical relationships between certain items in the financial statements. As with vertical analysis, a single period's financial statements are used, but all amounts are not expressed in terms of a single significant amount on a particular statement. Thus, many ratios can be computed from the same set of financial statements. The choice of ratios that should be prepared is limited only by the requirement that the items used to construct a ratio have a logical relationship to one another.

HORIZONTAL AND VERTICAL ANALYSIS: AN ILLUSTRATION

Illustrations 20.1 and 20.2 show comparative financial statements of The Knight Corporation for the years ended December 31, 1984, and 1985. These statements will serve as a basis for an illustration of horizontal and vertical analysis. The comparative statements can be analyzed to disclose certain relationships among the various items included in those statements. Management may use these relationships in making business decisions; investors and creditors also may use them when deciding whether to invest in or loan money to the firm.

Illustration 20.1:   Comparative balance sheets

THE KNIGHT CORPORATION
Comparative Balance Sheets
December 31, 1984 and 1985   *Exhibit A*

	December 31		Increase or decrease* 1985 over 1984		Percentage of total assets December 31	
	(1)	(2)	(3)	(4) Per-centage	(5)	(6)
	1985	1984	Dollars		1985	1984
Assets						
Current assets:						
Cash	$ 80,200	$ 55,000	$25,200	45.8	12.6	10.0
Accounts receivable, net	124,200	132,600	8,400*	6.3*	19.6	24.1
Notes receivable	55,000	50,000	5,000	10.0	8.7	9.1
Inventories	110,800	94,500	16,300	17.2	17.4	17.1
Prepaid expenses	3,600	4,700	1,100*	23.4*	0.6	0.9
Total current assets	$373,800	$336,800	$37,000	11.0	58.8R	61.1R
Property, plant, and equipment:						
Land	$ 21,000	$ 21,000	–0–	–0–	3.3	3.8
Building	205,000	160,000	$45,000	28.1	32.3	29.0
Less: Accumulated depreciation	(27,000)	(22,400)	(4,600)	21.0	(4.3)	(4.1)
Furniture and fixtures	83,200	69,800	13,400	19.2	13.1	12.7
Less: Accumulated depreciation	(20,800)	(14,100)	(6,700)	47.5	(3.3)	(2.6)
Total	$261,400	$214,300	$47,100	22.0	41.2R	38.9R
Total assets	$635,200	$551,100	$84,100	15.3	100.0	100.0
Liabilities and Stockholders' Equity						
Current liabilities:						
Accounts payable	$ 70,300	$ 64,600	$ 5,700	8.8	11.1	11.7
Notes payable	20,000	15,100	4,900	32.5	3.1	2.8R
Taxes accrued..............................	36,800	30,200	6,600	21.9	5.8	5.5
Total current liabilities	$127,100	$109,900	$17,200	15.7	20.0	20.0R
Long-term liabilities:						
Mortgage notes payable, land and building, 12%, 1987	43,600	60,800	17,200*	28.3*	6.9	11.0
Total liabilities	$170,700	$170,700	$ 0	0.0	26.9	31.0
Stockholders' equity:						
Common stock, par value $10 per share	$240,000	$200,000	$40,000	20.0	37.8	36.3
Retained earnings	224,500	180,400	44,100	24.4	35.3	32.7
Total stockholders' equity	$464,500	$380,400	$84,100	22.1	73.1	69.0
Total liabilties and stockholders' equity ...	$635,200	$551,100	$84,100	15.3	100.0	100.0

R Rounding difference.

Analysis of balance sheet

Examination of the comparative balance sheet reveals (among other items) the following:

Columns 1, 2, and 3 in Illustration 20.1 show the absolute dollar amounts for each item for December 31, 1984, and December 31, 1985, and the change

Illustration 20.2:   Comparative statements of income and retained earnings

THE KNIGHT CORPORATION
Comparative Statements of Income and Retained Earnings
For the Years Ended December 31, 1984 and 1985   *Exhibit B*

	Year ended December 31		Increase or decrease* 1985 over 1984		Percentage of net sales	
	(7)	(8)	(9)	(10)	(11)	(12)
				Per-		
	1985	*1984*	*Dollars*	*centage*	*1985*	*1984*
Net sales	$986,400	$765,500	$220,900	28.9	100.0	100.0
Cost of goods sold	623,200	500,900	122,300	24.4	63.2	65.4
Gross margin	$363,200	$264,600	$ 98,600	37.3	36.8	34.6
Operating expenses:						
Selling	$132,500	$ 84,900	$ 47,600	56.1	13.4	11.1
Administrative	120,300	98,600	21,700	22.0	12.2	12.9
Total operating expenses	$252,800	$183,500	$ 69,300	37.8	25.6	24.0
Net operating income	$110,400	$ 81,100	$ 29,300	36.0	11.2	10.6
Other expenses	3,000	2,800	200	7.1	0.3	0.4
Net income before federal income taxes ..	$107,400	$ 78,300	$ 29,100	37.2	10.9	10.2
Federal income taxes	48,300	31,700	16,600	52.4	4.9	4.1
Net income	$ 59,100	$ 46,600	$ 12,500	26.8	6.0	6.1[R]
Retained earnings, January 1	180,400	146,300	34,100	23.3		
	$239,500	$192,900	$ 46,600	24.2		
Dividends declared	15,000	12,500	2,500	20.0		
Retained earnings, December 31	$224,500	$180,400	$ 44,100	24.4		

[R] Rounding difference.

for the year. If the change between the two dates is an increase from 1984 to 1985, the change is shown as a positive figure. If the change is a decrease, it is so indicated by an asterisk (*).

Examples of the items highlighted by the first three columns are:

a.   Current assets have increased $37,000, consisting largely of a $25,200 increase in cash, while current liabilities have increased only $17,200.

b.   Total assets have increased $84,100, while liabilities have remained unchanged.

c.   The increase in total assets has been financed by the sale of common stock, $40,000, and by the retention of earnings, $44,100.

Column 4 in Illustration 20.1 expresses the dollar change in column 3 as a percentage of column 2. Frequently, percentage increases and decreases are more informative than absolute amounts, as is illustrated by the current asset and current liability changes. Although the absolute amount of current assets has increased more than twice the amount of current liabilities, the percentages reveal that current assets increased 11 percent, while current liabilities increased 15.7 percent. Thus, current liabilities are increasing at a rate faster than the current assets that will be used to pay them. But, in view of the substantial amount of cash possessed, the company is not likely to fail to pay its debts as they come due. The 28.3 percent decrease in mortgage notes payable will lead the analyst to conclude that interest charges will be lower in the coming years. The 20 percent increase in common shares outstanding will tend to reduce earnings per share.

Columns 5 and 6 express the dollar amounts of each item in columns 1 and 2 as percentages of total assets (equities). Vertical analysis of The Knight Corporation's balance sheet is used to disclose an account's relative significance to total assets (equities) which aids in assessing the importance of changes in that account. For example, although prepaid expenses declined $1,100 in 1985, a decrease of 23.4 percent, the account represents less than 1 percent of total assets and, therefore, probably would not be investigated further. The vertical analysis also shows that long-term debt financing decreased from 11 percent of total assets to 6.9 percent in 1985, a minus 4.1 percent. The percentage of stockholder financing to total assets of the company increased from 69.0 to 73.1, a plus 4.1 percent.

Analysis of income statement

The amounts in columns 7 and 8 in Illustration 20.2 are the dollar amounts for the years 1984 and 1985. The amounts and percentages in columns 9 through 12 are computed in the same manner as the balance sheet amounts in Illustration 20.1 except that the items in columns 11 and 12 are percentages of net sales. Examination of the comparative statements of net income and retained earnings shows the following:

a. Sales increased 28.9 percent in 1985.
b. Gross margin increased 37.3 percent in 1985.
c. Selling expenses increased 56.1 percent in 1985.
d. Federal income taxes rose by 52.4 percent in 1985.
e. Net income increased 26.8 percent, while dividends increased 20.0 percent.
f. Net income per dollar of sales remained virtually constant over the two years.

Considering both horizontal and vertical analysis information, the analyst would conclude that an increase in the gross margin rate from 34.6 percent to 36.8 percent, coupled with a 28.9 percent increase in sales, resulted in a 37.3 percent increase in gross margin in 1985. The increase in net income was held to 26.8 percent because selling expenses increased 56.1 percent and income taxes increased 52.4 percent. Predicting net income for 1986 would be aided if the analyst knew whether this increase in selling expenses is expected to recur. Other expenses remained basically the same, on a percentage-of-sales basis, over the two years.

Proper analysis does not stop upon the calculation of increases and decreases in amounts or percentages over several years. Such changes generally indicate areas worthy of further investigation. They are merely clues that may lead to significant findings. Accurate predictions depend upon a host of factors including economic and political conditions; management's plans regarding new products, plant expansion, promotional outlays; and the expected activities of competitors.

TREND PERCENTAGES

Trend percentages are also referred to as index numbers. They are used for comparison of financial information over time to a base year. Trend percentages are calculated by:

1. Selecting a base year.
2. Assigning a weight of 100 percent to the amounts appearing on the base year financial statements.
3. Expressing the amounts shown on the other years' financial statements as a percentage of base year amounts. The percentages are computed by dividing nonbase amounts by the base year amounts and then multiplying the result by 100.

As an example, the following information is given:

	1984	1985	1986	1987
Sales	$350,000	$367,500	$441,000	$485,000
Cost of goods sold	200,000	196,000	230,000	285,000
Gross margin	$150,000	$171,500	$211,000	$200,000
Operating expenses	145,000	169,000	200,000	192,000
Net income before taxes	$ 5,000	$ 2,500	$ 11,000	$ 8,000

Letting 1984 be the base year, trend percentages would be calculated for each year by dividing sales by $350,000; cost of goods sold by $200,000; gross margin by $150,000; operating expenses by $145,000; and net income before income taxes by $5,000. After all divisions have been made, each result would be multiplied by 100, and the resulting trends would appear as follows:

	1984	1985	1986	1987
Sales	100	105	126	139
Cost of goods sold	100	98	115	143
Gross margin	100	114	141	133
Operating expenses	100	117	138	132
Net income before taxes	100	50	220	160

Trend percentages indicate changes that are taking place in an organization and highlight direction of the changes. The percentages can provide clues as to which items need further investigation or analysis. In reviewing trend percentages, a manager or investor should pay close attention to the trends in related items, such as the cost of goods sold in relation to sales. Trend analysis that shows a constantly declining gross margin rate may be a signal that trouble lies ahead in diminished earnings or actual losses. The nature and direction of changes in trend analysis data may be seen more clearly when such data are presented graphically.

Expressing changes as percentages is usually straightforward as long as the amount in the base year is positive—that is, not zero or negative. A $30,000 increase in notes receivable cannot be expressed in percentages if the increase is from zero last year to $30,000 this year. Also, an increase in net income from a loss last year of $10,000 to earnings this year of $20,000 cannot be expressed in percentage terms.

RATIO ANALYSIS

Logical relationships exist between certain accounts or items in a firm's financial statements. These accounts may appear on the same statement or they may appear on two different statements. The dollar amounts of the related accounts or items are set up in fraction form and called ratios. These ratios can be broadly classified as (1) liquidity ratios, (2) equity or solvency ratios, (3) profitability tests, and (4) market tests.

Liquidity ratios

Liquidity ratios are used to indicate a firm's debt-paying ability, especially its short-term debt-paying ability. Thus, these ratios are designed to show the firm's general capacity to meet maturing current liabilities and its ability to generate cash to pay these liabilities.

Current or working capital ratio. Working capital is the excess of current assets over current liabilities. The ratio which relates these two categories is known as the *current* or *working capital ratio*. It indicates the ability of a company to pay its current liabilities from current assets and, in this way, shows the strength of the company's working capital position.

The current ratio is computed by dividing total current assets by total current liabilities:

$$\text{Current ratio} = \frac{\text{Current assets}}{\text{Current liabilities}}$$

The ratio usually is stated in terms of the number of dollars of current assets to one dollar of current liabilities (although the dollar signs usually are omitted). Thus, if current assets total $75,000 and current liabilities total $50,000, the ratio is expressed as 1.5:1, or the firm has $1.50 of current assets for each $1 of current liabilities.

The current ratio provides a better index of a firm's ability to pay current debts than does the absolute amount of working capital. To illustrate, assume that Company A and Company B have current assets and current liabilities on December 31, 1984, as follows:

	Company A	Company B
Current assets	$11,000,000	$200,000
Current liabilities	10,000,000	100,000
Working capital	$ 1,000,000	$100,000
Current ratio	1.1:1	2:1

Company A has 10 times as much working capital as Company B. But Company B has a superior debt-paying ability since it has two dollars of current assets for each dollar of current liabilities. Company A has only $1.10 of current assets for each $1 of current liabilities.

Short-term creditors are particularly interested in the current ratio. They expect to receive payment from conversion of inventories and accounts receivable into cash. Long-term creditors are also interested in the current ratio because a firm that is unable to pay short-term debts may be forced into bankruptcy. For this reason, many bond indentures contain a provision requiring the borrower to maintain at least a certain minimum current ratio. A firm can increase its current ratio by issuing long-term debt or capital stock or by selling noncurrent assets.

A firm must also guard against a current ratio that is too high, especially if caused by idle cash, slow-paying customers, and slow-moving inventory. Decreased net income and rates of return upon assets and stockholders' equity follow when too much capital that could be used profitably elsewhere is tied up in current assets.

Referring back to The Knight Corporation data in Illustration 20.1, the current ratios for the two years are as follows:

	December 31		Amount of
	1985	1984	increase
Current assets (a)	$373,800	$336,800	$37,000
Current liabilities (b)	127,100	109,900	17,200
Working capital (a − b)......	$246,700	$226,900	$19,800
Current ratio (a ÷ b)	2.94:1	3.06:1	

Thus, although Knight's working capital increased by $19,800, or 8.7 percent, its current ratio fell from 3.06:1 to 2.94:1, reflecting the fact that its current liabilities increased faster than its current assets.

Quick or acid-test ratio. The current ratio is not the only measure of a firm's short-term debt-paying ability. Another measure is the *quick* or *acid-test ratio,* which is the ratio of quick assets (cash, marketable securities, and net receivables) to current liabilities.

$$\text{Acid-test ratio} = \frac{\text{Quick assets}}{\text{Current liabilities}}$$

stockholders increased their proportionate equity in the firm's assets by additional investment in the company's common stock and by retention of income earned during the year.

The Knight Corporation's equity ratio increased from 69.0 percent in 1984 to 73.1 percent in 1985. The equity ratio must be interpreted carefully. From a creditor's point of view, a high proportion of owners' equity is desirable. A high percentage indicates the existence of a large protective buffer for creditors in the event the company suffers a loss. But from an owner's point of view, a high proportion of owners' equity may or may not be desirable. If borrowed funds can be used by the business to generate earnings in excess of the net after-tax cost of the interest on such borrowed funds, a lower percentage of owners' equity may be desirable.

Following is a brief illustration of the effect on The Knight Corporation if it were more highly leveraged (i.e., had a larger proportion of debt). Assume that Knight Corporation could have financed its present operations with $40,000 of 12 percent bonds instead of 4,000 shares of common stock. The effect on earnings for 1985 would be as follows, assuming a marginal federal income tax rate of 50 percent:

Net income as presently stated (Illustration 20.2)	$59,100
Deduct additional interest on debt (0.12 × $40,000)	4,800
	$54,300
Add reduced tax due to interest deduction (0.5 × $4,800)	2,400
Adjusted net income	$56,700

As shown, net income would be less. But there would be 4,000 fewer shares outstanding. As a result, earnings per share would be increased to $2.84 ($56,700/20,000) from $2.46 ($59,100/24,000). Since investors place heavy emphasis upon earnings per share amounts, many companies in recent years have introduced larger portions of debt into their capital structures to increase earnings per share. This practice is not without its dangers because financial leverage magnifies losses as well as earnings per share since there are fewer shares of stock over which to spread the loss.

It should also be pointed out that too low a percentage of owners' equity (too much debt) may be hazardous from the owners' standpoint. A period of business recession may result in operating losses and shrinkages in the values of assets (such as receivables and inventories) leading to an inability to meet fixed payments for interest and principal on the debt. This in turn may cause stockholders to lose control of the company. The company may be forced into liquidation.

Owners' equity/debt ratio. The relative equities of owners and creditors may be expressed in several ways. To say that creditors hold a 26.9 percent interest in the assets of The Knight Corporation on December 31, 1985, is equivalent to saying stockholders hold a 73.1 percent interest. In many cases, the relationship is expressed as a ratio—*owners' equity to debt ratio.* Such a ratio for The Knight Corporation would be 2.23:1 ($380,400/$170,700) on

December 31, 1984, and 2.72:1 ($464,500/$170,700) on December 31, 1985. This ratio is sometimes inverted and called the *debt/equity ratio.* Some analysts use only long-term debt rather than total debt in calculating these ratios.

Profitability tests

Profitability is a very important measure of a firm's operating success. Generally, there are two areas of concern when judging profitability: (1) relationships on the income statement which indicate a company's ability to recover costs and expenses, and (2) relationship of income to some balance sheet measure which indicates the relative ability to earn income on assets employed.

Earning power percentage (return on operating assets).   The best measure of earnings performance without regard to sources of assets is the relationship of net operating income to operating assets, which is known as the *earning power percentage.* There are two elements in the determination of this ratio: operating margin and turnover of operating assets.

Operating margin reflects the percentage of each dollar of net sales which becomes net operating income. Net operating income excludes extraordinary items, nonoperating revenues, such as interest revenue, and nonoperating expenses, such as interest expense and income taxes. The formula for operating margin is:

$$\text{Operating margin} = \frac{\text{Net operating income}}{\text{Net sales}}$$

Turnover of operating assets shows the dollars of sales for each dollar invested in operating assets. Year-end operating assets typically are used, even though an average would be better in theory. *Operating assets* are all assets actively used in producing operating revenues. Examples of nonoperating assets are land held for future use, a factory building rented to another company, and long-term bond investments. Total assets should not be used in evaluating earnings performance due to the inclusion of nonoperating assets that do not contribute to the generation of sales. The formula for the *turnover of operating assets* is:

$$\text{Turnover of operating assets} = \frac{\text{Net sales}}{\text{Operating assets}}$$

The earning power percentage of a firm then is equal to operating margin multiplied by turnover of operating assets. The more a company earns per dollar of sales and the more sales it makes per dollar invested in operating assets, the higher will be the return per dollar invested. Earning power may be expressed by the following formulas:

$$\text{Earning power} = \text{Operating margin} \times \text{Turnover of operating assets, } or$$

$$\text{Earning power} = \frac{\text{Net operating income}}{\text{Net sales}} \times \frac{\text{Net sales}}{\text{Operating assets}}$$

Since net sales appears as both a numerator and a denominator, it can be canceled out, and the formula for earning power percentage becomes:

$$\text{Earning power percentage} = \frac{\text{Net operating income}}{\text{Operating assets}}$$

But it is more useful for analytical purposes to leave the formula in the form which shows margin and turnover separately.

Securing desired earnings power. Companies that are to survive in the economy must attain some minimum level of earning power. But this minimum can be obtained in many different ways. To illustrate, consider a grocery store and a jewelry store, each with an earning power of 8 percent on operating assets. The grocery store normally would have a low margin and a high turnover, while the jewelry store would have a high margin and a low turnover:

	Margin ×	Turnover ×	Earning power percentage
Grocery store	1% ×	8.0 times	8
Jewelry store	20% ×	0.4 times	8

The earning power percentage figures for The Knight Corporation for 1985 and 1984 are calculated below.

	1985	1984	Amount of increase
Net operating income (*a*)	$110,400	$ 81,100	$ 29,300
Net sales (*b*)	$986,400	$765,500	$220,900
Operating margin (*a* ÷ *b* = *c*)	11.19%	10.59%	
Net sales (*d*)	$986,400	$765,500	$220,900
Total assets (all operating assets) (*e*)	$635,200	$551,100	$ 84,100
Turnover of operating assets (*d* ÷ *e* = *f*)	1.55:1	1.39:1	
Earning power percentage (*c* × *f*)	17.34%	14.72%	

Earning power percentage or rate of return on operating assets is designed to show the earning power of the company as a bundle of assets. By disregarding both nonoperating assets and nonoperating income, earning power percentage measures the profitability of the firm in carrying out its primary business functions.

Net income to net sales. Net income as a percentage of net sales (*net income to net sales*) is obtained by dividing net income for the period by net sales of the period:

$$\text{Net income to net sales} = \frac{\text{Net income}}{\text{Net sales}}$$

This ratio measures the proportion of the sales dollar that remains after deduction of all expenses. The computations for The Knight Company are:

	1985	1984	Amount of increase
Net income (a)	$ 59,100	$ 46,600	$ 12,500
Net sales (b)	$986,400	$765,500	$220,900
Ratio of net income to net sales (a ÷ b)	5.99%	6.09%	

Although the ratio of net income to net sales indicates the net amount of profit on each sales dollar, a great deal of care must be exercised in the use and interpretation of this ratio. The amount of net income includes all types of nonoperating items that may occur in a particular period; therefore, net income includes the effects of such things as extraordinary items and interest charges. Thus, a period which contains the effects of an extraordinary item will not be comparable to a period which contains no extraordinary items. Also, since interest expense is deductible in the determination of income while dividends are not, net income is affected by the methods used to finance the firm's assets.

Net income to average stockholders' equity. From the stockholders' point of view, an important measure of the income-producing ability of a company is the relationship of *net income to average stockholders' equity* or the *rate of return on average stockholders' equity.* The ratio also is often referred to simply as *return on equity (ROE).* Stockholders are interested in the ratio of operating income to operating assets as a measure of the efficient use of assets by management. But stockholders are even more interested in knowing what return was earned by the company on each dollar of owners' equity invested.

$$\text{Net income to average stockholders' equity} = \frac{\text{Net income}}{\text{Average stockholders' equity}}$$

The ratios for The Knight Company are shown below. Assume that total stockholders' equity on January 1, 1984, was $321,500.

	1985	1984	Amount of increase
Net income (a)	$ 59,100	$ 46,600	$ 12,500
Total stockholders' equity:			
January 1	$380,400	$321,500	$ 58,900
December 31	464,500	380,400	84,100
Total	$844,900	$701,900	$143,000
Average total stockholders' equity (b)	$422,450	$350,950	
Ratio of net income to stockholders' equity (a ÷ b)	13.99%	13.28%	

The increase in the ratio from 13.28 percent to 13.99 percent would be regarded favorably by stockholders. This ratio indicates that for each average dollar of capital invested by a stockholder, the company earned 14 cents in 1985.

Earnings per share.   Probably the measure used most widely to appraise a firm's operating ability is *earnings per share* of common stock (hereafter simply EPS). An EPS amount is usually computed for common stock and is equal to earnings available to common stockholders divided by weighted-average number of shares of common stock outstanding. The financial press regularly publishes actual and forecasted EPS amounts for many corporations, together with period-to-period comparisons. The Accounting Principles Board noted the significance attached to EPS by requiring that such amounts be reported on the face of the income statement.[2]

Calculation of EPS may be a fairly simple or a highly complex problem, depending upon the corporation's capital structure. A firm has a simple capital structure if it has no outstanding securities that can be exchanged for common stock such as convertible bonds, convertible preferred stocks, warrants, or options. If a firm has such securities outstanding, it has a complex capital structure. A firm with a simple capital structure reports a single EPS amount calculated as follows:

$$\text{EPS of common stock} = \frac{\text{Earnings available to common stockholders}}{\text{Weighted-average number of common shares outstanding}}$$

The numerator in the EPS fraction is equal to net income less the current year's preferred dividends, whether declared or not.

Weighted-average number of shares. The denominator in the EPS fraction is the weighted-average number of common shares outstanding for the period. If the number of shares outstanding changed during the period, the change in shares must be weighted for the fractional period. For example, assume that 20,000 shares were outstanding at the beginning of the year and that 4,000 shares were issued on June 30. The 4,000 shares are weighted by one half for the half year they were outstanding. The weighted-average number of shares outstanding for the year is 22,000: 20,000 shares outstanding all year, plus 4,000 shares outstanding for a half year, which is the equivalent of 2,000 shares outstanding all year. Another way of describing this situation is to say that 20,000 shares were outstanding for one-half year and 24,000 shares for one-half year, for an average of 22,000 shares for the year. If the company had purchased 400 shares of treasury stock on September 30, the calculation would read:

20,000 shares × ½ year (January–June)	=	10,000
24,000 shares × ¼ year (July–September)	=	6,000
23,600 shares × ¼ year (October–December)	=	5,900
Weighted-average number of common shares outstanding		21,900

[2] Accounting Principles Board, "Reporting Earnings per Share," *Opinion No. 15* (New York: AICPA, 1969), par. 12.

A weighted average for the common shares outstanding should be computed whenever shares are issued or acquired during a period. Such changes increase or decrease the capital invested in the company, which should affect earnings available to stockholders. Shares should be considered outstanding only during those periods that the related capital investment was available to help produce income.

EPS amounts for The Knight Corporation, which has no preferred stock outstanding, are shown below. The weighted-average number of shares for 1985 is computed under the assumption that 4,000 shares were issued on June 30.

	1985	1984	Amount of increase
Net income (a)	$59,100	$46,600	$12,500
Average number of shares of common stock outstanding (b)	22,000	20,000	2,000
EPS of common stock (a ÷ b)..............	$2.69	$2.33	

The better than 15 percent increase in EPS from $2.33 to $2.69 would probably be viewed quite favorably by The Knight Corporation's stockholders.

EPS and stock dividends or splits. Increases in shares outstanding as a result of a stock dividend or split do not require weighting for fractional periods. Such shares do not increase capital invested in the business and therefore do not affect earnings. All that is required is to restate all prior calculations of EPS using the increased number of shares. For example, a firm reported EPS for 1984 of $1 ($100,000/100,000 shares) and earned $150,000 in 1985. The only change in common stock over the two years was a two-for-one stock split on December 1, 1985, which doubled the shares outstanding to 200,000. EPS for 1984 would be restated at $0.50 ($100,000/200,000 shares) and would be $0.75 ($150,000/200,000 shares) for 1985.

Primary EPS and fully diluted EPS. In the merger wave of the 1960s, corporations often issued securities to finance their acquisitions of other companies. Many of the securities issued were "calls on common" or possessed "equity kickers." These terms mean that the securities were convertible into, or exchangeable for, shares of their issuers' common stock. As a result, many complex problems arose in computing EPS. *APB Opinion No. 15* provided guidelines for solving these problems. A company with a complex capital structure must present primary EPS and fully diluted EPS data. But, because of the complexities faced, further discussion and illustration of these two EPS amounts must be reserved for an intermediate accounting text.

Times interest earned ratio. Creditors, especially long-term creditors, want to know whether a borrower can meet its required interest payments when they become due. A ratio that provides some indication of this ability is the *times interest earned ratio* (or *interest coverage ratio*). It is computed as follows:

$$\text{Times interest earned ratio} = \frac{\text{Income before interest and taxes}}{\text{Interest expense}}$$

Analysts disagree on whether the denominator should be interest on long-term debt or all interest expense. We prefer the latter since failure to make any required interest payment is a serious matter. Assume that a company has income before interest expense and income taxes of $100,000, and interest expense for the period of $10,000. The times interest earned ratio is 10 to 1; it can also be said that the company earned its interest expense 10 times during the period. Income before interest and income taxes is used in the ratio since there would be no income taxes if interest expense is equal to or greater than income before interest and taxes. The ratio is a rough measure of cash flow from operations and cash flow out as interest on debt. Very low or negative interest coverage ratios suggest that the borrower could default on required interest payments. A firm is not likely to be able to continue interest payments over many periods if it fails to earn enough income to cover them. On the other hand, interest coverage of 10 to 20 times suggests the company is not likely to default on interest payments.

Times preferred dividends earned ratio. Preferred stockholders, like bondholders, must usually be satisfied with a fixed-dollar return on their investments. They are interested in the company's ability to make preferred dividend payments each year. This can be measured by computing the *times preferred dividends earned ratio.* It can be computed as follows:

$$\text{Times preferred dividends earned ratio} = \frac{\text{Net income}}{\text{Preferred dividends}}$$

Suppose a company has net income of $48,000 and has $100,000 (par value) of 8 percent preferred stock outstanding. The number of times the preferred dividends are earned would be:

$$\frac{\$48,000}{\$8,000} = 6 \text{ to } 1, \text{ or } 6 \text{ times}$$

The higher this rate, the higher is the probability that the preferred stockholders will receive their dividends each year.

Market tests

Certain ratios are computed using information from the financial statements and information about market price for the company's stock. These tests help investors and potential investors assess the relative merits of the various stocks in the marketplace.

Yield on common stock and price-earnings ratio. The *yield* on a stock investment is the annual earnings or dividends per share as a percentage of the current market price per share. Thus, a firm's earnings yield per share of common stock is calculated as follows:

$$\text{Earnings yield on common stock} = \frac{\text{EPS}}{\text{Current market price per share}}$$

Suppose, for example, that a company had EPS of common stock of $2 and that the quoted market price of the stock on the New York Stock Exchange was $30. The *earnings yield on common stock* would be:

$$\frac{\$2}{\$30} = 6\tfrac{2}{3} \text{ percent}$$

This ratio when inverted is called the *price-earnings ratio.* In the case just cited, the price-earnings ratio is:

$$\text{Price-earnings ratio} = \frac{\text{Current market price per share}}{\text{EPS}} = \frac{\$30}{\$2} = 15:1$$

Investors would say that this stock is selling at 15 times earnings or at a multiple of 15. They might have a multiple in mind as being the proper one that should be used to judge whether the stock was underpriced or over-priced. Different investors will have different estimates of the proper price-earnings ratio for a given stock and also different estimates of the future earnings prospects of the firm. These are two of the factors which cause one investor to sell stock at a particular price and another investor to buy at that price.

Dividend yield and payout ratios. The dividend paid per share of common stock is also of much interest to common stockholders. When the dividend is divided by the current market price per share, the result is called the *dividend yield.*

If the company referred to immediately above paid a $1.50 per share dividend, the dividend yield would be:

$$\text{Dividend yield on common stock} = \frac{\text{Dividend per share}}{\text{Current market price per share}} = \frac{\$1.50}{\$30.00} = 5 \text{ percent}$$

One additional step is to divide the dividend per share by the earnings available per share to determine the *payout ratio* on common stock as follows:

$$\text{Payout ratio} = \frac{\text{Dividend per share}}{\text{EPS}} = \frac{\$1.50}{\$2.00} = 75 \text{ percent}$$

A payout ratio of 75 percent means that the company paid out 75 percent of the EPS in the form of dividends. Some investors are attracted by the stock of companies that pay out a large percentage of their earnings. Other investors are attracted by the stock of companies that retain and reinvest a large percentage of their earnings. The tax status of the investor has a great deal to do with this. Investors in very high tax brackets often prefer to have the company reinvest the earnings with the expectation that this will result in share price appreciation that would be taxed at capital gains rates when the shares are sold. Dividends are taxed at ordinary income rates, which may be much higher than capital gains rates.

Yield on preferred stock. Preferred stockholders compute dividend yield in a manner similar to the computation of dividend yield for common stockholders. Suppose a company has 2,000 shares of $100 par value, 8 percent preferred stock outstanding that has a current market price of $110 per share. The dividend yield would be computed as follows:

$$\text{Dividend yield on preferred stock} = \frac{\text{Dividend per share}}{\text{Current market price per share}} = \frac{\$8}{\$110} = 7.27 \text{ percent}$$

Through the use of dividend yield rates, different preferred stocks having different annual dividends and different market prices can be compared.

FINAL CONSIDERATIONS IN FINANCIAL STATEMENT ANALYSIS

Standing alone, a single financial ratio may not be very informative. Greater insight can be obtained by computing and anlyzing several related ratios for a company. The ratios presented in this chapter are summarized in Illustration 20.3. A review of these ratios should make it apparent that some are directly related to others or that there may be several ratios which can provide similar information.

By comparing one company's financial data and ratios over time, an indication can be gained as to changes and trends of that company. But to evaluate these trends, standards for comparison are needed. Comparisons with standards provide a starting point for the analyst's thinking and lead to further investigation and, ultimately, to conclusions and business decisions.

Sources of comparative standards

The possible sources of comparative standards include:

1. Records of past performance and position of the company as gained from comparative financial statements of the past three to five years. Such records are often used by an investor contemplating purchase of common stock. For a present stockholder, the most common comparisons are likely to be EPS for the most recent quarter and year to date as compared with the same data for last year.
2. Trade associations, governmental agencies, such as the Federal Trade Commission, and financial reporting services, such as Dun & Bradstreet and Robert Morris Associates.
3. Ratios and financial data of a firm's major competitors.
4. The analyst's personal experiences and observations.
5. Traditional rules of thumb, which must be applied with caution because the firm may be unique. An example is the time-worn rule that a firm's current ratio should be at least 2:1.

Illustration 20.3: Summary of ratios

Ratio	Formula	Significance
Current ratio	Current assets ÷ Current liabilities	Test of debt-paying ability
Acid-test (quick) ratio	(Cash + Net receivables + Marketable securities) ÷ Current liabilities	Test of immediate debt-paying ability
Accounts receivable turnover	Net sales ÷ Average net accounts receivable	Test of quality of accounts receivable
Average collection period of accounts receivable (number of days' sales in accounts receivable)	Number of days in year ÷ Accounts receivable turnover ratio	Test of quality of accounts receivable
Inventory turnover	Cost of goods sold ÷ Average inventory	Test of whether or not a sufficient volume of business is being generated relative to inventory
Total assets turnover	Net sales ÷ Average total assets	Test of whether or not volume of business generated is adequate relative to amount of capital invested in business
Equity ratio	Owners' (Stockholders') equity ÷ Total equities	Index of long-run solvency and safety
Earning power percentage	Net operating income ÷ Operating assets	Measure of managerial effectiveness
Net income to stockholders' equity	Net income ÷ Average stockholders' equity	Measure of what a given company earned for its stockholders from all sources as a percentage of the stockholders' investment
EPS (of common stock)	Net income available to common stockholders ÷ Average number of shares of common stock outstanding	Tends to have an effect on the market price per share
Times interest earned ratio	Income before interest and taxes ÷ Interest expense	Indicates likelihood that bondholders will continue to receive their interest payments
Times preferred dividends earned ratio	Net income ÷ Preferred dividends	Indicates the probability that preferred stockholders will receive their dividend each year
Earnings yield on common stock	EPS ÷ Current market price per share	Useful for comparison with other stocks
Price-earnings ratio	Current market price per share ÷ EPS	Index of whether a stock is relatively cheap or expensive
Dividend yield	Dividend per share ÷ Current market price per share	Useful for comparison with other stocks
Payout ratio on common stock	Dividend per share ÷ EPS	Index of whether company pays out a large percentage of earnings as dividends or reinvests most of its earnings

Financial statement analysis must be carried out with knowledge of industry characteristics. Acceptable current ratios, gross margin rates, debt-to-equity ratios, and so on, vary widely depending upon environmental conditions within an industry. Even within an industry, legitimate variations may exist.

Need for comparable data

Analysts must be sure that their comparisons are valid—whether the comparison is of items for different periods or different companies. Consistent accounting practices must be followed if valid interperiod comparisons are to be made. Comparable interfirm comparisons are more difficult to secure. Accountants cannot do much more than disclose the fact that one firm is using Fifo and another is using Lifo. Such a disclosure alerts analysts that interfirm comparisons of, for example, inventory turnover ratios may not be strictly comparable.

Also, when comparing a firm's ratios to industry averages provided by an external source such as Dun & Bradstreet, the analyst must calculate the firm's ratio in the same manner as the reporting service. Thus, if Dun & Bradstreet uses sales (rather than cost of goods sold) to compute inventory turnover, so should the analyst. Net sales is used because cost of goods sold amounts are not computed and reported in the same manner by all companies. Ratios based on sales may lead to different conclusions from those obtained using cost of goods sold because gross margin rates may differ. For example, two firms, A and B, may both have $100 sales and $10 average inventory for an identical inventory turnover based on sales of 10 ($100/$10). But, if A's gross margin rate is 40 percent, its inventory turnover based on cost of goods sold is 6, ($100 − $40)/$10. If B's gross margin rate is 30 percent, its cost of goods sold is $70 and its inventory turnover is 7.

Influence of external factors

Financial analysis relies heavily upon informed judgment. Percentages and ratios are guides to aid comparison and are useful in uncovering potential strengths and weaknesses. But the financial analyst should seek the basic causes behind changes and established trends. Quite often, facts and conditions not disclosed by the financial statements may affect their interpretation. A single important event may have been largely responsible for a given relationship. For example, a new product may have been unexpectedly put on the market by competitors, making it necessary for the company under study to sacrifice its inventory of a product suddenly rendered obsolete. Such an event would affect the percentage of gross margin to net sales severely. Yet there may be little or no chance that such an event would happen again.

General business conditions within the business or industry of the company under study must be considered. A downward trend in earnings, for example, is less alarming if the industry trend or the general economic trend is also downward rather than limited to a single corporation.

Consideration should be given to the possible seasonal nature of the businesses under study. If the balance sheet date represents the seasonal peak in the volume of business, for example, the ratio of current assets to current liabilities may acceptably be much lower than if the balance sheet date is one in a season of low activity.

The potential investor should realize that acquiring the ability to make informed judgments is a long process and does not occur overnight. Using ratios and percentages mechanically is a sure road to wrong conclusions.

NEW TERMS INTRODUCED IN CHAPTER 20

Accounts receivable turnover
Net sales divided by average net accounts receivable.

Acid-test (quick) ratio
The ratio of cash, net receivables, and marketable securities to current liabilities.

Common-size statements
Show only percentages and no absolute dollar amounts.

Current ratio
The ratio of current assets to current liabilities.

Debt/equity ratio
Total debt divided by owners' equity.

Dividend yield
On common or preferred stock, current annual dividend per share divided by current market price per share.

Earning power percentage
(Net operating income ÷ Net sales) × (Net sales ÷ Operating assets). Result is equal to net operating income divided by operating assets; often called **rate of return on operating assets.**

Earnings per share (EPS)
Usually computed for common stock; net income less required preferred dividends, which equals earnings available to common stockholders, divided by weighted-average number of shares of common stock outstanding.

Earnings yield on common stock
Ratio of current EPS to current market price per share.

Equity ratio
The ratio of owners' equity to total equities (or total assets).

Horizontal analysis
Analysis of a firm's financial statements for two or more successive periods showing percentage and absolute changes from prior year.

Inventory turnover
Cost of goods sold divided by average inventory.

Net income to average stockholders' equity
Net income divided by average stockholders' equity; often called **rate of return on stockholders' equity,** or, simply, **return on equity (ROE).**

Net income to net sales
Net income divided by net sales.

Number of days' sales in accounts receivable
The number of days in a year (365) divided by the accounts receivable turnover. Also called the **average collection period for accounts receivable.**

Operating assets
All assets actively used in producing operating revenues.

Operating margin
Net operating income divided by net sales.

Owners' equity to debt ratio
Owners' equity divided by total debt; often used in inverted form and called the **debt/equity ratio.**

Payout ratio (on common stock)
The ratio of dividends per share to earnings per share.

Price-earnings ratio
The ratio of current market price of a share of stock to the EPS of the stock.

Quick ratio
Same as acid-test ratio.

Return on equity (ROE)
Net income divided by average stockholders' equity.

Times interest earned ratio
A ratio computed by dividing net income before interest expense and income taxes by interest expense (also called **interest coverage ratio**).

Times preferred dividends earned ratio
Net income divided by annual required preferred dividends whether declared or not.

Total assets turnover
Net sales divided by average total assets.

Trend percentages
Similar to horizontal analysis except that comparisons are in percentages and are related to a base year rather than the prior year.

Turnover
The relationship between the amount of an asset and some measure of its use. See accounts receivable turnover, inventory turnover, and total assets turnover.

Turnover of operating assets
Net sales divided by operating assets.

Vertical analysis
Consists of the study of a single period's financial statements by expressing each item as a percentage of a significant total, for example, percentages of sales calculations.

Working capital ratio
Same as current ratio.

Yield (on stock)
The annual earnings or dividends per share, expressed as a percentage of current market price per share; see earnings yield and dividend yield.

DEMONSTRATION PROBLEM 20–1

Comparative financial statements for the Roscoe Company for 1984 and 1985 are:

ROSCOE COMPANY
Comparative Income Statements
For the Years Ended December 31, 1984, and 1985
($000)

	1985	1984
Net sales	$800	$700
Cost of goods sold	497	427
Gross margin	$303	$273
Operating expenses	220	198
Net income before income taxes	$ 83	$ 75
Income taxes	33	30
Net income	$ 50	$ 45

ROSCOE COMPANY
Comparative Balance Sheets
December 31, 1984, and 1985
($000)

	1985	1984
Assets		
Cash	$ 23	$ 24
Accounts receivable	51	58
Inventory	85	63
Plant assets (net)	177	178
Total assets	$336	$323
Liabilities and Stockholders' Equity		
Current liabilities	$ 60	$ 52
Long-term liabilities	70	70
Common stock	180	180
Retained earnings	26	21
Total liabilities and stockholders' equity	$336	$323

Required:

a. Prepare comparative common-size income statements for 1984 and 1985.

b. Perform a horizontal analysis of the comparative balance sheets.

c. Comment on the results of (*a*) and (*b*).

Solution to demonstration problem 20–1

a.

ROSCOE COMPANY
Common-Size Comparative Income Statements
For the Years Ended December 31, 1984, and 1985

	1985	1984
Net sales	100.00	100.00
Cost of goods sold	62.13	61.00
Gross margin	37.87	39.00
Operating expenses	27.50	28.29
Net income before income taxes . .	10.37	10.71
Income taxes	4.12	4.28
Net income	6.25	6.43

b.

ROSCOE COMPANY
Comparative Balance Sheets
December 31, 1984, and 1985
($000)

	1985	1984	Increase or decrease* 1985 over 1984 Amount	Percent
Assets				
Cash	$ 23	$ 24	$ 1*	4.17*
Accounts receivable	51	58	7*	12.07*
Inventory	85	63	22	34.92
Plant assets (net)	177	178	1*	0.56
Total assets	$336	$323	$13	4.02
Liabilities and Stockholders' Equity				
Current liabilities	$ 60	$ 52	$ 8	15.38
Long-term liabilities	70	70	–0–	–0–
Common stock	180	180	–0–	–0–
Retained earnings	26	21	5	23.81
Total liabilities and stockholders' equity . .	$336	$323	$13	4.02

c. The $100,000 increase in sales yielded only a $30,000 increase in gross margin because the gross margin rate decreased from 39 percent to 37.87 percent. Although operating expenses increased from $198,000 to $220,000, they declined relatively from 28.29 percent to 27.50 percent of sales. This change together with the change in gross margin combined to hold net income to an increase of $5,000, which represents a decline of 0.18 percent in the rate of net income to sales. The significant change in the balance sheet was the 35 percent increase in inventory that was financed by decreases in cash and accounts receivable and by increases in current liabilities and in retained earnings. The company is in a less liquid position at the end of 1985 than at the end of 1984.

DEMONSTRATION PROBLEM 20–2

The balance sheet and supplementary data for the Turner Corporation are shown below:

TURNER CORPORATION
Balance Sheet
December 31, 1984

Assets

Cash		$ 50,000
Marketable securities		30,000
Accounts receivable		70,000
Inventory		150,000
Building	$400,000	
Less: Accumulated depreciation	100,000	300,000
Total assets		$600,000

Liabilities and Stockholders' Equity

Accounts payable	$ 30,000
Bank loans payable	10,000
Mortgage notes payable, due in 1987	40,000
Bonds payable, 10%, due December 31, 1989	100,000
Common stock, $100 par value	300,000
Retained earnings	120,000
Total liabilities and stockholders' equity	$600,000

Supplementary data:

1. 1984 net income: $60,000.
2. 1984 cost of goods sold: $540,000.
3. 1984 sales: $900,000.
4. Inventory, December 31, 1983: $100,000.
5. Interest expense: $13,000.
6. 1984 net income before interest and taxes: $130,000.
7. Accounts receivable on January 1, 1984: $50,000.
8. Total assets on January 1, 1984: $540,000.

Required:

Compute the following ratios:

a. Current ratio.

b. Acid-test ratio.

c. Accounts receivable turnover.

d. Inventory turnover.

e. Total assets turnover.

f. Equity ratio.

g.   EPS of common stock.

h.   Times interest earned ratio.

Solution to demonstration problem 20–2

a.   Current ratio:

$$\frac{\text{Current assets}}{\text{Current liabilities}} = \frac{\$300,000}{\$40,000} = 7.5:1$$

b.   Acid-test ratio:

$$\frac{\text{Quick assets}}{\text{Current liabilities}} = \frac{\$150,000}{\$40,000} = 3.75:1$$

c.   Accounts receivable turnover:

$$\frac{\text{Net sales}}{\text{Average accounts receivable}} = \frac{\$900,000}{\$60,000} = 15 \text{ times}$$

d.   Inventory turnover:

$$\frac{\text{Cost of goods sold}}{\text{Average inventory}} = \frac{\$540,000}{\$125,000} = 4.32 \text{ times}$$

e.   Total assets turnover:

$$\frac{\text{Net sales}}{\text{Average total assets}} = \frac{\$900,000}{\$570,000} = 1.58 \text{ times}$$

f.   Equity ratio:

$$\frac{\text{Stockholders' equity}}{\text{Total assets}} = \frac{\$420,000}{\$600,000} = 70 \text{ percent}$$

g.   EPS of common stock:

$$\frac{\text{Net income}}{\text{Number of shares of common stock outstanding}} = \frac{\$60,000}{3,000} = \$20$$

h.   Times interest earned:

$$\frac{\text{Net income before interest and taxes}}{\text{Interest expense}} = \frac{\$130,000}{\$13,000} = 10 \text{ to } 1, \text{ or } 10.0 \text{ times}$$

QUESTIONS

1.   Distinguish between horizontal and vertical analysis of financial statements.

2.   What are common-size financial statements? What item is assigned a value of 100 percent in the common-size income statement, and what item is assigned a value of 100 in the common-size balance sheet?

3.   How do trend percentages differ from comparative financial statements?

4.   What are the changes, absolute and percentage, if net income of $40,000 is earned in 1985 as compared to a net loss sustained in 1984 of $10,000? What are the changes if the net loss was sustained in 1985 after earning net income in 1984?

5. Explain the meaning of this statement: "With 1976 equal to 100, net sales increased from 225 in 1984 to 260 in 1985."

6. Of what significance is the equity ratio? What are the alternative ways of conveying the same information?

7. The higher the accounts receivable turnover rate, the better off is the company. Do you agree? Why?

8. Think of a situation where the current ratio is very misleading as an indicator of short-term debt-paying ability. Does the quick ratio offer a remedy to the situation you have described? Describe a situation where the quick ratio will not suffice either.

9. Before the John Company issued $10,000 of long-term notes (due more than a year from the date of issue) in exchange for a like amount of accounts payable, its acid-test ratio was 2:1. Will this transaction increase, decrease, or have no effect on (a) the current ratio and (b) the equity ratio?

10. Through the use of turnover ratios, explain why a firm might seek to increase the volume of its sales even though such an increase can be secured only at reduced prices.

11. Indicate which of the relationships illustrated in Chapter 20 would be used to judge:

a. The short-term debt-paying ability of the firm.
b. The overall efficiency of the firm without regard to the sources of assets.

c. The return to owners of a corporation.
d. The safety of bondholders' interest.
e. The safety of preferred stockholders' dividends.

12. Indicate how each of the following ratios or measures is calculated:

a. Payout ratio.
b. EPS of common stock.
c. Price-earnings ratio.
d. Yield on common stock.
e. Yield on preferred stock.
f. Times interest earned ratio.
g. Times preferred dividends earned ratio.
h. Return on stockholders' equity.

13. How is earning power on operating assets determined? Is it possible for two companies with "operating margins" of 5 percent and 1 percent, respectively, to both have an earning power of 20 percent on operating assets? How?

14. Cite some of the possible deficiencies in accounting information especially as regards its use in analyzing a particular company over a 10-year period.

15. A provision in a bond indenture requires the borrower to maintain positive working capital. Explain what this means and why such a provision is included in an indenture.

16. Explain why the EPS for 1983 must be adjusted in a three-year summary of earnings data (presented in 1985) for a 20 percent stock dividend distributed in June 1985.

EXERCISES

E–1. Income statement data for White Company for 1984 and 1985 are:

	1985	1984
Net sales	$725,000	$538,000
Cost of goods sold	508,000	349,000
Selling expenses	110,000	97,000
Administrative expenses	65,000	55,000
Income taxes	16,000	15,000

Prepare a horizontal and vertical analysis of the above income data in a form similar to that in Illustration 20.2. Comment on the results of this analysis.

E–2. A firm engaged in the following three independent transactions:

1. Merchandise purchased on account, $100,000.
2. Machinery purchased for cash, $100,000.
3. Issued capital stock for cash, $100,000.

   a.   Compute the current ratio after each of these transactions assuming current assets were $200,000 and the current ratio was 1:1 before the transactions occurred.

   b.   Repeat part (a) assuming current assets were $200,000 and the current ratio was 2:1.

   c.   Repeat part (a) assuming current assets were $200,000 and the current ratio was 1:2.

E–3.   A company has sales of $720,000 per year. Its average accounts receivable balance is $240,000.

   a.   What is the average number of days an account receivable is outstanding?

   b.   By how much would the capital invested in accounts receivable be reduced if the turnover could be increased to 6 without loss of sales?

E–4.   From the following partial income statement, calculate the inventory turnover for the period.

Net sales		$650,000
Cost of goods sold:		
Beginning inventory	$ 75,000	
Purchases	425,000	
Cost of goods available for sale	$500,000	
Less: Ending inventory	85,000	
Cost of goods sold		$415,000
Gross margin		$235,000
Operating expenses		105,000
Net operating income		$130,000

E–5.   The Edger Company had 60,000 shares of common stock outstanding on January 1, 1984. On April 1, 1984, it issued 20,000 additional shares for cash. The earnings available for common stockholders for 1984 were $400,000. What amount of EPS of common stock should the company report?

E–6.   A company paid interest of $6,000, incurred federal income taxes of $17,000, and had net income (after taxes) of $25,000. How many times was the bond interest earned?

E–7.   The Dell Company had 8,000 shares of $75 par value, 6 percent, preferred stock outstanding. Net income after taxes was $252,000. The market price per share was $90.

   a.   How many times were the preferred dividends earned?

   b.   What was the yield on the preferred stock assuming the regular preferred dividends were declared and paid?

E–8.   A company had 9,000 shares of $50 par value common stock outstanding. Net income was $45,000. Current market price per share is $75. Compute the price-earnings ratio.

E–9.   Klone, Inc., had net sales of $660,000, gross margin of $280,000, and operating expenses of $170,000. Total assets (all operating) were $550,000. Compute Klone's earning power percentage (rate of return on operating assets).

E-10. Box Company started 1985 with 50,000 shares of common stock outstanding. On March 31, it issued 8,000 shares for cash; and on September 30, it purchased 4,000 shares for cash. Compute the weighted-average number of common shares outstanding for the year.

E-11. Felix Company started 1984 with total stockholders' equity of $450,000. Its net income for 1984 was $120,000, and $20,000 of dividends were declared. Compute the rate of return on average stockholders' equity for 1984.

E-12. A company reported EPS of $2. ($200,000/100,000 shares) for 1983, ending the year with 100,000 shares outstanding. In 1984, the company earned net income of $330,000, issued 40,000 shares of common stock for cash on September 30, and distributed a 100 percent stock dividend on December 31, 1984. Compute EPS for 1984 and compute the adjusted EPS for 1983 that would be shown in the 1984 annual report.

PROBLEMS, SERIES A

P20-1-A. You are given the following data for a company:

	1984	1985	1986	1987
Sales	$700,000	$775,000	$910,000	$1,150,000
Cost of goods sold	450,000	475,000	530,000	750,000
Gross margin	$250,000	$300,000	$380,000	$ 400,000
Operating expenses	225,000	260,000	300,000	345,000
Net operating income	$ 25,000	$ 40,000	$ 80,000	$ 55,000

Required:

a. Prepare a statement showing the trend percentages for each item above, using 1984 as the base year.

b. Comment on the trends noted.

P20-2-A. The Swan Company currently uses the Fifo method to account for its inventory but is considering a switch to Lifo before the books are closed for the year. Selected data for the year are:

Inventory, January 1	$125,000
Inventory, December 31 (Fifo)	165,000
Current assets	315,000
Current liabilities	100,000
Total assets (all operating assets)	500,000
Net sales	335,000
Cost of goods sold (Fifo)	195,000
Operating expenses	80,000
Inventory, December 31 (Lifo)	135,000

Required:

a. Compute the current ratio, inventory turnover ratio, and earning power percentage assuming the company continues using Fifo.

b. Repeat part (a) assuming the company adjusts its accounts to the Lifo method for ending inventory.

20-3-A. Comparative income statements for the years ending December 31, 1984, and 1985, and comparative balance sheets for the Howard Company are as follows:

HOWARD COMPANY
Comparative Statements of Income
and Retained Earnings
For the Years Ended December 31, 1984, and 1985
($000)

	1985	1984
Net sales	$344,500	$298,000
Cost of goods sold	208,500	184,800
Gross margin	$136,000	$113,200
Operating expenses:		
Selling	$ 65,000	$ 53,400
Administrative	48,000	45,600
Total operating expenses	$113,000	$ 99,000
Net operating income	$ 23,000	$ 14,200
Interest expense	18,000	12,000
Income before income taxes	$ 5,000	$ 2,200
Income taxes	2,000	800
Net income	$ 3,000	$ 1,400
Retained earnings, January 1	2,200	1,000
	$ 5,200	$ 2,400
Dividends	300	200
Retained earnings, December 31	$ 4,900	$ 2,200

HOWARD COMPANY
Comparative Balance Sheets
December 31, 1984, and 1985
($000)

	1985	1984
Assets		
Current assets:		
Cash	$ 10,000	$ 15,200
Accounts receivable (net)	24,000	22,400
Inventory	57,800	58,000
Total current assets	$ 91,800	$ 95,600
Plant assets (net)	83,100	71,600
Total assets	$174,900	$167,200
Liabilities and		
Stockholders' Equity		
Current liabilities:		
Accounts payable and accruals	$ 40,000	$ 43,000
Notes payable	—	22,000
Total current liabilities	$ 40,000	$ 65,000
Bonds payable	30,000	—
Total liabilities	$ 70,000	$ 65,000
Stockholders' equity:		
Common stock	$100,000	$100,000
Retained earnings	4,900	2,200
Total stockholders' equity	$104,900	$102,200
Total liabilities and stockholders' equity	$174,900	$167,200

Required:

    a. Perform horizontal and vertical analysis of the above financial statements in a manner similar to that shown in Illustrations 20.1 and 20.2.

    b. Comment on the results of the analysis in part (*a*).

P20–4–A.   The following account balances are taken from the ledger of the Arnold Company:

	December 31, 1985	December 31, 1984
Allowance for doubtful accounts	$ 48,000	$ 38,000
Prepaid expenses	23,000	30,000
Accrued liabilities	140,000	124,000
Cash in Bank A	730,000	650,000
Bank overdraft in Bank B (credit balance)	–0–	25,000
Accounts payable	476,000	390,000
Merchandise inventory	895,000	958,000
Bonds payable, due in 1989	410,000	396,000
Marketable securities	145,000	98,000
Notes payable (due in six months)	200,000	130,000
Accounts receivable	605,000	580,000

Required:

    a. Compute the amount of working capital as of both year-end dates.

    b. Compute the current ratio as of both year-end dates.

    c. Compute the acid-test ratio as of both year-end dates.

    d. Comment briefly on the company's short-term financial position.

P20–5–A.   On December 31, 1985, the Trendy Company's current ratio was 3:1 before the following transactions were completed. Indicate (*a*) whether the amount of working capital will increase, decrease, or be unaffected by each of the transactions; and (*b*) whether the current ratio will increase, decrease, or be unaffected by each of the transactions. (Consider each transaction independently of all the others.)

Transactions:

1. Purchased merchandise on account.
2. Paid a cash dividend declared on November 15, 1985.
3. Sold equipment for cash.
4. Temporarily invested cash in marketable securities.
5. Sold obsolete merchandise for cash (at a loss).
6. Issued 10-year bonds for cash.
7. Wrote off goodwill to retained earnings.
8. Paid cash for inventory.
9. Purchased land for cash.
10. Returned merchandise which had not been paid for.
11. Wrote off an account receivable as uncollectible.
12. Accepted a 90-day note from a customer in settlement of customer's account receivable.
13. Declared a stock dividend on common stock.

P20–6–A.   From the following data of the Crater Company:

    a. Prepare comparative income statements that show for each item its percentage of net sales. Ignore income taxes.

    b. Prepare comparative balance sheets that show for each item its percentage of total assets.

c. Prepare a schedule that shows the percentage of each current asset to total current assets as of both year-end dates.

d. Compute the current ratios as of both dates.

e. Compute the acid-test ratios as of both dates.

f. Compute the percentage of stockholders' equity to total assets as of both dates.

THE CRATER COMPANY
Comparative Balance Sheets
December 31, 1984, and 1985

	December 31, 1985	December 31, 1984
Assets		
Cash	50,000	$ 32,000
Accounts receivable, net	90,000	46,000
Merchandise inventory	52,000	42,000
Plant assets, net	54,000	41,000
Total assets	$246,000	$161,000
Liabilities and Stockholders' Equity		
Accounts payable	$ 29,000	$ 20,000
Notes payable	37,000	21,000
Common stock	130,000	92,000
Retained earnings	50,000	28,000
Total liabilities and stockholders' equity	$246,000	$161,000
Other data:		
Sales	$380,000	$290,000
Gross margin	230,000	190,000
Selling and administrative expenses	120,000	106,000
Interest expense	4,000	1,400

Cash dividends of $84,000 were paid in 1985. In 1985, plant assets were increased by giving a note for $6,000 for machinery of the same cost. The note matures October 1, 1988. All other notes are short term.

P20–7–A.   The following balance sheet and supplementary data are for the Freedom Corporation for 1985:

FREEDOM CORPORATION
Balance Sheet
December 31, 1985

Assets

Current assets:		
Cash	$ 225,000	
Marketable securities	120,000	
Accounts receivable	195,000	
Inventory	165,000	$ 705,000
Property, plant, and equipment:		
Plant assets, cost	$3,400,000	
Less: Accumulated depreciation	250,000	3,150,000
Total assets		$3,855,000

Liabilities and Stockholders' Equity

Current liabilities:

Accounts payable	$ 170,000	
Bank loans payable	70,000	$ 240,000

Long-term liabilities:

Mortgage notes payable, due in 1988	$ 90,000	
Bonds payable, 6%, due December 31, 1987	430,000	520,000
Total liabilities		$ 760,000

Stockholders' equity:

Common stock, par value $50 per share	$2,200,000	
Paid-in capital in excess of par	80,000	
Retained earnings	815,000	3,095,000
Total liabilities and stockholders' equity		$3,855,000

Supplementary data:

1. 1985 net income, $300,000.
2. 1985 income before interest and taxes, $600,000.
3. 1985 cost of goods sold was $800,000.
4. 1985 net sales amounted to $1,500,000.
5. Inventory on December 31, 1984, was $145,000.
6. Total interest expense for the year was $25,800.

Required:

Calculate the following ratios. Where you would normally use the average amount for an item in a ratio, but the information is not available to do so, use the year-end balance. (Analysts sometimes have to do this.) Show computations.

    a. Current ratio.

    b. Percentage of net income to stockholders' equity.

    c. Turnover of inventory.

    d. Average collection period of accounts receivable (365 days in 1985).

    e. EPS of common stock.

    f. Times interest earned ratio.

    g. Stockholders' equity ratio.

    h. Percentage of net income to total assets.

    i. Turnover of total assets.

    j. Acid-test ratio.

P20–8–A. The Blank Company has net operating income of $125,000 and operating assets of $500,000. Its net sales are $1,000,000.

The accountant for the company computes the rate of earning power on operating assets after first computing the operating margin and the turnover of operating assets.

Required:

    a. Show the computations the accountant made.

    b. Indicate whether the operating margin and turnover will increase or decrease and then determine what the actual rate of earning power on operating assets would be after each of the following changes. The events are not interrelated; consider each separately, starting from the original earning power position. No other changes occurred.

1. Sales were increased by $40,000. There was no change in the amount of operating earnings and no change in operating assets.
2. Management found some cost savings in the manufacturing process. The amount of reduction in operating expenses was $10,000. The savings resulted from the use of less materials to manufacture the same quantity of goods. As a result, average inventory was $4,000 lower than it otherwise would have been. Operating income was not affected by the reduction in inventory.
3. The company invested $20,000 of cash (received on accounts receivable) in a plot of land it plans to use in the future (a nonoperating asset); earnings were not affected.
4. The federal income tax rate increased and caused income tax expense to increase by $5,000. The taxes have not yet been paid.
5. The company issued bonds and used the proceeds to buy $100,000 of machinery to be used in the business. Interest payments are $5,000 per year. Operating earnings increased by $25,000 (net sales did not change).

P20–9–A.

	1985	1984
Net sales	$840,000	$520,000
Income before interest and taxes	220,000	170,000
Net income	111,000	126,000
Interest expense	18,000	16,000
Stockholders' equity, December 31		
(on December 31, 1983, $400,000).	610,000	470,000
Common stock, par value $50,		
December 31	520,000	460,000

Additional shares of common stock were issued on January 1, 1985.

Required:

Compute the following for both 1984 and 1985:

a. EPS of common stock.

b. Percentage of net income to net sales.

c. Rate of return on average stockholders' equity.

d. Times interest earned ratio.

Compare and comment.

PROBLEMS, SERIES B

P20–1–B.   You are given the following data for a company:

	1984	1985	1986	1987
Sales	$450,000	$515,000	$600,000	$850,000
Cost of goods sold	300,000	325,000	450,000	650,000
Gross margin	$150,000	$190,000	$150,000	$200,000
Operating expenses	120,000	128,000	147,000	176,000
Net operating income	$ 30,000	$ 62,000	$ 3,000	$ 24,000

Required:

  a. Prepare a statement showing the trend percentages for each of the above items, using 1984 as the base year.

  b. Comment on the trends noted.

P20–2–B. The Larkley Company is considering switching from the Fifo method to the Lifo method of accounting for its inventory before it closes its books for the year. The January 1 inventory was $240,000. Following are data taken or compiled from the adjusted trial balance at the end of the year:

Inventory, December 31	$280,000	Current assets	$525,000
Current liabilities	200,000	Total assets (operating)	800,000
Net sales	700,000	Cost of goods sold	405,000
Operating expenses	215,000		

  If the switch to Lifo takes place, the December 31 inventory would be $250,000.

Required:

  a. Compute the current ratio, the inventory turnover ratio, and the earning power percentage (rate of return on operating assets) assuming the company continues its use of Fifo.

  b. Repeat part (*a*) assuming the company adjusts its accounts to the Lifo inventory method.

P20–3–B. Roscoe Company's comparative income statements for the years ended December 31, 1984, and 1985 and its comparative balance sheets as of the end of each of these years are as follows:

ROSCOE COMPANY
Comparative Statements of Income
and Retained Earnings
For the Years Ended December 31, 1984, and 1985
($000)

	1985	1984
Net sales	$824,500	$785,700
Cost of goods sold	523,100	501,100
Gross margin	$301,400	$284,600
Operating expenses:		
Selling	$121,100	$128,500
Administrative	112,200	103,900
Total operating expenses	$233,300	$232,400
Net operating income	$ 68,100	$ 52,200
Interest expense	18,400	12,000
Income before income taxes	$ 49,700	$ 40,200
Income taxes.................................	20,000	16,000
Net income	$ 29,700	$ 24,200
Retained earnings, January 1	75,000	60,800
	$104,700	$ 85,000
Dividends.....................................	10,700	10,000
Retained earnings, December 31	$ 94,000	$ 75,000

ROSCOE COMPANY
Comparative Balance Sheets
December 31, 1984, and 1985
($000)

	1985	1984
Assets		
Current assets:		
Cash	$ 20,400	$ 11,100
Accounts receivable (net)	58,100	56,500
Inventory	144,500	150,100
Total current assets	$223,000	$217,700
Plant assets (net)	188,000	179,000
Total assets	$411,000	$396,700
Liabilities and Stockholders' Equity		
Current liabilities:		
Accounts payable and accruals	$ 57,000	$121,700
Notes payable	40,000	100,000
Total current liabilities	$ 97,000	$221,700
Bonds payable	120,000	–0–
Total liabilities	$217,000	$221,700
Stockholders' equity:		
Common stock	$100,000	$100,000
Retained earnings	94,000	75,000
Total stockholders' equity	$194,000	$175,000
Total liabilities and stockholders' equity . .	$411,000	$396,700

Required:

a. Perform horizontal and vertical analysis of the above financial statements in a manner similar to that shown in Illustrations 20.1 and 20.2.

b. Comment on the results obtained.

P20–4–B. From the following data for the James Company, compute (*a*) the working capital; (*b*) the current ratio; and (*c*) the acid-test ratio, all as of both dates; and (*d*) comment briefly on the company's short-term financial position.

	December 31, 1985	December 31, 1984
Notes payable (due in 90 days)	$ 94,000	$ 75,000
Merchandise inventory	300,000	260,000
Cash	125,000	160,000
Marketable securities	62,000	37,500
Accrued liabilities	24,000	27,500
Accounts receivable	235,000	230,000
Accounts payable	140,000	90,000
Allowance for doubtful accounts	30,000	19,000
Bonds payable, due 1989	195,000	200,000
Prepaid expenses	8,000	9,200

P20–5–B. Rolley Products, Inc., has a current ratio on December 31, 1984, of 2:1 before the following transactions were completed. Indicate (*a*) whether the amount of working capital will increase, decrease, or be unaffected by each of the transactions; and (*b*) whether the current ratio will increase, decrease, or be unaffected by each of the transactions (consider each independently of all of the others).

Transactions:

1. Sold building for cash.
2. Exchanged old equipment for new equipment. (No cash was involved.)
3. Declared a cash dividend on preferred stock.
4. Sold merchandise on account (at a profit).
5. Retired mortgage notes which would have matured in 1992.
6. Issued stock dividend to common stockholders.
7. Paid cash for a patent.
8. Temporarily invested cash in government bonds.
9. Purchased inventory for cash.
10. Wrote off an account receivable as uncollectible.
11. Paid the cash dividend on preferred stock.
12. Purchased a computer and gave a two-year promissory note.
13. Collected accounts receivable.
14. Borrowed from bank on a 120-day promissory note.
15. Discounted a customer's note. A financial expense was involved.

P20–6–B. The following are comparative balance sheets of the Witten Corporation on December 31, 1984, and 1985:

WITTEN CORPORATION
Comparative Balance Sheets

	December 31, 1985	December 31, 1984
Assets		
Cash	$150,000	$170,000
Accounts receivable, net	130,000	150,000
Merchandise inventory	90,000	110,000
Plant assets, net	200,000	90,000
Total assets	$570,000	$520,000
Liabilities and Stockholders' Equity		
Accounts payable	$ 80,000	$ 50,000
Notes payable	70,000	86,000
Common stock	220,000	220,000
Retained earnings	200,000	164,000
Total liabilities and stockholders' equity	$570,000	$520,000
Other data:		
Sales	$690,000	$600,000
Gross margin	285,000	255,000
Selling and administrative expense	180,000	165,000
Interest expense	6,000	3,000
Cash dividends	63,000	22,500

During 1985, a note in the amount of $50,000 was given for equipment purchased at that price. Unlike the company's other notes, which are short term, the $50,000 note matures in 1989.

Required:

a. Prepare comparative income statements that show for each item its percentage of net sales. Ignore income taxes.

b. Prepare comparative balance sheets that show for each item its percentage of total assets.

c. Prepare a schedule that shows the percentage of each current asset to total current assets as of both year-end dates.

d. Compute the current ratios as of both dates.

e. Compute the acid-test ratios as of both dates.

f. Compute the percentage of stockholders' equity to total equity (or total assets) as of both dates.

P20–7–B. The following condensed balance sheet and supplementary data are for the Quartermain Company for 1985:

QUARTERMAIN COMPANY
Balance Sheet
December 31, 1985

Assets

Current assets:

Cash	$ 600,000	
Marketable securities	350,000	
Accounts receivable	750,000	
Inventory	620,000	$2,320,000

Property, plant, and equipment:

Plant assets, cost	4,000,000	
Less: Accumulated depreciation	750,000	3,250,000
Total assets		$5,570,000

Liabilities and Stockholders' Equity

Current liabilities:

Accounts payable	$ 400,000	
Bank loans payable (due in six months)	120,000	$ 520,000

Long-term liabilities:

Mortgage notes payable, due in 1991	$ 475,000	
Bonds payable, 8%, due December 31, 1999 ..	900,000	1,375,000
Total liabilities		$1,895,000

Stockholders' equity:

Common stock, par value $50 per share	$2,700,000	
Paid-in capital in excess of par	175,000	
Retained earnings	800,000	3,675,000
Total liabilities and stockholders' equity ..		$5,570,000

Supplementary data:

1. 1985 interest expense, $80,000.
2. 1985 net sales, $4,000,000.
3. 1985 cost of goods sold, $2,700,000.
4. 1985 net income $300,000.
5. 1985 income before interest and taxes, $700,000.
6. Inventory, December 31, 1984, $820,000.

Required:

Calculate the following ratios. Where you would normally use the average amount for an item in a ratio, but the information is not available to do so, use the year-end balance. (Analysts sometimes have to do this.) Show computations.

a. Current ratio.

b. Percentage of net income to stockholders' equity.

c. Turnover of inventory.

d. Average collection period of accounts receivable (365 days in 1985).

e. EPS of common stock.

f. Times interest earned ratio.

g. Stockholders' equity ratio.

h. Percentage of net income to total assets.

i. Turnover of total assets.

j. Acid-test ratio.

P20–8–B.

	Operating assets	Net operating income	Net sales
Company 1	$ 450,000	$ 60,000	$ 660,000
Company 2	2,700,000	195,000	6,000,000
Company 3	12,000,000	1,575,000	11,250,000

Required:

a. Determine the operating margin, turnover of operating assets, and earning power on operating assets for each company.

b. In the subsequent year the following changes took place (no other changes occurred):

Company 1 bought some new machinery at a cost of $50,000. Net operating income increased by $4,000 as a result of an increase in sales of $80,000.

Company 2 sold some equipment it was using which was relatively unproductive. The book value of the equipment sold was $200,000. As a result of the sale of the equipment, sales declined by $100,000 and operating earnings declined by $2,000.

Company 3 purchased some new retail outlets at a cost of $2,000,000. As a result, sales increased by $3,000,000 and operating income increased by $160,000.

1. Which company has the largest absolute change in—
    a. Operating margin ratio?
    b. Turnover of operating assets?
    c. Earning power on operating assets?

2. Which one realized the largest dollar change in operating income? Explain this in the light of the earning power changes.

P20–9–B.   You have managed to determine the following data:

	1985	1984
Net sales	$750,000	$525,000
Net income before interest and taxes	120,000	40,000
Net income	60,000	20,000
Interest expense	24,000	10,000
Stockholders' equity, January 1	750,000	500,000
Stockholders' equity, December 31	800,000	750,000
Common stock, par value $50, December 31 ...	400,000	240,000

Additional shares of common stock were issued on January 1, 1985.

Required:

Compute the following for both 1984 and 1985:

a.   EPS of common stock.

b.   Percentage of net income to net sales.

c.   Rate of return on stockholders' equity.

d.   Times interest earned ratio.

Compare and comment.

BUSINESS DECISION PROBLEM 20–1

Shown below are the comparative balance sheets of the Charles Corporation for December 31, 1985 and 1984.

CHARLES CORPORATION
Comparative Balance Sheets
December 31, 1985, and 1984

	December 31, 1985	December 31, 1984
Assets		
Cash	$100,000	$ 20,000
Accounts receivable	18,000	24,000
Inventory	80,000	84,000
Plant and equipment	56,000	60,000
Total assets	$254,000	$188,000
Liabilities and Stockholders' Equity		
Accounts payable	$ 20,000	$ 20,000
Common stock	140,000	140,000
Retained earnings	94,000	28,000
Total liabilities and stockholders' equity	$254,000	$188,000

Required:

a.   What was the net income for 1985 assuming no dividend payments?

b.   What was the primary source of the large increase in the cash balance from 1984 to 1985?

c.   What are the two main sources of assets for the Charles Corporation?

d.   What other comparisons and procedures would you use to complete the analysis of the balance sheet begun above?

BUSINESS DECISION PROBLEM 20–2

The information below was obtained from the annual reports of the Kramer Manufacturing Company:

	1982	1983	1984	1985
Net accounts receivable	$ 60,000	$120,000	$150,000	$ 200,000
Net sales	600,000	775,000	950,000	1,100,000

Required:

    a. If cash sales account for 30 percent of all sales and credit terms are always 1/10, n/60, determine all turnover ratios possible and the number of days' sales in accounts receivable at all possible dates. (The number of days' sales in accounts receivable should be based on year-end accounts receivable and net credit sales.)

    b. How effective is the company's credit policy?

BUSINESS DECISION PROBLEM 20–3

    Gloria White is interested in investing in one of three companies (X, Y, or Z) by buying its common stock. The companies' shares are selling at about the same price. The long-term capital structures of the companies are as follows:

	Company X	*Company Y*	*Company Z*
Bonds with a 10% interest rate			$ 750,000
Preferred stock with an 8% dividend rate		$ 750,000	
Common stock, $10 par	$1,500,000	750,000	750,000
Retained earnings	120,000	120,000	120,000
Total long-term equity	$1,620,000	$1,620,000	$1,620,000
Number of common shares outstanding	150,000	75,000	75,000

    Ms. White has consulted two investment advisors. One advisor believes that each of the companies will earn $125,000 per year before interest and taxes. The other advisor believes that each company will earn about $400,000 per year before interest and taxes.

Required:

    a. Compute each of the following, assuming first the estimate made by the first advisor is used and then the one made by the second advisor is used:

1. Earnings available for common stockholders assuming a 40 percent tax rate.
2. EPS of common stock.
3. Rate of return on total stockholders' equity.

    b. Which stock should Ms. White select if she believes the first advisor?

    c. Are the stockholders as a group (common and preferred) better off with or without the use of long-term debt in the above companies?

Part Seven

Accounting in manufacturing companies

765

Chapter 21

Income measurement in manufacturing companies

CHAPTER GOALS

After study of this chapter, you should be able to:

1. Name the three broad classifications of costs incurred by a manufacturing firm and the three basic components of manufacturing costs incurred to produce a product.

2. Describe the general pattern of the flow of costs through the accounting system of a manufacturing firm under periodic inventory procedure and under perpetual inventory procedure.

3. Describe the differences in financial reporting by a manufacturer and a merchandiser and prepare a statement of cost of goods manufactured, an income statement, and a balance sheet for a manufacturer.

4. Describe the difference between product costs and period costs and explain why proper classification is essential.

5. Prepare journal entries to account for the production activities of a manufacturer under both periodic and perpetual procedure.

6. Define and use correctly the new terms in the glossary.

Previous discussion of accounting for inventory and cost of goods sold has been limited to retailers and wholesalers. Attention is now focused on manufacturing companies. A manufacturing firm's activities are more extensive and complex than those of a retailer because a manufacturer's activities involve both the production and sale of a product.

RETAILER—MANUFACTURER ACCOUNTING DIFFERENCES

Perhaps the most important accounting difference between manufacturers and retailers relates to the difference in the nature of their activities. A retailer purchases goods which are already in their finished state and ready to be sold. On the other hand, a manufacturer must purchase materials and use equipment and the labor of its workers to process the materials into finished products that are to be sold to customers. Thus, while a retailer has only one type of inventory—merchandise available for sale—a manufacturer has three types—unprocessed *materials,* partially complete *work in process,* and ready-for-sale *finished goods.* Three different inventory accounts instead of one are necessary to show the cost of inventory in various stages of production.

A comparison of a retailer's and a manufacturer's cost of goods sold section of the income statement is shown in Illustration 21.1.

Illustration 21.1: Cost of goods sold comparison

Retailer		Manufacturer	
Merchandise inventory, January 1	$ 25,000	Finished goods inventory, January 1	$ 40,000
Cost of purchases	165,000	Cost of goods manufactured (from statement of cost of goods manufactured)	250,000
Cost of goods available for sale	$190,000	Cost of goods available for sale	$290,000
Merchandise inventory, December 31	30,000	Finished goods inventory, December 31	50,000
Cost of goods sold	$160,000	Cost of goods sold	$240,000

Note the following differences in the cost of goods sold schedules: (1) goods ready to be sold are referred to as *merchandise inventory* by a retailer and *finished goods* inventory by a manufacturer, and (2) *cost of purchases* for a retailer is equivalent to *cost of goods manufactured* by a manufacturer.

COST CLASSIFICATIONS

Manufacturing costs

Cost is a financial measure of the resources used or given up to achieve a stated purpose. The total cost of manufacturing a product includes the costs of (1) direct materials, (2) direct labor, and (3) manufacturing overhead.

These three elements of total cost are collectively referred to as *product cost, manufacturing cost,* or *factory cost.*

Direct materials.   *Direct materials* have three characteristics: (1) they are included in the finished product, (2) they are used only in the manufacture of the product, and (3) they are clearly and easily traceable to the product. For example, iron ore is a direct material to a steel company because the iron ore is clearly traceable to the finished product, steel. In turn, steel becomes a direct material to an automobile manufacturer.

The cost of direct materials includes the net invoice price of the actual quantity used plus delivery charges. Some firms also include storage and handling costs. The method of valuing inventories used (Fifo, Lifo, etc.) also affects the measurement of direct materials.

Some materials (such as glue and thread used in manufacturing furniture) may become part of the finished product but can be traced to the product only at great cost and effort. For this reason, these materials are referred to as indirect materials or supplies and are included in manufacturing overhead. *Indirect materials* are materials used in the manufacture of a product that cannot or will not, for practical reasons, be traced directly to the products being manufactured.

Direct labor.   *Direct labor* is the cost of labor by employees actually working on materials to convert them into finished goods. As with direct materials, the direct labor costs of a product include those labor costs that are clearly traceable to or readily identifiable with the finished product. This relationship can be established by showing that the direct labor cost varies proportionally with the number of units produced. Therefore, the labor of machinists, assemblers, cutters, and painters can be classified as direct labor.

Direct labor cost is usually measured by multiplying the number of hours of direct labor received by the hourly wage rate. Other costs associated with direct labor, such as employer's payroll taxes, pension costs, paid vacations, and other "fringe benefits" significantly increase the total wage and benefit cost. Although occasionally accounted for as direct labor, normally these benefit costs are included in manufacturing overhead because they can be traced to the product only at great cost and effort.

Some labor costs (materials handling costs for example) may not be accounted for as direct labor even though they vary directly with the number of units produced. These labor costs are described as indirect labor and are accounted for as manufacturing overhead. *Indirect labor* consists of the cost of services that cannot or will not, for practical reasons, be traced to the product being manufactured.

Manufacturing overhead.   There are many alternative names for the manufacturing overhead category, including factory indirect costs, factory burden, and manufacturing expense. *Manufacturing overhead* is a "catchall" classification, since it includes all manufacturing costs, except for those costs accounted for as direct materials and direct labor. *Manufacturing overhead*

Illustration 21.2:   Manufacturing overhead costs

Repairs and maintenance	Write-off of hand tools
Depreciation on factory	Utilities
buildings and equipment	Payroll taxes and fringe benefits
Insurance and taxes on factory	Overtime wage premiums on direct labor
property and inventories	Indirect labor:
Indirect materials:	Janitors
Lubricants	Supervisors
Adhesives	Engineers
Cleaners, etc.	Timekeepers
	Toolroom personnel
	Materials storeroom personnel, etc.
	Cost accountant

costs are manufacturing costs that must be incurred, but which cannot or will not be traced directly to specific units produced. As noted earlier, manufacturing overhead may include certain materials and labor costs that could theoretically be accounted for as direct materials or direct labor.

Manufacturing overhead contains a number of other costs that are related to the manufacturing process such as depreciation on machines, supervisors' salaries, and factory utility costs. Illustration 21.2 shows a summary of manufacturing overhead costs.

Note from the illustration that overtime wage premiums on direct labor are commonly included in manufacturing overhead rather than in direct labor cost. This is because the need for employees to work overtime normally results from an overall production backlog, not from the need to manufacture a given product line. For example, in a company that manufactures three products, employees may work overtime on any one of the three products, depending on the *arbitrary scheduling* of the production manager. Thus, the need for overtime is due to the combined time requirements of all three products and should not be charged to any one product unless that product was its sole cause.

Manufacturing cost terminology.   It is often useful for decision-making purposes to classify costs according to their relation to the finished product or the manufacturing process. For this reason, there are special terms to identify these classifications. The sum of direct materials costs and direct labor costs incurred to manufacture a product is called *prime cost.* The sum of direct labor costs and manufacturing overhead costs is called *conversion cost* because these costs are incurred in the conversion of the direct materials into finished goods. The relationship of these cost terms is shown in Illustration 21.3. Product costs will be discussed further in a later section.

Nonmanufacturing costs

Nonmanufacturing costs differ from manufacturing costs in that they are not incurred to produce the finished product. Nonmanufacturing costs are generally classified as either selling costs or administrative costs.

Illustration 21.3:   Cost relationships

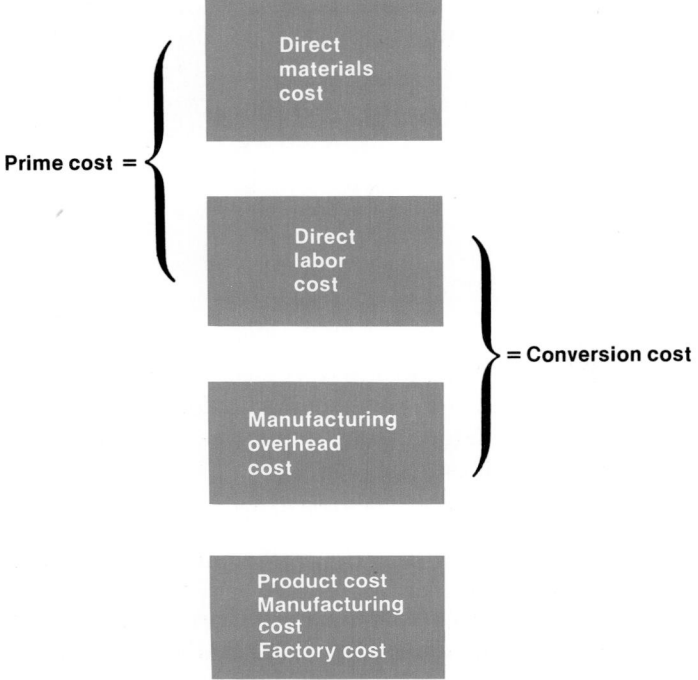

Selling costs. *Selling costs* are costs incurred to obtain customer orders and to get the finished product into the customer's possession. Advertising, market research, sales salaries and commissions, and delivery and storage of finished goods are examples of selling costs. The costs of delivery and storage of finished goods are considered to be selling costs since they are incurred *after* production has been completed. Therefore, the costs of storing *materials* are included in manufacturing overhead whereas the costs of storing *finished goods* are a part of selling costs. Keep in mind that retailers, wholesalers, manufacturers, and service organizations all have some type of selling costs.

Administrative costs. *Administrative costs* are nonmanufacturing costs that include the costs of top administrative functions and various staff departments such as accounting, data processing, and personnel. Examples of administrative costs are executive salaries, clerical salaries, office expenses, office rent, donations, research and development costs, and legal costs. As with selling costs, all organizations have administrative costs of some sort.

Period costs

Costs can also be classified as either period or product costs. *Period costs* are related more closely to periods of time than to products produced. These costs cannot be traced directly to the production of a specific product.

For this reason, period costs are expensed (deducted from revenues) in the period in which they are *incurred.* To illustrate, assume that a firm pays its sales manager a fixed salary. Even though the manager may be working on projects that will benefit future periods, the salary is expensed in the period in which it is incurred since it cannot be traced to the production of goods. It is important to remember that *all selling and nonfactory administrative costs are treated as period costs.*

Product costs

Product costs are incurred in the manufacture of products and include direct material, direct labor, and manufacturing overhead. These costs are attached to goods produced rather than related to periods of time. Product costs are considered to be *the cost of producing inventory,* just as the purchases of a retailer are the costs of *purchasing inventory.* Therefore, product costs are not expensed when incurred but are *expensed in the period the goods are sold.* If product costs are incurred at the end of period 1 and the goods are sold at the beginning of period 2, the costs involved are expensed against revenues of period 2.

Illustration 21.4 shows how period costs and product costs are reported in the financial statements. Selling and administrative expenses are reported in the income statement for the period in which they were incurred. These period costs are deducted from gross margin on sales to compute income before taxes.

The ending inventories of a manufacturing firm are reported on the balance sheet as materials inventory, work in process inventory, and finished

Illustration 21.4:   Statement analysis of period and product costs

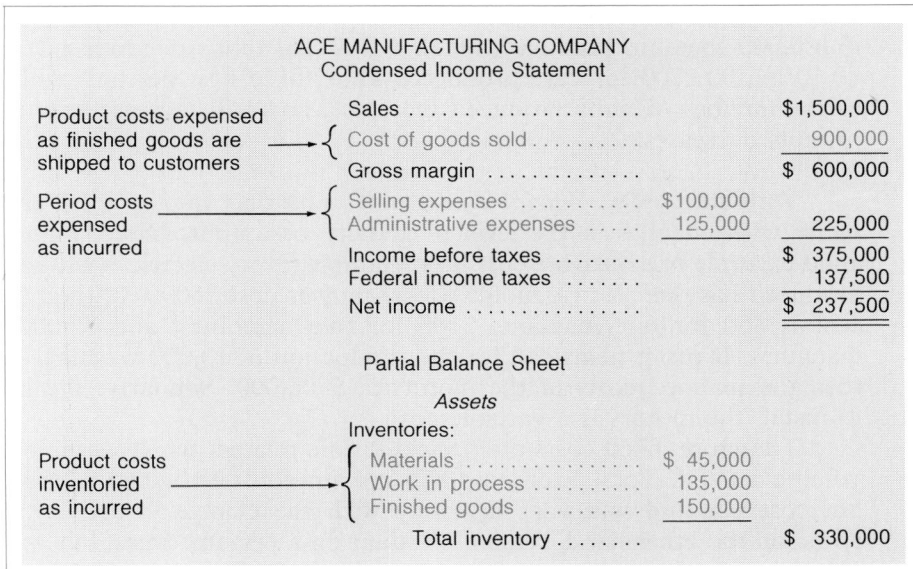

ACE MANUFACTURING COMPANY
Condensed Income Statement

Sales		$1,500,000
Cost of goods sold		900,000
Gross margin		$ 600,000
Selling expenses	$100,000	
Administrative expenses	125,000	225,000
Income before taxes		$ 375,000
Federal income taxes		137,500
Net income		$ 237,500

Product costs expensed as finished goods are shipped to customers

Period costs expensed as incurred

Partial Balance Sheet

Assets

Inventories:

Product costs inventoried as incurred

Materials	$ 45,000	
Work in process	135,000	
Finished goods	150,000	
Total inventory		$ 330,000

goods inventory. These inventories are assets, and the product costs they contain are expensed in the period the goods are sold to customers. As items of finished goods inventory are sold, their costs are reported as an expense (cost of goods sold) on the income statement for the period of sale.

Relationship of costs and production

In addition to classifying costs by their relationships to the manufacturing process or time periods, costs can be classified according to the degree to which they are affected by the level of manufacturing activity. Some costs may not be affected in total by the level of manufacturing activity at all, in which case they are considered *fixed costs;* other costs may vary directly with changes in total production levels and are called *variable costs.* The fixed cost and variable cost concepts will be used in many of the chapters which follow.

Fixed costs.   *Fixed costs remain constant in total amount over wide variations in the level of activity.* For example, the annual license for an automobile may cost $50 whether the auto is driven 1,000 or 100,000 miles during the year. The same may hold for the annual premium on an insurance policy for the auto. Property taxes, depreciation, rent, and executives' salaries are further examples of fixed costs. It may be helpful to consider fixed costs as time related, such as a one-year salary for the president, while variable costs are volume related, such as the number of motors necessary for some output of washing machines.

Fixed costs present a special problem in determining the unit cost of producing a certain product line. Since total fixed costs do not change with volume, cost *per unit* may vary widely if output varies. If a factory building is rented for $100,000 per year, then the rental cost per ton of output is $1 if 100,000 tons are produced, $0.50 if 200,000 tons are produced, and only $0.10 if 1,000,000 tons are produced. Thus, fixed cost per unit will decrease as the number of units produced increases, and will increase as the number of units decreases.

Variable costs.   *Variable costs* are costs that vary in total amount directly with changes in the level of activity or output. Direct materials is a good example of a variable cost. For example, every electric washing machine produced has one electric motor. If the motors cost $50 each, then the motor cost is $50 for one machine, $100 for two machines, and $5,000 for 100 machines. If profit plans call for the production of 10,000 washing machines, then the planned costs of the motors is $500,000. Similarly, the labor cost to install the motors is a variable cost.

Therefore, fixed costs are basically time related, while variable costs are volume related. Total fixed cost will remain constant with volume changes, but cost per unit will vary inversely with the change in activity. Variable costs, on the other hand, remain constant on a per unit basis, but will change in total in direct relation to the change in level of activity.

PERIODIC INVENTORY PROCEDURE

A manufacturer may use either periodic or perpetual inventory procedure. Periodic procedure will be covered first. Recall from Chapter 5 that under periodic inventory procedure the inventory accounts are brought to their proper balances only at the end of the accounting period by taking a physical inventory. Under perpetual inventory procedure, covered in Chapter 9, the inventory accounts are maintained at their proper balances throughout the period.

Accounts used for materials and other inventories

When a manufacturer uses periodic inventory procedure the Materials Purchases, Transportation-In, Materials Purchase Returns and Allowances, and Materials Inventory accounts are used in the same manner as they are used by a retailer. Purchases during the period are debited to the Materials Purchases account. Transportation charges incurred on purchases are debited to Transportation-In. And returns of purchased materials and allowances granted on purchases are credited to Materials Purchase Returns and Allowances. Each of these accounts is closed through Manufacturing Summary to Income Summary at the end of the accounting period. The Materials Inventory account contains the beginning inventory amount until year-end, when the ending inventory is entered in the account during the closing process.

In addition to materials, a manufacturer must account for unfinished goods still in various stages of production and completed goods which are yet to be sold. This is accomplished by use of Work in Process Inventory and Finished Goods Inventory accounts. As with Materials Inventory, when a periodic inventory system is in use these accounts will contain the beginning inventory amount until year-end, when a physical inventory is taken and the amount of ending inventory is entered in the accounts. The following T-accounts show how the accounts are used by a manufacturer using a periodic inventory system.

Materials Purchases		Transportation-In	
Purchases of materials entered here	Closed through Manufacturing Summary to Income Summary at end of period	Freight charges incurred on purchases entered here	Closed through Manufacturing Summary to Income Summary at end of period

Materials Purchase Returns and Allowances		Materials Inventory	
Closed through Manufacturing Summary to Income Summary at end of period	Cost of materials returned to suppliers and amount of any allowances granted on purchases entered here	Beg. Bal. xx End. Bal. xx Ending balance entered at end of period based on a physical inventory	Beginning balance closed through Manufacturing Summary to Income Summary at end of period

Work-in-Process Inventory		Finished Goods Inventory	
Beg. Bal. xx	Beginning balance closed through Manufacturing Summary to Income Summary at end of period	Beg. Bal. xx	Beginning balance closed to Income Summary at end of period.
End. Bal. xx Ending balance entered at end of period based on a physical inventory.		End. Bal. xx Ending balance entered at end of period based on a physical inventory.	

Estimation of inventory costs

When a periodic inventory system is in use, inventory quantities are determined at year-end by making a physical count of the materials, work in process, and finished goods on hand. Once the *quantity* of these inventories has been established, their *cost* must be estimated.

Cost of the materials on hand can be determined quite accurately by simply looking at purchase invoices to obtain purchase prices. Materials inventory cost is then calculated by multiplying the unit purchase price by the quantity of each type of item. Estimating the cost of work in process or finished goods inventory is more complicated. In order to obtain the cost per unit of these inventories, a manufacturer must:

1. *Estimate* direct material cost contained in each unit.
2. *Estimate* direct labor cost incurred for each unit.
3. *Estimate* manufacturing overhead applicable to each unit.

The sum of the three elements of unit cost represents the unit product cost, which is then multiplied by the number of units in work in process and finished goods inventories to obtain the total costs of these inventories.

Direct material cost. Direct material cost in each unit of work in process and finished goods can be established by referring to a materials specification list to determine the quantity of materials contained in each product. This quantity multiplied by the purchase invoice price represents the direct material cost per unit.

Direct labor cost. The direct labor cost in each unit of product is normally based on observations made by management to determine the normal amount of time it takes workers to complete the product. This amount of time multiplied by the hourly wage rate gives the direct labor cost per unit. In the case of products still in production, management estimates the percentage of completion of the good and determines the amount of direct labor cost applicable to work in process based on this percentage. Direct material and direct labor costs may be estimated in this manner because these costs are clearly traceable to the product.

Manufacturing overhead cost. Since manufacturing overhead costs are not clearly traceable, they must be allocated to the product based on a ***manufacturing overhead rate.*** The manufacturing overhead rate expresses manufacturing overhead costs as a percentage of some level of activity such as direct labor cost or direct labor-hours. The amount of direct labor costs is often used because manufacturing overhead costs often vary proportionately with the amount of direct labor used. Examples of this relationship would be that the more direct labor cost incurred, the more supervisors would be needed to supervise laborers or the more maintenance and repair work would be needed on the machines used by the direct laborers.

As an example of the computation of a manufacturing overhead rate and the cost of ending inventories of work in process and finished goods, assume the following information is available for a company:

Direct materials used (100,000 units)	$600,000
Direct labor (50,000 hours)	500,000
Manufacturing overhead	400,000
Ending inventories (determined by physical count):	
Work in process	8,000 units
Finished goods	2,000 units

The company manufactures only one product—product P. All direct materials are issued to production at the start of the manufacturing process. Each unit of product contains one unit of direct materials. Therefore, the direct material cost per unit is $600,000 ÷ 100,000 units = $6. The direct labor cost per hour is $500,000 ÷ 50,000 hours = $10. Management estimates that each completed unit of product contains two hours of direct labor, while each unit still in production contains an average of one hour of direct labor. Thus, the direct labor cost per unit is $20 for finished goods and $10 for work in process.

The manufacturing overhead rate expressed as a percentage of direct labor cost is computed as follows:

$$\frac{\text{Total manufacturing overhead cost}}{\text{Total direct labor cost}} = \text{Manufacturing overhead rate}$$

$$\frac{\$400,000}{\$500,000} = 0.80 = 80 \text{ percent}$$

The cost of the ending inventories of work in process and finished goods can now be determined as shown in Illustration 21.5.

Illustration 21.5: Computation of work in process and finished goods inventories of product P

	Estimated cost per unit					
Inventory	Direct materials +	Direct labor +	Manufacturing overhead (80 percent of direct labor cost)	= Total ×	Units in inventory =	Total ending inventory cost
Work in process	$6	$10	$ 8	$24	8,000	$192,000
Finished goods	6	20	16	42	2,000	84,000

THE WORK SHEET FOR A MANUFACTURING COMPANY
USING PERIODIC PROCEDURE

You may recall that the use of a work sheet assists in the preparation of adjusting and closing entries. Also, the completed work sheet contains all the information needed for the preparation of formal financial statements.

Remember that the major accounting difference between retailers and manufacturers is that retailers have only one type of inventory (merchandise) while manufacturers have three (materials, work in process, and finished goods). This difference is further complicated by the fact that Work in Process and Finished Goods inventories are each composed of direct materials, direct labor, and manufacturing overhead costs allocated to production. These factors contribute to the complexity of determining the periodic cost of goods sold for a manufacturer. For this reason, manufacturers prepare a *statement of cost of goods manufactured* to support the cost of goods sold figure on the income statement. An additional pair of columns for the statement of cost of goods manufactured is provided on the work sheet of a manufacturer to assist in the preparation of this statement.

The example in Illustration 21.6 shows how a work sheet is prepared for a manufacturing company and focuses on the production-related accounts. The Jernigan Manufacturing Company trial balance is taken from its ledger accounts at year-end. The administrative and selling expenses have been summarized in order to emphasize the firm's production activities. The beginning of the year inventory account balances for materials, work in process, and finished goods are $40,000, $84,000, and $56,000, respectively. The year-end inventory account balances are $38,000, $80,000, and $60,000, respectively. The required adjustments for the Jernigan Manufacturing Company work sheet are as follows:

1. The bad debts expense was estimated to be $1,500 for the year.
2. Depreciation on the factory building was $20,000.
3. Depreciation on the factory equipment was $46,000.
4. Expired insurance was $6,500. Of this amount, $6,000 applied to the factory building and equipment, and the remainder applied to administrative offices (administrative expense).
5. Accrued factory payroll since the last payday was distributed as follows: direct labor, $9,000; supervisors' salary, $3,000; janitorial and maintenance, $1,800; materials storeroom personnel, $700; and finished goods storeroom personnel (selling expense), $500. Employees who do not work directly in and around the factory were paid on December 31.

The Manufacturing Statement columns show the total manufacturing costs incurred during the period. The first element of total manufacturing cost is materials used in production. The beginning materials inventory plus materials purchases and related transportation costs represent the total cost of materials available for production. Therefore, materials inventory, materials purchases, and transportation-in are included in the Manufacturing Statement debit column of the work sheet. Materials remaining in inventory at the end of the period were not used, so the ending balance in materials inventory is included in the Manufacturing Statement credit column in order to remove that amount from the cost of materials issued to production.

Direct labor incurred in production and all manufacturing overhead costs incurred during the period are included in the Manufacturing Statement debit column because these items increase the cost of goods produced during the period.

The total manufacturing costs for the period are the costs put into production. To determine the cost of goods manufactured, add the beginning work in process inventory to total manufacturing costs for the period and subtract the ending work in process inventory. Thus, the beginning balance of Work in Process Inventory is included in the Manufacturing Statement debit column and the ending balance of Work in Process Inventory is included in the credit column. Note that the excess of total debits over total credits represents the *cost of goods manufactured and is the total cost of all goods completed during the period.*

Adjusting entries

Based on the work sheet shown in Illustration 21.6, the following adjusting entries are recorded for the Jernigan Manufacturing Company:

1.	Bad Debts Expense...	1,500	
	Allowance for Doubtful Accounts		1,500
	To record bad debt expense for the year.		
2.	Depreciation Expense—Factory Building	20,000	
	Accumulated Depreciation—Factory Building		20,000
	To record depreciation on factory building.		
3.	Depreciation Expense—Factory Equipment	46,000	
	Accumulated Depreciation—Factory Equipment		46,000
	To record depreciation on factory equipment.		
4.	Insurance Expense—Factory	6,000	
	Insurance Expense—Administration.........................	500	
	Prepaid Insurance		6,500
	To record and distribute expired insurance.		
5.	Direct Labor	9,000	
	Supervisors' Salaries	3,000	
	Indirect Labor	2,500	
	Selling Expenses	500	
	Accrued Payroll Payable		15,000
	To record and distribute accrued payroll.		

THE CLOSING ENTRIES

Closing entries for a manufacturing company using periodic inventory procedure are slightly different from closing entries prepared for a retailer. This difference is due to the use of a Manufacturing Summary account which records the cost of goods produced during the period. All of the items in the Manufacturing Statement columns are closed first; then entries are made to Income Summary and to record net income.

Illustration 21.6: Manufacturing work sheet

JERNIGAN MANUFACTURING COMPANY
Work Sheet for the Year Ended December 31, 1984

Account Titles	Trial Balance Debit	Trial Balance Credit	Adjustments Debit	Adjustments Credit	Manufacturing Statement Debit	Manufacturing Statement Credit	Income Statement Debit	Income Statement Credit	Balance Sheet Debit	Balance Sheet Credit
Cash	62,000								62,000	
Accounts receivable	160,000								160,000	
Allowance for doubtful accounts		500		(1) 1,500						2,000
Prepaid insurance	7,500			(4) 6,500					1,000	
Inventories:										
Materials	40,000				40,000	38,000			38,000	
Work in process	84,000				84,000	80,000			80,000	
Finished goods	56,000						56,000	60,000	60,000	
Factory building	400,000								400,000	
Accumulated depreciation—factory building		40,000		(2) 20,000						60,000
Factory equipment	460,000								460,000	
Accumulated depreciation—factory equipment		92,000		(3) 46,000						138,000
Land	32,000								32,000	
Accounts payable		60,000								60,000
Mortgage payable, 10 percent		200,000								200,000
Common stock—$5 par		600,000								600,000
Retained earnings, January 1		103,500								103,500
Sales		1,800,000						1,800,000		
Materials purchases	480,000				480,000					
Transportation-in	6,000				6,000					

Account	Dr	Cr	Adjustments Dr	Adjustments Cr	Cost of Goods Manufactured Dr	Cost of Goods Manufactured Cr	Income Statement Dr	Income Statement Cr
Direct labor	371,000		(5) 9,000		380,000			
Indirect labor	62,500		(5) 2,500		65,000			
Supervisors' salaries	127,000		(5) 3,000		130,000			
Maintenance and repairs	17,000				17,000			
Utilities expense	5,000				5,000			
Selling expenses	199,500		(5) 500				200,000	
Administrative expenses	184,500		(4) 500				185,000	
Interest expense	20,000						20,000	
Factory taxes	15,000				15,000			
Income tax expense	107,000						107,000	
	2,896,000	2,896,000						
Bad debts expense			(1) 1,500				1,500	
Depreciation expense—factory building			(2) 20,000		20,000			
Depreciation expense—factory equipment			(3) 46,000		46,000			
Insurance expense—factory			(4) 6,000		6,000			
Accrued payroll payable				(5) 15,000				15,000
			89,000	89,000	1,294,000	118,000	1,176,000	
Cost of goods manufactured						1,176,000	1,745,500	1,860,000
Net income							114,500	114,500
					1,294,000	1,294,000	1,860,000	1,860,000	1,293,000	1,293,000

(1) To record bad debts expense for the year.
(2) To record depreciation on factory building.
(3) To record depreciation expense on factory equipment.
(4) To record and distribute expired insurance.
(5) To record and distribute accrued payroll.

Closing the accounts in the Manufacturing Statement columns

The first closing entry closes all of the accounts appearing in the Manufacturing Statement debit column by crediting those accounts. The debit is to Manufacturing Summary for the subtotal of the Manufacturing Summary debit column ($1,294,000):

```
1984
Dec. 31  Manufacturing Summary ...........................   1,294,000
              Materials Inventory (beginning) ...................                40,000
              Work in Process Inventory (beginning) .............                84,000
              Materials Purchases ............................                  480,000
              Transportation-In ...............................                   6,000
              Direct Labor ....................................                 380,000
              Indirect Labor ...................................                 65,000
              Supervisors' Salaries ...........................                 130,000
              Maintenance and Repairs .......................                    17,000
              Utilities Expense ...............................                   5,000
              Factory Taxes ..................................                   15,000
              Depreciation Expense—Factory Building ............                 20,000
              Depreciation Expense—Factory Equipment ..........                  46,000
              Insurance Expense—Factory ......................                    6,000
         To close all accounts in the Manufacturing Statement debit
         column to Manufacturing Summary.
```

The second closing entry sets up the inventories which appear in the Manufacturing Statement credit column by debiting those accounts. The credit is to Manufacturing Summary for the subtotal of the Manufacturing Statement credit column ($118,000):

```
1984
Dec. 31  Materials Inventory (ending) .......................           38,000
         Work in Process Inventory (ending) .................           80,000
              Manufacturing Summary .......................                   118,000
         To set up the ending inventories of materials and work
         in process.
```

At this point in the closing process, the Manufacturing Summary account has a debit balance of $1,176,000. This amount represents the cost of goods manufactured during the period.

Closing the accounts in the Income Statement columns

The third closing entry closes all of the accounts in the Income Statement debit column by crediting those accounts. The debit is to the Income Summary account for the subtotal of the Income Statement debit column, $1,745,500.

```
1984
Dec. 31  Income Summary.................................   1,745,500
              Finished Goods Inventory (beginning) .............                56,000
              Selling Expenses .............................                   200,000
              Administrative Expenses .......................                  185,000
              Interest Expense ..............................                   20,000
              Income Tax Expense ..........................                    107,000
              Bad Debts Expense ...........................                      1,500
              Manufacturing Summary .......................                  1,176,000
         To close all of the accounts appearing in the Income
         Statement debit column to Income Summary.
```

The fourth closing entry establishes the ending finished goods inventory and closes the Sales revenue account by debiting those accounts. The credit is to the Income Summary account for the subtotal of the Income Statement credit column, $1,860,000.

```
1984
Dec. 31   Finished Goods Inventory (ending) ..................      60,000
              Sales ..........................................   1,800,000
                  Income Summary .............................                1,860,000
              To set up the ending Finished Goods Inventory and close
              Sales to the Income Summary account.
```

At this point in the closing process the Income Summary account has a credit balance of $114,500, which is the amount of net income on the work sheet. The fifth and last closing entry closes the Income Summary account by debiting Income Summary and crediting Retained Earnings:

```
1984
Dec. 31   Income Summary .................................     114,500
              Retained Earnings ............................                 114,500
              To close the Income Summary account to Retained Earn-
              ings.
```

FINANCIAL REPORTING BY MANUFACTURING COMPANIES

Typically, it would be difficult to determine from a statement of retained earnings and a statement of changes in financial position whether the reporting company was a merchandiser or a manufacturer. But you could determine this from an income statement or a balance sheet.

The statement of cost of goods manufactured

The *statement of cost of goods manufactured* is an accounting report showing the cost to manufacture and the cost of goods manufactured. Illustration 21.7 is the statement of cost of goods manufactured for the Jernigan Manufacturing Company for 1984. Note how this statement shows the costs incurred for materials, direct labor, and manufacturing overhead and describes this total as *cost of goods manufactured* (completed) during the period.

Careful attention should be given so that the terms *cost to manufacture* and *cost of goods manufactured* are not confused with one another. *Cost to manufacture* consists of the costs of all resources put into production during the period. *Cost of goods manufactured* consists of the costs of all goods *completed* during the period. It includes "cost to manufacture" and the change in Work in Process Inventory from the beginning to the end of the period.

In this illustration, all materials (both direct and indirect) are included in the Materials Inventory account. Therefore, materials used consists of both direct materials and indirect materials. These amounts could have been separated and the amount of indirect materials could have been shown as a line item included under manufacturing overhead.

Illustration 21.7: Statement of cost of goods manufactured

JERNIGAN MANUFACTURING COMPANY
Statement of Cost of Goods Manufactured
For the Year Ended December 31, 1984

Materials:			
Materials inventory, January 1		$ 40,000	
Materials purchases		480,000	
Transportation-in		6,000	
Materials available for use		$526,000	
Less: Materials inventory, December 31		38,000	
Materials used			$ 488,000
Direct labor			380,000
Manufacturing overhead:			
Indirect labor		$ 65,000	
Supervisors' salaries		130,000	
Maintenance and repairs		17,000	
Utilities expense		5,000	
Factory taxes		15,000	
Depreciation expense—factory building		20,000	
Depreciation expense—factory equipment		46,000	
Insurance expense—factory		6,000	
Total manufacturing overhead			$ 304,000
Cost to manufacture			$1,172,000
Add: Work in process inventory, January 1			84,000
			$1,256,000
Less: Work in process inventory, December 31			80,000
Cost of goods manufactured			$1,176,000

The income statement

Income statement preparation for a manufacturer may be considerably more complex than for a merchandiser. This is because in producing goods, a manufacturer incurs more types of costs than a merchandiser who buys goods which are ready for sale. In order to make the income statement more understandable to the readers of the financial statements, only the cost of goods manufactured is shown on the income statement. A statement of cost of goods manufactured is prepared to support this amount. Notice the relationship of the statement of cost of goods manufactured to the income statement: the cost of goods manufactured appears in the cost of goods sold section as an addition to the beginning inventory of finished goods to derive cost of goods available for sale. Cost of goods manufactured is shown in the same place that purchases would be presented on a merchandiser's income statement.

The income statement for the Jernigan Manufacturing Company is shown in Illustration 21.8. The various elements shown are taken directly from the work sheet in Illustration 21.6. When financial statements are released to the public, it is common practice to include previous years' income statements alongside the current year's for comparison.

Illustration 21.8: Income statement of a manufacturer

JERNIGAN MANUFACTURING COMPANY
Income Statement
For the Year Ended December 31, 1984

Operating revenues:		
Sales		$1,800,000
Cost of goods sold:		
Finished goods inventory, January 1	$ 56,000	
Cost of goods manufactured (see statement of cost of goods manufactured)	1,176,000	
Cost of goods available for sale	$1,232,000	
Less: Finished goods inventory, December 31, 1984	60,000	
Cost of goods sold		1,172,000
Gross margin		$ 628,000
Operating expenses:		
Selling	$ 200,000	
Administrative	185,000	
Other operating expenses	1,500	
Total operating expenses		386,500
Net income from operations		$ 241,500
Nonoperating revenues and expenses:		
Interest expense		20,000
Net income before income taxes		$ 221,500
Less: Income tax expense		107,000
Net income		$ 114,500

The balance sheet

The balance sheet for a manufacturer typically shows materials, work in process, and finished goods inventories separately. A merchandiser, in contrast, reports a single merchandise inventory amount. A manufacturer's balance sheet may also show greater detail in the property, plant, and equipment section than a merchandiser's balance sheet because of the significant investment in plant assets.

Illustration 21.9 shows the balance sheet for the Jernigan Manufacturing Company taken from the work sheet in Illustration 21.6.

PERPETUAL INVENTORY PROCEDURE—THE GENERAL COST ACCUMULATION MODEL

Up to this point, use of periodic inventory procedure has been illustrated. Periodic inventory systems are used in general accounting systems which are designed to determine the *total* cost of goods manufactured and the *total* cost of goods sold at the end of the accounting period so financial statements can be prepared. But in manufacturing companies, a primary accounting objective often is to measure the cost of manufacturing a product line on a *per-*

Illustration 21.9:   Balance sheet of a manufacturer

JERNIGAN MANUFACTURING COMPANY
Balance Sheet
December 31, 1984

Assets

Current assets:

Cash		$ 62,000
Accounts receivable	$160,000	
Less: Allowance for doubtful accounts	2,000	158,000
Prepaid insurance		1,000
Inventories:		
Materials	$ 38,000	
Work in process	80,000	
Finished goods	60,000	178,000
Total current assets		$ 399,000
Property, plant, and equipment:		
Land		$ 32,000
Factory building	$400,000	
Less: Accumulated depreciation	60,000	340,000
Factory equipment	$460,000	
Less: Accumulated depreciation	138,000	322,000
Total property, plant, and equipment		$ 694,000
Total assets		$1,093,000

Liabilities and Stockholders' Equity

Current liabilities:		
Accrued payroll payable	$ 15,000	
Accounts payable	60,000	75,000
Long-term liabilities		
Mortgage payable		200,000
Total liabilities		$ 275,000
Stockholders' equity:		
Common stock—$5 par value, 120,000 shares authorized,		
issued, and outstanding		$ 600,000
Retained earnings		218,000
Total stockholders' equity		$ 818,000
Total liabilities and stockholders' equity		$1,093,000

unit basis during the period so that timely cost control and product pricing decisions can be made. Unit product costs are measured under the principle that such costs consist of (1) direct materials, (2) direct labor, and (3) a fair share of manufacturing costs incurred. Unit product costs under perpetual procedure are determined during the period, rather than estimated at the end of the period, by transferring the cost of direct materials, direct labor, and manufacturing overhead to work in process and then finished goods inventory accounts as goods are processed. Unit costs are available throughout the period because they can be obtained quickly without having to take a physical inventory. Before proceeding with an explicit illustration of perpetual inventory procedure, it is important to first understand the basic pattern of cost accumulation under perpetual inventory procedure in a manufacturing environment.

Product and cost flows

Under perpetual procedure, accounting records are usually set up so that the flow of costs through the records will match the physical flow of products through the production process, as shown in Illustration 21.10.

The physical flow of the manufacturing process begins when materials are received from suppliers and placed in the materials storeroom. When needed for processing, the materials are moved from the materials storeroom to the production departments for processing. During production, the materials are processed by laborers and machines and become partially manufactured products. At any time during production, these partially manufactured products are collectively known as *work in process.* Eventually the products are completed, at which time they are known as *finished goods.* They are then moved to the finished goods storeroom for later delivery to customers.

The accounting flow of costs under perpetual procedure follows the physical flow of the manufacturing process. The accounting records show the flow of direct material costs from Materials Inventory into Work in Process Inventory. Here, the costs of direct labor and other factory services are added. When the products are completed and transferred, their costs are removed from Work in Process Inventory and assigned to Finished Goods Inventory. As the goods are sold, the related costs are transferred from Finished Goods Inventory to Cost of Goods Sold. The relationship between the physical flow and the accounting flow is shown graphically in Illustration 21.10.

Illustration 21.11 shows the same manufacturing cost flows and also shows the selling, administrative, and financing costs of a firm. These three expense categories along with the cost of goods sold are the total expenses of the firm and are deducted from sales to arrive at net income.

Illustration 21.10   Product and cost flows

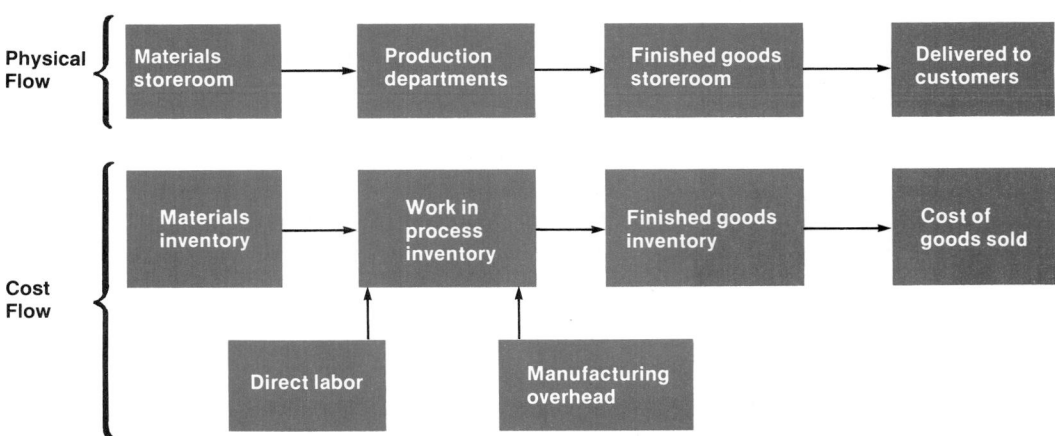

Illustration 21.11: A manufacturing company's total operations

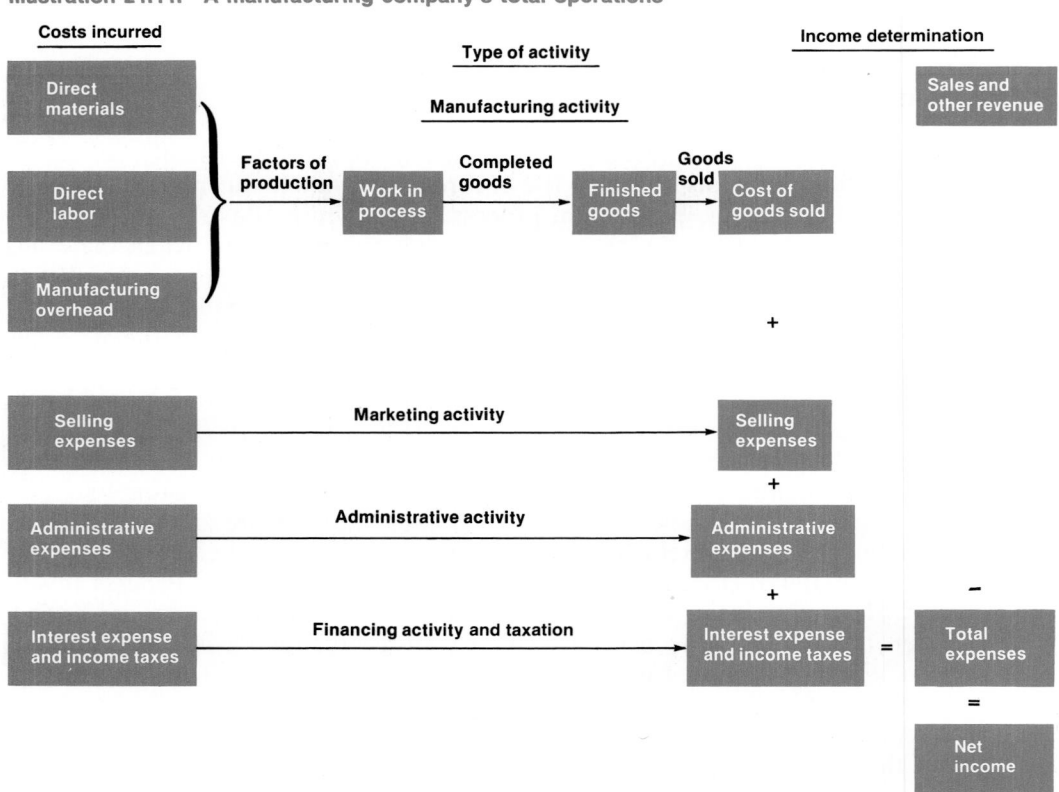

Manufacturing cost flows under perpetual procedure illustrated

Illustration 21.12 uses T-accounts to trace the flow of materials, labor, and overhead costs through the production process to finished goods inventory. The sale of finished goods inventory to customers and the closing of the revenue and expense accounts for the year are then illustrated. Examples of the journal entries necessary to record the above transactions are also included. Frequent reference should be made to Illustration 21.12.

Flow of direct and indirect materials cost. During July, $40,000 of materials and supplies were purchased on account; $28,000 of direct materials and $2,000 of indirect materials (supplies) were issued to production from the storeroom. The required entries (keyed numerically to the entries in the T-accounts in Illustration 21.12) are:

1.	Materials Inventory	40,000	
	Accounts Payable		40,000
	To record purchases of materials and supplies on account.		

```
2.  Work in Process Inventory ...................................    28,000
    Manufacturing Overhead ....................................     2,000
        Materials Inventory ....................................                30,000
    To record direct and indirect materials issued to production.
```

Note that purchases of both direct and indirect materials (supplies) are debited to Materials Inventory. But when materials are issued to production direct materials are debited to Work in Process Inventory, while indirect materials are recorded in Manufacturing Overhead because they are not easily traceable to specific products.

Flow of labor costs. Two groups of employees are likely to be involved in accounting for labor costs. One group is concerned with *payroll accounting*—that is, determining the total wages earned, the various deductions, and the net pay of each employee. The second group engages in *labor cost accounting*—that is, determining which accounts are to be charged with what amount of labor costs. Under such a procedure, an account common to both groups is needed to tie together the separate accounting activities. This account is called Payroll Summary. It is a temporarily established account called a clearing account that is debited when payrolls are prepared by the payroll department and credited when labor costs are distributed by the factory accounting department. Normally, the Payroll Summary account will have a zero balance at the end of any accounting period. During the period, the account will have a balance only because of the time lag between preparation and distribution of the payroll.

The factory payrolls for July amounted to $75,000—direct labor of $60,000 and indirect labor of $15,000. Payroll withholdings amounted to $3,500 social security taxes, $8,000 federal income taxes, and $500 union dues. The entries required are:

```
3.  Payroll Summary .........................................    75,000
        FICA Taxes Payable ...................................                 3,500
        Employees' Federal Income Taxes Payable ................                 8,000
        Employees' Union Dues Payable .........................                   500
        Accrued Payroll Payable...............................                63,000
    To record factory payroll and various withholdings.

4.  Work in Process Inventory ...................................    60,000
    Manufacturing Overhead ....................................    15,000
        Payroll Summary ......................................                75,000
    To distribute labor costs for July.
```

Accrued payroll shown in entry 3 will be paid in cash to the employees, while the amounts withheld will be paid at a later date on the employees' behalf to the federal government (social security taxes and federal income taxes) and the labor union (union dues). Entry 4 adds to Work in Process Inventory all labor cost traceable to the products being manufactured, while nontraceable labor costs are transferred to Manufacturing Overhead.

Flow of overhead costs. Indirect costs of operating the factory during the period included repairs of $1,000 paid in cash, property taxes of $1,500,

Illustration 21.12: Cost and revenue flowchart (perpetual inventory system)

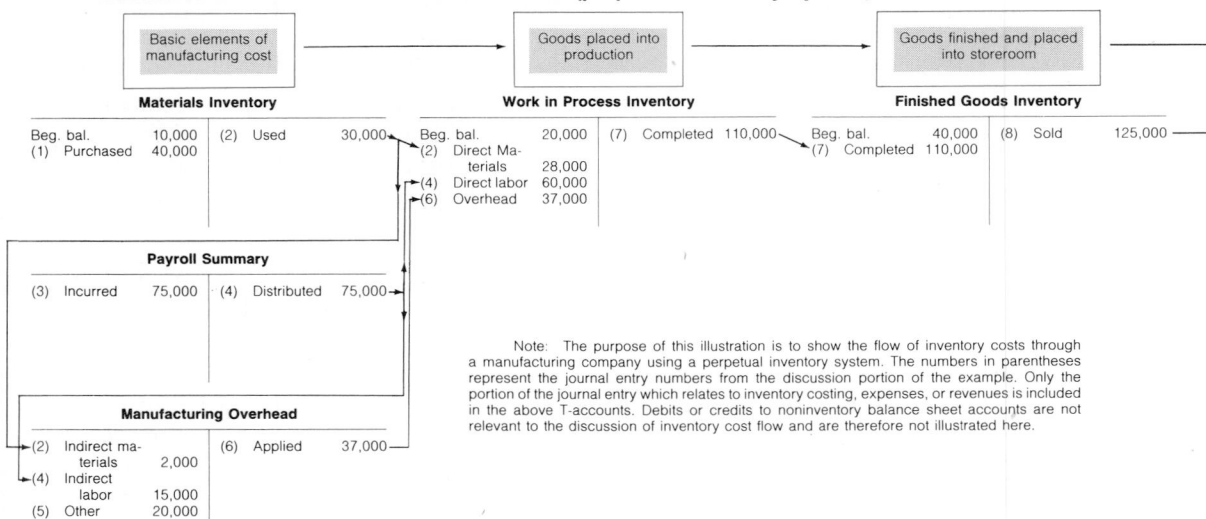

Note: The purpose of this illustration is to show the flow of inventory costs through a manufacturing company using a perpetual inventory system. The numbers in parentheses represent the journal entry numbers from the discussion portion of the example. Only the portion of the journal entry which relates to inventory costing, expenses, or revenues is included in the above T-accounts. Debits or credits to noninventory balance sheet accounts are not relevant to the discussion of inventory cost flow and are therefore not illustrated here.

equipment rent of $2,500, payroll taxes of $3,500, utilities of $4,000, insurance of $2,000, and factory building depreciation of $5,500. Entry 5 below shows the recording of these indirect costs.

5.	Manufacturing Overhead	20,000	
	Cash		1,000
	Accounts Payable		4,000
	Accrued Property Taxes Payable		1,500
	Prepaid Insurance		2,000
	Prepaid Rent		2,500
	Accumulated Depreciation—Factory Building		5,500
	Accrued Payroll Taxes Payable		3,500
	To record factory indirect costs for July.		

Manufacturing overhead costs are as much a part of a period's production cost as are the costs of direct materials and direct labor. Manufacturing overhead costs must, therefore, be added to the Work in Process Inventory account. This is done in entry 6 below.

6.	Work in Process Inventory	37,000	
	Manufacturing Overhead		37,000
	To assign overhead to work in process.		

As discussed in the next chapter, manufacturing overhead costs are generally assigned to production using overhead rates. For purposes of this illustra-

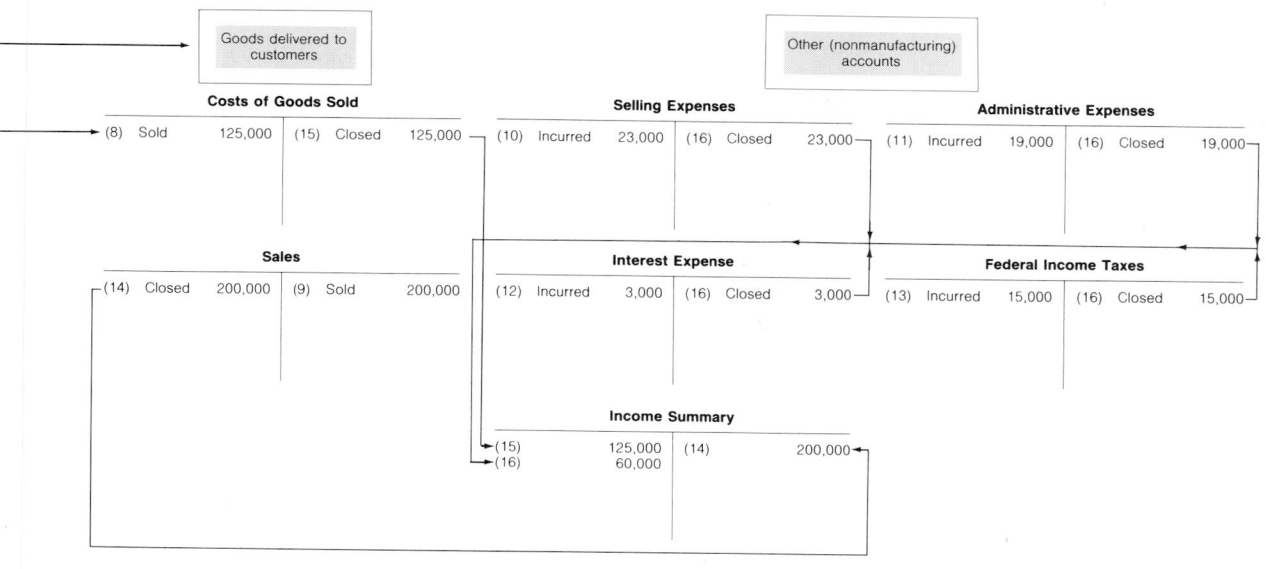

tion, it is assumed that *all* overhead incurred during July is assigned to production.

Flow of finished goods. As shown in Illustration 21.12, for product cost purposes Work in Process Inventory is charged with materials, labor, and overhead costs. When the goods are completed and transferred out of production, an entry is made to transfer their cost from Work in Process Inventory to Finished Goods Inventory. Assuming goods costing $110,000 were completed and transferred, the entry needed is:

7.	Finished Goods Inventory	110,000	
	Work in Process Inventory		110,000
	To record transfer of completed goods.		

Now assume that goods costing $125,000 were sold on account for $200,000. Entries are required to transfer the cost of the inventory out of finished goods to cost of goods sold and to record the sale. The required entries are:

8.	Costs of Goods Sold	125,000	
	Finished Goods Inventory		125,000
	To record cost of goods sold.		

9.   Accounts Receivable   200,000
     Sales   200,000
     To record sales on account.

To complete the explanation of the entries in Illustration 21.12, assume that selling expenses of $23,000, administrative expenses of $19,000, interest expense of $3,000, and federal income taxes of $15,000 were incurred in July. The required entries are:

10.   Selling Expenses   23,000
      Various asset and liability accounts   23,000
      To record selling expenses incurred in July.

11.   Administrative Expenses   19,000
      Various asset and liability accounts   19,000
      To record administrative expenses incurred in July.

12.   Interest Expense   3,000
      Accrued Interest Payable   3,000
      To record interest expense incurred in July.

13.   Federal Income Taxes   15,000
      Federal Income Taxes Payable   15,000
      To record estimated income taxes for July.

Subsidiary records or accounts would be kept for the various types of selling and administrative expenses incurred. The credits in entries 10 and 11 would be to accounts such as Cash, Accounts Payable, Salaries Payable, and Accumulated Depreciation.

Although the accounts are usually formally closed only at the end of the accounting year, entry 14 records the closing of the Sales revenue account for the month of July as an illustration of the annual entry:

14.   Sales   200,000
      Income Summary   200,000
      To close Sales revenue account.

Entries 15 and 16 are required to close the expense accounts:

15.   Income Summary   125,000
      Cost of Goods Sold   125,000
      To close Cost of Goods Sold account.

16.   Income Summary   60,000
      Selling Expenses   23,000
      Administrative Expenses   19,000
      Interest Expense   3,000
      Federal Income Taxes   15,000
      To close other expense accounts.

The closing process would, of course, be completed by recording net income in the Retained Earnings account.

17.   Income Summary   15,000
      Retained Earnings   15,000
      To close Income Summary.

Use of a work sheet under perpetual procedure

A manufacturing company using perpetual procedure can use the same work sheet as illustrated in Chapter 5. The work sheet has columns labeled Trial Balance, Adjustments, Adjusted Trial Balance, Income Statement, and Balance Sheet. The amounts shown in the trial balance for materials inventory, work in process inventory, and finished goods inventory will be the end of period balances. The amounts would be carried to the Balance Sheet debit column. The cost of goods sold amount will be included with the other expenses in the trial balance. All other steps in preparing the work sheet are as described in Chapter 5. Thus, the work sheet for a manufacturer using perpetual inventory procedure will not be illustrated here.

CONCLUSION

This chapter has shown that there are two different ways of dealing with inventories of manufacturers—periodic and perpetual. Under periodic procedure, the total cost of goods manufactured is determined at the end of the period when ending inventories are recorded. Information on unit costs and on the cost of product lines is not developed in the accounts. Under perpetual procedure, all three inventory accounts are constantly updated to reflect manufacturing activity as it transpires. Physical inventories are taken to confirm recorded inventories, thus providing control over inventories. Unit costs for goods produced are available when production of units is completed during the period. Perpetual procedure provides far more useful information but, as is shown in the next chapter, at the cost of maintaining considerably more detailed accounting records.

NEW TERMS INTRODUCED IN CHAPTER 21

Administrative costs
Nonmanufacturing costs that include the costs of top administrative functions and various staff departments such as accounting, data processing, and personnel.

Conversion cost
The sum of direct labor and manufacturing overhead costs.

Cost
A financial measure of the resources used or given up to achieve a stated purpose.

Cost of goods manufactured
Consists of the costs of all goods completed during the period; total manufacturing cost plus beginning work in process inventory minus ending work in process inventory.

Cost to manufacture
Consists of the cost of all resources put into production during the period; the sum of the costs of direct materials, direct labor, and manufacturing overhead placed in production in a period.

Direct labor
The services of labor by employees actually working on materials to convert them into finished goods.

Direct materials
Materials that are included in the finished product, are used only in the manufacture of the product, and are clearly and easily traceable to the product.

Factory cost
See manufacturing cost.

Finished goods (products)
Completed manufactured products to be sold; also the title of an inventory account maintained for such products.

Fixed costs
Remain constant in total amount over wide variations in the level of activity.

Indirect labor
Cost of services of factory employees that cannot or will not, for practical reasons, be traced to the products being manufactured.

Indirect materials
Materials used in the manufacture of a product that cannot or will not, for practical reasons, be traced directly to the products being manufactured.

Manufacturing cost
The cost incurred to produce or create a product. It includes direct materials, direct labor, and manufacturing overhead costs.

Manufacturing overhead
All costs incurred in manufacturing a product, except for those costs accounted for as direct materials and direct labor.

Manufacturing overhead rate
A means of allocating overhead to units of product; usually determined by dividing total manufacturing overhead by some measure of activity such as direct labor cost.

Materials
Unprocessed items that will be used in the manufacturing process.

Period costs
Costs related more closely to periods of time than to products produced. Period costs normally occur in the selling or administrative functions of a firm and are expensed in the period in which they are incurred.

Prime cost
The sum of the direct materials costs and direct labor costs incurred to manufacture a product.

Product costs
(See also manufacturing cost.) Costs incurred in the manufacture of products; include direct materials, direct labor, and manufacturing overhead. These costs are attached to the product and treated as an expense when the product is sold.

Selling costs
Costs incurred to obtain customer orders and get the finished product into the customer's possession.

Statement of cost of goods manufactured
An accounting report showing the cost to manufacture and the cost of goods manufactured.

Variable costs
Costs that vary in total amount directly with changes in the level of activity or output.

Work in process
Partially manufactured products; the title of an inventory account maintained for such products.

DEMONSTRATION PROBLEM

The data for completion of the work sheet of the Douglas Manufacturing Company are given below. The company uses a periodic inventory system.

1. The December 31, 1985, trial balance was taken from the general ledger of the company. (The inventories in the trial balance are those of January 1, 1985.)
2. The only entry in the Retained Earnings account during the year ended December 31, 1985, was a debit of $18,000 for the declaration of cash dividends.
3. The inventories at December 31, 1985, were as follows:

   a. Materials inventory $24,000
   b. Work in process inventory 44,000
   c. Finished goods inventory 34,000

   Adjustments are as follows:

1. The allowance for doubtful accounts is to be adjusted to 5 percent of the accounts receivable.
2. Accrued wages and salaries:

   Accrued direct labor $2,400
   Accrued sales salaries 4,000
   Accrued office and officers' salaries ... 6,000

3. Interest on the mortgage bonds was last paid on July 1.
4. Factory supplies used, $2,200.
5. Factory insurance expired during the period, $1,200.
6. Accrued factory taxes, $1,400.

7. Depreciation of factory building, $4,000.
8. Depreciation of machinery and equipment, $23,000.
9. Depreciation of office equipment, $1,000.

The Trial Balance columns of the work sheet and the proper totals of other columns on the work sheet have already been completed (see pp. 794–95).

Required:

Prepare the necessary adjusting entries for the work sheet and extend the amounts in the work sheet Trial Balance columns (plus or minus any adjustments) to their proper columns.

Solution to demonstration problem

The adjusting entries for the Douglas Manufacturing Company for the year ended December 31, 1985, are shown below:

1. Bad Debts Expense	3,800	
Allowance for Doubtful Accounts		3,800
To increase allowance to 5 percent of outstanding accounts receivable: 0.05 × $80,000 = $4,000; $4,000 − $200 = $3,800.		
2. Direct Labor	2,400	
Sales Salaries	4,000	
Office and Officers' Salaries	6,000	
Accrued Wages and Salaries Payable		12,400
To record accrual of salaries and wages.		
3. Mortgage Bond Interest Expense	1,500	
Accrued Bond Interest Payable		1,500
To record accrual of 6 months' interest on bonds ($100,000 × 0.03 × ½).		
4. Factory Supplies Expense	2,200	
Factory Supplies on Hand		2,200
To record factory supplies used.		
5. Factory Insurance Expense	1,200	
Prepaid Factory Insurance		1,200
To record expired factory insurance.		
6. Factory Taxes Expense	1,400	
Accrued Taxes Payable		1,400
To record the accrual of $1,400 of factory taxes.		
7. Depreciation Expense—Factory Building	4,000	
Accumulated Depreciation—Factory Building		4,000
To record depreciation on factory building.		
8. Depreciation Expense—Machinery and Equipment	23,000	
Accumulated Depreciation—Machinery and Equipment		23,000
To record depreciation on machinery and equipment.		
9. Depreciation Expense—Office Equipment	1,000	
Accumulated Depreciation—Office Equipment		1,000
To record depreciation on office equipment.		

The completed work sheet for the Douglas Manufacturing Company for the year ended December 31, 1985 is shown on pp. 796–97.

THE DOUGLAS MANUFACTURING COMPANY
Work Sheet for the Year Ended December 31, 1985

Account Titles	Trial Balance		Adjustments		Manufacturing Statement		Income Statement		Balance Sheet	
	Debit	Credit	Debit	Credit	Debit	Credit	Debit	Credit	Debit	Credit
Cash	31,000									
Accounts receivable	80,000									
Allowance for doubtful accounts		200								
Prepaid factory insurance	1,800									
Materials inventory	20,000									
Work in process inventory	42,000									
Finished goods inventory	28,000									
Factory supplies on hand	2,800									
Land	16,000									
Factory building	200,000									
Accumulated depreciation—building		20,000								
Machinery and equipment	230,000									
Accumulated depreciation—machinery and equipment		46,000								
Small tools	700									
Office equipment	18,000									
Accumulated depreciation—office equipment		2,600								
Accounts payable		29,400								
Income and FICA taxes withheld		2,600								
Mortgage bonds payable, 3 percent		100,000								
Common stock		300,000								
Retained earnings		103,600								
Sales		800,000								
Sales discounts	4,000									
Materials purchases	240,000									
Purchase returns		2,000								
Transportation-in	3,000									
Direct labor	184,000									
Supervisors' salaries	64,000									
Indirect labor	16,000									

Building maintenance and repairs	2,200	
Maintenance of machinery and equipment	6,400	
Heat, light, power	2,400	
Factory taxes expense	9,800	
Small tools expense	3,100	
General factory expense	5,600	
Advertising and sales promotion	21,600	
Sales salaries	60,000	
Sales travel expense	3,400	
Sales office expense	7,300	
Office and officers' salaries	90,000	
Stationery and supplies expense	2,200	
Office taxes, property and payroll	4,800	
General office operating expense	8,400	
Mortgage bond interest expense	1,500	
Gain on sale of plant assets		3,600
	1,410,000	1,410,000
Bad debts expense		
Factory insurance expense		
Accrued wages and salaries payable		
Accrued bond interest payable		
Factory supplies used		
Accrued taxes payable		
Depreciation expense—factory building		
Depreciation expense— machinery and equipment		
Depreciation expense— office equipment		
	50,500	50,500
Cost of goods manufactured		632,700 632,700
Net Income		837,600 837,600 678,900 678,900

THE DOUGLAS MANUFACTURING COMPANY
Work Sheet for the Year Ended December 31, 1985

Account Titles	Trial Balance Debit	Trial Balance Credit	Adjustments Debit	Adjustments Credit	Manufacturing Statement Debit	Manufacturing Statement Credit	Income Statement Debit	Income Statement Credit	Balance Sheet Debit	Balance Sheet Credit
Cash	31,000								31,000	
Accounts receivable	80,000								80,000	
Allowance for doubtful accounts		200		(1) 3,800						4,000
Prepaid factory insurance	1,800			(5) 1,200					600	
Materials inventory	20,000				20,000	24,000			24,000	
Work in process inventory	42,000				42,000	44,000			44,000	
Finished goods inventory	28,000						28,000	34,000	34,000	
Factory supplies on hand	2,800			(4) 2,200					600	
Land	16,000								16,000	
Factory building	200,000								200,000	
Accumulated depreciation—factory building		20,000		(7) 4,000						24,000
Machinery and equipment	230,000								230,000	
Accumulated depreciation—machinery and equipment		46,000		(8) 23,000						69,000
Small tools	700								700	
Office equipment	18,000								18,000	
Accumulated depreciation—office equipment		2,600		(9) 1,000						3,600
Accounts payable		29,400								29,400
Income and FICA taxes withheld		2,600								2,600
Mortgage bonds payable, 3 percent		100,000								100,000
Common stock		300,000								300,000
Retained earnings		103,600								103,600
Sales		800,000						800,000		
Sales discounts	4,000						4,000			
Materials purchases	240,000				240,000					
Purchase returns		2,000				2,000				
Transportation-in	3,000				3,000					
Direct labor	184,000		(2) 2,400		186,400					
Supervisors' salaries	64,000				64,000					
Indirect labor	16,000				16,000					

Account	Trial Balance Dr	Trial Balance Cr	Adjustments Dr	Adjustments Cr	Cost of Goods Manufactured Dr	Cost of Goods Manufactured Cr	Income Statement Dr	Income Statement Cr	Balance Sheet Dr	Balance Sheet Cr
Building maintenance and repairs	2,200				2,200					
Maintenance of machinery and equipment	6,400				6,400					
Heat, light, power	2,400				2,400					
Factory taxes expense	9,800		(6) 1,400		11,200					
Small tools expense	3,100				3,100					
General factory expense	5,600				5,600					
Advertising and sales promotion	21,600						21,600			
Sales salaries	60,000		(2) 4,000				64,000			
Sales travel expense	3,400						3,400			
Sales office expense	7,300						7,300			
Office and officers' salaries	90,000		(2) 6,000				96,000			
Stationery and supplies expense	2,200						2,200			
Office taxes, property, and payroll	4,800						4,800			
General office operating expense	8,400						8,400			
Mortgage bond interest expense	1,500		(3) 1,500				3,000			
Gain on sale of plant assets		3,600						3,600		
	1,410,000	1,410,000								
Bad debts expense			(1) 3,800				3,800			
Factory insurance expense			(5) 1,200		1,200					
Accrued wages and salaries payable				(2) 12,400						12,400
Accrued bond interest payable				(3) 1,500						1,500
Factory supplies used			(4) 2,200		2,200					
Accrued taxes payable				(6) 1,400						1,400
Depreciation expense—factory building			(7) 4,000		4,000					
Depreciation expense—machinery and equipment			(8) 23,000		23,000					
Depreciation expense—office equipment			(9) 1,000				1,000			
			50,500	50,500		70,000				
Cost of goods manufactured						562,700	562,700			
					632,700	632,700			810,200	837,600
Net income							27,400			27,400
							678,900	678,900	837,600	837,600

QUESTIONS

1. Identify the three elements of cost incurred in manufacturing a product and indicate the distinguishing characteristics of each.

2. Explain how the income statement of a manufacturing company differs from the income statement of a merchandising company.

3. Why might a firm claim that the total cost of employing a person is $10.30 per hour even though the employee's wage rate is $6.50 per hour? How should this difference be classified and why?

4. Identify the three broad classifications of costs incurred by manufacturing firms. Indicate why it is important that costs be correctly classified.

5. What is meant by the term *product cost?* State the general principle under which product costs are accumulated.

6. Why are certain costs referred to as period costs? What are the major types of period costs incurred by a manufacturer?

7. What is the general content of a statement of cost of goods manufactured? What is its relationship to the income statement?

8. What is the typical accounting for the overtime wage premium paid to a direct laborer? Why?

9. Explain the differences between fixed costs and variable costs.

10. Under perpetual inventory procedure what is the relationship between cost flows in the accounts and the flow of physical products through a factory?

EXERCISES

E-1.   Given below are some costs incurred by an electrical appliance manufacturer. Classify these costs as direct materials, direct labor, manufacturing overhead, selling, or administrative.

   a. President's salary.
   b. Cost of electrical wire.
   c. Cost of janitorial supplies.
   d. Wages of assembly-line workers.
   e. Cost of promotional displays.
   f. Plant supervisor's salary.
   g. Cost accountant's salary.
   h. Research and development costs.
   i. Cost of aluminum used for toasters.
   j. Cost of market research survey.

E-2.   Classify the costs listed in Exercise E-1 as either product costs or period costs.

E-3.   Which of the items in Exercise E-1 would most likely vary directly with the number of appliances produced? Which would be considered prime costs?

E-4.   The following data pertain to the Toy Company for the year ended December 31, 1984:

Materials inventory, January 1, 1984	$15,000
Materials inventory, December 31, 1984	20,000
Materials purchases	55,000
Direct labor	70,000

Work in process inventory, January 1, 1984	10,000
Work in process inventory, December 31, 1984	15,000
Manufacturing overhead	40,000
Finished goods inventory, January 1, 1984	25,000
Finished goods inventory, December 31, 1984	40,000

Compute the cost of goods manufactured. Compute the cost of goods sold.

E–5.   Fred Day was paid $294 for 46 hours as an assembly-line worker at a manufacturing plant. This sum consisted of 40 hours regular time at $6 per hour and 6 hours overtime at time and a half.

  a. Prepare the entry to distribute this labor cost to the accounts.
  b. Prepare the entry to distribute the labor cost to the accounts assuming Fred is a salesman.
  c. Prepare the entry assuming Fred is a factory supervisor.

E–6.   Compute the manufacturing overhead rate for the Carter Manufacturing Company based on direct labor costs, given the following information:

Direct labor costs	$300,000
Manufacturing overhead costs . . .	180,000

E–7.   The following data pertain to the WDB Company for the year ended December 31, 1984:

Estimated direct materials included in work in process inventory for product D	$11
Estimated direct materials included in finished goods inventory for product D	11
Estimated direct labor included in work in process inventory for product D	10
Estimated direct labor included in finished goods inventory for product D	16
Manufacturing overhead rate	75% of direct labor cost
Units of product D included in work in process inventory	300 units
Units of product D included in finished goods inventory	150 units

Compute the ending work in process inventory and finished goods inventory for product D.

E–8.   The Pedro Company uses perpetual inventory procedure. The following data are for the month of June:

1. Materials purchased on account, $52,000.
2. Direct materials issued, $60,000.
3. Repairs and maintenance on factory buildings, $6,000.
4. Factory depreciation, taxes, and utilities, $50,000.
5. Factory payroll for June, $36,000, including $3,200 of indirect labor.
6. Manufacturing overhead is assigned in full to production.
7. Cost of goods completed and transferred, $165,000.
8. Cost of goods sold, $160,000.
9. Sales for the month on account, $300,000.

The June 1 inventory account balances were:

Materials	$16,000
Work in process	40,000
Finished goods	12,000

Prepare a cost and revenue flowchart similar to the one in Illustration 21.12, incorporating the above data.

E–9.   Prepare journal entries to record the transactions in Exercise E–8.

PROBLEMS—SERIES A

P21–1–A.   The following data are from a work sheet prepared by the Foster Manufacturing Company at December 31, 1984:

	Manufacturing Statement	
	Debit	Credit
Inventories:		
Materials	35,000	60,000
Work in process	55,000	15,000
Materials purchases (net)	375,000	
Transportation-in	50,000	
Direct labor	250,000	
Indirect labor	100,000	
Supervisors' salaries	50,000	
Utilities (factory)	40,000	
Supplies used (factory)	30,000	
Depreciation expense—factory building..	80,000	
Depreciation expense—equipment	60,000	
Other manufacturing overhead	150,000	
	1,275,000	75,000
Cost of goods manufactured		1,200,000
	1,275,000	1,275,000

Required:

a.   Using this information, prepare a statement of cost of goods manufactured for Foster Manufacturing Company for the year ended December 31, 1984.

b.   Prepare all necessary closing entries, including the entry to set up the new balances in the inventory accounts and the entry to close the Manufacturing Summary account.

P21–2–A.   The following account balances were taken from the December 31, 1984, work sheet for the Skinner Company:

	Manufacturing Statement		Income Statement	
	Debit	Credit	Debit	Credit
Sales				900,000
Materials purchases	240,000			
Transportation-in	2,000			
Inventories:				
Materials	20,000	19,000		
Work in process	42,000	40,000		
Finished goods			28,000	30,000
Direct labor	190,000			
Utilities expense	2,500			
Maintenance and repairs	8,500			
Selling expenses			100,000	
Administrative expenses			92,500	
Income tax expense			50,000	
Insurance expense—factory	6,000			
Depreciation expense—factory				
building	10,000			
Depreciation expense—factory				
equipment	23,000			
	544,000	59,000		
Cost of goods manufactured		485,000	485,000	
	544,000	544,000	755,500	930,000
Net income			174,500	
			930,000	930,000

Required:

> *a.* Prepare a statement of cost of goods manufactured for the Skinner Company for 1984.

> *b.* Prepare an income statement for the Skinner Company for the year ended December 31, 1984.

P21–3–A. Refer to the information given in Problem P21–2–A.

Required:

> Give all necessary entries to set up the ending inventory balances and to close the books of the Skinner Company on December 31, 1984.

P21–4–A. The following account balances were taken in alphabetical order from the completed work sheet of Shields Manufacturing, Inc., at December 31, 1984:

Administrative salaries expense* ...	$ 20,000	Inventories, December 31:	
Advertising and promotion		Materials	$ 12,000
expense	24,000	Work in process	16,000
Depreciation expense—factory		Finished goods	26,000
equipment...................	14,000	Materials purchases	60,000
Depreciation expense—office		Materials purchase returns	2,000
equipment*	10,000	Other factory overhead	18,000
Depreciation expense—sales		Other selling expenses	10,000
fixtures	8,000	Rent—factory	8,000
Direct labor	130,000	Rent—selling and	
Factory supervision and		administrative*	30,000
inspection	12,000	Repairs and maintenance—	
Factory supplies used	12,000	factory......................	6,000
Indirect labor	10,000	Sales	440,000
Inventories, January 1:		Sales salaries	20,000
Materials	4,000	Transportation-in	8,000
Work in process	6,000		
Finished goods	36,000		

* These amounts are to be allocated 40 percent to general (nonfactory) administration and 60 percent to the sales department.

Required:

a. Prepare a statement of cost of goods manufactured for Shields Manufacturing, Inc., for 1984.

b. Prepare an income statement for the year ended December 31, 1984 (ignore taxes).

c. Prepare all necessary closing entries.

P21–5–A. On December 31, 1984, Popovich Products, Inc., made the following entries to adjust the inventory amounts and to close the temporary manufacturing accounts:

1.	Manufacturing Summary	237,000	
	Materials Purchases Returns	3,000	
	Materials Inventory (beginning)		8,000
	Work in Process Inventory (beginning)		4,500
	Materials Purchases		80,000
	Transportation-In		4,000
	Direct Labor...		60,000
	Indirect Labor		40,000
	Depreciation Expense—Building ..../.		10,000
	Depreciation Expense—Machinery		7,500
	Repairs and Maintenance..................................		6,000
	Factory Supplies Used		3,000
	Other Factory Overhead		17,000

To close the manufacturing accounts and to remove the beginning balances of materials and work in process.

2.	Materials Inventory (ending)...................................	12,000	
	Work in Process Inventory (ending)	2,500	
	Manufacturing Summary....................................		14,500

To record the ending inventories of materials and work in process.

Required:

a. Using the information given, prepare a statement of cost of goods manufactured for the year just ended.

b. To what account should the Manufacturing Summary be closed? Give the required entry.

P21–6–A.   The following trial balance and supplementary information pertain to the Williams Manufacturing Company for the year ended June 30, 1984:

	Debits	Credits
Cash	$ 11,500	
Accounts receivable	54,600	
Allowance for doubtful accounts		$ 200
Factory supplies on hand	11,700	
Office supplies on hand	850	
Materials inventory	19,000	
Work in process inventory	4,200	
Finished goods inventory	12,000	
Prepaid insurance—factory	6,750	
Factory machinery	45,000	
Accumulated depreciation—machinery		18,000
Factory building	350,000	
Accumulated depreciation—building		21,000
Office equipment	15,000	
Accumulated depreciation—office equipment		4,500
Accounts payable		40,500
Mortgage note payable (10 percent)		50,000
Common stock ($10 par value)		290,000
Retained earnings		12,400
Sales		497,300
Materials purchases (net)	75,000	
Direct labor	83,000	
Factory supervision	14,200	
Indirect labor	10,300	
Utilities—factory	23,100	
Machine maintenance	4,750	
Rent on factory equipment	2,000	
Property taxes—factory	2,800	
General factory costs	8,400	
Sales office salaries	40,500	
Selling expenses	39,200	
Officers' salaries	50,000	
Administrative expenses	27,000	
Interest expense	2,500	
Income taxes	20,550	
	$933,900	$933,900

Supplementary information:

Inventories, June 30, 1984:

Materials	$10,000
Work in process	8,000
Finished goods	15,000

Information needed for adjustments:

1. Estimated bad debts expense for the year: 1 percent of sales.
2. Factory insurance expired ... $ 5,550
3. Factory supplies used ... 11,175
4. Office supplies used ... 575

Depreciation rates per year are:

5. Factory building ... 2%
6. Factory machinery ... 20
7. Office equipment ... 15

8. Accrued factory payroll at June 30, 1984:

Direct labor	$ 1,950
Factory supervision	600
Indirect labor	300
	$ 2,850

9. Accrued salaries at June 30, 1984:

Officers' salaries	$ 1,300
Sales office salaries	850
	$ 2,150

Required:

Prepare the following for the year ended June 30, 1984:

a. Work sheet.

b. Statement of cost of goods manufactured.

c. Income statement.

d. Balance sheet.

e. Entries to set up the ending inventories and to close the accounts.

P21–7–A. The following information was taken from the December 31, 1984, statement of cost of goods manufactured of the Martin Corporation:

Direct materials used (100,000 units)	$300,000
Direct labor (100,000 hours)	450,000
Manufacturing overhead	396,000

All materials are issued to production at the beginning of the manufacturing process. Factory supervisors estimate that products still in production have received 1½ hours of direct labor per unit, while finished products have received 2 hours of direct labor per unit.

Required:

a. Compute the overhead rate for 1984 as a percentage of direct labor costs.

b. Estimate the per unit and total cost of the work in process and finished goods inventories. The year-end physical count showed 20,000 units still in production and 10,000 units in the finished goods storeroom.

P21–8–A. The Bliz Company uses perpetual inventory procedure. The operations for the quarter ended March 31, 1983, are summarized as follows:

1.	Materials purchased on account	$ 45,000
2.	Direct materials issued to production	55,000
3.	Indirect materials used (from materials inventory)	1,500
4.	Gross payroll costs incurred	68,000
5.	Payroll costs distributed:	
	Direct labor	50,000
	Indirect labor	18,000
6.	Other overhead costs incurred:	
	Depreciation of equipment	48,000
	Repairs and maintenance	7,500
	Utilities	12,500
	Other	6,500
7.	Selling expenses	35,000
8.	Administrative expenses	40,000
9.	Overhead costs actually incurred are assigned to production (determine from above data).	
10.	Cost of goods completed and transferred to finished goods inventory	200,000

11. Sales on account 270,000
12. Cost of goods sold 180,000

Inventory balances on January 1 were as follows:

Materials $15,500
Work in process...... 19,000
Finished goods 45,000

Required:

Using T-accounts, prepare a cost and revenue flowchart similar to Illustration 21.12. Key your entries using the numbers given.

P21–9–A. Assume each of the companies in this problem uses perpetual inventory procedure.

a. In June, Company A purchased on account $150,000 of direct materials and $40,000 of supplies. Also in June, $100,000 of direct materials and $20,000 of indirect materials (supplies) were issued by the storeroom to the production department.

Required:

Prepare the necessary journal entries.

b. Company B's payroll department records indicate that the week's payroll amounted to $50,000 (gross pay) with the following amounts withheld:

FICA taxes $1,800
Union dues 750
Federal income taxes...... 9,000

Further analysis reveals that of the $50,000, $35,000 was for direct labor. The indirect labor consists of the following wages and salaries:

Inspectors $3,500
Supervisors 4,500
Janitors 1,000
Timekeepers 2,000
Toolroom personnel 3,000
Storeroom personnel...... 1,000

Required:

Record the incurrence of the above labor costs and their distribution to the proper accounts.

c. In August, Company C incurred the following factory related costs: insurance, $1,000; depreciation of factory building, $2,500; rent of machinery, $1,500; payroll taxes, $3,800; utilities, $900; repairs, $450 (cash). The company assigns actual overhead costs to production at the end of each month.

Required:

Prepare journal entries to record and assign overhead costs.

d. In September, Company D completed production of goods costing $190,000 and transferred them to the finished goods storeroom. Also in September, Company D sold goods costing $175,000 to customers for $253,750, on account.

Required:

Prepare journal entries to record these transactions.

P21–10–A. The following data relate to the Watusi Company for the month of October 1984. The company uses perpetual inventory procedure.

1. Purchased materials on account, $70,000.
2. Materials issued to production, $80,000 (including $2,000 of indirect materials).
3. Factory payroll (gross) for the month, $92,000. Withholdings were $5,500 for FICA taxes and $16,000 for federal income taxes.
4. Payroll costs distributed: direct labor, $80,000; indirect labor, $12,000.
5. Other overhead costs incurred: factory depreciation, $70,000; property taxes, $16,000; repairs, $10,000; utilities, $8,000; and other, $6,000.
6. Selling expenses incurred, $60,000; administrative expenses incurred, $55,000.
7. Actual overhead costs were assigned to production.
8. Costs of goods completed and transferred, $260,000.
9. Sales on account, $400,000; cost of goods sold, $250,000.
10. Interest expense incurred, $300; federal income taxes payable, $17,500.

October 1 inventory balances were:

Materials	$18,000
Work in process	22,000
Finished goods	42,000

Required:

a. Prepare journal entries to record the above transactions.

b. Using T-accounts, compute the balance in each of the inventory accounts at the end of October.

c. Prepare an income statement for the Watusi Company for the month of October, 1984.

d. Prepare the closing entries for October 31, 1984.

PROBLEMS—SERIES B

P21–1–B. The Manufacturing Statement columns of a work sheet prepared by Woolwich Manufacturing, Inc., at June 30, 1984, contained the following adjusted amounts:

	Manufacturing Statement	
	Debit	Credit
Inventories:		
Materials	31,500	54,000
Work in process	50,000	26,000
Materials purchases	337,000	
Materials purchase returns		3,000
Transportation-in	35,000	
Direct labor	225,000	
Indirect labor	70,000	
Supervisors' salaries	45,000	
Factory building rent	12,000	
Factory utilities	36,000	
Factory supplies used	19,500	
Depreciation expense—machinery	50,000	
Other factory overhead	75,000	
	986,000	83,000
Cost of goods manufactured		903,000
	986,000	986,000

Required:

      a. Prepare a statement of cost of goods manufactured for Woolwich Manufacturing, Inc., for the year ended June 30, 1984.

      b. Prepare all necessary closing entries, including the entry to establish the ending inventory balances and the entry to close the Manufacturing Summary account.

P21–2–B. The information given below was taken from a work sheet prepared by the Hertha Company on December 31, 1984:

	Manufacturing Statement		Income Statement	
	Debit	Credit	Debit	Credit
Sales				1,850,000
Materials purchases	237,500			
Materials purchase returns		12,500		
Transportation-in	2,500			
Inventories:				
Materials	30,000	25,000		
Work in process	65,000	54,000		
Finished goods			90,000	75,000
Indirect materials	8,000			
Direct labor	280,000			
Overtime wages	16,000			
Payroll taxes—factory	85,000			
Utilities expense	8,500			
Maintenance and repairs	3,000			
Selling expenses			300,000	
Administrative expenses			450,000	
Property taxes—factory	2,200			
Income tax expense			100,000	
Insurance expense—factory	3,000			
Depreciation expense—factory building	15,000			
Depreciation expense—factory equipment	20,000			
	775,700	91,500		
Cost of goods manufactured		684,200	684,200	
	775,700	775,700	1,624,200	1,925,000
Net income			300,800	
			1,925,000	1,925,000

Required:

      a. Prepare a statement of cost of goods manufactured for the Hertha Company for the year ended December 31, 1984.

      b. Prepare an income statement for the Hertha Company for the year ended December 31, 1984.

P21–3–B.

Required:

      Using the information given for the Hertha Company in Problem P21–2–B, prepare all necessary entries to set up the ending inventory balances and to close the books for 1984.

P21–4–B.   The following account balances were taken from the completed work sheet of Toomer's Corner Manufacturing Company at December 31, 1984:

Direct labor	$200,000	Materials purchases	$120,000
Indirect labor	25,000	Transportation-in	6,000
Factory supervision	44,000	Insurance expense (70%	
Selling and administrative		applicable to factory)	10,000
salaries	100,000	Repairs and maintenance	
Factory supplies used	6,000	expense	1,500
Inventories, January 1:		Utilities expense (70%	
Materials	8,000	applicable to factory)	3,000
Work in process	20,000	Payroll taxes (factory)	30,000
Finished goods	18,000	Depreciation expense (80%	
Inventories, December 31:		applicable to factory)	40,000
Materials	12,000	Delivery expense	16,000
Work in process	25,000	Sales	740,000
Finished goods	22,000	Other selling and	
		administrative expenses	20,000

Required:

a.   Prepare a statement of cost of goods manufactured for 1984.

b.   Prepare an income statement for the year ended December 31, 1984 (ignore income taxes).

c.   Prepare all necessary closing entries.

P21–5–B.   The closing entries shown below were made on the books of Weitenbeck Producers, Inc., on December 31, 1984.

Manufacturing Summary	559,500	
Materials Inventory (beginning)		10,000
Work in Process Inventory (beginning)		15,000
Materials Purchases		140,000
Transportation-In		2,000
Direct Labor		220,000
Indirect Labor		60,000
Supervisors' Salaries		75,000
Maintenance and Repairs		3,000
Utilities Expense		2,000
Factory Taxes		1,500
Depreciation Expense—Factory Equipment		10,000
Depreciation Expense—Factory Building		18,000
Insurance Expense—Factory		3,000

To close all accounts in the Manufacturing Statement debit column to Manufacturing Summary.

Materials Inventory (ending)	12,000	
Work in Process Inventory (ending)	20,000	
Manufacturing Summary		32,000

To set up the ending inventories of materials and work in process.

Income Summary	920,000	
Finished Goods Inventory (beginning)		95,000
Selling Expenses		125,000
Administrative Expenses		130,000
Interest Expense		6,000
Income Tax Expense		36,000
Bad Debts Expense		500
Manufacturing Summary		527,500

To close all of the accounts appearing in the Income Statement debit column to Income Summary.

Finished Goods Inventory (ending)	30,000	
Sales	1,100,000	
Income Summary		1,130,000

To set up the ending Finished Goods Inventory and to close sales to the Income Summary account.

Required:

Using the information given in the entries, prepare the following for Weitenbeck Producers, Inc.:

    a.   Statement of cost of goods manufactured.

    b.   Income statement.

    c.   The required entry to close the Income Summary account.

P21–6–B.   Quincy Products, Inc., prepared the following trial balance and supplementary information on December 31, 1984, the end of its first year of operations:

	Debits	Credits
Cash	$ 45,070	
Accounts receivable	153,000	
Prepaid factory insurance	9,492	
Factory supplies on hand	14,916	
Office supplies on hand	6,430	
Factory machinery	362,000	
Factory equipment	66,800	
Office equipment	23,800	
Accounts payable		$ 35,000
Mortgage notes payable		80,000
Common stock		500,000
Sales		644,500
Sales returns	3,000	
Sales discounts	6,170	
Materials purchases	122,300	
Direct labor	175,160	
Factory supervision	32,500	
Indirect labor	17,000	
Heat, light, power—factory	33,564	
Machine maintenance	9,200	
Rent of factory	24,000	
Property taxes—factory	3,200	
General factory expense	11,520	
Sales office salaries	54,240	
Advertising expense	8,400	
Rent of sales office	4,800	
Officers' salaries	41,594	
Office salaries	22,034	
Miscellaneous office expense	5,310	
Rent of administrative office	2,200	
Interest expense	1,800	
	$1,259,500	$1,259,500

Supplementary information:

Inventories at December 31, 1984:

Materials	$17,800
Work in process	6,400
Finished goods	23,200

Information needed for adjustments:

1. Estimated bad debts expense for the year: 1 percent of net sales.
2. Factory insurance expired .... $ 2,292
3. Factory supplies used 13,066
4. Office supplies used 5,510

Depreciation rates:

5. Factory machinery 10%
6. Factory equipment 15
7. Office equipment 7
8. Accrued factory payroll at December 31, 1984:

Direct labor	$ 7,100
Factory supervision	950
	$ 8,050

9. Accrued salaries of December 31, 1984:

Sales office salaries	$ 2,000
Office salaries	1,140
	$ 3,140

10. Accrued rent of office (administrative) 200
11. Accrued interest on mortgage note 600

Required:

Using the information given, prepare the following for the year ended December 31, 1984.

a. Work sheet.

b. Statement of cost of goods manufactured.

c. Income statement (ignore income taxes).

d. Balance sheet.

e. Entries to set up the ending inventories and to close the accounts.

P21–7–B. The Busby Company incurred the following manufacturing costs for the first quarter of 1984:

Materials used	$192,300
Direct labor	310,000
Manufacturing overhead	248,000

The work in process and finished goods inventories were $32,400 and $134,000, respectively, on January 1, 1984. The production department provided the following information relating to the cost of the work in process and finished goods inventories on March 31, 1984:

		Estimated cost per unit	
	Units in inventory	Direct materials	Direct labor
Work in process:			
Product A	500	$4.00	$10.00
Product B	1,000	6.00	5.00
Finished goods:			
Product A	2,000	9.00	15.00
Product B	2,610	8.40	12.00

Required:

      a. Compute the manufacturing overhead rate, based on direct labor cost.

      b. Using the rate computed in (*a*), determine the cost of the inventories of work in process and finished goods at March 31, 1984.

      c. Compute the cost of goods manufactured and the cost of goods sold during the first quarter of 1984.

P21–8–B. The Ginseng Company uses perpetual inventory procedure. The following data are for the month of June:

1. Materials purchased on account, $48,000.
2. Direct materials issued, $56,000.
3. Repairs and maintenance on factory buildings, $6,000.
4. Factory depreciation, taxes, and utilities, $41,600.
5. Factory payroll for June, $36,000, including $3,200 of indirect labor.
6. Actual manufacturing overhead is assigned to production.
7. Cost of goods completed and transferred, $156,000.
8. Cost of goods sold, $160,000.
9. Sales for the month on account, $300,000.

      The June 1 inventory account balances were:

Materials	$16,000
Work in process	40,000
Finished goods	12,000

Required:

      Using T-accounts, prepare a cost and revenue flowchart similar to the one shown in Illustration 21.12. Key your entries using the numbers given.

P21–9–B. The Barry Company uses perpetual inventory procedure. Assume the inventories at August 1, 1984, were as follows:

Materials inventory	$22,000
Work in process inventory	32,000
Finished goods inventory	45,000

Required:

      a. Give the journal entries for the following transactions:

Transactions:

1. During August, $80,000 of materials were purchased on account and $65,000 were issued to production.
2. The factory payrolls (gross) for August were $95,000. Direct labor was $70,000, and indirect labor was $25,000. Payroll withholdings included $6,000 of social security taxes, $18,000 of federal income taxes, and $1,500 of union dues.
3. The indirect costs of production included machinery repairs of $1,500, equipment rental of $3,000, utilities of $10,000, payroll taxes of $6,000, amortization of prepaid insurance of $4,000, and factory building depreciation of $3,200.
4. Overhead was assigned in full to production.
5. Goods costing $140,000 were completed and transferred to finished goods inventory.
6. Goods costing $150,000 were sold on account for $220,000.

      b. Using T-accounts, compute the balance in each of the three inventory accounts at August 31, 1984.

P21–10–B. The Willow Manufacturing Company, which uses perpetual inventory procedure, had the following transactions for the month of May 1984:

Transactions:

1. Materials and supplies purchased on account, $24,000.
2. Materials issued to production, $28,000; indirect materials issued, $2,000.
3. Repairs and maintenance on factory equipment, $1,500.
4. Factory depreciation, $10,000; property taxes, $4,000; and utilities, $6,800.
5. Administrative salaries paid, $12,000.
6. Depreciation on administrative building, $5,000.
7. Factory payroll (gross), $18,000; withholdings: social security taxes, $1,100; federal income taxes, $3,200.
8. Factory payroll distribution: direct labor, $16,400; indirect labor, $1,600.
9. Advertising expense, $500; delivery expense, $350.
10. Sales salaries and commissions paid, $4,500.
11. Actual manufacturing overhead cost was assigned to production.
12. Cost of goods completed and transferred, $78,000.
13. Sales on account, $150,000; cost of goods sold, $80,000.
14. Other selling expenses, $280; other administrative expenses, $540 (including $40 of interest expense); all paid in cash.
15. Federal income taxes, 50 percent of net income from operations.

Required:

a.   Prepare journal entries to record the May transactions.

b.   Prepare an income statement for the Willow Manufacturing Company for the month of May 1984.

c.   Prepare closing entries at May 31, 1984.

BUSINESS DECISION PROBLEM

A number of costs that would affect business decisions in the factory operations of different companies are listed below. These costs may be fixed or variable with respect to some measure of volume or output and may be classified as direct materials (DM), direct labor (DL), or manufacturing overhead (MO).

1. Glue used to attach labels to bottles containing a patented medicine.
2. Compressed air used in operating machines turning out products.
3. Insurance on factory building and equipment.
4. A production department supervisor's salary.
5. Rent on factory machinery.
6. Iron ore and coke in a steel mill.
7. Oil, gasoline, and grease for forklift trucks.
8. Services of painters in building construction.
9. Cutting oils used in machining operations.
10. Cost of food in a factory employees' cafeteria.
11. Payroll taxes and fringe benefits related to direct labor.
12. The plant electricians' salaries.
13. Sand in a glass manufacturer.
14. Copy editor's salary in a book publisher.

Required:

a.   List the numbers 1 through 14 down the left side of a sheet of paper. After each number write the letters V (for variable) or F (for fixed) and either DM (for direct materials), DL (for direct labor), or MO (for manufacturing overhead) to show how you would classify the similarly numbered cost item given above.

b.   With which of your own answers given for part (*a*) could you take issue? Discuss.

Chapter 22

Job order and process cost systems

CHAPTER GOALS

After study of this chapter, you should be able to:

1. Describe and distinguish between the two major types of cost accumulation systems employed by manufacturing companies under perpetual inventory procedure.

2. Describe the documents used to accumulate product costs in a job order system and a process cost system.

3. Show how a predetermined overhead rate is computed and how it is used to assign overhead to production.

4. Discuss the determination of unit costs in a process cost system.

5. Prepare a production cost report for a process cost system and discuss its relationship to the Work in Process Inventory account.

6. Define and use correctly the terms in the chapter glossary.

The preceding chapter dealt with both periodic inventory procedure and perpetual inventory procedure for a manufacturer. This chapter expands the coverage of perpetual inventory procedure. Perpetual procedure is used when it is desirable to determine unit costs before taking a physical inventory at year-end.

It is a mistake to assume that a *precise* unit cost can be found. There are different techniques for finding a cost figure. Assumptions must be made regarding the use of Fifo, Lifo, or weighted-average inventory flows, the amount of depreciation charged against a given period, and other similar considerations. Reasonable types of cost allocations must be made. Also, for decision-making purposes, future costs rather than past costs must often be used. Finally, how a unit cost is determined is dependent on the type of cost accumulation system employed in the company.

Two major types of cost accumulation systems under perpetual procedure are found in practice: the *job order cost system* and the *process cost system*. In each system, *the goal is to determine before year-end the unit costs of the products being manufactured.* Unit costs may be used throughout the period to compute (1) cost of goods sold, (2) cost of work in process and finished goods ending inventories, (3) payments to be received under contracts based on "full" cost,[1] and (4) selling prices.

JOB ORDER COST SYSTEMS

Timely and useful information

A *job order cost system* is a cost accounting system in which the costs incurred to produce a product are accumulated according to the individual job. For example, a job may consist of 1,000 chairs, 10 sofas, 5 miles of highway, a single machine, a dam, or a building. A job cost system is generally used when the products being manufactured can be separately identified or when goods are produced to meet a customer's particular needs, such as constructing a house. Job costing is also used in other types of construction, motion pictures, and printing.

Under job order costing, an up-to-date record of the costs incurred on a job is kept in order to provide management with timely cost data. Reports to management can be revised as often as desired, even daily, on such matters as materials used, labor costs incurred, manufacturing overhead assigned, goods completed, total production costs incurred, and whether production costs are in line with expectations.

Up-to-date information for each job is made available by maintaining a job order cost sheet for each job. A *job order cost sheet* is a form used to summarize the costs of direct materials, direct labor, and manufacturing overhead incurred for a job. It is the *key document* in the system. The file of

---

[1] A "full" cost contract basically guarantees the manufacturer total recovery of the costs incurred in producing the product and, usually, a specified profit margin.

these cards for jobs not yet completed represents the subsidiary ledger for the Work in Process Inventory account.

Accounting for materials

As materials are received from vendors, they are placed in the materials storeroom. A *stores (or materials) card* is a record which shows the quantities and costs of each type of material received, issued to a job, and left on hand. A card is kept for each type of direct and indirect material maintained in inventory. The file of these cards serves as the subsidiary ledger for the Materials Inventory account. When materials are needed in production, a supervisor fills out a materials requisition. A *materials requisition* is a written order directing the stores clerk to issue certain materials to a production or service center. The requisition shows the types, quantities, and costs of the materials ordered from the storeroom and identifies the job to which the cost of those materials is to be assigned (Illustration 22.1).

The quantity of materials issued is entered in the issued column of the appropriate stores card (shown in Illustration 22.2, which appears later in this chapter). The requisitions are accumulated by job number; and at the end of the day, the total of direct materials issued for each job is entered on the job order cost sheet for that particular job order. When the material issued is classified by the firm as an indirect material, those requisitions are accumulated, and, at the end of the day, the total amount is charged to manufacturing overhead. Illustration 22.2 shows how the information from the materials requisition is used.

Illustration 22.1

MATERIALS REQUISITION				
		Req. No.		R4
Storekeeper: Issue Following to Bearer		Date	6/4/84	
		Dept. No.		1
Charge Job No. 201	Dept. Assembly			
Item	Quantity	Stock No.	Cost	Amount
DG	8,000	16	$3.00	$24,000
	Entered on Job Order Cost Sheet: *BN*		Signed: *ATP*	

Accounting for labor

Labor costs must be accumulated and recorded for each job. A *work (labor time) ticket* is a form or card that shows the amount of time taken by an employee to complete a given assignment. When an employee works on a particular job, the number of hours worked, employee number, job number, and any other important information are entered on the work ticket. The work ticket is shown in Illustration 22.2. At the end of the day, these work tickets are accumulated and the total direct labor costs for each job is entered in the job order cost sheet.

During the day, an employee may also be assigned work that is not directly related to a particular job, such as maintenance work. Recall that time spent on this type of activity is classified as indirect labor and is part of manufacturing overhead. The employee will still enter the nature of the tasks performed on a work ticket, and at the end of the day, these work tickets are accumulated and the total indirect labor cost is charged to manufacturing overhead. Thus, an employee fills out a work ticket for each task performed so that all of the daily hours are accounted for on one or more work tickets.

Accounting for manufacturing overhead

In order to exert some control over manufacturing overhead costs incurred, each production center or department must summarize its factory indirect costs. A *manufacturing overhead cost sheet* is the record used to summarize the various manufacturing overhead costs incurred. The file of manufacturing overhead cost sheets serves as the subsidiary ledger for the manufacturing overhead account. An example of the manufacturing overhead costs sheet can be found in Illustration 22.2.

Predetermined overhead rates. In most manufacturing operations, it is necessary to compute unit costs at the time a job is completed. The costs of direct materials and direct labor have already been entered on the job order cost sheet by way of materials requisitions and work tickets. Each job must then be assigned its share of the manufacturing overhead costs.

In the last chapter, a manufacturing overhead rate was illustrated using actual overhead costs for the period. Most manufacturing companies prefer the use of a *predetermined* overhead rate rather than waiting to accumulate all overhead costs during a period and developing an actual manufacturing overhead rate. A *predetermined overhead rate* is calculated by dividing *estimated* total overhead costs for a period by an *expected level* of activity, such as total estimated direct labor-hours or direct labor cost for the period. Predetermined overhead rates are usually set at the beginning of the year in which they will be used.

Reasons for using predetermined rates. In addition to the need for current information on unit costs, other reasons for using a predetermined overhead rate in manufacturing operations include:

1. Overhead cost are seldom incurred uniformly throughout the year (for example, heating costs will be larger during winter). No useful purpose is served by allocating less cost to a unit produced in the summer than to one produced in the winter. Use of a predetermined rate results in applying overhead based on direct labor cost or hours incurred or some other measure of activity rather than on actual overhead incurred in a particular month.
2. Some overhead costs are fixed costs. Thus, if the volume of goods produced varies from month to month, there will be sharp fluctuations in average unit cost unless a predetermined rate is used.
3. Total unit costs of production are known sooner. Using a predetermined rate, overhead costs can be assigned to production when direct materials and direct labor costs are assigned. Without use of a predetermined rate, unit costs would not be known until the end of the month or even later if bills for overhead costs have not arrived by then.

Computing predetermined overhead rates. Predetermined overhead rates are computed in the same basic manner as actual rates except *estimated* rather than *actual* levels of costs and activity are used. Costs are first estimated and charged to the various production centers. As a part of the budgeting process, an expected level of activity is estimated in terms of some specified base, such as direct labor-hours or machine-hours. The overhead rate can then be calculated by using the following formula:

$$\frac{\text{Estimated manufacturing overhead costs}}{\text{Expected level of activity (direct labor-hours)}} = \frac{\text{Predetermined}}{\text{overhead rate}}$$

To illustrate, assume that budgeted production center overhead for the period is $540,000. The expected level of activity is 60,000 direct labor-hours. The predetermined overhead rate would therefore be:

$$\frac{\$540,000}{60,000 \text{ hours}} = \$9 \text{ per direct labor-hour}$$

Overhead would be applied in this situation to the Work in Process Inventory account at the rate of $9 of overhead for each direct labor-hour worked on a job. The journal entry to apply overhead is:

```
Work in Process ............................................................ xx
    Manufacturing Overhead ............................................... xx
    To apply overhead using a predetermined overhead
    rate of $9 per direct labor-hour.
```

Sometimes separate rates are computed for variable overhead and fixed overhead. Later chapters illustrate how separate rates may be useful.

Underapplied or overapplied overhead.   When overhead is applied to production using predetermined rates, the manufacturing overhead account is credited with *estimated* amounts applied to work in process inventory. This follows because the rate is based on estimates when it is established. Under these circumstances, it is highly unlikely that the actual costs debited to the account will exactly equal the overhead applied and credited to the account. A *debit balance* will remain if actual overhead exceeds applied overhead, and overhead will be *underapplied* or *underabsorbed*. *Underapplied (underabsorbed) overhead* is the amount by which actual overhead costs incurred in a period exceed the overhead applied to production in that period. A *credit balance* will remain if applied overhead exceeds actual overhead, and overhead will be *overapplied* or *overabsorbed*. *Overapplied (overabsorbed) overhead* is the amount by which the overhead applied to production exceeds the actual overhead costs incurred in that same period.

To illustrate the use of predetermined overhead rates during a period, consider the following facts:

Estimated manufacturing overhead for year $48,000
Estimated level of activity for year . . . .   80,000 direct labor-hours
Predetermined overhead rate ($48,000 ÷ 80,000 hours) . . . $0.60 per direct labor-hour
Actual overhead costs incurred during year $45,000
Actual direct labor-hours worked . . . .   70,000 hours

The following journal entries are necessary to record the above information:

Work in Process   42,000
    Manufacturing Overhead   42,000
To apply overhead at predetermined rate of $0.60 per
direct labor-hour for 70,000 hours worked.

Manufacturing Overhead   45,000
    Various Accounts   45,000
To record actual overhead costs incurred during period.

Based on these two entries, the Manufacturing Overhead account will appear as follows:

Manufacturing Overhead

Actual costs	45,000	Applied to production	42,000
Balance	3,000		

The $3,000 debit balance is the amount of underapplied overhead during the period.

Reasons for underapplied or overapplied overhead.   Underapplied or overapplied overhead may be the result of unexpected events such as price changes, a severe winter, excessive repairs, or inefficient use of overhead items. For instance, underapplied overhead may be caused by incurring overhead costs at a higher level than the level used to calculate the rate. Excessive heating bills caused by a severe winter is one example. On the other hand, overapplied overhead may be the result of operating at a higher actual level of production (more direct labor-hours) than was used in setting the overhead rate. Recall that some manufacturing overhead costs are fixed costs which remain the same at any level of operation. Thus, total overhead costs do not increase in direct proportion to increases in direct labor-hours.

Disposition of underapplied or overapplied overhead. An under or overapplied overhead balance can be carried forward in monthly or quarterly (interim) financial statements if the probability exists that it will be reduced or offset by operations for the remainder of the year. At year-end, any remaining balance could be allocated to Work in Process Inventory, Finished Goods Inventory, and Cost of Goods Sold by recomputing the cost of production for the year using actual overhead rates and adjusting the three account balances to their appropriate actual amounts.

As an alternative, charging underapplied overhead off as a loss of the period has particular merit if it results from idle capacity or from unusual circumstances. But, as a practical matter, *underapplied or overapplied overhead is usually transferred to Cost of Goods Sold.* Little distortion of net income or of assets results from this treatment if the amount transferred is small or if most of the goods produced during the year were sold. Thus, the entry to dispose of the $3,000 of underapplied overhead in the previous example would read:

Cost of Goods Sold	3,000	
Manufacturing Overhead		3,000
To dispose of underapplied overhead.		

Summary of the basic records in job order systems

Illustration 22.2 shows the basic records or source documents used in a job order cost system:

1. The job order cost sheet summarizes all costs—direct materials, direct labor, and applied overhead—of producing a given job or batch of products. The job order cost sheet is the key document in the system and is used to control production costs by comparing actual costs with budgeted costs. One sheet is maintained for each job. The file of job order sheets for unfinished jobs is the subsidiary ledger for the Work in Process Inventory account. When the goods are completed and transferred, the job order cost sheets are transferred to a completed jobs file. The number of units and their unit costs are recorded on inventory cards supporting the Finished Goods Inventory account. An example of a job order cost sheet is shown in Illustration 22.2.

2. A stores (or materials) card is kept for each type of direct and indirect materials maintained in inventory. It shows the quantities (and costs) of each type of materials received, issued, and on hand for which the storekeeper is responsible. When a job is started, direct materials are ordered

Illustration 22.2: Basic records in a job order cost system

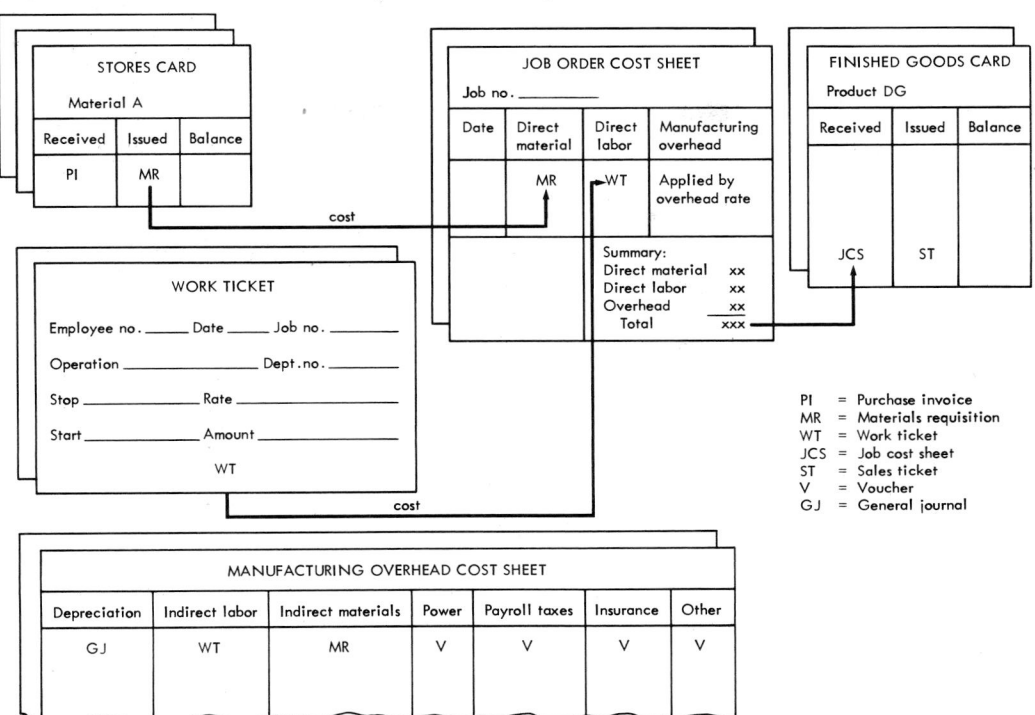

from the storeroom on a materials requisition, which shows the types and quantities of the materials ordered.

3. The work (or labor time) ticket shows who worked on what job for how many hours and at what wage rate. All of each employee's daily hours must be accounted for on one or more work tickets.
4. The manufacturing overhead cost sheet summarizes the various factory indirect costs incurred. One sheet is maintained for each production center.
5. A *finished goods card* is a running record of units and costs of products completed, sold, and on hand. A card is maintained for each type of product manufactured and sold.

The flow of manufacturing costs through the accounting system of a firm using a job order cost system is shown in Illustration 22.3. To gain a full understanding of a job order cost system, this illustration should be studied carefully and related to the documents shown in Illustration 22.2 and to the journal entries in the following example.

Job order costing—an example

This example will illustrate a job order cost system, emphasizing the tie-in between the general ledger accounts and the subsidiary records. The example covers the month of July. Beginning inventories on July 1 were:

Materials inventory (material A, $10,000; material B, $6,000; various indirect materials, $4,000)	$20,000
Work in process inventory (Job No. 106: direct materials, $4,200; direct labor, $5,000; and overhead, $4,000)	13,200
Finished goods inventory (500 units of product AB at a cost of $11 per unit)	5,500

The example assumes that Job No. 106, which was in process at the beginning of July, was completed in July. Of the two jobs started in July (Nos. 107 and 108), only Job. No. 107 was completed by the end of July. The transactions and journal entries to record these transactions are given below:

1. Purchased $10,000 of material A and $15,000 of material B on account.

Materials Inventory	25,000	
Accounts Payable		25,000
To record purchase of direct materials.		

2. Issued direct materials: material A to Job No. 106, $1,000; to Job No. 107, $8,000; to Job No. 108, $2,000; material B to Job No. 106, $2,000;

Illustration 22.3:   Job order cost system—cost flows

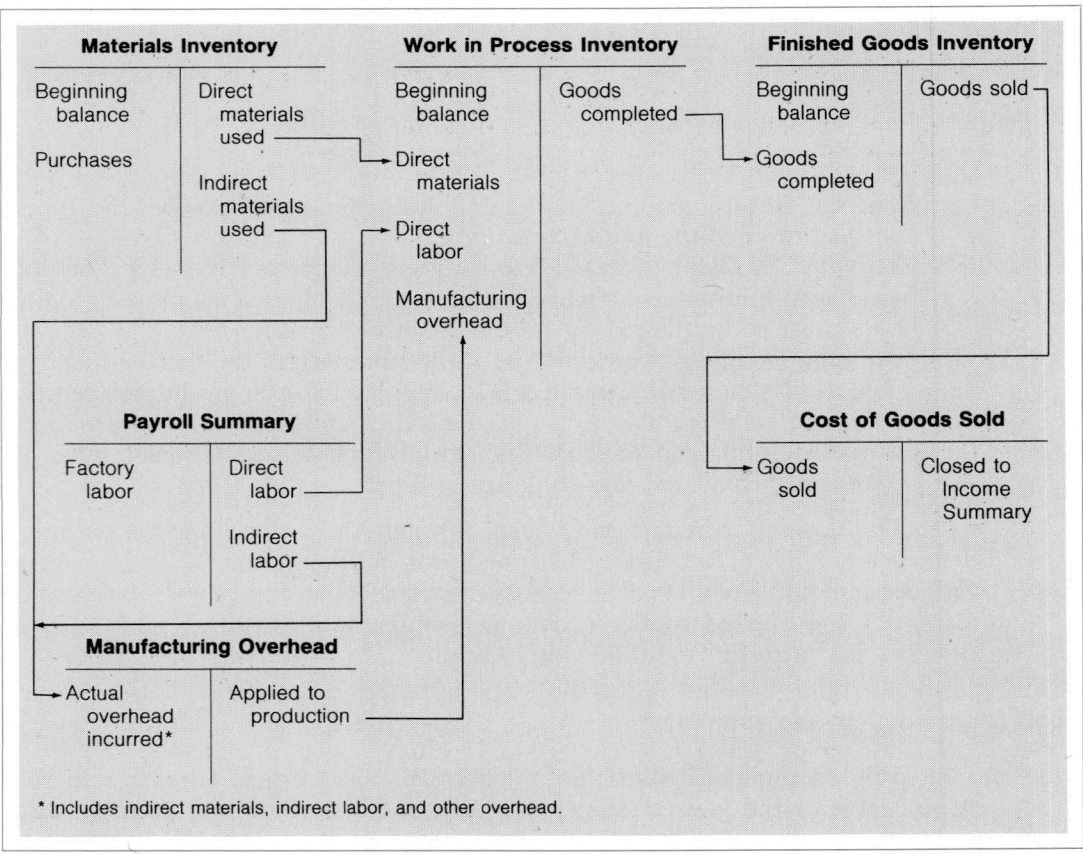

to Job No. 107, $6,000; to Job No. 108, $4,000. Indirect materials issued to all jobs, $1,000.

```
Work in Process Inventory .......................................   23,000
Manufacturing Overhead .........................................    1,000
     Materials Inventory .........................................              24,000
     To record direct and indirect materials issued.
```

3. **Factory payroll for the month, $25,000; social security and income taxes withheld, $4,000.**

```
Payroll Summary ..............................................   25,000
     Various liability accounts for taxes withheld ....................              4,000
     Accrued Wages Payable ......................................             21,000
     To record factory payroll for July.
```

4. **Factory payroll paid, $19,000.**

```
Accrued Wages Payable .........................................   19,000
     Cash ....................................................              19,000
     To record cash paid to factory employees in July.
```

5. **Payroll costs distributed: direct labor, $20,000 (Job No. 106, $5,000; Job No. 107, $12,000; and Job No. 108, $3,000); and indirect labor, $5,000.**

```
Work in Process Inventory .......................................   20,000
Manufacturing Overhead .........................................    5,000
     Payroll Summary ...........................................             25,000
     To distribute factory labor costs incurred.
```

6. **Other manufacturing overhead costs incurred:**

```
          Payroll taxes accrued ...........................  $ 3,000
          Repairs (on account) ............................    1,000
          Property taxes accrued ..........................    4,000
          Heat, light, and power (on account) ...............    2,000
          Depreciation .....................................    5,000
                                                             $15,000
```

```
Manufacturing Overhead .........................................   15,000
     Accounts Payable ...........................................              3,000
     Accrued Payroll Taxes Payable ...............................              3,000
     Accrued Property Taxes Payable .............................              4,000
     Accumulated Depreciation ...................................              5,000
     To record manufacturing overhead costs incurred.
```

7. **Manufacturing overhead applied to production (assume a predetermined rate of 80 percent of direct labor cost):**

```
          Job No. 106 (0.80 × $5,000) .....................  $ 4,000
          Job No. 107 (0.80 × $12,000) ...................    9,600
          Job No. 108 (0.80 × $3,000) .....................    2,400
                                                             $16,000
```

```
Work in Process Inventory .......................................   16,000
     Manufacturing Overhead .....................................             16,000
     To record application of overhead to production.
```

8. **Jobs completed and transferred to finished goods storeroom (see Illustration 22.4 for details):**

Job No. 106 (4,000 units of product DG @ $6.30) $25,200
Job No. 107 (10,000 units of product XY @ $3.56) 35,600
$60,800

Finished Goods Inventory 60,800
   Work in Process Inventory 60,800
   To record completed production for July.

9. Sales on account for the month: 500 units of product AB for $8,000, cost, $5,500; and 10,000 units of product XY for $62,000, cost, $35,600 (Job No. 107).

Accounts Receivable 70,000
   Sales 70,000
   To record sales on account for July.

Cost of Goods Sold 41,100
   Finished Goods Inventory 41,100
   To record cost of goods sold in July.

After the above entries have been posted, the Work in Process Inventory and Finished Goods Inventory accounts would appear (in T-account form) as follows:

Work in Process Inventory

July 1 balance	13,200	Completed	60,800
Direct materials used	23,000		
Direct labor cost incurred	20,000		
Overhead applied	16,000		
July 31 balance	11,400		

Finished Goods Inventory

July 1 balance	5,500	Sold	41,100
Completed	60,800		
July 31 balance	25,200		

On July 31, the Work in Process Inventory account has a balance of $11,400, which agrees with the total costs charged thus far to Job No. 108, as shown in Illustration 22.4. The balance consists of direct materials, $6,000; direct labor, $3,000; and manufacturing overhead, $2,400. Finished Goods Inventory has a balance on July 31 of $25,200, supported by the finished goods inventory card for Job No. 106 (Illustration 22.4), which shows that the units of product DG on hand have a total cost of $25,200.

Note that the ledger account entries given above are often made from summaries of costs and thus are recorded only at the end of the month. On the other hand, in order to keep management informed as to costs incurred, details of the various costs are recorded more frequently, often daily.

The above example should be studied until the advantages of using predetermined overhead rate are clear. Three jobs were worked on during the month. One (No. 106) was started last month and completed in July. One

Illustration 22.4: Supporting inventory cards and job order sheets

STORES CARD Material A				STORES CARD Material B		
Received	Issued	Balance		Received	Issued	Balance
$10,000		$10,000		$15,000		$ 6,000
		20,000				21,000
	$1,000	19,000			$2,000	19,000
	8,000	11,000			6,000	13,000
	2,000	9,000			4,000	9,000

JOB ORDER COST SHEET (Product DG)   Job No. 106

Date	Direct Materials	Direct Labor	Manufacturing Overhead
July 1	$ 4,200	$ 5,000	$4,000
July	A: 1,000	5,000	4,000
	B: 2,000	$10,000	$8,000
	$ 7,200		
	Job completed (4,000 units of product DG @ $6.30). Total cost, $25,200.		

JOB ORDER COST SHEET (Product XY)   Job No. 107

Date	Direct Materials	Direct Labor	Manufacturing Overhead
July	A: $ 8,000	$12,000	$9,600
	B: 6,000		
	$14,000		
	Job completed (10,000 units of product XY @ $3.56). Total cost, $35,600.		

JOB ORDER COST SHEET (Product OR)   Job No. 108

Date	Direct Materials	Direct Labor	Manufacturing Overhead
July	A: $ 2,000	$3,000	$2,400
	B: 4,000		
	Job incomplete (1,000 units of product OR). Cost to date, $11,400.		

FINISHED GOODS CARD Product AB			FINISHED GOODS CARD Product DG			FINISHED GOODS CARD Product XY		
Received	Issued	Balance	Received	Issued	Balance	Received	Issued	Balance
		$5,500	$25,200		$25,200	$35,600		$35,600
	$5,500	–0–					$35,600	–0–

(No. 107) was started and completed in July. And one (No. 108) was started but not finished in July. Each required different amounts of direct materials and direct labor. Under these conditions, there is simply no timely way to apply overhead to products without the use of a predetermined rate based on some level of activity. Note that the use of a predetermined overhead rate permits the computation of unit costs for Job Nos. 106 and 107 at the time of their completion rather than waiting until the end of the month. But this advantage is secured only at the expense of keeping more detailed records of the costs incurred. As discussed below, the other major cost accumulation system—process cost—requires far less record keeping, but the computation of unit costs is more complex.

PROCESS COST SYSTEMS

Many business firms manufacture huge quantities of a single product or similar products (paint, paper, chemicals, gasoline, rubber, and plastics) on a continuous basis over long periods of time. There is no separate job or specific batch of units; rather, production is ongoing over the year or even several years. Costs must be accumulated for each process which a product undergoes on its way to completion. The processes or departments serve as cost centers where costs are accumulated for the entire period (usually a month). These costs are divided by the number of units produced (tons, pounds, gallons, or feet) to get an average unit cost. The cost system used in these circumstances is called a process cost system. A *process cost system (process costing)* is a manufacturing cost system in which costs incurred to produce a product are accumulated according to the processes or departments a product goes through on its way to completion.

Basic system design

As shown in Illustration 22.5, process cost systems have the same cost flows as found in a job order system. Costs of the factors of production are first recorded in separate accounts for materials inventory, labor, and overhead. Costs are then transferred to work in process inventory. A process cost system usually has more than one work in process inventory account. An account is kept for each processing center in order to determine the unit cost of each process. All products manufactured may be subjected to processing in a specified *sequential* order, as depicted in Illustration 22.5; the products are started in Department A, processed, transferred to Department B, processed further, and then transferred to finished goods inventory.

Process costing illustrated

Assume that Ajax Company sells a chemical product that is processed in two departments. In Department A, basic materials are crushed, powdered, and blended. In Department B, the product is packaged, tested, and transferred to finished goods. Production and cost data for the month of June are:

	Department A	Department B
Units started, completed, and transferred	11,000	9,000
Units on hand at June 30, partially completed	–0–	2,000
Beginning inventory	$ –0–	$ –0–
Direct materials	16,500	1,100
Direct labor	5,500	5,900
Actual manufacturing overhead	4,500	5,600
Applied manufacturing overhead	4,400	5,900

Illustration 22.5: Cost flows in a process cost system

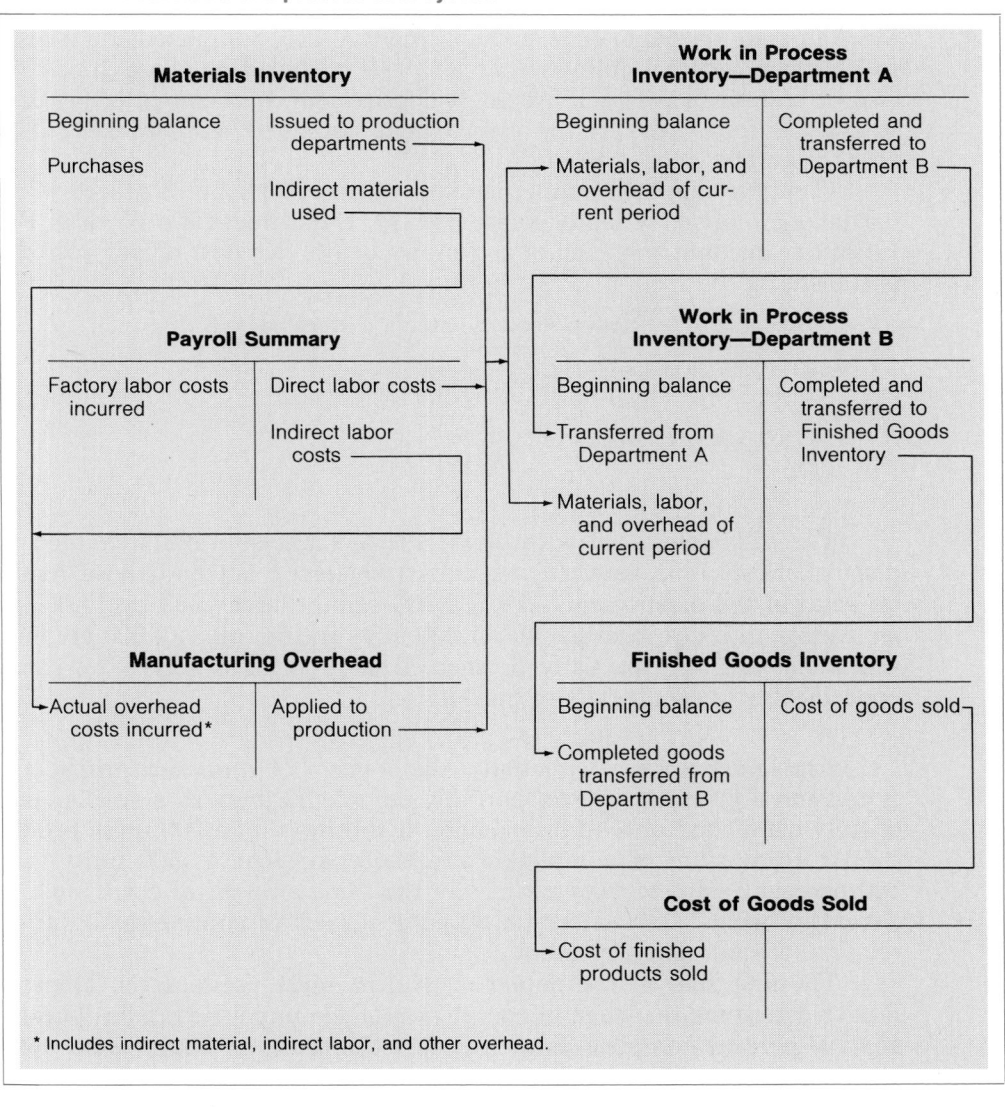

* Includes indirect material, indirect labor, and other overhead.

In Department A, manufacturing overhead is applied on the basis of a predetermined rate of 80 percent of direct labor cost. In Department B, manufacturing overhead is applied at the rate of 100 percent of direct labor cost.

From these data, the Work in Process Inventory—Department A account can be constructed and summarized as follows:

Work in Process Inventory—Department A

Direct materials	16,500	Transferred to Department B—	
Direct labor	5,500	11,000 units @ $2.40	26,400
Applied overhead (80 percent of			
direct labor cost)	4,400		
Total	26,400		

Since all units started in June in Department A were completed and transferred to Department B, it follows that all costs assigned to those goods should also be transferred. The unit cost in Department A is computed by dividing $26,400 of total costs by the 11,000 units completed and transferred to get an average unit cost of $2.40.

Computations are seldom this simple. One complication is faced whenever partially completed inventories are present. Department B's Work in Process Inventory account for June is as follows before the cost of completed units is transferred out:

Work in Process Inventory—Department B

Transferred in from Department A	26,400
Direct material	1,100
Direct labor	5,900
Overhead (100 percent of direct labor)	5,900
Total	39,300

The task now faced is to divide the $39,300 total costs charged to the department in June between the units transferred out and those remaining on hand in the department. The $39,300 cannot be divided by 11,000 to get an average unit cost because the 11,000 units are not alike; 9,000 are finished, and 2,000 are only partially finished. The problem is solved by using the concept of equivalent units of production.

Equivalent units. Essentially, the concept of *equivalent units* involves expressing a given number of partially completed units as a smaller number of fully completed units. For example, it follows that 1,000 units brought to a 50 percent state of completion are the equivalent of 500 units that are 100 percent complete. Approximately the same amount of costs must be incurred to bring 1,000 units to a 50 percent level of completion as would be required to complete 500 units.

The first step in computing equivalent units produced in Department B is to determine the stage of completion of the unfinished units. These units are 100 percent complete as to transferred-in costs or they would not have been transferred out of Department A. The units may have different stages of completion as to materials, labor, and overhead costs added in Department B. Units are often assumed to be at the same stage of completion regarding labor and overhead. This assumption is made because overhead is often applied to work in process on a direct labor basis (direct labor and overhead together are termed *conversion costs*). All direct materials are added at the start of processing in Department B. Thus, both ending inventory and units transferred out are 100 percent complete as to materials and equivalent production for materials is 11,000 units. Next, assume that the 2,000 units are, on the average, 50 percent complete as to conversion. Equivalent production for labor and overhead is 10,000 units—9,000 units transferred out fully complete and 2,000 brought to a 50 percent completion state, which is the equivalent of 1,000 fully complete units.

Basic data for this illustration come from the work in process T-account for Department B. With equivalent units of production known, unit costs of processing in Department B and total per unit can now be computed as follows:

	Transferred in	Materials	Conversion	Total
Costs to be accounted for:				
Charged to Department B	$26,400	$ 1,100	$11,800*	$39,300
Equivalent units	11,000	11,000	10,000†	
Unit costs	$2.40	$0.10	$1.18	$3.68

* Conversion costs consist of direct labor + overhead ($5,900 + $5,900).
† Units transferred (9,000) + equivalent units in ending inventory (1,000).

With unit cost computed, the $39,300 of costs charged to Department B in June can now be divided between costs transferred out and costs remaining in the department's ending inventory:

	Transferred in	Materials	Conversion	Total
Costs accounted for:				
Costs transferred out (9,000 units)	$21,600	$ 900	$10,620	$33,120
Cost of ending inventory (2,000 units)	4,800	200	1,180	6,180
Costs accounted for	$26,400	$1,100	$11,800	$39,300

The $33,120 total costs transferred out consists of $21,600 of Department A's cost (9,000 × $2.40), $900 of materials costs (9,000 × $0.10), and $10,620 of conversion costs (9,000 × $1.18) or $3.68 per unit. The 2,000 units of ending inventory in Department B are fully complete as to materials and 50 percent complete as to conversion. Ending inventory cost, then, consists of the following:

Costs from Department A (2,000 × $2.40)		$4,800
Costs added by Department B:		
Materials (2,000 × $0.10)	$ 200	
Conversion (2,000 × 0.5 × $1.18)	1,180	1,380
Total cost of ending inventory		$6,180

The units transferred out of Department B will be carried in finished goods inventory at a cost of $3.68 each until they are sold, at which time the costs will be charged to Cost of Goods Sold.

The June journal entries for the above activities are given below.

1.	Work in Process Inventory—Department A	16,500	
	Work in Process Inventory—Department B	1,100	
	Materials Inventory		17,600
	To record materials placed in production in June.		
2.	Payroll Summary	11,400	
	(Various withholding accounts and accrued		
	wages payable)		11,400
	To record factory payroll for June.		
3.	Work in Process Inventory—Department A	5,500	
	Work in Process Inventory—Department B	5,900	
	Payroll Summary		11,400
	To distribute factory labor costs (assumed that all such costs are chargeable directly to production departments).		
4.	Manufacturing Overhead	10,100	
	(Various accounts—cash, accounts payable, accruals, and		
	accumulated depreciation)		10,100
	To record actual overhead costs incurred in June.		
5.	Work in Process Inventory—Department A	4,400	
	Work in Process Inventory—Department B	5,900	
	Manufacturing Overhead		10,300
	To apply overhead to production using predetermined rates based on direct labor cost: Department A, 80 percent; and Department B, 100 percent.		
6.	Work in Process Inventory—Department B	26,400	
	Work in Process Inventory—Department A		26,400
	To record transfer of goods from Department A to Department B.		
7.	Finished Goods Inventory	33,120	
	Work in Process Inventory—Department B		33,120
	To record transfer of completed goods from Department B to finished goods.		

Assuming that 6,000 completed units were sold in June at a price of $10 per unit on account, the following entries would be required:

8.	Accounts Receivable	60,000	
	Sales		60,000
	To record sales on account.		
9.	Cost of Goods Sold	22,080	
	Finished Goods Inventory		22,080
	To record cost of goods sold in June, 6,000 units @ $3.68.		

When a processing center has both beginning and ending inventories, the computations for unit cost are more complex than when only ending inventory is involved. The key report in a process costing system is designed to make equivalent unit and unit cost computations easier; this report is called a production cost report. A *production cost report* shows the flow of units and costs through a processing center and how those costs are divided between the cost of units transferred out and the cost of units in ending inventory.

To illustrate the use of a production cost report and partially completed beginning and ending inventories, the following data are assumed for Department 3 of the A Company for the month of June 1984:

Units

Units in beginning inventory, complete as to materials, 60% complete as to conversion	6,000
Units transferred in from Department 2	18,000
Units completed and transferred out	16,000
Units in ending inventory, complete as to materials, 50% complete as to conversion	8,000

Costs

Cost of beginning inventory:		
Cost transferred in from preceding department in May	$12,000	
Materials added in May in Department 3	6,000	
Conversion costs (equal amounts of labor and overhead)	3,000	$21,000
Costs transferred in from preceding department in June		37,200
Costs added in Department 3 in June:		
Materials	$18,480	
Conversion (equal amounts of labor and overhead)	18,000	36,480
Total costs in beginning inventory and placed in production in Department 3 in June		$94,680

From the above data, the production cost report for Department 3 will be developed (Illustration 22.6). The report first uses information given in regard to units of product and then uses cost information to derive a unit cost and the total costs of goods transferred out and in ending inventory. This report will be discussed by explaining the four steps in its preparation.

The first step in the preparation of a production cost report is to trace the physical flow of actual units into and out of the department. The section entitled "UNITS" in Illustration 22.6 shows that 6,000 units were in the June beginning inventory and that 18,000 units were transferred in from the previous department, making a total of 24,000 units that must be accounted for. Of these 24,000 units, 16,000 units were completed and transferred out (either to the next processing department or to finished goods) and 8,000 remained partially completed in Department 3 at the end of the month.

Next, actual units are converted into equivalent units of production. The production cost report illustrated uses an *average* cost procedure; *equivalent units consist of the total units transferred out plus the equivalent units in ending inventory.* Since the units were fully complete as to costs transferred in and materials, equivalent units for these two cost elements are 24,000. But the units in ending inventory were only 50 percent complete as to conversion costs; therefore, equivalent units for conversion cost purposes consist

Illustration 22.6:   Production cost report

A COMPANY
Production Cost Report—Department 3
For the Month of June, 1984

	Actual Units	Equivalent units		
		Transferred in	Materials	Conversion
UNITS:				
Units in beginning inventory	6,000			
Units transferred in from Department 2	18,000			
Units to be accounted for	24,000			
Units completed and transferred	16,000	16,000	16,000	16,000
Units in ending inventory*	8,000	8,000	8,000	4,000
Units accounted for	24,000	24,000	24,000	20,000

* Inventory is complete as to materials added, 50 percent complete as to conversion.

	Transferred in	Materials	Conversion	Total
COSTS:				
Costs to be accounted for:				
Costs in beginning inventory	$12,000	$ 6,000	$ 3,000	$21,000
Costs transferred in from Department 2	37,200			37,200
Costs added in Department 3		18,480	18,000	36,480
Costs to be accounted for	$49,200	$24,480	$21,000	$94,680
Equivalent units (as above)	24,000	24,000	20,000	
Unit costs (per equivalent unit)	$2.05	$1.02	$1.05	$4.12
Costs accounted for:				
Costs in ending inventory	$16,400	$ 8,160	$ 4,200	$28,760
Costs transferred out	32,800	16,320	16,800	65,920
Costs accounted for	$49,200	$24,480	$21,000	$94,680

of 16,000 fully completed and transferred out units plus 4,000 (8,000 units at 50 percent complete) equivalent units of ending inventory or a total of 20,000 equivalent units.

Now that equivalent units have been computed, unit cost can be calculated. Costs are accumulated for each cost element of production: costs transferred in, materials, and conversion. Notice that the costs of beginning inventory and costs of the current month are totaled for each cost element. The summation of all costs charged to the department is referred to as "total costs to be accounted for"; these costs will appear either in ending inventory of Department 3 or will be transferred out. Total cost assignable to each cost element is divided by the appropriate number of equivalent units of production related to that cost element. Since all costs for each cost element are totaled before the division, the unit costs computed are averages across the current and the prior period. As shown in Illustration 22.6, average unit costs for June are as follows: transferred in cost, $2.05; materials, $1.02; and conversion, $1.05. These costs are monitored closely by management for cost control purposes in the event that there are extreme fluctuations from one month to the next.

Lastly, costs can be distributed to the units transferred out and those remaining in ending inventory. The units that were transferred out were fully complete as to all elements of production. Therefore, the 16,000 units can be multiplied times $4.12, the total cost per unit. This gives $65,920, the amount to be assigned to the next department as "cost transferred in" or to finished goods as the cost of current period production. The cost of ending inventory would be computed as follows:

8,000 equivalent units transferred in @ $2.05	$16,400
8,000 equivalent units of materials costs @ $1.02	8,160
4,000 equivalent units of conversion costs @ $1.05	4,200
Total cost of ending inventory	$28,760

The sum of the ending inventory cost and the cost of the units transferred out must equal the total costs for which the department is accountable. Thus, a built-in check is provided to determine whether the procedures of cost allocation have been properly followed. To illustrate this, ending inventory cost of $28,760 is added to cost transferred out of $65,920, and the total equals costs accountable for of $94,680 as shown in the production cost report.

NEW TERMS INTRODUCED IN CHAPTER 22

Equivalent units
A method of expressing a given number of partially completed units as a smaller number of fully completed units; for example, bringing 1,000 units to a 75 percent level of completion is viewed as the equivalent of bringing 750 units to the 100 percent level of completion.

Finished goods card
A running record of units and costs of products completed, sold, and on hand.

Job order cost sheet
A form used to summarize the costs of direct materials, direct labor, and manufacturing overhead incurred for a job. The job order sheets for all partially completed jobs form the subsidiary ledger for the Work in Process Inventory account.

Job order cost system (job costing)
A cost accounting system in which the costs incurred to produce a product are accumulated according to the individual job, such as a building, dam, 1,000 chairs, or 10 desks.

Manufacturing overhead cost sheet
A record that summarizes the various manufacturing overhead costs incurred.

Materials requisition
A written order directing the stores clerk to issue certain materials to a production or service center.

Overapplied (overabsorbed) overhead
The amount by which the overhead applied to production exceeds the actual overhead costs incurred in that same period.

Predetermined overhead rate
Is calculated by dividing estimated total overhead costs for a period by the expected level of activity, such as direct labor-hours or direct labor cost for the period. Predetermined overhead rates are usually set at the beginning of the year in which they will be used. The use of a predetermined rate is a means of applying manufacturing overhead to production such that unit costs can be determined immediately after production has been completed.

Process cost system (process costing)
A cost accounting system in which costs incurred to produce a product are accumulated according to the processes or departments a product goes through on its way to completion.

Production cost report
A report which shows how the costs charged to a department are divided between the cost of units transferred out and the cost of ending inventory.

Stores (or materials) card
A record which shows the quantities and costs of each type of material received, issued to a job, and left on hand.

Underapplied (underabsorbed) overhead
The amount by which actual overhead costs incurred in a period exceed the overhead applied to production in that period.

Work (labor time) ticket
A form or card that shows the amount of time taken by an employee to complete a given assignment; may be prepared for both direct and indirect labor.

DEMONSTRATION PROBLEM

Part 1. Heille Company employs a job order cost system. As of January 1, 1984, its records showed:

Materials and supplies .... $ 80,000
Work in process 172,000
Finished goods (50,000 units at $4) 200,000

The work in process inventory consists of two jobs:

No.	Materials	Labor	Manufacturing overhead	Total
212......	$30,000	$40,000	$20,000	$ 90,000
213......	34,000	32,000	16,000	82,000
	$64,000	$72,000	$36,000	$172,000

Summarized below are manufacturing data for the company for 1984:

1. Materials and supplies purchased on account, $330,000.
2. Factory payrolls accrued, $680,000; FICA taxes withheld, $34,000; and federal income taxes withheld, $60,000.
3. Manufacturing overhead costs incurred: depreciation, $20,000; heat, light, and power, $8,000; and miscellaneous, $12,000.
4. Direct materials and supplies requisitioned: for Job No. 212, $52,000; Job No. 213, $96,000; Job No. 214, $160,000; and indirect supplies requisitioned, $8,000.
5. Payrolls distributed: direct labor—Job No. 212, $80,000; Job No. 213, $160,000; Job No. 214, $240,000; factory supervision, $80,000; and indirect labor, $120,000.
6. Overhead is assigned to work in process at 50% of direct labor costs as in 1983.
7. Job Nos. 212 and 213 were completed.
8. The cost of goods sold for the year was $688,000.

Required:

Prepare general journal entries to record the above summarized data, as well as all closing entries for which you have sufficient information.

Part 2. AFA, Inc., uses a process cost system to accumulate the costs it incurs to produce aluminum awning stabilizers. The costs incurred in the finishing department are shown for the month of May. The May 1 inventory consisted of 30,000 units, fully complete as to materials, 80 percent complete as to conversion. Its total cost of $240,000 consisted of $180,000 of costs transferred in from the molding department, $25,000 of finishing department material costs, and $35,000 of conversion costs.

Costs from molding department (excluding costs in beginning
  inventory).. $600,000
Costs added in finishing department in May (excluding costs in
  beginning inventory):
    Materials .... $ 53,000
    Conversion   109,480   162,480
                                                                         $762,480

The finishing department received 100,000 units from the molding department; 106,000 units were completed and transferred; 24,000 units, complete as to materials and 60 percent complete as to conversion, were left in the May 31 inventory.

Required:

a. Prepare a production cost report for the finishing department for the month of May.

b. Compute the average unit cost for conversion for April in the finishing department.

Solution to demonstration problem

Part 1

HEILLE COMPANY
General Journal

1.	Materials Inventory	330,000	
	Accounts Payable		330,000
	To record materials purchased on account.		
2.	Payroll Summary	680,000	
	FICA Taxes Withheld		34,000
	Federal Income Taxes Withheld		60,000
	Accrued Payroll		586,000
	To record accrued factory payrolls.		
3.	Manufacturing Overhead	40,000	
	Accumulated Depreciation		20,000
	Accounts Payable (Accrued Expenses, Cash, etc.)		20,000
	To record incurrence of various manufacturing overhead costs.		
4.	Work in Process Inventory	308,000	
	Manufacturing Overhead	8,000	
	Materials Inventory		316,000
	To record requisitions of materials and supplies:		

        Job No. 212 .... $ 52,000
              213 96,000
              214 160,000
        Supplies 8,000
                            $316,000

5.	Work in Process Inventory	480,000	
	Manufacturing Overhead	200,000	
	Payroll Summary		680,000
	To distribute labor costs:		

    Direct labor to Work in Process:
        Job No. 212 .... $ 80,000
              213 160,000
              214 .... 240,000 $480,000
    Manufacturing overhead:
        Factory supervision .... $ 80,000
        Indirect labor 120,000   200,000
                              $680,000

6.	Work in Process Inventory	240,000	
	Manufacturing Overhead		240,000
	Overhead assigned: Job No. 212, $40,000; Job No. 213, $80,000; and Job No. 214, $120,000.		

7.	Finished Goods Inventory	680,000	
	Work in Process Inventory		680,000
	Completed jobs transferred:		

No. 212	$262,000
No. 213	418,000
	$680,000

8.	Cost of Goods Sold	688,000	
	Finished Goods Inventory		688,000
	To record cost of goods sold.		
	Cost of Goods Sold	8,000	
	Manufacturing Overhead		8,000
	To close underapplied manufacturing overhead.		
	Income Summary	696,000	
	Cost of Goods Sold		696,000
	To close Cost of Goods Sold expense account.		

Part 2

a.

AFA, INC.
Finishing Department
Production Cost Report
For the Month Ending May 31

	Actual units	Equivalent units		
		Transferred in	Materials	Conversion
UNITS:				
Units in May 1 inventory	30,000			
Units transferred in	100,000			
Units to be accounted for	130,000			
Units completed and transferred	106,000	106,000	106,000	106,000
Units in May 31 inventory*	24,000	24,000	24,000	14,400
Units accounted for	130,000	130,000	130,000	120,400

* Inventory is complete as to materials, 60% complete as to conversion.

	Transferred in	Materials	Conversion	Total
COSTS:				
Costs to be accounted for:				
Costs in May 1 inventory	$180,000	$ 25,000	$ 35,000	$ 240,000
Costs transferred in	600,000			600,000
Costs added in department		53,000	109,480	162,480
Costs to be accounted for . . .	$780,000	$ 78,000	$144,480	$1,002,480
Equivalent units (as above)	130,000	130,000	120,400	
Unit costs	$6.00	$0.60	$1.20	$7.80
Costs accounted for:				
Costs in May 31 inventory	$144,000	$ 14,400	$ 17,280	$ 175,680
Costs transferred out	636,000	63,600	127,200	826,800
Costs accounted for	$780,000	$ 78,000	$144,480	$1,002,480

b. The unit cost for conversion in the finishing department in April was $1.46 [$35,000 ÷ (0.8 × 30,000)].

QUESTIONS

1. What is the basic purpose of any costing system?

2. In what respects does a process cost system differ from a job order cost system? What factors should be taken into consideration in determining which type of system should be employed?

3. How is a predetermined overhead rate calculated? Why is the use of a predetermined rate necessary in a perpetual inventory cost system?

4. What is a job order sheet? Explain how it is used.

5. What is the reason, other than errors in estimating costs, for overapplied overhead?

6. What is meant by the term *equivalent units?* Of what use is the computation of the number of equivalent units of production?

7. Distinguish between the number of units completed and transferred during a period and the equivalent units for the same period.

8. What is the basic information reported in a production cost report?

9. Under what circumstances would the number of equivalent units of materials differ from the equivalent units of labor and overhead in the same department in the same period? Under what circumstances would they be the same?

10. In a process cost system, under what circumstances is the assignment of overhead to production applying a predetermined rate definitely preferable to assigning actual overhead incurred?

11. It requires less effort to operate a job cost system than a process cost system. Do you agree or disagree? Explain.

EXERCISES

E–1. In September, George Company worked only on Job No. 714, completing it on September 30. During the month, the company purchased and used $10,000 of direct materials and incurred $15,000 of direct labor costs. Assuming overhead is applied at the rate of 120 percent of direct labor costs, what is the total cost of Job No. 714? Prepare journal entries to record the above transactions, including the transfer of Job No. 714 to finished goods inventory.

E–2. As of August 1, Job. No. 210 had already accumulated $5,000 in total costs. During August, Job No. 210 required $7,000 of direct materials and $14,000 of direct labor. Overhead is applied to production at the rate of 80 percent of direct labor costs. Assuming completed Job No. 210 consisted of 800 units, what is the total cost per unit? Give the journal entries necessary to record the transfer of Job No. 210 to finished goods inventory and the ultimate sale of all 800 units at 150 percent of cost.

E–3. The Pylon Company builds desks to fit the specifications in each order received. It engaged in the following transactions during June:

Transactions:

1. Purchased precut wood for desk tops, $10,000.
2. Wood and other direct materials issued to production, $7,000.
3. Direct labor costs incurred, $5,000.
4. Overhead assigned to production, $6,000.
5. Job No. 312 is completed and transferred.

Job No. 312 was the only order worked on in June, and it consisted of 5,000 desks. The total costs assigned to Job. No. 312 in May amounted to $4,500.

    a. Journalize the transactions listed above.
    b. Compute the cost per unit of Job No. 312.

E–4. The Bud Company, which uses a job order cost system, engaged in the following activities during December:

1. Three jobs were started: Nos. 122, 123, and 124.
2. Direct materials issued:

        To Job 122 . . . . . . $5,000
            Job 123   7,000
            Job 124   4,000

3. Direct labor costs incurred:

For Job 122 . . . . . . 500 hours @ $7/hour
Job 123 . . . . . . 750 hours @ $6/hour
Job 124 . . . . . . 200 hours @ $8.50/hour

4. Assume overhead is applied at the rate of $4 per direct labor-hour.

Compute the cost of each job and give the necessary journal entry to record the transfer of Job No. 123 to Finished Goods Inventory.

E–5.   Z Company estimated its manufacturing overhead for 1984 at $400,000 ($100,000 fixed and $300,000 variable) based on an estimated activity of 200,000 direct labor-hours. At the end of 1984, manufacturing overhead was overapplied by $3,000, while actual direct labor-hours amounted to 202,000. Analyze the $3,000 as to the reasons for its existence. Give the journal entry required to reflect a practical disposition of the overhead balance.

E–6.   Assume that at the end of 1984, in Exercise E–5, the costs of the 202,000 actual direct labor-hours were lodged in the following accounts: Work in Process, 20,200 hours; Finished Goods, 50,500 hours; and Cost of Goods Sold, 131,300 hours. Give the journal entry to allocate the overhead balance to these accounts.

E–7.   In Department B, materials are added at the beginning of the process. The ending inventory was 20 percent complete as to conversion costs. Assume there were 500 units in beginning inventory, 6,000 units were started during the period and 4,000 units were transferred to finished goods inventory. Under the average method, what are the equivalent units of production for materials and conversion costs?

E–8.   The following cost data relate to Exercise E–7:

	Materials	Conversion	Total
Beginning inventory	$ 7,000	$ 3,500	$10,500
Incurred during year	22,250	21,250	43,500
Total costs to be accounted for	$29,250	$24,750	$54,000

Compute the cost of goods completed and transferred to Finished Goods Inventory and the cost of the ending work in process inventory.

PROBLEMS, SERIES A

P22–1–A.   The James Company has established the following budget for 1984:

	Assembling	Welding
Manufacturing overhead	$ 700,000	$ 900,000
Direct labor cost	1,200,000	1,500,000
Direct labor-hours	100,000	150,000
Machine-hours	52,000	150,000

James Company uses predetermined rates to apply manufacturing overhead, based on machine-hours in assembling and on direct labor costs in welding.

Required:

a. Compute the predetermined overhead rate for each department.

b. During May, the job cost sheet for Job No. 195 showed the following:

	Assembling	Welding
Direct materials used	$ 4,000	$16,000
Direct labor cost	12,000	5,000
Direct labor-hours	1,000	500
Machine-hours	480	300

Using the overhead rates computed in part (*a*), compute the total cost of Job No. 195.

P22–2–A.   Omaha Company intends to start a policy of using a predetermined rate to charge manufacturing overhead to production. Selected actual and budgeted production data and costs for 1984 are:

	Budgeted	Actual
Manufacturing overhead	$600,000	$607,000
Direct labor-hours	75,000	76,000
Machine-hours	60,000	59,000
Units of production	200,000	195,000

Required:

    a.   Compute three possible rates by which the overhead can be applied to production. Also compute the underapplied or overapplied overhead for 1984 under each rate.

    b.   Theoretically, what disposition should be made for financial reporting of the underapplied or overapplied overhead in part (*a*)?

P22–3–A.   Blake Corporation employs a job order cost system. Its manufacturing activities in July 1984, its first month of operation, are summarized as follows:

	Job number			
	201	202	203	204
Direct materials	$8,000	$5,800	$12,600	$6,000
Direct labor cost	$6,600	$6,000	$ 8,400	$2,400
Direct labor-hours	1,100	1,000	1,400	400
Units produced	200	100	1,000	300

Manufacturing overhead is applied at a rate of $2 per direct labor-hour for variable overhead and $3 per direct labor-hour for fixed overhead, for a total rate of $5 per direct labor-hour.

Job Nos. 201, 202, and 203 were completed in July.

Required:

    a.   Compute the amount of overhead charged to each job.

    b.   Compute the total and unit cost of each completed job.

    c.   Prepare the entry, in general journal form, to record the transfer of completed jobs to finished goods inventory.

    d.   Compute the balance in the July 31, 1984, Work in Process Inventory account and provide a schedule of the costs charged to each incomplete job to support this balance.

P22–4–A.   The Tiger Company's general ledger shows the following balances as of January 1, 1984:

Materials inventory	$50,000
Work in process inventory	22,500
Finished goods inventory	82,000

The work in process inventory consists of the following:

Job No. 1858:

Material	$16,500
Labor	2,000
Overhead	4,000
	$22,500

The following transactions took place in January:

Transactions:

1. Materials purchased on account, $140,000.
2. Materials issued during the month: direct, $100,000; indirect, $17,000. Of the direct materials issued, $14,000 were assigned to Job No. 1858, with the balance going equally to Job Nos. 1859 and 1860.
3. Gross payroll for January was $75,000; FICA taxes withheld amounted to $4,000; federal income taxes withheld totaled $8,500.
4. The $75,000 payroll consisted of $60,000 of direct labor (one third charged to each job) and $15,000 of indirect labor.
5. Manufacturing overhead is applied at 200 percent of direct labor cost.
6. Job No. 1858 was completed.

Required:

a. Prepare journal entries for the above transactions.

b. Compute the balance in ending Work in Process Inventory.

P22–5–A. The following data pertain to a production center of the Fox Company:

Work in process inventory, February 1, 10,000 units.

Direct materials	$10,500
Direct labor	5,000
Manufacturing overhead (150 percent of direct labor cost)	7,500
	$23,000
Units started in February	30,000
Costs incurred in February:	
Direct materials	$30,300
Direct labor	46,000
Overhead applied	?

The ending inventory consisted of 15,000 units (100 percent complete as to materials, 60 percent complete as to conversion).

Required:

Compute the following:

a. Number of units completed and transferred to finished goods inventory.

b. The equivalent units of production for materials and conversion costs (use the average method).

c. Cost per equivalent unit.

d. Cost of units completed and transferred.

e. Cost of ending inventory.

P22–6–A. Baker Company manufactures a product called Savem and determines product costs using a process cost system. Following are cost and production data for the handle department for the month of June:

	Units	Materials costs	Conversion costs
Inventory, June 1	20,000	$1,790	$2,200
Placed in production in June	60,000	5,410	9,560
Inventory, June 30	30,000	?	?

The June 30 inventory was complete as to materials and 20 percent complete as to conversion.

Required:

Prepare a production cost report.

P22–7–A.   Davis Company manufactures a product called DOG and determines product costs using a process cost system. Materials costing $22,000 were introduced at the start of processing, and $18,000 of conversion costs were incurred. During the period, 40,000 units of product were started and 38,000 were completed. At the end of the period, 2,000 units were still in process and were 40 percent complete as to conversion.

Required:

Prepare a production cost report.

P22–8–A.   Plaza Drug Company manufactures an ointment for relieving sore muscles. The product is moved through two departments, mixing and bottling. Production and cost data for the bottling department in December were as follows:

Work in process, December 1 (20,000 pints):
Costs transferred in	$10,000
Materials costs	4,000
Conversion costs	2,000

Costs incurred in December:
Transferred in (60,000 pints)	$30,800
Materials costs	12,800
Conversion costs	12,250

All materials are added at the beginning of the bottling process. Ending inventory consists of 15,000 pints, 100 percent complete as to materials and 40 percent complete as to conversion.

Required:

Prepare a production cost report for December.

PROBLEMS, SERIES B

P22–1–B.   The Doberman Company has established the following budget for 1984.

	Assembly	Packaging
Manufacturing overhead	$1,000,000	$1,400,000
Direct labor cost	1,800,000	2,200,000
Direct labor-hours . . . . : . . .	150,000	220,000
Machine-hours	75,000	200,000

Doberman Company uses predetermined rates to apply manufacturing overhead, based on machine-hours in assembly and on direct labor costs in packaging.

Required:

    a. Compute the predetermined overhead rate for each department.

    b. During June, the job cost sheet for Job No. 104 showed the following:

	Assembly	*Packaging*
Direct materials used	$ 6,000	$24,000
Direct labor cost	18,000	7,500
Direct labor-hours	1,500	750
Machine-hours	750	500

Using the overhead rates computed in (*a*), compute the total overhead cost of Job No. 104.

P22–2–B. Hauer applies overhead to production using a predetermined overhead rate based on machine-hours. Budgeted data for 1984 are:

Budgeted machine-hours 100,000
Budgeted overhead $580,000

Required:

    a. Compute the predetermined overhead rate.

    b. Assume that in 1984, actual overhead amounted to $665,000, and that 122,000 machine-hours were used. Compute the amount of underapplied or overapplied overhead for 1984.

P22–3–B. Jordan Corporation employs a job order cost system. Its manufacturing activities in June 1984, the first month of operation, are summarized as follows:

	Job number		
	101	*102*	*103*
Direct materials cost	$12,000	$8,000	$18,000
Direct labor cost	$10,000	$9,000	$12,000
Direct labor-hours	1,500	1,600	2,000
Units produced	300	150	1,500

Manufacturing overhead is applied at a rate of $3 per direct labor-hour for variable overhead and $4 per hour for fixed overhead.

Job Nos. 101 and 102 were completed in June.

Required:

    a. Compute the amount of overhead charged to each job.

    b. Compute the total and unit cost of each completed job.

    c. Prepare the entry, in general journal form, to record the transfer of completed jobs to Finished Goods Inventory.

    d. Compute the balance in the June 30, 1984, Work in Process Inventory account and provide a schedule of the costs charged to each incomplete job to support this balance.

P22–4–B. The Bozo Company engaged in the following activities during 1984:

Materials purchased $130,000
Factory payroll incurred (all direct, all employees
  paid $5 per hour) 105,000

The following jobs were worked on during 1984:

	Job No. 1	Job No. 2	Job No. 3
Direct materials	$34,000	$26,000	$40,000
Direct labor	50,000	40,000	15,000
Overhead (applied at $3.50 per direct labor-hour)	?	?	?

Job No. 1 was completed and sold (at 150 percent of cost), Job No. 2 was completed but not sold, and Job No. 3 was not completed.

Required:

Compute the balance in each inventory account (Materials, Work In Process, and Finished Goods) at December 31, 1984.

P22–5–B.   Hall Company uses a job order cost system, applying overhead at predetermined rates based on direct labor-hours in Department A and machine-hours in Department B. A job may be worked on in either Department A or Department B. Budgeted estimates for 1984 are:

	Department A	Department B
Direct labor cost	$60,000	$66,000
Manufacturing overhead	$72,000	$96,000
Direct labor-hours	12,000	16,000
Machine-hours	8,000	24,000

Detailed cost records show the following for Job No. 105 which was completed in 1984:

	Department A	Department B
Materials used	$5,000	$250
Direct labor cost	$4,000	$300
Direct labor-hours	100	50
Machine-hours	25	40

Required:

a.   Compute the predetermined overhead rates for 1984 for Departments A and B.

b.   Compute the amount of overhead applied to Job No. 105 in each department.

P22–6–B.   The following information relates to the Buffalo Company:

Units in beginning inventory	1,500
Cost of units in beginning inventory:	
Materials	$15,000
Conversion	7,000
Units placed in production	40,000
Costs incurred during current period:	
Materials	$92,000
Conversion	79,940
Units remaining in ending inventory (100 percent complete as to materials, 50 percent complete as to conversion)	2,500

Required:

Prepare a production cost report (use the average method).

P22–7–B.   Wynn Company employs a job order cost system. As of January 1, 1984, its records showed the following inventory balances:

```
Materials.............................  $ 45,000
Work in process .....................    86,000
Finished goods (25,000 units @ $4)......   100,000
```

The work in process inventory consisted of two jobs:

Job No.	Materials	Direct labor	Manufacturing overhead	Total
212.......	$15,000	$20,000	$10,000	$45,000
213.......	17,000	16,000	8,000	41,000
	$32,000	$36,000	$18,000	$86,000

Summarized below are production and sales data for the company for 1984.

1. Materials purchased, $160,000.
2. Factory payroll costs incurred, $340,000.
3. Factory indirect costs incurred (other than indirect labor and indirect materials): depreciation, $10,000; heat, light, and power, $4,000; and miscellaneous, $6,000.
4. Materials requisitioned: direct materials for Job No. 212, $26,000; for Job No. 213, $48,000; and for Job No. 214, $80,000; supplies (indirect materials) requisitioned, $4,000.
5. Factory payroll distributed: direct labor to Job No. 212, $40,000; to Job No. 213, $80,000; and to Job No. 214, $120,000; indirect labor, $100,000.
6. Overhead is assigned to work in process at the same rate per dollar of direct labor cost as in 1983.
7. Job Nos. 212 and 213 were completed.
8. Sales for the year amounted to $600,000; cost of goods sold, $344,000.

Required:

    a. Prepare journal entries to record the above transactions.

    b. Prepare all closing entries for which you have information.

    c. Set up T-accounts for Materials Inventory, Payroll Summary, Manufacturing Overhead, Work in Process Inventory, Finished Goods Inventory, and Cost of Goods Sold. Post those parts of the entries made in (*a*) and (*b*) that affect these accounts.

    d. Show that the total costs charged to incomplete jobs agrees with the balance in the Work in Process Inventory account.

P22–8–B. Strong Company uses a process cost system to account for the costs incurred in making its single product, a health food called Vita-Myte. This product is processed first in Department K and then in Department L. Materials are added in both departments. Production for May was as follows:

	Department K	Department L
Units started or transferred in	100,000	75,000
Units completed and transferred out	75,000	60,000
Stage of completion of May 31 inventory:		
Materials	100%	80%
Conversion............................	50%	40%
Direct materials costs	$ 60,000	$ 10,800
Conversion costs	$175,000	$118,800

There was no May 1 inventory in either department.

Required:

    a. Prepare a production cost report for Department K for May.

    b. Prepare a production cost report for Department L for May.

BUSINESS DECISION PROBLEM

The Plainsman Manufacturing Company manufactures one product, an orange industrial dye. The demand for this dye is highly seasonal, and because of this, Plainsman adjusts its production schedule so that it is in line with demand (the dye is susceptible to spoilage). The president of Plainsman, Doug Hertha, has received complaints from the sales department that it is having difficulty in setting a stable price for the dye. The sales department is under orders from Mr. Hertha to set prices on the basis of "cost plus 30 percent of cost." It complains that the cost figures it receives from the production manager vary widely from quarter to quarter, which in turn causes the selling price to fluctuate. In an attempt to settle the dispute, Mr. Hertha calls the production manager, William Benn, into his office for a conference. Mr. Benn reports that he has no choice but to change the cost every quarter, as to do otherwise would mean that a loss would result during periods of low demand. He tells Mr. Hertha that he has the numbers to back up this statement, and reminds Mr. Hertha that figures don't lie. As proof, he offers the following information:

	First quarter	Second quarter	Third quarter	Fourth quarter
Direct materials	$ 60,000	$ 24,000	$ 12,000	$ 48,000
Direct labor	75,000	30,000	15,000	60,000
Variable manufacturing overhead	15,000	6,000	3,000	12,000
Fixed manufacturing overhead	100,000	100,000	100,000	100,000
Total	$250,000	$160,000	$130,000	$220,000
Number of gallons to be produced	50,000	20,000	10,000	40,000
Cost per gallon	$5.00	$8.00	$13.00	$5.50

Mr. Hertha realizes that the root of the problem is manufacturing overhead. Overhead costs cannot be reduced enough to make a difference during the periods of low demand. He asks Mr. Benn to find a better way to allocate the manufacturing overhead costs to each gallon of dye produced in order to arrive at a more uniform cost figure per gallon.

Required:

a. How would you recommend to Mr. Benn that manufacturing overhead costs be assigned to production? How would this differ from his present method?

b. What benefits would be gained by using your recommended solution?

c. To justify your recommendation made in (a) above, recalculate the per gallon cost of the dye using your recommendation.

Part Eight

Planning, control, and decision making

849

Chapter 23

Control through standard costs

CHAPTER GOALS

After study of this chapter, you should be able to:

1. Discuss the concept of a standard cost system, specifically addressing how standards are set and the advantages achieved through their use.

2. Calculate the six variances from standard and prepare journal entries based on that information.

3. Discuss possible reasons for the existence of variances and how the isolation of these variances can support a management by exception philosophy.

4. Discuss theoretical and practical methods for disposing of variances from standard.

5. Discuss standard costs in relation to job order or process cost systems (covered in Appendix).

6. Define and use correctly the terms in the chapter glossary.

STANDARD COSTS

The job order and process cost systems discussed in Chapter 22 gathered actual historical cost data. Because these data say little about how efficiently operations were conducted, many firms find it helpful to introduce standard costs into their cost systems. Standard costs can be used in both job order cost and process cost systems as shown in the Appendix to this chapter.

Nature of standard costs

A *standard cost* is a carefully predetermined measure of what a cost *should be* under stated conditions. A standard cost is not merely an estimate of what a cost will be; it is more in the nature of a goal to be sought. If a standard is properly set, achieving it represents a reasonable level of performance.

Standards are set in many ways, but to be of any real value they should be more than mere estimates found by extending historical trends into the future. Usually, engineering and time and motion studies are undertaken to determine the amounts of material, labor, and other services required to produce a unit of product. Then total unit cost can be found. General economic conditions should be considered because they affect the cost of materials and the other services that must be purchased for a manufacturing company.

A standard cost is found for each manufactured unit of product by determining the standard costs of direct materials, direct labor, and manufacturing overhead needed to produce that unit. Standard direct materials cost per unit is made up of the standard amount of material required to produce that unit multiplied by the standard price of the material. For example, if the standard price of cloth is $3 per yard and the standard quantity of material required to produce a dress is 3 yards, standard direct materials cost per dress is $9 (3 × $3). Similarly, standard direct labor cost per unit consists of the standard number of hours of direct labor needed to produce that unit multiplied by the standard labor or wage rate.

The standard overhead cost of a unit is usually based on a predetermined overhead rate. This rate may be computed by dividing budgeted overhead costs for the year by estimated units of production during the year, or the standard overhead cost may be expressed as a rate per unit of some other measure of activity, such as direct labor-hours. For example, standard overhead may be expressed as $5 per direct labor-hour. The standard overhead rate may include both fixed and variable overhead.

In both standard and actual cost systems, overhead is assigned to production through use of a predetermined rate. The two systems differ in that an actual cost system collects *actual* costs for materials and labor, while a standard cost system gathers *standard* costs for these elements of production. The standard costs flow through the accounting system to determine a standard or "normal" cost for finished goods inventory. Actual costs incurred during the period will then be compared with standard costs to assist management in decision making and to determine whether proper cost controls exist over production activities.

Advantages of using standard costs

A number of benefits result from the use of a standard cost system. These include (1) cost control, (2) provision of useful information for managerial planning and decision making, (3) more reasonable inventory measurements, (4) cost savings in record keeping, and (5) possible reductions in the costs incurred.

Cost control is gained mainly by setting standards for each type of cost incurred—materials, labor, and overhead. The amount by which an actual cost differs from a standard cost is called a *variance.* These variances provide a starting point for judging the effectiveness of managers in controlling the costs for which they are held responsible. For example, in a certain center, it may be far more useful to know that actual direct materials costs of $52,015 exceeded standard cost by $6,015, than merely to know that actual direct materials costs amounts to $52,015. It is important for the manager to know that the materials cost exceeded standard cost by $6,015 so that the cause of the excess of actual cost over standard can be investigated and action taken.

Thus, a standard cost system highlights *exceptions* or variances—instances where things are not going as planned. Further investigation will show whether the exception is caused by factors under management's control or not. For example, the exception (the variance) may be caused by inefficient use of materials, or it may be the result of higher prices because of inflation. In either case, the standard cost system has served as an early warning system by highlighting a potential problem for management.

If management develops appropriate standards and succeeds in controlling costs, future actual costs should be fairly close to standard. When this is true, standard costs can be used in preparing budgets and in estimating costs for bidding on jobs.

Unit costs for batches of identical products may differ widely under an actual cost system. This difference may be caused by a machine malfunction during production of a given batch that resulted in more labor and overhead being charged to that batch. Under a standard cost system such costs would not be included in inventory. Rather, they would be charged to variance accounts after comparing actual costs with standard costs such as the ones discussed in the following section. Thus, in a standard cost system, all units of a given product are carried in inventory at the same unit cost. It seems logical that physically identical units produced in a given time period should be recorded at the same cost.

Although a standard cost system may seem to require more detailed record keeping than an actual cost system, actually the reverse is true. For example, in a job order system, detailed records must be kept of the various types of materials used on each job as well as the various types and quantities of labor services received. In a standard cost system, standard cost sheets may be printed in advance showing quantities, unit costs, and total costs for the materials, labor, and overhead needed to produce a given amount of a certain product. Thus, when a job is started, the job order sheet shows all the various costs that apply to it.

The use of standard costs may cause employees to become quite cost conscious and thus to seek improved methods of completing their tasks. This may result in cost savings.

COMPUTING VARIANCES

As noted above, a variance exists when standard costs differ from actual costs. It is logical to look upon a variance as favorable when actual costs are less than standard costs, and as unfavorable when actual costs exceed standard. But it does not follow automatically that these terms should be equated with good and bad, as will be explained later. Such an appraisal should be made only after the causes of the variance are known.

Variances cannot serve as essential elements in cost control until they have been isolated. Thus, attention is directed first to the computation of the dollar amount of a variance.

The discussion and illustrations that follow are based upon the activities of the Beta Company. The company manufactures and sells a single product, each unit of which has the following standard costs:

Materials—5 sheets at $6	$30
Direct labor—2 hours at $10	20
Manufacturing overhead—2 direct labor-hours at $5	10
Total standard cost per unit	$60

Additional data regarding the production activities of the company will be presented as needed.

Materials variances

The standard materials cost of any product is simply the standard *quantity* of materials that should be used multiplied by the *standard price* that should be paid for those materials. Actual costs may differ from standard costs for materials because of the *quantity* of materials used or the *price* paid for the materials, or both. This suggests the need to isolate two variances for materials—a *price variance* and a *usage variance*. But there are other reasons for isolating the variances. First, different individuals may be responsible for each—a purchasing agent for the price variance and a production manager for the usage variance. Second, the materials might not be purchased and used in the same period. The variance associated with the purchase should be isolated in the period of purchase, and that associated with usage should be isolated in the period of use. As a general rule, the sooner a variance can be isolated, the greater its value in cost control. Finally, it is unlikely that a single materials variance—the difference between the standard cost and the actual cost of the materials used—would be of any real value to management for effective cost control.

Materials price variance. The standard price for materials meeting certain engineering specifications is usually set by the purchasing and accounting departments. Consideration will be given to factors such as market conditions, vendors' quoted prices, and the optimum size of a purchase order. The *materials price variance (MPV)* is caused by paying a higher or lower price than the standard price for materials. The materials price variance (MPV) is the difference between actual price (AP) and standard price (SP) multiplied by the actual quantity (AQ) of materials purchased. In equation form, the materials price variance is:

$$MPV = (AP - SP) \times AQ \text{ purchased}$$

To illustrate, assume that the Beta Company was able, because of the entry into the market of a new foreign supplier, to purchase 60,000 sheets of material at a price of $5.90 each, for a total cost of $354,000. Since the standard price is $6 per sheet, the materials price variance using the above formula is:

$$
\begin{aligned}
MPV &= (AP - SP) \times AQ \text{ purchased} \\
MPV &= (\$5.90 - \$6.00) \times 60{,}000 \\
MPV &= -\$0.10 \times 60{,}000 \\
MPV &= -\$6{,}000 \text{ (favorable)}
\end{aligned}
$$

The materials price variance of $6,000 is considered favorable since the materials were acquired for a price less than standard. (Why it is expressed as a negative amount will be explained later.) If the actual price had exceeded standard price, the variance would be unfavorable because more costs would have been incurred than allowed by the standard. In T-account form the entry to record the purchase of the materials is:

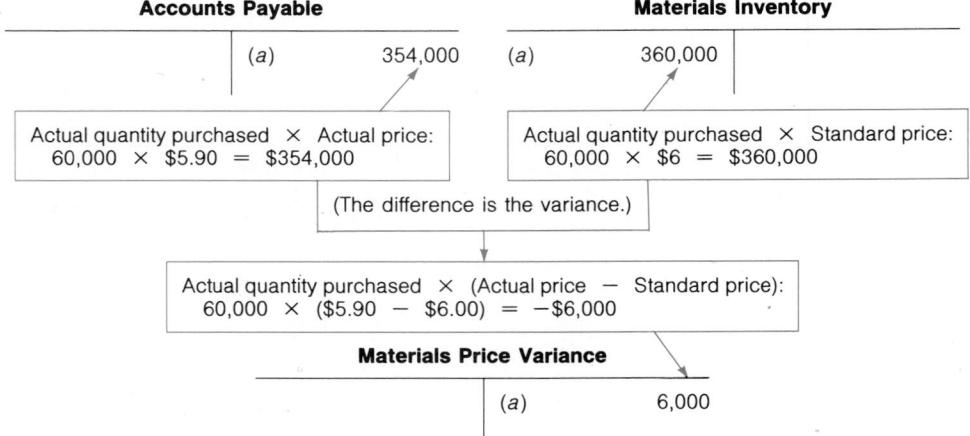

The general journal entry to record the purchase of materials is:

a. Materials Inventory 360,000
    Materials Price Variance.   6,000
    Accounts Payable   354,000
      To record the purchase of materials at less than standard cost.

Note that the Accounts Payable account shows the actual debt owed to suppliers, while the Materials Inventory account shows the *standard price* of the actual quantity of materials *purchased*. The Materials Price Variance account shows the difference between actual price and standard price multiplied by the actual quantity purchased.

Materials usage variance.   Since the standard quantity of materials to be used in making a product is largely a matter of physical requirements or product specifications, it is usually set by the engineering department. But if the quality of materials used varies with price, the accounting and purchasing departments may take part in special studies to find the "right" quality.

The *materials usage variance (MUV)* is caused by using more or less than the standard amount of materials to produce a product or complete a process. The variance shows only differences from standard caused by the quantity of materials used; it does not include price variances. Thus, the materials usage variance (MUV) is equal to actual quantity used (AQ) minus standard quantity allowed (SQ) multiplied by standard price (SP):

$$\text{MUV} = (\text{AQ used} - \text{SQ}) \times \text{SP}$$

To illustrate, assume that the Beta Company used 55,500 sheets of materials to produce 11,000 units of a product for which the standard quantity allowed is 55,000 sheets (5 × 11,000). Since the standard price of the material is $6 per sheet, the materials usage variance of $3,000 would be computed as follows:

$$\text{MUV} = (\text{AQ used} - \text{SQ}) \times \text{SP}$$
$$\text{MUV} = (55,500 - 55,000) \times \$6$$
$$\text{MUV} = 500 \times \$6$$
$$\text{MUV} = \$3,000 \text{ (unfavorable)}$$

The variance is unfavorable because more materials were used than the standard amount allowed to complete the job. If the standard quantity allowed had exceeded the quantity actually used, the materials usage variance would have been favorable. The recording in T-accounts of the use of materials is as follows:

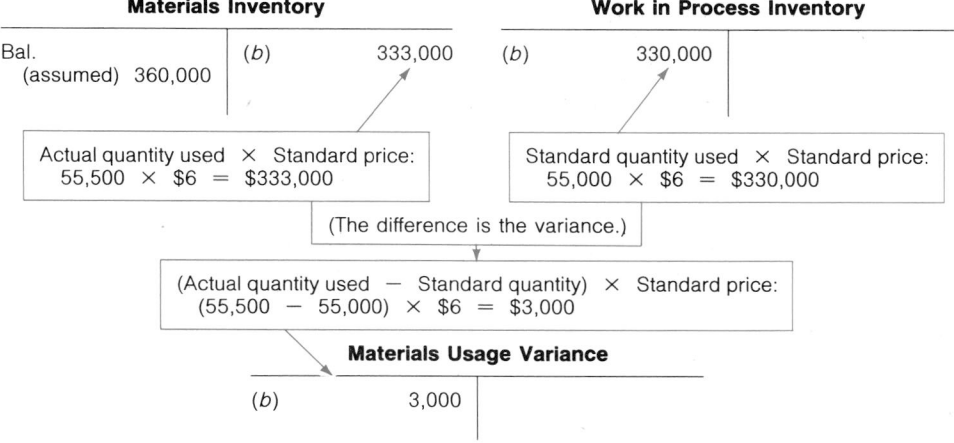

The general journal entry to record the use of materials is:

b. Work in Process Inventory   330,000
    Materials Usage Variance   3,000
        Materials Inventory   333,000
        To record the use of materials and to establish the materials usage
        variance.

The Materials Usage Variance shows the standard cost of the excess materials *used.* Note also that the Work in Process Inventory account contains standard quantities and standard prices.

The equations for both of the above materials variances were expressed so that positive amounts were unfavorable variances and negative amounts were favorable variances. Unfavorable variances are debits in variance accounts because they add to the costs incurred, which are recorded as debits. Similarly, favorable variances are shown as negative amounts because they are reductions in costs. Thus, favorable variances are recorded in variance accounts as credits. This format will be used in this text, but a word of caution is in order. Far greater understanding is achieved if a variance is determined to be favorable or unfavorable by reliance upon reason or logic. If more materials were used than standard, or if a price greater than standard was paid, the variance is unfavorable. If the reverse is true, the variance is favorable.

Labor variances

The standard labor cost of any product is equal to the standard quantity of labor time allowed multiplied by the wage rate that should be paid for this time. Here again it follows that the actual labor cost may differ from standard labor cost because of the *quantity* of labor used, the *wages* paid for labor, or both. Both of the labor variances relate to the same period because labor services cannot be purchased in one period, stored, and then used in the next period.

Labor rate variance. The *labor rate variance (LRV)* is caused by paying a higher or lower rate of pay than standard to produce a product or complete a process. The labor rate variance is similar to the materials price variance.

The labor rate variance (LRV) is computed by multiplying the difference between the actual rate (AR) paid and the standard rate (SR) allowed by the actual hours (AH) of labor services received:

$$LRV = (AR - SR) \times AH$$

To continue the Beta Company example, assume that the direct labor payroll of the company consisted of 22,200 hours at a total cost of $233,100 (an average actual hourly rate of $10.50). With a standard labor rate of $10 per hour, the labor rate variance is:

$$LRV = (AR - SR) \times AH$$
$$LRV = (\$10.50 - \$10.00) \times 22,200$$
$$LRV = \$0.50 \times 22,200$$
$$LRV = \$11,100 \text{ (unfavorable)}$$

The variance is positive and unfavorable because the actual rate paid exceeded the standard rate allowed. If the reverse were true, the variance would be favorable.

Labor efficiency variance. The *labor efficiency variance (LEV)* is caused by using more or less than the standard amount of labor-hours to produce a product or complete a process. The labor efficiency rate is quite similar to the materials usage variance. The standard amount of labor time (hours or minutes) needed to complete a product is usually set by the firm's engineering department. It may be based on time and motion studies and may be the subject of bargaining with the employees' union.

The labor efficiency variance (LEV) is computed by multiplying the difference between the actual hours (AH) required and the standard hours (SH) allowed by the standard rate (SR) per hour, or

$$LEV = (AH - SH) \times SR$$

To illustrate, assume that the 22,200 hours of direct labor time worked by Beta Company employees resulted in 11,000 units of production. These 11,000 units have a standard labor time of 22,000 hours (11,000 units at 2 hours per unit). Since the standard labor rate is $10 per hour, the labor efficiency variance is $2,000 (unfavorable), computed as follows:

$$
\begin{aligned}
LEV &= (AH - SH) \times SR \\
LEV &= (22,200 - 22,000) \times \$10 \\
LEV &= 200 \times \$10 \\
LEV &= \$2,000 \text{ (unfavorable)}
\end{aligned}
$$

The variance is unfavorable since more hours than standard were required to complete the period's production. If the reverse were true, the variance would be favorable.

A graphic illustration may aid in understanding the relationship between standard and actual labor cost and the computation of the labor variances. Illustration 23.1, which is deliberately not drawn to scale, is based on the following data relating to the Beta Company:

Standard labor time per unit	2 hours
Equivalent units produced in period	11,000 units
Standard labor rate per direct labor-hour	$10
Total direct labor wages paid (at average rate of $10.50 per hour) . .	$233,100
Actual direct labor hours received	22,200 hours

The standard labor time allowed for the period's output is 22,000 hours (11,000 units at 2 hours per unit). The standard labor cost is $10 per hour. The standard labor cost for the output achieved is therefore $220,000. The $220,000 is the amount of labor costs that will be assigned to inventory, regardless of the actual labor cost.

The unfavorable labor rate variance is the above-standard wages paid ($10.50 − $10.00 = $0.50 per hour) times the actual hours worked (22,200), or $11,100. Note that the labor rate variance includes the above-standard wages paid on the 200 extra (above-standard) hours used to secure the produc-

Illustration 23:1:   Computation of labor variance

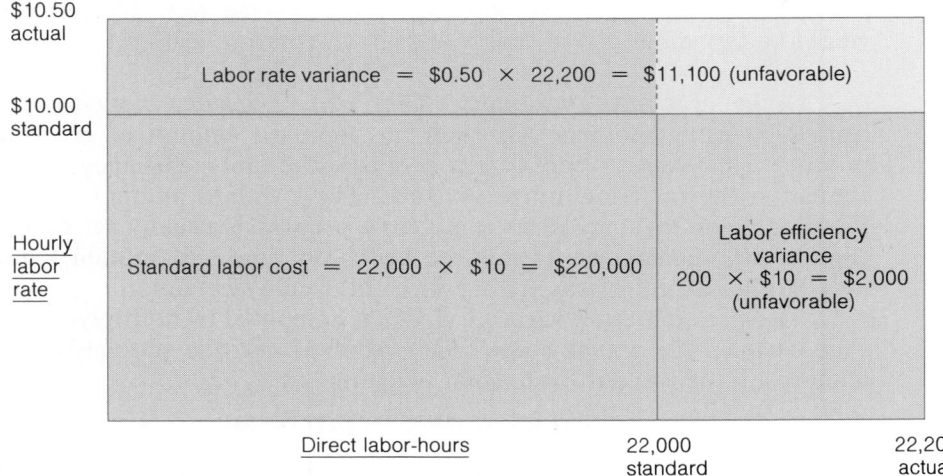

tion—the lightly-shaded area in the upper right-hand corner of Illustration
23.1. This variation from standard is actually caused by both extra hours
and above-standard wages. But, as shown, it is included in the labor rate
variance. The labor efficiency variance is the standard cost of the extra hours
of labor required [(22,200 − 22,000) × $10 = $2,000]. This variance is unfavorable because more hours of labor were used than are allowed by the standard.

The charging of Work in Process Inventory with direct labor cost and
recording of the two labor variances for the Beta Company would be as
shown in the T-accounts below.

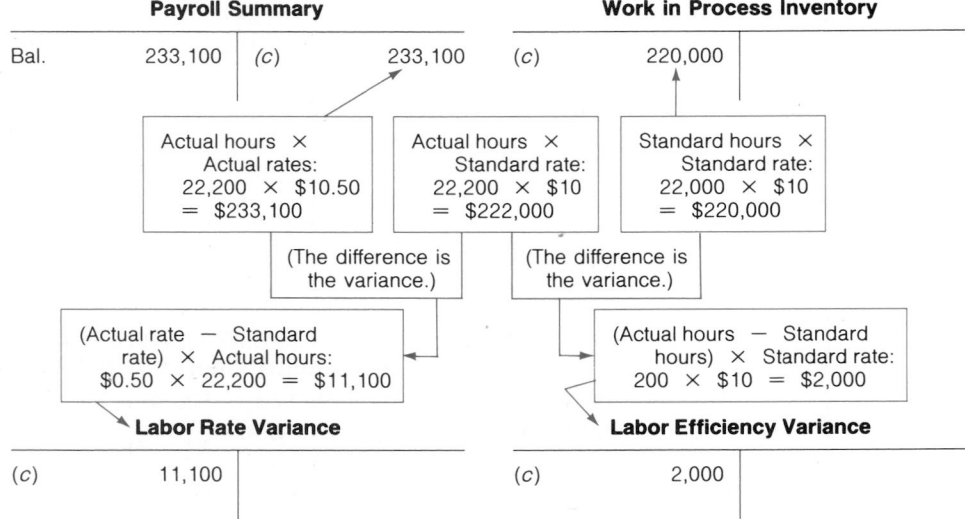

The general journal entry to charge the direct labor cost to work in process
is:

c.	Work in Process Inventory	220,000	
	Labor Rate Variance	11,100	
	Labor Efficiency Variance	2,000	
	Payroll Summary		233,100

To charge work in process with direct labor and to establish the two labor variances.

With the above entry, gross wages earned by direct-production employees ($233,100) are distributed as follows: $220,000 (the standard labor cost of production) to Work in Process Inventory and the balance to the two labor variance accounts. The unfavorable labor rate variance is not necessarily caused by paying employees more wages than they are entitled to receive; a more probable reason is that employees who worked on production had different pay rates than those used to compute the standard or that wage rates were increased since the standard was developed. Favorable rate variances, on the other hand, could be caused by using less skilled, and thereby, cheaper labor in the production process. Typically, the hours of labor employed are more likely to be under management's control than the rates that are paid. For this reason, labor efficiency variances are generally watched more closely than labor rate variances.

Summary of labor variances. The accuracy of the two labor variances can be checked readily by comparing their sum with the difference between actual and standard labor cost for a period. In the Beta Company illustration, this difference was:

Actual labor cost incurred (22,200 hours × $10.50)	$233,100	
Standard labor cost allowed (22,000 hours × $10)	220,000	
Total labor variance (unfavorable)	$ 13,100	

This $13,100 is made up of two labor variances, both unfavorable:

Labor efficiency variance (200 × $10)	$ 2,000	
Labor rate variance (22,200 × $0.50)	11,100	
Total labor variance (unfavorable) . . .	$13,100	

Overhead variances

In a cost system using standard costs, overhead is applied to the goods produced by means of a standard overhead rate. The rate is set prior to the start of the period through use of a flexible overhead budget. This budget is called a flexible (or variable) budget because it shows the budgeted amount of overhead for various levels of output or volume. Total budgeted overhead will vary as output varies because some overhead costs are variable. But since some overhead costs are fixed, total overhead will not vary in direct proportion with output.

The flexible budget for the Beta Company for the period is shown in Illustration 23.2. Note that it shows the overhead costs expected to be incurred at three levels of activity: 90 percent, 100 percent, and 110 percent of capacity. For product costing purposes, the expected level of activity must be estimated

Illustration 23.2: Flexible overhead budget

BETA COMPANY
Flexible Manufacturing Overhead Budget

	90%	100%	110%
Percent of capacity	90%	100%	110%
Direct labor-hours	18,000	20,000	22,000
Units of output	9,000	10,000	11,000
Variable overhead:			
Indirect materials	$ 7,200	$ 8,000	$ 8,800
Power	9,000	10,000	11,000
Royalties	1,800	2,000	2,200
Other	18,000	20,000	22,000
Total variable overhead	$36,000	$ 40,000	$ 44,000
Fixed overhead:			
Insurance	$ 4,000	$ 4,000	$ 4,000
Property taxes	6,000	6,000	6,000
Depreciation	20,000	20,000	20,000
Other	30,000	30,000	30,000
Total fixed overhead	$60,000	$ 60,000	$ 60,000
Total manufacturing overhead	$96,000	$100,000	$104,000
Standard overhead rate ($100,000 ÷ 20,000 hours)		$5	

and a rate set based on that level. *The level chosen is called the standard volume of output.* This standard volume of output may be expressed in terms of percent of capacity, units of output, and/or direct labor-hours. In our example it is assumed to be at 100 percent of capacity, at which level 10,000 units are expected to be produced and 20,000 direct labor-hours of services are expected to be used. The standard total overhead rate then is $5 ($100,000 ÷ 20,000 hours) per direct labor-hour. The $5 per hour overhead rate is used in applying overhead to production. Knowing the separate rates for variable and fixed overhead is sometimes useful for analysis purposes. The variable overhead rate is $2 ($40,000 ÷ 20,000 hours) per hour, and the fixed overhead rate is $3 ($60,000 ÷ 20,000 hours) per hour. If the expected volume had been 18,000 direct labor-hours (90 percent of capacity), the standard overhead rate would have been $5.33 ($96,000 ÷ 18,000 hours). If the standard volume had been 22,000 direct labor-hours (110 percent of capacity), the standard overhead would have been $4.73 ($104,000 ÷ 22,000 hours).

To continue the illustration, assume that Beta Company incurred $108,000 of actual manufacturing overhead costs in the period in which 11,000 units of product were produced. The standard number of direct labor-hours allowed for this production is 22,000 hours. The company had only expected to produce 10,000 units (standard production) and had used that level to determine the total overhead rate of $5 per direct labor-hour. The actual costs would be debited to Manufacturing Overhead and credited to a variety of accounts such as Accounts Payable, Accumulated Depreciation, Unexpired Insurance, Accrued Property Taxes Payable, and so on. The entry, in T-account form, to record the application of $110,000 of overhead to production (22,000 hours at $5 per hour) would be:

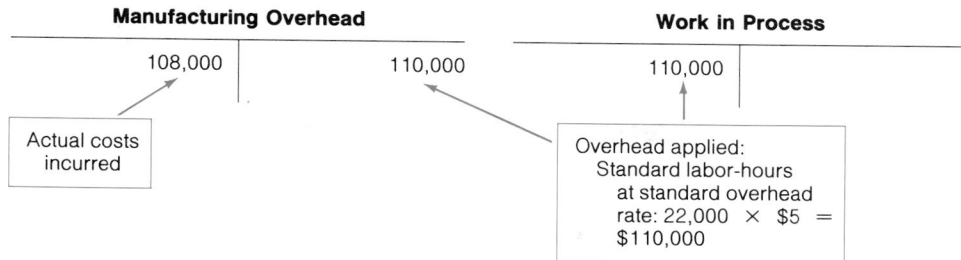

Manufacturing Overhead		Work in Process	
108,000	110,000	110,000	

Actual costs incurred

Overhead applied:
Standard labor-hours
at standard overhead
rate: 22,000 × $5 =
$110,000

The general journal entry to apply manufacturing overhead to production would be:

Work in Process 110,000
    Manufacturing Overhead 110,000
To apply manufacturing overhead to production (22,000 hours at $5 per hour).

    The above accounts show that manufacturing overhead has been overapplied to production by the $2,000 credit balance in the Manufacturing Overhead account. Such overapplication of overhead will occur whenever actual production is greater than standard production. Although various complex computations can be made for overhead variances, a simple approach will be used. This approach consists of the calculation of an overhead volume variance and an overhead budget variance. This is known as the two-variance approach to overhead variances.

    Overhead volume variance. The *overhead volume variance (OVV)* is caused by producing at a level other than that used in setting the standard overhead application rate. Because fixed overhead does not change over a wide range of activity, any deviation from planned production will cause the application rate to be incorrect. The overhead volume variance shows whether plant assets produced more or fewer goods than expected. The overhead volume variance is the difference between the budgeted amount of overhead (BOH) for the *actual volume achieved* and the applied overhead (applied OH) or

$$OVV = BOH - \text{Applied OH}$$

    In the Beta Company illustration, the 11,000 units produced in the period have a standard labor allowance of 22,000 hours. The flexible budget in Illustration 23.2 shows that the budgeted overhead for 22,000 direct labor-hours is $104,000. Overhead is applied to work in process on the basis of standard hours allowed for a particular amount of production, in this case 11,000 units or 22,000 hours at $5 per hour. The overhead volume variance then is:

$$OVV = BOH - \text{Applied OH}$$
$$OVV = \$104,000 - \$110,000$$
$$OVV = \$-6,000 \text{ (favorable)}$$

Notice that the amount of the overhead volume variance is related solely to fixed overhead. In Illustration 23.2, fixed overhead at all levels of activity is $60,000. Since Beta Company computed its overhead application rate on the basis of 20,000 direct labor-hours, the fixed overhead rate was $3 per direct labor-hour. Beta worked 2,000 (22,000 − 20,000) more standard hours than was expected. The overhead volume variance can also be calculated as follows:

$$\left(\begin{array}{c} \text{Number of hours} \\ \text{used in setting} \\ \text{predetermined} \\ \text{overhead rates} \end{array} - \begin{array}{c} \text{Number of standard} \\ \text{hours allowed} \\ \text{for production} \\ \text{level achieved} \end{array}\right) \times \begin{array}{c} \text{Fixed overhead} \\ \text{rate per hour} \end{array}$$

$$(20,000 \quad - \quad 22,000) \quad \times \quad \$3 \quad = \quad \$-6,000$$
$$\text{(favorable)}$$

The variance is favorable since the company achieved a higher level of production than was expected.

The overhead budget variance.   The *overhead budget variance (OBV)* (also called the spending or controllable variance) shows in one amount how efficiently operations were conducted in the sense of the prices paid for and the amounts of the overhead services used. This overhead variance is similar to a combined price and usage variance for materials or labor. The overhead budget variance (OBV) is equal to the difference between total actual overhead costs (Actual OH) and total budgeted overhead costs (BOH) for the *actual* output attained. Since the total actual overhead was $108,000 and the total budgeted overhead was $104,000 (from Illustration 23.2) for 11,000 units (22,000 standard direct labor-hours), the overhead budget variance is computed as follows:

$$\text{OBV} = \text{Actual OH} - \text{BOH}$$
$$\text{OBV} = \$108,000 - \$104,000$$
$$\text{OBV} = \$4,000 \text{ (unfavorable)}$$

The variance is unfavorable because actual overhead costs were $108,000 while, according to the flexible budget, they should have been $104,000.

Recording overhead variances.   If desired, a formal entry can be made in the accounts showing the two parts of the $2,000 net overhead variance. The T-account entry for the Beta Company would be as follows (the debits and credits are keyed with the letter [*f*]):

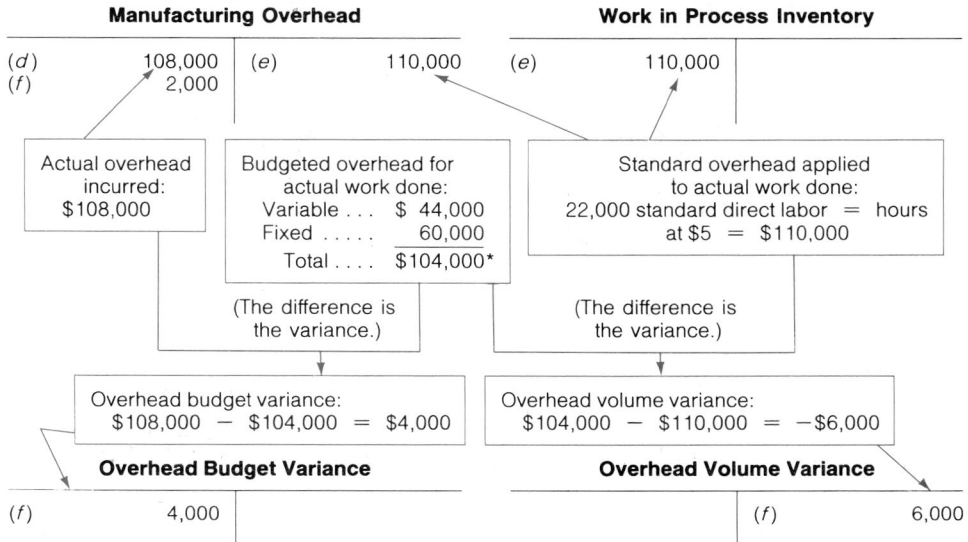

* From flexible budget. See Illustration 23.2.

The general journal entries related to overhead are as follows:

    d. Manufacturing Overhead 108,000
           Various Accounts   108,000
        To record actual overhead.

    e. Work in Process 110,000
           Manufacturing Overhead   110,000
        To record the application of overhead to work in process.

    f. Manufacturing Overhead 2,000
       Overhead Budget Variance 4,000
           Overhead Volume Variance   6,000
        To record the variances related to overhead and close the manufac-
        turing overhead account.

The first entry records the actual overhead costs incurred during the period by Beta Company. The second entry applies overhead to Work in Process at the rate of $5 per standard direct labor-hour (22,000). The final entry reduces the Manufacturing Overhead account balance to zero and recognizes the two variances calculated for overhead; these two variance accounts analyze the causes of the overapplied overhead for the period.

    Summary of overhead variances. The accuracy of the two overhead variances can be easily determined by comparing the sum of the volume and budget variances with the difference between the costs of actual and standard overhead. For the Beta Company example, the difference between actual and standard overhead was:

Actual overhead incurred $108,000
Standard overhead allowed (22,000 direct labor-hours × $5 per hour) .. 110,000
      Total overhead variance (favorable) .... −$ 2,000

This difference is made up of the two overhead variances:

Overhead budget variance—Unfavorable ($108,000 − $104,000)		$ 4,000
Overhead volume variance—Favorable [$104,000 − (22,000 × $5)] ...		−6,000
Total overhead variance		−$ 2,000

GOODS COMPLETED AND SOLD

To complete our Beta Company example, assume that 11,000 units were completed and transferred to finished goods, 10,000 units were sold on account at a price equal to 160 percent of standard cost, there was no beginning or ending work in process inventory, and there was no finished goods beginning inventory. In the T-accounts below, entry (g) shows the transfer of the standard cost of the units completed, $660,000 (11,000 × $60), from Work in Process Inventory to Finished Goods Inventory. Entry (h) records the sales for the period, $960,000, while entry (i) records the cost of goods sold, $600,000 (10,000 × $60).

Work in Process Inventory

(b) Materials	330,000	(g) Completed 660,000
(c) Labor	220,000	
(e) Overhead	110,000	

Finished Goods Inventory

(g) Completed	660,000	(i) Sold 600,000

Accounts Receivable

(h) 960,000	

Cost of Goods Sold

(i) Sold 600,000	

Sales

	(h) 960,000

In journal entry form, entries (g), (h), and (i) are:

g.	Finished Goods Inventory	660,000	
	Work in Process Inventory.............................		660,000
	To transfer the standard cost of units completed (11,000 × $60).		
h.	Accounts Receivable	960,000	
	Sales		960,000
	To record sales for the period.		
i.	Cost of Goods Sold	600,000	
	Merchandise Inventory		600,000
	To record cost of goods sold for the period.		

Work in Process Inventory has been debited with the standard cost of materials, labor, and overhead put into production. Therefore, the entry recording the transfer of the standard cost of the completed units, $660,000 (11,000 × $60), reduces Work in Process Inventory to a zero balance. Note that Finished Goods Inventory is debited with the standard cost of goods completed and credited with the standard cost of goods sold. Thus, ending inventory consists of the units actually on hand (1,000) at their standard cost of $60 each, or $60,000. Sales for the period amount to 10,000 units at $96 each (160 percent of $60). It is fairly common practice to at least partially base selling prices on standard costs.

INVESTIGATING VARIANCES FROM STANDARD

Once all variances have been computed, management must decide which ones should be investigated further. Since so many variances occur, they all cannot be investigated. Management needs some selection guides. Possible guides include (1) absolute size of the variance, (2) size of the variance relative to cost incurred, and (3) type of cost incurred, that is, whether it is considered controllable or noncontrollable. Statistical analysis may also be used in deciding which variances to investigate. For instance, the mean (average) value of actual costs could be determined for a period of time. It could be agreed that only future variances which deviate from the mean by more than a certain amount or percentage would be investigated. Management should seek the opinions of knowledgeable operating personnel in determining which selection guides to use.

Any analysis of variances is likely to disclose some variances that are controllable within the company and others that are not. Prices paid for materials purchased may be largely beyond the buyer's control or, on the other hand, the purchasing agent may be at fault for not getting competitive bids. Quantities used are generally controllable internally. Also, although separate variances are isolated, they are not always as independent as they may appear. An unfavorable labor rate variance may result from using higher paid employees in a certain task; but this may result in a favorable labor efficiency variance from greater productivity and possibly a favorable materials usage variance if the more highly skilled employees wasted less material. It follows that significant variances, both favorable and unfavorable, should be investigated.

DISPOSING OF VARIANCES FROM STANDARD

At the end of the year, variances from standard must be disposed of in the accounting records. The variances may be (1) viewed as losses due to inefficiency and closed to Income Summary; (2) allocated as adjustments to the recorded cost of Work in Process Inventory, Finished Goods Inventory, and Cost of Goods Sold; or (3) closed to Cost of Goods Sold. Theoretically, the alternative chosen should depend upon whether the standards set were reasonably attainable and whether the variances were controllable by company employees. For instance, an unfavorable materials usage or labor efficiency variance caused by carelessness or inefficiency may be considered a loss and closed to Income Summary because the standard was attainable and the variance was controllable. An unfavorable materials price variance caused by an unexpected price change may be considered an added cost and allocated to the inventory accounts and cost of goods sold because the standard was unattainable and the variance was uncontrollable. As a practical matter, and especially if they are small, the variances are usually closed to the Cost of Goods Sold account rather than allocated. This practice tends to reduce net income below the amount that would be reported if the variances were treated as cost elements and allocated to the inventory accounts and Cost of Goods Sold.

Entry (j) in the T-accounts below reflects this practical disposition of the variances in the continuing example of the Beta Company:

Materials Price Variance				Materials Usage Variance				Labor Rate Variance			
(j)	6,000	(a)	6,000	(b)	3,000	(j)	3,000	(c)	11,100	(j)	11,100

Labor Efficiency Variance				Overhead Budget Variance				Overhead Volume Variance			
(c)	2,000	(j)	2,000	(f)	4,000	(j)	4,000	(j)	6,000	(f)	6,000

Cost of Goods Sold		
(i)	600,000	
(j)	8,100	

In general journal entry form, entry (j) is

$j.$	Materials Price Variance	6,000	
	Overhead Volume Variance	6,000	
	Cost of Goods Sold	8,100	
	Materials Usage Variance		3,000
	Labor Efficiency Variance		2,000
	Overhead Budget Variance		4,000
	Labor Rate Variance		11,100
	To close variance accounts.		

Variances are not reported separately in statements released to the public, but simply included in the reported cost of goods sold amount. In statements prepared for internal use, the variances may be listed separately after cost of goods sold at standard cost.

APPENDIX: APPLYING STANDARD COSTS IN JOB ORDER AND PROCESS COST SYSTEMS

STANDARD COSTS IN A JOB COST SYSTEM

In a job order cost system, production quantities are known in advance; thus, some variances can be isolated much earlier than in a process cost system in which equivalent production is known only at the end of a period. This early isolation of variances is illustrated in the following example.

Assume that A Company accounts for the manufacture of its products in a job order cost system using standard costs. Its flexible budget monthly amounts (at a standard activity of 8,000 direct labor-hours) are variable overhead, $24,000, and fixed overhead, $16,000. These figures yield a standard overhead rate of $5 per direct labor-hour. The variable portion of this rate is $3 ($24,000 ÷ 8,000 hours), and the fixed portion is $2 ($16,000 ÷ 8,000 hours).

A Company had no work in process inventory as of June 1. During June, two jobs were started for which standard specifications were:

	Job 101	Job 102
Direct materials	$20,000	$50,000
Direct labor:		
2,000 hours at $4	8,000	
5,000 hours at $4		20,000
Overhead:		
2,000 hours at $5	10,000	
5,000 hours at $5		25,000
Total standard cost......	$38,000	$95,000

The A Company's activities for June 1984 are summarized as follows:

a. Materials with a standard cost of $79,500 were purchased on account at an actual price of $80,150.
b. Standard direct materials were issued for both jobs. In addition, excess materials were requisitioned: Job No. 101, $400; and Job No. 102, $700.
c. Analysis of the factory payrolls debited to Payroll Summary shows they consisted of $10,000 of indirect labor ($4,000 variable and $6,000 fixed), and 6,000 hours of direct labor (Job No. 101, 1,980 hours, and Job No. 102, 4,020 hours) at a cost of $24,600. Job No. 101 was completed.
d. Various overhead costs were incurred: variable, $14,500; and fixed, $10,200.
e. Standard overhead was assigned to production: Job No. 101, $10,000 (2,000 hours at $5 per hour), and Job No. 102, $20,100 (4,020 hours at $5 per hour). Even though Job 102 was incomplete at the end of the month, overhead needs to be assigned to it for valuation of Work in Process Inventory on the balance sheet.
f. Job No. 101 was completed and transferred to the finished goods storeroom.
g. Sales for the month—all units in Job No. 101 at a total price of $60,000.

The entries to record the above information and isolate the variances are as follows:

a. Materials Inventory 79,500
    Materials Price Variance 650
        Accounts Payable   80,150
    To record purchase of materials and to isolate materials price
    variance.

b. Work in Process Inventory 70,000
    Materials Usage Variance 1,100
        Materials Inventory   71,100
    To charge standard materials to production and to charge excess
    materials requisitioned to a variance account.

c. Work in Process Inventory 24,080
    Manufacturing Overhead 10,000
    Labor Rate Variance 600
        Labor Efficiency Variance   80
        Payroll Summary   34,600
    To distribute labor costs and to isolate labor
    variances:

    Job No. 101 (2,000 hours at $4) .... $ 8,000
    Job No. 102 (4,020 hours at $4)   16,080
        Total labor to Work in Process Inventory $24,080

    Labor efficiency variance on Job No. 101: (1,980 actual
    hours — 2,000 standard hours) × $4 = $—80
    (favorable). Labor rate variance: ($4.10 actual wage
    rate — $4.00 standard rate) × 6,000 hours = $600
    (unfavorable).

d. Manufacturing Overhead 24,700
        Accounts Payable (and various other accounts)   24,700
    To record incurrence of overhead costs.

e. Work in Process Inventory 30,100
        Manufacturing Overhead   30,100
    To apply standard overhead to production: Job No. 101—
    $10,000 (standard amount, job completed); Job No. 102—
    4,020 hours at $5 = $20,100 (based on standard labor,
    job incomplete).

f. Finished Goods Inventory 38,000
        Work in Process Inventory   38,000
    To record transfer of completed Job No. 101 at standard.

g. Accounts Receivable 60,000
        Sales   60,000
    To record sales for the month.

    Cost of Goods Sold 38,000
        Finished Goods Inventory   38,000
    To record cost of goods sold (Job No. 101, $38,000).

Note that in the above entries the materials and labor variances are isolated rather routinely in the recording process. But the overhead variances must be computed separately at the end of the period, unless standard production for the period is known earlier. For the A Company, the overhead variances are computed as follows:

Overhead budget variance:
Actual overhead (entries [c] and [d] above) $34,700
Budgeted overhead (from flexible budget)
  (6,020* standard hours at $3 variable
  overhead + $16,000 fixed overhead) 34,060
      Unfavorable overhead budget variance . . . . $ 640

Overhead volume variance:
Budgeted overhead [(6,020* hours × $3) + $16,000] $34,060
Standard overhead applied to production
  (6,020* hours at $5) 30,100
Unfavorable overhead volume variance 3,960
      Total unfavorable overhead variance $4,600

* 6,020 hours are used in the calculations because standard hours allowed for Job No. 101 are 2,000 and standard hours allowed this far on Job No. 202 are 4,020 for a total of 6,020 hours.

The following entry isolates the two overhead variances in the accounts:

Overhead Budget Variance 640
Overhead Volume Variance 3,960
    Manufacturing Overhead 4,600
To set up separate overhead variance accounts.

Note that the credit to Manufacturing Overhead of $4,600 reduces that account to a zero balance (for previous entries to the account, see entries [c], [d], and [e] above), thus proving the accuracy of the computations.

Typically, the overhead variances and the materials and labor variances will be summarized in a report prepared periodically for internal management. Such a report could be called a "Summary of Variances from Standard."

STANDARD COSTS IN A PROCESS COST SYSTEM

To provide a brief illustration of how standard costs might be incorporated into a process cost system, the following example is presented. Assume that P Company manufactures a product for which the standard specifications are:

Materials—2 pounds at $2 per pound $4.00
Direct labor—0.5 hours at $4 per hour 2.00
Overhead—0.5 hours at $3 per hour 1.50
    Total standard cost $7.50

The fixed overhead included in the standard cost is based upon a monthly flexible budget which shows budgeted variable overhead of $120,000 and budgeted fixed overhead of $60,000 at a standard activity level of 60,000 standard labor-hours. Thus the variable overhead rate is $2 per hour ($120,000 ÷ 60,000 hours), and the fixed overhead rate is $1 per hour ($60,000 ÷ 60,000 hours). Since each unit only requires one-half hour to produce, total overhead assignable per unit is $1.50 ($3 per hour × ½ hour).

One change in a standard cost system will be shown in this example. Work in Process will be charged with actual quantities and actual costs rather than the standard quantities and standard costs illustrated in the chapter. The variances will be calculated and placed in variance accounts at the end of the month. Alternatively, the materials price variance could be recorded when materials are purchased, and the labor rate variance could be recorded when direct labor is charged to Work in Process.

The entries to the Work in Process account for the month of May are summarized below.

Direct materials (180,500 pounds at $2.02)	$364,610
Direct labor (40,100 hours at $3.95)	158,395
Actual fixed overhead	58,700
Actual variable overhead	80,500
Total cost put into production	$662,205
Standard cost of units completed and transferred	
(70,000 at $7.50)	525,000
Balance, May 31, 1984	$137,205

Production records show that 70,000 units were completed and transferred and that 20,000 units of product remain in process at the end of the month. These units are complete as to materials and 50 percent complete as to conversion.

From the above information, the equivalent production for the period in terms of standard units of product can be computed as follows:

	Materials	Labor and overhead
Units started and finished	70,000	70,000
Equivalent units in ending inventory	20,000	10,000
Equivalent production	90,000	80,000

Now enough information is available to calculate all of the variances presented in the "Summary of Variances from Standard" shown in Illustration 23.3.

Since the actual price paid for materials was $0.02 per pound above standard, the materials price variance is the actual usage of 180,500 pounds multiplied by $0.02. Since the standard materials allowed for 90,000 equivalent units is 180,000 pounds (90,000 × 2), there is a materials usage variance of 500 pounds times $2. Both variances are unfavorable.

The average wage rate paid employees was $0.05 less than standard; thus a favorable rate variance of this amount multiplied by actual hours of 40,100 emerges. The standard labor allowed for the production of the period (80,000 × 0.5 hours) is 100 hours less than actual. Hence, an unfavorable labor efficiency variance was experienced.

Fixed overhead costs were $1,300 less than budget, while variable overhead costs exceeded their budgeted amount for the actual production in May by $500. Together they yield a net favorable variance of $800. Because the standard overhead applied to production of $120,000 is less than the budgeted overhead for the month of $140,000, there is an unfavorable volume variance of $20,000. These variances amount to $19,200 for overhead and $22,205 as the total variance (unfavorable) from standard for the month.

The variances shown in Illustration 23.3 can be formally recorded in

Illustration 23.3: Summary of variances from standard

```
                          P COMPANY
                 Summary of Variances from Standard
                     Month Ended May 31, 1984
Materials:
  Price variance (180,500 pounds × $0.02) .................  $  3,610
  Usage variance (500 pounds × $2) ......................     1,000
    Total unfavorable materials variance ...................            $  4,610
Labor:
  Rate variance (40,100 hours × $0.05) ...................  $ -2,005
  Efficiency variance (100 hours × $4) ....................       400
    Net favorable labor variance ..........................              -1,605
Overhead:
  Budget variance—fixed ($58,700 − $60,000) + variable
    ($80,500 − $80,000*) ...................................  $  -800
  Volume variance ($140,000 − $120,000) ..................    20,000
    Net unfavorable overhead variance ....................              19,200
        Total variance from standard for the month ...........          $22,205

* (40,000 hours × $2).
```

the accounts by the following entry, thus removing the month's variances from Work in Process Inventory:

```
Materials Price Variance .........................................  3,610
Materials Usage Variance .........................................  1,000
Labor Efficiency Variance ........................................    400
Overhead Volume Variance .........................................  20,000
    Labor Rate Variance ..........................................           2,005
    Overhead Budget Variance .....................................             800
    Work in Process Inventory.....................................          22,205
    To set up variances from standard for the month.
```

Subtracting the $22,205 from the previously given balance of $137,205 in the Work in Process Inventory account leaves a balance of $115,000, which is equal to the standard cost of the ending inventory. The standard cost of the ending inventory can be separately computed as follows:

```
Direct materials (20,000 units, 100%
  complete, unit cost $4) ...............................  $ 80,000
Direct labor (20,000 units, 50% complete, unit cost $2) ......    20,000
Overhead (20,000 units, 50% complete, unit cost $1.50) ......    15,000
    Total standard cost of ending inventory ..............   $115,000
```

NEW TERMS INTRODUCED IN CHAPTER 23[1]

Labor efficiency variance (LEV)
A variance from standard caused by using more or less than the standard amount of labor-hours to produce a product or complete a process; computed as (Actual labor-hours − Standard labor-hours) × Standard rate per hour.

Labor rate variance (LRV)
A variance from standard caused by paying a higher or lower average rate of pay than standard to produce a product or complete a process; computed as (Actual rate per hour − Standard rate per hour) × Actual hours worked.

Materials price variance (MPV)
A variance from standard caused by paying a higher or lower price than standard for materials purchased; computed as (Actual price − Standard price) × Actual quantity purchased.

Materials usage variance (MUV)
A variance from standard caused by using more or less than the standard amount of materials to produce a product or complete a process; computed as (Actual quantity used − Standard quantity allowed) × Standard price.

Overhead budget variance (OBV)
A variance from standard caused by incurring more or less than the standard overhead for the actual production volume achieved, as shown by a flexible budget; computed as Actual overhead − Budgeted overhead at actual production volume level.

Overhead volume variance (OVV)
A variance from standard caused by producing at a level other than that used in setting the standard overhead rates; computed as Budgeted overhead − Applied overhead.

Standard cost
A carefully predetermined measure of what a cost should be under stated conditions.

Variance
A deviation from standard; may be favorable or unfavorable. That is, actual costs may be less than or more than standard, and may relate to materials, labor, or manufacturing overhead.

DEMONSTRATION PROBLEM

The Baxter Company manufactures children's toys that are all identical. The standard cost of each toy is:

```
Direct materials:
    Three blocks of wood at $0.20 . . . . . .   $0.60
Direct labor (1 hour at $5) . . . . . . . . . .    5.00
Overhead:
    Fixed ($18,000 ÷ 60,000 units) . . . . .     0.30
    Variable . . . . . . . . . . . . . . . . . . . . . . . .    0.40
                                                            $6.30
```

The standard overhead rate is based on a volume of 60,000 units per month. In May, 50,000 units were manufactured. Detailed data relative to production are summarized as follows:

```
Materials purchased:
    160,000 blocks of wood at $0.22
Materials used:
    152,000 blocks of wood
Direct labor: 49,000 hours at $5.10
Fixed overhead: $18,200
Variable overhead: $20,350
```

From the above data, compute the six variances from standard for the month.

Solution to demonstration problem

Materials price variance:
   ($0.22 − $0.20) × 160,000 (unfavorable) $3,200
Materials usage variance:
   (152,000 − 150,000*) × $0.20 (unfavorable)   400
     Net materials variance (unfavorable) $3,600
Labor rate variance:
   ($5.10 − $5.00) × 49,000 (unfavorable) $4,900
Labor efficiency variance:
   (49,000 − 50,000) × $5.00 (favorable) ....   −5,000
     Total labor variance (favorable) ....   −100
Overhead budget variance:
   Actual ($18,200 + $20,350) $38,550
   Budgeted [$18,000 + (50,000 × $0.40)] 38,000
     Overhead budget variance (unfavorable) .... $ 550
Overhead volume variance:
   Budgeted − Applied [$38,000 − (50,000 × $0.70)]   3,000
     Total overhead variance (unfavorable)   3,550
       Total variance for month (unfavorable) $7,050

* 50,000 units × 3 blocks per unit.

QUESTIONS

1. Is a standard cost an estimated cost? What is the primary objective of employing standard costs in a cost system? What are some of the other advantages of using standard costs?

2. How can it be maintained that the use of standard costs permits the application of the principle of management by exception?

3. How do standards help in controlling production costs?

4. Compute the materials price and usage variances from the following data:

Standard—1,000 units at $20 per unit.
Purchased—1,200 units at $20.25; used—995 units.

5. What might be a plausible explanation for a given company having a substantial favorable materials price variance and a substantial unfavorable materials usage variance?

6. What is the usual cause of a favorable or unfavorable labor rate variance? What other labor variance is isolated in a standard cost system? Of the two variances, which is more likely to be under the control of management? Explain.

7. Identify the type of variance indicated by each situation below and whether it is favorable or unfavorable.

a. The cutting department of a company during the week ending July 15 cut 12 size S cogged wheels out of three sheets of 12-inch high-tempered steel. Usually three wheels of such size are cut out of each sheet.

b. A company purchased and installed a new expensive cutting machine to handle expanding orders. This purchase and the related depreciation had not been anticipated when the overhead rate was set.

c. Edwards, the band saw operator, was on vacation last week. Lands took his place for the normal 40-hour week. Edwards' wage rate is $5.40 per hour, while Lands's is $5.20 per hour. Production was at capacity last week and the week before.

8. Theoretically, how should variances from standard be disposed of? What is typically their practical disposition?

9. Why are variances typically isolated as soon as possible?

10. Is it correct to consider favorable variances as always being desirable? Explain.

EXERCISES

E–1. During January, the cutting department completed 1,000 units of a product that had a standard materials cost of 2,000 square feet at $0.60 per square foot. The actual material purchased consisted of 2,050 square feet at $0.55 per square foot at a total cost of $1,127.50. The actual material used this period was 2,020 square feet. Compute the materials price and usage variances, indicating whether each is favorable or unfavorable.

E–2. Compute the labor variances in the following situation:

Actual direct labor payroll (21,500 hours at $3.75)	$80,625
Standard labor allowed per unit, 3.5 hours at $4	$ 14
Production for month (in units)	5,500

E–3. During September, 150 units of a certain product were produced. This product has a standard labor cost of two hours at $3.50 per hour in Department 1 and one hour at $5 per hour in Department 2. Department 1 paid $950 for 295 hours, and Department 2 incurred a cost of $840 for 160 labor-hours. Compute the labor variances for each department.

E–4. The following data relate to the manufacturing activities of the Silver Company for the first quarter of 1984:

Standard activity (units)	25,000
Actual production (units)	20,000
Budgeted fixed overhead	$15,000
Variable overhead rate (per unit)	$2.00
Actual fixed overhead	$15,500
Actual variable overhead	$37,000

Compute the overhead budget variance and the overhead volume variance.

E–5. Assume that the actual production in Exercise E–4 was 22,000 units. What was the overhead volume variance?

E–6. The standard cost variance accounts of the Martin Company at the end of its fiscal year had the following balances:

Materials usage variance (unfavorable)	$2,000
Materials price variance (unfavorable)	2,500
Labor rate variance (favorable)	1,500
Labor efficiency variance (unfavorable)	5,500
Overhead volume variance (unfavorable)	3,000
Overhead budget variance (favorable)	500

Set up T-accounts for the above variances; enter the above balances in these accounts; then prepare one entry to record the closing of these variance accounts in the most practical manner.

E–7. Angle Company produces a product which has the following standard costs:

Direct materials—4 pounds at $5 per pound	$20
Direct labor—3 hours at $6 per hour	18
Manufacturing overhead—150% of direct labor	27
	$65

Assume Angle's purchasing agent took advantage of a special offer from one of its suppliers and purchased 80,000 pounds of material at $4.10 per pound. Assume 10,000 units were produced and 62,000 pounds of material were used. Compute the variances for materials. Comment on the purchasing agent's decision to take the special offer.

E-8.   The Grain Company manufactures a product which has a standard labor cost of two hours at $5 per hour. Assume that in producing 5,000 units, the foreman used a different crew from usual which resulted in a total labor cost of $46,000 for 8,000 hours. Compute the labor variances and comment on the foreman's decision to use a different crew.

PROBLEMS, SERIES A

P23-1-A.   The James Company has the following data for the month of April, when 1,100 finished units were produced:

Materials used: 3,600 pounds
Standard per finished unit: 3 pounds at $3 per pound
Materials purchased: 5,000 pounds at $3.25 per pound
Direct labor: 2,450 hours at a total cost of $9,800
Standard: $7.60 per finished unit, 2 hours per unit

Required:

a. Compute the materials and labor variances.

b. Prepare journal entries to record the transactions involving these variances.

P23-2-A.   Some of the records of Waverly Company's repair and maintenance division have been lost in a fire. Salvaged records indicate that actual labor-hours for the period were 4,000. The *total* labor variance was $3,000, favorable (the difference between actual hours times actual rate and standard hours times standard rate). The standard labor rate was $14 per hour and the labor rate variance was $1,200, unfavorable.

Required:

Compute the actual labor rate per hour.

P23-3-A.   During the month of December, the Jay Company produced 15,000 units of a product called Alpha. Alpha has a standard materials cost of two pieces per unit at $4 per piece. The actual material used consisted of 30,500 pieces at a cost of $115,900. Actual purchases of the materials amounted to 40,000 pieces at a cost of $152,000.

Required:

Using T-accounts, prepare entries for the purchase of materials and the issuance of materials to production.

P23-4-A.   The Entertainment Division of the Radio Company produced 5,000 stereos during the year ended December 31, 1984. The standard number of direct labor-hours per stereo is 2.5 at a standard rate of $4.50 per hour. During the year, 12,200 direct labor-hours were accumulated at a cost of $58,560.

Required:

a. Record the labor data in a journal entry and post the entry to T-accounts.

b. Record the journal entry to dispose of any variances and post the entry to the T-accounts.

P23–5–A.   The Rock Company computes its overhead rates based on a standard activity of 75,000 units. Fixed overhead for 1984 is budgeted at $60,000. Actual fixed overhead for 1984 was $58,000.

Required:

Compute the amount of overhead volume variance for the year under each of the following assumptions regarding actual output:

   a.   45,000 units.

   b.   75,000 units.

   c.   90,000 units.

P23–6–A.   The Calculator Company manufactures electronic games. The standard production volume is 25,000 direct labor-hours per month for 50,000 units. Fixed overhead is budgeted at $125,000, while variable overhead is budgeted at $2.20 per direct labor-hour.

In April, a total of 22,000 direct labor-hours were used in producing 45,000 units. The actual overhead for the month amounted to $119,000 fixed and $46,000 variable.

Required:

Compute the two overhead variances. Show all calculations.

P23–7–A.   The Tile Company produces ceramic figurines which, although different in shape and color, are similar enough to be considered one product for standard costing purposes. The standard cost of each figurine is:

Direct materials:
```
  1 pound of clay at $0.40 per pound . . . . . . . . . . . . . . . .$0.40
  2 ounces of coloring pigment at $1.25 per ounce . . . . . .  2.50
Direct labor (½ hour at $10 per hour) . . . . . . . . . . . . . . .  5.00
```
Overhead:
```
  Fixed (total budgeted fixed overhead of $21,000
    divided by standard output of 35,000 units) . . . . . . . . .  0.60 ($1.20 per direct
                                                                         labor-hour)
  Variable . . . . . . . . . . . . . . . . . . . . . . . . . . . . . . . . . . . .  0.80 ($1.60 per direct
                                                                         labor-hour)
    Total . . . . . . . . . . . . . . . . . . . . . . . . . . . . . . . . . . . .$9.30
```

In March, 25,000 units were manufactured and 21,000 units were sold. Production data are as follows:

```
Materials purchased:
  51,000 pounds of clay at $0.39 per pound
  105,000 ounces of pigment at $1.30 per ounce
Materials used:
  23,500 pounds of clay and 48,000 ounces of pigment
Direct labor: 12,000 hours at $10.20
Fixed overhead: $16,800
Variable overhead: $21,250
The total overhead rate is $2.80 per standard direct labor-hour.
```

Required:

Record the above data in journal entries, isolating variances as soon as possible.

P23–8–A. (*Based on the Appendix*)

The Merrill Company maintains a job order standard cost accounting system. The standard cost of the plastic material it uses is $4 per pound, while the standard labor cost is $3 per hour. Overhead is charged to the various jobs at the rate of $4 per direct labor-hour. This rate is based on a flexible budget at a standard volume of activity of 200,000 direct labor-hours that shows $400,000 of budgeted fixed overhead and $2 per standard direct labor-hour for variable overhead. Work in process inventory is charged with standard quantities and standard prices. There was no work in process inventory at May 1, 1984.

During May 1984, the following transactions and events occurred:

Transactions:

1. Purchased 200,000 pounds of plastic at $3.92.
2. Started the following jobs during the month:

Job No.	Standard units of material	Standard hours of labor
505	2,500	5,000
506	2,000	4,000
All others	120,500	211,000
	125,000	220,000

3. Materials issued during the month:

Job No.	Pounds
505	2,550
506	1,975
All others	121,475
	126,000

4. Of the direct labor cost charged to Payroll Summary, the following amounts relate to the various jobs:

Job No.	Actual hours	Standard hours	Actual cost
505	5,100	5,000	$ 15,120
506	4,080	4,000	11,880
All others	184,000	181,000	550,700
	193,180	190,000	$577,700

5. Appropriate overhead was charged to the various jobs.
6. Actual fixed overhead incurred, $408,000; actual variable overhead, $376,000.
7. Job Nos. 505 and 506 were completed along with other production having a standard cost of $1,580,000.

Required:

a. Prepare journal entries to record the above summarized data, isolating variances as soon as possible.

b. Compute and prepare journal entries to record the two overhead variances.

c. Assuming that the variances isolated are for the year ending May 31, 1984, prepare an entry that represents a practical disposition of these variances.

P23–9–A. (*Based on the Appendix*)

The Dent Manufacturing Company manufactures a product by processing it through three successive departments, A, B, and C. A process cost system incorporating standard costs is used. The standard cost of the product in Department A is:

Materials (20 pounds at $1.50) $30
Labor (3 hours at $6)   18
Fixed overhead   15
Variable overhead   12
                                              $75

Materials price variances are recorded at the time of purchase with the result that materials are charged to production at actual quantity and standard price. Work in process is charged for actual costs incurred for labor and overhead, and variances are isolated at the end of the period when production is known. Budgeted overhead at the standard volume of output of 25,000 units per month is $375,000 plus $12 per unit completed.

There was no beginning work in process inventory on June 1, 1984, in Department A. Following are summarized data for the month of June for Department A:

1. Materials purchased, 450,000 pounds at $1.56.
2. Materials requisitioned, 440,310 pounds.
3. Of the charges to Payroll Summary, $359,940 represents the cost of 59,940 hours of direct labor received in Department A.
4. Actual overhead costs charged to Work in Process Inventory: fixed, $378,000; and variable, $242,595.
5. Units completed and transferred to Department B, 18,000; 4,000 units remain on hand in the department, 100 percent complete as to materials (which are added only at the beginning of the processing in the department) and 50 percent complete as to processing.

Required:

  a. Prepare journal entries for the above summarized data. (In the illustration in the Appendix all variances were isolated at the end of the period. Use logic to isolate the materials price variances as required in this problem.)

  b. Compute the remaining five variances and give one journal entry to remove the variances from the Work in Process Inventory—Department A account.

  c. Can the overhead volume variance be logically related to the labor efficiency variance? Explain.

PROBLEMS, SERIES B

P23–1–B.   A certain product has a standard materials usage and cost of 2 pounds at $3.50 per pound. During the month, 1,100 pounds of material were purchased at $3.65 per pound. Production for the month totaled 500 units requiring 980 pounds of materials. Compute the materials variances.

P23–2–B.   During the month of March, a department completed 5,000 units of a product which had a standard material cost of 6,000 square feet at $0.30 per square foot. The actual material used consisted of 6,100 square feet at an actual cost of $1,708. The actual purchase of this material amounted to 9,000 square feet at a total cost of $2,520.

Required:

  Using T-accounts, prepare entries (*a*) for the purchase of the materials and (*b*) for the issuance of materials to production.

P23–3–B.   The O. Z. Company makes plastic garbage bags. One box of bags requires 1.5 hours of labor at an hourly rate of $3. Compute the labor variances assuming that 50,000 boxes were produced with 80,000 hours of labor at a total cost of $220,000.

P23–4–B.   The finishing department of the Merry Company produced 20,000 units during the month of November. The standard number of direct labor-hours per unit is two hours. The standard rate per hour is $7. During the month, 41,000 direct labor-hours were worked at a cost of $307,500.

Required:

    a.   Record the labor data in a journal entry and post to T-accounts.

    b.   Record the journal entry to dispose of any variances and post the entry to the T-accounts.

P23–5–B.   The monthly budgeted fixed overhead of the Buffalo plant of the ABC Company is absorbed into production using a rate based upon a standard volume of output of 100,000 units per month. The flexible budget for the month for overhead allows $75,000 for fixed overhead and $1 per unit of output for variable overhead. Actual overhead for the month consisted of $75,600 of fixed overhead with actual variable overhead given below.

Required:

    Compute the overhead budget variance and the overhead volume variance assuming actual production in units and actual variable overhead in dollars were:

    a.   75,000 and $76,000.

    b.   110,000 and $112,700.

P23–6–B.   The Table Company manufactures chalkboards for sale to various high schools and colleges. The expected volume of activity is 25,000 units. Standard direct labor-hours are 3 per unit. At the 25,000-unit level of output, fixed overhead is budgeted at $60,000 and variable overhead is budgeted at $1.10 per hour.

    In July, 77,000 direct labor-hours were worked to achieve the standard level of output of 25,000 units. Actual overhead for July consisted of $63,000 of fixed overhead and $90,000 of variable overhead.

Required:

    Compute the two overhead variances showing all computations.

P23–7–B.   Based on a standard volume of output of 80,000 units per month, the standard cost of the product manufactured by the Jasper Company is:

Direct materials (0.25 pounds)	$0.50
Direct labor (0.5 hours)	1.90
Variable overhead	1.25
Fixed overhead	0.75
Total	$4.40

    A total of 21,000 pounds of materials were purchased at $2.10 per pound. During the month of May, 82,000 units were produced with the following costs:

Direct materials used (20,650 pounds at $2.10)	$ 43,365
Direct labor (40,000 hours at $3.90)	156,000
Variable overhead	104,000
Fixed overhead	60,520

Required:

    Compute the materials price and usage variances, the labor rate and efficiency variances, and the overhead budget and volume variances.

P23–8–B. (Based on the Appendix)

The Bryant Manufacturing Company employs a job order standard cost accounting system. The standard cost of the material used is $0.80 per square foot, while the standard labor cost is $4 per hour. Overhead is assigned to jobs at the rate of $3 per standard direct labor-hour. Based upon a standard volume of activity of 60,000 direct labor-hours, the flexible budget allows $60,000 of fixed overhead and $2 of variable overhead per direct labor-hour for the month of June 1984.

Work in process is charged with standard quantities and standard prices. On June 1, 1984, one job (No. 201) was in process, to which the following standard costs have already been assigned:

Material (2,500 square feet)	$2,000
Labor (400 direct labor-hours)	1,600
Manufacturing overhead ($3 per standard direct labor-hours)	1,200
Total	$4,800

When completed, the standard quantities for Job No. 201 are 4,000 square feet of material and 500 hours of direct labor.

During the month of June 1984, the following transactions and events occurred:

Transactions:

1. Purchased 600,000 square feet of material at $0.78 per square foot.
2. Materials issued:

Job No.	Actual quantity (square feet)	Standard quantity (square feet)
201	1,600	1,500
All others	420,000	421,200
	421,600	422,700

3. The direct labor costs and hours for the month were:

Incurred on—	Actual hours	Standard hours	Actual cost
Job No. 201	104	100	$ 434
All other jobs	51,096	51,000	206,966
	51,200	51,100	$207,400

4. The appropriate amount of overhead was assigned to the jobs.
5. Actual overhead incurred during the month was $155,000.
6. Job No. 201 was completed during the month. Other production also completed during the month has a standard cost of $520,000.

Required:

a. Prepare general journal entries for each of the numbered transactions given above.

b. Compute and prepare general journal entries to record the overhead budget variance and the overhead volume variance for the month.

P23–9–B. (Based on the Appendix)

The Martinez Company employs a process cost system with standard costs to account for the product it manufactures in a two-step process through Departments I and II. The standard cost of this product in Department I is:

```
Direct materials (10 units at $8) . . . . . . .   $ 80
Direct labor (5 hours at $6) . . . . . . . . . .     30
Variable overhead (5 hours at $4) . . . . . .       20
Fixed overhead (5 hours at $2) . . . . . . . .      10
                                                  $140
```

The flexible overhead budget, based on 60,000 direct labor-hours as a standard volume of activity, allows $120,000 of fixed overhead plus $4 per direct labor-hour. Materials price variances are isolated at time of purchase, labor rate variances when direct labor is charged to Work in Process. Materials usage and labor efficiency variances are isolated at the end of the month when production is known. Standard overhead is assigned to production and overhead variances are isolated at the end of the month when production and actual costs are known.

There was no work in process inventory as of July 1, 1984; in Department I. Selected, summarized data for the month are:

1. Purchased 121,000 units of material for $963,160.
2. Direct materials requisitioned by Department I, 110,580 units.
3. Of the payroll costs for the month, 49,900 hours with a total cost of $299,760 are chargeable to Department I.
4. Total overhead costs incurred by the department for the month consist of $120,900 of fixed overhead and $201,100 of variable overhead.
5. A total of 9,000 units was completed during the month and 2,000 units remain in process, 100 percent complete as to materials and 50 percent complete as to labor and overhead.
6. Overhead is assigned to production on the basis of standard labor-hours.

Required:

    a. Prepare journal entries to record the above summarized data. (In the illustration in the Appendix all variances were isolated at the end of the period. Use logic to isolate them as required in this problem.)

    b. Compute the materials usage variance and the labor efficiency variance and prepare journal entries to remove them from work in process inventory.

    c. Compute and prepare journal entries to record the overhead budget variance and the overhead volume variance.

    d. Assuming the variances isolated are for the year ending July 31, 1984, prepare an entry that represents a practical disposition of these variances.

BUSINESS DECISION PROBLEM 23–1

Turn to Exercise E–6 in this chapter. For each of the variances listed give a possible reason for its existence.

BUSINESS DECISION PROBLEM 23–2

Bill Watts, the president of the Able Company, has a problem. It does not involve substantial dollar amounts but does involve the important question of responsibility for variances from standard costs. He has just received the following report:

Total materials costs for the month of May (6,900 pounds at $2.40 per pound)	$16,560
Unfavorable materials price variance ($2.40 − $2.00) × 6,900 pounds	(2,760)
Unfavorable materials usage variance (6,900 pounds − 6,000 pounds) × $2	(1,800)
Standard materials at standard price for the actual production in May	$12,000

Bill has discussed the unfavorable price variance with Marie Hatter, the purchasing officer. She agrees that under the circumstances she should be held responsible for most of the materials price variance. But she objects to the inclusion of $360 (900 pounds of excess materials used at $0.40 per pound). This, she argues, is the responsibility of the production department. If it had not been so inefficient in the use of materials, she would not have had to purchase the extra 900 pounds. On the other hand, Ron Sills, the production manager, agrees that he is basically responsible for the excess quantity of materials used. But he does not agree that the above materials usage variance should be revised to include the $360 of unfavorable price variance on the excess materials used. "That's Marie's responsibility," he says.

Bill now turns to you for help. Specifically, he wants you to tell him:

a.   Who is responsible for the $360 in dispute?

b.   If responsibility cannot be clearly assigned, in which materials variance should the accounting department include the variance? Why?

c.   Are there likely to be other circumstances where materials variances cannot be considered the responsibility of the person who is most likely to be considered responsible for them? Explain.

Prepare written answers to the three questions asked by Bill.

Chapter 24

Responsibility accounting; segmental analysis

CHAPTER GOALS

After study of this chapter, you should be able to:

1. Discuss the concept of responsibility accounting.
2. Prepare responsibility accounting reports.
3. Prepare a segmental income statement showing the contribution to indirect expenses using the contribution margin format.
4. Determine return on investment, margin, and turnover for a segment.
5. Determine the residual earnings of a segment.
6. Define and use correctly the new terms in the glossary.

RESPONSIBILITY ACCOUNTING

Responsibility accounting refers to an accounting system that collects, summarizes, and reports accounting data according to the responsibilities of individual managers. A responsibility accounting system provides information to evaluate each manager on revenue and expense items over which that manager has primary control (authority to influence). A responsibility accounting report contains only those items that are controllable by the responsible manager or, if both controllable and noncontrollable items are included, clearly segregates those items that are not controllable. This identification of controllable items is fundamental in responsibility accounting and reporting.

The business entity must be well organized so that responsibility is assignable to individual managers. Clear lines of authority and responsibility should exist throughout the organization. Various company managers, their responsibility levels, and lines of authority should be fully defined. The organization chart in Illustration 24.1 demonstrates lines of authority and responsibility that could be used as a basis for responsibility reporting. If clear areas of authority cannot be determined, it is very doubtful that responsibility accounting can be effectively implemented.

Lines of authority should follow a specified path. For example, a plant supervisor may report to a plant manager, who reports to a vice president of manufacturing, who is responsible to the president. The president is ultimately responsible to stockholders or their elected representatives, the board of directors. In a sense, the president is responsible for all revenue and expense items of the firm, since at the presidential level all items are controllable over some period of time. The president will usually delegate authority to various managers since he cannot keep fully informed of the day-to-day operating details of all areas of the business.

Reference is often made to management levels. The president is usually considered a first-level manager. Managers who report directly to the president are second-level managers. Notice on the organization chart in Illustration 24.1 that individuals at a specific management level are on a horizontal line across the chart. But not all managers at that level have equal authority and responsibility. The relative authority of certain types of managers will vary from firm to firm.

While the president may delegate much decision-making power, there are some revenue and expense items that may remain exclusively under the president's control. For example, large capital (plant and equipment) expenditures may be approved only by the president. Hence, depreciation, property taxes, and other related expenses should not be designated as a plant manager's responsibility since these costs are not primarily under that manager's control. The controllability criterion is crucial to the content of performance reports for each manager. For example, at the supervisor level, perhaps only direct materials and direct labor cost control are appropriate for measuring performance. At the plant manager level, many other costs, not controllable at a lower level, are controllable and therefore are included in the performance evaluation of the plant manager.

Illustration 24.1:   Illustration of a corporate functional organization chart including four levels
of management

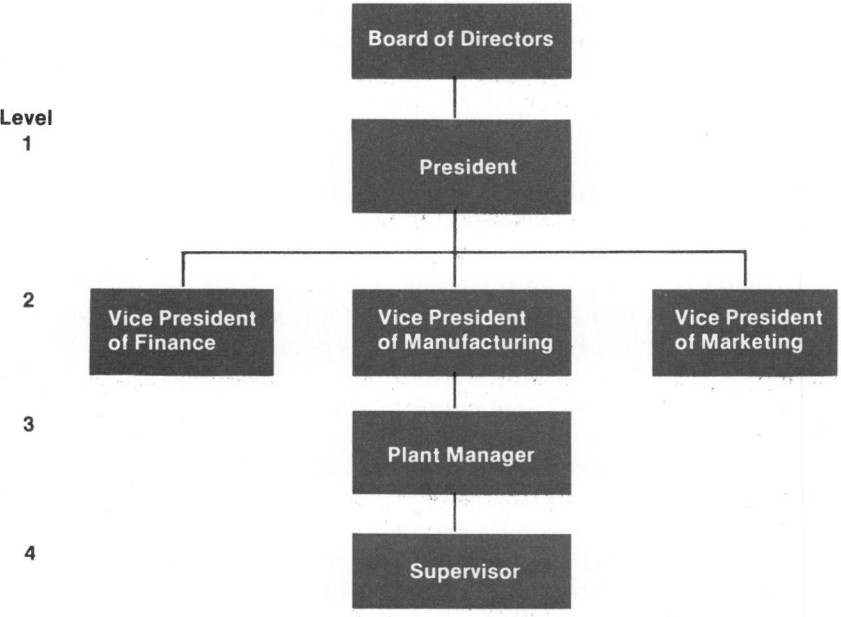

THE CONCEPT OF CONTROL

Theoretically, a manager should have absolute control over an item to be held responsible for it. Unfortunately, absolute controllability is rare. Quite frequently, external or internal factors beyond a manager's control may affect revenues or expenses under that manager's responsibility. For example, the imposition of a 10 percent excise tax by a governmental agency may decrease sales of certain items in a manager's segment. Although the manager has the authority and responsibility for segment sales, the decline in revenues was beyond that manager's control. Another example would be the excessive use of raw materials in a production process under the control of a particular manager. Although the manager has the authority to control such expenses, that manager should not be held responsible for excess costs if the purchasing department bought low-quality materials that created an unusual amount of spoilage.

Therefore, the theoretical requirement that a manager have absolute control over items for which that manager is held responsible often must be compromised since most revenue and expense items have some elements of noncontrollability in them. The manager is, then, usually held responsible for items where *relative* control is present. *Relative control* means that the manager has control over most of the factors which influence a given budget item. The use of relative control may lead to some motivational problems, since the manager is evaluated on results that may not reflect that manager's efforts. Nevertheless, most budget plans assign control on a relative control basis in order to develop and use segmental budgets.

RESPONSIBILITY REPORTS

A unique feature of a responsibility accounting system is the amount of detail in the various reports issued to different levels of management. For example, a performance report to a supervisor would include actual and budgeted dollar amounts of all revenue and expense items under that supervisor's control. The responsibility report issued to the plant manager would show only totals from all the supervisors' performance reports and any additional items under the plant manager's control, such as plant administrative expense. The vice president of manufacturing's report would contain totals from all the plants plus any additional items under the vice president's control. Because a responsibility accounting system selectively condenses data, the report to the president includes summary totals of the subordinate levels plus any additional items under the president's control.

The condensation of data as information flows upward to increasingly higher levels of management may seem to be a hindrance to performance analysis. Actually, this lack of detail results in "management by exception." *Management by exception* is the concept that upper level management does not need to examine operating details of subordinate levels unless there appears to be a problem. Since modern business enterprises are becoming increasingly complex, it has become necessary to filter and condense accounting data so that they may be analyzed quickly. Most executives do not have time to study detailed accounting reports, searching for problem areas. Reporting only summary totals highlights those areas that need attention so that the executive can make more efficient use of available time.

Reports issued under a responsibility accounting system are interrelated since totals from one level are carried forward in the report to the management level immediately above. Control reports submitted to the president include all revenue and expense items (in summary form) since the president is responsible for controlling the profitability of the entire firm.

The condensation of data that occurs at successive levels of management is justified on the basis that the appropriate manager will take the necessary corrective action. Thus, specific performance details need not be reported to supervisors. For example, if direct labor cost has been excessively high in a particular department, that departmental supervisor should seek to find and correct the cause of the problem. When the plant manager questions the unfavorable budget variance of the department, the supervisor can inform the manager that corrective action was taken. Hence, it is not necessary to report to the vice president of manufacturing that a particular department within one of the plants is not operating satisfactorily, since the matter has already been attended to. Alternatively, if a manager's entire plant has been performing poorly, summary totals reported to the vice president of manufacturing will disclose this situation and an investigation of the plant manager's problems may be indicated.

In preparing responsibility accounting reports, there are two basic ways of handling revenue or expense items that are noncontrollable by a particular manager. First, those items may be omitted entirely from reports until the management level at which they become controllable. As a result, responsibility reports at each level contain only those items that are controllable at that level. A second approach is to include all revenue and expense items that can be traced directly or allocated indirectly to a particular manager. This method represents a full-cost approach, which means *all* costs of a given area can be disclosed in a single report. When this approach is used, care must be taken to separate controllable from noncontrollable items in order to differentiate those items for which a manager can and should be held responsible.

Features of responsibility reports

In order for accounting reports to be of maximum benefit, they must be *timely*. That is, reports should be prepared as soon as possible after the end of the performance measurement period. Timely reporting allows prompt corrective action to be taken. Reports that are excessively delayed lose their effectiveness as control devices. For example, a report on the previous month's operations that is not received until the end of the current month is virtually useless for analyzing poor performance areas and taking corrective action.

Reports should also be issued *regularly*. Regular reports are desirable since trends can be spotted. Appropriate management action can be initiated before major problems occur. Regularity is also important so that managers will rely on the reports and become familiar with their contents.

Reports should be relatively simple. Care should be taken to avoid using confusing terminology. Results should be expressed in physical units where appropriate. It is also desirable to report both budgeted (expected) and actual amounts. A *budget variance* is the difference between the budgeted and actual amount of an item. Budget variances should be reported so that relative performance can be ascertained. Through careful analysis, significant deviations from budget are highlighted. Variance analysis allows management to spot problem areas quickly. The use of variances is helpful in applying the management-by-exception principle. Finally, in addition to the current period analysis, a year-to-date analysis is often included in the reports so that a manager can determine performance to date.

RESPONSIBILITY REPORTS—ILLUSTRATION

The following example shows how an organization's responsibility accounting reports are interrelated. The organization has four management levels. The illustrations focus on the president, vice president of manufacturing, plant manager, and supervisor (dye shop). (See Illustration 24.2.) A responsibility report would be prepared for each management level (Illustration 24.3).

Illustration 24.2:   Organization chart

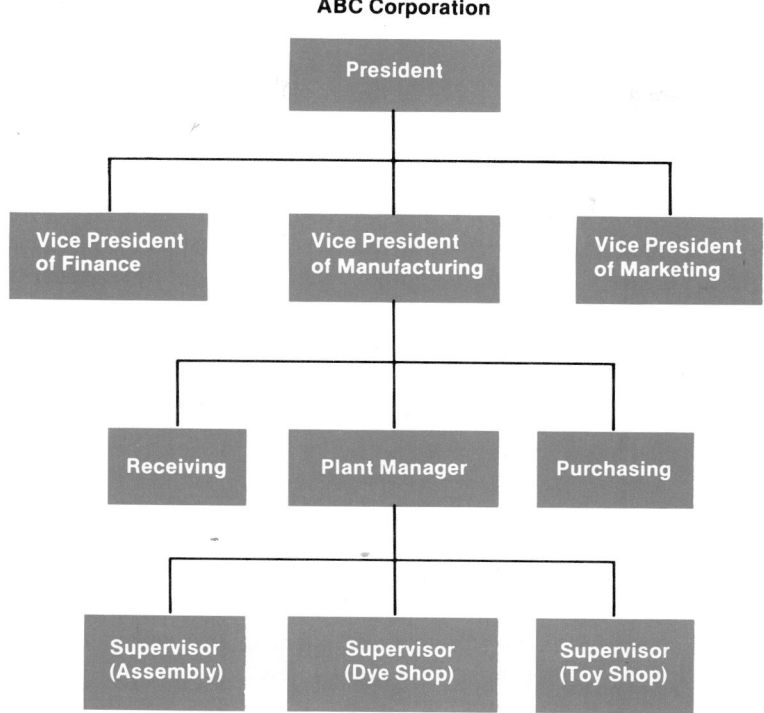

Illustration 24.3:   Responsibility reports

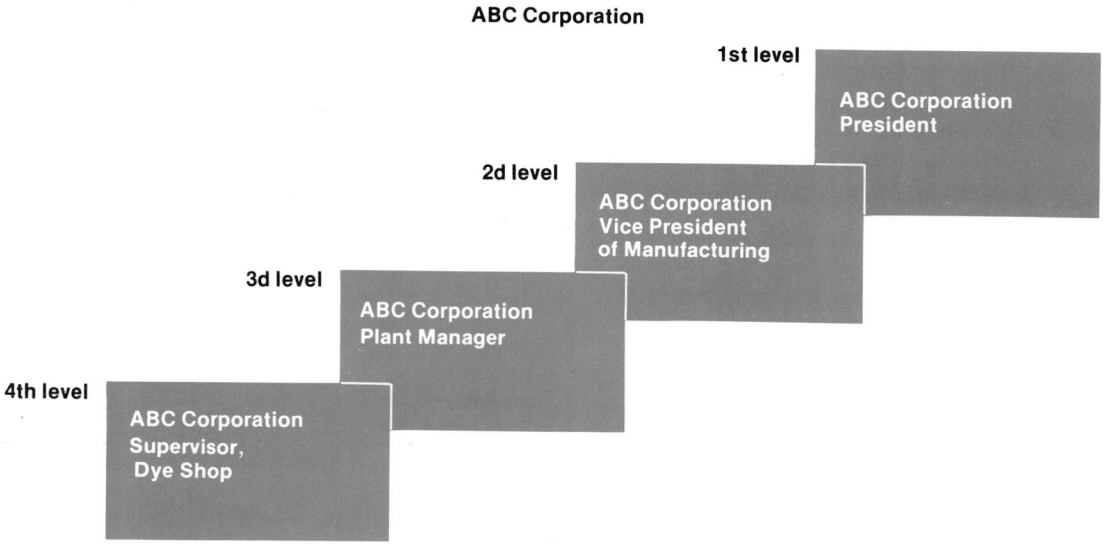

Illustration 24.4 shows the detailed information included in the responsibility reports. The reports contain only controllable expenses. Notice that only totals from the supervisor's responsibility report are included in the plant manager's report. In turn, only totals from the plant manager's report are included on the report to the vice president, and so on. Detailed data from the lower levels are summarized and reported at the next higher level. Also, controllable costs which were not included on lower level reports are introduced into the reports for levels 3, 2, and 1. For instance, the president's office expense and the vice presidents' salaries are first reported in the president's report because these expenses are not controllable at lower levels.

Based on an analysis of these reports, the dye shop supervisor probably will take immediate action to see why supplies and overtime were significantly over budget this month. The plant manager may ask the supervisor what the problems were and whether they are now under control. The vice president may ask the same question of the plant manager. The president may ask each vice president why the budget was exceeded this month and what corrective action has been taken.

RESPONSIBILITY CENTERS

Various references have been made to the segments of a business enterprise. A *segment* is a fairly autonomous unit or division of a company. Examples of segments are departments, product lines, and service centers. The segments of a business enterprise must be defined according to function or product line. For example, companies have traditionally been organized along functional lines. The segments or departments organized along functional lines perform a specified function (e.g., marketing, finance, purchasing, production, shipping). Recently, large firms have tended to organize segments according to product lines (e.g., electrical products division, shoe department, or food division). These segments are to a degree autonomous, self-contained units, each with various functional units contained within themselves.

A *responsibility center* is a segment of an organization for which a particular executive is responsible. There are three possible types of responsibility centers: expense (or cost) centers, profit (or earnings) centers, and investment centers. The characteristics of a specific segment and the extent of the responsible manager's authority will limit the selection of an appropriate reporting basis. The accounting system must be structured to gather and report information for each segment.

Expense or cost centers

An *expense center* is a company segment having only expense items and producing no direct revenue from the sale of goods or services. Examples of expense centers are service centers (e.g., the maintenance and accounting departments) or intermediate production facilities which produce parts for assembly into a finished product. *Managers of expense centers are held responsible only for specified expense items.*

Illustration 24.4: Responsibility reports for ABC Corporation

First level

ABC CORPORATION
President

Controllable expenses	Amount		Over or (under) budget	
	This month	Year to date	This month	Year to date
President's office expense	$ 1,000	$ 5,000	$ 100	$ 200
Vice president, manufacturing	18,800	93,000	600	800
Vice president, sales	8,700	19,000	400	800
Vice president, finance	4,000	15,000	800	900
Vice presidents' salaries	9,000	45,000	–0–	–0–
Total	$41,500	$177,000	$1,900	$2,700

Second level

ABC CORPORATION
Vice President of Manufacturing

Controllable expenses	Amount		Over or (under) budget	
	This month	Year to date	This month	Year to date
Vice president's office expense	$ 2,840	$ 9,500	$ (50)	$(800)
Plant departmental costs	7,880	43,000	250	500
Purchasing	380	2,500	100	200
Receiving	700	3,000	300	900
Salaries of plant manager and heads of purchasing and receiving	7,000	35,000	–0–	–0–
Total (include in report for next higher level)	$18,800	$93,000	$600	$ 800

Third level

ABC CORPORATION
Plant Manager

Controllable expenses	Amount		Over or (under) budget	
	This month	Year to date	This month	Year to date
Plant manager's office expense	$ 800	$ 9,100	$ (50)	$(100)
Dye shop costs	680	2,600	160	230
Toy shop costs	1,000	5,000	80	130
Assembly	400	1,300	60	240
Salaries of supervisors	5,000	25,000	–0–	–0–
Total (include in report for next higher level)	$7,880	$43,000	$250	$ 500

Fourth level

ABC CORPORATION
Supervisor, Dye Shop

Controllable expenses	Amount		Over or (under) budget	
	This month	Year to date	This month	Year to date
Repairs and maintenance	$200	$1,000	$ 10	$ 40
Supplies	180	850	80	95
Tools	100	300	(10)	81
Overtime	200	450	80	14
Total (include in report for next higher level)	$680	$2,600	$160	$230

The appropriate goal of an expense center is the *long-run* minimization of expense. Short-run minimization of expenses may not be appropriate. For example, a production supervisor could eliminate maintenance costs for a short period of time which would cause short-term costs to be lower. But, in the long run, total costs might be higher due to more frequent machine breakdowns.

Profit centers

Because managers are motivated when rewards are based on earnings, the calculation of segmental earnings has considerable appeal. Accordingly, in an increasing number of firms, the segments are organized as profit centers. A *profit center* has both revenues and expenses. Since segmental earnings are usually defined as segmental revenues minus related expenses, the manager must be able to *control* both of these categories. That is, the manager must have the authority to control selling price, sales volume, and all reported expense items. The manager's authority over all of these measured items is essential to proper performance evaluation. *Controllable profits of a segment* are shown when expenses under a manager's control are deducted from revenues under that manager's control.

Transfer prices. When a division or segment sells its output only to other segments within the company, a transfer price must be established between the two segments. A *transfer price* is an artificial price used when goods or services are transferred from one segment to another segment within the same company. This is necessary in order for the producing department to have a measured "revenue" from production. The transfer price is recorded as revenue of the producing segment and as a cost or expense of the receiving segment. This enables this type of producing division to become a profit center rather than an expense center.

No cash actually changes hands; rather, the transfer price is recorded as an internal accounting adjustment. Ideally, a transfer price should be the amount a part or service would cost if purchased from an outside party. Because such a "market" price might not be available, transfer prices often are determined on a cost plus profit margin basis. In other cases, transfer prices are negotiated between the two segments, possibly with the help of an arbitration board.

No matter how the transfer price is determined, it is essential that the manufacturing segment manager have some degree of control over setting the price. If the manager does not have any control over the transfer price and output volume, the use of a profit center may be undesirable for motivational purposes.

Investment centers

Closely related to the profit center concept is an investment center. An *investment center* is a segment of a company having revenues, expenses, and a specified investment base. When a segment is considered an investment center, it is evaluated on the basis of the rate of return that it can earn on its investment base. *Return on investment (ROI)* (also called rate of return) is computed by dividing segmental earnings by the appropriate investment base. For example, a segment that earns $100,000 on an investment base of $1,000,000 is said to have a ROI of 10 percent. Of course, there is a question as to the appropriate investment base that should be used in calculating ROI.

Normally, the assets available for use by the division make up the investment base of the division. But accountants disagree on whether depreciable assets should be included in the ROI calculation at original cost, original cost less accumulated depreciation, or current replacement cost. *Original cost* is the price paid to acquire an asset. *Original cost less accumulated depreciation* is the book value of the asset—the amount paid less total depreciation taken. *Current replacement cost* is the cost of replacing the present assets with similar assets in the same condition as those now in use. Each of these measures normally would generate different rates of return. Therefore, management must select and agree upon an appropriate measure of investment base prior to making ROI calculations or interdivision comparisons.

Even after the investment base is defined, problems may still remain since most segment managers have limited control over some of the items included in the investment bases of their segments. For instance, capital expenditure decisions are often made by top-level management rather than at the segment level. Therefore, the segment manager may have little control over the plant assets used by the segment. Another problem area may exist if the firm has a centralized credit and collection department. In this case, the manager may have little control over the amount of accounts receivable included as segment assets since the manager cannot change the credit-granting or collection policies of the company.

Usually the above problems are overcome by the logic that all segments are treated in the same manner and that inclusion of noncontrollable items in the investment base is therefore acceptable. Then comparisons between segments are at least based on consistent treatment of items. It is important, though, that the segment managers agree to this treatment in order to avoid adverse reaction or decreased motivation.

The logic for using investment centers as bases for performance evaluation is that segments with more resources should produce more profits than segments with fewer resources. By calculating rates of return for performance evaluation, the relative effectiveness of the segment can be measured. Thus, the segment with the highest percentage return is presumably the most effective in using its resources. But when the absolute amount of profits is used to measure performance, larger segments have a distinct advantage over smaller segments.

Typical investment centers are large, autonomous segments of large companies. The centers are often separated from one another by location, types of products, functions, and/or necessary management skills. Segments such as these often seem to be separate companies to an outside observer. But the investment center concept can be applied even in relatively small companies, wherever the manager has control over revenues, expenses, and assets.

SEGMENTAL ANALYSIS

So far, this chapter has described only the fundamentals of responsibility accounting. Now, the concept of investment centers will be explained in greater depth, and some aspects of segmental analysis will be discussed.

Decentralization refers to the extent to which management decision making is dispersed among lower levels of the organization. In other words, the extent of decentralization refers to the degree of control that segment managers have over the revenues, expenses, and assets of their segments. When a segment manager has control over these three elements, the investment center concept can be applied to the segment. Thus, the more decentralized the decision making is in an organization, the more applicable is the investment center concept to the segments of the company. The more centralized the decision making is, the more likely one is to find responsibility centers established as expense centers only.

Some of the advantages of decentralized decision making are:

1. Increased control over their segments trains managers for high-level positions in the company. The added responsibility and authority also represent "job enlargement" and often increase job satisfaction and motivation.
2. Top management can be more removed from day-to-day decision making at lower levels of the company and can manage by exception. When top management is not involved with routine problem solving, it can devote more time to long-range planning and to the most significant problem areas.
3. Decisions can be made at the point where problems arise. It is often difficult for members of top management to make appropriate decisions on a timely basis when they are not intimately involved with the problem they are trying to solve.
4. Since decentralization permits use of the investment center concept, performance evaluation criteria such as ROI and residual earnings can be used.

CONCEPTS USED IN SEGMENTAL ANALYSIS

The concepts of variable cost, fixed cost, direct cost, indirect cost, net income of a segment, and contribution to indirect expenses need to be understood before the investment center analysis can begin. Variable cost and fixed cost were discussed in Chapter 21. The other terms will now be discussed.

Direct cost and indirect cost

Costs may be either directly or indirectly related to a particular cost objective (or object). A *cost objective* is a segment, product, or other item for which costs may be accumulated. In other words, a cost is not "direct" or "indirect" in and of itself. It is only "direct" or "indirect" in relation to a given cost object.

A cost is a *direct cost* (*expense*) of a cost objective if it is specifically traceable to that cost object. It is an *indirect cost (expense)* of a cost object if it is not traceable to that object but has been allocated to it. A particular cost may be direct to one cost object and indirect to another. For instance, the salary of a segment manager may be a direct cost of that segment but an indirect cost of one of the products manufactured by that segment.

Since a direct cost is traceable to a cost object, the cost is likely to be eliminated if the cost object is eliminated. For instance, if the plastics segment of a business is closed down, the salary of the manager of that segment probably will be eliminated. Sometimes one may be able to think of a direct cost which would remain even if the cost object were eliminated, but this is the exception rather than the rule.

An indirect cost is not traceable to a particular cost object; therefore, it only becomes an expense of the cost object through an allocation process. For example, if depreciation expense on the company headquarters building is allocated to each of the segments of the company, that depreciation expense is an indirect cost of each segment. If any segment of the company is eliminated, an indirect cost is not likely to disappear; it will merely be allocated among the remaining segments. Again, it may be possible in a given situation to identify an indirect cost which would be eliminated if the cost object were eliminated, but this would be the exception to the general rule.

Since direct costs of a segment are clearly identified with that segment, these costs are often controllable by the segment manager. Since indirect costs become segment costs only through allocation, most of them are noncontrollable by the segment manager. But care must be taken not to equate direct costs with controllable costs. For example, the salary of a segment supervisor may be direct to that segment and yet noncontrollable by that supervisor because supervisors cannot specify their own salaries.

Net income format for a segment

The *net income of a segment* is the amount which remains after all the segment's expenses (direct and indirect) have been deducted from its revenues. The net income of a segment measures the contribution which that segment makes to overall company earnings. An income statement may be used to present this information. The format of such an income statement focuses on direct expenses and indirect expenses rather than cost of goods sold, operating expenses, and nonoperating expenses. An example of a segmental income statement is shown in Illustration 24.5.

Contribution margin is equal to sales revenue less variable expenses. Notice in Illustration 24.5 that all variable expenses are direct expenses. Some fixed expenses are direct, while others are indirect.

In determining the contribution that a segment makes to company profits, it is tempting to use segment net income since total net income is used in evaluating the performance of an entire company. The problem with using net income of a segment to evaluate the different segments is that certain indirect fixed expenses are allocated to the segment on an arbitrary basis. *Contribution to indirect expenses* is defined as the income of a segment when

Illustration 24.5: Segmental net income

| | Segment | | |
	A	B	Total
Sales	$1,000,000	$700,000	$1,700,000
Less: Variable expenses (all direct expenses)	500,000	410,000	910,000
Contribution margin	$ 500,000	$290,000	$ 790,000
Less: Direct fixed expenses	120,000	170,000	290,000
Contribution to indirect expenses	$ 380,000	$120,000	$ 500,000
Less: Indirect fixed expenses	90,000	160,000	250,000
Net income	$ 290,000	$ (40,000)	$ 250,000

only direct expenses of the segment are deducted from segmental revenues. Because this figure includes only items directly related to the segment, this amount is often considered more appropriate for evaluation purposes. The contribution to indirect expenses figure basically shows how much company profits would decrease if the segment were discontinued.

If management relied on segment net income to judge a segment, management might conclude that segment B in the above illustration should be eliminated since it shows a loss of $40,000. But this action would reduce overall company profits by $120,000, as shown below.

Reduction in corporate revenues		$700,000
Reduction in corporate expenses:		
Variable expenses	$410,000	
Direct fixed expenses	170,000	580,000
Reduction in corporate earnings		$120,000

Notice that the elimination of segment B did not eliminate the $160,000 of allocated fixed costs. These costs would merely need to be covered by segment A if segment B no longer existed.

Contribution to indirect expenses is, therefore, a useful figure for determining whether or not a segment should be retained. For this reason, and because the allocation of indirect fixed expenses is so arbitrary, many companies prepare an income statement (for internal use) with the format shown in Illustration 24.6.

This format stresses the direct costs of a particular segment and eliminates some of the problems of arbitrary indirect cost allocations. The income statement format shown in Illustration 24.6 is called the *contribution margin format;* it shows the contribution margin (Sales − Variable expenses) for each segment.

Arbitrary allocations of indirect fixed expenses. As stated above, indirect fixed expenses, such as depreciation on the corporate administration building or on the computer facilty maintained at company headquarters, can only be allocated to segments on some arbitrary basis.

Illustration 24.6: Segmental contribution to indirect expenses

	Segment A	Segment B	Total
	A	**B**	**Total**
Sales	$1,000,000	$700,000	$1,700,000
Less: Variable expenses	500,000	410,000	910,000
Contribution margin	$ 500,000	$290,000	$ 790,000
Less: Direct fixed expenses	120,000	170,000	290,000
Contribution to indirect expenses	$ 380,000	$120,000	$ 500,000
Less: Indirect fixed expenses			250,000
Net income			$ 250,000

For certain indirect expenses, allocation can be made on the basis of benefit received. For instance, assume segment A in Illustration 24.5 used 4,000 hours of a total of 10,000 hours of computer time used. Segment A could be charged with 40 percent of the computer facility cost, since this is proportional to the benefit received.

For certain other expenses, allocation is based on responsibility for incurrence. For instance, assume that segment A contracts with a magazine to run an advertisement which will benefit both segment A and various other segments of the company. Many companies would allocate the entire cost of the advertisement to segment A since it was responsible for incurring that portion of total advertising expense.

To illustrate the allocation of indirect expenses, based on some measure of benefit or responsibility for incurrence, assume that Daily Company operates two segments, X and Y. It allocates the following indirect expenses to its two segments using the designated allocation bases.

Expense	Allocation base
Home office building occupancy expense, $40,000	Net sales
Insurance expense, $25,000	Cost of direct plant assets
General administrative expenses, $30,000	Number of employees

The following additional data are provided:

	Segment X	Segment Y	Total
Sales (net)	$200,000	$300,000	$500,000
Direct plant assets	150,000	200,000	350,000
Number of employees	40	60	100

The allocation of indirect expenses is as shown in the following expense allocation schedule:

	Segment X	Segment Y	Total
Home office building occupancy expense	$16,000[1]	$24,000[2]	$40,000
Insurance expense	10,714[3]	14,286[4]	25,000
General administrative expenses	12,000[5]	18,000[6]	30,000

1. $\dfrac{\$200,000}{\$500,000} \times \$40,000 = \$16,000.$

2. $\dfrac{\$300,000}{\$500,000} \times \$40,000 = \$24,000.$

3. $\dfrac{\$150,000}{\$350,000} \times \$25,000 = \$10,714.$

4. $\dfrac{\$200,000}{\$350,000} \times \$25,000 = \$14,286.$

5. $\dfrac{40}{100} \times \$30,000 = \$12,000.$

6. $\dfrac{60}{100} \times \$30,000 = \$18,000.$

When neither "benefit" nor "responsibility" can be used to allocate indirect fixed expenses, some other reasonable, but arbitrary, basis must be found. Often, for lack of a better approach, expenses are allocated based on net sales. For instance, if segment X's net sales were 60 percent of total company sales, then 60 percent of a certain indirect expense would be allocated to segment X. Allocating expenses based on sales is not recommended because it reduces the incentive of a segment manager to increase sales since this would result in more indirect expenses being allocated to that segment.

To this point, the segmental analysis discussion has concentrated on the contribution to indirect expenses or segmental net income approaches and has excluded the investment center concept. Investment base will now be introduced into the analysis.

INVESTMENT CENTER ANALYSIS

Consideration of the investment base transforms the performance criteria into an investment center analysis. Recall that for a responsibility center to be treated as an investment center, the manager of that center must have control over revenues, expenses, and assets (investment). The following two criteria include the concept of investment base in the analysis. They are ROI (return on investment) and RE (residual earnings).

Return on investment (ROI)

It seems reasonable that a segment which has a large amount of assets should earn more (in an absolute sense) than a segment that has a small amount of assets. ROI gives consideration to this by calculating the return (earnings) as a percentage of the assets employed (investment):

$$\text{ROI} = \frac{\text{Earnings}}{\text{Investment}}$$

Illustration 24.7: Computation of return on investment (ROI)

		Segment			
		(1)	(2)	(3)	Total
a.	Earnings	$ 100,000	$ 500,000	$ 250,000	$ 850,000
b.	Investment	1,000,000	2,500,000	1,000,000	4,500,000
	Return on investment (a) ÷ (b) ..	10%	20%	25%	18.89%

To illustrate, assume the facts shown in Illustration 24.7 for a company with three segments.

If absolute dollars of earnings are used to evaluate performance, segment 2 appears to be doing twice as well as segment 3.

But the use of ROI as a criterion for evaluating the segments indicates that segment 3 is really performing the best (25 percent), segment 2 is next (20 percent), and segment 1 is performing the worst (10 percent). ROI is therefore a more useful indicator of the relative performance of segments than absolute earnings.

Although ROI appears to be a quite simple and straightforward computation, there are several alternative methods to make the calculation. These alternatives focus on what is meant by "earnings" and "investment." Illustration 24.8 shows various definitions and applicable situations for each type of computation. Also, before calculating ROI, an indication must be made of the valuation basis to be used for plant assets. As discussed earlier in the

Illustration 24.8: Possible definitions of "earnings" and "investment"

Situation	Definition of Earnings	Definition of Investment
1. Evaluation of the earning power of the company. Do not use for segments or segment managers due to inclusion of noncontrollable expenses.	Net income of the company.*	Total assets of the company.†
2. Evaluation of rate of earnings contribution of segment. Do not use for segment managers due to inclusion of noncontrollable expenses.	Contribution to indirect expenses.	Assets directly used by and identified with the segment.
3. Evaluation of earnings performance of segment manager.	"Controllable" earnings. This would begin with contribution to indirect expenses and would eliminate any revenues and direct expenses not under the control of the segment manager.	Assets under the control of the segment manager.

* Often *net operating income* is used; this is defined as earnings before interest and taxes.
† *Operating assets* are often used in the calculation. This definition excludes assets not used in normal operations.

chapter, possible valuation bases include original cost, cost less accumulated depreciation, and current replacement cost. Each of the valuation bases has merits and drawbacks.

The use of cost less accumulated depreciation as a valuation base is probably the most widely used and is easily determined. But since there are many types of depreciation methods, comparisons between segments or firms may be difficult. Also, as book value decreases, a constant income would result in a steadily increasing ROI. The use of original cost eliminates the problem of decreasing book value, but since the cost of old assets was less than the cost of new assets, income from old assets can be much less than income from new assets to realize the same ROI. Current replacement cost is difficult to use because replacement cost figures are often not available, but this base does eliminate some of the problems caused by the other two methods. Whichever valuation basis is adopted, all ROI calculations that are to be used for comparative purposes should be made consistently.

Expanded form of ROI computation. It is sometimes useful to break the ROI formula into its two component parts as follows:

$$\text{ROI} = \frac{\text{Earnings}}{\text{Sales}} \times \frac{\text{Sales}}{\text{Investment}}$$

The first part of the formula, Earnings/Sales, is called margin or return on sales. The *margin* refers to the percentage relationship of earnings or profits to sales. This percentage shows the number of cents of profit that are generated by each dollar of sales. The second part of the formula, Sales/Investment, is called turnover. *Turnover* shows the number of dollars of sales generated by each dollar of investment. Turnover measures how effectively each dollar of assets was used.

As was mentioned in Chapter 20, there are several ways to increase ROI. A manager may choose one of the following methods:

1. Concentrate on increasing profit margin while holding turnover constant. Pursuing this strategy would involve leaving selling prices constant and making every effort to increase efficiency and thereby reduce expenses.
2. Concentrate on increasing turnover by reducing the investment in assets while holding income and sales constant. For example, working capital could be decreased, thereby reducing the investment in assets.
3. Actions could possibly be taken which affect both margin and turnover. For example, disposing of nonproductive depreciable assets would decrease investment while also increasing earnings (through the reduction of depreciation expense). Thus, both margin and turnover would increase. An advertising campaign would probably increase sales and earnings. Turnover would increase, and margin might increase or decrease depending on the relative amounts of the increases in earnings and sales.

Illustration 24.9 shows possible outcomes of some of these strategies on ROI.

Illustration 24.9:   Strategies for increasing ROI

Past year return on investment:

$$ROI = Margin \times Turnover$$
$$ROI = \frac{Earnings}{Sales} \times \frac{Sales}{Investment}$$
$$ROI = \frac{\$100,000}{\$2,000,000} \times \frac{\$2,000,000}{\$1,000,000}$$
$$ROI = 5 \text{ percent} \times 2 \text{ times}$$
$$ROI = 10 \text{ percent}$$

1. Increase margin through reducing expenses by $40,000; no effect on sales or investment.

$$ROI = \frac{\$140,000}{\$2,000,000} \times \frac{\$2,000,000}{\$1,000,000}$$
$$ROI = 7 \text{ percent} \times 2 \text{ times}$$
$$ROI = 14 \text{ percent}$$

2. Increase turnover through reducing investment in assets by $200,000; no effect on sales or earnings.

$$ROI = \frac{\$100,000}{\$2,000,000} \times \frac{\$2,000,000}{\$800,000}$$
$$ROI = 5 \text{ percent} \times 2\frac{1}{2} \text{ times}$$
$$ROI = 12\frac{1}{2} \text{ percent}$$

3(a). Increase margin and turnover through disposing of nonproductive depreciable assets; earnings increased by $10,000; investment decreased by $200,000.

$$ROI = \frac{\$110,000}{\$2,000,000} \times \frac{\$2,000,000}{\$800,000}$$
$$ROI = 5.5 \text{ percent} \times 2.5 \text{ times}$$
$$ROI = 13.75 \text{ percent}$$

3(b). Increase margin and turnover through increased advertising; sales increased by $500,000 and earnings by $50,000; no effect on investment.

$$ROI = \frac{\$150,000}{\$2,500,000} \times \frac{\$2,500,000}{\$1,000,000}$$
$$ROI = 6 \text{ percent} \times 2\frac{1}{2} \text{ times}$$
$$ROI = 15 \text{ percent}$$

3(c). Increase turnover with a decrease in margin through increased advertising; sales increased by $500,000 and earnings by $12,500; no effect on investment.

$$ROI = \frac{\$112,500}{\$2,500,000} \times \frac{\$2,500,000}{\$1,000,000}$$
$$ROI = 4.5 \text{ percent} \times 2\frac{1}{2} \text{ times}$$
$$ROI = 11.25 \text{ percent}$$

Residual earnings

The use of ROI as the sole criterion for evaluating performance can result in what is termed suboptimization. *Suboptimization* occurs when a segment manager takes an action that is in the segment's best interest (i.e., raises that segment's ROI), but that action is not in the best interest of the company as a whole.

To prevent such suboptimization, companies sometimes use the concept of residual earnings. *Residual earnings (RE)* are defined as the amount of earnings a segment has in excess of the desired minimum ROI. Each company will set its own minimum desired ROI based on many factors including expected growth rate, debt coverage, industry technology, and desired returns to stockholders.

Residual earnings (RE) = Earnings − (Investment × Desired minimum ROI)

To illustrate, assume the manager of segment 3 in Illustration 24.10 has an opportunity to take on a project involving an investment of $100,000 that is estimated to return $22,000 or 22 percent on investment. Since the segment is already realizing a ROI of 25 percent, the manager may decide to reject the project. This is a valid decision from the manager's point of view because to accept the project will cause the segment's ROI to decline. But from a company standpoint ROI is 18.89 percent, and accepting the project would increase the overall company ROI.

When the concept of RE is applied to the segments as a measure of performance, the manager of segment 3 has shown increased achievement through the acceptance of the project and the company as a whole is better off. When RE are used to evaluate performance, the segment rated as the best is the segment with the greatest amount of RE rather than the one with the highest ROI. Segment managers will then take those actions which will increase their segments' RE.

When calculating RE for a *segment,* the earnings and investment definitions are contributions to indirect expenses and assets directly used by and identified with the segment. When calculating RE for a *manager* of a segment,

Illustration 24.10: Computation of residual earnings (RE)

		Segment 1	Segment 2	Segment 3	Total company
a.	Earnings	$ 100,000	$ 500,000	$ 250,000	$ 850,000
b.	Investment	1,000,000	2,500,000	1,000,000	4,500,000
c.	Rate of return on investment (ROI)	10%	20%	25%	18.89%
d.	Desired minimum ROI (10%)	$ 100,000	$ 250,000	$ 100,000	*
e.	Residual earnings	–0–	250,000	150,000	*

* The RE concept is generally not used for evaluating an entire company, since the problem of suboptimization, by definition, does not exist.

With acceptance of project by segment 3, the figures would be as follows:

		Segment 1	Segment 2	Segment 3	Total company
a.	Earnings	$ 100,000	$ 500,000	$ 272,000*	$ 872,000
b.	Investment	1,000,000	2,500,000	1,100,000†	4,600,000
c.	Rate of return on investment (ROI)	10%	20%	24.7%	18.96%
d.	Desired minimum ROI (10%)	$ 100,000	$ 250,000	$ 110,000	
e.	Residual earnings	–0–	250,000	162,000	

* $250,000 + (22 percent of $100,000).
† $1,000,000 original investment + $100,000 new investment.

the earnings and investment definitions should be earnings controllable by the manager and assets under the "control" of the segment manager.

In evaluating performance of a segment or a segment manager, comparisons should be made not only with the current budget and with other segments or managers within the company but also with past performance of that segment or manager and with similar segments or managers in other companies. Consideration must be given to general economic conditions, market conditions for the product being produced, and so on. A superior segment in Company A may be earning a return of 12 percent, which is above similar segments in other companies but below other segments in Company A. The other segments in Company A may be more profitable because of market conditions and the nature of the products rather than because of the performance of the segment managers. Careful judgment must be used whenever performance is evaluated.

SEGMENTAL REPORTING IN EXTERNAL FINANCIAL STATEMENTS

Formerly, segmental information was reported only to management for internal decision-making purposes. In December 1976, the Financial Accounting Standards Board issued *Statement of Financial Accounting Standards No. 14,* "Financial Reporting for Segments of a Business Enterprise." This *Statement* requires publicly held companies to publish certain segmental information in their annual financial statements. Thus, external users of financial statements now have segmental information to aid them in their decisions regarding these companies.

NEW TERMS INTRODUCED IN CHAPTER 24*

Budget variance
A difference between a budgeted and actual amount for an item.

Contribution margin
Sales revenues less variable expenses.

Contribution margin format
An income statement format for a segment which shows the contribution margin (Sales − Variable expenses).

Contribution to indirect expenses
The income of a segment when only direct expenses are deducted from segmental revenues.

Controllable profits of a segment
Earnings of a segment when expenses under the control of the manager are deducted from revenues under the control of the manager.

Cost objective
A segment, product, or other item for which costs may be accumulated.

Current replacement cost
The cost of replacing the present assets with similar assets in the same condition as those now in use.

Decentralization
The extent to which management decision making is dispersed among lower levels of the organization.

Direct cost (expense)
A cost which is directly traceable to a given cost object.

Expense center
A segment of a company having only expense items and no direct revenue from the sale of goods or services. Examples include the accounting department and the maintenance department.

* Some terms listed in earlier chapters are repeated here for your convenience.

Indirect cost (expense)
A cost that is not directly traceable to or has been allocated to a given cost object.

Investment center
A segment of a company having revenues, expenses, and an appropriate investment base.

Management by exception
The concept that upper level management does not need to examine operating details of subordinate levels unless there appears to be a problem (an exception).

Margin (as used in ROI)
Equal to $\dfrac{\text{Earnings}}{\text{Sales}}$.

Net income of a segment
The income of a segment when all of its expenses (direct and indirect) are deducted from its revenues.

Original cost
The price paid to acquire an asset.

Original cost less accumulated depreciation
Equal to the book value of an asset—the amount paid less total depreciation taken.

Profit center
Segment of a company having both revenue and expense items.

Relative control
Means the manager has control over most of the factors which influence a given budget item.

Residual earnings (RE)
The amount of earnings a segment has in excess of the desired minimum ROI. Residual earnings

are equal to Earnings − (Investment × Desired minimun ROI).

Responsibility accounting
Refers to an accounting system that collects, summarizes, and reports accounting data according to the responsibilities of the individual managers. The responsibility reports provide information needed to evaluate each manager on the basis of the revenue and expense items over which that manager has control.

Responsibility center
A segment of an organization for which a particular executive is responsible.

Return on investment (ROI)
Equal to $\dfrac{\text{Earnings}}{\text{Investment}}$ or $\dfrac{\text{Earnings}}{\text{Sales}} \times \dfrac{\text{Sales}}{\text{Investment}}$.

Segment
A fairly autonomous unit or division of a company.

Suboptimization
A situation that occurs when an individual within a company takes an action that benefits one segment but is not in the best interest of the company.

Transfer price
An artificial price used when goods or services are transferred from one segment to another segment within the same company.

Turnover
Equal to $\dfrac{\text{Sales}}{\text{Investment}}$.

DEMONSTRATION PROBLEM

The Corey Company has two segments. Results of operations for 1984 were as follows:

	Segment 1	Segment 2	Total
Sales	$50,000	$75,000	$125,000
Variable expenses	35,000	45,000	80,000
Fixed expenses:			
Direct	5,000	14,000	19,000
Indirect			7,000

The company has total operating assets of $175,000, of which $160,000 are identified with the segments as follows:

	Segment 1	Segment 2
Assets directly used by and identified with the segment	$60,000	$100,000

Required:

  a. Prepare a statement showing the contribution margin, contribution to indirect expenses for each segment, and the total income for the Corey Company.

  b. Determine the return on investment for evaluating each segment and then for the entire company

  c. Comment on the results of (*a*) and (*b*).

Solution to demonstration problem

a.

COREY COMPANY
Income Statement Showing Segmental
Contributions to Indirect Expenses
For the Year Ended December 31, 1984

	Segment 1	*Segment 2*	*Total*
Sales	$50,000	$75,000	$125,000
Less: variable expenses	35,000	45,000	80,000
Contribution margin	$15,000	$30,000	$ 45,000
Less: direct fixed expenses	5,000	14,000	19,000
Contribution to indirect expenses	$10,000	$16,000	$ 26,000
Less: indirect fixed expenses			7,000
Net income			$ 19,000

b. 1. $\text{ROI} = \dfrac{\text{Contribution to indirect expenses}}{\text{Assets directly used by and identified with the segment}}$

Segment 1   *Segment 2*

$$\text{ROI} = \frac{\$10,000}{\$60,000} = 16.67\% \qquad \text{ROI} = \frac{\$16,000}{\$100,000} = 16\%$$

2. $\text{ROI} = \dfrac{\text{Net operating income}}{\text{Operating assets}} = \dfrac{\$19,000}{\$175,000} = 10.9\%$

  c. In part (*a*), segment 2 showed a higher contribution to indirect expenses. But in (*b*), segment 1 showed a higher return on investment. This shows that when a segment is evaluated as a profit center, the center with the highest investment base will usually show the best results. But when the segment is evaluated as an investment center, the segment with the highest investment base will not necessarily show the highest return. The computations in (*b*) also demonstrate that the return on investment for the company as a whole will be lower than the segments because of the increased investment base.

QUESTIONS

1. What is the fundamental principle of responsibility accounting?

2. Hope Company manufactures refrigerators. Below are listed several costs that occur. Indicate whether or not the shop supervisor can control each of the listed items.

 a. Depreciation.
 b. Repairs.
 c. Small tools.
 d. Supplies.
 e. Bond interest.

3. List five important factors that should be considered in designing reports for a responsibility accounting system.

4. Describe a segment of a business enterprise that is best treated as an expense center. List four indirect expenses that may be allocated to such an expense center.

5. Name and describe three possible reporting bases for evaluating business segments.

6. What is the logic of using an investment center as a basis for performance evaluation?

7. How soon should accounting reports be prepared after the end of the performance measurement period? Explain.

8. Compare and contrast an expense center and an investment center.

9. Which categories of items must a segment manager have control over for the investment center concept to be applicable?

10. What connection is there between the extent of decentralization and the investment center concept?

11. Give some of the advantages of decentralization of decision making.

12. Differentiate between a direct cost and an indirect cost of a segment. What happens to each category if the segment to which they are related is eliminated?

13. Is it possible for a cost to be "direct" to one cost objective and "indirect" to another cost objective? Explain.

14. Describe some of the methods by which indirect expenses are usually allocated to a segment.

15. Give the general formula for return on investment (ROI). How may this be split into two components?

16. Give the three sets of definitions for "earnings" and "investment" which may be used in ROI calculations, explaining when each set is applicable.

17. Give the various valuation bases that could be used for plant assets in investment center calculations. Discuss some of the advantages and disadvantages of these methods.

18. In what way is the use of the residual earnings (RE) concept superior to use of ROI?

19. How are RE determined?

20. If the RE for segment manager A were $50,000 while the RE for segment manager B were $100,000, does this necessarily mean that B is a better manager than A? Explain.

21. What purpose is served by setting transfer prices?

EXERCISES

E–1. The following information refers to the toy shop of the Entertainment Company for the month of May:

	Amount	Over or (under) budget
Supplies	$ 50,000	$(10,000)
Repairs and maintenance	250,000	20,000
Overtime	100,000	10,000
Salary of supervisor	30,000	(5,000)
Salary of plant manager	40,000	–0–
Allocation of company accounting costs	30,000	10,000
Allocation of depreciation	20,000	(5,000)

Required:

Using the above information, prepare a responsibility report for the *supervisor* of the toy shop for the month of May. (Ignore year-to-date expenses.)

E–2.   Present the following information for segment A in the contribution margin format.

Sales $2,000,000
Variable selling and administrative expenses 150,000
Fixed direct manufacturing expenses 50,000
Variable manufacturing expenses 600,000
Fixed direct selling and administrative expenses 250,000

E–3.   Given the following data, prepare a schedule which shows contribution margin, contribution to indirect expenses, and net income of the segment:

Direct fixed expenses ..... $ 75,000
Indirect fixed expenses 60,000
Sales 520,000
Variable expenses 360,000

What would be the effect on company earnings if the segment were eliminated?

E–4.   Three segments (A, B, and C) of the Bob Company have net sales of $500,000, $300,000, and $100,000, respectively. A decision is made to allocate the pool of $40,000 of administrative overhead expenses of the home office to the segments, using net sales as a basis for allocation.

    a. How much should be allocated to each segment?

    b. If segment C is eliminated, how much will be allocated to A and B?

E–5.   Two segments (tires and batteries) showed the following data for the most recent year:

	Tires	*Batteries*
Contribution to indirect expenses	$ 250,000	$ 300,000
Assets directly used by and identified with the segment	750,000	1,300,000
Sales	2,000,000	4,000,000

    a. Calculate ROI for each segment in the most direct manner.

    b. Calculate ROI using the margin and turnover components.

E–6.   For segment B of the Dog Company, the following data are available:

Net income of the segment .... $ 20,000
Contribution to indirect expenses 50,000
Controllable earnings 30,000
Total assets related to the segment 250,000
Assets directly used by segment 150,000
Assets under the "control" of segment manager ... 100,000

Determine the ROI for evaluating (*a*) the earnings performance of the manager of segment B and (*b*) the rate of earnings contribution of the segment.

E–7.   Determine the effect of each of the following on the margin, turnover, and ROI of the tire segment in Exercise E–5. Consider each change independently of the others.

    a. Direct variable expenses were reduced by $10,000, and indirect expenses were reduced by $20,000. Sales and assets were unaffected.

    b. Assets used by the segment were reduced by $150,000, while earnings and sales were unaffected.

c. An advertising campaign increased sales by $200,000 and earnings by $50,000. Assets directly used by the segment were unaffected.

E–8. The Wheat Company has three segments: A, B, and C. Data concerning "earnings" and "investment" were as follows:

	A	*B*	*C*
Contribution to indirect expenses	$ 30,000	$ 60,000	$ 80,000
Assets directly used by and identified with the segment	200,000	400,000	900,000

Assuming that the minimum desired ROI is 10 percent, calculate the residual earnings (RE) of each of the segments. Do the results indicate that any of the segments should be eliminated?

E–9. Assume that for segment A in Exercise E–8, $10,000 of the direct expenses and $25,000 of the segmental assets are not under the control of the segment manager. Top management wishes to evaluate the segment manager's earnings performance. Calculate the manager's ROI and RE. (Because certain expenses and assets are not controllable by the segment manager, the minimum desired ROI is 15 percent.)

PROBLEMS, SERIES A

P24–1–A. You were given the following information for the Mayday Company for the year ended December 31, 1984. The company is organized according to functions.

Controllable expenses	Shop A supervisor Budget	Shop A supervisor Actual	Plant manager Budget	Plant manager Actual	Vice president of manufacturing Budget	Vice president of manufacturing Actual
Office expense	$3,000	$1,500	$ 6,000	$ 7,500	$15,000	$13,500
Supervision	4,500	6,000				
Supplies (manufacturing)	6,000	7,500				
Tools	7,500	9,000				
Shop B			13,500	15,000		
Shop C			16,500	18,000		
Purchasing					21,000	25,500
Receiving					22,500	22,500
Inspection					24,000	12,000

Required:

Prepare the responsibility accounting reports for three levels of management—supervisor, plant manager, and vice president of manufacturing.

P24–2–A. The Heights Corporation has three production plants (A, B, and C). These plants are treated as responsibility centers. The following summarizes the results for the month of April 1984:

Plant	Revenue	Expenses	Investment base (gross assets)
A	$ 300,000	$ 250,000	$ 1,200,000
B	400,000	150,000	1,600,000
C	2,100,000	1,600,000	11,000,000

Required:

      a.   If the plants are treated as earnings centers, which plant manager appears to have done the best job?

      b.   If the plants are treated as investment centers, which plant manager appears to have done the best job? (Assume that plant managers are evaluated in terms of rate of return on gross assets.)

      c.   Do the results of earnings center analysis and investment center analysis give different findings? If so, why?

P24–3–A.   Seaside, Inc., allocates expenses and revenues to the two segments that it operates. It extends credit to customers under a revolving charge plan whereby all account balances not paid within 30 days are charged interest at the rate of 1½ percent per month.

       Given below are selected revenue and expense accounts and some additional data needed to complete the allocation of the one revenue amount and the expenses.

Revenue and expenses (allocation bases)

Revolving charge service revenue (net sales)	$20,000
Home office building occupancy expense (net sales)	15,000
Buying expenses (net purchases)	50,000
General administrative expenses (number of employees in department)	25,000
Insurance expense (relative average inventory plus cost of equipment and fixtures in each department)	6,000
Depreciation expense on home office equipment (net sales)	10,000

Additional data:

	Segment R	Segment S	Total
Number of employees	3	7	10
Sales (net)	$100,000	$200,000	$300,000
Purchases (net)	80,000	120,000	200,000
Average inventory	20,000	40,000	60,000
Cost of equipment and fixtures	30,000	60,000	90,000

Required:

      a.   Prepare a schedule showing allocation of the above items to segments R and S.

      b.   Present criticisms of some of these allocation bases.

P24–4–A.   Bay, Inc., is a diamond importer which operates two segments, A and B. The revenue and expense data for 1984 were as follows:

	Segment A	Segment B	Total
Net sales	$700,000	$1,000,000	$1,700,000
Service charges revenue	10,000	30,000	40,000
Direct expenses:*			
Cost of goods sold	300,000	500,000	800,000
Selling	60,000	40,000	100,000
Administrative	20,000	12,000	32,000
Bad debts	10,000	10,000	20,000
Indirect expenses (all fixed):			
Selling			300,000
Administrative			250,000

* All the direct expenses are variable except $10,000 of the selling expenses for each segment.

Required:

   a. Prepare a schedule showing the contribution margin, the contribution to indirect expenses of each segment, and net income for the company as a whole. Do not allocate indirect expenses to the segments.

   b. Assume that indirect selling expenses are to be allocated to the segments on the basis of net sales and that indirect administrative expenses are to be allocated on the basis of direct administrative expenses. Prepare a statement (starting with the contribution to indirect expenses) which shows the net income of each segment.

   c. Comment on the appropriateness of the "earnings" amounts shown in parts (*a*) and (*b*) for determining the earnings contribution of the segments.

P24–5–A.   The Smith Corporation has three segments. Results of operations for 1984 were as follows:

	Segment 1	*Segment 2*	*Segment 3*	*Total*
Sales	$25,000,000	$15,000,000	$10,000,000	$50,000,000
Variable expenses ...	18,000,000	8,500,000	6,750,000	33,250,000
Fixed expenses:				
Direct	3,500,000	1,250,000	500,000	5,250,000
Indirect				2,500,000

   The following direct fixed expenses were not under the control of the segment manager: segment 1, $250,000; segment 2, $175,000; and segment 3, $200,000.
   For the company's total operating assets of $70,000,000, the following facts exist:

	Segment 1	*Segment 2*	*Segment 3*
Assets directly used by and identified with the segment	$35,000,000	$20,000,000	$10,000,000
Assets under the "control" of the segment manager	30,000,000	16,000,000	8,000,000

Required:

   a. Prepare a statement showing the contribution margin and the contribution to indirect expenses for each segment and the total earnings of the Smith Corporation.

   b. Determine the ROI for evaluating (1) the earning power of the entire company, (2) the rate of earnings contribution of each segment, and (3) the earnings performance of each segment manager.

   c. Comment on the results of part (*b*).

P24–6–A.   The Jones Company has three segments, R, S, and T. Data regarding these segments were as follows:

	Segment R	*Segment S*	*Segment T*
Contribution to indirect expenses	$ 600,000	$ 290,000	$100,000
Earnings controllable by the manager	660,000	315,000	120,000
Assets directly used by and identified with the segment ...	5,000,000	2,000,000	500,000
Assets under the "control" of the segment manager	4,800,000	1,900,000	450,000

Required:

   a. Calculate the ROI for each segment and each segment manager. Rank them from highest to lowest.

b. Assume the minimum desired rates of return are 10 percent for a segment and 12 percent for a segment manager. Calculate the RE for each segment and for each manager. Rank them from highest to lowest.

c. Repeat (*b*), but now assume that the desired minimum rates of return are 14 percent for a segment and 16 percent for a segment manager. Rank them from highest to lowest.

d. Comment on the rankings achieved.

P24–7–A. The Blade segment of the Sword Corporation reported the following data for 1984:

Contribution to indirect expenses	$ 1,050,000
Assets directly used by and identified with the segment ...	8,400,000
Sales	16,800,000

Required:

a. Determine the margin, turnover, and ROI for the segment in 1984.

b. Determine the effect on margin, turnover, and ROI of the segment in 1985 if each of the following changes were to occur. Consider each one separately, and assume that any items not specifically mentioned remain the same as in 1984.

1. A new labor contract with the union increased expenses by $300,000 for 1985.
2. A strike in early 1985 shut down operations for two months. Sales decreased by $4,500,000, cost of goods sold by $3,000,000, and other direct expenses by $900,000.
3. Introduction of a new product caused sales to increase by $6,000,000, cost of goods sold by $4,200,000, and other direct expenses by $450,000. Assets increased by $900,000.
4. An advertising campaign was launched. As a result, sales increased by $1,500,000, cost of goods sold by $1,050,000, and other direct expenses by $450,000.

P24–8—A. The following information is available for the Shepherd Company as a whole and for the Cane segment for the year ending December 31, 1984.

	Shepherd Company overall	Cane segment Project A	Project B	Total
Sales	$4,000,000	$500,000	$750,000	$1,250,000
Earnings	450,000	100,000	90,000	190,000
Investment	3,000,000	400,000	500,000	900,000

The Shepherd Company anticipates that the above relationships (margin, turnover, and ROI) will hold true for the coming year. The Cane segment intends to add project C in 1985, with the following projected data:

	Project C
Sales	$250,000
Earnings	25,000
Investment ...	150,000

Required:

a. Using the above information, determine the ROI for 1984 for the Shepherd Company, the Cane segment, and for projects A and B separately.

b. Using ROI information, should the manager of the Cane Segment undertake project C? What problems might be encountered in using ROI as a decision-making tool?

PROBLEMS, SERIES B

P24–1–B.   You were given the following information for the Macon Company for the year ended December 31, 1984:

Controllable expenses	Plant manager Budget	Plant manager Actual	Vice president of manufacturing Budget	Vice president of manufacturing Actual	President Budget	President Actual
Office expense	$ 4,500	$ 6,000	$ 7,500	$10,500	$ 15,000	$ 10,500
Printing shop	3,000	3,000				
Iron shop	1,500	1,350				
Toaster shop	12,000	12,000				
Purchasing			15,000	16,500		
Receiving			7,500	9,000		
Inspection			12,000	10,500		
Sales manager					120,000	105,000
Controller					90,000	75,000
Treasurer					60,000	45,000
Personnel manager ...					30,000	45,000

Required:

Prepare the responsibility accounting reports for three levels of management—plant manager, vice president of manufacturing, and president.

P24–2–B.   The Joy Corporation has three production plants (X, Y, and Z). These plants are treated as responsibility centers. The following summarizes the results for the month of March 1984:

Plant	Revenue	Expenses	Investment base (gross assets)
X	$1,500,000	$ 750,000	$15,000,000
Y	3,000,000	1,200,000	22,500,000
Z	4,500,000	1,650,000	48,000,000

Required:

a.   If the plants are treated as earnings centers, which plant manager appears to have done the best job?

b.   If the plants are treated as investment centers, which plant manager appears to have done the best job? (Assume that plant managers are evaluated in terms of ROI on gross assets.)

c.   Do the results of earnings center analysis and investment center analysis give different findings? If so, why?

P24–3–B.   Prince Company allocates all of its home office expenses to its two segments, A and B. Given below are selected expense account balances and additional data upon which allocations are based:

Expense (basis of allocation)

Home office building expense (net sales)	$12,000
Buying expenses (net purchases)	10,500
Bad debts (net sales)	2,250
Depreciation of home office equipment (net sales)	3,300
Advertising expense (indirect, allocated on basis of relative amounts of direct advertising)	13,500

Insurance expense (relative amounts of equipment
plus average inventory in department)   3,600

Additional data:

	Segment A	Segment B	Total
Purchases (net)	$38,000	$12,000	$ 50,000
Sales (net)	80,000	20,000	100,000
Equipment (cost)	15,000	10,000	25,000
Advertising (direct)	4,000	2,000	6,000
Average inventory	25,000	10,000	35,000

Required:

a. Prepare a schedule showing the amounts of each type of expense allocable to segments A and B using the above data and the bases of allocation.

b. Criticize some of these allocation bases.

P24–4–B.   Wine, Inc., is a company with two segments, 1 and 2. Its revenues and expenses for 1984 are as follows:

	Segment 1	Segment 2	Total
Sales (net)	$160,000	$240,000	$400,000
Direct expenses:*			
Cost of goods sold	75,000	165,000	240,000
Selling	22,800	12,000	34,800
Administrative:			
Bad debts	5,000	3,000	8,000
Insurance	4,000	2,000	6,000
Interest	800	400	1,200
Indirect expenses (all fixed):			
Selling			30,000
Administrative			42,000

* All the direct expenses are variable except insurance and interest, which are fixed.

Required:

a. Prepare a schedule showing the contribution margin, the contribution to indirect expenses of each segment, and net income for the company as a whole. Do not allocate indirect expenses to the segments.

b. Assume that indirect selling expenses are to be allocated on the basis of net sales and that indirect administrative expenses are to be allocated on the basis of direct administrative expenses. Prepare a statement (starting with the contribution to indirect expenses) which shows the net income of each segment.

c. Comment on the appropriateness of the "earnings" amounts shown in parts (a) and (b) for determining the earnings contribution of the segments.

P24–5–B.   The following data pertain to the operating revenues and expenses for the Bell Company for 1984:

	Segment C	Segment D	Total
Sales	$600,000	$300,000	$900,000
Variable expenses	400,000	160,000	560,000
Direct fixed expenses	50,000	40,000	90,000
Indirect fixed expenses			120,000

Of the direct fixed expenses, $10,000 of those shown for segment C and $9,000 of those shown for segment D are not under the control of the segment manager.

Regarding the company's total operating assets of $1,500,000 the following facts exist:

	Segment C	Segment D
Assets directly used by and identified with the segment	$600,000	$300,000
Assets under the "control" of the segment manager	500,000	250,000

Required:

    a. Prepare a statement showing the contribution margin and the contribution to indirect expenses for each segment and the total earnings of the Ben Company.

    b. Determine the ROI for evaluating (1) the earning power of the entire company, (2) the rate of earnings contribution of each segment, and (3) the earnings performance of each segment manager.

    c. Comment on the results of part (*b*).

P24–6–B.   The Aspen Company operates with three segments, K, L, and M. Data regarding these segments were as follows:

	Segment K	Segment L	Segment M
Contribution to indirect expenses	$ 90,000	$ 50,000	$ 40,000
Earnings controllable by the manager	125,000	75,000	64,000
Assets directly used by and identified with the segment	500,000	400,000	200,000
Assets under the "control" of the segment manager	440,000	355,000	180,000

Required:

    a. Calculate the ROI for each segment and each segment manager. Rank them from highest to lowest.

    b. Assume the minimum desired rates of return are 12 percent for a segment and 20 percent for a segment manager. Calculate the RE for each segment and each manager. Rank them from highest to lowest.

    c. Repeat (*b*), but now assume the desired minimum rates of return are 17 percent for a segment and 25 percent for a segment manager. Rank them from highest to lowest.

    d. Comment on the rankings achieved.

P24–7–B.   The manager of the Ski segment of the Huntsman Corporation was faced with the following data for the year 1984:

Contribution to indirect expenses	$ 750,000
Assets directly used by and identified with the segment	9,375,000
Sales	15,000,000

Required:

    a. Determine the margin, turnover, and ROI for the segment in 1984.

    b. Determine the effect on margin, turnover, and ROI of the segment in 1985 if each of the following changes were to occur. Consider each one separately and assume that any items not specifically mentioned remain the same as in 1984.

1. A campaign to control costs resulted in $150,000 of reduced expenses.
2. Certain nonproductive assets were eliminated. As a result "investment" decreased by $750,000 and expenses decreased by $60,000.
3. An advertising campaign resulted in increasing sales by $3,000,000, cost of goods sold by $2,-250,000 and advertising expense by $450,000.
4. An investment was made in productive assets costing $750,000. As a result sales increased by $300,000 and expenses increased by $45,000.

P24–8–B.   For the year ending December 31, 1984, the Cleanser Company reported the following information for the company as a whole and for one of its segments:

		Bathroom segment		
	Cleanser Company	Tile project	Bath project	Total
Sales	$8,000,000	$ 900,000	$400,000	$1,300,000
Earnings	1,500,000	400,000	50,000	450,000
Investment	6,000,000	1,200,000	140,000	1,340,000

The Cleanser Company anticipates that the above relationships (ROI, margin, turnover) will hold true for the upcoming year. The bathroom segment is faced with the possibility of adding a new project in 1985, with the following projected data:

	Sink project
Sales	$300,000
Earnings............	70,000
Investment	250,000

Required:

a.   Determine the ROI for the Cleanser Company, the bathroom segment, and for the two projects separately for the year ending December 31, 1984.

b.   Using the above information, determine if the manager of the bathroom segment should add the sink project if ROI is a deciding factor. What problem may be encountered?

P24–9–B.   Using the data provided in P24–8–B, determine the residual earnings for all three projects and for the bathroom segment with and without the sink project if the desired ROI is 25 percent (the ROI for the company as a whole). Should the sink project be added if RE is a deciding factor?

BUSINESS DECISION PROBLEM

Respond to each of the following situations.

a.   The Dexter Company manufactures swimsuits. The company's business is seasonal so that between August and December usually 10 skilled manufacturing employees are "laid off." In order to improve morale, the financial vice president suggested that these 10 employees not be laid off in the future. Instead it was suggested that they work in general labor from August to December but still be paid their manufacturing wages of $6 per hour. General labor personnel earn $3 per hour. What are the implications of this plan for the assignment of costs to the various segments of the business?

b.   The Piper Company builds new homes. Baker is in charge of the construction department. Among other things Baker hires and supervises the carpenters and other workers who build the homes. The Piper Company does not do its own foundation work. The construction of the foundation is done by subcontractors hired by Ruff of the procurement department.

The Piper Company was about to start the development of a 500-home community. Ruff hired the Low Company to build the foundations for the homes. On the day construction was to begin, the Low Company went out of business. Consequently, construction was delayed six weeks while Ruff hired a new subcontractor. Which department should be charged with the cost of the delay in construction? Why?

c. John Calachi is supervisor of Department 39 of the Farrow Company. The annual budget for the department is as follows:

	Annual budget for Department 39
Small tools	$ 9,000
Set up	10,000
Direct labor	11,000
Direct materials	20,000
Supplies	5,000
Supervision	30,000
Property taxes	5,000
Property insurance	1,000
Depreciation, machinery	2,000
Depreciation, building	2,000
Total	$95,000

Identify the budget items that are controllable by Calachi. Calachi's salary of $20,000 is included in supervision. The remaining $10,000 in supervision is the salary of the assistant supervisor who is directly responsible to Calachi.

Chapter 25

Budgeting

CHAPTER GOALS

After study of this chapter, you should be able to:

1. Define budget and name several kinds of budgets.
2. List several benefits of a budget.
3. List five general principles of budgeting.
4. Prepare an operating budget and its supporting budgets, such as the sales budget, production and purchases budgets, and other expense budgets.
5. Prepare flexible operating budgets.
6. Prepare a financial budget and its supporting budgets.
7. Define and use correctly the new terms in the glossary.

Time and wealth are scarce resources to all individuals and organizations, and use of these resources requires planning. But planning alone is insufficient. Control is also necessary to ensure that feasible plans are actually carried out. A tool widely used in planning and controlling the use of scarce resources is a *budget.*

There are many types of budgets. *Responsibility budgets,* which were examined in the preceding chapter, are designed to judge the performance of an individual manager. *Capital budgets,* covered in Chapter 27, evaluate long-term capital projects such as the addition of equipment or the relocation of a plant. This chapter examines the *master budget,* which consists of an *operating budget* and a *financial budget.* The **operating budget** helps plan future earnings and results in a projected income statement. The *financial budget* helps management plan the financing of assets and results in a projected balance sheet.

Purposes of budgets

A *budget* is a *plan* showing the firm's objectives and how management intends to acquire and use resources to attain those objectives. A budget also shows how management intends to *control* the acquisition and use of resources in the coming period(s). A budget formalizes management's plans in quantitative terms. It also forces all levels of management to think ahead, anticipate results, and take action to remedy possible poor results.

Budgets may also be used to *motivate* individuals so that they strive to achieve stated goals. Budget-to-actual comparisons may be used to evaluate individual performance. For instance, the standard variable cost of producing a given part in a given cost center is a budget figure with which actual cost can be compared to help evaluate the performance of that cost center's manager.

The preparation and use of budgets result in many other benefits. Business activities are better *coordinated;* managers *become aware of other managers' problems;* employees may become *cost conscious* and try to *conserve* resources; the organizational plan of the company may be *reviewed* more often and changed where necessary; and a breadth of *vision,* which might not otherwise be developed, is fostered. The planning process that results in a formal budget provides an opportunity for various levels of management to think through and commit future plans to writing. In addition, a properly prepared budget will allow management to follow the management-by-exception principle by devoting attention to activities that are deviating significantly from planned levels. For all these reasons, the expected results which are reflected in the budget must be clearly stated.

Considerations in preparing a budget

Uncertainty with regard to future developments is a poor excuse for failing to budget. In fact, the less stable the conditions, the more necessary and desirable is budgeting, although the process becomes more difficult. Obviously, stable operating conditions permit greater reliance on past experience as a basis for budgeting. But it must be emphasized that budgets are based on more than past results. Future plans must also be considered. The current year's expected activities are based on current conditions. As a result, budgeted performance is more useful than past performance as a basis for judging actual results.

A budget should describe management's assumptions relating to (1) the state of the economy over the planning horizon; (2) plans for adding, deleting, or changing product lines; (3) the nature of the industry's competition; and (4) the effects of existing or possible government regulations. If assumptions change during the budget period, the effects of the changes should be analyzed and included in the evaluation of performance.

Budgets are quantitative plans for the future. But they are based mainly on past experience adjusted for future expectations. Thus, accounting data related to the past play an important part in budget preparation. The accounting system and the budget are closely related. The details of the budget must agree with the company's ledger accounts. In turn, the accounts must be designed to assist in preparing the budget, financial statements, and interim financial reports to facilitate operational control.

Accounting data and budgeted projections should be compared often during the budget period and any differences investigated. Yet budgeting is not a substitute for good management. Rather, the budget is an important tool of managerial control. Managers make decisions in budget preparation to provide an operating guideline so that results can be measured against a plan of action.

SOME GENERAL PRINCIPLES OF BUDGETING

Budgeting involves coordinating financial and nonfinancial planning to satisfy organizational goals and objectives. Although there is no foolproof method for preparing an effective budget, the following aspects should be carefully considered.

Top-management support. All management levels must be aware of the budget's importance to the firm. Plans must be clearly stated. Overemphasis on pure mechanics of the budget process should be avoided. Overall broad objectives for the corporation must be decided upon and communicated throughout the organization.

Participation in goal setting. It is generally believed that employees are more likely to strive toward organizational goals if they participate in setting them. Employees may have significant information that would help the budget process. Also, the employees can be made aware of the interrelationships among budget items.

Responsibility accounting. Individuals should be informed of management's expectations. Only those costs over which an individual has predominant control should be used in evaluating that individual's performance. As noted in the previous chapter, responsibility reports often contain budget-to-actual comparisons.

Communication of results. People should be informed of their progress promptly and clearly. Effective communication implies (1) timeliness, (2) reasonable accuracy, and (3) understandability. Results should be communicated so that any necessary adjustments to performance can be made.

Flexibility. If the basic assumptions underlying the budget change during the year, the budget should be restated. In this way, efficiency at the actual level of operations can be analyzed relative to expected performance at that level.

BEHAVIORAL IMPLICATIONS

The term *budget* has negative connotations for many employees who feel they are *subjected* to a budget. Often in the past, management has imposed a budget without considering the opinions and feelings of the personnel affected. Such a dictatorial process may result in resistance to the budget. A number of reasons may underlie such resistance, including lack of understanding of the program, concern for status, and an expectation of increased pressure to perform. Employees may believe that the performance evaluation method is unfair or that the goals are unrealistic and unattainable. They may lack confidence in the way accounting figures are generated or prefer a less formal communication and evaluation system. Often these fears are completely unfounded. But if an employee believes these problems exist, it will be very difficult to accomplish the objectives of budgeting.

Problems encountered with such *imposed* budgets have led accountants and management to participating budgeting. *Participating budgeting* means active participation by all levels of management responsible for actual performance in setting operating goals for the coming period. Managers are more likely to understand, accept, and pursue goals if they are actively involved in formulating them.

Where do accountants fit into a participatory budget process? Accountants should be *compilers* or coordinators of the budget, not *preparers.* They should be on hand during the preparation process to present and explain significant financial data. Accountants must identify the relevant cost data that will enable management's objectives to be quantified in dollars, and they are responsible for meaningful budget reports. Accountants must continually strive to make the accounting system more responsive to managerial needs that will, in turn, increase confidence in the system.

The picture of budget participation up to this point has been fairly one-sided. Studies have shown that in many organizations budget participation does not work. Whether participation works or not depends on management's leadership style and on the organization's size and structure. Participation is not the answer to all the problems of budget preparation. It is one way to achieve better results in organizations which are receptive to the philosophy of participation.

THE MASTER BUDGET

A *master budget* consists of a projected income statement (operating budget) and a projected balance sheet (financial budget) showing the organization's objectives and proposed ways of attaining them. The rest of this chapter will concentrate on how to prepare a master budget. The master budget is emphasized because of its prime importance to financial planning and control in a business entity. Illustration 25.1 presents the major elements involved in preparing a master budget.

The preparation flow proceeds from top to bottom in Illustration 25.1. The end result is a projected income statement and a projected balance sheet prepared from elements contained in previously prepared budgets or schedules.

The budgeting process starts with management's plans and objectives for the next period. These plans result in various policy decisions concerning selling price, distribution network, advertising expenditures, and environmental influences from which sales forecasts for the period (in units by product or product line) are made. Multiplying units by selling price gives the sales budget in dollars. Projected cost of goods sold is based on expected production, sales volume, and inventory policy. Volume and inventory policies influence the preparation of the purchasing budget. Detailed budgets are made for each major type of manufacturing expense on both a cost center (responsibility) basis and in the aggregate.

The projected balance sheet is prepared using information contained in the operating budget. It is also influenced by policy decisions pertaining to dividends, inventory, credit, capital expenditures, and financing plans. The planning of capital expenditures will be described in Chapter 27. Financing by debt or stock issuances was discussed in earlier chapters.

This chapter cannot cover all areas of budgeting in detail; whole books are devoted to the subject. But the following presentation provides an overview of a budgeting procedure that has been used successfully by many business enterprises. Illustration 25.1 should be studied carefully as it provides a frame of reference for the following discussion.

Preparing the operating budget

Since the projected balance sheet depends on many items in the projected income statement, the logical starting point in preparing a master budget is the projected income statement or *operating budget*. (The projected balance sheet is called the *financial budget*.) Several supporting budgets are usually prepared before the operating budget. The sales budget is the first of these.

Illustration 25.1: A flowchart of the financial planning process (an overview)

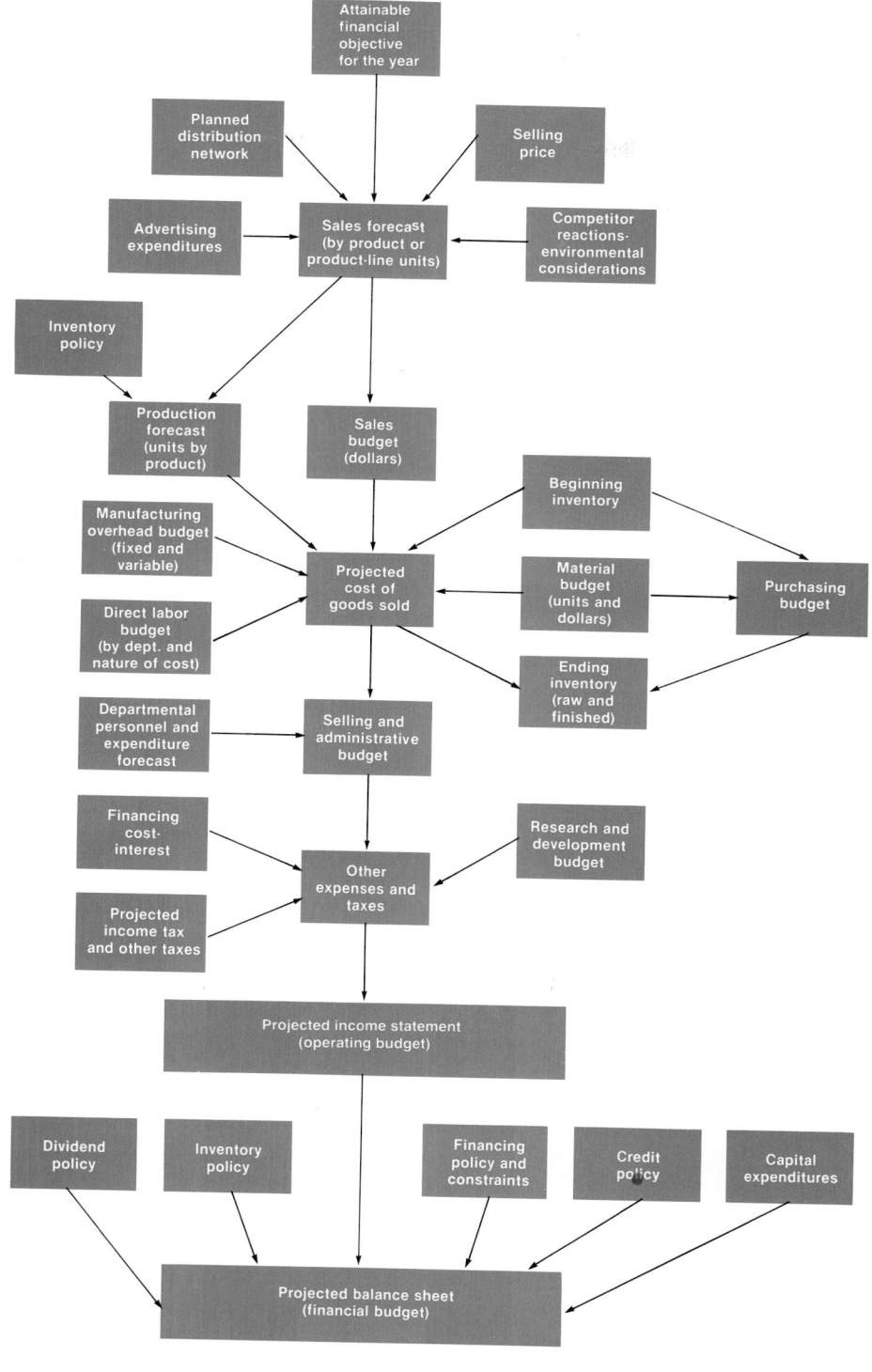

The sales budget. Preparing the sales budget is a critical step in the budgeting process. Most other budgets are derived from the sales budget, so if the sales budget is not properly prepared, the entire operating budget will be affected.

Generally, sales forecasts are based on a combination of past experience and future expectations. The expected general level of economic activity and prospects for the industry as a whole must be considered. These prospects may be influenced by population growth, per capita income, new construction, population migration, and so on. The firm's relative position in the industry must also be reviewed in light of any expected changes.

Allowances must be made for varying conditions that affect different products and territories or the strength of competitors. The effect of any changes in the expected level of advertising expenditures must be estimated. Quotas may be developed for salespersons based on sales analyses by territory, by customer, by product, and so on.

The sales manager is usually responsible for the sales budget, which is prepared first in units and then in dollars. The remaining budgets that support the operating budget are based on the sales budget in units.

The production budget. The *production budget* is geared to the sales budget and the company's inventory policy. The production budget is first developed in units. Unit costs can seldom be developed until production volume is known. The principal objective of the production budget is to coordinate in terms of time and quantity the production of goods and their sale. Careful scheduling is needed to maintain certain minimum quantities of inventory on hand while avoiding excessive inventory accumulation. Also, the cost of carrying inventory on hand must be compared with the higher unit costs frequently encountered in producing relatively small batches of a product.

The production budget is often subdivided into budgets for materials, labor, and overhead. Usually materials and labor will vary directly with production within a given *relevant range* of production. Overhead costs may not vary directly with production, but may be constant in total across the relevant range of production. For example, a certain cost may be $15,000 at 60–80 percent of capacity and $25,000 at the 80–90 percent level. The nature of these costs must be carefully analyzed at different levels of operation.

Selling, administrative, and other expense budgets (schedules). Departmental personnel and expenditure forecasts are used to budget the amounts of selling and administrative expenses. Other expenses such as interest expense, income tax expense, and research and development expenses are also estimated.

Preparing the financial budget

Preparing a projected balance sheet involves analyzing every balance sheet account. The beginning balance is taken from the balance sheet prepared at the end of the preceding period. Then, the effects of any planned activities upon each account are considered. Many accounts will be affected by items appearing in the operating budget and by either cash inflows or outflows. Cash inflows and outflows are usually shown in a cash budget.

The complexities encountered in preparing the financial budget often will require the preparation of work sheets. These schedules analyze such things as planned accounts receivable collections and balances, planned material purchases, planned inventories, changes in all accounts affected by operating costs, and the amount of federal income taxes payable. Dividend policy, financing policy and constraints, credit policy, and planned capital expenditures also affect amounts shown in the financial budget.

The preparation of a master budget for the Leed Company for 1984 will now be illustrated. If you follow the example closely, you should be able to prepare a master budget for an actual company.

THE MASTER BUDGET ILLUSTRATED

Preparing the operating budget in units for the Leed Company

The operating budget is first developed in units rather than dollars. Since revenues and most expenses vary with volume, they can be forecasted more easily after sales or production quantities are established. Assume that management forecasts sales for the year at 100,000 units. Quarterly sales are expected to be 20,000, 35,000, 20,000, and 25,000 units. Since it is company policy to stabilize production, the 100,000 units will be produced uniformly throughout the year at the rate of 25,000 units per quarter. To simplify the example, assume there are no beginning or ending work in process inventories (although it would be more realistic to assume that work in process inventories would remain stable throughout the year). The finished goods inventory on January 1, 1984, is 10,000 units.

From the above data, a schedule of budgeted sales and production in units is prepared as shown in Illustration 25.2.

Illustration 25.2: Planned sales and production in units

	Quarter ending	
	---	---
	March 31, 1984	June 30, 1984
Sales forecast	20,000	35,000
Production planned	25,000	25,000
Increase (decrease) in finished goods inventory	5,000	(10,000)
Planned beginning finished goods inventory	10,000*	15,000
Planned ending finished goods inventory	15,000	5,000

LEED COMPANY
Planned Sales and Production
(in units of product)

* Actual on January 1.

Notice that the ending inventory must be allowed to fluctuate if sales vary and a stable production policy is maintained. Thus, the finished goods inventory absorbs the difference between production and sales. Management has decided that it is less costly to deal with fluctuating inventories than with fluctuating production.

Preparing the operating budget in dollars

Next, dollars must be introduced into the analysis. A forecast of expected selling prices must be made and costs must be analyzed. The forecasted selling price and costs are shown in Illustration 25.3. Note that costs are classified according to whether they are variable or fixed and are budgeted accordingly. As noted earlier, *variable costs* vary in total directly with production or sales. *Fixed costs* are unaffected in total by the relative level of production or sales. Thus, variable costs are budgeted as a constant dollar amount *per unit,* while fixed costs are budgeted only in total. Individual budgets could be prepared for each of the identifiable operating units of the company and accumulated to form the overall budget. This is true for each budget area to be discussed in the remainder of the chapter.

Next, a schedule is prepared to forecast cost of goods sold. This schedule is shown in Illustration 25.4.

A separate budget is now prepared for all selling and administrative expenses. Several supporting schedules may be involved for items such as advertising expense, office expense, and payroll department expense. Total selling and administrative expenses for each of the first two quarters are entered into the operating budget, as shown in Illustration 25.5.

All of the items appearing in the operating budget have been discussed and explained except the income tax accrual. Income taxes are budgeted for Leed Company at an assumed rate of 50 percent of net income before taxes.

Illustration 25.3   Budget estimate of selling price and costs

LEED COMPANY
Budget Estimates of Selling Price and Costs
For the Quarters Ending March 31, and June 30, 1984

Forecasted selling price . . . . $	20
Manufacturing costs:	
Variable (per unit manufactured):	
Direct materials	2
Direct labor	6
Overhead	1
Fixed overhead (total each quarter)	75,000
Selling and administrative expenses:	
Variable (per unit sold)	2
Fixed (total each quarter)	100,000

Illustration 25.4: Planned cost of goods sold

LEED COMPANY
Planned Cost of Goods Sold

	Quarter ending	
	March 31, 1984	June 30, 1984
Beginning finished goods inventory	$130,000*	$180,000
Cost of goods manufactured:		
Direct materials (25,000 × $2)	$ 50,000	$ 50,000
Direct labor (25,000 × $6)	150,000	150,000
Variable overhead (25,000 × $1)	25,000	25,000
Fixed overhead (per Illustration 25.3)	75,000	75,000
Cost of goods manufactured (25,000 units at $12)	$300,000	$300,000
Goods available for sale	$430,000	$480,000
Ending finished goods inventory:		
(15,000 at $12)†	180,000	
(5,000 at $12)		60,000
Cost of goods sold	$250,000	$420,000

* Actual on January 1.
† First-in, first-out procedure assumed.

The operating budget illustrated

Illustration 25.5 shows the resulting operating budget. If the operating budget does not show the desired net income, new plans will have to be formulated and a new budget developed. The purpose of preparing an operating budget is to gain some knowledge of what the outcome of a period's activities will be before they actually occur.

The flexible operating budget

One of the basic principles of budgeting is to adjust the budget for changes in assumptions or in the level of operations. A technique known as flexible budgeting has been developed to cope with budgetary adjustments. This concept was introduced in Chapter 23. A *flexible operating budget* provides detailed information about budgeted expenses (and revenues) at various levels of output. For example, Illustration 25.6 shows a flexible budget for Leed Company's manufacturing overhead costs at various levels of output. In this example, supplies are considered a strictly variable cost. Supplies increase $500 for every 10 percent increase in capacity. In fact, there are probably few costs that vary in an exact linear relationship with output. Power, for example, is a semivariable cost. It varies with volume, but not in a direct relationship. For Leed Company it is assumed that beyond a minimum level, power varies directly with output at the rate of $1,000 for each 10 percent increase in volume. Insurance and maintenance are semivariable costs because they do not increase in proportion to increases in production volume. Deprecia-

Illustration 25.5: Projected statements

LEED COMPANY
Projected Income Statements
For Quarters Ending March 31 and June 30, 1984

	Quarter ending	
	March 31, 1984	June 30, 1984
Forecasted sales (20,000 and 35,000 at $20) (per Illustration 25.3)	$400,000	$700,000
Cost of goods sold (per Illustration 25.4)	250,000	420,000
Gross margin	$150,000	$280,000
Selling and administrative expenses:		
Variable (20,000 and 35,000 at $2) (per Illustration 25.3)	$ 40,000	$ 70,000
Fixed (per Illustration 25.3)	100,000	100,000
Total expenses	$140,000	$170,000
Net income before income taxes	$ 10,000	$110,000
Estimated federal income taxes (assumed to be 50%) ..	5,000	55,000
Net income	$ 5,000	$ 55,000

tion and supervision are fixed costs over this particular relevant range of activity.

A similar flexible budget may be prepared for selling and administrative expenses with supporting schedules for each expense item. Variable expenses are calculated for various levels of sales volume, while fixed costs remain constant within the relevant range.

When a flexible budget is used to appraise performance, the budgeted costs used in the appraisal are for the actual level of activity experienced.

Budget variances. A *budget variance* is the difference between an actual cost incurred at a certain level of operations and the budgeted amount *for that same level of operations.* Budget variances may be indicators of efficiency, since they emerge from a comparison of "what was" with "what should have been."

Actual costs must not be compared with budgeted costs for some *other* level of activity. To illustrate, assume that a departmental budget is prepared based on an expected production of 100,000 units—the 100 percent of capacity level in Illustration 25.6. At this level of production, the budgeted amount for supplies is $2,000, or $0.02 per unit. If by the end of the period $1,600 of supplies have been used, the first impression is that a favorable variance exists of $400. But if actual production for the period is only 90,000 units (90 percent of capacity), there is actually an unfavorable variance of $100. This is because, according to the flexible operating budget, at 90 percent of capacity only $1,500 of supplies should be used. Consequently, there appears to have been an inefficient use of supplies.

Using the same data in Illustration 25.6, maintenance may have been

Illustration 25.6: Flexible budget

Element of overhead	Volume (percent of capacity)			
	70 percent	80 percent	90 percent	100 percent
Supplies	$ 500	$ 1,000	$ 1,500	$ 2,000
Power	7,000	8,000	9,000	10,000
Insurance	4,500	4,500	5,000	5,000
Maintenance	5,800	6,200	7,200	8,000
Depreciation	40,000	40,000	40,000	40,000
Supervision	35,000	35,000	35,000	35,000
	$92,800	$94,700	$97,700	$100,000

LEED COMPANY

budgeted at $6,200 for a given period on the assumption that 80,000 units would be produced (80 percent of operating capacity). If actual maintenance costs were $6,800 for the period, this does not necessarily mean that an unfavorable variance of $600 was incurred. It depends on actual production volume. If 90,000 units were produced and maintenance costs were budgeted at $7,200 for that level of production, there was actually a favorable variance of $400 ($7,200 − $6,800).

The main advantage of flexible operating budgets is that performance can be appraised on two levels. First, the deviation from expected output can be analyzed. Then, given the actual level of operations, actual costs can be compared with expected costs for that level of output. The use of flexible budgets gives a valid basis for comparison when production volume differs from expectations.

Sometimes a flexible budget is presented for every 10 percent change in the level of operations. For instance, it may be presented for the 70, 80, 90, 100, and 110 percent levels of operations. Actual production may be somewhere between levels, say, 84 percent. For directly variable costs, the expected cost can be computed easily at any level. For *semivariable costs* (partially fixed and partially variable), the budgeted amount for any operating level other than those presented can be computed using the following formula:

Budgeted amount = Fixed portion of costs
 + (Variable portion of costs per unit × Units of output)

More complicated formulas are needed if the relationship between costs and volume above a minimum level of costs is not linear, that is, if costs do not vary proportionally with production.

Other semivariable costs may change only when a sufficiently large increase in production occurs, such as when one additional inspector must be added for every 20 percent increase in capacity used. Such semivariable costs usually can be read directly from the flexible budget.

Fixed costs are the same at any level of output over a relevant range.

The flexible budget and budget variances illustrated.   The Leed Company has prepared a detailed flexible budget for the quarter ending March

31, 1984, using the data in Illustration 25.3. The budget, based on expected sales of 20,000 units and expected production of 25,000 units, is shown in Illustration 25.7, together with actual results for the quarter.

Assume that (1) the actual selling price of all units was $20 per unit, (2) actual production was 25,000 units, and (3) actual sales were 19,000 units.

Comparing the original budget with actual results yields some useful information. It shows where actual performance deviated from planned performance. Sales were 1,000 units lower than expected, gross margin was $12,500 less than expected, and net income was $2,000 more than expected. The cost of goods manufactured section shows budgeted and actual costs for the 25,000 units produced. But the comparison does not show the expected expenditures for cost of goods sold and selling and administrative expenses for the actual level of sales attained. This information would be useful for expense control.

The company expected to sell 20,000 units but only sold 19,000. A valid analysis for expense control purposes can be made by using a flexible budget for 19,000 units for every item except those in the cost of goods manufactured section of the income statement. For the items in the cost of goods manufactured section, the budgeted and actual amounts are for 25,000 units since 25,000 units were manufactured (Illustration 25.8). In such analyses, if the number of units produced is equal to the number sold, beginning and ending inventories often are not shown. Instead, the budget may show the number of units actually sold times the budgeted unit cost of the materials, labor,

Illustration 25.7:   Comparison of expected budget and actual results

LEED COMPANY Comparison of Expected Budget and Actual Results For Quarter Ended March 31, 1984	Budget	Actual
Sales (budgeted 20,000 units, actual 19,000 units) . .	$400,000	$380,000
Cost of goods sold:		
Beginning finished goods inventory	$130,000	$130,000
Cost of goods manufactured (25,000 units):		
Direct materials	$ 50,000	$ 62,500
Direct labor	150,000	143,750
Variable overhead	25,000	31,250
Fixed overhead	75,000	75,000
Cost of goods manufactured	$300,000	$312,500
Goods available for sale	$430,000	$442,500
Ending finished goods inventory	180,000	200,000
Cost of goods sold	$250,000	$242,500
Gross margin	$150,000	$137,500
Selling and administrative expenses:		
Variable	$ 40,000	$ 28,500
Fixed	100,000	95,000
Total expenses	$140,000	$123,500
Net income before income taxes	$ 10,000	$ 14,000
Estimated federal income taxes (50%)	5,000	7,000
Net income	$ 5,000	$ 7,000

and overhead. The actual costs for materials, labor, and overhead are also shown for the number of units sold.

The flexible budget (Illustration 25.8) reveals some inefficiencies for items in the costs of goods manufactured section. For instance, direct materials cost $2.50 per unit ($62,500/25,000) instead of the $2 expected. Direct labor cost was only $5.75 per unit ($143,750/25,000) instead of the $6 expected. Variable overhead was $1.25 per unit ($31,250/25,000) instead of the $1 expected.

Net income was $5,000 more than expected at a sales level of 19,000 units. The main reason for the increase in net income was the lower than expected amounts of selling and administrative expenses. Variable selling and administrative expenses were only $1.50 per unit ($28,500/19,000) instead of the $2 expected; fixed selling and administrative expenses were only $95,000 instead of the $100,000 expected.

Preparing the financial budget for the Leed Company

To prepare a projected balance sheet, each balance sheet account must be analyzed. First, the beginning balance is taken from the balance sheet at the end of the preceding period. The balance sheet as of December 31, 1983,

Illustration 25.8: Comparison of flexible operating budget and actual results

	Budget	Actual	Budget variance over/under*
LEED COMPANY Comparison of Flexible Operating Budget and Actual Results For Quarter Ended March 31, 1984			
Sales (19,000 units)	$380,000	$380,000	–0–
Cost of goods sold:			
Beginning finished goods inventory	$130,000	$130,000	$ –0–
Cost of goods manufactured (25,000 units):			
Direct materials	$ 50,000	$ 62,500	12,500
Direct labor	150,000	143,750	6,250*
Variable overhead	25,000	31,250	6,250
Fixed overhead	75,000	75,000	–0–
Cost of goods manufactured	$300,000	$312,500	$12,500
Goods available for sale	$430,000	$442,500	$12,500
Ending finished goods inventory	192,000	200,000	8,000
Cost of goods sold (19,000 units)	$238,000	$242,500	$ 4,500
Gross margin	$142,000	$137,500	4,500*
Selling and administrative expenses:			
Variable	$ 38,000	$ 28,500	$ 9,500*
Fixed	100,000	95,000	5,000*
Total expenses	$138,000	$123,500	$14,500*
Net income before income taxes	$ 4,000	$ 14,000	$10,000
Estimated federal income taxes (50%)	2,000	7,000	5,000
Net income	$ 2,000	$ 7,000	$ 5,000

is shown in Illustration 25.9. Then the effects of planned activities on these balances are considered. Many accounts will be affected by items shown in the operating budget, by cash inflows and outflows, and by policy decisions of the firm.

The operating budget shown in Illustration 25.5 and the other illustrations previously given will be helpful in preparing Leed Company's financial budget for the first two quarters of 1984. The sources of the numbers given in the following illustrations will be discussed to explain how the financial budget should be prepared.

Accounts receivable. To prepare a financial budget, schedules other than the ones already prepared in connection with the operating budget must be prepared. The first of these is the accounts receivable schedule shown in Illustration 25.10. This schedule assumes that 60 percent of the current quarter's sales will be collected in that quarter and the remaining 40 percent will

Illustration 25.9: Balance sheet at beginning of period

LEED COMPANY
Balance Sheet
December 31, 1983

Assets

Current assets:

Cash		$ 130,000
Accounts receivable		200,000
Inventories:		
Materials	$ 40,000	
Finished goods	130,000	170,000
Prepaid expenses		20,000
Total current assets		$ 520,000

Property, plant, and equipment:

Land		$ 60,000
Buildings	$1,000,000	
Less: Accumulated depreciation	400,000	600,000
Equipment	$ 600,000	
Less: Accumulated depreciation	180,000	420,000
Total property, plant, and equipment		$1,080,000
Total assets		$1,600,000

Liabilities and Stockholders' Equity

Current liabilities:

Accounts payable	$ 80,000
Accrued liabilities	160,000
Federal income taxes payable	100,000
Total current liabilities	$ 340,000

Stockholders' equity:

Capital stock (100,000 shares of $10 par value)	$1,000,000
Retained earnings	260,000
Total stockholders' equity	$1,260,000
Total liabilities and stockholders' equity	$1,600,000

Illustration 25.10:   Planned accounts receivable collections and balances

LEED COMPANY
Planned Accounts Receivable Collections and Balances

	Quarter ending	
	March 31, 1984	June 30, 1984
Planned balance at beginning of quarter	$200,000*	$160,000
Planned sales for period (per Illustration 25.5)	400,000	700,000
Total	$600,000	$860,000
Projected collections during quarter (per discussion in text)	440,000	580,000
Planned balance at end of quarter	$160,000	$280,000

* Actual on January 1.

be collected in the following quarter. Thus, collections for the first quarter will be $440,000; that is, 60 percent of budgeted sales of $400,000 for the first quarter plus the uncollected sales of the previous quarter [0.6($400,000) + $200,000]. Second quarter collections will be $580,000 [0.6($700,000) + $160,000]. Several other simplifying assumptions have been made; for example, there are no sales returns or allowances, no discounts, and no uncollectible accounts. All sales are assumed to be on a credit basis.

Inventories.   A schedule of planned purchases and inventories should be prepared. Planned usage and cost per unit are taken from the production schedules. Assuming no work in process inventories, there will be only materials and finished goods inventories.

Illustration 25.11 shows planned purchases and inventories of materials. Materials inventory is normally maintained at a level of one half of next quarter's planned usage. The beginning inventory was greater than normal because of a strike threat in the supplier company. This threat has now passed,

Illustration 25.11:   Planned materials purchases and inventories

LEED COMPANY
Planned Materials Purchases and Inventories

	Quarter ending	
	March 31, 1984	June 30, 1984
Planned usage (25,000 × $2) (per Illustration 25.4)	$50,000	$50,000
Planned ending inventory (½ × 25,000 × $2) (per discussion in text)	25,000	25,000
Planned materials available for use	$75,000	$75,000
Inventory at beginning of quarter	40,000*	25,000
Planned purchases for the quarter	$35,000	$50,000

* Actual on January 1.

and the materials inventory will be reduced in the first quarter to the normal planned level.

The calculation of planned ending finished goods inventories is included in Illustration 25.4.

Accounts affected by operating costs. Individual schedules could be prepared for each of the accounts affected by operating costs. But for illustrative purposes a schedule will be prepared combining the analyses of all the accounts affected by material purchases or operating costs.

The following assumptions are made:

1. All purchases of materials are made on account.
2. Direct labor incurred is credited to accrued liabilities.
3. Manufacturing overhead incurred is credited to the following accounts:

	Quarter ending	
	March 31	June 30
Accounts Payable	$ 16,000	$ 13,000
Accrued Liabilities	60,000	64,000
Prepaid Expenses	6,000	5,000
Accumulated Depreciation—Building	5,000	5,000
Accumulated Depreciation—Equipment	13,000	13,000
Total	$100,000	$100,000

4. Selling and administrative expenses incurred are credited to the following accounts:

	Quarter ending	
	March 31	June 30
Accounts Payable	$ 5,000	$ 10,000
Accrued Liabilities	130,000	154,000
Prepaid Expenses	2,000	3,000
Accumulated Depreciation—Building	1,000	1,000
Accumulated Depreciation—Equipment	2,000	2,000
Total	$140,000	$170,000

5. Planned cash payments are as follows:

	Quarter ending	
	March 31	June 30
Accounts Payable	$ 80,000	$ 56,000
Accrued Liabilities	330,000	354,000
Prepaid Expenses	–0–	10,000
	$410,000	$420,000

Illustration 25.12 shows analyses of the accounts credited as a result of the above data. It provides a considerable amount of information needed in constructing financial budgets for the quarters ended March 31, 1984, and June 30, 1984. The balances on both dates for Accounts Payable, Accrued Liabilities, Prepaid Expenses, Accumulated Depreciation—Building, and Accumulated Depreciation—Equipment are computed in the schedule.

Illustration 25.12: Analyses of accounts credited for materials purchases and operating costs

LEED COMPANY
Analyses of Accounts Credited for Materials Purchases and Operating Costs

	Total	Accounts payable (Cr.)	Accrued liabilities (Cr.)	Prepaid expenses (Dr.)	Accumulated depreciation Building (Cr.)	Accumulated depreciation Equipment (Cr.)
Purchases or operating costs, quarter ending March 31:						
Materials (per Illustration 25.11)	$ 35,000	$ 35,000				
Direct labor (per Illustration 25.4)	150,000		$150,000			
Overhead (per Illustration 25.4)	100,000	16,000	60,000	$ 6,000 Cr.	$ 5,000	$ 13,000
Selling and administrative expenses (per Illustration 25.5)	140,000	5,000	130,000	2,000 Cr.	1,000	2,000
Total	$425,000	$ 56,000	$340,000	$ 8,000 Cr.	$ 6,000	$ 15,000
Beginning balances (per Illustration 25.9)		80,000	160,000	20,000 Dr.	400,000	180,000
		$136,000	$500,000	$12,000 Dr.	$406,000	$195,000
Planned cash payments		80,000	330,000			
Planned balances, March 31		$ 56,000	$170,000	$12,000 Dr.	$406,000	$195,000
Purchases or operating costs, quarter ending June 30:						
Materials (per Illustration 25.11)	$ 50,000	$ 50,000				
Direct labor (per Illustration 25.4)	150,000		$150,000			
Overhead (per Illustration 25.4)	100,000	13,000	64,000	$ 5,000 Cr.	$ 5,000	$ 13,000
Selling and administrative expenses (per Illustration 25.5)	170,000	10,000	154,000	3,000 Cr.	1,000	2,000
Total	$470,000	$ 73,000	$368,000	$ 8,000 Cr.	$ 6,000	$ 15,000
Total including March 31 balances		$129,000	$538,000	$ 4,000 Dr.	$412,000	$210,000
Planned cash payments		56,000	354,000	10,000 Dr.		
Planned balances, June 30		$ 73,000	$184,000	$14,000 Dr.	$412,000	$210,000

Federal income taxes payable. A separate schedule could be prepared showing the changes in the Federal Income Taxes Payable account. Balances reported in the financial budgets assume that one half of the $100,000 liability shown in the December 31, 1983, balance sheet is paid in each of the first two quarters of 1984 (Illustration 25.15). The accrual for the current quarter is added (Illustration 25.5). Thus, the balance on March 31, 1984, is $55,000 ($100,000 − $50,000 + $5,000). The balance on June 30, 1984, is $60,000 ($55,000 − $50,000 + $55,000). On June 30, the balance equals the accrual for the current year—$5,000 for the first quarter and $55,000 for the second quarter.

Cash budget. After the above analyses have been prepared, sufficient information should be available to prepare the cash budget and compute the balance in the Cash account on March 31 and June 30, 1984. To prepare a cash budget, information about cash receipts and cash disbursements is required.

Illustration 25.13:   Planned cash receipts

LEED COMPANY		
Planned Cash Receipts		
		Quarter ending
	March 31, 1984	***June 30, 1984***
Collections on accounts receivable:		
From preceding quarter's sales	$200,000	$160,000
From current quarter's sales	240,000 (0.6 × $400,000)	420,000 (0.6 × $700,000)
Total cash receipts (per Illustration 25.10) . .	$440,000	$580,000

Cash receipts. The cash receipts schedule can be prepared from the information used to compute the accounts receivable schedule. For example, information concerning the collection of sales can be obtained from the accounts receivable budget. A schedule of planned cash receipts for the Leed Company is shown in Illustration 25.13.

Cash disbursements. Cash is needed to pay for purchases, wages, rent, interest, income taxes, cash dividends, and other expenses. The amount of each cash disbursement may be obtained from other budgets or schedules. Illustration 25.14 shows the cash disbursements schedule for the Leed Company. The illustration shows where the information came from except for the payment of federal income taxes and dividends. Income taxes were discussed earlier and are assumed to be 50 percent of net income before taxes. It is assumed that $20,000 of dividends will be paid in the first quarter and $40,000 in the second quarter.

Once cash receipts and disbursements have been determined, a cash budget can be prepared, as shown in Illustration 25.15, for the Leed Company. The cash budget is a plan indicating expected inflows and outflows of cash. It helps management decide whether enough cash will be available for short-term needs. If the cash budget indicates a cash shortage at a certain date, the company may need to borrow money on a short-term basis. If the expected

Illustration 25.14:   Planned cash disbursements

LEED COMPANY		
Planned Cash Disbursements		
		Quarter ending
	March 31, 1984	***June 30, 1984***
Payment of accounts payable (per Illustration 25.12)	$ 80,000	$ 56,000
Payment of accrued liabilities (per Illustration 25.12)	330,000	354,000
Payment of federal income tax liability	50,000	50,000
Payment of dividends	20,000	40,000
Expenses prepaid (per Illustration 25.12)	–0–	10,000
Total cash disbursements	$480,000	$510,000

Illustration 25.15: Planned cash flows and cash balances

LEED COMPANY
Planned Cash Flows and Cash Balances

	Quarter ending	
	March 31, 1984	June 30, 1984
Planned balance at beginning of quarter	$130,000*	$ 90,000
Planned cash receipts:		
Collections of accounts receivable (per Illustration 25.13)	440,000	580,000
	$570,000	$670,000
Planned cash disbursements:		
Payment of accounts payable (per Illustration 25.12)	$ 80,000	$ 56,000
Payment of accrued liabilities (per Illustration 25.12)	330,000	354,000
Payment of federal income tax liability	50,000	50,000
Payment of dividends	20,000	40,000
Expenses prepaid (per Illustration 25.12)	–0–	10,000
Total disbursements	$480,000	$510,000
Planned balance at end of quarter	$ 90,000	$160,000

* Actual on January 1.

cash balance appears to be higher than necessary, the company may wish to invest the extra funds for short periods rather than leave the cash idle.

The financial budgets illustrated

The financial budgets for the quarters ended March 31, 1984, and June 30, 1984, are now complete and are shown in Illustration 25.16.

The financial budgets for the two quarters complete the preparation of the master budget. Management now has on hand information to help it appraise the policies it has adopted before implementing them. If the results of these policies, as shown by the master budget, are unsatisfactory, the policies can be changed before serious problems arise. For example, the Leed Company management had decided to stabilize production. The master budget shows that production can be stabilized even though sales fluctuate widely. But the planned ending inventory at June 30 may be considered somewhat low in view of the fluctuations in sales. Management now knows this in advance and can take action if necessary.

Purchases budget for a mechandising company

Throughout the chapter, discussion has centered on the preparation of operating and financial budgets for a manufacturer. Suppose a budget is being prepared for a retail merchandising business, such as a dress shop or a furniture store. In this case, a purchases budget will be prepared instead of a production budget. To compute the purchases for each quarter, the cost of the goods to be sold during the quarter and the inventory required at the end of the quarter must be estimated.

Illustration 25.16:   Projected balance sheet

LEED COMPANY
Projected Balance Sheet

	March 31, 1984	June 30, 1984
Assets		
Current assets:		
Cash (per Illustration 25.15)	$ 90,000	$ 160,000
Accounts receivable (per Illustration 25.10)	160,000	280,000
Inventories:		
Materials (per Illustration 25.11)	25,000	25,000
Finished goods (per Illustration 25.4)	180,000	60,000
Prepaid expenses (per Illustration 25.12)	12,000	14,000
Total current assets	$ 467,000	$ 539,000
Property, plant, and equipment:		
Land (per Illustration 25.9)	$ 60,000	$ 60,000
Buildings ($1,000,000 less accumulated depreciation		
of $406,000 and $412,000) (per Illustrations 25.9 and 25.12) ..	594,000	588,000
Equipment ($600,000 less accumulated depreciation		
of $195,000 and $210,000) (per Illustrations 25.9 and 25.12) ..	405,000	390,000
Total property, plant, and equipment.....................	$1,059,000	$1,038,000
Total assets	$1,526,000	$1,577,000
Liabilities and Stockholders' Equity		
Current liabilities:		
Accounts payable (per Illustration 25.12)	$ 56,000	$ 73,000
Accrued liabilities (per Illustration 25.12)	170,000	184,000
Federal income taxes payable (per discussion		
on page 935)	55,000	60,000
Total current liabilities	$ 281,000	$ 317,000
Stockholders' equity:		
Capital stock (100,000 shares of $10 par value)		
(per Illustration 25.9)	$1,000,000	$1,000,000
Retained earnings (see below)	245,000*	260,000†
Total stockholders' equity	$1,245,000	$1,260,000
Total liabilities and stockholders' equity	$1,526,000	$1,577,000

* $260,000 (per Illustration 25.9) + Income of $5,000 — Dividends of $20,000.
† $245,000 + Income of $55,000 — Dividends of $40,000.

The purchases budget can be derived from the sales budget and the company's inventory policy. Suppose the Strobel Furniture Company had prepared the sales budget shown in Illustration 25.17. Assume that the company likes to maintain sufficient inventory to cover one half of the next quarter's sales, and that cost of goods sold is 55 percent of sales. The ending inventory on December 31, 1983, was $8,250. The purchases budget can now be prepared. It is shown in Illustration 25.18. (The sales budget for the first quarter of 1985 is $40,000.) For the first quarter of 1984 notice that the ending inventory is one half of the second quarter's cost of goods sold [.5 × (55 percent of $80,000)].

Illustration 25.17

STROBEL FURNITURE COMPANY Sales Budget Quarter Ending			
March 31, 1984	**June 30, 1984**	**September 30, 1984**	**December 31, 1984**
$30,000	$80,000	$50,000	$90,000

Illustration 25.18

STROBEL FURNITURE COMPANY
Purchases Budget
Quarter Ending

	March 31, 1984	**June 30, 1984**	**September 30, 1984**	**December 31, 1984**
Ending inventory desired	$22,000	$13,750	$24,750	$11,000
Cost of goods sold	16,500	44,000	27,500	49,500
Total	$38,500	$57,750	$52,250	$60,500
Less: Beginning inventory ...	8,250	22,000	13,750	24,750
Purchases required	$30,250	$35,750	$38,500	$35,750

NEW TERMS INTRODUCED IN CHAPTER 25*

Budget
A plan showing a company's objectives and proposed ways of attaining the objectives. Two major types of budgets are (1) the master budget and (2) control or responsibility budgets.

Budgeting
The coordination of financial and nonfinancial planning to satisfy an organization's goals.

Budget variance
The difference between an actual cost incurred (or revenue earned) at a certain level of operations and the budgeted amount for that same level of operations.

Financial budget
The projected balance sheet portion of a master budget.

Fixed costs
Costs that are unaffected by the relative levels of production or sales.

Flexible operating budget
Provides detailed information about expenses and revenues at various levels of output.

Master budget
The projected income statement and projected balance sheet showing the organization's objectives and proposed ways of attaining them; includes supporting budgets for such areas as cash, sales, costs, and production; also called master profit plan. It is the overall plan of the enterprise as a whole and ideally consists of all of the various segmental budgets.

Operating budget
The projected income statement portion of a master budget.

Participatory budgeting
A method of preparing the budget that includes the participation of all levels of management responsible for actual performance.

Semivariable costs
Costs that vary with volume, but not in proportion to increases in volume.

Variable costs
Costs that vary directly with production and are a constant amount per unit of output over different levels of output or sales.

---

* Some terms defined in earlier chapters are repeated here for your convenience.

DEMONSTRATION PROBLEM

During January 1984, the Phoenix Company plans to sell 20,000 units at a price of $20 per unit. Selling expenses are estimated to be $40,000 plus 2 percent of sales revenue. General and administrative expenses are estimated to be $30,000 plus 1 percent of sales revenue. Income tax expense is estimated to be 40 percent of net operating income.

Phoenix plans to produce 25,000 units during January with estimated variable costs per unit as follows: $2 for material, $5 for labor, and $3 for variable overhead. The fixed overhead cost is estimated at $20,000 per month. The finished goods inventory at January 1, 1984, is 4,000 units with a cost per unit of $10. The company uses Fifo inventory procedure.

Required:

Prepare a projected income statement for January 1984.

Solution to demonstration problem

PHOENIX COMPANY
Projected Income Statement
For January 1984

Sales (20,000 × $20)		$400,000
Cost of goods sold (see Schedule 1)		212,800
Gross margin		$187,200
Selling expenses:		
Fixed	$ 40,000	
Variable (0.02 × $400,000)	8,000	
General and administrative expenses:		
Fixed	30,000	
Variable (0.01 × $400,000)	4,000	82,000
Net income before taxes		$105,200
Income taxes (40%)		42,080
Net income		$ 63,120

Schedule 1

PHOENIX COMPANY
Planned Cost of Goods Sold

Beginning finished goods inventory (4,000 × $10)		$ 40,000
Cost of goods manufactured:		
Direct materials (25,000 × $2)	$ 50,000	
Direct labor (25,000 × $5)	125,000	
Variable overhead (25,000 × $3)	75,000	
Fixed overhead	20,000	
Cost of goods manufactured (25,000 × $10.80)		270,000
Cost of goods available for sale		$310,000
Ending finished goods inventory (9,000 × $10.80)		97,200
Cost of goods sold		$212,800

QUESTIONS

1. What are three purposes of budgeting?

2. What is meant by the term *management by exception?* How does the concept relate to budgeting?

3. What are five basic principles which, if followed, should improve the possibility of preparing a meaningful budget? Why is each important?

4. What is the difference between an "imposed" budget and a "participatory" budget?

5. Define and explain a budget variance.

6. What are the two major budgets in the master budget? Which should be prepared first? Why?

7. Distinguish between a master budget and a responsibility budget.

8. The budget established at the beginning of a given period carried an item for supplies in the amount of $40,000. At the end of the period, the supplies used amounted to $44,000. Can it be concluded from these data that there was inefficient use of supplies or that care was not exercised in purchasing the supplies?

9. Management must make certain assumptions about the business environment when preparing a budget. What areas should be considered?

10. Why is budgeted performance better than past performance as a basis for judging actual results?

EXERCISES

E–1.   The Jewel Shoe Company has decided to produce 30,000 pairs of shoes at a uniform rate throughout 1984. The sales department of Jewel Shoe Company has estimated sales for 1984 according to the following schedule:

	Sales in units
First quarter	8,000
Second quarter	6,500
Third quarter	7,500
Fourth quarter	10,500
Total for 1984	32,500

If the December 31, 1983, inventory is estimated to be 4,000 pairs of shoes, prepare a schedule of planned sales and production (in units) for the first two quarters of 1984.

E–2.   Labor and materials of Michael Corporation are considered to be variable costs. Expected production for the year is 150,000 units. At that level of production, labor cost is budgeted at $562,500 and materials cost is expected to be $247,500. Prepare a flexible budget for labor and materials for possible production levels of 105,000, 120,000, and 135,000 units of product.

E–3.   Assume that in Exercise E–2 actual production was 120,000 units, material cost was $210,000, and labor cost was $400,000. What are the budget variances?

E–4.   The following data apply to the collection of accounts receivable for the Pete Company.

Current balance—February 28—$50,000 (of which $30,000 relates to February sales)
Planned sales for March—$250,000

Assumptions: 70 percent of sales are collected in the month of sale, 20 percent in the following month, and the remaining 10 percent in the second month after the sale. Prepare a schedule of planned collections and ending balance for accounts receivable as of March 31, 1984.

E–5.   The Bell Company expects to sell 60,000 units during the next quarter at a price of $20 per unit. Production costs (all variable) are $7.00 per unit. Selling and administrative expenses are: variable $5.00 per unit, and fixed $160,000 in total. What is budgeted net income? (Do not consider taxes.)

E–6.   Fixed production costs for the Oak Company are budgeted at $160,000 assuming 80,000 units of product. Actual sales for the period were 70,000 units, while actual production was 80,000 units. Actual fixed costs used in computing cost of goods sold were $140,000. What is the budget variance?

E–7.   The shoe department of Jack's Department Store has prepared a sales budget for the month of April calling for a sales volume of $20,000. The department expects to begin April with a $15,000 inventory and end the month with a $16,000 inventory. Its cost of goods sold averages 70 percent of sales.

Prepare a purchases budget for the department showing the amount of goods to be purchased during April.

E–8.   The Wooley Company projects sales of 50,000 units during May at $5 per unit. Variable production costs are $1.50 per unit. Variable selling and administrative expenses are $0.50 per unit; fixed costs are $95,000. Ignore income taxes. Compute the budgeted income before taxes.

PROBLEMS, SERIES A

P25–1–A.   The James Company prepares monthly operating and financial budgets. Estimates of sales (in units) are made for each month. Production is scheduled at a level high enough to take care of current needs and to carry into each month one half of that next month's unit sales. Direct materials, direct labor, and variable overhead are estimated at $3, $5, and $2 per unit; and total fixed overhead is budgeted at $200,000 per month. Sales for April, May, June, and July are estimated at 100,000, 120,000, 160,000, and 120,000 units. The inventory at April 1 consists of 50,000 units with a cost of $12 per unit.

Required:

a.   Prepare a schedule showing the budgeted production in units for April, May, and June 1984.

b.   Prepare a schedule showing the budgeted cost of goods sold for the same three months assuming that the Fifo method is used for inventories.

P25–2–A.   Following is a summary of operating data of the Iron Company for the year 1983:

Sales		$5,000,000
Cost of goods sold:		
Direct materials	$1,000,000	
Direct labor	900,000	
Variable manufacturing overhead	200,000	
Fixed manufacturing overhead	600,000	2,700,000
Gross margin		$2,300,000

Selling expenses:
Variable	$ 250,000	
Fixed	200,000	450,000
		$1,850,000

General and administrative expenses:
Variable	$ 100,000	
Fixed	900,000	1,000,000
Net operating income		$ 850,000

Sales volume for 1984 is budgeted at 90 percent of 1983 volume with no expectation of price change. The 1984 budget amounts for the various other costs and expenses differ from those reported in 1983 only for the expected volume change in the variable items. Assume there were no beginning or ending inventories in 1983 or 1984.

The actual operating data for 1984 are:

Sales	$3,900,000
Direct materials	910,000
Direct labor	825,000
Variable manufacturing overhead	175,000
Fixed manufacturing overhead	605,000
Variable selling expenses	330,000
Fixed selling expenses	195,000
Variable general and administrative expenses	92,000
Fixed general and administrative expenses	895,000

Required:

a.   Prepare a report comparing the operating budget for 1984 with the actual results for that year.

b.   Prepare a budget report which would be useful in pinpointing the responsibility for the poor showing in 1984. (Hint: Prepare budget data on a flexible budget basis.)

c.   Comment on the differences revealed by the two budget comparisons.

P25–3–A.   The following data are presented for the Smith Company for use in preparing its 1984 operating budget:

Plant capacity	1,000,000 units
Expected sales	900,000 units
Expected production	900,000 units
Forecasted sales price	$ 5.00 per unit

Manufacturing costs:
Variable (per unit):	
Direct material	2.00
Direct labor	1.00
Overhead	0.50
Fixed overhead	225,000

Selling and administrative expenses:
Variable (per unit)	0.25
Fixed	200,000

Assume no beginning inventory. Taxes are 40 percent of net income before taxes.

Required:

Part I.   Prepare an operating budget for the year ended December 31, 1984.

Part II.   The actual results for the Smith Company for the year ended December 31, 1984, were as follows: (Note: actual sales price was *$4.75 per unit*. Actual production [in units] was equal to actual sales [in units]).

Sales		$4,750,000
Cost of goods sold:		
Direct materials	$1,900,000	
Direct labor	1,050,000	
Variable overhead	600,000	
Fixed overhead	225,000	3,775,000
		$ 975,000
Selling and administrative expense:		
Variable	250,000	
Fixed	200,000	450,000
Net income before taxes		$ 525,000
Income tax at 40%		210,000
Net income		$ 315,000

Using a flexible operating budget, analyze the efficiency of operations. Comment on the results of 1984 and the company's sales policy.

P25–4–A.   The Control Company is in the process of preparing its master budget for the year ended December 31, 1984. Management is interested in the responsibility budget to be prepared for the sales department. The sales manager and general manager have met with all department heads and have given you the following estimates relating to next year's expectations:

1. The company presently employs 40 full-time salespersons with a base salary of $350 per month. In addition, it has eight regional managers with a base salary of $15,000 per year while the one sales manager draws $30,000 per year.
2. Current year sales are estimated at $9,000,000. The 40 full-time salespersons are given sales commissions of 5 percent on 70 percent of total sales, and 3 percent on 20 percent of sales, while the remaining 10 percent of sales are not subject to commission. Approximately one third of the sales are made in the first three months of the year.
3. Advertising commitments have been made with major magazines. These commitments are for $15,000 per month.
4. The company is planning a special in-store promotion during January–February–March. Special incentives are given to the retailers in the form of supplies, aids, and advertising assistance up to 2 percent of total gross sales during the month. Past history has shown the retailers to take advantage of about three fourths of these incentives.
5. A supplementary advertising campaign will also be used during the first quarter of 1984 and will average $30,000 for January and $20,000 during the next two months.
6. Salespersons' travel allowances average $150 per month per salesperson (excluding managers).
7. Selling supplies average 1 percent of gross sales.
8. Sales department clerical salaries are set at $2,500 per month. Rent for sales offices is $6,000 per month.
9. The sales department will conduct a special market test of a new product during the first quarter. Nonrecurring expenses of $45,000 associated with this test are expected to be incurred.

Required:

   Prepare a detailed operating expense budget for the sales department for the first quarter of 1984.

P25–5–A.   The Picture Manufacturing Company is in the process of preparing a schedule of planned cost of goods sold and ending inventory for the quarters ended March 31, 1984, and June 30, 1984. The following data relate to expected activity for the two quarters:

1. Expected sales:

March quarter	$400,000
June quarter	300,000
September quarter	600,000

2. Selling price per unit is $40.
3. The company policy is to carry a beginning of the period inventory equal to 20 percent of the next period's requirements. Beginning inventory at January 1, 1984, was 2,000 units at $25 per unit.
4. Cost of production is estimated at:

Direct materials	$ 6 per unit
Direct labor	14 per unit
Variable overhead	4 per unit
Fixed overhead	38,000 per quarter

5. There is no work in process inventory at the beginning or end of either period.
6. Inventory is computed on a Fifo basis.

Required:

Prepare a schedule of planned cost of goods sold for the quarters ended March 31 and June 30, 1984. (Hint: Prepare a production schedule in units first.)

P25–6–A. Gordon Company has a cash balance of $22,000 on May 1, 1984. Gordon Company's product sells for $45 per unit. Actual and projected sales are:

March, actual	$320,000
April, actual	200,000
May, estimated	225,000
June, estimated	240,000
July, estimated	190,000

All sales are on account. Generally, 45 percent of the accounts receivable are collected in the month of sale, 40 percent in the second month, and 15 percent in the third month.

Generally, 65 percent of purchases are due and payable in the month of purchase and the remainder the following month. Purchase cost per unit is $30. The company maintains an end-of-the-month inventory of 250 units plus 20 percent of the next month's unit sales.

Required:

Prepare schedules for May and June showing:

a. Planned accounts receivable collections and balances.

b. Planned materials purchases and inventories. Round all units to the nearest whole number.

P25–7–A. Refer to P25–6–A. In addition to the information given, selling and administrative expenses are $420,000 per year, distributed evenly throughout the year.

Required:

Prepare a monthly cash budget for May and June for the Gordon Company.

P25–8–A. The Sign Company has gathered the following budget information for the quarter ending September 30:

Sales	$180,000
Purchases	150,000
Salaries and wages	65,000
Rent	3,000
Supplies	2,000
Insurance	600
Other cash expenses	4,400

A cash balance of $12,000 is planned for July 1. Accounts receivable are expected to be $20,000 on July 1. All but one half of 1 percent of the July 1 balance will be collected in the quarter ending September 30. The company's sales collection pattern is 95 percent in the quarter of sale and 5 percent in the quarter after sale. Accounts payable will be $10,000 on July 1 and will be paid during the coming quarter. Seventy-five percent of purchases is paid for in the quarter of purchase. The remaining 25 percent is paid for in the quarter after purchase. Expenses are paid in the quarter of incurrence.

Required:

Prepare a cash budget for the quarter ending September 30.

P25–9–A.

NELSON CORPORATION
Post-Closing Trial Balance
December 31, 1983

	Debits	Credits
Cash	$ 20,000	
Accounts receivable	40,000	
Allowance for doubtful accounts		$ 3,000
Inventories	50,000	
Prepaid expenses	6,000	
Land	50,000	
Buildings and equipment	150,000	
Accumulated depreciation		20,000
Accounts payable		30,000
Accrued liabilities (including income taxes)		20,000
Capital stock		200,000
Retained earnings		43,000
	$316,000	$316,000

The Nelson Corporation, whose post-closing trial balance at December 31, 1983, appears above, is a rapidly expanding company. Sales in the last quarter of 1983 amounted to $200,000 and are projected at $250,000 and $400,000 for the first two quarters of 1984. This expansion has created a very tight cash position. Management is especially concerned about the probable cash balance at March 31, 1984, since a payment of $30,000 for some new equipment must be made upon delivery on April 2. The current cash balance of $20,000 is considered to be the minimum workable balance.

Additional data:

1. Purchases, all on account, are to be scheduled so that the inventory at the end of any quarter is equal to one third of the goods expected to be sold in the coming quarter. Cost of goods sold averages 60 percent of sales.
2. Selling expenses are budgeted at $10,000 fixed plus 8 percent of sales; $2,000 is expected to be incurred on account, $24,000 accrued, $2,800 from expired prepayments, and $1,200 from allocated depreciation.
3. Purchasing expenses are budgeted at $7,000 fixed plus 5 percent of purchases; $1,000 will be incurred on account, $13,000 accrued, $1,100 from expired prepayments, and $900 from allocated depreciation.
4. Administrative expenses are budgeted at $12,500 fixed plus 3 percent of sales; $2,000 will be incurred on account, $11,000 accrued, $1,100 from expired prepayments, $900 from allocated depreciation, while bad debts are equal to 2 percent of current sales.
5. Federal income taxes are budgeted at 50 percent of net operating income before taxes and are accrued in accrued liabilities. Payments on these taxes are included in the payments on accrued liabilities discussed below.
6. All December 31, 1983, accounts payable will be paid in the first quarter plus 80 percent of current credits to this account. All of the December 31, 1983, accrued liabilities will be paid in the first quarter except for $6,000. Of the current quarter's accrued liabilities, all but $24,000 will be paid during the quarter.

7. Cash outlays for various expenses normally prepaid will amount to $8,000 during the quarter.
8. All sales are made on account, and 80 percent of the sales are collected in the quarter in which made, and all of the remaining sales are collected in the following quarter except for 2 percent which is never collected. The allowance for doubtful accounts shows the estimated amount of accounts receivable at December 31, 1983, arising from 1983 sales which will not be collected.

Required:

a. Prepare an operating budget for the quarter ending March 31, 1984. Supporting schedules for planned purchases and operating expenses should be included.

b. Prepare a financial budget for March 31, 1984. Include supporting schedules analyzing accounts credited for purchases and expenses, showing planned cash flows and cash balance and showing planned collections on and balance of accounts receivable.

c. Will sufficient cash be on hand April 2 to pay for the new equipment?

PROBLEMS, SERIES B

P25–1–B. The Jay Corporation prepares monthly operating and financial budgets. The operating budgets for June and July are based on the following data:

	Units produced	Units sold
June	200,000	180,000
July	180,000	200,000

All sales are at $20 per unit. Direct materials, direct labor, and variable overhead are estimated at $2, $4, and $2 per unit, while total fixed overhead is budgeted at $360,000 per month. Operating expenses are budgeted at $400,000 plus 10 percent of sales, while federal income taxes are budgeted at 50 percent of net operating income. The inventory at June 1 consists of 100,000 units with a cost of $11.40 each.

Required:

a. Prepare monthly budget estimates of cost of goods sold assuming use of Fifo inventory procedure.

b. Prepare operating budgets for June and July. (Use a single amount for cost of goods sold—as derived above.)

P25–2–B. Net operating income for the Stage Company for 1983 was as follows:

Sales		$1,000,000
Cost of goods sold:		
Direct materials	$200,000	
Direct labor	150,000	
Variable overhead	60,000	
Fixed overhead	100,000	510,000
Gross margin		$ 490,000
Selling expenses:		
Variable	$ 60,000	
Fixed	90,000	150,000
		$ 340,000
General and administrative expenses:		
Variable	80,000	
Fixed	130,000	210,000
Net operating income		$ 130,000

An operating budget is prepared for 1984 with sales forecasted at a 20 percent increase solely from volume. Direct materials, direct labor, and all costs labeled variable above are completely variable. Fixed costs are expected to continue as above except for a $10,000 increase in fixed general and administrative expenses. Assume there were no beginning or ending inventories in 1983 or 1984.

Actual operating data for 1984 are:

Sales	$1,150,000
Direct materials	235,000
Direct labor	175,000
Variable overhead	67,500
Fixed overhead	102,500
Variable selling expense	69,000
Fixed selling expense	91,000
Variable general and administrative expense	95,000
Fixed general and administrative expense	135,000

Required:

a. Prepare a budget report comparing the 1984 operating budget with actual 1984 data.

b. Prepare a budget report which would be useful in appraising the performance of the various persons charged with responsibility for providing satisfactory earnings. (Hint: Prepare budget data on a flexible basis.)

c. Comment on the difference revealed by the two reports.

P25–3–B. The following data are presented for the Bay Company for use in preparing its 1984 operating budget:

Plant capacity	25,000 units
Expected sales volume	22,500 units
Expected production	22,500 units
Actual production	22,500 units
Forecasted sale price	$10.00 per unit
Actual selling price	$11.25 per unit

Manufacturing costs:
Variable (per unit):

Direct materials	3.00
Direct labor	0.50
Overhead	1.50
Fixed overhead	45,000

Selling and administrative expenses:

Variable (per unit)	0.75
Fixed	12,500

Assume no beginning or ending inventory. Taxes are 40 percent of net income before taxes.

Required:

Part I. Prepare an operating budget for the year ended December 31, 1984.

Part II. The actual results of the Bay Company for the year 1984 were as follows:

Sales		$225,000
Cost of goods sold:		
Direct materials	$65,000	
Direct labor	10,000	
Variable overhead	30,000	
Fixed overhead	40,000	145,000
Gross margin		$ 80,000

Selling and administrative expenses:

Variable	$20,000	
Fixed	15,000	35,000
Earnings before income tax		$ 45,000
Income taxes—at 50%		22,500
Net income		$ 22,500

Using a flexible operating budget, analyze the efficiency of operations and comment on the company's sales policy.

P25–4–B. The Johnson Company is in the process of preparing its master budget for the year ending December 31, 1984. You are responsible for compiling the detailed budget for selling and administrative expenses. The sales manager and general manager have met with all department heads and have given you the following estimates relating to next year's expectations:

1. Sales for the year are estimated at $7,600,000. About 80 percent of sales are subject to commission. Of the commission sales, approximately 60 percent have a commission of 10 percent going to the salespersons while the remaining 40 percent have a commission rate of 5 percent.
2. In addition to commissions, the company pays 30 salespersons a base salary of $250 per month, and 10 salespersons a base salary of $500 per month. Each of the nine regional sales offices has a manager with a base salary of $1,200 per month, who is not entitled to commissions.
3. Administrative salaries were $30,000 per month last year. A 5 percent increase has been granted for next year, beginning on June 1, 1984.
4. Office equipment of $600,000 is depreciated at the rate of 10 percent per year.
5. Building rent is $5,000 per month, of which 80 percent is allocable to administrative expenses and 20 percent to selling expenses.
6. Selling supplies used are estimated at 2 percent of sales.
7. Office supplies used are estimated at 1 percent of sales.
8. Advertising expense is budgeted at a base amount of $100,000 plus 3 percent of sales.
9. Other expenses include:
   Salesperson's travel—$1,200 per month.
   Other administrative expenses (telephone, etc.)—$600 per month.
   Assume there are no plans to add or terminate any employees.

Required:

Prepare a sales department operating expense budget and an administrative expense budget that will be useful in evaluating the two separate functions.

P25–5–B The Price Company wants to prepare a schedule of planned cost of goods sold and ending inventory for the quarters ending September 30, 1984, and December 31, 1984. The following data relate to the expected activity for the two quarters:

1. Expected sales for the next three quarters are $600,000 (September, 1984), $750,000 (December, 1984), and $408,000 (March 1985).
2. The selling price is $30 per unit.
3. Due to demand, the company wishes to carry a beginning-of-period inventory equal to 25 percent of the following quarter's expected requirements.
4. Inventory of finished goods on June 30, 1984, is 5,000 units at $24 per unit.
5. Cost of production is estimated at:

Direct materials	$4 per unit
Direct labor	8 per unit
Variable overhead	2 per unit
Fixed overhead	200,000 per quarter

6. There is no work in process inventory at the beginning or end of either period.
7. The company computes inventory on a Fifo basis.

Required:

Prepare a schedule of planned cost of goods sold for the quarters ending September 30, 1984, and December 31, 1984. (Hint: Prepare production schedules in units first.)

P25–6–B. Lee Company manufactures and sells bathroom fixtures. Estimated sales for the next three months are:

September 1984	$150,000
October 1984	225,000
November 1984	175,000

Sales for August were $160,000. All sales are on account. Lee Company estimates that 60 percent of the accounts receivable are collected in the month of sale with the remaining 40 percent collected the following month. The units sell for $25 a unit. The cash balance for September 1, 1984, is $34,000.

Generally, 60 percent of purchases are due and payable in the month of purchase with the remainder due the following month. Purchase cost per unit is $15. The company maintains an end-of-month inventory of 500 units plus 10 percent of next month's unit sales.

Required:

Prepare a cash receipts schedule for September and October and a purchases budget for August, September, and October.

P25–7–B. Refer to P25–6–B. In addition to the information given, selling and administrative expenses are $50,000 per month.

Required:

Prepare a monthly cash budget for September and October for the Lee Company.

P25–8–B. The Jones Company has gathered the following budget information for the quarter ending March 31:

Sales	$270,000
Purchases	225,000
Salaries and wages	97,500
Rent	4,500
Supplies	3,000
Insurance	900
Other cash expenses	6,600

A cash balance of $18,000 is planned for January 1. Accounts receivable are expected to be $30,000 on January 1. All but one half of 1 percent of the January 1 balance will be collected in the quarter ending March 31. The company's sales collection pattern is 95 percent in the quarter of sale and 5 percent in the quarter after sale. Accounts payable will be $15,000 on January 1 and will be paid during the coming quarter. Seventy-five percent of purchases is paid for in the quarter of purchase. The remaining 25 percent is paid for in the quarter after purchase. Expenses are paid in the quarter of incurrence.

Required:

Prepare a cash budget for the quarter ending March 31.

P25–9–B. Samson Corporation prepares annual budgets by quarters for its fiscal year ending June 30. Given below is its post-closing trial balance at December 31, 1983:

	Debits	Credits
Cash	23,000	
Accounts receivable	60,000	
Allowance for doubtful accounts		$ 2,000
Inventories	26,000	
Prepaid expenses	2,000	
Furniture and equipment	30,000	
Accumulated depreciation		2,000
Accounts payable		20,000
Accrued liabilities		6,000
Notes payable, 5% (due 1987)		80,000
Capital stock		50,000
Retained earnings (deficit)	19,000	
	$160,000	$160,000

All of the stock of Samson Corporation was recently acquired by Floyd White after the corporation had suffered losses for a number of years. After the purchase, White loaned substantial sums of money to the corporation, which still owes him $80,000 on a 5 percent note. Because of these past losses there are no accrued federal income taxes payable, but future earnings will be subject to taxation.

White is anxious to withdraw $20,000 from the corporation (as a payment on the note payable to him) but will not do so if it reduces the corporation's cash balance below $20,000. Thus, he is quite interested in the budgets for the quarter ending March 31, 1984.

Additional data:

1. Sales for the coming quarter are forecasted at $200,000; for the following quarter at $250,000. All sales are priced to yield a gross margin of 40 percent. Inventory is to be maintained on hand at the end of any quarter in an amount equal to 20 percent of the goods to be sold in the next quarter. All sales are on account, and 95 percent of the December 31, 1983, receivables plus 70 percent of the current quarter's sales will be collected during the quarter ending March 31, 1984.
2. Selling expenses are budgeted at $8,000 fixed plus 6 percent of sales; $4,000 will be incurred on account, $11,000 accrued, $4,500 from expiration of prepaid rent and unexpired insurance, and $500 from allocated depreciation.
3. Purchasing expenses are budgeted at $5,800 fixed plus 5 percent of purchases for the quarter; $1,500 will be incurred on account, $8,000 accrued, $2,300 from expired prepaid expenses, and $200 from allocated depreciation.
4. Administrative expenses are budgeted at $7,000 plus 2 percent of sales; $500 will be incurred on account, $6,000 accrued, $2,200 from expired prepayments, and $300 from allocated depreciation, while bad debts are estimated at 1 percent of sales.
5. Interest accrues at 5 percent on the notes payable and is credited to Accrued Liabilities.
6. All of the beginning balances in Accounts Payable and Accrued Liabilities will be paid during the quarter plus 80 percent of the current credits to Accounts Payable and all but $5,000 of the current accrued liabilities. A $3,000 insurance premium is to be paid prior to March 31, and a full year's rent of $24,000 is due on January 2.
7. Federal income taxes are budgeted at 50 percent of the net income before taxes. The taxes should be accrued separately, and no payments are due in the first quarter.

Required:

   a. Prepare an operating budget for the quarter ending March 31, 1984, including supporting schedules for planned purchases and operating expenses.

   b. Prepare a financial budget for March 31, 1984. A supporting schedule analyzing accounts credited for purchases and operating expenses, a schedule showing planned accounts receivable collections and balances, and a schedule showing planned cash flows and cash balances should be included.

   c. Will White be able to collect $20,000 on his note?

BUSINESS DECISION PROBLEM

The Scott Company has applied at a local bank for a short-term loan of $25,000, starting on October 1. The loan will be repaid with interest at 10 percent on December 31. The bank's loan officer has requested a cash budget from the company for the quarter ending December 31. The following budget information is needed to prepare the cash budget:

Sales	$108,000
Purchases	60,000
Salaries and wages to be paid . . .	21,000
Rent payments	1,200
Supplies (payments for)	800
Insurance payments	300
Other cash payments	3,700

A cash balance of $4,000 is planned for October 1. Accounts receivable are expected to be $8,000 on October 1. All of these accounts will be collected in the quarter ending December 31. In general, sales are collected as follows: 90 percent in the quarter of sale and 10 percent in the quarter after sale. Accounts payable will be $80,000 on October 1 and will be paid during the quarter ending December 31. All purchases are paid for in the quarter after purchase.

Required:

a.   Prepare a cash budget for the quarter ending December 31. Assume that the $25,000 loan will be made on October 1 and will be repaid with interest at 10 percent on December 31.

b.   Will the company be able to repay the loan on December 31? If the company desires a minimum cash balance of $3,000, will the company be able to repay the loan as planned?

Chapter 26
Short-term decision making

CHAPTER GOALS

After study of this chapter, you should be able to:

1. Describe different cost behavior patterns.
2. Compute the break-even point for a company.
3. List the assumptions underlying cost-volume-profit analysis.
4. Apply cost-volume-profit analysis to practical situations.
5. Make short-term decisions involving relevant costs.
6. Differentiate between and compute net income under absorption and direct costing.
7. Define and use correctly the new terms in the glossary.

The *short-run* is considered to be a time frame during which company management cannot change the effects of certain decisions that were made in the past. The short-run is often considered to be one year or less. In the short run, many costs, such as depreciation expense, are assumed to be fixed and unchangeable. But in the long run all costs are subject to change. Management must be careful to consider both short- and long-run effects of any decisions.

A very simple example of the conflicts between short-run and long-run decisions would be a company policy to reduce or eliminate machine maintenance for the next period. This reduction in expenses will cause an increase in short-run income, but future maintenance costs, and possibly materials and labor costs, may rise significantly.

This chapter discusses cost behavior patterns and short-run decision making. Management must attempt to classify all costs as either variable or fixed in order to understand how costs will react to changes in volume of production or sales.

COST BEHAVIOR PATTERNS

Illustration 26.1 shows four basic types of cost behavior patterns: variable, fixed, mixed (semivariable), and step. As discussed in earlier chapters, *variable costs* vary directly with changes in volume. A change in volume can mean either volume of production or volume of sales. In contrast, *fixed costs* remain constant over some relevant range of output and are often described as time-related costs. Depreciation, insurance, property taxes, and administrative salaries are examples of fixed costs.

Illustration 26.1: Four cost patterns

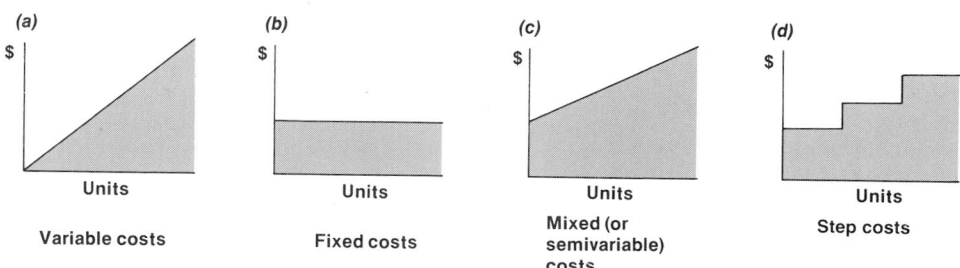

Mixed and step costs demonstrate both fixed and variable characteristics. A *mixed cost* contains a fixed portion of cost that will be incurred even when the plant is completely idle and a variable portion that will increase directly with volume. An example of a mixed cost is electricity. A certain amount of cost is incurred in order for the company to have electrical service. As the plant operates, each additional kilowatt-hour of usage generates an additional amount of cost. A mixed cost may be separated into its fixed and variable components, as shown in Illustration 26.2.

Illustration 26.2:   Separation of a mixed cost

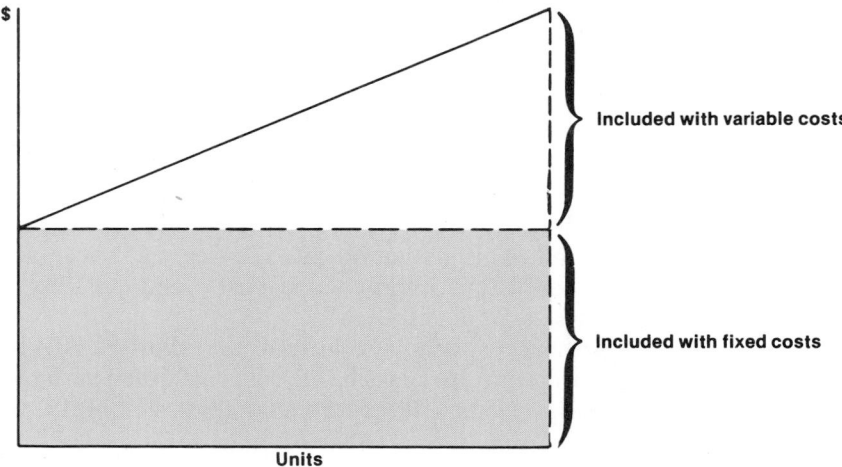

A *step cost* may be either a step variable or a step fixed cost. The major difference between the two types is the size of the "steps." In both cases, there is a fixed and variable component to the cost. An example of a step variable cost might be the cost of water for company usage. The utility company charges a flat fee for provision of service and an additional amount depending on the quantity of water used. Unlike the charge for electricity, which was on an hour-by-hour basis, the charge for water may be stated in increments as follows: $10 for the first 1,000 gallons or less; $5 additional for use of 1,001 to 5,000 gallons; $8 additional for use of 5,001 to 10,000 gallons; and so on. This type of cost is shown in Illustration 26.3.

A step fixed cost can be illustrated by a cost such as supervisors' salaries. At any level of production from 1 unit to 40,000 units, one supervisor is necessary at a salary of $20,000 per year. If the company produces at a level over 40,000 units but below 100,000 units, a second supervisor is needed at an additional cost of $20,000. A step fixed cost for supervisors' salaries is shown in Illustration 26.4.

For decision making, management must classify mixed and step costs as either variable or fixed. A mixed cost can be easily broken down into its two component elements. The fixed portion of a mixed cost will be included with other fixed costs, while the variable element can be shown as directly changing with volume. A step variable cost will be treated in the same manner as a mixed cost. The fixed portion of a step variable cost will be treated as a fixed cost, and the remaining cost will be treated as entirely variable.

Since a step fixed cost is fixed over a relatively wide range of activity, it can be treated as entirely fixed for decision-making purposes. This is done by estimating the level of operations and then treating the level of step fixed costs that is expected at that level of operations as a fixed cost for decision making.

Illustration 26.3: Separation of a step variable cost

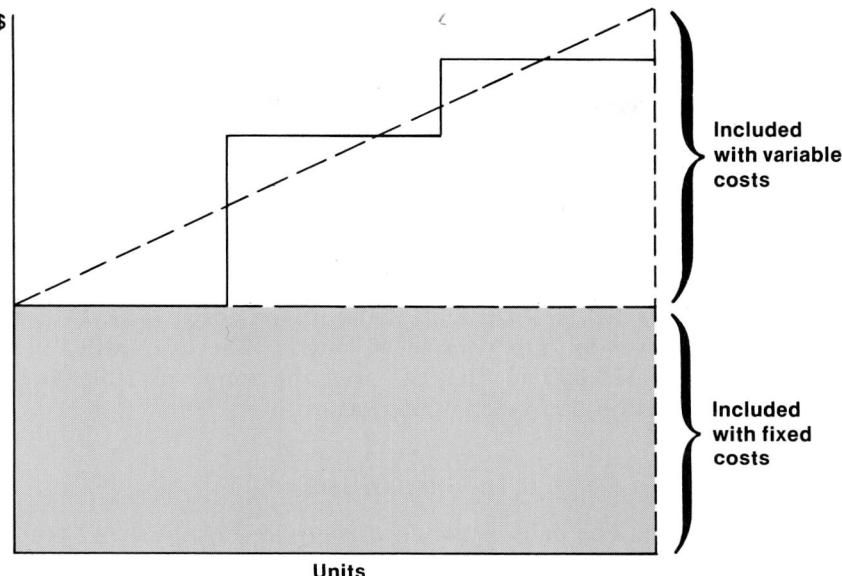

Even though step variable costs do not vary directly with changes in volume, they can be treated for planning purposes as though they were directly variable costs. The slanted dashed line represents the smoothing of the step variable costs into a directly variable cost.

Illustration 26.4: A step fixed cost

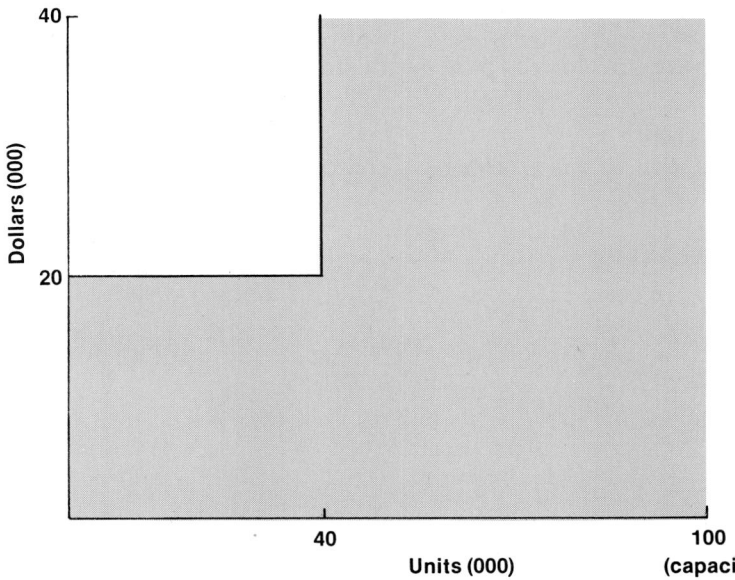

Methods for analyzing costs

There are several methods for breaking down a mixed or a step variable cost into its fixed and variable cost components. Two of these procedures are the scatter diagram and the high-low method.

The scatter diagram.   A *scatter diagram* shows plots of actual costs incurred for various levels of output or sales. The dots on the scatter diagram in Illustration 26.2 represent total actual maintenance costs for a firm's fleet of delivery trucks at various levels of past activity. A line is drawn through what appears visually to be the center of the pattern formed by the dots. In Illustration 26.5, the fixed element of the mixed cost is $23,000 since that is the amount of cost at zero volume of output. The line (called a regression line) rises from $23,000 to $63,000 over the range of 100,000 units. The variable cost portion can be computed as

$$\frac{\$63,000 \; - \; \$23,000}{100,000 \text{ units}}$$

or $0.40 per unit. The data in the chart suggest that the firm's truck maintenance costs can be estimated at $23,000 plus 40 cents for every mile driven.

A more sophisticated technique, called the *least squares method,* could be used to draw the regression line and divide mixed costs into their fixed and variable portions. This method is more precise, but since it involves statistical analysis, it will not be presented in this text.

The high-low method.   The high-low method is also widely used to identify the behavior of mixed costs. The *high-low method* uses only the highest and lowest plots on a scatter diagram to draw a line representing a total mixed cost.

To illustrate, the lowest plot in Illustration 26.5 is $38,000 of expense

Illustration 26.5: Scatter diagram

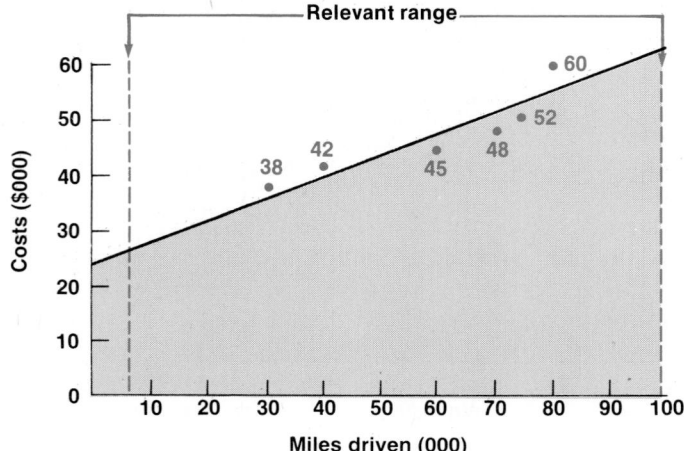

at 30,000 units of output and the highest plot is $60,000 at 80,000 units of output. The amount of variable cost per unit is found as follows:

$$\frac{\text{Change in cost}}{\text{Change in units}} = \frac{\$60,000 - \$38,000}{80,000 \text{ units} - 30,000 \text{ units}} = \frac{\$22,000}{50,000} = \$0.44 \text{ per unit}$$

The fixed portion is then found as follows:

Total cost at 80,000 units of output	$60,000
Less: Variable cost at that level of output (80,000 × $0.44)	35,200
Fixed cost at all levels of output within the relevant range	$24,800

The high-low method is less precise than the scatter diagram since it uses only two data points in the computation. Either or both points may not be representative of the data as a whole.

In summary, although there are four basic cost behavior patterns, management must attempt to classify all types of costs into only two categories: variable and fixed. This simplification is necessary in order to visualize the ways in which costs will react to changes in production volume or sales.

COST-VOLUME-PROFIT (CVP) ANALYSIS

Cost-volume-profit (CVP) analysis (sometimes called *break-even analysis*) is used to determine what effects any changes in a company's selling prices, costs, and/or volume will have on income in the short run. The starting point of such an analysis is the company's break-even point. A company is said to break even for a given period if sales revenue and costs charged to that period are exactly equal, thereby creating no income or incurring no loss. Thus, the *break-even point* is that level of operations at which revenues and costs are equal.

A careful and accurate cost-volume profit (CVP) analysis requires knowledge of costs and their behavior as volume changes. Management must be able to distinguish among different types of costs involved in its operations. Of course, the types and quantities of cost data accumulated depend on the costs of obtaining the data compared with the benefits of more refined information. Within this constraint, it is desirable to compute break-even points for each area of decision making within the company. Some important classifications of cost data for break-even analysis are by product, territory, salesperson, or class of customer.

A break-even point may be expressed in dollars of sales revenue or number of units produced or sold. No matter how break even is expressed, it is still the point of zero income or loss.

As an illustration, assume the Muffet Manufacturing Company produces a single product that sells for $20. Fixed costs per period total $40,000, while variable cost is $12 per unit. The *variable cost rate*, which expresses variable cost as a percentage of sales, would be 60 percent ($12 ÷ $20). The sales revenue needed to break even would be calculated as that point at which all costs are covered, but no income is generated. The break-even point can be expressed as:

$$\text{Sales} = \text{Fixed costs} + \text{Variable costs}$$

or

$$S = FC + VC$$

Substituting the amount of fixed costs and the variable cost rate in the formula gives the following:

$$
\begin{aligned}
S &= \$40,000 + 0.60S \\
S - 0.60S &= \$40,000 \\
0.40S &= \$40,000 \\
S &= \$40,000 \div 0.40 \\
S &= \$100,000
\end{aligned}
$$

Sales revenue at the break-even point is $100,000. To compute the break-even point in units, simply divide the $100,000 of sales by the $20 selling price per unit. This gives a break-even point in units of 5,000.

Alternatively, the break-even point in units could have been calculated first. The break-even point in units involves a concept known as contribution margin. *Contribution margin* is the amount by which revenue exceeds variable costs of producing that revenue; it can be calculated on a per unit or total sales volume basis. On a per unit basis, the contribution margin for Muffet Company is $8, which is the selling price of $20 less variable cost per unit of $12. Contribution margin indicates the amount of money or marginal income remaining after variable cost is covered. This remainder contributes to the coverage of fixed costs and the generation of net income. The break-even point in units is computed by dividing total fixed costs by the contribution margin per unit.

$$\text{BEP}_{\text{units}} = \frac{\text{Fixed costs}}{\text{Contribution margin per unit}}$$

$$\text{BEP}_{\text{units}} = \frac{\$40,000}{\$8}$$

$$= 5,000 \text{ units}$$

If the Muffet Company's production capacity is 20,000 units, then the break-even point is equal to 25 percent of capacity, (5,000/20,000 = 25 percent). An alternative method of finding the break-even point in sales dollars is to divide the total fixed costs by the contribution margin rate. The *contribution margin rate* expresses the contribution margin as a percentage of sales and is calculated by dividing the contribution margin per unit by the selling price per unit.

$$\text{BEP}_{\text{dollars}} = \frac{\text{Fixed costs}}{\text{Contribution margin rate}}$$

$$\text{BEP}_{\text{dollars}} = \frac{\$40,000}{0.40}$$

$$= \$100,000$$

In the Muffet Company example, contribution margin per unit was $8 and the contribution margin rate was 40 percent ($8/$20).

Break-even chart

A *break-even chart* is a graphical representation of the relationships between sales, costs, volume, and profit that also shows the break-even point. Illustration 26.6 presents the break-even chart for the Muffet Company. Each break-even chart or calculation is valid only for a specified relevant range of volume. The *relevant range* is the range of production or sales volume over which the basic cost behavior assumptions will hold true. For volumes outside these ranges, costs will behave differently and will alter the assumed relationships. For example, if more than 10,000 units were produced by the Muffet Company, it might be necessary to increase plant capacity, thus incurring additional fixed costs, or to work extra shifts, thus incurring overtime charges and other inefficiencies. In either case, the cost relationships first assumed are no longer valid. Illustration 26.6 is based on cost data for Muffet Company in a relevant range of output from 500 to 10,000 units.

The chart in Illustration 26.6 shows that the break-even volume of sales

Illustration 26.6: The break-even chart

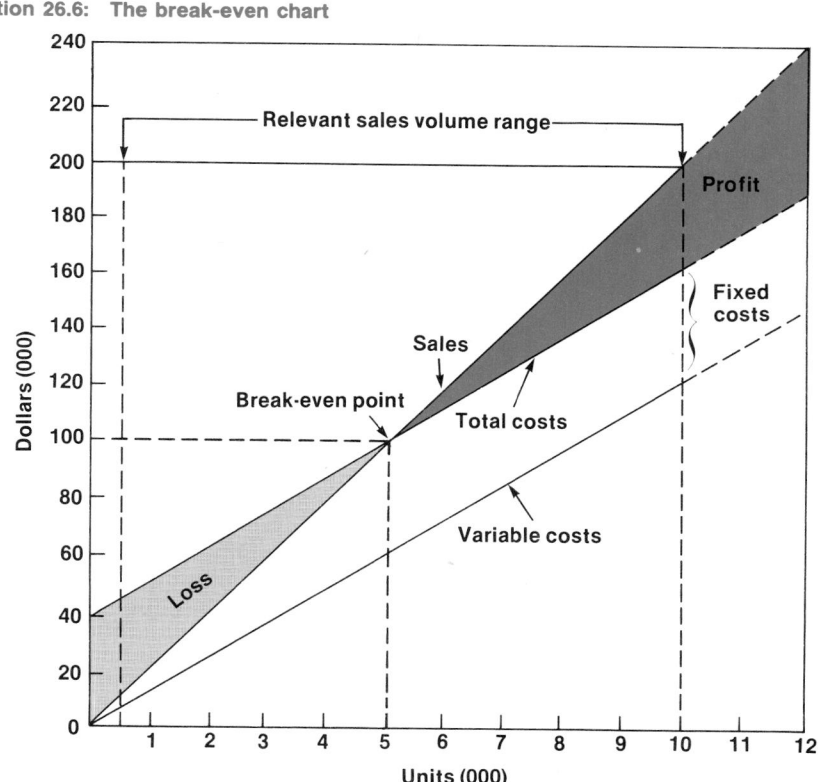

is $100,000 (5,000 units at $20). At this level of sales, fixed costs and variable costs are exactly equal to sales revenue, as shown:

Revenues	$100,000
Less: Variable costs	60,000
Contribution margin	$ 40,000
Less: Fixed costs	40,000
Net income	$ –0–

The break-even chart could also be re-labeled to indicate contribution margin, as shown in Illustration 26.7.

The break-even charts show that a period of complete idleness will produce a loss of $40,000 (the amount of fixed costs), while output of 10,000 units will produce net income of $40,000. Other points on the graphs show that sales of 7,500 units will result in $150,000 of revenue. At that point, total costs amount to $130,000, leaving net income of $20,000. In addition, net income at any level of output can be found by multiplying the contribution margin per unit by the number of units sold and subtracting total fixed costs from the result.

Illustration 26.7: Break-even chart showing that fixed costs equal contribution margin at break-even point

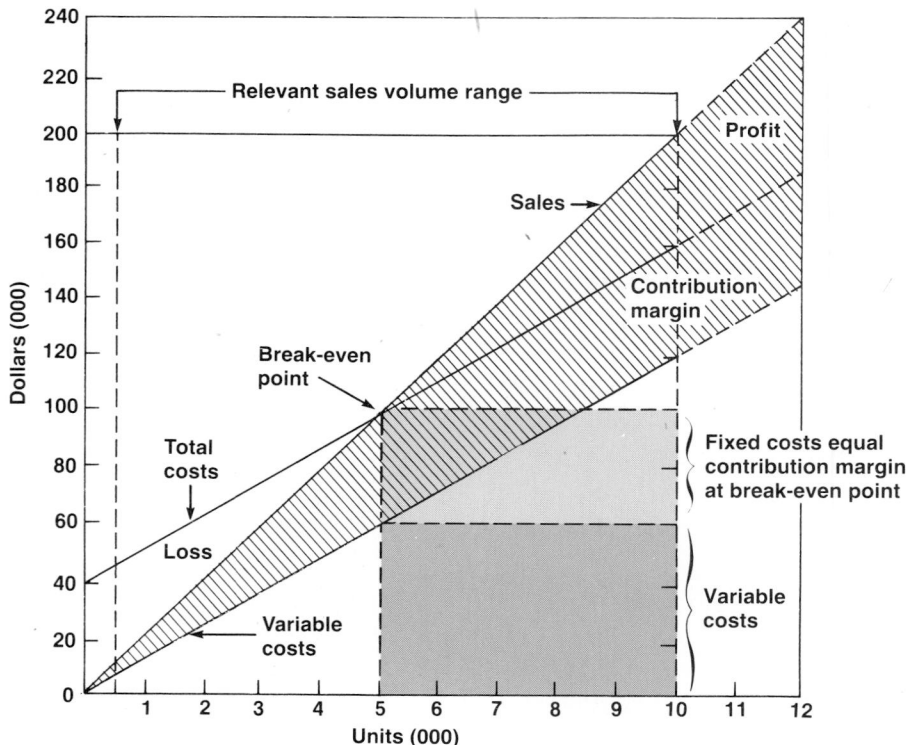

Changing the break-even point

Break-even points can be lowered or raised by changing selling price, variable cost per unit, or fixed costs. If the selling price is increased or the variable cost per unit is decreased, the break-even point will be lower because the contribution margin per unit is larger. This means that more of the selling price of each unit can be used to cover fixed costs. Similarly, if fixed costs are decreased, it takes fewer units sold to cover the smaller amount of fixed costs. Lowering the selling price, increasing variable cost per unit, or increasing fixed costs will raise the break-even point.

To illustrate the effects of changing the selling price, variable cost, or fixed cost, so as to lower the break-even point, assume that a company currently has a single product that sells for $60, variable cost per unit of $15 or 25 percent of selling price, and fixed costs of $27,000. The break-even point is $36,000 of sales revenue, computed as follows:

$$
\begin{aligned}
S &= FC + VC \\
S &= \$27,000 + 0.25S \\
0.75S &= \$27,000 \\
S &= \$36,000
\end{aligned}
$$

Increase selling price. If the company can increase its selling price to $75 while keeping variable costs and fixed costs the same, the variable cost rate becomes 20 percent, $15 ÷ $75 = 20 percent. The break-even point will decrease by $2,250:

$$
\begin{aligned}
S &= FC + VC \\
S &= \$27,000 + 0.20S \\
0.80S &= \$27,000 \\
S &= \$33,750
\end{aligned}
$$

Reduce fixed costs. If the company lowers its fixed costs to $24,000 without raising the selling price, the break-even point is still reduced:

$$
\begin{aligned}
S &= FC + VC \\
S &= \$24,000 + 0.25S \\
0.75S &= \$24,000 \\
S &= \$32,000
\end{aligned}
$$

Reduce variable cost. Finally, if the company can reduce the variable cost per unit to $12 and thus the variable cost rate to 20 percent of selling price, the break-even point can be lowered:

$$
\begin{aligned}
S &= FC + VC \\
S &= \$27,000 + 0.20S \\
0.80S &= \$27,000 \\
S &= \$33,750
\end{aligned}
$$

As shown, companies have a great deal of flexibility in the means of adjusting their break-even points. Of course, companies attempt to operate at a level of operations above the break-even point. And if the break-even point can be *lowered,* then the company can earn some income at a lower volume of operations than previously.

Margin of safety

If a company's current sales are above its break-even point, then the company is said to have a *margin of safety* equal to current sales less break-even sales. The margin of safety is the amount by which sales can decrease before a loss will be incurred. For example, assume a company currently has sales of $250,000 and break-even sales are $200,000.

The margin of safety is $50,000, computed as follows:

$$\text{Margin of safety} = \text{Current sales} - \text{Break-even sales}$$
$$= \$250,000 - \$200,000 = \$50,000$$

A *margin of safety rate* can also be specified and is equal to (Current sales − Break-even sales) ÷ Current sales. The margin of safety rate for the company discussed above is 20 percent, computed as follows:

$$\text{Margin of safety rate} = \frac{\text{Current sales} - \text{Break-even sales}}{\text{Current sales}}$$
$$= \frac{\$250,000 - \$200,000}{\$250,000}$$
$$= 20 \text{ percent}$$

Assumptions made in cost-volume-profit analysis

Certain assumptions are made for CVP analysis. These assumptions are sometimes criticized as being unrealistic in many situations, but even where there is truth to the criticisms, the assumptions are necessary in order to make the calculations. The assumptions are as follows:

1. Selling price and variable costs per unit remain constant throughout the relevant range. This means that more units can be sold at the same price and there is no change in technical efficiency as volume increases.
2. The number of units produced equals the number of units sold.
3. In multiproduct situations, the product mix is known in advance.
4. Costs can be accurately classified into their fixed and variable portions.

Cost-volume-profit analysis illustrated

An illustration will be used to analyze CVP relationships. First, the break-even point is calculated. Then the illustration demonstrates other uses of CVP analysis.

Calculation of break-even point. A major airline wishes to know the number of seats that must be sold on a certain flight for the flight to break even. To solve this problem, costs must first be identified and separated into fixed and variable categories.

The fixed costs are the same regardless of the number of seats filled. Fixed costs include items such as fuel required to fly the plane and crew (with no passengers) to destination; depreciation on the plane and facilities used on the flight; and salaries of crew members, gate attendants, and maintenance and refueling personnel. The variable costs will vary directly with the number of passengers. Variable costs would include meals and beverages provided to passengers, baggage handling costs, and the cost of the additional fuel required to fly the plane to its destination, each cost expressed on a per person basis.

Assume that after the various costs have been analyzed and classified as fixed or variable, the fixed costs for a given flight are $12,000. Variable costs are $25 per passenger and tickets are sold at $125; thus the variable cost rate is 20 percent ($25 $\div$ $125). This yields a contribution margin per ticket of $100 ($125 − $25). The contribution margin rate is 80 percent [($125 − $25) $\div$ $125].

The break-even point can be expressed in dollars or in number of passengers. The sales revenue needed to break even is computed as follows:

$$
\begin{aligned}
\text{Sales} &= \text{Fixed costs } + \text{ Variable costs} \\
S &= FC + VC \\
S &= \$12{,}000 + 0.20S \\
0.80S &= \$12{,}000 \\
S &= \$15{,}000
\end{aligned}
$$

The break-even point could have also been found using the contribution margin rate:

$$
\begin{aligned}
BEP_{\text{dollars}} &= \frac{\text{Fixed costs}}{\text{Contribution margin rate}} \\
&= \frac{\$12{,}000}{0.80} \\
&= \$15{,}000
\end{aligned}
$$

The break-even point in number of passengers may be found by dividing the break-even point in dollars ($15,000) by the selling price per unit ($125), giving 120 passengers. It may also be found as follows:

$$
\begin{aligned}
BEP_{\text{units}} &= \frac{\text{Fixed costs}}{\text{Contribution margin per unit}} \\
&= \frac{\$12{,}000}{\$125 - \$25} \\
&= 120 \text{ passengers}
\end{aligned}
$$

Calculating sales volume needed for desired net income. CVP analysis can also show the sales volume needed to generate some desired level of net income. A simple adjustment to the break-even formulas is all that is necessary. The income level is simply added to the total costs that need to be covered, and management can then determine necessary sales volume in dollars or units. For example, if the airline discussed above wishes to earn $8,000 of income on its flight, the company can calculate the amount of necessary sales revenue by the following formula:

$$\text{Sales} = \text{Fixed costs} + \text{Variable costs} + \text{Desired net income}$$

or

$$S = FC + VC + NI$$
$$S = \$12,000 + 0.20S + \$8,000$$
$$0.8S = \$20,000$$
$$S = \$25,000 \text{ (or 200 passengers)}$$

If the airline wants to know how many passenger tickets must be sold in order to earn $8,000, a modification of the break-even point formula could be used to achieve the desired calculation. Remembering that the contribution margin per ticket is $100, the number of tickets to be sold is as follows:

$$\text{Number of units} = \frac{\text{Fixed costs} + \text{Desired net income}}{\text{Contribution margin per unit}}$$
$$= \frac{\$12,000 + \$8,000}{\$100}$$
$$= \frac{\$20,000}{\$100}$$
$$= \underline{\underline{200}} \text{ passengers}$$

Calculating the effect on earnings of changing prices. The company could also use the formula to determine the results if one or more elements in the formula were changed. For example, the flight normally carries 150 passengers (sales of $18,750 and net income of $3,000) and a decision was made to increase ticket prices by 5 percent. If variable and fixed costs are assumed to remain constant and passenger load will not change, income will rise from $3,000 to $3,937.50 as shown:

$$S = FC + VC + NI$$
$$\$18,750 \, (1.05) = \$12,000 + 0.20 \, (\$18,750) + X$$
$$\$19,687.50 = \$12,000 + \$3,750 + X$$
$$\$19,687.50 = \$15,750 + X$$
$$\$3,937.50 = X$$

The reason variable costs remain constant at 20 percent of current sales in the above illustration is because a change in selling price has no effect on the variable costs associated with providing flight service. Income rose by the entire amount of the price increase ($19,687.50 − $18,750 = $937.50) because all variable and fixed costs were already being covered by the original selling price.

Calculating sales needed to maintain earnings when costs change. As a final example, the price of gasoline rises and causes both the fixed and variable costs to increase for the airline. Fixed costs are increased by $4,000 and variable costs by $6.25 per passenger. Variable costs are now 25 percent ($31.25/$125) of sales price. In order to maintain the current net income of $3,000 (on $18,750 of sales), the airline will need to increase sales revenue to $25,333 as shown below.

$$S = FC + VC + NI$$
$$S = \$16,000 + 0.25S + \$3,000$$
$$0.75S = \$19,000$$
$$S = \$25,333 \text{ (or 203 passengers)}$$

Other uses of CVP analysis. Management also can use its knowledge of CVP relationships to determine answers to such questions as whether to increase sales promotion costs in an effort to increase sales volume or to accept an order at a lower-than-usual price. In general, the careful study of break-even charts helps management plan future courses of action. Indeed, it has been said that to be successful, management must become "break-even minded."

Calculating the break-even point for a multiproduct firm

When computing the break-even point for a multiproduct firm, only dollars of sales will be used. In a multiproduct firm, a given product mix is assumed to be constant and unchanging for CVP purposes. *Product mix* relates to the proportion of the company's total sales attributable to each type of product sold by the company. To illustrate a multiproduct firm situation, assume the following historical data:

	Products							
	1		**2**		**3**		**Total**	
	Amount	Per-cent	Amount	Per-cent	Amount	Per-cent	Amount	Per-cent
Sales	$60,000	100	$30,000	100	$10,000	100	$100,000	100
Less: Variable costs	40,000	67	16,000	53	4,000	40	60,000	60
Contribution margin..........	$20,000	33	$14,000	47	$ 6,000	60	$ 40,000	40

The product mix for products 1, 2, and 3 is 60:30:10, respectively; that is, for each $60 of sales of product 1 there were $30 of sales of product 2 and $10 of sales of product 3. Variable costs are 60 percent of total sales. If the product mix is assumed to remain constant and fixed costs for the company are $50,000, break-even sales are $125,000:

$$S = FC + VC$$
$$S = \$50,000 + 0.60S$$
$$0.40S = \$50,000$$
$$S = \$125,000$$

The $125,000 of sales can be specified by product by multiplying total sales dollars by the percent of product mix of each of the three products. Therefore, the company will have to sell $75,000 (0.6 × $125,000) of product 1, $37,500 (0.3 × $125,000) of product 2, and $12,500 (0.1 × $125,000) of product 3 in order to break even.

If there is any change in the mix of products sold, the break-even point will also change; this is because of the shift between products of higher or lower contribution margins. Also, if historical patterns of selling prices or variable costs are not expected to hold true in the future, projected sales and variable expenses should be used to determine expected percentages of variable expenses to total sales.

DIFFERENTIAL ANALYSIS

Another tool of short-term decision making is differential analysis. *Differential analysis* involves analyzing a particular situation by reviewing the different costs and benefits which would arise from varying alternative solutions to the situation. *Relevant costs (or revenues)* in a given situation are future costs that differ between alternatives. The amount of the difference between relevant costs for two alternatives is called the *differential cost or expense.*[1] Future costs that do not differ between alternatives may be ignored since they will affect both alternatives similarly. Past costs are known as *sunk costs* and are also not relevant in decision making because the costs have already been incurred and, therefore, by their very nature cannot differ in the future no matter what alternative is chosen. Relevant revenues are those future revenues that differ between alternatives. *Differential revenue* is defined as the difference in revenues between two alternatives.

For certain decisions, revenues do not differ between alternatives. Under those circumstances, the decision should be to select the alternative with the least cost. In other situations, costs do not differ between alternatives. Accordingly, the alternative that results in the greatest revenue should be selected. In many decision situations, both future costs and future revenues differ between alternatives. In these situations, the alternative resulting in the greatest positive difference between future revenues and future expenses (costs) should be selected.

As an example of relevant, differential, and sunk costs, assume that Jack Bennett had invested $400 in a tiller so that he could till gardens for a fee of $1,500 during the summer. He is now offered the opportunity of working at a horse stable feeding horses and cleaning stalls for a salary of $1,200 for the summer. The additional costs that he would incur in tilling are $100 for transportation and $150 for supplies. The additional costs he will incur at the horse stable are $100 for transportation and $50 for supplies. If Jack works at the stable, the tiller would still be retained and be used by his

[1] Some authors equate relevant cost and differential cost. This text uses the term *relevant* to identify which costs should be considered in a situation and the term *differential* to identify the amount by which these costs differ.

parents and loaned to friends at no charge. The original tiller cost of $400 is not *relevant* to the decision because it is a *sunk* cost, nor is the cost of transportation relevant because it does not differ between alternatives. Therefore, the relevant costs and revenues are shown below:

	Performing tilling service	Working at horse stable	Differential
Revenues	$1,500	$1,200	$300
Costs	150	50	100
Net benefit in favor of tilling service			$200

In many situations, total variable costs differ between alternatives while total fixed costs do not. But one cannot assume that variable costs are always differential costs and fixed costs are never differential costs. For example, the differential cost between operating at a production level of 40,000 units versus a production level of 60,000 units might include increases in both variable and fixed costs. This increase in fixed costs could be the result of a step fixed cost such as that related to number of supervisors necessary for a particular production level.

The nature of fixed costs

Until now in this discussion, fixed costs have been treated as if they were all alike. But two types of fixed costs should be identified. They are *committed fixed costs* and *discretionary fixed costs*.

Committed fixed costs. *Committed fixed costs* relate to the basic facilities and organization structure that a company must have to continue operations. They are not changed in the short run without seriously disrupting operations. Examples of committed costs are depreciation on buildings and equipment and salaries of key executives. In the short run, costs such as these are viewed as being not subject to the discretion or control of management. They result from past decisions that "committed" the company for a period of several years. For instance, once a company constructs a building to house production operations, it is committed to the use of the building for many years. The depreciation on that building is not as subject to control by management as are some other types of fixed cost.

Discretionary fixed costs. In contrast to committed fixed costs, *discretionary fixed costs* are subject to management control from year to year. Each year management decides how much to spend on advertising, research and development, and employee training and development programs. Since these decisions are made each year, they are said to be under the "discretion" of management. Management is not locked in or committed to a certain level of expense for any more than one budget period. The next period it may change the level of expense or may eliminate it completely.

The philosophy of management can affect to some extent which fixed costs are committed and which are discretionary. For instance, during the recession of the mid 1970s, some companies terminated persons in the upper levels of management while other companies kept their "management team" intact. Thus, in some firms the salaries of top-level managers are discretionary while in others they are committed.

The discussion of committed fixed costs and discretionary fixed costs is relevant to CVP analysis. If a company's fixed costs are almost all committed fixed costs, it is going to have a more difficult time in reducing its break-even point for the next budget period than if most of its fixed costs are discretionary in nature. A company with a large proportion of discretionary fixed costs may be able to reduce fixed costs dramatically in a recessionary period. By doing this it may be able to "run lean" and show some earnings even when economic conditions are difficult. Its chances of long-run survival may be enhanced.

One other cost concept is necessary before discussing decision making and that is the concept of opportunity cost. An *opportunity cost* is the potential benefit that is forgone from *not* following the next best alternative course of action. For instance, assume that the two best uses of a plot of land are as a mobile home park (annual income of $100,000) and as a golf driving range (annual income of $60,000). The opportunity cost of utilizing the land as a mobile home park is $60,000, while the opportunity cost of utilizing the land as a driving range is $100,000. Opportunity costs are not recorded in the accounting records since they are the costs of *not* following a certain alternative.

Product pricing

Each possible price for a given product represents an alternative course of action. Relevant amounts for decision making are future total sales revenue and relevant costs (usually only future variable costs). These are the future amounts which vary between alternatives. Total fixed costs usually remain the same between pricing alternatives and, if so, may be ignored. In selecting a price for a product, the goal is to select that price at which total future revenues will exceed total future variable costs by the greatest amount or, in other words, that price which will result in the greatest *total* contribution margin.

A high price is not necessarily the price that will maximize earnings. There may be some good substitutes for the product. If a high price is set, the number of units sold may decline substantially as customers switch to lower priced competitive products. Thus, in the maximization of earnings, expected volume of sales at each price is as important as contribution margin per unit of product sold. In making any decision regarding the establishment of selling price, management should seek that combination of price and volume that will produce the largest *total* contribution margin. This is often difficult to do in an actual situation since management may have to estimate the number of units which can be sold at each price.

Assume that a company has fixed costs of $10,000 and variable production costs of $5 per unit. Estimates of product demand are as follows:

20,000 units at $4 per unit
15,000 units at $6 per unit
10,000 units at $8 per unit
 5,000 units at $10 per unit

What price should be set for the product? As shown below, the company should select a price of $8 per unit since this will result in the greatest total contribution margin ($30,000).

Choice	Contribution margin per unit*	×	Number of units	=	Total contribution margin
1	−$1		20,000		−$20,000
2	1		15,000		15,000
3	3		10,000		30,000
4	5		5,000		25,000

* Sales price − Variable cost.

Special orders

Sometimes management is faced with the opportunity to sell its product in two or more different markets at two or more different prices. Price discrimination is unlawful under the Robinson-Patman Act unless it is justified by differences in costs of delivery or selling. Since such cost differences often exist, a single product may be marketed at more than one selling price.

The desirability of keeping physical facilities and personnel working at capacity is obvious. Good business management requires keeping the cost of idleness at a minimum. When operations are at a level less than full capacity, additional business should be sought. Such additional business may be accepted at prices lower than average unit costs because the only relevant costs are the future *additional* costs that will be incurred. For the most part, the relevant costs will be variable costs, such as materials and labor.

To illustrate, assume that a given company produces and sells a single product which has a variable cost of $8 per unit. Annual capacity is 10,000 units, and annual fixed costs total $48,000. The selling price is $20 per unit, and production and sales are budgeted at 5,000 units. Thus, budgeted net income is $12,000, computed as follows:

Sales (5,000 units at $20)		$100,000
Costs:		
Fixed	$48,000	
Variable (5,000 at $8)	40,000	88,000
Net income		$ 12,000

An order for 3,000 units is received from a foreign distributor at a price of $10 per unit. This is only half the regular selling price per unit, and also less than the average cost per unit of $17.60 ($88,000 ÷ 5,000 units). But the $10 price offered exceeds variable cost per unit by $2. If the order is accepted, net income will be $18,000, computed as follows:

Sales (5,000 units at $20, 3,000 units at $10) ...		$130,000
Costs:		
Fixed	$48,000	
Variable (8,000 units at $8)	64,000	112,000
Net income		$ 18,000

To continue to operate at 50 percent of capacity would produce net income of only $12,000. Thus, a contribution margin of $2 per unit on the new units will result from acceptance of the order, and net income will increase by $6,000. Because the regular market is unlikely to be affected by the export of the product at a sharply reduced price, the order should be accepted.

Using the decision format illustrated earlier, the analysis would be as follows:

	(1) Accept order	(2) Reject order	Differential
Revenues	$130,000	$100,000	$30,000
Costs	64,000	40,000	24,000
Net benefit in favor of accepting order			$ 6,000

In summary, variable costs set a floor for the selling price in cost analyses. Even if price exceeds variable costs only slightly, the additional business may make a contribution to earnings. But "contribution pricing" of marginal business often brings only short-term increases in earnings. Such pricing should be appraised in light of the long-range effects on company and industry price structures. In the long run, full costs must be covered.

Elimination of products, segments, or customers

Periodically, management faces the question of eliminating or retaining certain products, segments, or customers. A special study of costs and revenues may assist in the solution of such problems. Since the income statement does not automatically associate costs with given products, segments, or customers, costs must be reclassified into those that would be changed by the elimination and those that would not. In effect, one must simply assume elimination and compare the reduction in revenues with the eliminated costs.

Usually costs such as materials, labor, and other variable costs will be eliminated and, therefore, become part of differential cost. The fixed costs will *normally* remain unaffected and are not relevant to the decision. If revenues lost from discontinuing the product, segment, or customer exceed the costs that would be eliminated, that item is making a positive contribution to profits and should, therefore, be retained unless a more profitable opportunity exists.

To illustrate, assume that elimination of product R is being considered. Product R provides revenues of $100,000 annually and incurs costs of $110,000, $80,000 variable and $30,000 fixed. Therefore, product R creates an apparent annual loss of $10,000. But careful cost analysis reveals that if product R were dropped, the reduction in costs would be $80,000. The $30,000 fixed costs would continue to be incurred and would need to be covered by the remaining products of the company. The analysis is as follows:

	(1) Retain product R	(2) Drop product R	Differential
Revenues	$100,000	–0–	$100,000
Costs	80,000	–0–	80,000
Net benefit of retaining Product R			$ 20,000

The illustration shows that product R, even though producing no net income itself, has been contributing $20,000 ($100,000 − $80,000) annually to covering fixed costs of the business. Its elimination could be a costly mistake unless there was a more profitable use for the released resources. For instance, if the released facilities could be used to produce an alternative product that would make a contribution to earnings of more than $20,000 per year, product R should be eliminated, and production of the alternative product should proceed. Earnings from the alternative product are an opportunity cost of retaining product R and vice versa.

Joint products

In some manufacturing situations several products result from a common raw material or manufacturing process; these are called *joint products*. An example is crude oil, from which a wide variety of fuels, solvents, lubricants, and residual petrochemicals are derived. *Joint costs* are those costs incurred up to the point where the joint products split off from each other. These costs are sunk costs in deciding whether to process a joint product further before selling it or to sell it in its condition at split off.

Assume that Company Y manufactures two products, A and B, from a common manufacturing process. Each of the products could be sold in its present form or could be processed further and sold at a higher price. Assume the following data:

Product	Selling price per unit at split-off point	Cost of further processing per unit	Selling price per unit after further processing
A	$10	$6	$21
B	12	7	18

The differential revenues and costs of further processing of the two products are as follows:

Product	Differential revenue of further processing	Differential cost of further processing	Net advantage (disadvantage) of further processing
A	$11	$6	$ 5
B	6	7	(1)

Based on this analysis, product A should be processed further since this will increase earnings by $5 per unit sold. Product B should not be processed further as this will decrease earnings by $1 per unit sold.

This same form of analysis should also be used in deciding whether *by-products,* the waste materials that result from the production of a product, should be discarded or processed further to be made salable. If the differential revenue of further processing exceeds the differential cost, then further processing should be done. If not, the waste material should be discarded.

Make-or-buy decisions

Another application of differential analysis is the make-or-buy decision. A *make-or-buy decision* concerns whether to manufacture or purchase a part or material used in the manufacture of another product. The price which would be paid for the part if it were purchased is compared with the *additional costs* that would be incurred if the part were manufactured. If almost all of the manufacturing costs are fixed and would exist in any case, it is likely that manufacture rather than purchase of the part or material would be more economical.

To illustrate, a company is manufacturing parts costing $6 for use in its final product. Cost components are materials, $3; labor, $1.50; fixed overhead costs, $1.05; and variable overhead costs, $0.45. The part could be purchased for $5.25. Since fixed overhead would presumably continue even if the part were purchased, manufacture of the part should be continued. The added costs of manufacturing amount to only $4.95 ($3.00 + $1.50 + $0.45). This is 30 cents per unit less than the purchase price of the part, as shown in the following analysis:

	(1) Make	(2) Buy	Differential
Revenues	$0	$0	$0
Costs	4.95	5.25	0.30
Net advantage of making			$0.30

The opportunity cost of not utilizing the space for some other purpose should also be considered. If the opportunity cost of not using this space in its best alternative use is more than 30 cents per unit times the number of units produced, then the part should be purchased from outside.

In certain situations, it may be possible to avoid portions of fixed costs by buying outside. If so, these fixed costs should be treated the same as variable costs in the analysis, since they would then be relevant costs.

In some cases, the relative cost to manufacture as opposed to purchase may be only a minor consideration. Other factors to be considered are competency of existing personnel to undertake manufacture of the part or material, availability of working capital, and cost of any borrowings that may be necessary.

ABSORPTION VERSUS DIRECT COSTING

As the final consideration in short-term decision making, a new or different form of income statement and product costing will be considered. Currently, the most commonly accepted theory and method of product costing is called absorption or full costing. *Absorption (or full) costing* holds that all production costs, including fixed manufacturing overhead, are accounted for as product costs and are allocated to the units of product produced during a period. *Direct (or variable) costing,* on the other hand, includes only variable manufacturing costs as product costs. All fixed manufacturing overhead is charged to expense in the period in which it is incurred. The difference between the income statements under the two methods is that absorption costing focuses on gross margin, while direct costing focuses on contribution margin.

The differences between absorption and direct costing can be seen by comparing the income statements that would result from applying each technique to the same data. Assume the Breaux Company had the following data related to manufacturing and sales activities for May 1984:

Beginning inventory		–0–
Production (units)		10,000
Sales (units)		9,000
Fixed costs:		
Manufacturing overhead		$ 6,000
Selling expenses		15,000
Administrative expenses		12,000

Variable costs (per unit):	
Direct materials	$2.00
Direct labor	1.00
Manufacturing overhead	0.30
Total	$3.30
Variable selling expenses (per unit)	$0.20
Selling price (per unit)	$8.00

Absorption costing

Under absorption costing, the fixed manufacturing overhead would be applied to the units of production at the rate of $0.60 per unit ($6,000/10,000 units). Therefore, the cost per unit of inventory is $3.90, the total of the direct materials, and direct labor, and the variable and fixed manufacturing overhead. All selling and administrative expenses are period costs. Illustration 26.8 contains the income statement for the company which would be prepared under absorption costing.

Generally, variable and fixed manufacturing costs do not appear as separate line items on the income statement; they are presented this way simply to illustrate that the fixed manufacturing costs are included as part of product cost and that some of these costs are included in ending inventory. Ending inventory is priced at "full cost" of $3.90 per unit, ($39,000/10,000). Also, no distinction is made between fixed and variable selling expenses. These are totaled and shown under operating expenses of the period.

Absorption costing is required for external financial statement presentation and also for tax purposes. But as shown throughout this chapter, a "full" cost approach is not necessarily the best approach for management decision making. Management often needs information on contribution margin rather than gross margin in order to decide on such things as break-even points and special order pricing. Direct costing presents this information in a more obvious and prominent form.

Illustration 26.8: Income statement under absorption costing

Sales (9,000 units at $8)		$72,000
Cost of goods sold:		
Variable costs of production (10,000 units at $3.30)	$33,000	
Fixed overhead costs	6,000	
Total costs of producing 10,000 units	$39,000	
Less: Inventory (1,000 units at $3.90)	3,900	35,100
Gross margin on sales		$36,900
Operating expenses:		
Selling ($15,000 fixed plus 9,000 at $0.20 each)	$16,800	
Administrative	12,000	28,800
Net income		$ 8,100

Direct costing

Under direct costing, all *variable* costs of production (direct materials, direct labor, and variable manufacturing overhead) are treated as product costs. All *fixed* manufacturing costs are considered period costs and are charged to expense. The logic behind this expensing of fixed overhead is that such costs would be incurred whether there was production or whether the plant was idle and, therefore, do not specifically relate to the manufacture of products. The direct costing income statement for Breaux Company for May 1984 is presented in Illustration 26.9.

Illustration 26.9: Income statement under direct costing

Sales (9,000 units at $8)		$72,000
Variable costs:		
Variable production costs incurred (10,000 units at $3.30)	$33,000	
Less: Inventory (1,000 units at $3.30)	3,300	29,700
Manufacturing margin		$42,300
Variable selling expenses (9,000 units at $0.20)		1,800
Contribution margin		$40,500
Fixed costs:		
Manufacturing overhead	$ 6,000	
Selling expenses	15,000	
Administrative expenses	12,000	33,000
Net income ·		$ 7,500

Notice in the direct or variable cost income statement that the goods in inventory are carried at $3.30 per unit rather than the $3.90 full cost. All variable costs are shown separately at the top of the statement as deductions from sales to disclose contribution margin for the month. All fixed costs are presented as period costs no matter what the source of the cost (manufacturing, selling, or administrative).

Comparing the two methods

Comparing the two income statements, there is a $600 difference in net income for the month and a $600 difference in ending inventory valuation. These differences are due to the treatment of fixed manufacturing overhead. Under absorption costing, each unit in ending inventory carries $0.60 of fixed overhead cost as part of product cost. There are 1,000 units in inventory at the end of the month; therefore, the $600 difference in inventory exists. Under direct costing, *all* the fixed manufacturing overhead is charged off during the period rather than being deferred and carried forward to the next period as part of inventory cost. Therefore, $6,000 of fixed overhead appears on the direct costing income statement as an expense rather than $5,400 ($0.60 per unit × 9,000 units sold) under absorption costing.

As a final point of emphasis, recognize that the difference between the two methods is *solely* in the treatment of fixed manufacturing overhead and income statement presentation. Selling and administrative expenses are treated the same way, as period costs, under both methods. The only difference in regard to these costs is their placement on the income statement and the segregation of variable and fixed selling and administrative expenses. Variable selling or administrative expenses are *not* part of product cost under either method.

Analysis is slightly more complicated when both beginning and ending inventories are involved. The difference in net income is found by determining whether the amount of fixed overhead included in inventory cost under absorption costing increased or decreased from the beginning to end of the period.

If that amount increased, net income under direct costing will be less than under absorption costing. If the amount of fixed overhead included in inventory decreased during the period, net income under direct costing will be greater than under absorption costing.

As a general rule, the difference in net incomes under the two methods can be related to the *change* in inventories. Assuming a relatively constant level of production, if inventories increase during the year, production exceeded sales and reported net income will be less under direct costing than under absorption costing. Conversely, if inventories decreased, sales exceeded production and net income will be larger under direct costing than under absorption costing.

Direct costing is not currently considered acceptable for income measurement, inventory valuation, or tax purposes. Currently accepted practice requires that *all* costs of producing a product be, to the extent possible, attached to that product and treated as expenses only when the product is sold. But the type of information accumulated under direct costing, especially the classification of costs as fixed and variable, is very useful to management in understanding relationships between costs, volume, and profits. Certainly the responsibility for and the control of costs are more readily secured through proper cost classification. Since direct costing is such a valuable management tool, its use is likely to increase.

NEW TERMS INTRODUCED IN CHAPTER 26*

Absorption (or full) costing
A concept of costing under which all production costs, including fixed factory overhead, are accounted for as product costs and allocated to the units produced during a period.

Break-even analysis
See cost-volume-profit analysis.

Break-even chart
A graphic presentation of the relationships between sales, costs, volume, and profit that also shows the break-even point.

Break-even point
That level of operations at which revenues for a period are equal to the costs assigned to that period so that there is no net income or loss.

By-products
The waste materials (which sometimes have a small market value compared to the main product) that result from the production of a product or products.

Committed fixed costs
Costs relating to the basic facilities and organization structure that a company must have to continue operations. An example is depreciation on the factory building.

Contribution margin
The amount by which revenue exceeds the variable costs incurred in generating that revenue.

Contribution margin rate
Contribution margin expressed as a percentage of selling price.

Cost-volume-profit (CVP) analysis
An analysis of the effects of changes in selling price, costs, and volume upon earnings (profits) in the short run. Also called break-even analysis.

Differential analysis
An analysis of the different costs and benefits that would arise from varying alternative solutions to a situation.

Differential cost or expense
The difference between the amounts of relevant costs for two alternatives.

Differential revenue
The difference between the amounts of relevant revenues for two alternatives.

* Some terms listed in earlier chapters are repeated here for your convenience.

Direct (or variable) costing
A concept of costing under which only variable manufacturing costs are accounted for as product costs and allocated to the units produced during a period. All fixed manufacturing overhead is charged to expense in the period in which it is incurred.

Discretionary fixed costs
Those fixed costs that are subject to management control from year to year. An example is advertising expense.

Fixed costs
Costs that remain constant (in total) over the entire range of output.

High-low method
A method used in dividing mixed costs into their fixed and variable portions. The high plot and low plot of actual costs are used to draw a line representing a total mixed cost.

Joint costs
Those costs incurred up to the point where joint products are split off from each other.

Joint products
Two or more products resulting from a common raw material or manufacturing process.

Least squares method
A method used for dividing mixed costs into their fixed and variable portions. It uses statistical techniques to draw the regression line representing a total mixed cost.

Make-or-buy decision
Concerns whether to manufacture or purchase a part or material used in the manufacture of another product.

Margin of safety
The difference between current sales and sales at the break-even point.

Margin of safety rate
Is equal to (Current sales − Break-even sales) ÷ Current sales.

Mixed cost
A cost that is partly fixed and partly variable so a minimum cost is incurred regardless of volume of output but total cost increases with output.

Opportunity cost
The potential benefit that is forgone from not following the next best alternative course of action.

Product mix
The proportion of the company's total sales attributable to each type of product sold by the company. Product mix may be defined either in terms of sales dollars or in terms of number of units sold.

Relevant (or revenues) costs
Costs (or revenues) that will differ in the future depending on which alternative course of action is selected.

Relevant range
The range of production or sales volume over which the basic cost behavior assumptions will hold true.

Scatter diagram
A diagram that shows plots of actual costs incurred for various levels of output or sales. It is used in dividing mixed costs into their fixed and variable portions.

Short run
The period of time over which it is assumed that plant capacity and certain costs are fixed; often determined to be one year or less.

Step cost
A cost that remains constant (in total) over a range of output (or sales) but then increases in steps at certain points over the entire range of output (or sales).

Sunk costs
Past costs about which nothing can be done; they are irrelevant to decisions.

Variable costs
Costs which vary (in total) directly with changes in volume.

Variable cost rate
Variable costs expressed as a percentage of selling price.

DEMONSTRATION PROBLEM 26–1

The Boston Company has fixed costs of $250,000 per year and variable costs of $6 per unit. Its product sells for $10 per unit. Full capacity is 100,000 units.

Required:

a.   Compute the break-even point in (1) sales dollars, (2) units, and (3) percentage of capacity.

b.   Compute the number of units the company must sell if it wishes to have net income of $120,000.

Solution to demonstration problem 26–1

Variable costs are 60 percent of sales ($6/$10).

a.   1.   Sales (S) = Fixed costs (FC) + Variable costs (VC)

$$S = \$250,000 + 0.6S$$
$$0.4S = \$250,000$$
$$S = \$250,000 \div 0.4$$
$$S = \underline{\underline{\$625,000}}$$

2.   Break-even point in units = $625,000 \div \$10 = \underline{\underline{62,500}}$

3.   Break-even point as percentage of capacity = $62,500 \div 100,000 = \underline{\underline{62.5}}$ percent

b.   Number of units = $\dfrac{\text{Fixed costs} + \text{Desired net income}}{\text{Contribution margin}}$

$$= \frac{\$250,000 + \$120,000}{\$10 - \$6}$$

$$= \frac{\$370,000}{\$4}$$

$$= \underline{\underline{92,500}}$$

DEMONSTRATION PROBLEM 26–2

The Detroit Division of the Orvis Company produces a single product which it sells for $10 each. Its production costs are $2 per unit variable costs and $330,000 per year of fixed overhead costs. Normal activity for fixed overhead absorption is 110,000 units per year. Thus, fixed overhead is applied at $3 per unit. Selling and administrative expenses are $25,000 plus $0.50 per unit sold.

On December 31, 1984, the division's finished goods inventory consisted of 20,000 units with a total cost of $100,000 ($40,000, variable; $60,000, fixed). Sales and production data for 1985 are:

Sales in units	100,000
Dollars of sales	$1,000,000
Production in units	110,000
Variable production costs	$ 220,000

Required:

a.   Prepare an income statement for the division for 1985 under absorption costing.

b.   Repeat part (*a*) under direct costing.

Solution to demonstration problem 26–2

a.   Income statement under absorption costing:

Sales (100,000 units at $10)			$1,000,000
Cost of goods sold:			
Variable production costs ($2 per unit)	$220,000		
Fixed overhead absorbed ($3 per unit)	330,000		
Cost of goods manufactured		$ 550,000	
Beginning finished goods inventory			
(absorption cost $5 per unit)		100,000	
Ending finished goods inventory			
(absorption cost $5 per unit)		(150,000)	
Cost of goods sold			500,000
Gross margin on sales			$ 500,000
Selling and administrative expenses			75,000
Net income			$ 425,000

b. Income statement under direct costing:

Sales (100,000 units at $10)			$1,000,000
Cost of goods sold:			
Direct cost of goods manufactured			
($2 per unit)	$220,000		
Beginning finished goods inventory			
(direct cost $2 per unit)	40,000		
Ending finished goods inventory			
(direct cost $2 per unit)	(60,000)		
Cost of goods sold		$ 200,000	
Manufacturing margin		$ 800,000	
Variable selling and administrative expenses		50,000	
Contribution margin		$ 750,000	
Period costs:			
Fixed manufacturing overhead	$330,000		
Fixed selling and administrative expenses	25,000		
Net income		355,000	
		$ 395,000	

QUESTIONS

1. Name and describe the four cost behavior patterns.

2. What are the various ways in which the cost line for a mixed cost can be determined? Describe each method.

3. What is meant by the term *break-even point?* What factors must be taken into consideration in determining it?

4. What are the different ways in which the break-even point may be expressed?

5. How is relevant range related to break-even analysis?

6. Why is break-even analysis considered appropriate only for short-run decisions?

7. What is the formula for calculating the break-even point in sales revenue?

8. What formula is used to solve for the break-even point in units? How can this formula be altered to calculate the number of units which must be sold to achieve a desired level of earnings?

9. Why might a business wish to lower its break-even point? How would it go about lowering the break-even point? What effect would you expect the mechanization and automation of production processes to have upon the break-even point?

10. How is the break-even point calculated for a multi-product firm?

11. What does the label "units" on the horizontal axis of the break-even chart mean?

12. Identify some types of decisions that can be made using differential analysis.

13. What is a committed fixed cost? Give some examples.

14. What is a discretionary fixed cost? Give some examples.

15. Give an example of a fixed cost that might be considered committed for one firm and discretionary for another.

16. What assumptions are made in cost-volume profit (CVP) analysis?

17. What essential feature distinguishes direct costing from absorption costing?

18. Under what specific circumstances would you expect net income to be larger under direct costing than under absorption costing? What is the specific reason for this difference?

EXERCISES

E–1. Use the high-low method to determine the fixed and variable components of a mixed cost, given the following observations:

Volume (units)	Cost
8,000	$10,000
16,000	16,000

E–2. Compute the break-even point in sales dollars if fixed costs are $110,000 and variable costs are 45 percent of sales.

E–3. The Pretenders Company sells each unit it produces for $10, with fixed costs of $40,000 and variable costs of $6 per unit. Find the break-even point in units.

E–4. The Magnet Company currently sells each unit it produces for $5. Variable cost is $1.50 per unit and fixed costs are $70,000. Compute the break-even point in both dollars and units under each of the following independent assumptions. Comment on why the break-even points are different.

    a. The costs and selling price are as given above.
    b. Fixed costs are increased to $77,000.
    c. Selling price is increased by 2 percent.
    d. Variable cost is increased to $1.80 per unit.

E–5. Consider a company which sells a product for $10 each with variable cost of $5 for each unit. Fixed costs are $500,000. The company currently sells 200,000 units per year. Should this company undertake an advertising campaign that will result in a $50,000 increase in fixed costs, a $1 per unit decrease in variable cost, and a 10 percent increase in sales? What would the margin of safety be before and after the campaign?

E–6. If a company has fixed costs of $65,000 and variable cost of $7 per unit, how many units would have to be sold at $10.50 each to break even? How many units would have to be sold to earn $50,000? If 30,000 units are 100 percent of capacity, what percentage of capacity do the two levels of output represent?

E–7. Big Gulp Company sells three products. Last year's sales were $50,000 for product A, $65,000 for product B, and $35,000 for product C. Variable costs were A, $30,000; B, $40,000; and C, $22,000. Fixed costs were $24,000. What was the margin of safety?

E–8. If the company in Exercise E–7 changes the product mix to 2:2:1 with total dollar sales being the same as last year, what will the new break-even point be? Comment on why it has changed.

E–9.   The Circus Company sells each unit it produces for $4. Calculate the break-even point in dollars given the following cost observations:

Volume (units)	Cost
2,000	$12,000
17,000	37,500

E–10.   Assume you had invested $240 in a lawn mower to set up a lawn mowing business for the summer. During the first week, you are presented with two opportunities. You can mow the grounds at a housing development (at a fee of $300) or you can help paint a garage (at a fee of $250). The additional costs you will incur are $50 and $20, respectively. These costs include $4 under each alternative for a pair of gloves that will last about one week. Prepare a schedule showing:

  a. The relevant revenues and expenses (costs).
  b. The differential revenue and expense.
  c. The net benefit or advantage of selecting one alternative over the other.

E–11.   The Lane Corporation is operating at 80 percent of capacity producing 8,000 units. Variable costs amount to $60 per unit. Wholesaler A offers to buy up to 2,000 units at $70 per unit. Wholesaler B proposes to buy 1,500 units at $75 per unit. Which offer, if any, should the Lane Corporation accept?

E–12.   Two companies, Halstead, Inc., and Kelsey and Company, are competitors. Halstead, Inc., has just installed the latest automated equipment so that its fixed costs are $60,000. Kelsey and Company operates a run-down plant with only $30,000 of fixed costs. Both companies have $100,000 in sales with gross margins of 20 percent. Compute gross margins for the two companies assuming a 10 percent drop in sales volume.

E–13.   In the situation described in Exercise E–12, which company can bid lower on a special order to regain lost sales? Why?

E–14.   Analysis of product A reveals that it is losing $5,000 annually. Ten thousand units of product A are sold at a price of $5 per unit each year. If variable costs are $4 per unit, what would be the increase (decrease) in company earnings if product A were eliminated?

E–15.   Department 1 of the Slate Company has revenues of $100,000, variable expenses of $40,000, direct fixed expenses of $20,000, and allocated, indirect fixed expenses of $50,000. If the department is eliminated, what will be the effect on earnings?

E–16.   The Lobek Company manufactures two joint products. At the split-off point they have sales values of:

Product 1 . . . . . $7/unit
Product 2 . . . . . $5/unit

After further processing costing $4 and $3, respectively, they can be sold for $15 and $7, respectively. Should further processing be done on both products? Why?

E-17.   The Synder Corporation currently is manufacturing 20,000 units per year of a part used in its final product. The cost of producing this part is $21.50 each. The variable portion of this cost consists of direct materials of $12, direct labor of $6.50, and manufacturing overhead of $1. The company could earn $20,000 per year from the space now used to manufacture this part. Assuming equal quality and availability, what is the maximum price Synder Corporation should pay to buy the part rather than make it?

E-18.   The following data relate to the Friday Company for the year ended December 31, 1984:

Costs of production:

Direct materials	$50,000
Direct labor	70,000
Manufacturing overhead:	
Variable	25,000
Fixed	50,000
Sales commissions (variable)	15,000
Sales salaries (fixed)	10,000
Administrative expense (fixed)	20,000
Units produced	25,000
Units sold (at $15 each)	20,000

     Without making any computations, would you expect net income to be higher under absorption or under direct costing? Compute the amount of net income and ending inventory under both methods.

E-19.   The following data are for a certain company for the year 1984:

Sales (20,000 units)	$200,000
Direct materials used (24,000 units at $3) ...	72,000
Direct labor cost incurred	24,000
Manufacturing overhead incurred:	
Variable	7,200
Fixed	9,600
Selling and administrative expenses:	
Variable	12,000
Fixed	40,000

     Assume that one unit of direct materials goes into each unit of finished goods. There is an ending inventory of finished goods of 4,000 units, and there are no other beginning or ending inventories. The variable and fixed overhead rates (based on normal activity of 24,000 units) were $0.30 and $0.40, respectively. Compute the net income before income taxes under (*a*) absorption costing and (*b*) direct costing.

E-20.   Given below are the costs of the finished goods inventories of the M Company:

Cost element	Beginning inventory	Ending inventory
Direct materials	$30,000	$3,000
Direct labor	50,000	5,200
Overhead:		
Variable	20,000	2,000
Fixed	15,000	2,000

     Assume the M Company uses absorption costing and there were no work in process inventories at the beginning or end of the year. State by how much M Company's net income before income taxes for the year would have differed if direct costing could have been used for tax purposes.

PROBLEMS, SERIES A

P26–1–A.   The Westly Company has identified various variable and fixed costs in its operations. There is a mixed cost which needs to be divided into its fixed and variable portions. Actual data pertaining to this cost are as follows:

Year	Units	Cost
1975	10,400	$12,800
1976	10,000	12,000
1977	11,000	13,000
1978	12,800	12,800
1979	14,200	13,000
1980	15,000	13,800
1981	16,400	14,200
1982	17,800	15,200
1983	18,800	16,000
1984	20,000	17,200

Required:

a.   Using the high-low method, determine the total amount of fixed costs and the amount of variable cost per unit. Draw the cost line.

b.   Prepare a scatter diagram, plot the actual costs, and visually fit a linear cost line to the points. Estimate the amount of total fixed costs and the amount of variable cost per unit.

P26–2–A.

a.   Determine the break-even point in sales dollars and units for a firm which has fixed costs of $60,000, variable costs of $6 per unit, and a selling price of $11 per unit.

b.   Y Company breaks even when sales are $100,000. In 1984, sales were $450,000 and variable costs were $270,000. Compute the amount of fixed costs.

c.   The Match Company had sales in 1984 of $140,000, variable costs of $77,000, and fixed costs of $35,000. At what level of sales did the firm break even?

d.   What would the break-even point in sales dollars have been in (c) above if variable costs had been 10 percent higher?

e.   What would the break-even point in sales dollars have been in (c) above if fixed costs had been 10 percent higher?

f.   Compute the break-even point in sales dollars for the Match Company under the assumptions of both (d) and (e) together.

P26–3–A.   The Fargo Company has plant capacity of 75,000 units. Variable costs are $300,000 at 100 percent capacity. Fixed costs are $200,000, but this is true only between 25,000 and 75,000 units.

Required:

a.   Prepare a break-even chart for the Fargo Company assuming it sells its product for $8 each. Indicate on the chart the relevant range, contribution margin, break-even point, and earnings.

b. Verify the break-even point on the chart by using the break-even sales formula given in ths chapter. Also calculate the break-even point in units.

c. How many units would have to be sold in order to earn $50,000 before taxes?

P26–4–A.   Following is a summary of operations in 1984 for two companies:

	Company C		Company D	
Sales		$500,000		$500,000
Expenses:				
Fixed	$100,000		$350,000	
Variable	300,000		50,000	
Total expenses ...		400,000		400,000
Net operating income		$100,000		$100,000

Required:

a. Compute the break-even point in sales dollars for each company.

b. Assume that without changes in selling price the sales of each company decreased by 25 percent. Present condensed income statements, similar to the ones above, showing the effect of the decrease in sales on the operating income of each company.

P26–5–A.   The Flour Company has plant capacity of 100,000 units, at which level variable costs are $600,000. Fixed costs are expected to be $180,000. Each unit sells for $10.

Required:

a. Determine the company's break-even point in sales dollars and units.

b. What level of sales would the firm need to attain in order to earn $120,000 before taxes?

c. If the selling price were raised to $12 per unit, what level of sales would the firm need to attain in order to earn $120,000 before taxes?

P26–6–A.

a. The Oscar Corporation sells its product for $6 per unit. Variable costs are $4.50 per unit and fixed costs are $225,000. Compute the break-even point in dollars and units.

b. The Sells Company had sales in 1984 of $600,000, and its variable costs were $240,000. If the company breaks even with sales of $175,000, what are the fixed costs?

c. What would the break-even point in sales dollars have been for the Sells Company in part (*b*) if variable costs had been 15 percent higher?

d. What would the break-even point in sales dollars have been in part (*b*) if fixed costs had been 10 percent lower?

e. What would the break-even point in sales dollars have been under the assumptions of both (*c*) and (*d*) together?

P26–7–A.   The Fred Corporation has fixed costs of $100,000. It sells three products. The cost and revenue data for these products are as follows:

	Products		
	1	*2*	*3*
Sales	$50,000	$75,000	$100,000
Variable costs	30,000	50,000	55,000

Required:

    a. Compute the break-even point in sales dollars.

    b. Assume the sales mix is expected to be in the ratio of 2:2:1 next year with total sales being the same as this year. What would the break-even point be in sales dollars?

P26–8–A. A state government has asked for bids on an order for 200,000 units of product X. The Rex Company, which has a production capacity of 1,000,000 units and is currently operating at 80 percent of capacity, is considering making a bid for the government contract. The Rex Company's fixed costs amount to $4,000,000, and its variable costs are $40 per unit.

Required:

    a. What is the minimum price to be bid by the company?

    b. Present two income statements, the first assuming that the bid is unsuccessful and that the price on regular sales is $60 per unit, and the second assuming that the contract is obtained at a bid price of $50 per unit, while regular sales are at $60 per unit.

P26–9–A. Bill Grant, the president of Grant's, Inc., is very concerned over the fact that he is unable to generate any net income from Department 3. He has devoted considerable time and a disproportionate part of the expenditures of the business to this department and it still shows a loss. He has reached the point where he is considering closing the department and expanding his other two departments equally into the space now occupied by Department 3. He believes that this move will neither increase the sales nor lower the costs of the other two departments but simply will relieve some overcrowding. In condensed form, the income statement for the year ended September 30, 1984, is:

	Dept. 1	Dept. 2	Dept. 3	Total
Net sales	$120,000	$80,000	$40,000	$240,000
Cost of goods sold	80,000	$50,000	$25,000	$155,000
Advertising expense	4,000	3,000	4,000	11,000
Sales salaries	10,000	7,000	3,000	20,000
Delivery expense	3,000	2,000	1,000	6,000
Buying expense	6,000	4,000	2,000	12,000
Occupancy expense	5,000	2,500	2,500	10,000
Administrative expense ...	7,500	5,000	3,500	16,000
Total expenses	$115,500	$73,500	$41,000	$230,000
Net income	$ 4,500	$ 6,500	$ (1,000)	$ 10,000

    For all departments, any direct expense would be eliminated if the department were eliminated. Indirect expenses would not be eliminated. Advertising expense is direct to the extent of $3,000 to each of the three departments while the balance is allocable equally to 1 and 3. All of the sales salaries and related expenses are direct. Delivery expense is all indirect and is allocated on the basis of sales; no reduction is expected if Department 3 is closed. Buying expenses are allocated on the basis of purchases ($90,000, $60,000, and $30,000). If Department 3 is discontinued, these expenses will be reduced by $2,000. Occupancy expenses are all indirect and fixed and are allocated on the basis of square feet of space occupied (10,000, 5,000, and 5,000). Departments 1 and 2 will each take equal amounts of the space formerly occupied by 3 if 3 is closed. Administrative expenses are direct to the extent of $4,000, $1,000, and $2,000 to 1, 2, and 3. The indirect expense is allocated on the basis of estimated direct administrative officer time spent on each department, which is in the ratio of 7:8:3.

Required:

　　a. Present an income statement for the year ended September 30, 1984, showing the net income for the remaining departments and the company that would have resulted if Department 3 had been closed during the year.

　　b. Should Department 3 be closed? Explain.

P26–10–A. The following data are for the Stein Company for the year 1984:

Sales (10,000 units)	$100,000
Direct materials used (12,000 units at $3)	36,000
Direct labor cost incurred	12,000
Variable manufacturing overhead incurred	3,600
Fixed manufacturing overhead incurred	4,800
Variable selling and administrative expenses . . .	6,000
Fixed selling and administrative expenses	20,000

　　One unit of direct materials goes into each unit of finished goods. The only beginning or ending inventory is the 2,000 units of finished goods on hand at the end of 1984. Variable and fixed overhead rates (based on 100 percent of capacity of 12,000 units) were $0.30 and $0.40, respectively.

Required:

　　Prepare an income statement under—

　　a. Direct costing.

　　b. Absorption costing.

PROBLEMS, SERIES B

P26–1–B. The May Company assigns to you the task of estimating maintenance costs on its production machinery. This cost is a mixed cost. You are supplied with the following data from past years:

Year	Units	Cost
1976	4,000	$5,000
1977	5,000	5,400
1978	4,500	5,500
1979	5,500	5,800
1980	5,000	5,800
1981	6,500	6,200
1982	7,000	6,700
1983	9,000	7,200
1984	10,000	8,000

Required:

　　a. Using the high-low method, determine the total amount of fixed costs and the amount of variable cost per unit.

　　b. Prepare a scatter diagram, plot the actual costs, and visually fit a linear cost line to the points. Estimate the amount of total fixed costs and the amount of variable cost per unit.

P26–2–B.   If a company has fixed costs of $250,000, variable cost of $3 per unit, and a selling price of $7, how many units must be sold to break even? How many units will it have to sell to earn $40,000 before taxes?

P26–3–B.   Compute the break-even point in sales dollars and units under each of the following independent assumptions. Selling price in each case is $25 per unit unless otherwise stated.

  a. Fixed costs are $100,000; variable cost is $17 per unit.

  b. Fixed costs are $100,000; variable cost is $15 per unit.

  c. Fixed costs are $80,000; variable cost is $15 per unit.

  d. Fixed costs are $80,000; selling price is $20, and variable cost is $15 per unit.

  e. Use the assumptions in (d) above to determine the level of sales required to achieve net income of $50,000.

P26–4–B.

  a. Assume that fixed costs of A Corporation are $400,000 per year, variable cost is $8 per unit, and selling price is $20 per unit. Determine the break-even point in sales dollars.

  b. B Company breaks even when sales amount to $4,000,000. In 1984, its sales were $6,000,000 and its variable costs amounted to $1,800,000. Determine the amount of its fixed costs.

  c. The sales of C Corporation in 1984 amounted to $80,000,000, its variable costs were $20,000,000, and its fixed costs were $40,000,000. At what level of sales would the C Corporation have exactly broken even?

  d. What would have been the net income of the C Corporation, in part (c) above, if sales volume had been 10 percent higher but selling prices had remained unchanged?

  e. What would have been the net income of the C Corporation, in part (c) above, if variable costs had been 10 percent lower?

  f. What would have been the net income of the C Corporation, in part (c) above, if fixed costs had been 10 percent lower?

  g. Determine the break-even point in sales dollars for the C Corporation on the basis of the data given in (e) above; in (f) above.

P26–5–B.   The operating results for two companies are presented below:

	Company 1	Company 2
Sales (20,000 units)	$200,000	$200,000
Variable costs	50,000	110,000
Contribution margin	$150,000	$ 90,000
Fixed costs	100,000	40,000
Net income	$ 50,000	$ 50,000

Required:

  a. Prepare a break-even chart for Company 1, indicating the break-even point, the contribution margin, and the areas of earnings and losses.

  b. Compute the break-even point of both companies in sales dollars and units.

c. Assume that without changes in selling price, the sales of each company decline by 20 percent. Prepare condensed income statements for both companies similar to the ones above.

P26–6–B.   The Easy Listening Company, a leading manufacturer of clock radios, incurred $210,000 of fixed costs while selling 20,000 radios at $50 each. Variable cost was $15 per radio.

A new machine used in the production of clock radios has recently become available and is more efficient than the machine currently being used. The new machine would reduce variable costs by 20 percent and can be leased on an annual basis for $8,000 per year.

Required:

a.   Compute the break-even point *in units* assuming use of the old machine.

b.   Compute the break-even point in units assuming use of the new machine.

c.   Assuming total sales remain at $1,000,000, compute expected net income assuming the new machine is leased.

d.   Should the new machine be leased? Why?

P26–7–B.

a.   Thomas Company reports sales of $400,000, variable costs of $240,000, and fixed costs of $60,000. If the company spends $40,000 on a sales promotion campaign, it is estimated that sales can be increased by $150,000. Should the company proceed with the campaign? (Show computations.)

b.   The following data pertain to the Flick Corporation:

Sales $200,000
Variable costs . . .   120,000
Fixed costs   40,000

The president is considering hiring an efficiency expert at $40,000 this year, who can reduce variable costs by 25 percent. Assuming that sales will remain at the same level, should the expert be hired?

P26–8–B.   The Braxton Company sells three products. It has fixed costs of $100,000. The sales and variable costs of these products for 1984 were as follows:

	Products		
	A	*B*	*C*
Sales	$100,000	$150,000	$250,000
Variable costs . . .	70,000	90,000	125,000

Required:

a.   Determine the break-even point in sales dollars for 1985 assuming that the product mix will remain as it was in 1984.

b.   Determine the break-even point in sales dollars for 1985 assuming that the product mix ratio for 1985 is expected to change to 50:30:20 while total sales remain the same.

P26–9–B.   The following data pertain to a given company:

		Product		
	Total	**1**	**2**	**3**
Sales	$1,000,000	$500,000	$300,000	$200,000
Manufacturing costs:				
Fixed	$ 150,000	$ 75,000	$ 35,000	$ 40,000
Variable	650,000	300,000	250,000	100,000
Total	$ 800,000	$375,000	$285,000	$140,000
Gross margin	$ 200,000	$125,000	$ 15,000	$ 60,000
Selling costs:				
Fixed	$ 25,000	$ 20,000	$ 4,000	$ 1,000
Variable	75,000	20,000	20,000	35,000
Administrative costs:				
Fixed	15,000	10,000	3,000	2,000
Variable	35,000	15,000	5,000	15,000
Total	$ 150,000	$ 65,000	$ 32,000	$ 53,000
Net income	$ 50,000	$ 60,000	$ (17,000)	$ 7,000

In view of the operating loss shown above for product 2, the company's management is considering dropping that product. All variable costs are direct costs and would be eliminated and all fixed costs are indirect costs and would not be eliminated.

Required:

Assuming product 2's volume would be lost to the company if it were dropped, would you recommend elimination of that product? Give supporting computations.

P26–10–B. Based upon the information given in Problem P26–9–B, assume that the product mix of the firm is technologically interchangeable. The company can delete one product and produce a given amount of the existing other products without changes in unit variable costs, selling prices, or total fixed costs.

Assume that dropping product 2 will allow the company to explore these alternatives:

1. Produce $275,000 more of product 3.
2. Produce $250,000 more of product 1.
3. Produce $100,000 more of product 1 and $200,000 more of product 3.
4. Produce $150,000 more of product 1 and $100,000 more of product 3.

Required:

a. What is the best alternative (show computations)?

b. Selecting the best alternative, show what the resulting sales and net income would be.

P26–11–B. Garcia Company employs an absorption cost system in accounting for the single product it manufactures. Following are selected data for the year 1984:

Sales (10,000 units)	$200,000
Direct materials used (12,000 units at $6)	72,000
Direct labor cost incurred	24,000
Variable manufacturing overhead	7,200
Fixed manufacturing overhead	9,600
Variable selling and administrative expenses	12,000
Fixed selling and administrative expenses	40,000

One unit of direct materials goes into each unit of finished goods. Overhead rates are based on a capacity of 12,000 units and are $0.60 and $0.80 per unit for variable and fixed overhead. The only beginning or ending inventory is the 2,000 units of finished goods on hand at the end of 1984.

Required:

a. Prepare an income statement for 1984 under variable costing.

b. Prepare an income statement for 1984 under absorption costing.

c. Explain the reason for the difference in net income between (*a*) and (*b*).

BUSINESS DECISION PROBLEM 26–1

The Woodson Company is operating at almost 100 percent of capacity. The company expects the demand for its product to increase by 25 percent next year (1985). In order to satisfy the demand for its product, the company is considering two alternatives. The first alternative will increase fixed costs by 15 percent but will have no effect on variable costs. The second alternative will not affect fixed costs but will cause variable costs to increase to 60 percent of the selling price of the company's product.

The Woodson Company's condensed income statement for 1984 is shown below:

Sales		$3,000,000
Costs:		
Variable	$1,350,000	
Fixed	550,000	1,900,000
Net income before taxes		$1,100,000

Required:

a. Determine the break-even point in sales dollars for 1985 under each of the alternatives.

b. Determine projected net income before taxes for 1985 under each of the alternatives.

c. Which alternative would you recommend? Why?

BUSINESS DECISION PROBLEM 26–2

When the plant of the Wilkerson Company is completely idle, fixed costs amount to $150,000. When the plant operates at levels of 50 percent of capacity and below, its fixed costs are $175,000, and at levels above 50 percent of capacity its fixed costs are $250,000. The company's variable costs at full capacity (100,000 units) amount to $375,000.

Required:

a. Assuming that the company's product sells at $12.50 per unit, what is the company's break-even point in sales dollars?

b. Using only the data given, at what level of sales would it be more economical to close the factory than to operate? In other words, at what level will operating losses approximate the losses incurred if the factory is closed down completely?

c. Assume that when the Wilkerson Company is operating at half its capacity, it decides to reduce the selling price from $12.50 per unit to $7.50 per unit in order to increase sales. At what percentage of capacity must the company operate in order to break even at the reduced sales price?

BUSINESS DECISION PROBLEM 26–3

The Why-not Company has recently been awarded a contract to sell 50,000 units of its product to the federal government. Why-not manufactures the components of the product rather than purchase them from outside suppliers. When the news of the contract was released to the public, the president of Why-not, Dana Wilson, received a call from the president of the How-come Corporation, Jeff Weitenbeck. Mr. Weitenbeck offered to sell to Why-not 50,000 units of one of the needed components, part N, for $6.25. After receiving the offer, Ms. Wilson calls you into her office and assigns to you the task of providing her a recommendation (along with any supporting information) on whether to accept or reject Mr. Weitenbeck's offer.

You first go to the company's records and obtain the following information concerning the production of part N.

	Costs at current production level (400,000 units)
Direct labor	$1,040,000
Direct materials	480,000
Manufacturing overhead	500,000
Total cost	$2,020,000

You calculate the unit cost of part N to be $5.05 ($2,020,000 ÷ 400,000). But you suspect that this unit cost may not hold true at all production levels. To find out, you consult the production manager. She tells you that in order to meet the increased production needs, equipment will have to be rented and the production workers will have to work some overtime. She estimated the machine rental to be $50,000 and the total overtime premiums to be $90,000. She provides you with the following cost information:

	Costs at increased production level (450,000 units)
Direct labor	$1,170,000
Direct materials	540,000
Manufacturing overhead (including equipment rental and overtime premiums)	690,000
Total cost	$2,400,000

The production manager advises you to reject the offer, as the unit cost of part N will only rise to $5.33 (2,400,000 ÷ 450,000), even with the additional costs of equipment rental and overtime premiums. This is much less than the $6.25 offered by Mr. Weitenbeck. You are still undecided, so you return to your office to consider the matter further.

Required:

a. Using the high-low method, compute the variable cost portion of manufacturing overhead. (Remember that the costs of equipment rental and overtime premiums are included in manufacturing overhead. Subtract these amounts before performing the calculation.)

b. Compute the total costs to manufacture the additional units of part N. (Note: Include overtime premiums as a part of direct labor.)

c. Compute the unit cost to manufacture the additional units of part N.

d. Will you advise Ms. Wilson to accept or reject Mr. Weitenbeck's offer?

BUSINESS DECISION PROBLEM 26–4

The general manager of the Chicago Division of the Burleson Company submitted its income statement for the year ended June 30, 1984 (prepared under absorption costing), with the comment that the division was at least profitable. The report showed that sales amounted to 80,000 units at $20 per unit and that the following costs had been incurred:

Direct materials $440,000
Direct labor   190,000
Manufacturing overhead   570,000
Selling and administrative   . . .   600,000

A total of 110,000 units was put into process during the year. Of the 30,000 units in the June 30, 1984, inventory, all materials costs had been incurred but the units were only 50 percent complete as to processing. There were no other finished goods or work in process inventories, either beginning or ending.

The Chicago Division's production process is highly automated and its costs are largely fixed—$475,000 of the overhead and $200,000 of the selling and administrative costs are fixed.

Upon receipt of the division's income statement, the company's controller made a few quick calculations and commented that the division actually operated at a loss. The general manager of the division took exception to this statement, causing a long argument.

Required:

a. Prepare the division's income statement under absorption costing. Include a schedule showing computation of the cost of the ending work in process Inventory. Assume fixed overhead is absorbed under expected activity and this equaled actual activity for the year.

b. Repeat part (*a*) under direct costing.

c. State exactly what caused the difference in net income between (*a*) and (*b*).

d. Who is right in this debate? Explain.

Chapter 27

Capital budgeting: Long-range planning

CHAPTER GOALS

After study of this chapter, you should be able to:

1. Determine the net cash benefits, after taxes, for both an asset addition and an asset replacement.
2. Evaluate projects using payback period, unadjusted rate of return, net present value, profitability index, and time-adjusted rate of return.
3. Determine, for project evaluation, the effect of an investment in working capital.
4. Define and use correctly the new terms in the glossary.

Effective planning for the future is essential to the continuation and success of a company. Decisions about short-run factors such as selling prices, costs, volume, and profits were considered in the preceding chapter. This chapter addresses decisions concerning long-term investments in capital assets, such as buildings and equipment. This part of the planning process is referred to as capital budgeting.

CAPITAL BUDGETING DEFINED

Capital budgeting is the process of considering alternative capital projects and selecting those alternatives that provide the most profitable return on available funds, within the framework of company goals and objectives. A *capital project* includes any long-range endeavor to purchase, build, lease, or renovate buildings, equipment, or other major items of property. Such decisions usually involve very large sums of money and usually bring about a large increase in fixed costs for a number of years in the future.

Once a firm builds a plant or undertakes some other capital expenditure, it becomes less flexible. Poor capital budgeting decisions can be very costly. If a poor capital budgeting decision is implemented, the firm can lose all or part of the funds originally invested. In addition, the capital budgeting decision affects other day-to-day decisions, such as whether to hire and train employees to work with new equipment. If the new equipment is not purchased, the decision to hire and train becomes irrelevant. Other actions taken within the company regarding the project, such as arranging for sources of supply for raw materials, are wasted if the capital budgeting decision is revoked. Poor capital budgeting decisions may also harm the firm's competitive position and image.

For all these reasons, firms must be very careful in their analyses of capital projects. Capital expenditures do not occur as often as ordinary expenditures (such as payroll or inventory purchases) but involve substantial sums of money that are then committed for a long period of time. Therefore, the means by which firms evaluate capital expenditure decisions need to be much more formal and detailed than would be necessary for ordinary purchase decisions.

Investment of funds in a poor alternative can create extensive problems within a company, other than the effect on net income. Workers who were hired for the project might be laid off if the project fails, creating morale and unemployment problems. Many of the fixed costs will still remain, even if the plant is closed or is not producing. Advertising efforts will have been wasted. Stock prices could be affected by the decline in earnings. On the other hand, failure to invest enough funds in a good project can also be costly. Ford's Mustang is an excellent example of this. If, at the time of the original capital budgeting decision, Ford had projected the Mustang's popularity, the company would have expended more funds on the project. Because of undercommitment of funds, Ford found itself short on production which, thereby, caused lost or postponed sales of the automobile.

Finally, the amount of funds available for investment is limited. Thus, once a capital investment decision is made, alternative investment opportunities are lost. The benefits or returns lost by rejecting the best alternative investment are an *opportunity cost.*

PROJECT SELECTION: A GENERAL VIEW

Some techniques will be discussed that are used to evaluate alternative proposals. The techniques include payback, unadjusted rate of return, net present value, profitability index, and time-adjusted rate of return. But first, some concepts used in these techniques need to be discussed.

Time value of money

Money received today is worth more than the same amount of money received at a future date such as a month or a year from now. This principle, which involves the use of compound interest, is known as the present value approach. Closely related to present value are the concepts of future worth and the present value of an annuity. These concepts were covered in the Appendix to Chapter 17. If you need to review these concepts, refer back to the Chapter 17 Appendix before continuing with this chapter.

Net cash benefits

The *net cash benefit* (as used in capital budgeting) is the net cash inflow expected from a project in a period. It is the difference between the periodic cash inflows and the periodic cash outflows for a proposed project.

Asset addition. Assume, for example, that a firm is considering the purchase of new equipment for $120,000. The equipment is expected to have a useful life of 15 years and no salvage value. The equipment is expected to produce cash inflows (revenue) of $75,000 per year and cash outflows (costs) of $50,000 per year. Ignoring depreciation and taxes, the annual net cash inflow is computed as follows:

Cash inflows	$75,000
Cash outflows	50,000
Net cash inflow . . .	$25,000

Depreciation and taxes. Although depreciation does not involve a cash outflow, it is deductible in arriving at federal taxable income. Thus, depreciation reduces the amount of cash outflow for income taxes. This reduction in cash outflows for income taxes is a tax saving made possible by a depreciation tax shield. A *tax shield* is the amount by which taxable income is reduced due to the deductibility of an item.

Thus, if depreciation is $8,000, the tax shield is $8,000. The tax shield results in a tax saving. The amount of the tax saving can be found by multiplying the tax rate by the amount of the depreciation tax shield. The formula is shown below:

$$\text{Tax rate} \times \text{Depreciation tax shield} = \text{Tax saving}$$

Using the data in the previous example and assuming straight-line depreciation of $8,000 per year and a 40 percent tax rate, the amount of the tax saving is $3,200 (40 percent × $8,000 depreciation tax shield). Now, considering taxes and depreciation, the annual net cash inflow from the $120,000 of equipment is computed as follows:

	To compute net income	To compute cash flow
Cash inflows	$75,000	$75,000
Cash outflows	50,000	50,000
Net cash inflow before taxes	$25,000	$25,000
Depreciation	8,000	
Taxable income	$17,000	
Tax at 40%	6,800	6,800
Net income after taxes	$10,200	
Net cash inflow (after taxes)		$18,200

Considering taxes and depreciation, the net cash inflow is $18,200 instead of the $25,000 computed previously.

Asset replacements.   Sometimes a firm has to decide whether to acquire new plant assets to replace existing ones. Such replacement decisions often occur when faster and more efficient machinery and equipment appear on the market.

The computation of net cash benefit is more complex for a replacement decision than for an acquisition decision because cash inflows and outflows for **two** items (the asset being replaced and the new asset) must be considered. To illustrate, assume that a company operates two machines that were purchased four years ago at a cost of $18,000 each. The estimated useful life of each machine is 12 years (with no salvage value). Each machine will produce 30,000 units of product each year. The annual cash costs (labor, repairs, etc.) of operating both machines total $14,000.

After the old machines have been used for four years, a new machine becomes available. The new machine can be acquired for $28,000 and has an estimated useful life of eight years (with no salvage value). The new machine will produce 60,000 units annually at a cash cost of $10,000.

There must be a $28,000 cash outflow in the first year to acquire the new machine. The additional annual cash inflow from replacement is computed as follows:

	To compute tax	To compute cash flow
Cash operating costs:		
Old machines	$14,000	
New machines	10,000	
Difference—additional taxable income	$ 4,000	$4,000
Depreciation:		
Old machines ($18,000 ÷ 12) × 2 ...	$ 3,000	
New machine ($28,000 ÷ 8)	3,500	
Difference—additional tax deduction	$ (500)	
Additional taxable income	$ 4,000	
Additional tax deduction	(500)	
Net increase in taxable income	$ 3,500	
Additional tax at 40%	1,400	1,400
Additional annual cash inflow		$2,600

Notice that the above figures concentrated only on the differences in costs for each of the two alternatives. Two other items also need to be considered that are relevant to the decision. First, the purchase of the new machine will create a $28,000 cash outflow immediately upon acquisition. Second, the two old machines can probably be sold, and the selling price or salvage value of the old machines will create a cash inflow in the period of disposal. Also, the above example used straight-line depreciation. If an accelerated depreciation method is used, the tax shield is larger in the early years and smaller in the later years of the asset's life.

Out-of-pocket and sunk costs.   There is an important distinction between out-of-pocket costs and sunk costs. An *out-of-pocket cost* is one that requires a future outlay of resources, usually cash. It can be avoided or changed in amount. Future labor and repair costs are examples of out-of-pocket costs.

Sunk costs are costs that have already been incurred. Nothing can be done about sunk costs at the present time; they cannot be avoided or changed in amount. The price paid for a machine becomes a sunk cost the minute it is acquired (before that moment it was an out-of-pocket cost). Its amount cannot be changed regardless of whether the machine is scrapped or used. Thus, depreciation is a sunk cost. Depletion and amortization of assets such as ore deposits and patents are also sunk costs. A sunk cost is a past cost, while an out-of-pocket cost is a future cost. Only the out-of-pocket costs (the future cash outlays) are relevant to capital budgeting decisions. Sunk costs are not.

Initial cost and salvage value.   Any cash outflows necessary to acquire an asset and place it in a position and condition for use are part of the *initial cost of the asset.* If an investment has a salvage value, that value should be treated as a cash inflow in the year of the asset's disposal.

    The cost of capital. The cost of capital is important in project selection. Certainly any acceptable proposal should offer a return that exceeds the cost of the funds used to finance it. The cost of capital, usually expressed as a rate, may be computed on an after-tax basis. *Cost of capital* is the cost of all sources of capital (debt and equity) employed by a firm. For convenience, most current liabilities, such as accounts payable and federal income taxes payable, are treated as being without cost. Everything else on the right (equity) side of the balance sheet has a cost. The subject of determining the cost of capital is a controversial topic in the literature of accounting and finance and will not be discussed here. Assumed rates for cost of capital will be used in the rest of the chapter.

PROJECT SELECTION: PAYBACK PERIOD

    The payback period of an outlay is often computed to help evaluate an investment proposal. The *payback period* is the period of time during which the net cash savings from an investment must continue in order to recover the initial net cash outlay. In effect, it answers the question: How long will it take the new machine to pay for itself? The formula for the payback period is:

$$\text{Payback period} = \frac{\text{Initial cash outlay}}{\text{Annual net cash inflows (or benefits)}}$$

    The payback period for the assets discussed previously can be computed as follows. In regard to the purchase of the $120,000 equipment, which has a net cash inflow of $18,200, the payback period is 6.6 years:

$$\text{Payback period} = \frac{\$120,000}{\$18,200} = 6.6 \text{ years}$$

The payback period for the replacement machine, with a $28,000 cash outflow in the first year and an annual cash inflow of $2,600, is 10.8 years:

$$\text{Payback period} = \frac{\$28,000}{\$2,600} = 10.8 \text{ years}$$

Remember that the payback period indicates how long it will take the machine to pay for itself. The replacement machine has a payback period of 10.8 years, but a useful life of only 8 years. Therefore, since the investment cannot pay for itself within its useful life, the machine should *not* be purchased to replace the two old machines.

    In each of the two examples above, the cash flows per year were uniform. When the annual returns are uneven, a cumulative calculation must be used to determine payback period, as shown in the following situation.

    The Neil Company is considering an investment proposal that costs $40,000 and is expected to last 10 years. The projected annual cash inflows are as follows:

Year	Investment	Annual net cash inflows	Cumulative net cash inflows
0	$40,000	—	—
1	—	$8,000	$ 8,000
2	—	6,000	14,000
3	—	7,000	21,000
4	—	5,000	26,000
5	—	8,000	34,000
6	—	6,000	40,000
7	—	3,000	43,000
8	—	2,000	45,000
9	—	3,000	48,000
10	—	1,000	49,000

The payback period in this example is six years—the time it takes to recover the $40,000 original investment.

When payback period is used to evaluate investment proposals, management may use one of the following rules to decide on project selection:

1. Select the investments with the shortest payback periods.
2. Select only those investments that have a payback period of less than a specified number of years.

Both decision rules focus on rapid return of invested capital. If capital can be recovered rapidly, it can be invested in other projects, thereby generating more cash inflows or profits.

Although it is used extensively in capital budgeting due to its simplicity and because cash flow is critical in many businesses, payback period analysis has several important limitations. First, it ignores the periods of time beyond the payback period. For example, the Allen Company is considering two alternative investments that each require an initial outlay of $30,000. Proposal Y will return $6,000 per year for five years, while proposal Z will return $5,000 per year for eight years. The payback period for Y is five years ($30,000/$6,000) and for Z is six years ($30,000/$5,000). But, if the goal is to maximize income, proposal Z should be selected rather than proposal Y, even though Z has a longer payback period. This is because Z will return a total of $40,000 while Y simply recovers investment cost.

Second, payback analysis also ignores the time value of money. For example, consider the following net cash receipts in the first three years expected from two capital proposals:

	Project A	Project B
First year	$15,000	$ 9,000
Second year	12,000	12,000
Third year	9,000	15,000
	$36,000	$36,000

Both projects have the same net cash receipts each year beyond the third year. If the cost of each project is $36,000, then each has a payback period of three years. But common sense indicates that the projects are not equal because money has a time value and can be reinvested to increase income. Since larger amounts of cash are received sooner under project A, it is the preferable project.

PROJECT SELECTION: UNADJUSTED RATE OF RETURN

The unadjusted rate of return is another method of evaluating investment projects. The **unadjusted rate of return** is an approximate calculation of the percentage return on investment of a capital project. It is computed by dividing the average annual income after taxes by the average amount of investment in the project. The average investment is computed as the original outlay divided by 2. The formula for unadjusted rate of return is:

$$\text{Unadjusted rate of return} = \frac{\text{Average annual income after taxes}}{\text{Average amount of investment}}$$

Notice that annual *income* rather than net cash inflows is used in the calculation. Also, some formulas use the initial investment as the denominator instead of the average investment.

As an example, the Thomas Company is considering two proposals that both have useful lives of three years. The firm does not have enough funds to undertake both projects. Information relating to the projects is shown below:

Proposal	Initial cost	Average annual before-tax net cash inflows	Average depreciation
1	$72,000	$45,000	$24,000
2	90,000	55,000	30,000

Assuming a 40 percent tax rate, the unadjusted rate of return is determined as follows:

	Proposal 1	Proposal 2
1. Average investment:		
Original outlay ÷ 2	$36,000	$45,000
Annual net cash inflow (before taxes)	$45,000	$55,000
Annual depreciation	24,000	30,000
Annual income (before taxes)	$21,000	$25,000
Income taxes at 40%	8,400	10,000
2. Average net income from investment	$12,600	$15,000
Rate of return (2) ÷ (1)	35%	33⅓%

From these calculations, if Thomas Company makes an investment decision solely on the basis of unadjusted rate of return, proposal 1 would be selected since it has a higher rate.

The unadjusted rate of return can also be computed with the following formula:

$$\text{Rate of return} = \frac{\left(\begin{array}{c}\text{Average annual before-} \\ \text{tax net cash inflow}\end{array} - \begin{array}{c}\text{Average annual} \\ \text{depreciation}\end{array}\right)(1 - \text{Tax rate})}{\text{Average investment}}$$

For proposal 1 above, the computation would be as follows:

$$\text{Rate of return} = \frac{(\$45,000 - \$24,000)(1 - 0.4)}{(\$72,000/2)} = \frac{(\$21,000)(0.6)}{\$36,000}$$

$$= \frac{\$12,600}{\$36,000} = 35 \text{ percent}$$

This formula would give the same rate of return of $33\frac{1}{3}$ percent for proposal 2 as shown in the schedule.

If the average annual after-tax net cash flow is given, the depreciation can be deducted to arrive at average net income. For instance, for proposal 2 above:

After-tax net cash inflow ($55,000 − $10,000) ...	$45,000
Deduct depreciation	30,000
Average net income	$15,000

The unadjusted rate of return, like payback period analysis, has several limitations. First, the length of time over which the return will be earned is not considered. Second, the rate allows a sunk cost, depreciation, to enter into the calculation. Since depreciation can be calculated in so many different ways, the rate of return can be manipulated by simply changing the method of depreciation used for the project. Lastly, this method also does not consider the timing of cash flows or the time value of money.

PROJECT SELECTION: NET PRESENT VALUE METHOD AND THE PROFITABILITY INDEX

Net present value method. The *net present value* method uses the concept of the time value of money. Management requires some minimum rate of return on its investments. This required rate of return should be the firm's cost of capital. Since it is difficult to determine the cost of capital, management often selects a target rate of return that it believes to be at or above the cost of capital.

Under the *net present value* method, the minimum rate of return is used to discount to the present all expected cash flows (after tax effects) from a proposed investment. The total present value of the expected cash flows is then compared with the investment amount. If the present value of the expected cash flows equals or exceeds the investment amount, the investment proposal is given further consideration. On the other hand, if the present value of the expected cash flows is less than the investment amount, the proposal is rejected.

To illustrate, the Morris Company is considering an investment that will cost $25,000. Net cash inflows after taxes for the next four years are expected to be $8,000, $7,500, $8,000, and $7,500, respectively. Management requires a minimum rate of return of 14 percent and wants to know if the project is acceptable. The following analysis is developed, using the tables in Appendix C at the end of the text.

	Net cash inflow (after taxes)	Present value of $1 at 14 percent (from Table 3)	Total present value
First year	$ 8,000	0.87719	$ 7,018
Second year	7,500	0.76947	5,771
Third year	8,000	0.67497	5,400
Fourth year	7,500	0.59208	4,441
Total	$31,000		$22,630
Cost of investment			25,000
Net present value			$ (2,370)

Since the present value of the benefits, $22,630 is less than the initial outlay of $25,000, the project is not acceptable. Its *net present value* is equal to the present value of the benefits less the present value of its cost (the investment amount), which in this instance is −$2,370 ($22,630 − $25,000).

In general, a proposed investment is acceptable if it has a positive net present value. In the previous example, if the expected benefits from the investment had been $10,000 per year for four years, the present value of the benefits would have been (from Appendix Table 4):

$$\$10,000 \times 2.91371 = \$29,137$$

This yields a net present value of $4,137 ($29,137 − $25,000). Since the net present value is positive, the investment proposal is acceptable. But there may be a competing project that has an even higher net present value. In general, when the net present value method is used to screen projects, those projects that have the highest net present values should be selected.

Profitability index. When investment projects costing different amounts are being compared, the net present value method does not provide a valid means to rank the projects in order of contribution to income or desirability. A profitability index provides this additional information to management. A *profitability index* is calculated as the present value of the expected net after-tax cash inflows or benefits from an investment divided by the initial cash outlay or cost:

$$PI = \frac{\text{PV of net cash benefits}}{\text{Initial cost}}$$

Only those proposals having a profitability index greater than or equal to 1.00 will be considered by management. Proposals with a profitability index of less than 1.00 will not yield the minimum rate of return because the present value of the projected cash inflows will be less than the initial cost.

To illustrate, assume that a company is considering two alternative capital outlay proposals that have the following initial costs and expected net cash benefits after taxes:

	Proposal X	Proposal Y
Initial cost	$7,000	$9,500
Expected net cash benefits (after taxes):		
Year 1	$5,000	$9,000
Year 2	4,000	6,000
Year 3	6,000	3,000

Management's minimum desired rate of return is 20 percent. The net present values and profitability indices can be computed as follows (using Appendix C, Table 3):

	Present value	
	Proposal X	Proposal Y
Year 1 (cash benefit in year 1 × 0.83333)	$ 4,167	$ 7,500
Year 2 (cash benefit in year 2 × 0.69444)	2,778	4,167
Year 3 (cash benefit in year 3 × 0.57870)	3,472	1,736
Total	$10,417	$13,403
Initial outlay	7,000	9,500
Net present value	$ 3,417	$ 3,903

	Proposal X	Proposal Y
Profitability index:	$\frac{\$10,417}{\$7,000} = 1.49$	$\frac{\$13,403}{\$9,500} = 1.41$

When net present values are compared, proposal Y appears to be more favorable than X because the net present value is higher. But after computing the profitability indices, proposal X is found to be a more desirable investment because it has the higher profitability index. The higher the profitability index, the more profitable the project. Proposal X is earning a higher rate of return on a smaller investment than proposal Y. The effect of each proposal on such intangible factors as employee morale and the future flexibility of the firm should also be considered.

PROJECT SELECTION: THE TIME-ADJUSTED RATE OF RETURN

The time-adjusted rate of return is also called the discounted or internal rate of return. The *time-adjusted rate of return* equates the present value of future expected net after-tax cash inflows from an investment to the cost of the investment. It is the rate at which the net present value of the project is zero. If the time-adjusted rate of return equals or exceeds the cost of capital or target rate of return, then the investment should be considered further. But if the proposal's time-adjusted rate of return is less than the minimum rate, the proposal should be rejected. If management is considering several competing investments and only one can be accepted, the project with the highest time-adjusted rate of return that is over the minimum allowable rate of return should be selected.

Present value tables can be used to approximate the time-adjusted rate of return. To illustrate, assume that the Young Company is considering a $90,000 investment that is expected to last 25 years with no salvage value. The investment will yield $15,000 per year after taxes. The first step in computing rate of return is to determine the payback period. In this case, payback period is six years ($90,000 ÷ $15,000). Next, examine Appendix C, Table 4, (present value of an annuity) to find the present value factor that is nearest in amount to the payback period of 6. Since the investment is expected to yield returns for 25 years, look at that row in the table. In that row, the factor nearest to 6 is 5.92745, which appears under the 16.5 percent interest column. If the annual return of $15,000 is multiplied by the 5.92745 factor, the result is $88,912, which is just below the $90,000 cost of the project. Thus, the actual rate of return is slightly less than 16.5 percent. It is less than 16.5 percent because as interest rates decrease, present values increase, since more investment is needed to generate the same income or earnings.

The above example involved level cash flows from year to year. What happens when cash flows are not level? In such instances, a trial and error procedure is necessary. For example, assume that a company is considering a $200,000 project that will last four years and yield the following returns (ignoring scrap value):

At the end of—	Net cash inflow (after taxes)
Year 1	$ 20,000
Year 2	40,000
Year 3	80,000
Year 4	150,000
Total	$290,000

The average annual net cash inflow is $72,500 ($290,000 ÷ 4). Based on this average net cash inflow, the payback period is 2.76 years ($200,000 ÷ $72,500). Looking in the four-year row of Appendix C, Table 4, we find that the factor 2.77048 is nearest to the payback period of 2.76. But in this case, cash flows are not level. The largest returns occur in the later years of the asset's life. Since the early returns have the largest present value, it is likely that the rate of return will be less than the 16.5 percent rate that corresponds to the present value factor of 2.77048. Thus, various interest rates are tried that are less than 16.5 percent. Several attempts may be necessary before the discount rate which yields a present value closest to the initial outlay of $200,000 is found. By trial and error the rate of return is found to be slightly higher than 12 percent. The following computation reveals why this is true:

	Return	Present value factor at 12 percent	Present value of net cash benefits
Year 1	$ 20,000	0.89286	$ 17,857
Year 2	40,000	0.79719	31,888
Year 3	80,000	0.71178	56,942
Year 4	150,000	0.63553	95,330
			$202,017

If the returns had been greater during the earlier years of the asset's life, the correct rate of return would have been higher than 16 percent.

Since the cost of capital is not a precise percentage, some financial theorists argue that the time-adjusted rate of return method is better than the net present value method. Under the time-adjusted rate of return method, the cost of capital is used only as a *cutoff point* in deciding which projects are acceptable for more consideration. Under the net present value method, the cost of capital is used in the calculation of the present value of the benefits. Thus, if the cost of capital percentage is wrong, the *ranking* of the projects will be affected. As a result, management may select projects that are really not as profitable as other projects.

No matter which of the two time value of money concepts is "better," these methods are both theoretically superior to the payback and unadjusted rate of return methods. But the time value of money methods are more difficult to compute. In reality, no single method should be used to make capital budgeting decisions. All aspects of the investment should be considered, including nonquantitative factors, such as employee morale (layoffs of workers due to higher efficiency of a new machine) and company flexibility (versatility of production of one machine over another). The firm will be committed to its investment in a capital project for a long period of time and should use the best selection techniques and judgment available.

INVESTMENTS IN WORKING CAPITAL

An investment in plant assets usually must be supported by an investment in working capital, such as accounts receivable and inventory. For example, an investment in plant assets often is expected to increase sales. The increased sales may require an increase in accounts receivable and inventory to support the higher sales level. The increases in the current assets—accounts receivable and inventory—are investments in working capital that usually are recovered in full at the end of a capital project's life. Such investments should be considered in capital budgeting decisions.

To illustrate, assume that a company is considering a capital project that will involve a $50,000 investment in machinery and a $40,000 investment in working capital. The machine, which will be used to produce a new product, has a useful life of eight years and no salvage value. The annual cash inflow (before taxes) is estimated at $25,000, with annual cash outflows (before taxes) of $5,000. The annual net cash flow from the proposal is computed below (assuming straight-line depreciation and a 40 percent tax rate):

	To compute tax	To compute cash flows
Cash inflows	$25,000	$25,000
Cash outflows	5,000	5,000
	$20,000	$20,000
Depreciation ($50,000/8)	6,250	
Taxable income	$13,750	
Tax at 40%	$ 5,500	5,500
Annual net cash inflow, years 1–8		$14,500

In addition to the $14,500 recovered each year for eight years, the $40,000 investment in working capital will be recovered in year 8.

The net present value of the proposal is computed as follows (assuming a 14 percent minimum desired rate of return):

Net cash inflow, years 1–8 ($14,500 × 4.63886)	$67,263
Recovery of investment in working capital ($40,000 × 0.35056)	14,022
Present value of net cash inflows	$81,285
Initial cash outlay ($50,000 + $40,000)	90,000
Net present value	$ (8,715)

The investment is not acceptable because it has a negative net present value. If the working capital investment had been ignored, the proposal would have had a rather large positive net present value of $17,263 ($67,263 − $50,000). Thus, it should be obvious that investments in working capital must be considered if correct capital budgeting decisions are to be made.

THE POSTAUDIT

The last step in the capital budgeting process is a postaudit review that should be performed by a person not involved in the capital budgeting decision-making process. Such a person can provide an impartial judgment on the project's worthiness. This step should be performed early in the project's life, but enough time should have passed for any operational "bugs" to have been worked out. Actual operating costs and revenues should be determined and compared with those estimated when the project was originally reviewed and accepted. This allows management to know if projections were accurate and if all items were considered in the projections.

The postaudit performs several functions. It lets management know if a particular project is performing as it was expected to in regard to costs and revenues. The review may provide additional factors for management to consider in upcoming capital budgeting decisions, such as costs which were forgotten in a particular project. Finally, since the capital budgeting process involves planning, all plans should be reviewed after implementation for control and feedback purposes under basic management principles.

NEW TERMS INTRODUCED IN CHAPTER 27

Capital budgeting
The term used to describe the planning and financing of plant assets.

Cost of capital
The cost of all sources of capital employed by a firm.

Initial cost of an asset
Any cash outflows necessary to acquire an asset and place it in a position and condition for its intended use.

Net cash benefit
The annual cash inflows from a proposal less the annual cash outflows related to the proposal.

Net present value
A project selection technique that discounts all expected cash flows (after taxes) to the present using a minimum rate of return determined by management. If the amount obtained by this process exceeds or equals the investment amount, the proposal is considered acceptable for further consideration.

Out-of-pocket cost
A cost requiring a future outlay of resources, usually cash.

Payback period
The period of time during which the net cash savings from an investment must continue in order to recover the initial cash outlay.

Opportunity cost
The benefits or returns lost by rejecting the best alternative investment.

Profitability index
The ratio of the present value of the expected net cash benefits (after taxes) from an investment divided by the initial cash outlay.

Sunk costs
Past commitments of funds about which nothing can be done at the present time.

Tax shield
The total amount by which taxable income is reduced due to the deductibility of an item.

Time-adjusted rate of return
A project selection technique that finds a rate of return that will equate the present value of future expected net cash inflows (after taxes) from an investment with the cost of the investment.

Unadjusted rate of return
The rate of return computed by dividing average future annual income (after taxes) from a project by the average amount of the investment.

DEMONSTRATION PROBLEM

The Logue Company is considering three different investments. Listed below are some data related to these investments:

Investment	Initial outlay	Expected after-tax net cash inflow per year	Expected life of proposals
A	$100,000	$20,000	10 years
B	120,000	17,600	15
C	150,000	21,000	20

Management requires a minimum return on investments of 14 percent.

Required:

Rank these proposals using the following selection techniques. (Ignore income taxes and salvage value.)

a. Unadjusted rate of return.

b. Payback period.

c. Time-adjusted rate of return.

d. Profitability index.

Solution to demonstration problem

a. Unadjusted rate of return:

Proposal	(a) Average investment	(b) Average annual after-tax net cash inflow	(c) Average depreciation	(b) − (c) = (d) Average annual earnings	(d/a) Rate of return
A	$50,000	$20,000	$10,000	$10,000	20%
B	60,000	17,600	8,000	9,600	16
C	75,000	21,000	7,500	13,500	18

The proposals in order of rank are A, C, and B.

b. Payback period:

Proposal	(a) Investment	(b) Annual after-tax cash flow	(a/b) Payback period
A..........	$100,000	$20,000	5.00 years
B..........	120,000	17,600	6.82
C..........	150,000	21,000	7.14

The proposals in order of rank are A, B, and C.

c. Time-adjusted rate of return:

Proposal	Rate	How found
A	15% (slightly above)	$100,000 ÷ $20,000 = Factor of 5 in 10-period row
B	12 (slightly below)	$120,000 ÷ $17,600 = Factor of 6.82 in 15-period row
C	13 (slightly below)	$150,000 ÷ $21,000 = Factor of 7.14 in 20-period row

The proposals in order of rank are A, C, and B. (But neither B nor C earns the minimum rate of return.)

d. Profitability index:

Proposal	(a) Annual after-tax net cash inflow	(b) Present value factor at 14 percent	a × b = (c) Present value of annual net cash inflow	(d) Initial outlay	(c/d) Profitability index
A	$20,000	5.21612	$104,322	$100,000	1.04
B	17,600	6.14217	108,102	120,000	0.90
C	21,000	6.62313	139,086	150,000	0.93

The proposals in order of rank are A, C, and B. (But neither B nor C should be considered acceptable since their profitability indices are less than one.)

QUESTIONS

1. How do capital expenditures differ from ordinary expenditures?

2. What effects can capital budgeting decisions have on a firm?

3. What effect does depreciation have on cash flow?

4. Give an example of an out-of-pocket cost and a sunk cost by describing a situation in which both are encountered.

5. A machine currently is being considered for purchase. The salesperson attempting to sell the machine says that it will pay for itself in five years. What is meant by this statement?

6. Discuss the limitations of the payback method.

7. What is the profitability index and of what value is it?

8. What is the time-adjusted rate of return of a capital investment?

9. What role does the cost of capital play in the time-adjusted rate of return method and in the net present value method?

10. What is the purpose of a postaudit? When should a postaudit be performed?

EXERCISES

E–1. The Acorn Athletic Club is considering investing $150,000 in some new sports equipment with an estimated useful life of 10 years and no salvage value. The equipment is expected to produce $60,000 in cash inflows and $40,000 in cash outflows annually. Straight-line depreciation is used by the company, which has a 40 percent tax rate. Determine the annual estimated income and net cash flow.

E–2. The Donald Manufacturing Company is considering replacing a four-year-old machine with a new, advanced model. The old machine was purchased for $20,000, has a useful life of 10 years with no salvage value, and has annual maintenance costs of $5,000. The new machine would cost $15,000 and produce the same output as the old machine. But annual maintenance costs would be only $2,000. The new machine would have a useful life of 10 years with no salvage value. Using straight-line depreciation and a 40 percent tax rate, compute the additional annual cash inflow if the old machine is replaced.

E–3. Given the following annual costs, compute the payback period for the new machine if its net cost is $70,000. (Ignore income taxes.)

	Old machine	*New machine*
Depreciation	$ 6,000	$14,000
Labor	24,000	21,000
Repairs	7,000	1,500
Other costs	4,000	1,200
	$41,000	$37,700

E–4. The Star Company is considering investing $50,000 in a new machine. The machine is expected to last five years and to have no salvage value. Annual after-tax net cash inflow from the machine is expected to be $14,000. Calculate the unadjusted rate of return.

E–5. Compute the profitability index for each of the following two proposals assuming a desired minimum rate of return of 20 percent. Based upon the profitability indices, which proposal is better?

	Proposal R	*Proposal T*
Initial outlay	$8,000	$10,300
Cash flow (after taxes):		
First year	5,000	6,000
Second year	4,500	6,000
Third year	3,000	4,000
Fourth year	–0–	2,500

E–6. The Jefferson Company is considering three alternative investment proposals. Using the information presented below, rank the proposals in order of desirability using (*a*) the payback method and (*b*) the unadjusted rate of return method. Assume the net cash inflows occur evenly throughout each year.

	M	*O*	*P*
Initial outlay	$120,000	$120,000	$120,000
Net cash inflow (after taxes):			
First year	$ –0–	$ 30,000	$ 30,000
Second year	60,000	90,000	60,000
Third year	60,000	30,000	90,000
Fourth year	30,000	60,000	150,000
	$150,000	$210,000	$330,000

E–7. The Jason Company is considering the purchase of a new machine. The machine can be bought for $90,000. It is expected to save $18,000 cash per year for 10 years. It has an estimated useful life of 10 years and an estimated salvage value of zero. Management will not make any investment unless at least an 18 percent rate of return can be earned. Using the net present value method, determine if the proposal is acceptable.

E–8. Assume the same situation described in Exercise E–7. Calculate the time-adjusted rate of return. (Ignore income taxes.)

E–9. Rank the following investments in order of their desirability using (*a*) the payback method, (*b*) the net present value method, and (*c*) the time-adjusted rate of return method. Management requires a minimum rate of return of 14 percent.

Investment	Initial outlay	Expected after-tax net cash inflow per year	Expected life of proposal
A	$20,000	$3,000	8
B	25,000	4,375	20
C	40,000	8,000	10

PROBLEMS, SERIES A

P27–1–A.   The Ironside Manufacturing Company is currently using three machines that it bought seven years ago to manufacture its product. Each machine produces 20,000 units annually. The machines originally cost $51,000 each and have a life of 17 years with no salvage value.

     The new assistant manager of the Ironside Manufacturing Company suggests that the company replace the three old machines with two technically superior machines for $45,000 each. Each new machine would produce 30,000 units annually and would have a life of 10 years with no salvage value.

     The new assistant manager points out that the cost of maintaining the new machines would be much lower. Each old machine costs $5,000 a year to maintain; each new machine would cost only $2,000 a year to maintain.

Required:

     Compute the increase in after-tax annual cash inflow that would result from replacing the old machines, assuming straight-line depreciation and a tax rate of 40 percent.

P27–2–A.   Refer to the information given in Problem P27–1–A. The new assistant manager of the Ironside Manufacturing Company also points out that the old machines could be sold for $25,000 each. Assume this would result in an after-tax cash inflow of $75,000. (The tax effect of the gain or loss on this sale should be ignored.)

Required:

     Using the net present value method, should the new machines be bought if the company's cost of capital is 14 percent?

P27–3–A.   The Garden Company is considering replacing 10 of its delivery vans that originally cost $20,000 each and on each of which $12,200 of depreciation has been taken. They were originally estimated to have useful lives of eight years and no salvage value. Each van travels an average of 150,000 miles per year. The 10 new vans, if purchased, will cost $24,000 each. Each van will be driven 150,000 miles per year and will have no salvage value at the end of its three-year estimated useful life. A trade-in allowance of $2,000 is available for each of the old vans.

     Following is a comparison of costs of operation per mile:

	Old vans	New vans
Fuel, lubricants, etc.	$0.101	$0.079
Tires	0.045	0.045
Repairs	0.073	0.058
Depreciation	0.017	0.053
Other operating costs (variable)	0.034	0.029
Operating cost per mile	$0.270	$0.264

Required:

Ignore income taxes. Use the payback method for parts (*a*) and (*b*).

a. Do you recommend replacing the old vans? Support your answer with computations, and disregard all factors not related to the cost data given above.

b. If the old vans were already fully depreciated, would your answer be different? Why?

c. Assume that all cash flows for operating costs fall at the end of each year, and that 18 percent is an appropriate rate for discounting purposes. Using a present value technique, present a schedule showing whether or not the new vans should be acquired.

P27-4-A. The Baseline Company has been using an old-fashioned forklift for many years. The forklift has a zero salvage value. The company is considering buying a modern forklift. The new forklift will cost $70,000. It will save $14,000 per year after taxes in cash operating costs. If the company decides not to buy the new forklift, it can use the old forklift for an indefinite period of time. The new forklift will have a useful life of 10 years.

Required:

a. Compute the time-adjusted rate of return for the new forklift.

b. The company is uncertain about the 10-year useful life. Compute the time-adjusted rate of return for the new forklift if its useful life is (1) 6 years, and (2) 15 years, instead of 10 years.

c. Suppose the forklift has a useful life of 10 years and the annual after-tax cost savings are only $12,000. Compute the time-adjusted rate of return.

d. Assume the annual after-tax cost savings will be $16,000 and that the useful life will be eight years. Compute the time-adjusted rate of return.

P27-5-A. The Rainy Company is considering three different investments involving depreciable assets with no salvage value. Listed below are some data related to these investments.

Investment	Initial outlay	Expected after-tax net cash inflow per year	Expected life of proposal
1	$ 30,000	$ 4,400	20 years
2	80,000	10,000	10
3	110,000	18,400	10

Management requires a minimum return on investments of 12 percent.

Required:

Rank these proposals using the following selection techniques.

a. Unadjusted rate of return.

b. Payback method.

c. Time-adjusted rate of return.

d. Profitability index.

P27-6-A. Ben's Moving Company has always purchased its trucks outright and sold them after three years. The company is ready to sell its present fleet of trucks and is trying to decide whether it should continue to purchase trucks or whether it should lease trucks.

If the trucks are purchased, the following costs will be incurred:

	Costs per fleet
Acquisition cost	$104,000
Repairs, first year	1,200
Repairs, second year	2,200
Repairs, third year	3,000
Other annual costs	3,200

At the end of three years, the trucks could be sold for a total of $32,000. Another fleet of trucks could be purchased then. The costs listed above, including the same acquisition cost, would also be incurred with respect to the second fleet of trucks. The second fleet could also be sold for $32,000 at the end of three years.

If the trucks are leased, the lease contract will run for six years. One fleet of trucks will be provided immediately, and a second fleet of trucks will be provided at the end of three years. The company will pay $42,000 per year under the lease contract. The lessor will bear the cost of all repairs.

Required:

Assume the company's cost of capital is 18 percent. Should the company buy or lease the trucks? (Ignore income taxes.)

P27–7–A.   DAC Manufacturing Company is considering adding a new electronic calculator to its line of products. The following information has been provided by various departments within the company:

1. Additional machinery and equipment will be needed to manufacture the calculator. The machinery and equipment will cost $150,000, have a 15-year useful life, and have a zero salvage value.
2. Sales of DAC calculators for the next 15 years have been projected as follows:

Year	Sales in units
1–5	750
6–10	500
11–15	250

3. Selling price per calculator will be $125.
4. Variable costs will be $50 per calculator. Fixed costs and straight-line depreciation will total $17,500 annually.
5. Advertising campaign costs will be:

Year	Advertising cost
1–5	$12,500
6–10	7,500
11–15	2,000

6. The company requires a 12 percent minimum rate of return on investments.

Required:

Using the net present value method, decide whether or not DAC Manufacturing Company should add the calculator to its line of products. (Ignore income taxes.)

P27–8–A.   The Pool Company is considering the purchase of equipment that will cost $400,000. It is estimated that the useful life of the equipment will be 10 years and that there will be a salvage value of $100,000 at that time. The company uses straight-line depreciation. It is estimated that the new equipment will have a net cash inflow before taxes of $100,000 annually. Assume a tax rate of 35 percent and that management requires a minimum return of 20 percent.

Required:

Using the net present value method determine whether or not the equipment is an acceptable investment.

P27–9–A.   The Bolt Company has an opportunity to sell a piece of equipment for $60,000. Such a sale will result in a tax-deductible loss of $4,000. If it is not sold, the equipment is expected to produce annual net cash benefits after taxes of $24,000 for the next 20 years. In 20 years it is expected that the equipment will have no salvage value. The company's management feels that currently it has other opportunities that will yield 12 percent. Assume a 30 percent income tax rate.

Required:

Should the company sell the equipment? Prepare a schedule to support your conclusion.

PROBLEMS, SERIES B

P27–1–B.   Keystone Company is considering purchasing a new machine that would cost $100,000 and have a useful life of 10 years with no salvage value. The new machine is expected to have annual cash inflows of $50,000 and annual cash outflows of $20,000. The machine will be depreciated using straight-line depreciation, and the tax rate is 40 percent.

Required:

a.   Determine the net after-tax cash inflow for the new machine.

b.   Determine the payback period for the new machine.

P27–2–B.   The Blue Star Company currently uses four machines to produce 200,000 units annually. The machines were bought three years ago for $25,000 each and have a useful life of 10 years with no salvage value. They cost a total of $14,000 a year to repair and maintain.

The company is considering replacing the four machines with one technologically superior machine that is capable of producing the 200,000 units annually by itself. The machine would cost $70,000 and have a useful life of seven years with no salvage value. Annual repair and maintenance costs are estimated at $7,000.

Required:

Assuming straight-line depreciation and a 40 percent tax rate, determine the annual additional after-tax cash inflow if the new machine is acquired.

P27–3–B.   The Jason Manufacturing Company owns five spinning machines that it uses in its manufacturing operations. Each of the machines was purchased four years ago at a cost of $80,000. Each machine has an estimated life of 10 years with no expected salvage value. A new machine has become available. One new machine has the same productive capacity as the five old machines combined. The new machine will cost $432,000, is estimated to last six years, and will have a salvage value at the end of that time of $48,000. A trade-in allowance of $16,000 is available for each of the old machines. The new machine can produce 400,000 units each year.

Operating costs per unit are compared below:

	Five old machines	New machine
Repairs	$0.453	$0.057
Depreciation	0.100	0.160
Power	0.126	0.069
Other operating costs	0.108	0.033
Operating costs per unit	$0.787	$0.319

Required:

Ignore income taxes. Use the payback method for parts (*a*) and (*b*).

a. Do you recommend replacing the old machines? Support your answer with computations. Disregard all factors except those reflected in the data given above.

b. If the old machines were already fully depreciated, would your answer be different? Why?

c. Using the net present value method with a discount rate of 20 percent, present a schedule showing whether or not the new machine should be acquired.

P27–4–B. The Greylord Canning Company has used a particular canning machine for several years. The machine has a zero salvage value. The company is considering buying a technologically improved machine at a cost of $116,000. The new machine will save $25,000 per year after taxes in cash operating costs. If the company decides not to buy the new machine, it can use the old machine for an indefinite period of time by incurring heavy repair costs. The new machine will have a useful life of eight years.

Required:

a. Compute the time-adjusted rate of return for the new machine.

b. The company thinks the estimated useful life of the new machine may be more or less than eight years. Compute the time-adjusted rate of return for the new machine if its useful life is (1) 5 years, and (2) 12 years, instead of eight years.

c. Suppose the new machine's useful life is eight years but the annual after-tax cost savings are only $20,000. Compute the time-adjusted rate of return.

d. Assume the annual after-tax cost savings from the new machine will be $22,000 and its useful life will be 10 years. Compute the time-adjusted rate of return.

P27–5–B. The Bulldog Company is considering three different investments involving depreciable assets with no salvage value. Listed below are some data related to these investments:

Investment	Initial outlay	Expected after-tax net cash inflow per year	Expected life of proposal
1	$ 70,000	$14,000	10 years
2	120,000	24,000	20
3	180,000	34,000	10

Management requires a minimum return on investments of 12 percent.

Required:

Rank these proposals using the following selection techniques. (Ignore income taxes and salvage value.)

     a. Unadjusted rate of return.

     b. Payback period.

     c. Time-adjusted rate of return.

     d. Profitability index.

P27–6–B.   The Outland Company has decided to computerize its accounting system. The company has two alternatives—it can lease a computer under a three-year contract, or it can purchase a computer outright.

    If the computer is leased, the lease payment will be $9,000 each year. The first lease payment will be due on the day the lease contract is signed. The other two payments will be due at the end of the first and second years. All repairs and maintenance will be provided by the lessor.

    If the computer is purchased outright the following costs will be incurred:

Acquisition cost	$21,000
Repairs and maintenance:	
First year	600
Second year	500
Third year	700

The computer is expected to have only a three-year useful life because of obsolescence and technological advancements. The computer will have no salvage value and will be depreciated on a double-declining-balance basis. The Outland Company's cost of capital is 16 percent.

Required:

    Show whether the Outland Company should lease or purchase the computer. (Ignore income taxes.)

P27–7–B.   The Timberline Sports Company is trying to decide whether or not to add tennis equipment to its existing line of football, baseball, and basketball equipment. Market research studies and cost analyses have provided the following information:

1. Additional machinery and equipment will be needed to manufacture the tennis equipment. The machines and equipment will cost $600,000, have a 10-year useful life, and have a $20,000 salvage value.
2. Sales of tennis equipment for the next 10 years have been projected as follows:

Year	Sales in dollars
1	$100,000
2	150,000
3	225,000
4	250,000
5	275,000
6–10 (each year)	300,000

3. Variable costs are 60 percent of selling price, and fixed costs and straight-line depreciation will total $118,000 per year.
4. The company will need to advertise its new product line to gain rapid entry into the market. Its advertising campaign costs will be:

Years	Advertising cost
1–3	$100,000 (each year)
4–10	50,000 (each year)

5. The company requires a 14 percent minimum rate of return on investments.

Required:

> Using the net present value method, decide whether or not the Timberline Sports Company should add the tennis equipment to its line of products. (Ignore income taxes.)

P27–8–B.   The Brooks Company is considering purchasing new equipment that will cost $300,000. It is estimated that the useful life of the equipment will be five years and that there will be a salvage value of $100,000. The company uses straight-line depreciation. It is estimated that the new equipment will have a net cash inflow (before taxes) of $43,000 annually. Assume a tax rate of 40 percent and that management requires a minimum return of 14 percent.

Required:

> Using the net present value method determine whether the equipment is an acceptable investment.

P27–9–B.   The Starlight Company has an opportunity to sell some equipment for $20,000. Such a sale will result in a tax-deductible loss of $2,000. If it is not sold, the equipment is expected to produce net cash inflows after taxes of $6,000 for the next 10 years. In 10 years it is expected that the equipment can be sold for its book value of $2,000. The company's management feels that currently it has other opportunities that will yield 18 percent. Assume a 40 percent tax rate.

Required:

> Should the company sell the equipment? Prepare a schedule to support your conclusion.

BUSINESS DECISION PROBLEM 27–1

The Biltmore Company wishes to invest $500,000 in capital projects which have a minimum expected rate of return of 14 percent. Five proposals are being evaluated. Acceptance of one proposal does *not* preclude acceptance of any of the other proposals. The company's criterion is to select proposals which have a minimum required rate of return of 14 percent.

The relevant information related to the five proposals is presented below:

Investment	Initial outlay	Expected after-tax net cash inflow per year	Expected life of proposal
A	$100,000	$30,000	5 years
B	200,000	40,000	8
C	250,000	55,000	10
D	300,000	52,000	12
E	100,000	21,000	10

Required:

> *a.*   Compute the net present value of each of the five proposals.
>
> *b.*   Which projects should be undertaken? Why? In what order should they be undertaken?

BUSINESS DECISION PROBLEM 27–2

The Rockford Company is considering a capital project that will involve a $150,000 investment in machinery and a $30,000 investment in working capital. The machine has a useful life of 10 years and no salvage value. The annual cash inflow (before taxes) is estimated at $60,000 with annual cash outflows (before taxes) of $20,000. The company uses straight-line depreciation. The income tax rate is 40 percent.

The company's new bookkeeper computed the net present value of the project using a minimum required rate of return of 16 percent (the company's cost of capital). The bookkeeper's computations are shown below:

Cash inflow	$ 60,000
Cash outflow	−20,000
Net cash inflow	$ 40,000
Present value factor at 16% for 10 years	×4.833
Present value of net cash inflow	$193,320
Initial outlay	150,000
Net present value	$ 43,320

Required:

  a. Are the bookkeeper's computations correct? If not, compute the correct net present value.

  b. Is this capital project acceptable to the company? Why or why not?

BUSINESS DECISION PROBLEM 27–3

The Bronson Company is trying to decide whether to purchase or lease a new factory machine. If the machine is purchased, the following costs will be incurred:

Acquisition cost	$200,000
Repairs and maintenance:	
Years 1–5	5,000
Years 6–10	10,000

The machine will be depreciated on a straight-line basis and will have no salvage value.

If the machine is leased, the lease payment will be $30,000 each year for 10 years. The first lease payment will be due on the day the lease contract is signed. All repairs and maintenance will be provided by the lessor.

The Bronson Company's cost of capital is 12 percent.

Required:

Do you recommend that the company lease or purchase the machine? Show computations to support your answer. (Ignore income taxes.)

Chapter 28

Personal and corporate income taxes

CHAPTER GOALS

After study of this chapter, you should be able to:

1. Compute gross income, adjusted gross income, and taxable income for personal tax returns.
2. Compute tax liability on personal returns, including the effects of tax credits.
3. Compute the tax liability for corporations.
4. Illustrate the use of tax loss carry-backs and carry-forwards.
5. Compute depreciation allowance for tax purposes using the Accelerated Cost Recovery System (ACRS).
6. Identify the nature of permanent and timing differences between taxable income and accounting pretax income.
7. Account for timing differences using interperiod tax allocation.
8. Define and use correctly the new terms in the glossary.

Income taxes play a significant role in both personal and business decisions. As decision alternatives are considered, the tax consequences of those decisions also need to be noted and weighed. The purpose of this chapter is to provide an introductory understanding of federal income taxes, both personal and corporate. This chapter can only provide a general overview of these taxes due to their complexity and the constantly changing nature of tax laws. Coverage in this chapter is based on tax laws in effect under the Economic Recovery Act of 1981 and the Tax Equity and Fiscal Responsibility Act of 1982. Recognize that some changes may have been made to the tax law since those acts were passed.

PERSONAL FEDERAL INCOME TAXES

The first part of this chapter develops the concept of taxable income and illustrates the measurement of the tax liability for individual taxpayers.

Who must file a return

In general, all U.S. citizens and resident aliens must file a federal tax return. More specifically, the determination of who must file a return depends upon filing status and income level. For 1982, the income levels at which a tax return must be filed are $3,300 for a single person, $4,300 if age 65 or older, $5,400 for a married couple filing a joint return, $6,400 if one spouse is age 65 or older, and $7,400 if both are age 65 or older.

Filing status. There are four basic filing statuses that can be used in filing an income tax return. These are single, married filing jointly, married filing separately, and head of household. All of these are self-explanatory except *head of household* who typically is an unmarried or legally separated person who maintains a residence for a person who qualifies as a dependent of the taxpayer.

Gross income

Illustration 28.1 contains a general model of the determination of taxable income. The model starts with gross (total) income. *Gross income* includes all income from whatever source derived, except income specifically exempted, such as social security benefits. Gross income includes wages, interest, dividends, tips, bonuses, gambling winnings, gains from property sales, and prizes (including noncash prizes). Even income generated illegally, such as by theft, must be included in gross income. The general rule is that every income item, unless specifically exempted by law, must be included in gross income.

Exclusions from gross income. Income items excluded are interest on state and municipal bonds, social security benefits, workmen's compensation insurance benefits, and several employee "fringe" benefits, such as employer-paid health insurance premiums. Also, gifts, inheritances, certain disability

Illustration 28.1:   Determination of taxable income for an individual taxpayer

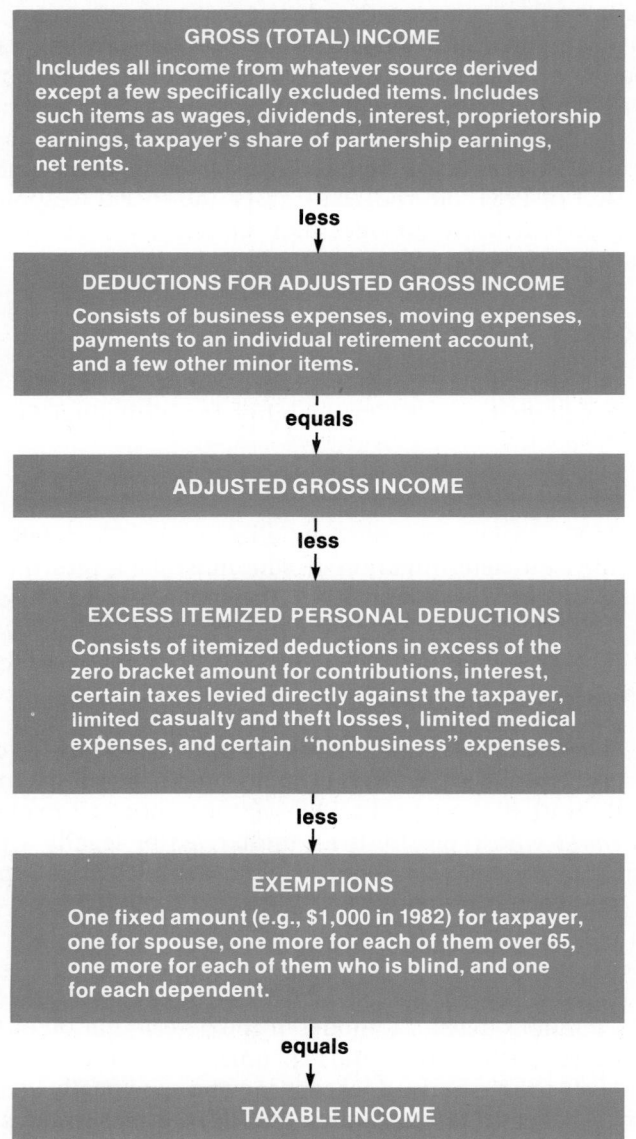

benefits, scholarships, and the proceeds from life insurance policies are excluded. The first $100 of dividend income ($200 on a joint return no matter which spouse earned the dividend) can be excluded.

Adjusted gross income

Taxpayers are allowed to deduct certain items from gross income in arriving at *adjusted gross income.* The computation of adjusted gross income is necessary in order to compute the allowable amounts of certain personal, itemized deductions.

Deductions for adjusted gross income to arrive at adjusted gross income consist basically of business expenses related to the production of income, moving expenses related to job or business, payments to individual retirement accounts (IRAs) or to Keogh retirement plans, alimony paid to an ex-spouse, and interest penalties assessed on certain investments for early withdrawals of funds.

Ordinary and necessary business expenses which would be deductible (to the extent that they are unreimbursed) in computing adjusted gross income would include any items which fall into the following three basic categories:

1. Expenses incurred by employees while away from home on business for travel, food, or accommodations.
2. Transportation expenses incurred as an employee, other than the normal cost of commuting to and from work.
3. Expenses incurred in moving to a new place of employment.

Employees can deduct contributions to an individual retirement account (IRA) from gross income. An IRA is a retirement savings account usually set up in a bank, savings and loan association, insurance company, mutual fund, or brokerage firm. The annual deduction is limited to the lesser of 100 percent of earnings or $2,000 for an individual, $4,000 for a married couple, if both have jobs, and $2,250 for a married couple in which only one spouse has earned income. Deductions cannot be based on unearned income, such as interest and dividends.

Since self-employed individuals are not covered by company-established retirement plans as employees are, they are allowed to establish their own retirement plan, called a Keogh plan (pronounced Key-oh). The distinction between an IRA and a Keogh plan is that while an IRA is available to anyone, a Keogh plan is available only to self-employed individuals. The annual deduction for a Keogh plan differs from that of an IRA and is limited to the lesser of 15 percent of earnings or $15,000. Substantive and rather complex new rules effective in tax years after 1982 regarding Keogh plans were introduced in the 1982 act. These rules include a new definition of earnings and a general limitation of $30,000 as a deductible item in computing adjusted gross income.

Taxable income

Taxpayers are allowed certain additional deductions and exemptions in arriving at *taxable income*. The *deductions from adjusted gross income* are called itemized or personal deductions and are specified by law. These itemized deductions are allowable only to the extent that they exceed a specified amount called the *zero bracket amount.* This amount is $2,300 for single and head of household returns, $3,400 for joint returns, and $1,700 for married persons filing separately. Itemized deductions *in excess* of the zero bracket amount are called *excess itemized deductions* and can be deducted from adjusted gross income. A taxpayer will only itemize deductions if those deductions exceed the zero bracket amount. The zero bracket amount is built into the tax rate schedules and tables.

Itemized deductions. The more common *itemized deductions* include:

1. *Taxes.* Real estate taxes, personal property taxes, state and local income taxes, and sales taxes are deductible. License fees and federal excise taxes are not deductible.

2. *Interest.* Virtually all interest paid on any type of personal debt is deductible.

3. *Charitable contributions.* Gifts to educational, religious, scientific, and charitable organizations are deductible if, in total, they do not exceed 50 percent of adjusted gross income. Donations to individuals, labor unions, and organizations that seek to influence legislation are not deductible.

4. *Medical expenses.* Within certain limits, unreimbursed hospital, medical, and dental expenses incurred by taxpayers and their dependents are deductible. Only that amount of medical costs that exceeds 5 percent of adjusted gross income is deductible. Drugs and medicines are included with these medical costs only to the extent that they exceed 1 percent of adjusted gross income. But, beginning in 1984, the *entire* cost of only *prescription* drugs and insulin will be included in medical costs.

An illustration will clarify the treatment of medical expenses. Assume that in 1983, a taxpayer with an adjusted gross income of $20,000 paid $550 of health insurance premiums, incurred other medical expenses of $700, and incurred medicine costs of $400. The medical deduction is:

Health insurance premiums		$ 550
Other unreimbursed medical expenses		700
Medicine costs	$400	
Less: 1% of adjusted gross income (0.01 × $20,000)	200	200
		$1,450
Less: 5% of adjusted gross income (0.05 × $20,000)		1,000
Medical deduction		$ 450

If the taxpayer had the same adjusted gross income and medical expenses for 1984, the allowed medical deduction would be $650. The requirement that medicine (prescription drug) costs exceed one percent of adjusted gross income before they can be included in medical expenses no longer applies.

5. *Casualty losses.* Casualty losses are sudden and unexpected losses resulting from theft, accidents, storms, fire, and similar events. They are deductible to the extent that *each* casualty loss exceeds $100, *and* the sum total of all unreimbursed casualty losses for the year exceeds 10 percent of adjusted gross income. Thus, to compute the deduction, subtract $100 from the dollar amount of *each* loss (ignore losses of less than $100) to obtain an adjusted casualty loss. From the sum of the adjusted casualty losses, subtract 10 percent of adjusted gross income. The positive difference is the casualty loss deduction.

6. *Other deductions.* In general, this category consists of expenses related to the taxpayer's business or profession that are not deductible from gross income. Included are the costs of professional publications and dues, union dues, safe-deposit box rentals, income tax preparer's fees, business entertainment, and job-related clothing and tools.

Exemptions

The final step to determine taxable income is to deduct the amount of income exempt from taxation. This is determined by multiplying the number of *exemptions* allowed the taxpayer by $1,000. Married persons filing jointly are both considered taxpayers even though only one spouse has income and are allowed one exemption each, plus one for each dependent. An additional exemption is allowed each taxpayer who is 65 or over or blind. Thus, a married couple with no dependents may be allowed up to six exemptions, three each—one for self, one for age 65 or over, and one for being blind.

A taxpayer is allowed an exemption for each person who (1) is closely related to the taxpayer or who lived as a member of the taxpayer's family for the entire year; (2) has an income of less than $1,000; (3) received more than half of his or her support from the taxpayer; and (4) who, if married, does not file a joint return with a spouse for the taxable year. The $1,000 income limitation does not apply to the taxpayer's children who are under 19 or who are enrolled as full-time students. Thus, student status may yield two exemptions: one on the parents' return and another on the student's own return.

Computing tax liability

As discussed above, the manner of calculating taxable income differs slightly depending upon whether deductions are itemized or not. If deductions are itemized, taxable income is equal to adjusted gross income less excess itemized deductions and exemptions; if deductions are not itemized, taxable income is equal to adjusted gross income less exemptions.

If taxable income is $50,000 or less, tax liability in most cases is determined by using *tax tables* provided by the Internal Revenue Service. Portions of the tax tables used for a recent year are shown in Illustration 28.2. Note there are four tax tables provided; the one to be used depends upon the taxpayer's filing status.

To illustrate use of the tables, assume Mr. and Mrs. Olson file a joint return showing taxable income of $24,610. Their income tax liability is found on the $24,600–$24,650 line in the "Married couple filing jointly" column. The amount is $4,457.

If taxable income is more than $50,000, *tax rate schedules* such as those in Illustration 28.3 must be used to compute the tax. Thus, the tax on $61,000 of taxable income reported by a married couple filing jointly is $17,705 + (0.49 × $1,000), or $18,195.

Illustration 28.2: Partial tax table

If line 34 (taxable income) is—		And you are—			
At least	But less than	Single	Married filing jointly *	Married filing separately	Head of a household
		Your tax is—			
24,500	24,550	5,695	4,428	7,067	5,254
24,550	24,600	5,714	4,442	7,091	5,271
24,600	24,650	5,733	4,457	7,115	5,289
24,650	24,700	5,752	4,472	7,139	5,307
24,700	24,750	5,772	4,488	7,164	5,325
24,750	24,800	5,791	4,504	7,188	5,342
24,800	24,850	5,810	4,520	7,212	5,360
24,850	24,900	5,829	4,536	7,236	5,378
24,900	24,950	5,849	4,551	7,260	5,396
24,950	25,000	5,868	4,567	7,285	5,413
25,000					
25,000	25,050	5,887	4,583	7,309	5,431
25,050	25,100	5,906	4,599	7,333	5,449
25,100	25,150	5,926	4,615	7,357	5,467
25,150	25,200	5,945	4,630	7,381	5,485
25,200	25,250	5,964	4,646	7,406	5,502
25,250	25,300	5,984	4,662	7,430	5,520
25,300	25,350	6,003	4,678	7,454	5,538
25,350	25,400	6,022	4,694	7,478	5,556
25,400	25,450	6,041	4,709	7,502	5,573
25,450	25,500	6,061	4,725	7,526	5,591
25,500	25,550	6,080	4,741	7,551	5,609
25,550	25,600	6,099	4,757	7,575	5,627
25,600	25,650	6,118	4,773	7,599	5,645
25,650	25,700	6,138	4,788	7,623	5,662
25,700	25,750	6,157	4,804	7,647	5,680
25,750	25,800	6,176	4,820	7,672	5,698
25,800	25,850	6,195	4,836	7,696	5,716
25,850	25,900	6,215	4,852	7,720	5,733
25,900	25,950	6,234	4,867	7,744	5,751
25,950	26,000	6,253	4,883	7,768	5,769
26,000					
26,000	26,050	6,272	4,899	7,793	5,787
26,050	26,100	6,292	4,915	7,817	5,805
26,100	26,150	6,311	4,931	7,841	5,822
26,150	26,200	6,330	4,946	7,865	5,840
26,200	26,250	6,349	4,962	7,889	5,858
26,250	26,300	6,369	4,978	7,914	5,876
26,300	26,350	6,388	4,994	7,938	5,893
26,350	26,400	6,407	5,010	7,962	5,911
26,400	26,450	6,426	5,025	7,986	5,929
26,450	26,500	6,446	5,041	8,010	5,947
26,500	26,550	6,465	5,057	8,035	5,965
26,550	26,600	6,484	5,073	8,059	5,982
26,600	26,650	6,503	5,089	8,083	6,000
26,650	26,700	6,523	5,104	8,107	6,018
26,700	26,750	6,542	5,120	8,131	6,036
26,750	26,800	6,561	5,136	8,156	6,053
26,800	26,850	6,580	5,152	8,180	6,071
26,850	26,900	6,600	5,168	8,204	6,089
26,900	26,950	6,619	5,183	8,228	6,107
26,950	27,000	6,638	5,199	8,252	6,124
27,000					
27,000	27,050	6,657	5,215	8,276	6,142
27,050	27,100	6,677	5,231	8,301	6,160
27,100	27,150	6,696	5,247	8,325	6,178
27,150	27,200	6,715	5,262	8,349	6,196
27,200	27,250	6,735	5,278	8,373	6,213

If line 34 (taxable income) is—		And you are—			
At least	But less than	Single	Married filing jointly *	Married filing separately	Head of a household
		Your tax is—			
27,250	27,300	6,754	5,294	8,397	6,231
27,300	27,350	6,773	5,310	8,422	6,249
27,350	27,400	6,792	5,326	8,446	6,267
27,400	27,450	6,812	5,341	8,470	6,284
27,450	27,500	6,831	5,357	8,494	6,302
27,500	27,550	6,850	5,373	8,518	6,320
27,550	27,600	6,869	5,389	8,543	6,338
27,600	27,650	6,889	5,405	8,567	6,356
27,650	27,700	6,908	5,420	8,591	6,373
27,700	27,750	6,927	5,436	8,615	6,391
27,750	27,800	6,946	5,452	8,639	6,409
27,800	27,850	6,966	5,468	8,664	6,427
27,850	27,900	6,985	5,484	8,688	6,444
27,900	27,950	7,004	5,499	8,712	6,462
27,950	28,000	7,023	5,515	8,736	6,480
28,000					
28,000	28,050	7,043	5,531	8,760	6,498
28,050	28,100	7,062	5,547	8,785	6,516
28,100	28,150	7,081	5,563	8,809	6,533
28,150	28,200	7,100	5,578	8,833	6,551
28,200	28,250	7,120	5,594	8,857	6,569
28,250	28,300	7,139	5,610	8,881	6,587
28,300	28,350	7,158	5,626	8,906	6,604
28,350	28,400	7,177	5,642	8,930	6,622
28,400	28,450	7,197	5,657	8,954	6,640
28,450	28,500	7,216	5,673	8,978	6,658
28,500	28,550	7,235	5,689	9,002	6,676
28,550	28,600	7,254	5,705	9,026	6,693
28,600	28,650	7,274	5,721	9,051	6,711
28,650	28,700	7,293	5,736	9,075	6,729
28,700	28,750	7,312	5,752	9,099	6,747
28,750	28,800	7,331	5,768	9,123	6,764
28,800	28,850	7,352	5,784	9,147	6,784
28,850	28,900	7,374	5,800	9,172	6,804
28,900	28,950	7,395	5,815	9,196	6,825
28,950	29,000	7,417	5,831	9,220	6,846
29,000					
29,000	29,050	7,439	5,847	9,244	6,867
29,050	29,100	7,461	5,863	9,268	6,887
29,100	29,150	7,482	5,879	9,293	6,908
29,150	29,200	7,504	5,894	9,317	6,929
29,200	29,250	7,526	5,910	9,341	6,950
29,250	29,300	7,547	5,926	9,365	6,970
29,300	29,350	7,569	5,942	9,389	6,991
29,350	29,400	7,591	5,958	9,414	7,012
29,400	29,450	7,613	5,973	9,438	7,032
29,450	29,500	7,634	5,989	9,462	7,053
29,500	29,550	7,656	6,005	9,486	7,074
29,550	29,600	7,678	6,021	9,510	7,095
29,600	29,650	7,700	6,037	9,535	7,115
29,650	29,700	7,721	6,052	9,559	7,136
29,700	29,750	7,743	6,068	9,583	7,157
29,750	29,800	7,765	6,084	9,607	7,178
29,800	29,850	7,786	6,100	9,631	7,198
29,850	29,900	7,808	6,116	9,656	7,219
29,900	29,950	7,830	6,133	9,680	7,240
29,950	30,000	7,852	6,151	9,704	7,261

If line 34 (taxable income) is—		And you are—			
At least	But less than	Single	Married filing jointly *	Married filing separately	Head of a household
		Your tax is—			
30,000					
30,000	30,050	7,873	6,169	9,729	7,281
30,050	30,100	7,895	6,187	9,756	7,302
30,100	30,150	7,917	6,206	9,783	7,323
30,150	30,200	7,939	6,224	9,809	7,344
30,200	30,250	7,960	6,242	9,836	7,364
30,250	30,300	7,982	6,261	9,863	7,385
30,300	30,350	8,004	6,279	9,889	7,406
30,350	30,400	8,025	6,297	9,916	7,426
30,400	30,450	8,047	6,315	9,943	7,447
30,450	30,500	8,069	6,334	9,969	7,468
30,500	30,550	8,091	6,352	9,996	7,489
30,550	30,600	8,112	6,370	10,023	7,509
30,600	30,650	8,134	6,388	10,049	7,530
30,650	30,700	8,156	6,407	10,076	7,551
30,700	30,750	8,177	6,425	10,103	7,572
30,750	30,800	8,199	6,443	10,129	7,592
30,800	30,850	8,221	6,461	10,156	7,613
30,850	30,900	8,243	6,480	10,183	7,634
30,900	30,950	8,264	6,498	10,209	7,655
30,950	31,000	8,286	6,516	10,236	7,675
31,000					
31,000	31,050	8,308	6,535	10,263	7,696
31,050	31,100	8,330	6,553	10,289	7,717
31,100	31,150	8,351	6,571	10,316	7,738
31,150	31,200	8,373	6,589	10,343	7,758
31,200	31,250	8,395	6,608	10,369	7,779
31,250	31,300	8,416	6,626	10,396	7,800
31,300	31,350	8,438	6,644	10,423	7,821
31,350	31,400	8,460	6,662	10,449	7,841
31,400	31,450	8,482	6,681	10,476	7,862
31,450	31,500	8,503	6,699	10,503	7,883
31,500	31,550	8,525	6,717	10,529	7,903
31,550	31,600	8,547	6,735	10,556	7,924
31,600	31,650	8,569	6,754	10,583	7,945
31,650	31,700	8,590	6,772	10,609	7,966
31,700	31,750	8,612	6,790	10,636	7,986
31,750	31,800	8,634	6,809	10,663	8,007
31,800	31,850	8,655	6,827	10,689	8,028
31,850	31,900	8,677	6,845	10,716	8,049
31,900	31,950	8,699	6,863	10,743	8,069
31,950	32,000	8,721	6,882	10,769	8,090
32,000					
32,000	32,050	8,742	6,900	10,796	8,111
32,050	32,100	8,764	6,918	10,823	8,132
32,100	32,150	8,786	6,936	10,849	8,152
32,150	32,200	8,808	6,955	10,876	8,173
32,200	32,250	8,829	6,973	10,902	8,194
32,250	32,300	8,851	6,991	10,929	8,215
32,300	32,350	8,873	7,010	10,956	8,235
32,350	32,400	8,894	7,028	10,982	8,256
32,400	32,450	8,916	7,046	11,009	8,277
32,450	32,500	8,938	7,064	11,036	8,297
32,500	32,550	8,960	7,083	11,062	8,318
32,550	32,600	8,981	7,101	11,089	8,339
32,600	32,650	9,003	7,119	11,116	8,360
32,650	32,700	9,025	7,137	11,142	8,380
32,700	32,750	9,046	7,156	11,169	8,401

Marginal and effective tax rates. A quick look at the tax rate schedules in Illustration 28.3 shows clearly that the rates are progressive. That is, the tax rates increase with successively higher amounts of taxable income. For example, the taxable income of a single taxpayer over $2,300 but not over $3,400 is taxed at a 12 percent rate. Income over $34,100 but not over $41,500 is taxed at a 44 percent rate. These percentages are called marginal tax rates. A *marginal tax rate* is the rate applied to the next dollar of income or each incremental amount of income. Such rates are important in decision making because they show the marginal effect of a decision. For example, assume that Joe Hardy, a single taxpayer in the 44 percent tax bracket, could earn $400 on a plumbing job if he would work on Sunday. But being in the 44 percent bracket means that Joe would have to pay $176, ($400 × 0.44), more income taxes if he takes the job, which means that he would net only $224

Illustration 28.3: Tax rate schedules

Tax rate schedule for single individuals

If taxable income is: Over—	But not over—	Income tax is: This amount		Of amount over—
–0–	$ 2,300		–0–	
$ 2,300	3,400	. . . . .	+ 12%	$ 2,300
3,400	4,400	$ 132	+ 14%	3,400
4,400	6,500	272	+ 16%	4,400
6,500	8,500	608	+ 17%	6,500
8,500	10,800	948	+ 19%	8,500
10,800	12,900	1,385	+ 22%	10,800
12,900	15,000	1,847	+ 23%	12,900
15,000	18,200	2,330	+ 27%	15,000
18,200	23,500	3,194	+ 31%	18,200
23,500	28,800	4,837	+ 35%	23,500
28,800	34,100	6,692	+ 40%	28,800
34,100	41,500	8,812	+ 44%	34,100
41,500	55,300	12,068	+ 50%	41,500
55,300	. . . . .	18,968	+ 50%	55,300

Tax rate schedule for married individuals filing joint returns and surviving spouses

If taxable income is: Over—	But not over—	Income tax is: This amount		Of amount over—
–0–	$ 3,400		–0–	
$ 3,400	5,500	. . . . .	+ 12%	$ 3,400
5,500	7,600	$ 252	+ 14%	5,500
7,600	11,900	546	+ 16%	7,600
11,900	16,000	1,234	+ 19%	11,900
16,000	20,200	2,013	+ 22%	16,000
20,200	24,600	2,937	+ 25%	20,200
24,600	29,900	4,037	+ 29%	24,600
29,900	35,200	5,574	+ 33%	29,900
35,200	45,800	7,323	+ 39%	35,200
45,800	60,000	11,457	+ 44%	45,800
60,000	85,600	17,705	+ 49%	60,000
85,600	. . . . .	30,249	+ 50%	85,600

from the job. Joe may decide he would rather watch a football game or go fishing. This type of analysis is a correct use of the marginal tax rate.

The effective tax rate rather than the marginal rate should be used as a measure of total taxes to be paid. The *effective tax rate* is the average rate of taxation of a given amount of taxable income. For example, if Joe Hardy earns $34,600 for the year, he is in the 44 percent bracket. But he does not pay $15,224, ($34,600 × 0.44), per year in taxes. Joe actually pays at a 26.1 percent rate computed as follows:

$$\text{Effective (average) tax rate} = \frac{\text{Total taxes paid}}{\text{Total taxable income}}$$

$$\text{Effective rate} = \frac{\$8,812 + [0.44(\$34,600 - \$34,100)]^*}{\$34,600}$$

$$\text{Effective rate} = \frac{\$9,032}{\$34,600} = 26.1 \text{ percent}$$

* These figures were taken from Illustration 28.3 for a single taxpayer.

Capital gains and losses

Taxpayers seek to report taxable income as long-term capital gains because of the favorable tax treatment of such gains. A gain—an excess of selling price over cost—is a *long-term capital gain* if it relates to a capital asset held for more than one year prior to sale. *Capital assets* are all items of property other than inventories, receivables, copyrights, certain governmental obligations, and real and depreciable property used in a trade or business. But gains in excess of losses from sales of business real or depreciable property are treated as capital gains. Losses on such property are deductible as ordinary business expense.

Taxation of capital gains

Some capital gains escape taxation. For example, a taxpayer, age 55 or older, may exclude from gross income up to $125,000 ($62,500 on a separate return) of any gain on sale of the taxpayer's home.

All other capital gains are short term or long term according to whether the capital asset sold was held for more than one year. Short-term capital gains are fully taxable; that is, 100 percent of such gains is included in adjusted gross income. But only 40 percent of a long-term capital gain is included in adjusted gross income; the remaining 60 percent escapes taxation.

The tax savings to a taxpayer in the 44 percent tax rate bracket from qualifying a $1,000 gain from sale of stock investments as long term rather than short term is $264. The tax on the gain, if short term, is $440, ($1,000 × 0.44). The tax on the gain, if long term, is $176, [$1,000 − (0.6 × $1,000)] × 0.44; $440 − $176 = $264. The effective tax rate on the gain, if long term, is 17.6 percent, ($176/$1,000). With a maximum marginal income tax rate of 50 percent, the maximum tax on a long-term capital gain is 20 percent, (0.5×0.4).

If a taxpayer has both short-term and long-term capital gains and losses, the following procedures are applied:

1. Offset short-term gains and losses into a single net short-term gain or loss.
2. Offset long-term gains and losses into a single net long-term gain or loss.

If net short-term gains exceed net long-term losses, the excess is included in adjusted gross income. If net long-term gains exceed net short-term losses, 40 percent of the excess is included in adjusted gross income. For example, if a taxpayer has $5,000 of net short-term gains and $2,000 of net long-term losses, the $3,000 difference is included in adjusted gross income. If the taxpayer has net long-term gains of $6,000 and a net short-term loss of $1,000, 40 percent of the $5,000 difference, or $2,000, is included in adjusted gross income. If there is both a net short-term gain and a net long-term gain, all of the short-term gain and 40 percent of the long-term gain is included in adjusted gross income. The tax law relative to net losses is more complex, containing certain limitations. Discussion of losses is left for a more advanced course.

Tax credits

A *tax credit* is a direct deduction from the amount of taxes to be paid, resulting largely from certain expenditures made by the taxpayer. Because tax credits reduce the amount of taxes to be paid dollar for dollar, they are much more valuable to the taxpayer than deductions. A tax credit of $100 saves $100 of cash; a $100 deduction, on the other hand, is worth only $100 times the taxpayer's marginal tax rate. The maximum value, then, of any deduction is 50 percent of the amount of the deduction since the highest marginal tax rate is now 50 percent.

Among a number of tax credits are the following:

A tax credit of 50 percent of contributions made to candidates for public office is allowed, up to a maximum of $50 ($100 if filing jointly).

If new or used equipment is acquired for a trade or business, 10 percent of its cost may be taken as an *investment tax credit (ITC)*. Thus, a $10,000 purchase of capital equipment yields a $1,000 tax credit. The 1982 act requires that the basis for an asset for depreciation purposes be reduced by one half of the tax credit. The basis in this case would be $9,500, ($10,000 − $500), on which depreciation would be computed.

A tax credit can be taken for part of the cost of home energy conservation items, such as insulation, storm windows and doors, caulking, and clock thermostats. The credit is 15 percent of qualified expenditures up to $2,000, or a maximum credit of $300 for all years, not for each year.

A tax credit is available for part of the cost of installing alternative energy equipment such as solar, wind, and geothermal equipment in the taxpayer's home. The credit is 30 percent of the first $2,000 of such costs, plus 20 percent of the next $8,000, with a maximum credit of $2,000 for all years.

There also are tax credits for persons with low earned income levels, for the elderly, for child and dependent care expenses, for income taxes paid to foreign countries, and for wages paid in work incentive programs.

Filing the tax return

Personal tax returns generally must be filed by April 15 of the year following the tax year. Extensions may be filed, but payment of any tax liability is still due on April 15. As discussed in Chapter 12, most taxpayers are also employees and are, therefore, on a pay-as-you-go tax system. In addition to taxes withheld by employers, the Tax Equity and Fiscal Responsibility Act of 1982 requires the withholding of 10 percent of all interest and dividends (effective June 30, 1983) paid to individuals and partnerships. Among those recipients of interest and dividends excluded from this requirement are:

1. Individuals whose tax liability was $600 or less ($1,000 for joint returns) for the preceeding year.
2. Persons over 65 with tax liabilities of $1,500 or less ($2,500 on a joint return) for the preceding year.
3. Persons whose interest receipts are $150 or less on an annualized basis.

The withholding does not apply to interest earned on tax exempt bonds or to interest earned on an IRA or Keogh plan which is then *reinvested* in those plans. Because of these withholding requirements, most taxpayers will have paid most, if not all, of their income taxes for the year by payroll and other withholdings. Also, taxpayers having income above a prescribed amount that is not subject to withholding must pay an *estimated tax*. This estimated tax must be paid in four installments. The taxes withheld and the estimated taxes paid are entered as offsets to the total tax liability on the tax return. Any remaining unpaid taxes are paid to the Internal Revenue Service when the return is filed. In some cases, tax withholdings and estimated taxes paid may have exceeded tax liability and the taxpayer can claim a refund.

COMPREHENSIVE ILLUSTRATION—PERSONAL INCOME TAXES

An actual tax return consists of a number of preprinted forms that are filled out by the taxpayer. Most taxpayers will file either Form 1040A, often called the short form, or Form 1040, the long form. A taxpayer who intends to itemize deductions cannot file a short form 1040A. Two common schedules included in the long form are Schedule A and Schedule B. Schedule A shows the itemized deductions, while Schedule B lists all dividend and interest income when dividend and interest income exceeds $400. As mentioned in Chapter 12, one copy of the taxpayer's Form W-2 is attached to the tax return. The

W-2 is issued by the employer and shows wages earned and taxes withheld during the period on these wages.

Illustration 28.4 shows a brief summary schedule of the tax return items for Lee and Dora Bowman, who are married and file a joint return. Lee is chief engineer for a manufacturing company; Dora is a full-time homemaker. Both taxpayers are under age 65; they have two dependent children, age 13 and 15. Dora owns a number of bonds and shares of stock, some of which she sold during the year, realizing $10,000 of long-term capital gains and $1,000 of short-term capital losses. Total income taxes withheld during the year amounted to $16,700. In addition, Lee and Dora paid estimated taxes of $800. Other information needed to compute the Bowman's tax liability and tax payment are shown in the illustration. The income tax of $17,635 is computed using the tax rate schedule in Illustration 28.3. These rates are used for illustrative purposes only and may have changed by the time you read this text.

Illustration 28.4: Joint tax return computations

Salary		$58,000
Interest income		4,000
Dividend income, net of $200 exclusion		6,000
Long-term capital gain ($10,000) less short-term capital loss ($1,000)	$ 9,000	
Less: 60 percent exclusion	5,400	3,600
Total		$71,600
Contribution to an individual retirement account		2,250
Adjusted gross income		$69,350
Excess itemized deductions:		
Medical expense ($3,618 − $3,468; total medical costs less 5% of adjusted gross income)	$ 150	
Charitable contributions	2,100	
Taxes (real estate on home, state income, sales)	5,670	
Casualty loss ($7,485 − $6,935; total adjusted casualty losses less 10% of adjusted gross income)	550	
Miscellaneous (professional dues, subscriptions, unreimbursed business entertainment expenses, etc.)	440	
	$ 8,910	
Zero bracket amount	3,400	
Excess itemized deductions		5,510
		$63,840
Exemptions (4 × $1,000)		4,000
Taxable income		$59,840
Income tax [$11,457 + (0.44 × $14,040)]		$17,635
Credit for political contribution ($250 × 0.5 = $125, limited to $100)		100
Total tax liability		$17,535
Income taxes withheld	$16,700	
Estimated taxes paid	800	17,500
Income taxes payable with return		$ 35

CORPORATE FEDERAL INCOME TAXATION

Business managers strive to maximize income in a company, while at the same time attempting to minimize taxes. In a sole proprietorship or partnership, business earnings flow directly to the owner or owners and thus affect personal tax returns. The corporation is considered by law as a taxpayer and, therefore, is the only form of business organization which pays federal income taxes.

Taxable income

Corporate income taxes are based on the amount of taxable income shown on Form 1120. Corporate taxable income is computed by subtracting all allowable deductions from the corporation's gross income. Corporate gross income is calculated much like the calculation for personal gross income; it basically includes all revenues from sales, services, or investments of the company. Allowable deductions from a corporate standpoint must meet four criteria. Such deductions must be business related, reasonable in amount, necessary, and legal.

Once taxable income is determined, a tax rate is applied to find the amount of tax liability. As of this writing, the graduated tax rates applicable to corporations for the years 1983 and beyond are:

Corporate taxable income	Tax rate
First $25,000	15%
Second $25,000	18
Third $25,000	30
Fourth $25,000	40
Over $100,000	46

To illustrate, assume a corporation had taxable income in 1984 of $60,000. The tax due would be $11,250, computed as follows:

Tax on first $25,000 (at 15%)	$ 3,750
Tax on second $25,000 (at 18%)	4,500
Tax on remaining $10,000 (at 30%)	3,000
	$11,250

As was noted with personal tax returns, tax credits are available. One tax credit particularly significant to the corporation is the investment tax credit. The *investment tax credit* (*ITC*) is a 10 percent credit to tax liability when certain qualifying machinery and equipment are purchased. Therefore, if the corporation in the above example had purchased $47,500 of qualifying plant assets during the year, it would have a $4,750 tax credit available. This ITC would be used to directly reduce the tax liability of $11,250, making the net tax due $6,500, ($11,250 − $4,750).

Tax loss carry-backs and carry-forwards

A tax law provision permits corporations to carry losses back three years and forward 15 years. This means that if a company has a loss in a given year, it can apply the loss against taxable income of other years and recover some or all of the taxes paid during those years. The company has the option of carrying the loss back or waiting until future years of income and carrying the loss forward. If the company elects to carry the loss back, the company must apply the loss to the oldest year first, then the next oldest, and so on until the loss has been used up or until there is no more prior year income which may be offset.

An illustration may be helpful. Assume the amounts of taxable income (or loss) shown below:

Year	Taxable income (or loss)	Taxes paid	Taxes recovered
1979	$ 15,000	$ 2,250	$2,250
1980	20,000	3,000	3,000
1981	5,000	750	750
1982	(100,000)	–0–	–0–
1983	40,000	–0–	–0–
1984	10,000	–0–	–0–
1985	30,000	3,000	–0–
1986	50,000	8,250	–0–
1987	60,000	11,250	–0–

The loss of $100,000 in 1982 would first be offset against the $15,000 of income in 1979, then the $20,000 in 1980, and next the $5,000 in 1981. The company would recover the $6,000 taxes previously paid. At this point it would have a $60,000 loss carry-forward. It would apply $40,000 of the loss toward taxable income in 1983 and therefore pay no taxes in that year. This leaves $20,000 of loss carry-forward remaining; $10,000 would be used to offset income in the next year (1984), and the other $10,000 would be used to reduce 1985 taxable income. If the loss carry-forward is not "used up" by the end of the 15th year, the remaining portion is lost.

Depreciation methods used for tax purposes

Tax depreciation is substantially different from depreciation used for accounting purposes. In accounting, depreciation methods are designed to match the expense of a capital investment against the revenue the investment produces. The depreciable period or useful life used for tax purposes is based on tax law and has no relationship to the actual useful life of the asset; thus, no attempt is made to match income and expenses.

Prior to 1981, several depreciation methods were available for tax purposes, including the sum-of-years'-digits method and the uniform-rate-on-declining-balance method. The Economic Recovery Tax Act of 1981 introduced a new depreciation system known as the Accelerated Cost Recovery System (ACRS). For the most part, this new system is mandatory for property placed in service after December 31, 1980.

The primary objective of the ACRS is capital retention through the rapid recovery of capital costs. Capital assets are rapidly depreciated, thus allowing high tax deductions early in the life of the asset. Under the ACRS, the concepts of useful life and salvage value are eliminated. Instead, capital assets are grouped into several different classes. Each class has an assigned life over which the assets are depreciated.

Personal property is any property that is movable since it is not attached to land. Examples are trucks and machinery. *Real property (real estate)* is land and any property attached to land, such as a building, which cannot be moved. For tangible personal property and real estate, ACRS provides classes of 3, 5, 10, and 15 years. The composition of these classes is as follows:

Class of investment	*Kinds of assets*
3 years	Automobiles, light-duty trucks, machinery, and equipment used in research and development
5 years	All other machinery and equipment, such as dies, drills, presses, etc., petroleum storage facilities, furniture, and fixtures
10 years	Some public utility property, coal conversion boilers and equipment, railroad tank cars
15 years	Most depreciable real estate and public utility property

Once the asset has been classified, the depreciation allowance for each year is determined by reference to the ACRS depreciation table located in the Appendix to this chapter.

These depreciation rules apply to both new and used property. Except for depreciable real property (such as a building), the first year percentage allowance is the same regardless of when the property was placed in service during the year.

To illustrate the application of the ACRS, assume that Bigwig Company acquired and placed in service a new machine on July 1, 1984, for $100,000. The machine falls into the five-year class under ACRS. Using the percentages taken from the five-year column of Table 28.1 in the Appendix, the depreciation allowance for the machine would be as follows:

Year	Cost	× Percent allowance	= Depreciation allowance
1984	100,000	0.15	15,000*
1985	100,000	0.22	22,000
1986	100,000	0.21	21,000
1987	100,000	0.21	21,000
1988	100,000	0.21	21,000
1989	100,000	–0–	

* 15 percent × 100,000 = 15,000.

Depreciation is an expense that does not require the outlay of additional capital or cash by the corporation. Therefore, tax depreciation is very desirable since it decreases taxable income and hence the corporation's tax liability. The great advantage of the new ACRS is the early write-off of capital assets for tax purposes. By providing accelerated depreciation for tax purposes, tax savings are provided in the early years of the asset's life. The tax savings in early years can be reinvested and thus increase the earnings per share available for common stockholders for the entire period.

INCOME TAX ALLOCATION

Taxable income and net income before income taxes (for simplicity, pretax income) for a corporation may differ sharply for a number of reasons. In fact, the tax return may show a loss, while the income statement shows positive pretax income. This raises questions as to what amount of income taxes should be shown on the income statement. The answer lies in the nature of the items causing the difference between taxable income and pretax income. For tax purposes, differences between taxable income and pretax income are classified into two categories: permanent differences and timing differences.

Permanent differences

Certain types of revenue and expense included in the computation of net income for book purposes are excluded from the computation of taxable income. *Permanent differences* between taxable incomes and financial statement pretax income are caused by tax law provisions that exclude an item of expense, revenue, gain, or loss as an element of taxable income. For instance, interest earned on state, county, or municipal bonds is included in book net income but is not subject to tax and therefore is not included in determining taxable income. The same is true for life insurance proceeds received by a corporation. Other items, which are expensed for book purposes, are not deductible for tax purposes. These items include premiums paid for officers' life insurance, costs of attempting to influence legislation, and amortization of goodwill. These are only a few of numerous items in which the tax treatment is completely different from the accounting treatment. These differences in treatment *never* change or reverse themselves. Therefore, they are called *permanent differences.* Such differences cause no accounting problem—the estimated actual amount of income taxes payable for the year is shown on the income statement even if this results in reporting only $1,000 of income tax expense on $100,000 of pretax income.

Timing differences

Other items of revenue and expense often are recognized for tax purposes at *different times* from those used in preparing income statements. *Timing differences* between taxable income and financial statement pretax income are caused by items that affect both taxable income and pretax income but in different periods. For example, interpretations of the tax code generally have held that revenue received in advance is taxable when received and that current expenses based on estimates of future costs (such as costs of performance under service contracts) are not deductible until actually incurred. Also, elective accounting methods may be used for tax purposes that are different from the ones used for financial statements. For example, a corporation may be using straight-line depreciation for book purposes and ACRS depreciation for tax purposes. Eventually these revenues and expenses are recognized in computing both business (book) income and taxable income. It is the timing of recognition that differs. Therefore, these variations between taxable income and net income are called timing differences. For a given corporation, the reconciliation between income before taxes and taxable income may appear as follows:

Net income before taxes per income statement......		$74,000
Add:		
Life insurance premiums paid	$ 700	
Service revenue received in advance	5,000	
Estimated expenses under service contracts	1,000	6,700
		$80,700
Deduct:		
Interest on New York State bonds	$3,000	
Difference in depreciation for tax purposes		
($8,000) and for book purposes ($6,000)	2,000	5,000
Taxable income		$75,700

As discussed above, timing differences include items which will be included in both taxable income and in pretax income, but in *different periods*. The items involved thus will have a tax effect. When this is true, generally accepted accounting principles require that *tax allocation* procedures be applied to prevent the presentation of possibly misleading information. *Interperiod tax allocation* is a procedure whereby the tax effects of an element of expense or revenue, loss or gain, which will affect taxable income are allocated to the period in which the item is recognized for accounting purposes, regardless of the period in which it is recognized for tax purposes.

To illustrate the tax allocation procedure required for timing differences, assume that (1) a firm acquires automobiles for $20,000 that have an estimated life of four years with no expected salvage value, (2) it uses the straight-line depreciation method for financial reporting purposes and the ACRS method for tax purposes (the automobiles fall into the three-year class), (3) net income before depreciation and income taxes is $15,000 for each year of the automobiles' lives, (4) there are no other items that cause differences between pretax income and taxable income, and (5) the tax rate is 40 percent (to simplify the illustration).

Under these circumstances, the actual tax liability for each year will be as shown in Illustration 28.5.

Illustration 28.5:   Calculation of tax liability

	1982	1983	1984	1985	Total
Income before depreciation and income taxes	$15,000	$15,000	$15,000	$15,000	$60,000
Depreciation (ACRS, three-year class method)	5,000	7,600	7,400	–0–	20,000
Taxable income	$10,000	$ 7,400	$ 7,600	$15,000	$40,000
Income taxes payable (40% of taxable income)	$ 4,000	$ 2,960	$ 3,040	$ 6,000	$16,000

If the amount of income taxes payable for each year is considered the tax expense for the year, net income for each year would be as shown in Illustration 28.6. It should be noted that the amount of taxable income to be shown on the corporation's tax return for each year (Illustration 28.5) is different from the amount of pre-tax income reported on the corporation's income statement (Illustration 28.6). To report this much year-to-year net income variance under the circumstances described would be considered quite misleading under generally accepted accounting principles. Generally accepted accounting principles contend that the income taxes should be $4,000 per year since the tax rate is 40 percent and each year has $10,000 of income before taxes. This contention is supported by drawing attention to the fact that the total income taxes paid for the four years will be $16,000, the same as income tax expense for accounting purposes (4 × $4,000). Any taxes not paid in the early years of the automobiles' lives will be paid later—note the $6,000 of taxes in 1985—when, as the accountant would say, the timing differences reverse. In this case, reversing occurs in 1985 when depreciation is less per tax return than for financial reporting purposes.

Illustration 28.6:   Net income with no tax allocation

	1982	1983	1984	1985	Total
Income before depreciation and income taxes	$15,000	$15,000	$15,000	$15,000	$60,000
Depreciation (straight-line method) ..	5,000	5,000	5,000	5,000	20,000
Income before income taxes	$10,000	$10,000	$10,000	$10,000	$40,000
Income taxes (computed in Illustration 28.5)	4,000	2,960	3,040	6,000	16,000
Net income	$ 6,000	$ 7,040	$ 6,960	$ 4,000	$24,000

Consequently, tax allocation procedures should be applied in the above circumstances. Under such procedures, the income statement for each of the four years would be as shown in Illustration 28.7.

Illustration 28.7: Net income with tax allocation

	Each year	Total for four years
Income before depreciation and income taxes	$15,000	$60,000
Depreciation expense	5,000	20,000
Income before income taxes	$10,000	$40,000
Income taxes expense	4,000	16,000
Net income	$ 6,000	$24,000

Income tax expense is reported on the income statement at $4,000 per year regardless of the taxes payable per the tax return for each year. The entries necessary in 1982, 1983, and 1984 to record income taxes on the company's books are:

	1982		1983		1984	
Federal Income Tax Expense	4,000		4,000		4,000	
Federal Income Taxes Payable		4,000		2,960		3,040
Deferred Federal Income Taxes Payable		–0–		1,040		960
To record income tax expense.						

The required entry for 1985 is:

Federal Income Tax Expense	4,000	
Deferred Federal Income Taxes Payable ...	2,000	
Federal Income Taxes Payable		6,000
To record income tax expense.		

Under tax allocation, reported net income is $6,000 per year. Note especially that reported income tax expense is $4,000 in each year, which seems logical when pretax income is $10,000 and the tax rate is 40 percent.

The entries are posted to T-accounts below. When payments are actually made to the federal government, the Federal Income Taxes Payable account is debited and Cash is credited for the amount of the payment.

Federal Income Tax Expense		Federal Income Taxes Payable		Deferred Federal Income Taxes Payable	
1982 4,000			1982 4,000	1985 2,000	1982 –0–
1983 4,000			1983 2,960		1983 1,040
1984 4,000			1984 3,040		1984 960
1985 4,000			1985 6,000		
16,000			16,000		–0–

Note again that the amount of tax expense recognized remained constant at $4,000 even though the tax liability increased from $2,960 for 1983 to $6,000 for 1985. The normalizing of the tax expense for each year was accomplished by entries in the Deferred Federal Income Taxes Payable account. As can be seen, the tax expense for the four years is $16,000, and the tax payments for the four years also sum to $16,000. The only difference is that the tax expense charged to each year is not the same amount as the actual liability for the year. Note, also, that in the simplified example the Deferred Federal Income Taxes Payable account has a zero balance at the end of four years.

Actual business experience has shown that once a Deferred Federal Income Taxes Payable account is established, it is seldom decreased or reduced to zero. The reason is that most businesses acquire new depreciable assets, at perhaps higher prices. The result is that depreciation for tax purposes continues to be greater than depreciation for financial reporting purposes, and the balance in the Deferred Federal Income Taxes Payable account also continues to grow. For this reason, many accountants seriously question the validity of tax allocation in circumstances such as those described above. But discussion of this controversial issue must be left to a more advanced text. In the above example, the Deferred Federal Income Taxes Payable account would be reported as a long-term liability on the balance sheet because the item causing its existence (the machine) is classified as a long-term asset.

APPENDIX: ACCELERATED COST RECOVERY SYSTEM DEPRECIATION ALLOWANCE TABLES

ACRS depreciation will, for the most part, be mandatory for assets (new or used) purchased and put into service *after* December 31, 1980. Table 28.1 gives the depreciation rates for such assets.

Table 28.1: Personal property placed in service after December 31, 1980

	Class of investment			
Ownership year	3 years (percent)	5 years (percent)	10 years (percent)	15-year utility property (percent)
1	25	15	8	5
2	38	22	14	10
3	37	21	12	9
4		21	10	8
5		21	10	7
6			10	7
7			9	6
8			9	6
9			9	6
10			9	6
11				6
12				6
13				6
14				6
15				6
	100	100	100	100

In using the ACRS table, keep in mind the following three rules:

1.   Ignore salvage value. Apply the percentage to the cost of the asset.
2.   If an asset is purchased and put into service at any time during the year, it will still receive a full year's depreciation (for tax purposes) for that calendar year.
3.   Ignore the estimated useful life of an asset. The number of years that the asset is to be depreciated is determined strictly by its classification, not its useful life.

NEW TERMS INTRODUCED IN CHAPTER 28

Adjusted gross income
Gross income less deductions for adjusted gross income such as business expenses, employee moving expenses, payments to an individual retirement account (IRA), and certain other deductions.

Capital assets
All items of property other than inventories in a trade or business, trade accounts and notes receivable, copyrights, government obligations due within one year and issued at a discount, and real or depreciable property used in a trade or business.

Deductions for adjusted gross income
Expenses of carrying on a trade, business, or practice of a profession, employee moving expenses, payments to an IRA or Keogh plan, forfeited interest penalty, and alimony paid.

Deductions from adjusted gross income
Excess itemized deductions and exemptions.

Effective tax rate
Average rate of taxation of a given amount of taxable income.

Estimated tax
A tax that must be paid in four installments by persons having amounts of income above a certain level that are not subject to withholding.

Excess itemized deductions
The amount by which itemized deductions exceed the zero bracket amount.

Exemptions
Fixed amount ($1,000 in 1982) the taxpayer may deduct from adjusted gross income for a taxpayer, the spouse, and one more for each if blind or over 65, plus one more for each dependent.

Gross income
All items of income from whatever source derived, except a few items specifically excluded by law.

Head of household
Certain unmarried or legally separated persons (and those married to nonresident aliens) who maintain a residence for a relative or dependent.

Interperiod tax allocation
A procedure whereby the tax effects of an element of expense or revenue, loss or gain, which will affect taxable income are allocated to the period in which the item is recognized for accounting purposes, irrespective of the period in which it is recognized for tax purposes.

Investment tax credit (ITC)
A direct reduction from tax liability equal to 10 percent of the cost of certain qualifying business machinery and equipment purchased.

Itemized deductions
Deductions from adjusted gross income for items such as contributions, interest paid, taxes, casualty losses, limited medical expenses, and other employment related expenses.

Long-term capital gains
Gains resulting from the sale of capital assets and certain other assets that were held more than one year prior to sale. Preferential tax treatment is accorded such gains.

Marginal tax rate
The tax rate that will be levied against the next dollar of taxable income.

Permanent differences
Differences between taxable income and financial statement pretax income caused by tax law provisions that exclude an item of expense, revenue, gain, or loss as an element of taxable income.

Personal property
Any property that is movable since it is not attached to land. Examples include trucks and machinery.

Real property (real estate)
Land and any property attached to land, such as a building, which cannot be moved.

Tax credit
A direct reduction from the amount of taxes to be paid, resulting largely from certain expenditures made.

Tax rate schedules
Schedules showing the taxes levied on base amounts of income, plus the tax rate to be applied to amounts in excess of the base. Used by taxpayers with taxable incomes in excess of $50,000, and certain others (Illustration 28.3).

Tax tables
Tables provided by the IRS from which taxpayers can look up the amount of income taxes levied upon their taxable incomes (Illustration 28.2).

Taxable income
Adjusted gross income less excess itemized deductions less exemptions.

Timing differences
Differences between taxable income and financial statement pretax income caused by items that affect both taxable income and pretax income but in different periods.

Total (gross) income
See gross income.

Zero bracket amount
An amount which is built into the tax tables as a deduction that all can take. Itemized deductions can be deducted from adjusted gross income only to the extent they exceed the zero bracket amount.

DEMONSTRATION PROBLEM 28–1

Lee Nash is a CPA employed by a CPA firm at an annual salary of $45,000. He is single and has no dependents. Other information concerning his 1983 finances includes:

Gain on sale of stock acquired in 1979	$ 6,000
Loss on sale of stock purchased in February of 1983	600
Interest received	1,500
Dividends received	2,440
Interest paid	600
Taxes paid:	
State income	1,800
Property taxes	750
Sales	900
Professional dues and subscriptions to professional journals	475
Business entertainment expenses	300
Charitable contributions	400
Health insurance premiums	500
Drugs and medicine	700
Other medical and dental expenses	2,470
Income taxes withheld	12,000

Required:

a. Compute the taxable income for Mr. Nash. (Prepare a schedule similar to Illustration 28.4.)

b. Using the tax rate schedule in Illustration 28.3, compute the additional taxes due or the refund claimable upon the filing of Lee's income tax return.

Solution to demonstration problem 28–1

Salary			$45,000
Interest income			1,500
Dividend income, less $100 exclusion			2,340
Long-term capital gain ($6,000) less short-term			
capital loss ($600)		$5,400	
Less: 60 percent exclusion		3,240	2,160
Adjusted gross income			$51,000
Excess itemized deductions:			
Interest paid		$ 600	
Taxes paid (state income, property, sales)		3,450	
Miscellaneous business expenses			
(entertainment, professional			
dues, journal subscriptions)		775	
Charitable contributions		400	
Health care:			
Health insurance premiums	$ 500		
Other medical and dental expenses	2,470		
Drugs and medicine $700			
Less: 1 percent of adjusted gross income 510	190		
	$3,160		
Less: 5 percent of adjusted gross income	2,550		
Medical deduction		610	
		$5,835	
Zero bracket amount		2,300	
Excess itemized deductions			3,535
			$47,465
Exemptions (1 × $1,000)			1,000
Taxable income			$46,465
Income tax [$12,068 + (0.50 × $4,965)			$14,550
Income taxes withheld			12,000
Additional tax due			$ 2,550

DEMONSTRATION PROBLEM 28–2

The records of the Vista Corporation show the following for the calendar year, 1984.

Sales	$385,000
Interest earned on—	
State of New Jersey bonds......................................	3,000
City of Miami bonds...	1,500
Essex County, Ohio, School District No. 2 bonds	375
Cost of goods sold and other expenses	315,000
Allowable extra depreciation for tax purposes	4,500
Dividends declared	15,000
Revenue received in advance, considered taxable income of this year	3,000
Contribution to influence legislation (included in	
"other expenses")	300

Required:

    a.   Present a schedule showing the computation of taxable income.

    b.   Compute the amount of the corporation's tax that was payable for the current year. (Use the rates mentioned in the text. Also assume the company acquired $100,000 of new equipment during the year and qualified for the full amount of investment credit as a reduction in taxes.)

c. Prepare the adjusting entry necessary to recognize federal income tax expense assuming income tax allocation procedures are followed. (The reduction in taxes caused by the investment credit is to be deducted from federal income tax expense and federal income tax currently payable.) The only permanent differences are the contribution to influence legislation and the nontaxable interest.

Solution to demonstration problem 28–2

a.

VISTA CORPORATION
Computation of Taxable Income and Income Taxes
For the Year 1984

Sales	$385,000
Cost of goods sold and other expenses	315,000
Reported income from operations	$ 70,000
Add: Revenue received in advance	3,000
Contribution to influence legislation	300
	$ 73,300
Less: Allowable additional depreciation	4,500
Taxable income	$ 68,800

b. Computation of tax liability:

15% of first $25,000	$ 3,750
18% on the next $25,000	4,500
30% on the remaining $18,800	5,640
Total tax before investment credit	$13,890
Less: Investment credit ($100,000 × 10%)	10,000
Total tax payable	$ 3,890

c.

Federal Income Tax Expense*	4,340	
Federal Income Taxes Payable		3,890
Deferred Federal Income Taxes Payable		450

To record federal income tax expense.

* Federal income tax expense is computed as follows:

Reported income from operations	$70,000
Add back permanent difference—contribution to influence legislature	300
Base for computing tax expense	$70,300
Computation of tax expense:	
$25,000 at 15%	$ 3,750
$25,000 at 18%	4,500
$20,300 at 30%	6,090
Tax on $70,300	$14,340
Deduct reduction in taxes caused by investment credit	10,000
Tax expense	$ 4,340

DEMONSTRATION PROBLEM 28–3

On January 1, 1984, the Warman Corporation purchased new equipment for $20,000. The equipment falls into the three-year class under ACRS, but will be depreciated for accounting purposes over four years using the straight-line method.

Required:

      a. Using Table 28.1 in the Appendix, compute the depreciation allowance for tax purposes for 1984, 1985, and 1986.

      b. Assuming that there are no other timing differences and that net income before depreciation and income taxes is $80,000 for each of the four years, prepare a schedule showing taxable income and income taxes payable (assume a 40 percent rate).

      c. Prepare a schedule showing net income with interperiod tax allocation for each of the four years.

      d. Give the required adjusting journal entry at year-end to record income tax expense for each of the four years.

Solution to demonstration problem 28–3

a.   1984: $20,000 × 0.25 = $5,000
      1985: $20,000 × 0.38 = $7,600
      1986: $20,000 × 0.37 = $7,400

b.

	1984	1985	1986	1987
Income before depreciation and income taxes ..	$80,000	$80,000	$80,000	$80,000
Depreciation	5,000	7,600	7,400	–0–
Taxable income	$75,000	$72,400	$72,600	$80,000
Income taxes payable (40%)	$30,000	$28,960	$29,040	$32,000

c.

	1984	1985	1986	1987
Income before depreciation and income taxes ..	$80,000	$80,000	$80,000	$80,000
Depreciation	5,000	5,000	5,000	5,000
Pretax income	$75,000	$75,000	$75,000	$75,000
Income tax expense (40%).................	30,000	30,000	30,000	30,000
Net income	$45,000	$45,000	$45,000	$45,000

d. 1984 Federal Income Tax Expense 30,000
               Federal Income Tax Payable   30,000
           To record federal income tax expense.

      1985 Federal Income Tax Expense 30,000
               Deferred Federal Income Taxes Payable   1,040
               Federal Income Tax Payable   28,960
           To record federal income tax expense.

      1986 Federal Income Tax Expense 30,000
               Deferred Federal Income Taxes Payable   960
               Federal Income Taxes Payable   29,040
           To record federal income tax expense.

      1987 Federal Income Tax Expense 30,000
         Deferred Federal Income Taxes Payable   2,000
               Federal Income Taxes Payable   32,000
           To record federal income tax expense.

QUESTIONS

1. How does one determine whether a particular cash receipt is includable in gross income? Name several items that might be considered income that are excluded from gross income. Why are they excluded?

2. Define the term *adjusted gross income* as it is used for personal income tax purposes.

3. For what kinds of expenditures may personal (itemized) deductions be taken on a personal income tax return? What effect does the zero bracket amount have on the total personal deductions that may be deducted from adjusted gross income?

4. What are exemptions and by how much does one reduce taxable income?

5. Why does a taxpayer wish a gain to qualify as a long-term capital gain and how will a gain so qualify?

6. What is a tax credit? Give several examples of tax credits.

7. Which is the most valuable to a taxpayer: (*a*) an investment tax credit of $1,000, (*b*) a $1,000 allowed deduction for a contribution to an IRA, or (*c*) an additional exemption which is currently worth $1,000? In your answer, rank the three items according to their probable value to a taxpayer.

8. What does a person mean when making the statement, "I'm in the 44 percent bracket"?

9. Which taxpayers are exempt from the interest and dividend withholding requirements? Which interest payments are exempt?

10. What is the estimated tax? How is it levied and paid?

11. H Corporation has suffered a loss for the current year. How can the corporation treat this loss for tax purposes?

12. How is depreciation for accounting purposes different from tax depreciation?

13. What is the primary objective of ACRS depreciation? How does it accomplish this objective?

14. Explain the difference in the causes of permanent and timing differences between taxable income and accounting pretax income. List two items which might be a cause for each type of difference.

15. When is interperiod tax allocation used?

16. A classmate states: "Why all the fuss about deferring revenue and recognizing expenses sooner for tax purposes? All net taxable income is taxed eventually anyway. It is only a matter of putting off the payment. I don't think these manipulations are worth the effort." Comment.

17. Classified among the long-term liabilities of the A Corporation is an account entitled "Deferred Federal Income Taxes Payable." Explain the nature of this account.

EXERCISES

E–1. Paul Daly is 65 years old; his wife is 58 years old and blind. They have three sons, ages 26, 29, and 32. The son who is 26 is a full-time student in medical school and earns $3,000 per year. His parents contribute $4,000 annually toward his living expenses. The other two sons are fully self-supporting. How many exemptions are Paul and his wife entitled to claim on their joint return?

E–2. John Franks has gross income of $45,000, deductions for adjusted gross income of $4,000, excess itemized deductions of $6,500, and six exemptions. He files a joint return with his wife who has no separate income. Compute their tax liability.

E–3. Identify the letters of those items listed below that would be included in gross income:

a. Tips received while working as a beautician.
b. Golf clubs won as a door prize while attending a conference.
c. Social security benefits.
d. Check received as reimbursement for medical expenses paid earlier this year.
e. Cash received as a beneficiary in an uncle's estate.
f. Cash received from proceeds of a life insurance policy on an aunt.
g. Employer paid $1,000 of health insurance premiums.
h. Gain on sale of personal asset, a sail boat.
i. Interest earned on an IRA.
j. Scholarship received from state university.

E–4. Using the following data, calculate the adjusted gross income for the joint return of Bruce and Helen Green:

Interest on New York City bonds	$ 4,000
Salary of Bruce	26,000
Dividend income—Bruce	300
Dividend income—Helen	80
Lottery prize	250
Long-term capital gain on sale of painting	4,000
Cash received as personal award for injury suffered in auto accident	800

E–5. The following data are for Ann Skilman, a single taxpayer:

Salary	$28,000
Contribution to an IRA	2,000
Contribution to candidate running for senate	60
Allowable itemized personal expenses	2,700
Income taxes withheld from salary	4,500

Using the tax table in Illustration 28.2, compute the amount of tax due or refund claimable.

E–6. Lucy Frances has three exemptions, even though she is unmarried. Her adjusted gross income was $20,100. Her itemized personal expenses amounted to $2,600. Compute her taxable income.

E–7. Given here are the capital gains and losses of two taxpayers, Harry and Sue. For each taxpayer, indicate the effect upon adjusted gross income for the year of their capital gains and losses.

	Harry	*Sue*
Long-term capital gains	$4,000	$ 500
Long-term capital losses	1,000	1,500
Short-term capital gains	500	3,000
Short-term capital losses	1,500	1,000

E–8. Joe Murdock has $25,000 of taxable income from other sources. He also has a capital gain of $6,000. Using the tax table in Illustration 28.2, compute the amount of income taxes Joe would save if the gain is a long-term rather than a short-term capital gain. Assume Joe is single.

E–9. Wuxtry Corporation has taxable income of $15,000, $30,000 and $45,000 in its first three years of operations. Determine the amount of federal income taxes it will incur each year assuming the first year of operations is 1983.

E–10.   Sutton Corporation had taxable income of $130,000 in 1984. Compute the tax liability of Sutton Corporation.

E–11.   Using the information in Exercise E–10, compute Sutton's tax liability assuming that during the year, $40,000 of plant assets were purchased which qualify for the investment tax credit.

E–12.   Gordon Company suffered a $60,000 loss in its fifth year of operations. Information from Gordon's previous tax returns shows the following information.

Year	Taxable income	Taxes paid
1.......	$30,000	$4,650
2.......	35,000	5,550
3.......	15,000	2,250
4.......	25,000	3,750

Assuming that Gordon elects to carry the loss back, determine the amount of taxes that can be recovered from each of the previous years.

E–13.   Sun Company purchased equipment which falls into the three-year class under ACRS. The equipment was purchased for $50,000 on July 1, 1983, and placed into service immediately. Compute the 1984 depreciation allowance for tax purposes (use Appendix Table 28.1).

E–14.   The pre-tax income of the R Corporation for a given year amounts to $200,000 while its taxable income is only $160,000. The difference is attributable entirely to additional depreciation taken for tax purposes. If the current income tax rate is 40 percent, give the entry to record the income taxes chargeable to the year and the tax liability for the year.

PROBLEMS, SERIES A

P28–1–A.   Elizabeth Powers is a professional model and is considered self-employed for tax purposes. She is single and has no dependents. She gathered the following information for your possible use in preparing her 1983 income tax return:

Business income	$50,000
Royalties received	2,000
Interest received (including $100 on New York City bonds)	1,300
Long-term capital gain	5,000
Contribution to a retirement account (Keogh plan)	7,000
Medical and dental expenses including $400 medical insurance premiums paid and $200 of drugs	3,896
Property taxes on residence	2,600
State sales tax	420
State income tax	4,200
Interest paid	6,500
Contributions to church and charitable organizations	2,800
Theft loss, excess over $100	2,100
Political contributions	200
Estimated taxes paid and income taxes withheld	8,000

Required:

Using the tax table in Illustration 28.2, compute the additional income taxes due, or the refund claimable, upon the filing of Ms. Power's income tax return.

P28–2–A.   Bob and Alice Jensen file a joint tax return. They have three children; the oldest is Dan who is 20 and a full-time student. Although Dan earned $2,500 in the current year, he still gets most of his support from his parents. Bob earned a salary of $34,000 in 1984. He also received $500 of interest and $80 of dividends. He sold some bonds held for three years at a gain of $3,000 and also sold some stock held for eight months at a loss of $500. Alice received $330 of interest from some City of Detroit bonds and $420 of dividends. Total income taxes withheld were $4,800. Among the personal expenditures of the Jensen family are the following:

Investment in an IRA	$2,000
State income taxes	1,200
Social security taxes withheld	2,212
Property taxes on residence	2,000
State sales tax	400
Charitable contributions	700
Contribution to political candidate	125
Interest paid	1,200
Medical costs, including $400 of health insurance premiums, cost of drugs and medicine of $500,	2,638
Miscellaneous items consisting of investment advice and subscriptions, and fee paid for income tax return preparation	260

Required:

Assuming the tax rate schedules in Illustration 28.3 are for 1984, prepare a schedule similar to Illustration 28.4 showing the taxes due or overpayment that would appear on the joint return for the Jensens.

P28–3–A.   The following data pertain to four individuals:

			Expenditures on—			
Individual	Tax status	Taxable income	Assets qualifying for the investment credit	Energy conservation	Qualified alternative energy equipment	Qualified political contributions
1	Single	$24,610	$5,000		$3,000	$220
2	Married filing jointly	54,000		4,000		250
3	Head of household	28,000		1,200		
4	Married filing separately	25,000	4,000		2,500	

Required:

Using the data given above and either the table in Illustration 28.2 or the schedules in Illustration 28.3, calculate the amount of federal income taxes now due. None of the individuals had ever before taken a credit for energy conservation or alternative energy equipment.

P28–4–A.   The following information relates to the activities of the Paradise Company for 1984:

Sales	$900,000
Interest income—	
State of Alabama Bonds	8,000
ABC Corporation Bonds	9,000

Cost of goods sold	675,000
Other expenses	125,000
Extra depreciation allowed for tax purposes	15,000
Amortization of goodwill, included in "other expenses"	1,100

In February 1984, Paradise purchased for $50,000 machinery qualifying Paradise for an investment tax credit.

Required:

a. Compute the taxable income for Paradise Company.

b. Calculate the tax liability for the current year (use the tax rates mentioned in the chapter).

P28–5–A. The Harvest Company has the following amounts of taxable income (loss) in the years indicated:

1983	40,000
1984	50,000
1985	30,000
1986 (see parts [a], [b], and [c] below)	
1987	15,000
1988	45,000
1989	20,000
1990	50,000
1991	75,000
1992	90,000

Assume that the rates for 1983 are in effect for the entire period.

Required:

a. If the loss in 1986 was $120,000, how much in back taxes would Harvest be eligible to recover?

b. Assuming that the loss in 1986 was $210,000, how much taxes would Harvest be required to pay for the years 1987–92?

c. If the 1986 loss was $350,000, how much taxes would be paid for the years 1987–92?

d. If after 15 years there is unused carry-forward remaining, what happens to it?

P28–6–A. The Samford Company purchased equipment for $80,000. It is estimated to have a useful life of six years and falls into the five-year category under ACRS.

Required:

For each year that the equipment is expected to be used, calculate the depreciation allowance for tax purposes assuming the equipment was purchased and put into use in 1984 (use Table 28.1 in the Appendix).

P28–7–A. The Telephone Company expects to have income before depreciation and income taxes of $200,000 each year for the period 1984–87. On January 1, 1984, the company acquired light-duty trucks for $160,000, which are expected to last four years and have no salvage value at the end of that period. For financial accounting purposes the company uses the straight-line depreciation method, and for tax purposes it uses the ACRS three-year class (see Appendix, Table 28.1). Assume that the tax rate is 40 percent (for the sake of simplicity) and that there are no other items which cause differences between pretax income and taxable income.

Required:

       a.   Prepare a schedule showing the actual tax liability for each year.

       b.   Calculate the income tax expense that should be shown each year assuming income tax allocation procedures are to be used.

       c.   Prepare journal entries to record the tax expense and tax liability for each year.

       d.   Show how the entries prepared in part (*c*) would be summarized in T-accounts. How would the amounts appearing in these accounts eventually be cleared from the accounts?

PROBLEMS, SERIES B

P28–1–B.   Alan Grimes is a systems analyst for a computer company at an annual salary of $50,000. He also provides consulting services from which he derived $16,000 of income after deducting related expenses. Alan is single and has no dependents. Other data for 1983 include:

Interest received	$ 2,500
Long-term capital gain from sale of securities	2,500
Contribution to a retirement (Keogh) plan	2,400
Interest paid	1,000
Medical and dental expenses, including medical insurance premium paid of	
$450, and drugs and medicine of $200	2,463
Taxes:	
State income	2,600
Property taxes on residence	2,200
Sales	500
Contributions to charitable organizations	600
Professional dues, subscriptions to professional publications,	
business entertainment, safe-deposit box rentals, etc....................	300
Casualty loss ($550 damage loss to automobile, less $200 deduct-	
ible amount paid by Alan)	350
Income taxes withheld	10,200
Estimated taxes paid	8,000

Required:

       Using the tax schedules in Illustration 28.3, present a schedule similar to Illustration 28.4 showing the computation of the additional taxes due, or the refund claimable upon the filing of Alan's income tax return for 1983.

P28–2–B.   Joy and Rob Bakke, who are married and the parents of two school-age children, file a joint tax return. They provide almost all of the support for Joy's mother, age 66, who lives with them. In 1984, Rob earned a salary of $43,000. They earned $800 of taxable interest during the year. They received $500 of dividends and realized a long-term capital gain of $5,000. Rob invested $2,000 in an IRA. Other data for the year are:

State income taxes paid	$1,900
State sales taxes paid	350
Property taxes paid on residence	2,000
Contributions (including estimated value, $200, of clothing	
donated to neighbors who suffered a loss from fire)..............	600
Interest paid (on mortgage, $4,500; on auto loan, $1,000)	5,500

Medical expenses paid (including health insurance premium of $500 and drugs and medicine of $300)	2,452
Miscellaneous expenses paid (all deductible)	200
Income tax withheld	8,000

Required:

Assuming the tax schedules in Illustration 28.3 are for 1984, prepare a schedule similar to Illustration 28.4 showing the additional taxes due or overpayment of taxes for 1984 that would appear on the Bakke's joint tax return for that year.

P28–3–B.   The following data are for four individual taxpayers:

			Expenditures on—		
Individual	Tax status	Taxable income	Assets qualifying for the investment credit	Energy conservation	Qualified alternative energy equipment
A	Married filing jointly	$66,000	5,000		3,000
B	Head of household	32,000		2,500	
C	Married filing separately	32,140			
D	Single	31,720	4,500	1,400	

Required:

Using the data given and either the table in Illustration 28.2, or the schedules in Illustration 28.3, calculate the amount of federal income tax due. None of the individuals had ever before taken a credit for energy conservation or alternative energy equipment.

P28–4–B.   The records of the Rawhide Corporation show the following for the year 1984:

Sales	$750,000
Interest earned on—	
State of New York bonds	6,000
City of Detroit bonds	3,000
Howard County, Ohio, School District No. 1 bonds	750
Cost of goods sold and other expenses	630,000
Loss on sale of asset	6,000
Gain on sale of asset	15,000
Allowable extra depreciation deduction for tax purposes	9,000
Dividends declared	30,000
Revenue received in advance, considered taxable income of this year	6,000
Contribution made to influence legislation (included in the $630,000 listed above)	600

Required:

a.   Present a schedule showing the computation of taxable income.

b.   Compute the corporation's tax for the current year. (Use the tax rates mentioned in this chapter.)

P28–5–B.   The Squash Company had the following amounts of taxable income (loss) in the years indicated.

1983	....	$30,000
1984	....	20,000
1985	....	60,000
1986	.... (see parts [a], [b], and [c] below)	
1987	....	40,000
1988	....	10,000
1989	....	50,000
1990	....	70,000
1991	....	80,000
1992	....	65,000

Assume that the rates for 1983 are in effect for the entire period.

Required:

a.   If the loss in 1986 were $110,000, how much would the company recover in back taxes?

b.   If the loss in 1986 were $180,000, how much would the company have to pay in taxes for the period 1987–92?

c.   If the loss in 1986 were $400,000, how much would the company have to pay in taxes for the period 1987–92?

d.   If there is a remaining unused carry-forward at the end of fifteen years, what happens to it?

P28–6–B.   The We-Haul Company purchased a van to use in making its local deliveries. Under ACRS, the van is classified as a three-year investment.

Required:

Assuming that the van cost $15,000, compute the depreciation allowance for each year assuming that the van was purchased and put into use in 1984 (use Appendix Table 28.1).

P28–7–B.   On January 1, 1984, Alexander Corporation acquired light-duty trucks for $100,000 which are expected to have a four-year life and no salvage value. The company uses the ACRS (three-year class) method of depreciation for tax purposes (see the Appendix, Table 28.1) and the straight-line method for book purposes. There are no other timing differences. Net income before depreciation and income taxes is $100,000 for each of the four years.

Required:

a.   Prepare a schedule showing taxable income and income taxes due for each of the four years (assuming a 40 percent tax rate for the sake of simplicity).

b.   Prepare a schedule showing income tax expense assuming income tax allocation procedures are used.

c.   Prepare the year-end adjusting entry required at the end of each of the four years to recognize federal income tax expense.

BUSINESS DECISION PROBLEM

J. W. Enterprises is considering whether or not to invest in a fleet of delivery vans, thereby expanding into a new business area for the company. Mike Livingston, president of J. W. Enterprises, estimates that the vans will generate new revenues equal to cash flows before income taxes of $150,000 per year for four years. The fleet of vans would cost $400,000 and would have an estimated useful life of four years. The vans will be classified as three-year life property under ACRS tax regulations. The vans will qualify for the 10 percent investment tax credit.

Required:

Assume the company is subject to a 40 percent income tax rate and that all cash flows, except the $400,000 cost, fall at the end of the year. Show whether this project is acceptable, assuming the company requires a minimum return of 15 percent. (Hint: Use the net present value method of appraising alternative investment projects, as discussed in Chapter 27. Recall that the tax basis of the vans must be reduced 5 percent when an investment tax credit is claimed.)

Appendix A
International accounting

WHY ACCOUNTING PRINCIPLES AND PRACTICES DIFFER AMONG NATIONS

In today's world we find it hardly surprising to discover a British bank in Atlanta, Coca-Cola in Paris, and French airplanes in Zaire. German auto parts are assembled in Spain and sold in the United States. Japan buys oil from Saudi Arabia and sells cameras in Italy. Soviet livestock eat American grain, and the British sip tea from Sri Lanka and China. Business has become truly international, but accounting, often described as the language of business, does not cross borders so easily. Accounting principles and reporting practices differ from country to country, and international decision making is made more difficult by the lack of a common communication system. If business is practiced at an international level, then accounting must find a way to provide its services at that level.

The problem is that accounting must first reflect the national economic and social environment in which it is practiced, and this environment is not the same in Bangkok as in Boston. Some economies, for example, are mainly agricultural. Others are based on manufacturing, trade, or service industries. Still others export natural resources, such as oil or gold, while a few derive most of their income from tourism. Accounting for inventories and natural resources, cost accounting techniques, and methods of foreign currency translation naturally have a different orientation, emphasis, and degree of refinement in these different economies.

Other accounting differences stem from the legal or political systems of nations. In centrally controlled economies, for instance, the state owns all or most of the property. It makes little sense to prescribe full disclosure of accounting procedures to protect investors when there is little or no private ownership of property. Some of these countries standardize their accounting methods and incorporate them into law. But in market-oriented economies, the development of accounting principles and reporting practices is left mainly to the private sector. Where uniformity exists, it occurs more by general agreement or consensus of interested parties than by governmental decree. In these economies, accounting principles and practices must be more flexible to serve the needs of business firms which differ widely in ownership, size, and complexity. In countries where business firms are predominately family owned, disclosure practices can be less complete than in countries where large, publicly-held corporations dominate.

The degree of development of the accounting profession and the general level of education of a country also influence accounting practices and procedures. Nations which lack a well-organized accounting profession may adopt almost wholesale the accounting methods of other countries. Commonwealth countries, for example, tend to follow British accounting standards; the former French colonies of Africa use French systems; Bermuda follows Canadian pronouncements; and the influence of the United States is widespread. At the same time, levels of expertise vary. There is little point in advocating statistical accounting and auditing techniques in countries where there is little knowledge or understanding of statistics. Accounting systems designed for electronic data processing are not helpful in countries where few or no businesses use computers.

Even in advanced countries, genuine differences of opinion exist regarding accounting theory and appropriate accounting methods. American standards, for example, require the periodic amortization of goodwill to expense, but British, German, and Dutch standards do not. Accounting methods also differ within nations. Most countries, including the United States, permit several depreciation methods and two or more inventory costing methods. Such flexibility is essential if accounting is to serve a useful purpose in economic, political, and social environments that are not uniform.

ATTEMPTED HARMONIZATION OF ACCOUNTING PRACTICES

The question arises whether financial statements that reflect the economic and social environment of, say, France, can also be useful to a potential American investor. Can some of the differences between French and American accounting be eliminated or at least explained so that French and American investors will understand each other's reports and find them useful when they make decisions?

Several organizations are working to achieve greater understanding and harmonization of different accounting practices. Examples include the United Nations Commission on Transnational Corporations, the Organization for Economic Cooperation and Development (OECD), the European Economic Community (EEC), the International Federation of Accountants (IFAC), and the International Accounting Standards Committee (IASC). These organizations study the information needs and accounting and reporting practices of different nations and issue pronouncements recommending specific practices and procedures for adoption by all members.

The IASC is making a significant contribution to the development of international accounting standards. It was founded in London in 1973 by the professional accountancy bodies of 10 countries: Australia, Canada, France, Germany, Ireland, Japan, Mexico, the Netherlands, the United Kingdom, and the United States. Since 1973, the professional bodies of more than 30 countries have joined the IASC as associate members. The IASC selects a topic for study from lists of problems submitted by the profession all over the world. After research and discussion by special committees, the IASC issues an exposure draft of a proposed standard for consideration by the profession and the business and financial communities. After about six months' further study of the topic in light of the comments received, the IASC issues the final international accounting standard. To date, 19 standards have been issued on topics as varied as *Disclosure of Accounting Policies* (IAS 1), *Depreciation Accounting* (IAS 4), *Statement of Changes in Financial Position* (IAS 7), and *Revenue Recognition* (IAS 18, effective January 1, 1984). Setting international standards is not easy. If they are too detailed or rigid, then the flexibility needed to reflect different national environments will be lost. On the other hand, if pronouncements are vague and allow too many alternative methods, then there is little point in setting international standards.

One major problem is the question of enforcement. There is no organization, nor is there likely to be, which can ensure compliance with international standards. Enforcement is left to national standard-setting bodies or legislatures, which may or may not adopt a recommended international standard. Generally, members commit themselves to support the objectives of the international body. They promise to use their best endeavors to see that international standards are formally adopted by local professional accountancy bodies, by government departments or other authorities that control the securities markets, and by the industrial, business, and financial communities of their respective countries.

The American Institute of Certified Public Accountants (AICPA), for example, issued a revised statement in 1975 reaffirming its support for the implementation of international standards adopted by the IASC. The AICPA's position is that international accounting standards must be specifically adopted by the Financial Accounting Standards Board (FASB), which is not a member of the IASC, in order to achieve acceptance in the United States. But if there is no significant difference between an international standard and U.S. practice, compliance with U.S. generally accepted accounting principles (GAAP) constitutes compliance with the international standard. Where a significant difference exists, the AICPA publishes the IASC standard together with comments on how it differs from U.S. GAAP and undertakes to urge the FASB to give early consideration to harmonizing the differences.[1] Significant support for IASC standards has resulted also from a resolution adopted by the World Federation of Stock Exchanges in 1975. The resolution binds members to require conformance with IASC standards in securities listing agreements.[2]

Although these developments are important for international harmonization of accounting, ultimately the success of international pronouncements depends on the willingness of the members of the issuing body to support them. In some cases, national legislation is required and may be slow or difficult to pass. The EEC, for example, issues "Directives" which must be accepted as compulsory objectives by the 10 member states (Belgium, Denmark, France, Germany, Greece, Ireland, Italy, Luxembourg, the Netherlands, and the United Kingdom) but which are translated into national legislation at the discretion of each member state. The EEC's important *Fourth Directive* was adopted in 1978 to regulate the preparation, content, presentation, audit, and publication of the accounts and reports of companies. It applies to all limited-liability companies (corporations) registered in the EEC, except for banks and insurance companies. Under the directive, member states were to introduce legislation by July 1980 so that accounts in all EEC countries would conform to the directive as of the fiscal year beginning January 1, 1982.

---

[1] American Institute of Certified Public Accountants, *CPA Letter,* August 1975.

[2] *CA Magazine,* January 1975, p. 52.

Yet by that date, only Belgium, Denmark, and the United Kingdom had passed the necessary legislation, although most of the other member countries were close to doing so.

The general movement toward international harmonization of accounting standards is increasing in other areas of society. The accounting profession, national standard-setting bodies, universities, academic societies, and multinational corporations have all shown an increased interest in international accounting problems in recent years. The AICPA has an International Practice Division as a formal part of its line organization. The American Accounting Association officially established an International Accounting Section in 1976. The University of Lancaster (England) and the University of Illinois have international accounting research centers which support research studies and conduct international conferences and seminars. Georgia State University received a Touche Ross & Co. grant to internationalize its accounting curriculum. Many universities currently offer courses in international business and accounting.

In the auditing area, progress is also being made. Several national accountancy organizations formed the International Federation of Accountants (IFAC) at the World Congress of Accountants held in Munich in 1977. The IFAC's Auditing Practices Committee issues international auditing guidelines which help to promote understanding of auditing standards and procedures around the world. Many large accountancy firms have permanently organized international departments and serve clients from offices established in many different countries. They provide regular information services to clients of different nationalities and conduct periodic studies of different accounting practices. Arthur Andersen & Co., for instance, issues a *European Review* three times a year, the principal purpose of which is "to discuss the development, content and impact on the business community of EEC pronouncements."[3] Price Waterhouse conducts periodic surveys to document and describe accounting principles and reporting practices in other countries.[4]

All this activity helps to increase the flow of information and our knowledge and understanding of the accounting and reporting practices in other parts of the world. Greater understanding improves the likelihood that unnecessary differences will be eliminated and general acceptance of international standards enhanced. Such a development will be very beneficial to international business and trade.

Some examples of the accounting methods used in different countries and of the concepts which underlie them will illustrate the difficulty of achieving international harmonization. The discussion will start with foreign currency translation, which is clearly a common problem in an international business environment.

---

[3] Arthur Andersen & Co., *European Review* no. 1, January 1981, p. 1.

[4] Price Waterhouse International, *International Survey of Accounting Principles and Reporting Practices*, 1979.

FOREIGN CURRENCY TRANSLATION

Foreign currency translation has two main components: accounting for transactions in a foreign currency and translating the financial statements of foreign enterprises into a different, common currency.

Accounting for transactions in a foreign currency

Suppose an American automobile dealership imports vehicles from Japan and promises to pay for them in yen 90 days after receiving them. If there is no change in the dollar-yen exchange rate between the date the goods are received and the date the invoice is paid, there is no problem. Both the purchase and the payment will be recorded at the same dollar value. But if the yen appreciates against the dollar during the 90-day period, the importer must pay more dollars for the yen needed on the settlement date.[5] Which exchange rate should the importer use to record payment of the invoice—the rate used on the purchase date or the one in effect now?

One approach to the problem is to regard the purchase of the automobiles and settlement of the invoice as two separate transactions and record them at two different exchange rates. The difference between the amount recorded in Accounts Payable on the purchase date and the decrease in Cash on the settlement date is considered an exchange gain or loss (a loss in this case). This approach is known as the "time-of-transaction" method and was the prescribed or predominant practice in 61 of 64 countries surveyed in 1979,[6] including the United States.[7] It is also the method recommended in the IASC's exposure draft, *Accounting for the Effects of Changes in Foreign Exchange Rates,* issued in March 1982.

The other approach is known as the "time-of-settlement" method and regards the transaction and its settlement as a single event. If this method is used, the amount recorded on the purchase date is regarded as an estimate of the settlement amount. Any fluctuations in the exchange rate between the purchase date and the settlement date are accounted for as part of the transaction and are not treated as a separate gain or loss. Consequently there is no effect on earnings.

Although the time-of-transaction method is widely used, the treatment of resulting exchange gains and losses is not uniform. If the gains or losses are realized, that is, if settlement is made within the same accounting period as the purchase, then most countries recognize such gains and losses in the income statement for that period. If the exchange gains or losses are unrealized,

---

[5] This example ignores the possibility that the importer might obtain a forward exchange contract, a discussion of which is beyond the scope of this text.

[6] Price Waterhouse International, *International Survey.* Data on the different methods used and on the number of countries using each method described in these examples are derived substantially from this publication.

[7] FASB *Statement of Financial Accounting Standards No. 8,* "Accounting for the Translation of Foreign Currency Transactions and Foreign Currency Financial Statements" (Stamford, Conn., 1975). The "time-of-transaction" method is also prescribed by FASB *Statement No. 52,* "Foreign Currency Translation" (Stamford, Conn., 1981) which supersedes FASB *Statement No. 8.*

that is, if they result from translating Accounts Payable (or Accounts Receivable for the vendor) at the balance sheet date, the treatment varies. Recording losses of this kind was the prescribed or predominant practice in 54 countries in 1979. But only 40 countries similarly recognized exchange gains in income, the remaining nations preferring to defer them until settlement. In the United States, under the provisions of FASB *Statement No. 52*, both realized and unrealized transaction gains and losses are recognized in earnings of the period in which the exchange rate changes.

Translating financial statements

Financial statements of foreign subsidiaries are translated into a single common unit of measure for purposes of consolidation. Considerable argument has arisen in recent years as to the correct way to do this; that is, which exchange rate should be used to translate items in the balance sheet and income statement, and what treatment is appropriate for any resulting exchange gains and losses? Items which are translated at the exchange rate in effect on the balance sheet date (the current rate) can suffer exchange gains and losses if the current rate differs from the rate in effect when those items were recorded (the historical rate). Items which are translated at the historical rate cannot suffer exchange gains or losses. If the current rate is used, a related question is: should the resulting exchange gains or losses be recognized immediately in income or deferred in some way?

The several methods commonly used to translate financial statements fall basically into two groups: translation of all items at the current rate and translation of some items at the current rate and others at the historical rates. The two groups are based on different concepts of both consolidation and international business.

The current-rate approach. The current- or closing-rate method translates all assets and liabilities at the exchange rate in effect on the balance sheet date. The main advantage of this method is its simplicity; it treats all items uniformly. The approach is based on the view that a foreign subsidiary is a separate unit from the domestic parent company. Multinational groups, therefore, consist of entities which operate independently but which contribute to a central fund of resources. There may also be an assumption that the assets used in a foreign operation are acquired largely out of local borrowings of the foreign subsidiary. Consequently, in consolidation it is believed that stockholders of the parent company are interested primarily in the parent company's net investment in the foreign subsidiary.

The current/historical-rates approach. This approach regards the parent company and its foreign subsidiaries as a single business undertaking. Assets owned by a foreign subsidiary are viewed as indistinguishable from assets owned by the parent company. Foreign assets should, therefore, be reflected in consolidated statements in the same way as similar assets of the parent company, that is, at historical cost in the parent company's currency.

Three translation methods are commonly used under this approach. The *current-noncurrent method* generally translates current assets and current liabilities at the current rate—the rate in effect on the balance sheet date, while noncurrent items are translated at their respective historical rates. Under the *monetary-nonmonetary method,* the current rate is used for monetary assets and liabilities, that is, for those that have a fixed, nominal value in terms of the foreign currency, while historical rates are applied to nonmonetary items. The *temporal method* is a variation of the monetary-nonmonetary method. Cash, receivables and payables, and other assets and liabilities carried at current prices (for example, marketable securities carried at current market value) are translated at the current rate of exchange. All other assets and liabilities are translated at historical rates.

Disagreement over the appropriate translation method seems likely to continue in view of the different concepts of parent-subsidiary relations on which they are founded. In 1979, only six countries prescribed a single method. The temporal method was required in Austria, Canada, Bermuda, Jamaica, and the United States (under FASB *Statement No. 8*), while Uruguay required the current-rate method. Since that time the United States has changed to the current-rate method (FASB *Statement No. 52*), and Canada is reconsidering its position, a decision which will also affect Bermuda. Apart from these 6 nations, 24 countries, including most of Europe, Japan, and Australia, followed predominantly the current-rate approach, while in 25 countries, including Germany, South Africa, and most of Central and South America, some variation of the current/historical-rates approach was common practice.

The treatment of exchange gains and losses produced by translating items at the current rate varies and is not strictly related to the translation method used. In 1979 the predominant practice in 42 nations, including much of Europe, Latin America, Japan, and the United States, was to recognize all gains and losses immediately in income. Eighteen of these countries used the current-rate-translation method and 23 followed one of the current/historical-rates methods. Alternative treatments of translation gains and losses included recording them directly in stockholders' equity (Australia), recognizing some of them immediately in income and deferring others (United Kingdom), and recognizing some in income and deferring and amortizing others over the remaining life of the items concerned (Canada and Bermuda).

Since issuance of FASB *Statement No. 52,* immediate recognition of translation gains and losses in income is not permitted in the United States. Instead, they are reported separately and accumulated in a separate component of stockholders' equity until the parent company's investment in the foreign subsidiary is sold or liquidated, at which time they are reported as part of the gain or loss on sale or liquidation of the investment.

INVENTORIES

Variations in accounting for inventories relate principally to the basis for determining cost, whether cost once determined should be increased or decreased to reflect the market value of the inventories, and whether the variable (direct) costing or the absorption (full) costing approach should be used to allocate overhead.

Determination of cost

Although other methods are occasionally used in some countries, discussion will be limited to the three principal bases for determining cost that are described in this text: first-in, first-out (FIFO), last-in, first-out (LIFO), and average cost.

The most frequently used methods in 1979 were FIFO and average cost. Each of these methods was predominant in 31 countries, although no country required the use of one method to the exclusion of the other. FIFO was more common in Europe, although Austria, France, Greece, and Portugal used an average method. FIFO also predominated in Australia, Canada, South Africa, and the United States. The average method was generally followed in Latin America, Japan, and much of Africa. LIFO was the principal method in only one country—Italy—although it was a common minority method in Japan, the United States, most of Latin America, and several European countries. LIFO was considered an unacceptable method in Australia, Brazil, France, Ireland, Malawi, Norway, Peru, and the United Kingdom. IASC's Statement No. 2, *Valuation and Presentation of Inventories in the Context of the Historical Cost System,* supports the preference of the majority of countries and recommends the use of FIFO or average cost.

Market value of inventories

Only seven countries in 1979 did not require or predominantly follow the principle that inventories should be carried at the lower of cost or market value. Five of these countries, including Japan, used cost, even when cost exceeded market value. In the other two countries—Portugal and Switzerland—most enterprises wrote down inventories to amounts below both cost and market value, a practice permitted by law.

The main difference in the countries that did use the lower of cost or market approach was in the interpretation of "market value." Forty-eight countries equated it with net realizable value, meaning estimated selling price in the ordinary course of business less costs of completion and necessary selling expenses. This view was essentially required in 22 countries, including Australia, France, Ireland, South Africa, and the United Kingdom. IASC Statement No. 2 also requires this interpretation. Austria, Greece, Italy, and Venezuela interpreted market value as replacement cost—the current cost of replacing the inventories in their present condition and location.

The United States defines market value as replacement cost, with the stipulation that it cannot exceed net realizable value or fall below net realizable value reduced by the normal profit margin. In 1979, Chile, the Dominican Republic, Mexico, Panama, and the Philippines also used this interpretation of market value.

Allocation of overhead

Recall from Chapter 22 that under direct (variable) costing, all variable manufacturing costs are charged to the product and all fixed costs (including fixed manufacturing costs) are charged to expense. Manufacturing overhead costs must, therefore, be separated into variable and fixed portions. The variable portion is assigned to production and included in inventory costs until the goods are sold, whereas the fixed portion is expensed immediately. Under absorption (full) costing, in contrast, all manufacturing costs, including fixed overhead costs, are applied to production and included in inventories.

Fifty-one countries in 1979 required or predominantly used absorption costing based on a level of normal capacity. IASC Statement No. 2 requires this approach. Ecuador, Ivory Coast, Malaysia, Morocco, and Senegal used direct costing, while in Botswana, the Netherlands, South Africa, and Switzerland there was no predominant practice. Chile, Denmark, India, and Malawi normally excluded all overhead—fixed and variable—from inventories.

In view of the importance of inventories and the wide variation in accounting for them, it is fortunate for users of financial statements that most countries require disclosure of information relating to the valuation of inventories. Only 8 of the countries surveyed in 1979 did not generally disclose whether the basis of valuation was cost, market, or the lower of cost or market, while all but 13 countries usually disclosed the basis for determining cost. IASC Statement No. 2 also recommends adequate disclosure.

ACCOUNTING FOR THE EFFECTS OF CHANGING PRICES

The final example of international differences will illustrate an opportunity for international harmonization that is almost unique. Accounting for the effects of inflation is still in its infancy, and it may be possible to achieve a general international approach to the problem before national practices become too varied and too entrenched.

In Chapter 13 two approaches to accounting for the effects of inflation on business enterprises were discussed: general price-level accounting and current-cost accounting. The FASB, in *Statement No. 33*, requires both methods.[8] The first approach attempts to reflect the effects of changes in general purchasing power on historical-cost financial statements, while the second is concerned with the impact of specific price changes.

A number of countries are addressing the problem of loss of relevance of historical-cost financial reporting in inflationary environments, and several have adopted one of the first two approaches. So far only the United States and Mexico require both. Some countries, usually those with the longest history of severe inflation, have issued standards which are mandatory for all enterprises, or at least for large or publicly held entities. In other countries, the

---

[8] FASB *Statement of Financial Accounting Standards No. 33*, "Financial Reporting and Changing Prices" (Stamford, Conn., FASB, 1979).

accounting profession recommends, but does not prescribe, a form of inflation-adjusted statements, usually as supplementary information. The accountancy bodies of several nations have issued exposure drafts but have not yet adopted formal standards. But few countries are prepared to abandon the historical-cost basis for their primary financial statements, at least until decision makers have had sufficient experience with inflation accounting to give an opinion on its utility. Exceptions to this view are Argentina, Brazil, and Chile, which now require incorporation of general price-level accounting in the primary financial statements of all enterprises.

The United Kingdom's standard prescribes provision of current-cost information either in the primary financial statements or as supplementary statements or additional information. New Zealand requires a supplementary income statement and balance sheet on a current-cost basis. Australia and South Africa recommend but do not yet require similar supplementary current-cost statements. Germany recommends incorporation of current-cost information in notes to the historical-cost financial statements, while in the Netherlands, some companies prepare the primary statements on a current-cost basis, and some provide only supplementary information.

The fact that, even with something as relatively new as inflation accounting, the accountancy bodies of various nations are adopting neither a uniform approach nor a uniform application of any approach highlights the difficulty of achieving international harmonization of accounting standards. Adoption of different approaches to inflation accounting by different countries will make the preparation of consolidated financial statements by multinational corporations especially difficult, while at the same time comparability of the financial reports of companies in different nations will be further reduced. But even if all countries adopted a similar approach, a major barrier to comparability would still remain: the price indices used in each country to compute adjustments for price changes are not comparable in composition, accuracy, frequency of publication, or timeliness.

Many accountants are reluctant to see inflation-adjusted statements replace historical-cost financial statements because they believe historical cost is the most objective basis of valuation. But business entities may be more likely to favor inflation accounting, once they become accustomed to it, because of its tax implications. Since inflation accounting generally leads to lower profit figures than those computed on a historical-cost basis, there is a strong incentive for companies to adopt inflation accounting in those countries where computation of the tax liability is based on reported net income. Governments, in contrast, may decide to prohibit the use of inflation accounting for tax purposes when a decline in tax revenues becomes apparent.

With regard to the general approach to accounting for inflation, the trend appears to be towards current-cost accounting and away from general price-level accounting. It has been suggested that, of the two approaches, governments prefer current-cost accounting, and this may influence the decisions of the accounting profession in some countries. As one British writer has pointed out,

No government wants to have the effects of its currency debasement measured by anyone—certainly not by every business enterprise in the country. Much better to point the finger at all those individual prices moving around because of the machinations of big business, big labour and big aliens.[9]

Whether current-cost accounting will become common practice or whether some combination of current-cost and general price-level accounting will gain favor, perhaps along the lines of FASB *Statement No. 33,* should depend on the usefulness to decision makers of the information provided by each approach. One thing is clear: unless inflation abates, more countries will adopt some form of inflation accounting. The opportunity to achieve a higher level of international harmonization while national standards are still at the development stage should not be missed.

We have attempted in these few pages to provide a broad and general picture of the variety of accounting principles and reporting practices that exist across the world. This variety is inevitable and necessary if accounting is to be useful within widely differing national business environments. At the same time, the information needs of international business must also be satisfied. It is a challenging problem and one that will receive increasing attention in the years to come.

SELECTED BIBLIOGRAPHY

Arthur Andersen & Co. (London). *European Review* nos. 1–5 (January 1981–May 1982).

Choi, Frederick D. S. and Gerhard G. Mueller. *An Introduction to Multinational Accounting.* Englewood Cliffs, N.J.: Prentice-Hall, Inc., 1978.

Hauworth, William P., II. "A Comparison of Various International Proposals on Inflation Accounting: A Practitioner's View." Monograph, 1980.

International Centre for Research in Accounting. *International Financial Reporting Standards: Problems and Prospects. ICRA Occasional Paper No. 13.* Lancaster, England: ICRA, University of Lancaster, 1977.

Price Waterhouse International. *International Survey of Accounting Principles and Reporting Practices,* 1979.

Stamp, Edward. *The Future of Accounting and Auditing Standards. ICRA Occasional Paper No. 18.* Lancaster, England: International Centre for Research in Accounting, University of Lancaster, 1979.

Stamp, Edward, and Maurice Moonitz. "International Auditing Standards—Parts I and II." *The CPA Journal* LII, nos. 6 and 7 (June–July 1982).

---

[9] P. H. Lyons, "Farewell to Historical Costs?" *CA Magazine,* February 1976, p. 23.

Appendix B

A set of consolidated financial statements and other financial data for Interlake, Inc. and subsidiaries

Presented in this appendix are 23 pages of the 1981 Annual Report of Interlake, Inc., and its consolidated subsidiaries. Included are (1) 1981 Financial Highlights; (2) sections described as Financial Report, Financial Developments, and Review of Business Segments in which management discusses and explains significant factors affecting results of operations and financial position; (3) Statement of Consolidated Income and Retained Earnings; (4) Consolidated Balance Sheet; (5) Statement of Changes in Consolidated Financial Position; (6) Notes to Consolidated Financial Statements; (7) Report of Independent Accountants; (8) selected data on the company's common stock; and (9) Supplementary Financial Information in which inflation-adjusted accounting information is disclosed and compared with required historical cost based data in a five-year summary. These items illustrate the financial reporting practices of a modern business corporation to its stockholders and to other external parties.

Particular attention should be paid to the rather substantial amounts of additional information and explanation presented in the Notes to Consolidated Financial Statements. For example, Note 1 discloses the accounting policies followed in developing the amounts reported in the various statements, such as the depreciation and inventory methods used as well as the consolidation principles employed.

A strong trend has developed in recent years toward making more informative disclosures in corporate annual reports. Many of these added disclosures result from FASB or SEC requirements. Examples include (1) a financial review and discussion by management of a summary of operations, (2) the disclosure of the details with respect to income taxes, and (3) the reporting statement acknowledging that management, not the independent accountants, is primarily responsible for the integrity of the financial information in the annual report.

The premise underlying many of these added disclosures is simply that management knows better than anyone else what happened and why. Therefore, it should be called to explain. These added disclosures reflect the fact that stockholders and others need information that is more timely and for periods of time less than a year in length. Users of financial statements may also need information related to segments of the enterprise such as revenues, earnings, and assets categorized by products or geographical areas.

Interlake, Inc. 1981 Financial Highlights

For The Year (In thousands)	1981	1980	% Change
Net sales	$1,016,605	$1,055,883	− 3.7
Net income	46,577	13,818	+237.1
Capital expenditures	37,393	31,276	+ 19.6
Cash dividends declared or paid	14,735	13,287	+ 10.9
At Year-End (In thousands)			
Working capital	$ 199,803	$ 181,145	+ 10.3
Current ratio	2.2 to 1	2.0 to 1	+ 10.0
Property, plant and equipment−net	263,296	254,855	+ 3.3
Long-term debt, less current maturities	126,618	133,020	− 4.8
Shareholders' equity	358,748	336,707	+ 6.5
Shares outstanding	6,179	6,089	+ 1.5
Per Share Statistics			
Net income	$ 7.59	$ 2.29	+231.4
Cash dividends declared or paid	2.40	2.20	+ 9.1
Shareholders' equity at year-end	58.06	55.30	+ 5.0

Sales and Earnings by Business Segments (In millions)	Sales		Earnings	
	1981	1980	1981	1980
Metals				
Investment/Die Castings	$ 108.5	$ 114.3	$ 14.1	$ 22.0
Metal Powders	87.7	70.9	16.9	8.9
Silicon Metal/Ferroalloys	95.7	84.5	8.9	6.2
Iron/Steel	344.2	325.2	19.3	(34.5)
Materials Handling				
Material Handling/Storage Products	277.4	350.5	9.7	22.6
Packaging	175.0	164.1	13.2	8.9
Corporate Items/Eliminations	(71.9)	(53.6)	(3.0)	(13.5)
	$1,016.6	$1,055.9	$ 79.1	$ 20.6

Contents

Financial Report

1981—A Very Good Year

In most ways 1981 was an excellent year for Interlake. Earnings were at record levels and sales topped the billion dollar mark for the third year in a row. Overall financial strength continued to improve.

Net sales were $1,017,000,000 and net income was $46,577,000, equivalent to $7.59 per share of common stock.

The year started on an optimistic note. The recovery from the brief, yet intense general recession of 1980 seemed to give economic strength to the first quarter of 1981. Still, everything never quite came together. The residential construction and automotive industries failed to show improvement and the prolonged recessions in these industries placed increasing strain on the rest of the economy. The result was a state of economic "sputter and spurt" which struck severely at some business areas, but offered opportunities in others. By the fourth quarter of 1981, a new recession was underway in the United States.

International economies were also under adverse pressure, especially in Europe.

Sales

Interlake's 1981 sales of $1,017,000,000 were approximately 4% below 1980 sales of $1,056,000,000. This decline can be attributed to loss of sales from plant operations which were discontinued in 1980 and to strengthening of the U.S. dollar which reduced the translated value of sales from foreign operations. Elsewhere, inflation inspired price increases helped buoy sales against real volume declines in some product areas.

Despite the loss of sales from discontinued plants, the iron and steel products group posted a 6% sales increase over 1980. New sales records were reported for Hoeganaes' metal powders and Globe's silicon metal/ferroalloys. Sales improved from 1980 for Acme's packaging products, but fell short of 1979's record. Material Handling and Storage Products' sales were off nearly 21% due in large part to strengthening of the dollar, but also due to poor market conditions. Arwood's investment/die castings sales declined approximately 5% as a result of sluggish domestic industrial activity, especially in the aerospace industry.

Net Income

Earnings showed substantial improvement from 1980. A rebound was to be expected due to the shutdown/disposal provision of $37,000,000 before taxes that was charged against 1980's results. Still, 1981's net income of $46,577,000 reflected an improvement which went beyond this expectation and exceeded the previous record of $39,735,000 established in 1979. Net income per share reached $7.59 in 1981 compared with 1980's earnings, before the shutdown/disposal provision, of $6.39 per share and net income per share of $2.29.

Earnings improvements in the iron and steel businesses, especially at the Chicago operation, played a large part in the overall income gain. Additional gains were reported by metal powders, silicon metal/ferroalloys, and packaging. Material Handling and Storage Products and Arwood's investment/die castings business showed earnings declines from 1980.

Financial Information

The following pages of this report include a review of the Company's business segments and important financial developments; financial statements; explanatory notes to the financial statements; and other supplementary information. The goal in presenting this material is to give the reader sufficient financial information to understand the Company's operations and financial condition. Sometimes this is more information than the casual reader really wants and there are occasions when mandated requirements of form and content produce technical items which may be overly complicated. With this in mind, we are including some additional commentary which we hope will make this financial report even more useful to you.

Management is responsible for the integrity of the financial information in this Annual Report and maintains a system of internal accounting controls that provides reasonable assurance as to the reliability of financial reporting and the protection of Company assets. Interlake's policy is to have a comprehensive system of internal accounting controls and organization arrangements which provides such assurance. This system includes reviews by five outside directors who constitute the Audit Review Committee of the Board of Directors and Price Waterhouse, our independent public accountants (whose report appears on page 49).

Financial Strength

As you read on, you will see that Interlake ended 1981 financially stronger than at any time in recent history and has the financial strength to support continued progress in the future.

Robert Jacobs

Robert Jacobs
*Executive Vice President-
Finance and Planning*

MR. JACOBS

Financial Developments

Billion Dollar Sales

Net sales topped the $1 billion mark for the third consecutive year. Although not quite to last year's level, the 1981 results were achieved against fairly difficult circumstances. Firstly, the economic climate has not been good and recessionary pressures have adversely influenced sales volumes and selling prices. In addition, the 1980 shutdown of steel facilities eliminated the equivalent of $69.5 million in sales. Finally, the increasing value of the U.S. dollar reduced the equivalent value of foreign sales by about $38 million. (Specific sales effects are discussed in the review of business segments.)

Record Earnings

Earnings for 1981 surpassed all previous records. While the year was not burdened with the shutdown/disposal provision that appeared in 1980, these results could not have been achieved without substantial benefits from reductions in production costs.

In many ways the results are a tribute to Interlake's diversification efforts. Packaging was the only business segment to establish a new operating income record. Investment/die castings and material handling/storage products both had earnings declines. But, without beating any records, iron/steel, metal powders, and silicon metal/ferroalloys attained improvements that supported Interlake's overall gain. (Specific operating income results

are discussed in the review of business segments.)

Dividend Increased

On August 27, 1981 the Board of Directors voted to increase Interlake's quarterly dividend from $.55 to $.65 per common share. This was done as a move to share the Company's earnings growth with shareholders and demonstrated confidence in Interlake's future, based on the Company's overall financial strength.

Dividends Reinvested

Interlake's dividend reinvestment plan was established in August, 1979. It offers shareholders an opportunity to reinvest their dividends in Interlake common stock at a 5% discount and without brokerage or service fees. Roughly 34% of the fourth quarter 1981 dividends were reinvested through this plan. This was a gratifying vote of confidence in the Company. (Requests for information on the Dividend Reinvestment and Voluntary Stock Purchase Plan can be obtained by writing the Corporate Secretary's Office.)

The Foreign Currency Translation Paradox

The value of the U.S. dollar rose in world money markets in 1981, a positive indicator of the economic strength of our country compared to other countries. However, there can also be negative aspects of a more valuable dollar. Three distinct and

significant effects impacted Interlake in 1981.

☐ First, when 1981 sales and earnings of our foreign operations are translated into equivalent U.S. dollars, they are lower than they would have been if translated at 1980 exchange rates. Sales from foreign operations were $38.0 million lower and operating profits dropped $4.1 million because of declining foreign exchange rates.

☐ Second, a new accounting standard was used in 1981 – Statement of Financial Accounting Standards No. 52, "Foreign Currency Translation." Under SFAS No. 52, balance sheet items formerly translated into U.S. dollars at historic rates are translated at current rates. Now, major items like property, plant and equipment and inventories are translated at current rates. Applying SFAS No. 52 at a time when foreign currency values were declining caused a downward adjustment in the translated dollar amount of all foreign balance sheet items at 1981 year end. The adjustment amounted to $13.0 million and was deferred in a new section of shareholders' equity according to SFAS No. 52.

☐ Third, because of the rising value of the U.S. dollar, foreign goods cost less to buy in 1981. Imports were more price competitive against U.S. produced goods and affected several of Interlake's domestic markets, most notably steel and ferroalloys. Again the paradox – a strengthening U.S. dollar limited demand for and the price of certain Interlake products.

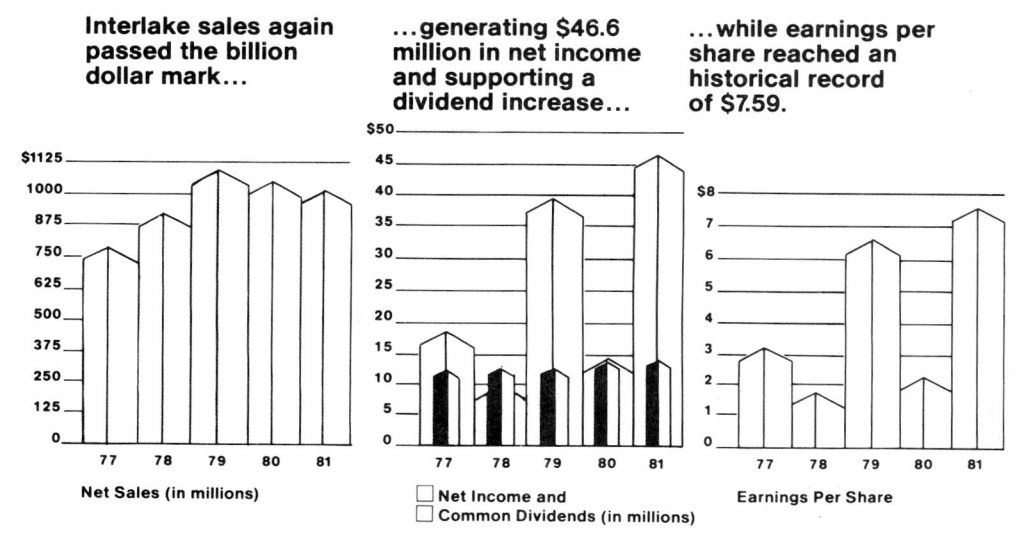

Interlake sales again passed the billion dollar mark...

Net Sales (in millions)

...generating $46.6 million in net income and supporting a dividend increase...

☐ Net Income and
☐ Common Dividends (in millions)

...while earnings per share reached an historical record of $7.59.

Earnings Per Share

Review of Business Segments

The Total is The Sum of The Parts

Interlake has followed a policy of diversification within two key business areas: metals and materials handling. The domestically-based metals business consists of Iron/Steel; Metal Powders; Investment/Die Castings; and Silicon Metal/Ferroalloys. The materials handling business functions worldwide through Material Handling/Storage Products and Packaging.

Each of these six business segments is distinct. Each has its own particular products, markets, and production processes. Furthermore, each faces demand level, pricing, and cost situations which can vary significantly.

The following review highlights the varying factors within each business segment in recent years so that the reader can gain a fuller appreciation of Interlake's overall operating results.

Investment/Die Castings Slip

Arwood was unable to match last year's record performances and suffered its first downturn since its acquisition in 1976.

SALES
(in millions)

$125

100

75

50

25

0

77 78 79 80 81

OPERATING INCOME
(in millions)

$25

20

15

10

5

0

77 78 79 80 81

This slippage was caused principally by slowdowns in the aerospace industry, which adversely affected investment castings, and by weakened overall economic conditions which acted as a damper to die castings' consumer-oriented products. Arwood's net sales fell by 5% from 1980, but were still 6% over 1979.

Slowdowns in both the commercial and military aviation sectors became pronounced in 1981 and had a severe effect on investment castings' volume. This was somewhat offset by the acquisition of ACC Castings Company in May and Duradyne Technologies in July. Still, investment castings' net sales declined 5% from 1980, although remaining 15% ahead of 1979.

The die castings business is oriented toward the consumer products markets which were recession hit in 1981 and 1980. As a result, die castings showed a second consecutive year of reduced sales as 1981 sales fell 6% behind 1980 and 10% behind 1979. Only the Garland, Texas plant ran counter to this trend by showing sales gains in 1980 and 1981.

Prior to 1981, steady sales growth and the efficiencies of higher volumes had boosted Arwood's operating income to a string of records. The process was thrown into reverse in 1981–with market resistance to higher selling prices and loss of volume efficiencies. The resulting squeeze on Arwood's earnings reduced operating income from 1979-1980 levels, but this business still posted its third best year.

Metal Powders More Evolution

Hoeganaes Corporation's metal powders business has grown on the strength of developing new applications for powder metallurgy. This has led to increasing use within the U.S. automotive industry–as measured by pounds per car manufactured–and a gradual spreading to other industries. In order to support this growth, a $31 million atomized steel powder plant was completed in 1979 at Gallatin, Tennessee and a $4 million expansion of Riverton, New Jersey research and development facilities was undertaken in 1981.

Metal powders enjoyed surging demand in 1978 and 1979. Shipments were far in excess of existing capacity–1978 volume being sustained by elimination of inventory reserves and 1979 supported by imports from Hoeganaes' original Swedish parent company.

The critical slump in the domestic automotive industry had an adverse impact on 1980 and a lingering effect throughout 1981.

The cumulative effect of higher selling prices allowed 1981 sales to surpass the previous record of 1979 by 5%–an improvement of 24% over 1980. Shipment volume, however, trailed 1979 and 1978 by 12%. Still, considering the state of the automotive industry, 1981's volume was very satisfying. It reflected further development of new applications and was sustained by significantly greater utilization of the Gallatin plant. Production levels in 1981 were nearly equivalent to the 1978-1979 period.

SALES
(in millions)

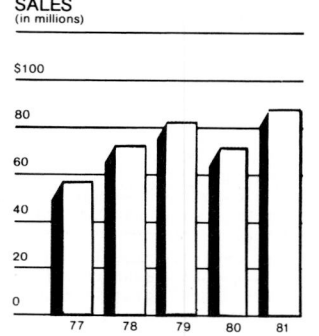

$100

80

60

40

20

0

77 78 79 80 81

OPERATING INCOME
(in millions)

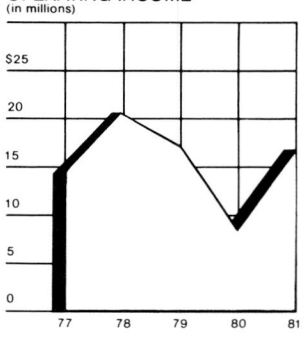

$25

20

15

10

5

0

77 78 79 80 81

Hoeganaes' operating income peaked in 1978. There was a 17% earnings drop in 1979 due to higher labor and materials costs, start-up expenses at Gallatin, and the unfavorable effect of importing powders to satisfy customer demands. This was followed by a 48% operating income decline in 1980 as shipping and production volumes fell sharply. The earnings recovery of 1981 came within 3% of the 1979 level with inferior market conditions and lower volumes. This was, in part, caused by the favorable effect of Gallatin operating efficiencies.

Review of Business Segments

Silicon Metal/Ferroalloys Hangs Tough

It's hard enough to put together a sales record, it's particularly tough in a poor economic environment, and almost impossible in a poor year that follows a poor year. Nevertheless, the silicon metal/ferroalloys business extended itself to a new sales high by gaining 13% over 1980 to top the old record of 1979 by 8%.

Silicon metal is sold primarily to the aluminum and chemical markets. The aluminum market continued to be hard hit by the depressed conditions in the automotive industry while the chemical market sustained favorable demand conditions. Competitive pressures intensified during the year, but shipping volume increased by 12%–almost reaching 1979 levels.

SALES
(in millions)

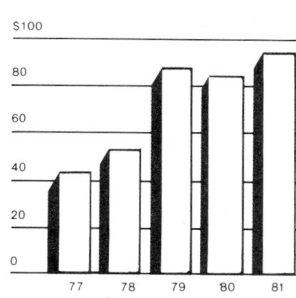

OPERATING INCOME
(in millions)

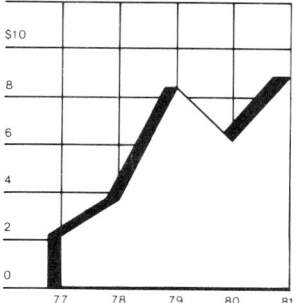

Ferroalloys consist mainly of ferrosilicon, magnesium ferrosilicon, and ferrochromes. All of these products are under some pressure from low-priced imports. This pressure has been most severe among ferrochromes and the number of domestic producers has been steadily shrinking. Low carbon ferrochrome shipments declined 29% in 1981 following a 21% decline in 1980. However, high carbon ferrochrome volume was up a marked 76% as some major users recognized the need to maintain domestic sources of supply.

Recent ferroalloys growth has come mainly from the 1977 introduction of magnesium ferrosilicon products and Globe's 1978 re-entry into the ferrosilicon market. Magnesium ferrosilicon sales volume increased by 44% in 1981, while ferrosilicon stayed within 1% of 1980 levels. Both products showed relatively stable volumes in 1980 versus 1979.

Operating income advanced to its highest level since the 1974 record year. To some extent the upward thrust came from higher sales volume, just as lower sales volume drove 1980 earnings downward. However, most of the year-to-year income gain came from efficiency and productivity improvement efforts.

Iron/Steel Rebounds

The iron and steel industry has faced turbulent conditions over the last several years and has been especially hard hit during the 1979-1981 period. Import pressures, deteriorating cost/price relationships, and massive capital investment requirements have raised questions as to the continuing survival of some companies.

Interlake's iron and steel business has also been severely tested during these years. In 1978, the Toledo, Ohio pig iron operation was closed as a result of declining sales due to a depressed market that was increasingly dominated by low-priced imported iron. In 1980, the Newport/Wilder steel plants were shut down. This followed a $16 million capital spending effort aimed at restoring profitability to these operations and was necessitated by the local union's rejection of a one year containment of labor costs. During the last five years, over $60 million has been invested at the Chicago plant to rehabilitate its facilities and restore a profitable operating base.

Iron and steel sales comparisons are muddied by the loss of volume from discontinued operations. On the surface sales fell by $97 million or 23% in 1980 and advanced a modest $19 million or 6% in 1981. However, sales of the continuing Chicago and Riverdale locations only declined by $36 million or 13% in 1980 and rebounded in 1981 with increases of $95 million or 38%.

Shipping volume from on-going locations fell by 15% in 1980, but picked up by 35% in 1981. The 1981 advance was especially pronounced at the Chicago iron plant where tonnage gains of 74% followed an 8% decline in 1980. A substantial portion of this gain resulted from spot sales to another steel company. This increase in plant volume had a significant favorable effect on unit production costs. The Riverdale steel operation recorded a 1981 tonnage increase of 13%, but remained 9% below 1979 shipping levels.

Iron and steel reported a profit for the first time since 1977 on the strength of improved operating levels at Chicago and Interlake's affiliated ore mining companies. This business segment's recent history has been burdened by pre-tax shutdown/disposal provisions of $37.0 million in 1980 and $15.7 million in 1978. Results in 1978 were depressed further by severe winter weather, an extended United Mine Workers' strike, and costs associated with major facility rehabilitation programs. The rehabilitation costs continued in 1979, but related benefits started to take hold that year and have grown in subsequent years. In 1980, productivity and efficiency gains were stressed and earnings were favorably influenced by the liquidation of LIFO inventories, but this progress was restricted by volume declines and inadequate selling price increases.

SALES
(in millions)

 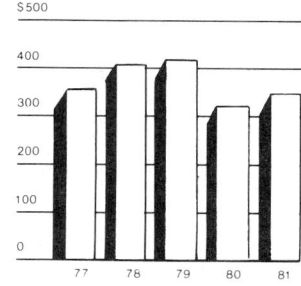

OPERATING INCOME
(in millions)

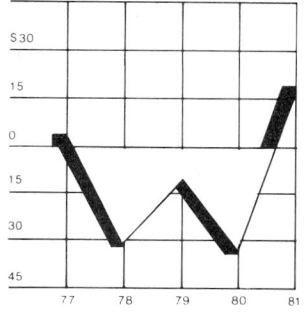

Material Handling/Storage Products Recession Plagued

The material handling/storage products business is highly dependent on our customers' capital expenditures for new facilities or upgrading old facilities. Unfortunately, the nearly worldwide recession in capital expenditure projects which began in 1980 lingered through 1981.

SALES
(in millions)

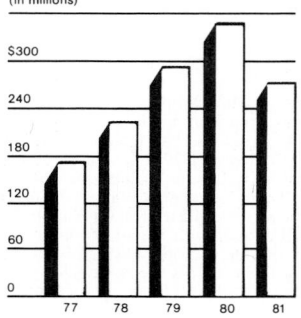

OPERATING INCOME
(in millions)

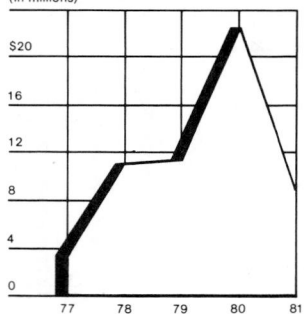

Truly international, the material handling/storage products business derived 72% of 1981 sales from outside the United States. The high value of the U.S. dollar had a significantly unfavorable impact on these sales. Over 80% of the decline in foreign operation sales was attributable to the strengthening of the U.S. dollar versus other currencies, especially the British pound. Ignoring currency swings, 1981 foreign sales trailed 1980 by 4% but were 9% ahead of 1979.

The European recession has been widespread and unremitting and while aggressive marketing was able to gain some headway in 1980, it could not stem the downward pressures of 1981. The only exception to this was France where a 6% French franc sales gain was achieved.

Australian and Canadian operations were able to continue their forward thrusts and each achieved a new sales record in 1981. Australian sales improved 29% from 1980 and were roughly 56% over 1979. Canadian sales beat 1980 by 5% and were 32% ahead of 1979.

Domestic sales suffered from recession induced reductions in capital spending in this country. Sales were off by 29% from 1980 and trailed 1979 by 16%. U.S. sales were boosted in 1980 by work on a major warehouse distribution center. This one million square foot center is the largest single systems order ever received by Interlake, but the major portion of this job was completed before 1981 and no similar projects were booked in 1981. The swing on this job alone accounted for 83% of the domestic sales decline from 1980.

The various declining economic climates pressed on sales volumes and selling prices and these factors, along with the rising value of the dollar, had a predictable influence on operating income. Material handling/storage products' earnings fell by 57% from 1980's peak and reached their lowest level since 1977. The only bright spots were Australia and England. Australia achieved record earnings, even in U.S. dollars, and England struggled for a gain in pound sterling income, but this was washed away by the declining value of the pound.

Packaging Earnings Record

Packaging sales resumed their upward path with a 7% gain from 1980 and operating income exceeded its 1978 peak by 19%.

Packaging products are used in nearly all industrial areas and sales are particularly sensitive to levels of economic activity. During 1981, sales were 7% over 1980 and came within 1.5% of 1979's record. The year-to-year sales gain was hampered by declining British pound exchange rates which left English sales with a 10% drop in dollars although they were up by 3% in pounds sterling. Canadian sales were up by 4% in U.S. dollars and 6% in Canadian dollars. Domestic sales were up 10%.

Metallic steel strapping is the major packaging product and has been hit hard by worldwide recessionary influences in the last two years. Overall metallic shipments were only 2% ahead of 1980 with domestic volume gaining 5% while Canada slipped 6% and England remained steady. This follows across-the-board volume declines in 1980 of 16% domestically, 2% in Canada, and 18% in England. Non-metallic strapping shipments have remained stable for the last two troubled years after gains of 13% in 1979 and 30% in 1978.

Operating income reversed its two-year slide as the relocated tool and machine plant in Sumter, South Carolina came on stream and operating costs at other facilities were reduced. Canadian operations continued their string of income records which began in 1978 and domestic operations bested their previous 1978 high.

SALES
(in millions)

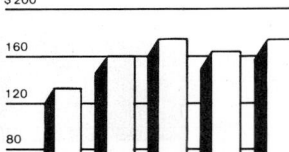

OPERATING INCOME
(in millions)

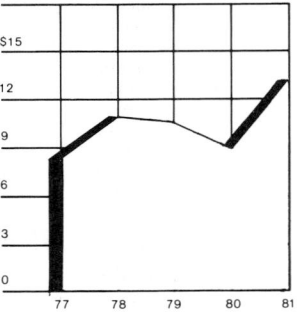

Financial Statements

What to look for when reading the Income Statement

The statement of income is often referred to as the statement of profit and loss. It is a summary of revenues and related costs and expenses which indicates the profitability of the Company.

MR. POLANEK

The statement focuses on the income producing activities of the Company and, therefore, reflects the results of operations for the fiscal year and provides the reader with a basis for assessing the Company's performance.

Revenue growth is usually one of the things the reader looks for. Interlake's revenues come mainly from the net sales of its various businesses and, while sales have been over the billion dollar level for the last three years, there has been slippage in the last two. As indicated in the financial comments and notes, this slippage is the result of discontinuing certain operations in 1980 and of recent turbulent economic conditions.

Other revenues include royalties, interest income and gains on sales of property and equipment. The big jump in 1981 was due to substantially higher interest income and gains on asset sales.

Operating profitability is the reader's primary concern and attention is usually concentrated in this area. On a pre-tax basis, earnings from on-going operations were $79,119,000 in 1981, $57,553,000 in 1980 and $45,177,000 in 1979. Although 1980 included benefits of $15,400,000 from liquidation of LIFO inventories, earnings from on-going operations reflect a strong pattern in light of the recent economic climate.

There are three key statistics which analysts frequently use to measure earnings performance.

INTERLAKE, INC.
Statement of Consolidated Income and Retained Earnings

For the Years Ended December 27, 1981, December 28, 1980 and December 30, 1979

	1981	1980	1979
	(In thousands except per share statistics)		
Sales and Revenues:			
Net sales	$1,016,605	$1,055,883	$1,104,588
Other revenues	16,706	7,880	7,847
	1,033,311	1,063,763	1,112,435
Costs and Expenses:			
Cost of products sold (excluding depreciation and taxes) (Note 1)	772,692	815,586	888,773
Depreciation, depletion and amortization	25,976	26,869	25,015
Selling and administrative expenses	111,442	116,523	106,871
Taxes other than income taxes	30,675	31,485	31,645
Interest expense (Note 1)	13,407	15,747	14,954
	954,192	1,006,210	1,067,258
Income Before Nonrecurring Item, Taxes on Income and Minority Interest	79,119	57,553	45,177
Shutdown/Disposal Provision (Note 6)	–	37,000	–
Income Before Taxes on Income and Minority Interest	79,119	20,553	45,177
Provision for Income Taxes (Notes 1 and 8)	30,953	5,998	3,129
	48,166	14,555	42,048
Minority Interest in Net Income of Subsidiary	1,589	737	2,313
Net Income for the Year	$ 46,577	$ 13,818	$ 39,735
Net Income Per Share of Common Stock (based on average shares of 6,134,310 in 1981, 6,038,764 in 1980, and 5,967,415 in 1979)	$7.59	$2.29	$6.66
Retained Earnings at Beginning of Year	$ 239,606	$ 239,075	$ 212,467
Net Income for the Year	46,577	13,818	39,735
	286,183	252,893	252,202
Deduct – Cash Dividends Declared or Paid ($2.40 per share in 1981 and $2.20 per share in 1980 and 1979)	(14,735)	(13,287)	(13,127)
Retained Earnings at End of Year	$ 271,448	$ 239,606	$ 239,075

(See notes to consolidated financial statements)

These are:
- Return on Sales – net income divided by net sales.
- Return on Investment – net income before interest and minority interest, divided by average investment less interest bearing items.
- Return on Equity – net income divided by average shareholders' equity.

These statistics confirm the strength of 1981's results.

	1981	1980	1979
Return on Sales	4.6%	1.3%	3.6%
Return on Investment	10.3%	4.1%	9.8%
Return on Equity	13.5%	4.2%	12.7%

Richard I. Polanek
Controller

INTERLAKE, INC.
Consolidated Balance Sheet

December 27, 1981 and December 28, 1980

Assets	1981	1980
	(In thousands)	
Current Assets:		
Cash	$ 5,599	$ 5,470
Certificates of deposit	29,367	15,282
Receivables, less allowances of $2,811,000 in 1981 and $3,677,000 in 1980	146,244	169,162
Inventories (Note 1)	171,445	163,706
Other current assets	19,559	15,912
Total current assets	372,214	369,532
Investments and Other Assets:		
Investments in and advances to associated companies (Notes 1, 9 and 11)	43,960	43,793
Other assets (Note 1)	30,747	35,438
	74,707	79,231
Property, Plant and Equipment, at cost (Notes 1 and 9):		
Land and mineral properties, less depletion	10,146	11,593
Buildings	103,474	97,363
Equipment	446,158	423,592
Construction in progress	17,679	16,790
	577,457	549,338
Depreciation and amortization	(314,161)	(294,483)
	263,296	254,855
Total Assets	$710,217	$703,618

Liabilities and Shareholders' Equity

	1981	1980
Current Liabilities:		
Accounts payable (Note 1)	$ 76,840	$ 59,269
Accrued liabilities	34,392	56,706
Accrued employment costs	26,036	27,838
Income taxes payable (Note 8)	14,946	15,874
Taxes other than income taxes	8,908	9,277
Debt due within one year (Note 2)	11,289	19,423
Total current liabilities	172,411	188,387
Long-Term Debt (Note 2)	126,618	133,020
Other Long-Term Liabilities:		
Noncurrent shutdown costs	10,022	12,145
Other	14,538	13,078
	24,560	25,223
Future Income Taxes (Note 1)	20,738	13,331
Minority Interest in Subsidiary	7,142	6,950
Commitments and Contingencies (Note 9)	–	–
Shareholders' Equity (Note 3):		
Common stock, par value $1 a share, authorized 20,000,000 shares, issued 6,997,642 shares in 1981 and 6,932,643 shares in 1980	115,412	112,860
Cost of common stock held in treasury (818,776 shares in 1981 and 843,493 shares in 1980) (Note 4)	(15,120)	(15,759)
Retained earnings (Note 5)	271,448	239,606
Accumulated foreign currency translation adjustments (Note 1)	(12,992)	–
	358,748	336,707
Total Liabilities and Shareholders' Equity	$710,217	$703,618

(See notes to consolidated financial statements)

Understanding the Balance Sheet—A Real Asset.

The purpose of a balance sheet is to summarize the financial position of a business on a specific date. It is a "snapshot" of how the Company stands on the last day of its fiscal year.

The asset section of the balance sheet shows the Company's assets—everything that the Company owns. This consists of property rights, physical goods, uncollected claims, and prepayments. Those items that can be converted into cash or will be consumed within a year are called current assets. The remaining assets are referred to as long-term or fixed assets, because they generally are investments intended to produce revenues and earnings and are not intended to be sold in the ordinary course of business.

The other section of the balance sheet lists the Company's liabilities and the equity investment of the shareholders—everything that the Company owes. Liabilities which will fall due within a year are called current liabilities.

MR. ANDERSON

The reader can gain insight into the financial vigor of an enterprise from its balance sheet. The primary considerations usually center around the firm's ability to pay its debts as they fall due (liquidity) and to take advantage of new opportunities (flexibility).

There are three key statistics which analysts frequently use to measure financial strength:
- Current Ratio—current assets divided by current liabilities.
- Quick Ratio—cash, cash equivalents and receivables divided by current liabilities.
- Debt to Equity Ratio—the proportion of total debt, including short-term borrowings, to shareholders' equity.

A review of these statistics demonstrates Interlake's solid financial strength:

	1981	1980	1979
Current Ratio	2.2/1	2.0/1	1.7/1
Quick Ratio	1.1/1	1.0/1	.9/1
Debt/Equity	28/72	31/69	35/65

Raymond T. Anderson, Treasurer

Financial Statements

Making Sense of Cash Flows

The statement of changes in financial position summarizes where the Company acquired its financial resources during the fiscal year and where it applied or used these resources. It is intended to give the reader a better understanding of the financing and investing activities of the Company.

The statement is designed to emphasize changes in working capital from the viewpoint of cash entering and leaving the Company on a permanent or long-term basis. The circulation of cash through the working capital components is treated separately because current asset and current liability balances are variable and will roll over in fairly brief time periods.

The Company's primary source of funds over the last three years has been cash generated by operations. This is different from net income, because some of the income and expense items do not involve cash movements during the current year. When net income is adjusted for non-cash items, it indicates working capital provided from operations or cash income.

Financial resources can also be acquired by selling properties which are no longer needed in the business, borrowing, or raising equity capital. The disposal of discontinued operations generated substantial funds in 1981, no major borrowings have occurred since 1978, and the dividend reinvestment program has been an increasing source of capital.

The focus of generating cash inflows is to maintain and expand the Company's productive base, repay creditors, and reward investors. Interlake's capital expenditures and investment activities have been significant, and fully funded by current operations. Debt is being retired at a rate that exceeds minimum requirements and dividend payments have been increased.

Interlake has substantial capital resources to meet future financial requirements. In addition to the Company's basic earning power and long-term debt borrowing strength, Interlake's liquidity is enhanced by bank credit lines totaling $136,000,000 and only $10,179,000 was borrowed against these lines at year end 1981. This includes a domestic credit agreement for $75 million. Interlake can borrow up to the full amount during the period ending July 1, 1984 and, at its option, may convert any balance to a five-year term loan.

INTERLAKE, INC.
Statement of Changes in Consolidated Financial Position

For the Years Ended December 27, 1981, December 28, 1980 and December 30, 1979

	1981	1980*	1979*
		(In thousands)	
Financial Resources Were Provided By:			
Net income	$ 46,577	$ 13,818	$ 39,735
Depreciation, depletion and amortization	25,976	26,869	25,015
Equity in earnings of affiliates and joint ventures, less dividends received	(1,828)	1,248	(923)
Shutdown/disposal provision— non-current portion	—	25,584	—
Future income taxes	7,407	(7,509)	3,941
Other long-term liabilities	(847)	1,934	1,680
Minority interest in net income of subsidiary, less dividend paid	192	(258)	715
Working capital provided from operations	77,477	61,686	70,163
Long-term borrowings	—	1,233	2,864
Disposals of property, plant and equipment	3,568	1,341	2,133
Disposal of shutdown facilities	13,860	—	—
Decrease in construction funds held by trustees	1,237	1,305	8,016
Dividend reinvestment plan	2,173	1,896	903
Other	3,197	(307)	1,166
	101,512	67,154	85,245
Financial Resources Were Used For:			
Capital expenditures	37,393	31,276	69,556
Reduction of long-term debt	6,402	3,716	3,640
Cash dividends declared	14,735	13,287	13,127
Acquisition of businesses, net of working capital acquired	9,896	—	—
Investment in tax leases, net of amortization	4,967	—	—
Change in exchange rates	9,461	—	—
	82,854	48,279	86,323
Increase (decrease) in working capital	$ 18,658	$ 18,875	$ (1,078)
Increase (Decrease) in Working Capital Comprises:			
Cash and short-term investments ...	$ 14,214	$ 9,944	$ (9,897)
Receivables	(22,918)	(11,528)	33,587
Inventories	7,739	(17,659)	21,694
Other current assets	3,647	5,298	(2,689)
Accounts payable and other accrued liabilities	6,914	19,469	(27,325)
Income taxes payable	928	(8,444)	8,421
Debt due within one year	8,134	21,795	(24,869)
	18,658	18,875	(1,078)
Working capital at beginning of year	181,145	162,270	163,348
Working capital at end of year	$199,803	$181,145	$162,270

* Certain amounts have been reclassified to conform to the presentation in 1981.

(See notes to consolidated financial statements)

Notes to Consolidated Financial Statements

THE NOTES COMPLETE THE PICTURE

The financial statements present summarized and condensed information. This provides the reader with a convenient overview of recent developments and that is frequently all that the reader desires. However, the statements do not present information in depth.

The notes are used to detail information that cannot reasonably be accommodated in the body of the financial statements. They amplify and explain the material that appears in the financial statements by clarifying content, furnishing details, and providing additional information.

For example, Note 1 explains the significant accounting policies which Interlake uses to prepare its financial information. In many areas, a company must choose between alternative accounting treatments and the statement information becomes clearer when the reader knows the choices that have been made.

Another illustration appears in Note 2. This note details the long-term debt information summarized in the balance sheet and elaborates on the nature of the debt and its repayment requirements through 1986. The note also provides extra information by describing credit arrangements which make additional resources available to the Company for future use.

As you can see, the financial statements furnish the central foreground to the Company's financial picture and the notes provide the background that completes the picture.

INTERLAKE, INC.—NOTES TO CONSOLIDATED FINANCIAL STATEMENTS

For the Years Ended December 27, 1981, December 28, 1980 and December 30, 1979.

NOTE 1—SUMMARY OF SIGNIFICANT ACCOUNTING POLICIES

Principles of Consolidation • The consolidated financial statements include the accounts of all majority-owned domestic and foreign subsidiaries. Investments in corporate joint ventures and companies owned 20% to 50% are accounted for by the equity method. Such investments are carried at cost plus equity in undistributed earnings.

Inventories • Inventories are stated at the lower of cost or market value. Cost is determined principally by the last-in, first-out (LIFO) method, which is less than current costs by $124,800,000 and $111,028,000, at December 27, 1981 and December 28, 1980, respectively.

Effective with the beginning of fiscal 1981, the Company extended the use of the LIFO method of accounting for the principal inventories of its foreign subsidiaries which previously used the FIFO (first-in, first-out) method. Management believes that the LIFO method provides a better matching of current costs with current revenues. The effect of the extension of LIFO for foreign inventories was to reduce net income $1.0 million or $.16 per share. There was no cumulative effect of this change on prior years' reported earnings.

During 1980, inventory quantities were reduced, resulting in a liquidation of LIFO inventory quantities carried at lower costs prevailing in prior years as compared with the cost of 1980 production. As a result, income before taxes was increased by $23,200,000, equivalent to $2.08 per share after applicable income taxes, of which $15,400,000, equivalent to $1.38 per share after applicable income taxes, was reflected in cost of products sold and the balance was included as a reduction of the 1980 shutdown/disposal provision (see Note 6).

December 27, 1981 and December 28, 1980 inventory amounts by category were:	December 27, 1981	December 28, 1980
Raw materials	$ 58,976,000	$ 56,644,000
Semi-finished and finished products	88,502,000	82,478,000
Supplies	23,967,000	24,584,000
	$171,445,000	$163,706,000

In 1981, 1980 and 1979 the Company made raw material purchases of $76,106,000, $57,631,000 and $51,025,000, respectively, from affiliated iron ore and coal mining interests. Included in accounts payable are amounts due affiliated companies for raw material purchases of $20,005,000, $10,755,000 and $13,169,000 at December 27, 1981, December 28, 1980 and December 30, 1979, respectively.

Property, Plant and Equipment and Depreciation • For financial reporting purposes, plant and equipment are depreciated principally on a straight-line method over the estimated useful lives of the assets. Depreciation claimed for income tax purposes is computed by use of accelerated methods. Income taxes applicable to differences between depreciation claimed for tax purposes and that reported in the financial statements are charged or credited to future income taxes, as appropriate. Provisions for depletion of mineral properties are based on tonnage rates which are expected to amortize the cost of such properties over the estimated amount of mineral deposits to be removed.

Upon sale or disposal of property, plant and equipment, it is the Company's policy to relieve the respective asset accounts of cost and, in the case of normal sales or disposals, to charge such original cost to accumulated depreciation and amortization, thereby not recognizing any gain or loss. Any proceeds from these sales or disposals are credited to accumulated depreciation and amortization. On an abnormal sale or disposal of property, plant and equipment, the original cost and the amount of depreciation actually credited to accumulated depreciation and amortization are removed from the accounts and any gain or loss on the disposal is credited or charged to income.

Notes to Consolidated Financial Statements

Expenditures for maintenance and repairs and minor renewals and betterments are charged to expense as incurred. Furnace relines and expenditures for renewals and betterments of a character calculated to extend the originally estimated useful life of any asset or materially increase its productivity are capitalized.

Goodwill • Other assets includes goodwill of $13,947,000 and $8,095,000 at December 27, 1981 and December 28, 1980, respectively Goodwill represents the excess of the purchase price over the fair value of the net assets of acquired companies and is being amortized on a straight-line method over a period of approximately thirty years.

Foreign Currency Translation • In the fourth quarter of 1981 the Company adopted, retroactive to the beginning of the year, Statement of Financial Accounting Standards No. 52, "Foreign Currency Translation." This Statement provides that adjustments for currency exchange rate changes are included in net income for those fluctuations that impact cash flows and are excluded for those that do not. Translation gains and losses are deferred in a separate component of shareholders' equity entitled "Accumulated foreign currency translation adjustments." Activity in this account during 1981 was as follows:

Opening balance	$ 2,583,000
Adjustments from translating foreign currency financial statements at current rates	(15,575,000)
Balance at December 27, 1981	$(12,992,000)

The opening balance represents the effect of translating certain assets and liabilities at December 28, 1980 (previously translated at historical exchange rates) at the exchange rates in effect at that date.

Adoption of this Statement had a minimal effect on 1981 net income. 1980 and 1979 net income included a net gain of $1.4 million or $.24 per share, and a net loss of $.7 million or $.12 per share, respectively, for foreign currency translation and hedging costs.

Investment Tax Credits • The full amount of investment tax credits claimed for tax purposes is reflected in income in the year in which the credits first become available.

Purchased Tax Benefits • In the fourth quarter of 1981, the Company entered into several agreements to purchase tax benefits through tax leases. The purchase price, which has been included in "other assets," is being amortized to income at a constant rate of return over the period benefited and resulted in a gain of $679,000 included in 1981 net income. The current liability for income taxes payable at December 27, 1981 has been reduced by $7,358,000 for such tax benefits to be reflected in the Company's 1981 U.S. Federal income tax return.

Pension Plans • The Company has various pension plans which cover substantially all employees. The provision for pension costs includes current costs plus interest on and amortization of unfunded prior service costs over periods not exceeding twenty-five years. The Company's policy is to fund pension costs accrued.

Interest Costs • In 1980, the Company adopted Statement of Financial Accounting Standards No. 34, "Capitalization of Interest Costs," which requires capitalization of interest costs as part of the historical cost of acquiring certain assets. Interest costs capitalized in 1981 and 1980 were immaterial.

NOTE 2—LONG-TERM DEBT AND CREDIT ARRANGEMENTS

Long-term debt of the Company consists of the following:

	December 27, 1981	December 28, 1980
	(In thousands)	
8.8% Debentures, due annually $2,500,000 1982 to 1995, and $5,000,000 in 1996	$ 34,997	$ 39,928
8-1/2% Senior Notes, due annually $3,000,000 1984 through 1998	45,000	45,000
Obligations under long-term lease agreements	16,150	16,650
11-1/4% Notes payable, due annually in varying installments from 1982 to 1998	9,711	9,909
Pollution control and industrial development loan agreements	18,350	18,350
Other	3,520	4,275
	127,728	134,112
Less– current maturities	1,110	1,092
	$126,618	$133,020

At December 27, 1981, 8.8% debentures with a face value of $5,003,000 were held in the treasury by the Company. $2,500,000 of these may be used in meeting the 1982 sinking fund requirement and have been applied as a reduction of debt due within one year.

The long-term lease obligations relate principally to capitalized pollution control facilities. The interest rates on these obligations vary from 6.00% to 7.88%. Principal payments began in 1981 and continue in varying annual amounts through 2002.

The Company borrowed funds under several loan agreements with state and county pollution control and industrial development authorities to finance certain environmental control and facility expansion and improvement projects. Interest rates on these obligations vary from 6% to 7-1/8% with the exception of a $1,000,000 loan at 65% of the prime rate. Principal payments of

$1,000,000, $1,700,000 and $3,500,000 are to be made in 1983, 1988 and 1993, respectively, then continue in varying amounts from 1998 to 2009.

The combined aggregate maturities and sinking fund requirements for long-term debt for the five years following 1981, after giving effect to debentures held by the Company and available for sinking fund requirements, are as follows:

1982	$1,110,000
1983	2,135,000
1984	6,499,000
1985	6,577,000
1986	6,815,000

The Company maintains formal and informal domestic and foreign short-term bank credit lines of $136,000,000 against which $10,179,000 was borrowed at December 27, 1981. Domestic borrowings bear interest at the prime rate. Foreign borrowings bear interest at varying rates which are generally the overseas equivalent of the prime rate. In connection with the domestic lines of credit, the Company has entered into informal arrangements to maintain average compensating balances of 5% for the unused portion of the informal lines and 5% for any borrowings under the formal lines.

NOTE 3—CAPITAL STOCK

The Company's authorized capital stock includes 2,000,000 shares of serial preferred stock at $1 par value per share, none of which has been issued.

The Company's 1979 Dividend Reinvestment and Voluntary Stock Purchase Plan allows shareholders to purchase shares of the Company's common stock at 95% of market for dividend reinvestments and at market for voluntary cash payments, subject to certain limitations. Shares issued in connection with the Plan totaled 64,999 shares or $2,173,000 in 1981, 76,590 shares or $1,896,000 in 1980 and 36,543 shares or $903,000 in 1979.

NOTE 4—STOCK INCENTIVE PLANS

The Company's 1975 stock option plan (as amended and restated in 1981) provides for the granting of options for the purchase of common stock to officers and other key employees at prices equal to the fair market value at the dates of grant. A maximum of 650,000 shares may be granted under the Plan until December 31, 1984. Options become exercisable one third annually, on a cumulative basis, starting one year from the date of grant and may be exercised until ten years have elapsed from the date of grant. The 1981 amendment and restatement of the plan, besides permitting the granting of options to purchase 275,000 additional shares, included in the above maximum, also provided that options may be exercised by the transfer to the Company of shares of Company common stock having a value equal to the total option price.

The Company's 1977 Stock Incentive Program consists of a Stock Appreciation Rights Plan under which a maximum of 300,000 shares of common stock may be issued, a Stock Awards Plan and a Restricted Stock Purchase Plan. Total shares issued for the latter two plans may not exceed 100,000. Stock Appreciation Rights (S.A.R.s) are issued concurrently with specific stock option grants and entitle the holders to receive the difference between option price and market price at the time of exercise of the S.A.R.s in cash, shares of common stock, or a combination of the two at the Company's discretion. An equivalent number of shares under option are surrendered upon exercise of S.A.R.s. Under the Stock Awards Plan, shares of common stock are issued at the date of the award and delivered to recipients 20% immediately and 20% on each of the four succeeding anniversary dates, subject to certain restrictions. The Board of Directors has not adopted a Restricted Stock Purchase Plan.

Notes to Consolidated Financial Statements

Changes in common shares under option and related S.A.R.s for the three years are summarized as follows:

	1981 Option Shares	1981 Average Option Price	1980 Option Shares	1980 Average Option Price	1979 Option Shares	1979 Average Option Price
Stock Options:						
Outstanding–beginning of year	263,814	$28.93	247,198	$29.99	200,249	$30.77
Granted	47,650	40.25	78,500	25.94	70,000	26.29
Exercised	(5,062)	25.09	(4,723)	23.75	(5,400)	18.43
Surrendered for exercised S.A.R.s	(8,214)	26.89	(9,874)	24.19	(5,150)	22.35
Canceled or expired	(14,851)	29.39	(47,287)	31.03	(12,501)	29.86
Outstanding–end of year	283,337	30.94	263,814	28.93	247,198	29.99
Exercisable–end of year	173,689	30.17	140,093	31.51	128,730	33.03
Available for grant	313,540		71,339		102,552	
Stock Appreciation Rights:						
Outstanding–beginning of year	139,941		136,932		109,250	
Granted	28,650	40.25	38,250	25.94	35,650	26.21
Exercised	(8,214)		(9,874)		(5,150)	
Canceled or expired	(1,100)		(25,367)		(2,818)	
Outstanding–end of year	159,277		139,941		136,932	

Treasury shares issued for exercised stock appreciation rights totaled 1,055 in 1981, 794 in 1980 and 405 in 1979. The Stock Awards Plan, activated in 1978, resulted in the awarding of 18,600 shares in 1981, 4,350 shares in 1980 and 1,650 shares in 1979 with total market value at dates awarded of $571,000, $113,000 and $44,000, respectively.

NOTE 5–RETAINED EARNINGS

Under the most restrictive terms of the Company's various loan agreements, the Company could not as of December 27, 1981 pay cash dividends or repurchase the Company's capital stock in amounts aggregating more than $94,600,000.

NOTE 6–SHUTDOWN/DISPOSAL PROVISION

In the third quarter of 1980, a provision was recorded for the closing of the Newport and Wilder, Kentucky steel making and related facilities. The provision of $37,000,000 was equivalent to $4.10 per share after applicable income taxes and covered estimated losses on the disposition of property, plant and equipment and inventories, and employee severance and other costs. Net sales of products from these facilities included in consolidated sales totaled $69,497,000 in 1980 and $102,564,000 in 1979. These facilities were sold in the second quarter of 1981 with no adjustment to the 1980 provision required.

NOTE 7–RETIREMENT BENEFITS

Pension costs totaled $17,024,000, $24,582,000 and $25,396,000 in 1981, 1980 and 1979, respectively. The decrease in 1981 was primarily attributable to an increase in the assumed rate of return on investments from 6% to 7% and to the exclusion of Newport and Wilder plant employees.

In addition to the above 1980 pension costs, the 1980 provision for the shutdown of the Newport and Wilder plants (see Note 6) included pension costs related to terminated employees.

A comparison of accumulated plan benefits and plan net assets for the Company's domestic defined benefit plans follows:

	December 27, 1981	December 28, 1980
	(In thousands)	
Actuarial present value of accumulated plan benefits:		
Vested	$ 80,500	$ 95,300
Non-vested	1,600	2,400
	$ 82,100	$ 97,700
Net assets available for plan benefits	$219,700	$219,400

The assumed rates of return used in determining the actuarial present value of accumulated plan benefits were 14.5% at December 27, 1981 and 12.4% at December 28, 1980 which were the Standard and Poor's average of AAA industrial and utility bond rates.

NOTE 8–INCOME TAXES

The provisions for taxes on income consist of:

	Currently Payable	Deferred	Total
		(In thousands)	
1981			
U.S. Federal	$ 13,863	$ 5,312	$ 19,175
Foreign	9,622	(947)	8,675
State and other	3,103	–	3,103
	$ 26,588	$ 4,365	$ 30,953
1980			
U.S. Federal	$ 7,521	$(13,019)	$ (5,498)
Foreign	8,153	714	8,867
State and other	2,629	–	2,629
	$ 18,303	$(12,305)	$ 5,998
1979			
U.S. Federal	$ (5,969)	$ 7,094	$ 1,125
Foreign	(1,199)	570	(629)
State and other	2,633	–	2,633
	$ (4,535)	$ 7,664	$ 3,129

The U.S. Federal income tax provisions were reduced by investment tax credits, net of recapture, of $2,409,000 in 1981, $1,142,000 in 1980 and $6,383,000 in 1979.

The deferred tax provisions result from timing differences in the recognition of income and expenses for tax and financial reporting purposes. Significant items and the tax effects thereof are as follows:

	1981	1980	1979
		(In thousands)	
Benefit on plant closing	$ (1,529)	$ (7,560)	$ 3,960
Retirement benefit costs	2,047	(1,915)	2,467
Equity in earnings of affiliated companies	(109)	(952)	144
Foreign translation and hedge contracts	(1,959)	(874)	93
Excess of tax over book depreciation	6,888	(68)	2,581
DISC operations	(430)	(30)	(414)
All other net	(543)	(906)	(1,167)
	$ 4,365	$(12,305)	$ 7,664

The effective income tax rates in 1981, 1980 and 1979 are reconciled to the federal statutory tax rates in the following table:

	1981	1980	1979
Statutory federal income tax rate	46.0%	46.0%	46.0%
Increase (reduction) in taxes resulting from:			
Tax effect of U.K. stock relief	(2.4)	(17.9)	(22.3)
Investment tax credit	(3.0)	(5.5)	(14.1)
Excess percentage over cost depletion	(2.2)	(4.4)	(3.9)
Earnings attributable to affiliated companies	(1.6)	(3.6)	(3.5)
State income taxes	2.1	6.9	3.1
Taxes on foreign income before stock relief	1.1	4.8	2.8
Non-deductible acquisition costs	.1	1.8	.7
All other net	(1.0)	1.1	(1.9)
	39.1%	29.2%	6.9%

The amounts included in consolidated income before taxes on income which represent income of foreign operations were $20,536,000, $27,764,000 and $17,458,000 for 1981, 1980 and 1979, respectively.

As of December 27, 1981, U.S. Federal income tax returns for the years 1976 through 1978 were in process of examination. All prior years have been examined and settled. All assessments have been paid including any applicable interest. The Company believes that adequate provision has been made for possible assessments of additional taxes.

Provision for U.S. taxes has not been made on approximately $71,000,000 of unremitted earnings of foreign subsidiaries, considered to be permanently reinvested at December 27, 1981.

Notes to Consolidated Financial Statements

NOTE 9–COMMITMENTS AND CONTINGENCIES

With respect to the Company's interest in two mining joint ventures, the Company is required to take its ownership proportion of production for which it is committed to pay its proportionate share of the operating costs of these projects, either directly or as a part of the product price. Such costs include, as a minimum and regardless of the quantity of ore received, annual interest and principal payments on the debt of these projects of approximately $4,000,000 through 1983, and lesser amounts thereafter.

The Company is involved, on a continuing basis, as a party to enforcement and other proceedings with governmental agencies relating to the application of environmental laws and regulations to certain of the Company's plants. In some of such proceedings, and in other ways pursuant to laws and regulations, government agencies have threatened or indicated imposition of penalties which, if such agencies prevailed, could involve sums material to the Company; these matters are routinely negotiated and, in the opinion of the Company, are not likely to result in the assessment of penalties material in amount. Several of such proceedings have been settled on the basis of Company commitments to meet certain emission standards and to install control facilities at substantial cost. The Company anticipates that capital expenditures for installation of environmentally-related facilities (including those agreed to in settlement of proceedings) will aggregate approximately $5,000,000 over the next three years.

NOTE 10–BUSINESS SEGMENT INFORMATION

The Company operates in six lines of business; four in metals and two in material handling products. Metals includes iron and steel, metal powders, investment castings and die castings, and silicon metal and ferroalloys. Materials handling consists of material handling and storage products and packaging. The accompanying tables present financial information by line of business for the years 1981, 1980 and 1979.

Sales between lines of business are primarily priced at market value for metal products and at distributor prices for material handling products. Operating profit consists of total sales and other revenues of a product line less all related operating expenses. Income and expenses which are not related to nor appropriately allocable to lines of business, primarily interest expense, are included in general corporate expense.

The liquidation of LIFO inventory quantities in 1980 increased income before taxes for iron and steel by $16.3 million (of which $7.8 million was included in the shutdown/disposal provision), for material handling and storage products $4.0 million, for packaging products $2.0 million, and for all other segments combined $.9 million.

The operating results of the iron and steel segment were impacted by the Newport and Wilder, Kentucky plant shutdowns in 1980 ($37.0 million); (see Note 6). Also, the packaging segment was adversely affected in 1980 by a $2.5 million provision for a plant relocation.

Total assets by line of business consist of those assets used directly in the operations of the product line. Corporate assets consist principally of cash, securities and investments in real property.

INFORMATION ABOUT THE COMPANY'S LINES OF BUSINESS

	Net Sales		Operating Profit (Loss)	Assets At Year-End (b)	Depreciation Depletion & Amortization	Capital Expenditures
	Customers (a)	Affiliates				
1981			(In millions)			
Iron/Steel						
Operations	$ 274.3	$ 69.9	$ 6.1	$ 166.3	$ 11.5	$ 6.7
Equity in uncon- solidated affiliates ..	–	–	13.2	43.7	–	–
	274.3	69.9	19.3	210.0	11.5	6.7
Metal Powders	87.7	–	16.9	83.0	3.0	4.2
Investment/Die Castings	108.5	–	14.1	66.3	1.9	8.9
Silicon Metal/ Ferroalloys	95.4	.3	8.9	54.3	2.2	3.4
Material Handling/ Storage Products	277.4	–	9.7	164.1	5.8	7.4
Packaging	173.3	1.7	13.2	78.8	1.4	6.8
Corporate Items/ Eliminations	–	(71.9)	(3.0)	53.7	.2	–
Consolidated	$1,016.6	$ –	$ 79.1	$ 710.2	$ 26.0	$ 37.4
1980						
Iron/Steel						
Operations	$ 274.4	$ 50.8	$ (41.8)	$ 198.4	$ 12.2	$ 7.6
Equity in uncon- solidated affiliates .	–	–	7.3	43.1	–	–
	274.4	50.8	(34.5)	241.5	12.2	7.6
Metal Powders	70.9	–	8.9	77.5	2.9	3.5
Investment/Die Castings	114.3	–	22.0	50.0	1.3	5.3
Silicon Metal/ Ferroalloys	83.4	1.1	6.2	45.0	2.1	1.1
Material Handling/ Storage Products	350.5	–	22.6	181.7	5.6	7.3
Packaging	162.4	1.7	8.9	71.8	2.4	6.5
Corporate Items/ Eliminations	–	(53.6)	(13.5)	36.1	.4	–
Consolidated	$1,055.9	$ –	$ 20.6	$ 703.6	$ 26.9	$ 31.3
1979						
Iron/Steel						
Operations	$ 362.2	$ 60.0	$ (16.6)	$ 229.1	$ 12.2	$ 32.9
Equity in uncon- solidated affiliates .	–	–	6.0	44.4	–	–
	362.2	60.0	(10.6)	273.5	12.2	32.9
Metal Powders	83.5	–	17.3	79.6	2.1	20.4
Investment/Die Castings	102.4	–	20.5	43.7	1.0	3.6
Silicon Metal/ Ferroalloys	87.5	1.2	8.5	48.6	2.1	.9
Material Handling/ Storage Products	294.3	.3	11.3	191.8	4.4	9.4
Packaging	174.7	2.5	10.5	74.4	2.8	2.4
Corporate Items/ Eliminations	–	(64.0)	(12.3)	22.0	.4	–
Consolidated	$1,104.6	$ –	$ 45.2	$ 733.6	$ 25.0	$ 69.6

	1981	1980	1979
(a) Includes sales in Iron/Steel operations of: Iron Products	$108.3	$ 61.0	$ 86.1
Steel Products	166.0	213.4	276.1
(b) Includes investment in unconsolidated affiliates in:			
Material Handling/Storage Products	–	.5	.6
Packaging	.3	.3	.2

INTERLAKE ANNUAL REPORT 1981

Notes to Consolidated Financial Statements

INFORMATION ABOUT THE COMPANY'S OPERATIONS BY GEOGRAPHIC AREAS

| | Net Sales | | Operating | |
	Customers	Inter-geographic	Profit (Loss)	Assets At Year-End
		(In millions)		
1981				
United States	$ 754.8	$ 3.4	$ 50.2	$ 444.3
Equity in unconsolidated affiliates	–	–	9.3	28.6
	754.8	3.4	59.5	472.9
Western Europe	182.6	.6	9.4	125.6
Equity in unconsolidated affiliates	–	–	–	–
	182.6	.6	9.4	125.6
All Other Foreign	79.2	–	8.8	42.6
Equity in unconsolidated affiliates	–	–	3.9	15.4
	79.2	–	12.7	58.0
Corporate Items/Eliminations	–	(4.0)	(2.5)	53.7
Consolidated	$1,016.6	$ –	$ 79.1	$ 710.2
1980				
United States	$ 752.1	$ 4.9	$ 2.0	$ 441.4
Equity in unconsolidated affiliates	–	–	5.4	30.1
	752.1	4.9	7.4	471.5
Western Europe	231.2	.7	15.7	144.8
Equity in unconsolidated affiliates	–	–	–	.4
	231.2	.7	15.7	145.2
All Other Foreign	72.6	.1	10.0	37.5
Equity in unconsolidated affiliates	–	–	1.9	13.3
	72.6	.1	11.9	50.8
Corporate Items/Eliminations	–	(5.7)	(14.4)	36.1
Consolidated	$1,055.9	$ –	$ 20.6	$ 703.6
1979				
United States	$ 842.9	$ 3.9	$ 34.8	$ 488.7
Equity in unconsolidated affiliates	–	–	2.4	33.3
	842.9	3.9	37.2	522.0
Western Europe	200.1	.8	9.4	142.5
Equity in unconsolidated affiliates	–	–	–	.6
	200.1	.8	9.4	143.1
All Other Foreign	61.6	.1	7.3	35.2
Equity in unconsolidated affiliates	–	–	3.6	11.3
	61.6	.1	10.9	46.5
Corporate Items/Eliminations	–	(4.8)	(12.3)	22.0
Consolidated	$1,104.6	$ –	$ 45.2	$ 733.6

The Company's interest in iron ore mining joint ventures in Minnesota and Labrador, Canada and coal mining joint ventures in West Virginia and Kentucky are accounted for by the equity method within the iron and steel business. Investments in material handling companies in Mexico and Japan are also accounted for on an equity basis.

Sales to the largest individual customers are not material in relation to consolidated sales, nor are sales to domestic or foreign government agencies. Transfers between geographic areas, which are virtually all in the material handling lines of business, are made at prices which approximate the prices of similar items sold to distributors. Operating profit by geographic area is the difference between total sales and other revenues attributable to the areas and related operating expenses. Income and expenses which are not related to nor appropriately allocable to geographic areas, primarily interest expense, are included in general Corporate expense. Export sales to unaffiliated customers included in the United States' sales are not material.

'All other foreign' includes operations in Canada, Mexico, Australia and Japan.

Total assets consist of those assets used directly in the operations in the geographic areas shown.

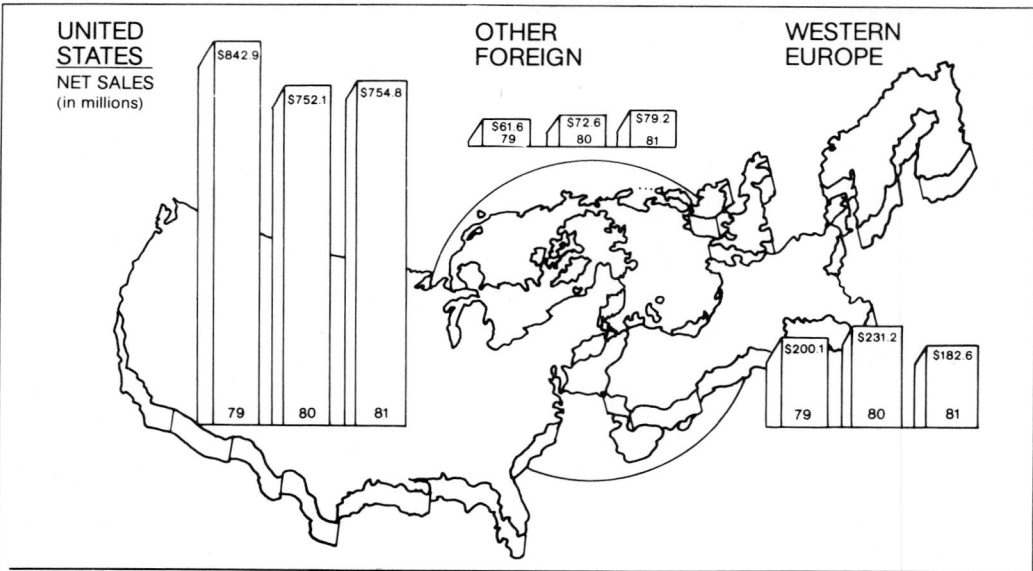

NOTE 11–INVESTMENTS IN IRON ORE INTERESTS

The Company holds investments in iron ore mining ventures, the principal investments being a 10% interest in Erie Mining Company and a 17.6% interest in Wabush Iron Company, Limited. Combined financial data of these companies is summarized below:

	1981	1980	1979
		(In thousands)	
Net working capital	$ 97,661	$ 70,298	$ 64,521
Capital assets, net of depreciation and depletion	195,277	208,660	223,813
Other assets	13,440	14,120	14,850
Long-term liabilities	94,564	103,865	113,821
Shareholders' equity	211,814	189,212	189,363
Revenues	467,557	339,114	394,989
Net income	114,871	59,886	75,784
Interlake's equity in net income, after consolidating eliminations	12,729	4,000	3,138

See Note 9 regarding the Company's obligations with respect to the long-term debt of these ventures.

Notes to Consolidated Financial Statements

NOTE 12–QUARTERLY RESULTS (UNAUDITED)

Quarterly results of operations for 1981, 1980 and 1979 were as follows:

	1st Quarter	2nd Quarter	3rd Quarter	4th Quarter
	(In millions except per share data)			
1981				
Net sales	$267.1	$267.2	$255.1	$227.2
Other revenues	3.5	4.9	4.1	4.2
Costs and expenses	252.4	249.8	239.1	212.9
Income before taxes on income and minority interest	18.2	22.3	20.1	18.5
Net income–Amount	10.2	12.4	12.3	11.7
–Per share	1.67	2.03	2.01	1.88
1980				
Net sales	$294.8	$277.7	$229.4	$254.0
Other revenues	2.7	1.8	1.4	2.0
Costs and expenses	278.9	273.0	263.9	227.4
Income (loss) before taxes on income and minority interest	18.6	6.5	(33.1)	28.6
Net income (loss)–Amount	11.3	5.6	(22.5)	19.4
–Per share	1.88	.94	(3.74)	3.21
1979				
Net sales	$264.5	$281.1	$271.6	$287.4
Other revenues	1.9	2.1	1.7	2.1
Costs and expenses	264.2	268.4	262.7	271.9
Income before taxes on income and minority interest	2.2	14.8	10.6	17.6
Net income–Amount	.8	9.7	15.6	13.6
–Per share	.14	1.62	2.62	2.28

In the fourth quarter of 1981 the Company adopted Statement of Financial Accounting Standards No. 52, "Foreign Currency Translation" with no material effect on quarterly results. Translation and hedging adjustments impacted 1980 and 1979 quarterly results as follows:

	Net Income (Loss)			
	1st Quarter	2nd Quarter	3rd Quarter	4th Quarter
	(In millions)			
1980	$2.5	$(3.8)	$1.3	$1.4
1979	(.2)	(.6)	.9	(.8)

The 1980 first quarter earnings reflected profitable operations in the iron and steel segment including the sale of certain facilities which increased net income by $.8 million. The low earnings in the first quarter of 1979 were primarily due to the iron and steel operations which were plagued by severe winter weather and by Chicago plant operating problems associated with a major facility rehabilitation program.

In the second quarter of 1981 vacant land adjacent to the Chicago coke plant was sold, increasing net income by $1.2 million. The second quarter of 1980 was severely affected by deteriorating economic conditions in the United States which affected most business segments.

The third quarter of 1980 was charged with a shutdown/disposal provision (see Note 6) which reduced net income by $24.7 million, or $4.10 per share, and a provision for relocation of a Packaging Division plant which reduced net income by $1.3 million, or $.22 per share.

The third quarter of 1979 benefited from the application of Statement of Financial Accounting Standards No. 31 regarding stock relief tax legislation in the United Kingdom which generated a tax credit of $7.4 million, or $1.24 per share, for the years 1973 through 1978. The third quarter of 1981 contained a stock relief tax credit of $1.5 million, or $.25 per share, compared to $.1 million, or $.01 per share, in the third quarter of 1980.

The fourth quarters of 1981, 1980 and 1979 contained stock relief tax credits of $.4 million, or $.07 per share, $3.0 million, or $.50 per share, and $1.5 million, or $.25 per share, respectively.

During the third and fourth quarters of 1980 inventory quantities were reduced resulting in a liquidation of LIFO inventory quantities carried at lower costs prevailing in prior years as compared with the cost of 1980 production. As a result, income before taxes was increased by $23.2 million, equivalent to $2.08 per share after applicable income taxes, of which $15.4 million, equivalent to $1.38 per share after applicable taxes, was reflected in cost of products sold ($5.0 million in the third quarter and $10.4 million in the fourth quarter) and the balance was included as a reduction of the shutdown/disposal provision (see Note 6).

Report of Independent Accountants

To the Board of Directors and Shareholders of Interlake, Inc.

In our opinion, the accompanying consolidated balance sheet and the related statement of consolidated income and retained earnings and the statement of changes in consolidated financial position present fairly the financial position of Interlake, Inc. and its subsidiaries at December 27, 1981 and December 28, 1980, and the results of their operations and the changes in their financial position for each of the three years in the period ended December 27, 1981, in conformity with generally accepted accounting principles consistently applied. Our examinations of these statements were made in accordance with generally accepted auditing standards and accordingly included such tests of the accounting records and such other auditing procedures as we considered necessary in the circumstances.

Chicago, Illinois
January 29, 1982   *Price Waterhouse*

INFORMATION FOR SPECIAL USES

The financial statements and notes combined with Price Waterhouse's independent opinion are the reader's primary source of financial information. Management's comments in respect to business segments and financial developments are intended to expand the reader's understanding of this information.

The supplementary information section is intended to relay information that may be helpful, but is not essential. This may include information that has a different perspective from that of the primary financial statements or is summarized in a different manner.

Like other major companies, Interlake is required to provide supplementary financial data adjusted for effects of changing prices. While the primary financial information is expressed in historical dollars, this supplementary presentation measures information in constant dollars and current costs. This information is being used by some technical readers for specialized analyses and the value of these studies has not been established. These are experimental approaches to the presentation of financial information and no one is really certain as to what it will actually accomplish or how useful it may be to the general reader.

The remaining schedules in this section furnish the reader with information on the market for the Company's common stock and a five-year summary of selected financial data.

MARKET FOR THE COMPANY'S COMMON STOCK AND RELATED SECURITY HOLDER MATTERS

The principal market for the Company's common stock is the New York Stock Exchange (ticker symbol IK). The Company's common stock is also listed on the Midwest Stock Exchange and is admitted to unlisted trading on the Pacific Coast Exchange and the Boston Exchange.

On December 27, 1981 the approximate number of record holders of the Company's common stock was 18,909.

High and low stock prices and dividends for the last two years were:

| | 1981 | | | 1980 | | |
| | Sales Price | | Per Share Cash Dividends | Sales Price | | Per Share Cash Dividends |
Calendar Quarter Ended	High	Low	Paid	High	Low	Paid
March 31	$ 34¼	$ 27½	$ .55	$ 33¾	$ 22½	$ .55
June 30	41¼	33⅞	.55	27¾	22⅝	.55
September 30	45	33	.65	29½	25⅜	.55
December 31	37	33¼	.65	31¼	25½	.55

The Company expects to continue its policy of paying regular cash dividends, although there is no assurance as to future dividends because they are dependent on future earnings, capital requirements, and financial condition. In addition, the payment of dividends is subject to the restrictions described in Note 5 to the accompanying financial statements.

Supplementary Financial Information

SUPPLEMENTARY FINANCIAL DATA ADJUSTED FOR EFFECTS OF CHANGING PRICES

The Financial Accounting Standards Board (FASB) has adopted supplementary disclosure requirements based on alternative measurements of traditonal financial information. In compliance with these requirements and the December 22, 1981 exposure draft on the proposed amendment of SFAS No. 33 for foreign currency translation, the historical cost (as reported) data has been adjusted to depict the effect of 1) general price level changes (constant dollar), and 2) price changes of specific assets (current cost).

Constant dollar adjustments bring historical cost data into units having the same general purchasing power by applying appropriate measures of the changes in the applicable general price level indexes.

Current cost adjustments to plant and equipment were determined by applying external price indexes closely related to the assets being measured to the historic acquisition costs of the assets; for land, current cost was primarily determined by reference to real estate tax assessments. Current cost of goods sold was determined by the LIFO (last-in, first-out) inventory method, which is principally the same method used by the Company in its primary financial statements, adjusted for any effect of prior-year LIFO layer liquidations.

Statement of Income Adjusted for Changing Prices

For The Year Ended December 27, 1981

	(In thousands)
Income as reported	$ 46,577
Constant dollar adjustments:	
–cost of goods sold	(5,682)
–depreciation and amortization expense	(16,739)
Income adjusted for general inflation	24,156
Adjustments to reflect the difference between constant dollar and current costs:	
–cost of goods sold	3,764
–depreciation and amortization expense	(3,884)
Income adjusted for changes in specific prices	$ 24,036
Gain from decline in purchasing power on net amounts owed	$ 10,621
Increase in general price level of inventories and property, plant and equipment held during the year	$ 66,254
Effect of increase in current cost*	52,309
Excess of increase in the general price level over the increase in current cost	$ 13,945
Aggregate foreign currency translation adjustments as reported	$(15,575)
–in constant dollars	$(19,860)
–in current cost	$(20,716)

* At December 27, 1981 current cost of inventory was $296.5 million and current cost of property, plant and equipment, net of accumulated depreciation was $462.4 million.

The constant dollar adjustments to reported income reflect the effect of general inflation on two principal categories of assets, resulting in:

- higher costs incurred to replace inventories sold during the year–an adjustment which is minimized because most inventories are valued by the LIFO method.
- higher depreciation expense that would arise if existing plant and equipment were replaced at higher constant dollar costs, reflecting assets with relatively long lives. The straight-line method was used for constant dollar depreciation for certain asset groupings depreciated in the primary financial statements on a basis which already reflected, in part, the effects of general inflation.

The current cost adjustments to reported income reflect the effect of price changes of specific assets, resulting in:

- higher costs of goods sold, as in the constant dollar adjustment–however, current costs for replacing inventories valued on the FIFO (first-in, first-out) method increased less than the general rate of inflation.
- higher depreciation expense, as in the constant dollar adjustment, with the additional amount attributed to a faster increase in specific prices for the related assets than the general rate of inflation.

Neither alternative measure for the effects of changing prices has been adjusted for the tax effects normally associated with incurring higher costs because the FASB standard does not permit such modifications and theoretical adjustments are not allowed for federal tax purposes.

Comparison of Selected Data Adjusted for Effects of Changing Prices

	1981	1980	1979	1978	1977
		(Dollar amounts in thousands except per share statistics)			
Net sales and other revenues					
–as reported	$1,033,311	$1,063,763	$1,112,435	$ 929,845	$ 773,058
–in constant dollars	1,033,311	1,174,105	1,393,870	1,296,263	1,160,226
Net income (loss)					
–as reported	46,577	13,818	39,735		
–in constant dollars	24,156	(32,405)	20,877		
–in current cost	24,036	(35,062)	19,627		
Net income (loss) per common share					
–as reported	7.59	2.29	6.66		
–in constant dollars	3.94	(5.36)	3.50		
–in current cost	3.92	(5.81)	3.28		
Cash dividends per common share					
–as declared	2.40	2.20	2.20	2.20	2.20
–in constant dollars	2.40	2.43	2.76	3.07	3.30
Market price per common share at year end					
–as reported	33.88	27.75	25.00	23.00	28.25
–in constant dollars	32.78	29.25	29.62	30.88	41.35
Net assets at year end					
–as reported	358,748	336,707	333,981		
–in constant dollars	645,537	652,337	698,681		
–in current cost	662,358	673,114	749,559		
Gain from decline in purchasing power on net amounts owed	10,621	20,823	24,386		
Excess of increase in the general price level over the increase in current cost	13,945	32,847	28,490		
Average consumer price index (1967 = 100.0)	272.4	246.8	217.4	195.4	181.5

In 1980, liquidation of LIFO inventory quantities required an adjustment to constant dollar and current cost amounts of cost of goods sold of $17.8 million and $17.0 million, respectively, in 1981 average dollars.

The shutdown/disposal provision in 1980 included the reduction of historical costs to expected realizable values. As such, the adjustments for the effects of changing prices were not necessary for assets related to this provision.

None of the preceding data includes current cost information on mineral properties held by joint ventures in which the Company holds investments accounted for by the equity method. The Company's share of estimated mineral reserves of these joint ventures as of December 27, 1981 were approximately 143 million net tons of iron ore and 20 million net tons of metallurgical coal. The prevailing average market prices per ton in 1981 for this iron ore and coal were $37.63 and $41.77, respectively. This information in and of itself is not meaningful without due consideration of the significant and ever-increasing costs of extraction, processing and shipping and associated capital expenditures.

Supplementary Financial Information

SELECTED FINANCIAL DATA

	1981	1980	1979	1978	1977
	(In thousands of dollars except per share data)				
For the Year					
Sales and revenues:					
Net sales	$1,016,605	$1,055,883	$1,104,588	$ 921,127	$ 766,614
Other revenues	16,706	7,880	7,847	8,718	6,444
	1,033,311	1,063,763	1,112,435	929,845	773,058
Income before nonrecurring					
item and taxes on income	79,119	57,553	45,177	31,626	34,284
Shutdown/disposal provision	–	37,000	–	15,682	–
Income before taxes on income	79,119	20,553	45,177	15,944	34,284
Provision for income taxes	30,953	5,998	3,129	3,100	14,010
	48,166	14,555	42,048	12,844	20,274
Minority interest in net income					
of subsidiaries	1,589	737	2,313	2,356	1,542
Net income	$ 46,577	$ 13,818	$ 39,735	$ 10,488	$ 18,732
Net income per common share	$ 7.59	$ 2.29	$ 6.66	$ 1.77	$ 3.17
Cash dividends per common share	2.40	2.20	2.20	2.20	2.20
At Year End					
Working capital					
–amount	$ 199,803	$ 181,145	$ 162,270	$ 163,348	$ 140,682
–current ratio	2.2 to 1	2.0 to 1	1.7 to 1	1.9 to 1	2.0 to 1
Total assets	710,217	703,618	733,559	658,415	559,568
Long-term debt, less current maturities	126,618	133,020	135,503	136,169	85,233
Common shareholders' equity					
–amount	358,748	336,707	333,981	306,311	308,400
–per common share	58.06	55.30	55.64	51.41	52.05

NOTE: 1978 was a 53-week year while all other periods were 52-week years.

Appendix C
Compound interest and annuity tables

Table 1: Future value of $1 at compound interest: 0.5%–10%

$$F_{1,n} = (1 + i)^n$$

Period	.5%	1%	1.5%	2%	2.5%	3%	3.5%	4%	4.5%	5%
1	1.00500	1.01000	1.01500	1.02000	1.02500	1.03000	1.03500	1.04000	1.04500	1.05000
2	1.01003	1.02010	1.03023	1.04040	1.05063	1.06090	1.07123	1.08160	1.09203	1.10250
3	1.01508	1.03030	1.04568	1.06121	1.07689	1.09273	1.10872	1.12486	1.14117	1.15762
4	1.02015	1.04060	1.06136	1.08243	1.10381	1.12551	1.14752	1.16986	1.19252	1.21551
5	1.02525	1.05101	1.07728	1.10408	1.13141	1.15927	1.18769	1.21665	1.24618	1.27628
6	1.03038	1.06152	1.09344	1.12616	1.15969	1.19405	1.22926	1.26532	1.30226	1.34010
7	1.03553	1.07214	1.10984	1.14869	1.18869	1.22987	1.27228	1.31593	1.36086	1.40710
8	1.04071	1.08286	1.12649	1.17166	1.21840	1.26677	1.31681	1.36857	1.42210	1.47746
9	1.04591	1.09369	1.14339	1.19509	1.24886	1.30477	1.36290	1.42331	1.48610	1.55133
10	1.05114	1.10462	1.16054	1.21899	1.28008	1.34392	1.41060	1.48024	1.55297	1.62889
11	1.05640	1.11567	1.17795	1.24337	1.31209	1.38423	1.45997	1.53945	1.62285	1.71034
12	1.06168	1.12683	1.19562	1.26824	1.34489	1.42576	1.51107	1.60103	1.69588	1.79586
13	1.06699	1.13809	1.21355	1.29361	1.37851	1.46853	1.56396	1.66507	1.77220	1.88565
14	1.07232	1.14947	1.23176	1.31948	1.41297	1.51259	1.61869	1.73168	1.85194	1.97993
15	1.07768	1.16097	1.25023	1.34587	1.44830	1.55797	1.67535	1.80094	1.93528	2.07893
16	1.08307	1.17258	1.26899	1.37279	1.48451	1.60471	1.73399	1.87298	2.02237	2.18287
17	1.08849	1.18430	1.28802	1.40024	1.52162	1.65285	1.79468	1.94790	2.11338	2.29202
18	1.09393	1.19615	1.30734	1.42825	1.55966	1.70243	1.85749	2.02582	2.20848	2.40662
19	1.09940	1.20811	1.32695	1.45681	1.59865	1.75351	1.92250	2.10685	2.30786	2.52695
20	1.10490	1.22019	1.34686	1.48595	1.63862	1.80611	1.98979	2.19112	2.41171	2.65330
21	1.11042	1.23239	1.36706	1.51567	1.67958	1.86029	2.05943	2.27877	2.52024	2.78596
22	1.11597	1.24472	1.38756	1.54598	1.72157	1.91610	2.13151	2.36992	2.63365	2.92526
23	1.12155	1.25716	1.40838	1.57690	1.76461	1.97359	2.20611	2.46472	2.75217	3.07152
24	1.12716	1.26973	1.42950	1.60844	1.80873	2.03279	2.28333	2.56330	2.87601	3.22510
25	1.13280	1.28243	1.45095	1.64061	1.85394	2.09378	2.36324	2.66584	3.00543	3.38635
26	1.13846	1.29526	1.47271	1.67342	1.90029	2.15659	2.44596	2.77247	3.14068	3.55567
27	1.14415	1.30821	1.49480	1.70689	1.94780	2.22129	2.53157	2.88337	3.28201	3.73346
28	1.14987	1.32129	1.51722	1.74102	1.99650	2.28793	2.62017	2.99870	3.42970	3.92013
29	1.15562	1.33450	1.53998	1.77584	2.04641	2.35657	2.71188	3.11865	3.58404	4.11614
30	1.16140	1.34785	1.56308	1.81136	2.09757	2.42726	2.80679	3.24340	3.74532	4.32194

5.5%	6%	6.5%	7%	7.5%	8%	8.5%	9%	9.5%	10%
1.05500	1.06000	1.06500	1.07000	1.07500	1.08000	1.08500	1.09000	1.09500	1.10000
1.11303	1.12360	1.13423	1.14490	1.15563	1.16640	1.17723	1.18810	1.19903	1.21000
1.17424	1.19102	1.20795	1.22504	1.24230	1.25971	1.27729	1.29503	1.31293	1.33100
1.23882	1.26248	1.28647	1.31080	1.33547	1.36049	1.38586	1.41158	1.43766	1.46410
1.30696	1.33823	1.37009	1.40255	1.43563	1.46933	1.50366	1.53862	1.57424	1.61051
1.37884	1.41852	1.45914	1.50073	1.54330	1.58687	1.63147	1.67710	1.72379	1.77156
1.45468	1.50363	1.55399	1.60578	1.65905	1.71382	1.77014	1.82804	1.88755	1.94872
1.53469	1.59385	1.65500	1.71819	1.78348	1.85093	1.92060	1.99256	2.06687	2.14359
1.61909	1.68948	1.76257	1.83846	1.91724	1.99900	2.08386	2.17189	2.26322	2.35795
1.70814	1.79085	1.87714	1.96715	2.06103	2.15892	2.26098	2.36736	2.47823	2.59374
1.80209	1.89830	1.99915	2.10485	2.21561	2.33164	2.45317	2.58043	2.71366	2.85312
1.90121	2.01220	2.12910	2.25219	2.38178	2.51817	2.66169	2.81266	2.97146	3.13843
2.00577	2.13293	2.26749	2.40985	2.56041	2.71962	2.88793	3.06580	3.25375	3.45227
2.11609	2.26090	2.41487	2.57853	2.75244	2.93719	3.13340	3.34173	3.56285	3.79750
2.23248	2.39656	2.57184	2.75903	2.95888	3.17217	3.39974	3.64248	3.90132	4.17725
2.35526	2.54035	2.73901	2.95216	3.18079	3.42594	3.68872	3.97031	4.27195	4.59497
2.48480	2.69277	2.91705	3.15882	3.41935	3.70002	4.00226	4.32763	4.67778	5.05447
2.62147	2.85434	3.10665	3.37993	3.67580	3.99602	4.34245	4.71712	5.12217	5.55992
2.76565	3.02560	3.30859	3.61653	3.95149	4.31570	4.71156	5.14166	5.60878	6.11591
2.91776	3.20714	3.52365	3.86968	4.24785	4.66096	5.11205	5.60441	6.14161	6.72750
3.07823	3.39956	3.75268	4.14056	4.56644	5.03383	5.54657	6.10881	6.72507	7.40025
3.24754	3.60354	3.99661	4.43040	4.90892	5.43654	6.01803	6.65860	7.36395	8.14027
3.42615	3.81975	4.25639	4.74053	5.27709	5.87146	6.52956	7.25787	8.06352	8.95430
3.61459	4.04893	4.53305	5.07237	5.67287	6.34118	7.08457	7.91108	8.82956	9.84973
3.81339	4.29187	4.82770	5.42743	6.09834	6.84848	7.68676	8.62308	9.66836	10.83471
4.02313	4.54938	5.14150	5.80735	6.55572	7.39635	8.34014	9.39916	10.58686	11.91818
4.24440	4.82235	5.47570	6.21387	7.04739	7.98806	9.04905	10.24508	11.59261	13.10999
4.47784	5.11169	5.83162	6.64884	7.57595	8.62711	9.81822	11.16714	12.69391	14.42099
4.72412	5.41839	6.21067	7.11426	8.14414	9.31727	10.65277	12.17218	13.89983	15.86309
4.98395	5.74349	6.61437	7.61226	8.75496	10.06266	11.55825	13.26768	15.22031	17.44940

Table 1 (*concluded*): Future value of $1 at compound interest: 10.5%–20%

Period	10.5%	11%	11.5%	12%	12.5%	13%	13.5%	14%	14.5%	15%
1	1.10500	1.11000	1.11500	1.12000	1.12500	1.13000	1.13500	1.14000	1.14500	1.15000
2	1.22103	1.23210	1.24323	1.25440	1.26563	1.27690	1.28822	1.29960	1.31102	1.32250
3	1.34923	1.36763	1.38620	1.40493	1.42383	1.44290	1.46214	1.48154	1.50112	1.52088
4	1.49090	1.51807	1.54561	1.57352	1.60181	1.63047	1.65952	1.68896	1.71879	1.74901
5	1.64745	1.68506	1.72335	1.76234	1.80203	1.84244	1.88356	1.92541	1.96801	2.01136
6	1.82043	1.87041	1.92154	1.97382	2.02729	2.08195	2.13784	2.19497	2.25337	2.31306
7	2.01157	2.07616	2.14252	2.21068	2.28070	2.35261	2.42645	2.50227	2.58011	2.66002
8	2.22279	2.30454	2.38891	2.47596	2.56578	2.65844	2.75402	2.85259	2.95423	3.05902
9	2.45618	2.55804	2.66363	2.77308	2.88651	3.00404	3.12581	3.25195	3.38259	3.51788
10	2.71408	2.83942	2.96995	3.10585	3.24732	3.39457	3.54780	3.70722	3.87307	4.04556
11	2.99906	3.15176	3.31149	3.47855	3.65324	3.83586	4.02675	4.22623	4.43466	4.65239
12	3.31396	3.49845	3.69231	3.89598	4.10989	4.33452	4.57036	4.81790	5.07769	5.35025
13	3.66193	3.88328	4.11693	4.36349	4.62363	4.89801	5.18736	5.49241	5.81395	6.15279
14	4.04643	4.31044	4.59037	4.88711	5.20158	5.53475	5.88765	6.26135	6.65697	7.07571
15	4.47130	4.78459	5.11827	5.47357	5.85178	6.25427	6.68248	7.13794	7.62223	8.13706
16	4.94079	5.31089	5.70687	6.13039	6.58325	7.06733	7.58462	8.13725	8.72746	9.35762
17	5.45957	5.89509	6.36316	6.86604	7.40616	7.98608	8.60854	9.27646	9.99294	10.76126
18	6.03283	6.54355	7.09492	7.68997	8.33193	9.02427	9.77070	10.57517	11.44192	12.37545
19	6.66628	7.26334	7.91084	8.61276	9.37342	10.19742	11.08974	12.05569	13.10039	14.23177
20	7.36623	8.06231	8.82058	9.64629	10.54509	11.52309	12.58686	13.74349	15.00064	16.36654
21	8.13969	8.94917	9.83495	10.80385	11.86323	13.02109	14.28608	15.66758	17.17573	18.82152
22	8.99436	9.93357	10.96597	12.10031	13.34613	14.71383	16.21470	17.86104	19.66621	21.64475
23	9.93876	11.02627	12.22706	13.55235	15.01440	16.62663	18.40369	20.36158	22.51781	24.89146
24	10.98233	12.23916	13.63317	15.17863	16.89120	18.78809	20.88818	23.21221	25.78290	28.62518
25	12.13548	13.58546	15.20098	17.00006	19.00260	21.23054	23.70809	26.46192	29.52141	32.91895
26	13.40971	15.07986	16.94910	19.04007	21.37793	23.99051	26.90868	30.16658	33.80202	37.85680
27	14.81772	16.73865	18.89824	21.32488	24.05017	27.10928	30.54135	34.38991	38.70331	43.53531
28	16.37359	18.57990	21.07154	23.88387	27.05644	30.63349	34.66443	39.20449	44.31529	50.06561
29	18.09281	20.62369	23.49477	26.74993	30.43849	34.61584	39.34413	44.69312	50.74101	57.57545
30	19.99256	22.89230	26.19667	29.95992	34.24330	39.11590	44.65559	50.95016	58.09846	66.21177

15.5%	16%	16.5%	17%	17.5%	18%	18.5%	19%	19.5%	20%
1.15500	1.16000	1.16500	1.17000	1.17500	1.18000	1.18500	1.19000	1.19500	1.20000
1.33402	1.34560	1.35722	1.36890	1.38063	1.39240	1.40422	1.41610	1.42802	1.44000
1.54080	1.56090	1.58117	1.60161	1.62223	1.64303	1.66401	1.68516	1.70649	1.72800
1.77962	1.81064	1.84206	1.87389	1.90613	1.93878	1.97185	2.00534	2.03926	2.07360
2.05546	2.10034	2.14600	2.19245	2.23970	2.28776	2.33664	2.38635	2.43691	2.48832
2.37406	2.43640	2.50009	2.56516	2.63164	2.69955	2.76892	2.83976	2.91211	2.98598
2.74204	2.82622	2.91260	3.00124	3.09218	3.18547	3.28117	3.37932	3.47997	3.58318
3.16706	3.27841	3.39318	3.51145	3.63331	3.75886	3.88818	4.02139	4.15856	4.29982
3.65795	3.80296	3.95306	4.10840	4.26914	4.43545	4.60750	4.78545	4.96948	5.15978
4.22493	4.41144	4.60531	4.80683	5.01624	5.23384	5.45989	5.69468	5.93853	6.19174
4.87980	5.11726	5.36519	5.62399	5.89409	6.17593	6.46996	6.77667	7.09654	7.43008
5.63617	5.93603	6.25045	6.58007	6.92555	7.28759	7.66691	8.06424	8.48037	8.91610
6.50977	6.88579	7.28177	7.69868	8.13752	8.59936	9.08528	9.59645	10.13404	10.69932
7.51879	7.98752	8.48326	9.00745	9.56159	10.14724	10.76606	11.41977	12.11018	12.83918
8.68420	9.26552	9.88300	10.53872	11.23487	11.97375	12.75778	13.58953	14.47167	15.40702
10.03025	10.74800	11.51370	12.33030	13.20097	14.12902	15.11797	16.17154	17.29364	18.48843
11.58494	12.46768	13.41346	14.42646	15.51114	16.67225	17.91480	19.24413	20.66590	22.18611
13.38060	14.46251	15.62668	16.87895	18.22559	19.67325	21.22904	22.90052	24.69575	26.62333
15.45460	16.77652	18.20508	19.74838	21.41507	23.21444	25.15641	27.25162	29.51143	31.94800
17.85006	19.46076	21.20892	23.10560	25.16271	27.39303	29.81035	32.42942	35.26615	38.33760
20.61682	22.57448	24.70839	27.03355	29.56618	32.32378	35.32526	38.59101	42.14305	46.00512
23.81243	26.18640	28.78527	31.62925	34.74026	38.14206	41.86043	45.92331	50.36095	55.20614
27.50335	30.37622	33.53484	37.00623	40.81981	45.00763	49.60461	54.64873	60.18134	66.24737
31.76637	35.23642	39.06809	43.29729	47.96327	53.10901	58.78147	65.03199	71.91670	79.49685
36.69016	40.87424	45.51433	50.65783	56.35684	62.66863	69.65604	77.38807	85.94045	95.39622
42.37713	47.41412	53.02419	59.26966	66.21929	73.94898	82.54240	92.09181	102.69884	114.47546
48.94559	55.00038	61.77318	69.34550	77.80767	87.25980	97.81275	109.58925	122.72511	137.37055
56.53216	63.80044	71.96576	81.13423	91.42401	102.96656	115.90811	130.41121	146.65651	164.84466
65.29464	74.00851	83.84011	94.92705	107.42321	121.50054	137.35111	155.18934	175.25453	197.81359
75.41531	85.84988	97.67373	111.06465	126.22227	143.37064	162.76106	184.67531	209.42916	237.37631

Table 2: Future value of an ordinary annuity of $1 per period: 0.5%–10% $F_{A_{i,n}} = \dfrac{(1 + i)^n - 1}{i}$

Period	.5%	1%	1.5%	2%	2.5%	3%	3.5%	4%	4.5%	5%
1	1.00000	1.00000	1.00000	1.00000	1.00000	1.00000	1.00000	1.00000	1.00000	1.00000
2	2.00500	2.01000	2.01500	2.02000	2.02500	2.03000	2.03500	2.04000	2.04500	2.05000
3	3.01502	3.03010	3.04522	3.06040	3.07562	3.09090	3.10622	3.12160	3.13702	3.15250
4	4.03010	4.06040	4.09090	4.12161	4.15252	4.18363	4.21494	4.24646	4.27819	4.31012
5	5.05025	5.10101	5.15227	5.20404	5.25633	5.30914	5.36247	5.41632	5.47071	5.52563
6	6.07550	6.15202	6.22955	6.30812	6.38774	6.46841	6.55015	6.63298	6.71689	6.80191
7	7.10588	7.21354	7.32299	7.43428	7.54743	7.66246	7.77941	7.89829	8.01915	8.14201
8	8.14141	8.28567	8.43284	8.58297	8.73612	8.89234	9.05169	9.21423	9.38001	9.54911
9	9.18212	9.36853	9.55933	9.75463	9.95452	10.15911	10.36850	10.58280	10.80211	11.02656
10	10.22803	10.46221	10.70272	10.94972	11.20338	11.46388	11.73139	12.00611	12.28821	12.57789
11	11.27917	11.56683	11.86326	12.16872	12.48347	12.80780	13.14199	13.48635	13.84118	14.20679
12	12.33556	12.68250	13.04121	13.41209	13.79555	14.19203	14.60196	15.02581	15.46403	15.91713
13	13.39724	13.80933	14.23683	14.68033	15.14044	15.61779	16.11303	16.62684	17.15991	17.71298
14	14.46423	14.94742	15.45038	15.97394	16.51895	17.08632	17.67699	18.29191	18.93211	19.59863
15	15.53655	16.09690	16.68214	17.29342	17.93193	18.59891	19.29568	20.02359	20.78405	21.57856
16	16.61423	17.25786	17.93237	18.63929	19.38022	20.15688	20.97103	21.82453	22.71934	23.65749
17	17.69730	18.43044	19.20136	20.01207	20.86473	21.76159	22.70502	23.69751	24.74171	25.84037
18	18.78579	19.61475	20.48938	21.41231	22.38635	23.41444	24.49969	25.64541	26.85508	28.13238
19	19.87972	20.81090	21.79672	22.84056	23.94601	25.11687	26.35718	27.67123	29.06356	30.53900
20	20.97912	22.01900	23.12367	24.29737	25.54466	26.87037	28.27968	29.77808	31.37142	33.06595
21	22.08401	23.23919	24.47052	25.78332	27.18327	28.67649	30.26947	31.96920	33.78314	35.71925
22	23.19443	24.47159	25.83758	27.29898	28.86286	30.53678	32.32890	34.24797	36.30338	38.50521
23	24.31040	25.71630	27.22514	28.84496	30.58443	32.45288	34.46041	36.61789	38.93703	41.43048
24	25.43196	26.97346	28.63352	30.42186	32.34904	34.42647	36.66653	39.08260	41.68920	44.50200
25	26.55912	28.24320	30.06302	32.03030	34.15776	36.45926	38.94986	41.64591	44.56521	47.72710
26	27.69191	29.52563	31.51397	33.67091	36.01171	38.55304	41.31310	44.31174	47.57064	51.11345
27	28.83037	30.82089	32.98668	35.34432	37.91200	40.70963	43.75906	47.08421	50.71132	54.66913
28	29.97452	32.12910	34.48148	37.05121	39.85980	42.93092	46.29063	49.96758	53.99333	58.40258
29	31.12439	33.45039	35.99870	38.79223	41.85630	45.21885	48.91080	52.96629	57.42303	62.32271
30	32.28002	34.78489	37.53868	40.56808	43.90270	47.57542	51.62268	56.08494	61.00707	66.43885

5.5%	6%	6.5%	7%	7.5%	8%	8.5%	9%	9.5%	10%
1.00000	1.00000	1.00000	1.00000	1.00000	1.00000	1.00000	1.00000	1.00000	1.00000
2.05500	2.06000	2.06500	2.07000	2.07500	2.08000	2.08500	2.09000	2.09500	2.10000
3.16802	3.18360	3.19922	3.21490	3.23062	3.24640	3.26222	3.27810	3.29402	3.31000
4.34227	4.37462	4.40717	4.43994	4.47292	4.50611	4.53951	4.57313	4.60696	4.64100
5.58109	5.63709	5.69364	5.75074	5.80839	5.86660	5.92537	5.98471	6.04462	6.10510
6.88805	6.97532	7.06373	7.15329	7.24402	7.33593	7.42903	7.52333	7.61886	7.71561
8.26689	8.39384	8.52287	8.65402	8.78732	8.92280	9.06050	9.20043	9.34265	9.48717
9.72157	9.89747	10.07686	10.25980	10.44637	10.63663	10.83064	11.02847	11.23020	11.43589
11.25626	11.49132	11.73185	11.97799	12.22985	12.48756	12.75124	13.02104	13.29707	13.57948
12.87535	13.18079	13.49442	13.81645	14.14709	14.48656	14.83510	15.19293	15.56029	15.93742
14.58350	14.97164	15.37156	15.78360	16.20812	16.64549	17.09608	17.56029	18.03852	18.53117
16.38559	16.86994	17.37071	17.88845	18.42373	18.97713	19.54925	20.14072	20.75218	21.38428
18.28680	18.88214	19.49981	20.14064	20.80551	21.49530	22.21094	22.95338	23.72363	24.52271
20.29257	21.01507	21.76730	22.55049	23.36592	24.21492	25.09887	26.01919	26.97738	27.97498
22.40866	23.27597	24.18217	25.12902	26.11836	27.15211	28.23227	29.36092	30.54023	31.77248
24.64114	25.67253	26.75401	27.88805	29.07724	30.32428	31.63201	33.00340	34.44155	35.94973
26.99640	28.21288	29.49302	30.84022	32.25804	33.75023	35.32073	36.97370	38.71350	40.54470
29.48120	30.90565	32.41007	33.99903	35.67739	37.45024	39.32300	41.30134	43.39128	45.59917
32.10267	33.75999	35.51672	37.37896	39.35319	41.44626	43.66545	46.01846	48.51345	51.15909
34.86832	36.78559	38.82531	40.99549	43.30468	45.76196	48.37701	51.16012	54.12223	57.27500
37.78608	39.99273	42.34895	44.86518	47.55253	50.42292	53.48906	56.76453	60.26384	64.00250
40.86431	43.39229	46.10164	49.00574	52.11897	55.45676	59.03563	62.87334	66.98891	71.40275
44.11185	46.99583	50.09824	53.43614	57.02790	60.89330	65.05366	69.53194	74.35286	79.54302
47.53800	50.81558	54.35463	58.17667	62.30499	66.76476	71.58322	76.78981	82.41638	88.49733
51.15259	54.86451	58.88768	63.24904	67.97786	73.10594	78.66779	84.70090	91.24593	98.34706
54.96598	59.15638	63.71538	68.67647	74.07620	79.95442	86.35455	93.32398	100.91430	109.18177
58.98911	63.70577	68.85688	74.48382	80.63192	87.35077	94.69469	102.72313	111.50116	121.09994
63.23351	68.52811	74.33257	80.69769	87.67931	95.33883	103.74374	112.96822	123.09377	134.20994
67.71135	73.63980	80.16419	87.34653	95.25526	103.96594	113.56196	124.13536	135.78767	148.63093
72.43548	79.05819	86.37486	94.46079	103.39940	113.28321	124.21473	136.30754	149.68750	164.49402

Table 2 (*concluded*):   **Future value of an ordinary annuity of $1 per period: 10.5%–20%**

Period	10.5%	11%	11.5%	12%	12.5%	13%	13.5%	14%	14.5%	15%
1 ...	1.00000	1.00000	1.00000	1.00000	1.00000	1.00000	1.00000	1.00000	1.00000	1.00000
2 ...	2.10500	2.11000	2.11500	2.12000	2.12500	2.13000	2.13500	2.14000	2.14500	2.15000
3 ...	3.32602	3.34210	3.35822	3.37440	3.39062	3.40690	3.42322	3.43960	3.45602	3.47250
4 ...	4.67526	4.70973	4.74442	4.77933	4.81445	4.84980	4.88536	4.92114	4.95715	4.99337
5 ...	6.16616	6.22780	6.29003	6.35285	6.41626	6.48027	6.54488	6.61010	6.67594	6.74238
6 ...	7.81361	7.91286	8.01338	8.11519	8.21829	8.32271	8.42844	8.53552	8.64395	8.75374
7 ...	9.63404	9.78327	9.93492	10.08901	10.24558	10.40466	10.56628	10.73049	10.89732	11.06680
8 ...	11.64561	11.85943	12.07744	12.29969	12.52628	12.75726	12.99273	13.23276	13.47743	13.72682
9 ...	13.86840	14.16397	14.46634	14.77566	15.09206	15.41571	15.74675	16.08535	16.43166	16.78584
10 ...	16.32458	16.72201	17.12997	17.54874	17.97857	18.41975	18.87256	19.33730	19.81425	20.30372
11 ...	19.03866	19.56143	20.09992	20.65458	21.22589	21.81432	22.42036	23.04452	23.68731	24.34928
12 ...	22.03772	22.71319	23.41141	24.13313	24.87913	25.65018	26.44711	27.27075	28.12197	29.00167
13 ...	25.35168	26.21164	27.10372	28.02911	28.98902	29.98470	31.01746	32.08865	33.19966	34.35192
14 ...	29.01361	30.09492	31.22065	32.39260	33.61264	34.88271	36.20482	37.58107	39.01361	40.50471
15 ...	33.06004	34.40536	35.81102	37.27971	38.81422	40.41746	42.09247	43.84241	45.67058	47.58041
16 ...	37.53134	39.18995	40.92929	42.75328	44.66600	46.67173	48.77496	50.98035	53.29282	55.71747
17 ...	42.47213	44.50084	46.63616	48.88367	51.24925	53.73906	56.35958	59.11760	62.02027	65.07509
18 ...	47.93170	50.39594	52.99932	55.74971	58.65541	61.72514	64.96812	68.39407	72.01321	75.83636
19 ...	53.96453	56.93949	60.09424	63.43968	66.98733	70.74941	74.73882	78.96923	83.45513	88.21181
20 ...	60.63081	64.20283	68.00508	72.05244	76.36075	80.94683	85.82856	91.02493	96.55612	102.44358
21 ...	67.99704	72.26514	76.82566	81.69874	86.90584	92.46992	98.41541	104.76842	111.55676	118.81012
22 ...	76.13673	81.21431	86.66062	92.50258	98.76908	105.49101	112.70149	120.43600	128.73249	137.63164
23 ...	85.13109	91.14788	97.62659	104.60289	112.11521	120.20484	128.91619	138.29704	148.39871	159.27638
24 ...	95.06985	102.17415	109.85364	118.15524	127.12961	136.83147	147.31988	158.65862	170.91652	184.16784
25 ...	106.05219	114.41331	123.48681	133.33387	144.02081	155.61956	168.20806	181.87083	196.69941	212.79302
26 ...	118.18767	127.99877	138.68780	150.33393	163.02341	176.85010	191.91615	208.33274	226.22083	245.71197
27 ...	131.59737	143.07864	155.63689	169.37401	184.40134	200.84061	218.82483	238.49933	260.02285	283.56877
28 ...	146.41510	159.81729	174.53513	190.69889	208.45151	227.94989	249.36618	272.88923	298.72616	327.10408
29 ...	162.78868	178.39719	195.60668	214.58275	235.50795	258.58338	284.03062	312.09373	343.04145	377.16969
30 ...	180.88149	199.02088	219.10144	241.33268	265.94644	293.19922	323.37475	356.78685	393.78246	434.74515

15.5%	16%	16.5%	17%	17.5%	18%	18.5%	19%	19.5%	20%
1.00000	1.00000	1.00000	1.00000	1.00000	1.00000	1.00000	1.00000	1.00000	1.00000
2.15500	2.16000	2.16500	2.17000	2.17500	2.18000	2.18500	2.19000	2.19500	2.20000
3.48902	3.50560	3.52222	3.53890	3.55562	3.57240	3.58922	3.60610	3.62302	3.64000
5.02982	5.06650	5.10339	5.14051	5.17786	5.21543	5.25323	5.29126	5.32951	5.36800
6.80945	6.87714	6.94545	7.01440	7.08398	7.15421	7.22508	7.29660	7.36877	7.44160
8.86491	8.97748	9.09145	9.20685	9.32368	9.44197	9.56172	9.68295	9.80568	9.92992
11.23897	11.41387	11.59154	11.77201	11.95533	12.14152	12.33064	12.52271	12.71779	12.91590
13.98101	14.24009	14.50415	14.77325	15.04751	15.32700	15.61181	15.90203	16.19776	16.49908
17.14807	17.51851	17.89733	18.28471	18.68082	19.08585	19.49999	19.92341	20.35632	20.79890
20.80602	21.32147	21.85039	22.39311	22.94997	23.52131	24.10749	24.70886	25.32580	25.95868
25.03095	25.73290	26.45570	27.19994	27.96621	28.75514	29.56737	30.40355	31.26433	32.15042
29.91075	30.85017	31.82089	32.82393	33.86030	34.93107	36.03734	37.18022	38.36088	39.58050
35.54692	36.78620	38.07134	39.40399	40.78585	42.21866	43.70424	45.24446	46.84125	48.49660
42.05669	43.67199	45.35311	47.10267	48.92337	50.81802	52.78953	54.84091	56.97529	59.19592
49.57548	51.65951	53.83638	56.11013	58.48496	60.96527	63.55559	66.26068	69.08547	72.03511
58.25968	60.92503	63.71938	66.64885	69.71983	72.93901	76.31338	79.85021	83.55714	87.44213
68.28993	71.67303	75.23307	78.97915	82.92080	87.06804	91.43135	96.02175	100.85079	105.93056
79.87486	84.14072	88.64653	93.40561	98.43194	103.74028	109.34615	115.26588	121.51669	128.11667
93.25547	98.60323	104.27321	110.28456	116.65753	123.41353	130.57519	138.16640	146.21244	154.74000
108.71007	115.37975	122.47829	130.03294	138.07260	146.62797	155.73160	165.41802	175.72387	186.68800
126.56013	134.84051	143.68721	153.13854	163.23531	174.02100	185.54194	197.84744	210.99002	225.02560
147.17695	157.41499	168.39560	180.17209	192.80149	206.34479	220.86720	236.43846	253.13308	271.03072
170.98937	183.60138	197.18087	211.80134	227.54175	244.48685	262.72763	282.36176	303.49403	326.23686
198.49272	213.97761	230.71571	248.80757	268.36155	289.49448	312.33225	337.01050	363.67536	392.48424
230.25910	249.21402	269.78381	292.10486	316.32482	342.60349	371.11371	402.04249	435.59206	471.98108
266.94926	290.08827	315.29813	342.76268	372.68167	405.27211	440.76975	479.43056	521.53251	567.37730
309.32639	337.50239	368.32233	402.03234	438.90096	479.22109	523.31215	571.52237	624.23135	681.85276
358.27198	392.50277	430.09551	471.37783	516.70863	566.48089	621.12490	681.11162	746.95647	819.22331
414.80414	456.30322	502.06127	552.51207	608.13264	669.44745	737.03300	811.52283	893.61298	984.06797
480.09878	530.31173	585.90138	647.43912	715.55585	790.94799	874.38411	966.71217	1068.86751	1181.88157

Table 3:   Present value of $1 at compound interest: 0.5%-7% $P_{i,n} = \dfrac{1}{(1 + i)^n}$

Period	.5%	1%	1.5%	2%	2.5%	3%	3.5%	4%	4.5%	5%	5.5%	6%	6.5%	7%
1 ...	0.99502	0.99010	0.98522	0.98039	0.97561	0.97087	0.96618	0.96154	0.95694	0.95238	0.94787	0.94340	0.93897	0.93458
2 ...	0.99007	0.98030	0.97066	0.96117	0.95181	0.94260	0.93351	0.92456	0.91573	0.90703	0.89845	0.89000	0.88166	0.87344
3 ...	0.98515	0.97059	0.95632	0.94232	0.92860	0.91514	0.90194	0.88900	0.87630	0.86384	0.85161	0.83962	0.82785	0.81630
4 ...	0.98025	0.96098	0.94218	0.92385	0.90595	0.88849	0.87144	0.85480	0.83856	0.82270	0.80722	0.79209	0.77732	0.76290
5 ...	0.97537	0.95147	0.92826	0.90573	0.88385	0.86261	0.84197	0.82193	0.80245	0.78353	0.76513	0.74726	0.72988	0.71299
6 ...	0.97052	0.94205	0.91454	0.88797	0.86230	0.83748	0.81350	0.79031	0.76790	0.74622	0.72525	0.70496	0.68533	0.66634
7 ...	0.96569	0.93272	0.90103	0.87056	0.84127	0.81309	0.78599	0.75992	0.73483	0.71068	0.68744	0.66506	0.64351	0.62275
8 ...	0.96089	0.92348	0.88771	0.85349	0.82075	0.78941	0.75941	0.73069	0.70319	0.67684	0.65160	0.62741	0.60423	0.58201
9 ...	0.95610	0.91434	0.87459	0.83676	0.80073	0.76642	0.73373	0.70259	0.67290	0.64461	0.61763	0.59190	0.56735	0.54393
10 ...	0.95135	0.90529	0.86167	0.82035	0.78120	0.74409	0.70892	0.67556	0.64393	0.61391	0.58543	0.55839	0.53273	0.50835
11 ...	0.94661	0.89632	0.84893	0.80426	0.76214	0.72242	0.68495	0.64958	0.61620	0.58468	0.55491	0.52679	0.50021	0.47509
12 ...	0.94191	0.88745	0.83639	0.78849	0.74356	0.70138	0.66178	0.62460	0.58966	0.55684	0.52598	0.49697	0.46968	0.44401
13 ...	0.93722	0.87866	0.82403	0.77303	0.72542	0.68095	0.63940	0.60057	0.56427	0.53032	0.49856	0.46884	0.44102	0.41496
14 ...	0.93256	0.86996	0.81185	0.75788	0.70773	0.66112	0.61778	0.57748	0.53997	0.50507	0.47257	0.44230	0.41410	0.38782
15 ...	0.92792	0.86135	0.79985	0.74301	0.69047	0.64186	0.59689	0.55526	0.51672	0.48102	0.44793	0.41727	0.38883	0.36245
16 ...	0.92330	0.85282	0.78803	0.72845	0.67362	0.62317	0.57671	0.53391	0.49447	0.45811	0.42458	0.39365	0.36510	0.33873
17 ...	0.91871	0.84438	0.77639	0.71416	0.65720	0.60502	0.55720	0.51337	0.47318	0.43630	0.40245	0.37136	0.34281	0.31657
18 ...	0.91414	0.83602	0.76491	0.70016	0.64117	0.58739	0.53836	0.49363	0.45280	0.41552	0.38147	0.35034	0.32189	0.29586
19 ...	0.90959	0.82774	0.75361	0.68643	0.62553	0.57029	0.52016	0.47464	0.43330	0.39573	0.36158	0.33051	0.30224	0.27651
20 ...	0.90506	0.81954	0.74247	0.67297	0.61027	0.55368	0.50257	0.45639	0.41464	0.37689	0.34273	0.31180	0.28380	0.25842
21 ...	0.90056	0.81143	0.73150	0.65978	0.59539	0.53755	0.48557	0.43883	0.39679	0.35894	0.32486	0.29416	0.26648	0.24151
22 ...	0.89608	0.80340	0.72069	0.64684	0.58086	0.52189	0.46915	0.42196	0.37970	0.34185	0.30793	0.27751	0.25021	0.22571
23 ...	0.89162	0.79544	0.71004	0.63416	0.56670	0.50669	0.45329	0.40573	0.36335	0.32557	0.29187	0.26180	0.23494	0.21095
24 ...	0.88719	0.78757	0.69954	0.62172	0.55288	0.49193	0.43796	0.39012	0.34770	0.31007	0.27666	0.24698	0.22060	0.19715
25 ...	0.88277	0.77977	0.68921	0.60953	0.53939	0.47761	0.42315	0.37512	0.33273	0.29530	0.26223	0.23300	0.20714	0.18425
26 ...	0.87838	0.77205	0.67902	0.59758	0.52623	0.46369	0.40884	0.36069	0.31840	0.28124	0.24856	0.21981	0.19450	0.17220
27 ...	0.87401	0.76440	0.66899	0.58586	0.51340	0.45019	0.39501	0.34682	0.30469	0.26785	0.23560	0.20737	0.18263	0.16093
28 ...	0.86966	0.75684	0.65910	0.57437	0.50088	0.43708	0.38165	0.33348	0.29157	0.25509	0.22332	0.19563	0.17148	0.15040
29 ...	0.86533	0.74934	0.64936	0.56311	0.48866	0.42435	0.36875	0.32065	0.27902	0.24295	0.21168	0.18456	0.16101	0.14056
30 ...	0.86103	0.74192	0.63976	0.55207	0.47674	0.41199	0.35628	0.30832	0.26700	0.23138	0.20064	0.17411	0.15119	0.13137
31 ...	0.85675	0.73458	0.63031	0.54125	0.46511	0.39999	0.34423	0.29646	0.25550	0.22036	0.19018	0.16425	0.14196	0.12277
32 ...	0.85248	0.72730	0.62099	0.53063	0.45377	0.38834	0.33259	0.28506	0.24450	0.20987	0.18027	0.15496	0.13329	0.11474
33 ...	0.84824	0.72010	0.61182	0.52023	0.44270	0.37703	0.32134	0.27409	0.23397	0.19987	0.17087	0.14619	0.12516	0.10723
34 ...	0.84402	0.71297	0.60277	0.51003	0.43191	0.36604	0.31048	0.26355	0.22390	0.19035	0.16196	0.13791	0.11752	0.10022
35 ...	0.83982	0.70591	0.59387	0.50003	0.42137	0.35538	0.29998	0.25342	0.21425	0.18129	0.15352	0.13011	0.11035	0.09366
36 ...	0.83564	0.69892	0.58509	0.49022	0.41109	0.34503	0.28983	0.24367	0.20503	0.17266	0.14552	0.12274	0.10361	0.08754
37 ...	0.83149	0.69200	0.57644	0.48061	0.40107	0.33498	0.28003	0.23430	0.19620	0.16444	0.13793	0.11579	0.09729	0.08181
38 ...	0.82735	0.68515	0.56792	0.47119	0.39128	0.32523	0.27056	0.22529	0.18775	0.15661	0.13074	0.10924	0.09135	0.07646
39 ...	0.82323	0.67837	0.55953	0.46195	0.38174	0.31575	0.26141	0.21662	0.17967	0.14915	0.12392	0.10306	0.08578	0.07146
40 ...	0.81914	0.67165	0.55126	0.45289	0.37243	0.30656	0.25257	0.20829	0.17193	0.14205	0.11746	0.09722	0.08054	0.06678
41 ...	0.81506	0.66500	0.54312	0.44401	0.36335	0.29763	0.24403	0.20028	0.16453	0.13528	0.11134	0.09172	0.07563	0.06241
42 ...	0.81101	0.65842	0.53509	0.43530	0.35448	0.28896	0.23578	0.19257	0.15744	0.12884	0.10554	0.08653	0.07101	0.05833
43 ...	0.80697	0.65190	0.52718	0.42677	0.34584	0.28054	0.22781	0.18517	0.15066	0.12270	0.10003	0.08163	0.06668	0.05451
44 ...	0.80296	0.64545	0.51939	0.41840	0.33740	0.27237	0.22010	0.17805	0.14417	0.11686	0.09482	0.07701	0.06261	0.05095
45 ...	0.79896	0.63905	0.51171	0.41020	0.32917	0.26444	0.21266	0.17120	0.13796	0.11130	0.08988	0.07265	0.05879	0.04761
46 ...	0.79499	0.63273	0.50415	0.40215	0.32115	0.25674	0.20547	0.16461	0.13202	0.10600	0.08519	0.06854	0.05520	0.04450
47 ...	0.79103	0.62646	0.49670	0.39427	0.31331	0.24926	0.19852	0.15828	0.12634	0.10095	0.08075	0.06466	0.05183	0.04159
48 ...	0.78710	0.62026	0.48936	0.38654	0.30567	0.24200	0.19181	0.15219	0.12090	0.09614	0.07654	0.06100	0.04867	0.03887
49 ...	0.78318	0.61412	0.48213	0.37896	0.29822	0.23495	0.18532	0.14634	0.11569	0.09156	0.07255	0.05755	0.04570	0.03632
50 ...	0.77929	0.60804	0.47500	0.37153	0.29094	0.22811	0.17905	0.14071	0.11071	0.08720	0.06877	0.05429	0.04291	0.03395
51 ...	0.77541	0.60202	0.46798	0.36424	0.28385	0.22146	0.17300	0.13530	0.10594	0.08305	0.06518	0.05122	0.04029	0.03173
52 ...	0.77155	0.59606	0.46107	0.35710	0.27692	0.21501	0.16715	0.13010	0.10138	0.07910	0.06178	0.04832	0.03783	0.02965
53 ...	0.76771	0.59016	0.45426	0.35010	0.27017	0.20875	0.16150	0.12509	0.09701	0.07533	0.05856	0.04558	0.03552	0.02771
54 ...	0.76389	0.58431	0.44754	0.34323	0.26358	0.20267	0.15603	0.12028	0.09284	0.07174	0.05551	0.04300	0.03335	0.02590
55 ...	0.76009	0.57853	0.44093	0.33650	0.25715	0.19677	0.15076	0.11566	0.08884	0.06833	0.05262	0.04057	0.03132	0.02420
56 ...	0.75631	0.57280	0.43441	0.32991	0.25088	0.19104	0.14566	0.11121	0.08501	0.06507	0.04987	0.03827	0.02941	0.02262
57 ...	0.75255	0.56713	0.42799	0.32344	0.24476	0.18547	0.14073	0.10693	0.08135	0.06197	0.04727	0.03610	0.02761	0.02114
58 ...	0.74880	0.56151	0.42167	0.31710	0.23879	0.18007	0.13598	0.10282	0.07785	0.05902	0.04481	0.03406	0.02593	0.01976
59 ...	0.74508	0.55595	0.41544	0.31088	0.23297	0.17483	0.13138	0.09886	0.07450	0.05621	0.04247	0.03213	0.02434	0.01847
60 ...	0.74137	0.55045	0.40930	0.30478	0.22728	0.16973	0.12693	0.09506	0.07129	0.05354	0.04026	0.03031	0.02286	0.01726

Period	.5%	1%	1.5%	2%	2.5%	3%	3.5%	4%	4.5%	5%	5.5%	6%	6.5%	7%
61 ..	0.73768	0.54500	0.40325	0.29881	0.22174	0.16479	0.12264	0.09140	0.06822	0.05099	0.03816	0.02860	0.02146	0.01613
62 ..	0.73401	0.53960	0.39729	0.29295	0.21633	0.15999	0.11849	0.08789	0.06528	0.04856	0.03617	0.02698	0.02015	0.01507
63 ..	0.73036	0.53426	0.39142	0.28720	0.21106	0.15533	0.11449	0.08451	0.06247	0.04625	0.03428	0.02545	0.01892	0.01409
64 ..	0.72673	0.52897	0.38563	0.28157	0.20591	0.15081	0.11062	0.08126	0.05978	0.04404	0.03250	0.02401	0.01777	0.01317
65 ..	0.72311	0.52373	0.37993	0.27605	0.20089	0.14641	0.10688	0.07813	0.05721	0.04195	0.03080	0.02265	0.01668	0.01230
66 ..	0.71952	0.51855	0.37432	0.27064	0.19599	0.14215	0.10326	0.07513	0.05474	0.03995	0.02920	0.02137	0.01566	0.01150
67 ..	0.71594	0.51341	0.36879	0.26533	0.19121	0.13801	0.09977	0.07224	0.05239	0.03805	0.02767	0.02016	0.01471	0.01075
68 ..	0.71237	0.50833	0.36334	0.26013	0.18654	0.13399	0.09640	0.06946	0.05013	0.03623	0.02623	0.01902	0.01381	0.01004
69 ..	0.70883	0.50330	0.35797	0.25503	0.18199	0.13009	0.09314	0.06679	0.04797	0.03451	0.02486	0.01794	0.01297	0.00939
70 ..	0.70530	0.49831	0.35268	0.25003	0.17755	0.12630	0.08999	0.06422	0.04590	0.03287	0.02357	0.01693	0.01218	0.00877
71 ..	0.70179	0.49338	0.34746	0.24513	0.17322	0.12262	0.08694	0.06175	0.04393	0.03130	0.02234	0.01597	0.01143	0.00820
72 ..	0.69830	0.48850	0.34233	0.24032	0.16900	0.11905	0.08400	0.05937	0.04204	0.02981	0.02117	0.01507	0.01074	0.00766
73 ..	0.69483	0.48366	0.33727	0.23561	0.16488	0.11558	0.08116	0.05709	0.04023	0.02839	0.02007	0.01421	0.01008	0.00716
74 ..	0.69137	0.47887	0.33229	0.23099	0.16085	0.11221	0.07842	0.05490	0.03849	0.02704	0.01902	0.01341	0.00947	0.00669
75 ..	0.68793	0.47413	0.32738	0.22646	0.15693	0.10895	0.07577	0.05278	0.03684	0.02575	0.01803	0.01265	0.00889	0.00625
76 ..	0.68451	0.46944	0.32254	0.22202	0.15310	0.10577	0.07320	0.05075	0.03525	0.02453	0.01709	0.01193	0.00835	0.00585
77 ..	0.68110	0.46479	0.31777	0.21766	0.14937	0.10269	0.07073	0.04880	0.03373	0.02336	0.01620	0.01126	0.00784	0.00546
78 ..	0.67772	0.46019	0.31308	0.21340	0.14573	0.09970	0.06834	0.04692	0.03228	0.02225	0.01536	0.01062	0.00736	0.00511
79 ..	0.67434	0.45563	0.30845	0.20921	0.14217	0.09680	0.06603	0.04512	0.03089	0.02119	0.01456	0.01002	0.00691	0.00477
80 ..	0.67099	0.45112	0.30389	0.20511	0.13870	0.09398	0.06379	0.04338	0.02956	0.02018	0.01380	0.00945	0.00649	0.00446
81 ..	0.66765	0.44665	0.29940	0.20109	0.13532	0.09124	0.06164	0.04172	0.02829	0.01922	0.01308	0.00892	0.00609	0.00417
82 ..	0.66433	0.44223	0.29497	0.19715	0.13202	0.08858	0.05955	0.04011	0.02707	0.01830	0.01240	0.00841	0.00572	0.00390
83 ..	0.66102	0.43785	0.29062	0.19328	0.12880	0.08600	0.05754	0.03857	0.02590	0.01743	0.01175	0.00794	0.00537	0.00364
84 ..	0.65773	0.43352	0.28632	0.18949	0.12566	0.08350	0.05559	0.03709	0.02479	0.01660	0.01114	0.00749	0.00504	0.00340
85 ..	0.65446	0.42922	0.28209	0.18577	0.12259	0.08107	0.05371	0.03566	0.02372	0.01581	0.01056	0.00706	0.00473	0.00318
86 ..	0.65121	0.42497	0.27792	0.18213	0.11960	0.07870	0.05190	0.03429	0.02270	0.01506	0.01001	0.00666	0.00445	0.00297
87 ..	0.64797	0.42077	0.27381	0.17856	0.11669	0.07641	0.05014	0.03297	0.02172	0.01434	0.00948	0.00629	0.00417	0.00278
88 ..	0.64474	0.41660	0.26977	0.17506	0.11384	0.07419	0.04845	0.03170	0.02079	0.01366	0.00899	0.00593	0.00392	0.00260
89 ..	0.64154	0.41248	0.26578	0.17163	0.11106	0.07203	0.04681	0.03048	0.01989	0.01301	0.00852	0.00559	0.00368	0.00243
90 ..	0.63834	0.40839	0.26185	0.16826	0.10836	0.06993	0.04522	0.02931	0.01903	0.01239	0.00808	0.00528	0.00346	0.00227
91 ..	0.63517	0.40435	0.25798	0.16496	0.10571	0.06789	0.04369	0.02818	0.01821	0.01180	0.00766	0.00498	0.00324	0.00212
92 ..	0.63201	0.40034	0.25417	0.16173	0.10313	0.06591	0.04222	0.02710	0.01743	0.01124	0.00726	0.00470	0.00305	0.00198
93 ..	0.62886	0.39638	0.25041	0.15856	0.10062	0.06399	0.04079	0.02606	0.01668	0.01070	0.00688	0.00443	0.00286	0.00185
94 ..	0.62573	0.39246	0.24671	0.15545	0.09816	0.06213	0.03941	0.02505	0.01596	0.01019	0.00652	0.00418	0.00269	0.00173
95 ..	0.62262	0.38857	0.24307	0.15240	0.09577	0.06032	0.03808	0.02409	0.01527	0.00971	0.00618	0.00394	0.00252	0.00162
96 ..	0.61952	0.38472	0.23947	0.14941	0.09343	0.05856	0.03679	0.02316	0.01462	0.00924	0.00586	0.00372	0.00237	0.00151
97 ..	0.61644	0.38091	0.23594	0.14648	0.09116	0.05686	0.03555	0.02227	0.01399	0.00880	0.00555	0.00351	0.00222	0.00141
98 ..	0.61337	0.37714	0.23245	0.14361	0.08893	0.05520	0.03434	0.02142	0.01338	0.00838	0.00526	0.00331	0.00209	0.00132
99 ..	0.61032	0.37341	0.22901	0.14079	0.08676	0.05359	0.03318	0.02059	0.01281	0.00798	0.00499	0.00312	0.00196	0.00123
100 ..	0.60729	0.36971	0.22563	0.13803	0.08465	0.05203	0.03026	0.01980	0.01226	0.00760	0.00473	0.00295	0.00184	0.00115
101 ..	0.60427	0.36605	0.22230	0.13533	0.08258	0.05052	0.03098	0.01904	0.01173	0.00724	0.00448	0.00278	0.00173	0.00108
102 ..	0.60126	0.36243	0.21901	0.13267	0.08057	0.04905	0.02993	0.01831	0.01122	0.00690	0.00425	0.00262	0.00162	0.00101
103 ..	0.59827	0.35884	0.21577	0.13007	0.07860	0.04762	0.02892	0.01760	0.01074	0.00657	0.00403	0.00247	0.00152	0.00094
104 ..	0.59529	0.35529	0.21258	0.12752	0.07669	0.04623	0.02794	0.01693	0.01028	0.00626	0.00382	0.00233	0.00143	0.00088
105 ..	0.59233	0.35177	0.20944	0.12502	0.07482	0.04488	0.02699	0.01627	0.00984	0.00596	0.00362	0.00220	0.00134	0.00082
106 ..	0.58938	0.34828	0.20635	0.12257	0.07299	0.04358	0.02608	0.01565	0.00941	0.00567	0.00343	0.00208	0.00126	0.00077
107 ..	0.58645	0.34484	0.20330	0.12017	0.07121	0.04231	0.02520	0.01505	0.00901	0.00540	0.00325	0.00196	0.00118	0.00072
108 ..	0.58353	0.34142	0.20029	0.11781	0.06947	0.04108	0.02435	0.01447	0.00862	0.00515	0.00308	0.00185	0.00111	0.00067
109 ..	0.58063	0.33804	0.19733	0.11550	0.06778	0.03988	0.02352	0.01391	0.00825	0.00490	0.00292	0.00174	0.00104	0.00063
110 ..	0.57774	0.33469	0.19442	0.11324	0.06613	0.03872	0.02273	0.01338	0.00789	0.00467	0.00277	0.00165	0.00098	0.00059
111 ..	0.57487	0.33138	0.19154	0.11101	0.06451	0.03759	0.02196	0.01286	0.00755	0.00445	0.00262	0.00155	0.00092	0.00055
112 ..	0.57201	0.32810	0.18871	0.10884	0.06294	0.03649	0.02122	0.01237	0.00723	0.00423	0.00249	0.00146	0.00086	0.00051
113 ..	0.56916	0.32485	0.18592	0.10670	0.06140	0.03543	0.02050	0.01189	0.00692	0.00403	0.00236	0.00138	0.00081	0.00048
114 ..	0.56633	0.32164	0.18318	0.10461	0.05991	0.03440	0.01981	0.01143	0.00662	0.00384	0.00223	0.00130	0.00076	0.00045
115 ..	0.56351	0.31845	0.18047	0.10256	0.05845	0.03340	0.01914	0.01099	0.00633	0.00366	0.00212	0.00123	0.00072	0.00042
116 ..	0.56071	0.31530	0.17780	0.10055	0.05702	0.03243	0.01849	0.01057	0.00606	0.00348	0.00201	0.00116	0.00067	0.00039
117 ..	0.55792	0.31218	0.17518	0.09858	0.05563	0.03148	0.01786	0.01016	0.00580	0.00332	0.00190	0.00109	0.00063	0.00036
118 ..	0.55514	0.30908	0.17259	0.09665	0.05427	0.03056	0.01726	0.00977	0.00555	0.00316	0.00180	0.00103	0.00059	0.00034
119 ..	0.55238	0.30602	0.17004	0.09475	0.05295	0.02967	0.01668	0.00940	0.00531	0.00301	0.00171	0.00097	0.00056	0.00032
120 ..	0.54963	0.30299	0.16752	0.09289	0.05166	0.02881	0.01611	0.00904	0.00508	0.00287	0.00162	0.00092	0.00052	0.00030

Table 3 (*continued*): Present value of $1 at compound interest: 7.5%–14%

Period	7.5%	8%	8.5%	9%	9.5%	10%	10.5%	11%	11.5%	12%	12.5%	13%	13.5%	14%
1	0.93023	0.92593	0.92166	0.91743	0.91324	0.90909	0.90498	0.90090	0.89686	0.89286	0.88889	0.88496	0.88106	0.87719
2	0.86533	0.85734	0.84946	0.84168	0.83401	0.82645	0.81898	0.81162	0.80436	0.79719	0.79012	0.78315	0.77626	0.76947
3	0.80496	0.79383	0.78291	0.77218	0.76165	0.75131	0.74116	0.73119	0.72140	0.71178	0.70233	0.69305	0.68393	0.67497
4	0.74880	0.73503	0.72157	0.70843	0.69557	0.68301	0.67073	0.65873	0.64699	0.63553	0.62430	0.61332	0.60258	0.59208
5	0.69656	0.68058	0.66505	0.64993	0.63523	0.62092	0.60700	0.59345	0.58026	0.56743	0.55493	0.54276	0.53091	0.51937
6	0.64796	0.63017	0.61295	0.59627	0.58012	0.56447	0.54932	0.53464	0.52042	0.50663	0.49327	0.48032	0.46776	0.45559
7	0.60275	0.58349	0.56493	0.54703	0.52979	0.51316	0.49712	0.48166	0.46674	0.45235	0.43846	0.42506	0.41213	0.39964
8	0.56070	0.54027	0.52067	0.50187	0.48382	0.46651	0.44989	0.43393	0.41860	0.40388	0.38974	0.37616	0.36311	0.35056
9	0.52158	0.50025	0.47988	0.46043	0.44185	0.42410	0.40714	0.39092	0.37543	0.36061	0.34644	0.33288	0.31992	0.30751
10	0.48519	0.46319	0.44229	0.42241	0.40351	0.38554	0.36845	0.35218	0.33671	0.32197	0.30795	0.29459	0.28187	0.26974
11	0.45134	0.42888	0.40764	0.38753	0.36851	0.35049	0.33344	0.31728	0.30198	0.28748	0.27373	0.26070	0.24834	0.23662
12	0.41985	0.39711	0.37570	0.35553	0.33654	0.31863	0.30175	0.28584	0.27083	0.25668	0.24332	0.23071	0.21880	0.20756
13	0.39056	0.36770	0.34627	0.32618	0.30734	0.28966	0.27308	0.25751	0.24290	0.22917	0.21628	0.20416	0.19278	0.18207
14	0.36331	0.34046	0.31914	0.29925	0.28067	0.26333	0.24713	0.23199	0.21785	0.20462	0.19225	0.18068	0.16985	0.15971
15	0.33797	0.31524	0.29414	0.27454	0.25632	0.23939	0.22365	0.20900	0.19538	0.18270	0.17089	0.15989	0.14964	0.14010
16	0.31439	0.29189	0.27110	0.25187	0.23409	0.21763	0.20240	0.18829	0.17523	0.16312	0.15190	0.14150	0.13185	0.12289
17	0.29245	0.27027	0.24986	0.23107	0.21378	0.19784	0.18316	0.16963	0.15715	0.14564	0.13502	0.12522	0.11616	0.10780
18	0.27205	0.25025	0.23028	0.21199	0.19523	0.17986	0.16576	0.15282	0.14095	0.13004	0.12002	0.11081	0.10235	0.09456
19	0.25307	0.23171	0.21224	0.19449	0.17829	0.16351	0.15001	0.13768	0.12641	0.11611	0.10668	0.09806	0.09017	0.08295
20	0.23541	0.21455	0.19562	0.17843	0.16282	0.14864	0.13575	0.12403	0.11337	0.10367	0.09483	0.08678	0.07945	0.07276
21	0.21899	0.19866	0.18029	0.16370	0.14870	0.13513	0.12285	0.11174	0.10168	0.09256	0.08429	0.07680	0.07000	0.06383
22	0.20371	0.18394	0.16617	0.15018	0.13580	0.12285	0.11118	0.10067	0.09119	0.08264	0.07493	0.06796	0.06167	0.05599
23	0.18950	0.17032	0.15315	0.13778	0.12402	0.11168	0.10062	0.09069	0.08179	0.07379	0.06660	0.06014	0.05434	0.04911
24	0.17628	0.15770	0.14115	0.12640	0.11326	0.10153	0.09106	0.08170	0.07335	0.06588	0.05920	0.05323	0.04787	0.04308
25	0.16398	0.14602	0.13009	0.11597	0.10343	0.09230	0.08240	0.07361	0.06579	0.05882	0.05262	0.04710	0.04218	0.03779
26	0.15254	0.13520	0.11990	0.10639	0.09446	0.08391	0.07457	0.06631	0.05900	0.05252	0.04678	0.04168	0.03716	0.03315
27	0.14190	0.12519	0.11051	0.09761	0.08626	0.07628	0.06749	0.05974	0.05291	0.04689	0.04158	0.03689	0.03274	0.02908
28	0.13200	0.11591	0.10185	0.08955	0.07878	0.06934	0.06107	0.05382	0.04746	0.04187	0.03696	0.03264	0.02885	0.02551
29	0.12279	0.10733	0.09387	0.08215	0.07194	0.06304	0.05527	0.04849	0.04256	0.03738	0.03285	0.02889	0.02542	0.02237
30	0.11422	0.09938	0.08652	0.07537	0.06570	0.05731	0.05002	0.04368	0.03817	0.03338	0.02920	0.02557	0.02239	0.01963
31	0.10625	0.09202	0.07974	0.06915	0.06000	0.05210	0.04527	0.03935	0.03424	0.02980	0.02596	0.02262	0.01973	0.01722
32	0.09884	0.08520	0.07349	0.06344	0.05480	0.04736	0.04096	0.03545	0.03070	0.02661	0.02307	0.02002	0.01738	0.01510
33	0.09194	0.07889	0.06774	0.05820	0.05004	0.04306	0.03707	0.03194	0.02754	0.02376	0.02051	0.01772	0.01532	0.01325
34	0.08553	0.07305	0.06243	0.05339	0.04570	0.03914	0.03355	0.02878	0.02470	0.02121	0.01823	0.01568	0.01349	0.01162
35	0.07956	0.06763	0.05754	0.04899	0.04174	0.03558	0.03036	0.02592	0.02215	0.01894	0.01621	0.01388	0.01189	0.01019
36	0.07401	0.06262	0.05303	0.04494	0.03811	0.03235	0.02748	0.02335	0.01987	0.01691	0.01440	0.01228	0.01047	0.00894
37	0.06885	0.05799	0.04888	0.04123	0.03481	0.02941	0.02487	0.02104	0.01782	0.01510	0.01280	0.01087	0.00923	0.00784
38	0.06404	0.05369	0.04505	0.03783	0.03179	0.02673	0.02250	0.01896	0.01598	0.01348	0.01138	0.00962	0.00813	0.00688
39	0.05958	0.04971	0.04152	0.03470	0.02903	0.02430	0.02036	0.01708	0.01433	0.01204	0.01012	0.00851	0.00716	0.00604
40	0.05542	0.04603	0.03827	0.03184	0.02651	0.02209	0.01843	0.01538	0.01285	0.01075	0.00899	0.00753	0.00631	0.00529
41	0.05155	0.04262	0.03527	0.02921	0.02421	0.02009	0.01668	0.01386	0.01153	0.00960	0.00799	0.00666	0.00556	0.00464
42	0.04796	0.03946	0.03251	0.02680	0.02211	0.01826	0.01509	0.01249	0.01034	0.00857	0.00711	0.00590	0.00490	0.00407
43	0.04461	0.03654	0.02996	0.02458	0.02019	0.01660	0.01366	0.01125	0.00927	0.00765	0.00632	0.00522	0.00432	0.00357
44	0.04150	0.03383	0.02761	0.02255	0.01844	0.01509	0.01236	0.01013	0.00832	0.00683	0.00561	0.00462	0.00380	0.00313
45	0.03860	0.03133	0.02545	0.02069	0.01684	0.01372	0.01119	0.00913	0.00746	0.00610	0.00499	0.00409	0.00335	0.00275
46	0.03591	0.02901	0.02345	0.01898	0.01538	0.01247	0.01012	0.00823	0.00669	0.00544	0.00444	0.00362	0.00295	0.00241
47	0.03340	0.02686	0.02162	0.01742	0.01405	0.01134	0.00916	0.00741	0.00600	0.00486	0.00394	0.00320	0.00260	0.00212
48	0.03107	0.02487	0.01992	0.01598	0.01283	0.01031	0.00829	0.00668	0.00538	0.00434	0.00350	0.00283	0.00229	0.00186
49	0.02891	0.02303	0.01836	0.01466	0.01171	0.00937	0.00750	0.00601	0.00483	0.00388	0.00312	0.00251	0.00202	0.00163
50	0.02689	0.02132	0.01692	0.01345	0.01070	0.00852	0.00679	0.00542	0.00433	0.00346	0.00277	0.00222	0.00178	0.00143
51	0.02501	0.01974	0.01560	0.01234	0.00977	0.00774	0.00615	0.00488	0.00388	0.00309	0.00246	0.00196	0.00157	0.00125
52	0.02327	0.01828	0.01438	0.01132	0.00892	0.00704	0.00556	0.00440	0.00348	0.00276	0.00219	0.00174	0.00138	0.00110
53	0.02164	0.01693	0.01325	0.01038	0.00815	0.00640	0.00503	0.00396	0.00312	0.00246	0.00194	0.00154	0.00122	0.00096
54	0.02013	0.01567	0.01221	0.00953	0.00744	0.00582	0.00455	0.00357	0.00280	0.00220	0.00173	0.00136	0.00107	0.00085
55	0.01873	0.01451	0.01126	0.00874	0.00680	0.00529	0.00412	0.00322	0.00251	0.00196	0.00154	0.00120	0.00094	0.00074
56	0.01742	0.01344	0.01037	0.00802	0.00621	0.00481	0.00373	0.00290	0.00225	0.00175	0.00137	0.00107	0.00083	0.00065
57	0.01621	0.01244	0.00956	0.00736	0.00567	0.00437	0.00338	0.00261	0.00202	0.00157	0.00121	0.00094	0.00073	0.00057
58	0.01508	0.01152	0.00881	0.00675	0.00518	0.00397	0.00305	0.00235	0.00181	0.00140	0.00108	0.00083	0.00065	0.00050
59	0.01402	0.01067	0.00812	0.00619	0.00473	0.00361	0.00276	0.00212	0.00162	0.00125	0.00096	0.00074	0.00057	0.00044
60	0.01305	0.00988	0.00749	0.00568	0.00432	0.00328	0.00250	0.00191	0.00146	0.00111	0.00085	0.00065	0.00050	0.00039

Period	7.5%	8%	8.5%	9%	9.5%	10%	10.5%	11%	11.5%	12%	12.5%	13%	13.5%	14%
61 ..	0.01214	0.00914	0.00690	0.00521	0.00394	0.00299	0.00226	0.00172	0.00131	0.00099	0.00076	0.00058	0.00044	0.00034
62 ..	0.01129	0.00847	0.00636	0.00478	0.00360	0.00271	0.00205	0.00155	0.00117	0.00089	0.00067	0.00051	0.00039	0.00030
63 ..	0.01050	0.00784	0.00586	0.00439	0.00329	0.00247	0.00185	0.00140	0.00105	0.00079	0.00060	0.00045	0.00034	0.00026
64 ..	0.00977	0.00726	0.00540	0.00402	0.00300	0.00224	0.00168	0.00126	0.00094	0.00071	0.00053	0.00040	0.00030	0.00023
65 ..	0.00909	0.00672	0.00498	0.00369	0.00274	0.00204	0.00152	0.00113	0.00085	0.00063	0.00047	0.00035	0.00027	0.00020
66 ..	0.00845	0.00622	0.00459	0.00339	0.00250	0.00185	0.00137	0.00102	0.00076	0.00056	0.00042	0.00031	0.00023	0.00018
67 ..	0.00786	0.00576	0.00423	0.00311	0.00229	0.00169	0.00124	0.00092	0.00068	0.00050	0.00037	0.00028	0.00021	0.00015
68 ..	0.00732	0.00534	0.00390	0.00285	0.00209	0.00153	0.00113	0.00083	0.00061	0.00045	0.00033	0.00025	0.00018	0.00014
69 ..	0.00680	0.00494	0.00359	0.00262	0.00191	0.00139	0.00102	0.00075	0.00055	0.00040	0.00030	0.00022	0.00016	0.00012
70 ..	0.00633	0.00457	0.00331	0.00240	0.00174	0.00127	0.00092	0.00067	0.00049	0.00036	0.00026	0.00019	0.00014	0.00010
71 ..	0.00589	0.00424	0.00305	0.00220	0.00159	0.00115	0.00083	0.00061	0.00044	0.00032	0.00023	0.00017	0.00012	0.00009
72 ..	0.00548	0.00392	0.00281	0.00202	0.00145	0.00105	0.00075	0.00055	0.00039	0.00029	0.00021	0.00015	0.00011	0.00008
73 ..	0.00510	0.00363	0.00259	0.00185	0.00133	0.00095	0.00068	0.00049	0.00035	0.00026	0.00018	0.00013	0.00010	0.00007
74 ..	0.00474	0.00336	0.00239	0.00170	0.00121	0.00086	0.00062	0.00044	0.00032	0.00023	0.00016	0.00012	0.00009	0.00006
75 ..	0.00441	0.00311	0.00220	0.00156	0.00111	0.00079	0.00056	0.00040	0.00028	0.00020	0.00015	0.00010	0.00008	0.00005
76 ..	0.00410	0.00288	0.00203	0.00143	0.00101	0.00071	0.00051	0.00036	0.00026	0.00018	0.00013	0.00009	0.00007	0.00005
77 ..	0.00382	0.00267	0.00187	0.00131	0.00092	0.00065	0.00046	0.00032	0.00023	0.00016	0.00012	0.00008	0.00006	0.00004
78 ..	0.00355	0.00247	0.00172	0.00120	0.00084	0.00059	0.00041	0.00029	0.00021	0.00014	0.00010	0.00007	0.00005	0.00004
79 ..	0.00330	0.00229	0.00159	0.00110	0.00077	0.00054	0.00038	0.00026	0.00018	0.00013	0.00009	0.00006	0.00005	0.00003
80 ..	0.00307	0.00212	0.00146	0.00101	0.00070	0.00049	0.00034	0.00024	0.00017	0.00012	0.00008	0.00006	0.00004	0.00003
81 ..	0.00286	0.00196	0.00135	0.00093	0.00064	0.00044	0.00031	0.00021	0.00015	0.00010	0.00007	0.00005	0.00004	0.00002
82 ..	0.00266	0.00182	0.00124	0.00085	0.00059	0.00040	0.00028	0.00019	0.00013	0.00009	0.00006	0.00004	0.00003	0.00002
83 ..	0.00247	0.00168	0.00115	0.00078	0.00054	0.00037	0.00025	0.00017	0.00012	0.00008	0.00006	0.00004	0.00003	0.00002
84 ..	0.00230	0.00156	0.00106	0.00072	0.00049	0.00033	0.00023	0.00016	0.00011	0.00007	0.00005	0.00003	0.00002	0.00002
85 ..	0.00214	0.00144	0.00097	0.00066	0.00045	0.00030	0.00021	0.00014	0.00010	0.00007	0.00004	0.00003	0.00002	0.00001
86 ..	0.00199	0.00134	0.00090	0.00060	0.00041	0.00028	0.00019	0.00013	0.00009	0.00006	0.00004	0.00003	0.00002	0.00001
87 ..	0.00185	0.00124	0.00083	0.00055	0.00037	0.00025	0.00017	0.00011	0.00008	0.00005	0.00004	0.00002	0.00002	0.00001
88 ..	0.00172	0.00114	0.00076	0.00051	0.00034	0.00023	0.00015	0.00010	0.00007	0.00005	0.00003	0.00002	0.00001	0.00001
89 ..	0.00160	0.00106	0.00070	0.00047	0.00031	0.00021	0.00014	0.00009	0.00006	0.00004	0.00003	0.00002	0.00001	0.00001
90 ..	0.00149	0.00098	0.00065	0.00043	0.00028	0.00019	0.00013	0.00008	0.00006	0.00004	0.00002	0.00002	0.00001	0.00001
91 ..	0.00139	0.00091	0.00060	0.00039	0.00026	0.00017	0.00011	0.00008	0.00005	0.00003	0.00002	0.00001	0.00001	0.00001
92 ..	0.00129	0.00084	0.00055	0.00036	0.00024	0.00016	0.00010	0.00007	0.00004	0.00003	0.00002	0.00001	0.00001	0.00001
93 ..	0.00120	0.00078	0.00051	0.00033	0.00022	0.00014	0.00009	0.00006	0.00004	0.00003	0.00002	0.00001	0.00001	0.00001
94 ..	0.00112	0.00072	0.00047	0.00030	0.00020	0.00013	0.00008	0.00005	0.00004	0.00002	0.00002	0.00001	0.00001	0.00000
95 ..	0.00104	0.00067	0.00043	0.00028	0.00018	0.00012	0.00008	0.00005	0.00003	0.00002	0.00001	0.00001	0.00001	0.00000
96 ..	0.00097	0.00062	0.00040	0.00026	0.00016	0.00011	0.00007	0.00004	0.00003	0.00002	0.00001	0.00001	0.00001	0.00000
97 ..	0.00090	0.00057	0.00037	0.00023	0.00015	0.00010	0.00006	0.00004	0.00003	0.00002	0.00001	0.00001	0.00000	0.00000
98 ..	0.00084	0.00053	0.00034	0.00021	0.00014	0.00009	0.00006	0.00004	0.00002	0.00002	0.00001	0.00001	0.00000	0.00000
99 ..	0.00078	0.00049	0.00031	0.00020	0.00013	0.00008	0.00005	0.00003	0.00002	0.00001	0.00001	0.00001	0.00000	0.00000
100 ..	0.00072	0.00045	0.00029	0.00018	0.00011	0.00007	0.00005	0.00003	0.00002	0.00001	0.00001	0.00000	0.00000	0.00000
101 ..	0.00067	0.00042	0.00026	0.00017	0.00010	0.00007	0.00004	0.00003	0.00002	0.00001	0.00001	0.00000	0.00000	0.00000
102 ..	0.00063	0.00039	0.00024	0.00015	0.00010	0.00006	0.00004	0.00002	0.00002	0.00001	0.00001	0.00000	0.00000	0.00000
103 ..	0.00058	0.00036	0.00022	0.00014	0.00009	0.00005	0.00003	0.00002	0.00001	0.00001	0.00001	0.00000	0.00000	0.00000
104 ..	0.00054	0.00033	0.00021	0.00013	0.00008	0.00005	0.00003	0.00002	0.00001	0.00001	0.00001	0.00000	0.00000	0.00000
105 ..	0.00050	0.00031	0.00019	0.00012	0.00007	0.00005	0.00003	0.00002	0.00001	0.00001	0.00000	0.00000	0.00000	0.00000
106 ..	0.00047	0.00029	0.00018	0.00011	0.00007	0.00004	0.00003	0.00002	0.00001	0.00001	0.00000	0.00000	0.00000	0.00000
107 ..	0.00044	0.00027	0.00016	0.00010	0.00006	0.00004	0.00002	0.00001	0.00001	0.00001	0.00000	0.00000	0.00000	0.00000
108 ..	0.00041	0.00025	0.00015	0.00009	0.00006	0.00003	0.00002	0.00001	0.00001	0.00000	0.00000	0.00000	0.00000	0.00000
109 ..	0.00038	0.00023	0.00014	0.00008	0.00005	0.00003	0.00002	0.00001	0.00001	0.00000	0.00000	0.00000	0.00000	0.00000
110 ..	0.00035	0.00021	0.00013	0.00008	0.00005	0.00003	0.00002	0.00001	0.00001	0.00000	0.00000	0.00000	0.00000	0.00000
111 ..	0.00033	0.00019	0.00012	0.00007	0.00004	0.00003	0.00002	0.00001	0.00001	0.00000	0.00000	0.00000	0.00000	0.00000
112 ..	0.00030	0.00018	0.00011	0.00006	0.00004	0.00002	0.00001	0.00001	0.00001	0.00000	0.00000	0.00000	0.00000	0.00000
113 ..	0.00028	0.00017	0.00010	0.00006	0.00004	0.00002	0.00001	0.00001	0.00000	0.00000	0.00000	0.00000	0.00000	0.00000
114 ..	0.00026	0.00015	0.00009	0.00005	0.00003	0.00002	0.00001	0.00001	0.00000	0.00000	0.00000	0.00000	0.00000	0.00000
115 ..	0.00024	0.00014	0.00008	0.00005	0.00003	0.00002	0.00001	0.00001	0.00000	0.00000	0.00000	0.00000	0.00000	0.00000
116 ..	0.00023	0.00013	0.00008	0.00005	0.00003	0.00002	0.00001	0.00001	0.00000	0.00000	0.00000	0.00000	0.00000	0.00000
117 ..	0.00021	0.00012	0.00007	0.00004	0.00002	0.00001	0.00001	0.00000	0.00000	0.00000	0.00000	0.00000	0.00000	0.00000
118 ..	0.00020	0.00011	0.00007	0.00004	0.00002	0.00001	0.00001	0.00000	0.00000	0.00000	0.00000	0.00000	0.00000	0.00000
119 ..	0.00018	0.00011	0.00006	0.00004	0.00002	0.00001	0.00001	0.00000	0.00000	0.00000	0.00000	0.00000	0.00000	0.00000
120 ..	0.00017	0.00010	0.00006	0.00003	0.00002	0.00001	0.00001	0.00000	0.00000	0.00000	0.00000	0.00000	0.00000	0.00000

Table 3 (*concluded*): Present value of $1: 14.5%–20%

Period	14.5%	15%	15.5%	16%	16.5%	17%	17.5%	18%	18.5%	19%	19.5%	20%
1	0.87336	0.86957	0.86580	0.86207	0.85837	0.85470	0.85106	0.84746	0.84388	0.84034	0.83682	0.83333
2	0.76276	0.75614	0.74961	0.74316	0.73680	0.73051	0.72431	0.71818	0.71214	0.70616	0.70027	0.69444
3	0.66617	0.65752	0.64901	0.64066	0.63244	0.62437	0.61643	0.60863	0.60096	0.59342	0.58600	0.57870
4	0.58181	0.57175	0.56192	0.55229	0.54287	0.53365	0.52462	0.51579	0.50714	0.49867	0.49038	0.48225
5	0.50813	0.49718	0.48651	0.47611	0.46598	0.45611	0.44649	0.43711	0.42796	0.41905	0.41036	0.40188
6	0.44378	0.43233	0.42122	0.41044	0.39999	0.38984	0.37999	0.37043	0.36115	0.35214	0.34339	0.33490
7	0.38758	0.37594	0.36469	0.35383	0.34334	0.33320	0.32340	0.31393	0.30477	0.29592	0.28736	0.27908
8	0.33850	0.32690	0.31575	0.30503	0.29471	0.28478	0.27523	0.26604	0.25719	0.24867	0.24047	0.23257
9	0.29563	0.28426	0.27338	0.26295	0.25297	0.24340	0.23424	0.22546	0.21704	0.20897	0.20123	0.19381
10	0.25819	0.24718	0.23669	0.22668	0.21714	0.20804	0.19935	0.19106	0.18315	0.17560	0.16839	0.16151
11	0.22550	0.21494	0.20493	0.19542	0.18639	0.17781	0.16966	0.16192	0.15456	0.14757	0.14091	0.13459
12	0.19694	0.18691	0.17743	0.16846	0.15999	0.15197	0.14439	0.13722	0.13043	0.12400	0.11792	0.11216
13	0.17200	0.16253	0.15362	0.14523	0.13733	0.12989	0.12289	0.11629	0.11007	0.10421	0.09868	0.09346
14	0.15022	0.14133	0.13300	0.12520	0.11788	0.11102	0.10459	0.09855	0.09288	0.08757	0.08258	0.07789
15	0.13120	0.12289	0.11515	0.10793	0.10118	0.09489	0.08901	0.08352	0.07838	0.07359	0.06910	0.06491
16	0.11458	0.10686	0.09970	0.09304	0.08685	0.08110	0.07575	0.07078	0.06615	0.06184	0.05782	0.05409
17	0.10007	0.09293	0.08632	0.08021	0.07455	0.06932	0.06447	0.05998	0.05582	0.05196	0.04839	0.04507
18	0.08740	0.04081	0.07474	0.06914	0.06399	0.05925	0.05487	0.05083	0.04711	0.04367	0.04049	0.03756
19	0.07633	0.07027	0.06471	0.05961	0.05493	0.05064	0.04670	0.04308	0.03975	0.03670	0.03389	0.03130
20	0.06666	0.06110	0.05602	0.05139	0.04715	0.04328	0.03974	0.03651	0.03355	0.03084	0.02836	0.02608
21	0.05822	0.05313	0.04850	0.04430	0.04047	0.03699	0.03382	0.03094	0.02831	0.02591	0.02373	0.02174
22	0.05085	0.04620	0.04199	0.03819	0.03474	0.03162	0.02879	0.02622	0.02389	0.02178	0.01986	0.01811
23	0.04441	0.04017	0.03636	0.03292	0.02982	0.02702	0.02450	0.02222	0.02016	0.01830	0.01662	0.01509
24	0.03879	0.03493	0.03148	0.02838	0.02560	0.02310	0.02085	0.01883	0.01701	0.01538	0.01390	0.01258
25	0.03387	0.03038	0.02726	0.02447	0.02197	0.01974	0.01774	0.01596	0.01436	0.01292	0.01164	0.01048
26	0.02958	0.02642	0.02360	0.02109	0.01886	0.01687	0.01510	0.01352	0.01211	0.01086	0.00974	0.00874
27	0.02584	0.02297	0.02043	0.01818	0.01619	0.01442	0.01285	0.01146	0.01022	0.00912	0.00815	0.00728
28	0.02257	0.01997	0.01769	0.01567	0.01390	0.01233	0.01094	0.00971	0.00863	0.00767	0.00682	0.00607
29	0.01971	0.01737	0.01532	0.01351	0.01193	0.01053	0.00931	0.00823	0.00728	0.00644	0.00571	0.00506
30	0.01721	0.01510	0.01326	0.01165	0.01024	0.00900	0.00792	0.00697	0.00614	0.00541	0.00477	0.00421
31	0.01503	0.01313	0.01148	0.01004	0.00879	0.00770	0.00674	0.00591	0.00518	0.00455	0.00400	0.00351
32	0.01313	0.01142	0.00994	0.00866	0.00754	0.00658	0.00574	0.00501	0.00438	0.00382	0.00334	0.00293
33	0.01147	0.00993	0.00861	0.00746	0.00648	0.00562	0.00488	0.00425	0.00369	0.00321	0.00280	0.00244
34	0.01001	0.00864	0.00745	0.00643	0.00556	0.00480	0.00416	0.00360	0.00312	0.00270	0.00234	0.00203
35	0.00875	0.00751	0.00645	0.00555	0.00477	0.00411	0.00354	0.00305	0.00263	0.00227	0.00196	0.00169
36	0.00764	0.00653	0.00559	0.00478	0.00410	0.00351	0.00301	0.00258	0.00222	0.00191	0.00164	0.00141
37	0.00667	0.00568	0.00484	0.00412	0.00352	0.00300	0.00256	0.00219	0.00187	0.00160	0.00137	0.00118
38	0.00583	0.00494	0.00419	0.00355	0.00302	0.00256	0.00218	0.00186	0.00158	0.00135	0.00115	0.00098
39	0.00509	0.00429	0.00362	0.00306	0.00259	0.00219	0.00186	0.00157	0.00133	0.00113	0.00096	0.00082
40	0.00444	0.00373	0.00314	0.00264	0.00222	0.00187	0.00158	0.00133	0.00113	0.00095	0.00080	0.00068
41	0.00388	0.00325	0.00272	0.00228	0.00191	0.00160	0.00134	0.00113	0.00095	0.00080	0.00067	0.00057
42	0.00339	0.00282	0.00235	0.00196	0.00164	0.00137	0.00114	0.00096	0.00080	0.00067	0.00056	0.00047
43	0.00296	0.00245	0.00204	0.00169	0.00141	0.00117	0.00097	0.00081	0.00068	0.00056	0.00047	0.00039
44	0.00259	0.00213	0.00176	0.00146	0.00121	0.00100	0.00083	0.00069	0.00057	0.00047	0.00039	0.00033
45	0.00226	0.00186	0.00153	0.00126	0.00104	0.00085	0.00071	0.00058	0.00048	0.00040	0.00033	0.00027
46	0.00197	0.00161	0.00132	0.00108	0.00089	0.00073	0.00060	0.00049	0.00041	0.00033	0.00028	0.00023
47	0.00172	0.00140	0.00114	0.00093	0.00076	0.00062	0.00051	0.00042	0.00034	0.00028	0.00023	0.00019
48	0.00150	0.00122	0.00099	0.00081	0.00066	0.00053	0.00043	0.00035	0.00029	0.00024	0.00019	0.00016
49	0.00131	0.00106	0.00086	0.00069	0.00056	0.00046	0.00037	0.00030	0.00024	0.00020	0.00016	0.00013
50	0.00115	0.00092	0.00074	0.00060	0.00048	0.00039	0.00031	0.00025	0.00021	0.00017	0.00014	0.00011
51	0.00100	0.00080	0.00064	0.00052	0.00041	0.00033	0.00027	0.00022	0.00017	0.00014	0.00011	0.00009
52	0.00088	0.00070	0.00056	0.00044	0.00036	0.00028	0.00023	0.00018	0.00015	0.00012	0.00009	0.00008
53	0.00076	0.00061	0.00048	0.00038	0.00031	0.00024	0.00019	0.00015	0.00012	0.00010	0.00008	0.00006
54	0.00067	0.00053	0.00042	0.00033	0.00026	0.00021	0.00017	0.00013	0.00010	0.00008	0.00007	0.00005
55	0.00058	0.00046	0.00036	0.00028	0.00022	0.00018	0.00014	0.00011	0.00009	0.00007	0.00006	0.00004
56	0.00051	0.00040	0.00031	0.00025	0.00019	0.00015	0.00012	0.00009	0.00007	0.00006	0.00005	0.00004
57	0.00044	0.00035	0.00027	0.00021	0.00017	0.00013	0.00010	0.00008	0.00006	0.00005	0.00004	0.00003
58	0.00039	0.00030	0.00023	0.00018	0.00014	0.00011	0.00009	0.00007	0.00005	0.00004	0.00003	0.00003
59	0.00034	0.00026	0.00020	0.00016	0.00012	0.00009	0.00007	0.00006	0.00004	0.00003	0.00003	0.00002
60	0.00030	0.00023	0.00018	0.00014	0.00010	0.00008	0.00006	0.00005	0.00004	0.00003	0.00002	0.00002

Period	14.5%	15%	15.5%	16%	16.5%	17%	17.5%	18%	18.5%	19%	19.5%	20%
61	0.00026	0.00020	0.00015	0.00012	0.00009	0.00007	0.00005	0.00004	0.00003	0.00002	0.00002	0.00001
62	0.00023	0.00017	0.00013	0.00010	0.00008	0.00006	0.00005	0.00003	0.00003	0.00002	0.00002	0.00001
63	0.00020	0.00015	0.00011	0.00009	0.00007	0.00005	0.00004	0.00003	0.00002	0.00002	0.00001	0.00001
64	0.00017	0.00013	0.00010	0.00007	0.00006	0.00004	0.00003	0.00003	0.00002	0.00001	0.00001	0.00001
65	0.00015	0.00011	0.00009	0.00006	0.00005	0.00004	0.00003	0.00002	0.00002	0.00001	0.00001	0.00001
66	0.00013	0.00010	0.00007	0.00006	0.00004	0.00003	0.00002	0.00002	0.00001	0.00001	0.00001	0.00001
67	0.00011	0.00009	0.00006	0.00005	0.00004	0.00003	0.00002	0.00002	0.00001	0.00001	0.00001	0.00000
68	0.00010	0.00007	0.00006	0.00004	0.00003	0.00002	0.00002	0.00001	0.00001	0.00001	0.00001	0.00000
69	0.00009	0.00006	0.00005	0.00004	0.00003	0.00002	0.00001	0.00001	0.00001	0.00001	0.00000	0.00000
70	0.00008	0.00006	0.00004	0.00003	0.00002	0.00002	0.00001	0.00001	0.00001	0.00001	0.00000	0.00000
71	0.00007	0.00005	0.00004	0.00003	0.00002	0.00001	0.00001	0.00001	0.00001	0.00000	0.00000	0.00000
72	0.00006	0.00004	0.00003	0.00002	0.00002	0.00001	0.00001	0.00001	0.00000	0.00000	0.00000	0.00000
73	0.00005	0.00004	0.00003	0.00002	0.00001	0.00001	0.00001	0.00001	0.00000	0.00000	0.00000	0.00000
74	0.00004	0.00003	0.00002	0.00002	0.00001	0.00001	0.00001	0.00000	0.00000	0.00000	0.00000	0.00000
75	0.00004	0.00003	0.00002	0.00001	0.00001	0.00001	0.00001	0.00000	0.00000	0.00000	0.00000	0.00000
76	0.00003	0.00002	0.00002	0.00001	0.00001	0.00001	0.00000	0.00000	0.00000	0.00000	0.00000	0.00000
77	0.00003	0.00002	0.00002	0.00001	0.00001	0.00001	0.00000	0.00000	0.00000	0.00000	0.00000	0.00000
78	0.00003	0.00002	0.00001	0.00001	0.00001	0.00000	0.00000	0.00000	0.00000	0.00000	0.00000	0.00000
79	0.00002	0.00002	0.00001	0.00001	0.00001	0.00000	0.00000	0.00000	0.00000	0.00000	0.00000	0.00000
80	0.00002	0.00001	0.00001	0.00001	0.00000	0.00000	0.00000	0.00000	0.00000	0.00000	0.00000	0.00000
81	0.00002	0.00001	0.00001	0.00001	0.00000	0.00000	0.00000	0.00000	0.00000	0.00000	0.00000	0.00000
82	0.00002	0.00001	0.00001	0.00001	0.00000	0.00000	0.00000	0.00000	0.00000	0.00000	0.00000	0.00000
83	0.00001	0.00001	0.00001	0.00000	0.00000	0.00000	0.00000	0.00000	0.00000	0.00000	0.00000	0.00000
84	0.00001	0.00001	0.00001	0.00000	0.00000	0.00000	0.00000	0.00000	0.00000	0.00000	0.00000	0.00000
85	0.00001	0.00001	0.00000	0.00000	0.00000	0.00000	0.00000	0.00000	0.00000	0.00000	0.00000	0.00000
86	0.00001	0.00001	0.00000	0.00000	0.00000	0.00000	0.00000	0.00000	0.00000	0.00000	0.00000	0.00000
87	0.00001	0.00001	0.00000	0.00000	0.00000	0.00000	0.00000	0.00000	0.00000	0.00000	0.00000	0.00000
88	0.00001	0.00000	0.00000	0.00000	0.00000	0.00000	0.00000	0.00000	0.00000	0.00000	0.00000	0.00000
89	0.00001	0.00000	0.00000	0.00000	0.00000	0.00000	0.00000	0.00000	0.00000	0.00000	0.00000	0.00000
90	0.00001	0.00000	0.00000	0.00000	0.00000	0.00000	0.00000	0.00000	0.00000	0.00000	0.00000	0.00000
91	0.00000	0.00000	0.00000	0.00000	0.00000	0.00000	0.00000	0.00000	0.00000	0.00000	0.00000	0.00000
92	0.00000	0.00000	0.00000	0.00000	0.00000	0.00000	0.00000	0.00000	0.00000	0.00000	0.00000	0.00000
93	0.00000	0.00000	0.00000	0.00000	0.00000	0.00000	0.00000	0.00000	0.00000	0.00000	0.00000	0.00000
94	0.00000	0.00000	0.00000	0.00000	0.00000	0.00000	0.00000	0.00000	0.00000	0.00000	0.00000	0.00000
95	0.00000	0.00000	0.00000	0.00000	0.00000	0.00000	0.00000	0.00000	0.00000	0.00000	0.00000	0.00000
96	0.00000	0.00000	0.00000	0.00000	0.00000	0.00000	0.00000	0.00000	0.00000	0.00000	0.00000	0.00000
97	0.00000	0.00000	0.00000	0.00000	0.00000	0.00000	0.00000	0.00000	0.00000	0.00000	0.00000	0.00000
98	0.00000	0.00000	0.00000	0.00000	0.00000	0.00000	0.00000	0.00000	0.00000	0.00000	0.00000	0.00000
99	0.00000	0.00000	0.00000	0.00000	0.00000	0.00000	0.00000	0.00000	0.00000	0.00000	0.00000	0.00000
100	0.00000	0.00000	0.00000	0.00000	0.00000	0.00000	0.00000	0.00000	0.00000	0.00000	0.00000	0.00000
101	0.00000	0.00000	0.00000	0.00000	0.00000	0.00000	0.00000	0.00000	0.00000	0.00000	0.00000	0.00000
102	0.00000	0.00000	0.00000	0.00000	0.00000	0.00000	0.00000	0.00000	0.00000	0.00000	0.00000	0.00000
103	0.00000	0.00000	0.00000	0.00000	0.00000	0.00000	0.00000	0.00000	0.00000	0.00000	0.00000	0.00000
104	0.00000	0.00000	0.00000	0.00000	0.00000	0.00000	0.00000	0.00000	0.00000	0.00000	0.00000	0.00000
105	0.00000	0.00000	0.00000	0.00000	0.00000	0.00000	0.00000	0.00000	0.00000	0.00000	0.00000	0.00000
106	0.00000	0.00000	0.00000	0.00000	0.00000	0.00000	0.00000	0.00000	0.00000	0.00000	0.00000	0.00000
107	0.00000	0.00000	0.00000	0.00000	0.00000	0.00000	0.00000	0.00000	0.00000	0.00000	0.00000	0.00000
108	0.00000	0.00000	0.00000	0.00000	0.00000	0.00000	0.00000	0.00000	0.00000	0.00000	0.00000	0.00000
109	0.00000	0.00000	0.00000	0.00000	0.00000	0.00000	0.00000	0.00000	0.00000	0.00000	0.00000	0.00000
110	0.00000	0.00000	0.00000	0.00000	0.00000	0.00000	0.00000	0.00000	0.00000	0.00000	0.00000	0.00000
111	0.00000	0.00000	0.00000	0.00000	0.00000	0.00000	0.00000	0.00000	0.00000	0.00000	0.00000	0.00000
112	0.00000	0.00000	0.00000	0.00000	0.00000	0.00000	0.00000	0.00000	0.00000	0.00000	0.00000	0.00000
113	0.00000	0.00000	0.00000	0.00000	0.00000	0.00000	0.00000	0.00000	0.00000	0.00000	0.00000	0.00000
114	0.00000	0.00000	0.00000	0.00000	0.00000	0.00000	0.00000	0.00000	0.00000	0.00000	0.00000	0.00000
115	0.00000	0.00000	0.00000	0.00000	0.00000	0.00000	0.00000	0.00000	0.00000	0.00000	0.00000	0.00000
116	0.00000	0.00000	0.00000	0.00000	0.00000	0.00000	0.00000	0.00000	0.00000	0.00000	0.00000	0.00000
117	0.00000	0.00000	0.00000	0.00000	0.00000	0.00000	0.00000	0.00000	0.00000	0.00000	0.00000	0.00000
118	0.00000	0.00000	0.00000	0.00000	0.00000	0.00000	0.00000	0.00000	0.00000	0.00000	0.00000	0.00000
119	0.00000	0.00000	0.00000	0.00000	0.00000	0.00000	0.00000	0.00000	0.00000	0.00000	0.00000	0.00000
120	0.00000	0.00000	0.00000	0.00000	0.00000	0.00000	0.00000	0.00000	0.00000	0.00000	0.00000	0.00000

Table 4: Present value of an ordinary annuity of $1 per period: 0.5%–7%

$$P_{A_{i,n}} = \frac{1 - \frac{1}{(1 + i)^n}}{i}$$

Period	.5%	1%	1.5%	2%	2.5%	3%	3.5%	4%	4.5%	5%	5.5%	6%	6.5%	7%
1	0.99502	0.99010	0.98522	0.98039	0.97561	0.97087	0.96618	0.96154	0.95694	0.95238	0.94787	0.94340	0.93897	0.93458
2	1.98510	1.97040	1.95588	1.94156	1.92742	1.91347	1.89969	1.88609	1.87267	1.85941	1.84632	1.83339	1.82063	1.80802
3	2.97025	2.94099	2.91220	2.88388	2.85602	2.82861	2.80164	2.77509	2.74896	2.72325	2.69793	2.67301	2.64848	2.62432
4	3.95050	3.90197	3.85438	3.80773	3.76197	3.71710	3.67308	3.62990	3.58753	3.54595	3.50515	3.46511	3.42580	3.38721
5	4.92587	4.85343	4.78264	4.71346	4.64583	4.57971	4.51505	4.45182	4.38998	4.32948	4.27028	4.21236	4.15568	4.10020
6	5.89638	5.79548	5.69719	5.60143	5.50813	5.41719	5.32855	5.24214	5.15787	5.07569	4.99553	4.91732	4.84101	4.76654
7	6.86207	6.72819	6.59821	6.47199	6.34939	6.23028	6.11454	6.00205	5.89270	5.78637	5.68297	5.58238	5.48452	5.38929
8	7.82296	7.65168	7.48593	7.32548	7.17014	7.01969	6.87396	6.73274	6.59589	6.46321	6.33457	6.20979	6.08875	5.97130
9	8.77906	8.56602	8.36052	8.16224	7.97087	7.78611	7.60769	7.43533	7.26879	7.10782	6.95220	6.80169	6.65610	6.51523
10	9.73041	9.47130	9.22218	8.98259	8.75206	8.53020	8.31661	8.11090	7.91272	7.72173	7.53763	7.36009	7.18883	7.02358
11	10.67703	10.36763	10.07112	9.78685	9.51421	9.25262	9.00155	8.76048	8.52892	8.30641	8.09254	7.88687	7.68904	7.49867
12	11.61893	11.25508	10.90751	10.57534	10.25776	9.95400	9.66333	9.38507	9.11858	8.86325	8.61852	8.38384	8.15873	7.94269
13	12.55615	12.13374	11.73153	11.34837	10.98318	10.63496	10.30274	9.98565	9.68285	9.39357	9.11708	8.85268	8.59974	8.35765
14	13.48871	13.00370	12.54338	12.10625	11.69091	11.29607	10.92052	10.56312	10.22283	9.89864	9.58965	9.29498	9.01384	8.74547
15	14.41662	13.86505	13.34323	12.84926	12.38138	11.93794	11.51741	11.11839	10.73955	10.37966	10.03758	9.71225	9.40267	9.10791
16	15.33993	14.71787	14.13126	13.57771	13.05500	12.56110	12.09412	11.65230	11.23402	10.83777	10.46216	10.10590	9.76776	9.44665
17	16.25863	15.56225	14.90765	14.29187	13.71220	13.16612	12.65132	12.16567	11.70719	11.27407	10.86461	10.47726	10.11058	9.76322
18	17.17277	16.39827	15.67256	14.99203	14.35336	13.75351	13.18968	12.65930	12.15999	11.68959	11.24607	10.82760	10.43247	10.05900
19	18.08236	17.22601	16.42617	15.67846	14.97889	14.32380	13.70984	13.13394	12.59329	12.08532	11.60765	11.15812	10.73471	10.33560
20	18.98742	18.04555	17.16864	16.35143	15.58916	14.87747	14.21240	13.59033	13.00794	12.46221	11.95038	11.46992	11.01851	10.59401
21	19.88798	18.85698	17.90014	17.01121	16.18455	15.41502	14.69797	14.02916	13.40472	12.82115	12.27524	11.76408	11.28498	10.83553
22	20.78406	19.66038	18.62082	17.65805	16.76541	15.93692	15.16712	14.45112	13.78442	13.16300	12.58317	12.04158	11.53520	11.06124
23	21.67568	20.45582	19.33086	18.29220	17.33211	16.44361	15.62041	14.85684	14.14777	13.48857	12.87504	12.30338	11.77014	11.27219
24	22.56287	21.24339	20.03041	18.91393	17.88499	16.93554	16.05837	15.24696	14.49548	13.79864	13.15170	12.55036	11.99074	11.46933
25	23.44504	22.02316	20.71961	19.52346	18.42438	17.41315	16.48151	15.62208	14.82821	14.09394	13.41393	12.78336	12.19788	11.65358
26	24.32402	22.79520	21.39863	20.12104	18.95061	17.87684	16.89035	15.98277	15.14661	14.37519	13.66250	13.00317	12.39237	11.82578
27	25.19803	23.55961	22.06762	20.70690	19.46401	18.32703	17.28536	16.32959	15.45130	14.64303	13.89810	13.21053	12.57500	11.98671
28	26.06769	24.31644	22.72672	21.28127	19.96489	18.76411	17.66702	16.66306	15.74287	14.89813	14.12142	13.40616	12.74648	12.13711
29	26.93302	25.06579	23.37608	21.84438	20.45355	19.18845	18.03577	16.98371	16.02189	15.14107	14.33310	13.59072	12.90749	12.27767
30	27.79405	25.80771	24.01584	22.39646	20.93029	19.60044	18.39205	17.29203	16.28889	15.37245	14.53375	13.76483	13.05868	12.40904
31	28.65080	26.54229	24.64615	22.93770	21.39541	20.00043	18.73628	17.58849	16.54439	15.59281	14.72393	13.92909	13.20063	12.53181
32	29.50328	27.26959	25.26714	23.46833	21.84918	20.38877	19.06887	17.87355	16.78889	15.80268	14.90420	14.08404	13.33393	12.64656
33	30.35153	27.98969	25.87895	23.98856	22.29188	20.76579	19.39021	18.14765	17.02286	16.00255	15.07507	14.23023	13.45909	12.75379
34	31.19555	28.70267	26.48173	24.49859	22.72379	21.13184	19.70068	18.41120	17.24676	16.19290	15.23703	14.36814	13.57661	12.85401
35	32.03537	29.40858	27.07559	24.99862	23.14516	21.48722	20.00066	18.66461	17.46101	16.37419	15.39055	14.49825	13.68696	12.94767
36	32.87102	30.10751	27.66068	25.48884	23.55625	21.83225	20.29049	18.90828	17.66604	16.54685	15.53607	14.62099	13.79057	13.03521
37	33.70250	30.79951	28.23713	25.96945	23.95732	22.16724	20.57053	19.14258	17.86224	16.71129	15.67400	14.73678	13.88786	13.11702
38	34.52985	31.48466	28.80505	26.44064	24.34860	22.49246	20.84109	19.36786	18.04999	16.86789	15.80474	14.84602	13.97921	13.19347
39	35.35309	32.16303	29.36458	26.90259	24.73034	22.80822	21.10250	19.58448	18.22996	17.01704	15.92866	14.94907	14.06499	13.26493
40	36.17223	32.83469	29.91585	27.35548	25.10278	23.11477	21.35507	19.79277	18.40158	17.15909	16.04612	15.04630	14.14553	13.33171
41	36.98729	33.49969	30.45896	27.79949	25.46612	23.41240	21.59910	19.99305	18.56611	17.29437	16.15746	15.13802	14.22115	13.39412
42	37.79830	34.15811	30.99405	28.23479	25.82061	23.70136	21.83488	20.18563	18.72355	17.42321	16.26300	15.22454	14.29216	13.45245
43	38.60527	34.81001	31.52123	28.66156	26.16645	23.98190	22.06269	20.37079	18.87421	17.54591	16.36303	15.30617	14.35884	13.50696
44	39.40823	35.45545	32.04062	29.07996	26.50385	24.25427	22.28279	20.54884	19.01838	17.66277	16.45785	15.38318	14.42144	13.55791
45	40.20720	36.09451	32.55234	29.49016	26.83302	24.51871	22.49545	20.72004	19.15635	17.77407	16.54773	15.45583	14.48023	13.60552
46	41.00219	36.72724	33.05649	29.89231	27.15417	24.77545	22.70092	20.88465	19.28837	17.88007	16.63292	15.52437	14.53543	13.65002
47	41.79322	37.35370	33.55319	30.28658	27.46748	25.02471	22.89944	21.04294	19.41471	17.98102	16.71366	15.58903	14.58725	13.69161
48	42.58032	37.97396	34.04255	30.67312	27.77315	25.26671	23.09124	21.19513	19.53561	18.07716	16.79020	15.65003	14.63592	13.73047
49	43.36350	38.58808	34.52468	31.05208	28.07137	25.50166	23.27656	21.34147	19.65130	18.16872	16.86275	15.70757	14.68161	13.76680
50	44.14279	39.19612	34.99969	31.42361	28.36231	25.72976	23.45562	21.48218	19.76201	18.25593	16.93152	15.76186	14.72452	13.80075
51	44.91820	39.79814	35.46767	31.78785	28.64616	25.95123	23.62862	21.61749	19.86795	18.33898	16.99670	15.81308	14.76481	13.83247
52	45.68975	40.39419	35.92874	32.14495	28.92308	26.16624	23.79576	21.74758	19.96933	18.41807	17.05848	15.86139	14.80264	13.86212
53	46.45746	40.98435	36.38300	32.49505	29.19325	26.37499	23.95726	21.87267	20.06634	18.49340	17.11705	15.90697	14.83816	13.88984
54	47.22135	41.56866	36.83054	32.83828	29.45683	26.57766	24.11330	21.99296	20.15918	18.56515	17.17255	15.94998	14.87151	13.91573
55	47.98145	42.14719	37.27147	33.17479	29.71398	26.77443	24.26405	22.10861	20.24802	18.63347	17.22517	15.99054	14.90282	13.93994
56	48.73776	42.71999	37.70588	33.50469	29.96486	26.96546	24.40971	22.21982	20.33303	18.69854	17.27504	16.02881	14.93223	13.96256
57	49.49031	43.28712	38.13387	33.82813	30.20962	27.15094	24.55045	22.32675	20.41439	18.76052	17.32232	16.06492	14.95984	13.98370
58	50.23911	43.84863	38.55554	34.14523	30.44441	27.33101	24.68642	22.42957	20.49224	18.81954	17.36712	16.09898	14.98577	14.00346
59	50.98419	44.40459	38.97097	34.45610	30.68137	27.50583	24.81780	22.52843	20.56673	18.87575	17.40960	16.13111	15.01011	14.02192
60	51.72556	44.95504	39.38027	34.76089	30.90866	27.67556	24.94473	22.62349	20.63802	18.92929	17.44985	16.16143	15.03297	14.03918

Period	.5%	1%	1.5%	2%	2.5%	3%	3.5%	4%	4.5%	5%	5.5%	6%	6.5%	7%
61 ...	52.46324	45.50004	39.78352	35.05969	31.13040	27.84035	25.06738	22.71489	20.70624	18.98028	17.48801	16.19003	15.05443	14.05531
62 ...	53.19726	46.03964	40.18080	35.35264	31.34673	28.00034	25.18587	22.80278	20.77152	19.02883	17.52418	16.21701	15.07458	14.07038
63 ...	53.92762	46.57390	40.57222	35.63984	31.55778	28.15567	25.30036	22.88729	20.83399	19.07508	17.55847	16.24246	15.09350	14.08447
64 ...	54.65435	47.10287	40.95785	35.92141	31.76369	28.30648	25.41097	22.96855	20.89377	19.11912	17.59096	16.26647	15.11127	14.09764
65 ...	55.37746	47.62661	41.33779	36.19747	31.96458	28.45289	25.51785	23.04668	20.95098	19.16107	17.62177	16.28912	15.12795	14.10994
66 ...	56.09698	48.14516	41.71210	36.46810	32.16056	28.59504	25.62111	23.12181	21.00572	19.20102	17.65096	16.31049	15.14362	14.12144
67 ...	56.81291	48.65857	42.08089	36.73343	32.35177	28.73305	25.72088	23.19405	21.05811	19.23907	17.67864	16.33065	15.15833	14.13219
68 ...	57.52529	49.16960	42.44423	36.99356	32.53831	28.86704	25.81727	23.26351	21.10824	19.27530	17.70487	16.34967	15.17214	14.14223
69 ...	58.23411	49.67020	42.80219	37.24859	32.72030	28.99712	25.91041	23.33030	21.15621	19.30981	17.72974	16.36762	15.18511	14.15162
70 ...	58.93942	50.16851	43.15487	37.49862	32.89786	29.12342	26.00040	23.39451	21.20211	19.34268	17.75330	16.38454	15.19728	14.16039
71 ...	59.64121	50.66190	43.50234	37.74374	33.07108	29.24604	26.08734	23.45626	21.24604	19.37398	17.77564	16.40051	15.20872	14.16859
72 ...	60.33951	51.15039	43.84467	37.98406	33.24008	29.36509	26.17134	23.51564	21.28808	19.40379	17.79682	16.41558	15.21945	14.17625
73 ...	61.03434	51.63405	44.18194	38.21967	33.40495	29.48067	26.25251	23.57273	21.32830	19.43218	17.81689	16.42979	15.22953	14.18341
74 ...	61.72571	52.11292	44.51422	38.45066	33.56581	29.59288	26.33092	23.62762	21.36680	19.45922	17.83591	16.44320	15.23900	14.19010
75 ...	62.41365	52.58705	44.84160	38.67711	33.72274	29.70183	26.40669	23.68041	21.40363	19.48497	17.85395	16.45585	15.24788	14.19636
76 ...	63.09815	53.05649	45.16414	38.89913	33.87584	29.80760	26.47989	23.73116	21.43888	19.50950	17.87104	16.46778	15.25623	14.20220
77 ...	63.77926	53.52127	45.48191	39.11680	34.02521	29.91029	26.55062	23.77996	21.47262	19.53285	17.88724	16.47904	15.26407	14.20767
78 ...	64.45697	53.98146	45.79498	39.33019	34.17094	30.00999	26.61896	23.82689	21.50490	19.55510	17.90260	16.48966	15.27142	14.21277
79 ...	65.13132	54.43709	46.10343	39.53940	34.31311	30.10679	26.68498	23.87201	21.53579	19.57628	17.91716	16.49968	15.27833	14.21755
80 ...	65.80231	54.88821	46.40732	39.74451	34.45182	30.20076	26.74878	23.91539	21.56534	19.59646	17.93095	16.50913	15.28482	14.22201
81 ...	66.46996	55.33486	46.70672	39.94560	34.58714	30.29200	26.81041	23.95711	21.59363	19.61568	17.94403	16.51805	15.29091	14.22617
82 ...	67.13428	55.77709	47.00170	40.14275	34.71916	30.38059	26.86996	23.99722	21.62070	19.63398	17.95643	16.52646	15.29663	14.23007
83 ...	67.79531	56.21494	47.29231	40.33603	34.84796	30.46659	26.92750	24.03579	21.64660	19.65141	17.96818	16.53440	15.30200	14.23371
84 ...	68.45304	56.64845	47.57863	40.52552	34.97362	30.55009	26.98309	24.07287	21.67139	19.66801	17.97932	16.54188	15.30704	14.23711
85 ...	69.10750	57.07768	47.86072	40.71129	35.09621	30.63115	27.03680	24.10853	21.69511	19.68382	17.98987	16.54895	15.31178	14.24029
86 ...	69.75871	57.50265	48.13864	40.89342	35.21582	30.70986	27.08870	24.14282	21.71781	19.69887	17.99988	16.55561	15.31622	14.24326
87 ...	70.40668	57.92342	48.41246	41.07198	35.33251	30.78627	27.13884	24.17579	21.73953	19.71321	18.00936	16.56190	15.32040	14.24604
88 ...	71.05142	58.34002	48.68222	41.24704	35.44635	30.86045	27.18728	24.20749	21.76032	19.72687	18.01835	16.56783	15.32431	14.24864
89 ...	71.69296	58.75249	48.94800	41.41867	35.55741	30.93248	27.23409	24.23797	21.78021	19.73987	18.02688	16.57342	15.32800	14.25106
90 ...	72.33130	59.16088	49.20985	41.58693	35.66577	31.00241	27.27932	24.26728	21.79924	19.75226	18.03495	16.57870	15.33145	14.25333
91 ...	72.96647	59.56523	49.46784	41.75189	35.77148	31.07030	27.32301	24.29546	21.81746	19.76406	18.04261	16.58368	15.33470	14.25545
92 ...	73.59847	59.96557	49.72201	41.91362	35.87462	31.13621	27.36523	24.32256	21.83489	19.77529	18.04987	16.58838	15.33774	14.25743
93 ...	74.22734	60.36195	49.97242	42.07218	35.97524	31.20021	27.40602	24.34861	21.85156	19.78599	18.05675	16.59281	15.34060	14.25928
94 ...	74.85307	60.75441	50.21913	42.22762	36.07340	31.26234	27.44543	24.37367	21.86753	19.79619	18.06327	16.59699	15.34329	14.26101
95 ...	75.47569	61.14298	50.46220	42.38002	36.16917	31.32266	27.48350	24.39776	21.88280	19.80589	18.06945	16.60093	15.34581	14.26262
96 ...	76.09522	61.52770	50.70168	42.52943	36.26261	31.38122	27.52029	24.42092	21.89742	19.81513	18.07531	16.60465	15.34818	14.26413
97 ...	76.71166	61.90862	50.93761	42.67592	36.35376	31.43808	27.55584	24.44319	21.91140	19.82394	18.08086	16.60816	15.35040	14.26555
98 ...	77.32503	62.28576	51.17006	42.81953	36.44269	31.49328	27.59018	24.46461	21.92479	19.83232	18.08612	16.61147	15.35249	14.26687
99 ...	77.93536	62.65917	51.39907	42.96032	36.52946	31.54687	27.62337	24.48520	21.93760	19.84031	18.09111	16.61460	15.35445	14.26810
100 ...	78.54264	63.02888	51.62470	43.09835	36.61411	31.59891	27.65543	24.50500	21.94985	19.84791	18.09584	16.61755	15.35629	14.26925
101 ...	79.14691	63.39493	51.84700	43.23368	36.69669	31.64942	27.68640	24.52404	21.96158	19.85515	18.10032	16.62033	15.35802	14.27033
102 ...	79.74817	63.75736	52.06601	43.36635	36.77726	31.69847	27.71633	24.54234	21.97281	19.86205	18.10457	16.62295	15.35964	14.27133
103 ...	80.34644	64.11619	52.28178	43.49642	36.85586	31.74609	27.74525	24.55995	21.98355	19.86862	18.10860	16.62542	15.36117	14.27228
104 ...	80.94173	64.47148	52.49437	43.62394	36.93255	31.79232	27.77318	24.57687	21.99382	19.87488	18.11241	16.62776	15.36260	14.27315
105 ...	81.53406	64.82325	52.70381	43.74896	37.00736	31.83720	27.80018	24.59315	22.00366	19.88083	18.11603	16.62996	15.36394	14.27398
106 ...	82.12344	65.17153	52.91016	43.87153	37.08035	31.88078	27.82626	24.60879	22.01307	19.88651	18.11946	16.63204	15.36521	14.27474
107 ...	82.70989	65.51637	53.11346	43.99170	37.15156	31.92308	27.85146	24.62384	22.02208	19.89191	18.12271	16.63400	15.36639	14.27546
108 ...	83.29342	65.85779	53.31375	44.10951	37.22104	31.96416	27.87581	24.63831	22.03070	19.89706	18.12579	16.63585	15.36750	14.27613
109 ...	83.87405	66.19583	53.51108	44.22501	37.28882	32.00404	27.89933	24.65222	22.03894	19.90196	18.12872	16.63759	15.36855	14.27676
110 ...	84.45180	66.53053	53.70550	44.33824	37.35494	32.04276	27.92206	24.66560	22.04684	19.90663	18.13148	16.63924	15.36953	14.27735
111 ...	85.02666	66.86191	53.89704	44.44926	37.41946	32.08035	27.94402	24.67846	22.05439	19.91108	18.13411	16.64079	15.37045	14.27789
112 ...	85.59867	67.19001	54.08576	44.55810	37.48240	32.11684	27.96523	24.69082	22.06162	19.91531	18.13659	16.64226	15.37131	14.27840
113 ...	86.16783	67.51486	54.27168	44.66480	37.54380	32.15227	27.98573	24.70272	22.06853	19.91934	18.13895	16.64364	15.37212	14.27888
114 ...	86.73416	67.83649	54.45486	44.76941	37.60371	32.18667	28.00554	24.71415	22.07515	19.92318	18.14119	16.64494	15.37289	14.27933
115 ...	87.29767	68.15494	54.63533	44.87197	37.66216	32.22007	28.02467	24.72514	22.08148	19.92684	18.14331	16.64617	15.37360	14.27975
116 ...	87.85838	68.47024	54.81313	44.97252	37.71918	32.25250	28.04316	24.73571	22.08754	19.93033	18.14531	16.64733	15.37428	14.28014
117 ...	88.41630	68.78242	54.98831	45.07110	37.77481	32.28398	28.06103	24.74588	22.09334	19.93364	18.14722	16.64843	15.37491	14.28050
118 ...	88.97144	69.09150	55.16089	45.16775	37.82908	32.31454	28.07829	24.75565	22.09889	19.93680	18.14902	16.64946	15.37550	14.28084
119 ...	89.52382	69.39753	55.33093	45.26250	37.88203	32.34421	28.09496	24.76505	22.10420	19.93981	18.15073	16.65043	15.37606	14.28116
120 ...	90.07345	69.70052	55.49845	45.35539	37.93369	32.37302	28.11108	24.77409	22.10929	19.94268	18.15235	16.65135	15.37658	14.28146

Table 4 (*continued*): Present value of an ordinary annuity of $1 per period: 7.5%–14%

Period	7.5%	8%	8.5%	9%	9.5%	10%	10.5%	11%	11.5%	12%	12.5%	13%	13.5%	14%
1	0.93023	0.92593	0.92166	0.91743	0.91324	0.90909	0.90498	0.90090	0.89686	0.89286	0.88889	0.88496	0.88106	0.87719
2	1.79557	1.78326	1.77111	1.75911	1.74725	1.73554	1.72396	1.71252	1.70122	1.69005	1.67901	1.66810	1.65732	1.64666
3	2.60053	2.57710	2.55402	2.53129	2.50891	2.48685	2.46512	2.44371	2.42262	2.40183	2.38134	2.36115	2.34125	2.32163
4	3.34933	3.31213	3.27560	3.23972	3.20448	3.16987	3.13586	3.10245	3.06961	3.03735	3.00564	2.97447	2.94383	2.91371
5	4.04588	3.99271	3.94064	3.88965	3.83971	3.79079	3.74286	3.69590	3.64988	3.60478	3.56057	3.51723	3.47474	3.43308
6	4.69385	4.62288	4.55359	4.48592	4.41983	4.35526	4.29218	4.23054	4.17029	4.11141	4.05384	3.99755	3.94250	3.88867
7	5.29660	5.20637	5.11851	5.03295	4.94961	4.86842	4.78930	4.71220	4.63704	4.56379	4.49230	4.42261	4.35463	4.28830
8	5.85730	5.74664	5.63918	5.53482	5.43344	5.33493	5.23919	5.14612	5.05564	4.96764	4.88205	4.79877	4.71774	4.63886
9	6.37889	6.24689	6.11906	5.99525	5.87528	5.75902	5.64632	5.53705	5.43106	5.32825	5.22848	5.13166	5.03765	4.94637
10	6.86408	6.71008	6.56135	6.41766	6.27880	6.14457	6.01477	5.88923	5.76777	5.65022	5.53643	5.42624	5.31952	5.21612
11	7.31542	7.13896	6.96898	6.80519	6.64730	6.49506	6.34821	6.20652	6.06975	5.93770	5.81016	5.68694	5.56786	5.45273
12	7.73528	7.53608	7.34469	7.16073	6.98384	6.81369	6.64996	6.49236	6.34058	6.19437	6.05348	5.91765	5.78666	5.66029
13	8.12584	7.90378	7.69095	7.48690	7.29118	7.10336	6.92304	6.74987	6.58348	6.42355	6.26976	6.12181	5.97943	5.84236
14	8.48915	8.24424	8.01010	7.78615	7.57185	7.36669	7.17018	6.98187	6.80133	6.62817	6.46201	6.30249	6.14928	6.00207
15	8.82712	8.55948	8.30424	8.06069	7.82818	7.60608	7.39382	7.19087	6.99671	6.81086	6.63289	6.46238	6.29893	6.14217
16	9.14151	8.85137	8.57533	8.31256	8.06226	7.82371	7.59622	7.37916	7.17194	6.97399	6.78479	6.60388	6.43077	6.26506
17	9.43396	9.12164	8.82519	8.54363	8.27604	8.02155	7.77939	7.54879	7.32909	7.11963	6.91982	6.72909	6.54694	6.37286
18	9.70601	9.37189	9.05548	8.75563	8.47127	8.20141	7.94515	7.70162	7.47004	7.24967	7.03984	6.83991	6.64928	6.46742
19	9.95908	9.60360	9.26772	8.95011	8.64956	8.36492	8.09515	7.83929	7.59644	7.36578	7.14652	6.93797	6.73946	6.55037
20	10.19449	9.81815	9.46334	9.12855	8.81238	8.51356	8.23091	7.96333	7.70982	7.46944	7.24135	7.02475	6.81890	6.62313
21	10.41348	10.01680	9.64363	9.29224	8.96108	8.64869	8.35376	8.07507	7.81149	7.56200	7.32565	7.10155	6.88890	6.68696
22	10.61719	10.20074	9.80980	9.44243	9.09688	8.77154	8.46494	8.17574	7.90269	7.64465	7.40058	7.16951	6.95057	6.74294
23	10.80669	10.37106	9.96295	9.58021	9.22089	8.88322	8.56556	8.26643	7.98447	7.71843	7.46718	7.22966	7.00491	6.79206
24	10.98297	10.52876	10.10410	9.70661	9.33415	8.98474	8.65662	8.34814	8.05782	7.78432	7.52638	7.28288	7.05279	6.83514
25	11.14695	10.67478	10.23419	9.82258	9.43758	9.07704	8.73902	8.42174	8.12361	7.84314	7.57901	7.32998	7.09497	6.87293
26	11.29948	10.80998	10.35409	9.92897	9.53203	9.16095	8.81359	8.48806	8.18261	7.89566	7.62578	7.37167	7.13213	6.90608
27	11.44138	10.93516	10.46460	10.02658	9.61830	9.23722	8.88108	8.54780	8.23552	7.94255	7.66736	7.40856	7.16487	6.93515
28	11.57338	11.05108	10.56645	10.11613	9.69707	9.30657	8.94215	8.60162	8.28298	7.98442	7.70432	7.44120	7.19372	6.96066
29	11.69617	11.15841	10.66033	10.19828	9.76902	9.36961	8.99742	8.65011	8.32554	8.02181	7.73717	7.47009	7.21914	6.98304
30	11.81039	11.25778	10.74684	10.27365	9.83472	9.42691	9.04744	8.69379	8.36371	8.05518	7.76638	7.49565	7.24153	7.00266
31	11.91664	11.34980	10.82658	10.34280	9.89472	9.47901	9.09271	8.73315	8.39795	8.08499	7.79234	7.51828	7.26126	7.01988
32	12.01548	11.43500	10.90008	10.40624	9.94952	9.52638	9.13367	8.76860	8.42866	8.11159	7.81541	7.53830	7.27864	7.03498
33	12.10742	11.51389	10.96781	10.46444	9.99956	9.56943	9.17074	8.80054	8.45619	8.13535	7.83592	7.55602	7.29396	7.04823
34	12.19295	11.58693	11.03024	10.51784	10.04526	9.60857	9.20429	8.82932	8.48089	8.15656	7.85415	7.57170	7.30745	7.05985
35	12.27251	11.65457	11.08777	10.56682	10.08699	9.64416	9.23465	8.85524	8.50304	8.17550	7.87036	7.58557	7.31934	7.07005
36	12.34652	11.71719	11.14081	10.61176	10.12511	9.67651	9.26213	8.87859	8.52291	8.19241	7.88476	7.59785	7.32982	7.07899
37	12.41537	11.77518	11.18969	10.65299	10.15992	9.70592	9.28700	8.89963	8.54072	8.20751	7.89757	7.60872	7.33904	7.08683
38	12.47941	11.82887	11.23474	10.69082	10.19171	9.73265	9.30950	8.91859	8.55670	8.22099	7.90895	7.61833	7.34718	7.09371
39	12.53899	11.87858	11.27625	10.72552	10.22074	9.75696	9.32986	8.93567	8.57103	8.23303	7.91906	7.62684	7.35434	7.09975
40	12.59441	11.92461	11.31452	10.75736	10.24725	9.77905	9.34829	8.95105	8.58389	8.24378	7.92806	7.63438	7.36065	7.10504
41	12.64596	11.96723	11.34979	10.78657	10.27146	9.79914	9.36497	8.96491	8.59541	8.25337	7.93605	7.64104	7.36621	7.10969
42	12.69392	12.00670	11.38229	10.81337	10.29357	9.81740	9.38006	8.97740	8.60575	8.26194	7.94316	7.64694	7.37111	7.11376
43	12.73853	12.04324	11.41225	10.83795	10.31376	9.83400	9.39372	8.98865	8.61502	8.26959	7.94947	7.65216	7.37543	7.11733
44	12.78003	12.07707	11.43986	10.86051	10.33220	9.84909	9.40608	8.99878	8.62334	8.27642	7.95509	7.65678	7.37923	7.12047
45	12.81863	12.10840	11.46531	10.88120	10.34904	9.86281	9.41727	9.00791	8.63080	8.28252	7.96008	7.66086	7.38258	7.12322
46	12.85454	12.13741	11.48877	10.90018	10.36442	9.87528	9.42739	9.01614	8.63749	8.28796	7.96451	7.66448	7.38554	7.12563
47	12.88794	12.16427	11.51038	10.91760	10.37847	9.88662	9.43656	9.02355	8.64349	8.29282	7.96846	7.66768	7.38814	7.12774
48	12.91902	12.18914	11.53031	10.93358	10.39130	9.89693	9.44485	9.03022	8.64887	8.29716	7.97196	7.67052	7.39043	7.12960
49	12.94792	12.21216	11.54867	10.94823	10.40301	9.90630	9.45235	9.03624	8.65369	8.30104	7.97508	7.67302	7.39245	7.13123
50	12.97481	12.23348	11.56560	10.96168	10.41371	9.91481	9.45914	9.04165	8.65802	8.30450	7.97785	7.67524	7.39423	7.13266
51	12.99982	12.25323	11.58119	10.97402	10.42348	9.92256	9.46529	9.04653	8.66190	8.30759	7.98031	7.67720	7.39580	7.13391
52	13.02309	12.27151	11.59557	10.98534	10.43240	9.92960	9.47085	9.05093	8.66538	8.31035	7.98250	7.67894	7.39718	7.13501
53	13.04474	12.28843	11.60882	10.99573	10.44055	9.93600	9.47588	9.05489	8.66850	8.31281	7.98444	7.68048	7.39839	7.13597
54	13.06487	12.30410	11.62103	11.00525	10.44799	9.94182	9.48043	9.05846	8.67130	8.31501	7.98617	7.68184	7.39947	7.13682
55	13.08360	12.31861	11.63229	11.01399	10.45478	9.94711	9.48456	9.06168	8.67382	8.31697	7.98771	7.68304	7.40041	7.13756
56	13.10103	12.33205	11.64266	11.02201	10.46099	9.95191	9.48829	9.06457	8.67607	8.31872	7.98907	7.68411	7.40124	7.13821
57	13.11723	12.34449	11.65222	11.02937	10.46666	9.95629	9.49166	9.06718	8.67809	8.32029	7.99029	7.68505	7.40198	7.13878
58	13.13231	12.35601	11.66104	11.03612	10.47183	9.96026	9.49472	9.06954	8.67990	8.32169	7.99137	7.68589	7.40262	7.13928
59	13.14633	12.36668	11.66916	11.04231	10.47656	9.96387	9.49748	9.07165	8.68152	8.32294	7.99232	7.68663	7.40319	7.13972
60	13.15938	12.37655	11.67664	11.04799	10.48088	9.96716	9.49998	9.07356	8.68298	8.32405	7.99318	7.68728	7.40369	7.14011

Period	7.5%	8%	8.5%	9%	9.5%	10%	10.5%	11%	11.5%	12%	12.5%	13%	13.5%	14%
61	13.17152	12.38570	11.68354	11.05320	10.48482	9.97014	9.50225	9.07528	8.68429	8.32504	7.99394	7.68786	7.40413	7.14044
62	13.18281	12.39416	11.68990	11.05798	10.48842	9.97286	9.50430	9.07683	8.68546	8.32593	7.99461	7.68837	7.40452	7.14074
63	13.19331	12.40200	11.69576	11.06237	10.49171	9.97532	9.50615	9.07822	8.68651	8.32673	7.99521	7.68882	7.40487	7.14100
64	13.20308	12.40926	11.70116	11.06640	10.49471	9.97757	9.50783	9.07948	8.68745	8.32743	7.99574	7.68922	7.40517	7.14123
65	13.21217	12.41598	11.70614	11.07009	10.49745	9.97961	9.50935	9.08061	8.68830	8.32807	7.99621	7.68958	7.40544	7.14143
66	13.22062	12.42221	11.71073	11.07347	10.49996	9.98146	9.51072	9.08163	8.68906	8.32863	7.99663	7.68989	7.40567	7.14160
67	13.22848	12.42797	11.71496	11.07658	10.50224	9.98315	9.51196	9.08255	8.68974	8.32913	7.99701	7.69017	7.40588	7.14176
68	13.23580	12.43330	11.71885	11.07943	10.50433	9.98468	9.51309	9.08338	8.69035	8.32958	7.99734	7.69042	7.40606	7.14189
69	13.24260	12.43825	11.72245	11.08205	10.50624	9.98607	9.51411	9.08413	8.69090	8.32999	7.99764	7.69063	7.40622	7.14201
70	13.24893	12.44282	11.72576	11.08445	10.50798	9.98734	9.51503	9.08480	8.69139	8.33034	7.99790	7.69083	7.40636	7.14211
71	13.25482	12.44706	11.72881	11.08665	10.50957	9.98849	9.51586	9.08541	8.69183	8.33066	7.99813	7.69100	7.40648	7.14221
72	13.26030	12.45098	11.73162	11.08867	10.51102	9.98954	9.51662	9.08595	8.69222	8.33095	7.99834	7.69115	7.40659	7.14229
73	13.26539	12.45461	11.73421	11.09052	10.51235	9.99049	9.51730	9.08644	8.69257	8.33121	7.99852	7.69128	7.40669	7.14236
74	13.27013	12.45797	11.73660	11.09222	10.51356	9.99135	9.51792	9.08688	8.69289	8.33143	7.99869	7.69140	7.40678	7.14242
75	13.27454	12.46108	11.73880	11.09378	10.51467	9.99214	9.51848	9.08728	8.69318	8.33164	7.99883	7.69150	7.40685	7.14247
76	13.27864	12.46397	11.74083	11.09521	10.51568	9.99285	9.51899	9.08764	8.69343	8.33182	7.99896	7.69160	7.40692	7.14252
77	13.28246	12.46664	11.74270	11.09653	10.51660	9.99350	9.51945	9.08797	8.69366	8.33198	7.99908	7.69168	7.40698	7.14256
78	13.28601	12.46911	11.74443	11.09773	10.51744	9.99409	9.51986	9.08826	8.69387	8.33213	7.99918	7.69175	7.40703	7.14260
79	13.28931	12.47140	11.74601	11.09883	10.51821	9.99463	9.52024	9.08852	8.69405	8.33226	7.99927	7.69181	7.40707	7.14263
80	13.29238	12.47351	11.74748	11.09985	10.51892	9.99512	9.52057	9.08876	8.69422	8.33237	7.99935	7.69187	7.40711	7.14266
81	13.29524	12.47548	11.74883	11.10078	10.51956	9.99556	9.52088	9.08897	8.69436	8.33247	7.99942	7.69192	7.40715	7.14268
82	13.29790	12.47729	11.75007	11.10163	10.52015	9.99597	9.52116	9.08916	8.69450	8.33257	7.99949	7.69197	7.40718	7.14270
83	13.30037	12.47897	11.75122	11.10241	10.52068	9.99633	9.52141	9.08934	8.69462	8.33265	7.99955	7.69201	7.40721	7.14272
84	13.30267	12.48053	11.75228	11.10313	10.52117	9.99667	9.52164	9.08949	8.69472	8.33272	7.99960	7.69204	7.40723	7.14274
85	13.30481	12.48197	11.75325	11.10379	10.52162	9.99697	9.52185	9.08963	8.69482	8.33279	7.99964	7.69207	7.40725	7.14275
86	13.30680	12.48331	11.75415	11.10440	10.52202	9.99724	9.52203	9.08976	8.69490	8.33285	7.99968	7.69210	7.40727	7.14277
87	13.30865	12.48455	11.75497	11.10495	10.52240	9.99749	9.52220	9.08987	8.69498	8.33290	7.99972	7.69212	7.40729	7.14278
88	13.31037	12.48569	11.75574	11.10546	10.52274	9.99772	9.52235	9.08998	8.69505	8.33294	7.99975	7.69214	7.40730	7.14279
89	13.31197	12.48675	11.75644	11.10593	10.52305	9.99793	9.52249	9.09007	8.69511	8.33299	7.99978	7.69216	7.40731	7.14280
90	13.31346	12.48773	11.75709	11.10635	10.52333	9.99812	9.52262	9.09015	8.69517	8.33302	7.99980	7.69218	7.40732	7.14280
91	13.31485	12.48864	11.75768	11.10675	10.52359	9.99829	9.52273	9.09023	8.69522	8.33306	7.99982	7.69219	7.40733	7.14281
92	13.31614	12.48948	11.75823	11.10711	10.52383	9.99844	9.52283	9.09029	8.69526	8.33309	7.99984	7.69221	7.40734	7.14282
93	13.31734	12.49026	11.75874	11.10744	10.52404	9.99859	9.52293	9.09036	8.69530	8.33311	7.99986	7.69222	7.40735	7.14282
94	13.31846	12.49098	11.75921	11.10774	10.52424	9.99871	9.52301	9.09041	8.69534	8.33314	7.99988	7.69223	7.40736	7.14283
95	13.31949	12.49165	11.75964	11.10802	10.52442	9.99883	9.52309	9.09046	8.69537	8.33316	7.99989	7.69224	7.40736	7.14283
96	13.32046	12.49227	11.76004	11.10827	10.52458	9.99894	9.52315	9.09050	8.69540	8.33318	7.99990	7.69225	7.40737	7.14283
97	13.32136	12.49284	11.76040	11.10851	10.52473	9.99903	9.52322	9.09054	8.69543	8.33319	7.99991	7.69225	7.40737	7.14284
98	13.32219	12.49337	11.76074	11.10872	10.52487	9.99912	9.52327	9.09058	8.69545	8.33321	7.99992	7.69226	7.40738	7.14284
99	13.32297	12.49386	11.76105	11.10892	10.52500	9.99920	9.52332	9.09061	8.69547	8.33322	7.99993	7.69226	7.40738	7.14284
100	13.32369	12.49432	11.76134	11.10910	10.52511	9.99927	9.52337	9.09064	8.69549	8.33323	7.99994	7.69227	7.40738	7.14284
101	13.32437	12.49474	11.76160	11.10927	10.52522	9.99934	9.52341	9.09067	8.69551	8.33324	7.99995	7.69227	7.40739	7.14284
102	13.32499	12.49513	11.76184	11.10942	10.52531	9.99940	9.52345	9.09069	8.69552	8.33325	7.99995	7.69228	7.40739	7.14285
103	13.32557	12.49549	11.76207	11.10956	10.52540	9.99945	9.52348	9.09071	8.69553	8.33326	7.99996	7.69228	7.40739	7.14285
104	13.32611	12.49582	11.76227	11.10969	10.52548	9.99950	9.52351	9.09073	8.69555	8.33327	7.99996	7.69228	7.40739	7.14285
105	13.32662	12.49613	11.76246	11.10981	10.52555	9.99955	9.52354	9.09075	8.69556	8.33328	7.99997	7.69229	7.40739	7.14285
106	13.32709	12.49642	11.76264	11.10991	10.52562	9.99959	9.52357	9.09077	8.69557	8.33328	7.99997	7.69229	7.40740	7.14285
107	13.32752	12.49668	11.76280	11.11001	10.52568	9.99963	9.52359	9.09078	8.69558	8.33329	7.99997	7.69229	7.40740	7.14285
108	13.32793	12.49693	11.76295	11.11010	10.52573	9.99966	9.52361	9.09079	8.69558	8.33329	7.99998	7.69229	7.40740	7.14285
109	13.32831	12.49716	11.76309	11.11019	10.52578	9.99969	9.52363	9.09080	8.69559	8.33330	7.99998	7.69230	7.40740	7.14285
110	13.32866	12.49737	11.76322	11.11026	10.52583	9.99972	9.52365	9.09082	8.69560	8.33330	7.99998	7.69230	7.40740	7.14285
111	13.32898	12.49756	11.76333	11.11033	10.52587	9.99975	9.52366	9.09082	8.69560	8.33330	7.99998	7.69230	7.40740	7.14285
112	13.32929	12.49774	11.76344	11.11040	10.52591	9.99977	9.52368	9.09083	8.69561	8.33331	7.99999	7.69230	7.40740	7.14285
113	13.32957	12.49791	11.76354	11.11046	10.52595	9.99979	9.52369	9.09084	8.69561	8.33331	7.99999	7.69230	7.40740	7.14285
114	13.32983	12.49807	11.76363	11.11051	10.52598	9.99981	9.52370	9.09085	8.69562	8.33331	7.99999	7.69230	7.40740	7.14286
115	13.33008	12.49821	11.76371	11.11056	10.52601	9.99983	9.52371	9.09085	8.69562	8.33332	7.99999	7.69230	7.40740	7.14286
116	13.33030	12.49834	11.76379	11.11060	10.52603	9.99984	9.52372	9.09086	8.69562	8.33332	7.99999	7.69230	7.40740	7.14286
117	13.33051	12.49846	11.76386	11.11065	10.52606	9.99986	9.52373	9.09086	8.69563	8.33332	7.99999	7.69230	7.40741	7.14286
118	13.33071	12.49858	11.76393	11.11069	10.52608	9.99987	9.52374	9.09087	8.69563	8.33332	7.99999	7.69230	7.40741	7.14286
119	13.33089	12.49868	11.76399	11.11072	10.52610	9.99988	9.52374	9.09087	8.69563	8.33332	7.99999	7.69230	7.40741	7.14286
120	13.33106	12.49878	11.76405	11.11075	10.52612	9.99989	9.52375	9.09088	8.69563	8.33332	7.99999	7.69230	7.40741	7.14286

Table 4 (*concluded*): Present value of an ordinary annuity of $1 per period: 14.5%–20%

Period	14.5%	15%	15.5%	16%	16.5%	17%	17.5%	18%	18.5%	19%	19.5%	20%
1	0.87336	0.86957	0.86580	0.86207	0.85837	0.85470	0.85106	0.84746	0.84388	0.84034	0.83682	0.83333
2	1.63612	1.62571	1.61541	1.60523	1.59517	1.58521	1.57537	1.56564	1.55602	1.54650	1.53709	1.52778
3	2.30229	2.28323	2.26443	2.24589	2.22761	2.20958	2.19181	2.17427	2.15698	2.13992	2.12309	2.10648
4	2.88410	2.85498	2.82634	2.79818	2.77048	2.74324	2.71643	2.69006	2.66412	2.63859	2.61346	2.58873
5	3.39223	3.35216	3.31285	3.27429	3.23646	3.19935	3.16292	3.12717	3.09208	3.05763	3.02382	2.99061
6	3.83600	3.78448	3.73407	3.68474	3.63645	3.58918	3.54291	3.49760	3.45323	3.40978	3.36721	3.32551
7	4.22358	4.16042	4.09876	4.03857	3.97979	3.92238	3.86631	3.81153	3.75800	3.70570	3.65457	3.60459
8	4.56208	4.48732	4.41451	4.34359	4.27449	4.20716	4.14154	4.07757	4.01519	3.95437	3.89504	3.83716
9	4.85771	4.77158	4.68789	4.60654	4.52746	4.45057	4.37578	3.30302	4.23223	4.16333	4.09627	4.03097
10	5.11591	5.01877	4.92458	4.83323	4.74460	4.65860	4.57513	4.49409	4.41538	4.33893	4.26466	4.19247
11	5.34140	5.23371	5.12951	5.02864	4.93099	4.83641	4.74479	4.65601	4.56994	4.48650	4.40557	4.32706
12	5.53834	5.42062	5.30693	5.19711	5.09098	4.98839	4.88918	4.79322	4.70037	4.61050	4.52349	4.43922
13	5.71034	5.58315	5.46055	5.34233	5.22831	5.11828	5.01207	4.90951	4.81044	4.71471	4.62217	4.53268
14	5.86056	5.72448	5.59355	5.46753	5.34619	5.22930	5.11666	5.00806	4.90333	4.80228	4.70474	4.61057
15	5.99176	5.84737	5.70870	5.57546	5.44747	5.32419	5.20567	5.09158	4.98171	4.87586	4.77384	4.67547
16	6.10634	5.95423	5.80840	5.66850	5.53422	5.40529	5.28142	5.16235	5.04786	4.93770	4.83167	4.72956
17	6.20641	6.04716	5.89472	5.74870	5.60878	5.47461	5.34589	5.22233	5.10368	4.98966	4.88006	4.77463
18	6.29381	6.12797	5.96945	5.81785	5.67277	5.53385	5.40075	5.27316	5.15078	5.03333	4.92055	4.81219
19	6.37014	6.19823	6.03416	5.87746	5.72770	5.58449	5.44745	5.31624	5.19053	5.07003	4.95443	4.84350
20	6.43680	6.25933	6.09018	5.92884	5.77485	5.62777	5.48719	5.35275	5.22408	5.10086	4.98279	4.86958
21	6.49502	6.31246	6.13868	5.97314	5.81532	5.66476	5.52101	5.38368	5.25239	5.12677	5.00652	4.89132
22	6.54587	6.35866	6.18068	6.01133	5.85006	5.69637	5.54980	5.40990	5.27628	5.14855	5.02638	4.90943
23	6.59028	6.39884	6.21704	6.04425	5.87988	5.72340	5.57430	5.43212	5.29644	5.16685	5.04299	4.92453
24	6.62907	6.43377	6.24852	6.07263	5.90548	5.74649	5.59515	5.45095	5.31345	5.18223	5.05690	4.93710
25	6.66294	6.46415	6.27577	6.09709	5.92745	5.76623	5.61289	5.46691	5.32780	5.19515	5.06853	4.94759
26	6.69252	6.49056	6.29937	6.11818	5.94631	5.78311	5.62799	5.48043	5.33992	5.20601	5.07827	4.95632
27	6.71836	6.51353	6.31980	6.13636	5.96250	5.79753	5.64084	5.49189	5.35014	5.21513	5.08642	4.96360
28	6.74093	6.53351	6.33749	6.15204	5.97639	5.80985	5.65178	5.50160	5.35877	5.22280	5.09324	4.96967
29	6.76064	6.55088	6.35281	6.16555	5.98832	5.82039	5.66109	5.50983	5.36605	5.22924	5.09894	4.97472
30	6.77785	6.56598	6.36607	6.17720	5.99856	5.82939	5.66901	5.51681	5.37219	5.23466	5.10372	4.97894
31	6.79288	6.57911	6.37755	6.18724	6.00734	5.83709	5.67576	5.52272	5.37738	5.23921	5.10771	4.98245
32	6.80601	6.59053	6.38749	6.19590	6.01489	5.84366	5.68150	5.52773	5.38175	5.24303	5.11106	4.98537
33	6.81747	6.60046	6.39609	6.20336	6.02136	5.84928	5.68638	5.53197	5.38545	5.24625	5.11386	4.98781
34	6.82749	6.60910	6.40354	6.20979	6.02692	5.85409	5.69054	5.53557	5.38856	5.24895	5.11620	4.98984
35	6.83623	6.61661	6.40999	6.21534	6.03169	5.85820	5.69407	5.53862	5.39119	5.25122	5.11816	4.99154
36	6.84387	6.62314	6.41558	6.22012	6.03579	5.86171	5.69708	5.54120	5.39341	5.25312	5.11980	4.99295
37	6.85054	6.62881	6.42041	6.22424	6.03930	5.86471	5.69965	5.54339	5.39528	5.25472	5.12117	4.99412
38	6.85637	6.63375	6.42460	6.22779	6.04232	5.86727	5.70181	5.54525	5.39686	5.25607	5.12232	4.99510
39	6.86146	6.63805	6.42823	6.23086	6.04491	5.86946	5.70368	5.54682	5.39820	5.25720	5.12328	4.99592
40	6.86590	6.64178	6.43136	6.23350	6.04713	5.87133	5.70526	5.54815	5.39932	5.25815	5.12408	4.99660
41	6.86978	6.64502	6.43408	6.23577	6.04904	5.87294	5.70660	5.54928	5.40027	5.25895	5.12475	4.99717
42	6.87317	6.64785	6.43643	6.23774	6.05068	5.87430	5.70775	5.55024	5.40107	5.25962	5.12532	4.99764
43	6.87613	6.65030	6.43847	6.23943	6.05208	5.87547	5.70872	5.55105	5.40175	5.26019	5.12579	4.99803
44	6.87872	6.65244	6.44024	6.24089	6.05329	5.87647	5.70955	5.55174	5.40232	5.26066	5.12618	4.99836
45	6.88098	6.65429	6.44176	6.24214	6.05433	5.87733	5.71026	5.55232	5.40280	5.26106	5.12651	4.99863
46	6.88295	6.65591	6.44308	6.24323	6.05522	5.87806	5.71086	5.55281	5.40321	5.26140	5.12679	4.99886
47	6.88467	6.65731	6.44423	6.24416	6.05598	5.87868	5.71137	5.55323	5.40355	5.26168	5.12702	4.99905
48	6.88618	6.65853	6.44522	6.24497	6.05664	5.87922	5.71180	5.55359	5.40384	5.26191	5.12721	4.99921
49	6.88749	6.65959	6.44608	6.24566	6.05720	5.87967	5.71217	5.55389	5.40409	5.26211	5.12738	4.99934
50	6.88864	6.66051	6.44682	6.24626	6.05768	5.88006	5.71249	5.55414	5.40429	5.26228	5.12751	4.99945
51	6.88964	6.66132	6.44746	6.24678	6.05809	5.88039	5.71275	5.55436	5.40447	5.26242	5.12762	4.99954
52	6.89052	6.66201	6.44802	6.24722	6.05845	5.88068	5.71298	5.55454	5.40461	5.26254	5.12772	4.99962
53	6.89128	6.66262	6.44850	6.24760	6.05876	5.88092	5.71318	5.55469	5.40474	5.26264	5.12780	4.99968
54	6.89195	6.66315	6.44892	6.24793	6.05902	5.88113	5.71334	5.55483	5.40484	5.26272	5.12786	4.99974
55	6.89253	6.66361	6.44928	6.24822	6.05924	5.88131	5.71348	5.55494	5.40493	5.26279	5.12792	4.99978
56	6.89304	6.66401	6.44959	6.24846	6.05944	5.88146	5.71360	5.55503	5.40500	5.26285	5.12797	4.99982
57	6.89348	6.66435	6.44987	6.24868	6.05960	5.88159	5.71370	5.55511	5.40507	5.26290	5.12801	4.99985
58	6.89387	6.66466	6.45010	6.24886	6.05974	5.88170	5.71379	5.55518	5.40512	5.26294	5.12804	4.99987
59	6.89421	6.66492	6.45030	6.24902	6.05987	5.88180	5.71386	5.55524	5.40516	5.26297	5.12807	4.99989
60	6.89451	6.66515	6.45048	6.24915	6.05997	5.88188	5.71393	5.55529	5.40520	5.26300	5.12809	4.99991

Period	14.5%	15%	15.5%	16%	16.5%	17%	17.5%	18%	18.5%	19%	19.5%	20%
61	6.89477	6.66534	6.45063	6.24927	6.06006	5.88195	5.71398	5.55533	5.40523	5.26303	5.12811	4.99993
62	6.89499	6.66552	6.45076	6.24937	6.06014	5.88200	5.71403	5.55536	5.40526	5.26305	5.12812	4.99994
63	6.89519	6.66567	6.45088	6.24946	6.06020	5.88206	5.71406	5.55539	5.40528	5.26307	5.12814	4.99995
64	6.89536	6.66580	6.45098	6.24953	6.06026	5.88210	5.71410	5.55542	5.40530	5.26308	5.12815	4.99996
65	6.89551	6.66591	6.45106	6.24960	6.06031	5.88214	5.71413	5.55546	5.40533	5.26309	5.12816	4.99996
66	6.89565	6.66601	6.45114	6.24965	6.06035	5.88217	5.71415	5.55546	5.40533	5.26310	5.12816	4.99997
67	6.89576	6.66609	6.45120	6.24970	6.06039	5.88219	5.71417	5.55547	5.40534	5.26311	5.12817	4.99998
68	6.89586	6.66617	6.45125	6.24974	6.06042	5.88222	5.71419	5.55548	5.40535	5.26312	5.12818	4.99998
69	6.89595	6.66623	6.45130	6.24978	6.06045	5.88224	5.71420	5.55549	5.40536	5.26313	5.12818	4.99998
70	6.89602	6.66629	6.45134	6.24981	6.06047	5.88225	5.71421	5.55550	5.40537	5.26313	5.12819	4.99999
71	6.89609	6.66634	6.45138	6.24983	6.06049	5.88227	5.71422	5.55551	5.40537	5.26314	5.12819	4.99999
72	6.89615	6.66638	6.45141	6.24986	6.06050	5.88228	5.71423	5.55552	5.40538	5.26314	5.12819	4.99999
73	6.89620	6.66642	6.45144	6.24988	6.06052	5.88229	5.71424	5.55552	5.40538	5.26314	5.12819	4.99999
74	6.89624	6.66645	6.45146	6.24989	6.06053	5.88230	5.71425	5.55553	5.40539	5.26314	5.12820	4.99999
75	6.89628	6.66648	6.45148	6.24991	6.06054	5.88231	5.71425	5.55553	5.40539	5.26315	5.12820	4.99999
76	6.89632	6.66650	6.45150	6.24992	6.06055	5.88231	5.71426	5.55554	5.40539	5.26315	5.12820	5.00000
77	6.89635	6.66653	6.45151	6.24993	6.06056	5.88232	5.71426	5.55554	5.40539	5.26315	5.12820	5.00000
78	6.89637	6.66654	6.45153	6.24994	6.06057	5.88232	5.71427	5.55554	5.40540	5.26315	5.12820	5.00000
79	6.89640	6.66656	6.45154	6.24995	6.06057	5.88233	5.71427	5.55554	5.40540	5.26315	5.12820	5.00000
80	6.89642	6.66657	6.45155	6.24996	6.06058	5.88233	5.71427	5.55555	5.40540	5.26315	5.12820	5.00000
81	6.89643	6.66659	6.45156	6.24996	6.06058	5.88234	5.71427	5.55555	5.40540	5.26315	5.12820	5.00000
82	6.89645	6.66660	6.45157	6.24997	6.06058	5.88234	5.71428	5.55555	5.40540	5.26315	5.12820	5.00000
83	6.89646	6.66661	6.45157	6.24997	6.06059	5.88234	5.71428	5.55555	5.40540	5.26316	5.12820	5.00000
84	6.89647	6.66661	6.45158	6.24998	6.06059	5.88234	5.71428	5.55555	5.40540	5.26316	5.12820	5.00000
85	6.89648	6.66662	6.45158	6.24998	6.06059	5.88234	5.71428	5.55555	5.40540	5.26316	5.12820	5.00000
86	6.89649	6.66663	6.45159	6.24998	6.06059	5.88234	5.71428	5.55555	5.40540	5.26316	5.12820	5.00000
87	6.89650	6.66663	6.45159	6.24998	6.06060	5.88235	5.71428	5.55555	5.40540	5.26316	5.12820	5.00000
88	6.89651	6.66664	6.45159	6.24999	6.06060	5.88235	5.71428	5.55555	5.40540	5.26316	5.12820	5.00000
89	6.89651	6.66664	6.45160	6.24999	6.06060	5.88235	5.71428	5.55555	5.40540	5.26316	5.12820	5.00000
90	6.89652	6.66664	6.45160	6.24999	6.06060	5.88235	5.71428	5.55555	5.40540	5.26316	5.12820	5.00000
91	6.89652	6.66665	6.45160	6.24999	6.06060	5.88235	5.71428	5.55555	5.40540	5.26316	5.12820	5.00000
92	6.89652	6.66665	6.45160	6.24999	6.06060	5.88235	5.71428	5.55555	5.40540	5.26316	5.12820	5.00000
93	6.89653	6.66665	6.45160	6.24999	6.06060	5.88235	5.71428	5.55555	5.40540	5.26316	5.12820	5.00000
94	6.89653	6.66665	6.45160	6.24999	6.06060	5.88235	5.71428	5.55555	5.40540	5.26316	5.12820	5.00000
95	6.89653	6.66666	6.45161	6.25000	6.06060	5.88235	5.71428	5.55555	5.40540	5.26316	5.12820	5.00000
96	6.89654	6.66666	6.45161	6.25000	6.06060	5.88235	5.71428	5.55555	5.40540	5.26316	5.12820	5.00000
97	6.89654	6.66666	6.45161	6.25000	6.06060	5.88235	5.71428	5.55555	5.40541	5.26316	5.12820	5.00000
98	6.89654	6.66666	6.45161	6.25000	6.06060	5.88235	5.71428	5.55556	5.40541	5.26316	5.12820	5.00000
99	6.89654	6.66666	6.45161	6.25000	6.06060	5.88235	5.71429	5.55556	5.40541	5.26316	5.12821	5.00000
100	6.89654	6.66666	6.45161	6.25000	6.06060	5.88235	5.71429	5.55556	5.40541	5.26316	5.12821	5.00000
101	6.89654	6.66666	6.45161	6.25000	6.06060	5.88235	5.71429	5.55556	5.40541	5.26316	5.12821	5.00000
102	6.89654	6.66666	6.45161	6.25000	6.06061	5.88235	5.71429	5.55556	5.40541	5.26316	5.12821	5.00000
103	6.89655	6.66666	6.45161	6.25000	6.06061	5.88235	5.71429	5.55556	5.40541	5.26316	5.12821	5.00000
104	6.89655	6.66666	6.45161	6.25000	6.06061	5.88235	5.71429	5.55556	5.40541	5.26316	5.12821	5.00000
105	6.89655	6.66666	6.45161	6.25000	6.06061	5.88235	5.71429	5.55556	5.40541	5.26316	5.12821	5.00000
106	6.89655	6.66666	6.45161	6.25000	6.06061	5.88235	5.71429	5.55556	5.40541	5.26316	5.12821	5.00000
107	6.89655	6.66666	6.45161	6.25000	6.06061	5.88235	5.71429	5.55556	5.40541	5.26316	5.12821	5.00000
108	6.89655	6.66666	6.45161	6.25000	6.06061	5.88235	5.71429	5.55556	5.40541	5.26316	5.12821	5.00000
109	6.89655	6.66667	6.45161	6.25000	6.06061	5.88235	5.71429	5.55556	5.40541	5.26316	5.12821	5.00000
110	6.89655	6.66667	6.45161	6.25000	6.06061	5.88235	5.71429	5.55556	5.40541	5.26316	5.12821	5.00000
111	6.89655	6.66667	6.45161	6.25000	6.06061	5.88235	5.71429	5.55556	5.40541	5.26316	5.12821	5.00000
112	6.89655	6.66667	6.45161	6.25000	6.06061	5.88235	5.71429	5.55556	5.40541	5.26316	5.12821	5.00000
113	6.89655	6.66667	6.45161	6.25000	6.06061	5.88235	5.71429	5.55556	5.40541	5.26316	5.12821	5.00000
114	6.89655	6.66667	6.45161	6.25000	6.06061	5.88235	5.71429	5.55556	5.40541	5.26316	5.12821	5.00000
115	6.89655	6.66667	6.45161	6.25000	6.06061	5.88235	5.71429	5.55556	5.40541	5.26316	5.12821	5.00000
116	6.89655	6.66667	6.45161	6.25000	6.06061	5.88235	5.71429	5.55556	5.40541	5.26316	5.12821	5.00000
117	6.89655	6.66667	6.45161	6.25000	6.06061	5.88235	5.71429	5.55556	5.40541	5.26316	5.12821	5.00000
118	6.89655	6.66667	6.45161	6.25000	6.06061	5.88235	5.71429	5.55556	5.40541	5.26316	5.12821	5.00000
119	6.89655	6.66667	6.45161	6.25000	6.06061	5.88235	5.71429	5.55556	5.40541	5.26316	5.12821	5.00000
120	6.89655	6.66667	6.45161	6.25000	6.06061	5.88235	5.71429	5.55556	5.40541	5.26316	5.12821	5.00000

Index

*This book had been set VideoComp, 11 and 10 point Times
Roman, leaded 1 point. Part and chapter numbers are
Helvetica Extra Light, part titles are 30 point Helvetica
Light, and chapter titles are 28 point Helvetica Light. The
size of the type page is 33 by 49 picas.*